A simple solution to take your course to the web

▶ Web Tutor features chats, discussion groups, testing, student progress tracking, and business law course materials. Web Tutor is perfect for distance learning courses or traditional courses that incorporate technology.

▶ **Chats and Discussion** enable instructors to teach the whole course or hold office hours without having to come on campus.

◀ *Ask your instructor for details*

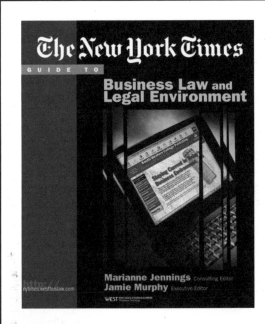

Daily law-related news updates from *The New York Times*

▶ *The New York Times Guide* is more than just a printed collection of articles. By purchasing the *Guide* you also gain access, via password, to an online collection of the most current and relevant *New York Times* articles that are continually posted as news breaks.

▶ Includes articles from CyberTimes, the online technology section of *The New York Times* on the Web.

◀ *http://nytimes.westbuslaw.com*

WEST'S LEGAL ENVIRONMENT OF BUSINESS

TEXT,
CASES,
ETHICAL, REGULATORY, INTERNATIONAL,
AND E-COMMERCE ISSUES

FOURTH EDITION

Frank B. Cross
Herbert D. Kelleher Centennial Professor in Business Law
University of Texas at Austin

Roger LeRoy Miller
Institute for University Studies
Arlington, Texas

WEST

THOMSON LEARNING

Australia   Canada   Mexico   Singapore   Spain   United Kingdom   United States

WEST

THOMSON LEARNING

WEST'S LEGAL ENVIRONMENT OF BUSINESS:
TEXT, CASES, ETHICAL, REGULATORY, INTERNATIONAL, AND E-COMMERCE ISSUES
by Frank B. Cross and Roger LeRoy Miller

Vice President/Team Director
Jack Calhoun

Senior Acquisitions Editor
Rob Dewey

Senior Developmental Editor
Jan Lamar

Marketing Manager
Mike Worls

Production Editor
Bill Stryker

Manufacturing Coordinator
Charlene Taylor

Internal Design
Bill Stryker

Copy Editor
Suzie DeFazio

Compositor
Parkwood Composition Service

Printer
Quebecor World

Library of Congress Cataloging-in-Publication Data
Cross, Frank B.
West's legal environment of business: text, cases, ethical,
regulatory, international, and e-commerce issues / Frank B.
Cross, Roger LeRoy Miller.—4th ed.
Includes bibliographic references and index.
ISBN 0–324–01572–0 (package)
ISBN 0–324–07294–5 (text)
1. Industrial laws and legislation—United States. 2. Trade
regulation—United States. 3. Commercial law—United
States. I. Title: Legal environment of business. II. Miller, Roger
LeRoy. III. Title
    KF1600.C76   2000
    346.7307—dc21   00–032076

This book is printed on acid-free paper.

Contents in Brief

Contents

UNIT TWO
The Public and International Environment 101

Chapter 5 ■ Constitutional Law 102

Chapter 6 ■ Administrative Law 120

Chapter 7 ■ Criminal Law 136

Chapter 8 ■ International and Comparative Law 159

UNIT THREE
The Private Environment 186

Chapter 9 ■ Contracts: Part 1 186

Chapter 10 ■ Contracts: Part II 212

CONCEPT SUMMARIES LIST

EXHIBITS LIST

EMERGING TRENDS IN TECHNOLOGY

Preface to the Instructor

The legal environment of business has universal applicability. A student entering virtually any field of business must have at least a passing understanding of business law in order to function in the real world. Additionally, students preparing for a career in accounting, government and political science, economics, and even medicine can fruitfully use much of the information they learn in a legal environment course.

Key Areas of Emphasis

To make sure that instructors and students alike can rely on the coverage, accuracy, and applicability of *West's Legal Environment of Business*, Fourth Edition, we emphasize the following throughout the text:

- **Cyberlaw and E-Commerce**—Technology is affecting not only the world around us but also business law and the legal environment. We are proud to include a trend-setting chapter on cyberlaw and e-commerce (Chapter 15). In addition, throughout the text there are special features entitled *Emerging Trends in Technology*. These features examine, for the most part, how the Internet has affected the law. Cyberlaw issues are also addressed in the CNN Update Video (discussed later in this Preface).

- **Access to Technology**—Every chapter ends with a feature entitled *Law on the Web*, in which students

are directed to useful online resources as well as Internet activities that they can perform to explore specific legal sources on the Web. Also, every *Focus on Legal Reasoning* (described below) and *Emerging Trends in Technology* presented in this text concludes with a brief section that refers students to relevant Web sites. Whenever possible, the citations to cases presented in the text are followed by a URL that students can use to access the case on an online database. Moreover, whenever a *Company Profile* is included in a case, the URL of the company's home page is indicated. To facilitate online research efforts by students, each student is provided with a complimentary booklet entitled *Online Legal Research*. As always, adopters of this book have free access to Westlaw®, which now includes two significant new features: *KeyCite* and *Court Link*. The latter allows access to the dockets of more than 180 federal courts and 250 state courts. Westlaw® is now also available on the Internet at http://www.westlaw.com. Finally, extensive online legal resources keyed to the text are found at the *West's Legal Environment of Business* Web site at http://wleb.westbuslaw.com (discussed below).

- **Limited Liability Companies and Limited Liability Partnerships**—Because these new forms of business organization are becoming increasingly important, we have included an entire chapter (Chapter 18) on their uses and restrictions.

■ **Comprehensiveness**—Virtually every important topic in the legal environment is covered in this book. Our comprehensive coverage gives instructors complete flexibility in choosing those areas of the law and legal environment that they wish to emphasize.

■ **Authoritativeness**—We have fully researched every aspect of business law and the legal environment included in this text. Instructors can rely on its accuracy and can find references to case and statutory law, as needed, for any authority. Complete parallel citations are given throughout the text. An extensive set of appendices includes the Uniform Commercial Code and other uniform codes and statutes. Accuracy is the watchword of *West's Legal Environment of Business*.

■ **Ethics**—In addition to the discussion of business ethics in Chapter 4 ("Ethics and Business Decision Making"), every unit ends with a *Focus on Ethics*. Additionally, selected cases within the text end with *Ethical Considerations*, and one chapter in every unit includes A *Question of Ethics* at the end of the *Questions and Case Problems* section.

■ **Critical Thinking and Legal Reasoning**—Your students' critical-thinking and legal-reasoning skills will be increased as they work through the numerous pedagogical devices within the book and its *Study Guide*. Questions concluding the *Emerging Trends* features and *Focus on Ethics* sections encourage critical thinking about the topics covered in those features. We have added two new features to the Fourth Edition, entitled *In Your Court* and *Focus on Legal Reasoning*, that will help your students develop skills in the areas of legal reasoning and analysis, as well as critical thinking. (These features will be described in more detail later in the Preface.) Finally, each unit also concludes with a *Cumulative Business Hypothetical*—a set of questions relating to topics covered throughout the unit.

■ **International and Comparative Law**—Chapter 8 ("International and Comparative Law") helps your students gain a background in the international and comparative aspects of the law, an increasingly important subject. Additionally, selected cases in the text end with *International Considerations*.

■ **AACSB Curriculum Requirements**—This text explicitly addresses the AACSB's broad array of curriculum requirements by focusing on the global, political, ethical, social, environmental, technological, and cultural context of many of the cases presented. Specifically, selected cases are preceded by a *Historical and [Social, Economic, Political, Technological, Environmental, or International] Setting*, which places the case in a particular political, ethical, social, or other setting. Additionally, *Company Profiles* precede many of the cases in this edition. Finally, the materials in Unit One (Chapters 1 through 4) explore virtually every facet of the AACSB's curriculum requirements. The AACSB's emphasis on the global and ethical context of the law is addressed throughout the rest of the text in features already mentioned: the *International* and *Ethical Considerations* that follow selected cases and the *Focus on Ethics* section found at the end of each unit.

West's Legal Environment of Business on the Web

When you visit our Web site at http://wleb.westbuslaw.com, you will find a broad array of teaching/learning resources, including the following:

■ A continually updated set of new cases, specifically keyed to each chapter in the text.
■ Current legal events updated regularly and keyed to chapters in this text.
■ Professors' Exchange: You will be able to e-mail your questions about *West's Legal Environment of Business* to Frank Cross.
■ A variety of classroom materials.
■ Internet Applications, which include at least one Internet activity for every chapter in the text.
■ Online quizzes.
■ Other contents will be added as we continue to improve our Web site to make it more useful for you and your students.

An Effective Case Format

To ensure that *West's Legal Environment of Business*, Fourth Edition, meets the needs of instructors and students alike, we have devoted significant efforts to finding cases that not only provide on-point illustrations of the principles of law discussed in the text but also are of high interest to students. Our selection includes classic, landmark cases as well as some of the most modern examples of business law. For those instructors who like to see the entire court opinions for cases presented in the text, we also offer a supplement called *Case Printouts to Accompany West's Legal Environment of Business, Fourth Edition*. This supplement contains the output from Westlaw® (without headnotes) for virtually every case that is included in each chapter. If the instructor wishes, the full court opinions may be copied and handed out to students.

BASIC CASE FORMAT

Each case in *West's Legal Environment of Business* is presented in the following basic format:

- *Case Title and Full Case Citation*—The case title and full case citation (including all parallel citations) are presented at the beginning of each case. When available, a URL for a Web site that includes the case is given.
- *Background and Facts*—This section contains a summary, in the authors' own words, of the events leading up to the lawsuit.
- *In the Language of the Court*—Following the summary of the background of the case, an excerpt from the actual court opinion is presented—in a contrasting type to differentiate it from the surrounding textual material. Whenever the court opinion contains a term or phrase that may be difficult for the student to understand, we provide a brief explanation of the term in brackets. When important phrases and sentences are italicized, bracketed notes clearly indicate that the emphasis was added by the authors, not by the court.
- *Decision and Remedy*—In this section, the authors summarize, in their own words, the outcome of the case.

ADDITIONAL SECTIONS IN THE CASES

Many cases include one of the following sections, which have already been described.

- *Company Profiles*—Numerous companies are profiled before appropriate cases. Each profile, which describes the history of the company involved in a particular case, is designed to give your students the real-world context of the case before the court. When available, the URL for the profiled company's Web site is given.
- *Historical and [Social or Other] Settings*—When appropriate, the global, political, ethical, social, environmental, technological, or cultural context of a case is presented in one of these settings.

- *Ethical Considerations*—These sections, as mentioned previously, discuss ethical aspects of the law or laws under consideration.
- *International Considerations*—As explained above, these sections let your students know how the particular issue at bar is treated in other countries.

Other Special Features of this Text

We have included in *West's Legal Environment of Business*, Fourth Edition, a number of additional pedagogical devices and special features, including those discussed here.

EMERGING TRENDS

Presented throughout this text are over two dozen features entitled *Emerging Trends in Technology*. These new features examine the effect of the Internet on the legal environment. Here are some examples of these features:

- Taxation Issues in Cyberspace (Chapter 5).
- Electronic Monitoring in the Workplace (Chapter 21).

CONCEPT SUMMARIES

Whenever key areas of the law need additional emphasis, we provide a *Concept Summary*. These summaries have always been a popular pedagogical tool in this text. There are now more than fifty of these summaries, including the following:

- Types of Crimes (Chapter 7).
- Equitable Remedies (Chapter 11).
- Violations of Virtual Property Rights (Chapter 15).

EXHIBITS

When appropriate, we have illustrated important aspects of the law in graphic or summary form in exhibits. In all, over forty exhibits are featured in *West's Legal Environment of Business*, Fourth Edition, including the following:

- Areas of the Law That May Affect Business Decision Making (Exhibit 1–3).
- Forms of Intellectual Property (Exhibit 14–1).
- Major Forms of Business Compared (Exhibit 18–2).

Vocabulary Stressed

In addition to including bracketed explanations of difficult terms and phrases within the court opinions presented in the text, we also boldface and fully define every important legal term when it is first introduced. Additionally, at the end of each chapter, all terms that were boldfaced within the chapter are listed in alphabetical order under the heading *Terms and Concepts to Review*. The page on which the term is defined is given after each term. For selected terms, particularly those of Latin origin, a special pronunciation guide has been included in footnotes within the chapters as well as in the Glossary at the end of the text.

Questions and Case Problems

Every chapter in this text ends with nine or ten questions and case problems. Normally, the first three to five of these are hypothetical questions. The remainder are actual case problems, many of which are from the late 1990s. Concluding each *Questions and Case Problems* section is a special problem entitled *In Your Court*. The problem poses a hypothetical situation and then asks a series of questions that require the student to engage in legal reasoning and analysis. In selected chapters, A *Question of Ethics* is also included at the end of the *Questions and Case Problems* section. Complete answers are given in a separate manual for all questions and case problems in the text.

Alternate Problem Sets with Answers

To expand the number of case problems available to instructors, for each chapter of *West's Legal Environment of Business*, Fourth Edition, we have created a set of five or more alternate case problems. These alternate case problems, along with their answers, are included at the end of the manual accompanying this text entitled *Answers to Questions and Case Problems and Alternate Problem Sets with Answers*. The alternate case problems and their answers are presented on perforated pages for easy removal and copying.

Special Unit-Ending Materials

Each of the eleven units in this text concludes with the following special features:

■ **Cumulative Business Hypothetical**—In addition to the hypotheticals in the *Questions and Case Problems* section, we include at the end of each unit a *Cumulative Business Hypothetical*. This feature first posits a scenario—such as a small business just getting under way—and then poses a series of questions for the student to answer. The questions provide an excellent means of reviewing legal concepts covered throughout the unit. Suggested answers for these hypotheticals are also included in the *Answers to Questions and Case Problems*.

■ **Extended Case Studies and Case Briefing Assignments**—Just following the *Cumulative Business Hypothetical* we present an extended case study entitled *Focus on Legal Reasoning*. The subtitle of each *Focus* gives the full case title of the case being studied. The feature then opens with an *Introduction* followed by a *Case Background*. We then present excerpts from court's majority and dissenting opinions (including legal sources cited by the justices). Following the excerpts, a series of questions ask the student to perform tasks involving legal research, legal analysis, critical thinking, and case briefing. The feature concludes with a *Going Online* section, in which students are referred to one or more Web sites for further study of the case or the issue it addresses.

■ **Focus on Ethics**—The unit-ending materials conclude with a *Focus on Ethics*. These sections address ethical aspects of the law discussed in the preceding unit. Each section is designed to elicit comments and discussion from the student-readers on ethical issues. For this reason, each *Focus* ends with a set of discussion questions.

Appendices

Because the majority of students keep their business law texts as a reference source, we have included a full set of appendices. In all, the following appendices are included in *West's Legal Environment of Business*, Fourth Edition:

A How to Brief Cases and Analyze Case Problems.
B The Constitution of the United States.
C The Administrative Procedure Act of 1946 (Excerpts).
D The Uniform Commercial Code (Excerpts).
E The National Labor Relations Act of 1914 (Excerpts).
F The Sherman Act of 1890 (Excerpts).

G The Clayton Act of 1914 (Excerpts).

H The Federal Trade Commission Act of 1914 (Excerpts).

I The Robinson-Patman Act of 1936 (Excerpts).

J Securities Act of 1933 (Excerpts).

K Securities Exchange Act of 1934 (Excerpts).

L Title VII of the Civil Rights Act of 1964 (Excerpts).

M Civil Rights Act of 1991 (Excerpts).

N Americans with Disabilities Act of 1990 (Excerpts).

O The Uniform Partnership Act.

P The Revised Uniform Partnership Act (Excerpts).

Q The Uniform Limited Liability Company Act (Excerpts).

R The General Agreement on Tariffs and Trade of 1994 (Excerpts).

S The North American Free Trade Agreement of 1993 (Excerpts).

T The Small Business Regulatory Enforcement Fairness Act of 1996 (Excerpts).

U Spanish Equivalents for Important Legal Terms in English.

Revised Appendix A. We have included in Appendix A a new section entitled "Analyzing Case Problems." This section contains tips for students on how they can "get started" when they are assigned to work on case problems. Included in the section is a discussion of the IRAC method of case analysis and an example of how students can apply this method when analyzing case problems.

The Most Complete Supplements Package Available Today

This edition of *West's Legal Environment of Business* is accompanied by an expansive number of teaching and learning supplements. For further information on the *West's Legal Environment of Business* teaching/learning package, contact your local West sales representative. An additional source of information is our *West's Legal Environment of Business* Web site at http://wleb.westbuslaw.com.

PRINTED SUPPLEMENTS

- *Online Legal Research* (free with every new copy of the text).

- *Instructor's Course Planning Guide and Media Handbook.*

- *Instructor's Manual* (also available in computerized form).

- *Study Guide* by William Eric Hollowell and text author Roger LeRoy Miller, including essay questions.

- A comprehensive *Test Bank* (co-written by text author Roger LeRoy Miller)—Contains approximately 1,000 multiple-choice questions with answers, over 1,000 true-false questions with answers, and short essay questions. Also available on software.

- *Answers to Questions and Case Problems and Alternate Problem Sets with Answers.*

- *Case Printouts.*

- *Handbook of Landmark Cases and Statutes in Business Law and the Legal Environment.*

- *Advanced Topics and Contemporary Issues: Expanded Coverage,* Third Edition, by Frank B. Cross.

- *Handbook on Critical Thinking and Writing in Business Law and the Legal Environment.*

- *A Guide to Personal Law.*

- *Law and Women's Issues.*

- *Instructor's Manual* for the *Drama of the Law* video series.

- *Quicken® Business Law Partner® CD-ROM and Applications.*

SOFTWARE AND VIDEO SUPPLEMENTS

- *Quicken® Business Law Partner® CD-ROM.*
- Computerized *Instructor's Manual.*
- ExamView Testing Software.
- Web Tutor on WebCT.
- *Lecture Outline System.*
- PowerPoint slides.
- Transparency Acetates.
- "The Legal Tutor on Contracts" software.
- "The Legal Tutor on Sales" software.
- Interactive Software—Contracts.
- Interactive Software—Sales.
- "You Be the Judge" software.
- Case-Problem Cases on Diskette.
- Westlaw®.
- West's Business Law and Legal Environment Audiocassette Library.
- Videocassettes, including those discussed next.

CNN *LEGAL ISSUES* Update Video

You can update your coverage of legal issues and cyberlaw, as well as spark a lively classroom discussion and foster a deeper understanding of business law, by using the *CNN Legal Issues* update video. This video is produced by Turner Learning, Inc., using the resources of CNN, the world's first twenty-four-hour, all-news network.

With the introduction of the *CNN Legal Issues* update video, West Legal Studies in Business is proud to be the educational partner of CNN for textbook/video integration for legal issues. By making use of the *CNN Legal Issues* update video, you can bring the power of CNN, the network known for providing live, in-depth coverage and analysis of breaking news events, to your classroom.

ADDITIONAL VIDEOS

South-Western's *Business Law* video series, a set of situational videos, covers a range of topics for the full business law course, including the Uniform Commercial Code, and employment law.

THE NEW YORK TIMES GUIDE TO LEGAL STUDIES IN BUSINESS

The New York Times Guide to Legal Studies in Business, by Marianne Jennings and Jamie Murphy, is more than just a printed collection of articles. The guide gives you access, via password, to an online collection of the most current and relevant *New York Times* articles that are continually posted as news breaks. Also included are articles from *CyberTimes,* the online technology section of the *New York Times* on the Web. Correlation guides for all South-Western legal studies in business texts are available on the South-Western *New York Times* Web site at **http:// nytimes.swcollege.com**. Ask your West sales representative about this great new supplement for your students.

For Users of the Third Edition

First of all, we want to thank you for helping make *West's Legal Environment of Business* the best-selling legal environment text in the United States today. Second, we want to make you aware of the numerous additions and changes that we have made in this edition. The major additions and changes are summarized below.

A NEW CHAPTER ON CYBERLAW AND E-COMMERCE

As discussed earlier in this Preface, this chapter ensures that your students will stay abreast of the important elements of the law that have been affected by the Internet, e-commerce, and technology in general. This chapter is guaranteed to make business law and the legal environment come alive for your students.

A NEW CHAPTER ON LIMITED LIABILITY COMPANIES AND LIMITED LIABILITY PARTNERSHIPS

As discussed earlier in this Preface, these new forms of business organization have taken on increasing importance. This chapter outlines their major characteristics and uses.

SIGNIFICANTLY REVISED CHAPTERS

—*Comparative Law*: The chapter on comparative law was combined with the chapter on international law. The combined chapter appears in the Fourth Edition as Chapter 8 ("International and Comparative Law").

—*Torts and Crimes*: Chapters 12 and 13 of the Third Edition ("Torts and Strict Liability" and "Torts and Crimes Related to Business") were reorganized for the Fourth Edition. In this edition, Chapter 12, "Torts and Strict Liability," includes a discussion of torts related to business. New to this edition, Chapter 7, entitled "Criminal Law," expands on the previous edition's coverage of crimes related to business.

—*Business Organizations*: Adding a new chapter on limited liability companies and limited partnerships (Chapter 18) prompted some reorganization of the Third Edition's Chapters 17 and 18 ("Business Organizations" and "Rights and Duties within the Corporation"). The discussion of partnership was expanded in the Fourth Edition's Chapter 17, "Sole Proprietorships, Partnerships, and Special Business Organizations." All of the material on corporations was moved to this edition's Chapter 19, "Corporations."

WHAT ELSE IS NEW?

In addition to the changes already noted, we have included in the Fourth Edition a number of new pedagogical features and have added some new supplements. The new features and elements are listed below.

New Features. We have added the following new features to the Eighth Edition, each of which has been described earlier in this Preface:

- *In Your Court.*
- *Focus on Legal Reasoning.*
- *Law on the Web.*

New *Emerging Trends.* All of the *Emerging Trends in Technology* and the *Emerging Trends in Business Law* are new to this edition.

New *Concept Summaries.* A number of new *Concept Summaries* have been added for this edition, including those listed earlier in the Preface.

New Exhibits. Several of the more than forty exhibits in this edition are new, including those listed earlier in the Preface.

New Cases. In all, over 70 percent of the cases in Fourth Edition are from the late 1990s. Many classic cases have been included also.

New Case Problems. Of the over 170 case problems in this text, more than a third are new to the Fourth Edition. The majority of these new case problems are from 1998 and 1999.

NEW SUPPLEMENTS AND SPECIAL RESOURCES

- *Online Legal Research.*
- Web Tutor on WebCT.
- *Internet Activities* (on the *West's Legal Environment of Business* Web site).
- A *Guide to Personal Law* as a separate paperback supplement.
- *The New York Times Guide to Legal Studies in Business.*

Acknowledgments for Previous Editions

Since we began this project a number of years ago, a sizable number of business law professors and others have helped us in various phases of the undertaking. The following reviewers offered numerous constructive criticisms, comments, and suggestions during the preparation of all previous editions.

Wm. Dennis Ames
Indiana University of Pennsylvania

Angela Cerino
Villanova University

David Cooper
Fullerton College

Gamewell Gant
Idaho State University

Arlene M. Hibschweiler
SUNY Fredonia

Marty Salley McGee
South Carolina State University

Kathleen A. Phillips
University of Houston

Brian Terry
Johnson and Wales University

Michael G. Walsh
Villanova University

Acknowledgments for the Fourth Edition

In preparing the Fourth Edition of *West's Legal Environment of Business*, we worked closely with the following reviewers, each of whom offered us valuable suggestions for how to improve the text:

Wm. Dennis Ames
Indiana University of Pennsylvania

Thomas M. Apke
California State University, Fullerton

Jane Bennett
Orange Coast College

Steven R. Donley
Cypress College

Joan Gabel
Georgia State University

Robert Mitchum
Arkansas State University, Beebe

Brian Terry
Johnson and Wales University

John Theis
Mesa State College

Glynda White
Community College Southern Nevada

As in all past editions, we owe a debt of extreme gratitude to the numerous individuals who worked directly with us or at West. We especially wish to thank Lavina Leed Miller for her management of the entire project, as well as for the application of her superb editorial skills. William Eric Hollowell, who also co-authored the *Instructor's Manual, Study Guide,* and *Test Bank,* helped with much of the research. We were fortunate to have the copyediting services of Suzie Franklin DeFazio. Literally dozens of individuals helped proofread the galleys and pages of this edition over many, many months. They include Lavina Leed Miller, William Eric Hollowell, Suzie Franklin DeFazio, Pat Lewis, and Roxanna Lee.

We continue to be the fortunate recipients of an incredibly skilled and dedicated editorial, production, and printing and manufacturing team at West. In particular, we wish to thank Rob Dewey and Jan Lamar for their helpful advice and guidance during all of the stages of this new edition. Jan Lamar also assisted us in making sure we addressed all reviewers' criticisms and suggestions, and she was instrumental in ensuring that the supplements came out on time. Kurt Gerdenich deserves a special note of appreciation for his incredibly masterful work on the *West's Legal Environment of Business* home page and just about everything else relating to technology for this text.

Our long-time textbook designer and production manager at West, Bill Stryker, came through again. He provided us with a visually stunning new edition and an error-free printing. His ability to turn around our materials quickly continues to amaze us. We thank him more than he can ever imagine.

Through the years, we have enjoyed a continuing correspondence with many of you who have found points on which you wish to comment. We continue to welcome all comments and promise to respond promptly. By incorporating your ideas, we can continue to write a business law text that is best for you and best for your students.

DEDICATION

To my parents and sisters.

F.B.C.

RLM dedicates this edition to
Richard Jaenicke,
who has given me more help
than I deserved, and has waited
too long for me to catch up
on Fox Creek. Thanks for all
the years of friendship.

R.L.M.

why?

UNIT ONE

The Foundations

CONTENTS

CHAPTER 1

Business and
Its Legal Environment

ONE OF THE IMPORTANT FUNCTIONS OF LAW in any society is to provide stability, predictability, and continuity so that people can be sure of how to order their affairs. If any society is to survive, its citizens must be able to determine what is legally right and legally wrong. They must know what sanctions will be imposed on them if they commit wrongful acts. If they suffer harm as a result of others' wrongful acts, they need to know how they can seek redress. By setting forth the rights, obligations, and privileges of citizens, the law enables individuals to go about their business with confidence and a certain degree of predictability. The stability and predictability created by the law provide an essential framework for all civilized activities, including business activities.

In this introductory chapter, we first look at the nature of law and then examine the foundation and fundamental characteristics of the American legal system. We next describe the basic sources of American law and some general classifications of law. We conclude with sections offering practical guidance on several topics, including how to find the sources of law discussed in this chapter (and referred to throughout the text), how to read and understand court opinions, and why a basic knowledge of the law is important for those who contemplate a career in business.

The legal environment of business includes the American court system, administrative agencies, and alternatives to litigation, as well as the laws and legal systems of other nations and the international community. The legal environment is a significant part of the world of business, influencing contracts, leases, creditor-debtor relations, employment relationships, real property transactions, business organizations, and the conduct of competitors. The remainder of this book addresses these and other topics with special emphasis on business ethics and on the effect of the legal environment in the area of electronic communications.

SECTION 1

What Is Law?

There have been and will continue to be different definitions of law. Although the definitions of law vary in their particulars, they all are based on the general observation that, at a minimum, **law consists of** *enforceable rules governing relationships among individuals and between individuals and their society.* These "enforceable rules" may consist of unwritten principles of behavior established by a nomadic tribe. They may be set forth in a law code, such as the Code of Hammurabi in ancient Babylon or the law code of one of today's European nations. They may consist of written laws and court decisions created by modern legislative and judicial bodies, as in the United States. Regardless of how such rules are created, they all have one thing in common: they establish rights, duties, and privileges that are consistent with the values and beliefs of their society or its ruling group.

While few legal philosophers and scholars would disagree with these general observations about the law, those who embark on a study of law will find that these broad statements leave unanswered some important questions concerning the nature of law. Part of the study of law, often referred to as **jurisprudence,** involves learning about different schools of jurisprudential thought and discovering how the approaches to law characteristic of each school can affect judicial decision making.

SCHOOLS OF JURISPRUDENTIAL THOUGHT

You may think that legal philosophy is far removed from the practical study of business law and the legal environment. In fact, it is not. As you will learn in the chapters of this text, how judges apply the law to specific disputes, including disputes relating to the business world, depends in part on their philosophical approaches to law. We look now at some of the significant schools of legal, or jurisprudential, thought that have evolved over time.

The Natural Law School. An age-old question about the nature of law has to do with the finality of a nation's laws, such as the laws of the United States at the present time. For example, what if a particular law is deemed to be a "bad" law by a substantial number of that nation's citizens? Must a citizen obey the law if it goes against his or her conscience to do so? Is there a higher or universal law to which individuals can appeal? One who adheres to the natural law tradition would answer this question in the affirmative. **Natural law** denotes a system of moral and ethical principles that are inherent in human nature and that people can discover through the use of their natural intelligence.

The natural law tradition is one of the oldest and most significant schools of jurisprudence. It dates back to the days of the Greek philosopher Aristotle (384–322 B.C.E.), who distinguished between natural law and the laws governing a particular nation. According to Aristotle, natural law applies universally to all humankind.

The notion that people have "natural rights" stems from the natural law tradition. Those who claim that a specific foreign government is depriving certain citizens of their human rights implicitly are appealing to a higher law that has universal applicability. The question of the universality of basic human rights also comes into play in the context of international business operations. Should rights extended to workers in this country, such as the right to be free of discrimination in the workplace, be applied to a U.S. firm doing business in another country that does not provide for such rights? This question is rooted implicitly in a concept of universal rights that has its origins in the natural law tradition.

The Positivist School. In contrast, **positive law,** or national law (the written law of a given society at a particular point in time), applies only to the citizens of that nation or society. Those who adhere to the **positivist school** believe that there can be no higher law than a nation's positive law. According to the positivist school, there is no such thing as "natural rights." Rather, human rights exist solely because of laws. If the laws are not enforced, anarchy will result. Thus, whether a law is "bad" or "good" is irrelevant. The law is the law and must be obeyed until it is changed—in an orderly manner through a legitimate lawmaking process. A judge with positivist leanings probably would be more inclined to defer to an existing law than would a judge who adheres to the natural law tradition.

The Historical School. The **historical school** of legal thought emphasizes the evolutionary process of law by concentrating on the origin and history of the legal system. Thus, this school looks to the past to discover what the principles of contemporary law should be. The legal doctrines that have withstood the passage of time—those that have worked in the past—are deemed best suited for shaping present laws. Hence, law derives its legitimacy and authority from adhering to the standards that historical development has shown to be workable. Adherents of the historical school are more likely than those of other schools to strictly follow decisions made in past cases.

Legal Realism. In the 1920s and 1930s, a number of jurists and scholars, known as legal realists, rebelled against the historical approach to law. **Legal realism** is based on the idea that law is just one of many institutions in society and that it is shaped by social forces and needs. The law is a human enterprise, and judges should take social and economic realities into account when deciding cases. Legal realists also believe that the law can never be applied with total uniformity. Given that judges are human beings with unique personalities, value systems, and intellects, obviously different judges will bring different reasoning processes to the same case.

Legal realism strongly influenced the growth of what is sometimes called the **sociological school** of jurisprudence. This school views law as a tool for promoting justice in society. In the 1960s, for example, the justices of the United States Supreme Court played a leading role in the civil rights movement by upholding long-neglected laws calling for equal treatment for all Americans, including African Americans and other minorities. Generally, jurists who adhere to this philosophy of law are more likely to depart from past decisions than are those jurists who adhere to the other schools of legal thought.

JUDICIAL INTERPRETATION OF THE LAW

Because of our common law tradition (which will be discussed shortly), the courts—and thus the personal views and philosophies of judges—play a paramount role in the American legal system. This is particularly true of the United States Supreme Court, which has the final say on how a particular law or legal principle should be interpreted and applied. Indeed, Oliver Wendell Holmes, Jr., once stated that law was a set of rules that allowed one to predict how a court would resolve a particular dispute—"the prophecies [predictions] of what the courts will do in fact, and nothing more pretentious, are what I mean by the law."

Clearly, judges are not free to decide cases solely on the basis of their personal philosophical views or their opinions on the issues before the court. A judge's function is not to make the laws—that is the function of the legislative branch of government—but to interpret and apply them. From a practical point of view, however, the courts play a significant role in defining what the law is. This is because laws enacted by legislative bodies tend to be expressed in general terms. Judges thus have some flexibility in interpreting and applying the law. It is because of this flexibility that different courts can, and often do, arrive at different conclusions in cases that involve nearly identical issues, facts, and applicable laws. This flexibility also means that each judge's unique personality, legal philosophy, set of values, and intellectual attributes necessarily frame the judicial decision-making process to some extent.

SECTION 2

The Common Law Tradition

Because of our colonial heritage, much of American law is based on the English legal system, which originated in medieval England and continued to evolve in the following centuries. A knowledge of this system is necessary to an understanding of the American legal system today.

EARLY ENGLISH COURTS

The origins of the English legal system—and thus the U.S. legal system as well—date back to 1066, when the Normans conquered England. William the Conqueror and his successors began the process of unifying the country under their rule. One of the means they used to this end was the establishment of the king's courts, or *curiae regis*. Before the Norman Conquest, disputes had been settled according to the local legal customs and traditions in various regions of the country. The king's courts sought to establish a uniform set of customs for the country as a whole. What evolved in these courts was the beginning of the **common law**—a body of general rules that prescribed social conduct and applied throughout the entire English realm.

Courts of Law and Remedies at Law. In the early English king's courts, the kinds of **remedies** (the legal means to recover a right or redress a wrong) that could be granted were severely restricted. If one person wronged another in some way, the king's courts could award as compensation one or more of the following: (1) land, (2) items of value, or (3) money. The courts that awarded this compensation became known as **courts of law,** and the three remedies were called **remedies at law.** (Today, the remedy at law normally takes the form of money **damages**—money given to a party whose legal interests have been injured.) Even though the system introduced uniformity in the settling of disputes, when a complaining party wanted a remedy other than economic compensation, the courts of law could do nothing, so "no remedy, no right."

Courts of Equity and Remedies in Equity. Equity is a branch of law, founded on what might be described as notions of justice and fair dealing, that seeks to supply a remedy when no adequate remedy at law is available. When individuals could not obtain an adequate remedy in a court of law because of strict technicalities, they petitioned the king for relief. Most of these petitions were decided by an adviser to the king, called a **chancellor,** who was said to be the "keeper of the king's conscience." When the chancellor thought that the claims were fair, new and unique remedies were granted. Eventually, formal chancery courts, or **courts of equity,** were established.

The remedies granted by equity courts became known as **remedies in equity,** or equitable remedies. These remedies include *specific performance* (ordering a party to perform an agreement as promised), an *injunction* (ordering a party to cease engaging in a specific activity or to undo some wrong or injury), and *rescission* (the cancellation of a contractual obligation). We discuss these and other equitable remedies in more detail at appropriate points in the chapters that follow. As a general rule, today's courts, like the early English courts, will not grant equitable remedies unless the remedy at law—money damages—is inadequate.

In fashioning appropriate remedies, judges often were (and continue to be) guided by so-called **equitable maxims**—propositions or general statements of equitable rules. Exhibit 1–1 lists some important equitable maxims. The last maxim listed in that exhibit—"Equity aids the vigilant, not those who rest on their rights"—merits special attention. It has become known as the equitable doctrine of **laches** (a term derived from the Latin *laxus,* meaning "lax" or "negligent"), and it can be used as a defense. A **defense** is an argument raised by the **defendant** (the party being sued) indicating why the **plaintiff** (the suing party) should not obtain the remedy sought. (Note that in equity proceedings, the party bringing a lawsuit is called the **petitioner,** and the party being sued is referred to as the **respondent.**)

The doctrine of laches arose to encourage people to bring lawsuits while the evidence was fresh. What constitutes a reasonable time, of course, varies according to the circumstances of the case. Time periods for different types of cases are now usually fixed by **statutes of limitations.** After the time allowed under a statute of limitations has expired, no action can be brought, no matter how strong the case was originally.

LEGAL AND EQUITABLE REMEDIES TODAY

The establishment of courts of equity in medieval England resulted in two distinct court systems: courts of law and courts of equity. The systems had different sets of judges and granted different types of remedies. Parties who sought legal remedies, or remedies at law, would bring their claims before courts of law. Parties seeking equitable relief, or remedies in equity, would bring their claims before courts of equity. During the nineteenth century, however, most states in the United States adopted rules of procedure that resulted in combined courts of law and equity—although some states, such as Arkansas, still retain the distinction. A party now may request both legal and equitable remedies in the same action, and the trial court judge may grant either or both forms of relief.

The distinction between legal and equitable remedies remains relevant to students of business law, however, because these remedies differ. To seek the proper remedy for a wrong, one must know what remedies are available. Additionally, certain vestiges of the procedures used when there were separate courts of law and equity still exist. For example, a party has the right to demand a jury trial in an action at law, but not in an action in equity. In the old courts of equity, the chancellor heard both sides of an issue and decided what should be done. Juries were considered inappropriate. In actions at law, however, juries

EXHIBIT 1–1 EQUITABLE MAXIMS

1. *Whoever seeks equity must do equity.* (Anyone who wishes to be treated fairly must treat others fairly.)

2. *Where there is equal equity, the law must prevail.* (The law will determine the outcome of a controversy in which the merits of both sides are equal.)

3. *One seeking the aid of an equity court must come to the court with clean hands.* (Plaintiffs must have acted fairly and honestly.)

4. *Equity will not suffer a wrong to be without a remedy.* (Equitable relief will be awarded when there is a right to relief and there is no adequate remedy at law.)

5. *Equity regards substance rather than form.* (Equity is more concerned with fairness and justice than with legal technicalities.)

6. *Equity aids the vigilant, not those who rest on their rights.* (Equity will not help those who neglect their rights for an unreasonable period of time.)

participated in determining the outcome of cases, including the amount of damages to be awarded. Exhibit 1–2 below summarizes the procedural differences (applicable in most states) between an action at law and an action in equity.

THE DOCTRINE OF *STARE DECISIS*

One of the unique features of the common law is that it is *judge-made* law. The body of principles and doctrines that form the common law emerged over time as judges decided actual legal controversies.

Case Precedents and Case Reporters.   When possible, judges attempted to be consistent and to base their decisions on the principles suggested by earlier cases. They sought to decide similar cases in a similar way and considered new cases with care, because they knew that their decisions would make new law. Each interpretation became part of the law on the subject and served as a legal **precedent**—that is, a decision that furnished an example or authority for deciding subsequent cases involving similar legal principles or facts.

By the early fourteenth century, portions of the most important decisions of each year were being gathered together and recorded in *Year Books,* which became useful references for lawyers and judges. In the sixteenth century, the *Year Books* were discontinued, and other forms of case publication became available. Today, cases are published, or "reported," in volumes called **reporters,** or *reports.* We describe today's case reporting system in detail later in this chapter.

Stare Decisis and the Common Law Tradition. The practice of deciding new cases with reference to former decisions, or precedents, became a cornerstone of the English and American judicial systems. The practice forms a doctrine called *stare decisis*[1] (a

---

1. Pronounced *ster*-ay dih-*si-ses.*

Latin phrase meaning "to stand on decided cases"). Under this doctrine, judges are obligated to follow the precedents established within their jurisdictions.

For example, suppose that the lower state courts in California have reached conflicting conclusions on whether drivers are liable for accidents they cause while merging into freeway traffic, even though the drivers looked and did not see any oncoming traffic and even though witnesses (passengers in their cars) testified to that effect. To settle the law on this issue, the California Supreme Court decides to review a case involving this fact pattern. The court rules that in such a situation, the driver who is merging into traffic is liable for any accidents caused by that driver's failure to yield to freeway traffic—regardless of whether that driver looked carefully and did not see an approaching vehicle.

The California Supreme Court's decision on this matter will influence the outcome of all future cases on this issue brought before the California state courts. Similarly, a decision on a given question by the United States Supreme Court (the nation's highest court) is binding on all courts. Case precedents, as well as statutes and other laws that must be followed, are referred to as **binding authorities.** (Nonbinding legal authorities on which judges may rely for guidance, such as precedents established in other jurisdictions, are referred to as *persuasive authorities.*)

The doctrine of *stare decisis* helps the courts to be more efficient, because if other courts have carefully analyzed a similar case, their legal reasoning and opinions can serve as guides. *Stare decisis* also makes the law more stable and predictable. If the law on a given subject is well settled, someone bringing a case to court can usually rely on the court to make a decision based on what the law has been in the past.

Departures from Precedent.   Although courts are obligated to follow precedents, sometimes a court will depart from the rule of precedent if it decides that the precedent should no longer be followed. If a court de-

---

EXHIBIT 1–2   PROCEDURAL DIFFERENCES BETWEEN AN ACTION AT LAW AND AN ACTION IN EQUITY

PROCEDURE	ACTION AT LAW	ACTION IN EQUITY
Initiation of lawsuit	By filing a complaint	By filing a petition
Parties	Plaintiff and defendant	Petitioner and respondent
Decision	By jury or judge	By judge (no jury)
Result	Judgment	Decree
Remedy	Monetary damages	Injunction, specific performance, or rescission

cides that a ruling precedent is simply incorrect or that technological or social changes have rendered the precedent inapplicable, the court might rule contrary to the precedent. Cases that overturn precedent often receive a great deal of publicity.[2]

Note that judges have some flexibility in applying precedents. For example, a trial court may avoid applying a Supreme Court precedent by arguing that the facts of the case before the court are distinguishable from the facts in the Supreme Court case. Therefore, the Supreme Court's ruling on the issue does not apply to the case before the court.

When There Is No Precedent. Occasionally, cases come before the courts for which no precedents exist. Such cases, called *cases of first impression*, often result when new practices or technological developments in society create new types of legal disputes. In the last several years, for example, the courts have had to deal with disputes involving transactions conducted via the Internet. When existing laws governing free speech, pornography, fraud, jurisdiction, and other areas were drafted, cyberspace did not exist. Although new laws are being created to govern such disputes, in the meantime the courts have to decide, on a case-by-case basis, what rules should be applied.

Generally, in deciding cases of first impression, courts may consider a number of factors, including persuasive authorities (such as cases from other jurisdictions, if there are any), legal principles and policies underlying previous court decisions or existing statutes, fairness, social values and customs, **public policy** (governmental policy based on widely held societal values), and data and concepts drawn from the social sciences. Which of these sources is chosen or receives the greatest emphasis depends on the nature of the case being considered and the particular judge or judges hearing the case. As mentioned previously, judges are not free to decide cases on the basis of their own personal views. In cases of first impression, as in all cases, judges must have legal reasons for ruling as they do on particular issues. When

a court issues a written opinion on a case (we discuss court opinions later in this chapter), the opinion normally contains a carefully reasoned argument justifying the decision.

STARE DECISIS AND LEGAL REASONING

Legal reasoning is the reasoning process used by judges in deciding what law applies to a given dispute and then applying that law to the specific facts or circumstances of the case. Through the use of legal reasoning, judges harmonize their decisions with those that have been made before—which the doctrine of *stare decisis* requires.

Students of the legal environment of business also engage in legal reasoning. For example, you may be asked to provide answers for some of the case problems that appear at the end of every chapter in this text. Each problem describes the facts of a particular dispute and the legal question at issue. If you are assigned a case problem, you will be asked to determine how a court would answer that question and why. In other words, you will need to give legal reasons for whatever conclusion you reach.[3] We look here at the basic steps involved in legal reasoning and then describe some forms of reasoning commonly used by the courts in making their decisions.

Basic Steps in Legal Reasoning. At times, the legal arguments set forth in court opinions are relatively simple and brief. At other times, the arguments are complex and lengthy. Regardless of the brevity or length of a legal argument, however, the basic steps of the legal reasoning process remain the same in all cases. These steps, which you also can follow when analyzing cases and case problems, form what is commonly referred to as the *IRAC method* of legal reasoning. IRAC is an acronym comprising the first letters of the following words: Issue, Rule, Application, and Conclusion. To apply the IRAC method, you would ask the following questions:

1. *What are the key facts and issues?* For example, suppose that a plaintiff comes before the court claiming *assault* (a wrongful and intentional action, or tort, in which one person makes another fearful of immediate physical harm). The plaintiff claims that the defendant threatened her while she was sleeping. Although the plaintiff was unaware that she was being

---

2. For example, when the United States Supreme Court held in the 1950s that racial segregation in the public schools was unconstitutional, it expressly overturned a Supreme Court precedent upholding the constitutionality of "separate-but-equal" segregation. The Supreme Court's departure from precedent received a tremendous amount of publicity as people began to realize the ramifications of this change in the law. See *Brown v. Board of Education of Topeka,* 347 U.S. 483, 74 S.Ct. 6896, 98 L.Ed. 873 (1954). (Legal citations are explained in the appendix at the end of this chapter.)

3. See Appendix A for further instructions on how to analyze case problems.

threatened, her roommate heard the defendant make the threat. The legal issue, or question, raised by these facts is whether the defendant's actions constitute the tort of assault, given that the plaintiff was not aware of those actions at the time they occurred.

2. *What rules of law apply to the case?* A rule of law may be a rule stated by the courts in previous decisions, a state or federal statute, or a state or federal administrative agency regulation. In our hypothetical case, the plaintiff **alleges** (claims) that the defendant committed a tort. Therefore, the applicable law is the common law of torts—specifically, tort law governing assault (see Chapter 12 for more detail on torts). Case precedents involving similar facts and issues thus would be relevant. Often, more than one rule of law will be applicable to a case.

3. *How do the rules of law apply to the particular facts and circumstances of this case?* This step is often the most difficult one, because each case presents a unique set of facts, circumstances, and parties. Although there may be similar cases, no two cases are ever identical in all respects. Normally, judges (and lawyers and law students) try to find **cases on point**—previously decided cases that are as similar as possible to the one under consideration. (Because of the difficulty—and importance—of this step in the legal reasoning process, we discuss it in more detail in the next subsection.)

4. *What conclusion should be drawn?* This step normally presents few problems. Usually, the conclusion is evident if the previous three steps have been followed carefully.

Forms of Legal Reasoning. Judges use many types of reasoning when following the third step of the legal reasoning process—applying the law to the facts of a particular case. Three common forms of reasoning are deductive reasoning, linear reasoning, and reasoning by analogy.

Deductive Reasoning. Deductive reasoning is sometimes called syllogistic reasoning because it employs a **syllogism**—a logical relationship involving a major premise, a minor premise, and a conclusion. For example, consider the hypothetical case presented earlier, in which the plaintiff alleged that the defendant committed assault by threatening her while she was sleeping. The judge might point out that "under the common law of torts, an individual must be *aware* of a threat of danger for the threat to constitute civil assault" (major premise); "the plaintiff in this case was unaware of the threat at the time it occurred" (minor premise);

and "therefore, the circumstances do not amount to a civil assault" (conclusion).

Linear Reasoning. A second important form of legal reasoning that is commonly employed might be thought of as "linear" reasoning, because it proceeds from one point to another, with the final point being the conclusion. An analogy will help make this form of reasoning clear. Imagine a knotted rope, with each knot tying together separate pieces of rope to form a tight length. As a whole, the rope represents a linear progression of thought logically connecting various points, with the last point, or knot, representing the conclusion. For example, suppose that a tenant in an apartment building sues the landlord for damages for an injury resulting from an allegedly dimly lit stairway. The court may engage in a reasoning process involving the following "pieces of rope":

1. The landlord, who was on the premises the evening the injury occurred, testifies that none of the other nine tenants who used the stairway that night complained about the lights.
2. The fact that none of the tenants complained is the same as if they had said the lighting was sufficient.
3. That there were no complaints does not prove that the lighting was sufficient but proves that the landlord had no reason to believe that it was not.
4. The landlord's belief was reasonable, because no one complained.
5. Therefore, the landlord acted reasonably and was not negligent in respect to the lighting in the stairway.

On the basis of this reasoning, the court concludes that the tenant is not entitled to compensation on the basis of the stairway's lighting.

Reasoning by Analogy. Another important type of reasoning that judges use in deciding cases is reasoning by *analogy*. To reason by **analogy** is to compare the facts in the case at hand to the facts in other cases and, to the extent that the patterns are similar, to apply the same rule of law to the present case. To the extent that the facts are unique, or "distinguishable," different rules may apply. For example, in case A, it is held that a driver who crosses a highway's center line is negligent. In case B, a driver crosses the line to avoid hitting a child. In determining whether case A's rule applies in case B, a judge would consider what the reasons were for the decision in A and whether B is sufficiently similar for those reasons to apply. If the judge holds that B's driver is not liable, that judge must indicate why case A's rule does not apply to the facts presented in case B.

THERE IS NO ONE "RIGHT" ANSWER

Many persons believe that there is one "right" answer to every legal question. In most situations involving a legal controversy, however, there is no single correct result. Good arguments can often be made to support either side of a legal controversy. Quite often, a case does not present the situation of a "good" person suing a "bad" person. In many cases, both parties have acted in good faith in some measure or have acted in bad faith to some degree.

Additionally, as already mentioned, each judge has his or her own personal beliefs and philosophy, which shape, at least to some extent, the process of legal reasoning. What this means is that the outcome of a particular lawsuit before a court can never be predicted with absolute certainty. In fact, in some cases, even though the weight of the law would seem to favor one party's position, judges, through creative legal reasoning, have found ways to rule in favor of the other party in the interests of preventing injustice.

CONCEPT SUMMARY 1.1

THE COMMON LAW TRADITION

SOURCE	DESCRIPTION
Origins of the Common Law	The American legal system is based on the common law tradition, which originated in medieval England. Following the conquest of England in 1066 by William the Conqueror, king's courts were established throughout England, and the common law was developed in these courts.
Legal and Equitable Remedies	The distinction between remedies at law (money or items of value, such as land) and remedies in equity (including specific performance, injunction, and rescission of a contractual obligation) originated in the early English courts of law and courts of equity, respectively.
Case Precedents and the Doctrine of *Stare Decisis*	In the king's courts, judges attempted to make their decisions consistent with previous decisions, called precedents. This practice gave rise to the doctrine of *stare decisis.* This doctrine, which became a cornerstone of the common law tradition, obligates judges to abide by precedents established in their jurisdictions.
Stare Decisis and Legal Reasoning	Legal reasoning refers to the reasoning process used by judges in applying the law to the facts and issues of specific cases. Legal reasoning involves becoming familiar with the key facts of a case, identifying the relevant legal rules, linking those rules to the facts, and forming a conclusion. In linking the legal rules to the facts of a case, judges may use deductive reasoning, linear reasoning, or reasoning by analogy.

SECTION 3

Sources of American Law

There are numerous sources of American law. *Primary sources of law,* or sources that establish the law, include the following:

1. The U.S. Constitution and the constitutions of the various states.

2. Statutory law—including laws passed by Congress, state legislatures, or local governing bodies.
3. Regulations created by administrative agencies, such as the Food and Drug Administration.
4. Case law and common law doctrines.

We describe each of these important sources of law in the following pages.

Secondary sources of law are books and articles that summarize and clarify the primary sources of law.

Examples are legal encyclopedias, treatises, articles in law reviews, and compilations of law, such as the *Restatements of the Law* (which will be discussed shortly). Courts often refer to secondary sources of law for guidance in interpreting and applying the primary sources of law discussed here.

CONSTITUTIONAL LAW

The federal government and the states have separate written constitutions that set forth the general organization, powers, and limits of their respective governments. **Constitutional law** is the law as expressed in these constitutions.

According to Article VI of the U.S. Constitution, the Constitution is the supreme law of the land. As such, it is the basis of all law in the United States. A law in violation of the Constitution, if challenged, will be declared unconstitutional and will not be enforced, no matter what its source. Because of its importance in the American legal system, we present the complete text of the U.S. Constitution in Appendix B.

The Tenth Amendment to the U.S. Constitution reserves all powers not granted to the federal government to the states. Each state in the union has its own constitution. Unless it conflicts with the U.S. Constitution or a federal law, a state constitution is supreme within the state's borders.

STATUTORY LAW

Laws enacted by legislative bodies at any level of government, such as the statutes passed by Congress or by state legislatures, make up the body of law generally referred to as **statutory law.** When a legislature passes a statute, that statute ultimately is included in the federal code of laws or the relevant state code of laws (these codes are discussed later in this chapter).

Statutory law also includes local **ordinances**— statutes (laws, rules, or orders) passed by municipal or county governing units to govern matters not covered by federal or state law. Ordinances commonly have to do with city or county land use (zoning ordinances), building and safety codes, and other matters affecting the local unit.

A federal statute, of course, applies to all states. A state statute, in contrast, applies only within the state's borders. State laws thus may vary from state to state. No federal statute may violate the U.S. Constitution, and no state statute or local ordinance may violate the U.S. Constitution or the relevant state constitution.

Uniform Laws. The differences among state laws were particularly notable in the 1800s, when conflicting state statutes frequently made trade and commerce among the states very difficult. To counter these problems, in 1892 a group of legal scholars and lawyers formed the National Conference of Commissioners (NCC) on Uniform State Laws to draft **uniform laws,** or model laws, for the states to consider adopting. The NCC still exists today and continues to issue uniform laws.

Each state has the option of adopting or rejecting a uniform law. *Only if a state legislature adopts a uniform law does that law become part of the statutory law of that state.* Note that a state legislature may adopt all or part of a uniform law as it is written, or the legislature may rewrite the law however the legislature wishes. Hence, even when a uniform law is said to have been adopted in many states, those states' laws may not be entirely "uniform."

The earliest uniform law, the Uniform Negotiable Instruments Law, had been completed by 1896 and adopted in every state by the early 1920s (although not all states used exactly the same wording). Over the following decades, other acts were drawn up in a similar manner. In all, over two hundred uniform acts have been issued by the NCC since its inception. The most ambitious uniform act of all, however, was the Uniform Commercial Code.

The Uniform Commercial Code. The Uniform Commercial Code (UCC), which was created through the joint efforts of the NCC and the American Law Institute,[4] was first issued in 1952. The UCC has been adopted in all fifty states,[5] the District of Columbia, and the Virgin Islands. The UCC facilitates commerce among the states by providing a uniform, yet flexible, set of rules governing commercial transactions. The UCC assures businesspersons that their contracts, if validly entered into, normally will be enforced.

As you will read in later chapters, from time to time the NCC revises the articles contained in the UCC

---

4. This institute was formed in the 1920s and consists of practicing attorneys, legal scholars, and judges.
5. Louisiana has not adopted Articles 2 and 2A (covering contracts for the sale and lease of goods), however.

and submits the revised versions to the states for adoption. During the 1990s, for example, four articles were revised (Articles 3, 4, 5, and 9). Additionally, new articles were added (Articles 2A and 4A). Because of its importance in the area of commercial law, we cite the UCC frequently in this text. We also present the UCC in Appendix C.

ADMINISTRATIVE LAW

An important source of American law is **administrative law**—which consists of the rules, orders, and decisions of administrative agencies. An **administrative agency** is a federal, state, or local government agency established to perform a specific function. Administrative law and procedures, which will be examined in detail in Chapter 6, constitute a dominant element in the regulatory environment of business. Rules issued by various administrative agencies now affect virtually every aspect of a business's operation, including the firm's capital structure and financing, its hiring and firing procedures, its relations with employees and unions, and the way it manufactures and markets its products.

At the national level, numerous **executive agencies** exist within the cabinet departments of the executive branch. The Food and Drug Administration, for example, is an agency within the Department of Health and Human Services. Executive agencies are subject to the authority of the president, who has the power to appoint and remove officers of federal agencies. There are also major **independent regulatory agencies** at the federal level, such as the Federal Trade Commission, the Securities and Exchange Commission, and the Federal Communications Commission. The president's power is less pronounced in regard to independent agencies, whose officers serve for fixed terms and cannot be removed without just cause.

There are administrative agencies at the state and local levels as well. Commonly, a state agency (such as a state pollution-control agency) is created as a parallel to a federal agency (such as the Environmental Protection Agency). Just as federal statutes take precedence over conflicting state statutes, so federal agency regulations take precedence over conflicting state regulations.

CASE LAW AND COMMON LAW DOCTRINES

As is evident from the earlier discussion of the common law tradition, another basic source of American law comprises the rules of law announced in court decisions. These rules of law include interpretations of constitutional provisions, of statutes enacted by legislatures, and of regulations created by administrative agencies. Today, this body of law is referred to variously as the common law, judge-made law, or **case law.**

The Relationship between the Common Law and Statutory Law. Common law doctrines and principles govern all areas not covered by statutory or administrative law. In a dispute concerning a particular employment practice, for example, if a statute regulates that practice, the statute will apply rather than the common law doctrine that applied prior to the enactment of the statute.

Even though the body of statutory law has expanded greatly since the beginning of this nation, thus narrowing the applicability of common law doctrines, there is a significant overlap between statutory law and the common law. For example, many statutes essentially codify existing common law rules, and thus the courts, in interpreting the statutes, often rely on the common law as a guide to what the legislators intended.

Additionally, how the courts interpret a particular statute determines how that statute will be applied. If you wanted to learn about the coverage and applicability of a particular statute, for example, you would, of course, need to locate the statute and study it. You would also need to see how the courts in your jurisdiction have interpreted the statute—in other words, what precedents have been established in regard to that statute. Often, the applicability of a newly enacted statute does not become clear until a body of case law develops to clarify how, when, and to whom the statute applies.

Restatements of the Law. The American Law Institute (ALI) has drafted and published compilations of the common law called *Restatements of the Law*, which generally summarize the common law rules followed by most states. There are *Restatements of the Law* in the areas of contracts, torts, agency, trusts, property, restitution, security, judgments, and conflict of laws. The *Restatements*, like other secondary sources of law, do not in themselves have the force of law but are an important source of legal analysis and opinion on which judges often rely in making their decisions.

Many of the *Restatements* are now in their second or third editions. For example, as you will read in Chapter 13, the ALI has recently published the first volume of the third edition of the *Restatement of the*

Law of Torts. We refer to the *Restatements* frequently in subsequent chapters of this text, indicating in parentheses the edition to which we are referring. For example, we refer to the second edition of the *Restatement of the Law of Contracts* simply as the *Restatement (Second) of Contracts.*

CONCEPT SUMMARY 1.2 — SOURCES OF AMERICAN LAW

SOURCE	DESCRIPTION
Constitutional Law	The law as expressed in the U.S. Constitution and the state constitutions. The U.S. Constitution is the supreme law of the land. State constitutions are supreme within state borders to the extent that they do not violate a clause of the U.S. Constitution or a federal law.
Statutory Law	Laws (statutes and ordinances) created by federal, state, and local legislatures and governing bodies. None of these laws may violate the U.S. Constitution or the relevant state constitution. Uniform statutes, when adopted by a state, become statutory law in that state.
Administrative Law	The rules, orders, and decisions of federal or state government administrative agencies.
Case Law and Common Law Doctrines	Judge-made law, including interpretations of constitutional provisions, of statutes enacted by legislatures, and of regulations created by administrative agencies. The common law—the doctrines and principles embodied in case law—governs all areas not covered by statutory or administrative law.

SECTION 4

Classifications of Law

Because the body of law is so large, one must break it down by some means of classification. A number of classification systems have been devised. For example, one classification system divides law into substantive law and procedural law. **Substantive law** consists of all laws that define, describe, regulate, and create legal rights and obligations. **Procedural law** consists of all laws that establish the methods of enforcing the rights established by substantive law.

Another classification system divides law into civil law and criminal law. **Civil law** is concerned with the duties that exist between persons or between citizens and their governments, excluding the duty not to commit crimes. Typically, in a civil case, a private party sues another private party (although the government can also sue a party for a civil law violation) to make that other party comply with a duty or pay for the damage caused by failure to comply with a duty. Much of the law that we discuss in this text is civil law. Contract law, for example, covered in Chapters 9 and 10, is civil law. The whole body of tort law (see Chapters 12 and 13) is civil law.

Criminal law, in contrast, is concerned with wrongs committed *against the public as a whole.* Criminal acts are defined and prohibited by local, state, or federal government statutes and prosecuted by public officials, such as a district attorney (D.A.), on behalf of the state, not by their victims or other private parties. (See Chapter 7 for a further discussion of the distinction between civil law and criminal law.)

Other classification systems divide law into federal law and state law, private law (dealing with relationships between private entities) and public law (addressing the relationship between persons and their governments), national law and international law, and so on.

SECTION 5

Businesspersons and the Law

Those entering into the world of business will find that laws and government regulations affect virtually all business activities—from hiring and firing decisions, to the manufacturing and marketing of products, to financing matters, and so on. To make good business decisions, a basic knowledge of the laws and regulations governing these activities is beneficial—if not essential. The study of the legal environment of business is thus a sound investment for anyone who wishes to succeed in today's business arena.

As you will note, each of the chapters in this text covers a specific area of the law and shows how the legal rules in that area of law affect businesses. While compartmentalizing the law in this fashion promotes conceptual clarity, it does not indicate the extent to which one area of law overlaps with another.

Consider an example. Net Systems, Inc., creates and maintains computer network systems for its clients, including business firms. Net Systems also markets software for customers who need an internal computer network but cannot afford an individually designed intranet. Mark is the president of Net Systems. Janet, an operations officer for Southwest Distribution Corporation (SDC), contacts Mark by e-mail about a possible contract concerning SDC's computer network. In deciding whether to enter into a contract with SDC, Mark needs to consider, among other things, the legal requirements for an enforceable contract. Are there different requirements for a

contract for services and a contract for products? What are the options if SDC **breaches** (breaks, or fails to perform) the contract? The answers to these questions are part of contract law and sales law.

Other questions might concern payment under the contract. How can Net Systems guarantee that it will be paid? If a payment is made with, for example, a check that is returned for insufficient funds, what are Net Systems's options? Answers to these questions can be found in the laws that relate to negotiable instruments (such as checks) and creditors' rights. Also, a dispute may occur over the rights to Net Systems's software, or there may be a question of liability if the software is defective. There may be an issue as to the authority of Mark or Janet to make a deal. A disagreement may arise from such circumstances as an accountant's evaluation of the contract. Resolutions of these questions may be found in areas of the law that relate to intellectual property, e-commerce, torts, product liability, agency, business organizations, or professional liability.

Finally, if any dispute cannot be resolved amicably, then the laws and the rules concerning courts and court procedures spell out the steps of a lawsuit. Exhibit 1–3 illustrates the various areas of law that may influence business decision making.

EXHIBIT 1–3   AREAS OF THE LAW THAT MAY AFFECT BUSINESS DECISION MAKING

TERMS AND CONCEPTS TO REVIEW

administrative agency 11

administrative law 11

allege 8

analogy 8

appellant 26

appellee 26

binding authority 6

breach 13

case law 11

case on point 8

chancellor 5

citation 17

civil law 12

common law 4

constitutional law 10

court of equity 5

court of law 4

criminal law 12

damages 4

defendant 5

defense 5

equitable maxims 5

executive agency 11

historical school 3

independent regulatory
    agency 11

jurisprudence 3

laches 5

law 2

legal realism 4

legal reasoning 7

natural law 3

opinion 26

ordinance 10

petitioner 5

plaintiff 5

positive law 3

positivist school 3

precedent 6

procedural law 12

public policy 7

remedy 4

remedy at law 4

remedy in equity 5

reporter 6

respondent 5

sociological school 4

stare decisis 6

statute of limitations 5

statutory law 10

substantive law 12

syllogism 8

uniform law 10

QUESTIONS AND CASE PROBLEMS

1–1. PHILOSOPHY OF LAW.   After World War II, which ended in 1945, an international tribunal of judges convened at Nuremberg, Germany. The judges convicted several Nazis of "crimes against humanity." Assuming that the Nazi war criminals who were convicted had not disobeyed any law of their country and had merely been following their government's (Hitler's) orders, what law had they violated? Explain.

1–2. STATUTORY VERSUS COMMON LAW.   How does statutory law come into existence? How does it differ from the common law? If statutory law conflicts with the common law, which law will govern?

1–3. READING CITATIONS.   First read the appendix to this chapter. Assume that you want to read the entire court opinion in the case of *Millennium Enterprises, Inc. v. Millennium Music, LP*, 33 F.Supp.2d 907 (D.Or. 1999). The case considers whether a South Carolina business

firm could be sued in Oregon based on the circumstance that its Web site could be accessed in Oregon. Explain specifically where you would find the court's opinion.

1–4. SOURCES OF AMERICAN LAW.   This chapter discussed a number of sources of American law. Which source of law takes priority in the following situations, and why?

(a) A federal statute conflicts with the U.S. Constitution.

(b) A federal statute conflicts with a state constitutional provision.

(c) A state statute conflicts with the common law of that state.

(d) A state constitutional amendment conflicts with the U.S. Constitution.

1–5. STARE DECISIS.   In the text of this chapter, we stated that the doctrine of *stare decisis* "became a cornerstone of the English and American judicial systems." What does *stare decisis* mean, and why has this doctrine been so fundamental to the development of our legal tradition?

1–6. COURT OPINIONS. What is the difference between a concurring opinion and a majority opinion? Between a concurring opinion and a dissenting opinion? Why do judges and justices write concurring and dissenting opinions, given the fact that these opinions will not affect the outcome of the case at hand, which has already been decided by majority vote?

1–7. COMMON LAW VERSUS STATUTORY LAW. Courts can overturn precedents and thus change the common law. Should judges have the same authority to overrule statutory law? Explain.

1–8. *STARE DECISIS.* "The judge's role is not to make the law but to uphold and apply the law." Do you agree or disagree with this statement? Discuss fully the reasons for your answer.

1–9. IN YOUR COURT

Arthur Rabe is suing Xavier Sanchez for breaching a contract in which Sanchez promised to sell Rabe a Van Gogh painting for $150,000. Assume that you are the judge in the trial court hearing the case and answer the following questions:

(a) In this lawsuit, who is the plaintiff and who is the defendant?
(b) Rabe wants Sanchez to perform the contract as promised. If you agree to Rabe's request, what remedy will you grant?
(c) Suppose that Rabe wants to cancel the contract because Sanchez fraudulently misrepresented the painting as an original Van Gogh when in fact it is a copy. If you agree to this request, what remedy will you grant?
(d) Will the remedy Rabe seeks in either situation be a remedy at law or a remedy in equity?
(e) Suppose that you find in Rabe's favor and grant one of these remedies. Sanchez then appeals the decision to a higher court. On appeal, which party will be the appellant (or petitioner), and which party will be the appellee (or respondent)?

LAW ON THE WEB

Today, business law professors and students can go online to access information on virtually every topic covered in this text. A good point of departure for online legal research is the Web site for *West's Legal Environment of Business,* Fourth Edition, at http://wleb.westbuslaw.com. There you will find numerous materials relevant to this text and to the legal environment of business generally, including links to various legal resources on the Web. Additionally, every chapter in this text ends with a *Law on the Web* feature that contains selected Web addresses.

You can access many of the sources of law discussed in Chapter 1 at the FindLaw Web site, which is probably the most comprehensive source of free legal information on the Internet. Go to

http://www.findlaw.com

The Legal Information Institute (LII) at Cornell Law School, which offers extensive information about U.S. law, is also a good starting point for legal research. The URL for this site is

http://www.law.cornell.edu

The Library of Congress offers extensive links to state and federal government resources at

http://www.loc.gov

Villanova University's Center for Information Law and Policy provides access to numerous legal resources, including opinions from the federal appellate courts. Go to http://www.law.vill.edu

The Virtual Law Library Index, created and maintained by the Indiana University School of Law, provides an index of legal sources categorized by subject at

http://www.law.indiana.edu

LEGAL RESEARCH EXERCISES ON THE WEB

The text's Web site also offers online research exercises. These exercises will help you find and analyze specific types of legal information available at specific Web sites. To access these exercises, go to this book's Web site at http://wleb.westbuslaw.com and click on "Internet Applications." When that page opens, select the relevant chapter to find the exercise or exercises relating to topics in that chapter. The following activity will direct you to some of the important sources of law discussed in Chapter 1:

Activity 1–1: Internet Sources of Law

APPENDIX TO CHAPTER 1

Finding and Analyzing the Law

This text includes numerous citations to primary sources of law—federal and state statutes, regulations issued by administrative agencies, and court cases. (A **citation** is a reference to a publication in which a legal authority—such as a statute or a court decision or other source—can be found.) In this appendix, we explain how you can use citations to find primary sources of law.

SECTION 1

Finding Statutory Law

When Congress passes laws, they are collected in a publication titled *United States Statutes at Large*. When state legislatures pass laws, they are collected in similar state publications. Most frequently, however, laws are referred to in their codified form—that is, the form in which they appear in the federal and state codes.

In these codes, laws are compiled by subject. The *United States Code* (U.S.C.) arranges all existing federal laws of a public and permanent nature by subject. Each of the fifty subjects into which the U.S.C. arranges the laws is given a title and a title number. For example, laws relating to commerce and trade are collected in Title 15, "Commerce and Trade." Titles are subdivided by sections. A citation to the U.S.C. includes title and section numbers. Thus, a reference to "15 U.S.C. Section 1" means that the statute can be found in Section 1 of Title 15. ("Section" may also be designated by the symbol §, and "Sections," by §§.) Sometimes a citation includes the abbreviation *et seq.*, as in "15 U.S.C. Sections 1 *et seq.*" The term is an abbreviated form of *et sequitur*, which in Latin means "and the following"; when used in a citation, it refers to sections that concern the same subject as the numbered section and follow it in sequence.

State codes follow the U.S.C. pattern of arranging law by subject. They may be called codes, revisions, compilations, consolidations, general statutes, or statutes, depending on the preferences of the states. In some codes, subjects are designated by number. In others, they are designated by name. For example, "13 Pennsylvania Consolidated Statutes Section 1101" means that the statute can be found in Title 13,

Section 1101, of the Pennsylvania code. "California Commercial Code Section 1101" means the statute can be found under the subject heading "Commercial Code" of the California code in Section 1101. Abbreviations may be used. For example, "13 Pennsylvania Consolidated Statutes Section 1101" may be abbreviated "13 Pa. C.S. §1101," and "California Commercial Code Section 1101" may be abbreviated "Cal. Com. Code §1101."

Commercial publications of these laws and regulations are available and are widely used. For example, West Group publishes the *United States Code Annotated* (U.S.C.A.). The U.S.C.A. contains the complete text of laws included in the U.S.C., plus notes on court decisions that interpret and apply specific sections of the statutes, as well as the text of presidential proclamations and executive orders. The U.S.C.A. also includes research aids, such as cross-references to related statutes, historical notes, and library references. A citation to the U.S.C.A. is similar to a citation to the U.S.C.: "15 U.S.C.A. Section 1."

SECTION 2

Finding Administrative Law

Rules and regulations adopted by federal administrative agencies are initially published in the *Federal Register*, a daily publication of the U.S. government. Later, they are incorporated into the *Code of Federal Regulations* (C.F.R.). Like the U.S.C., the C.F.R. is divided into fifty titles. Rules within each title are assigned section numbers. A full citation to the C.F.R. includes title and section numbers. For example, a reference to "17 C.F.R. Section 230.504" means that the rule can be found in Section 230.504 of Title 17.

SECTION 3

Finding Case Law

To understand how to read citations to court cases, we need first to look briefly at the court system. As will be discussed in Chapter 2, there are two types of courts in the United States, federal courts and state courts. Both the federal and state court systems consist of several levels, or tiers, of courts.

Trial courts, in which evidence is presented and testimony given, are on the bottom tier (which also includes lower courts handling specialized issues). Decisions from a trial court can be appealed to a higher court, commonly an intermediate *court of appeals*, or an *appellate court*. Decisions from these intermediate courts of appeals may be appealed to an even higher court, such as a state supreme court or the United States Supreme Court.

When reading the cases presented in this text, you will note that most of the state court cases are from state appellate courts. This is because most state trial court opinions are not published. Except in New York and a few other states that publish selected opinions of their trial courts, decisions from the state trial courts are merely filed in the office of the clerk of the court, where they are available for public inspection. Many of the federal trial (district) courts do publish their opinions, however, and you will find that several of the cases set forth in this book are from these courts, as well as the federal appellate courts.

STATE COURT DECISIONS

Written decisions of the state appellate, or reviewing, courts are published and distributed in volumes called *Reports*, which are numbered consecutively.

Reporters Containing State Court Decisions. Decisions of the appellate courts of a particular state are found in the reporters of that state. A few states—including those with intermediate appellate courts, such as California, Illinois, and New York—have more than one reporter for opinions given by their courts.

Additionally, state court opinions appear in regional units of the National Reporter System, published by West Group. Most lawyers and libraries have the West reporters because they report cases more quickly, and are distributed more widely, than the state-published reporters. In fact, many states have eliminated their own reporters in favor of West's National Reporter System. The National Reporter System divides the states into the following geographical areas: *Atlantic* (A. or A.2d), *South Eastern* (S.E. or S.E.2d), *South Western* (S.W. or S.W.2d), *North Western* (N.W. or N.W.2d), *North Eastern*

(N.E. or N.E.2d), *Southern* (So. or So.2d), and *Pacific* (P. or P.2d). (The *2d* in the preceding abbreviations refers to *Second Series*. In the near future, the designation *3d*, for *Third Series*, will be used for some of the regional reporters.) The states included in each of these regional divisions are indicated in Exhibit 1A–1, which illustrates West's National Reporter System.

Case Citations. After an appellate decision has been published, it is normally referred to (cited) by the name of the case (called the *style* of the case); the volume, name, and page of the state's official reporter (if different from West's National Reporter System); the volume, unit, and page number of the National Reporter; and the volume, name, and page number of any other selected reporter. (Citing a reporter by volume number, name, and page number, in that order, is common to all citations; often, as in this book, the year the decision was made will be included in parentheses, just following the citations to reporters.) When more than one reporter is cited for the same case, each reference is called a *parallel citation.*[1]

For example, consider the following case citation: *Crews v. Hollenbach*, 126 Md.App. 609, 730 A.2d 742 (1999). We see that the opinion in this case may be found in Volume 126 of the official *Maryland Appellate Reports*, on page 609. The parallel citation is to Volume 730 of the *Atlantic Reporter, Second Series*, page 742. In reprinting appellate opinions in this text, in addition to the reporter, we give the name of the court hearing the case and the year of the court's decision.

Sample citations to state court decisions are explained in Exhibit 1A–2, beginning on page 20.

FEDERAL COURT DECISIONS

Federal district (trial) court decisions are published unofficially in West's *Federal Supplement* (F.Supp. or F.Supp.2d), and opinions from the circuit courts of appeals are reported unofficially in West's *Federal*

---

1. Note that Wisconsin recently adopted a "public domain citation system" in which the format is somewhat different. For example, a Wisconsin Supreme Court decision might be designated "2000 WI 40," meaning that the case was decided in the year 2000 by the Wisconsin Supreme Court and was the fortieth decision issued by that court during that year. (Parallel citations to the *Wisconsin Reports* and West's *North Western Reporter* are still required when citing Wisconsin cases, but they must follow the public domain citation.)

EXHIBIT 1A–1   NATIONAL REPORTER SYSTEM — REGIONAL/FEDERAL

Regional Reporters	Coverage Beginning	Coverage
Atlantic Reporter (A. or A.2d)	1885	Connecticut, Delaware, Maine, Maryland, New Hampshire, New Jersey, Pennsylvania, Rhode Island, Vermont, and District of Columbia.
North Eastern Reporter (N.E. or N.E.2d)	1885	Illinois, Indiana, Massachusetts, New York, and Ohio.
North Western Reporter (N.W. or N.W.2d)	1879	Iowa, Michigan, Minnesota, Nebraska, North Dakota, South Dakota, and Wisconsin.
Pacific Reporter (P. or P.2d)	1883	Alaska, Arizona, California, Colorado, Hawaii, Idaho, Kansas, Montana, Nevada, New Mexico, Oklahoma, Oregon, Utah, Washington, and Wyoming.
South Eastern Reporter (S.E. or S.E.2d)	1887	Georgia, North Carolina, South Carolina, Virginia, and West Virginia.
South Western Reporter (S.W., S.W.2d, or S.W.3d)	1886	Arkansas, Kentucky, Missouri, Tennessee, and Texas.
Southern Reporter (So. or So.2d)	1887	Alabama, Florida, Louisiana, and Mississippi.

Federal Reporters		
Federal Reporter (F., F.2d, or F.3d)	1880	U.S. Circuit Courts from 1880 to 1912; U.S. Commerce Court from 1911 to 1913; U.S. District Courts from 1880 to 1932; U.S. Court of Claims (now called U.S. Court of Federal Claims) from 1929 to 1932 and since 1960; U.S. Courts of Appeals since 1891; U.S. Court of Customs and Patent Appeals since 1929; and U.S. Emergency Court of Appeals since 1943.
Federal Supplement (F.Supp. or F.Supp.2d)	1932	U.S. Court of Claims from 1932 to 1960; U.S. District Courts since 1932; and U.S. Customs Court since 1956.
Federal Rules Decisions (F.R.D.)	1939	U.S. District Courts involving the Federal Rules of Civil Procedure since 1939 and Federal Rules of Criminal Procedure since 1946.
Supreme Court Reporter (S.Ct.)	1882	U.S. Supreme Court since the October term of 1882.
Bankruptcy Reporter (Bankr.)	1980	Bankruptcy decisions of U.S. Bankruptcy Courts, U.S. District Courts, U.S. Courts of Appeals, and U.S. Supreme Court.
Military Justice Reporter (M.J.)	1978	U.S. Court of Military Appeals and Courts of Military Review for the Army, Navy, Air Force, and Coast Guard.

NATIONAL REPORTER SYSTEM MAP

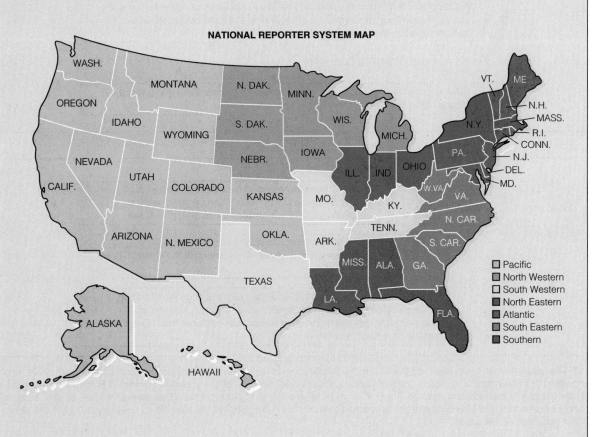

Legend:
- ☐ Pacific
- ☐ North Western
- ☐ South Western
- ■ North Eastern
- ■ Atlantic
- ☐ South Eastern
- ■ Southern

EXHIBIT 1A–2   HOW TO READ CITATIONS

State Courts

256 Neb. 170, 589 N.W.2d 318 (1999)[a]

> *N.W.* is the abbreviation for West s publication of state court decisions rendered in the *North Western Reporter* of the National Reporter System. *2d* indicates that this case was included in the *Second Series* of that reporter. The number 589 refers to the volume number of the reporter; the number 318 refers to the first page in that volume on which this case can be found.

> *Neb.* is an abbreviation for *Nebraska Reports,* Nebraska s official reports of the decisions of its highest court, the Nebraska Supreme Court.

75 Cal.App.4th 500, 89 Cal.Rptr.2d 146 (1999)

> *Cal.Rptr.* is the abbreviation for West s unofficial reports titled *California Reporter* of the decisions of California courts.

85 N.Y.2d 549, 650 N.E.2d 829, 626 N.Y.S.2d 982 (1995)

> *N.Y.S.* is the abbreviation for West s unofficial reports titled *New York Supplement* of the decisions of New York courts.

> *N.Y.* is the abbreviation for *New York Reports,* New York s official reports of the decisions of its court of appeals. The New York Court of Appeals is the state s highest court, analogous to other states supreme courts. In New York, a supreme court is a trial court.

236 Ga.App. 582, 512 S.E.2d 27 (1999)

> *Ga.App.* is the abbreviation for *Georgia Appeals Reports,* Georgia s official reports of the decisions of its court of appeals.

Federal Courts

___ U.S. ___, 119 S.Ct. 1961, 144 L.Ed.2d 319 (1999)

> *L.Ed.* is an abbreviation for *Lawyers' Edition of the Supreme Court Reports,* an unofficial edition of decisions of the United States Supreme Court.

> *S.Ct.* is the abbreviation for West s unofficial reports titled *Supreme Court Reporter* of decisions of the United States Supreme Court.

> *U.S.* is the abbreviation for *United States Reports,* the official edition of the decisions of the United States Supreme Court. Volume and page numbers are not included in this citation because they have not yet been assigned.

---

a. The case names have been deleted from these citations to emphasize the publications. It should be kept in mind, however that the name of a case is as important as the specific numbers of the volumes in which it is found. If a citation is incorrect, the correct citation may be found in a publication s index of case names. The date of a case is also important because, in addition to providing a check on error in citations, the value of a recent case as an authority is likely to be greater than that of an earlier case.

EXHIBIT 1A–2   HOW TO READ CITATIONS (CONTINUED)

Federal Courts (continued)

177 F.3d 114 (2d Cir. 1999)

> *2d Cir.* is an abbreviation denoting that this case was decided in the United States Court of Appeals for the Second Circuit.

38 F.Supp.2d 1233 (D.Colo. 1999)

> *D.Colo.* is an abbreviation indicating that the United States District Court for the District of Colorado decided this case.

English Courts

9 Exch. 341, 156 Eng.Rep. 145 (1854)

> *Eng.Rep.* is an abbreviation for *English Reports, Full Reprint,* a series of reports containing selected decisions made in English courts between 1378 and 1865.

> *Exch.* is an abbreviation for *English Exchequer Reports,* which included the original reports of cases decided in England s Court of Exchequer.

Statutory and Other Citations

18 U.S.C. Section 1961(1)(A)

> *U.S.C.* denotes *United States Code,* the codification of *United States Statutes at Large.* The number 18 refers to the statute s U.S.C. title number and 1961 to its section number within that title. The number 1 refers to a subsection within the section and the letter A to a subdivision within the subsection.

UCC 2—206(1)(b)

> *UCC* is an abbreviation for *Uniform Commercial Code.* The first number 2 is a reference to an article of the UCC and 206 to a section within that article. The number 1 refers to a subsection within the section and the letter b to a subdivision within the subsection.

Restatement (Second) of Contracts, Section 162

> *Restatement (Second) of Contracts* refers to the second edition of the American Law Institute s *Restatement of the Law of Contracts.* The number 162 refers to a specific section.

17 C.F.R. Section 230.505

> *C.F.R.* is an abbreviation for *Code of Federal Regulations,* a compilation of federal administrative regulations. The number 17 designates the regulation s title number, and 230.505 designates to a specific section within that title.

EXHIBIT 1A–2   HOW TO READ CITATIONS (CONTINUED)

Westlaw® Citations[b]

2000 WL 12345

> *WL* is an abbreviation for Westlaw®. The number 2000 is the year of the document that can be found with this citation in the Westlaw® database. The number 12345 is a number assigned to a specific document. A higher number indicates that a document was added to the Westlaw® database later in the year.

Uniform Resource Locators[c]

www.westlaw.com

> The suffix *com* is the top-level domain (TLD) for this Web site. The TLD *com* is an abbreviation for "commercial," which means that a for-profit entity hosts (maintains or supports) this Web site.

> *westlaw* is the host name—the part of the domain name selected by the organization that registered the name. In this case, West Group registered the name. This Internet site is the Westlaw database on the Web.

> *www* is an abbreviation for "World Wide Web." The Web is a system of Internet servers that support documents formatted in *HTML* (hypertext markup language). HTML supports links to text, graphics, and audio and video files.

www.uscourts.gov

> This is "The Federal Judiciary Home Page." The host is the Administrative Office of the U.S. Courts. The TLD *gov* is an abbreviation for "government." This Web site includes information and links from, and about, the federal courts.

www.law.cornell.edu/index.html

> This part of an URL points to a Web page or file at a specific location within the host's domain. This page, at this Web site, is a menu with links to documents within the domain and to other Internet resources.

> This is the host name for a Web site that contains the Internet publications of the Legal Information Institute (LII), which is a part of Cornell Law School. The LII site includes a variety of legal materials and links to other legal resources on the Internet. The TLD *edu* is an abbreviation for "educational institution" (a school or a university).

www.ipl.org.ref/RR

> *RR* is an abbreviation for this Web site's "Ready Reference Collection," which contains links to a variety of Internet resources.

> *ref* is an abbreviation for "Internet Public Library Reference Center," which is a map of the topics into which the links at this Web site have been categorized.

> *ipl* is an abbreviation for Internet Public Library, which is an online service that provides reference resources and links to other information services on the Web. The IPL is supported chiefly by the School of Information at the University of Michigan. The TLD *org* is an abbreviation for "organization (nonprofit)."

---

b. Many court decisions that are not yet published or that are not intended for publication can be accessed through Westlaw®, an online legal database.

c. The basic form for a URL is "service://hostname/path." The Internet service for all of the URLs in this text is *http* (hypertext transfer protocol). Most Web browsers will add this prefix automatically when a user enters a host name or a hostname/path.

Reporter (F., F.2d, or F.3d). Cases concerning federal bankruptcy law are published unofficially in West's *Bankruptcy Reporter* (Bankr.).

The official edition of all decisions of the United States Supreme Court for which there are written opinions is the *United States Reports* (U.S.), which is published by the federal government. The series includes reports of Supreme Court cases dating from the August term of 1791, although many of the Supreme Court's decisions were not reported in the early volumes.

Unofficial editions of Supreme Court cases include West's *Supreme Court Reporter* (S.Ct.), which includes cases dating from the Court's term in October 1882; and the *Lawyers' Edition of the Supreme Court Reports* (L.Ed. or L.Ed.2d), published by the Lawyers Cooperative Publishing Company (now a part of West Group). The latter contains many of the decisions not reported in the early volumes of the *United States Reports*.

Sample citations for federal court decisions are also listed and explained in Exhibit 1A–2.

OLD CASE LAW

On a few occasions, this text cites opinions from old, classic cases dating to the nineteenth century or earlier; some of these are from the English courts. The citations to these cases appear not to conform to the descriptions given above, because the reporters in which they were published were often known by the name of the person who compiled the reporter and have since been replaced.

CASE DIGESTS AND LEGAL ENCYCLOPEDIAS

The body of American case law consists of over five million decisions, to which more than forty thousand decisions are added each year. Because judicial decisions are published in chronological order, finding relevant precedents would be a Herculean task if it were not for secondary sources of law that classify decisions according to subject. Two important "finding tools" that are helpful when researching case law are case digests, such as West's *American Digest System*; and legal encyclopedias, such as *American Jurisprudence, Second Edition*, and *Corpus Juris Secundum*, both published by West Group.

SECTION 4

How to Read and Understand Case Law

The decisions made by the courts establish the boundaries of the law as it applies to business firms and business relationships. It thus is essential that businesspersons know how to read and understand case law. The cases that we present in this text have been condensed from the full text of the courts' opinions—that is, in each case we have summarized the background and facts, as well as the court's decision and remedy, in our own words and have included only selected portions of the court's opinion ("in the language of the court"). For those who wish to review court cases to perform research projects or to gain additional legal information, however, the following sections will provide useful insights into how to read and understand case law.

CASE TITLES

The title of a case, such as *Adams v. Jones*, indicates the names of the parties to the lawsuit. The *v.* in the case title stands for *versus*, which means "against." In the trial court, Adams was the plaintiff—the person who filed the suit. Jones was the defendant. If the case is appealed, however, the appellate court will sometimes place the name of the party appealing the decision first, so that the case may be called *Jones v. Adams* if Jones is appealing. Because some appellate courts retain the trial court order of names, it is often impossible to distinguish the plaintiff from the defendant in the title of a reported appellate court decision. You must carefully read the facts of each case to identify the parties. Otherwise, the discussion by the appellate court will be difficult to understand.

TERMINOLOGY

The following terms, phrases, and abbreviations are frequently encountered in court opinions and legal publications. Because it is important to understand what is meant by these terms, phrases, and abbreviations, we define and discuss them here.

Parties to Lawsuits. As mentioned previously, the party initiating a lawsuit is referred to as the *plaintiff* or *petitioner*, depending on the nature of the action, and the party against whom a lawsuit is brought is the *defendant* or *respondent*. Lawsuits frequently involve more than one plaintiff and/or defendant. When a case is appealed from the original court or jurisdiction to another court or jurisdiction, the party appealing the case is called the **appellant.** The **appellee** is the party against whom the appeal is taken. (In some appellate courts, the party appealing a case is referred to as the petitioner, and the party against whom the suit is brought or appealed is called the respondent.)

Judges and Justices.   The terms *judge* and *justice* are usually synonymous and represent two designations given to judges in various courts. All members of the United States Supreme Court, for example, are referred to as justices, and justice is the formal title usually given to judges of appellate courts, although this is not always the case. In New York, a *justice* is a judge of the trial court (which is called the Supreme Court), and a member of the Court of Appeals (the state's highest court) is called a *judge*. The term *justice* is commonly abbreviated to J., and *justices*, to JJ. A Supreme Court case might refer to Justice Kennedy as Kennedy, J., or to Chief Justice Rehnquist as Rehnquist, C.J.

Decisions and Opinions.   Most decisions reached by reviewing, or appellate, courts are explained in written **opinions.** The opinion contains the court's reasons for its decision, the rules of law that apply, and the judgment.

When all judges or justices unanimously agree on an opinion, the opinion is written for the entire court and can be deemed a *unanimous opinion*. When there is not a unanimous opinion, a *majority opinion* is written; it outlines the views of the majority of the judges or justices deciding the case. If a judge agrees, or concurs, with the majority's decision, but for different reasons, that judge may write a *concurring opinion*. A *dissenting opinion* is written by one or more judges who disagree with the majority's decision. The dissenting opinion is important because it may form the basis of the arguments used years later in overruling the precedential majority opinion.

Occasionally, a court issues a *per curiam* opinion. *Per curiam* is a Latin phrase meaning "of the court." In *per curiam* opinions, there is no indication of which judge or justice authored the opinion. This term may also be used for an announcement of a court's disposition of a case that is not accompanied by a written opinion. Sometimes, the cases presented

in this text are *en banc* decisions. When an appellate court reviews a case *en banc*, which is a French term (derived from a Latin term) for "in the bench," generally all of the judges sitting on the bench of that court review the case.

A SAMPLE COURT CASE

To illustrate the various elements contained in a court opinion, we present in Exhibit 1A–3 an annotated court opinion. The opinion is from an actual case that the U.S. Court of Appeals for the Second Circuit decided in 2000. Federal Express Corporation initiated the lawsuit against Federal Espresso, Inc., and others, claiming in part that the name "Federal Espresso" infringed on the Federal Express trademark. The court denied the plaintiff's request for a *preliminary injunction* (an injunction granted at the beginning of a suit to restrain the defendant from doing some act, the right to which is in dispute). Thus, the issue before the appellate court was whether the trial court erred in refusing to grant the injunction.

You will note that triple asterisks (*   *   *) and quadruple asterisks (*   *   *   *) frequently appear in the opinion. The triple asterisks indicate that we have deleted a few words or sentences from the opinion for the sake of readability or brevity. Quadruple asterisks mean that an entire paragraph (or more) has been omitted. Additionally, when the opinion cites another case or legal source, the citation to the case or other source has been omitted to save space and to improve the flow of the text. These editorial practices are continued in the other court opinions presented in this text.[2] In addition, whenever we present a court opinion that includes a term or phrase that may not be readily understandable, a bracketed definition or paraphrase has been added.

Knowing how to read and understand court opinions and the legal reasoning used by the courts is an essential step in undertaking accurate legal research. Yet a further step is "briefing," or summarizing, the case. Legal researchers routinely brief cases by reducing the texts of the opinions to their essential elements. Instructions on how to brief a case are given in Appendix A, which also includes a briefed version of the sample court case presented in Exhibit 1A–3.

---

2. We make an exception in the *Focus on Legal Reasoning* sections, however, in which we retain the court's citations to facilitate student research.

EXHIBIT 1A–3   A SAMPLE COURT CASE

**FEDERAL EXPRESS CORP. v.
FEDERAL ESPRESSO, INC.**
United States Court of Appeals, Second Circuit, 2000.
201 F.3d 168.

KEARSE, Circuit Judge.

* * * *

I. BACKGROUND

* * * Federal Express, incorporated in 1972, invented the overnight shipping business. It has used the name "Federal Express" since 1973. * * * Federal Express currently has 140,000 employees, ships 2.9 million packages per day, and has annual revenues of more than $11 billion.

Federal Express provides service in at least 210 countries * * *.

* * * *

In March 1994, defendants Anna Dobbs ("Dobbs") and David J. Ruston, her brother, formed a business called New York Espresso in Syracuse, New York, for the wholesale distribution of commercial espresso machines. In April 1994, Dobbs, her husband defendant John Dobbs, and Ruston decided to change the name of the business from New York Espresso to "Federal Espresso." * * *

* * * [I]n November 1995, Dobbs opened a coffee shop, called "Federal Espresso," [in] Syracuse * * *.

* * * *

Defendants opened a second store * * * in August 1997. * * * * * * Federal Express commenced the present action in August 1997. It principally asserted claims of * * * **trademark infringement** * * * and claims of **dilution** of the distinctive quality of its famous mark * * *; and it moved for a preliminary injunction.

* * * [T]he **district court denied the motion** * * *.

* * * *

II. DISCUSSION

* * * [A] party seeking a preliminary injunction must demonstrate (1) the likelihood of **irreparable injury** in the absence of such an injunction, and (2) * * * likelihood of success on the **merits** * * *.

* * * *

* * * The hallmark of [trademark] infringement * * * is **likelihood of confusion.**

Annotations (left margin):

This line gives the name of the judge who authored the opinion of the court.

The court divides the opinion into three parts, headed by roman numerals. The first part of the opinion summarizes the factual background of the case.

The unauthorized use or imitation of another's trademark.

A doctrine that protects a trademark from infringement by another party even when there is no competition or likelihood of confusion, such as when products are dissimilar.

A federal trial court in which a lawsuit is initiated.

The decision of the trial court, from which the appeal was taken.

The second major section of the opinion analyzes the issue before the court.

A wrong of a repeated and continuing nature for which damages are difficult to estimate.

The substance, elements, or grounds of a cause of action.

Likelihood of confusion occurs when a substantial number of ordinarily prudent purchasers are likely to be misled or confused as to the source of a product.

Exhibit 1A–3   A Sample Court Case (Continued)

A **presumption** is an assumption of fact that the law requires to be made from another fact.	* * * [P]roof of a likelihood of confusion would create a **presumption** of irreparable harm, and thus a plaintiff would not need to prove such harm independently. By the same token, however, if the plaintiff does not **show** likelihood of success on the merits, it cannot obtain a preliminary injunction without making an independent showing of likely irreparable harm.
To make apparent or clear, by evidence; to prove.	

As to Federal Express's claims of trademark infringement, we have no difficulty with the district court's ruling that Federal Express did not show likelihood of confusion and hence did not show that it was likely to succeed on the merits of those claims. * * * Accordingly, since Federal Express did not make any independent showing of likelihood of irreparable harm, the trademark infringement claims did not **warrant** the granting of a preliminary injunction.

To justify or call for; to deserve.

* * * *

The type of dilution pertinent to the present case is "blurring," a process that may occur where the defendant uses or modifies the plaintiff's trademark to identify the defendant's goods and services, raising the possibility that the mark will lose its ability to serve as a unique identifier of the plaintiff's product. * * *

* * * *

* * * Here, * * * the principal products—coffee and overnight delivery service—are dissimilar; there would seem to be little likelihood of confusion; and while Federal Express is a vast organization, operating in 210 countries, employing 140,000 persons., and grossing more than $11 billion annually, defendants are three individuals with two stores in Syracuse. * * * The court was entitled to conclude, given these facts and the tiny extent of the overlap among customers of Federal Express and Federal Espresso, that dilution was not **imminent** and that a preliminary injunction was not needed.

Impending; near at hand; on the point of happening.

* * * *

The final section of the opinion, in which the court gives its order.

III. CONCLUSION

* * * The order of the district court denying a preliminary injunction is affirmed.

CHAPTER 2

The Court System

TODAY IN THE UNITED STATES there are fifty-two court systems—one for each of the fifty states, one for the District of Columbia, and a federal system. Keep in mind that the federal courts are not superior to the state courts; they are simply an independent system of courts, which derives its authority from Article III, Section 2, of the U.S. Constitution. By the power given to it under Article I of the U.S. Constitution, Congress has extended the federal court system beyond the boundaries of the United States to U.S. territories such as Guam, the Virgin Islands, and Puerto Rico.[1] As we shall see, the United States Supreme Court is the final controlling voice over all of these fifty-two systems, at least when questions of federal law are involved.

Every businessperson will likely face a lawsuit at some time in his or her career. It is thus important for anyone involved in business to have an understanding of the American court systems, as well as the various methods of dispute resolution that can be pursued outside the courts. In this chapter, after examining the judiciary's general role in the American governmental scheme, we discuss some basic requirements that must be met before a party may bring a lawsuit

before a particular court. We then look at the court systems of the United States in some detail. We conclude the chapter with an overview of some alternative methods of settling disputes.

SECTION 1

The Judiciary's Role in American Government

As you learned in Chapter 1, the body of American law includes the federal and state constitutions, statutes passed by legislative bodies, administrative law, and the case decisions and legal principles that form the common law. These laws would be meaningless, however, without the courts to interpret and apply them. This is the essential role of the judiciary—the courts—in the American governmental system: to interpret the laws and apply them to specific situations.

As the branch of government entrusted with interpreting the laws, the judiciary can decide, among other things, whether the laws or actions of the other two branches are constitutional. The process for making such a determination is known as **judicial review.** The power of judicial review enables the judicial branch to act as a check on the other two branches of

1. In Guam and the Virgin Islands, territorial courts serve as both federal courts and state courts; in Puerto Rico, they serve only as federal courts.

27

government, in line with the checks and balances system established by the U.S. Constitution.[2]

The power of judicial review is not mentioned in the Constitution (although many constitutional scholars conclude that the founders intended the judiciary to have this power). Rather, this power was established by the United States Supreme Court in 1803 by its decision in *Marbury v. Madison*,[3] in which the Supreme Court stated, "It is emphatically the province and duty of the Judicial Department to say what the law is. . . . If two laws conflict with each other, the courts must decide on the operation of each. . . . So if the law be in opposition to the Constitution . . . [t]he Court must determine which of these conflicting rules governs the case. This is the very essence of judicial duty." Since the *Marbury v. Madison* decision, the power of judicial review has remained unchallenged. Today, this power is exercised by both federal and state courts.

SECTION 2

Basic Judicial Requirements

Before a lawsuit can be brought before a court, certain requirements must be met. These requirements relate to jurisdiction, venue, and standing to sue. We examine each of these important concepts here.

JURISDICTION

In Latin, *juris* means "law," and *diction* means "to speak." Thus, "the power to speak the law" is the literal meaning of the term **jurisdiction.** Before any court can hear a case, it must have jurisdiction over the person against whom the suit is brought or jurisdiction over the property involved in a lawsuit. The court must also have jurisdiction over the subject matter. Keep in mind throughout this discussion of jurisdiction that we are talking about jurisdiction over the *defendant* in a lawsuit.

Jurisdiction over Persons. Generally, a particular court can exercise *in personam* jurisdiction (personal jurisdiction) over residents of a certain geographical area. A state trial court, for example, normally has jurisdictional authority over residents of a particular area of the state, such as a county or district. A state's highest court (often called the state supreme court)[4] has jurisdictional authority over all residents within the state.

In some cases, under the authority of a state **long arm statute,** a court can exercise personal jurisdiction over nonresident defendants as well. Before a court can exercise jurisdiction over a nonresident defendant under a long arm statute, though, it must be demonstrated that the defendant had sufficient contacts, or *minimum contacts*, with the state to justify the jurisdiction.[5] For example, if an individual has committed a wrong within the state, such as injuring someone in an automobile accident or selling defective goods, a court can usually exercise jurisdiction even if the person causing the harm is located in another state. Similarly, a state may exercise personal jurisdiction over a nonresident defendant who is sued for breaching a contract that was formed within the state.

In regard to corporations,[6] the minimum-contacts requirement is usually met if the corporation does business within the state, advertises or sells its products within the state, or places its goods into the "stream of commerce" with the intent that the goods be sold in the state. Suppose that a business incorporated under the laws of Maine and headquartered in that state has a branch office or manufacturing plant in Georgia. Does this corporation have sufficient contacts with the state of Georgia to allow a Georgia court to exercise jurisdiction over the corporation? Yes, it does. If the Maine corporation advertises and sells its products in Georgia, or places goods within the stream of commerce with the expectation that the goods will be purchased by Georgia residents, those activities may also suffice to meet the minimum-contacts requirement.

In the following case, the issue was whether phone calls and letters constituted sufficient minimum contacts to give a court jurisdiction over a nonresident defendant.

---

2. In a broad sense, judicial review occurs whenever a court "reviews" a case or legal proceeding—as when an appellate court reviews a lower court's decision. When referring to the judiciary's role in American government, however, the term *judicial review* is used to indicate the power of the judiciary to decide whether the actions of the other two branches of government do or do not violate the Constitution.

3. 5 U.S. (1 Cranch) 137, 2 L.Ed. 60 (1803).

4. As will be discussed shortly, a state's highest court is often referred to as the state supreme court, but there are exceptions. For example, in New York the supreme court is a trial court.

5. The minimum-contacts standard was established in *International Shoe Co. v. State of Washington*, 326 U.S. 310, 66 S.Ct. 154, 90 L.Ed. 95 (1945).

6. In the eyes of the law, corporations are "legal persons"—entities that can sue and be sued. See Chapter 19.

CASE 2.1   Cole v. Mileti

United States
Court of Appeals,
Sixth Circuit, 1998.
133 F.3d 433.
http://www.law.emory.
edu/6circuit/jan98/
index.html[a]

HISTORICAL AND ECONOMIC SETTING   *A movie production company is expensive to operate. Over the two to five years it can take to produce a film, there are many expenses, including maintaining an office and hiring professionals of all kinds. Newcomers to the industry make many of the same mistakes that are the pitfalls of all businesses. For a novice producer or investor, there is the uncertainty of not knowing what you are doing and the danger of being outnegotiated by those who prey on a novice's ignorance. Finally, once a film is made, there is the audience, which may not choose to see it.*

BACKGROUND AND FACTS   *Nick Mileti, a resident of California, co-produced a movie called* Streamers *and organized a corporation, Streamers International Distributors, Inc., to distribute the film. Joseph Cole, a resident of Ohio, bought two hundred shares of Streamers stock. Cole also lent the firm $475,000, which he borrowed from Equitable Bank of Baltimore. The film was unsuccessful. Mileti agreed to repay Cole's loan in a contract arranged through phone calls and correspondence between California and Ohio. When Mileti did not repay the loan, the bank sued Cole, who in turn filed a suit against Mileti in a federal district court in Ohio. The court entered a judgment against Mileti. He appealed to the U.S. Court of Appeals for the Sixth Circuit, arguing in part that the district court's exercise of jurisdiction over him was unfair.[b]*

IN THE LANGUAGE OF THE COURT

MERRITT, Circuit Judge.

*   *   *   *

*   *   * [There is] a three-part test to determine whether specific jurisdiction exists over a nonresident defendant like Mileti. First, the defendant must purposefully avail himself of the privilege of conducting activities within the forum state [the state in which the court sits]; second, the cause of action must arise from the defendant's activities there; and third, the acts of the defendant or consequences caused by the defendant must have a substantial enough connection with the forum state to make its exercise of jurisdiction over the defendant fundamentally fair.

If, as here, a nonresident defendant transacts business by negotiating and executing a contract via telephone calls and letters to an Ohio resident, then the defendant has purposefully availed himself of the forum by creating a continuing obligation in Ohio. Furthermore, if the cause of action is for breach of that contract, as it is here, then the cause of action naturally arises from the defendant's activities in Ohio. Finally, when we find that a defendant like Mileti purposefully availed himself of the forum and that the cause of action arose directly from that contact, we presume the specific assertion of personal jurisdiction was proper.

DECISION AND REMEDY

The U.S. Court of Appeals for the Sixth Circuit held that the district court could exercise personal jurisdiction over Mileti. The appellate court reasoned that a federal district court in Ohio can exercise personal jurisdiction over a resident of California who does business in Ohio via phone calls and letters.

---

a. This page, which is part of the Web site of the Emory University School of Law, lists the published opinions of the U.S. Court of Appeals for the Sixth Circuit for January 1998. Scroll down the list of cases to the *Cole* case. To access the opinion, click on the case name.

b. As will be discussed shortly, federal courts can exercise jurisdiction over disputes between parties living in different states. This is called *diversity-of-citizenship* jurisdiction. When a federal court exercises diversity jurisdiction, the court normally applies the law of the state in which the court sits—in this case, the law of Ohio.

Jurisdiction over Property.   A court can also exercise jurisdiction over property that is located within its boundaries. This kind of jurisdiction is known as *in rem* **jurisdiction,** or "jurisdiction over the thing." For example, suppose a dispute arises over the ownership of a boat in dry dock in Fort Lauderdale, Florida. The boat is owned by an Ohio resident, over whom a Florida court normally cannot exercise personal jurisdiction. The other party to the dispute is a resident of Nebraska. In this situation, a lawsuit concerning the boat could be brought in a Florida state court on the basis of the court's *in rem* jurisdiction.

Jurisdiction over Subject Matter.   Jurisdiction over subject matter is a limitation on the types of cases a court can hear. In both the federal and state court systems, there are courts of *general* (unlimited) *jurisdiction* and courts of *limited jurisdiction.* A court of general jurisdiction can decide cases involving a broad array of issues. An example of a court of general jurisdiction is a state trial court or federal district court. An example of a state court of limited jurisdiction is a probate court. **Probate courts** are state courts that handle only matters relating to the transfer of a person's assets and obligations after that person's death, including issues relating to the custody and guardianship of children. An example of a federal court of limited subject-matter jurisdiction is a bankruptcy court. **Bankruptcy courts** handle only bankruptcy proceedings, which are governed by federal bankruptcy law (discussed in Chapter 16).

A court's jurisdiction over subject matter is usually defined in the statute or constitution creating the court. In both the federal and state court systems, a court's subject-matter jurisdiction can be limited not only by the subject of the lawsuit but also by how much money is in controversy, whether the case is a felony (a more serious type of crime) or a misdemeanor (a less serious type of crime), or whether the proceeding is a trial or an appeal.

Original and Appellate Jurisdiction.   The distinction between courts of original jurisdiction and courts of appellate jurisdiction normally lies in whether the case is being heard for the first time. Courts having original jurisdiction are courts of the first instance, or trial courts—that is, courts in which lawsuits begin, trials take place, and evidence is presented. In the federal court system, the *district courts* are trial courts. In the various state court systems, the trial courts are known by different names, as will be discussed shortly.

The key point here is that normally, any court having original jurisdiction is known as a trial court. Courts having appellate jurisdiction act as reviewing courts, or appellate courts. In general, cases can be brought before appellate courts only on appeal from an order or a judgment of a trial court or other lower court.

Jurisdiction of the Federal Courts.   Because the federal government is a government of limited powers, the jurisdiction of the federal courts is limited. Article III of the U.S. Constitution establishes the boundaries of federal judicial power. Section 2 of Article III states that "[t]he judicial Power shall extend to all Cases, in Law and Equity, arising under this Constitution, the Laws of the United States, and Treaties made, or which shall be made, under their Authority." In effect, this clause means that whenever a plaintiff's cause of action is based—at least in part—on the U.S. Constitution, a treaty, or a federal law, a **federal question** arises, and the case comes under the judicial authority of the federal courts. Any lawsuit involving a federal question can originate in a federal court. People who claim that their constitutional rights have been violated can begin their suits in a federal court.

Federal district courts can also exercise original jurisdiction over cases involving **diversity of citizenship.** This term applies whenever a federal court has jurisdiction over a case that does not involve a question of federal law. The most common type of diversity jurisdiction has two requirements:[7] (1) the plaintiff and defendant must be residents of different states, and (2) the dollar amount in controversy must exceed $75,000. For purposes of diversity jurisdiction, a corporation is a citizen of both the state in which it is incorporated and the state in which its principal place of business is located. A case involving diversity of citizenship can be filed in the appropriate federal district court. If the case starts in a state court, it can sometimes be transferred, or "removed," to a federal court. A large percentage of the cases filed in federal courts each year are based on diversity of citizenship.

Note that in a case based on a federal question, a federal court will apply federal law. In a case based on diversity of citizenship, however, a federal court will

---

7. Diversity jurisdiction also exists in cases between (1) a foreign country and citizens of a state or of different states and (2) citizens of a state and citizens or subjects of a foreign country. These bases for diversity jurisdiction are less commonly used.

apply the relevant state law (which is often the law of the state in which the court sits).

Exclusive versus Concurrent Jurisdiction. When both federal and state courts have the power to hear a case, as is true in suits involving diversity of citizenship, **concurrent jurisdiction** exists. When cases can be tried only in federal courts or only in state courts, **exclusive jurisdiction** exists. Federal courts have exclusive jurisdiction in cases involving federal crimes, bankruptcy, patents, and copyrights; in suits against the United States; and in some areas of admiralty law (law governing transportation on the seas and ocean waters). The states also have exclusive jurisdiction in certain subject matters—for example, divorce and adoption.

CONCEPT SUMMARY 2.1 — JURISDICTION

TYPE OF JURISDICTION	DESCRIPTION
Personal/Property	Exists when a defendant or a defendant's property is located within the territorial boundaries within which a court has the right and power to decide cases. Jurisdiction may be exercised over out-of-state defendants under state long arm statutes.
Subject Matter	Limits the court's jurisdictional authority to particular types of cases. 1. *Limited jurisdiction*—Exists when a court is limited to a specific subject matter, such as probate or divorce. 2. *General jurisdiction*—Exists when a court can hear cases involving a broad array of issues.
Original	Exists with courts that have the authority to hear a case for the first time (trial courts).
Appellate	Exists with courts of appeal and review; generally, appellate courts do not have original jurisdiction.
Federal	Arises in the following situations: 1. When a federal question is involved (when the plaintiff's cause of action is based at least in part on the U.S. Constitution, a treaty, or a federal law). 2. In diversity-of-citizenship cases between citizens of different states when the amount in controversy exceeds $75,000. (Diversity jurisdiction also exists in cases between a foreign country and citizens of a state or of different states and in cases between citizens of a state and citizens or subjects of a foreign country.)
Concurrent	Exists when both federal and state courts have authority to hear the same case.
Exclusive	Exists when only state courts or only federal courts have authority to hear a case.

VENUE

Jurisdiction has to do with whether a court has authority to hear a case involving specific persons, property, or subject matter. **Venue**[8] is concerned with the most appropriate location for a trial. For example, two state courts (or two federal courts) may have the authority to exercise jurisdiction over a case, but it may be more appropriate or convenient to hear the case in one court than in the other.

Basically, the concept of venue reflects the policy that a court trying a suit should be in the geographical neighborhood (usually the county) in which the incident leading to the lawsuit occurred or in which

---

8. Pronounced *ven-yoo*.

the parties involved in the lawsuit reside. Pretrial publicity or other factors, though, may require a change of venue to another community, especially in criminal cases in which the defendant's right to a fair and impartial jury has been impaired.

For example, a change of venue from Oklahoma City to Denver, Colorado, was ordered for the trials of Timothy McVeigh and Terry Nichols after they had been indicted in connection with the 1995 bombing of the federal building in Oklahoma City. As a result of the bombing, more than 160 persons were killed, and hundreds of others were wounded. In view of these circumstances, it was felt that to hold the trial in Oklahoma City could prejudice the rights of the defendants to a fair trial.

STANDING TO SUE

In order to bring a lawsuit before a court, a party must have **standing to sue**, or a sufficient "stake" in a matter to justify seeking relief through the court system. In other words, a party must have a legally protected and tangible interest at stake in the litigation in order to have standing. The party bringing the lawsuit must have suffered a harm or been threatened with a harm by the action about which he or she has complained. In some circumstances, a person can have standing to sue on be-

half of another person. For example, suppose that a child suffers serious injuries as a result of a defectively manufactured toy. Because the child is a minor, a lawsuit can be brought on his or her behalf by another person, such as the child's parent or legal guardian.

Standing to sue also requires that the controversy at issue be a **justiciable[9] controversy**—a controversy that is real and substantial, as opposed to hypothetical or academic. For instance, in the above example, the child's parent could not sue the toy manufacturer merely on the ground that the toy was defective. The issue would become justiciable only if the child had actually been injured due to the defect in the toy as marketed. In other words, the parent normally could not ask the court to determine what damages might be obtained if the child had been injured, because this would be merely a hypothetical question.

Meeting standing requirements is not always easy. In the following case, for example, an environmental organization sued a company for allegedly discharging pollutants into waterways beyond the amount allowed by the Environmental Protection Agency. At issue in the case was whether the organization had standing to sue under federal environmental laws.

---

9. Pronounced jus-*tish*-a-bul.

CASE 2.2	# Friends of the Earth, Inc. v. Crown Central Petroleum Corp.

United States
Court of Appeals,
Fifth Circuit, 1996.
95 F.3d 358.
http://www.ca5.
uscourts.gov/oparchdt.
cfm?Year-1996[a]

BACKGROUND AND FACTS   *Crown Central Petroleum Corporation does business as La Gloria Oil & Gas Company. Under a permit issued by the Environmental Protection Agency (EPA), La Gloria's oil refinery discharges storm-water run-off into Black Fork Creek. Black Fork Creek flows into Prairie Creek, which flows into the Neches River, which flows into Lake Palestine eighteen miles downstream. Friends of the Earth, Inc. (FOE), is a not-for-profit corporation dedicated to the protection of the environment. FOE filed a suit in a federal district court against La Gloria under the Federal Water Pollution Control Act.[b] FOE claimed that La Gloria had violated its EPA permit and that this conduct had directly affected "the health, economic, recreational, aesthetic and environmental interests of FOE's members" who used the lake. La Gloria filed a motion for summary judgment, arguing that FOE lacked standing to bring the suit. The court granted the motion, and FOE appealed.*

IN THE LANGUAGE
OF THE COURT

PATRICK E. HIGGINBOTHAM, Circuit Judge:
                  *   *   *   *

---

a. This is a page within the Web site of the U.S. Courts of the Fifth Judicial Circuit. Click on "1996." When the link opens, click on "September." When that link opens, click on "September 3." From the list of cases that appears, click on the the case name to access the opinion.
b. 33 U.S.C. Sections 1251–1387.

To demonstrate that FOE's members have standing, FOE must show that *   *   * the injury is "fairly traceable" to the defendant's actions *   *   * .
*   *   *   *

*   *   * FOE offered no competent evidence that La Gloria's discharges have made their way to Lake Palestine or would otherwise affect Lake Palestine. *   *   * FOE and its members relied solely on the truism that water flows downstream and inferred therefrom that any injury suffered downstream is "fairly traceable" to unlawful discharges upstream. At some point this common sense observation becomes little more than surmise. At that point certainly the requirements [for standing] are not met.

DECISION AND REMEDY   *The U.S. Court of Appeals for the Fifth Circuit affirmed the lower court's decision. FOE lacked standing to bring a suit against La Gloria.*

SECTION 3   STATE COURT SYSTEMS

The State and Federal Court Systems

As mentioned earlier in this chapter, each state has its own court system. Additionally, there is a system of federal courts. Although no two state court systems are exactly the same, the left-hand side of Exhibit 2–1 illustrates the basic organizational framework characteristic of the court systems in many states. The exhibit also shows how the federal court system is structured. We turn now to an examination of these court systems, beginning with the state courts.

STATE COURT SYSTEMS

Typically a state court system includes several levels, or tiers, of courts. As indicated in Exhibit 2–1, state courts may include (1) trial courts of limited jurisdiction, (2) trial courts of general jurisdiction, (3) intermediate appellate courts, and (4) the state's highest court (often called the state supreme court). Judges in the state court system are usually elected by the voters for specified terms.

Generally, any person who is a party to a lawsuit has the opportunity to plead the case before a trial court and then, if he or she loses, before at least one

EXHIBIT 2–1   THE STATE AND FEDERAL COURT SYSTEMS

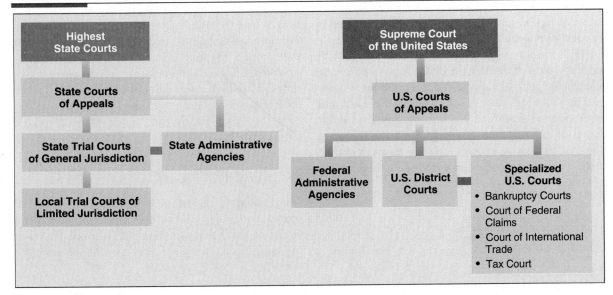

level of appellate court. Finally, if a federal statute or federal constitutional issue is involved in the decision of a state supreme court, that decision may be further appealed to the United States Supreme Court.

Trial Courts. Trial courts are exactly what their name implies—courts in which trials are held and testimony taken. State trial courts have either general or limited jurisdiction. Trial courts that have general jurisdiction as to subject matter may be called county, district, superior, or circuit courts.[10] State trial courts of general jurisdiction have jurisdiction over a wide variety of subjects, including both civil disputes and criminal prosecutions. In some states, trial courts of general jurisdiction may hear appeals from courts of limited jurisdiction.

Courts of limited jurisdiction as to subject matter are often called special inferior trial courts or minor judiciary courts. **Small claims courts** are inferior trial courts that hear only civil cases involving claims of less than a certain amount, such as $2,500 (the amount varies from state to state). Suits brought in small claims courts are generally conducted informally, and lawyers are not required. In a minority of states, lawyers are not even allowed to represent people in small claims courts for most purposes. Decisions of small claims courts may be appealed to a state trial court of general jurisdiction.

Other courts of limited jurisdiction include domestic relations courts, which handle only divorce actions and child custody cases; local municipal courts, which mainly handle traffic cases; and probate courts, as mentioned earlier.

Courts of Appeals. Every state has at least one court of appeals (appellate court, or reviewing court). A court of appeals may be an intermediate appellate court or the state's highest court. About three-fourths of the states have intermediate appellate courts. Generally, courts of appeals do not conduct new trials, in which evidence is submitted to the court and witnesses are examined. Rather, an appellate court panel of three or more judges reviews the record of the case on appeal, which includes a transcript of the trial proceedings, and then determines whether the trial court committed an error.

10. The name in Ohio and Pennsylvania is Court of Common Pleas; the name in New York is Supreme Court, Trial Division.

Appellate courts look at questions of law and procedure. Usually, they do not look at questions of fact. A **question of law** is a question concerning the application or interpretation of the law, on which only a judge, not a jury, can rule. A **question of fact** is a question about what really happened in regard to the dispute being tried. Questions of fact are decided by a trial judge (in a nonjury trial) or by a jury (in a jury trial) based on the evidence presented. Normally, an appellate court will defer to the trial court's judgment on questions of fact because the trial court judge and jury were in a better position to evaluate testimony. They directly observed witnesses' gestures, demeanor, and other nonverbal behavior during the trial. At the appellate level, the judges review the written transcript of the trial, which does not include these nonverbal elements.

An appellate court will tamper with a trial court's finding of fact only when the finding is clearly erroneous (that is, when it is contrary to the evidence presented at trial) or when there is no evidence to support the finding. For example, if at trial a jury concluded that a manufacturer's product had harmed the plaintiff but no evidence was submitted to the court to support that conclusion, the appellate court would hold that the trial court's decision was erroneous. The options exercised by appellate courts will be further discussed later in this chapter.

State Supreme (Highest) Courts. The highest state courts usually are called simply supreme courts, but they may be designated by other names. For example, in both New York and Maryland, the highest state court is called the court of appeals. In Maine and Massachusetts, the highest court is labeled the supreme judicial court. In West Virginia, the highest state court is the supreme court of appeals. The decisions of each state's highest court on all questions of state law are final. Only when issues of federal law are involved can a decision made by a state's highest court be overruled by the United States Supreme Court.

THE FEDERAL COURT SYSTEM

The federal court system is basically a three-tiered model consisting of (1) U.S. district courts (trial courts of general jurisdiction) and various courts of limited jurisdiction, (2) U.S. courts of appeals (intermediate courts of appeals), and (3) the United States Supreme Court.

Unlike state court judges, who are usually elected, federal court judges—including the justices of the Supreme Court—are appointed by the president of the United States, subject to confirmation by the U.S. Senate. Article III of the Constitution states that federal judges "hold their offices during good Behaviour." In effect, this means that federal judges have lifetime appointments. Although they can be impeached (removed from office) for misconduct, this is rarely done. In the entire history of the United States, only seven federal judges have been removed from office through impeachment proceedings.

U.S. District Courts. At the federal level, the equivalent of a state trial court of general jurisdiction is the district court. U.S. district courts have original jurisdiction in federal matters, and federal cases typically originate in district courts. There are other federal courts with original, but special (or limited), jurisdiction, such as the federal bankruptcy courts and others shown earlier in Exhibit 2–1.

There is at least one federal district court in every state. The number of judicial districts can vary over time, primarily owing to population changes and corresponding changes in caseloads. Currently, there are ninety-four federal judicial districts. Exhibit 2–2 on page 36 shows the boundaries of U.S. district courts, as well as the U.S. courts of appeals (discussed next).

U.S. Courts of Appeals. In the federal court system, there are thirteen U.S. courts of appeals—referred to as U.S. circuit courts of appeals. Twelve of the federal courts of appeals (including the Court of Appeals for the D.C. Circuit) hear appeals from the federal district courts located within their respective judicial "circuits," or geographical boundaries (shown in Exhibit 2–2). The court of appeals for the thirteenth circuit, called the Federal Circuit, has national appellate jurisdiction over certain types of cases, such as cases involving patent law and cases in which the U.S. government is a defendant. The decisions of a circuit court of appeals are binding on all courts within the circuit court's jurisdiction and are final in most cases, but appeal to the United States Supreme Court is possible.

United States Supreme Court. At the highest level in the three-tiered federal court system is the United States Supreme Court. According to the language of Article III of the U.S. Constitution, there is only one national Supreme Court. All other courts in the federal system are considered "inferior." Congress is empowered to create other inferior courts as it deems necessary. The inferior courts that Congress has created include the second tier in our model—the U.S. circuit courts of appeals—as well as the district courts and the various federal courts of limited, or specialized, jurisdiction.

The United States Supreme Court consists of nine justices. Although the Supreme Court has original, or trial, jurisdiction in rare instances (set forth in Article III, Section 2), most of its work is as an appeals court. The Supreme Court can review any case decided by any of the federal courts of appeals, and it also has appellate authority over cases involving federal questions that have been decided in the state courts. The Supreme Court is the final arbiter of the Constitution and federal law.

How Cases Reach the Supreme Court. To bring a case before the Supreme Court, a party requests the Court to issue a writ of *certiorari*. A **writ of *certiorari***[11] is an order issued by the Supreme Court to a lower court requiring the latter to send it the record of the case for review. The Court will not issue a writ unless at least four of the nine justices approve of it. This is called the **rule of four.**

Whether the Court will issue a writ of *certiorari* is entirely within its discretion. The Court is not required to issue one, and most petitions for writs are denied. (Thousands of cases are filed with the Supreme Court each year, yet it hears, on average, less than one hundred of these cases.[12]) A denial is not a decision on the merits of a case, nor does it indicate agreement with the lower court's opinion. Furthermore, denial of the writ has no value as a precedent. A denial of the writ simply means that the decision of the lower court remains the law within that court's jurisdiction.

---

11. Pronounced sur-shee-uh-*rah*-ree.

12. From the mid-1950s through the early 1990s, the Supreme Court reviewed more cases per year than it has in the last few years. In the Court's 1982–1983 term, for example, the Court issued written opinions in 151 cases. In contrast, during the Court's 1998–1999 term, the Court issued written opinions in only 75 cases.

EXHIBIT 2–2 U.S. DISTRICT COURTS AND COURTS OF APPEALS

Source: Administrative Office of The United States Courts, January 1983

Typically, the petitions granted by the Court involve cases that raise important constitutional questions or cases that conflict with other state or federal court decisions. For example, if federal appellate courts are rendering conflicting or inconsistent opinions on an important issue, such as how a particular federal statute should be applied to a specific factual situation, the Supreme Court may agree to review a case involving that issue. The Court can then render a definitive opinion on the matter, thus clarifying the law for the lower courts.

CONCEPT SUMMARY 2.2

TYPES OF COURTS

COURT	DESCRIPTION
Trial Courts	Trial courts are courts of original jurisdiction in which actions are initiated. 1. *State courts*—Courts of general jurisdiction can hear any case that has not been specifically designated for another court; courts of limited jurisdiction include domestic relations courts, probate courts, municipal courts, small claims courts, and others. 2. *Federal courts*—The federal district court is the equivalent of the state trial court. Federal courts of limited jurisdiction include the bankruptcy court and others shown in Exhibit 2–1 on page 33.
Intermediate Appellate Courts	Courts of appeals are reviewing courts; generally, appellate courts do not have original jurisdiction. About three-fourths of the states have intermediate appellate courts; in the federal court system, the U.S. circuit courts of appeals are the intermediate appellate courts.
Supreme Court	The highest state court is that state's supreme court, although it may be called by some other name. Appeal from state supreme courts to the United States Supreme Court is possible only if a federal question is involved. The United States Supreme Court is the highest court in the federal court system and the final arbiter of the Constitution and federal law.

SECTION 4

Judicial Procedures: Following a Case through the Courts

American and English courts follow the *adversary system of justice*. Although clients are allowed to represent themselves in court (called *pro se* representation),[13] most parties to lawsuits hire attorneys to represent them. Each lawyer acts as his or her client's advocate, presenting the client's version of the facts in such a way as to convince the judge (or the judge and jury, in a jury trial) that this version is correct.

Most of the judicial procedures that you will read about here are rooted in the adversarial framework of the American legal system. After a brief overview of judicial procedures, we illustrate the steps involved in a lawsuit with a hypothetical civil case.

PROCEDURAL RULES

The parties to a lawsuit must comply with the procedural rules of the court in which the lawsuit is filed. These rules specify what must be done at each stage of the litigation process. All civil trials held in federal

---

13. This right was definitively established in *Faretta v. California*, 422 U.S. 806, 95 S.Ct. 2525, 45 L.Ed.2d 562 (1975).

district courts are governed by the **Federal Rules of Civil Procedure (FRCP)**.[14] Each state also has rules of civil procedure that apply to all courts within that state. In addition, each court has its own local rules of procedure that supplement the federal or state rules.

Broadly speaking, there are three phases of the litigation process: pretrial, trial, and posttrial. Each phase involves specific procedures. Although civil lawsuits may vary greatly in terms of complexity, cost, and detail, they typically progress through the specific stages charted in Exhibit 2–3.

We now turn to our hypothetical civil case. The case arose from an automobile accident, which oc-

curred when a car driven by Antonio Carvello, a resident of New Jersey, collided with a car driven by Jill Kirby, a resident of New York. The accident took place at an intersection in New York City. Kirby suffered personal injuries, incurring medical and hospital expenses as well as lost wages for four months. In all, she calculated that the cost to her of the accident was $100,000.[15] Carvello and Kirby have been unable to agree on a settlement, and Kirby now must decide whether to sue Carvello for the $100,000 compensation she feels she deserves.

---

14. The United States Supreme Court's authority to promulgate these rules is set forth in 28 U.S.C. Sections 2071–2077.

15. We are ignoring in this example damages for pain and suffering or for permanent disabilities. Often in personal injury cases, plaintiffs seek such damages.

EXHIBIT 2–3   STAGES IN A TYPICAL LAWSUIT

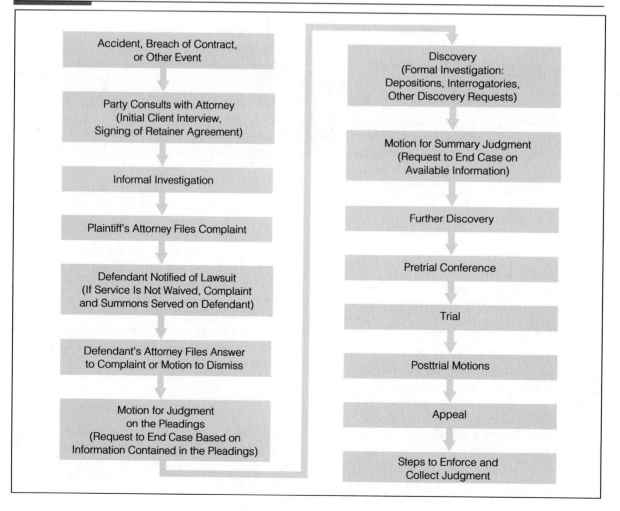

CONSULTING WITH AN ATTORNEY

The first step taken by virtually anyone contemplating a lawsuit is to obtain the advice of a qualified attorney. In the hypothetical Kirby-Carvello case, Kirby may consult with an attorney, who will advise her as to what she can expect to gain from a lawsuit, her probability of success if she sues, what procedures will be involved, and how long it may take to resolve the issue through the judicial process. Depending on the court hearing the case, the time costs of the litigation may be significant. Personal injury cases may take two to three years to resolve, and this is an important factor for Kirby to consider.

Legal Fees.   Another crucial factor that Kirby must consider is, of course, the cost of the attorney's time—the legal fees that she will have to pay to collect damages from the defendant, Carvello. Attorneys base their fees on such factors as the difficulty of a matter, the amount of time involved, the experience and skill of the attorney in the particular area of the law, and the cost of doing business. In the United States, legal fees range from $60 per hour to $450 per hour (the average fee per hour is between $140 and $160). Not included in attorneys' fees are various expenses relating to a case, often called "out-of-pocket" costs, that the attorneys must pay. These costs include court filing fees, travel expenses, the cost of expert witnesses and investigators, and so on.

A particular legal matter may include one type or a combination of several types of fees. *Fixed fees* may be charged for the performance of such services as drafting a simple will. *Hourly fees* may be computed for matters that will involve an indeterminate period of time. Any case brought to trial, for example, may involve an expenditure of time that cannot be precisely estimated in advance. *Contingency fees* are fixed as a percentage (usually between 25 and 40 percent) of a client's recovery in certain types of lawsuits, such as a personal injury lawsuit. If the lawsuit is unsuccessful, the attorney receives no fee. If Kirby retains an attorney on a contingency-fee basis, she normally will not have to pay any fees unless she wins the case. (She will, however, have to pay the court fees and any other expenses incurred by the attorney on her behalf.)

Many state and federal statutes allow for an award of attorneys' fees in certain legal actions, such as probate matters. In these cases, a judge sets the amount of the fee, based on such factors as the results obtained by the attorney and the fee customarily charged for similar services. In some situations, a client may receive an award of attorneys' fees as part of his or her recovery.

Settlement Considerations.   Frequently, the most important factor in determining the extent to which an attorney will pursue a resolution of a legal problem is how much time and money the client wishes to invest in the process. If the client decides that he or she can afford a lengthy trial and one or more appeals, the attorney may pursue those actions. Often, once a client learns the extent of the costs involved in litigating a claim, he or she may decide to settle the claim for a lower amount by using one of the methods of alternative dispute resolution discussed in Chapter 3, such as negotiation or mediation.

Another important factor in deciding whether to pursue litigation is the defendant's ability to pay the damages sought. Even if Kirby is awarded damages, it may be difficult to enforce the court's judgment. (We will discuss the problems involved in enforcing a judgment later in this chapter.)

PRETRIAL PROCEDURES

The pretrial litigation process involves the filing of the *pleadings*, the gathering of evidence (called *discovery*), and possibly other procedures, such as a pretrial conference and jury selection.

The Pleadings.   The *complaint* and *answer* (and other documents discussed below), taken together, are known as the **pleadings.** The pleadings notify each party of the claims of the other and specify the issues (disputed questions) involved in the case. Pleadings remove the element of surprise from a case. They allow lawyers to gather the most persuasive evidence and to prepare better arguments, thus increasing the probability that a just and true result will be forthcoming from the trial. The basic pleadings are the complaint and answer.

The Plaintiff's Complaint.   Kirby's action against Carvello will commence when her lawyer files a **complaint**[16] with the clerk of the trial court in the appropriate geographical area—the proper venue. (Typically, the lawyer or his or her assistant delivers the complaint in person to the trial court clerk. Increasingly, however, courts are experimenting with electronic filing—see this chapter's *Emerging Trends in Technology* for details.)

---

16. Sometimes, the document filed with the court is called a petition or a declaration instead of a complaint.

EMERGING TRENDS IN TECHNOLOGY

Filing Court Documents Electronically

In any litigation, a number of documents must be filed with the court. In complex litigation, this number may spiral into the hundreds or even thousands. Complaints and answers, claims and counterclaims, amendments to the pleadings, pretrial motions, discovery requests—all of these documents and more may have to be filed with the court during the pretrial phase of litigation. During and after the trial, other motions may need to be filed. Additionally, these documents must be made available to the other party or parties involved in the lawsuit. At the same time, today's courts are overloaded with work. Court dockets are packed, and record-keeping facilities are bulging.

ENTER TECHNOLOGY

One of the promises of today's communications technology, and particularly the Internet, is that it will help to reduce the mountains of paperwork typically involved in litigation. A number of courts have taken steps to reduce the burden of paperwork by allowing parties to a lawsuit to file court documents electronically. Filing documents with a court by electronic means may involve transferring the documents over the Internet, such as through an

e-mail system, or delivering them to the court on a computer disk or CD-ROM.

The federal court system first experimented with an electronic filing system in January 1996, in an asbestos case heard by the U.S. District Court for the Northern District of Ohio. In the same year, the Federal Rules of Civil Procedure were amended to change the definition of *filing* so that it permits the filing of papers by electronic means—the decision is left up to the individual federal courts. Currently, more than a dozen federal courts permit attorneys to file documents electronically in certain types of cases. At last count, more than 130,000 documents in approximately 10,000 cases had been filed electronically in federal courts.

State and local courts also are setting up electronic court filing systems. Since late 1997, the Pima County, Arizona, court system has been accepting pleadings via e-mail. In 1998, the supreme court of the state of Washington also began to accept online filings of litigation documents. Electronic filing projects are also being developed in other states, including Kansas, Virginia, Utah, and Michigan. Notably, the judicial branch of the state of Colorado recently decided to implement the first statewide court e-filing system in the United States. When implementation is complete, an Internet-based service will allow all Colorado civil courts to accept legal filings electronically. In California,

Florida, and a few other states, some court clerks offer docket information and other searchable databases online.

THERE ARE STILL HURDLES TO OVERCOME

Although electronic filing provides many benefits, there are numerous hurdles to overcome on the road to this "paperless" future. These hurdles involve both technological and human factors. For one thing, electronic filing typically is permissible only in cases specifically approved by the court and (usually) only if all parties involved in the case agree to the procedure. The parties' agreement to electronic filing is important because if certain hardware or software is required, one party may bear more of a burden than the other.

For example, in one case, an appellant filed a brief (an attorney's written argument supporting his or her client's position in a case) on a CD-ROM using an Internet browser interface. Every citation was in the form of a hyperlink. The brief also contained the entire trial record, including a transcript, and an audio-video appendix with deposition testimony. The federal court of appeals refused to accept the brief because the other party to the lawsuit did not have the equipment to "read" it and access the hypertext links included on the CD-ROM. In its written opinion, the court emphasized that although it did not wish to discourage electronic filing, it did not seem fair

EMERGING TRENDS IN TECHNOLOGY

Filing Court Documents Electronically,

continued

to impose such a burden on the other party.[a]

Software and hardware incompatibilities also pose problems. For example, when a state trial court judge in Mississippi was about to try a lawsuit brought by thousands of plaintiffs against twelve corporate defendants, the judge ordered the parties to file their documents electronically. The parties were to use specially designed software called LawPlus. Problems immediately surfaced. First, LawPlus used a proprietary system that relied on Microsoft Word, while practically all of the law firms involved used WordPerfect. As a result, the attorneys encountered constant problems with document conversion. Second, the system was modem based and very slow. Ultimately, LawPlus was abandoned, and the parties went back to using paper.[b]

---

a. *Yukiyo, Ltd. v. Watanabe,* 111 F.3d 883 (Fed.Cir. 1997).
b. For a discussion of this problem and other technological challenges faced by the judge in this case, see Wendy R. Leibowitz, "Courts in Tech Trenches," *The National Law Journal,* April 19, 1999, p. A25.

No doubt, ways to overcome these technological problems will be found in the coming years. Currently, for example, the Administrative Office of the U.S. Courts is looking for a new electronic database management system that will be set up in most federal courts and provide some uniformity. The system will provide electronic filing and document management capabilities, as well as case management features (details about cases that normally would be in paper files, appointment books, accounting systems, and personal computers).

IMPLICATIONS FOR THE BUSINESSPERSON

1. Clearly, the effects of electronic filing will be felt most directly by the legal profession and by the court systems. Nonetheless, businesspersons who are involved in litigation will benefit indirectly, through lower legal costs, by the time and cost savings resulting from electronic filing systems.
2. Businesspersons may also benefit from having pleadings, discovery documents, motions, supporting briefs, and other litigation materials available in electronic format. In an attempt to safeguard their reputations, a number of companies involved in lawsuits, including Microsoft Corporation, have posted such documents on their Web sites to inform the public of their side of the story.
3. The availability of pleadings and discovery materials on the Web may have a significant impact on businesses that are being sued in

similar cases. For example, in its landmark case against the tobacco industry, Minnesota's Blue Cross and Blue Shield put on the Web more than thirty million pages of documents that the state had collected from the tobacco companies during discovery. Shortly after the documents were posted, plaintiffs in other states— and even in other nations—began to use some of the documents to support their claims against tobacco companies.

FOR CRITICAL ANALYSIS

1. Is there any way to guarantee the security of documents that are filed via e-mail with a court? In other words, how can a court be sure of a document's origin or guarantee that a document hasn't been tampered with—by a computer hacker, for example?
2. Should private vendors be in charge of providing electronic filing systems for the courts, or should the government own and control any such systems to protect the integrity of public information?

RELEVANT WEB SITES

You can find a list of the courts that are experimenting with electronic filing at the following Web site, which is sponsored by Maryland Judge Arthur Ahalt: **http://www. mdlaw.net/efile.htm**. For an example of a hyperlinked court opinion, see the decision in *C.L.I.C. Electronics International, Inc. v. Casio, Inc.,* 975 F.Supp. 1343 (M.D.Fla 1997), at **http:// www.fedjudge.org/96-929.htm**.

In most states, the court would be one having general jurisdiction; in others, it might be a court having special jurisdiction with regard to subject matter. The complaint will contain (1) a statement alleging (asserting) the facts necessary for the court to take jurisdiction, (2) a short statement of the facts necessary to show that the plaintiff is entitled to a remedy, and (3) a statement of the remedy the plaintiff is seeking. A typical complaint is shown in Exhibit 2–4.

The complaint will state that Kirby was driving her car through a green light at the specified intersection, exercising good driving habits and reasonable care, when Carvello negligently drove his vehicle through a red light and into the intersection from a cross street, striking Kirby and causing serious personal injury and property damage. The complaint will go on to state that Kirby is seeking $100,000 in damages. (Note that in some state civil actions, the amount of damages sought is not specified.)

Service of Process. Before the court can exercise jurisdiction over the defendant (Carvello)—in effect, before the lawsuit can begin—the court must have proof that the defendant was notified of the lawsuit. The process of notifying the defendant of a lawsuit is called **service of process.** Service of process involves serving the defendant with a summons and a copy of the complaint—that is, delivering these items to the defendant. The **summons** notifies defendant Carvello that he is required to prepare an answer to the complaint and to file a copy of his answer with both the court and the plaintiff's attorney within a specified time period (twenty days in the federal courts).

The summons also informs Carvello that if he fails to answer or respond to the plaintiff's complaint within the required time period (unless he can provide a convincing reason to the court why he could not do so), the result will be a default judgment for the plaintiff. A **default judgment** in Kirby's favor would mean that she would be awarded the damages alleged in her complaint. A typical summons is shown in Exhibit 2–5 on page 44.

How service of process occurs depends on the rules of the court or jurisdiction in which the lawsuit is brought. Under the Federal Rules of Civil Procedure (FRCP), service of process in federal court cases may be effected by anyone who is not a party to the lawsuit and who is at least eighteen years of age. In state courts, the process server is often a county sheriff or deputy. Usually, the server effects the service by handing the summons to the defendant personally or by leaving it at the defendant's residence or place of business. In a few states, a summons can be served by mail if the defendant so agrees. When the defendant cannot be reached, special rules sometimes permit serving the summons by leaving it with a designated person, such as the secretary of state.

Serving Corporate Defendants. In cases involving corporate defendants, the summons and complaint may be served on an officer or *registered agent* (representative) of the corporation. The name of a corporation's registered agent can usually be obtained from the secretary of state's office in the state in which the company incorporated its business (and, usually, from the secretary of state's office in any state in which the corporation does business).

Waiver of Formal Service of Process. The FRCP allow formal service of process to be waived by defendants in federal cases, providing that certain procedures are followed. Kirby's attorney, for example, could mail to defendant Carvello a copy of the complaint, along with "Waiver of Service of Summons" forms for Carvello to sign. If Carvello signs and returns the forms within thirty days, formal service of process is waived. To encourage defendants to waive formal service of process, the FRCP provide that defendants who sign and return the waiver are not required to respond to the complaint for sixty days after the date on which the request for waiver of service was sent, instead of the twenty days allowed if formal service of process is undertaken.

The Defendant's Response. The defendant's response to the plaintiff's complaint may take the form of an **answer,** in which the defendant either admits the statements or allegations set out in the complaint or denies them and sets out any defenses that the defendant may have. If Carvello admits to all of Kirby's allegations in his answer, a judgment will be entered for Kirby. If Carvello denies Kirby's allegations, the matter will proceed further.

Carvello can also admit the truth of Kirby's complaint but raise new facts to show that he should not be held liable for Kirby's damages. This is called raising an **affirmative defense.** As will be discussed in subsequent chapters, there are affirmative defenses that can be raised by defendants

EXHIBIT 2–4   A TYPICAL COMPLAINT

```
            IN THE UNITED STATES DISTRICT COURT
        FOR THE  Southern  DISTRICT OF  New York

                                    CIVIL NO. 2-1047

        Jill Kirby
_____
                Plaintiff
    vs.                             COMPLAINT
      Antonio Carvello
_____
                Defendant.
```

The plaintiff brings this cause of action against the defendant, alleging as follows:

1. This action is between the plaintiff, who is a resident of the State of New York, and the defendant, who is a resident of the State of New Jersey. There is diversity of citizenship between the parties.

2. The amount in controversy, exclusive of interest and costs, exceeds the sum of $75,000.

3. On September 10th, 2001, the plaintiff, Jill Kirby, was exercising good driving habits and reasonable care in driving her car through the intersection of Boardwalk and Pennsylvania Avenue, New York City, New York, when the defendant, Antonio Carvello, negligently drove his vehicle through a red light at the intersection and collided with the plaintiff's vehicle.

4. As a result of the collision, the plaintiff suffered severe physical injury, which prevented her from working, and property damage to her car.

WHEREFORE, the plaintiff demands judgment against the defendant for the sum of $100,000 plus interest at the maximum legal rate and the costs of this action.

By _____*Joseph Roe*_____

Joseph Roe
Attorney for Plaintiff
100 Main Street
New York, New York

1/2/02

EXHIBIT 2–5   A TYPICAL SUMMONS

SUMMONS IN A CIVIL ACTION

United States District Court

FOR THE Southern **DISTRICT OF:** New York

CIVIL ACTION FILE NO. 2-1047

Jill Kirby

Plaintiff

v.

Antonio Carvello

Defendant

SUMMONS

To the above named Defendant:

You are hereby summoned and required to serve upon

Joseph Roe

100 Main Street

New York, New York

plaintiff's attorney, whose address is

an answer to the complaint which is herewith served upon you, within 20 days after service of this summons upon you, exclusive of the day of service. If you fail to do so, judgment by default will be taken against you for the relief demanded in the complaint.

Samuel Raeburn

Clerk of Court

Mary Doakes

Deputy Clerk.

Date: 1/10/02

[Seal of Court]

NOTE:—This summons is issued pursuant to Rule 4 of the Federal Rules of Civil Procedure.

in both civil and criminal cases. For example, a defendant accused of physically harming another might claim that he or she acted in self-defense. A defendant charged with breach of contract might defend on the ground (legal basis) of mistake or the fact that the contract was oral when it was required by law to be in writing. In the Kirby-Carvello case, assume that Carvello has obtained evidence that Kirby was not exercising good driving habits at the time the accident occurred (she was looking at a child in the back of her car instead of watching the road). Carvello could assert Kirby's own negligence as a defense. In some states, a plaintiff's contributory negligence operates as a complete defense. In most states, however, the plaintiff's own negligence constitutes only a partial defense (see Chapter 12).

Carvello could also deny Kirby's allegations and set forth his own claim that the accident occurred as a result of Kirby's negligence, and therefore Kirby owes Carvello money for damages to his car. This is appropriately called a **counterclaim.** If Carvello files a counterclaim, Kirby will have to submit an answer to the counterclaim.

Dismissals and Judgments before Trial.   Many actions for which pleadings have been filed never come to trial. The parties may, for example, negotiate a settlement of the dispute at any stage of the litigation process. There are also numerous procedural avenues for disposing of a case without a trial. Many of them involve one or the other party's attempts to get the case dismissed through the use of various motions.

A **motion** is a procedural request submitted to the court by an attorney on behalf of his or her client. When one party files a motion with the court, that party must also send to, or serve on, the opposing party a *notice of motion.* The notice of motion informs the opposing party that the motion has been filed. **Pretrial motions** include the motion to dismiss, the motion for judgment on the pleadings, and the motion for summary judgment.

Motion to Dismiss.   If the defendant challenges the sufficiency of the plaintiff's complaint, the defendant can present to the court a **motion to dismiss** for failure to state a claim for which relief (a remedy) can be granted, or a *demurrer.* (The rules of civil procedure in many states do not use the term *demurrer;* they use only *motion to dismiss.*) The motion to dismiss for failure to state a claim for which relief can be granted is

an allegation that even if the facts presented in the complaint are true, their legal consequences are such that there is no reason to go further with the suit and no need for the defendant to present an answer. If, for example, Kirby's complaint had alleged facts that excluded the possibility of negligence on Carvello's part, Carvello could move to dismiss the case.

Defendant Carvello could also file a motion to dismiss if he believed that he had not been properly served, that the complaint had been filed in the wrong court (for example, that the court lacked personal or subject-matter jurisdiction or the venue was improper), or for other specific reasons.

A motion to dismiss may be—and often is—filed with the court by a defendant instead of an answer. If the court denies the motion, the defendant generally is given an extension of time to file an answer (or further pleading). If the defendant fails to file the appropriate pleading, a judgment will normally be entered for the plaintiff. If the court grants the motion to dismiss, the defendant is not required to answer the complaint. The plaintiff generally is given time to file an amended complaint. If the plaintiff does not file this amended complaint, a judgment will be entered against the plaintiff solely on the basis of the pleadings, and the plaintiff will not be allowed to bring suit on the matter again.

If Kirby wishes to discontinue the suit because, for example, an out-of-court settlement has been reached, she can likewise move for dismissal. The court can also dismiss a case on its own motion.

Motion for Judgment on the Pleadings.   After the pleadings are closed—after the complaint, answer, and any other pleadings have been filed—either of the parties can file a **motion for judgment on the pleadings.** This motion may be filed when it appears from the pleadings that the plaintiff has failed to state a cause of action for which relief may be granted. The motion may also be filed when the pleadings indicate that no facts are in dispute and the only question is how the law applies to a set of agreed-on facts. For example, assume for a moment that in the Kirby-Carvello case, defendant Carvello admitted to all of Kirby's allegations in his answer and raised no affirmative defenses. In this situation, Kirby would file a motion for judgment on the pleadings in her favor.

The difference between this motion and a motion for summary judgment, discussed next, is that the party requesting the motion may support a motion for summary judgment with sworn statements and other materials that will be admissible as evidence at trial; on a motion for a judgment on the pleadings, however, a court may consider only what is contained in the pleadings.

Motion for Summary Judgment. The **motion for summary judgment** is similar to a motion for judgment on the pleadings in that the party filing the motion is asking the court to grant a judgment in its favor without a trial. As with a motion for judgment on the pleadings, a court will grant a motion for summary judgment only if it determines that no facts are in dispute and the only question is how the law applies to the facts.

To support a motion for summary judgment, one party can submit, prior to trial, sworn evidence obtained at any point prior to trial (including during the discovery stage of litigation—to be discussed shortly) that refutes the other party's factual claim. The evidence may consist of **affidavits** (sworn statements by parties or witnesses), as well as documents, such as a contract. The evidence must be *admissible* evidence—that is, evidence that the court would allow to be presented during the trial. Hearsay, for example,

normally would not be admissible. As mentioned, the use of this additional evidence is one of the features that distinguishes the motion for summary judgment from the motion to dismiss and the motion for judgment on the pleadings.

In the Kirby-Carvello accident, whether or not the light was red is a question of fact. Assume that during discovery, Carvello obtained undisputable evidence that the stoplight was not working when he drove through the intersection. Assume further that Carvello has evidence (a witness's testimony) that he was not exceeding the legal speed limit. Carvello could file a motion for summary judgment on the ground that there was no evidence in the record to support Kirby's claim. The court might grant Carvello's motion, because there would be no genuine factual dispute and Carvello would be entitled to judgment as a matter of law.

A motion for summary judgment can be made before or during a trial, but it will be granted only if, when the evidence is viewed in the light most favorable to the other party, it is clear that there are no factual disputes in contention. The following case illustrates this point.

CASE 2.3   Ausley v. Bishop

Court of Appeals of
North Carolina, 1999.
515 S.E.2d 72.
http://www.aoc.state.
nc.us/www/public/html/
opinions.html [a]

BACKGROUND AND FACTS   *In November 1994, Andrew Ausley, a state-certified real estate appraiser, hired Bryan Bishop, who wanted to become a certified appraiser, as an apprentice (a requirement for certification). Between November 1994 and April 1997, Bishop prepared and signed appraisal reports, as required by the North Carolina Appraisal Board. For each report, Bishop also prepared a log sheet. The board required that a supervising appraiser sign the log sheets. Ausley told Bishop to let his log sheets accumulate and he (Ausley) would sign them later. By April 1997, Bishop was qualified to receive an appraiser's license, subject only to Ausley signing the log sheets. Ausley said that before he'd sign them, he wanted Bishop to sign a new employment contract. Bishop agreed. Ausley signed the log sheets, and the state issued Bishop his license. That summer, to buy a house, Bishop applied for a mortgage with Robert Phillips of Southern Fidelity Mortgage, with whom Bishop also hoped to do business as an appraiser. In September, Ausley proposed renegotiating his contract with Bishop under terms that included reduced pay. Bishop refused and, a couple of days later, opened his own appraisal office. Ausley then told Phillips that Bishop had submitted false information to obtain his mortgage. Ausley also told others with whom Bishop had done, or hoped to do, business that Bishop had engaged in unethical behavior. After Bishop was seen leaving his old office at Ausley's place of business with a box, Ausley reported to the police that Bishop had stolen files. Ausley mentioned the police report to a person at*

---

a. This is a page within the official Web site of the North Carolina judicial branch. In the "Court of Appeals" column, click on "Reported Decisions© 1999." On that page, scroll down to "18 May 1999" and click on the case name to access the opinion.

Piedmont Home Equity, another of Bishop's potential clients. Finally, Ausley filed a suit in a North Carolina state court against Bishop, alleging, among other things, that Bishop breached (failed to perform) their contract. Bishop filed an answer that included a counterclaim charging Ausley with slander (wrongfully injuring Bishop's good reputation with false statements—see Chapter 12). Ausley filed a motion for summary judgment, which the court granted. Bishop appealed.

IN THE LANGUAGE OF THE COURT

EDMUNDS, Judge.

* * * *

A trial court's grant of summary judgment is fully reviewable by this Court. The standard of review for whether summary judgment is proper is whether the trial court properly concluded that there was no genuine issue of material fact and that the moving party [Ausley, in this case] was entitled to judgment as a matter of law. The record is to be viewed in the light most favorable to the non-movant [Bishop, in this case], giving it the benefit of all inferences reasonably arising therefrom. * * *

* * * *

* * * Defendant [Bishop] alleged in his counterclaim that plaintiff [Ausley] committed slander by communicating to defendant's personal mortgage lender statements to the effect that defendant had committed loan fraud. * * *

* * * Plaintiff admitted in his deposition that he made statements that impeached [discredited] defendant in his trade. During a line of questions pertaining to a form signed by plaintiff and submitted by defendant to mortgage broker Southern Fidelity to finance defendant's own home, plaintiff was asked, "Did you suggest, infer, or imply to Robert [Phillips] at Southern Fidelity that your signature was procured by fraud or some other unlawful means on that appraisal report?" Plaintiff responded, "Correct." * * * [Plaintiff] also admitted telling the same Robert Phillips at Southern Fidelity that "Mr. Bishop had not been truthful about his income in qualifying for the loan that Southern Fidelity brokered, arranged or gave to the Bishops," when there was evidence that plaintiff previously had verified defendant's income to Southern Fidelity. Additionally, defendant stated in his affidavit that "[plaintiff] contacted several of my clients and potential clients and advised them, untruthfully, that I had engaged in various unethical conduct." Because defendant was launching his own business as an appraiser, plaintiff's incorrect statements to defendant's clients and potential clients undoubtedly had the capacity to harm defendant in his trade or profession.

In a second episode, plaintiff admitted reporting to police that defendant had stolen client files. The evidence to support plaintiff's report was that defendant was seen leaving his old office at plaintiff's business with a box, and that later * * * files containing defendant's resumes and sample appraisal files were * * * missing from a file cabinet. Although the investigation subsequently was dropped without any charges being brought, plaintiff admitted communicating to at least one person at Piedmont Home Equity that he suspected defendant had taken files, and had called the police. Again, this statement to a potential client of defendant was capable of harming him in his trade or profession. We therefore conclude that defendant has forecast sufficient evidence of all essential elements of his claim to make a *prima facie* case[b] at trial to survive plaintiff's motion for summary judgment. We reverse as to this issue and remand for further proceedings.

DECISION AND REMEDY

The Court of Appeals of North Carolina held that Bishop had enough proof of his claim for it to go to trial. The court reversed the lower court's grant of summary judgment on this issue and remanded the case (sent it back to the trial court) for trial.

---

b. A *prima facie* case is one in which a party shows sufficient evidence of his or her claim to go to trial. The evidence should be enough to compel a conclusion in the charging party's favor unless the other party has evidence to disprove the claim.

Discovery.   Before a trial begins, the parties can use a number of procedural devices to obtain information and gather evidence about the case. Kirby, for example, will want to know how fast Carvello was driving, whether he had been drinking or was under the influence of any medication, whether he was wearing corrective lenses if he was required by law to do so while driving, and so on. The process of obtaining information from the opposing party or from witnesses prior to trial is known as **discovery.**

The Federal Rules of Civil Procedure and similar rules in the states set forth the guidelines for discovery activity. Discovery includes gaining access to witnesses, documents, records, and other types of evidence. The rules governing discovery are designed to make sure that a witness or a party is not unduly harassed, that privileged material is safeguarded, and that only information relevant to the case at hand—or likely to lead to the discovery of relevant information—is discoverable.

Of course, there are limits as to what a party can obtain as part of the discovery process. For example, a business firm in litigation with a competitor normally will not be given unrestricted access to the competitor's trade secrets, customer lists, and other confidential records. A court may order that only the firm's attorneys and certain experts can view such sensitive information.

Discovery prevents surprises by giving both parties access to evidence that might otherwise be hidden. This allows the litigants to learn as much as they can about what to expect at a trial before they reach the courtroom. Discovery also serves to narrow the issues so that trial time is spent on the main questions in the case. Currently, the trend is toward allowing more discovery and thus fewer surprises.[17]

Depositions and Interrogatories.   At a minimum, discovery involves the use of depositions, interrogatories, or both. A **deposition** is sworn testimony by a party to the lawsuit or by any witness, recorded by an authorized court official. The person deposed gives testimony and answers questions asked by the attorneys from both sides. The questions and answers are recorded, sworn to, and signed. These answers, of course, will help the attorneys prepare their cases.

Depositions also give attorneys the opportunity to evaluate how their witnesses will conduct themselves at trial. In addition, depositions can be employed in court to impeach (challenge the credibility of) a party or a witness who changes testimony at the trial. A deposition can also be used as testimony if the witness is not available at trial.

Interrogatories are written questions for which written answers are prepared and then signed under oath. Interrogatories are addressed only to parties directly involved in a lawsuit (plaintiffs or defendants), not to witnesses, and the parties can prepare their answers with the aid of attorneys. Whereas depositions are useful for eliciting candid responses from a party and answers not prepared in advance, interrogatories are designed to obtain accurate information about specific topics, such as how many contracts were signed, the specific dates on which certain contracts were signed, and so on.

Requests for Admissions.   One party can serve a written request to the other party for an admission of the truth of matters relating to the trial. Any fact admitted under such a request is conclusively established as true for the trial. For example, Kirby can ask Carvello to admit that his driver's license was suspended at the time of the accident. A request for admission shortens the trial, because the parties will not have to spend time proving facts on which they already agree.

Requests for Documents, Objects, and Entry upon Land.   A party can gain access to documents and other items not in his or her possession in order to inspect and examine them. Likewise, a party can gain "entry upon land" to inspect the premises. Carvello, for example, can gain permission to inspect and copy Kirby's repair bills.

Request for Examinations.   When the physical or mental condition of one party is in question, the opposing party can ask the court to order a physical or mental examination by an independent examiner. If the court is willing to make the order, the opposing party can obtain the results of the examination. Note that the court will make such an order only when the need for the information outweighs the right to privacy of the person to be examined.

Pretrial Conference.   After discovery has taken place and before the trial begins, the attorneys may meet with the trial judge in a **pretrial conference.**

---

17. This is particularly evident in the 1993 revision of the Federal Rules of Civil Procedure. The revised rules provide that each party must disclose to the other, on an ongoing basis, the types of evidence that will be presented at trial, the names of witnesses that may or will be called, and other relevant information.

The purpose of this conference is to clarify the issues that remain in dispute after discovery has taken place and to explore the possibility of settling the conflict without a trial. If a settlement is not possible at this time, the parties and the judge discuss the manner in which the trial will be conducted. In particular, the parties may attempt to establish ground rules to restrict such things as the number of expert witnesses or the admissibility of certain types of evidence. Once the pretrial conference concludes, both parties will have to turn their attention to the trial itself and, if the trial is to be a jury trial, to the selection of jurors who will hear the case.

The Right to a Jury Trial. The Seventh Amendment to the U.S. Constitution guarantees the right to a jury trial for cases at law in federal courts when the amount in controversy exceeds $20. Most states have similar guarantees in their own constitutions, although many states restrict the guarantee to a higher minimum amount. For example, Iowa requires the dollar amount of damages to be at least $1,000 before there is a right to a jury trial. The right to a trial by jury does not have to be exercised, and many cases are tried without a jury. If there is no jury, the judge determines the truth of the facts alleged in the case. In most states and in federal courts, one of the parties must request a jury, or the right is presumed to be waived.

Jury Selection. Prior to the commencement of any jury trial, a panel of jurors must be assembled. The clerk of the court will usually notify local residents by mail that they have been selected for jury duty. The process of selecting the names of these prospective jurors varies, but often they are randomly chosen by the court clerk from lists of registered voters or those within the state to whom driver's licenses have been issued. These persons then report to the courthouse on the date specified in the notice. There they are gathered into a single pool of jurors, and the process of selecting those jurors who will actually hear the case begins. Although some types of trials require twelve-person juries, most civil matters can be heard by six-person juries.

Voir Dire. The process by which the jury is selected is known as **voir dire.**[18] In most jurisdictions, voir dire consists of oral questions that attorneys for the plaintiff and the defendant ask a group of prospective jurors to determine whether a potential juror is biased or has any connection with a party to the action or with a prospective witness. Usually, jurors are questioned one at a time, although when large numbers of jurors are involved, the attorneys may direct their questions to groups of jurors instead to minimize the amount of time spent in jury selection. Sometimes, jurors are asked to fill out written questionnaires. Some trial attorneys use psychologists and other professionals to help them select jurors.

Challenges during Voir Dire. During *voir dire,* a party may challenge a certain number of prospective jurors *peremptorily*—that is, ask that these individuals not be sworn in as jurors without providing any reason. The total number of peremptory challenges allowed each side is determined by statute or by the court. Furthermore, a party may challenge any juror *for cause*—that is, provide a reason why an individual should not be sworn in as a juror. If the judge grants the challenge, the individual is asked to step down. A prospective juror may not be excluded from participation in the trial process, however, by use of discriminatory challenges, such as those based on racial criteria[19] or gender.[20]

After both sides have completed their challenges, those jurors who have been excused will be permitted to leave. The remaining jurors—those who have been found acceptable by the attorneys for both sides—will be seated in the jury box.

Alternate Jurors. Because unforeseeable circumstances or illness may necessitate that one or more of the sitting jurors be dismissed, the court, depending on the rules of the particular jurisdiction and the expected length of the trial, might choose to have two or three alternate jurors present throughout the trial. If a juror has to be excused in the middle of the trial, then an alternate may take his or her place without disrupting the proceedings. Once the jury members are seated, the judge will swear in the jury members, and the trial itself can begin.

---

18. Pronounced *vwahr deehr.* Literally, these French verbs mean "to see, to speak." During the *voir dire* phase of litigation, attorneys do in fact see the jurors speak. In legal language, however, the phrase refers to the process of interrogating jurors to learn about their backgrounds, attitudes, and so on.

19. *Batson v. Kentucky,* 476 U.S. 79, 106 S.Ct. 1712, 90 L.Ed.2d 69 (1986).

20. *J.E.B. v. Alabama ex rel. T.B.,* 511 U.S. 127, 114 S.Ct. 1419, 128 L.Ed.2d 89 (1994). (*Ex rel.* is an abbreviation of the Latin *ex relatione.* The phrase refers to an action brought on behalf of the state, by the attorney general, at the instigation of an individual who has a private interest in the matter.)

CONCEPT SUMMARY 2.3   PRETRIAL PROCEDURES

PROCEDURE	DESCRIPTION
Pleadings	1. *The plaintiff's complaint*—The plaintiff's statement of the cause of action and the parties involved, filed with the court by the plaintiff's attorney. After the filing, the defendant is notified of the suit through service of process. 2. *The defendant's response*—The defendant's response to the plaintiff's complaint may take the form of an answer, in which the defendant may admit to or deny the plaintiff's allegations. The defendant may raise an affirmative defense and/or assert a counterclaim.
Pretrial Motions	1. *Motion to dismiss*—A motion made by the defendant—often prior to filing an answer to the complaint—requesting the judge to dismiss the case for reasons that are provided in the motion (such as failure to state a claim for which relief can be granted). 2. *Motion for judgment on the pleadings*—May be made by either party; will be granted if no facts are in dispute and only questions of law are at issue. 3. *Motion for summary judgment*—May be made by either party; will be granted if no facts are in dispute and only questions of law are at issue. Unlike the motion for judgment on the pleadings, the motion for summary judgment may be supported by evidence outside the pleadings, such as testimony and other evidence obtained during the discovery phase of litigation.
Discovery	The process of gathering evidence concerning the case; involves (1) *depositions* (sworn testimony by either party or any witness); (2) *interrogatories* (in which parties to the action write answers to questions with the aid of their attorneys); and (3) requests for admissions, documents, examinations, or other information relating to the case.
Pretrial Conference	A pretrial hearing, at the request of either party or the court, to identify the matters in dispute after discovery has taken place and to explore the possibility of settling the dispute without a trial. If no settlement is possible, the parties plan the course of the trial.
Jury Selection	In a jury trial, the selection of members of the jury from a pool of prospective jurors. During a process known as *voir dire*, the attorneys for both sides may challenge prospective jurors either for cause or peremptorily (for no cause).

THE TRIAL

Various rules and procedures govern the trial phase of the litigation process. There are rules governing what kind of evidence will or will not be admitted during the trial, as well as specific procedures that the participants in the lawsuit must follow.

Rules of Evidence. Whether evidence will be admitted in court is determined by the **rules of evidence**—a series of rules that have been created by the courts to ensure that any evidence presented during a trial is fair and reliable. The Federal Rules of Evidence govern the admissibility of evidence in federal courts.

Evidence will not be admitted in court unless it is relevant to the matter in question. **Relevant evidence** is evidence that tends to prove or disprove a fact in question or to establish the degree of probability of a fact or action. For example, evidence that a suspect's gun was in the home of another person when a victim was shot would be relevant—because it would tend to prove that the suspect did not shoot the victim.

Even relevant evidence may not be admitted in court if its reliability is questionable or if its probative (proving) value is substantially outweighed by other important considerations of the court. For example, a video or a photograph that shows in detail the severity of a victim's injuries would be relevant evidence, but the court might exclude this evidence on the ground that it would emotionally inflame the jurors.

Generally, hearsay is not admissible as evidence. **Hearsay** is defined as any testimony given in court about a statement made by someone else. Literally, it is what someone heard someone else say. For example, if a witness in the Kirby-Carvello case testified in court concerning what he or she heard another observer say about the accident, that testimony would be hearsay—secondhand knowledge. Admitting hearsay into evidence carries many risks because, even though it may be relevant, there is no way to test its reliability.

Opening Statements. At the commencement of the trial, both attorneys are allowed to make **opening statements** concerning the facts that they expect to prove during the trial. The opening statement provides an opportunity for each lawyer to give a brief version of the facts and the supporting evidence that will be used during the trial.

Examination of Witnesses. Because Kirby is the plaintiff, she has the burden of proving that her claim is correct. Kirby's attorney begins the presentation of Kirby's case by calling the first witness for the plaintiff and examining (questioning) the witness. (For both attorneys, the types of questions and the manner of asking them are governed by the rules of evidence.) This questioning is called **direct examination.** After Kirby's attorney is finished, the witness is subject to **cross-examination** by Carvello's attorney. Then Kirby's attorney has another opportunity to question the witness in *redirect examination,* and Carvello's attorney may follow the redirect examination with a *recross-examination.* When both attorneys have finished with the first witness, Kirby's attorney calls the succeeding witnesses in the plaintiff's case, each of whom is subject to examination by the attorneys in the manner just described.

At the conclusion of the plaintiff's case, the defendant's attorney has the opportunity to ask the judge to direct a verdict for the defendant on the ground that the plaintiff has presented no evidence to support the plaintiff's claim. This is called a **motion for a directed verdict** (federal courts use the term *judgment as a matter of law* instead of *directed verdict*). In considering the motion, the judge looks at the evidence in the light most favorable to the plaintiff and grants the motion only if there is insufficient evidence to raise an issue of fact. (Motions for directed verdicts at this stage of trial are seldom granted.)

The defendant's attorney then presents the evidence and witnesses for the defendant's case. Witnesses are called and examined by the defendant's attorney. The plaintiff's attorney has the right to cross-examine them, and there may be a redirect examination and possibly a recross-examination. At the end of the defendant's case, either attorney can move for a directed verdict, and the test again is whether the jury can, through any reasonable interpretation of the evidence, find for the party against whom the motion has been made. After the defendant's attorney has finished introducing evidence, the plaintiff's attorney can present a **rebuttal,** which includes additional evidence to refute the defendant's case. The defendant's attorney can, in turn, refute that evidence in a **rejoinder.**

Closing Arguments. After both sides have rested their cases, each attorney presents a closing argument. In the **closing argument,** each attorney summarizes the facts and evidence presented during the trial, indicates why the facts and evidence support the client's claim, reveals the shortcomings of the points made by the opposing party during the trial, and generally urges a verdict in favor of the client. Each attorney's comments must be relevant to the issues in dispute.

Jury Instructions. After the closing arguments, the judge instructs the jury (assuming it is a jury trial) in the law that applies to the case. The instructions to the jury are often called *charges.* A charge is a document that includes statements of the applicable laws, as well as a review of the facts as they were presented during the case. Because the jury's role is to serve as the fact finder, the factual account contained in the charge is not binding on them. Indeed, the jurors may disregard the facts as noted in the charge entirely. They are not free to ignore the statements of law, however. The charge will help to channel the jurors' deliberations.

The Jury's Verdict. Following its receipt of instructions, the jury retires to the jury room to deliberate the case. In a civil case, the standard of proof is a *preponderance of the evidence.* That is, the plaintiff (Kirby in our hypothetical case) need not provide indisputable proof that she is entitled to a judgment. She need only show that her factual claim is more likely to be true than the defendant's. (In a criminal trial, the prosecution has a higher standard of proof to meet—it must prove its case *beyond a reasonable doubt.*)

Note that some civil claims must be proved by a "clear and convincing evidence" standard, under which the evidence must show that the truth of the party's claim is highly probable. This standard applies in suits involving charges of fraud, suits to establish the terms of a lost will, some suits relating to oral contracts, and other suits involving circumstances in which there is thought to be a particular danger of deception.

Once the jury has reached a decision, it may issue a **verdict** in favor of one party, which specifies the jury's factual findings and the amount of damages to be paid by the losing party. After the announcement of the verdict, which marks the end of the trial itself, the jurors will be discharged.

CONCEPT SUMMARY 2.4 TRIAL PROCEDURES

PROCEDURE	DESCRIPTION
Opening Statements	Each party's attorney is allowed to present an opening statement indicating what the attorney will attempt to prove during the course of the trial.
Examination of Witnesses	1. Plaintiff's introduction and direct examination of witnesses, cross-examination by defendant's attorney, possible redirect examination by plaintiff's attorney, and possible recross-examination by defendant's attorney. 2. Defendant's introduction and direct examination of witnesses, cross-examination by plaintiff's attorney, possible redirect examination by defendant's attorney, and possible recross-examination by plaintiff's attorney. 3. Possible rebuttal of defendant's argument by plaintiff's attorney, who presents more evidence. 4. Possible rejoinder by defendant's attorney to meet that evidence.
Closing Arguments	Each party's attorney argues in favor of a verdict for his or her client.
Jury Instructions	The judge instructs the jury as to how the law applies to the issue.
Jury Verdict	The jury renders its verdict, thus bringing the trial to an end.

POSTTRIAL MOTIONS

After the jury has rendered its verdict, either party may make a posttrial motion. The prevailing party usually files a motion for a judgment in accordance with the verdict. The nonprevailing party frequently files one of the motions discussed next.

Motion for a New Trial. At the end of the trial, a motion can be made to set aside an adverse verdict and any judgment and to hold a new trial. The **motion for a new trial** will be granted only if the judge (1) is convinced, after looking at all the evidence, that the jury was in error but (2) does not feel

it is appropriate to grant judgment for the other side. This will usually occur when the jury verdict is the obvious result of a misapplication of the law or a misunderstanding of the evidence presented at trial.

A new trial can also be granted on the grounds of newly discovered evidence, misconduct by the participants (such as the attorneys, the judge, or the jury) during the trial, or error by the judge. If a motion for a new trial is denied, the judge's denial may be appealed to a higher court. In the following case, the defendants filed a motion for a new trial based on the "improper and inflammatory" remarks made by the plaintiff's attorney.

CASE 2.4

LeBlanc v. American Honda Motor Co.

Supreme Court of
New Hampshire, 1997.
141 N.H. 579,
688 A.2d 556.
http://www.state.nh.us/
courts/supreme/
opinions/9701/honda.
htm^a

HISTORICAL AND SOCIAL SETTING   *One of the principles on which the United States was founded is that all persons are created equal and are entitled to have their individual dignity respected. There have been continual efforts by legislative enactments and judicial decisions to purge our society of racial and other prejudices. Despite these efforts, such biases still appear to influence decisions by many people who would deny equal respect to those of us of a different race, religion, or ethnic origin.*

BACKGROUND AND FACTS   *While riding on a snowmobile, Thomas LeBlanc was injured when the snowmobile collided with an off-road vehicle manufactured by American Honda Motor Company (a subsidiary of a Japanese corporation). LeBlanc sued Honda and the driver in a New Hampshire state court. During the trial, LeBlanc's lawyer, Vincent Martina, asked Honda's expert witness if he had ever wondered why the Honda vehicle was "red, white, and blue, the color of the American flag." During his closing argument, Martina told the jury that the case was not about "Pearl Harbor or the Japanese prime minister saying Americans are lazy and stupid. * * * What this case is about is not American xenophobia; it's about corporate greed." When the jury returned a verdict in favor of LeBlanc, Honda filed a motion for a new trial, which the court denied. Honda appealed to the Supreme Court of New Hampshire, arguing in part that Martina's remarks so tainted the proceedings as to deprive Honda of a fair trial.*

**IN THE LANGUAGE
OF THE COURT**

BROCK, Chief Justice.
  * * * * *
  * * * To justify a [new trial], remarks or * * * conduct must be more than merely inadmissible; they must constitute an irreparable injustice * * * .
  * * * * *
  * * * [A] new trial may be warranted where counsel attempts to appeal to the sympathies, passions, and prejudices of jurors grounded in race or nationality, by reference to the opposing party's religious beliefs or lack thereof, or by reference to a party's social or economic condition or status. Such an appeal was attempted in this case.
  * * * It is true that counsel's closing reference was brief. At the same time, when an elephant has passed through the courtroom one does not need a forceful reminder.

**DECISION
AND REMEDY**

The Supreme Court of New Hampshire reversed the decision in favor of LeBlanc and remanded the case for a new trial. The court held that remarks made during a trial to cultivate in the jury a racial and national bias constitute sufficient grounds for a new trial.

---

a. This is a page within the collection of New Hampshire Supreme Court opinions available at the Web site of the New Hampshire state government.

Motion for Judgment N.O.V.   If Kirby wins, and if Carvello's attorney has previously moved for a directed verdict, Carvello's attorney can now make a **motion for judgment** *n.o.v.* (from the Latin *non obstante veredicto*, meaning "notwithstanding the verdict"; federal courts use the term *judgment as a matter of law* instead of judgment *n.o.v.*). The standards for granting a judgment *n.o.v.* often are the same as those for granting a motion to dismiss or a motion for a directed verdict. Carvello can state that even if the evidence is viewed in the light most favorable to Kirby, a reasonable jury should not have found in Kirby's favor. If the judge finds this contention to be correct or decides that the law requires the opposite result, the motion will be granted. If the motion is denied, Carvello may then appeal the case. (Kirby may also appeal the case, even though she won at trial. She might appeal, for example, if she received a smaller money award than she had sought.)

THE APPEAL

Either party may appeal not only the jury's verdict but also any pretrial or posttrial motion. Many of the appellate court cases that appear in this text involve appeals of motions to dismiss, motions for summary judgment, or other motions that were denied by trial court judges. Note that few trial court decisions are reversed on appeal. In most appealed cases (approximately 90 percent), the trial court's decision is affirmed and thus becomes final.

Filing the Appeal.   If Carvello decides to appeal the verdict in Kirby's favor, then his attorney must file a *notice of appeal* with the clerk of the trial court within a prescribed period of time. Carvello then becomes the *appellant*. The clerk of the trial court sends to the reviewing court (usually an intermediate court of appeals) the *record on appeal*, which contains the following: (1) the pleadings, (2) a transcript of the trial testimony and copies of the exhibits, (3) the judge's rulings on motions made by the parties, (4) the arguments of counsel, (5) the instructions to the jury, (6) the verdict, (7) the posttrial motions, and (8) the judgment order from which the appeal is taken.

Carvello's attorney will file a **brief** with the reviewing court. The brief contains (1) a short statement of the facts; (2) a statement of the issues; (3) the rulings by the trial court that Carvello contends are erroneous and prejudicial (biased in favor of one of the parties); (4) the grounds for reversal of the judgment; (5) a statement of the applicable law; and (6) arguments on Carvello's behalf, citing applicable statutes and relevant cases as precedents. The attorney for the *appellee* (Kirby, in our hypothetical case) usually files an answering brief. Carvello's attorney can file a reply, although it is not required. The reviewing court then considers the case.

Appellate Review.   A court of appeals does not hear any evidence. Its decision concerning a case is based on the record on appeal and the briefs. The attorneys can present oral arguments, after which the case is taken under advisement. The court then issues a written opinion. In general, the appellate courts do not reverse findings of fact unless the findings are unsupported or contradicted by the evidence.

An appellate court has several options after reviewing a case: it can *affirm* the trial court's decision; it can *reverse* the trial court's judgment if it concludes that the trial court erred or that the jury did not receive proper instructions; or it can *remand* (send back) the case to the trial court for further proceedings consistent with its opinion on the matter. The court might also affirm or reverse a decision *in part*. For example, the court might affirm the jury's finding that Carvello was negligent but remand the case for further proceedings on another issue (such as the extent of Kirby's damages). An appellate court can also *modify* a lower court's decision. If the appellate court decided that the jury awarded an excessive amount in damages, for example, the court might reduce the award to a more appropriate, or fairer, amount.

Higher Appellate Courts.   If the reviewing court is an intermediate appellate court, the losing party may be allowed by the court to appeal the decision to the state supreme court. Such a petition corresponds to a petition for a writ of *certiorari* in the United States Supreme Court. If the petition is granted, new briefs must be filed before the state supreme court, and the attorneys may be allowed or requested to present oral arguments. Like the intermediate appellate courts, the supreme court may reverse or affirm the appellate court's decision or remand the case.

At this point, unless a federal question is at issue, the case has reached its end. If a federal question is involved, the losing party (or the winning party, if that party is dissatisfied with the relief obtained) may appeal the decision to the United States Supreme Court by petitioning the Court for a writ of *certiorari*. (As discussed earlier, the Supreme Court may or may not grant the writ, depending on the significance of the issue in dispute.)

CONCEPT SUMMARY 2.5

POSTTRIAL OPTIONS

PROCEDURE	DESCRIPTION
Posttrial Motions	1. *Motion for a new trial*—If the judge is convinced that the jury was in error, the motion will be granted. 2. *Motion for judgment n.o.v. ("notwithstanding the verdict")*—The party making the motion must have filed a motion for a directed verdict at the close of all the evidence during the trial; the motion will be granted if the judge is convinced that the jury was in error.
Appeal	Either party can appeal the trial court's judgment to an appropriate court of appeals. 1. *Filing the appeal*—The appealing party must file a notice of appeal with the clerk of the trial court, who forwards to the appellate court the record on appeal. Attorneys' briefs are filed. 2. *Appellate review*—The appellate court does not hear evidence but bases its opinion, which it issues in writing, on the record on appeal and the attorneys' briefs and oral arguments. The court may affirm or reverse all (or part) of the trial court's judgment and/or remand the case for further proceedings consistent with its opinion. Most decisions are affirmed on appeal. 3. In some cases, further review may be sought from a higher appellate court, such as a state supreme court. Ultimately, if a federal question is involved, the case may be appealed to the United States Supreme Court.

ENFORCING THE JUDGMENT

The uncertainties of the litigation process are compounded by the lack of guarantees that any judgment will be enforceable. Even if the jury awarded Kirby the full amount of damages requested ($100,000), for example, she might not, in fact, "win" anything at all. Carvello's auto insurance coverage might have lapsed, in which event the company would not pay any of the damages. Alternatively, Carvello's insurance policy might be limited to $50,000, meaning that Carvello would have to pay personally the remaining $50,000.

If Carvello did not have that amount of money available, then Kirby would need to go back to court and request that the court issue a *writ of execution*—an order, usually issued by the clerk of the court, directing the sheriff to seize and sell Carvello's nonexempt assets (certain assets are exempted by law from creditors' actions). The proceeds of the sale would then be used to pay the damages owed to Kirby. Any excess proceeds of the sale would be returned to Carvello. Alternatively, the nonexempt property itself could be transferred to Kirby in lieu of an outright payment. (Creditors' remedies, including those of judgment creditors, as well as exempt and nonexempt property, will be discussed in more detail in Chapter 16.)

The problem of collecting a judgment is less pronounced, of course, when a party is seeking to satisfy a judgment against a defendant, such as a major corporation, that has substantial assets that can be easily located. Usually, one of the factors considered before a lawsuit is initiated is whether the defendant has sufficient assets to cover the amount of damages sought, should the plaintiff win the case.

TERMS AND CONCEPTS TO REVIEW

affidavit 46	affirmative defense 42	answer 42

QUESTIONS AND CASE PROBLEMS

2–1. COURTS OF APPEALS. The defendant in a lawsuit is appealing the trial court's decision in favor of the plaintiff. On appeal, the defendant claims that the evidence presented at trial to support the plaintiff's claim was so scanty that no reasonable jury could have found for the plaintiff. Therefore, argues the defendant, the appellate court should reverse the trial court's decision. May an appellate court ever reverse a trial court's findings with respect to questions of fact? Discuss fully.

2–2. COURTS OF APPEALS. Appellate courts normally see only written transcripts of trial proceedings when they are reviewing cases. Today, in some states, videotapes are being used as the official trial reports. If the use of videotapes as official reports continues, will this alter the appellate process? Should it? Discuss fully.

2–3. DISCOVERY. In the past, the rules of discovery were very restrictive, and trials often turned on elements of surprise. For example, a plaintiff would not necessarily know until the trial what the defendant's defense was going to be. Within the last twenty-five years, however, new rules of discovery have substantially changed all this. Now each attorney can find out practically all the evidence that the other side will be presenting at trial, with the exception of certain information—namely, the opposing attorney's work product. Work product is not a clear concept. Basically, it includes all the attorney's thoughts on the case. Can you see any reason why such information should not be made available to the opposing attorney? Discuss fully.

2–4. MOTIONS. When and for what purpose are each of the following motions made? Which of them would be appropriate if a defendant claimed that the only issue between the parties was a question of law and that the law was favorable to the defendant's position?

(a) A motion for judgment on the pleadings.
(b) A motion for a directed verdict.
(c) A motion for summary judgment.
(d) A motion for judgment *n.o.v.*

2–5. PEREMPTORY CHALLENGES. During *voir dire*, the parties or their attorneys select those persons who will serve as jurors during the trial. The parties are prohibited, however, from excluding potential jurors on the basis of race or other discriminatory criteria. One issue concerns whether the prohibition against discrimination extends to potential jurors who have physical or mental disabilities. Federal law prohibits discrimination against an otherwise qualified person with a disability when that person could be accommodated without too much difficulty. Should this law also apply to the jury selection process? For example, should parties be prohibited from excluding blind persons, through either challenges for cause or peremptory challenges, from serving on juries? Discuss fully.

2–6. JURISDICTION. Marya Callais, a citizen of Florida, was walking one day near a busy street in Tallahassee, Florida, when a large crate flew off a passing truck and hit her, resulting in numerous injuries. She incurred a great deal of pain and suffering, plus significant medical expenses, and she could not work for six months. She wants to sue the trucking firm for $300,000 in damages. The firm's headquarters are in Georgia, although the company does business in Florida. In what court might Callais bring suit—a Florida state court, a Georgia state court, or a federal court? What factors might influence her decision?

2–7. MOTION TO DISMISS. Martin brought a civil rights action against his employer, the New York Department of Mental Hygiene, when it failed to promote him on several occasions. His complaint stated only that the defendant had discriminated against him on the basis of race by denying him "the authority, salary, and privileges commensurate with this position." The employer made a motion to dismiss the claim for failure to state a cause of action. Discuss whether the employer could be successful. [*Martin v. New York State Department of Mental Hygiene*, 588 F.2d 371 (2d Cir. 1978)]

2–8. MOTION FOR A NEW TRIAL. Washoe Medical Center, Inc., admitted Shirley Swisher for the treatment of a fractured pelvis. During her stay, Swisher suffered a fatal fall from her hospital bed. Gerald Parodi, the administrator of her estate, and others filed an action against Washoe in which they sought damages for the alleged lack of care in treating Swisher. During *voir dire*, when the plaintiffs' attorney returned a few minutes late from a break, the trial judge led the prospective jurors in a standing ovation. The judge joked with one of the prospective jurors, whom he had known in college, about his fitness to serve as a judge and personally endorsed another prospective juror's business. After the trial, the jury returned a verdict in favor of Washoe. The plaintiffs moved for a new trial, but the judge denied the motion. The plaintiffs then appealed, arguing that the tone set by the judge during *voir dire* prejudiced their right to a fair trial. Should the appellate court agree? Why or why not? [*Parodi v. Washoe Medical Center, Inc.*, 111 Nev. 365, 892 P.2d 588 (1995)]

2–9. STANDING. Blue Cross and Blue Shield insurance companies (the Blues) provide 68 million Americans with health-care financing. The Blues have paid billions of dollars for care attributable to illnesses related to tobacco use. In an attempt to recover some of this amount, the Blues filed a suit in a federal district court against tobacco companies and others, alleging fraud, among other things. The Blues claimed that beginning in 1953, the defendants conspired to addict millions of Americans, including members of Blue Cross plans, to cigarettes and other tobacco products. The conspiracy involved misrepresentation about the safety of nicotine and its addictive properties, marketing efforts targeting children, and agreements not to produce or market safer cigarettes. Their success caused lung, throat, and other cancers, as well as heart disease, stroke, emphysema, and other illnesses. The defendants asked the court to dismiss the case on the ground that the plaintiffs did not have standing to sue. Do the Blues have standing in this case? Why or why not? [*Blue Cross and Blue Shield of New Jersey, Inc. v. Philip Morris, Inc.*, 36 F.Supp.2d 560 (E.D.N.Y. 1999)]

2–10. DISCOVERY. Advance Technology Consultants, Inc. (ATC), contracted with RoadTrac, L.L.C., to provide software and client software systems for the products for global positioning satellite system (GPS) technology being developed by RoadTrac. RoadTrac agreed to provide ATC hardware with which ATC's software would interface. Problems soon arose, however. ATC claimed that RoadTrac's hardware was defective, making it difficult to develop the software. RoadTrac contended that its hardware was fully functional and that ATC simply failed to provide supporting software. ATC told RoadTrac that it considered their contract terminated. RoadTrac filed a suit in a Georgia state court against ATC, charging, among other things, breach of contract. During discovery, RoadTrac requested ATC's customer lists and marketing procedures. Before producing this material, ATC asked the court to limit RoadTrac's use of the information. Meanwhile, RoadTrac and ATC had become competitors in the GPS industry. How should the court rule regarding RoadTrac's discovery request? [*Advance Technology Consultants, Inc. v. RoadTrac, L.L.C.*, 236 Ga.App. 582, 512 S.E.2d 27 (1999)]

2–11. IN YOUR COURT

Ronald Metzgar placed his fifteen-month-old son Matthew, awake and healthy, in his playpen. Ronald left the room for five minutes and on his return found Matthew lifeless. A purple toy block had lodged in the boy's throat, choking him to death. Ronald called 911, but efforts to revive Matthew were to no avail. There was no warning of a choking hazard on the box containing the block. Matthew's parents sued Playskool, Inc., the manufacturer of the block, and others, alleging, among other things, that the manufacturer had been negligent in failing to warn of the block's hazard. Playskool filed a motion for summary judgment, arguing that the danger of a young child choking on a small block was obvious. Assume that you are the judge in the trial court hearing this case and answer the following questions:

(a) Is the question of whether a child could choke on one of the small blocks a question of fact or a question of law?

(b) Should you grant Playskool's request for summary judgment? Why or why not?

(c) Suppose that Matthew had not choked on the block but his father, concerned that Matthew *could have* choked on the block, filed a lawsuit against Playskool anyway. In the suit, the father asked the court to order Playskool to place a warning on the box as to the choking hazard so that other consumers would not be harmed. In this situation, would the father have standing to sue?

LAW ON THE WEB

For updated links to resources available on the Web, as well as a variety of other materials, visit this text's Web site at http://wleb.westbuslaw.com.

The decisions of the United States Supreme Court and of all of the U.S. courts of appeals are now published online shortly after the decisions are rendered (often within hours). You can find these decisions and obtain information about the federal court system by accessing the Federal Court Locator at

http://www.law.vill.edu

For information on the justices of the United States Supreme Court, links to opinions they have authored, and other information about the Supreme Court, go to

http://oyez.nwu.edu

The Web site for the federal courts offers information on the federal court system and links to all federal courts at

http://www.uscourts.gov

The National Center for State Courts (NCSC) offers links to the Web pages of all state courts. Go to

http://www.ncsc.dni.us/court/sites/courts.htm

If you are interested in learning more about the Federal Rules of Civil Procedure (FRCP) and the Federal Rules of Evidence (FRE), they can now be accessed via the Internet at the following Web site:

http://www.cornell.edu

For an example of a typical set of state rules governing attorney conduct, you can access Idaho's Rules of Professional Conduct Governing Lawyers at

http://www.law.cornell.edu:80/lawyers/ruletable.html

LEGAL RESEARCH EXERCISES ON THE WEB

Go to http://wleb.westbuslaw.com, the Web site that accompanies this text. Select "Internet Applications," and then click on "Chapter 2." There you will find the following Internet exercise that you can perform to learn more about the court procedures involved in civil lawsuits and in small claims courts:

Activity 2–1: The Judiciary's Role in American Government

Activity 2–2: Civil Procedure

CHAPTER 3

Alternative Dispute Resolution

TRIALS ARE COSTLY AND TIME consuming. It has been said that this is the result of "too many lawyers, too many lawsuits, and too many laws." In fact, since 1960, the number of lawyers has tripled, the number of lawsuits has tripled, and the number of laws has multiplied, while the numbers of judges and courts have not kept pace.

Although it is true that the number of lawsuits filed has grown rapidly, only 5 to 10 percent of lawsuits filed actually go to trial. Most cases are settled or dismissed long before the parties enter a courtroom. Moreover, the number of cases that are litigated does not appear to be growing any faster than the population. When compared with the large number of transactions that occur in our highly complex society, the rate of litigation appears low to some.

Nevertheless, in any individual case, it may be months before a hearing can even be scheduled. Depending on the complexity of the case, the extent of discovery proceedings required, and the delaying tactics of the opposing party, years may be spent in litigation. Even in the best of situations, the civil procedures discussed in Chapter 2 all require much time and money. As the cost and complexity of litigation have grown, businesspersons and other individuals have asked, "Is there a more appropriate way to resolve disputes?"

SECTION 1

The Search for Alternatives to Litigation

A number of solutions have been proposed, and some have been implemented, to reduce the congestion in our court system and to reduce the litigation costs facing all members of society. The enforcement of arbitration clauses, the use of court-referred arbitration and mediation, and the emergence of an increasing number of private forums for dispute resolution have all helped to reduce the caseload of the courts.

Another solution to the problem involves putting caps on damage awards, particularly for pain and suffering. Without the probability of obtaining multimillion-dollar judgments for pain and suffering, some potential litigants will be deterred from undertaking lawsuits to obtain damages. Another avenue of attack is to penalize those who bring frivolous lawsuits. Rule 11 of the Federal Rules of Civil Procedure allows for disciplinary sanctions against lawyers and litigants who bring frivolous lawsuits in federal courts.

Many courts require mediation or arbitration before a case goes to trial. There are proposals to reduce delay and expenses in federal civil cases further, and

59

proposals are being considered by the states as well. Some of the proposals can be viewed as case-management plans. One proposal, for example, would require each federal district court to implement procedures for placing cases on different tracks, with simple cases being handled more quickly than complex ones.

POLITICS AND LAW

Because reforms of any system affect individuals and groups differently, they seldom are accomplished easily and quickly. Reform of the court system is a prime example. At the federal level, members of Congress long have been concerned with bringing court costs and delay under control. These concerns gave rise to the enactment of legislation in the early 1990s that required the federal courts to develop a plan to cut costs and reduce delay within the federal judicial system.

NEW METHODS AND ARRANGEMENTS

The search for alternative means to resolve disputes has produced several distinct methods and arrangements. These range from neighbors' sitting down over a cup of coffee to work out their differences to huge multinational corporations' agreeing to resolve a dispute through a formal hearing before a panel of experts. All of these alternatives to traditional litigation make up what is broadly termed alternative dispute resolution.

Alternative dispute resolution (ADR) describes any procedure or device for resolving disputes other than the traditional judicial process. ADR is normally a less expensive and less time-consuming process than formal litigation. In some cases, it also has the advantage of being more private. Except in cases involving court-annexed arbitration (discussed later in this chapter), no public record of ADR proceedings is created; only the parties directly involved are privy to the information presented during the process. This is a particularly important consideration in many business disputes, because such cases may involve sensitive commercial information.

SECTION 2

Negotiation and Mediation

Alternative dispute resolution methods differ in the degree of formality involved and the extent to which third parties participate in the process. Generally, negotiation is the least formal method and involves no third parties. Mediation may be similarly informal but does involve the participation of a third party.

NEGOTIATION

In the process of **negotiation,** the parties come together informally, with or without attorneys to represent them. Within this informal setting, the parties air their differences and try to reach a settlement or resolution without the involvement of independent third parties. Because no third parties are involved and because of the informal setting, negotiation is the simplest form of ADR. Even if a lawsuit has been initiated, the parties may continue to negotiate their differences at any time during the litigation process and settle their dispute. Less than 10 percent of all corporate lawsuits, for example, end up in trial—the rest are settled beforehand.

Preparation for Negotiation. Because so many disputes are settled through negotiation, in spite of the informality of this means of dispute resolution, each party must carefully prepare his or her side of the case. The elements of the dispute should be considered, documents and other evidence should be collected, and witnesses should be prepared to testify. Negotiating from a well-prepared position improves the odds of obtaining a favorable result. Even if a dispute is not resolved through negotiation, preparation for negotiation will reduce the effort required to prepare for the next step in the dispute resolution process.

"Assisted Negotiation." To facilitate negotiation, various forms of what might be called "assisted negotiation" have been employed. Forms of ADR associated with the negotation process include mini-trials and early neutral case evaluation. Another form of assisted negotiation—the summary jury trial—is discussed later in this chapter.

A **mini-trial** is a private proceeding in which each party's attorney briefly argues the party's case before the other party. Typically, a neutral third party, who acts as an adviser and an expert in the area being disputed, is also present. If the parties fail to reach an agreement, the adviser renders an opinion as to how a court would likely decide the issue. The proceeding assists the parties in determining whether they should negotiate a settlement of the dispute or take it to court.

In **early neutral case evaluation,** the parties select a neutral third party (generally an expert in the subject matter of the dispute) to evaluate their respective positions. The parties explain their positions to the case evaluator however they wish. The evaluator then assesses the strengths and weaknesses of the parties' positions, and this evaluation forms the basis for negotiating a settlement.

Disputes may also be resolved in a friendly, nonadversarial manner through **conciliation,** in which a third party assists parties to a dispute in reconciling their differences. The conciliator helps to schedule negotiating sessions and carries offers back and forth between the parties when they refuse to face each other in direct negotiations. Technically, conciliators are not to recommend solutions. In practice, however, they often do. In contrast, a mediator is expected to propose solutions.

MEDIATION

Mediation is similar to negotiation. In the mediation process, as in negotiation, the parties themselves must reach agreement over their dispute. The major difference between negotiation and mediation is that the latter involves a third party, called a mediator. The **mediator** assists the parties in reaching a mutually acceptable agreement. The mediator talks face to face with the parties and allows them to discuss their disagreement, usually in an informal environment. The mediator's role, however, is limited to assisting the parties. The mediator does not decide a controversy; he or she only facilitates the process by helping the parties more quickly find common ground on which they can begin to reach an agreement for themselves.

Advantages of Mediation.   Few procedural rules are involved in the mediation process—far fewer than in a courtroom setting. The proceedings can be tailored to fit the needs of the parties—the mediator can be told to maintain a diplomatic role or be asked to express an opinion about the dispute, lawyers can be excluded from the proceedings, and the exchange of a few documents can replace the more expensive and time-consuming process of pretrial discovery. Disputes are often settled far more quickly in mediation than in formal litigation.[1]

There are other benefits. Because the parties reach agreement by mutual consent, the bitterness that often flows from the winner-take-all outcome of a formal trial decision is avoided. Hard feelings are also mini-

mized by the less stressful environment provided by mediation; the absence of the formal rules and adversarial tone of courtroom proceedings lessens the hostility the parties may feel toward one another. Minimizing hard feelings can be very important when the parties have to go on working with one another while the controversy is being resolved or after it has been settled. This is frequently the case when two businesses—say, a supplier and a purchaser—have a long-standing, mutually beneficial relationship that they would like to preserve despite their controversy. Similar considerations are found in the context of management and labor disputes; employee disciplinary matters and grievances are subjects that invite mediation as an alternative to formal litigation.

Another important benefit of mediation is that the mediator is selected by the parties. In litigation, the parties have no control over the selection of a judge. In mediation, the parties may select a mediator on the basis of expertise in a particular field as well as for fairness and impartiality. To the degree that the mediator has these attributes, he or she will more effectively aid the parties in reaching an agreement over their dispute.

Disadvantages of Mediation.   Mediation is not without disadvantages. A mediator is likely to charge a fee. (This can be split between the parties, though, and thus may represent less expense than would both sides' hiring lawyers.)

Informality and the absence of a third party referee can also be disadvantageous. (Remember that a mediator can only help the parties reach a decision, not make a decision for them.) Without a deadline hanging over the parties' heads, and without the threat of sanctions if they fail to negotiate in good faith, they may be less willing to make concessions or otherwise strive honestly and diligently to reach a settlement. This can slow the process or even cause it to fail.

SECTION 3

Arbitration

A third method of dispute resolution combines the advantages of third party decision making—as provided by judges and juries in formal litigation—with the speed and flexibility inherent in rules of procedure and evidence less rigid than those governing courtroom litigation. This is the process of **arbitration**—the settling of a dispute by an impartial third party (other than a court)

---

1. In Florida alone, as many as fifty thousand disputes that might have ended up in court are instead resolved through mediation each year. Florida's insurance commissioner used mediation to resolve hundreds of insurance claims stemming from 1992's Hurricane Andrew.

who renders a legally binding decision. The third party who renders the decision is called an **arbitrator.**

When a dispute arises, the parties can agree to settle their differences informally through arbitration rather than formally through the court system. Alternatively, the parties may agree ahead of time that, if a dispute should arise, they will submit to arbitration rather than bring a lawsuit. Both parties are obligated to follow the arbitrator's decision regardless of whether or not they agree with it; this is what is meant by saying the decision is legally binding.

The federal government and many state governments favor arbitration over litigation. The federal policy favoring arbitration is embodied in the Federal Arbitration Act (FAA) of 1925.[2] The FAA requires that courts give deference to all voluntary arbitration agreements in cases governed by federal law. Virtually any dispute can be the subject of arbitration. A voluntary agreement to arbitrate a dispute normally will be enforced by the courts if the agreement does not compel an illegal act or contravene public policy.

THE FEDERAL ARBITRATION ACT

The Federal Arbitration Act does not establish a set arbitration procedure. The parties themselves must agree on the manner of resolving their dispute. The FAA provides the means for enforcing the arbitration procedure that the parties have established for themselves.

Section 4 allows a party to petition a federal district court for an order compelling arbitration under an agreement to arbitrate a dispute. If the judge is "satisfied that the making of the agreement for arbitration or the

2. 9 U.S.C. Sections 1–15.

failure to comply therewith is not in issue, the court shall make an order directing the parties to proceed with arbitration in accordance with the terms of the agreement."

Under Section 9 of the FAA, the parties to the arbitration may agree to have the arbitrator's decision confirmed in a federal district court. Through confirmation, one party obtains a court order directing another party to comply with the terms of the arbitrator's decision. Section 10 establishes the grounds by which the arbitrator's decision may be set aside (canceled). The grounds for setting aside a decision are limited to misconduct, fraud, corruption, or abuse of power in the arbitration process itself; a court will not review the merits of the dispute or the arbitrator's judgment.

The FAA covers any arbitration clause in a contract that involves interstate commerce. Business activities that have even remote connections or minimal effects on commerce between two or more states are considered to be included. Thus, arbitration agreements involving transactions only slightly connected to the flow of interstate commerce may fall under the FAA, even if the parties, at the time of contracting, did not expect their arbitration agreement to involve interstate commerce.[3]

In the following case, an employer asked a court to issue an order compelling an ex-employee to submit to arbitration under an arbitration agreement that the parties had signed. Under that agreement, it was the employer's responsibility to establish the procedure and the rules for the arbitration. Those rules were the focus of the court's consideration of the employer's request.

3. *Allied-Bruce Terminix Cos., Inc. v. Dobson,* 513 U.S. 265, 115 S.Ct. 834, 130 L.Ed.2d 753 (1995).

CASE 3.1   Hooters of America, Inc. v. Phillips

United States
Court of Appeals,
Fourth Circuit, 1999.
173 F.3d 933.
http://www.law.emory.
edu/4circuit[a]

COMPANY PROFILE   *The first Hooters restaurant was opened in Clearwater, Florida, in 1983, by six friends, all of whom had business experience but none of whom had restaurant experience. The following year, they sold the rights to expand the business under the Hooters name to Hooters of America, Inc. (http://www.hooters.com). Today, Hooters of America owns or licenses more than two hundred restaurants in forty-two states, as well as Argentina, the Bahamas, Canada, Mexico, the United Kingdom, and other countries. The menu includes spicy chicken wings and sandwiches.*

BACKGROUND AND FACTS   *In 1989, Annette Phillips was hired by Hooters of Myrtle Beach (HOMB), a franchisee of Hooters of America, Inc., to work as a bartender at a*

a. In the "Listing by Month of Decision" section, click on "1999 Decisions". When the list opens, click on "April". On that page, scroll down the list of cases to the name of the case and click on it to access the opinion.

Hooters restaurant in Myrtle Beach, South Carolina. Five years later, Hooters implemented an alternative dispute resolution program. The company conditioned eligibility for raises, transfers, and promotions on an employee's signing an "agreement to arbitrate employment-related disputes," which specifically included claims of sexual harassment. The agreement stated that the arbitration was subject to "the company's rules and procedures for alternative resolution of employment-related disputes, as promulgated by the company from time to time." The employees were not given a copy of these rules. Phillips signed the agreement. In June 1996, Gerald Brooks, a Hooters' official and the brother of HOMB's principal owner, allegedly sexually harassed Phillips by grabbing and slapping her buttocks. After appealing to her manager for help and being told to "let it go," she quit her job. Phillips threatened to sue, claiming that the attack and the restaurant's failure to address it violated her rights. **b** *Hooters responded that she was required to submit her claim to arbitration. Phillips refused. Hooters filed a suit in a federal district court against Phillips to compel arbitration under Section 4 of the FAA. The court denied Hooters' request. The company appealed to the U.S. Court of Appeals for the Fourth Circuit.*

IN THE LANGUAGE OF THE COURT

WILKINSON, Chief Judge.

*   *   *   *

Hooters and Phillips agreed to settle any disputes between them not in a judicial forum, but in another neutral forum—arbitration. Their agreement provided that Hooters was responsible for setting up such a forum by promulgating arbitration rules and procedures. *   *   *

The Hooters rules when taken as a whole, however, are so one-sided that their *only possible purpose is to undermine the neutrality of the proceeding.* The rules require the employee to provide the company notice of her claim at the outset, including "the nature of the Claim" and "the specific act(s) or omissions(s) which are the basis of the Claim." Hooters, on the other hand, is not required to file any responsive pleadings or to notice its defenses. Additionally, at the time of filing this notice, the employee must provide the company with a list of all fact witnesses with a brief summary of the facts known to each. The company, however, is not required to reciprocate. [Emphasis added.]

The Hooters rules also provide a mechanism for selecting a panel of three arbitrators that is crafted to ensure a biased decision maker. The employee and Hooters each select an arbitrator, and the two arbitrators in turn select a third. Good enough, except that the employee's arbitrator and the third arbitrator must be selected from a list of arbitrators created exclusively by Hooters. This gives Hooters control over the entire panel and places no limits whatsoever on whom Hooters can put on the list. Under the rules, Hooters is free to devise lists of partial arbitrators who have existing relationships, financial or familial, with Hooters and its management. In fact, the rules do not even prohibit Hooters from placing its managers themselves on the list. Further, nothing in the rules restricts Hooters from punishing arbitrators who rule against the company by removing them from the list. Given the unrestricted control that one party (Hooters) has over the panel, the selection of an impartial decision maker would be a surprising result.

*   *   *   *.

In addition, the rules provide that upon 30 days notice Hooters, but not the employee, may cancel the agreement to arbitrate. Moreover, Hooters reserves the right to modify the rules, "in whole or in part," whenever it wishes and "without notice" to the employee. Nothing in the rules even prohibits Hooters from changing the rules in the middle of an arbitration proceeding.

DECISION AND REMEDY

The U.S. Court of Appeals for the Fourth Circuit held that Hooters' issuance of "so many biased rules" created "a sham system unworthy even of the name of arbitration," in violation of the parties' contract to arbitrate. The court affirmed the judgment of the lower court.

---

b. Phillips claimed specifically that Hooters violated her rights under Title VII of the Civil Rights Act of 1964. This law is discussed more fully in Chapter 22.

STATE ARBITRATION STATUTES

Virtually all states follow the federal approach to voluntary arbitration. Thirty-four states and the District of Columbia have adopted the Uniform Arbitration Act, which was drafted by the National Conference of Commissioners on Uniform State Laws in 1955. Those states that have not adopted the uniform act nonetheless follow many of the practices specified in it.

Under the uniform act, the basic approach is to give full effect to voluntary agreements to arbitrate disputes between private parties. The act supplements private arbitration agreements by providing explicit procedures and remedies for enforcing arbitration agreements. The uniform act does not, however, dictate the terms of the agreement. Moreover, under both federal and state statutes, the parties are afforded considerable latitude in deciding the subject matter of the arbitration and the methods for conducting the arbitration process. In the absence of a controlling statute, the rights and duties of the parties are established and limited by their agreement.

THE ARBITRATION PROCESS

The arbitration process begins with a *submission*. **Submission** is the act of referring a dispute to an arbitrator. The next step is the *hearing*, in which evidence and arguments are presented to the arbitrator. The process culminates in an *award*, which is the decision of the arbitrator.

The right to appeal the award to a court of law is limited. If the award was made under a voluntary arbitration agreement, a court normally will not set it aside even if it was the result of an erroneous determination of fact or an incorrect interpretation of law by the arbitrator.

This limitation is based on at least two grounds. First, if an award is not treated as final, then, rather than speeding up the dispute-resolution process, arbitration would merely add one more layer to the process of litigation. Second, the basis of arbitration—the freedom of parties to agree among themselves how to settle a controversy—supports treating an award as final. Having had the opportunity to frame the issues and to set out the manner for resolving the dispute, one party should not complain if the result was not what that party had hoped it would be.

Submission.   The parties may agree to submit questions of fact, questions of law, or both to the arbitrator. The parties may even agree to leave the interpretation of the arbitration agreement to the arbitrator. In the case of an existing agreement to arbitrate, the clause itself is the submission to arbitration.

The submission typically states the identities of the parties, the nature of the dispute to be resolved, the monetary amounts involved in the controversy, the place at which the arbitration is to take place, and the intention of the parties to be bound by the arbitrator's award. Exhibit 3–1 contains a sample submission form.

Most states require that an agreement to submit a dispute to arbitration be in writing. Moreover, because the goal of arbitration is speed and efficiency in resolving controversies, most states require that matters be submitted within a definite period of time, generally six months from the date on which the dispute arises.

The Hearing.   Because the parties are free to construct the method by which they want their dispute resolved, they must state the issues that will be submitted and the powers that the arbitrator will exercise. The arbitrator may be given power at the outset of the process to establish rules that will govern the proceedings. Typically, these rules are much less restrictive than those governing formal litigation. Regardless of who establishes the rules, the arbitrator will apply them during the course of the hearing.

Restrictions on the kind of evidence and the manner in which it is presented may be less rigid in arbitration, partly because the arbitrator is likely to be an expert in the subject matter involved in the controversy. Restrictions may also be less stringent because there is less fear that the arbitrator will be swayed by improper evidence. In contrast, evidence in a jury trial must sometimes be presented twice: once to the judge, outside the presence of the jury, to determine if the evidence may be heard by the jury, and—depending on the judge's ruling—again, to the jury.

In the typical hearing format, the parties begin as they would at trial by presenting opening arguments to the arbitrator and stating what remedies should or should not be granted. After the opening statements have been made, evidence is presented. Witnesses may be called and examined by both sides. After all the evidence has been presented, the

EXHIBIT 3–1   SAMPLE SUBMISSION FORM

American Arbitration Association
SUBMISSION TO DISPUTE RESOLUTION

Date: _____

The named parties hereby submit the following dispute for resolution under the _____
_____ Rules* of the American Arbitration Association:

Procedure Selected: ☐ Binding arbitration   ☐ Mediation settlement
                          ☐ Other _____
                                                 (Describe)

FOR INSURANCE CASES ONLY:

_____ _____ to _____ _____
Policy Number   Effective Dates   Applicable Policy Limits

_____   _____
Date of Incident   Location

Insured: _____   Claim Number: _____

Name(s) of Claimant(s)	Check if a Minor	Amount Claimed
_____	☐	_____
_____	☐	_____

Nature of Dispute and/or Injuries Alleged (attach additional sheets if necessary):

Place of Hearing: _____

We agree that, if binding arbitration is selected, we will abide by and perform any award rendered hereunder and that a judgment may be entered on the award.

To Be Completed by the Claimant	*To Be Completed by the Respondent*
_____	_____
Name of Party	Name of Party
_____	_____
Address	Address
_____	_____
City, State, and ZIP Code	City, State, and ZIP Code
( ) _____	( ) _____
Telephone Fax	Telephone Fax
_____	_____
Signature†	Signature†
_____	_____
Name of Party's Attorney or Representative	Name of Party's Attorney or Representative
_____	_____
Address	Address
_____	_____
City, State, and ZIP Code	City, State, and ZIP Code
( ) _____	( ) _____
Telephone Fax	Telephone Fax
_____	_____
Signature†	Signature†

Please file three copies with the AAA.

* If you have a question as to which rules apply, please contact the AAA.
† Signatures of all parties are required for arbitration.

Form G1-7/90

parties give their closing arguments. On completion of the closing arguments, the arbitrator closes the hearing.

The Award.   After each side has had an opportunity to present evidence and to argue its case, the arbitrator reaches a decision. The final decision of the arbitrator is called an **award,** even if no money is conferred on a party as a result of the proceedings. Under most statutes, the arbitrator must render an award within thirty days of the close of the hearing.

In most states, the award need not state the arbitrator's findings regarding factual questions in the case. Nor must the award state the conclusions that the arbitrator reached on any questions of law that may have been presented. All that is required for the award to be valid is that it completely resolve the controversy.

Most states do, however, require that the award be in writing, regardless of whether any conclusions of law or findings of fact are included. If the arbitrator does state his or her legal conclusions and factual findings, then a letter or an opinion will be drafted containing the basis for the award. Even when there is no statutory requirement that the arbitrator state the factual and legal basis for the award, the parties may impose the requirement in their submission or in their pre-dispute agreement to arbitrate.

ENFORCEMENT OF AGREEMENTS TO SUBMIT TO ARBITRATION

The role of the courts in the arbitration process is limited. One important role is played at the prearbitration stage. A court may be called on to order one party to an arbitration agreement to submit to arbitration under the terms of the agreement. The court in this role is essentially interpreting a contract. The court must determine what the parties have committed themselves to before ordering that they submit to arbitration.

The Issue of Arbitrability.   When a dispute arises as to whether or not the parties have agreed in an arbitration clause to submit a particular matter to arbitration, one party may file suit to compel arbitration. The court before which the suit is brought will not decide the basic controversy but must decide the issue of arbitrability—that is, whether the issue is one that must be resolved through arbitration. If the court finds that the subject matter in controversy is covered by the agreement to arbitrate, then a party may be compelled to arbitrate the dispute involuntarily.

Although the parties may agree to submit the issue of arbitrability to an arbitrator, the agreement must be explicit; a court will never *infer* an agreement to arbitrate. Unless a court finds an *explicit* agreement to have the arbitrator decide whether a dispute is arbitrable, the court will decide the issue. This is an important initial determination, because no party will be ordered to submit to arbitration unless the court is convinced that the party has consented to do so.

Compulsory Arbitration.   Are violations of rights granted by statutes appropriate subjects for arbitration? For example, should a court order the arbitration of a claim involving an alleged violation of a federal statute protecting an employee from employment discrimination?

In one important case, the United States Supreme Court held that a claim brought under the Age Discrimination in Employment Act (ADEA) of 1967 could be subject to compulsory arbitration.[4] The plaintiff in the case, Robert Gilmer, had been discharged from his employment at the age of sixty-two. Gilmer sued his employer, claiming that he was a victim of age discrimination. The employer argued that Gilmer had to submit the dispute to arbitration because he had agreed, as part of a required registration application to be a securities representative with the New York Stock Exchange, to arbitrate "any dispute, claim, or controversy" relating to his employment. The Supreme Court held that Gilmer, by agreeing to arbitrate any dispute, had waived his right to sue. (For a fuller discussion of the ADEA, see Chapter 22.)

Note that Gilmer had waived his *own* rights in a broadly worded arbitration clause. In the following case, the Supreme Court addresses the question of whether a union, in an equally broadly worded arbitration clause, can waive the rights of the employees whom it represents.

---

4. *Gilmer v. Interstate/Johnson Lane Corp.*, 500 U.S. 20, 111 S.Ct. 1647, 114 L.Ed.2d 26 (1991).

CASE 3.2   Wright v. Universal Maritime Service Corp.

Supreme Court of the
United States, 1998.
525 U.S. 70,
119 S.Ct. 391,
142 L.Ed.2d 361.
http://supct.law.
cornell.edu/supct/html/
97-156.ZS.html[a]

BACKGROUND AND FACTS   *Ceasar Wright was a longshoreman and a member of the International Longshoremen's Association (ILA). The ILA supplies workers to Universal Maritime Service Corporation and other members of the South Carolina Stevedores Association (SCSA). A collective bargaining agreement (CBA) between the ILA and the SCSA provided for the arbitration of "matters under dispute" in one clause and "all matters affecting wages, hours, and other terms and conditions of employment" in another. Still another clause stated that "[a]nything not contained in this Agreement shall not be construed as being part of this Agreement." Wright suffered a job-related injury that resulted in a disability. When a physician approved Wright's return to work, the SCSA members refused to hire him because of the disability. Wright filed a suit in a federal district court against Universal and others, on the ground that they had discriminated against him in violation of the Americans with Disabilities Act (ADA) of 1990 (see Chapter 42). The defendants argued that the suit should be dismissed because Wright had not submitted his claim to arbitration. The district court ruled in the defendants' favor, and the U.S. Court of Appeals for the Fourth Circuit affirmed this ruling. Wright appealed to the United States Supreme Court.*

IN THE LANGUAGE OF THE COURT

Justice SCALIA delivered the opinion of the Court.

*   *   *   *

*   *   * In [a previous case] we stated that a union could waive its officers' statutory right *   *   * to be free of antiunion discrimination, but we held that such a waiver must be *clear and unmistakable.* *   *   * [Emphasis added.]

*   *   * [T]he right to a federal judicial forum is of sufficient importance to be protected against a less-than-explicit union waiver in a CBA. The CBA in this case does not meet that standard. Its arbitration clause is very general, providing for arbitration of "[m]atters under dispute"—which could be understood to mean matters in dispute under the contract. And the remainder of the contract contains no explicit incorporation of statutory antidiscrimination requirements. The Fourth Circuit relied upon the fact that the equivalently broad arbitration clause in *Gilmer v. Interstate/Johnson Lane Corp.*—applying to "any dispute, claim or controversy"—was held to embrace federal statutory claims. But *Gilmer* involved an individual's waiver of his own rights, rather than a union's waiver of the rights of represented employees—and hence the "clear and unmistakable" standard was not applicable.

*   *   *   *

We hold that the collective-bargaining agreement in this case does not contain a clear and unmistakable waiver of the covered employees' rights to a judicial forum for federal claims of employment discrimination. We do not reach the question whether such a waiver would be enforceable.

DECISION AND REMEDY

The Supreme Court held that the arbitration clause in the CBA did not clearly waive the union members' right to have a court rule on federal claims of employment discrimination. Thus, Wright was not required to submit his claim to arbitration. The Court did not decide whether such a waiver would be enforceable if it were clear. The Court vacated the judgment of the lower court and remanded the case.

---

a. This page is part of the Supreme Court Collection of cases maintained by the Legal Information Institute, which is part of Cornell Law School. In the right-hand frame, in the "Arranged by party name" list, in the "1998" links, click on "1st party." On that page, scroll down to the case name and click on it to access the case.

International Arbitration and Public Policy   *International standards for the recognition of arbitration agreements and awards were set by the 1958 United Nations Convention on the Recognition and Enforcement of Foreign Arbitral Awards,[b] which has been signed by seventy-three countries, including the United States. Article V(2) of the convention creates an exception to enforcement of arbitration clauses that are "contrary to the public policy" of the relevant country. Thus, the resolution of a case will depend on the strength of a public policy in a given country. International organizations that handle arbitration matters include the United Nations Commission on International Trade Laws, the London Court of International Arbitration, the Euro-Arab Chamber of Commerce, the International Chamber of Commerce in Paris, and the International Trademark Association.*

b. June 10, 1958, 21 U.S.T. 2517 (the New York Convention).

SETTING ASIDE AN ARBITRATION AWARD

After the arbitration has been concluded, the losing party may appeal the arbitrator's award to a court, or the winning party may seek a court order compelling the other party to comply with the award. The scope of review in either situation is much more restricted than in an appellate court's review of a trial court decision. The court does not look at the merits of the underlying dispute, and the court will not add to or subtract from the remedies provided by the award. The court's role is limited to determining whether there exists a valid award. If so, the court will order the parties to comply with the terms. The general view is that because the parties were free to frame the issues and set the powers of the arbitrator at the outset, they cannot complain about the result.

Fact Findings and Legal Conclusions.   The arbitrator's fact findings and legal conclusions are nor-

mally final. That the arbitrator may have erred in a ruling during the hearing or made an erroneous fact finding is normally no basis for setting aside an award: the parties agreed that the arbitrator would be the judge of the facts. Similarly, no matter how obviously the arbitrator was mistaken in a conclusion of law, the award is normally nonetheless binding: the parties agreed to accept the arbitrator's interpretation of the law. A court will not look at the merits of the dispute, the sufficiency of the evidence presented, or the arbitrator's reasoning in reaching a particular decision.

This approach is consistent with the underlying view of all voluntary arbitration—that its basis is really contract law. If the parties freely contract with one another, courts will not interfere simply because one side feels that it received a bad bargain. Any party challenging an award must face the presumption that a final award is valid. But is an award final or binding if the parties did not agree that it would be? That was the issue in the following case.

CASE 3.3   Orlando v. Interstate Container Corp.

United States
Court of Appeals,
Third Circuit, 1996.
100 F.3d 296.

BACKGROUND AND FACTS   *Joseph Orlando, an employee of Interstate Container Corporation, underwent heart bypass surgery. For several months, he did not work but collected disability benefits, in part as provided by a collective bargaining agreement.[a] When his condition improved, he asked to return to work, but Interstate denied his request. He filed a complaint with the company, which, under the collective bargaining agreement, went to arbitration, culminating in an arbitrator's decision in Interstate's favor. The agreement did not state that the arbitrator's decision would be "final" or "binding,"*

a. A collective bargaining agreement is a contract negotiated by employees and their employer concerning the terms and conditions of employment. See Chapter 23.

however. In Orlando's subsequent suit against Interstate, a federal district court ruled that the decision was not binding. Interstate appealed.

IN THE LANGUAGE OF THE COURT

WEIS, Circuit Judge.

*   *   *   *

[Interstate] argues that because the contract makes arbitration mandatory, it must necessarily be final as well. That argument finds support in the policy favoring arbitration as a means of resolving disputes, but fails to meet the requirement of authorization by agreement of the parties. *   *   *

*   *   *   *

*   *   * [W]e must give full credit to the language the parties have chosen to include—or not include—in their agreement.

Collective bargaining agreements almost invariably explain that arbitration proceedings will be "final," "binding," or "exclusive," or use other words to that effect. This agreement was drafted by parties well-versed in labor matters and cognizant [aware] of that convention. The omission of any indication that arbitration proceedings should be final and binding leads us to conclude that, if we nevertheless declared them to be so, we would not be enforcing the will of the parties, as expressed in their agreement.

DECISION AND REMEDY

The U.S. Court of Appeals for the Third Circuit affirmed the lower court's decision. The award was not final or binding because the parties did not agree that it would be.

Public Policy and Illegality. In keeping with contract law principles, no award will be enforced if compliance with the award would result in the commission of a crime or would conflict with some greater social policy mandated by statute. A court will not overturn an award, however, simply because the arbitrator was called on to resolve a dispute involving a matter of significant public concern.[5] For an award to be set aside, it must call for some action on the part of the parties that would conflict with or in some way undermine public policy.[6]

Defects in the Arbitration Process. There are some bases for setting aside an award when there is a defect in the arbitration process. These bases are typified by those set forth in the Federal Arbitration Act. Section 10 of the act provides four grounds on which an arbitration award may be set aside:

1. The award was the result of corruption, fraud, or other "undue means."
2. The arbitrator exhibited bias or corruption.
3. The arbitrator refused to postpone the hearing despite sufficient cause, refused to hear evidence perti-

nent and material to the dispute, or otherwise acted to substantially prejudice the rights of one of the parties.
4. The arbitrator exceeded his or her powers or failed to use them to make a mutual, final, and definite award.

The first three bases for setting aside the award include actions or decisions that are more than simply mistakes in judgment. Each requires some "bad faith" on the part of the arbitrator. Bad faith actions or decisions are ones that affect the integrity of the arbitration process. The honesty and impartiality, rather than the judgment, of the arbitrator are called into question.

Sometimes it is difficult to make the distinction between honest mistakes in judgment and actions or decisions made in bad faith. A bribe is clearly the kind of "undue means" included in the first basis for setting aside an award. Letting only one side argue its case is likewise a clear violation of the second basis.

Meetings between the arbitrator and one party outside the presence of the other party also taint the arbitration process. Although meetings might not involve the kind of corruption that results from taking a bribe, they do affect the integrity of the process; the third basis for setting aside an award is meant to protect against this.

Not every refusal by an arbitrator to admit certain evidence is grounds for setting aside an award under the

---

5. See, for example, *Faherty v. Faherty*, 97 N.J. 99, 477 A.2d 1257 (1984).
6. See, for example, *Meehan v. Nassau Community College*, 647 N.Y.S.2d 865 (App.Div. 2 Dept. 1996).

third basis. As noted, to provide a basis for overturning an award, the arbitrator's decision must be more than an error in judgment, no matter how obviously incorrect that judgment might appear to another observer. The decision must be so obviously wrong or unfair as to imply bias or corruption. Otherwise, the decision normally cannot be a basis for setting aside an award.

The fourth basis for setting aside an award is that the arbitrator exceeded his or her powers in arbitrating the dispute. This issue involves the question of arbitrability. An arbitrator exceeds his or her powers and authority by attempting to resolve an issue that is not covered by the agreement to submit to arbitration.

In the following case, a party to an arbitration proceeding asked a court to set aside the award.

CASE 3.4   Garvey v. Roberts

United States
Court of Appeals,
Ninth Circuit, 2000.
203 F.3d 580.
http://www.ce9.
uscourts.gov[a]

BACKGROUND AND FACTS   *In 1986, 1987, and 1988, the Major League Baseball Players Association complained that the Major League Baseball Clubs had engaged in collusion to underpay some of the players. The grievance was submitted to arbitration before a panel chaired by Thomas Roberts. During a hearing in 1986, Ballard Smith, the president of the San Diego Padres, testified that there had been no collusion. Roberts' panel rejected this testimony as false. The Association and the Clubs entered into a settlement agreement, under which the Clubs set up a fund of $280 million to be distributed to players who suffered losses due to the collusion and the Association established a framework for evaluating each player's claim. A player could challenge the Association's recommendation in binding arbitration. Steve Garvey, who had played for the Padres between 1983 and 1987 under a contract, filed a claim for damages, alleging that the Padres would have extended his contract for the 1988 and 1989 seasons but for the collusion. Roberts, the arbitrator in Garvey's case, denied the claim. Roberts cited Smith's testimony in the 1986 hearing that the Padres were not interested in extending Garvey's contract. Roberts rejected Smith's admission, in a 1996 letter, that he had not told the truth during those hearings and that he had made Garvey an offer that was withdrawn due to the collusion. Garvey filed a suit in a federal district court against Roberts and the Association to have the arbitrator's award set aside. The court ruled in the defendants' favor. Garvey appealed to the U.S. Court of Appeals for the Ninth Circuit.*

IN THE LANGUAGE
OF THE COURT

REINHARDT, Circuit Judge.
        *   *   *   *

*   *   * We overturn an arbitrator's award only when it is clear from the arbitral opinion or award that the arbitrator *   *   * disregarded what the parties put before him and instead followed his own whims or biases.
        *   *   *   *

Under ordinary circumstances, we would accept a conclusion by the arbitrator that Smith told the truth in his 1986 testimony and lied in his 1996 letter even if that conclusion were clearly erroneous. We are presented, however, with the extraordinary circumstance in which the arbitrator's own rulings make clear that, more than being simply erroneous, his finding is completely inexplicable and borders on the irrational. *   *   *
        *   *   * [At] the collusion proceedings *   *   *, the panel of arbitrators headed by Arbitrator Roberts had previously ruled that the 1986 testimony by the owners, including Smith, was untruthful. The owners' testimony during those hearings had been designed for the sole purpose of convincing the arbitrators that no collusion had taken

---

a. In the right column, click on "Appeals Court Decisions". On the page, click on "2000". In the expanded list, click on "February". In that list, scroll to the name of the case and click on it to access the opinion.

place, and the arbitrators had concluded that the owners' testimony was not true. In light of that conclusion, Arbitrator Roberts' determination in Garvey's individual claim proceeding that Smith's (false) 1986 collusion testimony somehow precluded the crediting of his (truthful) confession in 1996 is, to say the least, bizarre.

The owners' mendacity [lies] in their 1980's collusive efforts to depress the ballplayers' income was in many ways as damaging to baseball as the Black Sox scandal of 1919.[b] The scope of the owners' deceit and fabrications in their 1980's effort to cheat their employees out of their rightful wages was wholly unprecedented, as was the financial injury suffered by the ballplayers. That the arbitrator would in these circumstances rely on Smith's statements made in the collusion hearing, and on the basis of those false statements reject Smith's later effort to remedy the injury he had caused, surpasses understanding. The only inference that can fairly be drawn from the arbitrator's current crediting of Smith's earlier perjurious testimony is that the arbitrator was attempting to dispense his own brand of industrial justice. For this reason, we decline to enforce his award.

DECISION AND REMEDY   *The U.S. Court of Appeals for the Ninth Circuit reversed the ruling of the lower court and remanded the case with directions to set aside the arbitrator's award. The arbitrator had improperly attempted "to dispense his own brand of industrial justice" by granting credibility to testimony that he had earlier declared to be false.*

---

b. In the 1919 World Series, the Chicago White Sox lost to the Cincinnati Reds under circumstances that led to the indictment of eight Chicago players—named the "Black Sox"—on charges of accepting bribes from gamblers to lose the games.

Waiver. Although a defect in the arbitration process is sufficient grounds for setting aside an award, a party sometimes forfeits the right to challenge an award by failing to object to the defect in a timely manner. The party must object when he or she learns of the problem. After making the objection, the party can still proceed with the arbitration process and still challenge the award in court after the arbitration proceedings have concluded. If, however, a party makes no objection and proceeds with the arbitration process, then a later court challenge to the award may be denied on the ground that the party *waived* the right to challenge the award on the basis of the defect.

Frequently, this occurs when a party fails to object that an arbitrator is exceeding his or her powers in resolving a dispute because the subject matter is not arbitrable or because the party did not agree to arbitrate the dispute. The question of arbitrability is one for the courts to decide. If a party does not object on this issue at the first demand for arbitration, however, a court may consider the objection waived.

Conflicts of Law. Parties are afforded wide latitude in establishing the manner in which their disputes will be resolved. Nevertheless, an agreement to arbitrate may be governed by the Federal Arbitration Act (FAA) or one of the many state arbitration acts, even though the parties do not refer to a statute in their agreement. Recall that the FAA covers any arbitration clause in a contract that involves interstate commerce. Frequently, however, transactions involving interstate commerce also have substantial connections to particular states, which may in turn have their own arbitration acts. In such situations, unless the FAA and state arbitration law are nearly identical, the acts may conflict. How are these conflicts to be resolved?

As a general principle, the supremacy clause and the commerce clause of the U.S. Constitution are the bases for giving federal law preeminence; when there is a conflict, state law is preempted by federal law. Thus, in cases of arbitration, the strong federal policy favoring arbitration can override a state's laws that might be more favorable to normal litigation.

Choice of Law. Notwithstanding federal preemption of conflicting state laws, the Federal Arbitration Act has been interpreted as allowing the parties to choose a particular state law to govern their arbitration agreement. The parties may choose to have the laws of a specific state govern their agreement by including in the agreement a *choice-of-law clause.* The FAA does not mandate any particular set of rules that parties must follow in arbitration; the parties are free to agree on the manner best suited to their needs. Consistent with this view that arbitration is at heart a contractual matter between private parties, the United States Supreme Court has upheld arbitration agreements containing choice-of-law provisions.

DISADVANTAGES OF ARBITRATION

Arbitration has some disadvantages. The result in any particular dispute can be unpredictable, in part because arbitrators do not need to follow any previous cases in rendering their decisions. Unlike judges, arbitrators do not have to issue written opinions or facilitate a participant's appeal to a court. Arbitrators must decide disputes according to whatever rules have been provided by the parties, regardless of how unfair those rules may be. In some cases, arbitration can be nearly as expensive as litigation. In part, this is because both sides must prepare their cases for presentation before a third-party decision maker, just as they would have to do to appear in court. Discovery is usually not available in arbitration, however, which means that during the hearing the parties must take the time to question witnesses whom, in a lawsuit, they would not need to call.[7]

SECTION 4

The Integration of ADR and Formal Court Procedures

Because of the congestion within the judicial system, many jurisdictions at both the state and federal levels are integrating alternative dispute resolution into the formal legal process. Utilizing methods such as arbitration and mediation within the traditional framework may relieve the logjams afflicting most of the nation's court systems.

COURT-MANDATED ADR

Increasingly, courts are requiring that parties attempt to settle their differences through some form of ADR

before proceeding to trial. For example, several federal district courts encourage nonbinding arbitration for cases involving amounts less than $100,000. Less than 10 percent of the cases referred for arbitration ever go to trial. Today, about half of all federal courts have adopted formal rules regarding the use of ADR, and many other courts without such rules use ADR procedures.

Most states have adopted programs that allow them to refer certain types of cases for negotiation, mediation, or arbitration. Typically—as in California and Hawaii—court systems have adopted mandatory mediation or nonbinding arbitration programs for certain types of disputes, usually involving less than a specified threshold dollar amount.[8] Only if the parties fail to reach an agreement, or if one of the parties disagrees with the decision of a third party mediating or arbitrating the dispute, will the case be heard by a court. South Carolina was the first state to institute a voluntary arbitration program at the appellate court level. In the South Carolina system, litigants must waive a court hearing when requesting arbitration. All decisions by the arbitrators are final and binding.

COURT-ANNEXED ARBITRATION

Court-annexed arbitration differs significantly from the voluntary arbitration process discussed above. There are some disputes that courts will not allow to go to arbitration. Most states, for example, do not allow court-annexed arbitration in disputes involving title to real estate or in cases in which a court's equity powers are involved.

A Fundamental Difference. The fundamental difference between voluntary arbitration and court-annexed arbitration is the finality and reviewability of the award. With respect to court-annexed arbitration, either party may reject the award for any reason. In the event that one of the parties does reject the award, the case will proceed to trial, and the court will hear the case *de novo*—that is, the court will reconsider all the evidence and legal questions as though no arbitration had occurred.

Everyone who has a recognizable cause of action or against whom such an action is brought is entitled to have the issue decided in a court of law. Because court-annexed arbitration is not voluntary, there must be some safeguard against using it in a way that denies

---

7. One notable dispute concerning computer chip technology lasted more than seven years and cost the participants more than $100 million. See *Advanced Micro Devices, Inc. v. Intel Corp.,* 9 Cal.4th 362, 885 P.2d 994, 36 Cal.Rptr.2d 581 (1994).

8. Hawaii, for example, has a program of mandatory, nonbinding arbitration for disputes involving less than $150,000.

an individual his or her day in court. This safeguard is provided by permitting either side to reject the award regardless of the reason for so doing.

The party rejecting the award may be penalized, however. Many statutes providing for court-annexed arbitration impose court costs and fees on a party who rejects an arbitration award but does not improve his or her position by going to trial. Thus, for example, if a party rejects an arbitration award, and the award turns out to be more favorable to that party than the subsequent jury verdict, the party may be compelled to pay the costs of the arbitration or some fee for the costs of the trial.

In court-annexed arbitration, discovery of evidence occurs before the hearing. After the hearing has commenced, a party seeking to discover new evidence must usually secure approval from the court that mandated the arbitration. This is intended to prevent the parties from using arbitration as a means of previewing each other's cases and then rejecting the arbitrator's award.

The Role of the Arbitrator. Notwithstanding the differences between voluntary and court-annexed arbitration, the role of the arbitrator is essentially the same in both types of proceedings. The arbitrator determines issues of both fact and law. The arbitrator also makes all decisions concerning applications of the rules of procedure and evidence during the hearing.

Which Rules Apply. Regarding the rules of evidence, there are differences among the states. Most states impose the same rules of evidence on an arbitration hearing as on a trial. Other states, such as New Jersey, allow all evidence relevant to the dispute regardless of whether the evidence would be admissible at trial. Still other jurisdictions, such as Washington, leave it to the arbitrator to decide what evidence is admissible.

Waiver. Once a court directs that a dispute is to be submitted to court-annexed arbitration, the parties must proceed to arbitration. As noted above, either side may reject the award that results from the arbitration for any reason. If a party fails to appear at or participate in the arbitration proceeding as directed by the court, however, that failure constitutes a waiver of the right to reject the award.

Court-Related Mediation

Mediation is proving to be more popular than arbitration as a court-related method of ADR. No federal court has adopted an arbitration program since 1991, while mediation programs continue to increase in number in both federal and state courts. Today, more court systems offer or require mediation, rather than arbitration, as an alternative to litigation.

Mediation is often used in disputes relating to employment law, environmental law, product liability, and franchises. One of the most important business advantages of mediation is the lower cost, which can be 25 percent (or less) of the expense of litigation. Another advantage is the speed with which a dispute can go through mediation (possibly one or two days) compared with arbitration (possibly months) or litigation (possibly years).

Part of the popularity of mediation is that its goal, unlike that of litigation and some other forms of ADR, is for opponents to work out a resolution that benefits both sides. The rate of participants' satisfaction with the outcomes in mediated disputes is high. In New Hampshire, for example, where mediation is mandatory for all civil cases in most state trial courts, as many as 70 percent of the participants report satisfaction with the results.

Summary Jury Trials

Another means by which the courts have integrated alternative dispute resolution methods into the traditional court process is through the use of summary jury trials. A **summary jury trial** is a mock trial that occurs in a courtroom before a judge and jury. Evidence is presented in an abbreviated form, along with each side's major contentions. The jury then presents a verdict.

The fundamental difference between a traditional trial and a summary jury trial is that in the latter, the jury's verdict is only advisory. The goal of a summary jury trial is to give each side an idea of how it would fare in a full-blown jury trial with a more elaborate and detailed presentation of evidence and arguments. At the end of the summary jury trial, the presiding judge meets with the parties and may encourage them to settle their dispute without going through a standard jury trial.

ADR and Mass Torts

A *tort* is a civil wrong that does not arise from a breach of contract. (Torts are discussed in detail in Chapter 12. Breach of contract is discussed in Chapter 10.) *Mass tort* is the term applied to civil lawsuits that share

EMERGING TRENDS IN TECHNOLOGY

ADR Goes Online

Given the increasing use of the World Wide Web for commercial transactions, it should come as no surprise that alternative dispute resolution (ADR) services are now available online as well. For some time, ADR resources have been available on the Web. For example, if you go to the Web site of the American Arbitration Association (AAA), you will find information on ADR methods, AAA rules, and sample AAA forms that can be downloaded or printed out for use in submitting a dispute to arbitration before the AAA. You can also find articles on topics ranging from how to draft an arbitration clause to creating a company ADR policy. Today, however, a number of Web sites are going even further: they offer parties to a dispute an opportunity to settle, mediate, or otherwise resolve their dispute using online forums.

ONLINE SETTLEMENTS

Traditionally, the parties to a dispute had a number of options for settling their differences. One option, of course, was coming to an agreement themselves. Another was enlisting the help of their attorneys in trying to work out a reasonable settlement. Still another alternative was to mediate or arbitrate the dispute. Indeed, if their contract contained an

arbitration clause, then the dispute would have to be arbitrated. Finally, the parties could take their dispute to court. Today, various Web sites offer yet another option: settling disputes by the click of a mouse.

Consider the services offered by clickNsettle.com (at **http://www.clickNsettle.com**), a subsidiary of National Arbitration & Mediation. At clickNsettle.com's Web site, disputing parties may be able to settle their dispute for only a small fee (currently ranging from $75 to $275). The settlement process is conducted through a series of confidential "bids," similar to those used in online auctions. First, the claimant submits a claim against the defendant to clickNsettle.com, which then notifies the defendant of the claim via e-mail. The defendant submits three amounts that it is willing to pay to settle the claim, following which the claimant submits an amount that he or she considers reasonable. If the claimant's amount falls within a specified range of one of the three amounts stated by the defendant, the matter is settled. If it does not, the claimant can submit two more amounts, or "bids."

Other online ADR providers use similar processes. For example, cyber$ettle.com (at **http://www.cybersettle.com**) gives disputing parties three opportunities, or "rounds," to settle their dispute. One demand and one offer can be entered for each round. The amount demanded in a particular round is compared to the amount

offered for that round. If an offer is within 30 percent, or $5,000, of the amount demanded, then cyber$ettle lets the parties know that a settlement has been reached, and a written confirmation of the settlement is sent to the parties. If, in all three rounds, the offer differs from a demand by more than 30 percent, or $5,000, no settlement is reached, and the parties are so notified.

One of the appealing aspects of these types of online settlement proceedings is that offers and demands normally are made separately, in confidence, and are never disclosed. Additionally, these sites can be accessed at any time, and little waiting is involved. Once a demand or offer is submitted, the computer program determines if a settlement has—or has not—been reached. If no settlement is reached, the parties can try some other form of ADR, such as mediation, before taking their case to court.

CYBERMEDIATION

People who wish to mediate their disputes can now go online to one of a number of Web sites that offer mediation services. Indeed, cybermediation is becoming an increasingly popular Web business. Through the use of e-mail, "chat rooms," videoconferencing, and other technologies, online mediators assist parties in finding acceptable resolutions to their disputes.

One of the first Web-based mediation services appeared in

such features as scientific or technological complexity and a large number of participants. Such cases often feature a high degree of emotional involvement on the part of the claimants, who may suffer from severe or life-threatening injuries, and on the part of the defendants, whose financial existence may be at stake.

EMERGING TRENDS IN TECHNOLOGY

ADR Goes Online, continued

1996, when the Virtual Magistrate (VM) Web page was launched. The aim of VM was to settle disputes, such as domain-name disputes, arising from online activities. This early effort in cybermediation was not very successful, however—the VM handled only one case. The VM project may ultimately succeed in its mission, though. Currently, the American Arbitration Association, one of the sponsors of the VM project, and other organizations are working with this enterprise to update its site.

As with traditional mediation, Web businesses that offer commercial mediation services typically charge the parties a fee. For example, one such service, Internet Neutral (at **http://www. internetneutral.com**), requires each party to pay a minimum fee of $250 when a request to mediate a dispute is submitted to the Internet Neutral Web site. The fee covers approximately two hours of mediation session time and two hours for reading and preparation. If the mediation continues for more than four hours, there is an hourly fee of $125 per hour, which is split by the parties. During a mediation session, the parties sit before their computers and use two "chat conference rooms." One of these rooms is used for private conversations between the party

and the mediator; the other room is used for private conversations involving both parties and the mediator. Videoconferences may also be held.

A well-known nonprofit mediation center on the Web is the Online Ombuds Office, at **http:// www.aaron.sbs.umass.edu/ center/ombuds/default.htm**. This office was established in 1997 as the dispute-resolution arm of the Center for Information Technology and Dispute Resolution at the University of Massachusetts. The Online Ombuds Office offers online mediation services to disputing parties at no cost. Although the office is primarily interested in mediating disputes that arise out of online activities, it will handle other disputes as well. In a pilot project conducted in early 1999, the Online Ombuds Office mediated 175 disputes at a major Internet auction site, eBay. Consumers who had complaints about their purchases could contact the Online Ombuds Office to have their disputes mediated. The parties communicated with a mediator via e-mail to try to resolve the claim.

IMPLICATIONS FOR THE BUSINESSPERSON

1. The proliferation of online ADR forums and online settlement services may lead to significant savings for businesspersons. The low cost of online settlement processes makes them a particularly attractive option for

businesspersons who wish to settle a dispute quickly and confidentially.

2. For those who do business on a global level, online ADR may be particularly beneficial. One of the risks of engaging in any international business transaction is that if a dispute arises, one (and often both) of the parties will be required to travel to a distant forum to have the dispute resolved, either through ADR or in a court. Because the Internet is a global network, parties from different countries can resolve their disputes through online ADR without leaving their offices.

FOR CRITICAL ANALYSIS

1. What might be some disadvantages of online dispute settlement or mediation?
2. In arbitration, and particularly in formal arbitration proceedings, the parties often present various forms of evidence to the arbitrator. Does this mean that online arbitration is not feasible?

RELEVANT WEB SITES

To learn more about online settlement and mediation services, go to any or all of the Web sites mentioned in this feature. If you are interested in seeing a transcript of the mediation of an actual dispute (between a Web site developer and a newspaper), go to **http:// aaron.sbs.umass.edu/center/ ombuds/narrative1.html**.

Examples of mass torts include litigation involving Agent Orange, the Dalkon Shield, the prescription drug DES, heart valves, and asbestos.

In the 1990s, there was an explosion in the number of mass torts. For example, more than 300,000 claims were filed in asbestos-related litigation—in the mid-1990s, new claims were filed at the rate of 5,000 every month. Such claims are overwhelming our civil justice system. In attempts to clear the courts, some judges in mass tort cases turn to methods of alternative dispute resolution, including mediation, arbitration, mini-trials, and summary jury trials. ADR may be used to assess the validity or the value of the claims or to sort out or resolve the scientific, technological, or medical issues. ADR may be used to settle large numbers of claims in a speedy, efficient, cost-effective manner. Once a settlement is reached, a neutral third party may coordinate payments to claimants. There may even be provision for an ADR appeals process.

SECTION 5

ADR Forums and Services

Services facilitating dispute resolution outside the courtroom are provided by both government agencies and private organizations.

NONPROFIT ORGANIZATIONS

The major source of private arbitration services is the American Arbitration Association (AAA). Most of the largest law firms in the nation are members of this association. Founded in 1926, the AAA now settles more than 80,000 disputes a year and has offices in every state. Cases brought before the AAA are heard by an expert or a panel of experts—of whom usually about half are lawyers—in the area relating to the dispute. To cover its costs, this nonprofit organization charges a fee, paid by the party filing the claim. In addition, each party to the dispute pays a price for each hearing day, as well as a special additional fee in cases involving personal injuries or property loss.

In addition to the AAA, hundreds of other state and local nonprofit organizations provide arbitration services. For example, the Arbitration Association of Florida provides ADR services in that state. The Better Business Bureau (BBB) offers ADR programs to aid in the resolution of certain types of disagreements. The BBB's programs include a mediation program called ComputerCare, through which buyers and sellers of computer equipment and software can settle their disputes. Many industries—including the insurance, automobile, and securities industries—also now have mediation or arbitration programs to facilitate timely and inexpensive settlement of claims.

FOR-PROFIT ORGANIZATIONS

Those who seek to settle their disputes quickly can turn to private, for-profit organizations to act as mediators or arbitrators. The leading firm in this private system of justice is JAMS/Endispute, which is based in Santa Ana, California. The private system of justice includes hundreds of firms throughout the country offering dispute-resolution services by hired judges. Procedures in these private courts are fashioned to meet the desires of the clients seeking their services. For example, the parties might decide on the date of the hearing, the presiding judge, whether the judge's decision will be legally binding, and the site of the hearing—which could be a conference room, a law-school office, or a leased courtroom complete with flag and Bible. The judges may follow procedures similar to those of the federal courts and use similar rules. Each party to the dispute may pay a filing fee and a designated fee for a half-day hearing session or a special, one-hour settlement conference.

There are also international organizations, such as the International Chamber of Commerce, that provide forums for the arbitration of disputes between parties to international contracts. These organizations, as well as some of the advantages and disadvantages of arbitrating disputes in the international context, will be discussed in Chapter 8.

Finally, a growing number of firms are offering dispute-resolution services online. See this chapter's *Emerging Trends in Technology* on pages 74–75 for a discussion of this latest development in ADR.

TERMS AND CONCEPTS TO REVIEW

alternative dispute resolution (ADR) 60	arbitration 61	award 66
	arbitrator 62	conciliation 61

early neutral case evaluation 60

mediation 61

mediator 61

mini-trial 60

negotiation 60

submission 64

summary jury trial 73

QUESTIONS AND CASE PROBLEMS

3–1. ARBITRATION. In an arbitration proceeding, the arbitrator need not be a judge or even a lawyer. How, then, can the arbitrator's decision have the force of law and be binding on the parties involved?

3–2. CHOICE OF LAW. Two private U.S. corporations enter into a joint-venture agreement to conduct mining operations in the newly formed Middle Eastern nation of Euphratia. As part of the agreement, the companies include an arbitration clause and a choice-of-law provision. The first states that any controversy arising out of the performance of the agreement will be settled by arbitration. The second states that the agreement is to be governed by the laws of the location of the venture, Euphratia. A dispute arises, and the parties discontinue operations. One of the parties claims sole ownership to the Euphratian mines and orders the other party to remove its equipment from the mines. The other party disputes the claim of sole ownership and seeks an order from a U.S. federal court compelling the parties to submit to arbitration over the ownership issue and alleged breaches of the joint-venture agreement. How should the court rule if the laws of Euphratia state that, whereas arbitration agreements are to be enforced generally, matters of ownership of natural resources can only be resolved in a Euphratian court of law? Does it matter that two U.S. companies engaged in international commerce would be governed by the Federal Arbitration Act?

3–3. CONFIRMATION OF AWARD. Two brothers, both of whom are certified public accountants (CPAs), form a professional association to provide tax-accounting services to the public. They also agree, in writing, that any disputes that arise between them over matters concerning the association will be submitted to an independent arbitrator, whom they designate to be their father, who is also a CPA. A dispute arises, and the matter is submitted to the father for arbitration. During the course of arbitration, which occurs over several weeks, the father asks the older brother, who is visiting one evening, to explain a certain entry in the brothers' association accounts. The younger brother learns of the discussion at the next meeting for arbitration; he says nothing about it, however. The arbitration is concluded in favor of the older brother, who seeks a court order compelling the younger brother to comply with the award. The younger brother seeks to set aside the award, claiming that the arbitration process was tainted by bias because "Dad always liked

my older brother best." The younger brother also seeks to have the award set aside on the basis of improper conduct in that matters subject to arbitration were discussed between the father and older brother without the younger brother's being present. Should a court confirm the award or set it aside? Why?

3–4. CALCULATION OF AWARD. After resolving their dispute, the two brothers encountered in Problem 4–3 above decide to resume their tax-accounting practice according to the terms of their original agreement. Again a dispute arises, and again it is decided by the father (now retired except for numerous occasions on which he acts as an arbitrator) in favor of the older brother. The older brother files a petition to enforce the award. The younger brother seeks to set aside the award and offers evidence that the father, as arbitrator, made a gross error in calculating the accounts that were material to the dispute being arbitrated. If the court is convinced that the father erred in the calculations, should the award be set aside? Why?

3–5. COMPELLING ARBITRATION. In 1981, AT&T laid off seventy-nine workers in the Chicago area, purportedly because of a slowdown in economic activity. The Communications Workers of America, a union representing some AT&T workers, argued that there was no lack of work and objected to the layoffs as violations of the terms of a collective bargaining agreement between the union and AT&T. The agreement provided that "differences arising with respect to the interpretation of this contract or the performance of any obligation" under the agreement would be resolved through arbitration. The agreement reserved to AT&T the free exercise of managerial functions such as hiring and firing employees. The agreement conditioned such decision making on compliance with the terms of the contract but expressly excluded disputes over those decisions from arbitration. AT&T relied on this exclusion to avoid the union's demand for arbitration over the layoffs. The union sought a court order to compel arbitration. The court held that the issue of whether the dispute over the layoffs was subject to arbitration should be decided by the arbitrator and ordered the parties to submit the question to the arbitrator. An appellate court affirmed the holding, and AT&T appealed to the United States Supreme Court. How should the Court rule? Discuss fully. [*AT&T Technologies v. Communications Workers of America*, 475 U.S. 643, 106 S.Ct. 1415, 89 L.Ed.2d 648 (1990)]

3–6. ARBITRATION. Randall Fris worked as a seaman on an Exxon Shipping Co. oil tanker for eight years without incident. One night, he boarded the ship for duty while intoxicated, in violation of company policy. This policy also allowed Exxon to discharge employees who were intoxicated and thus unfit for work. Exxon discharged Fris. Under a contract with Fris's union, the discharge was submitted to arbitration. The arbitrators ordered Exxon to reinstate Fris on an oil tanker. Exxon filed a suit against the union, challenging the award as contrary to public policy, which opposes having intoxicated persons operate seagoing vessels. Can a court set aside an arbitration award on the ground that the award violates public policy? Should the court set aside the award in this case? Explain. [*Exxon Shipping Co. v. Exxon Seamen's Union*, 11 F.3d 1189 (3d Cir. 1993)]

3–7. ARBITRATION. Phillip Beaudry, who suffered from mental illness, worked in the Department of Income Maintenance for the state of Connecticut. Beaudry was fired from his job when it was learned that he had misappropriated approximately $1,640 in state funds. Beaudry filed a complaint with his union, Council 4 of the American Federation of State, County, and Municipal Employees (AFSCME), and eventually the dispute was submitted to an arbitrator. The arbitrator concluded that Beaudry had been dismissed without "just cause," because Beaudry's acts were caused by his mental illness and "were not willful or volitional or within his capacity to control." Because Beaudry was disabled, the employer was required, under state law, to transfer him to a position that he was competent to hold. The arbitrator awarded Beaudry reinstatement, back pay, seniority, and other benefits. The state appealed the decision to a court. What public policies must the court weigh in making its decision? How should the court rule? [*State v. Council 4, AFSCME*, 27 Conn.App. 635, 608 A.2d 718 (1992)]

3–8. ARBITRATOR'S AUTHORITY. Hembree purchased a home from Broadway Realty and Trust Co. In the contract of sale, the buyer and seller agreed to arbitrate any claim or controversy "arising out of or relating to this contract." Hembree later claimed that the roof was defective, and the case was arbitrated. The arbitrator decided in favor of Hembree on the basis that the seller had breached an implied warranty. The seller appealed the arbitrator's decision, claiming that the arbitrator had exceeded his authority, because only claims arising out of or relating to the contract were to be arbitrated, and an implied warranty claim did not arise out of or relate to "this contract." Discuss whether the arbitrator was within his authority in addressing the implied warranty claim. [*Hembree v. Broadway Realty and Trust Co.*, 151 Ariz. 418, 728 P.2d 288 (1986)]

3–9. ARBITRATION. Stephanie Prince was an employee of Coca-Cola Bottling Co. of New York, Inc. (CNY), and a member of the Soft Drink and Brewery Workers Union. An agreement between CNY and the Union set out a procedure to follow in the event of a dispute between an employee and CNY relating to "any matter whatsoever including, the meaning, interpretation, application or violation of this Agreement." In this context, the agreement mentioned some employment laws but did not mention federal discrimination laws. After the Union was notified, and if the grievance was not resolved within thirty days, the dispute was to be submitted to arbitration. Prince reported to the Union, which told CNY, that she was being sexually harassed by her supervisors, Michael Drake and Leonard Erlanger. When no action was taken and Prince was subject to retaliatory behavior by Drake and Erlanger, she filed a complaint with the Equal Employment Opportunity Commission. The supervisors retaliated again by ordering her to leave the workplace and "stay home." Prince filed a suit in a federal district court against CNY and the supervisors, alleging, among other things, violations of federal discrimination law. CNY responded that its agreement with the Union required Prince to submit her claim to arbitration. Is CNY right? In whose favor should the court rule? Why? [*Prince. v. Coca-Cola Bottling Co. of New York, Inc.*, 37 F.Supp.2d 289 (S.D.N.Y. 1999)]

3–10. ARBITRATION. New York State revised its New Car Lemon Law to allow consumers who complained of purchasing a "lemon" to have their disputes arbitrated before a professional arbitrator appointed by the New York attorney general. Before this revision, the Lemon Law allowed for arbitration of disputes, but the forum in which arbitration took place was sponsored by trade associations within the automobile industry, and consumers often complained of unfair awards. The revised law also provided that consumers could choose between two options: arbitration before a professional arbitrator and suing the manufacturer in court. Manufacturers, however, were compelled to arbitrate claims, if a consumer chose to do so, and could not resort to the courts. Trade associations representing automobile manufacturers and importers brought an action seeking a declaration that the alternative arbitration mechanism of the Lemon Law was unconstitutional because it deprived them of their right to trial by jury. How will the court decide? Discuss. [*Motor Vehicle Manufacturers Association of the United States v. State*, 75 N.Y.2d 175, 550 N.E.2d 919, 551 N.Y.S.2d 470 (1990)]

3–11. IN YOUR COURT

Linda Bender, in her application for registration as a stockbroker with A. G. Edwards & Sons, Inc., agreed to submit any disputes with her employer to arbitration. Bender later sued her supervisor and employer (the defendants) for sexual harassment in violation of Title VII of the Civil Rights Act of 1964, which prohibits, among other things, employment discrimination based on gender. The defendants requested the court to compel arbitration. Assume that you are the judge hearing this case and answer the following questions:

(a) Does the right to a postarbitration judicial forum equate to the right to initial access to a judicial forum in employment disputes? Should you grant the defendants' request? Why or why not?

(b) Should the fact that reviewing courts rarely set aside arbitrators' awards have any bearing on the arbitrability of certain types of claims, such as those brought under Title VII?

LAW ON THE WEB

For updated links to resources available on the Web, as well as a variety of other materials, visit this text's Web site at http://wleb.westbuslaw.com. Here we list selected Web sites that offer information relevant to the topics covered in this chapter.

For information on alternative dispute resolution, go to the American Arbitration Association's Web site at

http://www.adr.org

LEGAL RESEARCH EXERCISES ON THE WEB

Go to http://wleb.westbuslaw.com, the Web site that accompanies this text. Select "Internet Applications," and then click on "Chapter 3." There you will find the following Internet research exercise that you can perform to learn more about alternative dispute resolution:

Activity 3–1: Alternative Dispute Resolution

CHAPTER 4

Ethics and Business Decision Making

THE PURPOSE OF ORGANIZING a business, no matter what business form is chosen for the enterprise, normally is to make a profit. Generally, profit-making activities are encouraged by the laws, because the flourishing of trade and commerce confers benefits on society as a whole. At the same time, businesspersons should not let their profit-making activities exceed the ethical boundaries established by society. In the past, these boundaries were often regarded as being coterminous with the law—that is, if something was legal, it was ethical. In today's rights-conscious world, however, a business firm that decides it has no duties other than those prescribed by law may find it difficult to survive. If a firm's behavior is perceived as unethical—even though it may be legal—that firm may suffer negative publicity, lost profits, and even government sanctions.

In this chapter, we first examine the nature of business ethics and some commonly used approaches to ethical reasoning. We then look at the ethical component of business decision making in some detail. Throughout the chapter, we include specific examples of ethical issues that commonly arise in the business world.

SECTION 1

The Nature of Business Ethics

Before we examine the nature of business ethics, we need to discuss what is meant by ethics generally. **Ethics** can be defined as the study of what constitutes right or wrong behavior. It is the branch of philosophy that focuses on morality and the way in which moral principles are derived or the way in which a given set of moral principles applies to one's conduct in daily life. Ethics has to do with questions relating to the fairness, justness, rightness, or wrongness of an action. What is fair? What is just? What is the right thing to do in this situation? These are essentially ethical questions.

Often, moral principles serve as the guiding force in an individual's personal ethical system. Although the terms *ethical* and *moral* often are used interchangeably, these terms refer to slightly different concepts. Whereas ethics has to do with the philosophical, rational basis for conduct, morals are often defined as *universal* rules or guidelines (such as those rooted in religious precepts) that determine our actions and character. Morals generally are "revealed" truths—that is, they are revealed to us by our family, influential mentors, or religious sources, such as the Bible (for Christians) or the Koran (for Muslims). Ethics, in contrast, is a reasoned set of principles of conduct. These principles may be based either on moral truths or on premises derived through logic and reasoning.

DEFINING BUSINESS ETHICS

Business ethics focuses on what constitutes right or wrong behavior in the business world and on how moral and ethical principles are applied by businesspersons to situations that arise in their daily activities in the workplace. Note that business ethics is not a separate *kind* of ethics. The ethical standards that guide our behavior as, say, mothers, fathers, or students apply equally well to our activities as businesspersons. Business decision makers, though, often must address more complex ethical issues and conflicts in the workplace than they do in their personal lives.

CONFLICTING DUTIES

One of the reasons that ethical decision making is more complex in the business context than in our personal lives is because business firms are perceived to owe duties to a number of groups. These groups include the firm's owners (in a corporation, the shareholders), its employees, its suppliers, those who use its products or services (consumers), the community in which it operates, and, according to many, society at large. When these duties come into conflict, which often occurs, difficult choices must be made.

For example, suppose that Jemico, Inc., decides to reduce its costs by downsizing and restructuring its operations. Among other things, this would allow the com-

pany to cut back on its overhead by consolidating various supervisory and managerial positions. The question for Jemico is, which employees should be retained and which should be let go? Should the firm retain highly paid employees who have worked for—and received annual raises from—the firm for years? Alternatively, in the interests of cutting costs, should it retain (or hire) younger, less experienced persons at lower salaries?

Jemico would not necessarily be acting illegally if it pursued the second option. Unless a fired employee can prove that the employer has breached an employment contract or violated the Age Discrimination in Employment Act (ADEA) of 1967, he or she will not have a cause of action against the employer. As you will learn in Chapter 22, the ADEA prohibits discrimination against workers forty years of age and older on the basis of their age.

In deciding this issue, remember that Jemico must keep its eye on its profit margin. If it does not, the firm may fail, and the shareholders will lose their investments. Furthermore, why should the firm retain highly paid employees if it can obtain essentially the same work output for a lower cost from less highly paid employees? Does Jemico owe an ethical duty to employees who have served the firm loyally over a long period of time? Most people would say yes. Should this duty take precedence over Jemico's duty to the firm's owners to maintain or increase the profitability of the firm? What if the firm faced imminent bankruptcy if it could not lower its operational costs? What if longtime employees were willing to take a slight reduction in pay to help the firm through its financial difficulties? What if they were not?

In the following case, an employer was confronted with a dwindling market and decreasing sales. The employer decided to reduce its costs of doing business by eliminating some of its obligations to its employees.

CASE 4.1   Varity Corp. v. Howe

Supreme Court of the
United States, 1996.
516 U.S. 489,
116 S.Ct. 1065,
134 L.Ed.2d 130.

BACKGROUND AND FACTS *Varity Corporation manufactures and sells farm implements. In 1986, Varity set up a subsidiary, Massey Combines Corporation (MCC), to market its self-propelled combines and four-wheel-drive tractors. The sales of both products were at an all-time low. Varity convinced current and former employees who were, or had been, involved with the products to accept a transfer to MCC of their jobs and retirement benefit plans. Varity did not tell those employees that it expected MCC to fail. Within two years, MCC did fail. Among other consequences, some retirees stopped receiving benefits. The retirees and other former employees sued Varity in a federal district court under the Employee Retirement Income Security Act of 1974 (ERISA), a federal act regulating employer-provided pension plans (see Chapter 21). They claimed that Varity owed them a fiduciary duty, which it had breached. The court ruled in their* *favor, the U.S. Court of Appeals for the Eighth Circuit affirmed, and Varity appealed the case to the United States Supreme Court.*

IN THE LANGUAGE OF THE COURT

Justice *BREYER* delivered the opinion of the Court.

*   *   *   *

*   *   * ERISA requires a "fiduciary" to "discharge his duties with respect to a [retirement benefit] plan solely in the interest of the participants and beneficiaries." To participate knowingly and significantly in deceiving a plan's beneficiaries in order to save the employer money at the beneficiaries' expense, is not to act "solely in the interest of the participants and beneficiaries." As other courts have held, "[l]ying is inconsistent with the duty of loyalty owed by all fiduciaries *   *   * ."

DECISION AND REMEDY

The United States Supreme Court affirmed the decision of the lower court. Varity had violated its fiduciary duty to its employees with respect to their retirement benefits.

PUBLIC OPINION AND BUSINESS ETHICS

Another factor complicating business ethics is the increasingly important role played by public opinion in determining what is or is not ethical business behavior. In the last two decades, and particularly since the advent of the Internet, the actions of business firms have been much more closely scrutinized by the media and various interest groups (groups supporting human rights, animal rights, the environment, consumers, employees, and so on) than they ever were in the past. What this means is that if a corporation undertakes or continues an action deemed to be unethical by one or more of these groups, the firm's "unethical" behavior will probably become widely known. In the interests of preserving their good reputations, business firms thus pay attention to public opinion. If they do not, they may lose customers, be boycotted by investors concerned about ethical issues, and, ultimately, lose profits.

Business ethics thus has a practical element. As a manager, you might personally be convinced that there is nothing unethical about a certain business action. If a highly vocal interest group believes otherwise, though, you might want to reassess your decision with a view toward preserving the firm's goodwill and reputation in the community. If you decide to pursue the action regardless of public opinion, you may violate your ethical (and legal) duty to act in the firm's best interests. You should keep this practical concern with public opinion in mind as you read through the remaining pages in this chapter.

SECTION 2

Approaches to Ethical Reasoning

Each individual, when faced with a particular ethical dilemma, engages in **ethical reasoning**—that is, a reasoning process in which the individual links his or her moral convictions or ethical standards to the particular situation at hand. Businesspersons do likewise when making decisions with ethical implications.

How do business decision makers decide whether a given action is the "right" one for their firms? What ethical standards should be applied? Broadly speaking, ethical reasoning relating to business traditionally has been characterized by two fundamental approaches. One approach defines ethical behavior in terms of duty, which also implies certain rights. The other approach determines what is ethical in terms of the consequences, or outcome, of any given action. We examine each of these approaches here.

DUTY-BASED ETHICS

Duty-based ethical standards often are derived from revealed truths, such as religious precepts. They can also be derived through philosophical reasoning.

Religious Ethical Standards. In the Judeo-Christian tradition, which is the dominant religious tradition in the United States, the Ten Commandments of the Old Testament establish fundamental rules for moral action. Other religions have their own sources of revealed truth. Religious rules generally are absolute with respect to the behavior of their adherents. For example, the commandment "Thou shalt not steal" is an absolute mandate for a person, such as a Jew or a Christian, who believes that the Ten Commandments reflect revealed truth. Even a benevolent motive for stealing (such as Robin Hood's) cannot justify the act, because the act itself is inherently immoral and thus wrong.

Ethical standards based on religious teachings also involve an element of *compassion*. Therefore, for example, even though it might be profitable for a firm to lay off a less productive employee, if that employee would find it difficult to find employment elsewhere and his or her family would suffer as a result, this potential suffering would be given substantial weight by the decision makers. Compassionate treatment of others is also mandated—to a certain extent, at least—by the Golden Rule of the ancients ("Do unto others as you would have them do unto you"), which has been adopted by most religions.

Kantian Ethics. Duty-based ethical standards may also be derived solely from philosophical reasoning. The German philosopher Immanuel Kant (1724–1804), for example, identified some general guiding principles for moral behavior based on what he believed to be the fundamental nature of human beings. Kant held that it is rational to assume that human beings are qualitatively different from other physical objects occupying space. Persons are endowed with moral integrity and the capacity to reason and conduct their affairs rationally. Therefore, their thoughts and actions should be respected. When human beings are treated merely as a means to an end, they are being treated as the equivalent of objects and are being denied their basic humanity.

A central postulate in Kantian ethics is that individuals should evaluate their actions in light of the consequences that would follow if *everyone* in society acted in the same way. This **categorical imperative** can be applied to any action. For example, say that you are deciding whether to cheat on an examination. If you have adopted Kant's categorical imperative, you will decide not to cheat, because if everyone cheated, the examination would be meaningless.

The Principle of Rights. Duty-based ethical standards imply that human beings have basic rights, because a duty cannot exist without a corresponding right. For example, the commandment "Thou shalt

not kill" implies that individuals have a right to live. Additionally, religious ethics may involve a rights component because of the belief—characteristic of many religions—that an individual is "made in the image of God" or "Allah." This belief confers on the individual great dignity as a person. For one who holds this belief, not to respect that dignity—and the rights and status that flow from it—would be morally wrong. Kantian ethics also implies fundamental rights based on the personal dignity of each individual. Just as individuals have a duty not to treat others as means to an end, so individuals have a right to have their status and moral integrity as human beings treated with respect.

The principle that human beings have certain fundamental rights (to life, freedom, and the pursuit of happiness, for example) is deeply embedded in Western culture. As discussed in Chapter 1, the natural law tradition embraces the concept that certain actions (such as killing another person) are morally wrong because they are contrary to nature (the natural desire to continue living). Those who adhere to this **principle of rights,** or "rights theory," believe that a key factor in determining whether a business decision is ethical is how that decision affects the rights of others. These others include the firm's owners, its employees, the consumers of its products or services, its suppliers, the community in which it does business, and society as a whole.

OUTCOME-BASED ETHICS: UTILITARIANISM

"Thou shalt act so as to generate the greatest good for the greatest number." This is a paraphrase of the major premise of the utilitarian approach to ethics. **Utilitarianism** is a philosophical theory developed by Jeremy Bentham (1748–1832) and then advanced, with some modifications, by John Stuart Mill (1806–1873)—both British philosophers. In contrast to duty-based ethics, utilitarianism is outcome oriented. It focuses on the consequences of an action, not on the nature of the action itself or on any set of preestablished moral values or religious beliefs.

Under a utilitarian model of ethics, an action is morally correct, or "right," when, among the people it affects, it produces the greatest amount of good for the greatest number. When an action affects the majority adversely, it is morally wrong. Applying the utilitarian theory thus requires (1) a determination of which individuals will be affected by the action in question; (2) a **cost-benefit analysis**—an assessment of the negative and positive effects of alternative actions on these individuals; and (3) a choice among alternative actions that will produce maximum societal utility (the greatest positive net benefits for the greatest number of individuals).

The utilitarian approach to decision making commonly is employed by businesses, as well as by individuals. Weighing the consequences of a decision in terms of its costs and benefits for everyone affected by it is a useful analytical tool in the decision-making process. At the same time, utilitarianism is often criticized because its objective, calculated approach to problems tends to reduce the welfare of human beings to plus and minus signs on a cost-benefit worksheet and to "justify" human costs that many find totally unacceptable.

For example, from a utilitarian standpoint it might be ethically acceptable to test drugs or medicines on human beings because presumably a majority of the population would benefit from the experiments. If, however, one accepts the principle that each individual has basic human rights, then an action that deprives an individual or group of individuals of these rights—even for the greater good of society—is ethically unacceptable.

SECTION 3

Ethical Decision Making

Most major companies today ask three questions about any action before it is undertaken: Is the action profitable? Is it legal? Is it ethical? The first prong of this test for business decision making—determining whether a given course of action will be profitable—is foremost. After all, for-profit firms remain in business only if they make a profit. If the action would not be profitable, it probably will not be undertaken. If the action would be profitable, then the decision makers need to evaluate whether it also would be legal and ethical.

IS THE
CONTEMPLATED ACTION LEGAL?

In today's business world, legal compliance usually is regarded as the **moral minimum.** In other words, the minimal acceptable standard for ethical business behavior is compliance with the law.

It may seem that answering a question concerning the legality of a given action should be simple. Either something is legal or it is not. In fact, one of the major challenges businesspersons face is that the legality of a particular action is not always clear. In part, this is because there are so many laws regulating business that it is possible to violate one of them without realizing it. There are also numerous "gray areas" in the law, making it difficult to predict with certainty how a court may apply a given law to a particular action.

Laws Regulating Business. Today's business firms are subject to extensive government regulation. As mentioned in Chapter 1, virtually every action a firm undertakes—from the initial act of going into business to hiring and firing personnel to selling products in the marketplace—is subject to statutory law and to numerous rules and regulations issued by administrative agencies. Furthermore, these rules and regulations are changed or supplemented frequently.

Determining whether a planned action is legal thus requires the decision makers to keep abreast of the law. Normally, large business firms have attorneys on their staffs to assist them in making key decisions. Small firms must also seek legal advice before making important business decisions—because the consequences of just one violation of a regulatory rule may be costly.

Ignorance of the law will not excuse a business owner or manager from liability for violating a statute or regulation. In one typical case, the court imposed criminal fines, as well as imprisonment, on a company's supervisory employee for violating a federal environmental act—even though the employee was totally unaware of what was required under the provisions of that act.[1]

In the following case, a company was alleged to have infringed on another's service mark "willfully or in bad faith." (Service marks, which are used in the sale or advertising of services, will be discussed in Chapter 14.) In its defense, the company offered what it called a "credible, innocent explanation" for its continued use of the mark.

---

1. *United States v. Hanousek,* 176 F.3d 1116 (9th Cir. 1999). This case will be presented as Case 7.1 in Chapter 7.

CASE 4.2

New York State Society of Certified Public Accountants v. Eric Louis Associates, Inc.

United States
District Court,
Southern District of
New York, 1999.
79 F.Supp.2d 331.

BACKGROUND AND FACTS   *The New York State Society of Certified Public Accountants (the Society) has more than 30,000 members. The Society sets standards for certified public accountants (CPAs) and protects the interests of its members and the public with respect to the practice of accountancy. Since 1984, the Society has used the service mark "NYSSCPA" on its business cards and other promotional material. In 1994, the Society registered the domain name "nysscpa.org." and, since 1997, has operated a Web site at this Internet address. Eric Louis Associates, Inc. (ELA), is a small firm engaged in the job placement of accountants and other professionals. Brian Elias was ELA's founder and president. In January 1999, ELA registered the domain name "nysscpa.com" and began operating a Web site at that address, using "NYSSCPA" as a meta tag.[a] ELA's home page stated that it was "not affiliated with" the Society, but clicking on a hyperlink from that page to the Society's site framed that site within ELA's site. On March 25, the Society wrote a letter to ELA, demanding that ELA stop using the "nysscpa.com" domain name and stop framing the Society's Web site. ELA agreed to do so if the Society would pay it $20,000 or provide, free of charge, an exhibitor's booth at the annual NYSSCPA conference for the next five years. On April 6, the Society sent a second letter, refusing ELA's offer and repeating its demands. When ELA did nothing, the Society filed a suit against ELA in a federal district court, which held that ELA had infringed the Society's mark. The next question was whether the infringement was willful or in bad faith, which would entitle the Society to collect its attorneys' fees from ELA.*

IN THE LANGUAGE
OF THE COURT

SAND, J. [Judge]
*   *   *   *

   Our *   *   * determination that Defendant intentionally copied Plaintiff's mark takes us a considerable way toward determining that this copying was tinged with bad faith. *   *   * [T]he "nysscpa.com" domain name clearly was not selected because it reflected some characteristic of ELA. Rather, it appears that ELA adopted it with the intention of capitalizing on plaintiff's reputation and goodwill. As Mr. Elias [testified], ELA was a small, young company in the business of placing CPA's and other financial professionals. It was thus presented with the challenge of making such professionals aware of its services. The web site was presumably created for this purpose. What better way to attract CPA's to this site than to give it the "nysscpa.com" domain name, and embed the "NYSSCPA" meta-tag in the site's [source] code. *   *   *
*   *   *   *

   This brings us, finally, to the question of whether Defendant has offered a credible innocent explanation of its adoption of Plaintiff's mark. *   *   *
*   *   *   *

   Consider first Mr. Elias's response to the Society's March 25th cease and desist demand. Even if Mr. Elias genuinely believed that ELA had done nothing wrong prior to this date, this demand put him on notice that ELA's use of the "nysscpa.com" domain name and the "NYSSCPA" meta-tag was potentially illegal. If Mr. Elias had then consulted an attorney and been advised that ELA's actions were arguably legal, ELA could plausibly maintain that its continued infringement *   *   * of the Society's mark subsequent to the cease and desist demand was not willful. But Mr.

---

a. A *meta tag* is a key word in the source code used to create Web pages. A meta tag prompts a search engine to include the meta tag's Web site in the search engine's results. Meta tags and the lawfulness of their use will be discussed in Chapter 15.

Elias chose a quite different course of conduct. Not only did he fail to seek the advice of counsel, but he proceeded to act on his uninformed belief that registration of the "nysscpa.com" domain name had given him certain rights by attempting to sell the name to the Society.

*   *   *   *

Even if we assume, however, that Mr. Elias had not crossed this line on March 26, with his offer to sell the domain name to Plaintiff, he surely crossed it by April 6, 1999: the date Defendant received Plaintiff's second cease and desist demand. *   *   * Defendant responded to this second cease and desist demand by continuing its two-pronged strategy of neither ceasing and desisting nor seeking the advice of counsel. On this date, therefore—at the latest—Mr. Elias's belief that ELA's actions were not violative of Plaintiff's trademark rights ceased being reasonable. As such, on this date—at the latest—Defendant's conduct commenced being willful and tinged with bad faith.

Decision and Remedy	*The court held that the Society was entitled to collect from ELA the attorneys' fees the Society owed for work done after April 6. ELA's conduct was willful and in bad faith after that date because, on learning that it may not have had any rights to the Society's service mark, ELA did not stop its use of the mark or seek the advice of counsel.*

"Gray Areas" in the Law.   In many situations, business firms can predict with a fair amount of certainty whether a given action would be legal. For example, firing an employee solely because of that person's race or gender would clearly violate federal laws prohibiting employment discrimination. In some situations, though, the legality of a particular action may be less clear.

For example, suppose that a firm decides to launch a new advertising campaign. How far can the firm go in making claims for its product or services? Federal and state laws prohibit firms from engaging in "deceptive advertising." At the federal level, the test for deceptive advertising normally used by the Federal Trade Commission is whether an advertising claim would deceive a "reasonable consumer."[2] At what point, though, would a reasonable consumer be deceived by a particular ad?

Another gray area in the law has to do with product misuse. As will be discussed in Chapter 13, product-liability laws require manufacturers and sellers to warn

consumers of the kinds of injuries that might result from the foreseeable misuse of their products. An exception to this rule is made when a risk associated with a product is "open and obvious." Sharp knives, for example, can obviously injure their users. Sometimes, a business has no way of predicting how a court might rule in deciding whether a particular risk is open and obvious or whether consumers should be warned of the risk.

In short, whether a given action will be deemed legal or illegal often depends on how an administrative agency or a court in a particular jurisdiction decides to interpret and apply the law to the facts and issues of a particular case. Business decision makers thus need to proceed with caution and evaluate the action and its consequences from an ethical perspective. Generally, if a company can demonstrate that it acted in good faith and responsibly in the circumstances, it has a better chance of successfully defending its action in court or before an administrative law judge.

Even courts often disagree on certain issues. In the following case, for example, the trial court and the appellate court arrived at different conclusions on whether a warning on an aerosol can of butane adequately warned consumers of the danger of inhaling the contents of the can.

---

2. See Chapter 24 for a discussion of the Federal Trade Commission's role in regulating deceptive trade practices, including misleading advertising.

CASE 4.3   Pavlik v. Lane Ltd./Tobacco Exporters International

United States
Court of Appeals,
Third Circuit, 1998.
135 F.3d 876.
http://www.findlaw.
com/casecode/courts/
3rd.html[a]

HISTORICAL AND ETHICAL SETTING   *It is human nature to play Monday morning quarterback—to second-guess the choices that others make after the consequences of those choices become fact. Sometimes, such hindsight consists of superimposing what one person believes is common knowledge onto another's set of beliefs and knowledge. This can occur when adults assume that children know what adults know—that an oven is hot, for example. A child has to be warned that an oven is hot, and even then he or she may not appreciate the danger, or the seriousness of the danger, depending on the context of the warning. Judges, in particular, have to avoid the temptation to impose their own assumptions about what is common knowledge onto the parties in the cases that come before them.*

BACKGROUND AND FACTS   *Butane is a fuel for cigarette lighters. Zeus brand butane is distributed in small aerosol cans by Lane Limited/Tobacco Exporters International (Lane). On each can is the warning "DO NOT BREATHE SPRAY." Twenty-year-old Stephen Pavlik died from intentionally inhaling the contents of one of the cans. His father, George Pavlik, filed a suit in a federal district court against Lane and others, claiming in part that the statement on the can did not adequately warn users of the hazards of butane inhalation. The court issued a summary judgment in the defendants' favor, reasoning in part that Stephen must have been aware of the dangers of inhaling butane and that a more specific warning would not have affected his conduct. George Pavlik appealed to the U.S. Court of Appeals for the Third Circuit.*

IN THE LANGUAGE OF THE COURT

BECKER, Chief Judge.

*   *   *   *

*   *   * [A]n otherwise properly designed product may still be unreasonably dangerous (and therefore "defective") for strict liability purposes if the product is distributed without sufficient warnings to apprise the ultimate user of the latent dangers in the product.

*   *   *   *

*   *   * [W]e have serious doubts that the Zeus warning sufficiently warns users of the potentially fatal consequences of butane inhalation, and we are not convinced of its adequacy *   *   * . More specifically, the "DO NOT BREATHE SPRAY" warning appears to give the user no notice of the serious nature of the danger posed by inhalation, intentional or otherwise, and no other language on the Zeus can does so. Yet, we similarly cannot find that such a directive is inadequate as a matter of law, and so we must leave the question for the jury.

DECISION AND REMEDY   *The U.S. Court of Appeals for the Third Circuit held that it was not clear that Stephen was fully aware of the dangers of inhaling butane, based on the label on the Zeus cans. The court reversed the judgment of the lower court and remanded the case for trial.*

a. In the "Browsing" section, in the "1998" row, click on "Feb." When that page opens, scroll down the list to the *Pavlik* case name and click on it to access the opinion.

IS THE CONTEMPLATED ACTION ETHICAL?

Even if a company is certain of the legality of a particular action, that does not necessarily mean that the action is ethical. For example, suppose that a corporation that markets baby formula in developing countries has learned that mothers in those countries often mix the formula with impure water, to make the formula go further. As a result, babies there are suffering from malnutrition, diarrhea, and even death. Although the corporation is not violating any law, many would contend that it should suspend sales of the formula in those countries.[3]

Typically, in deciding whether a given action would be ethical, a firm's decision makers are guided not only by their own ethical principles and reasoning processes but also by their company's ethical policies and code of conduct.

Ethical Codes and Corporate Compliance Programs. Virtually all large corporations today have established ethical policies or codes of conduct to help guide their executives and managers (and all company personnel) in making decisions. Typically, an ethical code, or code of conduct, will indicate the company's commitment to legal compliance, as well as to the welfare of its employees, suppliers, consumers, and others who may be affected by the company's decisions and practices.

For example, look at the fold-out exhibit in this chapter showing Costco's Code of Ethics. This code clearly indicates Costco's commitment to legal compliance, as well as to the welfare of its members (those who belong to its clubs and purchase its products), its employees, and its vendors (suppliers). The code also details some specific ways in which the interests and welfare of these groups will be protected. If you look closely at the exhibit, you will also see that Costco acknowledges that by protecting these groups' interests, it will realize its "ultimate goal"—which is to reward its shareholders (those who own the company). Costco's code can guide management and supervisory personnel as they make decisions involving the ethical rights and obligations of each group.

In a large corporation, an ethical code usually is just one part of a comprehensive corporate compliance program. Other components of such a program may include a corporate ethics committee, ethical training programs, and internal audits (to monitor compliance with applicable laws and the company's standards of conduct). Some companies also have a special office to which employees can report—in person or perhaps anonymously via an 800 number—suspected improper conduct, including any legal, ethical, or policy violations that may occur.

By making ethical and legal conduct a top priority, ethical codes and compliance programs help business managers to conduct their firms' affairs responsibly. Still, questions often arise for which there are no clear-cut answers, particularly when they involve conflicting goals. For example, suppose that a company's employees are pressuring management for a wage increase. If the company agrees to increase employees' wages, this will cut into the firm's profits and thus adversely affect the shareholder-owners' interests. The decision to be made here involves not a choice between an ethical and an unethical action but rather a choice between two conflicting goals.

Determining Ethical Priorities. An ethical issue involving conflicting duties can only be resolved by establishing which duties should take priority over others. For example, suppose that the Wellsen Company, a glue-manufacturing firm, learns that thousands of children in several Latin American countries have been inhaling its glue. As a result, many of the children may suffer severe health consequences in the future, including kidney disease and brain damage. Consumer activists have launched a media campaign against Wellsen, accusing it of being unethical by marketing its glue in those countries. What is the right thing to do in this situation? Should Wellsen cease selling its glue in the countries in question even though selling it is legal and profitable?

Assume that Wellsen decides to pull out of those markets. Whose interests would be adversely affected? First of all, the interests of the company's shareholder-owners would be—because the decision probably would result in lower profits. The interests of employees, particularly those with jobs at stake, would also be adversely affected by the decision. Additionally, those firms that supply Wellsen with the materials it needs in the glue-manufacturing process would see decreased profits, at least temporarily, because Wellsen would need fewer materials. Finally, what about the interests of the majority of the consumers in the Latin American countries, who do not misuse the glue? These consumers would also be adversely affected, because they could no longer purchase the glue for home or business purposes.

Clearly, if equal ethical weight were attached to the interests of each group, the right decision would be to continue marketing the product in Latin American countries. Indeed, from a utilitarian perspective, this action might be deemed the most

---

3. This situation faced the Nestlé Company in the 1970s. That company had concluded, on the basis of a cost-benefit analysis, that it was ethically justified in continuing to market its baby formula in developing countries. Nestlé was severely criticized for its behavior.

ethical, because the action would benefit the majority of those affected by the decision. From a duty-based (or rights-based) perspective, however, it would be difficult to justify a decision to continue selling a product that was harming some human beings, regardless of the fact that the harm was caused by product misuse.

SECTION 4

Maximum versus Optimum Profits

Today's corporate decision makers are, in a sense, poised on a fulcrum between profitability and ethical responsibility. If they emphasize profits at the expense of perceived ethical responsibilities to other groups, they may become the target of negative media exposure and even lawsuits. If they go too far in the other direction (keep an unprofitable plant open so that the employees do not lose their jobs, invest too heavily in charitable works or social causes, and so on), their profits will suffer and they may have to go out of business.

Striking the right balance on this fulcrum is difficult, and usually some profits must be sacrificed in the process. Instead of maximum profits, many firms today aim for **optimum profits**—the maximum profits a firm can realize while staying within legal *and* ethical limits. In the Wellsen Company's situation, if the decision makers base their reasoning on duty/rights-based ethical standards, they may conclude that they have an ethical duty to pull out of the Latin American markets. In other words, they may decide to settle for optimum profits rather than maximum profits.

Even from a utilitarian perspective, it might be wise to discontinue sales in the Latin American countries in question. Although utilitarian reasoning may lead to the conclusion that there is nothing unethical about continuing sales in those areas—because it would benefit the majority of persons affected by such a decision—Wellsen's reputation could suffer irreparable damage if it did so. In the long run, a decision to continue the sales thus could be an unprofitable one.

Note that in a utilitarian cost-benefit analysis of the ethical issue facing the Wellsen Company, the "cost" of potentially decreased profits in the long run was acknowledged primarily because of the media campaign against Wellsen. In other words, if consumer activists had not created widespread public awareness of Wellsen's actions, the outcome of the utilitarian analysis of the issue would probably be a decision to continue marketing the glue in the Latin American countries.

SECTION 5

The Ever-Changing Ethical Landscape

Society's determination of what constitutes ethical business behavior changes over time. Consider the ethical landscape of business as it existed seventy-five years ago. At that time, a corporation was perceived to have one major duty: to serve the interests of its shareholders (basically, make profitable decisions) and to act within legal limits when doing so. In other words, in the corporate decision-making process, only two questions normally were asked: Is it profitable? Is it legal? The third question (Is it ethical?) was largely answered by the first two.

Indeed, most of the ethical and social issues discussed in this chapter and elsewhere in this text either did not exist or were of little public concern at that time. Technological innovations, the communications revolution, pressing environmental problems, and social movements resulting in greater rights for minorities, women, and consumers have all dramatically changed the society in which we live and, consequently, the business and ethical landscape of the United States. Today, society expects business leaders to acknowledge and fulfill ethical duties to all persons and groups that are affected by the decisions and activities of their firms.

Moreover, the global dimension of business activity today has led to ethical issues that were of little concern to American firms—or to the American public—in the past. We look next at some of these issues.

MONITORING THE EMPLOYMENT PRACTICES OF FOREIGN SUPPLIERS

Many U.S. businesses now contract with companies in developing nations to produce goods, such as shoes and clothing, because the wage rates in those nations are significantly lower than in the United States. Yet what if a foreign company exploits its workers—by hiring women and children at below-minimum-wage rates, for example, or by requiring its employees to work long hours in a workplace full of health hazards? What if the company's supervisors routinely engage in workplace conduct that is offensive to women?

Given today's global communications network, few companies can assume that their actions in other nations will go unnoticed by "corporate watch" groups that discover and publicize unethical corporate behavior. As a result, American businesses today usually take steps to avoid such adverse publicity—either by refusing to deal with certain suppliers or by making arrangements to monitor their suppliers' workplaces to make sure that the workers are not being mistreated.

THE FOREIGN CORRUPT PRACTICES ACT

Another ethical problem in international business dealings has to do with the legitimacy of certain side payments to government officials. In the United States, the majority of contracts are formed within the private sector. In many foreign countries, however, decisions on most major construction and manufacturing contracts are made by government officials because of extensive government regulation and control over trade and industry. Side payments to government officials in exchange for favorable business contracts are not unusual in such countries, nor are they considered to be unethical. In the past, U.S. corporations doing business in developing countries largely followed the dictum, "When in Rome, do as the Romans do."

In the 1970s, however, the U.S. press, and government officials as well, uncovered a number of business scandals involving large side payments by U.S. corporations—such as Lockheed Aircraft—to foreign representatives for the purpose of securing advantageous international trade contracts. In response to this unethical behavior, in 1977 Congress passed the Foreign Corrupt Practices Act (FCPA), which prohibits U.S. businesspersons from bribing foreign officials to secure advantageous contracts.

Prohibition against the Bribery of Foreign Officials. The first part of the FCPA applies to all U.S. companies and their directors, officers, shareholders, employees, and agents. This part prohibits the bribery of most officials of foreign governments if the purpose of the payment is to get the official to act in his or her official capacity to provide business opportunities.

The FCPA does not prohibit payment of substantial sums to minor officials whose duties are ministerial. These payments are often referred to as "grease," or facilitating payments. They are meant to ensure that administrative services that might otherwise be performed at a slow pace are sped up. Thus, for example, if a firm makes a payment to a minor official to speed up an import licensing process, the firm has not violated the FCPA. Generally, the act, as amended, permits payments to foreign officials if such payments are lawful within the foreign country. The act also does not prohibit payments to private foreign companies or other third parties unless the U.S. firm knows that the payments will be passed on to a foreign government in violation of the FCPA.

Accounting Requirements. The second part of the FCPA is directed toward accountants, because in the past bribes were often concealed in corporate financial records. All companies must keep detailed records that "accurately and fairly" reflect the company's financial activities. In addition, all companies must have an accounting system that provides "reasonable assurance" that all transactions entered into by the company are accounted for and legal. These requirements assist in detecting illegal bribes. The FCPA further prohibits any person from making false statements to accountants or false entries in any record or account.

Penalties for Violations. In 1988, the FCPA was amended to provide that business firms that violate the act may be fined up to $2 million. Individual officers or directors who violate the FCPA may be fined up to $100,000 (the fine cannot be paid by the company) and may be imprisoned for up to five years.

OTHER NATIONS DENOUNCE BRIBERY

For twenty years, the FCPA was the only law of its kind in the world, despite attempts by U.S. political leaders to convince other nations to pass similar legislation. That situation is now changing. In 1997, the Organization for Economic Cooperation and Development, to which twenty-six of the world's leading industrialized nations belong, signed a convention (treaty) that made the bribery of foreign public officials a serious crime. Each signatory is obligated to enact legislation within its nation in accordance with the treaty. The agreement will not only improve the ethical climate in international trade but also level the playing field for U.S businesspersons.

TERMS AND CONCEPTS TO REVIEW

business ethics 81	ethical reasoning 82	optimum profits 89
categorical imperative 83	ethics 80	principle of rights 83
cost-benefit analysis 84	moral minimum 84	utilitarianism 83

QUESTIONS AND CASE PROBLEMS

4–1. BUSINESS ETHICS. Some business ethicists maintain that whereas personal ethics has to do with "right" or "wrong" behavior, business ethics is concerned with "appropriate" behavior. In other words, ethical behavior in business has less to do with moral principles than with what society deems to be appropriate behavior in the business context. Do you agree with this distinction? Do personal and business ethics ever overlap? Should personal ethics play any role in business ethical decision making?

4–2. BUSINESS ETHICS. If a firm engages in "ethical" behavior solely for the purpose of gaining profits from the goodwill it generates, the "ethical" behavior is essentially a means toward a self-serving end (profits and the accumulation of wealth). In this situation, is the firm acting unethically in any way? Which should carry greater weight on the ethical scales in this situation: motive or conduct?

4–3. ETHICAL REASONING. Susan Whitehead serves on the city planning commission. The city is planning to build a new subway system, and Susan's brother-in-law, Jerry, who owns the Custom Transportation Co., has submitted the lowest bid for the system. Susan knows that Jerry could complete the job for the estimated amount, but she also knows that once Jerry completes this job, he will probably sell his company and quit working. Susan is concerned that Custom Transportation's subsequent management might not be as easy to work with if revisions need to be made on the subway system after its completion. She is torn as to whether she should tell the city about the potential changes in Custom Transportation's management. If the city knew about the instability of Custom Transportation, it might prefer to give the contract to one of Jerry's competitors, whose bid was only slightly higher than Jerry's. Does Susan have an ethical obligation to disclose the information about Jerry to the city planning commission? How would you apply duty-based ethical standards to this question? What might be the outcome of a utilitarian analysis? Discuss fully.

4–4. ETHICAL DECISION MAKING. Assume that you are a high-level manager for a shoe manufacturer. You know that your firm could increase its profit margin by producing shoes in Indonesia, where you could hire women for $40 a month to assemble them. You also know, however, that a competing shoe manufacturer recently was accused by human rights advocates of engaging in exploitative labor practices because the manufacturer sold shoes made by Indonesian women working for similarly low wages. You personally do not believe that paying $40 a month to Indonesian women is unethical, because you know that in that impoverished country, $40 a month is a better-than-average wage rate. Assuming that the decision is yours to make, should you have the shoes manufactured in Indonesia and make higher profits for your company? Or should you avoid the risk of negative publicity and the consequences of that publicity for the firm's reputation and subsequent profits? Are there other alternatives? Discuss fully.

4–5. ETHICAL DECISION MAKING. Shokun Steel Co. owns many steel plants. One of its plants is much older than the others. Equipment at the old plant is outdated and inefficient, and the costs of production at that plant are now twice what they are at any of Shokun's other plants. The price of steel cannot be increased because of competition, both domestic and international. The plant is located in Twin Firs, Pennsylvania, which has a population of about forty-five thousand, and currently employs over a thousand workers. Shokun is contemplating whether to close the plant. What factors should the firm consider in making its decision? Will the firm violate any ethical duties if it closes the plant? Analyze these questions from the two basic perspectives on ethical reasoning discussed in this chapter.

4–6. EMPLOYMENT RELATIONSHIPS. Matt Theurer, an eighteen-year-old high school senior, worked part-time at a McDonald's restaurant in Oregon. Theurer volunteered to work an extra shift one day, in addition to his regular shifts (one preceding and one following the extra shift). After working about twelve hours during a twenty-four-hour period, Theurer told the manager that he was tired and asked to be excused from his next regularly scheduled shift so that he could rest. The manager agreed. While driving home from work, Theurer fell asleep at the wheel and crashed into a van driven by Frederic Faverty. Theurer died, and Faverty was severely injured. Faverty sued McDonald's, alleging, among other things, that McDonald's had been negligent in permitting Theurer to drive a car when it should have known that he was too tired to drive safely. Do employers have a duty to prevent fatigued employees from driving home from work? Should such a duty be imposed on them? How should the court decide this issue? How would you decide the issue if you were the judge? [*Faverty v. McDonald's Restaurants of Oregon, Inc.*, 133 Or.App. 514, 892 P.2d 703 (1994)]

4–7. LAWS REGULATING BUSINESS. Valdak Corp. operated a car wash that used an industrial dryer to spin-dry towels. The dryer was equipped with a device that was supposed to keep it locked while it spun, but the device often did not work. An employee reached into the dryer while it was spinning, and his arm was cut off above the elbow. The Occupational Safety and Health Administration (OSHA) cited Valdak for, among other things, a willful violation of a machine-guarding regulation and assessed a $28,000 penalty. Valdak appealed the decision, and ultimately the case was reviewed by a federal appellate court. On appeal, Valdak argued, in part, that it did not know about the specific regulation and thus could not be cited for a "willful" violation of it. What will the court decide, and why? [*Valdak Corp. v. Occupational Safety and Health Review Commission*, 73 F.3d 1466 (8th Cir. 1966)]

4–8. CONSUMER WELFARE. Isuzu Motors America, Inc., does not warn its customers of the danger of riding unrestrained in the cargo beds of its pickup trucks. Seventeen-year-old Donald Josue was riding unrestrained in the bed of an Isuzu truck driven by Iaone Frias. When Frias lost control of the truck, it struck a concrete center divider. Josue was ejected, and his consequent injuries rendered him a paraplegic. Josue filed a suit in a Hawaii state court against Isuzu, asserting a variety of legal claims based on its failure to warn of the danger of riding in the bed of the truck. Should Isuzu be held liable for Josue's injuries? Why or why not? [*Josue v. Isuzu Motors America, Inc.*, 87 Haw. 413, 958 P.2d 535 (1998)]

4–9. ETHICAL CONDUCT. Richard and Suzanne Weinstein owned Elm City Cheese Co. Elm City sold its products to three major customers that used the cheese as a "filler" to blend into their cheeses. In 1982, Mark Federico, a certified public accountant, became Elm City's accountant and the Weinsteins' personal accountant. The Weinsteins had known Federico since he was seven years old, and even before he became their accountant he knew the details of Elm City's business. Federico's duties went beyond typical accounting work, and when the Weinsteins were absent, Federico was put in charge of operations. In 1992, Federico was made a

vice president of the company, and a year later he was placed in charge of day-to-day operations. He also continued to serve as Elm City's accountant. The relationship between Federico and the Weinsteins deteriorated, and in 1995, he resigned as Elm City's employee and as its accountant. Less than two years later, Federico opened Lomar Foods, Inc., to make the same products as Elm City by the same process and to sell the products to the same customers. Federico located Lomar closer to Elm City's suppliers. Elm City filed a suit in a Connecticut state court against Federico and Lomar, alleging, among other things, misappropriation of trade secrets. Elm City argued that it was entitled to punitive damages because Federico's conduct was "willful and malicious." Federico responded in part that he did not act willfully and maliciously because he did not know that Elm City's business details were trade secrets. Were Federico's actions "willful and malicious"? Were they ethical? Explain. [*Elm City Cheese Co. v. Federico*, 251 Conn. 59, ___ A.2d ___ (1999)]

4–10. IN YOUR COURT

Francis Rogowski fell asleep at the wheel of his Mazda pickup truck and collided head-on with a large tree. To recover for the cost of his injuries, Rogowski sued the manufacturer of the pickup, Mazda Motor of America, Inc. Rogowski claimed, among other things, that Mazda should have warned him that the seat belts would not protect him from all injuries if he were in an accident. Assume that you are the judge in the trial court hearing this case and answer the following questions:

(a) The major issue before your court is whether the danger not warned of by Mazda (that the seat belts would not protect Rogowski from all injuries if he were in an accident) was open and obvious. If the danger was open and obvious, then Mazda had no duty to warn consumers of this danger under product-liability laws. How will you rule on this issue? Why?

(b) Compare this case to Case 4.3 (*Pavlik v. Lane Ltd./Tobacco Exporters International*), which involved a similar issue. What did the court decide in that case, and for what reasons? Does the court's decision in that case differ from your conclusion regarding Rogowski's claim? Explain.

4–11. A QUESTION OF ETHICS

Three-year-old Randy Welch climbed up to a shelf and picked up a disposable butane cigarette lighter. Randy then used the lighter to ignite a flame, which set fire to his pajama top. Welch and his parents brought a product-liability suit against the lighter's manufacturer, Scripto-Tokai Corp., for damages. One of the questions raised in this case was whether the risks attending the lighter were sufficiently "open and obvious" that the manufacturer did not need to warn of those risks. [*Welch v. Scripto-Tokai Corp.*, 651 N.E.2d 810 (Ind.App. 1995)]

(a) If you were the judge, how would you decide this issue? Explain your reasoning.

(b) Generally, how can a court decide what kinds of risks should be open and obvious for the ordinary consumer? How can a business decision maker decide such questions?

LAW ON THE WEB

For updated links to resources available on the Web, as well as a variety of other materials, visit this text's Web site at http://wleb.westbuslaw.com.

The Web site of DePaul University's Institute for Business and Professional Ethics includes several examples of the types of ethical issues that can arise in the business context. Go to

http://condor.depaul.edu/ethics/biz17.html

You can find articles on issues relating to shareholders and corporate accountability at the Corporate Governance Web site. Go to

http://www.corpgov.net

Numerous online groups focus on the activities of various corporations from an ethical perspective. A good starting point for locating these kinds of Web sites is Baobab's Corporate Power Information Center at

http://www.baobabcomputing.com/corporatepower

LEGAL RESEARCH EXERCISES ON THE WEB

Go to http://wleb.westbuslaw.com, the Web site that accompanies this text. Select "Internet Applications," and then click on "Chapter 4." There you will find the following Internet research exercises that you can perform to learn more about ethics and business decision making:

Activity 4–1: Ethics in Business

Activity 4–2: Environmental Self-Audits

UNIT ONE — CUMULATIVE BUSINESS HYPOTHETICAL

MicroWare, Inc., which has its headquarters in Sunnyvale, California, is one of the leading software manufacturers in the United States. The company invests millions of dollars in researching and developing new software applications and games, which are sold worldwide. It also has a large service department and has taken great pains to offer its customers excellent support services.

1. Olway Toy Mart, Inc., a Kansas retailer that sells MicroWare computer games, wants to sue MicroWare for allegedly breaching a contract. If Olway brought suit in a Kansas state court, could that court exercise jurisdiction over MicroWare? Explain.

2. Suppose that in its contract with MicroWare, Olway agreed to submit any dispute that arose between the two companies to binding arbitration. Following the arbitration hearing, the arbitrator concludes that MicroWare did not breach the contract. Olway is unsatisfied with the arbitrator's award. Can Olway appeal the arbitrator's decision to a court?

3. One of MicroWare's best-selling products is a computer game that involves some extremely violent actions. Groups of parents, educators, and consumer activists have bombarded MicroWare with letters and e-mail messages requesting the company to discontinue its sales of the product. MicroWare executives are concerned with the public outcry, but at the same time they realize that the game is MicroWare's major source of profits. If it ceased marketing the game, the company could go bankrupt. If you were a MicroWare decision maker, what would your decision be in this situation? How would you justify your decision from an ethical perspective?

FOCUS ON LEGAL REASONING
Friends of the Earth, Inc. v. Laidlaw Environmental Services (TOC), Inc.

INTRODUCTION

To bring a lawsuit to a court, a plaintiff must have standing to sue, or simply standing—a sufficient stake in a controversy to justify seeking relief from the court. Standing, and the difficulties that some parties have in meeting the requirement, is discussed in Chapter 2. Generally, a party bringing a suit must have been injured or otherwise suffered harm by the action about which he or she complains. In this *Focus on Legal Reasoning*, we examine *Friends of the Earth, Inc. v. Laidlaw Environmental Services, Inc.*,[1] a recent decision that dealt with the issue of standing under federal environmental laws.

_____
1. __ U.S. __, 120 S.Ct. 693, 145 L.Ed.2d 610 (2000).

CASE BACKGROUND

Laidlaw Environmental Services (TOC), Inc., bought a facility in Roebuck, South Carolina, that included a wastewater treatment plant. The South Carolina Department of Health and Environmental Control (DHEC) granted Laidlaw a National Pollutant Discharge Elimination System (NPDES) permit under the federal Clean Water Act (see Chapter 25). The permit allowed Laidlaw to dump its water into the North Tyger River, but limited, among other things, the amount of pollution in the water. Laidlaw exceeded the limits in its discharge of mercury, an extremely toxic substance, and other pollutants.

Friends of the Earth, Inc. (FOE), and other environmental organizations filed a suit in a federal district court against Laidlaw, asking the court to assess a fine based on the firm's noncompliance with the NPDES permit. The court determined that Laidlaw had gained a total economic benefit of $1,092,581 as a result of its actions, but the court concluded that a fine of $405,800 was appropriate.

FOE appealed this amount to the U.S. Court of Appeals for the Fourth Circuit. Meanwhile, Laidlaw closed the Roebuck facility, dismantled it, and put it up for sale. The court assumed for the sake of argument that FOE had standing but remanded the case to the lower court with instructions to dismiss the suit because Laidlaw had stopped all discharges. FOE appealed to the United States Supreme Court.

MAJORITY OPINION

Justice *GINSBURG* delivered the opinion of the Court.
 * * * *

 * * * [B]ecause we hold that the Court of Appeals erred in [remanding the case with instructions to dismiss], we have an obligation to assure ourselves that FOE had * * * standing at the outset of the litigation. * * *

 In *Lujan v. Defenders of Wildlife,* 504 U.S. 555, 112 S.Ct. 2130, 119 L.Ed.2d 351 (1992), we held that, to satisfy [the] standing requirements, a plaintiff must show * * * it has suffered an "injury in fact" * * *.

 Laidlaw contends * * * that FOE lacked standing * * * because the plaintiff organizations failed to show that any of their members had sustained or faced the threat of any "injury in fact" from Laidlaw's activities. In support of this contention Laidlaw points to the District Court's finding, made in the course of setting the [fine], that there had been "no demonstrated proof of harm to the environment" from Laidlaw's mercury discharge violations.

 The relevant showing for * * * standing, however, is not injury to the environment but injury to the plaintiff. To insist upon the former rather than the latter as part of the standing inquiry (as the dissent in essence does) is to raise the standing hurdle higher than the necessary showing for success on the merits in an action alleging noncompliance with an NPDES permit. Focusing properly on injury to the plaintiff, the District Court found that FOE had demonstrated sufficient injury to establish standing. For example, FOE member Kenneth Lee Curtis averred in affidavits that he lived a half-mile from Laidlaw's facility; that he occasionally drove over the North Tyger River, and that it looked and smelled polluted; and that he would like to fish, camp, swim, and picnic in and near the river between 3 and 15 miles downstream from the facility, as he did when he was a teenager, but would not do so because he was concerned that the water was polluted by Laidlaw's discharges. * * *

Other members presented evidence to similar effect. * * *

* * * [E]nvironmental plaintiffs adequately allege injury in fact when they aver that they use the affected area and are persons for whom the aesthetic and recreational values of the area will be lessened by the challenged activity.

* * * *

* * * Unlike the dissent, we see nothing "improbable" about the proposition that a company's continuous and pervasive illegal discharges of pollutants into a river would cause nearby residents to curtail their recreational use of that waterway and would subject them to other economic and aesthetic harms. The proposition is entirely reasonable, the District Court found it was true in this case, and that is enough for injury in fact.

DISSENTING OPINION

Justice *SCALIA,* * * * dissenting.

* * * *

The Court [states that] "[t]he relevant showing for purposes of * * * standing * * * is not injury to the environment but injury to the plaintiff." This statement is correct, as far as it goes. We have certainly held that a demonstration of harm to the environment is not enough to satisfy the injury-in-fact requirement unless the plaintiff can demonstrate how he personally was harmed. E.g., *Lujan [v. Defenders of Wildlife.]* In the normal course, however, a lack of demonstrable harm to the environment will translate, as it plainly does here, into a lack of demonstrable harm to citizen plaintiffs. While it is perhaps possible that a plaintiff could be harmed even though the environment was not, such a plaintiff would have the burden of articulating and demonstrating the nature of that injury. Ongoing "concerns" about the environment are not enough, for it is the reality of the threat of repeated injury that is relevant to the standing inquiry, not the plaintiff's subjective apprehensions. At the very least, in the present case, one would expect to see evidence supporting the affidavits' bald assertions regarding decreasing recreational usage and [other negative effects], as well as evidence for the improbable proposition that Laidlaw's violations, even though harmless to the environment, are somehow responsible for these effects. Plaintiffs here have made no attempt at such a showing, but rely entirely upon unsupported and unexplained affidavit allegations of "concern."

LEGAL REASONING AND ANALYSIS

1. **Legal Reasoning.** The majority and the dissent in this case agree on the standing requirement of an injury to the plaintiff. On what point do they disagree? With whom do you agree and why?

2. **Legal Analysis.** The majority and dissent both cite, in their opinions, *Lujan v. Defenders of Wildlife,* 504 U.S. 555, 112 S.Ct. 2130, 119 L.Ed.2d 351 (1992), (see the *Law on the Web* feature at the end of Chapter 2 for instructions on how to access federal court opinions). How do the facts, issues, and holdings in that case compare to the facts and issues in the *Friends of the Earth* case? Do the principles for which the *Lujan* case is cited support the position of the majority or the dissent in the *Friends of the Earth* case?

3. **Social Considerations.** Why should the defendant in this case be assessed a fine for something that it had ceased doing?

4. **Implications for Business.** What does the holding in this case say to business firms that may be in violation of environmental laws?

5. **Case Briefing Assignment.** Using the guidelines for briefing cases given in Appendix A of this text, brief the *Friends of the Earth* case.

GOING ONLINE

Lex Mundi, an association of independent law firms, maintains a Web site that contains, at **http://www.hg.org/litg.html**, links to a variety of sources for civil procedure materials, including international and national documents. For example, in the "U.S. Law, Regulations & Agencies" section are links to federal court rules, including the Federal Rules of Civil Procedure, and federal and state court cases.

Ethics and the Legal Environment of Business

As you learned in Chapter 4, which is devoted entirely to ethics and business decision making, *ethics* can be defined as the study of what constitutes right or wrong behavior. *Business ethics,* as the term implies, focuses on what constitutes right or wrong behavior in the business world.

Business ethics and business law are closely intertwined concepts, because ultimately the law rests on social beliefs about right and wrong behavior in the business world. Thus, business-persons, merely by complying with the law, are acting ethically. Mere legal compliance (the "moral minimum" in terms of business ethics), however, is often not enough. This is because the law does not—and cannot—provide the answers for all ethical questions. Rather, the law assumes that those in business will behave ethically in their day-to-day dealings. If they do not, the courts will not come to their assistance.

The main question facing many businesspersons is this: How can they know what constitutes ethical conduct in a particular situation? Furthermore, at what point does unethical conduct cross the line separating unethical from illegal conduct? Often, as mentioned, the laws do not make this line clear—this is left for the courts to decide on a case-by-case basis. In other words, in some cases, business-persons learn too late that they have violated not just business ethical standards but also the law.

In preparing for a career in business, you will find that a background in business ethics and a commitment to ethical behavior are just as important as a knowledge of the specific laws that are covered in this text. No textbook, however, can provide answers for the many ethical questions that arise in the business context. Nor can it anticipate the types of ethical questions that will arise in the future, as technology continues to transform the workplace and business relationships. The most we can do is provide examples of the types of ethical issues that businesspersons have faced in the past and that they are facing today. The *Focus on Ethics* sections in this book survey some of the important ethical issues that arise in various areas of business activity.

In this *Focus,* we look first at some obstacles to ethical behavior in the business context. We then examine a concept that has become a significant element of the legal environment of business: corporate social responsibility.

OBSTACLES TO ETHICAL BUSINESS BEHAVIOR

People sometimes behave unethically in the business context, just as they do in their private lives. Some businesspersons knowingly engage in unethical behavior because they think that they can "get away with it"—that no one will ever learn of their unethical actions. Examples of this kind of unethical behavior include padding expense accounts, casting doubts on the integrity of a rival co-worker to gain a job promotion, stealing company supplies or equipment, and so on. Obviously, these acts are unethical, and many of them are illegal as well. In other situations, businesspersons who would choose to act ethically may be deterred from doing so because of situational circumstances or external pressures.

Ethics and the Corporate Environment

Individuals in their personal lives normally are free to decide ethical issues as they wish and to follow through on those decisions. In the business world, and particularly in the corporate environment, rarely is such a decision made by one person. If you are an officer or a manager of a large company, for example, you will find that the decision as to what is right or wrong for the company is not totally yours to make. Your input may weigh in the decision, but ultimately a corporate decision is a collective undertaking.

Additionally, collective decision making, because it places emphasis on consensus and unity of opinion, tends to hinder individual ethical assertiveness. For example, suppose that a director has ethical misgivings about a planned corporate venture that promises to be highly profitable. If the other directors have no such misgivings, the director who does may be swayed by the enthusiasm of the others for the project and downplay his or her own criticisms.

Furthermore, just as no one person makes a collective decision, so no one person (normally) is held accountable for the decision. The corporate enterprise thus tends to shield corporate personnel from both personal exposure to the consequences of their decisions (such as direct experience with someone who suffers harm from a corporate product) and personal accountability for those decisions.

Ethics and Management

Much unethical business behavior occurs simply because management does not always make it clear what ethical standards and behaviors are expected of the firm's employees. Although most firms now issue ethical policies or codes of conduct, these policies and codes are not always effective in creating an ethical workplace. At times, this is because the firm's ethical policies are not communicated clearly to employees or do not bear on the real ethical issues confronting decision makers. Additionally, particularly in a large corporation, unethical behavior in one corporate department may simply escape the attention of those in control of the corporation or the corporate officials responsible for implementing and monitoring the company's ethics program.

Another deterrent to ethical behavior exists when corporate management, by its own conduct, indicates that ethical considerations take second place. If management makes no attempt to deter unethical behavior—through reprimands or employment terminations, for example—it will be clear to employees that management is not all that serious about ethics. Likewise, if a company gives promotions or salary increases to those who obviously use unethical tactics to increase the firm's profits, then employees who do not resort to such tactics will be at a disadvantage. An employee in this situation may decide that because "everyone else does it," he or she might as well do it too.

Of course, an even stronger deterrent to ethical behavior occurs when employers engage in blatantly unethical or illegal conduct and expect their employees to do so as well. An employee in this situation faces two options, neither of which is satisfactory: participate in the conduct or "blow the whistle" on (inform authorities of) the employer's actions—and, of course, risk being fired. (See Chapter 21 for a more detailed discussion of this ethical dilemma and its consequences for employees.)

CORPORATE SOCIAL RESPONSIBILITY

Perhaps no concept is more riddled with ethical perplexities than that of corporate social responsibility—the idea that corporations can and should act ethically and be accountable to society for their actions. We discussed some of the ethical (and legal) duties that corporations owe to their employees and to the users of their products in Chapter 4. Here we look at some problematic aspects of a corporation's responsibilities to other groups, including corporate shareholders, other "stakeholders" in the firm, the community in which the corporation operates, and society at large.

Duty to Shareholders

Corporate directors and officers have a duty to act in the shareholders' interest. Because of the nature of the relationship between corporate directors and officers and the shareholder-owners, the law holds directors and officers to a high standard of care in business decision making (see Chapter 19). Traditionally, it was perceived that this duty to shareholders took precedence over all other corporate duties and that the primary goal of corporations

should be profit maximization. Milton Friedman, the Nobel Prize–winning economist and a proponent of the profit-maximization view, saw "one and only one" social responsibility of a corporation: "to use its resources and engage in activities designed to increase its profits, so long as it stays within the rules of the game."[1] The "rules of the game" are the "basic rules of society, both those embodied in law and those embodied in ethical custom."[2]

Those who support the profit-maximization view of social responsibility contend that the duty to maximize profits must outweigh any other duty when obligations conflict—to the extent, of course, that in maximizing shareholders' profits a firm does not violate the "basic rules of society." The question here is, what are these basic rules?

Duty to Stakeholders

Increasingly, the traditional duty to shareholders is being balanced against a corporation's duty to other groups affected by corporate decisions. In the last decade or so, for example, about half of the states have enacted statutes that allow corporate decision makers to take into consideration not only the welfare of shareholders but also the welfare of *stakeholders*— employees, customers, suppliers, communities, and any group that has a stake in the corporation. Some of the statutes, such as those of Indiana and Pennsylvania, allow corporate management to place the interests of stakeholders above those of shareholders.

The reasoning behind these statutes—and behind what has come to be called "the stakeholder

---

1. *Capitalism and Freedom* (Chicago: University of Chicago Press, 1962), p. 133.
2. Milton Friedman, "Does Business Have Social Responsibility?" *Bank Administration,* April 1971, pp. 13–14.

view of corporate social responsibility"—is that in some circumstances, other groups may have a greater stake in company decisions than the shareholders do. Consider an example. A heavily indebted corporation is facing imminent bankruptcy. The shareholder-investors have little to lose in this situation, because their stock is already next to worthless. The corporation's creditors will be first in line for any corporate assets remaining. Because in this situation it is the creditors who have the greatest "stake" in the corporation, under the stakeholder view, corporate directors and officers should give greater weight to the creditors' interests than to those of the shareholders.

Duty to the Community

In some circumstances, the community in which a business enterprise is located has a substantial stake in the firm. Assume, for example, that a company employs two thousand workers at one of its plants. If the company decides that it would be profitable to close the plant or move it to another location, the employees—and the community—would suffer as a result. Today, to be considered socially responsible (and, in some circumstances, to comply with laws governing plant shutdowns), a corporation must take both employees' needs and community needs into consideration when making such a decision.

Another ethical question sometimes arises when a firm moves into a community. Does the company have an obligation to evaluate first how its presence will affect that community? This question has surfaced in regard to the expansion of Wal-Mart Stores, Inc., into small towns. Generally, most people in such areas welcome the lower prices and wider array of goods that Wal-Mart

offers relative to other, smaller stores in the vicinity. A vocal minority of people in some communities, however, claim that smaller stores often find it impossible to compete with Wal-Mart's prices and thus are forced to go out of business. Many of these smaller stores have existed for years and, according to Wal-Mart's critics, enhance the quality of community life. These critics claim that it is unethical of Wal-Mart to disregard a town's interest in the quality and character of life for its residents.

In the past decade, beginning in Oklahoma, Wal-Mart has been consolidating some of its smaller stores into large "superstores." In the process of this consolidation, Wal-Mart is closing stores in some of the very towns in which it drove its smaller competitors out of business. This development raises yet another ethical question: Does a store such as Wal-Mart have an obligation to continue operations in a community once it has forced its competitors to close their doors?

Duty to Society

Perhaps the most disputed area in the controversy surrounding corporate social responsibility is the nature of a corporation's duty to society at large. Generally, the question turns less on whether corporations owe a duty to society than on how that duty can best be fulfilled.

Those who contend that corporations should first and foremost attend to the goal of profit maximization would argue that it is by generating profits that a firm can best contribute to society. Society benefits by profit-making activities, because profits can only be realized when a firm markets products or services that are desired by society. These products and services enhance the standard of living, and the profits accumulated by successful

business firms generate national wealth. Our laws and court decisions promoting trade and commerce reflect the public policy that the fruits of commerce (wealth) are desirable and good. Because our society values wealth as an ethical goal, corporations, by contributing to that wealth, automatically are acting ethically.

Those arguing for profit maximization as a corporate goal also point out that it would be inappropriate to use the power of the corporate business world to fashion society's goals by promoting social causes. Determinations as to what exactly is in society's best interest involve questions that are essentially political, and therefore the public, through the political process, should have a say in making those determinations. The legislature—not the corporate board room—is thus the appropriate forum for such decisions.

Critics of the profit-maximization view believe that corporations should become actively engaged in seeking and furthering solutions to social problems. Because so much of the wealth and power of this country is controlled by business, business in turn has a responsibility to society to use that wealth and power in socially beneficial ways. Corporations should therefore promote human rights, strive for equal treatment of minorities and women in the workplace, take care to preserve the environment, and generally not profit from activities that society has deemed unethical. The critics also point out that it is ethically irresponsible to leave decisions concerning social welfare up to the government, because many social needs are not being met sufficiently through the political process.

It Pays to Be Ethical

Most corporations today have learned that it pays to be ethically responsible—even if it means less profit in the short run (and it often does). Today's corporations are subject to more intensive scrutiny— by both government agencies and the public—than corporations of the past. If a corporation fails to conduct its operations ethically or to respond quickly to an ethical crisis, its goodwill and reputation (and thus future profits) will likely suffer as a result.

There are other reasons as well for a corporation to behave ethically. For example, companies that demonstrate a commitment to ethical behavior—by implementing ethical programs, complying with environmental regulations, and promptly investigating product complaints, for example—often receive more lenient treatment from government agencies and the courts.

Additionally, investors may shy away from a corporation's stock if the corporation is perceived to be socially irresponsible. Since the 1970s, certain investment funds have guaranteed to the purchasers of their shares that they will invest only in companies that are ethical. For example, some funds invest money only in corporations that are "environmentally kind."

DISCUSSION QUESTIONS

1. What might be some other deterrents to ethical behavior in the business context, besides those discussed in this *Focus?*

2. Can you think of a situation in which a business firm may be acting ethically but not in a socially responsible manner? Explain.

3. Why are consumers and the public generally more concerned with ethical and socially responsible business behavior today than they were, say, fifty years ago?

4. Suppose that an automobile manufacturing company has to choose between two alternatives: contributing $1 million annually to United Way or reinvesting the $1 million in the company. In terms of ethics and social responsibility, which is the better choice?

5. Using the Internet, a small handful of activists can bring significant pressure to bear on a corporation that, in the opinion of those activists, is acting unethically. What are the implications of this development for corporate ethical decision making?

UNIT TWO

The Public and International Environment

CONTENTS

CHAPTER 5

Constitutional Law

THE U.S. CONSTITUTION IS THE SUPREME law in this country.[1] As mentioned in Chapter 1, neither Congress nor any state may pass a law that conflicts with the Constitution. Laws that govern business have their origin in the lawmaking authority granted by this document.

Before the Constitution was written, a *confederal form* of government existed. The Articles of Confederation, which went into effect in 1781, established a confederation of independent states and a central government of very limited powers. The central government could handle only those matters of common concern expressly delegated to it by the member states, and the national congress had no authority to make laws directly applicable to individuals unless the member states explicitly supported such laws. In short, *the sovereign power*[2] to govern rested essentially with the states. The Articles of Confederation clearly reflected the central tenet of the American Revolution—that a national government should not have unlimited power.

After the Revolutionary War, however, the states began to pass laws that hampered national commerce and foreign trade by preventing the free movement of goods and services. Consequently, in 1787, the Constitutional Convention assembled to **amend** (change, alter) the Articles of Confederation. Instead, the delegates to the Convention created the Constitution and a completely new type of federal government, which they believed was much better equipped than its predecessor to resolve the problems of the nation.

SECTION 1

The Constitutional Powers of Government

The U.S. Constitution established a federal form of government. A **federal form of government** is one in which the states form a union and the sovereign power is divided between a central governing authority and the member states. The Constitution delegates certain powers to the national government, and the states retain all other powers. The relationship between the national government and the state governments is a partnership—neither partner is superior to the other except within the particular area of exclusive authority granted to it under the Constitution.

To prevent the possibility that the national government might use its power arbitrarily, the Constitution provided for three branches of government. The legislative branch makes the laws, the executive branch enforces the laws, and the judicial branch interprets the

---

1. See Appendix B for the full text of the U.S. Constitution.
2. Sovereign power refers to that supreme power to which no other authority is superior or equal.

laws. Each branch performs a separate function, and no branch may exercise the authority of another branch.

Each branch, however, has some power to limit the actions of the other two branches. Congress, for example, can enact legislation relating to spending and commerce, but the president can veto that legislation. The executive branch is responsible for foreign affairs, but treaties with foreign governments require the advice and consent of members of the Senate. Although Congress determines the jurisdiction of the federal courts, the federal courts have the power to hold acts of the other branches of the federal government unconstitutional.[3] Thus, with this system of **checks and balances,** no one branch of government can accumulate too much power.

THE COMMERCE CLAUSE

Article I, Section 8, of the U.S. Constitution expressly permits Congress "[t]o regulate Commerce with foreign Nations, and among the several States, and with the Indian Tribes." This clause, referred to as the **commerce clause,** has had a greater impact on business than any other provision in the Constitution. This power was delegated to the federal government to ensure the uniformity of rules governing the movement of goods through the states.

One of the questions posed for the courts by the commerce clause is whether the word *among* in the phrase "among the several States" meant *between* the states or *between and within* the states. For some time, the federal government's power under the commerce clause was interpreted to apply only to commerce between the states (*interstate* commerce) and not commerce within the states (*intrastate* commerce). In 1824, however, in *Gibbons v. Ogden,*[4] the United States Supreme Court held that commerce within the states could also be regulated by the national government as long as the commerce concerned more than one state.

The Breadth of the Commerce Clause. As a result of the Supreme Court's interpretation of the commerce clause in *Gibbons v. Ogden,* the national government exercised increasing authority over all areas of economic affairs throughout the land. In a 1942 case,[5]

for example, the Court held that wheat production by an individual farmer intended wholly for consumption on his own farm was subject to federal regulation. The Court reasoned that the home consumption of wheat reduced the demand for wheat and thus could have a substantial effect on interstate commerce. In *McLain v. Real Estate Board of New Orleans, Inc.,*[6] a 1980 case, the Supreme Court acknowledged that the commerce clause had "long been interpreted to extend beyond activities actually in interstate commerce to reach other activities, while wholly local in nature, which nevertheless substantially affect interstate commerce."

Today, at least theoretically, the power over commerce authorizes the national government to regulate every commercial enterprise in the United States. The breadth of the commerce clause permits the national government to legislate in areas in which there is no explicit grant of power to Congress. Only rarely has the Supreme Court limited the regulatory reach of the national government under the commerce authority. One of these occasions was in 1995, in *United States v. Lopez.*[7] In that case, the Court held—for the first time in sixty years—that Congress had exceeded its regulatory authority under the commerce power when it passed the Gun-Free School Zones Act in 1990. The Court stated that the act, which banned the possession of guns within one thousand feet of any school, was unconstitutional because it attempted to regulate an area that had "nothing to do with commerce, or any sort of economic enterprise."

Generally, today's Supreme Court has indicated a willingness to rein in the constitutional powers of the national government to a far greater extent than the Court has during the past six decades. In addition to restricting the national government's regulatory reach under the commerce clause, the Court issued a number of decisions in the late 1990s that significantly enhanced the sovereign powers of the states within the federal system.[8]

The Regulatory Powers of the States. A problem that frequently arises under the commerce clause concerns a state's ability to regulate matters within its own borders. The U.S. Constitution does not expressly exclude state regulation of commerce, and there is no

---

3. As discussed in Chapter 2, the power of judicial review was established by the United States Supreme Court in *Marbury v. Madison,* 5 U.S. (1 Cranch) 137, 2 L.Ed. 60 (1803).

4. 22 U.S. (9 Wheat.) 1, 6 L.Ed. 23 (1824).

5. *Wickard v. Filburn,* 317 U.S. 111, 63 S.Ct. 82, 87 L.Ed. 122 (1942).

6. 444 U.S. 232, 100 S.Ct. 502, 62 L.Ed.2d 441 (1980).

7. 514 U.S. 549, 115 S.Ct. 1624, 131 L.Ed.2d 626 (1995).

8. See, for example, *Printz v. United States,* 521 U.S. 898, 117 S.Ct. 2365, 138 L.Ed.2d 914 (1997); and *Alden v. Maine,* 527 U.S. 706, 119 S.Ct. 2240, 144 L.Ed.2d 636 (1999).

doubt that states have a strong interest in regulating activities within their borders. As part of their inherent sovereignty, states possess **police powers.** The term does not relate solely to criminal law enforcement but rather refers to the broad right of state governments to regulate private activities to protect or promote the public order, health, safety, morals, and general welfare. Fire and building codes, antidiscrimination laws, parking regulations, zoning restrictions, licensing requirements, and thousands of other state statutes covering virtually every aspect of life have been enacted pursuant to states' police powers.

When state regulations impinge on interstate commerce, courts must balance the state's interest in the merits and purposes of the regulations against the burden placed by the regulations on interstate commerce. Generally, state laws enacted pursuant to a state's police powers carry a strong presumption of validity. If state laws *substantially* interfere with interstate commerce, however, they will be held to violate the commerce clause of the Constitution.

In *Raymond Motor Transportation, Inc. v. Rice,*[9] for example, the United States Supreme Court invalidated Wisconsin administrative regulations limiting the length of trucks traveling on the state's highways. The Court weighed the burden on interstate commerce against the benefits of the regulations and concluded that the challenged regulations "place a substantial burden on interstate commerce and they cannot be said to make more than the most speculative contribution to highway safety." Because courts balance the interests involved, it is extremely difficult to predict the outcome in a particular case.

The commerce clause also limits the states' ability to impose sales taxes on out-of-state businesses. In today's online world, this limitation has serious implications for state budgets—see this chapter's *Emerging Trends in Technology* on pages 106 and 107 for a discussion of this issue.

THE SUPREMACY CLAUSE AND FEDERAL PREEMPTION

Article VI of the Constitution provides that the Constitution, laws, and treaties of the United States are "the supreme Law of the Land." This article, commonly referred to as the **supremacy clause,** is important in the ordering of state and federal relationships. When there is a direct conflict between a federal law and a state law, the state law is rendered invalid. Because some powers are *concurrent* (shared by the federal government and the states), however, it is necessary to determine which law governs in a particular circumstance.

Federal Preemption. When Congress chooses to act exclusively in an area in which the federal government and the states have concurrent powers, it is said to have *preempted* the area. When federal **preemption** occurs, a valid federal statute or regulation will take precedence over a conflicting state or local law or regulation on the same general subject.

Whether the federal government has preempted a certain area can have important implications for businesspersons. For example, for some time it was not clear whether tobacco companies that complied with federal cigarette-labeling requirements could be sued under state laws requiring cigarette manufacturers to sufficiently warn consumers of the potential dangers associated with cigarette smoking. In a 1992 case, *Cipollone v. Liggett Group, Inc.,*[10] the United States Supreme Court held that the Federal Cigarette Labeling and Advertising Act of 1965, which requires specific warnings to be included on cigarette packages, preempted the state laws requiring warnings. The Court stated, however, that there was no indication that Congress had intended to preempt state laws that fall *outside* the scope of the federal law, such as laws governing fraudulent misrepresentation.

Determining Congressional Intent. In *Cipollone* and other cases involving preemption issues, the courts must decide whether Congress, when enacting a particular statute, *intended* to preempt the area and thus preclude plaintiffs from bringing claims under state law. In determining congressional intent, courts look at the wording of the statute itself, as well as at the legislative history of the statute (such as congressional committee reports on the topic).

For example, in *Tebbetts v. Ford Motor Co.,*[11] a plaintiff alleged that a 1988 Ford Escort was defectively designed because it did not contain an air bag on the driver's side. The defendant-manufacturer contended that it had complied with federal safety regulations authorized by the National Traffic and Motor Vehicle Safety Act (NTMVSA) of 1966 and that those regulations preempted recovery under state product-safety laws. The court interpreted House and Senate reports on the issue, as well as a clause included in the

---

9. 434 U.S. 429, 98 S.Ct. 787, 54 L.Ed.2d 664 (1978).

10. 505 U.S. 504, 112 S.Ct. 2608, 120 L.Ed.2d 407 (1992).
11. 665 A.2d 345 (N.H. 1995).

act itself, to mean that not all state law claims were preempted by the federal regulations. (The relevant clause stated that "[c]ompliance with any Federal motor vehicle safety standard issued under this [act] does not exempt any person from any liability under common law.") Thus, the plaintiff in *Tebbetts* was not precluded by the NTMVSA from suing Ford under state product-liability laws (see Chapter 13).

Generally, it is difficult to predict whether a defendant will be subject to liability under state laws notwithstanding the defendant's compliance with federally mandated product-safety standards. Courts differ in their interpretations of congressional intent, and the outcomes in cases involving similar facts can thus also differ.

THE TAXING AND SPENDING POWERS

Article I, Section 8, provides that Congress has the "Power to lay and collect Taxes, Duties, Imposts, and Excises." Section 8 further provides that "all Duties, Imposts and Excises shall be uniform throughout the United States." The requirement of uniformity refers to uniformity among the states, and thus Congress may not tax some states while exempting others.

Traditionally, if Congress attempted to regulate indirectly, by taxation, an area over which it had no authority, the tax would be invalidated by the courts. Today, however, if a tax measure is reasonable, it is generally held to be within the national taxing power. Moreover, the expansive interpretation of the commerce clause almost always provides a basis for sustaining a federal tax.

Under Article I, Section 8, Congress has the power "to pay the Debts and provide for the common Defence and general Welfare of the United States." Through the spending power, Congress disposes of the revenues accumulated from the taxing power. Congress can spend revenues not only to carry out its enumerated powers but also to promote any objective it deems worthwhile, so long as it does not violate the Bill of Rights. For example, Congress could not condition welfare payments on the recipients' agreement not to criticize government policies. The spending power necessarily involves policy choices, with which taxpayers may disagree.

SECTION 2

Business and the Bill of Rights

The importance of a written declaration of the rights of individuals eventually caused the first Congress of the United States to submit twelve amendments to the Constitution to the states for approval. The first ten of these amendments, commonly known as the **Bill of Rights,** were adopted in 1791 and embody a series of protections for the individual against various types of interference by the federal government.[12] The protections guaranteed by these ten amendments are summarized in Exhibit 5–1 (page 108).[13] Some of these constitutional protections apply to business entities as well. For example, corporations exist as separate legal entities, or *legal persons*, and enjoy many of the same rights and privileges as *natural persons* do.

As originally intended, the Bill of Rights limited only the powers of the national government. Over time, however, the United States Supreme Court "incorporated" most of these rights into the protections against state actions afforded by the Fourteenth Amendment to the Constitution. That amendment, passed in 1868 after the Civil War, provides in part that "[n]o State shall . . . deprive any person of life, liberty, or property, without due process of law." Starting in 1925, the Supreme Court began to define various rights and liberties guaranteed in the national Constitution as constituting "due process of law," which was required of state governments under the Fourteenth Amendment. Today, most of the rights and liberties set forth in the Bill of Rights apply to state governments as well as the national government. In other words, neither the federal government nor state governments can deprive individuals of those rights and liberties.

The rights secured by the Bill of Rights are not absolute. As you can see in Exhibit 5–1, many of the rights guaranteed by the first ten amendments are described in very general terms. For example, the Fourth Amendment prohibits *unreasonable* searches and seizures, but it does not define what constitutes an unreasonable search or seizure. Similarly, the Eighth Amendment prohibits excessive bail or fines, but no definition of *excessive* is contained in that amendment. Ultimately, it is the United States Supreme Court, as the final interpreter of the Constitution, that defines our rights and determines their boundaries.

FREEDOM OF SPEECH

A democratic form of government cannot survive unless people can freely voice their political opinions

---

12. Another of these proposed amendments was ratified 203 years later (in 1992) and became the Twenty-seventh Amendment to the Constitution. See Appendix B.
13. See the Constitution in Appendix B for the complete text of each amendment.

EMERGING TRENDS IN TECHNOLOGY

Taxation Issues in Cyberspace

Every year, consumers purchase more goods and services—ranging from automobiles to software to CDs to objects of art—from online merchants. Business-to-business sales are also increasing at a rapid rate. It is estimated that Internet sales will climb from $20 billion today to about $250 billion in 2005.

The potential tax revenues from today's burgeoning e-commerce have not escaped the attention of state governments. In fact, most states have extended their telecommunications tax laws to cover at least some of the components of e-commerce. For example, about a dozen states have imposed some form of access tax on Internet services, such as a fee added to the Internet subscription charge. Some jurisdictions attempt to tax the transfer of data downloaded by users. Some states, including Texas and New York, impose sales taxes on a broad array of e-commerce components, including software that is downloaded electronically and Internet access.

Not surprisingly, Internet companies, various business coalitions, and other groups have resisted such taxation. Some argue that the taxes so far imposed are unfair and discriminatory. Consider that in some places a newspaper customer pays no tax if the paper is physically delivered to the subscriber's doorstep. Yet the same customer must pay a tax if he or she downloads the electronic version of the paper posted on the Web. Others claim that attempts to tax Internet transactions will constrain the growth of e-commerce. Still others believe that if cyberspace is to be subject to taxation, the states must at least develop a more uniform taxation scheme.

THE PROBLEM FACING THE STATES

For most state governments, sales taxes are important sources of income. Typically, between 35 and 40 percent of state revenues are obtained through sales taxes. Today, however, the states are facing declining sales tax revenues. In part, this is because of the growth in direct-marketing sales made via mail order or the Internet. In a direct-marketing transaction, a seller, such as a mail-order house, sells goods directly to consumers located around the country. The problem for the states is that their ability to impose tax obligations on out-of-state sellers is limited.

This limitation was established by the United States Supreme Court long before the rise of the Internet. In 1967, the Court held that it was a violation of the commerce clause for a state to impose tax obligations on a business located outside the state's borders *unless* the business had a "nexus" with—a substantial physical presence in—the taxing state.[a] Generally, the nexus requirement is satisfied if a business has outlets, sales representatives, or other significant property in the taxing state. In a 1992 case, *Quill Corp. v. North Dakota*,[b] the Supreme Court held specifically that mail-order firms that lack this required nexus are exempt from state taxes. The reasoning in the *Quill* case can be extended to online direct marketing, meaning that it is impossible for a state to collect taxes from online merchants who have no physical presence in the state.

Because of these tax rulings, state governments claim that they are losing billions of dollars each year.

a. *National Bellas Hess, Inc. v. Department of Revenue of the State of Illinois,* 386 U.S. 753, 87 S.Ct. 1389, 18 L.Ed.2d 505 (1967).
b. 504 U.S. 298, 112 S.Ct. 1904, 119 L.Ed.2d 91 (1992).

and criticize government actions or policies. Freedom of speech, particularly political speech, is thus a prized right, and traditionally the courts have protected this right to the fullest extent possible.

Symbolic speech—gestures, movements, articles of clothing, and other forms of expressive conduct—is also given substantial protection by the courts. For example, in a 1989 case, *Texas v. Johnson,*[14] the United States Supreme Court ruled that state laws that prohibited the burning of the American flag as part of a peaceful protest violated the freedom of expression protected by the First Amendment. Congress responded by passing the Flag Protection Act of 1989, which was ruled un-

14. 491 U.S. 397, 109 S.Ct. 2533, 105 L.Ed.2d 342 (1989).

EMERGING TRENDS IN TECHNOLOGY

Taxation Issues in Cyberspace,

continued

THE INADEQUACY OF EXISTING TAX LAWS

Clearly, the nexus requirements set forth by the Supreme Court have become inadequate in today's electronic age. As a result, the states are proposing new theories of nexus that would enable them to impose taxes on direct-marketing transactions. For example, one proposal is that nexus requirements be changed to require merely an "economic" presence in the state (via the Internet) rather than a "physical presence." At the same time, the Clinton administration favored a tax-free Internet, as have business groups generally.

THE INTERNET TAX FREEDOM ACT

In response to pressure from various groups to take action, Congress passed the Internet Tax Freedom Act of 1998, which President Clinton signed into law on October 21, 1998. The act imposed a three-year moratorium

on all new taxes directed specifically at Web-based activities. (It did not, however, affect any state taxation systems that were already in place by March 1998.) During the three-year moratorium, which will expire on October 21, 2001, the act calls for a study and a report to Congress on various methods of Internet taxation. A central issue to be examined is how taxes might be imposed on Web-based activities without significantly constraining e-commerce.

IMPLICATIONS FOR THE BUSINESSPERSON

1. To date, retailers engaged in e-commerce have held a clear advantage over those who sell their goods through traditional outlets, at least with respect to sales taxes. The moratorium on Internet taxation means that this advantage will continue to exist until October 2001. Additionally, the moratorium offers a window of opportunity for entrepreneurs or existing firms to take advantage of the commercial capabilities of the Internet until that date.
2. It seems unrealistic to assume that online commerce will forever remain largely untaxed, as it is now. Therefore, business representatives and groups should

consider the merits of working in conjunction with tax agencies to help ensure that whatever rules are developed will be fair and consistent.

FOR CRITICAL ANALYSIS

1. Is it unfair for states to impose sales taxes on goods sold through traditional outlets—such as those located in downtown areas or shopping malls—but not on similar goods sold by online direct marketers? Would your answer be the same if you knew that the taxation of goods sold online would stifle the growth of e-commerce?
2. If new tax laws should be applied to e-commerce, what enforcement problems might arise? (Hint: Remember, the Internet is a global network.)

RELEVANT WEB SITES

You can find a "plain English" summary of the Internet Tax Freedom Act at **http://www. house.gov/chriscox/nettax**. For a Web site focusing on Internet taxation issues, go to **http://www. nettaxfairness.org**.

---

constitutional by the Supreme Court in 1990.[15] Congress and George Bush, who was then president, pledged immediately to work for a constitutional amendment to "protect our flag"—an effort that has yet to be successful. In a subsequent case,

the Supreme Court ruled that a city statute banning bias-motivated disorderly conduct (including, in this case, the placing of a burning cross in another's front yard as a gesture of hate) was an unconstitutional restriction of speech.[16]

---

15. *United States v. Eichman*, 496 U.S. 310, 110 S.Ct. 2804, 110 L.Ed.2d 287 (1990).

16. *R.A.V. v. City of St. Paul, Minnesota*, 505 U.S. 377, 112 S.Ct. 2538, 120 L.Ed.2d 305 (1992).

EXHIBIT 5–1   PROTECTIONS GUARANTEED BY THE BILL OF RIGHTS

First Amendment: Guarantees the freedoms of religion, speech, and the press and the rights to assemble peaceably and to petition the government.	**Sixth Amendment:** Guarantees the accused in a criminal case the right to a speedy and public trial by an impartial jury and with counsel. The accused has the right to cross-examine witnesses against him or her and to solicit testimony from witnesses in his or her favor.
Second Amendment: Guarantees the right to keep and bear arms.	
Third Amendment: Prohibits, in peacetime, the lodging of soldiers in any house without the owner's consent.	**Seventh Amendment:** Guarantees the right to a trial by jury in a civil case involving at least twenty dollars.[a]
Fourth Amendment: Prohibits unreasonable searches and seizures of persons or property.	**Eighth Amendment:** Prohibits excessive bail and fines, as well as cruel and unusual punishment.
Fifth Amendment: Guarantees the rights to indictment by grand jury, to due process of law, and to fair payment when private property is taken for public use; prohibits compulsory self-incrimination and double jeopardy (trial for the same crime twice if the first trial ends in acquittal or conviction).	**Ninth Amendment:** Establishes that the people have rights in addition to those specified in the Constitution.
	Tenth Amendment: Establishes that those powers neither delegated to the federal government nor denied to the states are reserved for the states.

a. Twenty dollars was forty days' pay for the average person when the Bill of Rights was written.

Governments can and do place restraints on free speech, of course, but such restraints are permissible only when they are necessary to protect other substantial interests and rights. It is up to the courts—and ultimately, the United States Supreme Court—to determine the point at which laws restricting free speech can be justified by the need to protect other rights.

Commercial Speech.   Speech and communications—primarily advertising—made by business firms are called *commercial speech*. Although commercial speech is protected by the First Amendment, it is not protected as extensively as noncommercial speech. A state may restrict certain kinds of advertising, for ex-

ample, in the interest of preventing consumers from being misled by the advertising practices. States also have a legitimate interest in the beautification of roadsides, and this interest allows states to place restraints on billboard advertising.

Generally, a restriction on commercial speech will be considered valid as long as it meets the following three criteria: (1) it must seek to implement a substantial government interest, (2) it must directly advance that interest, and (3) it must go no further than necessary to accomplish its objective. At issue in the following case was whether a government agency's decision to prohibit the inclusion of a certain illustration on beer labels unconstitutionally restricted commercial speech.

CASE 5.1   Bad Frog Brewery, Inc. v. New York State Liquor Authority

United States
Court of Appeals,
Second Circuit, 1998.
134 F.3d 87.
http://www.tourolaw.
edu/2ndCircuit/
January98/97-79490.
html[a]

HISTORICAL AND CULTURAL SETTING   *Hand gestures signifying insults have been in use throughout the world for centuries. Hand gestures regarded as insults in some countries include an extended right thumb, an extended little finger, raised index and middle fingers, and gestures effected with two hands. A gesture using the extended middle finger of either hand (sometimes referred to as "giving the finger" or "flipping the bird") is generally acknowledged to convey an obscene, offensive message: a suggestion to have intercourse with one's self. This gesture is said to have been used by Diogenes (a Greek philosopher in the fourth century B.C.E. who was known for his disregard of social niceties) to insult Demosthenes (a Greek statesman and contemporary of Diogenes).[b]*

a. This page is part of a Web site maintained by the Touro College Jacob D. Fuchsberg Law Center in Huntington, New York.
b. Betty J. Bauml and Franz H. Bauml, *Dictionary of Worldwide Gestures*, 2d ed. (Lanham, Md.: Scarecrow Press, 1997), p. 159.

BACKGROUND AND FACTS *Bad Frog Brewery, Inc., makes and sells alcoholic beverages. Some of the beverages feature labels that display a drawing of a frog making the gesture generally known as "giving the finger." Bad Frog's authorized New York distributor, Renaissance Beer Company, applied to the New York State Liquor Authority (NYSLA) for brand label approval, as required by state law before the beer could be sold in New York. The NYSLA denied the application, in part because "the label could appear in grocery and convenience stores, with obvious exposure on the shelf to children of tender age." Bad Frog filed a suit in a federal district court against the NYSLA, asking for, among other things, an injunction against the denial of Bad Frog's application. The court granted summary judgment in favor of the NYSLA. Bad Frog appealed to the U.S. Court of Appeals for the Second Circuit.*

IN THE LANGUAGE OF THE COURT

JON O. NEWMAN, Circuit Judge:

* * * *

* * * [T]o support its asserted power to ban Bad Frog's labels [NYSLA advances] * * * the State's interest in "protecting children from vulgar and profane advertising" * * * .

[This interest is] substantial * * * . States have a compelling interest in protecting the physical and psychological well-being of minors * * * .

* * * *

* * * NYSLA endeavors to advance the state interest in preventing exposure of children to vulgar displays by taking only the limited step of barring such displays from the labels of alcoholic beverages. In view of the wide currency of vulgar displays throughout contemporary society, including comic books targeted directly at children, barring such displays from labels for alcoholic beverages cannot realistically be expected to reduce children's exposure to such displays to any significant degree.

* * * If New York decides to make a substantial effort to insulate children from vulgar displays in some significant sphere of activity, at least with respect to materials likely to be seen by children, NYSLA's label prohibition might well be found to make a justifiable contribution to the material advancement of such an effort, but its currently isolated response to the perceived problem, applicable only to labels on a product that children cannot purchase, does not suffice. * * * [A] state must demonstrate that its commercial speech limitation is part of a substantial effort to advance a valid state interest, not merely the removal of a few grains of offensive sand from a beach of vulgarity.

* * * *

* * * Even if we were to assume that the state materially advances its asserted interest by shielding children from viewing the Bad Frog labels, it is plainly excessive to prohibit the labels from all use, including placement on bottles displayed in bars and taverns where parental supervision of children is to be expected. Moreover, to whatever extent NYSLA is concerned that children will be harmfully exposed to the Bad Frog labels when wandering without parental supervision around grocery and convenience stores where beer is sold, that concern could be less intrusively dealt with by placing restrictions on the permissible locations where the appellant's products may be displayed within such stores.

DECISION AND REMEDY *The U.S. Court of Appeals for the Second Circuit reversed the judgment of the district court and remanded the case for the entry of a judgment in favor of Bad Frog. The NYSLA's ban on the use of the labels lacked a "reasonable fit" with the state's interest in shielding minors from vulgarity, and the NYSLA did not adequately consider alternatives to the ban.*

Corporate Political Speech. Political speech that otherwise would fall within the protection of the First Amendment does not lose that protection simply because its source is a corporation. For example, in *First* *National Bank of Boston v. Bellotti,*[17] national banking associations and business corporations sought United

---

17. 435 U.S. 765, 98 S.Ct. 1407, 55 L.Ed.2d 707 (1978).

States Supreme Court review of a Massachusetts statute that prohibited corporations from making political contributions or expenditures that individuals were permitted to make. The Court ruled that the Massachusetts law was unconstitutional because it violated the right of corporations to freedom of speech. Similarly, the Court has held that a law forbidding a corporation from using bill inserts to express its views on controversial issues violates the First Amendment.[18] Although in 1990 a more conservative Supreme Court reversed this trend somewhat,[19] corporate political speech continues to be given significant protection under the First Amendment.

Unprotected Speech. The United States Supreme Court has made it clear that certain types of speech will not be protected under the First Amendment. Speech that harms the good reputation of another, or defamatory speech (see Chapter 12), is not protected under the First Amendment. Speech that violates criminal laws (threatening speech, pornography, and so on) is not constitutionally protected. Other unprotected speech includes "fighting words" (speech that is likely to incite others to respond violently). Many people think that the "hate speech" exchanged between members of different groups on college campuses should be included in the category of "fighting words." Courts, however, have been reluctant to uphold university codes banning hate speech, concluding that the codes go too far in restricting the free speech of students.[20]

Another category of unprotected speech is obscene speech. Numerous state and federal statutes make it a crime to disseminate obscene materials. The United States Supreme Court has grappled from time to time with the problem of trying to establish an operationally effective definition of obscene speech. Frequently, this determination is left to state and local authorities, who customarily base their definitions of obscenity on community standards. Generally, obscenity is still a constitutionally unsettled area. In the interest of preventing the abuse of children, however, the Supreme Court has upheld state laws prohibiting the sale and possession of child pornography.[21] In the interest of protecting women against sexual harassment on the job, at least one court has banned lewd speech and pornographic pinups in the workplace.[22]

In recent years, obscenity issues have also arisen in relation to television shows, movies, the lyrics and covers of music albums, and the content of monologues by "shock" comedians. In addition, as will be discussed in Chapter 15, a challenging legal issue today is how to regulate the availability of obscene materials on the Internet.

FREEDOM OF RELIGION

The First Amendment states that the government may neither establish any religion nor prohibit the free exercise of religious practices. The first part of this constitutional provision is referred to as the **establishment clause,** which has to do with the separation of church and state. The second part of the provision is known as the **free exercise clause.**

The Establishment Clause. The establishment clause prohibits the government from establishing a state-sponsored religion, as well as from passing laws that promote (aid or endorse) religion or that show a preference for one religion over another. Establishment clause issues often involve such matters as the legality of allowing or requiring school prayers, the teaching of evolutionary versus creationist theory, and state and local government aid to religious organizations and schools.

Federal or state laws that do not promote or place a significant burden on religion are constitutional even if they have some impact on religion. "Sunday closing laws," for example, make the performance of some commercial activities on Sunday illegal. These statutes, also known as "blue laws" (from the color of the paper on which an early Sunday law was written), have been upheld on the ground that it is a legitimate function of government to provide a day of rest. The United States Supreme Court has held that the closing laws, although originally of a religious character,

---

18. *Consolidated Edison Co. v. Public Service Commission,* 447 U.S. 530, 100 S.Ct. 2326, 65 L.Ed.2d 319 (1980).
19. See *Austin v. Michigan Chamber of Commerce,* 494 U.S. 652, 110 S.Ct. 1391, 108 L.Ed.2d 652 (1990), in which the Court upheld a state law prohibiting corporations from using general corporate funds for independent expenditures in state political campaigns.
20. See, for example, *Doe v. University of Michigan,* 721 F.Supp. 852 (1989); and *The UWM Post v. Board of Regents of the University of Wisconsin System,* 774 F.Supp. 1163 (E.D.Wis. 1991).

21. See *Osborne v. Ohio,* 495 U.S. 103, 110 S.Ct. 1691, 109 L.Ed.2d 98 (1990).
22. *Robinson v. Jacksonville Shipyards, Inc.,* 760 F.Supp. 1486 (M.D.Fla. 1991).

have taken on the secular purpose of promoting the health and welfare of workers.[23] Even though closing laws admittedly make it easier for Christians to attend religious services, the Court has viewed this effect as an incidental, not a primary, purpose of Sunday closing laws.

The First Amendment does not require a complete separation of church and state. On the contrary, it affirmatively mandates accommodation of all religions and forbids hostility toward any.[24] An ongoing challenge for the courts is determining the extent to which governments can accommodate a religion without appearing to promote that religion, which would violate the establishment clause. For example, in *Lynch v. Donnelly*,[25] the United States Supreme Court held that a municipality could include religious symbols, such as a Nativity scene, or crèche, in its annual holiday display as long as the religious symbols constituted just one part of a display in which other, nonreligious symbols (such as reindeer and candy-striped poles) were also featured. The Court has applied this same reasoning in subsequent cases and continues to face such issues.[26]

The Free Exercise Clause. The free exercise clause guarantees that no person can be compelled to do something that is contrary to his or her religious beliefs. For this reason, if a law or policy is contrary to a person's religious beliefs, exemptions are often made to accommodate those beliefs. When, however, religious practices work against public policy and the public welfare, the government can act. For example, children of Jehovah's Witnesses are not required to say the Pledge of Allegiance at school, but their parents cannot prevent these children from accepting medical treatment (such as blood transfusions) if the children's lives are in danger.

For business firms, an important issue involves the accommodation that businesses must make for the religious beliefs of their employees. For example, if an employee's religion prohibits him or her from working on a certain day of the week or at a certain type of job,

the employer must make a reasonable attempt to accommodate these religious requirements. Employers must reasonably accommodate an employee's religious belief even if the belief is not based on the tenets or dogma of a particular church, sect, or denomination. The only requirement is that the belief be religious in nature and sincerely held by the employee.[27] (See Chapter 22 for a further discussion of religious freedom in the employment context.)

SELF-INCRIMINATION

The Fifth Amendment guarantees that no person "shall be compelled in any criminal case to be a witness against himself." Thus, in any federal proceeding, an accused person cannot be compelled to give testimony that might subject him or her to any criminal prosecution. Nor can an accused person be forced to testify against himself or herself in state courts, because the due process clause of the Fourteenth Amendment (discussed later in this chapter) incorporates the Fifth Amendment provision against self-incrimination.

The Fifth Amendment's guarantee against self-incrimination extends only to natural persons. Because a corporation is a legal entity and not a natural person, the privilege against self-incrimination does not apply to it. Similarly, the business records of a partnership do not receive Fifth Amendment protection.[28] When a partnership is required to produce these records, it must give the information even if it incriminates the persons who constitute the business entity. In contrast, sole proprietors and sole practitioners (those who fully own their businesses) who have not incorporated cannot be compelled to produce their business records. These individuals have full protection against self-incrimination, because they function in only one capacity; there is no separate business entity.

In the following case, a state's investigation into the commercial practices of a certain corporation led the state's attorney general to issue a subpoena for the firm's business records. On the basis of the privilege against self-incrimination, the corporation refused to provide the records unless it was guaranteed immunity from prosecution.

---

23. *McGowan v. Maryland,* 366 U.S. 420, 81 S.Ct. 1101, 6 L.Ed.2d 393 (1961).

24. *Zorach v. Clauson,* 343 U.S. 306, 72 S.Ct. 679, 96 L.Ed. 954 (1952).

25. 465 U.S. 668, 104 S.Ct. 1355, 79 L.Ed.2d 604 (1984).

26. See, for example, *County of Allegheny v. American Civil Liberties Union,* 492 U.S. 573, 109 S.Ct. 3086, 106 L.Ed.2d 472 (1989); and *Capitol Square Review and Advisory Board v. Pinette,* 515 U.S. 753, 115 S.Ct. 2440, 132 L.Ed.2d 650 (1995).

27. *Frazee v. Illinois Department of Employment Security,* 489 U.S. 829, 109 S.Ct. 1514, 103 L.Ed.2d 914 (1989).

28. The privilege has been applied to some small family partnerships. See *United States v. Slutsky,* 352 F.Supp. 1005 (S.D.N.Y. 1972).

CASE 5.2

Verniero v. Beverly Hills Ltd., Inc.

Superior Court of
New Jersey, Appellate
Division, 1998.
316 N.J.Super. 121,
719 A.2d 713.
http://lawlibrary.rutgers.
edu/search.shtml[a]

BACKGROUND AND FACTS   *The New Jersey Division of Consumer Affairs, under the state Consumer Affairs Act, investigated the marketing practices of Beverly Hills Limited, Inc. On the division's behalf, Peter Verniero, the state's attorney general, served a subpoena on Beverly Hills. The subpoena ordered the firm to provide certain business records, including its marketing agreements with other companies and documents relating to the firm's status as a corporation. Beverly Hills and its attorney responded that it was entitled to "exemption from both civil and criminal punishment in the event demanded documents would in any way result in self-incrimination" and demanded a guarantee of immunity before turning over its records. They cited N.J.S.A. [New Jersey Statutes Annotated] 56:8-7, which provides a privilege against self-incrimination for "a person who is entitled by law to, and does assert such privilege," when ordered to produce documents. Verniero filed a suit in a New Jersey state court to enforce the subpoena against Beverly Hills, arguing that the corporation had no privilege against self-incrimination. The court ruled in favor of Beverly Hills. Verniero appealed to a state intermediate appellate court.*

IN THE LANGUAGE OF THE COURT

SKILLMAN, J.A.D. [Judge, Appellate Division]

*   *   *   *

The Fifth Amendment to the United States Constitution provides that "[n]o person *   *   * shall be compelled to be a witness against himself." Although the New Jersey Constitution does not contain a similar privilege, New Jersey has a common law privilege against self-incrimination which is now codified in [N.J.S.A. 2A:84-17 through 2A:84-19]. It is firmly established that *a corporation may not invoke either the Fifth Amendment or the New Jersey privilege against self-incrimination*. Moreover, a custodian of corporate records may not rely upon his or her personal privilege against self-incrimination as a basis for refusing to produce corporate records. [Emphasis added.]

Beverly Hills is admittedly a corporation, and the subpoena issued by the Division only sought the production of Beverly Hills' records. Therefore, it is clear that neither Beverly Hills nor [its attorney] could invoke the Fifth Amendment or the New Jersey privilege against self-incrimination incorporated in N.J.S.A. 2A:84-17 to 19 as a basis for refusing to produce the records.

*   *   *   *

N.J.S.A. 56:8-7 *   *   * only confers immunity upon a person who is "entitled by law to *   *   * assert [the] privilege" against self-incrimination. Thus, a person claiming immunity under N.J.S.A. 56:8-7 must identify some "law" other than N.J.S.A. 56:8-7 as the source of a privilege against self-incrimination. By construing N.J.S.A. 56:8-7 to provide immunity from prosecution to a party who is not entitled to invoke the privilege against self-incrimination, the trial court effectively read the words "entitled by law to *   *   * assert such privilege" out of the statute. *   *   *

DECISION AND REMEDY   *The state intermediate appellate court held that a corporation could not invoke a privilege against self-incrimination as a basis for refusing to produce documents in response to a subpoena. The court reversed the judgment of the lower court and remanded the case for the entry of an order compelling Beverly Hills to comply with the subpoena.*

---

a. Rutgers University School of Law in Camden, New Jersey, maintains this Web site. On this page, scroll down to the "Find Case by Citation" box. Select "N.J.Super." from the choices on the menu in the "Reporter" box. Enter "316" in the "Volume" box and "121" in the "Page" box. Click on "Submit Form" to access the case.

SEARCHES AND SEIZURES

The Fourth Amendment protects the "right of the people to be secure in their persons, houses, papers, and effects." Before searching or seizing private property, law enforcement officers must obtain a **search warrant**—an order from a judge or other public official authorizing the search or seizure.

Search Warrants and Probable Cause. To obtain a search warrant, the officers must convince a judge that they have reasonable grounds, or probable cause, to believe a search will reveal a specific illegality. **Probable cause** requires law enforcement officials to have trustworthy evidence that would convince a reasonable person that the proposed search or seizure is more likely justified than not. Furthermore, the Fourth Amendment prohibits *general* warrants. It requires a particular description of that which is to be searched or seized. General searches through a person's belongings are impermissible. The search cannot extend beyond what is described in the warrant.

There are exceptions to the requirement for a search warrant, as when it is likely that the items sought will be removed before a warrant can be obtained. For example, if a police officer has probable cause to believe an automobile contains evidence of a crime and it is likely that the vehicle will be unavailable by the time a warrant is obtained, the officer can search the vehicle without a warrant.

Searches and Seizures in the Business Context. Constitutional protection against unreasonable searches and seizures is important to businesses and professionals. As federal and state regulation of commercial activities increased, frequent and unannounced government inspections were conducted to ensure compliance with the regulations. Such inspections were at times extremely disruptive. In *Marshall v. Barlow's, Inc.*,[29] the United States Supreme Court held that government inspectors do not have the right to enter business premises without a warrant, although the standard of probable cause is not the same as that required in nonbusiness contexts. The existence of a general and neutral enforcement plan will justify issuance of the warrant.

Lawyers and accountants frequently possess the business records of their clients, and inspecting these documents while they are out of the hands of their true owners also requires a warrant. A warrant is not required, however, for the seizure of spoiled or contaminated food. In addition, warrants are also not required for searches of businesses in such highly regulated industries as liquor, guns, and strip mining. General manufacturing is not considered to be one of these highly regulated industries, however.

Of increasing concern to many government employers is how to maintain a safe and efficient workplace without jeopardizing the Fourth Amendment rights of employees "to be secure in their persons." Requiring government employees to undergo random drug tests, for example, may be held to violate the Fourth Amendment. In Chapter 21, we will discuss Fourth Amendment issues in the employment context, as well as employee privacy rights in general, in greater detail.

SECTION 3

Other Constitutional Protections

Other constitutional guarantees of great significance to Americans are mandated by the *privileges and immunities clause* and the *full faith and credit clause* of Article IV of the Constitution, the *due process clauses* of the Fifth and Fourteenth Amendments, and the *equal protection clause* of the Fourteenth Amendment.

THE PRIVILEGES AND IMMUNITIES CLAUSE

Article IV, Section 2, of the Constitution provides that the "Citizens of each State shall be entitled to all Privileges and Immunities of Citizens in the several States." This clause is often referred to as the interstate **privileges and immunities clause**.[30] When a citizen of one state engages in basic and essential activities in another state (the "foreign state"), such as transferring property, seeking employment, or accessing the court system, the foreign state must have a *substantial reason* for treating the nonresident differently from its own residents. The foreign state must also establish that its reason for the discrimination is

---

29. 436 U.S. 307, 98 S.Ct. 1816, 56 L.Ed.2d 305 (1978).

30. The terms *privilege* and *immunity* are commonly used synonymously with regard to the interpretation of this clause. Generally, the terms refer to certain rights, benefits, or advantages enjoyed by individuals.

substantially related to the state's ultimate purpose in adopting the legislation or activity.[31]

Charging nonresidents $2,500 for a shrimp-fishing license, for example, while residents are charged only $25 for the same license, may be considered unconstitutional discrimination against nonresidents who are pursuing the essential activity of making a living.[32] Similarly, attempting to limit the practice of law to residents only (on the premise that it would help reduce the state's unemployment rate) may unconstitutionally restrict a nonresident's professional pursuit without substantial justification.[33]

The Fourteenth Amendment provides that "[n]o State shall make or enforce any law which shall abridge the privileges or immunities of citizens of the United States." This clause also protects all individuals, as citizens of the United States, from *state* action that might infringe on their privileges or immunities.[34]

THE FULL FAITH AND CREDIT CLAUSE

Article IV, Section 1, of the Constitution provides that "Full Faith and Credit shall be given in each State to the public Acts, Records, and judicial Proceedings of every other State." This clause, which is referred to as the **full faith and credit clause,** applies only to civil matters. It ensures that rights established under deeds, wills, contracts, and the like in one state will be honored by other states. It also ensures that any judicial decision with respect to such property rights will be honored and enforced in all states.

The full faith and credit clause originally was included in the Articles of Confederation to promote mutual friendship among the people of the various states. In fact, it has contributed to the unity of American citizens, because it protects their legal rights as they move about from state to state. It also protects the rights of those to whom they owe obligations, such as judgment creditors. This is extremely important for the conduct of business in a country with a very mobile citizenry.

---

31. *Supreme Court of New Hampshire v. Piper,* 470 U.S. 274, 105 S.Ct. 1272, 84 L.Ed.2d 205 (1985).
32. *Toomer v. Witsell,* 334 U.S. 385, 68 S.Ct. 1156, 92 L.Ed. 1460 (1948).
33. *Hicklin v. Orbeck,* 437 U.S. 518, 98 S.Ct. 2482, 57 L.Ed.2d 397 (1978).
34. Unlike the due process and equal protection clauses (to be discussed shortly), the privileges and immunities clause of the Fourteenth Amendment does not apply to the individual rights found in the Bill of Rights.

DUE PROCESS

Both the Fifth and the Fourteenth Amendments provide that no person shall be deprived "of life, liberty, or property, without due process of law." The **due process clause** of these constitutional amendments has two aspects—procedural and substantive. Note that the due process clause applies to "legal persons" (that is, corporations) as well as to individuals.

Procedural Due Process. *Procedural* due process requires that any government decision to take life, liberty, or property must be made equitably. For example, fair procedures must be used in determining whether a person will be subjected to punishment or have some burden imposed on him or her. Fair procedure has been interpreted as requiring that the person have at least an opportunity to object to a proposed action before a fair, neutral decision maker (which need not be a judge). Thus, for example, if a driver's license is construed as a property interest, some sort of opportunity to object to its suspension or termination by the state must be provided.

Substantive Due Process. *Substantive* due process focuses on the content, or substance, of legislation. If a law or other governmental action limits a *fundamental right*, it will be held to violate substantive due process unless it promotes a *compelling* or *overriding state interest.* Fundamental rights include interstate travel, privacy, voting, and all First Amendment rights. Compelling state interests could include, for example, the public's safety. Thus, laws designating speed limits may be upheld even though they affect interstate travel, if they are shown to reduce highway fatalities, because the state has a compelling interest in protecting the lives of its citizens.

In all other situations, a law or action does not violate substantive due process if it rationally relates to any legitimate government purpose. It is almost impossible for a law or action to fail this "rational basis" test. Under this test, virtually any business regulation will be upheld as reasonable—the United States Supreme Court has upheld insurance regulations, price and wage controls, banking controls, and controls of unfair competition and trade practices against substantive due process challenges.

Suppose that a state legislature enacted a law imposing a fifteen-year term of imprisonment without a trial on all businesspersons who appeared in their own television commercials. This law would be unconstitutional on both substantive and procedural grounds. Substantive review would invalidate the legislation because it abridges freedom of speech, a fundamental right. Procedurally, the law is constitutionally invalid because it imposes a penalty without giving the accused a chance to defend his or her actions.

EQUAL PROTECTION

Under the Fourteenth Amendment, a state may not "deny to any person within its jurisdiction the equal protection of the laws." The United States Supreme Court has used the due process clause of the Fifth Amendment to make the **equal protection clause** applicable to the federal government. Equal protection means that the government must treat similarly situated individuals in a similar manner.

Both substantive due process and equal protection require review of the substance of the law or other governmental action rather than review of the procedures used. When a law or action limits the liberty of all persons to do something, it may violate substantive due process; when a law or action limits the liberty of some persons but not others, it may violate the equal protection clause. Thus, for example, if a law prohibits all persons from buying contraceptive devices, it raises a substantive due process question; if it prohibits only unmarried persons from buying the same devices, it raises an equal protection issue.

In an equal protection inquiry, when a law or action distinguishes between or among individuals, the basis for the distinction—that is, the classification—is examined by the courts. The courts may use one of three standards: strict scrutiny, intermediate scrutiny, or the "rational basis" test.

Strict Scrutiny. If a law or action prohibits or inhibits some persons from exercising a fundamental right, the law or action will be subject to "strict scrutiny" by the courts. Under this standard, the classification must be necessary to promote a *compelling state interest*. Also, if the classification is based on a *suspect trait*—such as race, national origin, or citizenship status—the classification must be necessary to promote a compelling state interest. Compelling state interests include remedying past unconstitutional or illegal discrimination but do not include correcting the general effects of "society's" discrimination. Thus, for example, if a city gives preference to minority applicants in awarding construction contracts, the city normally must identify the past unconstitutional or illegal discrimination against minority construction firms that it is attempting to correct. Generally, few laws or actions survive strict-scrutiny analysis by the courts.

Intermediate Scrutiny. Another standard, that of "intermediate scrutiny," is applied in cases involving discrimination based on gender or legitimacy. Laws using these classifications must be *substantially related to important government objectives*.

For example, an important government objective is preventing illegitimate teenage pregnancies. Therefore, because males and females are not similarly situated in this regard—only females can become pregnant—a law that punishes men but not women for statutory rape will be upheld, even though it treats men and women unequally. A state law requiring illegitimate children to bring paternity suits within six years of their births, however, will be struck down if legitimate children are allowed to seek support from their parents at any time. An important objective behind statutes of limitations is to prevent persons from bringing stale or fraudulent claims, but distinguishing between support claims on the basis of legitimacy has no relation to this objective.

The "Rational Basis" Test. In matters of economic or social welfare, the classification will be considered valid if there is any conceivable *rational basis* on which the classification might relate to a legitimate government interest. It is almost impossible for a law or action to fail the rational basis test. Thus, for example, a city ordinance that in effect prohibits all pushcart vendors except a specific few from operating in a particular area of the city will be upheld if the city provides a rational basis—perhaps regulation and reduction of traffic in the particular area—for the ordinance. In contrast, a law that provides unemployment benefits only to people over six feet tall would violate the guarantee of equal protection. There is no rational basis for determining the distribution of unemployment compensation on the basis of height. Such a distinction could not further any legitimate government objective.

Is there a rational basis for a city ordinance that provides free garbage collection for the owners of some residences but requires the owners of other dwellings to pay for the same service? That was the question in the following case.

CASE 5.3   WHS Realty Co. v. Town of Morristown

Superior Court of
New Jersey,
Appellate Division, 1999.
323 N.J.Super. 553,
733 A.2d 1206.

BACKGROUND AND FACTS   *The Town of Morristown enacted an ordinance that provided for free garbage collection for all residential dwellings with three or fewer units and condominium developments in which no more than 50 percent of the units were owned by one person or entity. Excluded from the ordinance were all multifamily dwellings with four or more units. WHS Realty Company owned an apartment complex that consisted of 140 units and thus did not receive the free service. WHS filed a suit in a New Jersey state court against Morristown, claiming in part that the ordinance violated the Constitution's equal protection clause. Morristown argued, among other things, that the ordinance was rationally related to fostering home ownership. The court determined that the ordinance was unconstitutional, finding it was not rationally related to the fostering of home ownership or any other legitimate state interest. The court ordered Morristown to collect garbage and recyclable materials from WHS's apartment complex according to the terms applied to condominium complexes. Morristown appealed.*

IN THE LANGUAGE
OF THE COURT

HAVEY, P.J.A.D. [Presiding Judge, Appellate Division]
    *   *   *   *

A municipality is not mandated to provide for municipal garbage removal. *   *   *

However, once the service is provided by a municipality, *   *   * [t]here is a violation of equal protection of the laws unless the service is available to all persons in like circumstances upon the same terms and conditions. Persons situated alike shall be treated alike.
    *   *   *   *

*   *   * [T]here is nothing about the mechanics or costs of solid waste collection that justifies differentiating between apartment complexes and other residents within the community. As the trial court observed during an early stage of the proceedings, "people are people," and the type and quality of solid waste generated by all types of residential dwellings is the same. *   *   *
    *   *   *

The Town defendants nevertheless argue that the *   *   * ordinance is rationally related to fostering home ownership. *   *   *
    *   *   *   *

*   *   * Here, *   *   * the facts established that approximately 42% of the dwelling units receiving garbage collection service are not occupied by their owners. Only 27% and 11.7% of the two- and three-family dwelling units are owner-occupied. If the disputed classification in fact promotes home ownership, particularly among the two- and three-family owners, there is no question that the percentages of owner-occupancy would be significantly higher. The low percentages of owner-occupants necessarily indicate that the disputed classification is irrational.
    *   *   * [T]he only service involved is collection of solid waste, which, according to the [facts], costs approximately $400 per residential unit per year. *   *   * The Town performed no studies or surveys indicating that people are more inclined to purchase a home if free garbage collection service is provided. No interviews of homeowners were conducted.
    *   *   *   *

The Town defendants also advance, as a rational basis for the ordinance, the fact that condominiums are taxed differently than apartment units. *   *   *
    *   *   *   *

*   *   * We conclude that the methodology of taxing apartment complexes and condominium units is not a rational basis for upholding the ordinance.

DECISION
AND REMEDY

The state intermediate appellate court affirmed the ruling of the lower court. The appellate court held that the ordinance violated the equal protection clause because it was not rationally related to any legitimate governmental interest. The court remanded the case, however, for a determination of the amount of damages, if any, to be paid to WHS.

PRIVACY RIGHTS

A personal right to privacy is held to be so fundamental as to be applicable at both the state and the federal levels. Although there is no specific guarantee of a right to privacy in the Constitution, such a right has been derived from guarantees found in the First, Third, Fourth, Fifth, and Ninth Amendments. Invasion of another's privacy is also a tort, or civil wrong (see Chapter 12), and over the last several decades legislation has been passed at the federal level to protect the privacy of individuals in numerous areas of concern.

Privacy rights often relate to emotionally charged issues, such as abortion, assisted suicide for terminally ill people, and gay and lesbian relationships. In the business world, issues of privacy often arise in the employment context, a topic we examine in Chapter 21.

TERMS AND CONCEPTS TO REVIEW

amend 102

Bill of Rights 105

checks and balances 103

commerce clause 103

due process clause 114

equal protection clause 115

establishment clause 110

federal form of government 102

free exercise clause 110

full faith and credit clause 114

police powers 104

preemption 104

privileges and immunities clause 113

probable cause 113

search warrant 113

supremacy clause 104

symbolic speech 106

QUESTIONS AND CASE PROBLEMS

5–1. COMMERCE CLAUSE. A Georgia state law requires the use of contoured rear-fender mudguards on trucks and trailers operating within Georgia state lines. The statute further makes it illegal for trucks and trailers to use straight mudguards. In approximately thirty-five other states, straight mudguards are legal. Moreover, in Florida, straight mudguards are explicitly required by law. There is some evidence that suggests that contoured mudguards might be a little safer than straight mudguards. Discuss whether this Georgia statute violates any constitutional provisions.

5–2. COMMERCIAL SPEECH. A mayoral election is about to be held in a large U.S. city. One of the candidates is Luis Delgado, and his campaign supporters wish to post campaign signs on lampposts and utility posts throughout the city. A city ordinance, however, prohibits the posting of any signs on public property. Delgado's supporters contend that the city ordinance is unconstitutional because it violates their right to free speech. Do you agree? In your answer, discuss what factors a court might consider in determining the constitutionality of the ordinance.

5–3. FREEDOM OF RELIGION. A business has a backlog of orders, and to meet its deadlines, management decides to run the firm seven days a week, eight hours a day. One of the employees, Abe Placer, refuses to work on Saturday on religious grounds. His refusal to work means that the firm may not meet its production deadlines and may therefore suffer a loss of future business. The firm fires Placer and replaces him with an employee who is willing to work seven days a week. Placer claims that his employer, in terminating his employment, has violated his constitutional right to the free exercise of his religion. Do you agree? Why or why not?

5–4. GOVERNMENT POWERS. The framers of the Constitution feared the twin evils of tyranny and anarchy. Discuss how specific provisions of the Constitution and the Bill of Rights reflect these fears and protect against both of these extremes.

5–5. FREEDOM OF RELIGION. Thomas worked in the nonmilitary operations of a large firm that produced both military and nonmilitary goods. When the company discontinued the production of nonmilitary goods, Thomas was transferred to a plant producing war materials. Thomas left his job, claiming that it violated his religious principles to participate in the manufacture of materials to be used in destroying life. In effect, he argued, the transfer to the war-materials plant forced him to quit his job. He was denied unemployment compensation by the state because he had not been effectively "discharged" by the employer but had voluntarily terminated his employment. Did the state's denial of unemployment benefits to Thomas violate the free exercise clause of the First Amendment? Explain. [*Thomas v. Review Board of the Indiana Employment Security Division*, 450 U.S. 707, 101 S.Ct. 1425, 67 L.Ed.2d 624 (1981)]

5–6. COMMERCE CLAUSE. South Dakota Disposal Systems, Inc. (SDDS), applied to the South Dakota Department of Water and Natural Resources (DWNR) for a permit to operate a solid waste disposal facility (Lonetree). It was estimated that 90 to 95 percent of the waste would come from out of state. The DWNR determined that Lonetree would be environmentally safe and issued a permit. Later, a public referendum was held. The state attorney general issued a pamphlet to accompany the referendum that urged the public to vote against "the out-of-state dump" because "South Dakota is not the nation's dumping grounds." The measure was defeated. SDDS filed a suit against the state, challenging the referendum as a violation of, among other things, the commerce clause. Was the referendum unconstitutional? Why or why not? [*SDDS, Inc. v. State of South Dakota*, 47 F.3d 263 (8th Cir. 1995)]

5–7. EQUAL PROTECTION. With the objectives of preventing crime, maintaining property values, and preserving the quality of urban life, New York City enacted an ordinance to regulate the locations of commercial establishments that featured adult entertainment. The ordinance expressly applied to female, but not male, topless entertainment. Adele Buzzetti owned the Cozy Cabin, a New York City cabaret, that featured female topless dancers. Buzzetti and an anonymous dancer filed a suit in a federal district court against the city, asking the court to block the enforcement of the ordinance. The plaintiffs argued in part that the ordinance violated the equal protection clause. Under the equal protection clause, what standard applies to the court's consideration of this ordinance? Under this test, how should the court rule? Why? [*Buzzetti v. City of New York*, 140 F.3d 134 (2d Cir. 1998)]

5–8. FREEDOM OF SPEECH. The City of Tacoma, Washington, enacted an ordinance that prohibited the playing of car sound systems at a volume that would be "audible" at a distance greater than fifty feet. Dwight Holland was arrested and convicted for violating the ordinance. The conviction was later dismissed, but Holland filed a civil suit in a Washington state court against the city. He claimed in part that the ordinance violated his freedom of speech under the First Amendment. On what basis might the court conclude that this ordinance is constitutional? (Hint: In playing a sound system, was Holland actually expressing himself?) [*Holland v. City of Tacoma*, 90 Wash.App. 533, 954 P.2d 290 (1998)]

5–9. FREEDOM OF SPEECH. The members of Greater New Orleans Broadcasting Association, Inc., operate radio and television stations in New Orleans. They wanted to broadcast ads for private, for-profit casinos that are legal in Louisiana. A federal statute banned casino advertising, but other federal statutes exempted ads for tribal, government, nonprofit, and "occasional and ancillary" commercial casinos. The association filed a suit in a federal district court against the federal government, asking the court to hold that the statute, as it applied to their ads, violated the First Amendment. The government argued that the ban should be upheld, because "[u]nder appropriate conditions, some broadcast signals from Louisiana broadcasting stations may be heard in neighboring states including Texas and Arkansas," where private casino gambling is unlawful. What is the test for whether a regulation of commercial speech violates the First Amendment? How might it apply in this case? How should the court rule? [*Greater New Orleans Broadcasting Association, Inc. v. United States*, 527 U.S. 173, 119 S.Ct. 1923, 144 L.Ed.2d 161 (1999)]

5–10. IN YOUR COURT

A state legislature enacted a statute that required any motorcycle operator or passenger on the state's highways to wear a protective helmet. Jim Alderman, a licensed motorcycle operator, sued the state to block enforcement of the law. Alderman asserted, among other things, that the statute violated the equal protection clause, because it placed requirements on motorcyclists that were not imposed on other motorists. Assume that you are the judge in the trial court hearing this case and answer the following questions:

(a) What type of government interest must be served in order to justify discriminatory classifications under each of the three standards of scrutiny, or "tests," discussed in this chapter?

(b) Which standard, or test, applies to this case? Why?

(c) Applying this standard, or test, is the helmet statute constitutional? Why or why not?

LAW ON THE WEB

For updated links to resources available on the Web, as well as a variety of other materials, visit this text's Web site at http://wleb.westbuslaw.com.

For an online version of the Constitution that provides hypertext links to amendments and other changes, go to

http://www.law.cornell.edu/constitution/constitution.overview.html

An ongoing debate in the United States is whether the national government exercises too much regulatory control over intrastate affairs. To find current articles on this topic, go to

http://www.vote-smart.org/issues/FEDERALISM_STATES_RIGHTS

For discussions of current issues involving the rights and liberties contained in the Bill of Rights, go to the Web site of the American Civil Liberties Union at

http://www.aclu.org

Summaries and the full texts of constitutional law decisions by the United States Supreme Court are included at the following site:

http://oyez.nwu.edu

LEGAL RESEARCH EXERCISES ON THE WEB

Go to http://wleb.westbuslaw.com, the Web site that accompanies this text. Select "Internet Applications," and then click on "Chapter 5." There you will find the following Internet research exercises that you can perform to learn more about free speech issues:

Activity 5–1: Flag Burning

Activity 5–2: Begging and the First Amendment

CHAPTER 6

Administrative Law

GOVERNMENT AGENCIES ESTABLISHED to adminis- ter the law have a tremendous impact on the day-to-day operation of the government and the economy. In the early years of our nation, the United States had a relatively simple, nonindustrial economy that required little regulation. Because often the purpose of administrative agencies is to create and enforce such regulations, there were relatively few such agencies. Today, however, there are rules covering virtually every aspect of a business's operation. Consequently, agencies have multiplied.

At the federal level, the Securities and Exchange Commission regulates the firm's capital structure and financing, as well as its financial reporting. The National Labor Relations Board oversees relations between the firm and any unions with which it may deal. The Equal Employment Opportunity Commission also regulates employer-employee relationships. The Environmental Protection Agency and the Occupational Safety and Health Administration affect the way the firm manufactures its products. The Federal Trade Commission influences the way it markets these products.

Added to this layer of federal regulation is a second layer of state regulation that, when not preempted by federal legislation, may cover many of the same activities or regulate independently those activities not covered by federal regulation. Finally, agency regulations at the county or municipal level also affect certain types of business activities.

Administrative agencies issue rules, orders, and decisions. These regulations make up the body of *administrative law.* You were introduced briefly to some of the main principles of administrative law in Chapter 1. In the following pages, we look at these principles in much greater detail.

SECTION 1

Agency Creation and Powers

Because Congress cannot possibly oversee the actual implementation of all the laws it enacts, it must delegate such tasks to others, particularly when the issues relate to highly technical areas, such as air and water pollution. By delegating some of its authority to make and implement laws to administrative agencies, Congress can monitor indirectly a particular area in which it has passed legislation without becoming bogged down in the details relating to enforcement— details that are often best left to specialists.

ENABLING LEGISLATION

To create an administrative agency, Congress passes **enabling legislation,** which specifies the name, purposes, functions, and powers of the agency being created. The enabling legislation for the Federal Trade Commission (FTC), for example, is the Federal Trade

Commission Act of 1914.[1] The act prohibits unfair methods of competition and deceptive trade practices. It also describes the procedures that the FTC must follow to charge persons or organizations with violations of the act, and it provides for judicial review of agency orders. The act grants the FTC the power to do the following:

1. Create "rules and regulations for the purpose of carrying out the Act."
2. Conduct investigations of business practices.
3. Obtain reports from interstate corporations concerning their business practices.
4. Investigate possible violations of federal antitrust statutes.[2]
5. Publish findings of its investigations.
6. Recommend new legislation.
7. Hold trial-like hearings to resolve certain kinds of trade disputes that involve FTC regulations or federal antitrust laws.

The commission that heads the FTC is composed of five members, each of whom the president appoints, with the advice and consent of the Senate, for a term of seven years. The president designates one of the commissioners to be chairperson. Various offices and bureaus within the FTC undertake different administrative activities for the agency. Exhibit 6–1 illustrates the organization of the FTC.

---

1. 15 U.S.C. Sections 41–58.
2. The FTC shares enforcement of the Clayton Act with the Antitrust Division of the U.S. Department of Justice.

Federal administrative agencies may exercise only those powers that Congress has delegated to them in enabling legislation. Through similar enabling acts, state legislatures create state administrative agencies.

TYPES OF AGENCIES

As discussed in Chapter 1, there are two basic types of administrative agencies: executive agencies and independent regulatory agencies. Federal *executive agencies* include the cabinet departments of the executive branch, which were formed to assist the president in carrying out executive functions, and the subagencies within the cabinet departments. The Occupational Safety and Health Administration, for example, is a subagency within the Department of Labor. Exhibit 6–2 on the next page lists the cabinet departments and their most important subagencies.

All administrative agencies are part of the executive branch of government, but *independent regulatory agencies* are outside the major executive departments. The Federal Trade Commission and the Securities and Exchange Commission are examples of independent regulatory agencies. These and other selected independent regulatory agencies, as well as their principal functions, are listed in Exhibit 6–3 on page 123.

The significant difference between the two types of agencies lies in the accountability of the regulators. Agencies that are considered part of the executive branch are subject to the authority of the president, who has the power to appoint and remove federal officers. In theory, this power is less pronounced in

EXHIBIT 6–1   ORGANIZATION OF THE FEDERAL TRADE COMMISSION

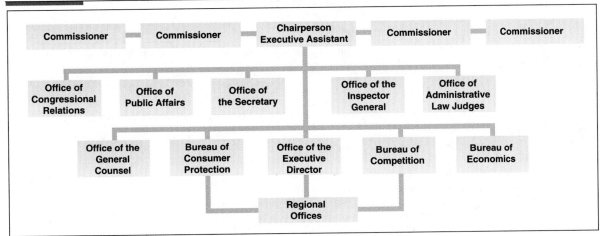

EXHIBIT 6–2   EXECUTIVE DEPARTMENTS AND IMPORTANT SUBAGENCIES

DEPARTMENT	DATE FORMED	IMPORTANT SUBAGENCIES
State	1789	Passport Office; Bureau of Diplomatic Security; Foreign Service; Bureau of Human Rights and Humanitarian Affairs; Bureau of Consular Affairs; Bureau of Intelligence and Research
Treasury	1789	Internal Revenue Service; Bureau of Alcohol, Tobacco, and Firearms; U.S. Secret Service; U.S. Mint; Customs Service
Interior	1849	U.S. Fish and Wildlife Service; National Park Service; Bureau of Indian Affairs; Bureau of Land Management
Justice	1870[a]	Federal Bureau of Investigation; Drug Enforcement Administration; Bureau of Prisons; U.S. Marshals Service; Immigration and Naturalization Service
Agriculture	1889	Soil Conservation Service; Agricultural Research Service; Food Safety and Inspection Service; Federal Crop Insurance Corporation; Farmers Home Administration
Commerce	1913[b]	Bureau of the Census; Bureau of Economic Analysis; Minority Business Development Agency; Patent and Trademark Office; National Oceanic and Atmospheric Administration; U.S. Travel and Tourism Administration
Labor	1913[b]	Occupational Safety and Health Administration; Bureau of Labor Statistics; Employment Standards Administration; Office of Labor-Management Standards; Employment and Training Administration
Defense	1949[c]	National Guard; Defense Investigative Service; National Security Agency; Joint Chiefs of Staff; Departments of the Air Force, Navy, Army
Housing and Urban Development	1965	Assistant Secretary for Community Planning and Development; Government National Mortgage Association; Assistant Secretary for Housing—Federal Housing Commissioner; Assistant Secretary for Fair Housing and Equal Opportunity
Transportation	1967	Federal Aviation Administration; Federal Highway Administration; National Highway Traffic Safety Administration; U.S. Coast Guard; Federal Transit Administration
Energy	1977	Office of Civilian Radioactive Waste Management; Bonneville Power Administration; Office of Nuclear Energy; Energy Information Administration; Office of Conservation and Renewable Energy
Health and Human Services	1980[d]	Food and Drug Administration; Health Care Financing Administration; Public Health Service
Education	1980[e]	Office of Special Education and Rehabilitation Services; Office of Elementary and Secondary Education; Office of Postsecondary Education; Office of Vocational and Adult Education
Veterans' Affairs	1989	Veterans Health Administration; Veterans Benefits Administration; National Cemetery System

a.   Formed from the Office of the Attorney General (created in 1789).
b.   Formed from the Department of Commerce and Labor (created in 1903).
c.   Formed from the Department of War (created in 1789) and the Department of the Navy (created in 1798).
d.   Formed from the Department of Health, Education, and Welfare (created in 1953).
e.   Formed from the Department of Health, Education, and Welfare (created in 1953).

EXHIBIT 6–3   SELECTED INDEPENDENT REGULATORY AGENCIES

NAME	DATE FORMED	PRINCIPAL DUTIES
Federal Reserve System Board of Governors (Fed)	1913	Determines policy with respect to interest rates, credit availability, and the money supply.
Federal Trade Commission (FTC)	1914	Prevents businesses from engaging in unfair trade practices; stops the formation of monopolies in the business sector; protects consumer rights.
Securities and Exchange Commission (SEC)	1934	Regulates the nation's stock exchanges, in which shares of stock are bought and sold; enforces the securities laws, which require full disclosure of the financial profiles of companies that wish to sell stock and bonds to the public.
Federal Communications Commission (FCC)	1934	Regulates all communications by telegraph, cable, telephone, radio, satellite, and television.
National Labor Relations Board (NLRB)	1935	Protects employees' rights to join unions and bargain collectively with employers; attempts to prevent unfair labor practices by both employers and unions.
Equal Employment Opportunity Commission (EEOC)	1964	Works to eliminate discrimination in employment based on religion, gender, race, color, disability, national origin, or age; investigates claims of discrimination.
Environmental Protection Agency (EPA)	1970	Undertakes programs aimed at reducing air and water pollution; works with state and local agencies to help fight environmental hazards. (It has been suggested recently that its status be elevated to that of a department.)
Nuclear Regulatory Commission (NRC)	1975	Ensures that electricity-generating nuclear reactors in the United States are built and operated safely; regularly inspects operations of such reactors.

regard to independent agencies, whose officers serve for fixed terms and cannot be removed without just cause. In practice, however, the president's ability to exert influence over independent agencies is often considerable.

AGENCY POWERS AND THE CONSTITUTION

Administrative agencies occupy an unusual niche in the American legal scheme, because they exercise powers that are normally divided among the three branches of government. Notice that in the FTC's enabling legislation, discussed above, the FTC's grant of power incorporates functions associated with the legislative branch (rulemaking), the executive branch (enforcement of the rules), and the courts (**adjudication,** or the formal resolution of disputes).

The constitutional principle of checks and balances allows each branch of government to act as a check on the actions of the other two branches. Furthermore, the Constitution authorizes only the legislative branch to create laws. Yet administrative agencies, to which the Constitution does not specifically refer, make **legislative rules,** or *substantive rules,* that are as legally binding as laws that Congress passes.

Courts generally hold that Article I of the U.S. Constitution authorizes delegating such powers to administrative agencies. In fact, courts generally hold that Article I is the basis for all administrative law. Section 1 of that article grants all legislative powers to Congress and requires Congress to oversee the implementation of all laws. Article I, Section 8, gives Congress the power to make all laws necessary for executing its specified powers. The courts interpret these passages, under what is referred to as the **delegation doctrine,** as granting Congress the power to establish administrative agencies that can create rules for implementing those laws.

The three branches of government exercise certain controls over agency powers and functions, as will be discussed later in this chapter, but in many ways administrative agencies function independently. For this reason, administrative agencies, which constitute the **bureaucracy,** are sometimes referred to as the "fourth branch" of the U.S. government.

SECTION 2

Administrative Process

The three functions mentioned previously—rulemaking, enforcement, and adjudication—make up what is known as the **administrative process.** Administrative process involves the administration of law by administrative agencies, in contrast to **judicial process,** which comprises the administration of law by the courts.

All federal agencies must follow specific procedural requirements in their rulemaking, adjudication, and other functions. Sometimes, Congress specifies certain procedural requirements in an agency's enabling legislation. In the absence of any directives from Congress concerning a particular agency procedure, the Administrative Procedure Act (APA) of 1946[3] applies. The APA is such an integral part of the administrative process that its application will be examined as we go through the basic functions carried out by administrative agencies. In addition, agency procedures are guided indirectly by the courts' interpretation of APA requirements.

RULEMAKING

A major function of an administrative agency is **rulemaking**—the formulation of new regulations. In an agency's enabling legislation, Congress confers the agency's power to make rules. For example, the Occupational Safety and Health Act of 1970 authorized the Occupational Safety and Health Administration (OSHA) to develop and issue rules governing safety in the workplace. In formulating any new legislative rule, OSHA has to follow specific rulemaking procedures required under the APA.

Note that administrative agencies also make *interpretive rules.* These rules are not legally binding on the public but simply indicate how an agency plans to interpret and enforce its statutory authority. For example, the Equal Employment Opportunity Commission periodically issues interpretive rules, usually referred to as enforcement guidelines, indicating how it plans to interpret and apply a provision of a certain statute, such as the Americans with Disabilities Act. When making interpretive rules, an agency need not follow the requirements of the APA.

The most commonly used rulemaking procedure is called **notice-and-comment rulemaking.** This procedure involves three basic steps: notice of the proposed rulemaking, a comment period, and the final rule.

Notice of the Proposed Rulemaking. When a federal agency decides to create a new rule, the agency publishes a notice of the proposed rulemaking proceedings in the *Federal Register,* a daily publication of the executive branch that prints government orders, rules, and regulations. The notice states where and when the proceedings will be held, the agency's legal authority for making the rule (usually its enabling legislation), and the terms or subject matter of the proposed rule.

Comment Period. Following the publication of the notice of the proposed rulemaking proceedings, the agency must allow ample time for persons to comment in writing on the proposed rule. The purpose of this comment period is to give interested parties the opportunity to express their views on the proposed rule in an effort to influence agency policy. The comments may be in writing or, if a hearing is held, may be given orally. The agency need not respond to all comments, but it must respond to any significant comments that bear directly on the proposed rule. The agency responds by either modifying its final rule or explaining, in a statement accompanying the final rule, why it did not make any changes. In some circumstances, particularly when the procedure being used in a specific instance is less formal, an agency may accept comments after the comment period is closed. The agency should summarize these *ex parte* (private, "off-the-record") comments in the record for possible review.

The Final Rule. After the agency reviews the comments, it drafts the final rule and publishes it in the *Federal Register.* The final rule is later compiled with

---

3. 5 U.S.C. Sections 551–706.

the rules and regulations of other federal administrative agencies in the *Code of Federal Regulations* (C.F.R.). Final rules have binding legal effect unless the courts later overturn them.

In the following case, AT&T Corporation and other established local telephone service providers asked the United States Supreme Court to overturn a Federal Communications Commission (FCC) rule issued to implement part of the Telecommunications Act of 1996. The Court considered how the FCC interpreted certain terms in the act when it formulated its rule. This illustrates the interpretation and application of statutory terms that any agency must make in its rulemaking.

CASE 6.1   AT&T Corp. v. Iowa Utilities Board

Supreme Court of the
United States, 1999.
525 U.S. 366,
119 S.Ct. 721,
142 L.Ed.2d 835.
http://supct.law.
cornell.edu/supct/
supct.January.1999.
html[a]

HISTORICAL AND TECHNOLOGICAL SETTING   *Until the 1990s, local telephone service was thought to be a natural monopoly. States typically granted an exclusive franchise in each local service area to a local exchange carrier (LEC), which owns, among other things, the local loops (wires connecting telephones to switches), the switches (equipment directing calls to their destinations), and the transport trunks (wires carrying calls between switches) that constitute a local exchange network. When technological advances made competition among multiple providers of local service seem possible, however, Congress enacted the Telecommunications Act of 1996 to end the state-sanctioned monopolies.*

BACKGROUND AND FACTS   *The Telecommunications Act required existing LECs to, among other things, share elements of their networks (loops, switches, and trunks) with their new competitors. The act ordered the Federal Communications Commission (FCC) to issue rules to implement this requirement. In deciding which elements to make available, the FCC was directed to consider whether access to each element was "necessary" and whether a lack of access would "impair" a competitor's ability to provide service. The FCC concluded that access was "necessary" even if a competitor could substitute an element from another source, and that "impairment" occurred if access was denied and a competitor had any increase in cost or decrease in quality. The FCC issued Rule 319, requiring the LECs to give their new competitors access to seven specific network elements.[b] The LECs, including AT&T Corporation, and others filed suits in courts across the United States to challenge the FCC's new rules, including Rule 319. The suits were combined into a single case in the U.S. Court of Appeals for the Eighth Circuit, which held, among other things, that the FCC's interpretations of "necessary" and "impair" were reasonable. The LECs appealed to the United States Supreme Court.*

IN THE LANGUAGE OF THE COURT   Justice *SCALIA* delivered the opinion of the Court.

*   *   *   *

*   *   * [T]he [Telecommunications] Act requires the FCC to apply some limiting standard, rationally related to the goals of the Act, which it has simply failed to do. *   *   * [I]t is hard to imagine when [an LEC's] failure to give access to the element[s] would not constitute an "impairment" under [the FCC's] standard. *   *   * [T]hat judgment allows [competitors], rather than the [FCC], to determine whether access to [the] elements is necessary, and whether the failure to obtain access to [the] elements would impair the ability to provide services. The [FCC] cannot, consistent with the statute, [ignore] the availability of elements outside the [LEC's] network. That failing alone

---

a. This page is part of the database of United States Supreme Court opinions maintained by the Legal Information Institute of Cornell Law School. On this page, click on the case title to access the opinion.
b. 47 C.F.R. Section 51.319. The seven elements included "the local loop, the network interface device, switching capability, interoffice transmission facilities, signaling networks and call-related databases, operations support systems functions, and operator services and directory assistance."

would require [Rule 319] to be set aside. In addition, however, the [FCC's] assumption that any increase in cost (or decrease in quality) imposed by denial of a network element renders access to that element "necessary," and causes the failure to provide that element to "impair" the [competitor's] ability to furnish its desired services, is simply not in accord with the ordinary and fair meaning of those terms. [A competitor] whose anticipated annual profits from the proposed service are reduced [by only 1 percent] of [its] investment has perhaps been "impaired" in its ability to amass earnings, but has not * * * been "impair[ed] * * * in its ability to provide the services it seeks to offer"; and it cannot realistically be said that the network element enabling it to [increase] its profits [by 1 percent] is "necessary." In a world of perfect competition, in which all carriers are providing their service at marginal [incremental] cost, the [FCC's] total equating of increased cost (or decreased quality) with "necessity" and "impairment" might be reasonable; but it has not established the existence of such an ideal world.

DECISION AND REMEDY *The United States Supreme Court concluded that the FCC did not interpret the terms of the Telecommunications Act in a "reasonable fashion" and vacated Rule 319. The Court indicated that the FCC should consider the availability, to competitors, of elements outside the LECs' networks.*

INVESTIGATION

Administrative agencies conduct investigations of the entities that they regulate. One type of agency investigation occurs during the rulemaking process to obtain information about a certain individual, firm, or industry. The purpose of such an investigation is to ensure that the rule issued is based on a consideration of relevant factors rather than being arbitrary and capricious. After final rules are issued, agencies conduct investigations to monitor compliance with those rules. A typical agency investigation of this kind might begin when a citizen reports a possible violation.

Inspections. Many agencies gather information through on-site inspections. Sometimes, inspecting an office, a factory, or some other business facility is the only way to obtain the evidence needed to prove a regulatory violation. Administrative inspections and tests cover a wide range of activities, including safety inspections of underground coal mines, safety tests of commercial equipment and automobiles, and environmental monitoring of factory emissions. An agency may also ask a firm or individual to submit certain documents or records to the agency for examination.

Normally, business firms comply with agency requests to inspect facilities or business records, because it is in any firm's interest to maintain a good relationship with regulatory bodies. In some instances, however, such as when a firm thinks an agency's request is unreasonable and may be detrimental to the firm's interest, the firm may refuse to comply with the

request. In such situations, an agency may resort to the use of a subpoena or a search warrant.

Subpoenas. There are two basic types of subpoenas. The subpoena *ad testificandum* ("to testify") is an ordinary subpoena. It is a writ, or order, compelling a witness to appear at an agency hearing. The subpoena *duces tecum*[4] ("bring it with you") compels an individual or organization to hand over books, papers, records, or documents to the agency. An administrative agency may use either type of subpoena to obtain testimony or documents.

There are limits on what an agency can demand. To determine whether an agency is abusing its discretion in its pursuit of information as part of an investigation, a court may consider such factors as the following:

1. The purpose of the investigation. An investigation must have a legitimate purpose. An improper purpose is, for example, harassment.
2. The relevance of the information being sought. Information is relevant if it reveals that the law is being violated or if it assures the agency that the law is not being violated.
3. The specificity of the demand for testimony or documents. A subpoena must, for example, adequately describe the material being sought.
4. The burden of the demand on the party from whom the information is sought. In responding to a

---

4. Pronounced *doo*-cheez *tee*-kum.

request for information, a party must bear the costs of, for example, copying the documents that must be handed over; a business is generally protected from revealing such information as trade secrets, however.

In the following case, former bank directors challenged the right of an administrative agency to subpoena their personal financial records. The court considered the extent of the agency's investigative powers.

CASE 6.2   Federal Deposit Insurance Corp. v. Wentz

United States
Court of Appeals,
Third Circuit, 1995.
55 F.3d 905.
http://www.findlaw.
com/casecode/courts/
3rd.html[a]

HISTORICAL AND ECONOMIC SETTING *Congress created the Federal Deposit Insurance Corporation (FDIC) in 1933 to help prevent commercial bank failures and to protect bank customers' accounts. In 1992, nearly five hundred banks failed. More than half of all bank failures can be attributed to agricultural loans, when the failure of farms leads to default on the loans. Fraud also often plays a role. When a bank fails, the FDIC covers each depositor's loss up to $100,000 and then sells the bank's assets, or takes other steps, to regain some of those funds.*

BACKGROUND AND FACTS *Sidney Wentz and Natalie Koether were directors of Howard Savings Bank of Livingston, New Jersey, when it was declared insolvent in October 1992. The Federal Deposit Insurance Corporation (FDIC) was appointed receiver. In April 1993, the FDIC issued subpoenas duces tecum to Wentz, Koether, and others, seeking, among other things, their personal financial records. The directors refused to comply. The FDIC asked a federal district court to enforce the subpoenas, arguing that the records were needed to assess whether any bank losses might be due to breach of the directors' fiduciary duties. The court ordered the directors to produce only those records showing additions to or reductions in their assets. The directors appealed, contending that this order intruded on their privacy.*

**IN THE LANGUAGE
OF THE COURT**

WEIS, Circuit Judge.

*   *   *   *

When personal documents of individuals, as contrasted with business records of corporations, are the subject of an administrative subpoena, privacy concerns must be considered. * * * [R]elevant factors [include] such matters as the type of record requested, the information that it might contain, the potential for harm and subsequent nonconsensual disclosure, the adequacy of safeguards to prevent unauthorized disclosure, the degree of need for access, * * * and the presence of recognizable public interests justifying access.

*   *   *   *

The FDIC has shown a reasonable need for gaining access to the directors' records in order to determine whether they reveal breaches of fiduciary duties through the improper channeling of bank funds for personal benefit. Moreover, the directors have not produced any evidence to show that the information contained in their personal financial records is of such a high degree of sensitivity that the intrusion could be considered severe or that the [directors] are likely to suffer any adverse effects from disclosure to [FDIC] personnel. Finally, we observe that regulatory provisions have been promulgated to guard against subsequent unauthorized disclosure of the subpoenaed information.

**DECISION
AND REMEDY**

The U.S. Court of Appeals for the Third Circuit affirmed the district court's order. The directors were required to produce their records.

a. In the "Browsing" section, in the "1995" row, click on "June." When that page opens, scroll down the list to "FDIC v WENTZ" and click on it to access the opinion.

Search Warrants. The Fourth Amendment protects against unreasonable searches and seizures by requiring that in most instances a physical search for evidence must be conducted under the authority of a search warrant. An agency's search warrant is an order directing law enforcement officials to search a specific place for a specific item and present it to the agency. Although it was once thought that administrative inspections were exempt from the warrant requirement, the United States Supreme Court held in *Marshall v. Barlow's, Inc.,*[5] that the requirement does apply to the administrative process.

Agencies can conduct warrantless searches in several situations. Warrants are not required to conduct searches in highly regulated industries. Firms that sell firearms or liquor, for example, are automatically subject to inspections without warrants. Sometimes, a statute permits warrantless searches of certain types of hazardous operations, such as coal mines. Also, a warrantless inspection in an emergency situation is normally considered reasonable.

ADJUDICATION

After conducting an investigation of a suspected rule violation, an agency may begin to take administrative action against an individual or organization. Most administrative actions are resolved through negotiated settlements at their initial stages, without the need for formal adjudication.

Negotiated Settlements. Depending on the agency, negotiations may take the form of a simple conversation or a series of informal conferences. Whatever form the negotiations take, their purpose is to rectify the problem to the agency's satisfaction and eliminate the need for additional proceedings.

Settlement is an appealing option to firms for two reasons: to avoid appearing uncooperative and to avoid the expense involved in formal adjudication proceedings and in possible later appeals. Settlement is also an attractive option for agencies. To conserve their own resources and avoid formal actions, administrative agencies devote a great deal of effort to giving advice and negotiating solutions to problems.

Formal Complaints. If a settlement cannot be reached, the agency may issue a formal complaint

against the suspected violator. If the Environmental Protection Agency (EPA), for example, finds that a factory is polluting groundwater in violation of federal pollution laws, the EPA will issue a complaint against the violator in an effort to bring the plant into compliance with federal regulations. This complaint is a public document, and a press release may accompany it. The factory charged in the complaint will respond by filing an answer to the EPA's allegations. If the factory and the EPA cannot agree on a settlement, the case is heard in a trial-like setting before an **administrative law judge (ALJ).** The adjudication process is described below and illustrated graphically in Exhibit 6–4.

The Role of the Administrative Law Judge. The ALJ presides over the hearing and has the power to administer oaths, take testimony, rule on questions of

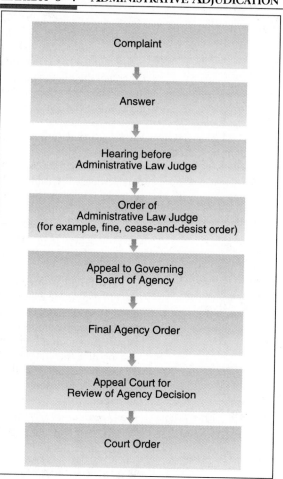

EXHIBIT 6–4 THE PROCESS OF FORMAL ADMINISTRATIVE ADJUDICATION

- Complaint
- Answer
- Hearing before Administrative Law Judge
- Order of Administrative Law Judge (for example, fine, cease-and-desist order)
- Appeal to Governing Board of Agency
- Final Agency Order
- Appeal Court for Review of Agency Decision
- Court Order

---

5. 436 U.S. 307, 98 S.Ct. 1816, 56 L.Ed.2d 305 (1978).

evidence, and make determinations of fact. Although formally, the ALJ works for the agency prosecuting the case (in our example, the EPA), the law requires an ALJ to be an unbiased adjudicator (judge).

Certain safeguards prevent bias on the part of the ALJ and promote fairness in the proceedings. For example, the APA requires that the ALJ be separate from an agency's investigative and prosecutorial staff. The APA also prohibits *ex parte* (private) communications between the ALJ and any party to an agency proceeding, such as the EPA or the factory. Finally, provisions of the APA protect the ALJ from agency disciplinary actions unless the agency can show good cause for such an action.

Hearing Procedures.   Hearing procedures vary widely from agency to agency. Administrative agencies generally exercise substantial discretion over the type of hearing procedure that will be used. Frequently, disputes are resolved through informal adjudication proceedings. For example, the parties, their counsel, and the ALJ may simply meet at a table in a conference room for the dispute-settlement proceedings.

A formal adjudicatory hearing, in contrast, resembles a trial in many respects. Prior to the hearing, the parties are permitted to undertake extensive discovery (involving depositions, interrogatories, and requests for documents or other information, as described in Chapter 2). During the hearing, the parties may give testimony, present other evidence, and cross-examine adverse witnesses. A significant difference between a trial and an administrative agency hearing, though, is that normally much more information, including hearsay (secondhand information) can be introduced as evidence during an administrative hearing.

Agency Orders.   Following a hearing, the ALJ renders an **initial order,** or decision, on the case. Either party can appeal the ALJ's decision to the board or commission that governs the agency. If the factory is dissatisfied with the ALJ's decision, for example, it can appeal the decision to the commission that governs the EPA. If the factory is dissatisfied with the commission's decision, it can appeal the decision to a federal court of appeals. If no party appeals the case, the ALJ's decision becomes the **final order** of the agency. The ALJ's decision also becomes final if a party appeals and the commission and the court decline to review the case. If a party appeals the case and the case is reviewed, the final order comes from the commission's decision or (if that decision is appealed to a federal appellate court) that of the court.

In the following case, an ALJ fined a company $2,000 for violating federal regulations governing mine safety. The company eventually asked a federal appellate court to review the order.

CASE 6.3

Buck Creek Coal, Inc. v. Federal Mine Safety and Health Administration

United States
Court of Appeals,
Seventh Circuit, 1995.
52 F.3d 133.
http://www.ca7.
uscourts.gov[a]

IN THE LANGUAGE
OF THE COURT

BACKGROUND AND FACTS   *Buck Creek Coal, Inc., operates a coal mine in Sullivan County, Indiana. When James Holland, an inspector for the Mine Safety and Health Administration (MSHA), inspected the mine, he noted an accumulation of loose coal and coal dust in the feeder area, where mined coal is transferred from mine shuttle cars to conveyor belts. Holland issued a citation, charging Buck Creek with violations of federal regulations that require mine operators to keep feeder areas clean. After hearing evidence from both sides, an ALJ found that the evidence supported Holland's conclusions and fined Buck Creek $2,000. Buck Creek asked the Federal Mine Safety and Health Review Commission to review the ALJ's conclusions. When the commission declined, Buck Creek sought review in the courts.*

ILANA DIAMOND ROVNER, Circuit Judge.

  *   *   *   *

   *   *   * [The ALJ] made these findings, based primarily on the testimony of Inspector Holland: "[T]here were substantial accumulations of loose coal, coal fines and

---

a. In the left column, click on "Judicial Opinions." On that page, in the "Case Numbers:" section, type "94" in the "Year" box and "2084" in the "Number" box, and click "Request Opinion" to access the case.

float coal dust, in the feeder area *   *   * . A heated roller turning in that combustible material could easily be an ignition source which could in turn cause a fire. *   *   * [I]n the event of a fire, smoke and gas inhalation by miners in the area would cause a reasonably serious injury requiring medical attention." *   *   * [N]o further evidence was necessary to support the ALJ's conclusion. First, *   *   * Inspector Holland [is] a federal mine inspector with 32 years of mining experience who specializes in mine ventilation. Nor was anything more than Inspector Holland's opinion necessary to support the common sense conclusion that a fire burning in an underground coal mine would present a serious risk of smoke and gas inhalation to miners who are present. *   *   * [F]ire is one of the primary safety concerns that has motivated federal regulation of the coal mining industry.

Nor has Buck Creek identified any evidence that tends to undermine the ALJ's conclusion. *   *   * Buck Creek has relied mainly on *   *   * testimony [that] pertained to Buck Creek's fire safety systems. *   *   * The fact that Buck Creek has safety measures in place *   *   * does not mean that fires do not pose a serious safety risk to miners. Indeed, the precautions are *   *   * in place *   *   * precisely because of the significant dangers associated with coal mine fires.

DECISION AND REMEDY   *The U.S. Court of Appeals for the Seventh Circuit denied Buck Creek's petition for review. The ALJ's conclusions became the final order of the agency. Buck Creek was ordered to pay the fine.*

SECTION 3

Limitations on Agency Powers

Combining the functions normally divided among the three branches of government into an administrative agency concentrates considerable power in a single organization. Because of this concentration of authority, one of the major policy objectives of the government is to control the risks of arbitrariness and overreaching by administrative agencies without hindering the effective use of agency power to deal with particular problem areas, as Congress intends.

The judicial branch of the government exercises control over agency powers through the courts' review of agency actions. The executive and legislative branches of government also exercise control over agency authority.

JUDICIAL CONTROLS

The APA provides for judicial review of most agency decisions, as described above. Agency actions are not automatically subject to judicial review, however. Parties seeking review must demonstrate that they meet certain requirements. The party bringing the action must have *standing to sue* the agency (the party must have a direct stake in the outcome of the judicial

proceeding), and there must be an *actual controversy* at issue. These are basic judicial requirements that must be met before a court will hear a case, as discussed in Chapter 2. Furthermore, the party must have *exhausted all possible administrative remedies*. Each agency has its "chain of review," and the party must follow agency appeal procedures before a court will deem that administrative remedies have been exhausted.

Recall from Chapter 2 that appellate courts normally defer to the decisions of trial courts on questions of fact. In reviewing administrative actions, the courts are similarly reluctant to question the factual findings of agencies. In reviewing an administrative agency's decision, a court normally will consider the following types of issues:

1. Whether the agency has exceeded its authority under its enabling legislation.
2. Whether the agency has properly interpreted laws applicable to the agency action under review.
3. Whether the agency has violated any constitutional provisions.
4. Whether the agency has acted in accordance with procedural requirements of the law.
5. Whether the agency's actions were arbitrary, capricious, or an abuse of discretion.
6. Whether any conclusions drawn by the agency are not supported by substantial evidence.

EXECUTIVE CONTROLS

The executive branch of government exercises control over agencies both through the president's power to appoint federal officers and through the president's veto power. The president may veto enabling legislation presented by Congress or congressional attempts to modify an existing agency's authority.

LEGISLATIVE CONTROLS

Congress also exercises authority over agency powers. Through enabling legislation, Congress gives power to an agency. Of course, an agency may not exceed the power that Congress has delegated to it. Through subsequent legislation, Congress can take away that power or even abolish an agency altogether. Legislative authority is required to fund an agency, and enabling legislation usually sets certain time and monetary limits on the funding of particular programs. Congress can always revise these limits.

In addition to its power to create and fund agencies, Congress has the authority to investigate the implementation of its laws and the agencies that it has created. Individual legislators may also affect agency policy through their "casework" activities, which involve attempts to help their constituents deal with agencies.

Congress also has the power to "freeze" the enforcement of most federal regulations before the regulations take effect. Under the Small Business Regulatory Enforcement Fairness Act of 1996,[6] all federal agencies must submit final rules to Congress before the rules become effective. If, within sixty days, Congress passes a joint resolution of disapproval concerning a rule, enforcement of the regulation is frozen while the rule is reviewed by congressional committees.

Another legislative check on agency actions is the Administrative Procedure Act, discussed earlier in this chapter. Additionally, the laws discussed in the next section provide certain checks on the actions of administrative agencies.

SECTION 4

Public Accountability

As a result of growing public concern over the powers exercised by administrative agencies, Congress passed several laws to make agencies more accountable through public scrutiny. We discuss here the most significant of these laws.

FREEDOM OF INFORMATION ACT

Enacted in 1966, the Freedom of Information Act (FOIA)[7] requires the federal government to disclose certain "records" to "any person" on request, even if no reason is given for the request. The FOIA exempts certain types of records. For other records, though, a request that complies with the FOIA procedures need only contain a reasonable description of the information sought (see Exhibit 6–5 on the next page). An agency's failure to comply with a request may be challenged in a federal district court. The media, industry trade associations, public-interest groups, and even companies seeking information about competitors rely on these FOIA provisions to obtain information from government agencies.

Under a 1996 amendment to the FOIA, all federal government agencies now have to make their records available electronically—on the Internet, on computer disks, and in other electronic formats. As of November 1, 1996, any document created by an agency must be available on computer within a year after its creation. Agencies must also provide a clear index to all of their documents.

GOVERNMENT-IN-THE-SUNSHINE ACT

Congress passed the Government-in-the-Sunshine Act,[8] or open meeting law, in 1976. It requires that "every portion of every meeting of an agency" be open to "public observation." The act also requires the establishment of procedures to ensure that the public is provided with adequate advance notice of scheduled meetings and agendas. Like the FOIA, the sunshine act contains certain exceptions. Closed meetings are permitted when (1) the subject of the meeting concerns accusing any person of a crime, (2) an open meeting would frustrate implementation of agency actions, or (3) the subject of the meeting involves matters relating to future litigation or rulemaking. Courts interpret these exceptions to allow open access whenever possible.

---

6. 5 U.S.C. Sections 801–808.

7. 5 U.S.C. Section 552.
8. 5 U.S.C. Section 552b.

EXHIBIT 6–5   SAMPLE LETTER REQUESTING INFORMATION FROM AN EXECUTIVE DEPARTMENT OR AGENCY

Date

Agency Head or FOIA Officer
Title
Name of Agency
Address of Agency
City, State, Zip

Re: Freedom of Information Act Request.

Dear _____ :

   Under the provisions of the Freedom of Information Act, 5 U.S.C. Section 552, I am requesting access to

_____

[identify the records as clearly as possible].
   [Optional] I am requesting this information because _____

_____

[state the reason for your request if you think it will assist you in obtaining the information].

   If there are any fees for searching for, or copying, the records I have requested, please inform me before you fill the request [or:] please supply the records without informing me if the fees do not exceed $ _____ .

   [or:] As you know, the act permits you to reduce or waive fees when the release of the information is considered as "primarily benefiting the public." I believe that this request fits that category, and I therefore ask that you waive any fees.

   If all or any part of this request is denied, please cite the specific exemption(s) that you think justifies your refusal to release the information, and inform me of the appeal procedures available to me under the law.

   I would appreciate your handling this request as quickly as possible, and I look forward to hearing from you within 10 days, as the law stipulates.

                                           Sincerely,
                                           [Signature]
                                         Name
                                         Address
                                         City, State, Zip

SOURCE: U.S. Congress, House Committee on Government Operations, *A Citizen's Guide on How to Use the Freedom of Information Act and the Privacy Act Requesting Government Documents*, 95th Congress, 1st session, 1977.

REGULATORY FLEXIBILITY ACT

Concern over the effects of regulation on the efficiency of businesses, particularly smaller ones, led Congress to pass the Regulatory Flexibility Act in 1980.[9] Under this act, whenever a new regulation will have a "significant impact upon a substantial number of small entities," the agency must conduct a regulatory flexibility analysis. The analysis must measure the cost that the rule would impose on small businesses and must consider less burdensome alternatives. The act also contains provisions to alert small businesses—

through advertising in trade journals, for example—about forthcoming regulations. The act reduces some record-keeping burdens for small businesses, especially with regard to hazardous waste management.

SMALL BUSINESS REGULATORY ENFORCEMENT FAIRNESS ACT

As mentioned above, the Small Business Regulatory Enforcement Fairness Act (SBREFA) of 1996 allows Congress to review new federal regulations for at least sixty days before they take effect. This period gives opponents of the rules time to present their arguments to Congress.

---

9. 5 U.S.C. Sections 601–612.

The SBREFA also authorizes the courts to enforce the Regulatory Flexibility Act. This helps to ensure that federal agencies, such as the Internal Revenue Service, will consider ways to reduce the economic impact of new regulations on small businesses. Federal agencies are required to prepare guides that explain in "plain English" how small businesses can comply with federal regulations.

At the Small Business Administration, the SBREFA set up the National Enforcement Ombudsman to receive comments from small businesses about their dealings with federal agencies. Based on these comments, Regional Small Business Fairness Boards rate the agencies and publicize their findings.

Finally, the SBREFA allows small businesses to recover their expenses and legal fees from the government when an agency makes demands for fines or penalties that a court considers excessive.

SECTION 5

State Administrative Agencies

Although most of this chapter deals with federal administrative agencies, state agencies play a significant role in regulating activities within the states. Many of the factors that encouraged the proliferation of federal agencies also fostered the expanding presence of state agencies. For example, one reason for the growth of administrative agencies at all levels of government is the inability of Congress and state legislatures to oversee the implementation of their laws. Another is the greater technical competence of the agencies.

PARALLEL AGENCIES

Commonly, a state creates an agency as a parallel to a federal agency to provide similar services on a more localized basis. Such parallel agencies include the federal Social Security Administration and the state welfare agency, the Internal Revenue Service and the state revenue department, and the Environmental Protection Agency and the state pollution-control agency. Not all federal agencies have parallel state agencies, however. For example, the Federal Bureau of Investigation and the Nuclear Regulatory Commission have no parallel agencies at the state level.

CONFLICTS BETWEEN PARALLEL AGENCIES

If the actions of parallel state and federal agencies conflict, the actions of the federal agency will prevail. For example, if the Federal Aviation Administration specifies the hours during which airplanes may land at and depart from airports, a state or local government cannot issue inconsistent laws or regulations governing the same activities. The priority of federal laws over conflicting state laws is based on the supremacy clause of the U.S. Constitution. Remember from Chapter 4 that this clause, which is found in Article VI of the Constitution, states that the Constitution and "the Laws of the United States which shall be made in Pursuance thereof . . . shall be the supreme Law of the Land."

TERMS AND CONCEPTS TO REVIEW

adjudication 123

administrative law judge (ALJ) 128

administrative process 124

bureaucracy 124

delegation doctrine 124

enabling legislation 120

final order 129

initial order 129

judicial process 124

legislative rule 123

notice-and-comment rulemaking 124

rulemaking 124

QUESTIONS AND CASE PROBLEMS

6–1. RULEMAKING PROCEDURES. Assume that the Food and Drug Administration (FDA), using proper procedures, adopts a rule describing its future investigations. This new rule covers all future cases in which the FDA wants to regulate food additives. Under the new rule, the FDA is not to regulate food additives without giving food companies an opportunity to cross-examine witnesses. Some time later, the FDA wants to regulate methylisocyanate, a food additive. The FDA undertakes an informal rulemaking procedure, without cross-examination, and regulates methylisocyanate. Producers protest, saying that the FDA promised them the opportunity for cross-examination. The FDA responds that the Administrative Procedure Act does not require such cross-examination and that it is free to withdraw the promise made in its new rule. If the producers challenge the FDA in a court, on what basis would the court rule in their favor?

6–2. RULEMAKING AND ADJUDICATION POWERS. For decades, the Federal Trade Commission (FTC) resolved fair trade and advertising disputes through individual adjudications. In the 1960s, the FTC began promulgating rules that defined fair and unfair trade practices. In cases involving violations of these rules, the due process rights of participants were more limited and did not include cross-examination. Although anyone found violating a rule would receive a full adjudication, the legitimacy of the rule itself could not be challenged in the adjudication. Any party charged with violating a rule was almost certain to lose the adjudication. Affected parties complained to a court, arguing that their rights before the FTC were unduly limited by the new rules. What will the court examine to determine whether to uphold the new rules?

6–3. RULEMAKING PROCEDURES. The Department of Commerce issued a flammability standard that required all mattresses, including crib mattresses, to pass a test that involved contact with a burning cigarette. The manufacturers of crib mattresses petitioned the department to exempt their product from the test procedure, but the department refused to do so. The crib manufacturers sued the department and argued that applying such a rule to crib mattresses was arbitrary and capricious because infants do not smoke. On what basis might the court hold that the rule is not arbitrary and capricious? [*Bunny Bear, Inc. v. Peterson*, 473 F.2d 1002 (1st Cir. 1973)]

6–4. RULEMAKING PROCEDURES. The Atomic Energy Commission (AEC) was engaged in rulemaking proceedings for nuclear reactor safety. An environmental group sued the commission, arguing that its proceedings were inadequate. The commission had carefully complied with all requirements of the Administrative Procedure Act. The environmentalists argued, however, that the very haz-ardous and technical nature of the reactor safety issue required elaborate procedures above and beyond those set forth in the act. A federal court of appeals agreed and overturned the AEC rules. The commission appealed the case to the United States Supreme Court. How should the Court rule? Discuss. [*Vermont Yankee Nuclear Power Corp. v. Natural Resources Defense Council, Inc.*, 435 U.S. 519, 98 S.Ct. 1197, 55 L.Ed.2d 460 (1978)]

6–5. EXECUTIVE CONTROLS. In 1982, the president of the United States appointed Matthew Chabal, Jr., to the position of U.S. marshal. U.S. marshals are assigned to the federal courts. In the fall of 1985, Chabal received an unsatisfactory annual performance rating, and he was fired shortly thereafter by the president. Given that U.S. marshals are assigned to the federal courts, are these appointees members of the executive branch? Did the president have the right to fire Chabal without consulting Congress about the decision? [*Chabal v. Reagan*, 841 F.2d 1216 (3d Cir. 1988)]

6–6. ARBITRARY AND CAPRICIOUS TEST. In 1977, the Department of Transportation (DOT) adopted a passive-restraint standard (known as Standard 208) that required new cars to have either air bags or automatic seat belts. By 1981, it had become clear that all of the major auto manufacturers would install automatic seat belts to comply with this rule. The DOT determined that most purchasers of cars would detach their automatic seat belts, thus making them ineffective. Consequently, the department repealed the regulation. State Farm Mutual Automobile Insurance Co. and other insurance companies sued in the District of Columbia Circuit Court of Appeals for a review of the DOT's repeal of the regulation. That court held that the repeal was arbitrary and capricious because the DOT had reversed its rule without sufficient support. The motor vehicle manufacturers, who initially had wanted to avoid the costs associated with implementing Standard 208, then appealed this decision to the United States Supreme Court. What will result? Discuss fully. [*Motor Vehicle Manufacturers Association v. State Farm Mutual Automobile Insurance Co.*, 463 U.S. 29, 103 S.Ct. 2856, 77 L.Ed.2d 443 (1983)]

6–7. JUDICIAL REVIEW. American Message Centers (AMC) provides answering services to retailers. Calls to a retailer are automatically forwarded to AMC, which pays for the calls. AMC obtains telephone service at a discount from major carriers, including Sprint. Sprint's tariff (a public document setting out rates and rules relating to Sprint's services) states that the "subscriber shall be responsible for the payment of all charges for service." When AMC learned that computer hackers had obtained the access code for AMC's lines and had made nearly $160,000 in long-distance calls, it asked Sprint to absorb the cost. Sprint refused. AMC filed a complaint with the Federal Communications Commission (FCC), claiming in part that Sprint's tariff was vague and ambiguous, in violation of the Communications Act of 1934 and FCC rules. These laws require that a carrier's tariff "clearly and definitely" specify any "exceptions or conditions which in any way affect the rates named in the tariff." The FCC rejected AMC's complaint. AMC appealed the FCC's decision to a federal appellate court, claiming that the FCC's decision to reject AMC's complaint was arbitrary and capricious. What should the court decide? Discuss fully. [*American Message Centers v. Federal Communications Commission*, 50 F.3d 35 (D.C.Cir. 1995)]

6–8. RULEMAKING. The Occupational Safety and Health Administration (OSHA) is part of the U.S. Department of Labor. OSHA issued a "Directive" under which each employer in selected industries was to be inspected unless it adopted a "Comprehensive Compliance Program (CCP)"—a safety and health program designed to meet standards that in some respects exceeded those otherwise required by law. The Chamber of Commerce of the United States objected to the Directive and filed a petition for review with the U.S. Court of Appeals for the District of Columbia Circuit. The Chamber claimed, in part, that OSHA did not use proper rulemaking procedures in issuing the Directive. OSHA argued that it was not required to follow those procedures because the Directive itself was a "rule of procedure." OSHA claimed that the rule did not "alter the rights or interests of parties, although it may alter the manner in which the parties present themselves or their viewpoints to the agency."

What are the steps of the most commonly used rulemaking procedure? Which steps are missing in this case? In whose favor should the court rule? Why? [*Chamber of Commerce of the United States v. U.S. Department of Labor*, 74 F.3d 206 (D.C.Cir. 1999)]

6–9. IN YOUR COURT

Assume that the Securities and Exchange Commission (SEC) has a rule that it will enforce statutory provisions prohibiting insider trading only when the insiders make monetary profits for themselves. Then the SEC makes a new rule, declaring that it has the statutory authority to bring an enforcement action against an individual even if he or she does not personally profit from the insider trading. In making the new rule, the SEC does not conduct a rulemaking proceeding but simply announces its new decision. A securities organization objects and says that the new rule was unlawfully developed without opportunity for public comment. The organization challenges the rule in an action that ultimately is reviewed by a federal appellate court. Assume that you are a judge on the appellate court reviewing this case and answer the following questions:

(a) Should the SEC's new rule be invalidated under the Administrative Procedure Act? Why or why not?

(b) Is the SEC's new rule a legislative rule or an interpretive rule? Why is this distinction important to the outcome of this case?

LAW ON THE WEB

For updated links to resources available on the Web, as well as a variety of other materials, visit this text's Web site at http://wleb.westbuslaw.com.

The Federal Web Locator permits searches for the names of federal administrative agencies and provides links to agency-related information. Go to

http://www.infoctr.edu/fwl

The Web site of the U.S. Government Printing Office, called GPO Access, offers free online access to all of its databases, including the *Federal Register*, at

http://www.access.gpo.gov/su_docs

LEGAL RESEARCH EXERCISES ON THE WEB

Go to http://wleb.westbuslaw.com, the Web site that accompanies this text. Select "Internet Applications," and then click on "Chapter 6." There you will find the following Internet research exercise that you can perform to learn more about how to obtain information from government agencies:

Activity 6–1: The Freedom of Information Act

CHAPTER 7

Criminal Law

THE LAW IMPOSES VARIOUS sanctions in attempting to ensure that individuals engaging in business in our society can compete and flourish. These sanctions include those imposed by civil law, such as damages for various types of tortious conduct (discussed in Chapters 12 and 13); damages for breach of contract (to be discussed in Chapter 10); and the equitable remedies discussed in Chapter 1. Additional sanctions are imposed under criminal law. Indeed, many statutes regulating business provide for criminal as well as civil penalties. Therefore, criminal law joins civil law as an important element in the legal environment of business.

In this chapter, after examining some essential differences between criminal law and civil law, we look at how crimes are classified, the basic requirements that must be met for criminal liability to be established, the various types of crimes, and the defenses that can be raised to avoid criminal liability. The chapter concludes with a discussion of criminal procedures.

SECTION 1

Civil Law and Criminal Law

Recall from Chapter 1 that *civil law* pertains to the duties that exist between persons or between citizens and their governments. Criminal law, in contrast, has to do with crime. A **crime** can be defined as a wrong

against society proclaimed in a statute and punishable by a fine and/or imprisonment—or, in some cases, death. As mentioned in Chapter 1, because crimes are *offenses against society as a whole*, they are prosecuted by a public official, such as a district attorney (D.A.) or an attorney general (A.G.), not by victims.

MAJOR DIFFERENCES BETWEEN CIVIL LAW AND CRIMINAL LAW

Because the state has extensive resources at its disposal when prosecuting criminal cases, there are numerous procedural safeguards to protect the rights of defendants. One of these safeguards is the higher standard of proof that applies in a criminal case. As you can see in Exhibit 7–1 on the next page, which summarizes some of the key differences between civil law and criminal law, in a civil case the plaintiff usually must prove his or her case by a *preponderance of the evidence*. Under this standard, the plaintiff must convince the court that, based on the evidence presented by both parties, it is more likely than not that the plaintiff's allegation is true.

In a criminal case, in contrast, the state must prove its case **beyond a reasonable doubt.** Every juror in a criminal case must be convinced, beyond a reasonable doubt, of the defendant's guilt. The higher standard of proof in criminal cases reflects a fundamental social value—a belief that it is worse to convict an

136

EXHIBIT 7–1 CIVIL AND CRIMINAL LAW COMPARED

ISSUE	CIVIL LAW	CRIMINAL LAW
Area of concern	Rights and duties between individuals	Offenses against society as a whole
Wrongful act	Harm to a person or to a person's property	Violation of a statute that prohibits some type of activity
Party who brings suit	Person who suffered harm	The state
Standard of proof	Preponderance of the evidence	Beyond a reasonable doubt
Remedy	Damages to compensate for the harm or an equitable remedy	Punishment (fine and/or imprisonment)

innocent individual than to let a guilty person go free. We will look at other safeguards later in the chapter, in the context of criminal procedure.

The sanctions imposed on criminal wrongdoers are also harsher than those that are applied in civil cases. As will be discussed in Chapter 12, the purpose of tort law is to allow persons harmed by the wrongful acts of others to obtain compensation, or money damages, from the wrongdoer or to enjoin (prevent) a wrongdoer from undertaking or continuing a wrongful action. Rarely are tortfeasors subject to punitive damages—damages awarded simply to *punish* the wrongdoer. In contrast, criminal sanctions are designed to punish those who commit crimes in order to deter others from committing similar acts in the future.

CIVIL LIABILITY FOR CRIMINAL ACTS

Some torts, such as assault and battery, provide a basis for a criminal prosecution as well as a tort action. For example, Jonas is walking down the street, minding his own business, when suddenly a person attacks him. In the ensuing struggle, the attacker stabs Jonas several times, seriously injuring him. A police officer restrains and arrests the wrongdoer. In this situation, the attacker may be subject both to criminal prosecution by the state and to a tort lawsuit brought by Jonas to compensate Jonas for his injuries. Exhibit 7–2 (page 138) illustrates how the same wrongful act can result in both a civil (tort) action and a criminal action against the wrongdoer.

SECTION 2

Classification of Crimes

Depending on their degree of seriousness, crimes are classified as felonies or misdemeanors.

FELONIES

Felonies are serious crimes punishable by death or by imprisonment in a federal or state penitentiary for one year or longer.[1] The Model Penal Code[2] provides for four degrees of felony:

1. Capital offenses, for which the maximum penalty is death.
2. First degree felonies, punishable by a maximum penalty of life imprisonment.
3. Second degree felonies, punishable by a maximum of ten years' imprisonment.
4. Third degree felonies, punishable by up to five years' imprisonment.

Although criminal laws vary from state to state, some general rules apply when grading crimes by degree. For example, most jurisdictions punish a burglary that involves a forced entry into a home at night more harshly than a burglary that takes place during the day and involves a nonresidential building or structure. A homicide—the taking of another's life—is classified according to the degree of intent involved.

For example, first degree murder requires that the homicide be premeditated and deliberate, instead of being a spontaneous act of violence. When no premeditation or deliberation is present but the offender

---

1. Some states, such as North Carolina, consider felonies to be punishable by incarceration for at least two years.
2. The American Law Institute issued the Official Draft of the Model Penal Code in 1962. The Model Penal Code is not a uniform code. Uniformity in criminal law among the states is not as important as uniformity in other areas of the law. Crime varies with local circumstances, and it is appropriate that punishments vary accordingly. The Model Penal Code contains four parts: (1) general provisions, (2) definitions of special crimes, (3) provisions concerning treatment and corrections, and (4) provisions on the organization of correction.

EXHIBIT 7–2   TORT LAWSUIT AND CRIMINAL PROSECUTION FOR THE SAME ACT

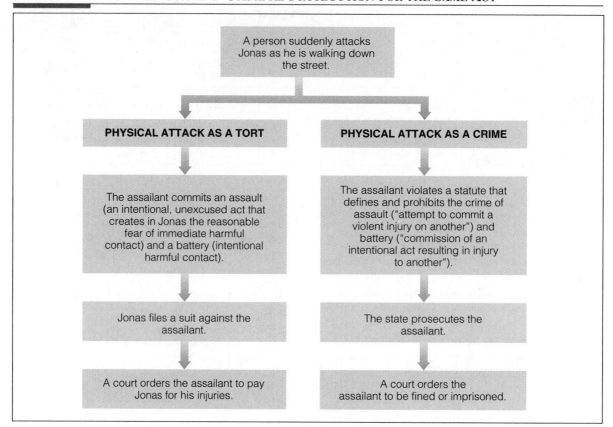

acts with *malice aforethought* (that is, with wanton disregard of the consequences of his or her actions for the victim), the homicide is classified as second degree murder. A homicide that is committed without malice toward the victim is known as *manslaughter*. *Voluntary manslaughter* occurs when the intent to kill may be present, as in a crime committed in the heat of passion, but malice is lacking. A homicide is classified as *involuntary manslaughter* when it results from an act of negligence, such as when a drunk driver causes the death of another person, and there is no intent to kill.

MISDEMEANORS AND PETTY OFFENSES

Under federal law and in most states, any crime that is not a felony is considered a **misdemeanor.** Misdemeanors are crimes punishable by a fine or by incarceration (imprisonment) for up to one year. If confined, the guilty party goes to a local jail instead of a penitentiary. Disorderly conduct and trespass are common misdemeanors. Some states have several classes of misdemeanors. For example, in Illinois, misdemeanors are either Class A (confinement for up to a year), Class B (not more than six months), or Class C (not more than thirty days). Whether a crime is a felony or a misdemeanor can also determine if the case is tried in a magistrate's court (for example, by a justice of the peace) or a general trial court.

In most jurisdictions, **petty offenses** are considered to be a subset of misdemeanors. Petty offenses are minor violations, such as violations of building codes or driving under the influence of alcohol. Even for petty offenses, however, a guilty party can be put in jail for a few days, fined, or both, depending on state law.

Probation and community service are often imposed on those who commit misdemeanors, especially juveniles. Also, most states have decriminalized all but the most serious traffic offenses. These infractions are treated as civil proceedings, and civil fines are imposed. In many states, "points" are assessed against the violator's driving record.

S E C T I O N   3

The Essentials of Criminal Liability

Two elements must exist for a person to be convicted of a crime: (1) the performance of a prohibited act and (2) a specified state of mind, or intent, on the part of the actor. Additionally, to establish criminal liability, there must be a *concurrence* between the act and the intent. In other words, these two elements must occur together.

For example, suppose that a woman plans to kill her husband by poisoning him. On the day she plans to do so, she is driving her husband home from work and swerves to avoid hitting a cat crossing the road. The car crashes into a tree as a result, killing her husband. Even though she had planned to murder her husband, the woman would not be guilty of murder in this situation because she had not planned to kill him by driving the car into a tree.

The Criminal Act

Every criminal statute prohibits certain behavior. Most crimes require an act of *commission*; that is, a person must *do* something in order to be accused of a crime. In criminal law, a prohibited act is referred to as the **actus reus**,[3] or guilty act. In some cases, an act of omission can be a crime, but only when a person has a legal duty to perform the omitted act. Failure to file a tax return is an example of an omission that is a crime.

The *guilty act* requirement is based on one of the premises of criminal law—that a person should be punished for harm done to society. Thus, for a crime to exist, the guilty act must cause some harm to a person or to property. Thinking about killing someone or about stealing a car may be wrong, but the thoughts do no harm until they are translated into action. Of course, a person can be punished for *attempting* murder or robbery, but only if substantial steps toward the criminal objective have been taken. Additionally, the punishment for an attempt to commit a crime is normally less severe than it would be if the act had been completed.

State of Mind

A wrongful mental state (**mens rea**)[4] is as necessary as a wrongful act in establishing guilt. The mental state,

or requisite intent, required to establish guilt of a crime is indicated in the applicable statute or law. Murder, for example, involves the guilty act of killing another human being, and the guilty mental state is the desire, or intent, to take another's life. For theft, the guilty act is the taking of another person's property, and the mental state involves both the awareness that the property belongs to another and the desire to deprive the owner of it.

A guilty mental state can be attributed to acts of negligence or recklessness as well. *Criminal negligence* involves the mental state in which the defendant deviates from the standard of care that a reasonable person would use under the same circumstances. The defendant is accused of taking an unjustified, substantial, and foreseeable risk that resulted in harm. Under the Model Penal Code, a defendant is negligent even if he or she was not actually aware of the risk but *should have been aware* of it.[5] The Model Penal Code defines *criminal recklessness* as "consciously disregard[ing] a substantial and unjustifiable risk."[6] In other words, a defendant is reckless if he or she is *actually aware* of the risk. A defendant who commits an act recklessly is more blameworthy than one who is criminally negligent.

S E C T I O N   4

Corporate Criminal Liability

As will be discussed in Chapter 19, a corporation is a legal entity created under the laws of a state. Both the corporation as an entity and the individual directors and officers of the corporation are potentially subject to liability for criminal acts.

Liability of the Corporate Entity

At one time, it was thought that a corporation could not incur criminal liability because, although a corporation is a legal person, it can act only through its agents (corporate directors, officers, and employees). Therefore, the corporate entity itself could not "intend" to commit a crime. Under modern criminal law, however, a corporation may be held liable for crimes. Obviously, corporations cannot be imprisoned, but they can be fined or denied certain legal privileges (such as a license).

---

3. Pronounced *ak*-tuhs *ray*-uhs.
4. Pronounced *mehns ray*-uh.

5. Model Penal Code Section 2.02(2)(d).
6. Model Penal Code Section 2.02(2)(c).

The Model Penal Code provides that a corporation may be convicted of a crime in the following situations:

1. The criminal act by the corporation's agent or employee is within the scope of his or her employment, and the purpose of the statute defining the act as a crime is to impose liability on the corporation.
2. The crime consists of a failure to perform a specific affirmative duty imposed on corporations by law.
3. The crime was authorized, requested, commanded, committed, or recklessly tolerated by one of the corporation's high managerial agents.[7]

As implied by the first statement in the above list, corporate criminal liability is vicarious—the corporation as an entity may be liable for the criminal acts of its employees when the acts are committed within the scope of employment. Thus, the corporation that is found to be criminally responsible for an act committed by an employee can be fined for that offense. Through the fine, stockholders and other employees suffer because of the vicarious liability of the corporation. The justification for such criminal liability involves a showing that the corporation could have prevented the act or that there was authorized consent to or knowledge of the act by persons in supervisory positions within the corporation.

LIABILITY OF CORPORATE OFFICERS AND DIRECTORS

Corporate directors and officers are personally liable for the crimes they commit, regardless of whether the crimes were committed for their private benefit or on the corporation's behalf. Additionally, corporate directors and officers may be held liable for the actions of employees under their supervision. Under what has become known as the "responsible corporate officer" doctrine, a court may impose criminal liability on a corporate officer regardless of whether he or she participated in, directed, or even knew about a given criminal violation.

For example, in *United States v. Park*,[8] the chief executive officer of a national supermarket chain was held personally liable for sanitation violations in corporate warehouses, in which the food was exposed to contamination by rodents. The court imposed personal liability on the corporate officer not because he intended the crime or even knew about it. Rather, liability was imposed because the officer was in a "responsible relationship" to the corporation and had the power to prevent the violation. Since the *Park* decision, courts have applied this "responsible corporate officer" doctrine on a number of occasions to hold corporate officers liable for their employees' statutory violations.

The following case illustrates that corporate officers and supervisors who oversee operations causing environmental harm may be held liable under the criminal provisions of environmental statutes. (The statute involved in this case—the federal Clean Water Act—will be discussed at some length in Chapter 25.)

---

7. Model Penal Code Section 2.07.

8. 421 U.S. 658, 95 S.Ct. 1903, 44 L.Ed.2d 489 (1975).

CASE 7.1   United States v. Hanousek

United States
Court of Appeals,
Ninth Circuit, 1999.
176 F.3d 1116.
http://www.ca9.
uscourts.gov[a]

BACKGROUND AND FACTS *Edward Hanousek worked for Pacific & Arctic Railway and Navigation Company (P&A) as a roadmaster of the White Pass & Yukon Railroad in Alaska. Hanousek was responsible "for every detail of the safe and efficient maintenance and construction of track, structures and marine facilities of the entire railroad," including special projects. One project was a rock quarry, known as "6-mile," above the Skagway River. Next to the quarry, and just beneath the surface, ran a high-pressure oil pipeline owned by Pacific & Arctic Pipeline, Inc., P&A's sister company. When the quarry's*

---

a. The U.S. Court of Appeals for the Ninth Circuit maintains this Web site. Click on the "OPINIONS" oval. From that page, click on the "CLICK HERE: GO TO OPINIONS" box. On the next page, click on the "1999" icon, and when the menu opens, click on "March." Scroll down to "USA V HANOUSEK" and click on the case name to access the case.

backhoe operator punctured the pipeline, an estimated 1,000 to 5,000 gallons of oil were discharged into the river. Hanousek was charged with, among other things, negligently discharging a harmful quantity of oil into a navigable water of the United States in violation of the criminal provisions of the Clean Water Act (CWA). After a trial in a federal district court, a jury convicted Hanousek, and the court imposed a sentence of six months' imprisonment, six months in a halfway house, six months' supervised release, and a fine of $5,000. Hanousek appealed to the U.S. Court of Appeals for the Ninth Circuit, arguing in part that the statute under which he was convicted violated his right to due process because he was not aware of what the CWA required.

IN THE LANGUAGE OF THE COURT

DAVID R. THOMPSON, Circuit Judge.

*   *   *   *

The criminal provisions of the CWA [Clean Water Act] constitute public welfare legislation. Public welfare legislation is designed to protect the public from potentially harmful or injurious items and may render criminal a type of conduct that a reasonable person should know is subject to stringent public regulation and may seriously threaten the community's health or safety.

It is well established that a public welfare statute may subject a person to criminal liability for his or her ordinary negligence without violating due process. [Emphasis added.]

*   *   * [W]here   *   * dangerous or deleterious devices or products or obnoxious waste materials are involved, the probability of regulation is so great that anyone who is aware that he is in possession of them or dealing with them must be presumed to be aware of the regulation.

Hanousek argues that   *   *   * he was simply the roadmaster of the White Pass & Yukon railroad charged with overseeing a rock-quarrying project and was not in a position to know what the law required under the CWA.   *   *   * In the context of a public welfare statute, as long as a defendant knows he is dealing with a dangerous device of a character that places him in responsible relation to a public danger, he should be alerted to the probability of strict regulation.   *   *   * Hanousek   *   *   * does not dispute that he was aware that a high-pressure petroleum products pipeline owned by Pacific & Arctic's sister company ran close to the surface next to the railroad tracks at 6-mile, and does not argue that he was unaware of the dangers a break or puncture of the pipeline by a piece of heavy machinery would pose. Therefore, Hanousek should have been alerted to the probability of strict regulation.

In light of [the fact] that the criminal provisions of the CWA constitute public welfare legislation, and the fact that a public welfare statute may impose criminal penalties for ordinary negligent conduct without offending due process, we conclude that [the CWA] does not violate due process by permitting criminal penalties for ordinary negligent conduct.

DECISION AND REMEDY

The U.S. Court of Appeals for the Ninth Circuit affirmed Hanousek's conviction. A corporate manager who has responsibility for operations with the potential to cause harm can be held criminally liable for harm that results even if he or she does not actually know of the specific statute under which liability may be imposed.

SECTION 5

Types of Crimes

The number of actions that are designated as criminal is nearly endless. Federal, state, and local laws provide for the classification and punishment of hundreds of thousands of different criminal acts. Generally, though, criminal acts can be grouped into six broad categories: violent crime (crimes against persons), property crime, public order crime, white-collar crime, organized crime, and computer crime.

VIOLENT CRIME

Some types of crime are called *violent crimes,* or crimes against persons, because they cause others to suffer harm or death. Murder is a violent crime. So is sexual assault, or rape. Assault and battery, which can be civil wrongs, are also classified as violent crimes. **Robbery**—defined as the taking of money, personal property, or any other article of value from a person by means of force or fear—is also a violent crime. Typically, states have more severe penalties for *aggravated robbery*—robbery with the use of a deadly weapon.

Each of these violent crimes is further classified by degree, depending on the circumstances surrounding the criminal act. These circumstances include the intent of the person committing the crime, whether a weapon was used, and (in cases other than murder) the level of pain and suffering experienced by the victim.

Property Crime

The most common type of criminal activity is property crime, or those crimes in which the goal of the offender is some form of economic gain or the damaging of property. Robbery is a form of property crime, as well as a violent crime, because the offender seeks to gain the property of another. We look here at a number of other crimes that fall within the general category of property crime.

Burglary.   At common law, **burglary** was defined as breaking and entering the dwelling of another at night with the intent to commit a felony. Originally, the definition was aimed at protecting an individual's home and its occupants. Most state statutes have eliminated some of the requirements found in the common law definition. The time at which the breaking and entering occurs, for example, is usually immaterial. State statutes frequently omit the element of breaking, and some states do not require that the building be a dwelling. *Aggravated burglary*—which is defined as burglary with the use of a deadly weapon, burglary of a dwelling, or both—incurs a greater penalty.

Larceny.   Any person who wrongfully or fraudulently takes and carries away another person's personal property is guilty of **larceny**. Larceny includes the fraudulent intent to deprive an owner permanently of property. Many business-related larcenies entail fraudulent conduct. Whereas robbery involves force or fear, larceny does not. Therefore, picking pockets is larceny, not robbery.

In most states, the definition of property that is subject to larceny statutes has been expanded to cover relatively new forms of theft. For example, stealing computer programs may constitute larceny even though the "property" consists of magnetic impulses. Stealing computer time may also be considered larceny. So, too, may the theft of natural gas. Trade secrets may be subject to larceny statutes. Intercepting cellular phone calls to obtain another's phone card number—and then using that number to place long-distance calls, often overseas—is a form of property theft. These types of larceny are covered by "theft of services" statutes in many jurisdictions.

The common law makes a distinction between grand and petit larceny based on the value of the property taken. Many states have abolished this distinction, but in those that have not, grand larceny (theft above a certain amount) is a felony and petit larceny, a misdemeanor.

Arson.   The willful and malicious burning of a building (and in some states, personal property) owned by another is the crime of **arson**. At common law, arson applied only to burning down another person's house. The law was designed to protect human life. Today, arson statutes have been extended to cover the destruction of any building, regardless of ownership, by fire or explosion.

Every state has a special statute that covers a person's burning a building for the purpose of collecting insurance. If Shaw owns an insured apartment building that is falling apart and sets fire to it himself or pays someone else to do so, he is guilty not only of arson but also of defrauding insurers, which is an attempted larceny. Of course, the insurer need not pay the claim when insurance fraud is proved.

Receiving Stolen Goods.   It is a crime to receive stolen goods. The recipient of such goods need not know the true identity of the owner or the thief. All that is necessary is that the recipient knows or should know that the goods are stolen, which implies an intent to deprive the owner of those goods.

Forgery.   The fraudulent making or altering of any writing in a way that changes the legal rights and liabilities of another is **forgery**. If, without authorization, Severson signs Bennett's name to the back of a check made out to Bennett, Severson is committing forgery. Forgery also includes changing trademarks, falsifying public records, counterfeiting, and altering a legal document.

Obtaining Goods by False Pretenses. It is a criminal act to obtain goods by false pretenses—for example, to buy groceries with a check, knowing that one has insufficient funds to cover it. Using another's credit-card number to obtain goods is another example of obtaining goods by false pretenses. Statutes dealing with such illegal activities vary widely from state to state. For example, in some states an intent to defraud must be proved before a person is criminally liable for writing a bad check. Some states define the theft and use of another's credit card as a separate crime, while others consider credit-card crime as a form of forgery.

PUBLIC ORDER CRIME

Historically, societies have always outlawed activities that are considered contrary to public values and morals. Today, the most common public order crimes include public drunkenness, prostitution, gambling, and illegal drug use. These crimes are sometimes referred to as *victimless crimes* because they harm only the offender. From a broader perspective, however, they are deemed detrimental to society as a whole because they often create an environment that may give rise to property and violent crimes.

WHITE-COLLAR CRIME

Crimes occurring in the business context are popularly referred to as white-collar crimes. Although there is no official definition of **white-collar crime,** the term is commonly used to mean an illegal act or series of acts committed by an individual or business entity using some nonviolent means to obtain a personal or business advantage. Usually, this kind of crime takes place in the course of a legitimate business occupation. The crimes discussed next normally occur only in the business environment and thus fall into the category of white-collar crimes. Note, though, that certain property crimes, such as larceny and forgery, may also fall into this category if they occur within the business context.

Embezzlement. When a person entrusted with another person's property or funds fraudulently appropriates that property or those funds, **embezzlement** occurs. Typically, embezzlement involves an employee who steals funds from his or her employer. Banks face this problem, and so do a number of businesses in which corporate officers or accountants "doctor" the

books to cover up the fraudulent conversion of funds for their own benefit. Embezzlement is not larceny, because the wrongdoer does not physically take the property from the possession of another, and it is not robbery, because no force or fear is used.

It does not matter whether the accused takes the money from the victim or from a third person. If, as the financial officer of a large corporation, Carlson pockets a certain number of checks from third parties that were given to her to deposit into the corporate account, she is embezzling.

Ordinarily, an embezzler who returns what has been taken will not be prosecuted, because the owner usually will not take the time to make a complaint, give depositions, and appear in court. That the accused intended eventually to return the embezzled property, however, does not constitute a sufficient defense to the crime of embezzlement.

Mail and Wire Fraud. One of the most potent weapons against white-collar criminals is the Mail Fraud Act of 1990.[9] Under this act, it is a federal crime to use the mails to defraud the public. Illegal use of the mails must involve (1) mailing or causing someone else to mail a writing—something written, printed, or photocopied—for the purpose of executing a scheme to defraud and (2) contemplating or organizing a scheme to defraud by false pretenses. If, for example, Johnson advertises by mail the sale of a cure for cancer that he knows to be fraudulent because it has no medical validity, he can be prosecuted for fraudulent use of the mails.

Federal law also makes it a crime (wire fraud) to use wire, radio, or television transmissions to defraud.[10] Violators may be fined up to $1,000, imprisoned for up to five years, or both. If the violation affects a financial institution, the violator may be fined up to $1 million, imprisoned for up to thirty years, or both.

Bribery. Basically, three types of bribery are considered crimes: commercial bribery, bribery of public officials, and bribery of foreign officials. As an element of the crime of bribery, intent must be present and proved. The bribe can be anything the recipient considers to be valuable. Realize that the *crime of bribery occurs when the bribe is offered.* It does not matter whether the person to whom the bribe is offered accepts the bribe or

---

9. 18 U.S.C. Sections 1341–1342.

10. 18 U.S.C. Section 1343.

agrees to perform whatever action is desired by the person offering the bribe. *Accepting a bribe* is a separate crime.

Typically, people make commercial bribes to obtain proprietary information, cover up an inferior product, or secure new business. Industrial espionage sometimes involves commercial bribes. For example, a person in one firm may offer an employee in a competing firm some type of payoff in exchange for trade secrets or pricing schedules. So-called kickbacks, or payoffs for special favors or services, are a form of commercial bribery in some situations.

The attempt to influence a public official to act in a way that serves a private interest is a crime. Bribing foreign officials to obtain favorable business contracts is also a crime. This crime was discussed in detail in Chapter 4, along with the Foreign Corrupt Practices Act of 1977, which was passed to curb the use of bribery by American businesspersons in securing foreign contracts.

Bankruptcy Fraud. Today, federal bankruptcy law (see Chapter 16) allows individuals and businesses to be relieved of oppressive debt through bankruptcy proceedings. Numerous white-collar crimes may be committed during the many phases of a bankruptcy action. A creditor, for example, may file a false claim against the debtor, which is a crime. Also, a debtor may fraudulently transfer assets to favored parties before or after the petition for bankruptcy is filed. For example, a company-owned automobile may be "sold" at a bargain price to a trusted friend or relative. Closely related to the crime of fraudulent transfer of property is the crime of fraudulent concealment of property, such as the hiding of gold coins.

Insider Trading. An individual who obtains "inside information" about the plans of publicly held corporations can often make stock-trading profits by using the information to guide decisions relating to the purchase or sale of corporate securities. *Insider trading* is a violation of securities law and will be considered more fully in Chapter 29. At this point, it may be said that one who possesses inside information and who has a duty not to disclose it to outsiders may not profit from the purchase or sale of securities based on that information until the information is available to the public.

The Theft of Trade Secrets. As will be discussed in Chapter 14, trade secrets constitute a form of intellectual property that for many businesses can be ex-

tremely valuable. The Economic Espionage Act of 1996[11] makes the theft of trade secrets a federal crime. The act also makes it a federal crime to buy or possess another person's trade secrets, knowing that the trade secrets were stolen or otherwise acquired without the owner's authorization.

Violations of the act can result in steep penalties. The act provides that an individual who violates the act can be imprisoned for up to ten years and fined up to $500,000. If a corporation or other organization violates the act, it can be fined up to $5 million. Additionally, the law provides that any property acquired as a result of the violation and any property used in the commission of the violation is subject to criminal forfeiture—meaning that the government can take the property. A theft of trade secrets conducted via the Internet, for example, could result in the forfeiture of every computer, printer, or other device used to commit or facilitate the violation.

ORGANIZED CRIME

White-collar crime takes place within the confines of the legitimate business world. Organized crime, in contrast, operates *illegitimately* by satisfying the public's demand for illegal goods and services. For organized crime, the traditional preferred markets are gambling, prostitution, illegal narcotics, pornography, and loan sharking (lending money at higher than legal interest rates), along with more recent ventures into counterfeiting and credit-card scams.

Money Laundering. The profits from organized crime and other illegal activities amount to billions of dollars a year, particularly the profits from illegal drug transactions and, to a lesser extent, from racketeering, prostitution, and gambling. Under federal law, banks, savings and loan associations, and other financial institutions are required to report currency transactions of over $10,000. Consequently, those who engage in illegal activities face difficulties in depositing their cash profits from illegal transactions.

As an alternative to simply placing cash from illegal transactions in bank deposits, wrongdoers and racketeers have invented ways to launder "dirty" money to make it "clean." This **money laundering** is done through legitimate businesses. For example, a successful drug dealer might become a partner with a restaurateur. Little by little, the restaurant shows an

---

11. 18 U.S.C. Sections 1831–1839.

increasing profit. As a shareholder or partner in the restaurant, the wrongdoer is able to report the "profits" of the restaurant as legitimate income on which federal and state taxes are paid. The wrongdoer can then spend those monies without worrying about whether his or her lifestyle exceeds the level possible with his or her reported income.

The Federal Bureau of Investigation estimates that organized crime alone has invested tens of billions of dollars in as many as a hundred thousand business establishments in the United States for the purpose of money laundering. Globally, it is estimated that $300 billion in illegal money moves through the world banking system every year.

RICO. In 1970, in an effort to curb the apparently increasing entry of organized crime into the legitimate business world, Congress passed the Racketeer Influenced and Corrupt Organizations Act (RICO).[12] The act, which was enacted as part of the Organized Crime Control Act, makes it a federal crime to (1) use income obtained from racketeering activity to purchase any interest in an enterprise, (2) acquire or maintain an interest in an enterprise through racketeering activity, (3) conduct or participate in the affairs of an enterprise through racketeering activity, or (4) conspire to do any of the preceding activities.

Racketeering activity is not a new type of substantive crime created by RICO; rather, RICO incorporates by reference twenty-six separate types of federal crimes and nine types of state felonies[13] and declares that if a person commits two of these offenses, he or she is guilty of "racketeering activity." The act provides for both civil and criminal liability.

Civil Liability under RICO. The penalties for violations of the RICO statute are harsh. In the event of a violation, the statute permits the government to seek civil penalties, including the divestiture of a defendant's interest in a business (called forfeiture) or the dissolution of the business. Perhaps the most controversial aspect of RICO is that in some cases, private individuals are allowed to recover three times their actual losses (treble damages), plus attorneys' fees, for business injuries caused by a violation of the statute.

The broad language of RICO has allowed it to be applied in cases that have little or nothing to do with organized crime, and an aggressive trial attorney may attempt to show that any business fraud constitutes

"racketeering activity." In its 1985 decision in *Sedima, S.P.R.L. v. Imrex Co.*,[14] the United States Supreme Court interpreted RICO broadly and set a significant precedent for subsequent applications of the act. Plaintiffs have used the RICO statute in numerous commercial fraud cases because of the inviting prospect of being awarded treble damages if they win. The most frequent targets of civil RICO lawsuits are insurance companies, employment agencies, commercial banks, and stockbrokerage firms.

One of the requirements of RICO is that there be more than one offense—there must be a "pattern of racketeering activity." What constitutes a "pattern" has been the subject of much litigation. According to the interpretation of some courts, a pattern must involve, among other things, continued criminal activity. This is known as the "continuity" requirement. Part of this requirement is that the activity occur over a "substantial" period of time.

Criminal Liability under RICO. Many criminal RICO offenses, such as gambling, arson, and extortion, have little, if anything, to do with normal business activities. But securities fraud (involving the sale of stocks and bonds) and mail and wire fraud also may constitute criminal RICO violations, and RICO has become an effective tool in attacking these white-collar crimes in recent years. Under the criminal provisions of RICO, any individual found guilty of a violation is subject to a fine of up to $25,000 per violation, imprisonment for up to twenty years, or both.

COMPUTER CRIME

The American Bar Association defines **computer crime** as any act that is directed against computers and computer parts, that uses computers as instruments of crime, or that involves computers and constitutes abuse. A variety of different types of crime can be committed with or against computers, including the cyber crimes discussed in Chapter 15. The dependence of businesses on computer operations has left firms vulnerable to sabotage, fraud, embezzlement, and the theft of proprietary data, such as trade secrets or other intellectual property (discussed in Chapter 14).

Many computer crimes fall into the broad category of financial crimes. Computer networks provide opportunities for employees and others to commit crimes that can involve serious economic losses. For

12. 18 U.S.C. Sections 1961–1968.
13. See 18 U.S.C. Section 1961(1)(A).
14. 473 U.S. 479, 105 S.Ct. 3275, 87 L.Ed.2d 346 (1985).

example, employees of accounting and computer departments can transfer monies among accounts with little effort and often with less risk than that involved in transactions evidenced by paperwork. The potential for crime in the area of financial transactions is great; most monetary losses from computer crime are suffered in this area.

The theft of computer equipment and the theft of goods with the aid of computers (such as by manipulating inventory records to disguise the theft of goods) are subject to the same criminal and tort laws as thefts of other physical property. In many jurisdictions, the unauthorized use of computer data or services is considered larceny. Other computer crimes include vandalism and destructive programming. A knowledgeable individual, such as an angry employee whose job has just been terminated, can do a considerable amount of damage to computer data and files. Destructive programming in the form of "viruses" presents an ongoing problem for businesspersons and other computer users today.

CONCEPT SUMMARY 7.1 TYPES OF CRIMES

CRIME CATEGORY	DEFINITION AND EXAMPLES
Violent Crime	1. *Definition*—Crimes that cause others to suffer harm or death. 2. *Examples*—Murder, assault and battery, sexual assault (rape), and robbery.
Property Crime	1. *Definition*—Crimes in which the goal of the offender is some form of economic gain or the damaging of property; the most common form of crime. 2. *Examples*—Burglary, larceny, arson, receiving stolen goods, forgery, and obtaining goods by false pretenses.
Public Order Crime	1. *Definition*—Crimes contrary to public values and morals. 2. *Examples*—Public drunkenness, prostitution, gambling, and illegal drug use.
White-Collar Crime	1. *Definition*—An illegal act or series of acts committed by an individual or business entity using some nonviolent means to obtain a personal or business advantage; usually committed in the course of a legitimate occupation. 2. *Examples*—Embezzlement, mail and wire fraud, bribery, bankruptcy fraud, insider trading, and the theft of trade secrets.
Organized Crime	1. *Definition*—A form of crime conducted by groups operating illegitimately to satisfy the public's demand for illegal goods and services (such as narcotics or pornography). 2. *Money laundering*—The establishment of legitimate enterprises through which "dirty" money (obtained through criminal activities, such as organized crime) can be "laundered" (made to appear as legitimate income). 3. *RICO*—The Racketeer Influenced and Corrupt Organizations Act (RICO) of 1970 makes it a federal crime to (a) use income obtained from racketeering activity to purchase any interest in an enterprise, (b) acquire or maintain an interest in an enterprise through racketeering activity, (c) conduct or participate in the affairs of an enterprise through racketeering activity, or (d) conspire to do any of the preceding activities. RICO provides for both civil and criminal liability.
Computer Crime	1. *Definition*—Any act that is directed against computers and computer parts, that uses computers as instruments of crime, or that involves computers and constitutes abuse. 2. *Examples*—Virtually all crimes involving computer use or abuse, including financial crimes (such as embezzlement), the theft of computer equipment, the theft of goods or services with the aid of computers, and destructive programming (such as viruses).

SECTION 6

Defenses to Criminal Liability

In certain circumstances, the law may allow a person to be excused from criminal liability because he or she lacks the required mental state. Criminal defendants may also be relieved of criminal liability if they can show that their criminal actions were justified, given the circumstances. Among the most important defenses to criminal liability are infancy, intoxication, insanity, mistake, consent, duress, justifiable use of force, necessity, entrapment, and the statute of limitations. Also, in some cases, defendants are given *immunity* from prosecution and thus relieved, at least in part, of criminal liability for their actions. We look next at each of these defenses.

Note that procedural violations (such as obtaining evidence without a valid search warrant) may operate as defenses also—because evidence obtained in violation of a defendant's constitutional rights may not be admitted in court. If the evidence is suppressed, then there may be no basis for prosecuting the defendant.

INFANCY

The term *infant*, as used in the law, refers to any person who has not yet reached the age of majority (see Chapter 9). In all states, certain courts handle cases involving children who are alleged to have violated the law. In some states, juvenile courts handle children's cases exclusively. In most states, however, courts that handle children's cases also have jurisdiction over other matters, such as traffic offenses.

Originally, juvenile court hearings were informal, and lawyers were rarely present. Since 1967, however, when the United States Supreme Court ordered that a child charged with delinquency must be allowed to consult with an attorney before being committed to a state institution,[15] juvenile court hearings have become more formal. In some states, a child will be treated as an adult and tried in a regular court if he or she is above a certain age (usually fourteen) and is guilty of a felony, such as rape or murder.

INTOXICATION

The law recognizes two types of intoxication, whether from drugs or from alcohol: involuntary and voluntary. *Involuntary intoxication* occurs when a person either is physically forced to ingest or inject an intoxicating substance or is unaware that a substance contains drugs or alcohol. Involuntary intoxication is a defense to a crime if its effect was to make a person incapable of understanding that the act committed was wrong or incapable of obeying the law.

Using voluntary drug or alcohol intoxication as a defense is based on the theory that extreme levels of intoxication may negate the state of mind that a crime requires. Many courts are reluctant to allow *voluntary intoxication* as a defense to a crime, however. After all, the defendant, by definition, voluntarily chose to put himself or herself into an intoxicated state.

INSANITY

Just as a child is often judged incapable of the state of mind required to commit a crime, so also may be someone suffering from a mental illness. Thus, insanity may be a defense to a criminal charge. The courts have had difficulty deciding what standards should be used to measure sanity for the purposes of a criminal trial. One of the oldest standards, or tests, for insanity is the *M'Naghten* test,[16] which is still used in about one-third of the states. Under this test, which is sometimes called the "right-wrong" test, a criminal defendant is not responsible if, at the time of the offense, he or she did not know the nature and quality of the act or did not know that the act was wrong.

Several other jurisdictions use the less restrictive irresistible-impulse test to determine sanity. Under this test, a person may be found insane even if he or she was aware that a criminal act was wrong, providing that some "irresistible impulse" resulting from a mental deficiency drove him or her to commit the crime.

Today, almost all federal courts and about half of the states use the relatively liberal standard set forth in the Model Penal Code:

> A person is not responsible for criminal conduct if at the time of such conduct as a result of mental disease or defect he lacks *substantial capacity* either to appreciate the wrongfulness of his conduct or to conform his conduct to the requirements of the law.[17] [Emphasis added.]

---

15. *In re Gault*, 387 U.S. 1, 87 S.Ct. 1428, 18 L.Ed.2d 527 (1967).

16. A rule derived from *M'Naghten's Case*, 8 Eng.Rep. 718 (1843).
17. Model Penal Code Section 4.01.

This "substantial-capacity" standard is considerably easier to meet than the *M'Naghten* test or the irresistible-impulse test.

Under any of these tests, it is extremely difficult to prove insanity. For this reason, the insanity defense is rarely used. It is raised in only about 1 percent of felony cases and is unsuccessful in about three-fourths of those cases.

MISTAKE

Everyone has heard the saying "Ignorance of the law is no excuse." Ordinarily, ignorance of the law or a mistaken idea about what the law requires is not a valid defense. In some states, however, that rule has been modified. People who claim that they honestly did not know that they were breaking a law may have a valid defense if (1) the law was not published or reasonably made known to the public or (2) the people relied on an official statement of the law that was erroneous.

A *mistake of fact*, as opposed to a *mistake of law*, operates as a defense if it negates the mental state necessary to commit a crime. If, for example, Oliver Wheaton mistakenly walks off with Julie Tyson's briefcase because he thinks it is his, there is no theft. Theft requires knowledge that the property belongs to another.

CONSENT

What if a victim consents to a crime or even encourages the person intending a criminal act to commit it? Depending on the circumstances, the law may allow **consent** as a defense. In each case, one question is whether the law forbids an act committed against the victim's will or forbids the act without regard to the victim's wish. The law forbids murder, prostitution, and drug use whether the victim consents or not. Also, if the act causes harm to a third person who has not consented, there is no escape from criminal liability. Consent or forgiveness given after a crime has been committed is not really a defense, although it can affect the likelihood of prosecution. Consent operates as a defense most successfully in crimes against property.

DURESS

Duress exists when the *wrongful threat* of one person induces another person to perform an act that he or she would not otherwise have performed. In such a situation, duress is said to negate the mental state necessary to commit a crime. For duress to qualify as a defense, the following requirements must be met:

1. The threat must be of serious bodily harm or death.
2. The harm threatened must be greater than the harm caused by the crime.
3. The threat must be immediate and inescapable.
4. The defendant must have been involved in the situation through no fault of his or her own.

One crime that cannot be excused by duress is murder. It is difficult to justify taking a life as a result of duress even if one's own life is threatened.

JUSTIFIABLE USE OF FORCE

Probably the most well-known defense to criminal liability is **self-defense.** Other situations, however, also justify the use of force: the defense of one's dwelling, the defense of other property, and the prevention of a crime. In all of these situations, it is important to distinguish between the use of deadly and nondeadly force. *Deadly force* is likely to result in death or serious bodily harm. *Nondeadly force* is force that reasonably appears necessary to prevent the imminent use of criminal force.

Generally speaking, people can use the amount of nondeadly force that seems necessary to protect themselves, their dwellings, or other property or to prevent the commission of a crime. Deadly force can be used in self-defense if there is a *reasonable belief* that imminent death or grievous bodily harm will otherwise result, if the attacker is using unlawful force (an example of lawful force is that exerted by a police officer), and if the defender has not initiated or provoked the attack. Deadly force can be used to defend a dwelling only if the unlawful entry is violent and the person believes deadly force is necessary to prevent imminent death or great bodily harm or—in some jurisdictions—if the person believes deadly force is necessary to prevent the commission of a felony in the dwelling.

What if deadly force results from a mechanical device, such as a spring gun rigged to go off when a trespasser enters through a doorway? A leading case on this issue is *Katco v. Briney,* presented on the next page.

CASE 7.2   Katco v. Briney

Supreme Court of Iowa, 1971.
183 N.W.2d 657.

BACKGROUND AND FACTS *In 1957, Bertha Briney inherited her parents' farm. Over the next ten years, the unoccupied farmhouse was broken into a number of times, resulting in the loss of some household items, in broken windows, and in the "messing up of the property in general." In June 1967, the Brineys set a shotgun trap in one of the bedrooms. Wire was rigged from the gun's trigger to the doorknob so that the gun would fire when the door was opened. On the night of July 16, Marvin Katco and Marvin McDonough broke into the house looking for antique bottles and jars. When Katco opened the bedroom door, he detonated the shotgun and was hit in the right leg above the ankle bone. Much of his leg, including part of the tibia, was blown away. He spent forty days in the hospital, a year on crutches, and a year in a special brace. He pleaded guilty to criminal charges of larceny, paid a $50 fine, and was paroled for good behavior from a sixty-day jail sentence. Katco sued the Brineys in an Iowa state court for damages. The trial court instructed the jury that "one may use reasonable force in the protection of his property, but * * * one may not use such means of force as will take human life or inflict great bodily injury." The jury returned a verdict for Katco for $30,000. The Brineys appealed.*

IN THE LANGUAGE OF THE COURT

MOORE, Chief Justice.

*   *   *   *

The overwhelming weight of authority, both textbook and case law, supports the trial court's statement of the applicable principles of law.

*   *   *   *

Restatement of Torts, [S]ection 85, states: "The value of human life and limb, not only to the individual concerned but also to society, so outweighs the interest of a possessor of land in excluding from it those whom he is not willing to admit thereto that a possessor of land has * * * no privilege to use force intended or likely to cause death or serious harm against another whom the possessor sees about to enter his premises or meddle with his [property], unless the intrusion threatens death or serious bodily harm to the occupiers or users of the premises. * * * *A possessor of land cannot do indirectly and by a mechanical device that which, were he present, he could not do immediately and in person.* * * * " [Emphasis added.]

*   *   *   *

In *Hooker v. Miller,* we held [a] defendant vineyard owner liable for damages resulting from a spring gun shot although plaintiff was a trespasser and there to steal grapes. [In the opinion,] this statement is made: "This court has held that a mere trespass against property * * * is not a sufficient justification to authorize the use of a deadly weapon by the owner in its defense; and that if death results in such a case it will be murder, though the killing be actually necessary to prevent the trespass." * * *

*   *   *   *

In addition to civil liability many jurisdictions hold a land owner criminally liable for serious injuries or homicide caused by spring guns or other set devices.

DECISION AND REMEDY

The Supreme Court of Iowa affirmed the trial court's decision. The Brineys were liable for Katco's injuries.

NECESSITY

Sometimes criminal defendants can be relieved of liability by showing that a criminal act was necessary to prevent an even greater harm. According to the Model Penal Code, the defense of **necessity** is justiable if "the harm or evil sought to be avoided by such conduct is greater than that sought to be prevented by the law defining the offense charged."[18] For example, in one case a convicted felon was threatened by an acquaintance with a gun. The felon grabbed the gun and fled the scene, but subsequently he was arrested under a statute that prohibits convicted felons from possessing firearms. In this situation, the necessity defense succeeded because the defendant's crime avoided a "greater evil."[19]

ENTRAPMENT

Entrapment is a defense designed to prevent police officers or other government agents from encouraging crimes in order to apprehend persons wanted for criminal acts. In the typical entrapment case, an undercover agent *suggests* that a crime be committed and somehow pressures or induces an individual to commit it. The agent then arrests the individual for the crime. For entrapment to be considered a defense, both the suggestion and the inducement must take place. The defense is intended not to prevent law enforcement agents from setting a trap for an unwary criminal but rather to prevent them from pushing the individual into that trap. The crucial issue is whether a person who committed a crime was predisposed to commit the crime or did so because the agent induced it.

STATUTE OF LIMITATIONS

With some exceptions, such as for the crime of murder, statutes of limitations apply to crimes just as they do to civil wrongs. In other words, criminal cases must be prosecuted within a certain number of years. If a criminal action is brought after the statutory time period has expired, the accused person can raise the statute of limitations as a defense. The running of the time period in a statute of limitations may be tolled—that is, suspended or stopped temporarily—if the defendant is a minor or is not in the jurisdiction. When the defendant reaches the age of majority or returns, the statute revives—that is, its time period begins to run or to run again.

---

18. Model Penal Code Section 3.02.
19. *United States v. Paolello*, 951 F.3d 537 (3d Cir. 1991).

IMMUNITY

At times, the state may wish to obtain information from a person accused of a crime. Accused persons are understandably reluctant to give information if it will be used to prosecute them, and they cannot be forced to do so. The privilege against self-incrimination is granted by the Fifth Amendment to the Constitution, which reads, in part, "nor shall [any person] be compelled in any criminal case to be a witness against himself." In cases in which the state wishes to obtain information from a person accused of a crime, the state can grant *immunity* from prosecution or agree to prosecute for a less serious offense in exchange for the information. Once immunity is given, the person can no longer refuse to testify on Fifth Amendment grounds, because he or she now has an absolute privilege against self-incrimination.

Often a grant of immunity from prosecution for a serious crime is part of the **plea bargaining** between the defending and prosecuting attorneys. The defendant may be convicted of a lesser offense, while the state uses the defendant's testimony to prosecute accomplices for serious crimes carrying heavy penalties.

SECTION 7

Criminal Procedures

Criminal law brings the force of the state, with all of its resources, to bear against the individual. Criminal procedures are designed to protect the constitutional rights of individuals and to prevent the arbitrary use of power on the part of the government.

The U.S. Constitution provides specific safeguards for those accused of crimes. The United States Supreme Court has ruled that most of these safeguards apply not only in federal but also in state courts by virtue of the due process clause of the Fourteenth Amendment. These safeguards include the following:

1. The Fourth Amendment protection from unreasonable searches and seizures.
2. The Fourth Amendment requirement that no

warrant for a search or an arrest be issued without probable cause.

3. The Fifth Amendment requirement that no one be deprived of "life, liberty, or property without due process of law."

4. The Fifth Amendment prohibition against **double jeopardy** (trying someone twice for the same criminal offense).[20]

5. The Fifth Amendment requirement that no person be required to be a witness against (incriminate) himself or herself.

6. The Sixth Amendment guarantees of a speedy trial, a trial by jury, a public trial, the right to confront witnesses, and the right to a lawyer at various stages in some proceedings.

7. The Eighth Amendment prohibitions against excessive bail and fines and cruel and unusual punishment.

THE EXCLUSIONARY RULE

Under what is known as the **exclusionary rule,** all evidence obtained in violation of the constitutional rights spelled out in the Fourth, Fifth, and Sixth Amendments normally is not admissible at trial. All evidence derived from the illegally obtained evidence is known as the "fruit of the poisonous tree," and such evidence normally must also be excluded from the trial proceedings. For example, if a confession is obtained after an illegal arrest, the arrest is the "poisonous tree," and the confession, if "tainted" by the arrest, is the "fruit."

The purpose of the exclusionary rule is to deter police from conducting warrantless searches and from other misconduct. The rule is sometimes criticized because it can lead to injustice. Many a defendant has "gotten off on a technicality" because law enforcement personnel failed to observe procedural requirements based on the above-mentioned constitutional amendments. Even though a defendant may be obviously guilty, if the evidence of that guilt is obtained improperly (without a valid search warrant, for example), it cannot be used against the defendant in court.

Over the last several decades, however, the United States Supreme Court diminished the scope of the exclusionary rule by creating some exceptions to its applicability. For example, in 1984 the Court held that if illegally obtained evidence would have been "inevitably" discovered and obtained by the police using lawful means, the evidence will be admissible at trial.[21] In another case decided in the same year, the Court held that a police officer who used a technically incorrect search warrant form to obtain evidence had acted in good faith and therefore the evidence was admissible. The Court thus created the "good faith" exception to the exclusionary rule.[22] Additionally, the courts can exercise a certain amount of discretion in determining whether evidence has been obtained improperly, thus somewhat balancing the scales.

THE MIRANDA RULE

In regard to criminal procedure, one of the questions many courts faced in the 1950s and 1960s was not whether suspects had constitutional rights—that was not in doubt—but how and when those rights could be exercised. Could the right to be silent (under the Fifth Amendment's prohibition against self-incrimination) be exercised during pretrial interrogation proceedings, or only during the trial? Were confessions obtained from suspects admissible in court if the suspects had not been advised of their right to remain silent and other constitutional rights?

To clarify these issues, the United States Supreme Court issued a landmark decision in 1966 in *Miranda v. Arizona*, presented on the next page. The procedural rights required by the Court in this case are familiar to virtually every American.

---

20. The prohibition against double jeopardy means that once a criminal defendant is found not guilty of a particular crime, the government may not reindict the person and retry him or her for the same crime. The prohibition against double jeopardy does not preclude a *civil* suit's being brought against the same person by the crime victim to recover damages. For example, a person found not guilty of assault and battery in a criminal case may be sued by the victim in a civil tort case for damages. Additionally, a state's prosecution of a crime will not prevent a separate federal prosecution of the same crime, and vice versa. For example, a defendant found not guilty of violating a state law can be tried in federal court for the same act, if the act is defined as a crime under federal law.

21. *Nix v. Williams,* 467 U.S. 431, 104 S.Ct. 2501, 81 L.Ed. 377 (1984).

22. *Massachusetts v. Sheppard,* 468 U.S. 981, 104 S.Ct. 3424, 82 L.Ed.2d 737 (1984).

CASE 7.3   Miranda v. Arizona

Supreme Court of the
United States, 1966.
384 U.S. 436,
86 S.Ct. 1602,
16 L.Ed.2d 694.

BACKGROUND AND FACTS   *On March 13, 1963, Ernesto Miranda was arrested at his home for the kidnapping and rape of an eighteen-year-old woman. Miranda was taken to a Phoenix, Arizona, police station and questioned by two officers. Two hours later, the officers emerged from the interrogation room with a written confession signed by Miranda. A paragraph at the top of the confession stated that the confession had been made voluntarily, without threats or promises of immunity, and "with full knowledge of my legal rights, understanding any statement I make may be used against me." Miranda was at no time advised that he had a right to remain silent and a right to have a lawyer present. The confession was admitted into evidence at the trial, and Miranda was convicted and sentenced to prison for twenty to thirty years. Miranda appealed the decision, claiming that he had not been informed of his constitutional rights. The Supreme Court of Arizona held that Miranda's constitutional rights had not been violated and affirmed his conviction. The* Miranda *case was subsequently consolidated with three other cases involving similar issues and reviewed by the United States Supreme Court.*

IN THE LANGUAGE
OF THE COURT

Mr. Chief Justice WARREN delivered the opinion of the Court.

The cases before us raise questions which go to the roots of our concepts of American criminal jurisprudence; the restraints society must observe consistent with the Federal Constitution in prosecuting individuals for crime. *   *   *

At the outset, if a person in custody is to be subjected to interrogation, he must first be informed in clear and unequivocal terms that he has the right to remain silent. *   *   *

The warning of the right to remain silent must be accompanied by the explanation that anything said can and will be used against the individual in court. This warning is needed in order to make him aware not only of the privilege, *but also of the consequences of forgoing it.* *   *   * [Emphasis added.]

The circumstances surrounding in-custody interrogation can operate very quickly to overbear the will of one merely made aware of his privilege by his interrogators. Therefore the right to have counsel present at the interrogation is indispensable to the protection of the Fifth Amendment privilege under the system we delineate today.

*   *   *   *

In order fully to apprise a person interrogated of the extent of his rights under this system then, it is necessary to warn him not only that he has the right to consult with an attorney, but also that if he is indigent [without funds] a lawyer will be appointed to represent him. *   *   * The warning of a right to counsel would be hollow if not couched in terms that would convey to the indigent—the person most often subjected to interrogation—the knowledge that he too has a right to have counsel present.

DECISION
AND REMEDY

The Supreme Court held that Miranda could not be convicted of the crime on the basis of his confession because his confession was inadmissible as evidence. For any statement made by a defendant to be admissible, the defendant must be informed of certain constitutional rights prior to police interrogation. If the accused waives his or her rights to remain silent and to have counsel present, the government must demonstrate that the waiver was made knowingly, voluntarily, and intelligently.

INTERNATIONAL
CONSIDERATIONS

The Right to Remain Silent in Great Britain   *The right to remain silent has long been a legal hallmark in Great Britain as well as in the United States. In 1994, however, the British Parliament passed an act that provides that a criminal defendant's silence may be interpreted as evidence of the defendant's guilt. British police officers are now required, when making arrests, to inform the suspects, "You do not have to say anything. But if you do not mention now something which you later use in your defense, the court* *may decide that your failure to mention it now strengthens the case against you. A record will be made of everything you say, and it may be given in evidence if you are brought to trial."*

Exceptions to the *Miranda* Rule. As part of a continuing attempt to balance the rights of accused persons against the rights of society, the Supreme Court has made a number of exceptions to the *Miranda* ruling. In 1984, for example, the Court recognized a "public safety" exception to the *Miranda* rule. The need to protect the public warranted the admissibility of statements made by the defendant (in this case, indicating where he placed the gun) as evidence in a trial, even when the defendant had not been informed of his *Miranda* rights.[23]

In 1986, the Court further held that a confession need not be excluded even though the police failed to inform a suspect in custody that his attorney had tried to reach him by telephone.[24] In an important 1991 decision, the Court stated that a suspect's conviction will not be automatically overturned if the suspect was coerced into making a confession. If the other evidence admitted at trial was strong enough to justify the conviction without the confession, then the fact that the confession was obtained illegally can be, in effect, ignored.[25] In yet another case, in 1994, the Supreme Court ruled that a suspect must unequivocally and assertively state his right to counsel in order to stop police questioning. Saying, "Maybe I should talk to a lawyer" during an interrogation after being taken into custody is not enough. The Court held that police officers are not required to decipher the suspect's intentions in such situations.[26]

Section 3501 of the Omnibus Crime Control Act of 1968. In 1999, the U.S. Court of Appeals for the Fourth Circuit stunned the nation's legal establishment by enforcing a long-forgotten provision, Section 3501, of the Omnibus Crime Control Act of 1968. Congress passed the act two years after the Supreme Court's *Miranda* decision in an attempt to reinstate a rule that had been in effect for 180 years before *Miranda*—namely, that statements by defendants can be used against them as long as they are voluntarily made.

The Justice Department immediately disavowed Section 3501 as unconstitutional and continues to hold this position. The Fourth Circuit, however, could see no reason not to enforce the provision. According to that court, Congress has the "unquestioned power to establish the rules of procedure and evidence in federal courts," and there is no explicit constitutional requirement that defendants be told of their rights to counsel and to remain silent.[27] Not surprisingly, the Fourth Circuit's decision has led to substantial controversy, which will likely continue until the Supreme Court (which has agreed to review the case) issues its decision on the matter.

Videotaped Interrogations. There are no guarantees that *Miranda* will survive indefinitely—particularly in view of the numerous exceptions that are made to the rule and the Fourth Circuit's decision on the issue. Additionally, law enforcement personnel are increasingly using videotapes to record interrogations. According to some scholars, the videotaping of *all* custodial interrogations would satisfy the Fifth Amendment's prohibition against coercion and in the process render the *Miranda* warnings unnecessary.

CRIMINAL PROCESS

As mentioned earlier in this chapter, a criminal prosecution differs significantly from a civil case in several respects. These differences reflect the desire to safeguard the rights of the individual against the state. Exhibit 7–3 page 154 summarizes the major steps in processing a criminal case. We discuss below in more detail three phases of the criminal process—arrest, indictment or information, and trial.

Arrest. Before a warrant for arrest can be issued, there must be probable cause for believing that the individual in question has committed a crime. As discussed in

23. *New York v. Quarles*, 467 U.S. 649, 104 S.Ct. 2626, 81 L.Ed.2d 550 (1984).

24. *Moran v. Burbine*, 475 U.S. 412, 106 S.Ct. 1135, 89 L.Ed.2d 410 (1986).

25. *Arizona v. Fulminante*, 499 U.S. 279, 111 S.Ct. 1246, 113 L.Ed.2d 302 (1991).

26. *Davis v. United States*, 512 U.S. 452, 114 S.Ct. 2350, 129 L.Ed.2d 362 (1994).

27. *United States v. Dickerson*, 97 F.3d 4750 (4th Cir. 1999).

EXHIBIT 7–3   MAJOR STEPS IN PROCESSING A CRIMINAL CASE

BOOKING
After arrest, at the police station, the suspect is searched, photographed, fingerprinted, and allowed at least one telephone call. After the booking, charges are reviewed, and if they are not dropped, a complaint is filed and a judge or magistrate examines the case for probable cause.

INITIAL APPEARANCE
The suspect appears before the judge, who informs the suspect of the charges and of his or her rights. If the suspect requests a lawyer, one is appointed. The judge sets bail (conditions under which a suspect can obtain release pending disposition of the case).

PRELIMINARY HEARING
In a proceeding in which both sides are represented by counsel, the judge determines whether there is probable cause to believe that the suspect committed the crime, based on the evidence.

GRAND JURY REVIEW
The federal government and about half of the states require grand jury indictments for at least some felonies. In those states, a grand jury determines whether the evidence justifies a trial on the charges sought by the prosecutor.

PROSECUTORIAL REVIEW
In jurisdictions that do not require grand jury indictments, a prosecutor issues an information. An information is similar to an indictment: both are charging instruments that replace the complaint.

ARRAIGNMENT
The suspect is brought before the trial court, informed of the charges, and asked to enter a plea.

PLEA BARGAIN
A plea bargain is a prosecutor's promise of concessions (or promise to seek concessions) in return for the defendant's guilty plea. Concessions include a reduced charge and/or a lesser sentence.

GUILTY PLEA
In more jurisdictions, most cases that reach the arraignment stage do not go to trial but are resolved by a guilty plea, often as the result of a plea bargain. The judge sets the case for sentencing.

TRIAL
If the defendant refuses to plead guilty, he or she proceeds to either a jury trial (in most instances) or a bench trial.

Chapter 5, *probable cause* can be defined as a substantial likelihood that the person has committed or is about to commit a crime. Note that probable cause involves a likelihood, not just a possibility. Arrests may sometimes be made without a warrant if there is no time to get one, but the action of the arresting officer is still judged by the standard of probable cause.

Indictment or Information. Individuals must be formally charged with having committed specific crimes before they can be brought to trial. If issued by a grand jury, such a charge is called an **indictment**.[28] A **grand jury** does not determine the guilt or innocence of an accused party; rather, its function is to determine, after hearing the state's evidence, whether a reasonable basis (probable cause) exists for supposing that a crime has been committed and whether a trial ought to be held.

Usually, grand juries are called in cases involving serious crimes, such as murder. For lesser crimes, an individual may be formally charged with a crime by an **information,** or criminal complaint. An information will be issued by a magistrate (a public official vested with judicial authority) if the magistrate determines that there is sufficient evidence to justify bringing the individual to trial.

Trial. At a criminal trial, the accused person does not have to prove anything; the entire burden of proof is on the prosecutor (the state). As discussed at the beginning of this chapter, the burden of proof in a criminal case is higher than that in a civil case. The prosecution must show that, based on all the evidence, the defendant's guilt is established *beyond a reasonable doubt*. If there is any reasonable doubt that a criminal defendant did not commit the crime with which he or she has been charged, then the verdict must be "not guilty." Note that giving a verdict of "not guilty" is not the same as stating that the defendant is innocent; it merely means that not enough evidence

---

28. Pronounced in-*dyte*-ment.

was properly presented to the court to prove guilt beyond all reasonable doubt.

Courts have complex rules about what types of evidence may be presented and how the evidence may be brought out in criminal cases, especially in jury trials. These rules are designed to ensure that evidence presented at trials is relevant, reliable, and not prejudicial against the defendant.

FEDERAL SENTENCING GUIDELINES

Traditionally, persons who had committed the same crime might have received very different sentences, depending on the judge hearing the case, the jurisdiction in which it was heard, and many other factors. In 1984, however, Congress passed the Sentencing Reform Act. This act created the U.S. Sentencing Commission, which was charged with the task of standardizing sentences for federal crimes. The commission's guidelines, which became effective in 1987, established a range of possible penalties for each federal crime. Judges must select a sentence from within this range when sentencing criminal defendants, taking into consideration the defendant's criminal record, the seriousness of the offense, and other factors specified in the guidelines.

The commission also created specific guidelines for the punishment of crimes committed by corporate employees (white-collar crimes). These guidelines, which went into effect in 1991, established stiffer penalties for mail and wire fraud, commercial bribery and kickbacks, and money laundering, as well as for criminal violations of securities laws (see Chapter 29), employment laws (see Chapters 21 and 22), and antitrust laws (see Chapters 27 and 28). The guidelines allow judges to take into consideration a number of factors when selecting from the range of possible penalties for a specified crime. These factors include the defendant company's history of past violations, the extent of management's cooperation with federal investigators, and the extent to which the firm has undertaken specific programs and procedures to prevent criminal activities by its employees.

TERMS AND CONCEPTS TO REVIEW

actus reus 139	beyond a reasonable doubt 136	computer crime 145
arson 142	burglary 142	consent 148

QUESTIONS AND CASE PROBLEMS

7–1. TYPES OF CRIMES. The following situations are similar (in all of them, Juanita's television set is stolen), yet three different crimes are described. Identify the three crimes, noting the differences among them.

(a) While passing Juanita's house one night, Sarah sees a portable television set left unattended on Juanita's lawn. Sarah takes the television set, carries it home, and tells everyone she owns it.

(b) While passing Juanita's house one night, Sarah sees Juanita outside with a portable television set. Holding Juanita at gunpoint, Sarah forces her to give up the set. Then Sarah runs away with it.

(c) While passing Juanita's house one night, Sarah sees a portable television set in a window. Sarah breaks the front-door lock, enters, and leaves with the set.

7–2. TYPES OF CRIMES. Which, if any, of the following crimes necessarily involves illegal activity on the part of more than one person?

(a) Bribery.
(b) Forgery.
(c) Embezzlement.
(d) Larceny.
(e) Receiving stolen property.

7–3. DOUBLE JEOPARDY. Armington, while robbing a drugstore, shot and seriously injured a drugstore clerk, Jennings. Armington was subsequently convicted in a criminal trial of armed robbery and assault and battery. Jennings later brought a civil tort suit against Armington for damages. Armington contended that he could not be tried again for the same crime, as that would constitute double jeopardy, which is prohibited by the Fifth Amendment to the Constitution. Is Armington correct? Explain.

7–4. RECEIVING STOLEN PROPERTY. Rafael stops Laura on a busy street and offers to sell her an expensive wristwatch for a fraction of its value. After some questioning by Laura, Rafael admits that the watch is stolen property, although he says he was not the thief. Laura pays for and receives the wristwatch. Has Laura committed any crime? Has Rafael? Explain.

7–5. ENTRAPMENT. Suppose that in the hypothetical situation discussed in Problem 8–4, Rafael is an undercover police officer. As soon as Laura pays for and receives the wristwatch, Rafael arrests her for the crime of receiving stolen property. At trial, Laura contends that she was a victim of entrapment. What should be the result of the trial? Discuss fully.

7–6. EMBEZZLEMENT. Faulkner, a truck driver, was hauling a load of refrigerators from San Diego to New York for the trucking company that employed him. He departed from his assigned route and stopped in Las Vegas, where he attempted to display and sell some of the refrigerators to a firm. Although the refrigerators never left the truck, to display them he had to break the truck's seals, enter the cargo department, and open two refrigerator cartons. The store owner refused to purchase the appliances, and when Faulkner left the store, he was arrested. He was later convicted under federal law for the embezzlement of an interstate shipment. Faulkner appealed, claiming that the charge of embezzlement should not apply because the property had not been physically removed from the owner's possession. Will the appellate court agree with Faulkner? Explain. [*United States v. Faulkner*, 638 F.2d 129 (9th Cir. 1981)]

7–7. CRIMINAL LIABILITY. In January 1988, David Ludvigson was hired as chief executive officer of Leopard Enterprises, a group of companies that owned funeral homes and cemeteries in Iowa and sold "pre-need" funeral contracts. Under Iowa law, 80 percent of the funds obtained under such a contract must be set aside in trust until the death of the person for whose benefit the funds were paid. Shortly after Ludvigson was hired, the firm began having financial difficulties. Ludvigson used money from the funeral contracts to pay operating expenses until the company went bankrupt and was placed in receivership. Ludvigson was charged and found guilty on five counts of second degree theft stemming from the misappropriation of these funds. He appealed, alleging, among other things, that he was not guilty of any crime, because he had not intended to permanently deprive any of the clients of their trust funds. Furthermore, because none of the victims whose trust funds were used to cover operating expenses was denied services, no injury was done. Will the court agree with Ludvigson? Explain. [*State v. Ludvigson*, 482 N.W.2d 419 (Ia. 1992)]

7–8. CRIMINAL LIABILITY. On the grounds of a school, Gavin T., a fifteen-year-old student, was eating lunch. He threw a half-eaten apple toward the outside wall of a classroom some distance away. The apple sailed through a slowly closing door and struck a teacher who was in the room. The teacher was knocked to the floor and lost consciousness for a few minutes. Gavin was charged, in a California state court, with assault by "any means of force likely to produce great bodily injury." The court found that he did not intend to hit the teacher but only intended to see the apple splatter against the outside wall. To send a "message" to his classmates that his actions were wrong, however, the court convicted him of the charge. Should Gavin's conviction be reversed on appeal? Why or why not? [*In re Gavin T.*, 66 Cal.App.4th 238, 77 Cal.Rptr.2d 701 (1998)]

7–9. FIFTH AMENDMENT. The federal government was investigating a corporation and its employees. The alleged criminal wrongdoing, which included the falsification of corporate books and records, occurred between 1993 and 1996 in one division of the corporation. In 1999, the corporation pled guilty and agreed to cooperate in an investigation of the individuals who might have been involved in the improper corporate activities. "Doe I," "Doe II," and "Doe III" were officers of the corporation during the period in which the illegal activities occurred and worked in the division where the wrongdoing took place. They were no longer working for the corporation, however, when, as part of the subsequent investigation, the government asked them to provide specific corporate documents in their possession. All three asserted the Fifth Amendment privilege against self-incrimination. The government asked a federal district court to order the three to produce the records. Corporate employees can be compelled to produce corporate records in a criminal proceeding, because they hold the records as representatives of the corporation, to which the Fifth Amendment privilege against self-incrimination does not apply. Should *former employees* also be compelled to produce corporate records in their possession? Why or why not? [*In re Three Grand Jury Subpoenas* Duces Tecum *Dated January 29, 1999*, 191 F.3d 173 (2d Cir. 1999)]

7–10. IN YOUR COURT

Britt was convicted of second degree homicide for the shooting death of his neighbor, Cavell. The victim was killed by a .44 caliber revolver that was part of a trap set by Britt to prevent forcible entry into his home from the back door. The booby trap was set to discharge if the door was opened a distance of two to four inches. The relevant Louisiana law reads as follows: "A homicide is justifiable . . . when committed by a person lawfully inside a dwelling against a person who is attempting to make an unlawful entry into the dwelling or who has made an unlawful entry into the dwelling and the person committing the homicide reasonably believes that the use of deadly force is necessary to prevent the entry or to compel the intruder to leave the premises. The homicide shall be justifiable even though the person committing the homicide does not retreat from the encounter." Britt argued on appeal that the shooting of Cavell was justified because, had Britt been present, he would have been authorized to use deadly force and to use a mechanical contrivance. Assume that you are a judge on the Louisiana appellate court reviewing this case and answer the following questions:

(a) Applying the statutory language cited above to the facts of this case, what would your decision be on the issue raised by Britt on appeal? Why?

(b) Compare this case to Case 7.2 (*Katco v. Briney*). How are the two cases similar? How do they differ? Would the court's reasoning in the *Katco* case be relevant to your decision in the *Britt* case? Why or why not?

LAW ON THE WEB

For updated links to resources available on the Web, as well as a variety of other materials, visit this text's Web site at http://wleb.westbuslaw.com.

The Bureau of Justice Statistics in the U.S. Department of Justice offers an impressive collection of statistics on crime at the following Web site:

http://www.ojp.usdoj.gov/bjs

For summaries of famous criminal cases and documents relating to these trials, go to Court TV's Web site at

http://www.courttv.com/index.html

If you would like to learn more about criminal procedures, the following site offers an "Anatomy of a Murder: A Trip through Our Nation's Legal Justice System":

http://tqd.advanced.org/2760/home.htm

At the above site, you can also find a glossary of terms used in crminal law, view actual forms that are filled out during the course of an arrest, and learn about some controversial issues in criminal law.

Many state criminal codes are now online. To find your state's code, go to

http://www.findlaw.com

and select "State" under the link to "Laws: Cases and Codes."

You can learn about some of the constitutional questions raised by various criminal laws and procedures by going to the Web site of the American Civil Liberties Union at

http://www.aclu.org

The text of the U.S. Sentencing Guidelines Manual is online at

http://www.ussc.gov

LEGAL RESEARCH EXERCISES ON THE WEB

Go to http://wleb.westbuslaw.com, the Web site that accompanies this text. Select "Internet Applications," and then click on "Chapter 7." There you will find the following Internet research exercise that you can perform to learn more about criminal procedures:

Activity 7–1: Revisiting *Miranda*

CHAPTER 8

International and Comparative Law

INTERNATIONAL BUSINESS TRANSACTIONS are not unique to the modern world. Indeed, since ancient times independent peoples and nations have traded their goods and wares with one another. What is new in our day is the dramatic growth in world trade and the emergence of a global business community. Today, nearly every major business considers the potential of international markets for its products or services. It is no longer uncommon for a U.S. corporation to have investments or manufacturing plants in a foreign country or for a foreign corporation to have operations in the United States. Because the exchange of goods, services, and ideas on a worldwide level is now routine, students of business law should be familiar with the laws pertaining to international business transactions.

Laws affecting the international legal environment of business include both international law and national law. **International law** can be defined as a body of law—formed as a result of international customs, treaties, and organizations—that governs relations among or between nations. **National law** is the law of a particular nation, such as the United States, Japan, Germany, or Brazil. In this chapter, we examine how both international law and national law frame business operations in the international context.

SECTION 1

International Law

The major difference between international law and national law is the fact that government authorities can enforce national law. What government, however, can enforce international law? By definition, a *nation* is a sovereign entity—which means that there is no higher authority to which that nation must submit. If a nation violates an international law, the most that other countries or international organizations can do (when persuasive tactics fail) is resort to coercive actions—from severance of diplomatic relations and boycotts to, as a last resort, war—against the violating nation.

In essence, international law is the result of centuries-old attempts to reconcile the traditional need of each country to be the final authority over its own affairs with the desire of nations to benefit economically from trade and harmonious relations with one another. Sovereign nations can, and do, voluntarily agree to be governed in certain respects by international law for the purpose of facilitating international trade and commerce, as well as civilized discourse. As a result, a body of international law has evolved. In this section, we examine the primary sources and characteristics of that body of law, as well as some important legal principles and doctrines that have been developed over time to facilitate dealings among nations.

SOURCES OF INTERNATIONAL LAW

Basically, there are three sources of international law: international customs, treaties and international agreements, and international organizations and conferences. We look at each of these sources here.

International Customs. One important source of international law consists of the international customs that have evolved among nations in their relations with one another. In Article 38(1) of the Statute of the International Court of Justice, an international custom is referred to as "evidence of a general practice accepted as law." The legal principles and doctrines that you will read about shortly are rooted in international customs and traditions that evolved over time in the international arena.

Treaties and International Agreements. Treaties and other explicit agreements between or among foreign nations provide another important source of international law. A **treaty** is an agreement or contract between two or more nations that must be authorized and ratified by the supreme power of each nation. Under Article II, Section 2, of the U.S. Constitution, the president has the power "by and with the Advice and Consent of the Senate, to make Treaties, provided two-thirds of the Senators present concur."

A *bilateral* agreement, as the term implies, occurs when two nations form an agreement that will govern their commercial exchanges or other relations with one another. *Multilateral* agreements are those formed by several nations. For example, regional trade associations such as the European Union (EU) and the trading unit established by the North American Free Trade Agreement (NAFTA), both of which are discussed later in this chapter, are the result of multilateral trade agreements. Other regional trade associations that have been created through multilateral agreements include the Association of Southeast Asian Nations (ASEAN) and the Andean Common Market (ANCOM).

International Organizations and Conferences. International organizations and conferences further contribute to international law. In international law,

the term **international organization** generally refers to an organization composed mainly of nations and usually established by treaty.

The United States is a member of more than one hundred multilateral and bilateral organizations, including at least twenty through the United Nations (see Exhibit 8–1). These organizations adopt resolutions, declarations, and other types of standards that often require a particular behavior of nations. The General Assembly of the United Nations, for example, has adopted numerous nonbinding resolutions and declarations that embody principles of international law. Disputes with respect to these resolutions and declarations may be brought before the International Court of Justice. That court, however, normally has authority to settle legal disputes only when nations voluntarily submit to its jurisdiction.

The United Nations Commission on International Trade Law has made considerable progress in establishing uniformity in international law as it relates to trade and commerce. One of the commission's most significant creations to date is the 1980 Convention on Contracts for the International Sale of Goods (CISG). The CISG is similar to Article 2 of the Uniform Commercial Code in that it is designed to settle disputes between parties to sales contracts. It spells out the duties of international buyers and sellers that will apply if the parties have not agreed otherwise in their contracts. The CISG only governs sales contracts between trading partners in nations that have ratified the CISG, however.

LEGAL PRINCIPLES AND DOCTRINES

Over time, a number of legal principles and doctrines have evolved and have been employed—to a greater or lesser extent—by the courts of various nations to resolve or reduce conflicts that involve a foreign element. The three important legal principles discussed below are based primarily on courtesy and respect and are applied in the interests of maintaining harmonious relations among nations.

The Principle of Comity. Under what is known as the principle of **comity,** one nation will defer and give effect to the laws and judicial decrees of another country, as long as those laws and judicial decrees are consistent with the law and public policy of the accommodating nation. For example, assume that a Swedish seller and an American buyer have formed a contract, which the buyer breaches. The seller

EXHIBIT 8–1   MULTILATERAL INTERNATIONAL ORGANIZATIONS IN WHICH THE UNITED STATES PARTICIPATES

NAME	PURPOSE
Customs Cooperation Council	Established in 1950. Supervises the application and interpretation of an international code classifying goods and customs tariffs.
International Bank for Reconstruction and Development	Popularly known as the World Bank; a specialized agency of the United Nations since 1947. Promotes growth, trade, and balance of trade by facilitating and providing technical assistance, particularly in agriculture, energy, transportation, and telecommunications.
International Center for the Settlement of Investment Disputes	Established in 1966. Conciliates and arbitrates disputes between private investors and governments of other countries.
International Civil Aviation Organization	Established in 1947 and became a specialized agency of the United Nations seven months later. Develops international civil aviation by issuing rules and policies for safe and efficient airports and air navigation.
International Court of Justice (World Court)	Established in 1922 and became one of the principal organs of the United Nations in 1945. Jurisdiction comprises all cases that are referred to it. Decides disputes in accord with the rules of international law.
International Maritime Organization	Established in 1948. Promotes cooperation in the areas of government regulation, practices and technical matters of all kinds affecting shipping in international trade, the adoption of standards of maritime safety and efficiency, and the abolition of discrimination and unnecessary restrictions.
International Monetary Fund (IMF)	Created in 1944 at the United Nations Monetary and Financial Conference. Promotes economic stability by aiding the growth of international trade and the stability of currency exchange rates, as well as by providing for a system of international monetary assistance.
International Telecommunications Satellite Organization	Established in 1964. Operates an international public communications satellite system on a commercial, nondiscriminatory basis.
Permanent Court of Arbitration	Established in 1899 to facilitate the settlement of international disputes. The court has jurisdiction over all cases that it is requested to arbitrate.
United Nations (UN)	Established in 1945 to maintain international peace and security. Promotes international cooperation.
World Intellectual Property Organization	Established in 1967 and became a specialized agency of the United Nations in 1974. Promotes protection of intellectual property throughout the world.
World Trade Organization (WTO)	Established in 1994 during the final round of negotiations of the General Agreement on Tariffs and Trade (GATT). The GATT was created in 1947 and was the first global commercial agreement in history. It became the principal instrument for regulating international trade and limiting tariffs and other barriers to world trade on particular commodities and other items. GATT ceased to exist in 1995, when the WTO came into existence to regulate worldwide trade.

sues the buyer in a Swedish court, which awards damages. The buyer's assets, however, are in the United States and cannot be reached unless the judgment is enforced by a U.S. court of law. In such a situation, if a U.S. court determined that the procedures and laws applied in the Swedish court were consistent with U.S. national law and policy, the U.S. court would likely defer to, and enforce, the foreign court's judgment.

The Act of State Doctrine. The **act of state doctrine** is a judicially created doctrine that provides that the judicial branch of one country will not examine the validity of public acts committed by a recognized foreign government within its own territory. This doctrine is premised on the theory that the judicial branch should not "pass upon the validity of foreign acts when to do so would vex the harmony of our international relations with that foreign nation."[1]

The act of state doctrine can have important consequences for individuals and firms doing business with, and investing in, other countries. For example, this doctrine is frequently employed in cases involving **expropriation,** which occurs when a government seizes a privately owned business or privately owned goods for a proper public purpose and awards just compensation. When a government seizes private property for an illegal purpose and without just compensation, the taking is referred to as a **confiscation.** The line between these two forms of taking is sometimes blurred because of differing interpretations of what is illegal and what constitutes just compensation. To illustrate: Tim Flaherty, an American businessperson, owns a mine in Brazil. The government of Brazil seizes the mine for public use and claims that the profits Tim has already realized from the mine constitute just compensation. Tim disagrees, but the act of state doctrine may prevent Tim's recovery in a U.S. court of law.

When applicable, both the act of state doctrine and the doctrine of *sovereign immunity*, which we discuss next, tend to shield foreign nations from the jurisdiction of U.S. courts. What this means is that, generally, firms or individuals who own property overseas have little legal protection against government actions in the countries in which they operate.

The Doctrine of Sovereign Immunity. When certain conditions are satisfied, the doctrine of **sovereign immunity** exempts foreign nations from the jurisdiction of the U.S. courts. In 1976, Congress codified this rule in the Foreign Sovereign Immunities Act (FSIA).[2] The FSIA also modified previous applications of the doctrine in certain respects by expanding the rights of plaintiff creditors against foreign nations.

The FSIA exclusively governs the circumstances in which an action may be brought in the United States against a foreign nation. Section 1605 of the FSIA sets forth the major exceptions to the jurisdictional immu-

nity of a foreign state. A foreign state is not immune from the jurisdiction of the courts of the United States when the state has "waived its immunity either explicitly or by implication" or when the state has engaged in actions that are taken "in connection with a commercial activity carried on in the United States by the foreign state" or that have "a direct effect in the United States."

Issues frequently arise as to whether particular entities fall within the category of foreign state. Under Section 1603 of the FSIA, a foreign state is defined to include both a political subdivision of a foreign state and an instrumentality of a foreign state (an agency or entity acting for the state). The question of what is a commercial activity has also been the subject of dispute, because the particulars of what constitutes a commercial activity are not defined in the act. Rather, it is left up to the courts to decide whether a particular activity is governmental or commercial in nature.

SECTION 2

Doing Business Internationally

A U.S. domestic firm can engage in international business transactions in a number of ways. Here, we look at the ways in which businesspersons typically extend their business operations into the international arena, laws regulating international business activities, and dispute settlement in the international context.

TYPES OF INTERNATIONAL BUSINESS OPERATIONS

Most U.S. companies make the initial foray into international business through exporting. There are several other alternatives, however, including those discussed here.

Exporting. The simplest way of entering into international business operations is to seek out foreign markets for domestically produced products. In other words, U.S. firms can **export** their goods and services to foreign markets. Exporting can take two forms: direct exporting and indirect exporting. In *direct exporting*, a U.S. company signs a sales contract with a foreign purchaser that provides for the conditions of shipment and payment for the goods. If business develops sufficiently

---

1. *Libra Bank Ltd. v. Banco Nacional de Costa Rica, S.A.,* 570 F.Supp. 870 (S.D.N.Y. 1983).
2. 28 U.S.C. Sections 1602–1611.

in foreign countries, a U.S. company may, through the appointment of a foreign agent or a foreign distributor, develop a specialized marketing organization in the foreign market. This is called *indirect exporting*.

When a U.S. firm desires a limited involvement in an international market, it will typically establish an agency relationship with a foreign firm. In an agency relationship, one person (the agent) agrees to act on behalf of, or instead of, another (the principal)—see Chapter 20. The foreign agent is thereby empowered to enter into contracts in the agent's country on behalf of the U.S. principal.

When a substantial market exists in a foreign country, a U.S. firm may wish to appoint a distributor located in that country. The U.S. firm and the distributor enter into a **distribution agreement,** which is a contract between the seller and the distributor setting out the terms and conditions of the distributorship—for example, price, currency of payment, guarantee of supply availability, and method of payment. The terms and conditions primarily involve contract law. Disputes concerning distribution agreements may involve jurisdictional or other issues, however.

Manufacturing Abroad. An alternative to direct or indirect exporting is the establishment of foreign manufacturing facilities. Typically, U.S. firms want to establish manufacturing plants abroad if they believe that by doing so they will reduce costs—particularly for labor, shipping, and raw materials—and thereby be able to compete more effectively in foreign markets. Apple Computer, IBM, General Motors, and Ford are some of the many U.S. companies that have established manufacturing facilities abroad. Foreign firms have done the same in the United States. Sony, Nissan, and other Japanese manufacturers have established U.S. plants to avoid import duties that the U.S. Congress may impose on Japanese products entering this country.

An American firm can conduct manufacturing operations in other countries in several ways. They include licensing and franchising, as well as investing in a wholly owned subsidiary or a joint venture.

Licensing. A U.S. firm can obtain business from abroad by licensing a foreign manufacturing company to use its copyrighted, patented, or trademarked intellectual property or trade secrets. Like any other licensing agreement (see Chapter 15), a licensing agreement with a foreign-based firm calls for a payment of royalties on some basis—such as so many cents per unit produced or a certain percentage of profits from units sold in a particular geographical territory. For example, the Coca-Cola Bottling Company licenses firms worldwide to use (and keep confidential) its secret formula for the syrup used in that soft drink, in return for a percentage of the income gained from the sale of Coca-Cola by those firms.

The licensing of intellectual property rights benefits all parties to the transaction: the firm that receives the license can take advantage of an established reputation for quality, and the firm that grants the license receives income from the foreign sales of its products, as well as establishing a global reputation. Also, once a firm's trademark is known worldwide, the demand for other products manufactured or sold by that firm may increase—obviously an important consideration.

Franchising. Franchising is a well-known form of licensing. As explained in Chapter 17, a franchise can be defined as an arrangement in which the owner of a trademark, trade name, or copyright (the franchisor) licenses another (the franchisee) to use the trademark, trade name, or copyright, under certain conditions or limitations, in the selling of goods or services. In return, the franchisee pays a fee, which is usually based on a percentage of gross or net sales. Examples of international franchises include McDonald's, Holiday Inn, Avis, and Hertz.

Investing in a Wholly Owned Subsidiary or a Joint Venture. One way to expand into a foreign market is to establish a wholly owned subsidiary firm in a foreign country. The European subsidiary would likely take the form of a *société anonyme* (S.A.), which is similar to a U.S. corporation. In German-speaking nations, it would be called an *Aktiengesellschaft* (A.G.). When a wholly owned subsidiary is established, the parent company, which remains in the United States, retains complete ownership of all the facilities in the foreign country, as well as total authority and control over all phases of the operation.

The expansion of a U.S. firm into international markets can also take the form of a joint venture. In a joint venture, the U.S. company owns only part of the operation; the rest is owned either by local owners in the foreign country or by another foreign entity. In a joint venture, responsibilities, as well as profits and liabilities, are shared by all of the firms involved in the venture. (See Chapter 17 for a more detailed discussion of joint ventures.)

THE REGULATION OF INTERNATIONAL BUSINESS ACTIVITIES

Doing business abroad can affect the economies, foreign policy, domestic politics, and other national interests of the countries involved. For this reason, nations impose laws to restrict or facilitate international business. Controls may also be imposed by international agreements.

Investing. Investing in foreign nations involves a risk that the foreign government may expropriate the investment property. As mentioned earlier in this chapter, expropriation occurs when property is taken and the owner is paid just compensation for what is taken. This does not violate generally observed principles of international law. Such principles are normally violated, however, when property is confiscated by a government without compensation (or without adequate compensation).

Few remedies are available for confiscation of property by a foreign government. Claims are often resolved by lump-sum settlements after negotiations between the United States and the taking nation. For example, investors whose claims arose out of confiscations following the Russian Revolution in 1917 were offered a lump-sum settlement by the Union of Soviet Socialist Republics in 1974. Still outstanding are $2 billion in claims against Cuba for confiscations that occurred in 1959 and 1960.

To counter the deterrent effect that the possibility of confiscation may have on potential investors, many countries guarantee compensation to foreign investors if property is taken. A guarantee can be in the form of national constitutional or statutory laws or provisions in international treaties. As further protection for foreign investments, some countries provide insurance for their citizens' investments abroad.

Export Control. The U.S. Constitution provides in Article I, Section 9, that "No Tax or Duty shall be laid on Articles exported from any State." Thus, Congress cannot impose any export taxes. Congress can, however, use a variety of other devices to control exports. Congress may set export quotas on various items, such as grain being sold abroad. Under the Export Administration Act of 1979,[3] restrictions can

be imposed on the flow of technologically advanced products and technical data. A controversial control in recent years has been the U.S. Department of Commerce's attempt to restrict the export of encryption software (discussed in Chapter 15).

Devices to stimulate exports and thereby aid domestic businesses include export incentives and subsidies. The Revenue Act of 1971, for example, gave tax benefits to firms marketing their products overseas through certain foreign sales corporations, exempting income produced by the exports.[4] Under the Export Trading Company Act of 1982,[5] U.S. banks are encouraged to invest in export trading companies. An export trading company consists of exporting firms joined together to export a line of goods. The Export-Import Bank provides financial assistance, consisting primarily of credit guaranties given to commercial banks that in turn loan funds to U.S. exporting companies.

Import Control. All nations have restrictions on imports, and the United States is no exception. Restrictions include strict prohibitions, quotas, and tariffs. Under the Trading with the Enemy Act of 1917,[6] for example, no goods may be imported from nations that have been designated enemies of the United States. Other laws prohibit the importation of illegal drugs, books that urge insurrection against the United States, and agricultural products that pose dangers to domestic crops or animals.

Quotas are limits on the amounts of goods that can be imported. At one time, the United States had legal quotas on the numbers of automobiles that could be imported from Japan. Currently, Japan "voluntarily" restricts the numbers of automobiles exported to the United States. **Tariffs** are taxes on imports. A tariff is usually a percentage of the value of the import, but it can be a flat rate per unit (such as per barrel of oil). Tariffs raise the prices of goods, causing some consumers to purchase less expensive, domestically manufactured goods.

The United States has specific laws directed at what it sees as unfair international trade practices. **Dumping,** for example, is the sale of imported goods at "less than fair value." *Fair value* is usually determined by the price of those goods in the exporting

---

3. 50 U.S.C. App. Sections 2401–2420.

4. 26 U.S.C. Sections 991–994.
5. 15 U.S.C. Sections 4001, 4003.
6. 12 U.S.C. Section 95a.

country. Dumping is designed to undersell U.S. businesses and obtain a larger share of the U.S. market. To prevent this, an extra tariff—known as an *antidumping duty*—may be assessed on the imports.

The procedure for imposing antidumping duties involves two U.S. government agencies: the International Trade Commission (ITC) and the International Trade Administration (ITA). The ITC is an independent agency that makes recommendations to the president concerning temporary import restrictions. The ITC assesses the effects of dumping on domestic businesses.

The ITA is part of the Department of Commerce and decides whether imports were sold at less than fair value. The ITA determination establishes the amount of antidumping duties, which are set to equal the difference between the price charged in the United States and the price charged in the exporting country. A duty may be retroactive to cover past dumping.

In the following case, the United States Supreme Court considered a challenge to tariff classifications imposed on clothing assembled from U.S. components and then "permapressed" in Mexico.

CASE 8.1   # United States v. Haggar Apparel Co.

Supreme Court of the
United States, 1999.
526 U.S. 380,
119 S.Ct. 1392,
143 L.Ed.2d 480.
http://www.supct.law.
cornell.edu/supct[a]

COMPANY PROFILE   *Haggar Apparel Company (**http://www.haggar.com**) is a leading maker of men's clothing. Haggar's products, including its "wrinkle-free" pants, are sold in more than seven thousand stores in the United States. These stores include seventy Haggar outlet stores. Haggar also makes lower-priced brands, private-label clothing, and women's wear, through Jerell, Inc., its Selena and Stonebridge brands, and Haggar Canada. Haggar's products are sold all over the world, with wholly owned subsidiaries in Canada, Great Britain, and Japan. Haggar has plants in the United States, the Dominican Republic, and Mexico.*

BACKGROUND AND FACTS   *Haggar Apparel Company buys fabric in the United States, has it treated with a chemical resin, has it cut, and then ships it to Mexico with thread, buttons, and zippers to make pants. The trousers are then sewn, permapressed, and shipped back to the United States. Permapressing is designed to maintain a garment's crease in the desired place and to avoid other creases or wrinkles that detract from its appearance. Permapressing is a baking process that activates the chemical resin to impart the permapress quality. To obtain that quality, extra steps would be needed if the baking were delayed until the garments were shipped back to the United States. Under a federal agency regulation, goods with U.S. components that are assembled abroad and reshipped to the United States are exempt from a duty that is charged against other incoming goods. The U.S. Customs Service levied a duty on Haggar's pants, however, under a regulation that deems all permapressing operations to be an additional step in manufacture, not part of or incidental to the assembly process. Haggar filed a suit in the U.S. Court of International Trade against the federal government, seeking a refund of the duty. Haggar argued that its permapressing was part of the assembly process. The court ruled in Haggar's favor, and the U.S. Court of Appeals for the Federal Circuit affirmed this ruling. The government appealed to the United States Supreme Court.*

IN THE LANGUAGE
OF THE COURT

Justice *KENNEDY* delivered the opinion of the Court.
　　　*　　*　　*　　*

　　*　　*　　* [Haggar] says the regulation binds Customs Service employees when they classify imported merchandise under the tariff schedules but does not bind the importers themselves. The statutory scheme does not support this limited view of the force

---

a. In the right column, in the "Arrayed by party name" section, in the "1999" row, click on "2nd party." Scroll down the list of cases to "Haggar Apparel Co., United States v." and click on it to access a syllabus of the case. On that page, click on the appropriate link to read the full opinion.

and effect of the regulation. The Customs Service (which is within the Treasury Department) is charged [by statute] with the classification of imported goods under the proper provision of the tariff schedules in the first instance. * * * In addition, the Secretary [of the Treasury] is directed by statute to "establish and promulgate such rules and regulations not inconsistent with the law * * * as may be necessary to secure a just, impartial and uniform appraisement of imported merchandise and the classification and assessment of duties thereon at the various ports of entry." The Secretary, in turn, has delegated to the Commissioner of Customs the authority to issue generally applicable regulations, subject to the Secretary's approval.

Respondent [Haggar] relies on the specific direction to the Secretary to make rules of classification for "the various ports of entry" to argue that the statute authorizes promulgation of regulations that do nothing more than ensure that customs officers in field offices around the country classify goods according to a similar and consistent scheme. The regulations issued under the statute have no bearing, says respondent, on the rights of the importer. We disagree. The phrase in question is explained by the simple fact that *classification decisions must be made at the port where goods enter.* We shall not assume Congress was concerned only to ensure that customs officials at the various ports of entry make uniform decisions but that it had no concern for uniformity once the goods entered the country and judicial proceedings commenced. *The tariffs do not mean one thing for customs officers and another for importers.* * * * [Emphasis added.]

* * * *

* * * Particularly in light of the fact that the agency utilized the notice-and-comment rulemaking process[b] before issuing the regulations, the argument that they were not intended to be entitled to judicial deference implies a sufficient departure from conventional contemporary administrative practice that we ought not to adopt it absent a different statutory structure and more express language to this effect in the regulations themselves.

DECISION AND REMEDY   *The Supreme Court vacated the judgment of the lower court and remanded the case for further proceedings. Congress authorized the Treasury Department and the Customs Service to administer the tariff regulations, which were the product of notice-and-comment rulemaking. The Court held that without language to the contrary in the enabling statutes or the regulations, the tariff classifications were entitled to "judicial deference."*

---

b. Notice-and-comment rulemaking was discussed in Chapter 6.

International Organizations and Agreements. Over the last decade, countries competing for international trade have become more evenly matched competitors than in earlier years. In part, this is due to the increased use and success of international and regional organizations, such as the World Trade Organization, the European Union, and the North American Free Trade Agreement.

The World Trade Organization. The origins of the World Trade Organization (WTO) date to 1947, when the General Agreement on Tariffs and Trade (GATT) was formed for the purpose of minimizing trade barriers among nations. In subsequent decades, the GATT became the principal instrument for regulating international trade and over time negotiated tariff reductions on a broad range of products.

In 1994, in a final round of GATT negotiations, called the "Uruguay Round," representatives from over one hundred nations signed agreements relating to investment policies, dispute resolution, and other topics. One of these agreements, the Trade-Related Aspects of Intellectual Property Rights Agreement (TRIPS), will be discussed in Chapter 14. The Uruguay Round also established the World Trade Organization (WTO), which replaced the GATT beginning in 1995. Each member country of the WTO agreed to grant **most-favored-nation status** to other member countries. This means that each WTO member must treat other WTO members at least as well as it treats the country that receives its most favorable treatment with regard to imports or exports. (Excerpts from the agreements made during the Uruguay Round of the GATT are presented in Appendix P at the end of this text.)

The European Union (EU). The European Union (EU) arose out of the 1957 Treaty of Rome, which created the Common Market, a free trade zone comprising the nations of Belgium, France, (then) West Germany, Italy, the Netherlands, and Luxembourg. Since 1957, more nations have been added. In 1995, the EU became a single integrated European trading unit made up of fifteen European nations.

The EU has its own governing authorities. One is the Council of Ministers, which coordinates economic policies and includes one representative from each nation. The EU also has a commission that proposes regulations to the council and an elected assembly, which oversees the commission. The EU also has its own court, the European Court of Justice, which can review each nation's judicial decisions and is the ultimate authority on EU law.

The EU has gone far toward creating a new body of law to govern all of the member nations—although some of its efforts to create uniform laws have been confounded by nationalism. The council and the commission issue regulations, or directives, that define EU law in various areas, and these requirements normally are binding on all member countries. EU directives govern such issues as environmental law, product liability, anticompetitive practices, and laws governing corporations. The EU directive on product liability, for example, states that a "producer of an article shall be liable for damages caused by a defect in the article, whether or not he knew or could have known of the defect." Liability extends to anyone who puts a trademark or other identifying feature on an article, and liability may not be excluded, even by contract.

The North American Free Trade Agreement (NAFTA). The North American Free Trade Agreement (NAFTA), which was signed in 1993 and became effective on January 1, 1994, created a regional trading unit consisting of Mexico, the United States, and Canada. The primary goal of NAFTA is to eliminate tariffs among these three nations on substantially all goods over a period of fifteen to twenty years.

NAFTA gives the three countries a competitive advantage by retaining tariffs on goods imported from countries outside the NAFTA trading unit. Additionally, NAFTA provides for the elimination of barriers that traditionally have prevented the cross-border movement of services, such as financial and transportation services. For example, NAFTA provides that, with some exceptions, U.S. firms do not have to relocate in Mexico or Canada to provide services in those countries. NAFTA also attempts to eliminate citizenship requirements for the licensing of accountants, attorneys, physicians, and other professionals. Appendix Q at the end of this text presents excerpts from NAFTA.

DISPUTE SETTLEMENT IN THE INTERNATIONAL CONTEXT

Businesspersons who engage in international business transactions normally take special precautions to protect themselves in the event that a party with whom they are dealing in another country breaches an agreement. Recall from Chapter 3 that the arbitration of civil disputes is becoming an increasingly attractive alternative to costly litigation through the court system. This is true on the international level as well. For example, arbitration clauses are frequently found in contracts governing the international sale of goods. By means of such clauses, the parties agree in advance to be bound by the decision of a specified third party in the event of a dispute.

The third party may be a neutral entity (such as the International Chamber of Commerce), a panel of individuals representing both parties' interests, or some other group or organization. The United Nations Convention on the Recognition and Enforcement of Foreign Arbitral Awards[7]—which has been implemented in more than fifty countries, including the United States—assists in the enforcement of arbitration clauses, as do provisions in specific treaties among nations. The American Arbitration Association (discussed in Chapter 3) provides arbitration services for international as well as domestic disputes.

When no arbitration clause is contained in a sales contract, a contract dispute may end in litigation. If the contract includes forum-selection and choice-of-law clauses, a court in the specified forum country will hear the lawsuit according to that country's law. If no forum or choice of law has been designated, however, legal proceedings will be more complex and attended by much more uncertainty. For example, litigation may take place in two or more countries, with each country applying its own choice-of-law rules to determine which substantive law will be applied to the particular transactions.

Furthermore, even if a plaintiff wins a favorable judgment in a lawsuit litigated in the plaintiff's country, there is no guarantee that the court's judgment will be enforced by judicial bodies in the defendant's country. As discussed earlier in this chapter, under

---

7. June 10, 1958, 21 U.S.T. 2517, T.I.A.S. No. 6997 (the "New York Convention").

the principle of comity, the judgment may be enforced in the defendant's country, particularly if the defendant's country is the United States and the foreign court's decision is consistent with U.S. national law and policy. Other nations, however, may not be as accommodating as the United States, and the plaintiff may be left empty-handed.

SECTION 3

Comparative Law

When doing business in a foreign nation, a company generally will be subject to the jurisdiction and laws of that nation. Therefore, businesspersons will find it helpful to become familiar with the legal systems and laws of foreign nations in which they conduct commercial transactions. We look at some similarities and differences in national legal systems, laws, and cultural and business traditions in this section on **comparative law,** which can be defined as the study and comparison of legal systems and laws across nations.

COMPARATIVE LEGAL SYSTEMS

The legal systems of foreign nations differ, in widely varying degrees, from that of the United States. Additionally, a number of nations have specialized commercial law courts to deal with business disputes (in the United States, some jurisdictions are establishing similar courts). France instituted such courts in 1807, and most nations with commercial codes have done likewise. The United Kingdom also has special commercial courts overseen by judges with expertise in business law.

Common Law and Civil Law Systems.   Legal systems around the globe generally are divided into *common law* and *civil law* systems. As discussed in Chapter 1, in a common law system, the courts independently develop the rules governing certain areas of law, such as torts and contracts. These common law rules apply to all areas not covered by statutory law. Although the common law doctrine of *stare decisis* obligates judges to follow precedential decisions in their jurisdictions, courts may modify or even overturn precedents when deemed necessary. Additionally, if there is no case law to guide a court, the court may create a new rule of law. Common law systems exist today in countries that were once a part

of the British Empire (such as Australia, India, and the United States).

In contrast to Great Britain and the other common law countries, most of the European nations base their legal systems on Roman civil law, or "code law." The term *civil law,* as used here, refers not to civil as opposed to criminal law but to *codified* law—an ordered grouping of legal principles enacted into law by a legislature or other governing body. In a **civil law system,** the only official source of law is a statutory code. Courts are required to interpret the code and apply the rules to individual cases, but courts may not depart from the code and develop their own laws. In theory, the law code will set forth all the principles needed for the legal system.

Today, civil law systems are followed in most of the continental European countries, as well as in the Latin American, African, and Asian countries that were once colonies of the continental European nations. Japan and South Africa also have civil law systems. Components of the civil law system are found in the Islamic courts of predominantly Muslim countries. In the United States, the state of Louisiana, because of its historical ties to France, has, in part, a civil law system. Exhibit 8–2 (p. 170) lists some of the nations that use common law systems and some that use civil law systems.

Legal Systems Compared.   Common law and civil law systems are not wholly distinct. For example, although the United States has a common law system, crimes are defined by statute as in civil law systems. Civil law systems also may allow considerable room for judges to develop law. There is also some variation within common law and civil law systems. The judges of different common law nations have produced differing common law principles. Although the United States and India both derived their legal traditions from England, the common law principles governing contract law vary in some respects between the two countries.

Similarly, the laws of nations that have civil law systems differ considerably. For example, the French code tends to set forth general principles of law, while the German code is far more specific and runs to thousands of sections. In some Middle Eastern countries, codes are grounded in the religious law of Islam, called **sharia.** The religious basis of these codes makes them far more difficult to alter.

Foreign laws may apply to international transactions of U.S. companies, even in those cases heard in U.S. courts, as the following case illustrates.

CASE 8.2   Universe Sales Co., Ltd. v. Silver Castle, Ltd.

United States
Court of Appeals,
Ninth Circuit, 1999.
182 F.3d 1036.
http://www.ce9.
uscourts.gov[a]

BACKGROUND AND FACTS   *Universe Sales Company, Ltd., sold sportswear and had been paying royalties on products to Offshore Sportswear, Inc. (Sportswear). After a general dispute, Universe claimed to have discovered that Sportswear did not own the trademarks on the products under Japanese law, which applied to the contract. Universe sued to recover the royalties as unjust enrichment. The parties presented evidence to a federal district court. Sportswear presented as evidence the declaration of a Japanese attorney, Mitsuhiro Kamiya, who specialized in trademark and contract law. Kamiya declared that Universe owed royalties under Japanese contract law regardless of the trademark's ownership at the time the license agreement was executed. The district court did not give credit to the affidavit and granted summary judgment for Universe. Sportswear appealed.*

IN THE LANGUAGE OF THE COURT

BRUNETTI, Circuit Judge:

*   *   *   *

*   *   * We agree with Sportswear's arguments regarding the district court's failure properly to take the Kamiya declaration into account.

The Kamiya declaration states that Japanese contract law, not Japanese trademark law, is controlling in this situation. Under Japanese contract law, explains the declaration, the License Agreement is both valid and enforceable, and as such requires that Universe make royalty payments to Sportswear. According to the declaration, under Japanese contract law a "licensee will be unable to cancel the license agreement or refuse to pay royalties strictly on the grounds that the licensor was not the registered owner of the licensed trademark when the license agreement was executed. In other words, only if the licensor cannot acquire proper title from the registered owner of the licensed trademark . . . will the license agreement be terminable." Here, the declaration states, Sportswear can and has obtained proper title of the two trademarks at issue, and therefore is entitled to collect royalty payments from Universe.

The Kamiya declaration is admissible pursuant to Federal Rule of Civil Procedure Rule 44.1, which provides, in relevant part: "The court, in determining foreign law, may consider any relevant material or source, including testimony, whether or not submitted by a party or admissible under the Federal Rules of Evidence." *   *   *

In this case, the expert testimony of Kamiya, in the form of a declaration with attached exhibits, was submitted by Sportswear. *   *   * [T]he declaration reasons that Japanese contract law applies, and under that body of law, Universe is obligated to pay royalties to Sportswear. Although Universe had numerous opportunities to present evidence that would rebut this portion of Kamiya's declaration regarding Japanese law, Universe introduced nothing. Also, the district court performed no independent research of Japanese law. The district court should have considered the fact that the Kamiya declaration states that Japanese contract law is controlling. The district court then could have instructed the parties to present further evidence regarding the interpretation of Japanese law on that point; or, the district court may have performed its own research. Because the Kamiya declaration stands as an unrebutted presentation and interpretation of Japanese law, the district court erred in granting summary judgment to Universe.

DECISION AND REMEDY

The court reversed the grant of summary judgment for Universe, granted summary judgment for Offshore Sportswear, and remanded the case to the district court to consider any remaining issues.

---

a. In the "Info Links" column, click on the "Appeals Court Decisions" icon. On that page, click on "1999" to open the menu. Click on "June," then scroll down the list to the name of the case, and click on it to access the opinion.

EXHIBIT 8–2	THE LEGAL SYSTEMS OF NATIONS
CIVIL LAW	**COMMON LAW**
Argentina	Australia
Austria	Bangladesh
Brazil	Canada
Chile	Ghana
China	India
Egypt	Israel
Finland	Jamaica
France	Kenya
Germany	Malaysia
Greece	New Zealand
Indonesia	Nigeria
Iran	Singapore
Italy	United Kingdom
Japan	United States
Mexico	Zambia
Poland	
South Korea	
Sweden	
Tunisia	
Venezuela	

Judges and Procedures. Judges play similar roles in virtually all countries: their primary function is the resolution of litigation. The characteristics and qualifications of judges, which are typically set forth in the nation's constitution, can vary widely, however. The U.S. judge normally does not actively participate in a trial, but many foreign judges involve themselves closely in the proceedings, such as by questioning witnesses.

The procedures employed in resolving cases also vary substantially from country to country. A knowledge of a nation's legal procedures is important for a person conducting business transactions in that nation. For example, an American businessperson was on trial in Saudi Arabia for assaulting and slandering a co-worker, an offense for which he might have been jailed or deported. He initially was required to present two witnesses to his version of events, but he had only one. Fortunately, he became aware that he could "demand the oath." In this procedure, he swore before God that he had neither kicked nor slandered the complainant. After taking the oath, he was promptly adjudged not guilty, as lying under oath is one of the most serious sins under Islamic law. Had he failed to demand the oath, he almost certainly would have been found guilty.

NATIONAL LAWS COMPARED

A businessperson engaging in business operations abroad would be wise to learn about the relevant national laws that may affect those operations. Virtually all nations have laws governing torts, contracts, employment, and other areas. Even when the basic principles are fundamentally similar (as in contract law), there are significant variations in the practical application and effect of these laws across countries. This section summarizes some of the similarities and differences among national laws relating to tort law, contracts, and employment relationships.

Tort Law. Tort law, which allows persons to recover damages for harms or injuries caused by the wrongful actions of others (see Chapter 12), may vary widely among nations. Common law nations have developed a body of judge-made law regarding what kinds of actions constitute negligence or some other tort that permits recovery. Civil law nations must authorize such recovery in their codes. Exhibit 8–3 shows how the civil law codes of several nations define what constitutes a tort.

Even when the statutory language is similar, the application of tort law varies among nations. For example, which party has the burden of proof in a tort lawsuit differs among countries. In the United States, the burden of proof is on the plaintiff. In Russia, the defendant has the burden of proving that he or she was not at fault. Statutes of limitations (deadlines for filing a lawsuit) in other countries also vary considerably. Generally, the limitations period is longer in other countries than it is in the United States. Additionally, national tort laws vary with respect to certain concepts, including failures to act and damages.

Failures to Act. National tort laws differ considerably with respect to liability for omissions, or failures to act. In some situations, a failure to act will not be regarded as a tort. For example, in the United States, tort law imposes no "duty to rescue," and a person normally is not liable for failing to rescue another person in distress. German law is basically similar. In some countries, though, the failure to rescue another in distress is regarded as negligence.

Damages. National tort laws also differ in the way in which damages in tort cases are calculated. For example, Swiss law and Turkish law permit a court to reduce damages if an award of full damages would

EXHIBIT 8–3 CIVIL CODE TORT DEFINITIONS

Brazil: He who, by a voluntary act or omission, by negligence or carelessness, violates another's right, or causes him harm, is bound to compensate for the damage.

Egypt: Every culpable act that causes damage to another obliges the person who did it to compensate for it.

The Netherlands: Every unlawful act by which damage is caused to another obliges the person by whose fault the damage occurred to compensate for it.

Spain: He who by act or omission causes damage to another, either by fault or negligence, is obliged to compensate for the damage caused.

Tunisia: Every act a person does without lawful justification that causes willful and voluntary damage—material or moral—to another obliges the person who did it to compensate for the aforesaid damage, when it is shown that the act is the direct cause.

Uruguay: Every unlawful act a person does which causes damage to another imposes on the person whose malice, fault, or negligence brought it about the obligation to compensate for it. When the unlawful act was done maliciously, i.e., with the intention of causing harm—it amounts to a delict [an intentional tort, discussed in Chapter 6, or a crime], when the intention to cause harm is not present, the unlawful act amounts to a quasi-delict [a tort or a crime caused by negligence]. In either case, the unlawful act can be negative or positive according to whether the breach of duty consists of an act or omission.

SOURCE: Andre Tunc, *International Encyclopedia of Comparative Law*, Vol. XI, Chapter 2, pp. 5–6.

cause undue hardship for a party who was found negligent. In some nations of northern Africa, different amounts of damages are awarded depending on the type of tortious action committed and the degree of intent involved. In the United States, the calculation of actual (compensatory) damages does not depend on whether the tort was negligent or intentional.

Contract Law. Because international business transactions typically involve contracts, businesspersons should familiarize themselves with the contract law of the countries in which they do business. To a degree, the United Nations Convention on Contracts for the International Sale of Goods (CISG) has simplified matters for parties to international sales contracts.

For many transactions, however, the CISG may not be applicable. For one thing, the CISG applies only to transactions involving firms in countries that have signed the convention, or agreement, and parties (in nonsignatory nations) that have stipulated in their contracts that the CISG will govern any dispute. When transactions involve firms in countries that are not signatory to the CISG, the contract parties need to determine which nation's law will govern any disputes that may arise under the contract. Additionally, even when the CISG would apply, it does so only if the parties have not agreed otherwise in their contract. For example, parties may agree in their contract that German law or U.S. law or some other nation's law will govern any contract dispute that arises. For these reasons, the contract laws of individual nations remain important to businesspersons involved in international contracts.

Generally, the laws of other nations governing contracts are similar to those in the United States. You will learn in Chapter 9 that for a valid contract to be formed, four requirements must be met—agreement, consideration, capacity, and legality. These requirements will be discussed at length in Chapters 9 and 10. Additionally, a valid contract may be unenforceable if genuineness of assent was lacking or if the contract was not in the proper form—such as in writing when the law requires that type of contract to be in writing. Many of these requirements exist under other nations' laws as well, but there are some significant differences.

Agreement. The requirement of agreement (offer and acceptance) is common among countries, although what is considered an offer varies by jurisdiction. In the United States, an offer, once made, normally can be revoked (canceled, or taken back) by the offeror at any time prior to the offer's acceptance. Many nations, however, require that an offer must remain open for some minimum period of time. For example, the German Civil Code, which has detailed provisions governing offer and acceptance, requires that a written contractual offer must be held open for a reasonable time, unless the offer specifically states otherwise. Unlike those in the United States, oral contractual offers (those made in person or by telephone) in Germany must be accepted immediately, or they terminate.

Mexico has some special rules for offer and acceptance. If a time for acceptance is not stated in an offer, the offer is deemed to be held open for three days, plus whatever time is necessary for the offer and acceptance to be sent through the mails. If acceptance is desired sooner, the offeror must state the time for acceptance in the offer.

In the United States, a contract's terms must be sufficiently definite that the parties (and a court) can determine whether the contract has been formed (see Chapter 9). For contracts for the sale of goods, however, the Uniform Commercial Code (UCC) has substantially relaxed common law requirements in respect to definiteness of contract terms (see Chapter 11). Mexico also has adopted a commercial code, which, like the UCC, liberalizes the traditional requirements of definiteness in mercantile transactions. Under contract law in some countries, such as Saudi Arabia, however, there are strict requirements about the definiteness of a contract's terms. If the terms of an offer are too vague or indefinite, acceptance of that offer normally will not create a valid contract.

Consideration. In contrast to contract law in the United States, contract law in most civil law countries does not require consideration in order for a contract to be legally binding on the parties. German law, for example, does not require the exchange of consideration. An agreement to make a gift may thus be enforceable by the donee (the gift's recipient). In the United States, because consideration is required for a valid contract, promises to make gifts normally are not enforceable (because the donee does not give consideration for the gift—see Chapter 9).

In other countries, such as Saudi Arabia, consideration is required. Similarly, in India, consideration normally is required, although some contracts may be lawful even when the consideration consists of "past consideration" (that is, consideration that consists of an action that occurred in the past). As will be noted in Chapter 9, in the United States past consideration is no consideration.

Remedies for Breach of Contract. The types of remedies available for breach of contract vary widely throughout the world. In many countries, as in the United States, the normal remedy is damages—money given to the nonbreaching party to compensate that party for the losses incurred owing to the breach (see Chapter 10). The calculation of damages resulting from a breach of contract, however, may differ from one country to another, as does the calculation of damages under tort law.

National contract laws also differ as to whether and when equitable remedies, such as specific performance (discussed in Chapter 10), will be granted. Germany's typical remedy for a breach of contract is specific performance, which means that the party must go forward and perform the contract. Damages are available only after certain procedures have been employed to seek performance. In contrast, in the United States, the equitable remedy of specific performance will usually not be granted unless the remedy at law (money damages) is inadequate and the subject matter of the contract is unique.

Defenses. As in the United States, contract law in most nations allows parties to defend against contractual liability by claiming that certain requirements for contract enforceability are lacking. For example, many nations, including the United States, have laws requiring that certain types of contracts must be in writing. If such contracts are not in writing, they will not be enforced. In Saudi Arabia, the law strongly encourages parties to put all contracts in writing, and any written contract should be formally witnessed by two males or a male and a female. In that country, it may be difficult to enforce an oral contract.

Another common defense is the assertion that a contract was entered into because of a mistake, fraud, or duress, and thus genuineness of assent to the contract's terms was lacking. In some countries, a party may claim that a contract was not formed because the consideration supporting the contract was inadequate—that is, not *enough* value or money was given in exchange for a contractual promise. Indian courts, for example, look to the adequacy of consideration when determining whether the parties' assent to the contract was truly genuine and therefore whether the contract should be enforced. In the United States, in contrast, courts rarely inquire into the adequacy of consideration. Normally, only in cases in which the consideration is so grossly inadequate as to "shock the conscience of the court" will a court refuse to enforce a contract on this basis.

Employment Law. Employment law is particularly important in many foreign nations. The United States traditionally left the details of the employment relationship to a negotiation between the employer and the employee. Under the common law *employment-at-will doctrine* (discussed in Chapter 21), employers are free to hire and fire employees "at will," meaning that an employee can be fired for any reason or no reason at all. Today, this common law doctrine is less applicable in the United States, because the workplace is regulated extensively by federal and state statutory law. Employment relationships in other nations also are subject to government regulation.

Modifications to the At-Will Doctrine. Many other countries, similar to the United States, have modified their traditional at-will employment rules. In France, for example, the concept of employment at will can be traced back to the original Napoleonic Code. Over the years, the French have modified this doctrine considerably. French courts developed the doctrine of *abus de droit* (abuse of rights), which prohibited employers from firing workers for illness, pregnancy, unionization, political beliefs, the exercise of certain rights, or even personal dislike. French courts also began requiring employers to follow customary procedures before terminating workers. French employee-discharge laws were codified in the Dismissal Law of 1973, which also established procedural requirements that employers must follow when discharging workers (to be discussed shortly).

Under the Polish labor code, employment continues to be predominantly "at will." Either party may terminate the employment relationship at any time. Advance notice is generally required, however, and notice requirements vary, depending on the length of the worker's tenure with the employer. An employer may terminate an employee immediately and without notice if the worker has committed a criminal offense, lost a license or other employment qualification, seriously breached his or her duties, or failed to appear regularly at the job site. An employer cannot immediately discharge an employee for the last reason if the employee's absence was due to child-care needs, infectious disease, or entitled sick leave.

Wages and Benefits. One of the reasons U.S. businesspersons decide to establish business operations, such as factories, in other countries is to cut production costs by taking advantage of lower wage rates. Although workers' wages may be lower in some countries than in the United States, typically workers in other countries have many paid holidays, plus vacation time. In addition, employers in other countries may be subject to a variety of requirements not found in the United States.

In Mexico, for example, workers have a right to an annual bonus equal to fifteen days' salary and paid at the end of the year. Mexican law requires a minimum amount of paid vacation time (six days in the first year

of employment) and also requires that companies give workers a 25 percent bonus above their ordinary pay rates during those vacations. For example, if a worker's ordinary pay is $200 per week, the vacation pay is $250 per week. Mexican employers also must periodically give training courses to workers. In some countries, such as Egypt, fringe benefits for employees account for as much as 40 percent of an employer's payroll costs.

Equal Employment Opportunity. National laws around the globe vary widely with respect to equal employment opportunity. In the United States, employers are prohibited from discriminating against employees or job applicants on the basis of race, color, national origin, gender, religion, age, or disability. U.S. laws prohibiting discrimination on these bases also apply to all U.S. employees working for U.S. employers abroad. Generally, a U.S. employer must abide by U.S. laws prohibiting employment discrimination *unless* to do so would violate the laws of the country in which the employer's workplace is located. This "foreign laws exception" usually allows U.S. employers abroad to avoid being subjected to conflicting laws.

Some other countries also prohibit discriminatory practices. For example, in Indonesia, the Ministry of Manpower, which implements employment laws and regulations, prohibits discrimination in the workplace. Mexican law forbids employers from discriminating against employees on the basis of race, religion, or gender. The Japanese constitution prohibits discrimination based on race, religion, nationality, or gender.

In contrast, some countries, such as Egypt and Turkey, have no laws requiring equal employment opportunity. In Argentina, racial, religious, or other discrimination is not a political issue or a practice prohibited by law. Similarly, in Brazil, equal opportunity is not a factor in employment relationships.

Generally, in those countries that do prohibit employment discrimination, employers retain some flexibility in hiring and firing managerial personnel. In Mexico, for example, employers traditionally have been allowed to hire and fire "confidential" employees—managerial employees—at their discretion. In Italy, workers classified as managers are also less protected by the law than rank-and-file employees are.

Employment Termination. In many countries, employers find it difficult, and often quite costly, to discharge employees. Employment laws may prohibit the firing of employees for discriminatory reasons, and other laws may also come into play. For example, in France, if an employment contract is for an indefinite term, the employer can fire the worker only for genuine and serious cause or for economic reasons. The law also establishes procedural requirements. Before terminating a worker for cause, the employer must undertake a conciliatory session with labor court mediators. The employer has the burden of proving to the labor court that the cause of the dismissal was serious.

In Egypt, employers commonly use fixed-period employment contracts, which are automatically terminated at the end of the contract period. If an employee continues to work after the end of the contract period and no new contract is created, the employment contract becomes indefinite. It is very difficult to discharge an employee with an indefinite contract. The employee must first commit a serious offense, whereupon the employer must submit a proposal for termination to a committee consisting of representatives of the union, the employer, and the government. Employees may appeal adverse decisions of this committee.

Taiwanese law places clear restrictions on the termination of employment. An employer must provide a reason for discharging an employee. An employer may discharge an employee with advance notice and severance pay for a number of economic reasons or if the worker is incapable of performing the assigned work. Employers may fire employees without notice or severance pay only for certain reasons, such as violence, imprisonment, or extensive absenteeism.

CULTURAL AND BUSINESS TRADITIONS

The ability to conduct business successfully in a foreign nation requires not only a knowledge of that nation's laws but also some familiarity with its cultural traditions, economy, and business climate. One obvious cultural difference among nations is language. For example, Rolls-Royce changed the name of its "Silver Mist" in Germany, because in that country, *mist* translates as "manure." In Japan, Esso had difficulty selling gasoline in part because *Esso* sounds like the Japanese word for stalled car. Pepsi's "Come Alive with Pepsi" campaign was translated in Taiwan as "Pepsi brings your ancestors back from the grave."

The meaning of nonverbal language (body movements, gestures, facial expressions, and the like) also varies from culture to culture. In the United States, for example, a nod of the head indicates "yes," while in some countries, such as Greece, the same gesture means "no."

There are also some important ethical differences. In Islamic countries, for example, the consumption of alcohol and certain foods is forbidden by the Koran (the sacred book of the Islamic religion). It would be thoughtless and imprudent to invite a Saudi Arabian business contact out for a drink. Additionally, in many foreign nations, gift giving is a common practice among contracting companies or between companies and government. To Americans, such gift giving may look suspiciously like an unethical (and possibly illegal) bribe. This has been an important source of friction in international business, particularly after the U.S. Congress passed the Foreign Corrupt Practices Act (FCPA) in 1977 (discussed in Chapter 4). The act prohibits American business firms from offering certain side payments to foreign officials to secure favorable contracts.

The role played by women in other countries may present some troublesome ethical problems for U.S. firms doing business internationally. Equal employment opportunity is a fundamental public policy in the United States, and Title VII of the Civil Rights Act of 1964 (discussed in Chapter 22) prohibits discrimination against women in the employment context. Some other countries, however, largely reject any professional role for women, which may cause difficulties for American women conducting business transactions in those countries. For example, when the World Bank sent a delegation including women to negotiate with the Central Bank of Korea, the Koreans were surprised and offended. They thought that the presence of women meant that the Koreans were not being taken seriously.

TERMS AND CONCEPTS TO REVIEW

abus de droit 173   act of state doctrine 161   civil law system 168

comity 160	expropriation 162	*sharia* 168
comparative law 168	international law 159	sovereign immunity 162
confiscation 162	international organization 160	tariff 164
distribution agreement 163	most-favored-nation status 166	treaty 160
dumping 164	national law 159	
export 162	quota 164	

QUESTIONS AND CASE PROBLEMS

8–1. COMPARATIVE EMPLOYMENT LAWS. Assume that you are the president of a manufacturing company that intends to expand overseas. Shipping costs and tariffs for your product are uniformly low. Your manufacturing process, however, is highly labor intensive. How would the employment laws of various nations influence your decision on where to situate a new manufacturing plant?

8–2. WOMEN AND BUSINESS. Joe Henderson is the president of an Asian branch of a U.S. bank. His top vice president is a woman, Betty Carter. He would like to take her with him to an important meeting at which he will undertake loan negotiations with a huge overseas company. He has been advised, however, that he will lose respect in the eyes of the foreign company—and perhaps the company's business—if she accompanies him. He talks with her, and she informs him that she does not mind deferring to men at social activities, if local customs demand such deference, but that at the corporate meetings, she will expect business as usual and will not alter her behavior simply because she is a woman. What should Henderson do? Discuss.

8–3. INTERNATIONAL BUSINESS CONTRACTS. In 1995, France implemented a law making the use of the French language mandatory in certain legal documents. Documents relating to securities offerings, such as prospectuses, for example, must be written in French. So must instruction manuals and warranties for goods and services offered for sale in France. Additionally, all agreements entered into with French state or local authorities, with entities controlled by state or local authorities, and with private entities carrying out a public service (such as providing utilities) must be written in French. What kinds of problems might this law pose for U.S. businesspersons who wish to form contracts with French persons or business firms?

8–4. LEGAL SYSTEMS. As China and the formerly Communist nations move toward free enterprise, they must develop a new set of business laws. If you could start from scratch, what kind of business law system would you adopt, a civil law system or a common law system? What kind of business regulations would you impose?

8–5. ACT OF STATE DOCTRINE. W. S. Kirkpatrick & Co. learned that the Republic of Nigeria was interested in contracting for the construction and equipping of a medical center in Nigeria. Kirkpatrick, with the aid of a Nigerian citizen, secured the contract as a result of bribing Nigerian officials. Nigerian law prohibits both the payment and the receipt of bribes in connection with the awarding of government contracts, and the U.S. Foreign Corrupt Practices Act (FCPA) of 1977 expressly prohibits U.S. firms and their agents from bribing foreign officials to secure favorable contracts. Environmental Tectonics Corp., International (ETC), an unsuccessful bidder for the contract, learned of the bribery and sued Kirkpatrick in a federal district court for damages. The district court granted summary judgment for Kirkpatrick, because resolution of the case in favor of ETC would require imputing to foreign officials an unlawful motivation (the obtaining of bribes) and accordingly might embarrass the Nigerian government or interfere with the conduct of U.S. foreign policy. Was the district court correct in assuming that the act of state doctrine barred ETC's action against Kirkpatrick? What should happen on appeal? Discuss fully. [*W. S. Kirkpatrick & Co. v. Environmental Tectonics Corp., International*, 493 U.S. 400, 110 S.Ct. 701, 107 L.Ed.2d 816 (1990)]

8–6. SOVEREIGN IMMUNITY. George Janini and other former professors and employees of Kuwait University (the plaintiffs) were terminated from their positions following Iraq's invasion of Kuwait in August 1990. Following the invasion, the government of Kuwait issued a decree stating, among other things, that "contracts concluded between the Government and those non-Kuwaiti workers who worked for it . . . shall be considered automatically abrogated because of the impossibility of enforcement due to the Iraqi invasion." The plaintiffs sued Kuwait University in a U.S. court, alleging that their termination breached their employment contracts, which required nine months' notice before termination. The plaintiffs sought back pay and other benefits to which they were entitled under their contracts. The university claimed that, as a government-operated institution, it was immune from the jurisdiction of U.S. courts under the doctrine of sovereign immunity. What exceptions are made to this doctrine? Will an exception apply to the university's activities with respect to the plaintiffs? Discuss fully. [*Janini v. Kuwait University*, 43 F.3d 1534 (D.C. Cir. 1995)]

8–7. DISCRIMINATION CLAIMS.   Radio Free Europe and Radio Liberty (RFE/RL), a U.S. corporation doing business in Germany, employs more than three hundred U.S. citizens at its principal place of business in Munich, Germany. The concept of mandatory retirement is deeply embedded in German labor policy, and a contract formed in 1982 between RFE/RL and a German labor union contained a clause that required workers to be retired when they reached the age of sixty-five. When William Mahoney and other American employees (the plaintiffs) reached the age of sixty-five, RFE/RL terminated their employment as required under its contract with the labor union. The plaintiffs sued RFE/RL for discriminating against them on the basis of age, in violation of the U.S. Age Discrimination in Employment Act of 1967. Will the plaintiffs succeed in their suit? Discuss fully. [*Mahoney v. RFE/RL, Inc.*, 47 F.3d 447 (D.C. Cir. 1995)]

8–8. SOVEREIGN IMMUNITY.   Nuovo Pignone, Inc., is an Italian company that designs and manufactures turbine systems. Nuovo sold a turbine system to Cabinda Gulf Oil Co. (CABGOC). The system was manufactured, tested, and inspected in Italy, then sent to Louisiana for mounting on a platform by CABGOC's contractor. Nuovo sent a representative to consult on the mounting. The platform went to a CABGOC site off the coast of West Africa. Marcus Pere, an instrument technician at the site, was killed when a turbine within the system exploded. Pere's widow filed a suit in a federal district court against Nuovo and others. Nuovo claimed sovereign immunity on the ground that its majority shareholder at the time of the explosion was Ente Nazionale Idrocaburi, which was created by the government of Italy to lead its oil and gas exploration and development. Is Nuovo exempt from suit under the doctrine of sovereign immunity? Is it subject to suit under the "commercial activity" exception? Why or why not? [*Pere v. Nuovo Pignone, Inc.*, 150 F.3d 477 (5th Cir. 1998)]

8–9. DUMPING.   In response to a petition filed on behalf of the U.S. pineapple industry, the U.S. Commerce Department initiated an investigation of canned pineapple fruit imported from Thailand. The investigation concerned Thai producers of the canned fruit, including The Thai Pineapple Public Co. The Thai producers also turned out products, such as pineapple juice and juice concentrate, outside the scope of the investigation. These products use separate parts of the same fresh pineapple, and so they share raw material costs. The Commerce Department had to calculate the Thai producers' cost of production, for the purpose of determining fair value and antidumping duties, and in so doing, had to allocate a portion of the shared fruit costs to the canned fruit. These allocations were based on the producers' own financial records, which were consistent with Thai generally accepted accounting principles. The result was a determination that more than 90 percent of the canned fruit sales were below the cost of production. The producers filed a suit in the U.S. Court of International Trade against the federal government, challenging this allocation. The producers argued that their records did not reflect actual production costs, which instead should be based on the weight of fresh fruit used to make the products. Did the Commerce Department act reasonably in determining the cost of production? Why or why not? [*The Thai Pineapple Public Co. v. United States*, 187 F.3d 1362 (Fed.Cir. 1999)]

8–10. IN YOUR COURT

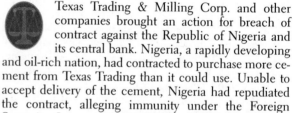

Texas Trading & Milling Corp. and other companies brought an action for breach of contract against the Republic of Nigeria and its central bank. Nigeria, a rapidly developing and oil-rich nation, had contracted to purchase more cement from Texas Trading than it could use. Unable to accept delivery of the cement, Nigeria had repudiated the contract, alleging immunity under the Foreign Sovereign Immunities Act (FSIA) of 1976, because the buyer of the cement was the Nigerian government. Assume that you are the judge in the trial court hearing this case and answer the following questions:

(a) What section of the FSIA is particularly applicable to this dispute?
(b) Given the provisions of that section, should the doctrine of sovereign immunity remove the dispute from the jurisdiction of U.S. courts? Explain your reasoning.

LAW ON THE WEB

For updated links to resources available on the Web, as well as a variety of other materials, visit this text's Web site at http://wleb.westbuslaw.com.

An extensive collection of URLs offering access to various international organizations is offered by the Villanova University School of Law at

http://vill.law.edu/compass/international/index.htm

The University of Arizona College of Law has an online collection of various resources relating to international law, as well as to the national laws of some foreign countries. You can access this collection by going to

http://www.law.arizona.edu/library/intlinks.html

The Library of Congress's Global Legal Information Network has information on the national laws of more than thirty-five countries, as well as a comprehensive Guide to Law Online. You can access this site at

http://lcweb2.loc.gov/glin/lawhome.html

LEGAL RESEARCH EXERCISES ON THE WEB

Go to http://wleb.westbuslaw.com, the Web site that accompanies this text. Select "Internet Applications," and then click on "Chapter 8." There you will find the following Internet research exercises that you can perform to learn more about international organizations and trade:

Activity 8–1: The World Trade Organization

Activity 8–2: Overseas Business Opportunities

UNIT TWO—CUMULATIVE HYPOTHETICAL PROBLEM

JB Mediquip, Inc., is in the business of manufacturing hospital equipment. JB does business throughout the world and has manufacturing plants in two other countries.

1. JB agrees to sell fifty hospital beds to a health-care facility operated on a military base in Zamboria, a foreign country. The health-care facility is owned and operated by the Zamborian government. JB ships the beds, but the health-care facility refuses to pay for them. To recover the price of the beds, JB sues the health-care facility in a U.S. district court. Zamboria moves to dismiss JB's action, contending that a U.S. court cannot exercise jurisdiction over the matter. On what ground might Zamboria base its assertion? Is Zamboria correct?

2. The Occupational Safety and Health Administration (OSHA) has proposed a new safety rule governing the handling of certain metals in the workplace, including those used by JB in its manufacturing operations. JB concludes that the rule, which will involve substantial compliance costs, will not significantly increase workplace safety. JB sends a letter to OSHA indicating its objections to the proposed rule and enclosing research reports and other data supporting those objections. Does OSHA have any obligation to consider these objections? What procedures must OSHA follow when it makes new rules, such as this one?

3. The head of JB's accounting department, Roy Olson, has to pay his daughter's college tuition within a week, or his daughter will not be able to continue taking classes. The payment due is over $20,000. Roy will be able to make the payment in two months but cannot do so until then. The college refuses to wait that long. In desperation, Roy—through a fictitious bank account and some clever accounting—"borrows" funds from JB. Before Roy can pay back the borrowed funds, an auditor discovers what Roy has done. JB's president alleges that Roy has "stolen" company funds and informs the police of the theft. Has Roy committed a crime? If so, what crime? Explain.

FOCUS ON LEGAL REASONING
Kimel v. Florida Board of Regents

INTRODUCTION

Congress can regulate commerce under the Constitution's commerce clause, as explained in Chapter 5. For example, under the commerce clause, in 1967 Congress enacted the Age Discrimination in Employment Act (ADEA) to prohibit discrimination in the employment context of persons forty years of age and older. (The ADEA is discussed in detail in Chapter 22.) Private employers are clearly subject to the ADEA. In this *Focus on Legal Reasoning*, we examine *Kimel v. Florida Board of Regents*[1] a recent decision that considered whether

states, as employers, are also subject to the ADEA.

CASE BACKGROUND

In April 1995, a group of current and former faculty and librarians of Florida State University and Florida International University, including J. Daniel Kimel, Jr., filed a suit against the Florida Board of Regents in a federal district court. The plaintiffs, all over age forty, alleged that the board refused to require the two state universities to allocate funds to provide previously agreed on adjustments to the salaries of eligible university employees. The plaintiffs contended in part that the failure to allocate the funds violated the ADEA. The plaintiffs asked for back pay, liquidated damages, and

permanent salary adjustments. The board filed a motion to dismiss the suit, arguing in effect that Congress did not have the authority to subject the states to the ADEA. The court held in part that the ADEA was a proper exercise of congressional authority under the Fourteenth Amendment, and denied the motion.

The board appealed to the U.S. Court of Appeals for the Eleventh Circuit, which combined the board's appeal with two other cases that concerned the same issue. The appellate court disagreed with the lower court, holding that the states could not be sued under the ADEA. Kimel and the other plaintiffs appealed to the United States Supreme Court.

---

1. __U.S.__, 120 S.Ct. 631, 145 L.Ed.2d 522 (2000).

MAJORITY OPINION

Justice *O'Connor* delivered the opinion of the Court.

* * * *

* * * Older persons, * * * unlike those who suffer discrimination on the basis of race or gender, have not been subjected to a history of purposeful unequal treatment. Old age also does not define a discrete and insular minority because all persons, if they live out their normal life spans, will experience it. Accordingly, age is not a suspect classification under the Equal Protection Clause [of the Fourteenth Amendment].

States may discriminate on the basis of age without offending the Fourteenth Amendment if the age classification in question is rationally related to a legitimate state interest. * * *

* * * [I]n *Gregory v. Ashcroft,* 501 U.S. 452, 111 S.Ct. 2395, 115 L.Ed.2d 410 (1991), we upheld a provision of the Missouri Constitution that required judges to retire at age 70. Noting that the Missouri provision was based on a generalization about the

effect of old age on the ability of individuals to serve as judges, we acknowledged that "[i]t is far from true that all judges suffer significant deterioration in performance at age 70," "[i]t is probably not true that most do," and "[i]t may not be true at all." Nevertheless, because Missouri's age classification was subject only to rational basis review, we held that the State's reliance on such imperfect generalizations was entirely proper under the Equal Protection Clause. * * *

* * * The [ADEA], through its broad restriction on the use of age as a discriminating factor, prohibits substantially more state employment decisions and practices than would likely be held unconstitutional under the applicable equal protection, rational basis standard. * * *

* * * *

A review of the ADEA's legislative record * * * reveals that Congress had virtually no reason to believe that state and local governments were unconstitutionally discriminating against their employees on the basis of age. * * * In light of the indiscriminate scope of the Act's substantive requirements, and the lack of evidence of widespread and unconstitutional age discrimination by the States, we hold that the ADEA is not a valid exercise of Congress' power under * * * the Fourteenth Amendment.

DISSENTING OPINION

Justice stevens * * * dissenting * * * .

* * * *

Congress' power to regulate the American economy includes the power to regulate both the public and the private sectors of the labor market. Federal rules outlawing discrimination in the workplace, like the regulation of wages and hours or health and safety standards, may be enforced against public as well as private employers. In my opinion, Congress' power to authorize federal remedies against state agencies that violate federal statutory obligations is coextensive with its power to impose those obligations on the States in the first place.

LEGAL REASONING AND ANALYSIS

1. **Legal Reasoning.** The majority and the dissent seem to disagree in their interpretations of the Constitution. What conclusions do they reach? What reasoning do they apply to reach those conclusions? With whom do you agree and why?

2. **Legal Analysis.** The majority cites, in its opinion, *Gregory v. Ashcroft*, 501 U.S. 452, 111 S.Ct. 2395, 115 L.Ed.2d 410 (1991) (see the Law on the Web feature at the end of Chapter 2 for instructions on how to access federal court opinions). How do the facts, issues, and holding in that case contrast with the facts and issues in the *Kimel* case? Do the law and reasoning of the *Gregory* case support the position of the majority in the *Kimel* case?

3. **Social Considerations.** Considering that most states have their own laws against age discrimination, what is the practical impact of the decision in the *Kimel* case?

4. **Implications for Employees.** What does the holding in this case say to employees of states that may not have strong antidiscrimination laws?

5. **Case Briefing Assignment.** Using the guidelines for briefing cases given in Appendix A of this text, brief the *Kimel* case.

GOING ONLINE

The Web site Jurist, at http://jurist.law.pitt.ed/sg_con.htm, links to resources on constitutional law, including the latest opinions of the United States Supreme Court and current congressional bills and legislation. The University of Pittsburgh School of Law in Pittsburgh, Pennsylvania, maintains this site.

The Public and International Environment

No other areas of law are as dynamic and engender as much controversy as those relating to the public and international environment. This stems from the fact that the law of the public and international environment, more than any other area, involves searching, ethical questions. All areas of law touch on ethical considerations. But many laws have as their basis practical necessity or commercial need. The law of the public environment, however, concerns issues such as the protection of freedom of speech, the promotion of racial equality, and government regulation of behavior for the public welfare versus individual rights. The law of the international environment involves such questions as the influence of foreign and international laws, the impact of divergent cultures, and the effect of different legal, political, and economic systems.

Little guidance is provided by considerations of practicality in resolving these issues. Moreover, these issues do not merely involve questions of ethics; they are in large measure purely ethical questions. In resolving them, one must rely on basic notions of fairness and justice. Yet conceptions of fairness, justice, and equality differ among individuals. Moreover, each individual's conception is a product of his or her circumstances; as circumstances change over time, so, too, basic conceptions change. Not surprisingly, at any moment in history, there is seldom a broad social consensus over legal issues in the public and international environment.

FREE SPEECH AND THE CORPORATION

Free speech is regarded as one of the basic rights of a democratic society. Yet it has never been considered an absolute right. The right of free speech must be balanced against other important rights and the advancement of other important social goals. In that sense the proper extent of freedom of speech, in its many forms, involves ethical considerations.

Because freedom of speech is not absolute, not all forms of expression are protected. Pornography, for example, is not protected by the First Amendment. Nor are utterances protected that would induce an immediate threat of violence or injury. Even within the context of protected speech, the Supreme Court has historically looked to the nature of the speech involved in determining the extent of the protection afforded. Commercial speech, for example, is afforded less protection from government restriction than is noncommercial speech. The lesser degree of protection means in practical terms that it is easier for government to show that the interest it seeks to promote by regulating the speech is more important than protecting the right of speech. But in balancing such conflicting rights and goals, value judgments must be made.

Judging the Source

The nature of the speech involved may be a legitimate concern in assessing the extent of freedom of speech, but is it legitimate to consider the source of the speech? For example, should it make a difference that the speaker, through either a spokesperson or an advertisement, is a corporation? Most corporate "speech" has as its primary purpose the promotion of a product; that is, it is commercial in nature and, as discussed, is afforded a lesser degree of protection. But what if the speech is political in nature? Should it matter in that case that the speaker is a corporation? This issue was addressed by the United States Supreme Court in *First National Bank of Boston v. Bellotti,* a case referred to in Chapter 5. Although the justices deciding the case were applying their concepts of the free speech clause of the First Amendment, the case raises some ethical questions, which are implicit in the Court's decision and in the opinions of the dissenting justices.

First National Bank of Boston v. Bellotti concerned a Massachusetts law that forbade corporations from using their resources to try to influence public opinion on issues submitted to a referendum vote when those issues did not materially relate to the corporation's business. Controversy arose when five corporations announced their intentions to mount a campaign in opposition to a proposed state individual income tax, which was to be submitted to a referendum vote. The state threatened to fine the corporations and punish their executives if the corporations entered the political debate. The corporations sought protection by asking the courts to declare the Massachusetts law unconstitutional. Ultimately, the case was appealed to the United States Supreme Court.

A divided Court decided in favor of the corporations. The majority held that free speech protections extended to corporations and that the Massachusetts law violated those constitutional protections. In deciding the case, the majority recast the issue involved. For the majority, the issue was *not* whether corporations were protected by the free speech clause but, rather, whether the speech involved was protected. Because the speech was political in nature, the majority concluded that the speech could not be restricted in the manner employed by the state. To the majority, it did not matter that the speaker was a corporation. And indeed, as the majority viewed the case, it was not protecting the corporation. Instead, it believed that the political nature of the speech meant that it should be heard.

The Ethical Dimensions

The majority's reasoning has some strong points. After all, political debate is the fundamental ingredient of the democratic political process. One of the few areas of virtually uniform agreement over First Amendment rights is that the authors of the Constitution definitely had the public exchange of political views in mind when they constructed the free speech clause. But there are other considerations, largely of an ethical nature, involved when the speaker is a corporation.

There are ethical considerations in a corporation's using its extensive resources to influence the political process. Certainly, bribing officials is wrong both ethically and legally. But other forms of corporate spending that

influence the political process also might be abusive. One concern is that a corporation can "leverage" political power through its economic skills. Corporations acquire resources through skills in marketing, management, and technology. Yet these skills, however beneficial to society's material well-being they may be, do not involve political ideas or necessarily indicate a concern for the public welfare. Should the resources garnered in the economic arena be redeployed in the political arena? Is it fair to allow economic skill to be translated into political power? These were concerns raised in dissent to the majority's opinion in Bellotti, but they are as much ethical issues as legal ones.

Notwithstanding these concerns, there are ethical as well as practical considerations that support the majority's view. Recall that the Massachusetts law challenged in *Bellotti* did not ban corporate expenditures on referendum issues that materially related to the corporation's business. The issue was a state individual income tax. The very fact that the corporations would not be materially affected by a state *individual* income tax might imply that their political participation was motivated solely by concern for the public welfare rather than their self-interest. Even if they were concerned that the proposed tax might affect the economy of the state and thus the profitability of their businesses, that does not in itself make their views less worthy to be heard. After all, on economic matters, the corporate view of the issues would seem to be extremely relevant. Possibly the corporate view should be heard for that reason alone. And if the corporations choose to subsidize with their own resources the dissemination of important views, maybe they should be praised rather than condemned.

ETHICS AND THE ADMINISTRATIVE PROCESS

In Chapter 5 we noted some of the other constitutional protections that apply in the context of business. We looked in Chapter 6 at how some of those protections apply in the administrative process. As noted in Chapter 6, effective governmental regulation necessitates the gathering of relevant information. Often that information can be obtained only by an on-site inspection of business premises or a first-hand examination of business records. When regulatory need conflicts with constitutional principles, not only are legal issues raised, but ethical ones as well.

Recall that the Fourth Amendment protection from unreasonable searches and seizures applies in the context of business. Within the context of administrative law, this protection has been interpreted as requiring that information sought by a regulatory agency be relevant to the matter under scrutiny. Furthermore, any demand for information must be reasonably specific and not unduly burdensome to the business providing the information.

The Need to Know

The ideals embodied in the Fourth Amendment are deeply ingrained in America's political culture. The image of midnight raids in which innocent families watch helplessly as gruff, heavily armed officers ransack their homes is often invoked when one thinks of a "search and seizure." Protection against such abhorrent practices is fundamental to the American ideal of liberty.

But are the same ideals felt as strongly in other contexts? What about in the business context, especially with regard to agency regulation? Even though the first

181

significant degree of federal economic regulation can be traced as far back as the first half of the nineteenth century, Americans continue to hold extremely ambivalent feelings toward the very idea of government regulation. Americans are prone to look to government to address every new ill society encounters, but then stridently resent, as governmental intrusion, the regulatory schemes designed to cure those ills.

Whatever the sentiments Americans hold regarding government regulation, most accept and many welcome it as an important part of modern society. In accepting such regulation, Americans also accept the fact that regulators must gather information. For example, the Securities and Exchange Commission desires information about proposed stock offerings. The Environmental Protection Agency may request to make an inspection of a chemical plant to ensure compliance with hazardous waste disposal regulations.

Despite acceptance of the need for regulators to gather information, an inherent conflict exists between the regulatory need for information and the individual's right of privacy. Specifically, how much latitude should be afforded to regulators in gathering information and overseeing private activities?

The United States Supreme Court has attempted to resolve the conflict by balancing the regulators' need to know against individual and corporate expectations of freedom from excessive government prying. An important consideration in resolving the conflict is the less intrusive nature of regulatory searches of businesses: most people simply do not have the same degree of concern about protecting places of business as they do about protecting the family dwelling. As a result, the standards for conducting regulatory

investigations and searches are different than those imposed when ordinary police investigations and searches are conducted. For example, even though there may be no suspicion of a regulatory violation, an agency may conduct an investigation or search the premises of a business merely to be assured that no violation is occurring. Within industries subject to a history of extensive regulation, searches may be made even without a warrant. Still, though, as noted in Chapter 6 and above, government is restricted in obtaining private information for regulatory purposes only.

The Ethics of Legal Avoidance

In the face of an agency investigation, a business may prevent or delay agency efforts by asserting legal challenges to the nature or manner of the investigation. There remains, however, the question of whether—in an ethical rather than legal sense—business should challenge any such investigation. We would be expected to challenge an unreasonable search of our homes. We would owe it to our families to challenge such abuse. Arguably, it would be one's civic duty to challenge it to protect future abuse of other families in our communities as well. Regulatory investigations may be somehow different, though.

Most regulatory investigations have as their objective ensuring compliance with existing regulatory schemes or gathering information for future ones. Such schemes are designed for the public welfare. Though individuals may disagree about the effectiveness of the scheme or the individual motives of the regulators, society generally accepts the underlying purpose of the regulation—the promotion of public welfare. In such instances, businesses may have an ethical duty not to use legal means to avoid agency action. Indeed, they

may have an ethical duty to aid in regulation by compliance, even though they may have a legal right to delay or avoid it.

ETHICS AND INTERNATIONAL LAW

Differences in the laws and customs of the various nations of the globe present unique ethical issues for firms engaged in international business transactions. Some of these issues were discussed in Chapter 8. Here, we look at a few other problems, focusing particularly on some ethical issues relating to international doctrines and to U.S. laws as they apply to international transactions.

Intellectual Property Rights

The licensing of technology allows U.S. owners of intellectual property (such as patents, trademarks, and copyrights) to benefit from sales of their products in other countries. Much intellectual property, however, is "pirated"—that is, unauthorized copies of the property (such as a software program) are made and sold. In 1994, to protect intellectual property rights on a worldwide basis, more than one hundred nations signed the international agreement on Trade-Related Aspects of Intellectual Property Rights (TRIPS), which is administered by the World Trade Organization. These nations pledged to pass and enforce laws protecting patents, copyrights, and trademarks (see the discussion of TRIPS in Chapter 14).

The attempted enforcement of intellectual property rights on a worldwide basis, however, raises some ethical concerns. For example, in a developing country, the welfare of small business firms and consumers may be enhanced by the ability to purchase pirated (less expensive) copies of high-tech products. Although the owners of the pirated intellectual property lose out, they might have received nothing anyway, if no authorized copies (at higher prices) could have been sold in the poorer country. Therefore, if a developing country's government is somewhat slack in curbing the piracy of intellectual property, it may be because this laxity is in the developing country's interests.

Furthermore, laws governing intellectual property rights are necessarily somewhat arbitrary. For example, if the United States grants copyright protection for a longer period of time than Japan, does this mean that U.S. law is "right" and Japanese law is "wrong"?

Sovereign Immunity

Sometimes, the application of the doctrine of sovereign immunity may lead to seemingly inequitable results. The economy of the United States is primarily controlled by private interests, whereas the economies of many foreign countries, particularly developing nations, are extensively controlled by government. When a U.S. firm does business with a foreign firm in a developing country, therefore, the chances are that the U.S. firm will work closely with foreign government officials. Should a dispute arise between the parties, the question then becomes whether the U.S. firm can bring a lawsuit against the foreign firm. If the foreign defendant raises the defense of sovereign immunity, alleging that it is a government-controlled operation, then it may be immune from liability. The ethical issue in these situations is whether it is fair that U.S. firms be left without any legal recourse when they suffer damages as a result of actions controlled by foreign governments.

Consider, for example, the situation that arose in *Antares Aircraft, L.P. v. Federal Republic of Nigeria*.[1] In that case, Antares Aircraft, a New York limited partnership, had one asset—a DC-8-55 aircraft registered in Nigeria. Antares was required by the Nigerian government to leave the plane at the airport in Lagos, Nigeria, until certain fees (which had been incurred by a previous owner of the plane) were paid. Antares paid the $100,000 in fees, but the Nigerian government did not release the plane until five months later. In the meantime, the plane had been damaged by exposure to the elements.

Antares filed suit against the Nigerian government for the tort of conversion, alleging that the Nigerian government had wrongfully detained the plane. Antares argued that the Nigerian government's actions fell within the commercial-activity exception to the Foreign Sovereign Immunities Act (FSIA) and therefore the Nigerian government was not immune from the jurisdiction of U.S. courts.

Although the court agreed with Antares that the fees collected by the Nigerian government were connected with a commercial activity, it found that the activity did not have a "direct effect" in the United States—in which case the commercial-activity exception to the FSIA did not apply. The court therefore held that the Nigerian government was immune from liability. The court stated that "the detention of Antares's sole asset affected the financial well-being of the American partnership. However, the fact that an American individual or firm suffers some financial loss from a foreign tort cannot, standing alone, suffice to trigger the [commercial-activity] exception."

Because the FSIA does not define exactly what types of activities on the part of a foreign government fall under the

1. 999 F.2d 33 (2d Cir. 1993).

commercial-activity exception, the courts exercise considerable discretion in deciding such issues. Although the majority on the court hearing the *Antares* case concluded that the loss suffered by Antares was not sufficiently significant to constitute a "direct effect in the United States," other courts might have concluded differently.

Certainly, the dissenting judge in *Antares* believed that the detention of the plane did have a direct effect in the United States. The partners lived in the United States and lost money because of a foreign government's interference with their property. The dissent concluded that the partnership's loss should be sufficient to establish an exception to immunity under the FSIA.

The Foreign Corrupt Practices Act

Since its passage by Congress in 1977, the Foreign Corrupt Practices Act (FCPA) has been the target of substantial criticism. Many U.S. firms have complained that the act places them at a competitive disadvantage relative to foreign firms.

For example, assume that your company wants to do business with a foreign firm. A foreign official promises your company the contract, but only if you agree to "contribute," say, $500,000 to the official's bank account in another country. You say no to the deal because you know that the FCPA prohibits you from making such a "bribe." If you agreed to the deal, you could face harsh criminal penalties, including imprisonment. A company from another nation, which has been competing for the contract, faces no such prohibition, however. That company agrees to pay the $500,000 and gets the contract.

As discussed in Chapter 8, for several years, the United States has been encouraging other nations to pass similar antibribery laws, and progress is clearly being made. Even if all nations had laws similar to the FCPA, however, a further issue would remain: How do you prove that a bribe has been tendered (or a side payment requested)?

The crime of bribery occurs not only when a bribe is accepted but also when a bribe is offered. When someone refuses to take a bribe, sometimes the only proof that the bribe was offered or solicited is the word of the person who refused. What would prevent a foreign government from retaliating if a U.S. firm's representative accused a foreign official of requesting a bribe but could not otherwise prove that the bribery occurred?

DISCUSSION QUESTIONS

1. You serve as chief executive officer of a large corporation. The state in which your company is headquartered has scheduled a statewide referendum on whether to allow casino gambling to be conducted within the state. Your company is in no way involved in gambling or in the sale of products used in the gaming industry, but you believe that evidence supports the inference that casino gambling, though potentially lucrative for those who operate the casinos, will hurt the state's economy. Some members of the board of directors have expressed similar concerns to you in casual conversation. Should you authorize the use of your company's resources to mount an opposition campaign to the proposal? Why or why not?

2. What if, in the situation described in question 1, you knew of no conclusive evidence to support or refute the proposition that casino gambling had any effect on the overall economy of the state? Suppose, though, you had a strong moral conviction that gambling was wrong. How would that change the ethical dimensions of the question of whether you should authorize the use of corporate resources to oppose the gambling initiative?

3. The United States banned the pesticide DDT, primarily because of its adverse effects on wildlife. In Asia, however, DDT has been a critical component of the mosquito control necessary to combat malaria. Should the ban in the United States prevent U.S. firms from manufacturing DDT and shipping it to an Asian country, where it could be used to save lives? Should the U.S. chemical manufacturer be required to produce the DDT in the same country that uses the chemical?

4. What are some of the implications of the doctrine of sovereign immunity for businesspersons doing business internationally? Should the courts make more exceptions to this doctrine?

5. The Foreign Corrupt Practices Act was passed in an attempt to ensure more ethical conduct on the part of U.S. businesspersons doing business abroad. Do you think that the act is fair to U.S. firms in view of the fact that other countries do not—at least as yet—have similar laws? The act permits so-called grease payments to minor government officials to expedite such things as paperwork. Do such payments amount to bribes? Should the act prohibit these kinds of payments as well?

UNIT THREE

The Private Environment

CONTENTS

CHAPTER 9

Contracts: Part 1

THE NOTED LEGAL SCHOLAR Roscoe Pound once said that "[t]he social order rests upon the stability and predictability of conduct, of which keeping promises is a large item."[1] A **promise** is an assurance that one will or will not do something in the future. A **contract** is "a promise or a set of promises for the breach of which the law gives a remedy, or the performance of which the law in some way recognizes as a duty."[2] Put simply, a contract is an agreement (based on a promise or an exchange of promises) that can be enforced in court.

Like other types of law, contract law reflects our social values, interests, and expectations at a given point in time. It shows, for example, to what extent our society allows people to make promises or commitments that are legally binding. It distinguishes between promises that create only *moral* obligations (such as a promise to take a friend to lunch) and promises that are legally binding (such as a promise to pay for merchandise purchased). Contract law also

demonstrates what excuses our society accepts for breaking certain types of promises. In addition, it indicates what promises are considered to be contrary to public policy—against the interests of society as a whole—and therefore legally invalid. When a promise is made by a child or a mentally incompetent person, for example, a question will arise as to whether the promise should be enforced. Resolving such questions is the essence of contract law.

The common law governs all contracts except when it has been modified or replaced by statutory law, such as the Uniform Commercial Code (UCC),[3] or by administrative agency regulations. Contracts relating to services, real estate, employment, insurance, and so on generally are governed by the common law of contracts. Contracts for the sale and lease of goods, however, are governed by the UCC—to the extent that the UCC has modified general contract law. The relationship between general contract law and the law governing sales and leases of goods will be explored in detail in Chapter 11. In the discussion of general contract law that follows, we indicate in footnotes the areas in which the UCC has significantly altered common law contract principles.

---

1. R. Pound, *Jurisprudence*, Vol. 3 (St. Paul: West Publishing Co., 1959), p. 162.

2. *Restatement (Second) of Contracts.* The *Restatement of the Law of Contracts* is a nonstatutory, authoritative exposition of the common law of contracts compiled by the American Law Institute in 1932. The *Restatement*, which is now in its second edition (a third edition is being drafted), will be referred to throughout this chapter and Chapter 10.

---

3. See Chapter 1 and Chapter 11 for further discussions of the significance and coverage of the Uniform Commercial Code. Article 2 of the UCC is presented in Appendix C at the end of this book.

SECTION 1

Elements of a Contract

The many topics that will be discussed in these two chapters on contract law require an understanding of the basic elements of a contract and the way in which a contract is created. The following list briefly describes these elements. Each element will be explained more fully in this chapter and Chapter 10.

1. *Agreement.* An agreement to form a contract includes an *offer* and an *acceptance*. One party must offer to enter into a legal agreement, and another party must accept the terms of the offer.

2. *Consideration.* Any promises made by the parties to the contract must be supported by legally sufficient and bargained-for *consideration* (something of value received or promised, such as money, to convince a person to make a deal).

3. *Contractual capacity.* Both parties entering into the contract must have the contractual *capacity* to do so; the law must recognize them as possessing characteristics that qualify them as competent parties.

4. *Legality.* The contract's purpose must be to accomplish some goal that is legal and not against public policy.

These four elements constitute what are normally known as the requirements that must be met for a valid contract to exist. If any of these elements is lacking, no contract will have been formed. Even if all of these elements exist, however, a contract may be unenforceable if the following requirements are not met. These requirements typically are raised as *defenses* to the enforceability of an otherwise valid contract.

1. *Genuineness of assent.* The apparent consent of both parties must be genuine. For example, if a contract was formed as a result of fraud, undue influence, mistake, or duress, the contract may not be enforceable.

2. *Form.* The contract must be in whatever form the law requires; for example, some contracts must be in writing to be enforceable.

(Standard contract forms are now available online at numerous Web sites—see this chapter's *Emerging Trends in Technology* on page 188 for information on some of these sites.)

SECTION 2

The Objective Theory of Contracts

Sometimes, parties claim that they should not be bound in contract because they did not *intend* to form an agreement that would be legally binding. Although the element of intent is of prime importance in determining whether a contract has been formed, it is not the party's *subjective* intent that a court looks to in deciding the issue. In contract law, intent is determined by what is called the *objective theory of contracts*, not by the personal or subjective intent, or belief, of a party. The theory is that intention to enter into a legally binding agreement, or contract, is judged by outward, objective facts as interpreted by a *reasonable* person, rather than by the party's own secret, subjective intentions. Objective facts include (1) what the party said when entering into the contract, (2) how the party acted or appeared (intent may be manifested by conduct as well as by oral or written words), and (3) the circumstances surrounding the transaction.

Consider an example. Jaffe has just purchased a new car for $28,000. A number of his neighbors are admiring his car, and one neighbor, Logan, states that he would like to own a car exactly like Jaffe's. Jaffe, in front of all of his neighbors, says to Logan, "I'll sell you this car for $20,000 in cash." Logan agrees to buy the car, and they put the agreement in writing and sign it. Jaffe immediately tells everyone that his agreement to sell the car to Logan was only a joke. Is the agreement legally binding? In other words, do Jaffe and Logan have a contract?

The answer depends on whether the circumstances (Jaffe's just having purchased a new car, the price of the new car, and the fact that Jaffe agreed in writing to sell the car) and Jaffe's words would, to a reasonable person, manifest Jaffe's intention to form a contract. It is not Jaffe's inner belief or intent to make a joke that determines the answer. If a person in Logan's position could reasonably believe that Jaffe intended to form the contract with him, Jaffe would be legally required to sell the car to Logan.

SECTION 3

Types of Contracts

There are many types of contracts. The categories into which contracts are placed involve legal distinctions as to formation, enforceability, and performance.

EMERGING TRENDS IN TECHNOLOGY

Online Contract Forms

Before the printing press, every contract form had to be handwritten. Since the advent of printing, however, most standard contract forms have been readily available at low cost. The introduction of computers into legal practice obviated the need to use preprinted forms and further allowed attorneys to customize contract forms for each given situation. This procedure has been both simplified and expanded by the inclusion of contract forms on simple-to-use CD-ROMs, such as Quicken's *Business Law Partner*. Now the Internet has made available an even larger variety of contract forms, as well as other legal and business forms.

For example, the 'Lectric Law Library has a collection of forms at **www.lectlaw.com/form.html**. In addition to actual forms, there are comments on how the forms should be used and filled out. The site includes forms for the assignment of a contract, a contract for sale of a motor vehicle, and many others. Another excellent online resource for various types of forms is FindForms, at **http://www. findforms.com**.

Other online forms collections can be found at LegalWiz.com (go

to **http://www.legalwiz.com/forms. htm**), a Web site that provides free legal forms, including a form that can be used to sell personal property. At **http://www.legaldocs. com** you will find an electronic forms book that offers hundreds of standardized legal forms, some of which are free. Washburn University School of Law has a Web page containing links to an extensive number of forms archives at **http://www.washlaw. edu/legalformslegalforms.html**. Finally, many law firms post legal forms, including contract forms, on their Web sites as well. For example, see the Web sites of Linsey Law Offices (at **http://www. linseylaw.com**) and Bornstein & Naylor (at **http://www.netset. com/~mb/free.htm**).

IMPLICATIONS FOR THE BUSINESSPERSON

1. Businesspersons should be aware that online contract forms for specific types of contracts are *standardized*—meaning that they contain the terms and conditions that typically appear in such contracts. In other words, such forms should be carefully scrutinized to ensure that they contain terms and conditions specific to the needs of particular contracting parties.
2. The expanding number of forms collections on the Web means that

businesspersons can "shop around" for the forms that most closely meet their needs.
3. Businesspersons who engage in online commerce can post their own customized contract forms on their Web sites for prospective customers or others to review or use. For example, an online merchant may include an offer to purchase or sell certain goods or services and provide a means by which the offer can be accepted— such as by clicking on a box stating "I agree" (see the *Emerging Trends in Technology* in Chapter 11 for further information on online offers).

FOR CRITICAL ANALYSIS

1. Does the availability of contract forms on the Web mean that one need not consult an attorney when forming a contract?
2. Do the downloading and use of contract forms—or any other types of business forms—from Web sites raise any copyright issues?

RELEVANT WEB SITES

In addition to the Web sites mentioned within this feature, FindLaw's forms site, at **http:// www.findlaw.com/16forms/index. html**, provides hyperlinks to a broad array of online collections of contract forms.

BILATERAL VERSUS UNILATERAL CONTRACTS

Every contract involves at least two parties. The *offeror* is the party making the offer. The *offeree* is the party to whom the offer is made. Whether the contract is classified as *unilateral* or *bilateral* depends on what the offeree must do to accept the offer and to bind the offeror to a contract. If to accept the offer the offeree must only *promise* to perform, the contract is a *bilateral contract*. Hence, a bilateral contract is a "promise for a promise." No performance, such as payment of money or delivery of goods, need take place for a bilateral contract to be formed. The contract comes into existence at the moment the promises are exchanged.

For example, Jeff offers to buy Ann's digital camera for $200. Jeff tells Ann that he will give her the money for the camera next Friday, when he gets paid. Ann accepts Jeff's offer and promises to give him the camera when Jeff pays her on Friday. Jeff and Ann have formed a bilateral contract.

In a *unilateral contract*, in contrast, the offer is phrased so that the offeree can accept the offer only by completing the contract performance. Hence, a unilateral contract is a "promise for an act."[4] A classic example of a unilateral contract is as follows: O'Malley says to Parker, "If you carry this package across the Brooklyn Bridge, I'll give you $10." Only on Parker's complete crossing with the package does she fully accept O'Malley's offer to pay $10. If she chooses not to undertake the walk, there are no legal consequences. Contests, lotteries, and other competitions involving prizes are examples of offers for unilateral contracts. If a person complies with the rules of the contest—such as by submitting the right lottery number at the right place and time—a unilateral contract is formed, binding the organization offering the prize to a contract to perform as promised in the offer.

EXPRESS VERSUS IMPLIED CONTRACTS

An *express contract* is one in which the terms of the agreement are fully and explicitly stated in words, oral or written. A signed lease for an apartment or a house is an express written contract. If a classmate calls you on the phone and agrees to buy your textbooks from last semester for $75, an express oral contract has been made.

A contract that is implied from the conduct of the parties is called an *implied-in-fact contract* or an implied contract. This type of contract differs from an express contract in that the *conduct* of the parties, rather than their words, creates and defines the terms of the contract. (Note that a contract may be a mixture of an express contract and an implied-in-fact contract. In other words, a contract may contain some express terms, while others are implied.) Normally, if the following conditions exist, a court will hold that an implied contract was formed:

1. The plaintiff furnished some service or property.
2. The plaintiff expected to be paid for that service or property, and the defendant knew or should have known that payment was expected.
3. The defendant had a chance to reject the services or property and did not.

For example, suppose that you need an accountant to complete your tax return this year. You look through the Yellow Pages and find an accountant at an office in your neighborhood, so you drop by to see her. You go into the accountant's office and explain your problem, and she tells you what her fees are. The next day you return and give her secretary all the necessary information and documents—canceled checks, W-2 forms, and so on. You say nothing expressly to the secretary; rather, you walk out the door. In this situation, you have entered into an implied-in-fact contract to pay the accountant the usual and reasonable fees for her services. The contract is implied by your conduct and by hers. She expects to be paid for completing your tax return, and by bringing in the records she will need to do the work, you have implied an intent to pay her.

QUASI CONTRACTS— CONTRACTS IMPLIED IN LAW

Quasi contracts, or contracts *implied in law*, are wholly different from actual contracts. Whereas express contracts and implied-in-fact contracts are actual contracts formed by the words or conduct of the parties, quasi contracts are fictional contracts created by courts and imposed on parties in the interests of fairness and justice. Quasi contracts are therefore equitable, rather than contractual, in nature. Usually, quasi contracts are imposed to avoid the *unjust enrichment* of one party at the expense of another. Under the doctrine of quasi contract, a plaintiff may recover in *quantum meruit*,[5] a Latin phrase meaning

---

4. Clearly, a contract cannot be "one sided," because, by definition, an agreement implies the existence of two or more parties. Therefore, the phrase *unilateral contract*, if read literally, is a contradiction in terms. As traditionally used in contract law, however, the phrase refers to the kind of contract that results when only one promise is being made (the promise made by the offeror in return for the offeree's performance).

---

5. Pronounced *kwahn*-tuhm *mehr*-oo-wit.

"as much as he deserves." *Quantum meruit* essentially describes the extent of compensation owed under a contract implied in law.

For example, suppose that a vacationing doctor is driving down the highway and encounters Potter lying unconscious on the side of the road. The doctor renders medical aid that saves Potter's life. Although the injured, unconscious Potter did not solicit the medical aid and was not aware that the aid had been rendered, Potter received a valuable benefit, and the requirements for a quasi contract were fulfilled. In such a situation, the law will impose a quasi contract, and Potter normally will have to pay the doctor for the reasonable value of the medical services rendered.

EXECUTED VERSUS EXECUTORY CONTRACTS

Contracts are also classified according to the degree to which they have been performed. A contract that has been fully performed on both sides is called an *executed contract*. A contract that has not been fully performed on either side is called an *executory contract*. If one party has fully performed but the other has not, the contract is said to be executed on the one side and executory on the other, but the contract is still classified as executory.

For example, assume that you agree to buy ten tons of coal from the Northern Coal Company. Further assume that Northern has delivered the coal to your steel mill, where it is now being burned. At this point, the contract is executed on the part of Northern and executory on your part. After you pay Northern for the coal, the contract will be executed on both sides.

VALID, VOID, VOIDABLE, AND UNENFORCEABLE CONTRACTS

A *valid contract* has the elements necessary to entitle at least one of the parties to enforce it in court. Those elements, as mentioned earlier, consist of (1) an agreement consisting of an offer and an acceptance of that offer, (2) supported by legally sufficient consideration, (3) made by parties who have the legal capacity to enter into the contract, and (4) made for a legal purpose.

A *void contract* is no contract at all. The terms *void* and *contract* are contradictory. A void contract produces no legal obligations on the part of any of the

parties. For example, a contract can be void because the purpose of the contract was illegal.

A *voidable contract* is a valid contract but one that can be avoided at the option of one or both of the parties. The party having the option can elect either to avoid any duty to perform or to *ratify* (make valid) the contract. If the contract is avoided, both parties are released from it. If it is ratified, both parties must fully perform their respective legal obligations.

As a general rule, but subject to exceptions, contracts made by minors are voidable at the option of the minor. Contracts entered into under fraudulent conditions are voidable at the option of the defrauded party. In addition, contracts entered into under duress or undue influence are voidable.

An *unenforceable contract* is one that cannot be enforced because of certain legal defenses against it. It is not unenforceable because a party failed to satisfy a legal requirement of the contract; rather, it is a valid contract rendered unenforceable by some statute or law. For example, certain contracts must be in writing, and if they are not, they will not be enforceable except in certain exceptional circumstances.

SECTION 4

Agreement

An essential element for contract formation is **agreement**—the parties must agree on the terms of the contract and manifest to each other their **mutual assent** to the same bargain. Ordinarily, agreement is evidenced by two events: an *offer* and an *acceptance*. One party offers a certain bargain to another party, who then accepts that bargain. The agreement does not necessarily have to be in writing. Both parties, however, must manifest their assent to the same bargain. Once an agreement is reached, if the other elements of a contract are present (consideration, capacity, and legality—discussed in subsequent chapters), a valid contract is formed, generally creating enforceable rights and duties between the parties.

Note that not all agreements are contracts. John and Kevin may agree to play golf on a certain day, but a court would not hold that their agreement is an enforceable contract. A *contractual* agreement only arises when the terms of the agreement impose legally enforceable obligations on the parties.

In today's world, contracts are frequently formed via the Internet. For a discussion of some important factors to be considered in online offers and acceptances, see the *Emerging Trends in Technology* in Chapter 11.

REQUIREMENTS OF THE OFFER

As mentioned earlier, the parties to a contract are the *offeror*, the one who makes an offer or proposal to another party, and the *offeree*, the one to whom the offer or proposal is made. An **offer** is a promise or commitment to do or refrain from doing some specified thing in the future. Under the common law, three elements are necessary for an offer to be effective:

1. The offeror must have a serious intention to become bound by the offer.
2. The terms of the offer must be reasonably certain, or definite, so that the parties and the court can ascertain the terms of the contract.
3. The offer must be communicated by the offeror to the offeree, resulting in the offeree's knowledge of the offer.

Once an effective offer has been made, the offeree has the power to accept the offer. If the offeree accepts, an agreement is formed (and thus a contract, if other essential elements are present).

Intention. The first requirement for an effective offer is a serious intent on the part of the offeror. Serious intent is not determined by the *subjective* intentions, beliefs, and assumptions of the offeror. As discussed in Section 2, courts generally adhere to the *objective theory of contracts* in determining whether a contract has been formed.

Offers made in obvious anger, jest, or undue excitement do not meet the intent test, because a reasonable person would realize that a serious offer was not being made. Because these offers are not effective, an offeree's acceptance does not create an agreement. For example, suppose that you and three classmates ride to school each day in Davina's new automobile, which has a market value of $20,000. One cold morning, the four of you get into the car, but Davina cannot get the car started. She yells in anger, "I'll sell this car to anyone for $500!" You drop $500 in her lap. Given these facts, a reasonable person, taking into consideration Davina's frustration and the obvious difference in worth between the market value of the car and the proposed purchase price, would declare that her offer was not made with serious intent and that you did not have an agreement.

The concept of intention can be further clarified through an examination of the types of expressions and statements that are not offers.

Expressions of Opinion. An expression of opinion is not an offer. It does not evidence an intention to enter into a binding agreement. Consider an example. Hawkins took his son to McGee, a doctor, and asked McGee to operate on the son's hand. McGee said that the boy would be in the hospital three or four days and that the hand would *probably* heal a few days later. The son's hand did not heal for a month, but the father did not win a suit for breach of contract. The court held that McGee had not made an offer to heal the son's hand in three or four days. He had merely expressed an opinion as to when the hand would heal.[6]

Statements of Intention. If Arif says, "I *plan* to sell my stock in Novation, Inc., for $150 per share," a contract is not created if John "accepts" and tenders the $150 per share for the stock. Arif has merely expressed his intention to enter into a future contract for the sale of the stock. If John accepts and tenders the $150 per share, no contract is formed, because a reasonable person would conclude that Arif was only *thinking about* selling his stock, not *promising* to sell it.

Preliminary Negotiations. A request or invitation to negotiate is not an offer. It only expresses a willingness to discuss the possibility of entering into a contract. Included are statements such as "Will you sell Blythe Estate?" or "I wouldn't sell my car for less than $1,000." A reasonable person in the offeree's position would not conclude that these statements evidenced an intention to enter into a binding obligation. Likewise, when construction work is done for the government and private firms, contractors are invited to submit bids. The *invitation* to submit bids is not an offer, and a contractor does not bind the government or private firm by submitting a bid. (The bids that the contractors submit are offers, however, and the government or private firm can bind the contractor by accepting the bid.)

---

6. *Hawkins v. McGee,* 84 N.H. 114, 146 A. 641 (1929).

Agreements to Agree. During preliminary negotiations, the parties may form an agreement to agree to a material term of a contract at some future date. Traditionally, such "agreements to agree" were not considered to be binding contracts. More recent cases illustrate the view that agreements to agree serve valid commercial purposes and can be enforced if the parties clearly intended to be bound by such agreements.

For example, suppose Zahn Consulting leases office space from Leon Properties, Inc. Their lease agreement includes a clause permitting Zahn to extend the lease at an amount of rent to be agreed on when the lease is extended. Under the traditional rule, because the amount of rent is not specified in the lease clause itself, the clause would be too indefinite in its terms to enforce. Under the current view, a court could hold that the parties intended the future rent to be a reasonable amount and could enforce the clause.[7] In other words, under the current view, the emphasis is on the parties' intent rather than on form.

Advertisements, Catalogues, Price Lists, and Circulars. In general, advertisements, mail-order catalogues, price lists, and circulars are treated not as offers to contract but as invitations to negotiate. Suppose that Loeser advertises a used paving machine. The ad is mailed to hundreds of firms and reads, "Used Loeser Construction Co. paving machine. Builds curbs and finishes cement work all in one process. Price $42,350." If Star Paving calls Loeser and says, "We accept your offer," no contract is formed. Any reasonable person would conclude that Loeser was not promising to sell the paving machine but rather was soliciting offers to buy it. If such an ad were held to constitute a legal offer, and fifty people accepted the offer, there would be no way for Loeser to perform all fifty of the resulting contracts. He would have to breach forty-nine contracts. Obviously, the law seeks to avoid such unfairness.

Price lists are another form of invitation to negotiate or trade. A seller's price list is not an offer to sell at that price; it merely invites the buyer to offer to buy at that price. In fact, the seller usually puts "prices subject to change" on the price list. Only in rare circumstances will a price quotation be construed as an offer.[8]

Although most advertisements and the like are treated as invitations to negotiate, this does not mean that an advertisement can never be an offer. If the advertisement makes a promise so definite in character that it is apparent that the offeror is binding himself or herself to the conditions stated, the advertisement is treated as an offer.[9]

Definiteness of Terms. The second requirement for an effective offer involves the definiteness of its terms. An offer must have terms that are reasonably definite so that, if a contract is formed, a court can determine if a breach has occurred and can provide an appropriate remedy. What specific terms are required depends, of course, on the type of contract. Generally, a contract must include the following terms, either expressed in the contract or capable of being reasonably inferred from it:

1. The identification of the parties.
2. The identification of the object or subject matter of the contract (also the quantity, when appropriate), including the work to be performed, with specific identification of such items as goods, services, and land.
3. The consideration to be paid.
4. The time of payment, delivery, or performance.

Courts sometimes are willing to supply a missing term in a contract when the parties have clearly manifested an intent to form a contract. If, in contrast, the parties have attempted to deal with a particular term of the contract but their expression of intent is too vague or uncertain to be given any precise meaning, the court will not supply a "reasonable" term, because to do so might conflict with the intent of the parties. In other words, the court will not rewrite the contract.[10]

If some terms are not specified in the words of a document, a court may nonetheless find that an enforceable contract exists if the terms can be made definite in light of the surrounding circumstances. The following case illustrates this point.

---

7. *Restatement (Second) of Contracts*, Section 33. See also UCC 2–204, 2–305.

8. See, for example, *Fairmount Glass Works v. Grunden-Martin Woodenware Co.*, 106 Ky. 659, 51 S.W. 196 (1899).

9. See, for example, *Lefkowitz v. Great Minneapolis Surplus Store, Inc.*, 251 Minn. 188, 86 N.W.2d 689 (1957).

10. See Chapter 11 and UCC 2–204. Article 2 of the UCC specifies different rules relating to the definiteness of terms used in a contract for the sale of goods. In essence, Article 2 modifies general contract law by requiring less specificity.

CASE 9.1   R. K. Chevrolet, Inc. v. Hayden

Supreme Court of
Virginia, 1997.
253 Va. 50,
480 S.E.2d 477.
**http://www.courts.state.
va.us/opin.htm**[a]

HISTORICAL AND SOCIAL SETTING   *Employment contracts are often considered to be a disadvantage to an employer. Such contracts sometimes work to an employer's advantage, however. An employer invests time and money in hiring and training its employees. An employment contract helps to ensure that the employer will get something in return for this investment. An employment contract can also help to ensure that confidential information to which employees are given access will not be disclosed to unauthorized persons.*

BACKGROUND AND FACTS   *R. K. Chevrolet, Inc., an automobile dealership, employed James Hayden as an assistant manager in its used-car department. Hayden's father owned and operated Coastal Chevrolet, one of R. K. Chevrolet's competitors. In May 1992, after Hayden had worked for R. K. Chevrolet for more than a year, he signed the following document:*

> Contract Between James J. Hayden & R. K. Chevrolet, GEO
> May 12, 1992
> I, James J. Hayden, willingly enter into a two year contract of employment with R. K. Chevrolet, Inc., GEO. The only reason allowable for Mr. Hayden to leave in this time frame, under this contract, is the untimely death of his father. Therefore, with the above exception, James J. Hayden agrees to work continuously at R. K. Chevrolet, Inc., GEO for at least two years in good faith.

Nine months later, Hayden quit without notice. After his departure, R. K. Chevrolet did not realize anticipated profits of $348,832 in its used-car department. The dealership filed a suit in a Virginia state court against Hayden, seeking, among other things, damages for breach of contract. Hayden argued that there was no contract because, in part, the terms were too indefinite. The court ruled in Hayden's favor. The dealership appealed.

**IN THE LANGUAGE
OF THE COURT**

STEPHENSON, Justice.

*   *   *   *

*   *   * *Even if some terms of a contract are uncertain, it may be read in the light of the surrounding circumstances, and, if from such reading, its meaning may be determined, the contract will be enforced.* *   *   * [Emphasis added.]

The trial court concluded that a number of terms were missing from the alleged contract. The court stated that "[t]he document is dated on May the 12th of 1992, but it does not say that it will continue until May the 12th of 1994." The document does state, however, that Hayden agreed to work continuously at R.K. "for at least two years." We think a jury, in the light of the surrounding circumstances, reasonably could conclude that the two-year period commenced on the date the document was executed.

The trial court also stated that there was nothing in the document to indicate what Hayden's position would be. Hayden, however, signed the document as the used car manager, and it is clear from the evidence adduced that he intended to serve in that capacity for the two-year term.

The court further noted that the document did not specify the amount of time Hayden was to work. Again, Hayden was already working as the used car manager when he signed the document, and a jury reasonably could find that he would continue to work the hours in a day and the days in a week that he had been working.

---

a. This page, which is part of a Web site maintained by the state of Virginia, includes links to, among other things, some of the "Supreme Court of Virginia Opinions." Under that heading, click on the box for the format in which you want to view the opinion. From that page, scroll down the list of cases to the *R.K. Chevrolet v. Hayden* case and click on the number (960943) to download the opinion.

Finally, the trial court stated that the document made no mention of what Hayden's compensation would be. From the surrounding circumstances, however, a jury reasonably could have concluded that Hayden's salary would be that which he was receiving at the time he signed the document.

DECISION AND REMEDY	*The Supreme Court of Virginia held that the terms were sufficiently definite to create an enforceable contract. The court reversed the decision of the lower court and remanded the case for a new trial.*

Communication. A third requirement for an effective offer is communication of the offer to the offeree, resulting in the offeree's knowledge of the offer. Ordinarily, one cannot agree to a bargain without knowing that it exists. Suppose that Estrich advertises a reward for the return of his lost dog. Hoban, not knowing of the reward, finds the dog and returns it to Estrich. Hoban cannot recover the reward, because she did not know it had been offered.[11]

TERMINATION OF THE OFFER

The communication of an effective offer to an offeree gives the offeree the power to transform the offer into a binding, legal obligation (a contract) by an acceptance. This power of acceptance, however, does not continue forever. It can be terminated either by the action of the parties or by operation of law.

Termination by Action of the Parties. An offer can be terminated by the action of the parties in any of three ways: by revocation, by rejection, or by counteroffer.

Revocation of the Offer by the Offeror. The offeror's act of withdrawing an offer is known as **revocation.** Unless an offer is irrevocable, the offeror usually can revoke the offer (even if he or she has promised to keep it open), as long as the revocation is communicated to the offeree before the offeree accepts. Revocation may be accomplished by express repudiation of the offer (for example, with a statement such as "I withdraw my previous offer of October 17") or by performance of acts inconsistent with the

existence of the offer, which are made known to the offeree.

The general rule followed by most states is that a revocation becomes effective when the offeree or offeree's agent (a person acting on behalf of the offeree) actually receives it. Therefore, a letter of revocation mailed on April 1 and delivered at the offeree's residence or place of business on April 3 becomes effective on April 3.

Irrevocable Offers. Although most offers are revocable, some can be made irrevocable. One type of irrevocable offer involves the option contract. Increasingly, courts also refuse to allow an offeror to revoke an offer when the offeree has changed position because of justifiable reliance on the offer. (In some circumstances, an offer for the sale of goods made by a merchant may also be considered irrevocable—see the discussion of the "merchant's firm offer" in Chapter 11.)

An *option contract* is created when an offeror promises to hold an offer open for a specified period of time in return for a payment (consideration) given by the offeree. An option contract takes away the offeror's power to revoke the offer for the period of time specified in the option. If no time is specified, then a reasonable period of time is implied.

When the offeree justifiably relies on an offer to his or her detriment, the court may hold that this *detrimental reliance* makes the offer irrevocable. In this situation, the doctrine of **promissory estoppel** comes into play. To *estop* means to bar, impede, or preclude someone from doing something. Thus, promissory estoppel means that the promisor (the offeror) is barred from revoking the offer, in this case because the offeree has already changed her actions in reliance on the offer. We look again at the doctrine of promissory estoppel later in this chapter, in the context of consideration.

---

11. A few states allow recovery of the reward, but not on contract principles. Because Estrich wanted his dog to be returned, and Hoban returned it, these few states would allow Hoban to recover on the basis that it would be unfair to deny her the reward just because she did not know it had been offered.

Detrimental reliance on the part of the offeree can also involve partial performance by the offeree in response to an offer looking toward formulation of a unilateral contract. As discussed earlier in this chapter, the offer to form a unilateral contract invites acceptance only by full performance; merely promising to perform does not constitute acceptance. Injustice can result if an offeree expends time and money in partial performance, and then the offeror revokes the offer before performance can be completed. Many courts will not allow the offeror to revoke the offer after the offeree has performed some substantial part of his or her duties.[12] In effect, partial performance renders the offer irrevocable, giving the original offeree reasonable time to complete performance. Of course, once the performance is complete, a unilateral contract exists.

Rejection of the Offer by the Offeree. The offer may be rejected by the offeree, in which case the offer is terminated. Any subsequent attempt by the offeree to accept will be construed as a new offer, giving the original offeror (now the offeree) the power of acceptance. A rejection is ordinarily accomplished by words or conduct evidencing an intent not to accept the offer. As with revocation, rejection of an offer is effective only when it is actually received by the offeror or the offeror's agent.

Merely inquiring about an offer does not constitute rejection. Suppose that a friend offers to buy your CD-ROM library for $300, and you respond, "Is that your best offer?" or "Will you pay me $375 for it?" A reasonable person would conclude that you had not rejected the offer but had merely made an inquiry for further consideration of the offer. You can still accept and bind your friend to the $300 purchase price. When the offeree merely inquires as to the firmness of the offer, there is no reason to presume that he or she intends to reject it.

Counteroffer by the Offeree. A rejection of the original offer and the simultaneous making of a new offer is called a **counteroffer.** Suppose that Duffy offers to sell her home to Wong for $170,000. Wong responds, "Your price is too high. I'll offer to purchase your house for $160,000." Wong's response is a counteroffer, because it terminates Duffy's offer to sell at $170,000 and creates a new offer by Wong to purchase at $160,000.

At common law, the **mirror image rule** requires the offeree's acceptance to match the offeror's offer exactly—to mirror the offer. Any material change in, or addition to, the terms of the original offer automatically terminates that offer and substitutes the counteroffer. The counteroffer, of course, need not be accepted; but if the original offeror does accept the terms of the counteroffer, a valid contract is created.[13]

Termination by Operation of Law. The power of the offeree to transform the offer into a binding, legal obligation can be terminated by operation of law through the occurrence of the following events:

1. Lapse of time.
2. Destruction of the specific subject matter of the offer.
3. Death or incompetence of the offeror or the offeree.
4. Supervening illegality of the proposed contract.

An offer terminates automatically by law when the period of time specified in the offer has passed. For example, suppose Alejandro offers to sell his camper to Kelly if she accepts within twenty days. Kelly must accept within the twenty-day period, or the offer will lapse (terminate). The time period specified in an offer normally begins to run when the offer is actually received by the offeree, not when it is sent or drawn up. When the offer is delayed (through the misdelivery of mail, for example), the period begins to run from the date the offeree would have received the offer, but only if the offeree knows or should know that the offer is delayed.[14]

If no time for acceptance is specified in the offer, the offer terminates at the end of a *reasonable* period of time. What constitutes a reasonable period of time depends on the subject matter of the contract, business and market conditions, and other relevant circumstances. An offer to sell farm produce, for example, will terminate sooner than an offer to sell farm equipment because farm produce is perishable and subject to greater fluctuations in market value.

---

12. *Restatement (Second) of Contracts,* Section 45.

13. The mirror image rule has been greatly modified in regard to sales contracts. Section 2–207 of the UCC provides that a contract is formed if the offeree makes a definite expression of acceptance (such as signing the form in the appropriate location), even though the terms of the acceptance modify or add to the terms of the original offer (see Chapter 11).

14. *Restatement (Second) of Contracts,* Section 49.

ACCEPTANCE

Acceptance is a voluntary act (either words or conduct) by the offeree that shows assent (agreement) to the terms of an offer. The acceptance must be unequivocal and communicated to the offeror. To exercise the power of acceptance effectively, the offeree must accept unequivocally. This is the *mirror image rule* previously discussed. If the acceptance is subject to new conditions or if the terms of the acceptance materially change the original offer, the acceptance may be deemed a counteroffer that implicitly rejects the original offer. An acceptance may be unequivocal even though the offeree expresses dissatisfaction with the contract. For example, "I accept the offer, but I wish I could have gotten a better price" is an effective acceptance. So, too, is "I accept, but can you shave the price?" In contrast, the statement "I accept the offer but only if I can pay on ninety days' credit" is not an unequivocal acceptance and operates as a counteroffer, rejecting the original offer.

Certain terms when added to an acceptance will not qualify the acceptance sufficiently to constitute rejection of the offer. Suppose that in response to an offer to sell a piano, the offeree replies, "I accept; please send a written contract." The offeree is requesting a written contract but is not making it a condition for acceptance. Therefore, the acceptance is effective without the written contract. If the offeree replies, "I accept if you send a written contract," however, the acceptance is expressly conditioned on the request for a writing, and the statement is not an acceptance but a counteroffer. (Notice how important each word is!)

Silence as Acceptance.　Ordinarily, silence cannot constitute acceptance, even if the offeror states, "By your silence and inaction you will be deemed to have accepted this offer." This general rule applies because an offeree should not be obligated to act affirmatively to reject an offer when no consideration has passed to the offeree to impose such a duty.

In some instances, however, the offeree does have a duty to speak, in which case his or her silence or inaction will operate as an acceptance. For example, silence may be an acceptance when an offeree takes the benefit of offered services even though he or she had an opportunity to reject them and knew that they were offered with the expectation of compensation.

Silence can also operate as acceptance when the offeree has had prior dealings with the offeror.

Suppose that a merchant routinely receives shipments from a certain supplier and always notifies the supplier when defective goods are rejected. In this situation, silence regarding a shipment will constitute acceptance. Additionally, if a person solicits an offer specifying that certain terms and conditions are acceptable, and the offeror makes the offer in response to the solicitation, the offeree has a duty to reject—that is, a duty to tell the offeror that the offer is not acceptable. Failure to reject (silence) operates as an acceptance.

Communication of Acceptance.　Whether the offeror must be notified of the acceptance depends on the nature of the contract. In a bilateral contract, communication of acceptance is necessary because acceptance is in the form of a promise (not performance) and the contract is formed when the promise is made (rather than when the act is performed). The offeree must communicate the acceptance to the offeror. Communication of acceptance is not necessary, however, if the offer dispenses with the requirement. Additionally, if the offer can be accepted by silence, no communication is necessary.

Because in a unilateral contract the full performance of some act is called for, acceptance is usually evident, and notification is therefore unnecessary. Exceptions do exist, however. When the offeror requests notice of acceptance or has no adequate means of determining whether the requested act has been performed, or when the law requires notice of acceptance, then notice is necessary.

Mode and Timeliness of Acceptance.　Acceptance in bilateral contracts must be timely. The general rule is that acceptance in a bilateral contract is timely if it is made before the offer is terminated. Problems arise, however, when the parties involved are not dealing face to face. In such cases, acceptance takes effect, thus completing formation of the contract, at the time the acceptance is communicated via the mode expressly or impliedly authorized by the offeror.

This rule traditionally has been referred to as the **mailbox rule,** also called the "deposited acceptance rule," because once an acceptance has been deposited into a mailbox, it is "out of the offeree's possession." Under this rule, if the authorized mode of communication is the mail, then an acceptance becomes valid when it is dispatched by mail (even if it is never received by the offeror). Thus, whereas a revocation becomes effective only when it is received by the offeree, an acceptance becomes effective on *dispatch*, providing that *authorized* means of communication are used.

An authorized means of communication may be either expressly authorized—that is, expressly stipulated in the offer—or impliedly authorized by the facts and circumstances surrounding the situation or by law. When an offeror specifies how acceptance should be made (for example, by overnight delivery), *express authorization* is said to exist, and the contract is not formed unless the offeree uses that specified mode of acceptance. Moreover, both offeror and offeree are bound in contract the moment this means of acceptance is employed. If overnight delivery is expressly authorized as the only means of acceptance, a contract is created as soon as the offeree delivers the message to the express delivery company. The contract would still exist even if the delivery company failed to deliver the message.

Many offerors, for one reason or another, do not indicate their preferred method of acceptance. When the offeror does not specify expressly that the offeree is to accept by a certain means, or that the acceptance will be effective only when received, acceptance of an offer may be made by any medium that is *reasonable under the circumstances*.[15] Several factors determine whether the acceptance was reasonable: the nature of the circumstances as they existed at the time the offer was made, the means used by the offeror to transmit the offer to the offeree, and the reliability of the offer's delivery.

An acceptance sent by means not expressly or impliedly authorized is normally not effective until it is received by the offeror. If an acceptance is timely sent and timely received, however, despite the means by which it is transmitted, it is considered to have been effective on its dispatch.

SECTION 5

Consideration

The fact that a promise has been made does not mean the promise can or will be enforced. No promise is enforceable without consideration. **Consideration** is usually defined as the value (such as money) given in return for a promise (such as the promise to sell a stamp collection on receipt of payment).

Often, consideration is broken down into two parts: (1) something of *legal value* must be given in exchange for the promise, and (2) there must be a *bargained-for* exchange. The "something of legal value" may consist of a return promise that is bargained for. If it consists of performance, that performance may be (1) an act (other than a promise); (2) a forbearance (a refraining from action); or (3) the creation, modification, or destruction of a legal relation.[16]

The following case is one of the classics of contract law. The issue before the court was whether refraining from certain behavior at the request of another is sufficient consideration to support a promise to pay a sum of money.

---

15. *Restatement (Second) of Contracts*, Section 30.

16. *Restatement (Second) of Contracts*, Section 71.

CASE 9.2   Hamer v. Sidway

Court of Appeals
of New York,
Second Division, 1891.
124 N.Y. 538,
27 N.E. 256.

BACKGROUND AND FACTS   *William E. Story, Sr., was the uncle of William E. Story II. In the presence of family members and guests invited to a family gathering, the elder Story promised to pay his nephew $5,000 if he would refrain from drinking, using tobacco, swearing, and playing cards or billiards for money until he reached the age of twenty-one. (Note that in 1869, when this contract was formed, it was legal in New York to drink and play cards for money prior to the age of twenty-one.) The nephew agreed and fully performed his part of the bargain. When he reached the age of twenty-one, he wrote and told his uncle that he had kept his part of the agreement and was therefore entitled to $5,000. The uncle replied that he was pleased with his nephew's performance, writing, "I have no doubt but you have, for which you shall have five thousand dollars, as I promised you. I had the money in the bank the day you was twenty-one years old that I intend for you, and you shall have the money certain. . . . P.S. You can consider this money on interest." The nephew received his uncle's letter and thereafter consented that the money should remain with his uncle according to the terms and conditions of the* *letter. The uncle died about twelve years later without having paid his nephew any part of the $5,000 and interest. The executor of the uncle's estate (Sidway, the defendant in this action) did not want to pay the $5,000 (with interest) to Hamer, a third party to whom the nephew had transferred his rights in the note, claiming that there had been no valid consideration for the promise. The court disagreed with the executor and reviewed the doctrine of detriment and benefit as valid consideration under the law.*

IN THE LANGUAGE
OF THE COURT

PARKER, J. [Justice]

*   *   *   *

*   *   * Courts will not ask whether the thing which forms the consideration does in fact benefit the promisee or a third party, or is of any substantial value to any one. It is enough that something is promised, done, forborne, or suffered by the party to whom the promise is made as consideration for the promise made to him. *In general a waiver of any legal right at the request of another party is a sufficient consideration for a promise.* Any damage, or suspension, or forbearance of a right will be sufficient to sustain a promise. *   *   * Now, applying this rule to the facts before us, the promisee used tobacco, occasionally drank liquor, and he had a legal right to do so. That right he abandoned for a period of years upon the strength of the promise of the testator that for such forbearance he would give him $5,000. We need not speculate on the effort which may have been required to give up the use of those stimulants. It is sufficient that he restricted his lawful freedom of action within certain prescribed limits upon the faith of his uncle's agreement, and now, having fully performed the conditions imposed, it is of no moment whether such performance actually proved a benefit to the promisor, and the court will not inquire into it; but, were it a proper subject of inquiry, we see nothing in this record that would permit a determination that the uncle was not benefited in a legal sense. [Emphasis added.]

DECISION
AND REMEDY

The court ruled that the nephew had provided legally sufficient consideration by giving up smoking, drinking, swearing, and playing cards or billiards for money until he reached the age of twenty-one and was therefore entitled to the money.

ETHICAL
CONSIDERATIONS

The Hamer v. Sidway *case is a good illustration of the distinction between benefits to the promisor and detriment to the promisee. Here the court did not inquire as to whether a benefit had flowed to the promisor but required only that there had been a legally sufficient detriment to the promisee. The court did note, however, that arguably the promisor had also benefited by the contract—to the extent that the uncle considered it a benefit that his nephew had given up various vices, protected the family's reputation, and so on.*

ADEQUACY OF CONSIDERATION

Adequacy of consideration refers to the fairness of the bargain. In general, a court will not question the adequacy of consideration if the consideration is legally sufficient. Under the doctrine of freedom of contract, parties are normally free to bargain as they wish. If people could sue merely because they had entered into an unwise contract, the courts would be overloaded with frivolous suits.

Extreme Cases. In extreme cases, a court may consider the adequacy of consideration in terms of its amount or worth because inadequate consideration may indicate fraud, duress, undue influence, or a lack of bargained-for exchange. It may also reflect a party's

incompetence (for example, an individual might have been too intoxicated or simply too young to make a contract). Suppose that Dylan has a house worth $100,000 and he sells it for $50,000. A $50,000 sale could indicate that the buyer unduly pressured Dylan into selling the house at that price or that Dylan was defrauded into selling the house at far below market value. (Of course, it might also indicate that Dylan was in a hurry to sell and that the amount was legally sufficient.)

Preexisting Duty. Under most circumstances, a promise to do what one already has a legal duty to do does not constitute legally sufficient consideration, because no legal detriment is incurred.[17] The preex-

---

17. See *Foakes v. Beer*, 9 App.Cas. 605 (1884).

isting legal duty may be imposed by law or may arise out of a previous contract. A sheriff, for example, cannot collect a reward for providing information leading to the capture of a criminal if the sheriff already has a legal duty to capture the criminal. Likewise, if a party is already bound by contract to perform a certain duty, that duty cannot serve as consideration for a second contract. To illustrate, suppose that Bauman-Bache, Inc., begins construction on a seven-story office building and after three months demands an extra $75,000 on its contract. If the extra $75,000 is not paid, it will stop working. The owner of the land, having no one else to complete construction, agrees to pay the extra $75,000. The agreement is not enforceable, because it is not supported by legally sufficient consideration; Bauman-Bache was under a preexisting contract to complete the building.

Past Consideration. Promises made in return for actions or events that have already taken place are unenforceable. These promises lack consideration in that the element of bargained-for exchange is missing. In short, you can bargain for something to take place now or in the future but not for something that has already taken place. Therefore, **past consideration** is no consideration.

Suppose, for example, that Elsie, a real estate agent, does her friend Judy a favor by selling Judy's house and not charging any commission. Later, Judy says to Elsie, "In return for your generous act, I will pay you $3,000." This promise is made in return for past consideration and is thus unenforceable; in effect, Judy is stating her intention to give Elsie a gift.

PROMISSORY ESTOPPEL

As discussed in the context of irrevocable offers, under the doctrine of *promissory estoppel*, a person who has reasonably and substantially relied on the promise of another may be able to obtain some measure of recovery. This doctrine is applied in a wide variety of contexts in which a promise is otherwise unenforceable, such as when a promise is not supported by consideration. Under this doctrine, a court may enforce an otherwise unenforceable promise to avoid the injustice that would therefore result. For the doctrine to be applied, the following elements are required:

1. There must be a clear and definite promise.
2. The promisee must justifiably rely on the promise.
3. The reliance normally must be of a substantial and definite character.
4. Justice will be better served by enforcement of the promise.

If these requirements are met, a promise may be enforced even though it is not supported by consideration. In essence, the promisor will be *estopped* (prevented) from asserting the lack of consideration as a defense. For example, suppose that your uncle tells you, "I'll pay you $150 a week so you won't have to work anymore." In reliance on your uncle's promise, you quit your job, but your uncle refuses to pay you. Under the doctrine of promissory estoppel, you may be able to enforce such a promise.[18]

In the following case, an individual sought to recover damages under the doctrine of promissory estoppel from a prospective employer that reneged on its promise of employment.

---

18. *Ricketts v. Scothorn,* 57 Neb. 51, 77 N.W. 365 (1898).

CASE 9.3   Goff-Hamel v. Obstetricians & Gynecologists, P.C.

Supreme Court of Nebraska, 1999.
256 Neb. 19,
588 N.W.2d 798.
http://www.findlaw.com/
11stategov/ne/neca.
html[a]

BACKGROUND AND FACTS *Julie Goff-Hamel worked for Hastings Family Planning. After eleven years, Goff-Hamel was earning $24,000, plus benefits: six weeks' paid maternity leave, six weeks' vacation, twelve paid holidays, twelve sick days, educational reimbursement, and medical and dental insurance. In July 1993, representatives of Obstetricians & Gynecologists, P.C.,[b] (Obstetricians)—including part owner Dr. George Adam and personnel consultant Larry Draper—asked Goff-Hamel to work for Obstetricians. Adam told Goff-Hamel that the position was full-time, at a salary of $10 per hour, and included two weeks' paid vacation, three or four paid holidays, uniforms, and an educational*

---

a. On this page, click on "1999," and on that page, click on "January." Scroll down to the case name, and click on "19990129" to access the opinion.

b. *P.C.* is an abbreviation for "professional corporation," which is a special form for a business entity. Corporations are discussed in more detail in Chapter 19.

stipend. A retirement plan would start after the end of the second year, retroactive to the end of the first year. The job did not include health insurance. Goff-Hamel agreed to start in October and gave notice to Hastings in August. She was given uniforms for her new job and a copy of her work schedule. The day before she was scheduled to start, Draper told her that she need not report to work and that Janel Foote, the wife of Dr. Terry Foote, a part owner, opposed her hiring. Goff-Hamel filed a suit in a Nebraska state court against Obstetricians, seeking damages in part on the basis of detrimental reliance. The court concluded that because she was to be employed at will,[c] her employment could be terminated at any time—which included before she began working—and issued a summary judgment in favor of Obstetricians. Goff-Hamel appealed to the Nebraska Supreme Court.

IN THE LANGUAGE OF THE COURT

WRIGHT, J. [Justice].
*   *   *   *

Other jurisdictions which have addressed the question of whether a cause of action for promissory estoppel can be stated in the context of a prospective at-will employee are split on the issue. Some have held that an employee can recover damages incurred as a result of resigning from the former at-will employment in reliance on a promise of other at-will employment. They have determined that when a prospective employer knows or should know that a promise of employment will induce an employee to leave his or her current job, such employer shall be liable for the reliant's damages. *   *   * [T]hey have concluded that the employee would have continued to work in his or her prior employment if it were not for the offer by the prospective employer. Although damages have not been allowed for wages lost from the prospective at-will employment, damages have been allowed based upon wages from the prior employment and other damages incurred in reliance on the job offer.

In contrast, other jurisdictions have held as a matter of law that a prospective employee cannot recover damages incurred in reliance on an unfulfilled promise of at-will employment, concluding that reliance on a promise consisting solely of at-will employment is unreasonable as a matter of law because the employee should know that the promised employment could be terminated by the employer at any time for any reason without liability. These courts have stated that an anomalous result occurs when recovery is allowed for an employee who has not begun work, when the same employee's job could be terminated without liability 1 day after beginning work.
*   *   *   *

*   *   * [W]e conclude under the facts of this case that promissory estoppel can be asserted in connection with the offer of at-will employment and that the trial court erred in granting Obstetricians summary judgment. *A cause of action for promissory estoppel is based upon a promise which the promisor should reasonably expect to induce action or forbearance on the part of the promisee [and] which does in fact induce such action or forbearance.* *   *   * [Emphasis added.]
*   *   *   *

The facts are not disputed that Obstetricians offered Goff-Hamel employment. Apparently, at the direction of the spouse of one of the owners, Obstetricians refused to honor its promise of employment. It is also undisputed that Goff-Hamel relied upon Obstetricians' promise of employment to her detriment in that she terminated her employment of 11 years. Therefore, under the facts of this case, the trial court should have granted summary judgment in favor of Goff-Hamel on the issue of liability.

DECISION AND REMEDY

The Nebraska Supreme Court reversed the judgment of the trial court. The state supreme court held that promissory estoppel can be asserted in connection with an offer of at-will employment. The court remanded the case for a determination of the amount of damages to which Goff-Hamel was entitled.

---

c. *Employment at will* is an employment relationship that either party may terminate at any time for any reason. Employment at will is explained in more detail in Chapter 21.

SECTION 6

Capacity

Although the parties to a contract must assume certain risks, the law indicates that neither party should be allowed to benefit from the other party's lack of *contractual capacity*—the legal ability to enter into a contractual relationship. Courts generally presume the existence of contractual capacity, but there are some situations in which capacity is lacking or may be questionable. In many situations, a party may have the capacity to enter into a valid contract but also have the right to avoid liability under it.

Minors usually are not legally bound by contracts. Subject to certain exceptions, the contracts entered into by a minor are voidable at the option of that minor. The minor has the option of *disaffirming* (renouncing) the contract and setting aside the contract and all legal obligations arising from it. An adult who enters into a contract with a minor, however, cannot avoid his or her contractual duties on the ground that the minor can do so. Unless the minor exercises the option to disffirm the contract, the adult party is bound by it.

Intoxication is a condition in which a person's normal capacity to act or think is inhibited by alcohol or some other drug. If the person was sufficiently intoxicated to lack mental capacity, then the transaction is voidable at the option of the intoxicated person even if the intoxication was purely voluntary.

If a person has been adjudged mentally incompetent by a court of law and a guardian has been appointed, any contract made by the mentally incompetent person is void—no contract exists. Only the guardian can enter into binding legal duties on the incompetent person's behalf.

SECTION 7

Legality

A contract to do something that is prohibited by federal or state statutory law is illegal and, as such, void from the outset and thus unenforceable. Also, a contract that calls for a tortious act or an action contrary to public policy is illegal and unenforceable. It is important to note that a contract or a clause in a contract may be illegal even in the absence of a specific statute prohibiting the action promised by the contract.

Although contracts involve private parties, some are not enforceable because of the negative impact they would have on society. Contracts in restraint of trade (anticompetitive agreements) usually adversely affect the public (which favors competition in the economy) and typically violate one or more federal or state statutes.[19] Many such contracts involve a type of restraint called a *covenant not to compete*, or a restrictive covenant.

Basically, a restriction on competition must be reasonable—that is, not any greater than necessary to protect a legitimate business interest. The following case illustrates this point.

---

19. Such as the Sherman Act, the Clayton Act, and the Federal Trade Commission Act (see Chapters 27 and 28).

CASE 9.4   Brunswick Floors, Inc. v. Guest

Court of Appeals of
Georgia, 1998.
506 S.E.2d 670.

HISTORICAL AND SOCIAL SETTING   *The value of a business frequently depends on the goodwill between key employees and customers. To enhance this value, a business will invest its key employees with training, experience, customer lists, trade secrets, and other valuable information. It can be devastating when a key employee quits, or is fired, and goes into business to compete with his or her former employer. A covenant not to compete can protect goodwill, and other assets, by at least prohibiting an employee from stealing existing customers. A covenant not to compete is enforceable if its provisions are reasonable, if it is part of a valid contract, and if it is related to the protection of a legitimate interest. As much as a business might wish, however, legitimate interests do not include preventing competition.*

BACKGROUND AND FACTS   *Brian Guest was a floor covering installer for Brunswick Floors, Inc. Guest signed a covenant not to compete that prohibited him for two years* *after termination of employment from engaging in the floor covering business in virtually any way, within an eighty-mile radius of Brunswick's location. After Guest quit Brunswick, he went to work as an independent flooring contractor. Brunswick filed a suit in a Georgia state court against Guest based on the covenant not to compete. The court ruled in part that the covenant unduly restricted Guest's right to earn a living. Brunswick appealed.*

IN THE LANGUAGE OF THE COURT

RUFFIN, Judge.

* * * * *

* * * [A]n employer is permitted to include in * * * a covenant [not to compete] the territory in which the employee has in fact performed work, thus protecting itself from the unfair appropriation of good will and information acquired in the course of that work. In contrast, [a] restriction relating to the area in which the employer does business is generally unenforceable due to overbreadth, unless the employer can show a legitimate business interest that will be protected by such an expansive geographic description.

In this case, the covenant restricts Guest from working within an 80 mile radius of Brunswick Floors' location * * * . The 80 mile radius relates to the area in which the employer, Brunswick Floors, and not the employee, Guest, did business. * * *

[Robert] Blake [the president of Brunswick] testified that "if our employees start * * * working for our competitors, then certainly our market share would face, you know, diminishing status." *Avoidance of competition, however, is not a legitimate business interest.* [Emphasis added.]

Brunswick Floors contends the training and money expended on Guest legitimizes their interest. * * * Here, Guest's minimal training does not outweigh the substantial harm imposed by prohibiting him from installing carpet in an 80 mile radius. Thus, we find this to be an overbroad territorial limitation.

We also find the scope of activity prohibited in the non-compete provision is overbroad. * * * This imposes a greater limitation on the employee than is necessary because [Guest] is prohibited from being an officer or director or owning stock in other companies, activities which are very different from [his] work as [a floor covering installer].

DECISION AND REMEDY

The Court of Appeals of Georgia held that a covenant not to compete is unenforceable if it bars an employee from engaging in the employer's business in virtually any way within the area in which the employer does business. The court affirmed the decision of the lower court.

SECTION 8

Genuineness of Assent

A contract has been entered into by two parties, each with full legal capacity and for a legal purpose. The contract is also supported by consideration. Nonetheless, the contract may be unenforceable if the parties have not genuinely assented to its terms. Lack of **genuineness of assent** can be used as a defense to the contract's enforceability.

Genuineness of assent may be lacking because of a mistake, misrepresentation, undue influence, or duress—in other words, because there is no true "meeting of the minds."

MISTAKES

We all make mistakes, and it is therefore not surprising that mistakes are made when contracts are formed. It is important to distinguish between *mistakes of fact* and *mistakes of value or quality*. Only a mistake of fact allows a contract to be avoided.

Mistakes of fact occur in two forms—*unilateral* and *mutual (bilateral)*. A unilateral mistake is made by only one of the contracting parties; a mutual, or bilateral, mistake is made by both.

Unilateral Mistakes. A unilateral mistake occurs when one contracting party makes a mistake as to some *material fact*—that is, a fact important to the subject matter of the contract. The general rule is that a unilateral mistake does not afford the mistaken party any right to relief from the contract. For example, DeVinck intends to sell his motor home for $17,500. When he learns that Benson is interested in buying a used motor home, DeVinck faxes Benson an offer to sell the vehicle to him. When typing the fax, however, DeVinck mistakenly keys in the price of $15,700. Benson immediately sends DeVinck a fax, accepting DeVinck's offer. Even though DeVinck intended to sell his motor home for $17,500, his unilateral mistake falls on him. He is bound in contract to sell the motor home to Benson for $15,700.

There are at least two exceptions to this general rule.[20] First, if the *other* party to the contract knows or should have known that a mistake of fact was made, the contract may not be enforceable. In the above example, if Benson knew that DeVinck intended to sell his motor home for $17,500, then DeVinck's unilateral mistake (stating $15,700 in his offer) may render the resulting contract unenforceable. The second exception arises when a unilateral mistake of fact was due to a mathematical mistake in addition, subtraction, division, or multiplication and was made inadvertently and without gross (extreme) negligence. If a contractor's bid was low because he or she made a mistake in addi-

tion when totaling the estimated costs, any contract resulting from the bid may be rescinded. Of course, in both situations, the mistake must still involve some *material* fact.

Bilateral Mistakes. When both parties are mistaken about the same material fact, the contract can be rescinded by either party.[21] To illustrate: Assume that at Umberto's art gallery, Keeley buys a painting of a landscape. Both Umberto and Keeley believe that the painting is by the artist Van Gogh. Later, Keeley discovers that the painting is a very clever fake. Because neither Umberto nor Keeley was aware of this material fact when they made their deal, Keeley can rescind the contract and recover the purchase price of the painting.

A word or term in a contract may be subject to more than one reasonable interpretation. In that situation, if the parties to the contract attach materially different meanings to the term, their mutual mistake of fact may allow the contract to be rescinded because there has been no "meeting of the minds," or true assent, which is required for a contract to arise. The classic case on mutual mistake involved a ship named *Peerless* that was to sail from Bombay with certain cotton goods on board. More than one ship named *Peerless* sailed from Bombay that winter, however.

---

20. The *Restatement (Second) of Contracts*, Section 153, liberalizes the general rule to take into account the modern trend of allowing avoidance even though only one party has been mistaken.

21. *Restatement (Second) of Contracts*, Section 152.

CASE 9.5   Raffles v. Wichelhaus

Court of Exchequer,
England, 1864.
159 Eng.Rep. 375.

BACKGROUND AND FACTS   *The defendant, Wichelhaus, purchased a shipment of Surat cotton from the plaintiff, Raffles, "to arrive 'Peerless' from Bombay." The defendant expected the goods to be shipped on the* Peerless *sailing from Bombay, India, in October. The plaintiff expected to ship the goods on a different* Peerless, *which sailed from Bombay in December. By the time the goods arrived and the plaintiff tried to deliver them, the defendant was no longer willing to accept them.*

IN THE LANGUAGE
OF THE COURT

PER CURIAM [by the whole court].

*   *   *   *

[The defendants asserted that the] ship mentioned in the *   *   * agreement was meant and intended by the defendants to be the ship called the "Peerless," which sailed from Bombay *   *   * in October; and that the plaintiff was not ready and willing and did not offer to deliver to the defendants any bales of cotton which arrived by the last mentioned ship, but instead thereof was only ready and willing and offered to deliver to the defendants 125 bales of Surat cotton which arrived by another and different ship, which was also called the "Peerless," and which sailed from Bombay * * * in December.

      *   *   *   *

There is nothing on the face of the contract to show that any particular ship called the "Peerless" was meant; but the moment it appears that two ships called the "Peerless" were about to sail from Bombay there is latent ambiguity, and parol evidence[a] may be given for the purpose of shewing [showing] that the defendant meant one "Peerless" and the plaintiff another. That being so, there was no consensus *ad idem* [on the point], and therefore no contract.

DECISION AND REMEDY   *The judgment was for the defendant, Wichelhaus. The court held that no mutual assent existed, because the parties had attached materially different meanings to an essential term of the written contract (the ship that was to transport the goods). This being so, oral testimony would have been needed to determine whether the parties had actually meant the same ship. If both had meant the same ship, then the contract would have been enforceable.*

---

a. With respect to contracts, *parol evidence* is evidence that the document itself does not furnish but that other sources (such as, in this case, oral testimony) provide.

FRAUDULENT MISREPRESENTATION

In the context of contract law, fraud may affect the genuineness of the innocent party's consent to the contract. Thus, the transaction is not voluntary in the sense of involving "mutual assent." When an innocent party is fraudulently induced to enter into a contract, the contract normally can be avoided because that party has not *voluntarily* consented to its terms.[22] Normally, the innocent party can either rescind the contract and be restored to his or her original position or enforce the contract and seek damages for any injuries resulting from the fraud.

The word *fraudulent* means many things in the law. Generally, fraudulent misrepresentation refers only to misrepresentation that is consciously false and is intended to mislead another. The perpetrator of the fraudulent misrepresentation knows or believes that the assertion is false or knows that he or she does not have a basis (stated or implied) for the assertion.[23]

What is at issue is whether the defendant believed that the plaintiff was substantially certain to be misled as a result of the misrepresentation. Dantzler, for example, makes a statement to the ABC Credit Rating Company about his financial condition that he knows is untrue. Dantzler realizes that ABC will publish this information for its subscribers. Marchetti, a subscriber, receives the published information. Relying on that information, Marchetti is induced to make a contract to lend money to Dantzler. Dantzler's statement is a fraudulent misrepresentation, and the contract is voidable by Marchetti.

Typically, fraudulent misrepresentation consists of the following elements:

1. A misrepresentation of a material fact must occur.
2. There must be an intent to deceive.
3. The innocent party must justifiably rely on the misrepresentation.

To collect damages, a party must also have been injured. To obtain rescission of a contract, or to defend against the enforcement of a contract on the basis of fraudulent misrepresentation, in most states a party need not have suffered an injury.

NONFRAUDULENT MISREPRESENTATION

If a plaintiff seeks to rescind a contract because of *fraudulent* misrepresentation, the plaintiff must prove that the defendant had the intent to deceive.

---

22. *Restatement (Second) of Contracts*, Sections 163 and 164.
23. *Restatement (Second) of Contracts*, Section 162.

Most courts also allow rescission in cases involving *nonfraudulent* misrepresentation—that is, innocent or negligent misrepresentation—if all of the other elements of misrepresentation exist.

UNDUE INFLUENCE

Undue influence arises from special kinds of relationships in which one party can greatly influence another party, thus overcoming that party's free will. Minors and elderly people, for example, are often under the influence of guardians. If the guardian induces a young or elderly ward to enter into a contract that benefits the guardian, undue influence may have been exerted. Undue influence can arise from a number of confidential or fiduciary relationships:[24] attorney-client, physician-patient, guardian-ward, parent-child, husband-wife, or trustee-beneficiary. The essential feature of undue influence is that the party being taken advantage of does not, in reality, exercise free will in entering into a contract. A contract entered into under excessive or undue influence lacks genuine assent and is therefore voidable.[25]

DURESS

Assent to the terms of a contract is not genuine if one of the parties is *forced* into the agreement. Forcing a party to do something, including entering into a contract, through fear created by threats is legally defined as *duress*. In addition, blackmail or extortion to induce consent to a contract constitutes duress. Duress is both a defense to the enforcement of a contract and a ground for the rescission of a contract.

Generally, the threatened act must be wrongful or illegal. Threatening to exercise a legal right is not ordinarily illegal and usually does not constitute duress. Suppose that Donovan injures Jaworski in an auto accident. The police are not called. Donovan has no automobile insurance, but she has substantial assets. Jaworski is willing to settle the potential claim out of court for $3,000. Donovan refuses. After much arguing, Jaworski loses her patience and says, "If you don't pay me $3,000 right now, I'm going to sue you for $35,000." Donovan is frightened and gives Jaworski a check for $3,000. Later in the day, she stops payment on the check. Jaworski comes back to sue her for the

$3,000. Although Donovan argues that she was the victim of duress, the threat of a civil suit is normally not considered duress.

Economic need is generally not sufficient to constitute duress, even when one party exacts a very high price for an item that the other party needs. If the party exacting the price also creates the need, however, *economic duress* may be found. The Internal Revenue Service, for example, assessed a large tax and penalty against Weller. Weller retained Eyman, the accountant who had filed the tax returns on which the assessment was based, to resist the assessment. Two days before the deadline for filing a reply with the Internal Revenue Service, Eyman declined to represent Weller unless he signed a very high contingency-fee agreement for his services. The agreement was unenforceable.[26] Although Eyman had threatened only to withdraw his services, something that he was legally entitled to do, he was responsible for delaying the withdrawal until the last days. Because it would have been impossible at that late date to obtain adequate representation elsewhere, Weller was forced either to sign the contract or to lose his right to challenge the IRS assessment.

ADHESION CONTRACTS AND UNCONSCIONABILITY

Questions concerning genuineness of assent may arise when the terms of a contract are dictated by a party with overwhelming bargaining power and the signer must agree to those terms or go without the commodity or service in question. Such contracts are often referred to as *adhesion contracts*. An adhesion contract is written *exclusively* by one party (the dominant party, usually the seller or the creditor) and presented to the other party (the adhering party, usually the buyer or the borrower) on a take-it-or-leave-it basis. In other words, the adhering party has no opportunity to negotiate the terms of the contract.

Standard-form contracts often contain fine-print provisions that shift a risk naturally borne by one party to the other. Such contracts are used by a variety of businesses and include life insurance policies, residential leases, loan agreements, and employment agency contracts. To avoid enforcement of the contract or of a particular clause, the aggrieved party must show that the parties had substantially unequal bargaining positions

---

24. A fiduciary relationship is one involving a high degree of trust and confidence.

25. *Restatement (Second) of Contracts*, Section 177.

26. *Thompson Crane & Trucking Co. v. Eyman*, 123 Cal.App.2d 904, 267 P.2d 1043 (1954).

and that enforcement would be manifestly unfair or oppressive. If the required showing is made, the contract or particular term is deemed **unconscionable**[27]— that is, generally speaking, so one sided under the circumstances as to be unfair—and not enforced. Technically, unconscionability under Section 2–302 of the Uniform Commercial Code (UCC) applies only to contracts for the sale of goods. Many courts, however, have broadened the concept and applied it in other situations.

The great degree of discretion permitted a court to invalidate or strike down a contract or clause as being unconscionable has met with resistance. As a result, some states have not adopted Section 2–302 of the UCC. In those states, the legislature and the courts prefer to rely on traditional notions of fraud, undue influence, and duress. On the one hand, this gives certainty to contractual relationships, because parties know they will be held to the exact terms of their contracts. On the other hand, public policy does require that there be some limit on the power of individuals and businesses to dictate the terms of contracts.

SECTION 9

The Statute of Frauds

At early common law, parties to a contract were not allowed to testify. This led to the practice of hiring third party witnesses. As early as the seventeenth century, the English recognized the many problems presented by this practice and enacted a statute to help deal with it. The statute, passed by the English Parliament in 1677, was known as "An Act for the Prevention of Frauds and Perjuries." The act established that certain types of contracts, to be enforceable, had to be evidenced by a writing and signed by the party against whom enforcement was sought.

MODERN STATUTES OF FRAUDS

Today, almost every state has a statute, modeled after the English act, that stipulates what types of contracts must be in writing. Although the statutes vary slightly from state to state, all states require certain types of contracts to be in writing or evidenced by a written memorandum signed by the party against whom enforcement is sought, unless certain exceptions apply. In this text, we refer to these statutes collectively as

27. Pronounced un-*kon*-shun-uh-bul.

the **Statute of Frauds.** The actual name of the Statute of Frauds is misleading because it neither applies to fraud nor invalidates any type of contract. Rather, it denies *enforceability* to certain contracts that do not comply with its requirements. The following types of contracts are said to fall "within" or "under" the Statute of Frauds and therefore require a writing:

1. Contracts involving interests in land.
2. Contracts that cannot by their terms be performed within one year from the date of formation.
3. Collateral, or secondary, contracts, such as promises to answer for the debt or duty of another and promises by the administrator or executor of an estate to pay a debt of the estate personally—that is, out of his or her own pocket.
4. Promises made in consideration of marriage.
5. Under the Uniform Commercial Code (UCC), contracts for the sale of goods priced at $500 or more.

PROMISSORY ESTOPPEL AND THE STATUTE OF FRAUDS

In some states, an oral contract that would otherwise be unenforceable under the Statute of Frauds may be enforced under the doctrine of promissory estoppel, based on detrimental reliance. Section 139 of the *Restatement (Second) of Contracts* provides that in these circumstances, an oral promise can be enforceable notwithstanding the Statute of Frauds if the reliance was foreseeable to the person making the promise and if injustice can be avoided only by enforcing the promise.

SECTION 10

Third Party Rights

Once it has been determined that a valid and legally enforceable contract exists, attention can turn to the rights and duties of the parties to the contract. A contract is a private agreement between the parties who have entered into it, and traditionally these parties alone have rights and liabilities under the contract. This principle is referred to as *privity of contract*. A *third party*—one who is not a direct party to a particular contract—normally does not have rights under that contract.

There are exceptions to the rule of privity of contract. One exception allows a party to a contract to transfer the rights or duties arising from the contract to another person through an *assignment* (of rights) or a *delegation* (of duties). Another exception involves a *third party beneficiary contract*—a contract in which the parties to the contract intend that the contract benefit a third party.

ASSIGNMENTS

In a bilateral contract, the two parties have corresponding rights and duties. One party has a *right* to require the other to perform some task, and the other has a *duty* to perform it. The transfer of contractual *rights* to a third party is known as an **assignment.** When rights under a contract are assigned unconditionally, the rights of the *assignor* (the party making the assignment) are extinguished. The third party (the *assignee*, or party receiving the assignment) has a right to demand performance from the other original party to the contract. The assignee takes only those rights that the assignor originally had.

As a general rule, all rights can be assigned. Exceptions are made, however, in some circumstances. If a statute expressly prohibits assignment of a particular right, that right cannot be assigned. When a contract is *personal* in nature, the rights under the contract cannot be assigned unless all that remains is a money payment.[28] A right cannot be as-

signed if assignment will materially increase or alter the risk or duties of the obligor (the other original party owing performance under the contract).[29] If a contract stipulates that a right cannot be assigned, then *ordinarily* the right cannot be assigned.

There are several exceptions to the rule that a contract can, by its terms, prohibit any assignment of the contract. These exceptions are as follows:

1. A contract cannot prevent an assignment of the right to receive money. This exception exists to encourage the free flow of money and credit in modern business settings.
2. The assignment of rights in real estate often cannot be prohibited, because such a prohibition is contrary to public policy. Prohibitions of this kind are called restraints against **alienation** (transfer of land ownership).
3. The assignment of *negotiable instruments* (which include checks and promissory notes) cannot be prohibited.
4. In a contract for the sale of goods, the right to receive damages for breach of contract or for payment of an account owed may be assigned even though the sales contract prohibits such assignment.

In the following case, the central issue was whether a covenant not to compete contained in an employment contract could be assigned.

---

28. *Restatement (Second) of Contracts*, Sections 317 and 318.

29. UCC 2–210(2).

CASE 9.6 Reynolds and Reynolds Co. v. Hardee

United States District Court, Eastern District of Virginia, 1996. 932 F.Supp. 149.

COMPANY PROFILE   *There is a $23 billion market in North America for business forms and related services. Reynolds and Reynolds Company (**http://www.reynoldsandreynolds.com**) provides business forms and electronic-document management systems for general and specialized business markets. Reynolds's products include traditional business forms, laser-print products, labels, digital printing, and mailers. Reynolds's services include document management, storage, and distribution. These products and services help business firms with accounting, inventory control, and sales. Reynolds's customers include 110 of the "Fortune 500" companies.*

BACKGROUND AND FACTS   *Thomas Hardee worked for Jordan Graphics, Inc., as a sales representative under an employment contract that included a covenant not to compete. Reynolds and Reynolds Company contracted to buy most of Jordan's assets. On the day of the sale, Jordan terminated Hardee's employment. Reynolds offered Hardee a new contract that contained a more restrictive covenant not to compete. Hardee rejected the offer and began selling in competition with Reynolds. Reynolds filed a suit in a federal district court against Hardee, seeking, among other things, to enforce the covenant not to compete that was in the contract between Hardee and Jordan.*

Hardee filed a motion to dismiss the case, asserting that Reynolds was not an assignee of that contract and could not enforce it.

IN THE LANGUAGE OF THE COURT

REBECCA BEACH SMITH, District Judge.

* * * *

* * * [C]ontracts for personal services are not assignable, unless both parties agree to the assignment. Defendant's [Hardee's] Employment Agreement with Jordan [was] clearly a contract for personal services, based on trust and confidence. Defendant's position involved direct sales to clients; he acted as Jordan's agent in its dealings with customers. A person in such a position must necessarily obtain the trust and confidence of his or her employer. Defendant also placed considerable trust in Jordan by even agreeing to the non-compete clause, namely trusting that Jordan would not fire him and then invoke the covenant not to compete.

* * * *

* * * Without question, an employment contract of the sort involved in this case is not assignable * * *.

DECISION AND REMEDY

The court found that Reynolds was not an assignee of the contract between Hardee and Jordan and thus could not enforce it. The court dismissed this part of Reynolds's claim.

DELEGATIONS

Just as a party can transfer rights through an assignment, a party can also transfer duties. The transfer of contractual *duties* to a third party is known as a **delegation.** Normally, a delegation of duties does not relieve the party making the delegation (the *delegator*) of the obligation to perform in the event that the party to whom the duty has been delegated (the *delegatee*) fails to perform. No special form is required to create a valid delegation of duties. As long as the delegator expresses an intention to make the delegation, it is effective; the delegator need not even use the word *delegate*.

As a general rule, any duty can be delegated. Delegation is prohibited, however, in the following circumstances:

1. When special trust has been placed in the obligor.
2. When performance depends on the personal skill or talents of the *obligor* (the person contractually obligated to perform).
3. When performance by a third party will vary materially from that expected by the obligee (the one to whom performance is owed) under the contract.
4. When the contract expressly prohibits delegation.

If a delegation of duties is enforceable, the *obligee* (the one to whom performance is owed) must accept performance from the *delegatee* (the one to whom the duties have been delegated). The obligee can legally refuse performance from the delegatee only if the duty is one that cannot be delegated.

A valid delegation of duties does not relieve the delegator of obligations under the contract.[30] Thus, if the delegatee fails to perform, the delegator is still liable to the obligee.

THIRD PARTY BENEFICIARIES

Another exception to the doctrine of privity of contract exists when the original parties to the contract intend at the time of contracting that the contract performance directly benefit a third person. In this situation, the third person becomes a **third party beneficiary** of the contract. As an **intended beneficiary** of the contract, the third party has legal rights and can sue the promisor directly for breach of the contract.

The benefit that an **incidental beneficiary** receives from a contract between two parties is unintentional. Because the benefit is *unintentional*, an incidental beneficiary cannot sue to enforce the contract. For example, Bollow contracts with Coolidge to build a recreational facility on Coolidge's land. Once the facility is constructed, it will greatly enhance the property values in the neighborhood. If Bollow subsequently refuses to build the facility, Tran, Coolidge's neighbor, cannot enforce the contract against Bollow because Tran is an incidental beneficiary.

---

30. *Crane Ice Cream Co. v. Terminal Freezing & Heating Co.,* 147 Md. 588, 128 A. 280 (1925).

TERMS AND CONCEPTS TO REVIEW

acceptance 196	genuineness o f assent 202	promise 186
agreement 190	incidental beneficiary 208	promissory estoppel 194
alienation 207	intended beneficiary 208	quasi contract 189
assignment 207	mailbox rule 196	revocation 194
consideration 197	mirror image rule 195	Statute of Frauds 206
contract 186	mutual assent 190	third party beneficiary 208
counteroffer 195	offer 191	unconscionable 206
delegation 208	past consideration 199	

QUESTIONS AND CASE PROBLEMS

9–1. BILATERAL VERSUS UNILATERAL CONTRACTS. Zdanis contacts Joe, who does lawn maintenance work, and makes the following offer: "After my lawn is mowed, I'll pay you $25." Joe responds by saying, "I accept your offer." Is there a contract? Is this an offer to form a bilateral or a unilateral contract? What is the legal significance of the distinction?

9–2. OFFER AND ACCEPTANCE. Ball writes Sullivan and inquires how much Sullivan is asking for a specific forty-acre tract of land Sullivan owns. In a letter received by Ball, Sullivan states, "I will not take less than $60,000 for the forty-acre tract as specified." Ball immediately sends Sullivan a telegram stating, "I accept your offer for $60,000 for the forty-acre tract as specified." Discuss whether Ball can hold Sullivan to a contract for sale of the land.

9–3. ASSENT. Discuss whether either of the following contracts will be unenforceable on the ground that genuineness of assent is lacking.

(a) Simmons finds a stone in his pasture that he believes to be quartz. Jenson, who also believes that the stone is quartz, contracts to purchase it for $10. Just before delivery, the stone is discovered to be a diamond worth $1,000.

(b) Jacoby's barn is burned to the ground. He accuses Goldman's son of arson and threatens to bring a criminal action unless Goldman agrees to pay him $5,000. Goldman agrees to pay.

9–4. ASSIGNMENT. Marsala is a student attending college. He signs a one-year lease agreement that runs from September 1 to August 31. The lease agreement specifies that the lease cannot be assigned without the landlord's consent. In late May, Marsala decides not to go to summer school and assigns the balance of the lease (three months) to a close friend, Fred. The landlord ob-

jects to the assignment and denies Fred access to the apartment. Marsala claims Fred is financially sound and should be allowed the full rights and privileges of an assignee. Discuss fully whether the landlord or Marsala is correct.

9–5. OFFER. Air Jamaica Vacations (AJV) requested bids from printing firms to produce travel brochures. Moore Graphic Services responded with an offer quoting prices and terms for an agreement to produce between 100,000 and 250,000 brochures. The offer stated that sales tax would be charged and requested that AJV indicate its acceptance by signing and returning the offer. Moore then contacted one of its vendors, Starr Printing Co., about producing the brochures and sent AJV samples of the work to be performed. Meanwhile, AJV returned the offer with some modified terms, including a handwritten notation, "no tax." Moore then told Starr it was putting "the job" on hold and told AJV that it could not perform "the job" because of the dispute about the tax. Starr printed the brochures and demanded payment. AJV refused, claiming in part that the brochures were of "poor quality." Starr filed a suit in a federal district court against AJV. AJV filed a suit against Moore, claiming breach of contract for giving the job to Starr. Moore filed a motion for summary judgment, on the ground that there was no contract. Did Moore and AJV have a contract? Why or why not? [*Starr Printing Co. v. Air Jamaica*, 45 F.Supp.2d 625 (W.D.Tenn. 1999)]

9–6. PREEXISTING DUTY. New England Rock Services, Inc., agreed to work as a subcontractor on a sewer project on which Empire Paving, Inc., was the general contractor. For drilling and blasting a certain amount of rock, Rock Services was to be paid $29 per cubic yard or on a time-and-materials basis, whichever was less. From the beginning, Rock Services experienced problems. The primary obstacle was a heavy concentration of water, which, according to the custom in the industry, Empire should have controlled but did not. Rock Services was compelled to use more costly and time-consuming methods than anticipated, and it was unable to complete the work on time. The subcontractor asked Empire to pay for the rest of the project on a time-and-materials basis. Empire signed a modification of the original agreement. On completion of the work, Empire refused to pay Rock Services the balance due under the modification. Rock Services filed a suit in a Connecticut state court against Empire. Empire claimed that the modification lacked consideration and was thus not valid and enforceable. Is Empire right? Why or why not? [*New England Rock Services, Inc. v. Empire Paving, Inc.*, 53 Conn.App. 771, 731 A.2d 784 (1999)]

9–7. CONTRACTS BY MINORS. Sergei Samsonov is a Russian and one of the top hockey players in the world. When Samsonov was seventeen years old, he signed a contract to play hockey for two seasons with the Central Sports Army Club, a Russian club known by the abbreviation CSKA. Before the start of the second season, Samsonov learned that because of a dispute between CSKA coaches, he would not be playing in Russia's premier hockey league. Samsonov hired Athletes and Artists, Inc. (A&A), an American sports agency, to make a deal with a U.S. hockey team. Samsonov signed a contract to play for the Detroit Vipers (whose corporate name was, at the time, Arena Associates, Inc.). Neither A&A nor Arena knew about the CSKA contract. CSKA filed a suit in a federal district court against Arena and others, alleging, among other things, wrongful interference with a contractual relationship. What effect will Samsonov's age have on the outcome of this suit? [*Central Sports Army Club v. Arena Associates, Inc.*, 952 F.Supp. 181 (S.D.N.Y. 1997)]

9–8. FRAUDULENT MISREPRESENTATION. In 1987, United Parcel Service Co. and United Parcel Service of America, Inc. (together known as "UPS"), decided to change its parcel delivery business from relying on contract carriers to establishing its own airline. During the transition, which took sixteen months, UPS hired 811 pilots. At the time, UPS expressed a desire to hire pilots who remained throughout that period with its contract carriers, which included Orion Air. A UPS representative met with more than fifty Orion pilots and made promises of future employment. John Rickert, a captain with Orion, was one of the pilots. Orion ceased operation after the UPS transition, and UPS did not hire Rickert, who obtained employment about six months later as a second officer with American Airlines, but at a lower salary. Rickert filed a suit in a Kentucky state court

against UPS, claiming, in part, fraud based on the promises made by the UPS representative. UPS filed a motion for a directed verdict. What are the elements for a cause of action based on fraudulent misrepresentation? In whose favor should the court rule in this case, and why? [*United Parcel Service, Inc. v. Rickert*, 996 S.W.2d 464 (Ky. 1999)]

9–9. THIRD PARTY BENEFICIARY. John Castle and Leonard Harlan, who headed Castle Harlan, Inc., an investment firm, entered into an agreement with the federal government to buy Western Empire Federal Savings and Loan. Under the agreement, Castle Harlan was to invest a nominal amount in the bank and arrange for others to invest much more, in exchange for, among other things, a promise that for two years, Western Empire would not be subject to certain restrictions in federal regulations. The government's enforcement of other regulations against Western Empire led to its going out of business. Castle, Harlan, and the other investors filed a suit in the U.S. Court of Federal Claims against the government, alleging breach of contract. The government filed a motion to dismiss all of the plaintiffs except Castle and Harlan, on the ground that the others did not sign the contract between the government and Castle and Harlan. Is the government correct? Should the court dismiss the claims brought by the other investors? Why or why not? [*Castle v. United States*, 42 Fed.Cl. 859 (1999)]

9–10. IN YOUR COURT

Grant Borman, who was engaged in a construction project, leased a crane from Allied Equipment, Inc., and hired Crosstown Trucking Co. to deliver the crane to the construction site. Crosstown, while the crane was in its possession and without permission from either Borman or Allied Equipment, used the crane to install a transformer for a utility company, which paid Crosstown for the job. Crosstown then delivered the crane to Borman's construction site at the appointed time of delivery. When Allied Equipment learned of the unauthorized use of the crane by Crosstown, it sued Crosstown for damages, seeking to recover in quasi contract the rental value of Allied's use of the crane. Assume that you are the judge in the trial court hearing this case and answer the following questions:

(a) Should a quasi contract be imposed on the parties in this situation so that Allied can recover damages from Crosstown?

(b) If so, what amount should Allied be able to recover in *quantum meruit* for Crosstown's unauthorized use of the crane?

LAW ON THE WEB

For updated links to resources available on the Web, as well as a variety of other materials, visit this text's Web site at http://wleb.westbuslaw.com.

The 'Lectric Law Library provides information on contract law, including a definition of a contract, the elements required for a contract, and so on. Go to

http://www.lectlaw.com

Then go to the Laypeople's Law Lounge, and scroll down to Contracts.

You can find articles and information on various areas of law—including contracts—at the Law Office's Web site. Go to

http://lawoffice.com

Select the topic of Business and Commercial Law from the Law Knowledgebase list on the right-hand side of the home page.

To find recent cases on contract law decided by the United States Supreme Court and the federal appellate courts, access Cornell University's School of Law site at

http://www.law.cornell.edu/topics/contracts.html

Professor Eric Talley of the University of Southern California provides an interesting discussion of the history and current applicability of the Statute of Frauds, both internationally and in the United States, at the following Web site:

http://www-bcf.usc.edu/~etalley/frauds.html

You can find a summary of the law governing assignments, as well as "SmartAgreement" forms that you can use for various types of contracts, at

http://www.smartagreements.com/gen1/lp75.htm

LEGAL RESEARCH EXERCISES ON THE WEB

Go to http://wleb.westbuslaw.com, the Web site that accompanies this text. Select "Internet Applications," and then click on "Chapter 9." There you will find the following Internet research exercises that you can perform to learn more about contracts:

Activity 9–1: Minors and the Law

Activity 9–2: The Statute of Frauds

CHAPTER 10

Contracts: Part II

JUST AS RULES ARE NECESSARY TO determine when a legally enforceable contract exists, so also are they required to determine when one of the parties can justifiably say, "I have fully performed, so I am now discharged from my obligations under this contract." The legal environment of business requires the identification of some point at which the parties can reasonably know that their duties are at an end.

Performance is the most common form of discharge. Duties can be discharged in other ways. A breach of contract, for example, will discharge the duty of the nonbreaching party to perform. A party is in breach of contract whenever he or she fails to perform part or all of the duties under the contract. In this chapter, we will discuss some of the important ways in which contracts can be discharged. We will also discuss the remedies available on a breach of contract to a nonbreaching party.

SECTION 1

Performance and Discharge

The most common way to **discharge,** or terminate, one's contractual duties is by the **performance** of those duties. For example, a buyer and seller have a contract for the sale of a 2000 Buick for $28,000. This contract will be discharged on the performance by the parties of their obligations under the contract—the buyer's payment of $28,000 to the seller and the seller's transfer of possession of the Buick to the buyer.

The duty to perform under a contract may be *conditioned* on the occurrence or nonoccurrence of a certain event, or the duty may be *absolute.* In the first part of this chapter, we look at conditions of performance and the degree of performance required. We then examine some other ways in which a contract can be discharged, including discharge by agreement of the parties and discharge by operation of law.

CONDITIONS

In most contracts, promises of performance are not expressly conditioned or qualified. Instead, they are *absolute promises.* They must be performed, or the parties promising the acts will be in breach of contract. For example, Jerome contracts to sell Alfonso a painting for $3,000. The parties' promises—Jerome's transfer of the painting to Alfonso and Alfonso's payment of $3,000 to Jerome—are unconditional. The payment does not have to be made if the painting is not transferred.

In some situations, however, performance is contingent on the occurrence or nonoccurrence of a certain event. A **condition** is a possible future event, the occurrence or nonoccurrence of which will trigger the performance of a legal obligation or terminate an existing obligation under a contract.[1] If this condition is not satisfied, the obligations of the parties are discharged. Suppose that Alfonso, in the previous example, offers to purchase Jerome's painting only if an independent appraisal indicates that it is worth at least $3,000. Jerome accepts Alfonso's offer. Their obligations (promises) are conditioned on the outcome of the appraisal. Should the condition not be satisfied (for example, if the appraiser deems the value of the painting to be only $1,500), the parties' obligations to each other are discharged and cannot be enforced.

DISCHARGE BY PERFORMANCE

The great majority of contracts are discharged by performance. The contract comes to an end when both parties fulfill their respective duties by performing the acts they have promised. Performance can also be accomplished by **tender.** Therefore, a seller who places goods at the disposal of a buyer has tendered delivery and can demand payment. A buyer who offers to pay for goods has tendered payment and can demand delivery of the goods. Once performance has been tendered, the party making the tender has done everything possible to carry out the terms of the contract. If the other party then refuses to perform, the party making the tender can sue for breach of contract.

Types of Performance.

There are two basic types of performance—*complete performance* and *substantial performance*. A contract may stipulate that performance must meet the personal satisfaction of either the contracting party or a third party. Such a provision must be considered in determining whether the performance rendered satisfies the contract.

Complete Performance.

When a party performs exactly as agreed, there is no question as to whether the contract has been performed. When a party's performance is perfect, it is said to be complete.

Conditions expressly stated in a contract must be fully satisfied for complete performance to take place.

For example, most construction contracts require the builder to meet certain specifications. If the specifications are conditions, complete performance is required to avoid material breach. (Material breach will be discussed shortly.) If the conditions are met, the other party to the contract must then fulfill his or her obligation to pay the builder. If the specifications are not conditions and if the builder, without the other party's permission, fails to comply with the standards, performance is not complete. What effect does such a failure have on the other party's obligation to pay? The answer is part of the doctrine of substantial performance.

Substantial Performance.

A party who in good faith performs substantially all of the terms of a contract can enforce the contract against the other party under the doctrine of substantial performance. Note that good faith is required, which means that the failure to fully perform must not be willful. Willfully failing to comply with the terms is a breach of the contract.

Generally, performance that provides a party with the important and essential benefits of a contract, in spite of any omission or deviation from the terms, is substantial performance.

Determining whether performance has provided the "important and essential benefits" of a contract requires taking into consideration all of the facts. For example, in a construction contract, these facts would include the intended purpose of the structure and the expense required to bring the structure into compliance with the contract. Thus, the exact point at which performance is considered substantial varies from case to case.

Because substantial performance is not perfect, the other party is entitled to damages to compensate for the failure to comply with the contract. The measure of the damages is the cost to bring the object of the contract into compliance with its terms, if that cost is reasonable under the circumstances. If the cost is unreasonable, the measure of damages is the difference in value between the performance that was rendered and the performance that would have been rendered if the contract had been performed completely.

The following classic case on substantial performance emphasizes that there is no exact formula for deciding when a contract has been substantially performed. The case also indicates some of the factors that courts consider in deciding whether a contract has been materially breached or substantially performed.

---

[1]. The *Restatement (Second) of Contracts*, Section 224, defines a condition as "an event, not certain to occur, which must occur, unless its nonoccurrence is excused, before performance under a contract becomes due."

CASE 10.1   Jacobs & Young, Inc. v. Kent

Court of Appeals of
New York, 1921.
230 N.Y. 239,
129 N.E. 889.

BACKGROUND AND FACTS   *The plaintiff, Jacobs & Young, Inc., was a builder that had contracted with the defendant, George Kent, to construct a country residence for the defendant. A specification in the building contract required that "[a]ll wrought-iron pipe must be well galvanized, lap welded pipe of the grade known as 'standard pipe' of Reading manufacture." The plaintiff installed substantially similar pipe that was not of Reading manufacture. When the defendant became aware of the difference, he ordered the plaintiff to remove all of the plumbing and replace it with the Reading type. To do so would have required removing finished walls that encased the plumbing—an expensive and difficult task. The plaintiff explained that the plumbing was of the same quality, appearance, value, and cost as Reading pipe. When the defendant refused to pay the plaintiff the $3,483.46 still owed for the work, the plaintiff sued to compel payment. The trial court ruled in favor of the defendant. The plaintiff appealed, and the appellate court reversed the trial court's decision. The defendant then appealed to the Court of Appeals of New York, the state's highest court.*

IN THE LANGUAGE OF THE COURT

CARDOZO, Justice.
*   *   *   *

*   *   * The courts never say that one who makes a contract fills the measure of his duty by less than full performance. They do say, however, that an omission, both trivial and innocent, will sometimes be atoned for by allowance of the resulting damage, and will not always be the breach of a condition[.] *   *   *

*   *   * Where the line is to be drawn between the important and the trivial cannot be settled by a formula. *   *   * We must weigh the purpose to be served, the desire to be gratified, the excuse for deviation from the letter, [and] the cruelty of enforced adherence. Then only can we tell whether literal fulfillment is to be implied by law as a condition. *   *   *

*   *   * [W]e think the measure of the allowance is not the cost of replacement, which would be great, but the difference in value, which would be either nominal or nothing. *   *   * The owner is entitled to the money which will permit him to complete, unless the cost of completion is grossly and unfairly out of proportion to the good to be attained.

DECISION AND REMEDY

The Court of Appeals of New York, holding that the plaintiff had substantially performed the contract, affirmed the appellate court's decision. The builder was entitled to the amount owed to it, less the difference in value between the specified and substituted pipe (which the court stated would be "nominal or nothing").

Material Breach of Contract.   A **breach of contract** is the nonperformance of a contractual duty. The breach is *material*[2] when performance is not at least substantial—in other words, when there has been a failure of consideration. In such cases, the nonbreaching party is excused from the performance of contractual duties and has a cause of action to sue for damages caused by the breach.

If the breach is *minor* (not material), the nonbreaching party's duty to perform can sometimes be suspended until the breach has been remedied, but the duty to perform is not entirely excused. Once the minor breach has been cured, the nonbreaching party must resume performance of the contractual obligations undertaken. Any breach entitles the nonbreaching party to sue for damages, but only a material breach discharges the nonbreaching party from the contract. The policy underlying these rules allows

2. *Restatement (Second) of Contracts,* Section 241.

contracts to go forward when only minor problems occur but allows them to be terminated if major difficulties arise.

Does preventing an employee from working constitute a breach of contract if the employer continues to pay her salary? That was the issue in the following case.

CASE 10.2   Van Steenhouse v. Jacor Broadcasting of Colorado, Inc.

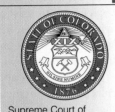

Supreme Court of
Colorado, 1998.
958 P.2d 464.
**http://www.findlaw.
com/11stategov/co/
coca.html**[a]

BACKGROUND AND FACTS *Jacor Broadcasting of Colorado, Inc., owns and operates Newsradio 85 KOA. In June 1991, Andrea Van Steenhouse signed a three-year agreement to perform as a radio talk-show host for KOA. She was to receive a base salary and a performance bonus, depending on how many people tuned into her show. In January 1994, Jacor replaced her show with Rush Limbaugh's program. Jacor paid Van Steenhouse her base salary for the rest of the term of their agreement but did not employ her as a talk-show host. Van Steenhouse filed a suit in a Colorado state court against Jacor and others, claiming, among other things, breach of contract. The court ruled that Jacor materially breached the contract and awarded Van Steenhouse an amount representing the bonus she could have received if she had not been taken off the air. The state intermediate appellate court affirmed the judgment. Jacor appealed to the Supreme Court of Colorado.*

**IN THE LANGUAGE
OF THE COURT**

Chief Justice VOLLACK delivered the Opinion of the Court.
    *   *   *   *

Ordinarily, an employment agreement does not obligate an employer to furnish work for an employee. However, such an obligation may be inferred depending on the circumstances under which the agreement for employment is made or the nature of the employment. In particular, *an obligation to furnish work arises if the employee materially benefits from performing the duties described in the agreement* *   *   *. [W]hen an employer fails to furnish the kind of work specified in an employment agreement, the employee has a cause of action for breach of contract. [Emphasis added.]
    *   *   *   *

*   *   * [I]n this case *   *   * Jacor breached the Agreement by depriving Van Steenhouse of the opportunity to perform as a talk show host on KOA. *   *   * As a result, Van Steenhouse lost the opportunity to build and maintain her professional marketability. In addition, Van Steenhouse lost the opportunity to earn a 1994 performance bonus.

Jacor deprived Van Steenhouse of these benefits by refusing to broadcast her show [as] specified by the clear terms of the Agreement. Accordingly, we hold that Van Steenhouse stated a valid claim for breach of contract.

**DECISION
AND REMEDY**

The Supreme Court of Colorado held that an employee's claim for breach of contract can be based solely on an employer's failure to provide an opportunity to work. The court affirmed this part of the lower court's decision.

a. In the "Supreme Court" list, in the "1998" row, click on "April." On that page, scroll down the list of cases to the *Van Steenhouse* case, and click on the name to access the opinion.

Time for Performance. If no time for performance is stated in the contract, a *reasonable time* is implied.[3] If a specific time is stated, the parties must usually perform by that time. Unless time is expressly stated to be vital, however, a delay in performance will not destroy the performing party's right to payment. When time is expressly stated to be vital, or when it is construed to be "of the essence," the parties normally must perform within the stated time period. The time element becomes a condition.

3. See UCC 2–204.

DISCHARGE BY AGREEMENT

Any contract can be discharged by agreement of the parties. The agreement can be contained in the original contract, or the parties can form a new contract for the express purpose of discharging the original contract.

Discharge by Rescission. *Rescission* is the process by which a contract is canceled or terminated and the parties are returned to the positions they occupied prior to forming it. For **mutual rescission** to take place, the parties must make another agreement, which must also satisfy the legal requirements for a contract. There must be an *offer*, an *acceptance*, and *consideration.*

Ordinarily, in an executory contract in which neither party has yet performed, if the parties agree to rescind the original contract, their promises not to perform the acts stipulated in the original contract will be legal consideration for the second contract. The rescission agreement is generally enforceable even if made orally. An exception applies under the Uniform Commercial Code (UCC) to agreements rescinding a contract for the sale of goods regardless of price when the contract requires written rescission.[4]

When one party has fully performed, an agreement to call off the original contract normally will not be enforceable. Because the performing party has received no consideration for the promise to call off the original bargain, additional consideration will be necessary.

In sum, contracts that are *executory on both sides* (contracts on which neither party has performed) can be rescinded solely by agreement.[5] But contracts that are *executed on one side* (contracts on which one party has performed) can be rescinded only if the party who has performed receives consideration for the promise to call off the deal.

Discharge by Novation. A contractual obligation may also be discharged through novation. A **novation** occurs when both of the parties to a contract agree to substitute a third party for one of the original parties. The requirements of a novation are as follows:

1. A previous valid obligation.
2. An agreement of all the parties to a new contract.

3. The extinguishment of the old obligation (discharge of the prior party).
4. A new contract that is valid.

For example, suppose that Union Corporation contracts to sell its pharmaceutical division to British Pharmaceuticals, Ltd. Before the transfer is completed, Union, British Pharmaceuticals, and a third company, Otis Chemicals, execute a new agreement to transfer all of British Pharmaceutical's rights and duties in the transaction to Otis Chemicals. As long as the new contract is supported by consideration, the novation will discharge the original contract (between Union and British Pharmaceuticals) and replace it with the new contract (between Union and Otis Chemicals).

A novation expressly or impliedly revokes and discharges a prior contract.[6] The parties involved may expressly state in the new contract that the old contract is now discharged. If the parties do not expressly discharge the old contract, it will be impliedly discharged because of the change or because of the new contract's different terms, which are inconsistent with the old contract's terms.

Discharge by Substituted Agreement. A *compromise*, or settlement agreement, that arises out of a genuine dispute over the obligations under an existing contract will be recognized at law. Such an agreement will be substituted as a new contract, and it will either expressly or impliedly revoke and discharge the obligations under any prior contract. In contrast to a novation, a substituted agreement does not involve a third party. Rather, the two original parties to the contract form a different agreement to substitute for the original one.

Discharge by Accord and Satisfaction. For a contract to be discharged by accord and satisfaction, the parties must agree to accept performance that is different from the performance originally promised. An *accord* is defined as an executory contract to perform some act to satisfy an existing contractual duty.[7] The duty has not yet been discharged. A *satisfaction* is the performance of the accord agreement. An accord and its satisfaction discharge the original contractual obligation.

4. UCC 2–209(2), (4).
5. Certain sales made to a consumer at home can be rescinded by the consumer within three days for no reason at all. This three-day "cooling-off" period is designed to aid consumers who are susceptible to high-pressure door-to-door sales tactics. See Chapter 24 and 15 U.S.C. Section 1635(a).

6. It is this immediate discharge of the prior contract that distinguishes a novation from both an accord and satisfaction, discussed in the next subsection, and an assignment, discussed in Chapter 9. In an assignment, the original party to the contract (the assignor) remains liable under the original contract if the assignee fails to perform the contractual obligations. In contrast, in a novation, the original party's obligations are completely discharged.
7. *Restatement (Second) of Contracts*, Section 281.

Once the accord has been made, the original obligation is merely suspended. The obligor (the one owing the obligation) can discharge the obligation by performing the obligation agreed to in the accord or the original obligation. If the obligor refuses to perform the accord, the obligee (the one to whom performance is owed) can bring action on the original obligation or seek a decree compelling specific performance on the accord.

DISCHARGE BY OPERATION OF LAW

Under certain circumstances, contractual duties may be discharged by operation of law. These circumstances include material alteration of the contract, the running of the statute of limitations, bankruptcy, and the impossibility or impracticability of performance.

Alteration of the Contract. To discourage parties from altering written contracts, the law operates to allow an innocent party to be discharged when the other party has materially altered a written contract without consent. For example, contract terms such as quantity or price might be changed without the knowledge or consent of all parties. If so, the party who was unaware of the alteration can treat the contract as discharged or terminated.[8]

Statutes of Limitations. As mentioned earlier in this text, statutes of limitations restrict the period during which a party can sue on a particular cause of action. After the applicable limitations period has passed, a suit can no longer be brought. For example, the limitations period for bringing suits for breach of oral contracts is usually two to three years; for written contracts, four to five years; and for recovery of amounts awarded in judgments, ten to twenty years, depending on state law.

Section 2–725 of the UCC deals with the statute of limitations applicable to contracts for the sale of goods. For purposes of applying this section, the UCC does not distinguish between oral and written contracts. Section 2–725 provides that an action for the breach of any contract for sale must be commenced within four years after the cause of that action has accrued. The cause of action accrues when the breach occurs, regardless of the aggrieved party's lack of knowledge of the breach. By original agreement, the parties can reduce this four-year period to one year. They cannot, however, extend it beyond the four-year limitation period.

Technically, the running of a statute of limitations bars access only to *judicial* remedies; it does not extinguish the debt or the underlying obligation. The statute precludes access to the courts for collection. If, however, the party who owes the debt or obligation agrees to perform (that is, makes a new promise to perform), the cause of action barred by the statute of limitations will be revived. For the old agreement to be restored by a new promise in this manner, many states require that the promise be in writing or that there be evidence of partial performance.

Bankruptcy. A proceeding in bankruptcy attempts to allocate the assets the debtor owns to the creditors in a fair and equitable fashion. Once the assets have been allocated, the debtor receives a discharge in bankruptcy. A discharge in bankruptcy will ordinarily bar enforcement of most of a debtor's contracts by the creditors. Partial payment of a debt *after* discharge in bankruptcy will not revive the debt. (Bankruptcy will be discussed in Chapter 16.)

Impossibility or Impracticability of Performance. After a contract has been made, performance may become impossible in an objective sense. This is known as **impossibility of performance** and may discharge a contract.[9]

Objective Impossibility of Performance. Objective impossibility ("It can't be done") must be distinguished from *subjective impossibility* ("I'm sorry, I simply can't do it"). Examples of subjective impossibility include cases in which goods cannot be delivered on time because of freight car shortages[10] and cases in which money cannot be paid on time because the bank is closed.[11] In effect, the party in each of these cases is saying, "It is impossible for me to perform," not "It is impossible for anyone to perform." Accordingly, such excuses do not discharge a contract, and the nonperforming party is normally held in

---

8. The contract is voidable, and the innocent party can also treat the contract as in effect, either on the original terms or on the terms as altered. A buyer who discovers that a seller altered the quantity of goods in a sales contract from 100 to 1,000 by secretly inserting a zero can purchase either 100 or 1,000 of the items.

9. *Restatement (Second) of Contracts*, Section 261.
10. *Minneapolis v. Republic Creosoting Co.*, 161 Minn. 178, 201 N.W. 414 (1924).
11. *Ingham Lumber Co. v. Ingersoll & Co.*, 93 Ark. 447, 125 S.W. 139 (1910).

breach of contract. Three basic types of situations, however, generally qualify as grounds for the discharge of contractual obligations based on impossibility of performance:[12]

1. *When one of the parties to a personal contract dies or becomes incapacitated prior to performance.* For example, Fred, a famous dancer, contracts with Ethereal Dancing Guild to play a leading role in its new ballet. Before the ballet can be performed, Fred becomes ill and dies. His personal performance was essential to the completion of the contract. Thus, his death discharges the contract and his estate's liability for his nonperformance.

2. *When the specific subject matter of the contract is destroyed.* For example, A-1 Farm Equipment agrees to sell Gudgel the green tractor on its lot and promises to have it ready for Gudgel to pick up on Saturday. On Friday night, however, a truck veers off the nearby highway and smashes into the tractor, destroying it beyond repair. Because the contract was for this specific tractor, A-1's performance is rendered impossible owing to the accident.

3. *When a change in law renders performance illegal.* An example is a contract to build an apartment building, when the zoning laws are changed to prohibit the construction of residential rental property at this location. This change renders the contract impossible to perform.

Commercial Impracticability. Courts may excuse parties from their performance obligations when the performance becomes much more difficult or expensive than originally contemplated at the time the contract was formed. For someone to invoke successfully the doctrine of **commercial impracticability**, however, the anticipated performance must become *extremely* difficult or costly.[13] For example, in one case, a court held that a contract was discharged because a party would have had to pay ten times more than the original estimate to excavate a certain amount of gravel.[14] Caution should be used in invoking commercial impracticability. The added burden of performing must be *extreme* and, more important, *must not have been within the cognizance of the parties when the contract was made.*

Frustration of Purpose. A theory closely allied with the doctrine of commercial impracticability is the doctrine of **frustration of purpose.** In principle, a contract will be discharged if supervening circumstances make it impossible to attain the purpose both parties had in mind when making the contract. The origins of the doctrine lie in the old English "coronation cases." A coronation procession was planned for Edward VII when he became king of England following the death of his mother, Queen Victoria. Hotel rooms along the coronation route were rented at exorbitant prices for that day. When the king became ill and the procession was canceled, a flurry of lawsuits resulted. Hotel and building owners sought to enforce the room-rent bills against would-be parade observers, and would-be parade observers sought to be reimbursed for rental monies paid in advance on the rooms. Would-be parade observers were excused from their duty of payment because the purpose of the room contracts had been "frustrated."

Temporary Impossibility. An occurrence or event that makes performance temporarily impossible operates to suspend performance until the impossibility ceases. Then, ordinarily, the parties must perform the contract as originally planned. If, however, the lapse of time and the change in circumstances surrounding the contract make it substantially more burdensome for the parties to perform the promised acts, the contract is discharged.

The leading case on the subject, *Autry v. Republic Productions,*[15] involved an actor who was drafted into the army in 1942. Being drafted rendered the actor's contract temporarily impossible to perform, and it was suspended until the end of the war. When the actor got out of the army, the value of the dollar had so changed that performance of the contract would have been substantially burdensome to the actor. Therefore, the contract was discharged.

Section 2

Breach of Contract and Remedies

When one party breaches a contract, the other party—the nonbreaching party—can choose one or more of several remedies. A *remedy* is the relief provided for an innocent party when the other party has breached the

---

12. *Restatement (Second) of Contracts,* Sections 262–266; UCC 2–615.
13. *Restatement (Second) of Contracts,* Section 264.
14. *Mineral Park Land Co. v. Howard,* 172 Cal. 289, 156 P. 458 (1916).

15. 30 Cal.2d 144, 180 P.2d 888 (1947).

contract. It is the means employed to enforce a right or to redress an injury.

The most common remedies available to a nonbreaching party include damages, rescission and restitution, specific performance, and reformation. As discussed in Chapter 1, a distinction is made between *remedies at law* and *remedies in equity*. Today, the remedy at law is normally money damages, which are discussed in the first part of this chapter. Equitable remedies include rescission and restitution, specific performance, and reformation, all of which will be examined later in the chapter. Usually, a court will not award an equitable remedy unless the remedy at law is inadequate.

DAMAGES

A breach of contract entitles the nonbreaching party to sue for money (damages). Damages are designed to compensate a party for harm suffered as a result of another's wrongful act. In the context of contract law, damages compensate the nonbreaching party for the loss of the bargain.[16]

Often, courts say that innocent parties are to be placed in the position they would have occupied had the contract been fully performed.[17] For example, in the famous case of the "hairy hand," a doctor promised to make a boy's scarred hand "a hundred percent perfect." Skin was taken from the boy's chest and grafted onto his thumb and fingers. The hand became infected, and the boy was hospitalized for three months. Use of the hand was greatly restricted, and hair grew out of the grafted skin. In hearing a suit against the doctor, the court explained that the amount of damages was to be determined by the difference between the value to the boy of the "perfect" hand that the doctor had promised and the value of the hand in its condition after the operation.[18]

Types of Damages. There are basically four broad categories of damages:

1. Compensatory (to cover direct losses and costs).

2. Consequential (to cover indirect and foreseeable losses).
3. Punitive (to punish and deter wrongdoing).
4. Nominal (to recognize wrongdoing when no monetary loss is shown).

Compensatory Damages. Damages compensating the nonbreaching party for the *loss of the bargain* are known as *compensatory damages*. These damages compensate the injured party only for damages actually sustained and proved to have arisen directly from the loss of the bargain caused by the breach of contract. They simply replace what was lost because of the wrong or damage. To illustrate: Wilcox contracts to perform certain services exclusively for Hernandez during the month of March for $2,000. Hernandez cancels the contract and is in breach. Wilcox is able to find another job during the month of March but can earn only $1,000. He can sue Hernandez for breach and recover $1,000 as compensatory damages. Wilcox can also recover from Hernandez the amount that he spent to find the other job. Expenses that are caused directly by a breach of contract—such as those incurred to obtain performance from another source—are known as *incidental damages*.

The measurement of compensatory damages varies by type of contract. In a contract for the sale of goods, the usual measure of compensatory damages is an amount equal to the difference between the contract price and the market price.[19] For example, suppose that Chrysler Corporation contracts to buy ten model UTS 400 network servers from an XEXO Corporation dealer for $8,000 each. The dealer, however, fails to deliver the ten servers to Chrysler. The market price of the servers at the time the buyer learns of the breach is $8,150. Chrysler's measure of damages is therefore $1,500 (10 × $150) plus any incidental damages (expenses) caused by the breach. In a situation in which the buyer breaches and the seller has not yet produced the goods, compensatory damages normally equal lost profits on the sale, not the difference between the contract price and the market price.

Ordinarily, because each parcel of land is unique, the remedy for a seller's breach of a contract for a sale of real estate is specific performance—that is, the buyer is awarded the parcel of property for which he

---

16. Bear in mind that although a nonbreaching party may succeed in obtaining damages from a court from the breaching party, the court's judgment may be difficult to enforce. As discussed in Chapter 2, the breaching party may not have sufficient funds or assets to pay the damages awarded.
17. *Restatement (Second) of Contracts*, Section 347; UCC 1–106(1).
18. *Hawkins v. McGee*, 84 N.H. 114, 146 A. 641 (1929).

19. That is, the amount is the difference between the contract price and the market price at the time and place at which the goods were to be delivered or tendered. See UCC 2–708 and UCC 2–713.

or she bargained (specific performance is discussed more fully later in this chapter). When this remedy is unavailable (for example, when the seller has sold the property to someone else), or when the breach is on the part of the buyer, the measure of damages is ordinarily the same as in contracts for the sale of goods—that is, the difference between the contract price and the market price of the land. The majority of states follow this rule.

A minority of states follow a different rule when the seller breaches the contract and the breach is not deliberate.[20] In such a case, these states allow the prospective purchaser to recover any down payment plus any expenses incurred (such as fees for title searches, attorneys, and escrows). This minority rule effectively places purchasers in the position they occupied prior to the sale.

Consequential Damages. Foreseeable damages that result from a party's breach of contract are called **consequential damages,** or *special damages.* They differ from compensatory damages in that they are caused by special circumstances beyond the contract

itself. They flow from the consequences, or results, of a breach.

For example, if a seller fails to deliver goods, and the seller knows that a buyer is planning to resell these goods immediately, consequential damages will be awarded for the loss of profit from the planned resale. The buyer will also recover compensatory damages for the difference between the contract price and the market price of the goods.

To recover consequential damages, the breaching party must know (or have reason to know) that special circumstances will cause the nonbreaching party to suffer an additional loss. This rule was enunciated in the classic case of *Hadley v. Baxendale*, which is presented below. This case established the rule that when damages are awarded, compensation is given only for those injuries that the defendant could *reasonably have foreseen* as a probable result of the usual course of events following a breach.

In reading through the following case, realize that in the mid-1800s in England, it was customary for large flour mills to have more than one crankshaft in the event the main one broke and had to be repaired. Also, in those days it was common knowledge that flour mills did indeed have spare crankshafts. It is against this background that the parties in the case presented here argued their respective positions on whether the damages resulting from the loss of profits while the crankshaft was repaired were reasonably foreseeable.

---

20. "Deliberate" breaches include the seller's failure to transfer the land because the market price has gone up. "Nondeliberate" breaches include the seller's failure to transfer the land because an unknown easement (another's right of use over the property) has rendered title unmarketable. See Chapter 26.

CASE 10.3   Hadley v. Baxendale

| Court of Exchequer, 1854. 156 Eng.Rep. 145. | **BACKGROUND AND FACTS**   *The Hadleys (the plaintiffs) ran a flour mill in Gloucester. The crankshaft attached to the steam engine in the mill broke, causing the mill to shut down. The shaft had to be sent to a foundry located in Greenwich so that the new shaft could be made to fit the other parts of the engine. Baxendale, the defendant, was a common carrier that transported the shaft from Gloucester to Greenwich. The freight charges were collected in advance, and Baxendale promised to deliver the shaft the following day. It was not delivered for a number of days, however. As a consequence, the mill was closed for a number of days. The Hadleys sued to recover the profits lost during that time. Baxendale contended that the loss of profits was "too remote" to be recoverable. The court held for the plaintiffs, and the jury was allowed to take into consideration the lost profits. The defendant appealed.* |

IN THE LANGUAGE   ALDERSON, B.
OF THE COURT   *   *   *   *

     *   *   * Where two parties have made a contract which one of them has broken, the damages which the other party ought to receive in respect of such breach of contract should be such as may fairly and reasonably be considered either arising naturally, i.e., according to the usual course of things, from such breach of contract itself, or such as may reasonably be supposed to have been in the contemplation of both parties, at the

time they made the contract, as the probable result of the breach of it. Now, if the special circumstances under which the contract was actually made were communicated by the plaintiffs to the defendants, and thus known to both parties, the damages resulting from the breach of such a contract, *which they would reasonably contemplate*, would be the amount of injury which would ordinarily follow from a breach of contract under these special circumstances so known and communicated. * * * Now, in the present case, if we are to apply the principles above laid down, we find that the only circumstances here communicated by the plaintiffs to the defendants at the time the contract was made, were, that the article to be carried was the broken shaft of a mill, and that the plaintiffs were the millers of that mill. * * * [S]pecial circumstances were here never communicated by the plaintiffs to the defendants. It follows, therefore, that the loss of profits here cannot reasonably be considered such a consequence of the breach of contract as could have been fairly and reasonably contemplated by both the parties when they made this contract. [Emphasis added.]

DECISION AND REMEDY	*The Court of Exchequer ordered a new trial. According to the court, the plaintiffs would have to have given express notice of the special circumstances that caused the loss of profits to collect consequential damages.*

Mitigation of Damages.   In most situations, when a breach of contract occurs, the innocent injured party is held to a duty to mitigate, or reduce, the damages that he or she suffers. Under this **mitigation of damages** doctrine, the duty owed depends on the nature of the contract.

For example, some states require a landlord to use reasonable means to find a new tenant if a tenant abandons the premises and fails to pay rent. If an acceptable tenant becomes available, the landlord is required to lease the premises to this tenant to mitigate the damages recoverable from the former tenant. The former tenant is still liable for the difference between the amount of the rent under the original lease and the rent received from the new tenant. If the landlord has not used the reasonable means necessary to find a new tenant, presumably a court can reduce the award made by the amount of rent he or she could have received had such reasonable means been used.

In the majority of states, persons whose employment has been wrongfully terminated owe a duty to mitigate damages suffered because of their employers' breach of the employment contract. The damages they receive are their salaries less the incomes they would have received in similar jobs that they could have obtained by reasonable means. The employer must prove both that such a job existed and that the employee could have been hired. As the following case illustrates, however, the employee is under no duty to take a job of a different type and rank.

CASE 10.4   Parker v. Twentieth Century-Fox Film Corp.

Supreme Court of California, 1970.
3 Cal.3d 176,
474 P.2d 689,
89 Cal.Rptr. 737.

COMPANY PROFILE   *Daryl Zanuck and Joseph Schenk formed the Twentieth Century Company in 1933 to make movies. Two years later, they merged with the Fox Film Company, which had been founded by William Fox, and became Twentieth Century-Fox Film Corporation (**http://www.fox.com**). Today, Twentieth Century-Fox produces movies and television shows as part of the News Corporation Limited, which is headquartered in Australia. The News Corporation also has interests in the production and distribution of newspapers, magazines, books, television programs, and films in Great Britain, Hong Kong, New Zealand, and other countries.*

BACKGROUND AND FACTS   *Twentieth Century-Fox Film Corporation planned to produce a musical,* Bloomer Girl, *and contracted with Shirley MacLaine Parker to play the* *leading female role. According to the contract, Fox was to pay Parker $53,571.42 per week for fourteen weeks, for a total of $750,000. Fox later decided not to produce* Bloomer Girl *and tried to substitute for the existing contract another contract under which Parker would play the leading role in* Big Country, *a Western movie, for the same amount of money guaranteed by the first contract. Fox gave Parker one week in which to accept the new contract. Parker filed suit against Fox to recover the amount of compensation guaranteed in the first contract because, she maintained, the two roles were not at all equivalent. The* Bloomer Girl *production was a musical, to be filmed in California, and could not be compared with a "Western type" production that was, according to tentative plans, to be produced in Australia. When the trial court held for Parker, Fox appealed.*

<table>
<tr><td>In the Language
of the Court</td><td>BURKE, Justice.
*   *   *   *

The general rule is that the measure of recovery by a wrongfully discharged employee is the amount of salary agreed upon for the period of service, less the amount which the employer affirmatively proves the employee has earned or with reasonable effort might have earned from other employment. However, before projected earnings from other employment opportunities not sought or accepted by the discharged employee can be applied in mitigation, the employer must show that the other employment was comparable, or substantially similar, to that of which the employee has been deprived *   *   * .

*   *   *   *

*   *   * The mere circumstance that "Bloomer Girl" was to be a musical review calling upon plaintiff's talents as a dancer as well as an actress, and was to be produced in the City of Los Angeles, whereas "Big Country" was a straight dramatic role in a "Western Type" story taking place in an opal mine in Australia, demonstrates the difference in kind between the two employments; the female lead as a dramatic actress in a western style motion picture can by no stretch of imagination be considered the equivalent of or substantially similar to the lead in a song-and-dance production.</td></tr>
<tr><td>Decision
and Remedy</td><td>*The Supreme Court of California affirmed the trial court's ruling. Parker could not be required to accept Fox's offer of the Western-movie role to mitigate the damages she had incurred as a result of the breach of contract.*</td></tr>
</table>

Liquidated Damages versus Penalties.   Unliquidated damages are damages that have not been calculated or determined. **Liquidated damages,** in contrast, are damages that are certain in amount. A liquidated damages provision in a contract specifies a certain amount to be paid in the event of a *future* default or breach of contract. For example, a provision requiring a construction contractor to pay $300 for every day he or she is late in completing the construction is a liquidated damages provision.

Liquidated damages differ from penalties. **Penalties** specify a certain amount to be paid in the event of a default or breach of contract and are designed to *penalize* the breaching party. Liquidated damages provisions are enforceable; penalty provisions are not.

To determine if a particular provision is for liquidated damages or for a penalty, two questions must be answered:

1. When the contract was entered into, was it apparent that damages would be difficult to estimate in the event of a breach?
2. Was the amount set as damages a reasonable estimate and not excessive?[21]

If the answers to both questions are yes, the provision will be enforced. If either answer is no, the provision will not be enforced. Section 2–718(1) of the Uniform Commercial Code (UCC) specifically permits the inclusion of liquidated damages clauses in contracts for the sale of goods as long as both of these tests are met. In construction contracts, it is difficult to estimate the amount of damages that would be caused by a delay in completing construction, so liquidated damages clauses are often used.

---

21. *Restatement (Second) of Contracts,* Section 356(1).

RESCISSION AND RESTITUTION

As discussed earlier in this chapter, *rescission* is essentially an action to undo, or terminate, a contract—to return the contracting parties to the positions they occupied prior to the transaction. When fraud, a mistake, duress, undue influence, misrepresentation, or lack of capacity to contract is present, unilateral rescission is available.[22] Rescission may also be available by statute.[23] The failure of one party to perform entitles the other party to rescind the contract. The rescinding party must give prompt notice to the breaching party. Generally, to rescind a contract, both parties must make **restitution** to each other by returning goods, property, or money previously conveyed.[24] If the goods or property received can be restored *in specie*—that is, if the actual goods or property can be returned—they must be. If the goods or property have been consumed, restitution must be made in an equivalent amount of money.

Essentially, *restitution* refers to the plaintiff's recapture of a benefit conferred on the defendant through which the defendant has been unjustly enriched. For example, Katie pays $10,000 to Bob in return for Bob's promise to design a house for her. The next day Bob calls Katie and tells her that he has taken a position with a large architectural firm in another state and cannot design the house. Katie decides to hire another architect that afternoon. Katie can obtain restitution of the $10,000.

Restitution may be appropriate when a contract is rescinded, but the right to restitution is not limited to rescission cases. Restitution may be sought in actions for breach of contract, tort actions, and other actions at law or in equity. Usually, restitution of money or property transferred by mistake or because of fraud can be awarded. An award in a case may include restitution of money or property obtained through embezzlement, conversion, theft, copyright infringement, or misconduct by a party in a confidential or other special relationship.

---

22. In *unilateral* rescission, only one party wants to undo the contract. In *mutual* rescission, both parties agree to undo the contract. Mutual rescission discharges the contract; unilateral rescission is generally available as a remedy for breach of contract.

23. The Federal Trade Commission and many states have rules or statutes allowing consumers to unilaterally rescind contracts made at home with door-to-door salespersons. Rescission is allowed within three days for any reason or for no reason at all. See, for example, California Civil Code Section 1689.5.

24. *Restatement (Second) of Contracts*, Section 370.

SPECIFIC PERFORMANCE

The equitable remedy of **specific performance** calls for the performance of the act promised in the contract. This remedy is quite attractive to the nonbreaching party for three reasons:

1. The nonbreaching party need not worry about collecting the money damages awarded by a court (see the discussion in Chapter 2 of some of the difficulties that may arise when trying to enforce court judgments).
2. The nonbreaching party need not spend time seeking an alternative contract.
3. The performance is more valuable than the money damages.

Normally, however, specific performance will not be granted unless the party's legal remedy (money damages) is inadequate.[25] For this reason, contracts for the sale of goods rarely qualify for specific performance. The legal remedy, money damages, is ordinarily adequate in such situations, because substantially identical goods can be bought or sold in the market. If the goods are unique, however, a court of equity will decree specific performance. For example, paintings, sculptures, or rare books or coins are so unique that money damages will not enable a buyer to obtain substantially identical substitutes in the market.

Sale of Land.   Specific performance is granted to a buyer in a contract for the sale of land. The legal remedy for breach of a land sales contract is inadequate, because every parcel of land is considered to be unique. Money damages will not compensate a buyer adequately, because the same land in the same location obviously cannot be obtained elsewhere. Only when specific performance is unavailable (for example, when the seller has sold the property to someone else) will money damages be awarded instead.

Contracts for Personal Services.   Personal-service contracts require one party to work personally for another party. Courts of equity normally refuse to grant specific performance of personal-service contracts. If a contract is not deemed personal, the remedy at law may be adequate if substantially identical service (for example, lawn mowing) is available from other persons.

---

25. *Restatement (Second) of Contracts*, Section 359.

In individually tailored personal-service contracts, courts will not order specific performance by the party who was to be employed because public policy strongly discourages involuntary servitude.[26] Moreover, the courts do not want to have to monitor a continuing service contract if supervision would be difficult—as it would be if the contract required the exercise of personal judgment or talent. For example, if you contracted with a brain surgeon to perform brain surgery on you and the surgeon refused to perform, the court would not compel (and you certainly would not want) the surgeon to perform under those circumstances. A court cannot assure meaningful performance in such a situation.[27]

REFORMATION

Reformation is an equitable remedy used when the parties have *imperfectly* expressed their agreement in writing. Reformation allows the contract to be rewritten to reflect the parties' true intentions. It applies most often when fraud or mutual mistake (for example, a clerical error) is present.

Reformation is almost always sought so that some other remedy may then be pursued. For example, if Gregory contracts to buy a certain parcel of land from Cavendish but their contract mistakenly refers to a parcel of land different from the one being sold, the contract does not reflect the parties' intentions. Accordingly, a court can reform the contract so that it conforms to the parties' intentions and accurately refers to the parcel of land being sold. Gregory can then, if necessary, show that Cavendish has breached the contract as reformed. She can at that time request an order for specific performance.

Two other examples deserve mention. The first involves two parties who have made a binding oral contract. They further agree to put the oral contract in writing, but in doing so, they make an error in stating the terms. Normally, the courts will allow into evidence the correct terms of the oral contract, thereby reforming the written contract. The second example deals with written agreements (covenants) not to compete (see

Chapter 9). If the covenant is for a valid and legitimate purpose (such as the sale of a business) but the area or time restraints of the covenant are unreasonable, some courts will reform the restraints by making them reasonable and will enforce the entire contract as reformed. Other courts, however, will throw out the entire restrictive covenant as illegal.

RECOVERY BASED ON QUASI CONTRACT

As stated in Chapter 9, quasi contract is a legal theory under which an obligation is imposed in the absence of an agreement. The courts use this theory to prevent unjust enrichment. Hence, quasi contract provides a basis for relief when no enforceable contract exists. The legal obligation arises because the law considers that a promise to pay for benefits received is implied by the party accepting the benefits. Generally, when one party has conferred a benefit on another party, justice requires the party receiving the benefit to pay the reasonable value for it. The party conferring the benefit can recover in *quantum meruit*, which means "as much as he deserves."

Quasi-contractual recovery is useful when one party has partially performed under a contract that is unenforceable. It can be used as an alternative to a suit for damages and will allow the party to recover the reasonable value of the partial performance, measured in some cases according to the benefit received and in others according to the detriment suffered.

To recover on a quasi contract, the party seeking recovery must show the following:

1. The party conferred a benefit on the other party.
2. The party conferred the benefit with the reasonable expectation of being paid.
3. The party did not act as a volunteer in conferring the benefit.
4. The other party (the party receiving the benefit) would be unjustly enriched by retaining the benefit without making payment.

For example, suppose that Watson contracts to build two oil derricks for Energy Industries. The derricks are to be built over a period of three years, but the parties do not make a written contract. Enforcement of the contract will therefore be barred by the Statute of Frauds.[28] Watson completes one derrick, and then Energy Industries informs him that it will not pay for

---

26. The Thirteenth Amendment to the U.S. Constitution prohibits involuntary servitude, and thus a court will not order a person to perform under a personal-service contract. A court may grant an order (injunction) prohibiting that person from engaging in similar contracts in the future for a period of time, however.
27. Similarly, courts often refuse to order specific performance of construction contracts because courts are not set up to operate as construction supervisors or engineers.

28. Contracts that by their terms cannot be performed within one year must be in writing to be enforceable. See Chapter 9.

the derrick. Watson can sue in quasi contract because he conferred a benefit on Energy Industries with the expectation of being paid, and allowing Energy Industries to retain the derrick without paying would enrich the company unjustly. Therefore, Watson should be able to recover in *quantum meruit* the reasonable value of the oil derrick. The reasonable value is ordinarily equal to the fair market value.

ELECTION OF REMEDIES

In many cases, a nonbreaching party has several remedies available. The party must choose which remedy to pursue. The purpose of the doctrine of *election of remedies* is to prevent double recovery.

Suppose that McCarthy agrees in writing to sell his land to Tally. Then McCarthy changes his mind and repudiates the contract. Tally can sue for compensatory damages *or* for specific performance. If Tally could seek compensatory damages in addition to specific performance, she would recover twice for the same breach of contract. The doctrine of election of remedies requires Tally to choose the remedy she wants, and it eliminates any possibility of double recovery. In other words, the election doctrine represents the legal embodiment of the adage "You can't have your cake and eat it, too."

The doctrine has often been applied in a rigid and technical manner, leading to some harsh results. For example, suppose that Wilson is fraudulently induced to buy a parcel of land for $150,000. He spends an additional $10,000 moving onto the land and then discovers the fraud. Instead of suing for damages, Wilson sues to rescind the contract. The court allows Wilson to recover only the purchase price of $150,000. The court denies recovery of the additional $10,000 because the seller, Martin, did not receive the $10,000 and is therefore not required to reimburse Wilson for his moving expenses. So Wilson suffers a net loss of $10,000 on the transaction. If Wilson had elected to sue for damages instead of seeking the remedy of rescission and restitution, he could have recovered the $10,000 as well as the $150,000.[29]

Because of such problems, the UCC expressly rejects the doctrine of election of remedies.[30] Remedies under the UCC are not exclusive but cumulative in nature and include all the available remedies for breach of contract.

---

29 See, for example, *Carpenter v. Mason*, 181 Wis. 114, 193 N.W. 973 (1923).
30. See UCC 2–703 and UCC 2–711.

WAIVER OF BREACH

Under certain circumstances, a nonbreaching party may be willing to accept a defective performance of the contract. This knowing relinquishment of a legal right (that is, the right to require satisfactory and full performance) is called a **waiver**. When a waiver of a breach of contract occurs, the party waiving the breach cannot take any later action on it. In effect, the waiver erases the past breach; the contract continues as if the breach had never occurred. Of course, the waiver of breach of contract extends only to the matter waived and not to the whole contract.

Businesspersons often waive breaches of contract to get whatever benefit is still possible out of the contract. For example, a seller contracts with a buyer to deliver to the buyer ten thousand tons of coal on or before November 1. The contract calls for the buyer's payment to be made by November 10 for coal delivered. Because of a coal miners' strike, coal is scarce. The seller breaches the contract by not tendering delivery until November 5. The buyer may be well advised to waive the seller's breach, accept delivery of the coal, and pay as contracted.

Ordinarily, the waiver by a contracting party will not operate to waive subsequent, additional, or future breaches of contract. This is always true when the subsequent breaches are unrelated to the first breach. For example, an owner who waives the right to sue for late completion of a stage of construction does not waive the right to sue for failure to comply with engineering specifications on the same job. A waiver will be extended to subsequent defective performance if a reasonable person would conclude that similar defective performance in the future will be acceptable. Therefore, a *pattern of conduct* that waives a number of successive breaches will operate as a continued waiver. To change this result, the nonbreaching party should give notice to the breaching party that full performance will be required in the future.

The party who has rendered defective or less-than-full performance remains liable for the damages caused by the breach of contract. In effect, the waiver operates to keep the contract going. The waiver prevents the nonbreaching party from calling the contract to an end or rescinding the contract. The contract continues, but the nonbreaching party can recover damages caused by defective or less-than-full performance.

CONTRACT PROVISIONS LIMITING REMEDIES

A contract may include provisions stating that no damages can be recovered for certain types of breaches or that damages must be limited to a maximum amount. The contract may also provide that the only remedy for breach is replacement, repair, or refund of the purchase price. Provisions stating that no damages can be recovered are called *exculpatory clauses*. Provisions that affect the availability of certain remedies are called *limitation-of-liability clauses*.

Whether these contract provisions and clauses will be enforced depends on the type of breach that is excused by the provision. For example, a provision excluding liability for fraudulent or intentional injury will not be enforced. Likewise, a clause excluding liability for illegal acts or violations of law will not be enforced. A clause excluding liability for negligence may be enforced in certain cases, however. When an exculpatory clause for negligence is contained in a contract made between parties who have roughly equal bargaining positions, the clause usually will be enforced.

TERMS AND CONCEPTS TO REVIEW

breach of contract 214

commercial
    impracticability 218

condition 212

consequential damages 220

discharge 212

frustration of purpose 218

impossibility of
    performance 217

liquidated damages 222

mitigation of damages 221

mutual rescission 216

novation 216

penalty 222

performance 212

reformation 224

restitution 223

specific performance 223

tender 213

waiver 225

QUESTIONS AND CASE PROBLEMS

10–1. IMPOSSIBILITY OF PERFORMANCE. In the following situations, certain events take place after the formation of contracts. Discuss which of these contracts are discharged because the events render the contracts impossible to perform.
    (a) Jimenez, a famous singer, contracts to perform in your nightclub. He dies prior to performance.
    (b) Raglione contracts to sell you her land. Just before title is to be transferred, she dies.
    (c) Oppenheim contracts to sell you one thousand bushels of apples from her orchard in the state of Washington. Because of a severe frost, she is unable to deliver the apples.
    (d) Maxwell contracts to lease a service station for ten years. His principal income is from the sale of gasoline. Because of an oil embargo by foreign oil-producing nations, gasoline is rationed, cutting sharply into Maxwell's gasoline sales. He cannot make his lease payments.

10–2. TIME FOR PERFORMANCE. Murphy contracts to purchase from Lone Star Liquors six cases of French champagne for $1,200. The contract states that delivery is to be made at the Murphy residence "on or before June 1, to be used for daughter's wedding reception on June 2." The champagne is carried regularly in Lone Star's stock. On June 1, Lone Star's delivery van is involved in an accident, and the champagne is not delivered that day. On the morning of June 2, Murphy discovers the nondelivery. Unable to reach Lone Star because its line is busy, Murphy purchases the champagne from another dealer. That afternoon, just before the wedding reception, Lone Star tenders delivery of the champagne at Murphy's residence. Murphy refuses tender, and Lone Star sues for breach of contract. Discuss fully the result.

10–3. LIQUIDATED DAMAGES. Cohen contracts to sell his house and lot to Windsor for $100,000. The terms of the contract call for Windsor to pay 10 percent of the purchase price as a deposit toward the purchase price, or a down payment. The terms further stipulate that should the buyer breach the contract, the deposit will be retained by Cohen as liquidated damages. Windsor pays the deposit, but because her expected financing of the $90,000 balance falls through, she breaches the contract. Two weeks later Cohen sells the house and lot to

Ballard for $105,000. Windsor demands her $10,000 back, but Cohen refuses, claiming that Windsor's breach and the contract terms entitle him to keep the deposit. Discuss who is correct.

10–4. SPECIFIC PERFORMANCE. In which of the following situations would specific performance be an appropriate remedy? Discuss fully.

(a) Thompson contracts to sell her house and lot to Cousteau. Then, on finding another buyer willing to pay a higher purchase price, she refuses to deed the property to Cousteau.

(b) Amy contracts to sing and dance in Fred's nightclub for one month, beginning May 1. She then refuses to perform.

(c) Hoffman contracts to purchase a rare coin owned by Erikson, as Erikson is breaking up his coin collection. At the last minute, Erikson decides to keep his coin collection intact and refuses to deliver the coin to Hoffman.

(d) There are three shareholders of the ABC Corp.: Panozzo, who owns 48 percent of the stock; Chang, who owns another 48 percent; and Ryan, who owns 4 percent. Ryan contracts to sell her 4 percent to Chang. Later, Ryan refuses to transfer the shares to Chang.

10–5. PERFORMANCE. Steven McPheters, a house builder and developer, hired Terry Tentinger, who did business as New Horizon Construction, to do some touching up and repainting on one of McPheters's new houses. Tentinger worked two days, billed McPheters $420 (a three-man crew for fourteen hours at $30 per hour), and offered to return to the house to remedy any defects in his workmanship at no cost. McPheters objected to the number of hours on the bill—although he did not express dissatisfaction with the work—and offered Tentinger $250. Tentinger refused to accept this amount and filed a suit in an Idaho state court to collect the full amount. McPheters filed a counterclaim, alleging that Tentinger failed to perform the job in a workmanlike manner, resulting in $2,500 in damages, which it would cost $500 to repair. Tentinger's witnesses testified that although some touch-up work needed to be done, the job had been performed in a workmanlike manner. McPheters presented testimony indicating that the workmanship was so defective as to render it commercially unreasonable. On what basis could the court rule in Tentinger's favor? Explain fully. [*Tentinger v. McPheters*, 132 Idaho 620, 977 P.2d 234 (Idaho App. 1999)]

10–6. RESCISSION. Jeffrey Stambovsky was a resident of New York City. While looking at houses in the village of Nyack, New York, Stambovsky came across a riverfront Victorian house that he liked. He purchased it, only to discover later that the house had a local reputation for being haunted. The seller, Helen Ackley, had promoted this reputation herself by reporting to the *Reader's Digest* in 1977 and to the local press in 1982 that the house was haunted. By 1989, the house was included in a five-home walking tour of Nyack because of the purported presence of ghosts in the house. There was even a newspaper article describing it as "a riverfront Victorian (with ghost)." Stambovsky brought an action to rescind the contract, contending that the house's reputation for being haunted impaired the value of the property. What will the court decide? Discuss fully. [*Stambovsky v. Ackley*, 169 A.D.2d 254, 572 N.Y.S.2d 672 (1991)]

10–7. LIQUIDATED DAMAGES VERSUS PENALTIES. The Ivanovs, who were of Russian origin, agreed to purchase the Sobels' home for $300,000. A $30,000 earnest money deposit was placed in the trust account of Kotler Realty, Inc., the broker facilitating the transaction. Tiasia Buliak, one of Kotler's salespersons, negotiated the sale because she spoke fluent Russian. To facilitate the closing without the Ivanovs' having to be present, Buliak suggested they form a Florida corporation, place the cash necessary to close the sale in a corporate account, and give her authority to draw checks against it. The Ivanovs did as Buliak had suggested. Before the closing date of the sale, Buliak absconded with all of the closing money, which caused the transaction to collapse. Subsequently, because the Ivanovs had defaulted, Kotler Realty delivered the $30,000 earnest money deposit in its trust account to the Sobels. The Ivanovs then sued the Sobels, seeking to recover the $30,000. Was the clause providing that the seller could retain the earnest money if the buyer defaulted an enforceable liquidated damages clause or an unenforceable penalty clause? Discuss. [*Ivanov v. Sobel*, 654 So.2d 991 (Fla.App.3d 1995)]

10–8. MITIGATION OF DAMAGES. Patricia Fair worked in a Red Lion restaurant. The employee manual provided that "[d]uring a medical leave of absence, every effort will be made to keep a position available for the employee's return." After sustaining an injury that was unrelated to her work, Fair was given a month's medical leave. On her return, she asked for, and was granted, additional time to submit a physician's release to return to work. She provided the release within the extra time, but before she went back to work she was terminated, effective as of her original return date. When she attempted to resolve the matter, Red Lion offered to reinstate her in her old job. Her response was to set several conditions for a return, including a different job. Red Lion said no, and Fair did not return. Fair filed a suit in a Colorado state court against Red Lion, alleging in part breach of contract. Red Lion argued that by rejecting its offer of reinstatement, Fair failed to mitigate her damages. Assuming that Red Lion was in breach of contract, did Fair fail to mitigate her damages? Explain. [*Fair v. Red Lion Inn, L.P.*, 943 P.2d 431 (Colo. 1997)]

10–9. DAMAGES. In December 1992, Beys Specialty Contracting, Inc., contracted with New York City's Metropolitan Transportation Authority (MTA) for construction work. Beys subcontracted with Hudson Iron Works, Inc., to perform some of the work for $175,000. Under the terms of the subcontract, within seven days after the MTA approved Hudson's work and paid Beys, Beys would pay Hudson. The MTA had not yet approved any of Hudson's work when Beys submitted to the MTA invoices dated May 20 and June 21, 1993. Without proof that the MTA had paid Beys on those invoices, Hudson submitted to Beys an invoice dated September 10, claiming that the May 20 and June 21 invoices incorporated its work. Beys refused to pay, Hudson stopped working, and Beys paid another contractor $25,083 more to complete the job than if Hudson had completed its subcontract. Hudson filed a suit in a New York state court to collect on its invoice. Beys filed a counterclaim for the additional money spent to complete Hudson's job. In whose favor should the court rule, and why? What might be the measure of damages, if any? [*Hudson Iron Works, Inc. v. Beys Specialty Contracting, Inc.*, 691 N.Y.S.2d 132 (N.Y.A.D., 2 Dept. 1999)]

10–10. IN YOUR COURT

Charles Kloss had worked for Honeywell, Inc., for over fifteen years when Honeywell decided to transfer the employees at its Ballard facility to its Harbour Pointe facility. Honeywell planned to hire a medical person at the

Harbour Pointe facility and promised Kloss that if he completed a nursing program and became a registered nurse (RN), the company would hire him for the medical position. When Kloss graduated from his RN program, however, Honeywell did not assign him to a nursing or medical position. Instead, the company gave Kloss a job in its maintenance department. Shortly thereafter, Kloss left the company and eventually sued Honeywell for damages (lost wages) resulting from Honeywell's breach of the employment contract. Assume that you are the judge in the trial court hearing this case and answer the following questions:

(a) One of the issues you will need to decide in this case is whether Kloss, by voluntarily leaving the maintenance job at Honeywell, had failed to mitigate his damages. How will you rule on this issue? Explain your reasoning.

(b) Review Case 10.4 (*Parker v. Twentieth Century-Fox Film Corp.*). Does the court's reasoning in that case on the issue of mitigation of damages apply to Kloss's situation as well? Why or why not?

LAW ON THE WEB

For updated links to resources available on the Web, as well as a variety of other materials, visit this text's Web site at http://wleb.westbuslaw.com.

For a summary of how contracts may be discharged and other principles of contract law, go to

> http://www.lawyers.com/site/aboutlaw/contract.html#contract10

Law Guru can lead you to other sources of law relating to contract performance and discharge. Go to

> http:lawguru.com/lawlinks.html

For a summary of how contracts may be breached and other information on contract law, go to

> http://www.lawyers.com/site/aboutlaw/contract.html#contract10

The following sites offer information on contract law, including breach of contract and remedies:

> http://www.nolo.com/Chunkcm/CM9.html

> http://www.law.cornell.edu/topics/contracts.html

LEGAL RESEARCH EXERCISES ON THE WEB

Go to http://wleb.westbuslaw.com, the Web site that accompanies this text. Select "Internet Applications," and then click on "Chapter 10." There you will find the following Internet research exercise that you can perform to learn more about breach of contract and damages:

Activity 10–1: Contract Damages and Contract Theory

CHAPTER 11

Sales and Leases

WHEN WE TURN TO CONTRACTS for the sale and lease of goods, we move away from common law principles and into the area of statutory law. State statutory law governing sales and lease transactions is based on the Uniform Commercial Code (UCC), which, as mentioned in Chapter 1, has been adopted as law by all states.[1] Relevant sections of the UCC are noted in the following discussion of sales and lease contracts. You should refer to Appendix C in the back of the book, which presents the most recent version of Article 2 of the UCC, while examining these notations.

We open this chapter with a look at the scope of the UCC's Article 2 (on sales) and Article 2A (on leases). Article 2 of the UCC sets out the requirements of sales contracts and how they are formed. It also addresses the sometimes sticky concept of when title passes and who bears the risk of loss for goods in the process of being sold—for example, goods en route from the seller to the buyer—along with the concept of insurable interest. Article 2 regulates performance and obligations required under sales contracts. It also delineates when a breach by either the buyer or the seller occurs and what remedies normally may be sought. A sale of goods usually carries with it at least one type of warranty; sales warranties, express and implied, likewise are governed by the UCC. Article 2A covers similar issues for lease contracts.

---

1. Louisiana has not adopted Articles 2 and 2A, however.

SECTION 1

The Scope of Article 2—The Sale of Goods

Article 2 of the UCC governs **sales contracts,** or contracts for the sale of goods. To facilitate commercial transactions, Article 2 modifies some of the common law contract requirements that were discussed in the previous chapters. To the extent that it has not been modified by the UCC, however, the common law of contracts also applies to sales contracts. For example, the common law requirements for a valid contract—agreement (offer and acceptance), consideration, capacity, and legality—that were discussed in Chapter 9 are also applicable to sales contracts. Thus, you should reexamine these common law principles when studying the law of sales.

In general, the rule is that whenever there is a conflict between a common law contract rule and the UCC, the UCC controls. In other words, when a UCC provision addresses a certain issue, the UCC governs; when the UCC is silent, the common law governs.

In regard to Article 2, you should keep in mind two things. First, Article 2 deals with the sale of *goods*; it does not deal with real property (real estate), services, or intangible property such as stocks and bonds. Thus, if the subject matter of a dispute is goods, the

UCC governs. If it is real estate or services, the common law applies. Second, in some cases, the rules may vary quite a bit, depending on whether the buyer or the seller is a *merchant*. We look now at how the UCC defines a *sale*, *goods*, and *merchant status*.

The fold-out exhibit in this chapter, which shows an actual sales contract used by Starbuck's Coffee Company, illustrates many of the terms and clauses that are typically contained in contracts for the sale of goods.

WHAT IS A SALE?

Section 2–102 of the UCC states that Article 2 "applies to transactions in goods." This implies a broad scope—covering gifts, bailments (temporary deliveries of personal property), and purchases of goods. In this chapter, however, we treat Article 2 as being applicable only to an actual sale (as would most authorities and courts). The UCC defines a **sale** as "the passing of title from the seller to the buyer for a price," where *title* refers to the formal right of ownership of property [UCC 2–106(1)]. The price may be payable in money or in other goods, services, or realty (real estate).

WHAT ARE GOODS?

To be characterized as a *good*, an item of property must be *tangible*, and it must be *movable*. **Tangible property** has physical existence—it can be touched or seen. Intangible property—such as corporate stocks and bonds, patents and copyrights, and ordinary contract rights—have only conceptual existence and thus do not come under Article 2. A *movable* item can be carried from place to place. Hence, real estate is excluded from Article 2.

WHO IS A MERCHANT?

Article 2 governs the sale of goods in general. It applies to sales transactions between all buyers and sellers. In a limited number of instances, however, the UCC presumes that in certain phases of sales transactions involving merchants, special business standards ought to be imposed because of the merchants' relatively high degree of commercial expertise.[2] Such standards do not apply to the casual or inexperienced seller or buyer ("consumer").

In general, a person is a **merchant** when he or she, acting in a mercantile capacity, possesses or uses an expertise specifically related to the goods being sold. This basic distinction is not always clear-cut. For example, courts in some states have determined that farmers may be merchants, while courts in other states have determined that the drafters of the UCC did not intend to include farmers as merchants.

SECTION 2

The Scope of Article 2A—Leases

In the past few decades, leases of personal property (goods) have become increasingly common. Consumers and business firms lease automobiles, industrial equipment, items for use in the home (such as floor polishers), and many other types of goods. Until Article 2A was added to the UCC, no specific body of law addressed the legal problems that arose when goods were leased, rather than sold. In cases involving leased goods, the courts generally applied a combination of common law rules, real estate law, and principles expressed in Article 2 of the UCC.

Article 2A of the UCC was created to fill the need for uniform guidelines in this area. Article 2A covers any transaction that creates a lease of goods, as well as subleases of goods [UCC 2A–102, 2A–103(k)]. Article 2A is essentially a repetition of Article 2, except that it applies to leases of goods, rather than sales of goods, and thus varies to reflect differences between sales and lease transactions.

Article 2A defines a **lease agreement** as the bargain of the lessor and lessee, as found in their language and as implied by other circumstances [UCC 2A–103(k)]. A **lessor** is one who sells the right to the possession and use of goods under a lease [UCC 2A–103(p)]. A **lessee** is one who acquires the right to the possession and use of goods under a lease [UCC 2A–103(o)]. Article 2A applies to all types of leases of goods, including commercial leases and consumer leases.

SECTION 3

The Formation of Sales and Lease Contracts

In regard to the formation of sales and lease contracts, the UCC modifies the common law in several ways. We look here at how Article 2 and Article 2A

---

2. The provisions that apply only to merchants deal principally with the Statute of Frauds, firm offers, confirmatory memoranda, warranties, and contract modification. These special rules reflect expedient business practices commonly known to merchants in the commercial setting. They will be discussed later in this chapter.

of the UCC modify common law contract rules. Remember that parties to sales contracts are free to establish whatever terms they wish. The UCC comes into play when the parties have not, in their contract, provided for a contingency that later gives rise to a dispute. The UCC makes this very clear time and again by its use of such phrases as "unless the parties otherwise agree" and "absent a contrary agreement by the parties."

OFFER

In general contract law, the moment a definite offer is met by an unqualified acceptance, a binding contract is formed. In commercial sales transactions, the verbal exchanges, the correspondence, and the actions of the parties may not reveal exactly when a binding contractual obligation arises. The UCC states that an agreement sufficient to constitute a contract can exist even if the moment of its making is undetermined [UCC 2–204(2), 2A–204(2)].

Open Terms. According to contract law, an offer must be definite enough for the parties (and the courts) to ascertain its essential terms when it is accepted. The UCC states that a sales or lease contract will not fail for indefiniteness even if one or more terms are left open as long as (1) the parties intended to make a contract and (2) there is a reasonably certain basis for the court to grant an appropriate remedy [UCC 2–204(3), 2A–204(3)].

Although the UCC has radically lessened the requirement of definiteness of terms, keep in mind that if too many terms are left open, a court may find that the parties did not intend to form a contract. (This is also true with respect to online offers—see this chapter's *Emerging Trends in Technology* on pages 232 and 233 for some suggestions on how online sellers can protect themselves against potential problems by including specific terms and provisions in their offers.)

Open Price Term. If the parties have not agreed on a price, the court will determine a "reasonable price at the time for delivery" [UCC 2–305(1)]. If either the buyer or the seller is to determine the price, the price is to be fixed in good faith [UCC 2–305(2)].

Sometimes the price fails to be fixed through the fault of one of the parties. In that case, the other party can treat the contract as canceled or fix a reasonable price. For example, Johnson and Merrick enter into a contract for the sale of goods and agree that Johnson will fix the price. Johnson refuses to fix the price.

Merrick can either treat the contract as canceled or set a reasonable price [UCC 2–305(3)].

Open Payment Term. When parties do not specify payment terms, payment is due at the time and place at which the buyer is to receive the goods [UCC 2–310(a)]. The buyer can tender payment using any commercially normal or acceptable means, such as a check or credit card. If the seller demands payment in cash, however, the buyer must be given a reasonable time to obtain it [UCC 2–511(2)]. This is especially important when the contract states a definite and final time for performance.

Open Delivery Term. When no delivery terms are specified, the buyer normally takes delivery at the seller's place of business [UCC 2–308(a)]. If the seller has no place of business, the seller's residence is used. When goods are located in some other place and both parties know it, delivery is made there. If the time for shipment or delivery is not clearly specified in the sales contract, then the court will infer a "reasonable" time for performance [UCC 2–309(1)].

Open Quantity Term. Normally, if the parties do not specify a quantity, a court will have no basis for determining a remedy. The UCC recognizes two exceptions in requirements and output contracts [UCC 2–306(1)].

In a **requirements contract,** the buyer agrees to purchase and the seller agrees to sell all or up to a stated amount of what the buyer *needs* or *requires.* There is implicit consideration in a requirements contract, for the buyer gives up the right to buy from any other seller, and this forfeited right creates a legal detriment. Requirements contracts are common in the business world and are normally enforceable. If, however, the buyer promises to purchase only if the buyer *wishes* to do so, or if the buyer reserves the right to buy the goods from someone other than the seller, the promise is illusory (without consideration) and unenforceable by either party.

In an **output contract,** the seller agrees to sell and the buyer agrees to buy all or up to a stated amount of what the seller *produces.* Again, because the seller essentially forfeits the right to sell goods to another buyer, there is implicit consideration in an output contract.

The UCC imposes a *good faith limitation* on requirements and output contracts. The quantity under such contracts is the amount of requirements or the amount of output that occurs during a *normal*

EMERGING TRENDS IN TECHNOLOGY

Online Offers

Today, numerous sales contracts are being formed online. Consumers purchase books, compact discs, software, airline tickets, clothing, computers, and a host of other goods via the Internet. Although the medium through which sales contracts are generated has changed, the age-old problems attending contract formation have not. Disputes concerning contracts formed online continue to center around contract terms and whether the parties voluntarily assented to those terms. Sellers doing business via the Internet can protect themselves against contract disputes and legal liability by creating offers that clearly spell out the terms that will govern their transactions if the offers are accepted.

DRAFTING AND DISPLAYING THE OFFER

Online offers should not be casually drafted. Rather, they must be carefully constructed and address all key terms and conditions so that, on their acceptance, the resulting contract clearly spells out the obligations of the parties. All important terms should be conspicuous and easily viewed by potential buyers. The seller's Web site should include a hypertext link to a page containing the full contract so that potential buyers are made aware of the terms to which they are assenting. At a minimum, the offer (contract) should include the following provisions:

■ A provision specifying the remedies available to the buyer if the goods turn out to be defective or if the contract is otherwise breached (any limitation of remedies should be clearly spelled out).
■ A forum-selection clause (indicating the forum, or location, for the resolution of any dispute that may arise under the contract). This clause will help to avert future jurisdictional problems, which often arise in online transactions, and help to ensure that the seller will not be required to appear in court in a distant state.
■ The statute of limitations governing the transaction (that is, the time period within which a legal action can be brought over a dispute concerning the contract).
■ A clause that clearly indicates the buyer's agreement to the terms of the offer.

■ A provision specifying how payment for the goods and of any applicable taxes must be made.
■ A statement of the seller's refund and return policies.
■ Disclaimers of liability for certain uses of the goods. For example, an online seller of business forms may add a disclaimer that the seller does not accept responsibility for the buyer's reliance on the forms rather than on an attorney's advice.
■ How the information gathered about the buyer will be used by the seller. (See the *Emerging Trends in Technology* in Chapter 12, concerning privacy rights in cyberspace, for more information on this topic.)

The contract generally must be displayed online in a readable format such as 12-point typeface. All provisions should be reasonably clear. For example, if a seller is offering certain goods priced according to a complex price schedule, that schedule must be fully provided and explained.

ONLINE ACCEPTANCE

An online offer should include some mechanism by which the customer may accept the offer. Typically, online sellers include

production year. The actual quantity purchased or sold cannot be unreasonably disproportionate to normal or comparable prior requirements or output [UCC 2–306].

Merchant's Firm Offer. Under regular contract principles, an offer can be revoked at any time before acceptance. The major common law exception is an

option contract, in which the offeree pays consideration for the offeror's irrevocable promise to keep the offer open for a stated period. The UCC creates a second exception, which applies only to firm offers for the sale or lease of goods made by a merchant (regardless of whether or not the offeree is a merchant). A **firm offer** arises when a merchant-offeror gives assurances *in a signed writing* that the offer will remain

EMERGING TRENDS IN TECHNOLOGY

Online Offers,
continued

boxes containing the words "I agree" or "I accept the terms of the offer" that offerees can click on to indicate acceptance. Electronic "click-on" acceptances have raised several legal issues. One issue is whether the agreement meets the signature requirements of the Statute of Frauds—because a point-and-click agreement is not actually signed by the recipient. A similar issue arises with agreements that are included in virtually all shrink-wrapped software. When the purchaser opens the software package, he or she agrees to abide by the terms of the limited license agreement.

Increasingly, the courts are holding that limited licenses included with shrink-wrapped software, as well as their equivalents on the Internet ("click-on" acceptances), are binding on the buyer. Section 2–204 of the UCC provides that any contract for the sale of goods "may be made in any manner sufficient to show agreement, including conduct by both parties which recognizes the existence of a contract." Thus, a

buyer's failure to object to terms contained within a shrink-wrapped software package (or an online offer) may constitute an acceptance of the terms by conduct.[a]

IMPLICATIONS FOR THE BUSINESSPERSON

1. Online offerors, when drafting their offers, should keep in mind some of the unique issues that can arise in the electronic-contracting environment and include terms and conditions in their offers that specifically address these issues. For example, because the Internet has no physical boundaries, jurisdictional issues often arise in Web-based business dealings. Including a forum-selection clause in the offer can help to prevent such problems.
2. Any businessperson engaging in the online sale of goods should make sure that offerees are instructed, in clear language, that by clicking "I agree" or "I accept" on a computer screen box they are

binding themselves (or their employers) in contract.

FOR CRITICAL ANALYSIS

1. Are there any significant differences between the types of terms and provisions that should be included in online offers as opposed to traditional (offline) offers?
2. What if a Web user claims that he or she clicked on a box stating "I agree" (to the terms and conditions of a contract) by mistake? What steps might online offerors take to reduce the likelihood that such "mistaken" acceptances will occur?

RELEVANT WEB SITES

For an overview of some cases dealing with click-on acceptances, go to **http://www.netlitigation. com/ecommerce.htm**. You can find a more detailed summary of *ProCD, Inc. v. Zeidenberg* (see footnote a in this feature), a landmark case on this issue, at **http://www.ccosta.com/ artprocd.htm**.

---

a. See, for example, *ProCD, Inc. v. Zeidenberg*, 86 F.3d 1447 (7th Cir. 1996); and *Hill v. Gateway 2000, Inc.*, 105 F.3d 1147 (7th Cir. 1997).

---

open. The merchant's firm offer is irrevocable without the necessity of consideration[3] for the stated period or, if no definite period is stated, a reasonable period (neither to exceed three months) [UCC 2–205, 2A–205].

---

3. If the offeree pays consideration, then an option contract (not a merchant's firm offer) is formed.

ACCEPTANCE

Acceptance of an offer to buy, sell, or lease goods generally may be made in any reasonable manner and by any reasonable means. The UCC generally takes the position that if the offeree's response indicates a *definite* acceptance of the offer, a contract is formed, even if the acceptance includes terms additional to or different from those contained in the offer [UCC 2–207(1)].

Promise to Ship or Prompt Shipment. The UCC permits acceptance of an offer to buy goods for current or prompt shipment by either a prompt *promise* to ship the goods to the buyer or the prompt shipment of conforming goods (that is, goods that accord with the contract's terms) to the buyer [UCC 2–206(1)(b)]. The prompt shipment of *nonconforming goods* constitutes both an *acceptance* (a contract) and a *breach* of that contract. This rule does not apply if the seller seasonably (within a reasonable amount of time) notifies the buyer that the nonconforming shipment is offered only as an *accommodation*, or as a favor. The notice of accommodation must clearly indicate to the buyer that the shipment does not constitute an acceptance and that, therefore, no contract has been formed.

Communication of Acceptance. Under the common law, because a unilateral offer invites acceptance by a performance, the offeree need not notify the offeror of performance unless the offeror would not otherwise know about it. The UCC is more stringent than the common law, stating that when the beginning of the requested performance is a reasonable mode of acceptance, an offeror who is not notified of acceptance within a reasonable time may treat the offer as having lapsed before acceptance [UCC 2–206(2), 2A–206(2)].

Additional Terms. If the acceptance includes terms additional to or different from those contained in the offer and one (or both) of the parties is a *nonmerchant*, the contract is formed according to the terms of the original offer submitted by the original offeror and not according to the additional terms of the acceptance [UCC 2–207(2)]. In contracts *between merchants*, the additional terms automatically become part of the contract unless (1) the original offer expressly limited acceptance to its terms, (2) the new or changed terms materially alter the contract, or (3) the offeror objects to the new or changed terms within a reasonable period of time [UCC 2–207(2)].

SECTION 4

Consideration

The common law rule that a contract requires consideration also applies to sales and lease contracts. Unlike the common law, however, the UCC does not require a contract modification to be supported by new consideration. The UCC states that an agreement modifying a contract for the sale or lease of goods "needs no consideration to be binding" [UCC 2–209(1), 2A–208(1)].

Of course, any contract modification must be made in good faith [UCC 1–203]. For example, Jim agrees to lease certain goods to Louise for a stated price. Subsequently, a sudden shift in the market makes it difficult for Jim to lease the items to Louise at the given price without suffering a loss. Jim tells Louise of the situation, and Louise agrees to pay an additional sum for the goods. Later, Louise reconsiders and refuses to pay more than the original price. Under the UCC, Louise's promise to modify the contract needs no consideration to be binding. Hence, Louise is bound by the modified contract.

In this example, a shift in the market is a *good faith* reason for contract modification. What if there really was no shift in the market, however, and Jim knew that Louise needed the goods immediately but refused to deliver them unless Louise agreed to pay an additional sum of money? This sort of extortion of a modification without a legitimate commercial reason would be ineffective, because it would violate the duty of good faith. Jim would not be permitted to enforce the higher price.

SECTION 5

The Statute of Frauds

The UCC contains Statute of Frauds provisions covering sales and lease contracts. Under these provisions, sales contracts for goods priced at $500 or more and lease contracts requiring payments of $1,000 or more must be in writing to be enforceable [UCC 2–201(1), 2A–201(1)].

SUFFICIENCY OF THE WRITING

The UCC has greatly relaxed the requirements for the sufficiency of a writing to satisfy the Statute of Frauds. A writing or a memorandum will be sufficient as long as it indicates that the parties intended to form a contract and as long as it is signed by the party (or agent of the party) against whom enforcement is sought. The contract normally will not be enforceable beyond the quantity of goods shown in the writing, however. All other terms can be proved in court by oral testimony. For leases, the writing must reasonably identify and describe the goods leased and the lease term.

SPECIAL RULES FOR CONTRACTS BETWEEN MERCHANTS

Once again, the UCC provides a special rule for merchants. The rule, however, applies only to sales (under Article 2); there is no corresponding rule that applies to leases (under Article 2A).[4] Merchants can satisfy the requirements of a writing for the Statute of Frauds if, after the parties have agreed orally, one of the merchants sends a signed written confirmation to the other merchant. The communication must indicate the terms of the agreement, and the merchant receiving the confirmation must have reason to know of its contents. Unless the merchant who receives the confirmation gives written notice of objection to its contents within ten days after receipt, the writing is sufficient against the receiving merchant, even though he or she has not signed anything [UCC 2–201(2)].

EXCEPTIONS

The UCC defines three exceptions to the writing requirements of the Statute of Frauds. An oral contract for the sale of goods priced at $500 or more or the lease of goods involving payments of $1,000 or more will be enforceable despite the absence of a writing in the following circumstances [UCC 2–201(3), 2A–201(4)].

Specially Manufactured Goods. An oral contract is enforceable if (1) it is for goods that are specially manufactured for a particular buyer or specially manufactured or obtained for a particular lessee, (2) these goods are not suitable for resale or lease to others in the ordinary course of the seller's or lessor's business, and (3) the seller or lessor has substantially started to manufacture the goods or has made commitments for the manufacture or procurement of the goods. In these situations, once the seller or lessor has taken action, the buyer or lessee cannot repudiate the agreement claiming the Statute of Frauds as a defense.

Admissions. An oral contract for the sale or lease of goods is enforceable if the party against whom enforcement is sought admits in pleadings, testimony, or other court proceedings that a sales or lease contract was made. In this situation, the contract will be enforceable even though it was oral, but enforceability will be limited to the quantity of goods admitted.

Partial Performance. An oral contract for the sale or lease of goods is enforceable if payment has been made and accepted or goods have been received and accepted. This is the "partial performance" exception. The oral contract will be enforced at least to the extent that performance *actually* took place.

SECTION 6

Title, Risk, and Insurable Interest

Before the creation of the Uniform Commercial Code (UCC), *title*—the right of ownership—was the central concept in sales law, controlling all issues of rights and remedies of the parties to a sales contract. There were numerous problems with this concept. For example, frequently it was difficult to determine when title actually passed from seller to buyer, and therefore it was also difficult to predict which party a court would decide had title at the time of a loss. Because of such problems, the UCC divorced the question of title as completely as possible from the question of the rights and obligations of buyers, sellers, and third parties (such as subsequent purchasers, creditors, or the tax collector).

In some situations, title is still relevant under the UCC, and the UCC has special rules for locating title. In most situations, however, the UCC has replaced the concept of title with three other concepts: (1) identification, (2) risk of loss, and (3) insurable interest.

In lease contracts, of course, title to the goods is retained by the lessor-owner of the goods. Hence, the UCC's provisions relating to passage of title do not apply to leased goods. Other concepts discussed in this chapter, though, including identification, risk of loss, and insurable interest, relate to lease contracts as well as to sales contracts.

IDENTIFICATION

Before any interest in specific goods can pass from the seller or lessor to the buyer or lessee, two conditions must prevail:

1. The goods must be in existence.
2. They must be identified as the specific goods designated in the contract.

---

4. According to the Comments accompanying UCC 2A–201 (Article 2A's Statute of Frauds), the "between merchants" provision was not included because "the number of such transactions involving leases, as opposed to sales, was thought to be modest."

Identification is a designation of goods as the subject matter of a sales or lease contract. Title and risk of loss cannot pass to the buyer from the seller unless the goods are identified to the contract [UCC 2–105(2)]. (As mentioned, title to leased goods remains with the lessor—or, if the owner is a third party, with that party. The lessee does not acquire title to leased goods.) Identification is significant because it gives the buyer or lessee the right to insure (or obtain an insurable interest in) the goods and the right to recover from third parties who damage the goods.

Once the goods are in existence, the parties can agree in their contract on when identification will take place. If they do not so specify, however, and if the contract calls for the sale or lease of specific and ascertained goods that are already in existence, identification takes place at the time the contract is made. If a sale involves unborn animals to be born within twelve months after contracting, identification takes place when the animals are conceived. If a lease involves any unborn animals, identification occurs when the animals are conceived. If a sale involves crops that are to be harvested within twelve months (or the next harvest season occurring after contracting, whichever is longer), identification takes place when the crops are planted or begin to grow. In a sale or lease of any other future goods, identification occurs when the goods are shipped, marked, or otherwise designated by the seller or lessor as the goods to which the contract refers. Goods that are part of a larger mass are identified when the goods are marked, shipped, or somehow designated by the seller or lessor as the particular goods to pass under the contract.

WHEN TITLE PASSES

Once goods exist and are identified, the provisions of UCC 2–401 apply to the passage of title. Unless an agreement is explicitly made,[5] title passes to the buyer at the time and the place the seller performs the *physical delivery* of the goods [UCC 2–401(2)].

Shipment and Destination Contracts. In the absence of agreement, delivery arrangements can determine when title passes from the seller to the buyer. In a **shipment contract,** the seller is required or authorized to ship goods by carrier, such as a trucking company. Under a shipment contract, the seller is required only to deliver the goods into the hands of a carrier, and title passes to the buyer at the time and place of shipment [UCC 2–401(2)(a)]. *Generally, all contracts are assumed to be shipment contracts if nothing to the contrary is stated in the contract.*

In a **destination contract,** the seller is required to deliver the goods to a particular destination, usually directly to the buyer, although sometimes the buyer designates that the goods should be delivered to another party. Title passes to the buyer when the goods are *tendered* at that destination [UCC 2–401(2)(b)]. A tender of delivery is the seller's placing or holding of conforming goods at the buyer's disposition (with any necessary notice), enabling the buyer to take delivery [UCC 2–503(1)].

Delivery without Movement of the Goods. When the contract of sale does not call for the seller's shipment or delivery of the goods (when the buyer is to pick up the goods), the passage of title depends on whether the seller must deliver a *document of title,* such as a bill of lading or a warehouse receipt, to the buyer. A *bill of lading* is a receipt for goods that is signed by a carrier and that serves as a contract for the transportation of the goods. A *warehouse receipt* is a receipt issued by a warehouser for goods stored in a warehouse.

When a document of title is required, title passes to the buyer *when and where the document is delivered.* Thus, if the goods are stored in a warehouse, title passes to the buyer when the appropriate documents are delivered to the buyer. The goods never move. In fact, the buyer can choose to leave the goods at the same warehouse for a period of time, and the buyer's title to those goods will be unaffected.

When no documents of title are required, and delivery is made without moving the goods, title passes at the time and place the sales contract is made, if the goods have already been identified. If the goods have not been identified, title does not pass until identification occurs. Consider an example. Rogers sells lumber to Bodan. It is agreed that Bodan will pick up the lumber at the yard. If the lumber has been identified (segregated, marked, or in any other way distinguished from all other lumber), title passes to Bodan when the contract is signed. If the lumber is still in storage bins at the mill, title does not pass to Bodan until the particular pieces of lumber to be sold under this contract are identified [UCC 2–401(3)].

---

5. In many sections of the UCC, the words "unless otherwise explicitly agreed" appear, meaning that any explicit agreement between the buyer and the seller determines the rights, duties, and liabilities of the parties, including when title passes.

RISK OF LOSS

Under the UCC, risk of loss does not necessarily pass with title. When risk of loss passes from a seller or lessor to a buyer or lessee is generally determined by the contract between the parties. Sometimes, the contract states expressly when the risk of loss passes. At other times, it does not, and a court must interpret the existing terms to ascertain whether the risk has passed.

Delivery with Movement of the Goods. When there is no specification in the agreement, the following rules apply to cases involving movement of the goods (carrier cases). In a shipment contract, if the seller or lessor is required or authorized to ship goods by carrier (but not required to deliver them to a particular destination), risk of loss passes to the buyer or lessee when the goods are duly delivered to the carrier [UCC 2–509(1)(a), 2A–219(2)(a)]. In a destination contract, the risk of loss passes to the buyer or lessee when the goods are tendered to the buyer or lessee at the specified destination [UCC 2–509(1)(b), 2A–219(2)(b)].

Specific terms in the contract help determine when risk of loss passes to the buyer. These terms, which are listed and defined in Exhibit 11–1 on page 238, relate generally to the determination of which party will bear the costs of delivery, as well as which party will bear the risk of loss. The following case illustrates these principles.

CASE 11.1   Windows, Inc. v. Jordan Panel System Corp.

United States
Court of Appeals,
Second Circuit, 1999.
177 F.3d 114.
**www.law.pace.edu/
lawlib/legal/us-legal/
judiciary/second-
circuit.html**[a]

BACKGROUND AND FACTS *Windows, Inc., is a fabricator and seller of windows, based in South Dakota. Jordan Systems, Inc., is a construction subcontractor, which contracted to install window wall panels at an air cargo facility at John F. Kennedy Airport in New York City. Jordan ordered custom-made windows from Windows. The contract specified that the windows were to be shipped properly packaged for cross-country motor freight transit and "delivered to New York City." Windows built the windows and arranged to ship them to Jordan by Consolidated Freightways Corporation. During the shipment, much of the glass was broken and many of the frames were gouged and twisted. Jordan employees disassembled the window frames to salvage as much of the shipment as possible. Jordan made a claim with Consolidated for the damages, including labor costs from the salvage efforts and other costs from Jordan's inability to perform its contracts on schedule. Jordan also ordered a new shipment from Windows, which was delivered without incident. Jordan did not pay Windows for either shipment. As part of the ensuing litigation, a federal district court heard Jordan's claim against Windows for incidental and consequential damages resulting from the damaged shipment. When the court granted Windows's motion for summary judgment, Jordan appealed to the U.S. Court of Appeals for the Second Circuit.*

**IN THE LANGUAGE
OF THE COURT**

LEVAL, Circuit Judge:

    *   *   *   *

    *   *   * [A] shipment contract arises [under UCC 2–504] where "the seller is required * * * to send the goods to the buyer and the contract does not require him to deliver them at a particular destination." Under a shipment contract, the seller must "put the goods in the possession of such a carrier and make such a contract for their transportation as may be reasonable having regard to the nature of the goods and other circumstances of the case."

    Where the terms of an agreement are ambiguous, there is a strong presumption under the U.C.C. favoring shipment contracts. Unless the parties "expressly specify" that the contract requires the seller to deliver to a particular destination, the contract is generally construed as one for shipment. [Emphasis added.]

---

a. This Web site is a joint project of Touro and Pace University School of Law with the cooperation of the U.S. Court of Appeals for the Second Circuit. In the "1999" column, click on "April." When that page opens, scroll down the list of cases to the case name and click on "Opinion" to access the case.

*   *   *   *

To overcome the presumption favoring shipment contracts, the parties must have explicitly agreed to impose on Windows the obligation to effect delivery at a particular destination. The language of this contract does not do so. Nor did Jordan use any commonly recognized industry term indicating that a seller is obligated to deliver the goods to the buyer's specified destination.

Given the strong presumption favoring shipment contracts, and the absence of explicit terms satisfying both requirements for a destination contract, we conclude that the contract should be deemed a shipment contract.

Under the terms of its contract, Windows thus satisfied its obligations to Jordan when it put the goods, properly packaged, into the possession of the carrier for shipment. Upon Windows' proper delivery to the carrier, Jordan assumed the risk of loss, and cannot recover incidental or consequential damages from the seller caused by the carrier's negligence.

This allocation of risk is confirmed by the terms of [UCC] 2–509(1)(a), entitled "Risk of Loss in the Absence of Breach." It provides that where the contract "does not require [the seller] to deliver [the goods] at a particular destination, the risk of loss passes to the buyer when the goods are duly delivered to the carrier." *   *   * Jordan does not contest the court's finding that Windows duly delivered conforming goods to the carrier. Accordingly, as Windows had already fulfilled its contractual obligations at the time the goods were damaged and Jordan had assumed the risk of loss, there was no "seller's breach" as is required for a buyer to claim incidental and consequential damages *   *   * . Summary judgment for Windows was therefore proper.

DECISION AND REMEDY   *The U.S. Court of Appeals for the Second Circuit affirmed the lower court's decision. The contract was a shipment contract, and thus, when the seller (Windows) put the goods into the hands of the carrier (Consolidated), the risk of loss passed to the buyer (Jordan).*

Delivery without Movement of the Goods. The UCC also addresses situations in which the seller or lessor is required neither to ship nor to deliver the goods. Frequently, the buyer or lessee is to pick up the goods from the seller or lessor, or the goods are to be held by a bailee. A *bailment* is a temporary delivery of personal property, without passage of title, into the care of another, called a *bailee*. Under the UCC, a bailee is a party who, by a bill of lading, warehouse receipt, or other document of title, acknowledges possession of goods and contracts to deliver them. A warehousing company, for example, or a trucking company that normally issues documents of title for the goods it receives is a bailee.

Exhibit 11–1   Contract Terms—Definitions

F.O.B. (free on board)—Indicates that the selling price of goods includes transportation costs (and that the seller carries risk of loss) to the specific F.O.B. place named in the contract. The place can be either the place of initial shipment (for example, the seller's city or place of business) or the place of destination (for example, the buyer's city or place of business) [UCC 2–319(1)].

F.A.S. (free alongside)—Requires that the seller, at his or her own expense and risk, deliver the goods alongside the ship before risk passes to the buyer [UCC 2–319(2)].

C.I.F. or **C.&F.** (cost, insurance, and freight or just cost and freight)—Requires, among other things, that the seller "put the goods in possession of a carrier" before risk passes to the buyer [UCC 2–320(2)]. (These are basically pricing terms, and the contracts remain shipment contracts, not destination contracts.)

Delivery ex-ship (delivery from the carrying vessel)—Means that risk of loss does not pass to the buyer until the goods leave the ship or are otherwise properly unloaded [UCC 2–322].

Goods Held by the Seller. If the goods are held by the seller, a document of title is usually not used. If the seller is a merchant, risk of loss to goods held by the seller passes to the buyer when the buyer *actually takes physical possession of the goods* [UCC 2–509(3)]. If the seller is not a merchant, the risk of loss to goods held by the seller passes to the buyer on tender of delivery [UCC 2–509(3)].

In respect to leases, the risk of loss passes to the lessee on the lessee's receipt of the goods if the lessor is a merchant. Otherwise, the risk passes to the lessee on tender of delivery [UCC 2A–219(c)].

Goods Held by a Bailee. When a bailee is holding goods for a person who has contracted to sell them and the goods are to be delivered without being moved, the goods are usually represented by a negotiable or nonnegotiable document of title (a bill of lading or a warehouse receipt). Risk of loss passes to the buyer when (1) the buyer receives a negotiable document of title for the goods, (2) the bailee acknowledges the buyer's right to possess the goods, or (3) the buyer receives a nonnegotiable document of title *and* has had a *reasonable time* to present the document to the bailee and demand the goods. Obviously, if the bailee refuses to honor the document, the risk of loss remains with the seller [UCC 2–503(4)(b), 2–509(2)].

With respect to leases, if goods held by a bailee are to be delivered without being moved, the risk of loss passes to the lessee on acknowledgment by the bailee of the lessee's right to possession of the goods [UCC 2A–219(2)(b)].

Conditional Sales. Buyers and sellers sometimes form sales contracts that are conditioned either on the buyer's approval of the goods or on the buyer's resale of the goods. Under such contracts, the buyer is in possession of the goods. Sometimes, however, problems arise as to whether the buyer or seller should bear the loss if, for example, the goods are damaged or stolen while in the possession of the buyer.

Sale or Return. A **sale or return** (sometimes called a *sale and return*) is a type of contract by which the buyer purchases the goods but has a conditional right to return the goods (undo the sale) within a specified time period. When the buyer receives possession at the time of sale, title and risk of loss pass to the buyer. Title and risk of loss remain with the buyer until the buyer returns the goods to the seller within the time period specified. If the buyer fails to return the goods within this time period, the sale is finalized. The return of the goods is made at the buyer's risk and expense. Goods held under a sale-or-return contract are subject to the claims of the buyer's creditors while they are in the buyer's possession.

The UCC treats a **consignment** as a sale or return. Under a consignment, the owner of goods (the *consignor*) delivers them to another (the *consignee*) for the consignee to sell or to keep. If the consignee sells the goods, the consignee must pay the consignor for them. If the consignee does not sell or keep the goods, they may simply be returned to the consignor. While the goods are in the possession of the consignee, the consignee holds title to them, and creditors of the consignee will prevail over the consignor in any action to repossess the goods [UCC 2–326(3)].

Sale on Approval. Usually, when a seller offers to sell goods to a buyer and permits the buyer to take the goods on a trial basis, a **sale on approval** is made. The term *sale* here is a misnomer, as only an *offer* to sell has been made, along with a bailment created by the buyer's possession.

Therefore, title and risk of loss (from causes beyond the buyer's control) remain with the seller until the buyer accepts (approves) the offer. Acceptance can be made expressly, by any act inconsistent with the *trial* purpose or the seller's ownership, or by the buyer's election not to return the goods within the trial period. If the buyer does not wish to accept, the buyer may notify the seller of that fact within the trial period, and the return is made at the seller's expense and risk [UCC 2–327(1)]. Goods held on approval are not subject to the claims of the buyer's creditors until acceptance.

Risk of Loss When a Sales or Lease Contract Is Breached. There are many ways to breach a sales or lease contract, and the transfer of risk operates differently depending on which party breaches. Generally, the party in breach bears the risk of loss.

When the Seller or Lessor Breaches. If the goods are so nonconforming that the buyer has the right to reject them, the risk of loss does not pass to the buyer until the defects are *cured* (that is, until the goods are repaired, replaced, or discounted in price by the seller) or until the buyer accepts the goods in spite of their defects (thus waiving the right to reject). For example, a buyer orders blue file cabinets from a seller, F.O.B. seller's plant. The seller ships black file cabinets instead. The black cabinets (nonconforming goods) are damaged in transit. The risk of loss falls on the seller. Had the seller shipped blue cabinets (conforming goods) instead, the risk would have fallen on the buyer [UCC 2–510(2)].

If a buyer accepts a shipment of goods and later discovers a defect, acceptance can be revoked. Revocation allows the buyer to pass the risk of loss back to the seller, at least to the extent that the buyer's insurance does not cover the loss [UCC 2–510(2)].

In regard to leases, Article 2A states a similar rule. If the lessor or supplier tenders goods that are so nonconforming that the lessee has the right to reject them, the risk of loss remains with the lessor or the supplier until cure or acceptance [UCC 2A–220(1)(a)]. If the lessee, after acceptance, revokes his or her acceptance of nonconforming goods, the revocation passes the risk of loss back to the seller or supplier, to the extent that the lessee's insurance does not cover the loss [UCC 2A–220(1)(b)].

When the Buyer or Lessee Breaches. The general rule is that when a buyer or lessee breaches a contract, the risk of loss *immediately* shifts to the buyer or lessee. There are three important limitations to this rule [UCC 2–510(3), 2A–220(2)]:

1. The seller or lessor must already have identified the contract goods.
2. The buyer or lessee bears the risk for only a *commercially reasonable time* after the seller or lessor has learned of the breach.
3. The buyer or lessee is liable only to the extent of any deficiency in the seller's or lessor's insurance coverage.

INSURABLE INTEREST

Parties to sales and lease contracts often obtain insurance coverage to protect against damage, loss, or destruction of goods. Any party purchasing insurance, however, must have a sufficient interest in the insured item to obtain a valid policy. Insurance laws—not the UCC—determine sufficiency. The UCC is helpful, however, because it contains certain rules regarding insurable interests in goods.

A buyer or lessee has an **insurable interest** in identified goods. The moment the contract goods are *identified* by the seller or lessor, the buyer or lessee has a special property interest that allows the buyer or lessee to obtain necessary insurance coverage for those goods even before the risk of loss has passed [UCC 2–501(1), 2A–218(1)].

A seller has an insurable interest in goods as long as he or she retains title to the goods. Even after title passes to a buyer, however, a seller who has a security interest in the goods, which is a legal right to secure payment, still has an insurable interest and can insure the goods [UCC 2–501(2)]. Hence, both a buyer and a seller can have an insurable interest in identical goods at the same time. Of course, the buyer or seller must sustain an actual loss to have the right to recover from an insurance company. In regard to leases, the lessor retains an insurable interest in leased goods until an option to buy has been exercised by the lessee and the risk of loss has passed to the lessee [UCC 2A–218(3)].

SECTION 7

Performance of Sales and Lease Contracts

To understand the obligations of the parties under a sales or lease contract, it is necessary to know the duties and obligations each party has assumed under the terms of the contract. Keep in mind that "duties and obligations" under the terms of the contract include those specified by the agreement, by custom, and by the UCC.

In the performance of a sales or lease contract, the basic obligation of the seller or lessor is to *transfer and deliver conforming goods*. The basic obligation of the buyer or lessee is to *accept and pay for conforming goods* in accordance with the contract [UCC 2–301, 2A–516(1)]. Overall performance of a sales or lease contract is controlled by the agreement between the parties. When the contract is unclear and disputes arise, the courts look to the UCC.

THE GOOD FAITH REQUIREMENT

The obligations of good faith and commercial reasonableness underlie every sales and lease contract within the UCC. These obligations can form the basis for a suit for breach of contract later on. The UCC's good faith provision, which can never be disclaimed, reads as follows: "Every contract or duty within this Act imposes an obligation of good faith in its performance or enforcement" [UCC 1–203]. Good faith means honesty in fact. In the case of a merchant, it means honesty in fact and the observance of reasonable commercial standards of fair dealing in the trade [UCC

2–103(1)(b)]. In other words, merchants are held to a higher standard of performance or duty than nonmerchants are.

OBLIGATIONS OF THE SELLER OR LESSOR

The major obligation of the seller or lessor under a sales or lease contract is to tender conforming goods to the buyer or lessee. **Tender of delivery** requires that the seller or lessor have and hold *conforming* goods at the disposal of the buyer or lessee and give the buyer or lessee whatever notification is reasonably necessary to enable the buyer or lessee to take delivery [UCC 2–503(1), 2A–508(1)]. **Conforming goods** are goods that conform exactly to the description of the goods in the contract.

Tender must occur at a *reasonable hour* and in a *reasonable manner*. For example, a seller cannot call the buyer at 2:00 A.M. and say, "The goods are ready. I'll give you twenty minutes to get them." Unless the parties have agreed otherwise, the goods must be tendered for delivery at a reasonable hour and kept available for a reasonable period of time to enable the buyer to take possession of them [UCC 2–503(1)(a)].

All goods called for by a contract must be tendered in a single delivery unless the parties agree otherwise [UCC 2–612, 2A–510] or the circumstances are such that either party can rightfully request delivery in lots [UCC 2–307].

If the contract does not designate the place of delivery for the goods, and the buyer is expected to pick them up, the place of delivery is the *seller's place of business* or, if the seller has none, the *seller's residence* [UCC 2–308]. If the contract involves the sale of *identified goods,* and the parties know when they enter into the contract that these goods are located somewhere other than at the seller's place of business (such as at a warehouse), then the *location of the goods* is the place for their delivery [UCC 2–308].

The Perfect Tender Rule. As previously noted, the seller or lessor has an obligation to ship or tender *conforming goods,* and this entitles the buyer or lessee to accept and pay for the goods according to the terms of the contract. Under the common law, the seller was obligated to deliver goods in conformity with the terms of the contract in every detail. This was called the **perfect tender rule.** The UCC preserves the perfect tender doctrine by stating that if goods or tender of delivery fail *in any respect* to conform to the contract, the buyer or lessee has the right to accept the goods, reject the entire shipment, or accept part and reject part [UCC 2–601, 2A–509].

Exceptions to the Perfect Tender Rule. Because of the rigidity of the perfect tender rule, several exceptions to the rule have been created, some of which we discuss here.

Agreement of the Parties. Exceptions to the perfect tender rule may be established by agreement. If the parties have agreed, for example, that defective goods or parts will not be rejected if the seller or lessor is able to repair or replace them within a reasonable period of time, the perfect tender rule does not apply.

Cure. The UCC does not specifically define the term **cure,** but it refers to the right of the seller or lessor to repair, adjust, or replace defective or nonconforming goods [UCC 2–508, 2A–513]. When any tender of delivery is rejected because of nonconforming goods and the time for performance has not yet expired, the seller or lessor can notify the buyer or lessee promptly of the intention to cure and can then do so *within the contract time for performance* [UCC 2–508(1), 2A–513(1)]. Once the time for performance under the contract has expired, the seller or lessor can still exercise the right to cure if he or she had *reasonable grounds to believe that the nonconforming tender would be acceptable to the buyer or lessee* [UCC 2–508(2), 2A–513(2)].

The right to cure substantially restricts the right of the buyer or lessee to reject goods. For example, if a lessee refuses a tender of goods as nonconforming but does not disclose the nature of the defect to the lessor, the lessee cannot later assert the defect as a defense if the defect is one that the lessor could have cured. Generally, buyers and lessees must act in good faith and state specific reasons for refusing to accept goods [UCC 2–605, 2A–514].

Substitution of Carriers. When an agreed-on manner of delivery (such as the use of a particular carrier to transport the goods) becomes impracticable or unavailable through no fault of either party, but a commercially reasonable substitute is available, this substitute performance is sufficient tender to the buyer and must be used [UCC 2–614(1)].

Commercial Impracticability. Occurrences unforeseen by either party when a contract was made may make performance commercially impracticable.

When this occurs, the rule of perfect tender no longer holds. According to UCC 2–615(a) and 2A–405(a), delay in delivery or nondelivery in whole or in part is not a breach when performance has been made impracticable "by the occurrence of a contingency the nonoccurrence of which was a basic assumption on which the contract was made." The seller or lessor must, however, notify the buyer or lessee as soon as practicable that there will be a delay or nondelivery.

An increase in cost resulting from inflation does not in and of itself excuse performance, as this kind of risk is ordinarily assumed by a seller or lessor conducting business. The unforeseen contingency must be one that would have been impossible to contemplate in a given business situation.

Destruction of Identified Goods. Sometimes, an unexpected event, such as a fire, totally destroys goods through no fault of either party and before risk passes to the buyer or lessee. In such a situation, if the *goods were identified at the time the contract was formed*, the parties are excused from performance [UCC 2–613, 2A–221]. If the goods are only partially destroyed, however, the buyer or lessee can inspect them and either treat the contract as void or accept the damaged goods with a reduction of the contract price.

Assurance and Cooperation. Two other exceptions to the perfect tender doctrine apply equally to parties to sales and lease contracts: the right of assurance and the duty of cooperation.

The UCC provides that if one of the parties to a contract has "reasonable grounds" to believe that the other party will not perform as contracted, he or she may *in writing* "demand adequate assurance of due performance" from the other party. Until such assurance is received, he or she may "suspend" further performance without liability. What constitutes "reasonable grounds" is determined by commercial standards. If such assurances are not forthcoming within a reasonable time (not to exceed thirty days), the failure to respond may be treated as a *repudiation* of the contract [UCC 2–609, 2A–401].

Sometimes the performance of one party depends on the cooperation of the other. The UCC provides that when such cooperation is not forthcoming, the other party can suspend his or her own performance without liability and hold the uncooperative party in breach or proceed to perform the contract in any reasonable manner [see UCC 2–311(3)(b)].

OBLIGATIONS OF THE BUYER OR LESSEE

Once the seller or lessor has adequately tendered delivery, the buyer or lessee is obligated to accept the goods and pay for them according to the terms of the contract.

Payment. In the absence of any specific agreements, the buyer or lessee must make payment at the time and place the buyer or lessee *receives* the goods [UCC 2–310(a), 2A–516(1)]. When a sale is made on credit, the buyer is obliged to pay according to the specified credit terms (for example, 60, 90, or 120 days), not when the goods are received. The credit period usually begins on the *date of shipment* [UCC 2–310(d)]. Under a lease contract, a lessee must make the lease payment specified in the contract [UCC 2A–516(1)].

Payment can be made by any means agreed on between the parties—cash or any other method generally acceptable in the commercial world. If the seller demands cash when the buyer offers a check, credit card, or the like, the seller must permit the buyer reasonable time to obtain legal tender [UCC 2–511].

Acceptance. A buyer or lessee can manifest assent to the delivered goods in the following ways, each of which constitutes acceptance:

1. There is an acceptance if the buyer or lessee, after having had a reasonable opportunity to inspect the goods, signifies agreement to the seller or lessor that the goods are either conforming or are acceptable in spite of their nonconformity [UCC 2–606(1)(a), 2A–515(1)(a)].
2. Acceptance is presumed if the buyer or lessee has had a reasonable opportunity to inspect the goods and has failed to reject them within a reasonable period of time [UCC 2–602(1), 2–606(1)(b), 2A–515(1)(b)].
3. In sales contracts, the buyer will be deemed to have accepted the goods if he or she performs any act inconsistent with the seller's ownership. For example, any use or resale of the goods generally constitutes an acceptance. Limited use for the sole purpose of testing or inspecting the goods is not an acceptance, however [UCC 2–606(1)(c)].

If some of the goods delivered do not conform to the contract and the seller or lessor has failed to cure, the buyer or lessee can make a *partial* acceptance [UCC 2–601(c), 2A–509(1)]. The same is true if the nonconformity was not reasonably discoverable before acceptance.[6] A buyer or lessee cannot accept less than a single commercial unit, however. A *commercial unit* is defined by the UCC as a unit of goods that, by commercial usage, is viewed as a "single whole" for purposes of sale, division of which would materially impair the character of the unit, its market value, or its use [UCC 2–105(6), 2A–103(c)]. A commercial unit can be a single article (such as a machine), a set of articles (such as a suite of furniture or an assortment of sizes), a quantity (such as a bale, a gross, or a carload), or any other unit treated in the trade as a single whole.

ANTICIPATORY REPUDIATION

What if, before the time for contract performance, one party clearly communicates to the other the in-

---

6. If the nonconformity was not reasonably discoverable before acceptance, the buyer or lessee may be able to revoke the acceptance.

tention not to perform? Such an action is a breach of the contract by *anticipatory repudiation*. When anticipatory repudiation occurs, the nonbreaching party has a choice of two responses. He or she can treat the repudiation as a final breach by pursuing a remedy; or he or she can wait, hoping that the repudiating party will decide to honor the obligations required by the contract despite the avowed intention to renege [UCC 2–610, 2A–402]. In either situation, the nonbreaching party may suspend performance.

Should the latter course be pursued, the UCC permits the breaching party (subject to some limitations) to "retract" his or her repudiation. This can be done by any method that clearly indicates an intent to perform. Once retraction is made, the rights of the repudiating party under the contract are reinstated [UCC 2–611, 2A–403].

The concept of anticipatory repudiation is further illustrated in the following case.

CASE 11.2 ## Banco International, Inc. v. Goody's Family Clothing

United States
District Court,
Eastern District of
Tennessee, 1999.
54 F.Supp.2d 765.

BACKGROUND AND FACTS *In April 1994, Banco International, Inc., and Goody's Family Clothing contracted for the manufacture of 62,748 custom-made, private-label windsuits (jogging suits) and their delivery in three shipments, for $749,103.60. The first shipment had to be at Goody's distribution center in Knoxville, Tennessee, by September 30 in time for holiday season sales, or the order was subject to cancellation. Banco sent to Goody's what Banco claimed were production samples but which Goody's learned had been produced by another manufacturer. Goody's also learned that a third party had the fabric and other materials that were needed to make the windsuits and would not release them to Banco without payment of a debt. By August 23, Banco had not started production, despite the representations of Muhammed Akhtar, the president and owner of Banco, to the contrary. On that day, Goody's canceled the contract. Akhtar acknowledged that Banco was behind schedule but said it could meet the delivery dates for the first two shipments if it shipped by air and the deadline for the third shipment by shipping by sea. Had Goody's asked how production could be accomplished so quickly, Akhtar later said he would have responded that it was "none of Goody's business." Goody's did not accept Akhtar's assurances. Banco filed a suit in a federal district court against Goody's, alleging breach of contract. Goody's argued that there was an anticipatory repudiation, or breach, of the contract by Banco.*

IN THE LANGUAGE OF THE COURT MURRIAN, Magistrate J. [Judge]

* * * *

* * * *It is not necessary for [anticipatory] repudiation that performance be made literally and utterly impossible.* Repudiation can result from action which reasonably indicates a rejection of the continuing obligation. [Emphasis added.]

Banco's failure to start actual production of the windsuits prior to cancellation of the contract on August 23, 1994, Banco's apparent inability to gain possession and control of the fabric and other raw materials necessary to perform the contract, Banco's false representations about production, and Banco's failure to give Goody's adequate assurances that it could perform the contract in a timely manner during the days following cancellation are the primary actions by Banco which reasonably indicated to Goody's that Banco had rejected its continuing obligation under the contract. These actions justified Goody's suspension of its own performance and cancellation of the contract.

In all contracts governed by Article 2 of the Uniform Commercial Code there is a continuing obligation of good faith and reasonableness. In this case, Goody's came to realize by August 23, 1994, that Mr. Akhtar had not been truthful with Goody's about the status of production of the windsuits; Goody's had reason to believe that the production samples were not production samples at all; Banco did not have possession of the fabric and raw materials to perform the contract; and, as far as Goody's knew, Banco had no prospects of obtaining possession and control of those raw materials. In the days subsequent to the cancellation, Banco's proffered "reasonable assurances" consisted of more promises from Mr. Akhtar (whose credibility had been severely damaged) but without an explanation of just how Banco proposed to perform because Mr. Akhtar believed it was "none of Goody's business."

* * * It was this apparent inability to perform without a substantial breach of the contract that justified Goody's in canceling the contract and in refusing Banco's proffered "reasonable assurances" of performance.

I find that Goody's was justified in reasonably concluding that Banco could not deliver the windsuits to it by the date set in the first purchase order between the parties. Additionally, the failure to deliver the goods by that date would have substantially impaired the value of those goods to Goody's.

DECISION AND REMEDY *The court entered a judgment in Goody's favor. Goody's was not liable for canceling the purchase orders because of Banco's anticipatory repudiation of their contract. This repudiation was indicated by Banco's failure to start performance within a reasonable time to meet the contract deadlines and by Banco's misrepresentations concerning the status of its performance.*

SECTION 8

Remedies for Breach of Sales and Lease Contracts

Sometimes, however, circumstances make it difficult for a person to carry out the performance promised in a contract, in which case the contract may be breached. When breach occurs, the aggrieved party looks for remedies. These remedies range from retaining the goods to requiring the breaching party's performance under the contract. The general purpose of these remedies is to put the aggrieved party "in as good a position as if the other party had fully performed." Remedies under the Uniform Commercial Code (UCC) are *cumulative* in nature. In other words, an innocent party to a breached sales or lease contract is not limited to one, exclusive remedy. (Of course, a party still may not recover twice for the same harm.)

REMEDIES OF THE SELLER OR LESSOR

A buyer or lessee breaches a sales or lease contract by any of the following actions: (1) wrongfully rejecting tender of the goods; (2) wrongfully revoking acceptance of the goods; (3) failing to make payment on or before delivery of the goods; or repudiating the contract. On the buyer's or lessee's breach, the seller or lessor is afforded several distinct remedies under the UCC. These include the right to stop or withhold delivery of the goods and the right to recover damages or to recover the purchase price of the goods.

The Right to Recover the Purchase Price or Lease Payments Due. Under the UCC, an unpaid seller or lessor who is unable to resell or dispose of the goods can bring an action to recover the purchase price or the payments due under the lease contract, plus incidental damages but only under one of the following circumstances:

1. When the buyer or lessee has accepted the goods and has not revoked acceptance.

2. When conforming goods have been lost or damaged after the risk of loss has passed to the buyer or lessee.

3.. When the buyer or lessee has breached after the goods have been identified to the contract and the sellor or lessor is unable to resell or otherwise dispose of the goods [UCC 2-709(1), 2A-529(1)].

If a seller or lessor sues under these circumstances, the goods must be held for the buyer or lessee. The seller or lessor can resell or dispose of the goods at any time prior to collection of the judgment from the buyer or lessee, but in that situation the net proceeds from the sale must be credited to the buyer or lessee. This is an example of the duty to mitigate damages.

The Right to Recover Damages. If a buyer or lessee repudiates a contract or wrongfully refuses to accept the goods, a seller or lessor can maintain an action to recover the damages sustained. Ordinarily, the amount of damages equals the difference between the contract price or lease payments and the market price or lease payments at the time and place of tender of the goods, plus incidental damages [UCC 2–708(1), 2A–528(1)]. The time and place of tender are frequently given by such terms as F.O.B., F.A.S., C.I.F., and the like (see Exhibit 11–1 on page 238), which determine whether there is a shipment or destination contract.

If the difference between the contract price or payments due under the lease contract and the market price or payments due under the lease contract is too small to place the seller or lessor in the position that he or she would have been in if the buyer or lessee had fully performed, the proper measure of damages is the lost profits of the seller or lessor, including a reasonable allowance for overhead and other expenses [UCC 2–708(2), 2A–528(2)].

REMEDIES OF THE BUYER OR LESSEE

A seller or lessor breaches a sales or lease contract by failing to deliver conforming goods or repudiating the contract prior to delivery. On the breach, the buyer or lessee has a choice of several remedies under the UCC. These remedies include the right to reject nonconforming or improperly delivered goods;

to *cover* (that is, to buy the goods elsewhere and recover from the seller the extra cost of obtaining the substitute goods); to recover damages; and, in certain circumstances, to obtain specific performance of the contract.

The Right to Obtain Specific Performance. A buyer or lessee can obtain specific performance when the goods are unique or when the remedy at law is inadequate [UCC 2–716(1), 2A–521(1)]. Ordinarily, an award of money damages is sufficient to place a buyer or lessee in the position he or she would have occupied if the seller or lessor had fully performed. When the contract is for the purchase of a particular work of art or a similarly unique item, however, money damages may not be sufficient. Under these circumstances, equity will require that the seller or lessor perform exactly by delivering the particular goods identified to the contract (a remedy of specific performance).

The Right to Recover Damages. If a seller or lessor repudiates the sales contract or fails to deliver the goods, or if the buyer is justified in rejecting goods that the seller or lessor tenders, then the buyer or lessee has several options under the UCC. The buyer or lessee may cancel the contract and recover as much of the price as has been paid to the seller or lessor. Following cancellation, the buyer or lessee may either (1) cover by obtaining goods from another seller or lessor and seeking reimbursement for the extra costs incurred or (2) recover damages for breach of the contract.

If the buyer or lessee elects to sue for damages, the measure of recovery is the difference between the contract price (or lease payments) and the market price of the goods (or lease payments that could be obtained for the goods) at the time the buyer (or lessee) *learned* of the breach. The market price or market lease payments are determined at the place where the seller or lessor was supposed to deliver the goods. The buyer or lessee can also recover incidental and consequential damages less the expenses that were saved as a result of the breach [UCC 2–713, 2A–519].

The Right to Reject the Goods. If either the goods or the tender of the goods by the seller or lessor fails to conform to the contract in any respect, the buyer or lessee can reject the goods. If some of the goods conform to the contract, the buyer or lessee can keep the conforming goods and reject the rest [UCC 2–601, 2A–509]. The buyer or lessee must reject the goods within a reasonable amount of time after delivery or tender of delivery, and the seller or lessor must be notified *seasonably*—that is, in a timely fashion or at the proper time [UCC 2–602(1), 2A–509(2)].

If a *merchant buyer* or *lessee* rightfully rejects goods, and the seller or lessor has no agent or business at the place of rejection, the buyer or lessee is required to follow any reasonable instructions received from the seller or lessor with respect to the goods controlled by the buyer or lessee. The buyer or lessee is entitled to reimbursement for the care and cost entailed in following the instructions [UCC 2–603, 2A–511]. The same requirements hold if the buyer or lessee rightfully revokes his or her acceptance of the goods at some later time [UCC 2–608(3), 2A–517(5)].

If no instructions are forthcoming and the goods are perishable or threaten to decline in value quickly, the buyer or lessee can resell the goods in good faith, taking appropriate reimbursement and a selling commission (not to exceed 10 percent of the gross proceeds) from the proceeds [UCC 2–603(1), (2); 2A–511(1)]. If the goods are not perishable, the buyer or lessee may store them for the seller or lessor or reship them to the seller or lessor [UCC 2–604, 2A–512].

The Right to Recover Damages for Accepted Goods. A buyer or lessee who has accepted nonconforming goods may also keep the goods and recover for any loss "resulting in the ordinary course of events . . . as determined in any manner which is reasonable" [UCC 2–714(1), 2A–519(3)]. The buyer or lessee, however, must notify the seller or lessor of the breach within a reasonable time after the defect was or should have been discovered.

When the goods delivered are not as warranted, the measure of damages equals the difference between the value of the goods as accepted and their value if they had been delivered as warranted unless special circumstances show proximately caused damages of a different amount, plus incidental and consequential damages [UCC 2–714, 2A–519].

Who qualifies as a "buyer" under these provisions? Is a party who does not actually purchase a product, but who is injured by its alleged defects, required to give notice of those defects within a reasonable time in order to recover for those injuries? This was an important question in the following case.

CASE 11.3 Yates v. Pitman Manufacturing, Inc.

Supreme Court of Virginia, 1999.
257 Va. 601,
514 S.E.2d 605.
http://www.courts.state.va.us/opin.html[a]

BACKGROUND AND FACTS. *In 1982, Pitman Manufacturing, Inc., made and sold a construction crane to Shelton Witt Equipment, a distributor. At the time, Pitman certified that the outrigger on the crane could be seen from its "actuating location." In 1991, Koch Carbon owned the crane and was using it to deliver equipment to Baldwin Coal Corporation. Ira Stiltner, a Koch employee, activated the outrigger from the front of the truck. At the time, he could not see the outrigger or Eddie Yates, a Baldwin employee, who was simultaneously releasing restraining chains from the crane truck's bed. Without warning, the outrigger dropped onto Yates's foot. Yates filed a suit in a Virginia state court against Pitman, seeking $3 million in damages for his injuries on the basis of breach of warranty (see Chapter 23). One of the issues was whether Yates had provided reasonable notice, under UCC 2–607(3), to Pitman of its breach of warranty. Yates argued in part that he did not have to give the notice, because he was not the purchaser of the crane. The court entered a judgment in Pitman's favor. Yates appealed to the Virginia Supreme Court.*

---

a. In the "Supreme Court of Virginia" section, click on the version in which you want to read this opinion. To view the opinion in text format, click on "Opinions in Text Format." On that page, scroll down the list of cases to the *Yates* case and click on the docket number ("981474") to access the opinion.

IN THE LANGUAGE
OF THE COURT

STEPHENSON, Senior Justice.

* * * *

First, we consider whether the trial court erred in holding that Yates was required to provide Pitman with notice of breach of warranty as a prerequisite to recovery therefor. The issue is one of first impression for [an issue never before examined by] this Court.

To resolve the issue, we look to [Virginia] Code [Section] 8.2–607(3) [Virgina's version of UCC 2–607(3)], the only provision of the Sales title of the Uniform Commercial Code (the UCC) that requires notice to be given to a seller of goods. The section provides, in pertinent part, the following:

> Where a tender has been accepted * * * the buyer must within a reasonable time after he discovers or should have discovered any breach notify the seller of breach or be barred from any remedy.

It is firmly established that, when a statute is clear and unambiguous, a court must accept its plain meaning and not resort to extrinsic evidence or rules of construction. The pertinent language in Code [Section] 8.2–607(3) is unambiguous and clearly states that "the buyer must * * * notify the seller of [the] breach." Thus, accepting the statute's plain meaning, it is apparent that the notice of breach is required from the "buyer" of the goods. [Emphasis added.]

In the present case, Yates was not the buyer of the crane unit. Therefore, the notice requirement of Code [Section] 8.2–607(3) does not preclude Yates from maintaining a breach of warranty action.

We hold, therefore, that only buyers, i.e., those who buy or contract to buy goods from a seller, must give notice of breach of warranty to the seller as a prerequisite to recovery. Consequently, the trial court erred in ruling that Yates was required to have given Pitman such notice.

DECISION
AND REMEDY

The Virginia Supreme Court reversed the judgment of the lower court and remanded the case for further proceedings consistent with this decision. Yates did not have to give the notice under UCC 2–607(3) to recover for his injuries, because he was not a "buyer."

CONTRACTUAL PROVISIONS AFFECTING REMEDIES

The parties to a sales or lease contract can vary their respective rights and obligations by contractual agreement. For example, a seller and buyer can expressly provide for remedies in addition to those provided in the UCC. They can also specifiy remedies in lieu of those provided in the UCC, or they can change the measure of damages. The seller can stipulate that the buyer's only remedy on the seller's breach be repair or replacement of the item, or the seller can limit the buyer's remedy to return of the goods and refund of the purchase price. In sales and lease contracts, an agreed-on remedy is in addition to those provided in the UCC unless the parties expressly agree that the remedy is exclusive of all others [UCC 2–719(1), 2A–503(1)].

If the parties state that a remedy is exclusive, then it is the sole remedy. When circumstances cause an exclusive remedy to fail in its essential purpose, however, it is no longer exclusive [UCC 2–719(2), 2A–503(2)]. For example, a sales contract that limits the buyer's remedy to repair or replacement fails in its essential purpose if the item cannot be repaired and no replacements are available.

SECTION 9

Sales and Lease Warranties

Warranty is an age-old concept. In sales and lease law, a warranty is an assurance by one party of the existence of a fact on which the other party can rely. Article 2 (on sales) and Article 2A (on leases) of the

Uniform Commercial Code (UCC) designate several types of warranties that can arise in a sales or lease contract. These warranties include warranties of title, express warranties, and implied warranties.

Because a warranty imposes a duty on the seller or lessor, a breach of warranty is a breach of the seller's or lessor's promise. If the parties have not agreed to limit or modify the remedies available to the buyer or lessee and if the seller or lessor breaches a warranty, the buyer or lessee can sue to recover damages from the seller or lessor. Under some circumstances, a breach can allow the buyer or lessee to rescind (cancel) the agreement.[7]

WARRANTY OF TITLE

Title warranty arises automatically in most sales contracts. UCC 2–312 imposes three types of warranties of title. In most cases, sellers warrant that they have good and valid title to the goods sold and that transfer of the title is rightful [UCC 2–312(1)(a)].

A second warranty of title provided by the UCC protects buyers who are *unaware* of any encumbrances (claims, charges, or liabilities—usually called *liens*[8]) against goods at the time the contract is made [UCC 2–312(1)(b)]. This warranty protects buyers who, for example, unknowingly purchase goods that are subject to a creditor's security interest (see Chapter 16). If a creditor legally repossesses the goods from a buyer *who had no actual knowledge of the security interest,* the buyer can recover from the seller for breach of warranty. (The buyer who has *actual knowledge of a security interest* has no recourse against a seller.) Article 2A affords similar protection for lessees. Section 2A–211(1) provides that during the term of the lease, no claim of any third party will interfere with the lessee's enjoyment of the leasehold interest.

A merchant seller is also deemed to warrant that the goods delivered are free from any copyright, trademark, or patent claims of a third person [UCC 2–312(3), 2A–211(2)].

In an ordinary sales transaction, the title warranty can be disclaimed or modified only by *specific language* in a contract. For example, sellers may assert that they are transferring only such rights, title, and interest as they have in the goods. In a lease transaction, the disclaimer must "be specific, be by a writing,

and be conspicuous" [UCC 2A–214(4)]. In certain cases, the circumstances surrounding the sale are sufficient to indicate clearly to a buyer that no assurances as to title are being made. The classic example is a sheriff's sale, when buyers know that the goods have been seized to satisfy debts, and the sheriff cannot guarantee title [UCC 2–312(2)].

EXPRESS WARRANTIES

A seller or lessor can create an **express warranty** by making representations concerning the quality, condition, description, or performance potential of the goods. Under UCC 2–313 and 2A–210, express warranties arise when a seller or lessor indicates any of the following:

1. That the goods conform to any *affirmation or promise* of fact that the seller or lessor makes to the buyer or lessee about the goods. Such affirmations or promises are usually made during the bargaining process. Statements such as "these drill bits will *easily* penetrate stainless steel—and without dulling" are express warranties.
2. That the goods conform to any *description* of them. For example, a label that reads "Crate contains one 150-horsepower diesel engine" or a contract that calls for the delivery of a "wool coat" creates an express warranty that the content of the goods sold conforms to the description.
3. That the goods conform to any *sample or model* of the goods shown to the buyer or lessee.

Express warranties can be found in a seller's or lessor's advertisement, brochure, or promotional materials, in addition to being made orally or in an express warranty provision in a sales or lease contract. To create an express warranty, a seller or lessor does not have to use formal words such as *warrant* or *guarantee*. It is only necessary that a reasonable buyer or lessee would regard the representation as part of the basis of the bargain [UCC 2–313(2), 2A–210(2)].

Basis of the Bargain. The UCC requires that for an express warranty to be created, the affirmation, promise, description, or sample must become part of the "basis of the bargain" [UCC 2–313(1), 2A–210(1)]. Just what constitutes the basis of the bargain is hard to say. The UCC does not define the concept, and it is a question of fact in each case whether a representation was made at such a time and in such a way that it induced the buyer or lessee to enter into the contract.

---

7. Rescission restores the parties to the positions they were in before the contract was made.

8. Pronounced *leens.* Liens will be discussed in detail in Chapter 16.

Therefore, if an express warranty is not intended, the marketing agent or salesperson should not promise too much. In the following case, the issue was whether statements made by the sellers of a used car to the buyer were part of the basis of the bargain for the purchase of the car.

CASE 11.4   Felley v. Singleton

Appellate Court
of Illinois,
Second District, 1999.
302 Ill.App.3d 248,
705 N.E.2d 930,
235 Ill.Dec. 747.
http://www.state.il.us/
court[a]

BACKGROUND AND FACTS   *Brian Felley went to the home of Thomas and Cheryl Singleton to look at a used car that the Singletons offered for sale. The car was a 1991 Ford Taurus with about 126,000 miles on it. They discussed the car's transmission, tires, brakes, and maintenance. The Singletons told Felley that they had experienced no brake problems and that, except for a bad or missing grommet, the car was in good mechanical condition. After test-driving the car, Felley bought it for $5,800. Two days later, Felley noticed a problem with the clutch. Over the next few days, the clutch problem worsened to the point where Felley was unable to shift the gears, and he paid $942.76 for its repair. The car developed serious brake problems within the same month. Felley paid $1,400.27 for brake work. Robert Hanover, a technician at Car X Muffler, later said that because problems such as those with the car's clutch and brakes take considerable time to develop, they probably existed when Felley bought the car. Felley filed a suit in an Illinois state court against the Singletons, asserting that their telling him that the car was in good mechanical condition was a primary consideration in his decision to buy it. The court concluded that the Singletons' statements were affirmations of fact that constituted an express warranty and became part of the basis of the bargain for Felley's purchase of the car. The Singletons appealed to a state intermediate appellate court.*

IN THE LANGUAGE
OF THE COURT

Presiding Justice *BOWMAN* delivered the opinion of the court:

    *   *   *   *

In defendants' view, their statements to plaintiff cannot fairly be viewed as entering into the bargain. Defendants assert that they are not automobile dealers or mechanics with specialized knowledge of the brake and clutch systems of the car and therefore their statements were merely expressions of a vendor's opinion that did not constitute an express warranty.

    *   *   *   *

    *   *   * *[A]ffirmations of fact made during a bargaining process regarding the sale of goods are presumed to be part of the basis of the bargain unless clear affirmative proof to the contrary is shown;* *   *   * a showing of reliance on the affirmations by the buyer is not necessary for the creation of an express warranty; and *   *   * the seller has the burden to establish by clear affirmative proof that the affirmations did not become part of the basis of the bargain. *   *   * [T]he seller may be held accountable for breach of warranty where affirmations are a basis of the bargain and the goods fail to conform to the affirmations. [Emphasis added.]

    *   *   * [I]n the context of a used car sale, representations by the seller such as the car is "in good mechanical condition" are presumed to be affirmations of fact that become part of the basis of the bargain. Because they are presumed to be part of the basis of the bargain, such representations constitute express warranties, regardless of the buyer's reliance on them, unless the seller shows by clear affirmative proof that the representations did not become part of the basis of the bargain.

In this case, it is undisputed that plaintiff asked defendants about the car's mechanical condition and that defendants responded that the car was in good mechanical condition. Under the foregoing principles, defendants' representations are presumed to be affirmations of fact that became a part of the basis of the bargain. Nothing in the record

---

a. This Web site is maintained by the Office of the Reporter of Decisions of the Illinois Judicial System. In the "Appellate Court" section, in the "Second District Opinions" row, click on "1999." When that page opens, in the "January" box, click on the case name to read the opinion.

indicates that defendants made a clear and affirmative showing that their representations did not become part of the basis of the bargain. Based on this record, we cannot say that the trial court's findings that defendants' representations were affirmations of fact that became a part of the basis of the bargain and created an express warranty were against the manifest weight of the evidence.

DECISION AND REMEDY   *The state intermediate appellate court affirmed the decision of the lower court. The Singletons' statements to Felley were afffirmations of fact that became part of the basis of the bargain and created an express warranty. Because of the Singletons' breach of that warranty, they were ordered to pay damages in the amount of Felley's paid repair bills.*

Statements of Opinion and Value. If the seller or lessor merely makes a statement that relates to the value or worth of the goods, or makes a statement of opinion or recommendation about the goods, the seller or lessor is not creating an express warranty [UCC 2–313(2), 2A–210(2)].

For example, a seller claims that "this is the best used car to come along in years; it has four new tires and a 150-horsepower engine just rebuilt this year." The seller has made several *affirmations of fact* that can create a warranty: the automobile has an engine; it has a 150-horsepower engine; the engine was rebuilt this year; there are four tires on the automobile; and the tires are new. The seller's *opinion* that the vehicle is "the best used car to come along in years," however, is known as "puffing" and creates no warranty. (*Puffing* is an expression of opinion by a seller or lessor that is not made as a representation of fact.) A statement relating to the value of the goods, such as "it's worth a fortune" or "anywhere else you'd pay $10,000 for it," usually does not create a warranty.

Although the ordinary seller or lessor can give an opinion that is not a warranty, if the seller or lessor is an expert and gives an opinion as an expert to a layperson, then a warranty may be created. For example, Saul is an art dealer and an expert in seventeenth-century paintings. If Saul states to Lauren, a purchaser, that in his opinion a particular painting is a Rembrandt, Saul has warranted the accuracy of his opinion.

It is not always easy to determine what constitutes an express warranty and what constitutes puffing. The reasonableness of the buyer's or lessee's reliance appears to be the controlling criterion in many cases. For example, a salesperson's statements that a ladder will "never break" and will "last a lifetime" are so clearly improbable that no reasonable buyer should rely on them. Additionally, the context within which

a statement is made might be relevant in determining the reasonableness of a buyer's or lessee's reliance. For example, a reasonable person is more likely to rely on a written statement made in an advertisement than on a statement made orally by a salesperson.

IMPLIED WARRANTIES

An **implied warranty** is one that *the law derives* by inference from the nature of the transaction or the relative situations or circumstances of the parties. Under the UCC, merchants impliedly warrant that the goods they sell or lease are merchantable and, in certain circumstances, fit for a particular purpose. In addition, an implied warranty may arise from a course of dealing or usage of trade. We examine these three types of implied warranties in the following subsections.

Implied Warranty of Merchantability. An **implied warranty of merchantability** automatically arises in every sale or lease of goods made *by a merchant* who deals in goods of the kind sold or leased [UCC 2–314, 2A–212]. Thus, a merchant who is in the business of selling ski equipment makes an implied warranty of merchantability every time the merchant sells a pair of skis, but a neighbor selling his or her skis at a garage sale does not.

To be *merchantable*, goods must be "reasonably fit for the ordinary purposes for which such goods are used." They must be of at least average, fair, or medium-grade quality. The quality must be comparable to quality that will pass without objection in the trade or market for goods of the same description. To be merchantable, the goods must also be adequately packaged and labeled as provided by the agreement, and they must conform to the promises or affirmations of fact made on the container or label, if any.

An implied warranty of merchantability also imposes on the merchant liability for the safe performance of the product. It makes no difference whether the merchant knew of or could have discovered a defect that makes the product unsafe—he or she is liable in either situation. Of course, merchants are not absolute insurers against *all* accidents arising in connection with the goods. For example, a bar of soap is not unmerchantable merely because a user could slip and fall by stepping on it.

Implied Warranty of Fitness for a Particular Purpose. The **implied warranty of fitness for a particular purpose** arises when any *seller or lessor* (merchant or nonmerchant) knows the particular purpose for which a buyer or lessee will use the goods *and* knows that the buyer or lessee is relying on the skill and judgment of the seller or lessor to select suitable goods [UCC 2–315, 2A–213].

A "particular purpose" of the buyer or lessee differs from the "ordinary purpose for which goods are used" (merchantability). Goods can be merchantable but unfit for a particular purpose. For example, suppose that you need a gallon of paint to match the color of your living room walls—a light shade somewhere between coral and peach. You take a sample to your local hardware store and request a gallon of paint of that color. Instead, you are given a gallon of bright blue paint. Here, the salesperson has not breached any warranty of implied merchantability—the bright blue paint is of high quality and suitable for interior walls—but he or she has breached an implied warranty of fitness for a particular purpose.

A seller or lessor does not need to have actual knowledge of the buyer's or lessee's particular purpose. It is sufficient if a seller or lessor "has reason to know" the purpose. The buyer or lessee, however, must have *relied* on the skill or judgment of the seller or lessor in selecting or furnishing suitable goods for an implied warranty to be created.

For example, Bloomberg leases a computer from Future Tech, a lessor of technical business equipment. Bloomberg tells the clerk that she wants a computer that will run a complicated new engineering graphics program at a realistic speed. Future Tech leases Bloomberg an Architex One computer with a CPU speed of only 233 megahertz, even though a speed of at least 500 megahertz would be required to run Bloomberg's graphics program at a "realistic speed." Bloomberg, after realizing that it takes her forever to run her program, wants her money back.

Here, because Future Tech has breached the implied warranty of fitness for a particular purpose, Bloomberg normally will be able to recover. The clerk knew specifically that Bloomberg wanted a computer with enough speed to run certain software. Furthermore, Bloomberg relied on the clerk to furnish a computer that would fulfill this purpose. Because Future Tech did not do so, the warranty was breached.

Implied Warranty Arising from Course of Dealing or Trade Usage. Implied warranties can also arise (or be excluded or modified) as a result of course of dealing, course of performance, or usage of trade [UCC 2–314(3), 2A–212(3)]. In the absence of evidence to the contrary, when both parties to a sales or lease contract have knowledge of a well-recognized trade custom, the courts will infer that both parties intended for that custom to apply to their contract. For example, if it is an industry-wide custom to lubricate a new car before it is delivered and a dealer fails to do so, the dealer can be held liable to a buyer for damages resulting from the breach of an implied warranty. (This, of course, would also be negligence on the part of the dealer.)

Warranty Disclaimers. Because each type of warranty is created in a special way, the manner in which warranties can be disclaimed or qualified by a seller or lessor varies with the type of warranty.

Express Warranties. As already stated, any affirmation of fact or promise, description of the goods, or use of samples or models by a seller or lessor creates an express warranty. Obviously, then, express warranties can be excluded if the seller or lessor carefully refrains from making any promise or affirmation of fact relating to the goods, describing the goods, or using a sample or model.

The UCC does permit express warranties to be negated or limited by specific and unambiguous language, provided that this is done in a manner that protects the buyer or lessee from surprise. Therefore, a written disclaimer in language that is clear and conspicuous, and called to a buyer's or lessee's attention, could negate all oral express warranties not included in the written sales or lease contract [UCC 2–316(1), 2A–214(1)]. This allows the seller or lessor to avoid false allegations that oral warranties were made, and it ensures that only representations made by properly authorized individuals are included in the bargain.

Implied Warranties. Generally speaking, unless circumstances indicate otherwise, the implied warranties of merchantability and fitness are disclaimed by the expressions "as is," "with all faults," and other similar expressions that in common understanding for *both* parties call the buyer's or lessee's attention to the fact that there are no implied warranties [UCC 2–316(3)(a), 2A–214(3)(a)].

The UCC also permits a seller or lessor to specifically disclaim an implied warranty either of fitness or of merchantability [UCC 2–316(2), 2A–214(2)]. To disclaim an implied warranty of fitness for a particular purpose, the disclaimer must be in writing and be conspicuous. The word *fitness* does not have to be mentioned in the writing; it is sufficient if, for example, the disclaimer states, "THERE ARE NO WARRANTIES THAT EXTEND BEYOND THE DESCRIPTION ON THE FACE HEREOF."

A merchantability disclaimer must be more specific; it must mention *merchantability*. It need not be written; but if it is, the writing must be conspicuous [UCC 2–316(2), 2A–214(4)]. The conspicuousness of a disclaimer of implied warranties was at issue in the following case.

CASE 11.5   Borden, Inc. v. Advent Ink Co.

Superior Court of
Pennsylvania, 1997.
701 A.2d 255.

BACKGROUND AND FACTS   *Borden, Inc., sold Aquablak, a dispersion ingredient used in water-based inks, to Advent Ink Company. On the front of the sales invoice, in red capital letters, was the phrase "SEE REVERSE SIDE." On the reverse side was a list of nineteen conditions of sale, the first of which was a disclaimer of warranties, including the implied warranty of merchantability. On the Aquablak label, beneath Borden's name, phone number, advertising slogan, and other brief statements, was another disclaimer of all warranties. Advent used the Aquablak to make ink that caused problems in the printing equipment of one of its customers. Advent lost the customer's account, which cost the firm over $1 million in profits and caused it to go out of business. When Advent did not pay for the Aquablak, Borden filed a suit in a Pennsylvania state court against Advent to recover the amount. Advent counterclaimed that the Aquablak had not complied with the implied warranties of merchantability and fitness for a particular purpose. Against this claim, Borden filed a motion for summary judgment, pointing to its disclaimers. Advent responded that the disclaimers were not sufficiently conspicuous. The court granted the motion in favor of Borden. Advent appealed.*

**IN THE LANGUAGE
OF THE COURT**

SAYLOR, Judge:
    *   *   *   *

    *   *   * [T]he print on the reverse side of the invoice is no larger than one-sixteenth inch in height. All of the type appears to be bold-faced. Although the disclaimer of warranties is the first of nineteen numbered paragraphs, *   *   * nevertheless there is nothing to indicate that the first paragraph is any more significant than, for example, the seventh ("WEIGHTS") *   *   * .

Even more important, the reference on the front of the invoice to the terms on the reverse side is even less informative *   *   * . The reference *   *   * simply states "SEE REVERSE SIDE"; there is absolutely no indication that among the terms on the reverse side is an exclusion of warranties, including *   *   * the implied warranty of merchantability *   *   * *so commonly taken for granted that its exclusion from a contract is recognized as a matter threatening surprise* *   *   * . [Emphasis added.]
    *   *   *   *

    *   *   * Finally, while the heading "DISCLAIMER" and the disclaimer itself are printed in capitals, so too are the preceding lines of text, and they are printed in larger sizes of type. Taking into account all of these factors, we conclude that this disclaimer, like that on the invoice, is inconspicuous and therefore ineffective.

**DECISION
AND REMEDY**

The Superior Court of Pennsylvania held that the disclaimers were so inconspicuous as to be ineffective. The court affirmed the lower court's decision on other grounds, however.

TERMS AND CONCEPTS TO REVIEW

conforming goods 241

consignment 239

cure 241

destination contract 236

express warranty 248

firm offer 232

identification 236

implied warranty 250

implied warranty of fitness for a
    particular purpose 251

implied warranty of
    merchantability 250

insurable interest 240

lease agreement 230

lessee 230

lessor 230

merchant 230

output contract 231

perfect tender rule 241

requirements contract 231

sale 230

sale on approval 239

sale or return 239

sales contract 229

shipment contract 236

tangible property 230

tender of delivery 241

QUESTIONS AND CASE PROBLEMS

11–1. OFFERS BETWEEN MERCHANTS. A. B. Zook, Inc., is a manufacturer of washing machines. Over the telephone, Zook offers to sell Radar Appliances one hundred model Z washers at a price of $150 per unit. Zook agrees to keep this offer open for ninety days. Radar tells Zook that the offer appears to be a good one and that it will let Zook know of its acceptance within the next two to three weeks. One week later, Zook sends and Radar receives notice that Zook has withdrawn its offer. Radar immediately thereafter telephones Zook and accepts the $150-per-unit offer. Zook claims, first, that no sales contract was ever formed between it and Radar and, second, that if there is a contract, the contract is unenforceable. Discuss Zook's contentions.

11–2. ACCOMMODATION SHIPMENTS. Flint, a retail seller of television sets, orders one hundred Color-X sets from manufacturer Martin. The order specifies the price and that the television sets are to be shipped by Humming Bird Express on or before October 30. The order is received by Martin on October 5. On October 8, Martin writes Flint a letter indicating that the order was received and that the sets will be shipped as directed, at the specified price. This letter is received by Flint on October 10. On October 28, Martin, in preparing the shipment, discovers it has only ninety Color-X sets in stock. Martin ships the ninety Color-X sets and ten television sets of a different model, stating clearly on the invoice that the ten are being shipped only as an accommodation. Flint claims Martin is in breach of contract. Martin claims the shipment was not an acceptance, and therefore no contract was formed. Explain who is correct and why.

11–3. RISK OF LOSS. On May 1, Sikora goes into Carson's retail clothing store to purchase a suit. Sikora finds a suit he likes for $190 and buys it. The suit needs alteration. Sikora is to pick up the altered suit at Carson's store on May 10. Consider the following separate sets of circumstances:

(a) One of Carson's major creditors obtains a judgment on the debt Carson owes and has the court issue a writ of execution (a court order to seize a debtor's property to satisfy a debt) to collect on that judgment all clothing in Carson's possession. Discuss Sikora's rights in the suit under these circumstances.

(b) On May 9, through no fault of Carson's, the store burns down, and all contents are a total loss. Between Carson and Sikora, who suffers the loss of the suit destroyed by fire? Explain.

11–4. REMEDIES OF THE BUYER OR LESSEE. McDonald has contracted to purchase five hundred pairs of shoes from Vetter. Vetter manufactures the shoes and tenders delivery to McDonald. McDonald accepts the shipment. Later, on inspection, McDonald discovers that ten pairs of the shoes are poorly made and will have to be sold to customers as seconds. If McDonald decides to keep all five hundred pairs of shoes, what remedies are available to her? Discuss.

11–5. COMMERCIAL IMPRACTICABILITY. E+E (US) Inc., Manley-Regan Chemicals Division, agreed to sell to Rockland Industries, Inc., three containers of antimony oxide for $1.80 per pound. At the time, both parties knew that there was a global shortage of the chemical, with rising prices, and that Manley-Regan would obtain its supply from GFI Chemicals, Inc. When GFI could not deliver, Manley-Regan told Rockland that it could not fulfill the contract. Rockland bought an equivalent amount of the chemical elsewhere at an increased price and filed a suit in a federal district court against Manley-Regan to recover the difference between the cost of the cover and the contract price. Manley-Regan argued that the failure of delivery by GFI, its sole source for the oxide, excused its failure to perform on the ground of commercial impracticability. Will the court agree? Why or why not? [*Rockland Industries, Inc. v. E+E (US) Inc., Manley-Regan Chemicals Division*, 991 F.Supp. 468 (D.Md. 1998)]

11–6. ACCEPTANCE.   OSHI Global Co. designs and sells novelty items, including a small children's plastic toy referred to as the "Number 89 Frog," a realistic replica of a frog that squeaks when it is squeezed. At a trade show in Chicago, Michael Osaraprasop, the owner of OSHI, sold a quantity of the frogs to Jay Gilbert, the president of S.A.M. Electronics, Inc. Gilbert asked Osaraprasop to design, make, and sell to S.A.M. a larger version of the frog with a motion sensor that would activate a "ribbit" sound. Osaraprasop agreed. OSHI delivered fourteen containers of the frogs, a number of which S.A.M. resold to its customers. When some of the buyers complained that the frogs were defective, S.A.M. had them repaired. S.A.M. refused to pay OSHI for any of the frogs and wrote a letter claiming to revoke acceptance of them. S.A.M. filed a suit in a federal district court against OSHI and others, alleging in part breach of contract, to which OSHI responded with a similar claim against S.A.M. OSHI argued that by reselling some of the frogs from the fourteen containers, S.A.M. had accepted all of them and must pay. In whose favor will the court rule? Discuss fully. [*S.A.M. Electronics, Inc. v. Osaraprasop*, 39 F.Supp.2d 1074 (N.D.Ill. 1999)]

11–7. LIMITATION OF REMEDIES.   Destileria Serralles, Inc., a distributor of rum and other products, operates a rum bottling plant in Puerto Rico. Figgie International, Inc., contracted with Serralles to provide bottle-labeling equipment capable of placing a clear label on a clear bottle of "Cristal" rum within a raised glass oval. The contract stated that Serralles's remedy, in case of a breach of contract, was limited to repair, replacement, or refund. When the equipment was installed in the Serralles plant, problems arose immediately. Figgie attempted to repair the equipment, but when it still did not work properly several months later, Figgie refunded the purchase price and Serralles returned the equipment. Serralles asked Figgie to pay for Serralles's losses caused by the failure of the equipment and by the delay in obtaining alternative machinery. Figgie filed a suit in a federal district court, asserting that it owed nothing to Serralles because its remedy for breach was limited to repair, replacement, or refund. Serralles responded that the limitation "fail[ed] of its essential purpose." In whose favor will the court resolve this dispute? Why? [*Figgie*

International, Inc. v. Destileria Serralles, Inc., 190 F.3d 252 (4th Cir. 1999)]

11–8. IMPLIED WARRANTIES.   Marilyn Keaton entered an A.B.C. Drug store to buy a half-gallon bottle of liquid bleach. The bottles were stacked at a height above her eye level. She reached up, grasped the handle of one of the bottles, and began pulling it down from the shelf. The cap was loose, however, causing bleach to splash into her face, injuring her eye. Keaton filed a suit in a Georgia state court against A.B.C., alleging, in part, breach of the implied warranty of merchantability. She claimed that the bleach had not been adequately packaged. A.B.C. argued, in part, that Keaton had failed to exercise care for her own safety. Had A.B.C. breached the implied warranty of merchantability? Discuss. [*Keaton v. A.B.C. Drug Co.*, 266 Ga. 385, 467 S.E.2d 558 (1996)]

11–9. EXPRESS WARRANTIES.   Ronald Anderson, Jr., a self-employed construction contractor, went to a Home Depot store to buy lumber for a construction project. It was raining, so Anderson bought a tarp to cover the bed of his pickup truck. To secure the tarp, Anderson bought a bag of cords made by Bungee International Manufacturing Corp. The printed material on the Bungee bag included the words "Made in the U.S.A." and "Premium Quality." To secure the tarp at the rear of the passenger's side, Anderson put one hook into the eyelet of the tarp, stretched the cord over the utility box, and hooked the other end in the drainage hole in the bottom of the box. As Anderson stood up, the upper hook dislodged and hit him in the left eye. Anderson filed a suit in a federal district court against Bungee and others, alleging in part breach of express warranty. Anderson alleged that the labeling on the bag of cords was an express warranty that "played some role in [his] decision to purchase this product." Bungee argued that, in regard to the cords' quality, the statements were puffery. Bungee filed a motion for summary judgment on this issue. Will the court grant the motion? Why or why not? [*Anderson v. Bungee International Manufacturing Corp.*, 44 F.Supp.2d 534 (S.D.N.Y. 1999)]

11–10. IN YOUR COURT

Benes contracts to purchase from Glover one hundred cases of Knee High Corn to be shipped F.O.B. Glover's warehouse by Reliant Truck Lines. Glover, by mistake, delivers one hundred cases of Green Valley Corn to Reliant Truck Lines. While in transit, the Green Valley Corn is stolen. Glover demands payment for the corn, but Benes refuses to pay, claiming that Glover should bear the loss. Glover argues that the risk of loss passed to Benes when Glover delivered the corn to Reliant Truck Lines. Assume that you are the judge in the trial court hearing this case and answer the following questions:

(a) A threshold issue in many cases is whether a contract is a shipment contract or a destination contract. Which is it in this case?

(b) Compare this case with Case 11.1 (*Windows, Inc. v. Jordan Panel System Corp.*). Are the facts and issues in both cases similar? Should the court's reasoning in Case 11.1 apply to the Benes-Glover dispute? Why or why not? Would your answer be any different if Glover had shipped Knee High Corn?

(c) How will you rule in the case now before your court? Summarize your reasoning.

LAW ON THE WEB

For updated links to resources available on the Web, as well as a variety of other materials, visit this text's Web site at http://wleb.westbuslaw.com.

For information about the National Conference of Commissioners (NCC) on Uniform State Laws and links to online uniform acts, go to

http://www.nccusl.org

The NCC, in association with the University of Pennsylvania Law School, now offers an official site for in-process and final drafts of uniform and model acts. For an index of in-process drafts, go to

http://www.law.upenn.edu/bll/ulc/ulc.htm

For an index of final drafts, go to

http://www.law.upenn.edu/bll/ulc/ulc_final.htm

Cornell University's Legal Information Institute offers online access to the UCC, as well as to UCC articles as enacted by particular states and proposed revisions to articles, at

http://www.law.cornell.edu/ucc/ucc.table.html

For an example of an "as is" clause, see the warranty disclaimer provided by the University of Minnesota for one of its research software products at

http://www.cmrr.drad.umn.edu/stimulate/stimUsersGuide/node7.html

GM's performance parts warranty policies (on automobile parts) are online at

http://www.gmperformanceparts.com/WARRANTY.htm

LEGAL RESEARCH EXERCISES ON THE WEB

Go to http://wleb.westbuslaw.com, the Web site that accompanies this text. Select "Internet Applications," and then click on "Chapter 11." There you will find the following Internet research exercise that you can perform to learn more about sales contracts:

Activity 11–1: Sales and Leases

CHAPTER 12

Torts and Strict Liability

PART OF DOING BUSINESS TODAY—and, indeed, part of everyday life—is the risk of being involved in a lawsuit. The list of circumstances in which businesspersons can be sued is long and varied. An employee injured on the job may attempt to sue the employer because of an unsafe working environment. A consumer who is injured while using a product may attempt to sue the manufacturer because of a defect in the product. At issue in these examples is alleged wrongful conduct by one person that causes injury to another. Such wrongful conduct is covered by the law of **torts** (the word *tort* is French for "wrong").

Of course, a tort is not the only type of wrong that exists in the law. Crimes also involve wrongs. A crime, however, is an act so reprehensible that it is considered a wrong against the state or against society as a whole, as well as against the individual victim. Therefore, the *state* prosecutes and punishes (through fines and/or imprisonment—and possibly death) persons who commit criminal acts. A tort action, in contrast, is a civil action in which one party brings a suit against another to obtain compensation (money damages) or other relief for the harm suffered. Some wrongs, however, provide a basis for both a criminal prosecution and a tort action—see Chapter 7.

Many of the lawsuits brought by or against business firms are based on the tort theories discussed in this chapter. Some of the torts examined here can occur in any context, including the business environment.

Others traditionally have been referred to as **business torts,** which are defined as wrongful interferences with the business rights of others. Included in business torts are such vaguely worded concepts as *unfair competition* and *wrongfully interfering with the business relations of others.* Because so many of today's lawsuits against businesses involve product liability (liability for defective products), we devote all of Chapter 13 to a discussion of those tort theories.

SECTION 1

The Basis of Tort Law

The basic purpose of tort law is to provide remedies for the invasion of various *protected interests.* Society recognizes an interest in personal physical safety, and tort law provides remedies for acts that cause physical injury or that interfere with physical security and freedom of movement. Society recognizes an interest in protecting property, and tort law provides remedies for acts that cause destruction or damage to property. Society also recognizes an interest in protecting certain intangible interests, such as personal privacy, family relations, reputation, and dignity, and tort law provides remedies for invasion of these interests.

In the remainder of this chapter, we examine two broad classifications of torts: *intentional torts* and *unintentional torts* (torts involving negligence). The

256

classification of a particular tort depends largely on how the tort occurs (intentionally or negligently) and the surrounding circumstances. (Under the doctrine of strict liability discussed in the following chapter, liability may be imposed regardless of fault.)

SECTION 2

Intentional Torts against Persons and Business Relationships

An **intentional tort,** as the term implies, requires *intent.* The **tortfeasor** (the one committing the tort) must intend to commit an act, the consequences of which interfere with the personal or business interests of another in a way not permitted by law. An evil or harmful motive is not required—in fact, the actor may even have a beneficial motive for committing what turns out to be a tortious act. In tort law, intent only means that the actor intended the consequences of his or her act or knew with substantial certainty that certain consequences would result from the act. The law generally assumes that individuals intend the *normal* consequences of their actions. Thus, forcefully pushing another—even if done in jest and without any evil motive—is an intentional tort (if injury results), because the object of a strong push can ordinarily be expected to go flying.

Intentional torts against persons and business relationships include assault and battery, false imprisonment, infliction of emotional distress, defamation, invasion of the right to privacy, appropriation, misrepresentation, and wrongful interference.

ASSAULT AND BATTERY

Any intentional, unexcused act that creates in another person a reasonable apprehension or fear of immediate harmful or offensive contact is an **assault.** Note that apprehension is not the same as fear. If a contact is such that a reasonable person would want to avoid it, and if there is a reasonable basis for believing that the contact will occur, then the plaintiff suffers apprehension whether or not he or she is afraid. The interest protected by tort law concerning assault is the freedom from having to expect harmful or offensive contact. The arousal of apprehension is enough to justify compensation.

The *completion* of the act that caused the apprehension, if it results in harm to the plaintiff, is a

battery, which is defined as an unexcused and harmful or offensive physical contact *intentionally* performed. For example, Ivan threatens Jean with a gun, then shoots her. The pointing of the gun at Jean is an assault; the firing of the gun (if the bullet hits Jean) is a battery. The interest protected by tort law concerning battery is the right to personal security and safety.

Essentially, any unpermitted, offensive contact, whether harmful or not, is a battery. The contact may be merely an unwelcome kiss or smoke intentionally blown in one's face. The contact can involve any part of the body or anything attached to it—for example, a hat or other item of clothing, a purse, or a chair or an automobile in which one is sitting. Whether the contact is offensive is determined by the *reasonable person standard.*[1] The contact can be made by the defendant or by some force the defendant sets in motion—for example, a rock thrown, food poisoned, or a stick swung. If the plaintiff shows there was contact, and the jury agrees that the contact was offensive, the plaintiff has a right to compensation. There is no need to establish that the defendant acted out of malice; in fact, proving a motive is never necessary.

A number of legally recognized defenses can be raised by a defendant who is sued for assault, battery, or both:

1. *Consent.* When a person consents to the act that damages him or her, there is generally no liability for the damage done.
2. *Self-defense.* An individual who is defending his or her life or physical well-being can claim self-defense. In a situation of either *real* or *apparent* danger, a person may normally use whatever force is *reasonably* necessary to prevent harmful contact (see Chapter 7 for a more detailed discussion of self-defense).
3. *Defense of others.* An individual can act in a reasonable manner to protect others who are in real or apparent danger.
4. *Defense of property.* Reasonable force may be used in attempting to remove intruders from one's home, although force that is likely to cause death or great bodily injury normally cannot be used just to protect property.

---

1. The reasonable person standard is an objective test of how a reasonable person would have acted under the same circumstances. See the subsection entitled "The Duty of Care and Its Breach" later in this chapter.

FALSE IMPRISONMENT

False imprisonment is defined as the intentional confinement or restraint of another person's activities without justification. It involves interference with the freedom to move without restriction. The confinement can be accomplished through the use of physical barriers, physical restraint, or threats of physical force. Moral pressure does not constitute false imprisonment. Furthermore, it is essential that the person being restrained not comply with the restraint willingly. In other words, the person being restrained must not agree to the restraint.

Businesspersons are often confronted with suits for false imprisonment after they have attempted to confine a suspected shoplifter for questioning. Under the privilege to detain granted to merchants in some states, a merchant can use the defense of *probable cause* to justify delaying a suspected shoplifter. Probable cause exists when the evidence to support the belief that a person is guilty outweighs the evidence against that belief. The detention, however, must be conducted in a *reasonable* manner and for only a *reasonable* length of time.

INTENTIONAL INFLICTION OF EMOTIONAL DISTRESS

The tort of *intentional infliction of emotional distress* can be defined as an intentional act that amounts to extreme and outrageous conduct resulting in severe emotional distress to another. For example, a prankster telephones an individual and says that the individual's spouse has just been in a horrible accident. As a result, the individual suffers intense mental pain or anxiety. The caller's behavior is deemed to be extreme and outrageous conduct that exceeds the bounds of decency accepted by society and is therefore **actionable** (capable of serving as the ground for a lawsuit).

Emotional distress claims pose several problems. One major problem is that such claims must be subject to some limitation, or the courts could be flooded with lawsuits alleging emotional distress. A society in which individuals are rewarded if they are unable to endure the normal emotional stresses of day-to-day living is obviously undesirable. Therefore, the law usually focuses on the nature of the acts that fall under this tort. Indignity or annoyance alone is usually not sufficient to support a lawsuit based on intentional infliction of emotional distress.

Many times, however, repeated annoyances (such as those experienced by a person who is being stalked), coupled with threats, are enough. In a business context, for example, the repeated use of extreme methods to collect an overdue debt may be actionable. Also, an event causing an unusually severe emotional reaction, such as the severe distress of a woman incorrectly informed that her husband and two sons have been killed, may be actionable. Because it is difficult to prove the existence of emotional suffering, a court may require that the emotional distress be evidenced by some physical symptom or illness or a specific emotional disturbance that can be documented by a psychiatric consultant or other medical professional.

In the following case, the court looks at one of the requirements that plaintiffs must meet to establish an emotional distress claim.

CASE 12.1   Roach v. Stern

Supreme Court of
New York,
Appellate Division,
Second Department,
1998.
675 N.Y.S.2d 133.

BACKGROUND AND FACTS *Deborah Roach—known as "Debbie Tay"—was a frequent guest on* The Howard Stern Show, *on which she discussed her purported sexual encounters with female aliens. Tay used her notoriety to launch her own cable television show. After her death from a drug overdose at the age of twenty-seven, her sister Melissa Driscol had the body cremated and gave a portion of the remains to Tay's friend Chaunce Hayden. Shortly afterward, Tay's brother, Jeff Roach, learned that Hayden was to appear on Stern's show and asked the producer to cancel the appearance. Hayden went on as planned, and during his appearance, the participants in the program handled and joked about Tay's remains. For example, Stern held up bone fragments while he guessed whether they came from Tay's skull or ribs. Tay's brother and sister filed a suit in a New York state court against Stern and others, seeking $8 million in damages for, among other things, intentional infliction of emotional distress. The defendants filed a motion to dismiss, contending that the conduct at issue was not particularly shocking, in light* *of Stern's reputation for vulgar humor and Tay's actions during her guest appearances on his show. The court granted the motion, and the plaintiffs appealed.*

IN THE LANGUAGE
OF THE COURT

MEMORANDUM BY THE COURT.

* * * * *

* * * In order to impose liability for this intentional tort, the conduct complained of must be so outrageous in character, and so extreme in degree, as to go beyond all possible bounds of decency, and to be regarded as atrocious, and utterly intolerable in a civilized community. *The element of outrageous conduct is rigorous, and difficult to satisfy, and its purpose is to filter out trivial complaints and assure that the claim of severe emotional distress is genuine.* * * * [Emphasis added.]

Upon our review of the allegations in the case at bar, we conclude that the Supreme Court erred in determining that the element of outrageous conduct was not satisfied * * * . Although the defendants contend that the conduct at issue was not particularly shocking, in light of Stern's reputation for vulgar humor and Tay's actions during her guest appearances on his program, a jury might reasonably conclude that the manner in which Tay's remains were handled, for entertainment purposes and against the express wishes of her family, went beyond the bounds of decent behavior.

We further conclude that the remaining elements necessary to establish a cause of action to recover damages for the intentional infliction of emotional distress were also sufficiently pleaded in the complaint.

DECISION
AND REMEDY

The state intermediate appellate court reversed the decision of the lower court and remanded the case for trial. The court held that a jury could reasonably conclude the manner in which Tay's remains were handled could constitute intentional infliction of emotional distress.

DEFAMATION

As discussed in Chapter 5, the freedom of speech guaranteed by the First Amendment is not absolute. In interpreting the First Amendment, the courts must balance the vital guarantee of free speech against other pervasive and strong social interests, including society's interest in preventing and redressing attacks on reputation.

Defamation of character involves wrongfully hurting a person's good reputation. The law imposes a general duty on all persons to refrain from making false, defamatory statements of fact about others. Breaching this duty orally involves the tort of **slander;** breaching it in writing involves the tort of **libel.** The tort of defamation also arises when a false statement of fact is made about a person's product, business, or title to property. We deal with these torts later in this chapter.

The Publication Requirement. The basis of the tort of defamation is the publication of a statement or statements that hold an individual up to contempt, ridicule, or hatred. *Publication* here means that the

defamatory statements are communicated to persons other than the defamed party. If Thompson writes Andrews a private letter falsely accusing him of embezzling funds, the action does not constitute libel. If Peters falsely states that Gordon is dishonest and incompetent when no one else is around, the action does not constitute slander. In neither case was the message communicated to a third party.

The courts have generally held that even dictating a letter to a secretary constitutes publication, although the publication may be privileged (a concept that will be explained shortly). Moreover, if a third party overhears defamatory statements by chance, the courts usually hold that this also constitutes publication. Defamatory statements made via the Internet are actionable as well (see Chapter 15). Note also that any individual who repeats (republishes) defamatory statements normally is liable even if that person reveals the source of the statements.

Damages for Defamation. Once a defendant's liability for libel is established, "general damages" are presumed as a matter of law. General damages are designed to compensate the plaintiff for nonspecific harms such as disgrace or dishonor in the eyes of the community, humiliation, injured reputation, emotional distress, and so on—harms that are difficult to measure. In other words, to recover damages in a libel case, the plaintiff need not prove that he or she was actually injured in any way as a result of the libelous statement.

In a case alleging slander, however, the plaintiff must prove "special damages" to establish the defendant's liability. The plaintiff must show that the slanderous statement caused the plaintiff to suffer actual economic or monetary losses. Unless this initial hurdle of proving special damages is overcome, a plaintiff alleging slander normally cannot go forward with the suit and recover any damages. This requirement is imposed in cases involving slander because slanderous statements have a temporary quality. In contrast, a libelous (written) statement has the quality of permanence, can be circulated widely, and usually results from some degree of deliberation on the part of the author.

Exceptions to the burden of proving special damages in cases alleging slander are made for certain types of slanderous statements. If a false statement constitutes "slander *per se*," no proof of special damages is required for it to be actionable. The following four types of utterances are considered to be slander *per se*:

1. A statement that another has a loathsome communicable disease.
2. A statement that another has committed improprieties while engaging in a profession or trade.
3. A statement that another has committed or has been imprisoned for a serious crime.
4. A statement that an unmarried woman is unchaste.

Defenses to Defamation.   Truth is almost always a defense against a defamation charge. In other words, if a defendant in a defamation case can prove that the allegedly defamatory statement of fact was actually true, normally no tort has been committed. Other defenses to defamation may exist if the speech is privileged or concerns a public figure.

Privileged Speech.   In some circumstances, a person will not be liable for defamatory statements because he or she enjoys a **privilege**, or immunity. Privileged communications are of two types: absolute and qualified. Only in limited cases, such as in judicial and legislative proceedings, is *absolute* privilege granted. For example, statements made by attorneys and judges in the courtroom during a trial are absolutely privileged.

So are statements made by legislators during congressional floor debate, even if the legislators make such statements maliciously—that is, knowing them to be untrue. An absolute privilege is granted in these situations because judicial and legislative personnel deal with matters that are so much in the public interest that the parties involved should be able to speak out fully and freely and without restriction.

In other situations, a person will not be liable for defamatory statements because he or she has a *qualified*, or conditional, privilege. For example, statements made in written evaluations of employees are qualifiedly privileged. Generally, if the communicated statements are made in good faith and the publication is limited to those who have a legitimate interest in the communication, the statements fall within the area of qualified privilege. The concept of conditional privilege rests on the common law assumption that in some situations, the right to know or speak is equal in importance to the right not to be defamed. If a communication is conditionally privileged, to recover damages, the plaintiff must show that the privilege was abused.

Public Figures.   In general, false and defamatory statements that are made about **public figures** (public officials who exercise substantial governmental power and any persons in the public limelight) and published in the press are privileged if they are made without "actual malice." To be made with **actual malice**, a statement must be made *with either knowledge of falsity or a reckless disregard of the truth.*[2]

Statements made about public figures, especially when they are communicated via a public medium, are usually related to matters of general public interest; they refer to people who substantially affect all of us. Furthermore, public figures generally have some access to a public medium for answering disparaging falsehoods about themselves; private individuals do not. For these reasons, public figures have a greater burden of proof in defamation cases (they must prove actual malice) than do private individuals.

INVASION OF PRIVACY

A person has a right to solitude and freedom from prying public eyes—in other words, to privacy. As mentioned in Chapter 5, the courts have held that certain

---

2. *New York Times Co. v. Sullivan*, 376 U.S. 254, 84 S.Ct. 710, 11 L.Ed.2d 686 (1964).

amendments to the U.S. Constitution imply a right to privacy. Some state constitutions explicitly provide for privacy rights. Additionally, a number of federal and state statutes have been enacted to protect individual privacy rights in specific areas. Tort law also safeguards these rights through the tort of *invasion of privacy*. Four acts qualify as invasion of privacy:

1. *The use of a person's name, picture, or other likeness for commercial purposes without permission.* For example, using without permission someone's picture to advertise a product or someone's name to enhance a company's reputation invades the person's privacy. (This tort, which is usually referred to as the tort of *appropriation*, will be examined shortly.)
2. *Intrusion on an individual's affairs or seclusion.* For example, invading someone's home or illegally searching someone's briefcase is an invasion of privacy. This tort has been held to extend to eavesdropping by wiretap, unauthorized scanning of a bank account, compulsory blood testing, and window peeping.
3. *Publication of information that places a person in a false light.* This could be a story attributing to someone ideas not held or actions not taken by that person. (The publication of such a story could involve the tort of defamation as well.)
4. *Public disclosure of private facts about an individual that an ordinary person would find objectionable.* A newspaper account of a private citizen's sex life or financial affairs could be an actionable invasion of privacy.

A pressing issue in today's online world has to do with the privacy rights of Internet users. For an exploration of this issue, see this chapter's *Emerging Trends in Technology* on pages 262 and 263.

APPROPRIATION

The use of another person's name, likeness, or other identifying characteristic, without permission and for the benefit of the user, constitutes the tort of **appropriation.** Under the law, normally an individual's right to privacy includes the right to the exclusive use of his or her identity. For example, in a case involving a Ford Motor Company television commercial in which a Bette Midler "sound-alike" sang a song that Midler had made famous, the court held that Ford "for their own profit in selling their product did appropriate part of her identity."[3]

---

3. *Midler v. Ford Motor Co.,* 849 F.2d 460 (9th Cir. 1988).

A court ruled similarly in a case brought by Vanna White, the hostess of the popular television game show *Wheel of Fortune,* against Samsung Electronics America, Inc. Without White's permission, Samsung included in an advertisement for Samsung videocassette recorders a depiction of a robot dressed in a wig, gown, and jewelry, posed in a setting that resembled the *Wheel of Fortune* set, in a stance for which White is famous. The court held in White's favor, holding that the tort of appropriation does not require the use of a celebrity's name or likeness. The court stated that Samsung's robot ad left "little doubt" as to the identity of the celebrity that the ad was meant to depict.[4]

Cases of wrongful appropriation, or misappropriation, may also involve the rights of those who invest time and money in the creation of a special system, such as a method of broadcasting sports events. Commercial misappropriation may also occur when a person takes and uses the property of another for the sole purpose of capitalizing unfairly on the goodwill or reputation of the property owner.

FRAUDULENT MISREPRESENTATION

A misrepresentation leads another to believe in a condition that is different from the condition that actually exists. This is often accomplished through a false or an incorrect statement. Misrepresentations may be innocently made by someone who is unaware of the facts. The tort of **fraudulent misrepresentation,** or *fraud,* however, involves intentional deceit for personal gain. The tort includes several elements:

1. A misrepresentation of material facts or conditions with knowledge that they are false or with reckless disregard for the truth.
2. An intent to induce another party to rely on the misrepresentation.
3. A justifiable reliance on the misrepresentation by the deceived party.
4. Damages suffered as a result of that reliance.
5. A causal connection between the misrepresentation and the injury suffered.

For fraud to occur, more than mere **puffery,** or *seller's talk,* must be involved. Fraud exists only when a person represents as a fact something he or she knows is untrue. For example, it is fraud to claim that the roof of a building does not leak when one knows

---

4. *White v. Samsung Electronics America, Inc.,* 971 F.2d 1395 (9th Cir. 1992).

EMERGING TRENDS IN TECHNOLOGY

The Protection of Privacy Rights in Cyberspace

You may not know it, but when you surf the Web you usually do not do so anonymously. When you visit a Web site, the site's owner or operator often knows where you are located, the kind of computer you have, the name of your Internet service provider, and other details. In fact, a 1998 Federal Trade Commission (FTC) survey of 1,400 Web sites found that although more than 85 percent of the sites collected personal information on visitors, only 14 percent of these sites informed visitors of their information-collecting practices.

Ironically, at a time when the value of personal information is higher than ever, the ability of individuals to control how that information is used is at a low

point. A growing concern today is how to protect Internet users' privacy rights without impeding the development of e-commerce and the flow of information online.

THE VALUE OF PERSONAL INFORMATION

In February 1999, Free-PC, a company based in Pasadena, California, announced that it would distribute 10,000 free Compaq computers immediately (and some 90,000 more computers in the future). Within days, the company received more than 1.2 million applications. What did Free-PC expect to get in return? The answer is—information. Those who received the computers had to disclose their ages, incomes, hobbies, and a variety of other details about their lives. They also had to permit their online travels to be tracked.

Online companies realize that profits can be made by gathering and using personal customer information, selling it to third parties, or sharing it with partners.

A user's name and everything connected to it have become valuable commodities to be purchased, sold, and otherwise exchanged for a profit in today's electronic marketplace.

WEB SITE PRIVACY POLICIES AND GUIDELINES

To ward off possible government action, as well as to avoid liability under existing laws, most online businesses are now taking steps to create and implement Web site privacy policies. Web site privacy guidelines are available from a number of online privacy groups and other organizations, including the Online Privacy Alliance, the Internet Alliance, and the Direct Marketing Association. Some organizations, including the Better Business Bureau, have even developed a "seal of approval" that Web-based businesses can display at their sites if they follow the organization's privacy guidelines.

Online privacy guidelines generally recommend that

it does. Facts are objectively ascertainable, whereas seller's talk is not. "I am the best architect in town" is seller's talk. The speaker is not trying to represent something as fact, because the term *best* is a subjective, not an objective, term.

Normally, the tort of fraudulent misrepresentation occurs only when there is reliance on a *statement of fact.* Sometimes, however, reliance on a *statement of opinion* may involve the tort of fraudulent misrepresentation if the individual making the statement of opinion has a superior knowledge of the subject matter. For example, when a lawyer, in a state in which he or she is licensed to practice, makes a statement of opinion about the law, a court would construe re-

liance on such a statement to be equivalent to reliance on a statement of fact.

Fraudulent misrepresentation was already examined in Chapter 9, in the context of contract law. A growing problem in the online era is fraudulent misrepresentation in Internet transactions, a topic we examine in Chapter 24.

WRONGFUL INTERFERENCE

Torts involving wrongful interference with another's business rights generally fall into two categories—interference with a contractual relationship and interference with a business relationship.

EMERGING TRENDS IN TECHNOLOGY

The Protection of Privacy Rights in Cyberspace,

continued

businesses post a notice on their Web sites about the type of information being collected, how it will be used, and the parties to whom it will be disclosed. Other recommendations include allowing Web site visitors to access and correct or remove personal information and giving visitors an "opt-in" or "opt-out" choice. For example, if a user selects an "opt-out" policy, the personal data collected by the site owner would be kept private. Ultimately, new technology may make privacy a structural component of the Internet. For example, software is currently being developed by Microsoft and other firms that

would enable Web browsers to display a warning if a user visits a Web site that does not have a privacy policy or that collects data the user does not wish to disclose.

Because of these and other efforts, the FTC recently proposed to Congress that pending legislative action be postponed for a time to see if the online industry can regulate itself. For self-regulation to be effective, however, online companies and privacy organizations will need to agree on uniform privacy policy standards and devise appropriate enforcement mechanisms. These obstacles may be difficult—if not impossible—to overcome.

IMPLICATIONS FOR THE BUSINESSPERSON

1. Any company involved in e-commerce today should consider creating and implementing a Web site privacy policy to avoid liability for violating the privacy rights of Web site visitors.
2. Online businesses should also consider joining an online privacy

organization, both to obtain guidelines for privacy policies and to promote further self-regulation of e-commerce.

FOR CRITICAL ANALYSIS

1. Is self-regulation by the online industry a realistic option, or will the government inevitably have to step in to further protect online privacy rights?
2. What benefits do Internet users derive from disclosing personal information to Web merchants?

RELEVANT WEB SITES

To obtain a free privacy analysis of your computer (and learn what information you disclose simply by visiting the site), go to **http://www. Privacy.net**. Free-PC describes its business operations at **http://www. free-pc.com/about.tp**. For information on the Online Privacy Alliance, go to **http://www. privacyalliance.org**.

Wrongful Interference with a Contractual Relationship. The body of tort law relating to *wrongful interference with a contractual relationship* has increased greatly in recent years. A landmark case in this area involved an opera singer, Joanna Wagner, who was under contract to sing for a man named Lumley for a specified period of years. A man named Gye, who knew of this contract, nonetheless "enticed" Wagner to refuse to carry out the agreement, and Wagner began to sing for Gye. Gye's action constituted a tort, because it interfered with the contractual relationship between Wagner and Lumley. (Of course, Wagner's refusal to carry out the

agreement also entitled Lumley to sue Wagner for breach of contract.)[5]

In principle, any lawful contract can be the basis for an action of this type. The plaintiff must prove that the defendant actually knew of the contract's existence and *intentionally induced* the breach of the contractual relationship, not merely that the defendant reaped the benefits of a broken contract. For example, suppose that Carlin has a contract with Sutter that calls for Sutter to do gardening work on Carlin's large estate every week for fifty-two weeks at

---

5. *Lumley v. Gye*, 118 Eng.Rep. 749 (1853).

a specified price per week. Mellon, who needs gardening services, contacts Sutter and offers to pay Sutter a wage that is substantially higher than that offered by Carlin—although Mellon knows nothing about the Sutter-Carlin contract. Sutter breaches his contract with Carlin so that he can work for Mellon. Carlin cannot sue Mellon, because Mellon knew nothing of the Sutter-Carlin contract and was totally unaware that the higher wage he offered induced Sutter to breach that contract.

Three elements are necessary for wrongful interference with a contractual relationship to occur:

1. A valid, enforceable contract must exist between two parties.
2. A third party must know that this contract exists.
3. This third party must *intentionally* cause one of the two parties to the contract to breach the contract, and the interference must be for the purpose of advancing the economic interest of the third party.

The contract may be between a firm and its employees or a firm and its customers, suppliers, competitors, or other parties. Sometimes a competitor of a firm draws away a key employee. If the original employer can show that the competitor induced the

breach of the employment contract—that is, that the employee would not normally have broken the contract—damages can be recovered.

In a famous case in the 1980s, Texaco, Inc., was found to have wrongfully interfered with an agreement between the Pennzoil Company and the Getty Oil Company. After Pennzoil had agreed to purchase a portion of Getty Oil, Texaco made an offer to purchase Getty Oil, and Getty Oil accepted Texaco's offer. Pennzoil then successfully sued Texaco for wrongful interference with Pennzoil's contractual relationship with Getty Oil.[6]

The following case illustrates the elements of the tort of wrongful interference with a contractual relationship in the context of an agreement not to compete (agreements not to compete were discussed in further detail in Chapter 9).

---

6. *Texaco, Inc. v. Pennzoil Co.,* 725 S.W.2d 768 (Tex.App.—Houston [1st Dist.] 1987, writ ref'd n.r.e.). (Generally, a complete Texas Court of Appeals citation includes a writ-of-error history showing the Texas Supreme Court's disposition of the case. In this case, "writ ref'd n.r.e." is an abbreviation for "writ refused, no reversible error," which means that Texas's highest court refused to grant the appellant's request to review the case, because the court did not consider there to be any reversible error.)

CASE 12.2   Kallok v. Medtronic, Inc.

Supreme Court of Minnesota, 1998.
573 N.W.2d 356.
http://www.courts.state.
mn.us/library/archive/
sctjl.html[a]

COMPANY PROFILE   *Medtronic, Inc. (**http://www.medtronic.com**), is the world's leading manufacturer of implantable biomedical devices. The company was started in 1949 by Earl Bakken, who was then a graduate student at the University of Minnesota, and Palmer Hermundslie, who worked in a lumberyard. The company's initial focus was the repair of hospital laboratory equipment. Today, Medtronic's most important products relate to cardiovascular and neurological health. Medtronic makes the most often prescribed heart pacemakers, as well as heart valves, implantable neurostimulation and drug-delivery systems, catheters used in angioplasties, and other products. Medtronic sells these products in more than 120 countries.*

BACKGROUND AND FACTS   *Michael Kallok signed a series of noncompete agreements when he worked for Medtronic, Inc., a medical device manufacturer. The agreements restricted his ability to work for Medtronic's competitors, including Angeion Corporation. When Kallok later approached Angeion for a job, he told it about the agreements. Angeion consulted with its attorneys, who advised that Kallok would not breach the agreements by accepting a job with Angeion. Angeion did not tell the attorneys all of the details of the agreements, however. After Kallok resigned from Medtronic to work for*

---

a. This page lists, in alphabetical order, Minnesota Supreme Court opinions and orders that have been issued since May 2, 1996, with first party names beginning with the letter J, K, or L. Scroll down the list to the *Kallok* case and click on the docket number to access the opinion. This page is part of the Web site for the "Minnesota State Court System" maintained by the Minnesota state government.

Angeion, he and Angeion filed a suit in a Minnesota state court against Medtronic, asserting that the noncompete agreements were unenforceable. Medtronic counterclaimed, alleging wrongful interference by Angeion. Angeion argued that its hiring of Kallok was justified because it consulted attorneys first. The court held Angeion liable and, among other things, awarded Medtronic damages. The plaintiffs appealed. The state intermediate appellate court took away the award. Medtronic appealed to the Minnesota Supreme Court.

IN THE LANGUAGE OF THE COURT

ANDERSON, Justice.
    *   *   *   *

Medtronic easily established the *   *   * elements [of a cause of action for tortious interference with a contractual relationship]. First, as Kallok signed valid noncompete agreements, it is evident that a contract existed between him and Medtronic. Second, Angeion knew of the existence of Kallok's noncompete agreements before it hired him. *   *   * Third, *   *   * Angeion *   *   * procured the breach of his noncompete agreements by offering him the *   *   * position that he eventually accepted.
    *   *   * Angeion, however, asserts that *   *   * its actions were justified because it consulted with its outside legal counsel before hiring Kallok *   *   * . We conclude that Angeion's argument lacks merit.
    *   *   * Angeion did not fully inform its outside counsel about Kallok's background at Medtronic or the intricacies of his noncompete agreements. Had Angeion candidly provided its attorneys with all relevant information *   *   * Angeion would have understood that hiring Kallok would cause him to breach his noncompete agreements with Medtronic. *   *   *
    *   *   *   *
    *   *   * As a result, Medtronic was forced into court to protect the legitimate interest embodied in Kallok's noncompete agreements. *   *   * We hold that the [trial] court *   *   * correctly allowed Medtronic to recover from Angeion the *   *   * expenses it incurred in enforcing its noncompete agreements with Kallok.

DECISION AND REMEDY

The Minnesota Supreme Court reversed the decision of the lower court. The state supreme court reinstated Medtronic's award of damages for Angeion's interference with the noncompete agreements between Medtronic and Kallok.

Wrongful Interference with a Business Relationship. Individuals devise countless schemes to attract business, but they are forbidden by the courts to interfere unreasonably with another's business in their attempts to gain a share of the market. There is a difference between *competitive practices* and *predatory behavior*. The distinction usually depends on whether a business is attempting to attract customers in general or to solicit only those customers who have already shown an interest in the similar product or service of a specific competitor.

For example, if a shopping center contains two shoe stores, an employee of Store A cannot be positioned at the entrance of Store B for the purpose of diverting customers to Store A. This type of activity constitutes the tort of wrongful interference with a business relationship, often referred to as interference with a prospective (economic) advantage, and it is commonly considered to be an unfair trade practice. If this type of activity were permitted, Store A would reap the benefits of Store B's advertising.

Generally, a plaintiff must prove the following elements to recover damages for the tort of wrongful interference with a business relationship:

1. There was an established business relationship.
2. The tortfeasor, by use of predatory methods, *intentionally* caused this business relationship to end.
3. The plaintiff suffered damages as a result of the tortfeasor's actions.

Defenses to Wrongful Interference. A person will not be liable for the tort of wrongful interference with a contractual or business relationship if it can be shown that the interference was justified, or permissible. Bona fide competitive behavior is a permissible interference even if it results in the breaking of a contract.

For example, if Jerrod's Meats advertises so effectively that it induces Sam's Restaurant to break its contract with Burke's Meat Company, Burke's Meat Company will be unable to recover against Jerrod's Meats on a wrongful interference theory. After all, the public policy that favors free competition in advertising definitely outweighs any possible instability that such competitive activity might cause in contractual relations. Therefore, although luring customers away from a competitor through aggressive marketing and advertising strategies obviously interferes with the competitor's relationship with its customers, such activity is permitted by the courts.

SECTION 3

Intentional Torts against Property

Intentional torts against property include trespass to land, trespass to personal property, and conversion. These torts are wrongful actions that interfere with individuals' legally recognized rights with regard to their land or personal property. The law distinguishes real property from personal property (see Chapter 46). *Real property* is land and things permanently attached to the land. *Personal property* consists of all other items, which are basically movable. Thus, a house and lot are real property, whereas the furniture inside a house is personal property. Money and securities are also personal property.

TRESPASS TO LAND

The tort of **trespass to land** occurs any time a person, without permission, enters onto, above, or below the surface of land that is owned by another; causes anything to enter onto the land; or remains on the land or permits anything to remain on it. Note that actual harm to the land is not an essential element of this tort, because the tort is designed to protect the right of an owner to exclusive possession. Common types of trespass to land include walking or driving on the land; shooting a gun over the land; throwing rocks or spraying water on a building that belongs to someone else; building a dam across a river, thus causing water to back up on someone else's land; and placing part of one's building on an adjoining landowner's property.

In the past, the right to land gave exclusive possession of a space that extended from "the center of the earth to the heavens," but this rule has been relaxed. Today, reasonable intrusions are permitted. Thus, aircraft can normally fly over privately owned land. Society's interest in air transportation preempts the individual's interest in the airspace.

Trespass Criteria, Rights, and Duties. Before a person can be a trespasser, the real property owner (or other person in actual and exclusive possession of the property) must establish that person as a trespasser. For example, "posted" trespass signs expressly establish as a trespasser a person who ignores these signs and enters onto the property. Any person who enters onto another's property to commit an illegal act (such as a thief entering a lumberyard at night to steal lumber) is established impliedly as a trespasser, without posted signs.

A guest in one's home is not a trespasser—unless he or she has been asked to leave but refuses. A *licensee* (a person who has a revocable right to come onto another person's land—see Chapter 26) who is asked to leave and refuses to do so is also a trespasser. For example, one who purchases a ticket to a play has a right to enter the theater, but the theater manager may revoke (take back) that right—if the playgoer becomes rowdy during the play's performance, for instance.

At common law, a trespasser is liable for damages caused to the property and generally cannot hold the owner liable for injuries that the trespasser sustains on the premises. This common law rule is being abandoned in many jurisdictions in favor of a "reasonable duty" rule that varies depending on the status of the parties. For example, a landowner may have a duty to post a notice that the property is patrolled by guard dogs. Also, under the "attractive nuisance" doctrine, a landowner may be held liable for injuries sustained by young children on the landowner's property if the children were attracted to the premises by some object, such as a swimming pool or an abandoned building. Finally, an owner can remove a trespasser from the premises—or detain a trespasser on the premises for a reasonable time—through the use of reasonable force without being liable for assault and battery or false imprisonment.

Defenses against Trespass to Land. Trespass to land involves wrongful interference with another person's real property rights. If it can be shown that the trespass was warranted, however, as when a trespasser enters to assist someone in danger, a defense exists.

TRESPASS TO PERSONAL PROPERTY

Whenever any individual, without consent, harms the personal property of another or otherwise interferes with the personal property owner's right to exclusive possession and enjoyment of that property, **trespass to personal property**—also called *trespass to personalty*—occurs. Trespass to personal property involves intentional meddling. If Kelly takes Ryan's business law book as a practical joke and hides it so that Ryan is unable to find it for several days prior to a final examination, Kelly has engaged in a trespass to personal property.

If it can be shown that trespass to personal property was warranted, then a complete defense exists. Most states, for example, allow automobile repair shops to hold a customer's car (under what is called an *artisan's lien*, discussed in Chapter 16) when the customer refuses to pay for repairs already completed.

CONVERSION

Conversion is defined as any act that deprives an owner of personal property without that owner's permission and without just cause. Conversion is the civil side of crimes related to theft. A store clerk who steals merchandise from the store commits a crime and engages in the tort of conversion at the same time. When conversion occurs, the lesser offense of trespass to personal property usually occurs as well. If the initial taking of the property was a trespass, retention of that property is conversion. If the initial taking of the property was permitted by the owner or for some other reason is not a trespass, failure to return it may still be conversion.

Even if a person mistakenly believed that he or she was entitled to the goods, a tort of conversion may still have occurred. In other words, good intentions are not a defense against conversion; in fact, conversion can be an entirely innocent act. Someone who buys stolen goods, for example, has committed the tort of conversion even if he or she did not know the goods were stolen.

A successful defense against the charge of conversion is that the purported owner does not in fact own the property or does not have a right to possess it that is superior to the right of the holder. Necessity is another possible defense against conversion. If Abrams takes Mendoza's cat, Abrams is guilty of conversion. If Mendoza sues Abrams, Abrams must return the cat or pay damages. If, however, the cat had rabies and Abrams took the cat to protect the public, Abrams has a valid defense—necessity.

CONCEPT SUMMARY 12.1 — INTENTIONAL TORTS

CATEGORY	NAME OF TORT
Intentional Torts against Persons and Business Relationships	1. *Assault and battery*—Any unexcused and intentional act that causes another person to be apprehensive of immediate harm is an assault. An assault resulting in physical contact is battery.
	2. *False imprisonment*—An intentional confinement or restraint of another person's movement without justification.
	3. *Intentional infliction of emotional distress*—An intentional act that amounts to extreme and outrageous conduct resulting in severe emotional distress to another.
	4. *Defamation (libel or slander)*—A false statement of fact, not made under privilege, that is communicated to a third person and that causes damage to a person's reputation. For public figures, the plaintiff must also prove that the statement was made with actual malice.
	5. *Invasion of privacy*—Publishing or otherwise making known or using information relating to a person's private life and affairs, with which the public had no legitimate concern, without that person's permission or approval.

CONCEPT SUMMARY 12.1

INTENTIONAL TORTS *(continued)*

CATEGORY	NAME OF TORT
Intentional Torts against Persons and Business Relationships (continued)	6. *Appropriation*—The use of another person's name, likeness, or other identifying characteristic, without permission and for the benefit of the user. 7. *Fraudulent misrepresentation (fraud)*—A false representation made by one party, through misstatement of facts or through conduct, with the intention of deceiving another and on which the other reasonably relies to his or her detriment. 8. *Wrongful interference with a contractual or a business relationship*—The knowing, intentional interference by a third party with an enforceable contractual relationship or an established business relationship between other parties for the purpose of advancing the economic interests of the third party.
Intentional Torts against Property	1. *Trespass to land*—The invasion of another's real property without consent or privilege. Specific rights and duties apply once a person is expressly or impliedly established as a trespasser. 2. *Trespass to personal property*—The intentional interference with an owner's right to use, possess, or enjoy his or her personal property without the owner's consent. 3. *Conversion*—The wrongful taking and use of another person's personal property for the benefit of the tortfeasor or another. 4. *Disparagement of property*—Any economically injurious falsehood that is made about another's product or property; an inclusive term for the torts of *slander of quality* and *slander of title*.

DISPARAGEMENT OF PROPERTY

Disparagement of property occurs when economically injurious falsehoods are made not about another's reputation but about another's product or property. *Disparagement of property* is a general term for torts that can be more specifically referred to as *slander of quality* or *slander of title*.

Slander of Quality. Publishing false information about another's product, alleging it is not what its seller claims, constitutes the tort of **slander of quality.** This tort has also been given the name **trade libel.** The plaintiff must prove that actual damages proximately resulted from the slander of quality. That is, it must be shown not only that a third person refrained from dealing with the plaintiff because of the improper publication but also that the plaintiff suffered damages because the third person refrained from

dealing with him or her. The economic calculation of such damages—they are, after all, conjectural—is often extremely difficult.

It is possible for an improper publication to be both a slander of quality and a defamation. For example, a statement that disparages the quality of a product may also, by implication, disparage the character of a person who would sell such a product. In one case, for instance, the claim that a product that was marketed as a sleeping aid contained "habit-forming drugs" was held to constitute defamation.[7]

Slander of Title. When a publication falsely denies or casts doubt on another's legal ownership of property, and when this results in financial loss to the

---

7. *Harwood Pharmacal Co. v. National Broadcasting Co.*, 9 N.Y.2d 460, 174 N.E.2d 602, 214 N.Y.S.2d 725 (1961).

property's owner, the tort of **slander of title** may exist. Usually, this is an intentional tort in which someone knowingly publishes an untrue statement about another's ownership of certain property with the intent of discouraging a third person from dealing with the person slandered. For example, it would be difficult for a car dealer to attract customers after competitors published a notice that the dealer's stock consisted of stolen autos.

Section 4

Negligence

In contrast to intentional torts, in torts involving **negligence,** the tortfeasor neither wishes to bring about the consequences of the act nor believes that they will occur. The actor's conduct merely creates a risk of such consequences. If no risk is created, there is no negligence. Moreover, the risk must be foreseeable; that is, it must be such that a reasonable person engaging in the same activity would anticipate the risk and guard against it. In determining what is reasonable conduct, courts consider the nature of the possible harm. A very slight risk of a dangerous explosion might be unreasonable, whereas a distinct possibility of someone's burning his or her fingers on a stove might be reasonable.

To succeed in a negligence action, the plaintiff must prove the following:

1. That the defendant owed a duty of care to the plaintiff.
2. That the defendant breached that duty.
3. That the plaintiff suffered a legally recognizable injury.
4. That the defendant's breach caused the plaintiff's injury.

We discuss here each of these four elements of negligence.

The Duty of Care and Its Breach

Central to the tort of negligence is the concept of a **duty of care.** This concept arises from the notion that if we are to live in society with other people, some actions can be tolerated and some cannot; some actions are right and some are wrong; and some actions are reasonable and some are not. The basic principle underlying the duty of care is that people are free to act as they please so long as their actions do not infringe on the interests of others.

The law of torts defines and measures the duty of care by the **reasonable person standard.** In determining whether a duty of care has been breached, for example, the courts ask how a reasonable person would have acted in the same circumstances. The reasonable person standard is said to be (though in an absolute sense it cannot be) objective. It is not necessarily how a particular person would act. It is society's judgment on how an ordinarily prudent person should act. If the so-called reasonable person existed, he or she would be careful, conscientious, prudent, even tempered, and honest. That individuals are required to exercise a reasonable standard of care in their activities is a pervasive concept in business law, and many of the issues dealt with in subsequent chapters of this text have to do with this duty.

In negligence cases, the degree of care to be exercised varies, depending on the defendant's occupation or profession, his or her relationship with the plaintiff, and other factors. Generally, whether an action constitutes a breach of the duty of care is determined on a case-by-case basis. The outcome depends on how the court judge (or jury, if it is a jury trial) decides a reasonable person in the position of the defendant would act in the particular circumstances of the case. In the following subsections, we examine the degree of care typically expected of landowners and professionals.

Duty of Landowners. Landowners are expected to exercise reasonable care to protect from harm individuals coming onto their property. As mentioned earlier in this chapter, in some jurisdictions, landowners are held to have a duty to protect even trespassers against certain risks. Landowners who rent or lease premises to tenants are expected to exercise reasonable care to ensure that the tenants and their guests are not harmed in common areas, such as stairways, entryways, and laundry rooms.

Retailers and other firms that explicitly or implicitly invite persons to come onto their premises are usually charged with a duty to exercise reasonable care to protect these **business invitees.** For example, if you entered a supermarket, slipped on a wet floor, and sustained injuries as a result, the owner of the supermarket would be liable for damages if, when you slipped, there was no sign warning that the floor was wet. A court would hold that the business owner was negligent because the owner failed to exercise a reasonable degree of care in protecting the store's customers against foreseeable risks about which the owner knew or *should have known.* That a patron might slip on the wet floor and be injured as a result was a foreseeable risk, and the owner should have taken care to avoid this risk or warn the customer of it.[8]

Some risks, of course, are so obvious that an owner need not warn of them. For example, a business owner does not need to warn customers to open a

door before attempting to walk through it. Other risks, however, even though they may seem obvious to a business owner, may not be so in the eyes of another, such as a child. For example, a hardware store owner may not think it is necessary to warn customers that, if climbed, a stepladder leaning against the back wall of the store could fall down and harm them. It is possible, though, that a child could tip the ladder over while climbing it and be hurt as a result.

In the following case, the court had to decide whether a store owner should be held liable for a customer's injury on the premises. The question was whether the owner had notice of the condition that led to the customer's injury.

---

8. A business owner can warn of a risk in a number of ways—for example, by placing a sign, traffic cone, sawhorse, board, or the like near a hole in the business's parking lot. See *Hartman v. Walkertown Shopping Center, Inc.,* 113 N.C.App. 632, 439 S.E.2d 787 (1994).

CASE 12.3   Martin v. Wal-Mart Stores, Inc.

United States
Court of Appeals,
Eighth Circuit, 1999.
183 F.3d 770.

BACKGROUND AND FACTS *Harold Martin was shopping in the sporting goods department of a Wal-Mart store. There was one employee in the department at that time. In front of the sporting goods section, in the store's main aisle (which the employees referred to as "action alley"), there was a large display of stacked cases of shotgun shells. On top of the cases were individual boxes of shells. Shortly after the sporting goods employee walked past the display, Martin did so, but Martin slipped on some loose shotgun shell pellets and fell to the floor. He immediately lost feeling in, and control of, his legs. Sensation and control returned, but during the next week, he lost the use of his legs several times for periods of ten to fifteen minutes. Eventually, sensation and control did not return to the front half of his left foot. Doctors diagnosed the condition as permanent. Martin filed a suit against Wal-Mart in a federal district court, seeking damages for his injury. The jury found in his favor, and the court denied Wal-Mart's motion for a directed verdict. Wal-Mart appealed to the U.S. Court of Appeals for the Eighth Circuit.*

IN THE LANGUAGE
OF THE COURT

BEAM, Circuit J. [Judge]
        *   *   *   *

        *   *   * [T]he traditional rule *   *   * required a plaintiff in a slip and fall case to establish that the defendant store had either actual or constructive notice of the dangerous condition. The defendant store [was] deemed to have actual notice if it [was] shown that an employee created or was aware of the hazard. Constructive notice could be established by showing that the dangerous condition had existed for a sufficient length of time that the defendant should reasonably have known about it.
        *   *   *   *

        *   *   * [R]etail store operations have evolved since the traditional liability rules were established. In modern self-service stores, customers are invited to traverse the same aisles used by the clerks to replenish stock, they are invited to retrieve merchandise from displays for inspection, and to place it back in the display if the item is not selected for purchase. Further, a customer is enticed to look at the displays, thus reducing the chance that the customer will be watchful of hazards on the floor. *   *   * [C]ustomers may take merchandise into their hands and may then lay articles that no longer interest them down in the aisle. *   *   * The risk of items creating dangerous conditions on the floor, previously created by employees, is now created by other customers as a result of the store's decision to employ the self-service mode of operation. *   *   * Thus, in slip and fall cases in self-service stores, the inquiry of whether the danger existed long enough that

the store should have reasonably known of it (constructive notice) is made in light of the fact that the store has notice that certain dangers arising through customer involvement are likely to occur, and the store has a duty to anticipate them.

*   *   *   *   *

Wal-Mart *   *   * claims that Martin *   *   * failed to establish that Wal-Mart had actual or constructive notice of the pellets in the action aisle. We disagree. We find there is substantial evidence of constructive notice in the record. Martin slipped on shotgun shell pellets on the floor which were next to a large display of shotgun shells immediately abutting the sporting goods department. The chance that merchandise will wind up on the floor (or merchandise will be spilled on the floor) in the department in which that merchandise is sold or displayed is exactly the type of foreseeable risk [that is part of the self-service exception to the traditional rule]. Under [this exception], Wal-Mart has notice that merchandise is likely to find its way to the floor and create a dangerous condition, and *it must exercise due care to discover this hazard and warn customers or protect them from the danger.* *   *   * Even assuming that the hazard was created by a customer, a jury could easily find, given that it had notice that merchandise is often mishandled or mislaid by customers in a manner that can create dangerous conditions, that, had Wal-Mart exercised due care under the circumstances, it would have discovered the shotgun pellets on the floor. [Emphasis added.]

DECISION AND REMEDY *The U.S. Court of Appeals for the Eighth Circuit affirmed the judgment of the lower court. There was sufficient evidence for a jury to find that Wal-Mart had constructive notice of the pellets on the floor in the main aisle.*

Duty of Professionals. If an individual has knowledge, skill, or intelligence superior to that of an ordinary person, the individual's conduct must be consistent with that status. Professionals—including physicians, dentists, psychiatrists, architects, engineers, accountants, and lawyers, among others—are required to have a standard minimum level of special knowledge and ability. Therefore, in determining what constitutes reasonable care in the case of professionals, the court takes their training and expertise into account. In other words, an accountant cannot defend against a lawsuit for negligence by stating, "But I was not familiar with that general principle of accounting."

If a professional violates his or her duty of care toward a client, the client may bring a **malpractice** suit against the professional. For example, a patient might sue a physician for *medical malpractice.* A client might sue an attorney for *legal malpractice.*

No Duty to Rescue. Although the law requires individuals to act reasonably and responsibly in their relations with others, if a person fails to come to the aid of a stranger in peril, that person will not be considered negligent under tort law. For example, assume that you are walking down a city street and notice that a pedestrian is about to step directly in front of an oncoming bus. You realize that the person has not seen the bus and is unaware of the danger. Do you have a legal duty to warn that individual? No. Although most people would probably concede that in this situation, the observer has an *ethical* or *moral* duty to warn the other, tort law does not impose a general duty to rescue others in peril. Duties may be imposed in regard to certain types of peril, however. For example, most states require a motorist involved in an automobile accident to stop and render aid. Failure to do so is both a tort and a crime.

THE INJURY REQUIREMENT AND DAMAGES

To recover damages (receive compensation), the plaintiff in a tort lawsuit must prove that he or she suffered a *legally recognizable* injury. That is, the plaintiff must have suffered some loss, harm, wrong, or invasion of a protected interest. This is true in lawsuits for intentional torts as well as lawsuits for negligence. Essentially, the purpose of tort law is to compensate for legally recognized harms and injuries resulting from wrongful acts. If no harm or injury results from a given negligent action, there is nothing to compensate—and no tort exists.

For example, if you carelessly bump into a passerby, who stumbles and falls as a result, you may be liable in tort if the passerby is injured in the fall. If the person is unharmed, however, there normally can be no suit for damages, because no injury was suffered. Although the passerby might be angry and suffer emotional distress, few courts recognize negligently inflicted emotional distress as a tort unless it results in some physical disturbance or dysfunction.

As already mentioned, the purpose of tort law is not to punish people for tortious acts but to compensate the injured parties for damages suffered. **Compensatory damages** are intended to compensate, or reimburse, a plaintiff for actual losses—to make the plaintiff whole. Occasionally, however, punitive damages are also awarded in tort lawsuits. **Punitive damages,** or *exemplary damages,* are intended to punish the wrongdoer and deter others from similar wrongdoing. Punitive damages are rarely awarded in lawsuits for ordinary negligence and usually are given only in cases involving intentional torts. They may be awarded, however, in suits involving *gross negligence,* which can be defined as an intentional failure to perform a manifest duty in reckless disregard of the consequences of such a failure for the life or property of another.

CAUSATION

Another element necessary to a tort is *causation.* If a person breaches a duty of care and someone suffers injury, the wrongful activity must have caused the harm for a tort to have been committed.

Causation in Fact and Proximate Cause. In deciding whether the requirement of causation is met, the court must address two questions:

1. *Is there causation in fact?* Did the injury occur because of the defendant's act, or would it have occurred anyway? If an injury would not have occurred without the defendant's act, then there is causation in fact. **Causation in fact** can usually be determined by use of the *but for* test: "but for" the wrongful act, the injury would not have occurred.

2. *Was the act the proximate cause of the injury?* Theoretically, causation in fact is limitless. One could claim, for example, that "but for" the creation of the world, a particular injury would not have occurred. Thus, as a practical matter, the law has to establish limits, and it does so through the concept of proximate cause. **Proximate cause,** or *legal cause,* exists when the connection between an act and an injury is strong enough to justify imposing liability. Consider an example. Ackerman carelessly leaves a campfire burning. The fire not only burns down the forest but also sets off an explosion in a nearby chemical plant that spills chemicals into a river, killing all the fish for a hundred miles downstream and ruining the economy of a tourist resort. Should Ackerman be liable to the resort owners? To the tourists whose vacations were ruined? These are questions of proximate cause that a court must decide.

Foreseeability. Questions of proximate cause are linked to the concept of foreseeability, because it would be unfair to impose liability on a defendant unless the defendant's actions created a foreseeable risk of injury. Probably the most cited case on the concept of foreseeability as a requirement for proximate cause—and as a measure of the extent of the duty of care generally—is the *Palsgraf* case. The question before the court was as follows: Does the defendant's duty of care extend only to those who may be injured as a result of a foreseeable risk, or does it extend also to persons whose injuries could not reasonably be foreseen?

CASE 12.4   Palsgraf v. Long Island Railroad Co.

Court of Appeals of New York, 1928. 248 N.Y. 339, 162 N.E. 99.

BACKGROUND AND FACTS   *The plaintiff, Palsgraf, was waiting for a train on a station platform. A man carrying a package was rushing to catch a train that was moving away from a platform across the tracks from Palsgraf. As the man attempted to jump aboard the moving train, he seemed unsteady and about to fall. A railroad guard on the car reached forward to grab him, and another guard on the platform pushed him from behind to help him board the train. In the process, the man's package, which (unknown to the railroad guards) contained fireworks, fell on the railroad tracks and exploded. There was nothing about the package to indicate its contents. The repercussions of the explosion caused scales at the other end of the train platform to fall on Palsgraf, causing injuries for which she sued the railroad company. At the trial, the jury found that the railroad* *guards had been negligent in their conduct. The railroad company appealed. The appellate court affirmed the trial court's judgment, and the railroad company appealed to New York's highest state court.*

IN THE LANGUAGE OF THE COURT

CARDOZO, C.J. [Chief Justice].

*   *   *   *

The conduct of the defendant's guard, if a wrong in its relation to the holder of the package, was not a wrong in its relation to the plaintiff, standing far away. Relatively to her it was not negligence at all. *   *   *

*   *   *   *

*   *   * What the plaintiff must show is "a wrong" to herself; i.e., a violation of her own right, and not merely a wrong to someone else[.] *   *   * *The risk reasonably to be perceived defines the duty to be obeyed[.]* *   *   * Here, by concession, there was nothing in the situation to suggest to the most cautious mind that the parcel wrapped in newspaper would spread wreckage through the station. If the guard had thrown it down knowingly and willfully, he would not have threatened the plaintiff's safety, so far as appearances could warn him. His conduct would not have involved, even then, an unreasonable probability of invasion of her bodily security. Liability can be no greater where the act is inadvertent. [Emphasis added.]

*   *   * One who seeks redress at law does not make out a cause of action by showing without more that there has been damage to his person. If the harm was not willful, he must show that the act as to him had possibilities of danger so many and apparent as to entitle him to be protected against the doing of it though the harm was unintended. *   *   * The victim does not sue *   *   * to vindicate an interest invaded in the person of another. *   *   * He sues for breach of a duty owing to himself.

*   *   * [To rule otherwise] would entail liability for any and all consequences, however novel or extraordinary.

DECISION AND REMEDY

Palsgraf's complaint was dismissed. The railroad had not been negligent toward her, because injury to her was not foreseeable. Had the owner of the fireworks been harmed, and had he filed suit, there could well have been a different result.

INTERNATIONAL CONSIDERATIONS

Differing Standards of Proximate Cause *The concept of proximate cause is common among countries around the globe, but its application differs from country to country. French law uses the phrase "adequate cause." An event breaks the chain of adequate cause if the event is both unforeseeable and irresistible. England has a "nearest cause" rule that attributes liability based on which event was nearest in time and space. Mexico bases proximate cause on the foreseeability of the harm but does not require that an event be reasonably foreseeable.*

DEFENSES TO NEGLIGENCE

The basic defenses to liability in negligence cases are (1) assumption of risk, (2) superseding cause, and (3) contributory negligence.

Assumption of Risk. A plaintiff who voluntarily enters into a risky situation, knowing the risk involved, will not be allowed to recover. This is the defense of **assumption of risk.** For example, a driver entering an automobile race knows there is a risk of being injured or killed in a crash. The driver has assumed the risk of injury. The requirements of this defense are (1) knowledge of the risk and (2) voluntary assumption of the risk.

The risk can be assumed by express agreement, or the assumption of risk can be implied by the plaintiff's knowledge of the risk and subsequent conduct. Of course, the plaintiff does not assume a risk different from or greater than the risk normally carried by the activity. In our example, the race driver assumes the risk of being injured in the race but not the risk that the banking in the curves of the racetrack will give way during the race because of a construction defect.

Risks are not deemed to be assumed in situations involving emergencies. Neither are they assumed when a statute protects a class of people from harm and a member of the class is injured by the harm. For example, courts have generally held that an employee cannot assume the risk of an employer's violation of safety statutes passed for the benefit of employees.

In the following case, a gas company worker was severely injured in a natural gas explosion that occured during an attempt to repair a gas leak. The question before the court is whether the worker should be barred from recovering for the injury by the defense of assumption of risk.

CASE 12.5   Crews v. Hollenbach

Court of Special
Appeals of Maryland,
1999.
126 Md.App. 609,
730 A.2d 742.

BACKGROUND AND FACTS   *Maryland Cable Partners, Limited Partnership,[a] hired Excalibur Cable Communications, Inc., to install cable lines in Bowie, Maryland. Byers Engineering Company was retained to locate the buried utility lines in the area where the cable lines were to be buried. Excalibur hired Honcho & Sons, Inc., to do the excavation. While Honcho's employee John Hollenbach was digging a hole, he struck a natural gas line owned by Washington Gas Company. Neither the police nor the fire department was promptly notified. Eventually, someone who smelled gas a mile and a half away contacted the fire department. Washington Gas was notified more than two hours later and dispatched a crew to fix the leak. The foreman was Lee James Crews. While Crews and his co-workers were attempting to repair the leak, an explosion occurred, severely injuring Crews. He filed a suit in a Maryland state court against Hollenbach and the others. The defendants filed a motion for summary judgment, claiming that Crews had assumed the risk of a gas explosion by virtue of his occupation. The court granted the motion. Crews appealed to a state intermediate appellate court.*

IN THE LANGUAGE OF THE COURT

HOLLANDER, Judge.

*   *   *   *

Appellant complains that there are issues relevant to whether he * * * assumed the risk, which the trial court did not consider and that the record did not address, such as the nature of the risk, whether appellant had a choice to respond to the scene, and whether appellant knew that the gas had been leaking for some two hours when he arrived at the scene. It is clear to us that these matters, including the apparent delay of some two hours in reporting the gas leak, do not defeat the application of the doctrine of * * * assumption of risk.

There is no basis to conclude that a gas company is always promptly advised about a possible gas leak. Indeed, it seems just as likely that a gas company would not immediately learn about a gas leak, for any number of reasons. To illustrate, a line could develop a leak in the middle of the night, and no one might realize it until hours later. * * * When a gas leak repairman accepts a position with the gas company, he does not assume only those risks associated with the least dangerous gas leak, or one that is reported within minutes of the occurrence. Rather, he assumes the dangers associated with gas leaks generally. * * *

*   *   *   *

*   *   * [T]he risk of an explosion from a gas leak is precisely within the scope of dangers intrinsic to the occupation of a gas leak repairman, much like a helicopter crash for a helicopter rescue team, an animal bite for a veterinarian, or a fireman's fall down an elevator shaft [while fighting a fire]. As appellant acknowledged in his deposition, "any type of gas leak or odor is always dangerous," because a fire could always "start behind natural gas." Thus, * * * appellant had reason to anticipate the danger. Indeed,

---

a. A limited partnership is a special form of a business organization. See Chapter 18.

Crews admitted that when working on a volatile natural gas leak "anything can set it off, gravels [sic] or rocks that hit together, hitting metal."

Crews "accept[ed] that responsibility when * * * [he] first got hired." Clearly, there was a direct causal relationship between the performance of appellant's duties as a gas leak repairman and the cause of his injury. Because appellant knew that his occupation carried with it certain risks, *he may not now be heard to complain when one of those job-related foreseeable risks materialized.* Under such circumstances, we agree with the trial court that appellant was barred from recovery. [Emphasis added.]

DECISION AND REMEDY *The state intermediate appellate court affirmed the ruling of the lower court. The appellate court held that Crews accepted the responsibility as a gas leak repairman to fix leaks in the face of dangers, including an explosion. By virtue of his employment, Crews was thus barred from recovering for his injury by the defense of assumption of risk.*

Superseding Cause. An unforeseeable intervening event may break the causal connection between a wrongful act and an injury to another. If so, it acts as a *superseding cause*—that is, it relieves a defendant of liability for injuries caused by the intervening event. For example, suppose that Derrick, while riding his bicycle, negligently hits Julie, who is walking on a sidewalk. As a result of the impact, Julie falls and fractures her hip. While she is waiting for help to arrive, a small aircraft crashes nearby and explodes, and some of the fiery debris hits her, causing her to sustain severe burns. Derrick will be liable for damages caused by Julie's fractured hip, but normally he will not be liable for the wounds caused by the plane crash—because the risk of a plane crashing nearby and injuring Julie was not foreseeable.

Contributory Negligence. Traditionally, under the common law, if a plaintiff's own negligence contributed to his or her injury, the defendant could raise the defense of **contributory negligence.** Contributory negligence on the part of the plaintiff was a complete defense to liability for negligence. Today, contributory negligence can be used as a defense in only a very few states.

In those jurisdictions that do allow the defense of contributory negligence, the *last clear chance* doctrine can excuse the effect of a plaintiff's negligence. The last clear chance doctrine allows the plaintiff to recover full damages despite his or her failure to exercise care. This rule operates when, through his or her own negligence, the plaintiff is endangered (or his or her property is endangered) by a defendant who has an opportunity to avoid causing damage but fails to take advantage of that opportunity. For example, if Murphy walks across the street against the light, and Lewis, a motorist, sees her in time to avoid hitting her

but hits her anyway, Lewis (the defendant) is not permitted to use Murphy's (the plaintiff's) prior negligence as a defense. The defendant negligently missed the opportunity to avoid injuring the plaintiff.

Neither the complete defense of contributory negligence nor the last clear chance doctrine applies in states that have adopted a comparative negligence standard, as the majority of states have done. Under the doctrine of **comparative negligence,** both the plaintiff's negligence and the defendant's negligence are taken into consideration, and damages are awarded accordingly. Some jurisdictions have adopted a "pure" form of comparative negligence that allows the plaintiff to recover damages even if his or her fault is greater than that of the defendant. For example, if the plaintiff was 80 percent at fault and the defendant was 20 percent at fault, the plaintiff may recover 20 percent of his or her damages. Many states' comparative negligence statutes, however, contain a "50 percent" rule, under which the plaintiff recovers nothing if he or she was more than 50 percent at fault.

SPECIAL NEGLIGENCE DOCTRINES AND STATUTES

There are a number of special doctrines and statutes relating to negligence that are important. We examine a few of them here.

Res Ipsa Loquitur. Generally, in lawsuits involving negligence, the plaintiff has the burden of proving that the defendant was negligent. In certain situations, the courts may presume that negligence has occurred, in which case the burden of proof rests on the defendant—that is, the defendant must prove that he or she was *not* negligent. The presumption of the defendant's negligence is known as the doctrine of *res ipsa loquitur,*[9] which translates as "the facts speak for themselves."

This doctrine is applied only when the event creating the damage or injury is one that ordinarily does not occur in the absence of negligence. For example, if a person undergoes knee surgery and following the surgery has a severed nerve in the knee area, that person can sue the surgeon under a theory of *res ipsa loquitur.* In this case, the injury would not have occurred but for the surgeon's negligence.[10] For the doctrine of *res ipsa loquitur* to apply, the event must have been within the defendant's power to control, and it must not have been due to any voluntary action or contribution on the part of the plaintiff.

Negligence *Per Se*. Certain conduct, whether it consists of an action or a failure to act, may be treated as **negligence *per se*** ("in or of itself"). Negligence *per se* may occur if an individual violates a statute or an ordinance providing for a criminal penalty and that violation causes another to be injured. The injured person must prove (1) that the statute clearly sets out what standard of conduct is expected, when and where it is expected, and of whom it is expected; (2) that he or she is in the class intended to be protected by the statute; and (3) that the statute was designed to prevent the type of injury that he or she suffered. The standard of conduct required by the statute is the duty that the defendant owes to the plaintiff, and a violation of the statute is the breach of that duty.

For example, a statute may require a landowner to keep a building in safe condition and may also subject the landowner to a criminal penalty, such as a fine, if the building is not kept safe. The statute is meant to protect those who are rightfully in the building. Thus, if the owner, without a sufficient excuse, violates the statute and a tenant is thereby injured, then a majority of courts will hold that the owner's unexcused violation of the statute conclusively establishes a breach of a duty of care—that is, that the owner's violation is negligence *per se.*

"Danger Invites Rescue" Doctrine. Under the "danger invites rescue" doctrine, if a person commits an act that endangers another, the person committing the act will be liable for any injuries the other party suffers as well as any injuries suffered by a third person in an attempt to rescue the endangered party. For example, suppose that Ludlam, while driving down a street, fails to see a stop sign because he is trying to stop a squabble between his two young children in the car's back seat. Salter, on the curb near the stop sign, realizes that Ludlam is about to hit a pedestrian walking across the street at the intersection. Salter runs into the street to push the pedestrian out of the way, and Ludlum's vehicle hits Salter instead. In this situation, Ludlam will be liable for Salter's injury, as well as for any injuries the other pedestrian sustained. Rescuers can injure themselves, or the persons rescued, or even bystanders, but the original wrongdoers will still be liable.

Special Negligence Statutes. A number of states have enacted statutes prescribing duties and responsibilities in certain circumstances. For example, most states now have what are called **Good Samaritan statutes.** Under these statutes, persons whom others aid voluntarily cannot turn around and sue the "Good Samaritans" for negligence. These laws were passed largely to protect physicians and medical personnel who voluntarily render their services in emergency situations to those in need, such as individuals hurt in car accidents.

Many states have also passed **dram shop acts,** under which a tavern owner or bartender may be held liable for injuries caused by a person who became intoxicated while drinking at the bar or who was already intoxicated when served by the bartender. Some states have statutes that impose liability on *social hosts* (persons hosting parties) for injuries caused by guests who became intoxicated at the hosts' homes. Under these statutes, it is unnecessary to prove that the tavern owner, bartender, or social host was negligent. Sometimes, the definition of a "social host" is fashioned broadly. For example, in a New York case, the court held that the father of a minor who hosted a "bring your own keg" party could be held liable for injuries caused by an intoxicated guest.[11]

SECTION 5

Strict Liability

Under the tort doctrine of **strict liability,** liability for injury is imposed for reasons other than fault. The

---

9. Pronounced *rihz ihp*-suh *low*-kwuh-duhr.

10. *Edwards v. Boland*, 41 Mass.App.Ct. 375, 670 N.E.2d 404 (1996).

11. *Rust v. Reyer*, 693 N.E.2d 1074, 670 N.Y.S.2d 822 (1998).

CONCEPT SUMMARY 12.2

NEGLIGENCE

TERM	DESCRIPTION
Definition of Negligence	The careless performance of a legally required duty or the failure to perform a legally required act.
Elements of Negligence	1. The defendant owed a duty of care to the plaintiff. 2. The defendant breached that duty. 3. The plaintiff suffered a legally recognizable injury. 4. The defendant's breach of the duty of care caused the plaintiff's injury.
Defenses to Negligence	1. Assumption of risk. 2. Superseding cause. 3. Contributory negligence.
Special Negligence Doctrines and Statutes	1. *Res ipsa loquitur*—A doctrine under which a plaintiff need not prove negligence on the part of the defendant because "the facts speak for themselves." 2. *Negligence per se*—A type of negligence that may occur if a person violates a statute or an ordinance providing for a criminal penalty and the violation causes another to be injured. 3. *Special negligence statutes*—State statutes that prescribe duties and responsibilities in certain circumstances, the violation of which will impose civil liability. Good Samaritan statutes and dram shop acts are examples of special negligence statutes.

modern concept of strict liability traces its origins, in part, to the 1868 English case of *Rylands v. Fletcher.*[12] In the coal-mining area of Lancashire, England, the Rylands, who were mill owners, had constructed a reservoir on their land. Water from the reservoir broke through a filled-in shaft of an abandoned coal mine nearby and flooded the connecting passageways in an active coal mine owned by Fletcher. Fletcher sued the Rylands, and the court held that the defendants (the Rylands) were liable, even though the circumstances did not fit within existing tort liability theories.

In justifying its decision, the court compared the situation to the trespass of dangerous animals: "the true rule of law is, that the person who for his own purposes brings on his land and collects and keeps there anything likely to do mischief if it escapes, must keep it at his peril, and, if he does not do so, is *prima facie* [at first sight; on the face of it] answerable for all the damage which is the natural consequence of its escape."

The doctrine that emerged from *Rylands v. Fletcher* was liberally applied by British courts.

12. L.R. 3 H.L. 330 (1868).

Initially, few U.S. courts accepted this doctrine, presumably because the courts were worried about its effect on the expansion of American businesses. Today, however, the doctrine of strict liability is the norm rather than the exception.

ABNORMALLY DANGEROUS ACTIVITIES

The influence of *Rylands v. Fletcher* can be seen in the strict liability rule for abnormally dangerous activities, which is one application of the strict liability doctrine. Abnormally dangerous activities have three characteristics:

1. The activity involves potential harm, of a serious nature, to persons or property.
2. The activity involves a high degree of risk that cannot be completely guarded against by the exercise of reasonable care.
3. The activity is not commonly performed in the community or area.

Clearly, the primary basis of liability is the creation of an extraordinary risk. For example, even if blasting with dynamite is performed with all reasonable care, there is still a risk of injury. Balancing that risk against the potential for harm, it seems reasonable to ask the person engaged in the activity to pay for any injury it causes. Although there is no fault, there is still responsibility because of the dangerous nature of the undertaking.

OTHER APPLICATIONS OF STRICT LIABILITY

Persons who keep wild animals are strictly liable for any harm inflicted by the animals. The basis for apply-ing strict liability is the fact that wild animals, should they escape from confinement, pose a serious risk of harm to persons in the vicinity. An owner of domestic animals (such as dogs, cats, cows, or sheep) may be strictly liable for harm caused by those animals if the owner knew, or should have known, that the animals were dangerous or had a propensity to harm others.

A significant application of strict liability is in the area of product liability, which we discuss in Chapter 13. Strict liability is also applied in certain types of *bailments* (a bailment exists when goods are transferred temporarily into the care of another).

TERMS AND CONCEPTS TO REVIEW

actionable 258	disparagement of property 268	puffery 261
actual malice 260	dram shop act 276	punitive damages 272
appropriation 261	duty of care 269	reasonable person standard 269
assault 257	fraudulent misrepresentation 261	*res ipsa loquitur* 276
assumption of risk 273		slander 259
battery 257	Good Samaritan statute 276	slander of quality 268
business invitee 269	intentional tort 257	slander of title 269
business tort 256	libel 259	strict liability 276
causation in fact 272	malpractice 271	tort 256
comparative negligence 275	negligence 269	tortfeasor 257
compensatory damages 272	negligence *per se* 276	trade libel 268
contributory negligence 275	privilege 260	trespass to land 266
conversion 267	proximate cause 272	trespass to personal property 266
defamation 259	public figure 260	

QUESTIONS AND CASE PROBLEMS

12–1. NEGLIGENCE. In which of the following situations will the acting party be liable for the tort of negligence? Explain fully.

(a) Shannon goes to the golf course on Sunday morning, eager to try out a new set of golf clubs she has just purchased. As she tees off on the first hole, the head of her club flies off and injures a nearby golfer.

(b) Shannon goes to the golf course on Sunday morning. While she is teeing off at the eleventh hole, her golf ball veers off toward a roadway next to the golf course and shatters the windshield of a car.

(c) Shannon's doctor gives her some pain medication and tells her not to drive after she takes it, as the medication induces drowsiness. In spite of the doctor's warning, Shannon decides to drive to the store while on the medication. Owing to her lack of alertness, she fails to stop at a traffic light and crashes into another vehicle, causing a passenger in that vehicle to be injured.

12–2. Causation. Ruth carelessly parks her car on a steep hill, leaving the car in neutral and failing to engage the parking brake. The car rolls down the hill, knocking down an electric line. The sparks from the broken line ignite a grass fire. The fire spreads until it reaches a barn one mile away. The barn houses dynamite, and the burning barn explodes, causing part of the roof to fall on and injure a passing motorist, Jim. Can Jim recover damages from Ruth? Why or why not?

12–3. Wrongful Interference. Lothar owns a bakery. He has been trying to obtain a long-term contract with the owner of Martha's Tea Salons for some time. Lothar starts a local advertising campaign on radio and television and in the newspaper. This advertising campaign is so persuasive that Martha decides to break the contract she has had with Harley's Bakery so that she can patronize Lothar's bakery. Is Lothar liable to Harley's Bakery for the tort of wrongful interference with a contractual relationship? Is Martha liable for this tort? For anything?

12–4. Duty of Care. As pedestrians exited at the close of an arts and crafts show, Jason Davis, an employee of the show's producer, stood near the exit. Suddenly and without warning, Davis turned around and collided with Yvonne Esposito, an eighty-year-old woman. Esposito was knocked to the ground, fracturing her hip. After hip-replacement surgery, she was left with a permanent physical impairment. Esposito filed a suit in a federal district court against Davis and others, alleging negligence. What are the factors that indicate whether Davis owed Esposito a duty of care? What do those factors indicate in these circumstances? [*Esposito v. Davis*, 47 F.3d 164 (5th Cir. 1995)]

12–5. Strict Liability. Gina is standing on a street corner waiting for a ride to work. Gomez has just purchased a new car manufactured by Optimal Motors. Gomez is driving down the street when suddenly the steering mechanism breaks, causing him to run over Gina. Gina suffers permanent injuries. Gomez's total income per year has never exceeded $15,000. Gina files suit against Optimal under the theory of strict liability in tort. Optimal claims that it is not liable because (1) due care was used in the manufacture of the car, (2) Optimal is not the manufacturer of the steering mechanism (Smith is), and (3) strict product liability applies only to users or consumers, and Gina is neither. Discuss the validity of the defenses claimed by Optimal.

12–6. Negligence Per Se. A North Carolina Department of Transportation regulation prohibits the placement of telephone booths within public rights of way. Despite this regulation, GTE South, Inc., placed a booth in the right of way near the intersection of Hillsborough and Sparger Roads in Durham County. Laura Baldwin was using the booth when an accident at the intersection caused a dump truck to cross the right of

way and smash into the booth. To recover for her injuries, Baldwin filed a suit in a North Carolina state court against GTE and others. Was Baldwin within the class of persons protected by the regulation? If so, did GTE's placement of the booth constitute negligence *per se*? Explain. [*Baldwin v. GTE South, Inc.*, 335 N.C. 544, 439 S.E.2d 108 (1994)]

12–7. Tort Theories. On the morning of October 2, 1989, a fire started by an arsonist broke out in the Red Inn in Provincetown, Massachusetts. The inn had smoke detectors, sprinklers, and an alarm system, all of which alerted the guests, but there were no emergency lights or clear exits. Attempting to escape, Deborah Addis and James Reed, guests at the inn, found the first-floor doors and windows locked. Ultimately, they forced open a second-floor window and jumped out. To recover for their injuries, they filed a suit in a Massachusetts state court against Tamerlane Corp., which operated the inn under a lease, and others (including Duane Steele, who worked for the owner of the inn). Under what tort theory discussed in this chapter might Addis and Reed recover damages from Tamerlane and the others? What must they prove to recover damages under this theory? Discuss fully. [*Addis v. Steele*, 38 Mass.App.Ct. 433, 648 N.E.2d 773 (1995)]

12–8. Duty of Landowners. The Oklahoma State Board of Cosmetology inspected the equipment of the Poteau Beauty College and found it to be in satisfactory condition. A month later, Marilyn Sue Weldon, a student at Poteau, was injured when a salon chair failed to work properly. Weldon had washed the hair of a woman with the chair in a reclining position. The chair did not spring back, and due to a previous injury, the client had to be helped into an upright position. The chair was close to a manicure table, and in maneuvering around the table, Weldon twisted her back. Weldon filed a suit in an Oklahoma state court against Poteau and others, claiming in part that the college was negligent. Assuming that Weldon was an invitee, what duty did Poteau, as the owner of the premises, owe to her? On what basis might the court rule that Poteau was not liable? [*Weldon v. Dunn*, 962 P.2d 1273 (Okla.Sup. 1998)]

12–9. Misappropriation. The United States Golf Association (USGA) was founded in 1894. In 1911, the USGA developed the Handicap System, which was designed to enable individual golfers of different abilities to compete fairly with one another. The USGA revised the system and implemented new handicap formulas between 1987 and 1993. The USGA permits any entity to use the system free of charge as long as it complies with the USGA's procedure for peer review through authorized golf associations of the handicaps issued to individual golfers. In 1991, Arroyo Software Corp. began marketing software known as EagleTrak, which incorporated the USGA's system, and used its name in Arroyo's ads without the USGA's permission. Arroyo's EagleTrak did not incorporate any means for obtaining peer review of handicap computations. The USGA filed a suit in a

California state court against Arroyo, alleging, among other things, misappropriation. The USGA asked the court to stop Arroyo's use of its system. Should the court grant the injunction? Why or why not? [*United States Golf Association v. Arroyo Software Corp.*, 69 Cal.App.4th 607, 81 Cal.Rptr.2d 708 (1999)]

12–10. IN YOUR COURT

Flora Gonzalez visited a Wal-Mart store. While walking in a busy aisle from the store's cafeteria toward a refrigerator, Gonzalez stepped on some macaroni that came from the cafeteria. She slipped and fell, sustaining injuries to her back, shoulder, and knee. She filed a suit against Wal-Mart, alleging that the store was negligent. She presented evidence that the macaroni had "a lot of dirt" and tracks through it and testified that the macaroni "seemed like it had been there awhile." Assume that you are the judge in the trial court hearing this case and answer the following questions:

   (a) What is the nature of the duty owed by businesses, such as Wal-Mart in this case, to their patrons?

   (b) Did Wal-Mart breach that duty in this case?

   (c) In deciding whether Wal-Mart should be held liable for Gonzalez's injuries, does it matter that she was walking in a busy aisle when she stepped on the macaroni?

   (d) Compare the facts in this case to the facts in Case 12.3 *(Martin v. Wal-Mart Stores, Inc.)*. What are the similarities and differences between the fact patterns in these two cases? If the facts are quite

similar in both cases, are you obligated, under the doctrine of *stare decisis*, to apply the ruling in Case 12.3 to the *Gonzalez* case? Why or why not?

12–11. A QUESTION OF ETHICS

Patsy Slone, while a guest at the Dollar Inn, a hotel, was stabbed in the thumb by a hypodermic needle concealed in the tube of a roll of toilet paper. Slone, fearing that she might have been exposed to the virus that causes acquired immune deficiency syndrome (AIDS), sued the hotel for damages to compensate her for the emotional distress she suffered after the needle stab. An Indiana trial court held for Slone and awarded her $250,000 in damages. The hotel appealed, and one of the issues before the court was whether Slone had to prove that she was actually exposed to AIDS to recover for emotional distress. The appellate court held that she did not and that her fear of getting AIDS was reasonable in these circumstances. [*Slone v. Dollar Inn, Inc.*, 395 N.E.2d 185 (Ind.App. 1998)]

   (a) Should the plaintiff in this case have been required to show that she was actually exposed to the AIDS virus in order to recover for emotional distress? Should she have been required to show that she actually acquired the AIDS virus as a result of the needle stab?

   (b) In some states, plaintiffs are barred from recovery in emotional distress cases unless the distress is evidenced by some kind of physical illness. Is this fair?

LAW ON THE WEB

For updated links to resources available on the Web, as well as a variety of other materials, visit this text's Web site at http://wleb.westbuslaw.com.

   You can find cases and articles on torts, including business torts, in the tort law library at the Internet Law Library's Web site. Go to

http://www.lawguru-com/ilawlib

LEGAL RESEARCH EXERCISES ON THE WEB

Go to http://wleb.westbuslaw.com, the Web site that accompanies this text. Select "Internet Applications," and then click on "Chapter 12." There you will find the following Internet research exercises that you can perform to learn more about privacy rights in an online world and the elements of negligence:

Activity 12–1: Privacy Rights in Cyberspace

Activity 12–2: Negligence and the *Titanic*

CHAPTER 13

Product Liability

PRODUCT LIABILITY REFERS TO THE liability incurred by manufacturers and sellers of products when product defects cause injury or property damage to consumers, users, or **bystanders** (people in the vicinity of the product). Product liability encompasses the tort theories of negligence and misrepresentation, which were discussed in Chapter 12, as well as strict liability. For example, if a product is defective because of the manufacturer's negligence, an injured user of the product can sue the manufacturer for negligence in a product liability suit. If a user is injured by a product as a result of the seller's fraudulent misrepresentation of the nature of that product, the basis of the product liability suit is fraud. In the last several decades, the doctrine of strict liability often has been applied in product liability suits.

In this chapter, we examine each of these bases for product liability. Product liability can also be based on warranty theory, a topic we treated in Chapter 11.

SECTION 1

Product Liability Based on Negligence

In Chapter 12, *negligence* was defined as the failure to exercise the degree of care that a reasonable, prudent person would have exercised under the circumstances.

If a manufacturer fails to exercise "due care" to make a product safe, a person who is injured by the product may sue the manufacturer for negligence.

Due care must be exercised in designing the product, in selecting the materials, in using the appropriate production process, in assembling and testing the product, and in placing adequate warnings on the label informing the user of dangers of which an ordinary person might not be aware. The duty of care also extends to the inspection and testing of any purchased components that are used in the final product sold by the manufacturer. A manufacturer's negligence *per se*—which occurs when a manufacturer violates a duty imposed by statute, such as a labeling statute (see Chapter 12)—may also serve as a ground for a tort action for damages.

A product-liability action based on negligence does not require the injured plaintiff and the negligent defendant-manufacturer to be in **privity of contract.** That is, the plaintiff and the defendant need not be directly involved in a contractual relationship. A manufacturer is liable for its failure to exercise due care to *any person* who sustains an injury proximately caused by a negligently made (defective) product. Relative to the long history of the common law, this exception to the privity requirement is a fairly recent development, dating to the early part of the twentieth century.[1]

---

1. A landmark case in this respect is *MacPherson v. Buick Motor Co.*, 217 N.Y. 382, 111 N.E. 1050 (1916).

SECTION 2

Product Liability Based on Misrepresentation

When a fraudulent misrepresentation has been made to a user or consumer and that misrepresentation ultimately results in an injury, the basis of liability may be the tort of fraud. In this situation, the misrepresentation must have been made knowingly or with reckless disregard for the facts. An example is the intentional concealment of a product's defects. In contrast to actions based on negligence and strict liability, in a suit based on fraudulent misrepresentation, the plaintiff does not have to show that the product was defective or that it malfunctioned in any way.[2]

Nonfraudulent misrepresentation, which occurs when a merchant *innocently* misrepresents the character or quality of goods, can also provide a basis of liability. In this situation, the plaintiff does not have to prove that the misrepresentation was made knowingly. A famous example involved a drug manufacturer and a victim of addiction to a prescription medicine called Talwin. The manufacturer, Winthrop Laboratories, a division of Sterling Drug, Inc., innocently indicated to the medical profession that the drug was not physically addictive. Using this information, a physician prescribed the drug for his patient, who developed an addiction that turned out to be fatal. Even though the addiction was a highly uncommon reaction resulting from the victim's unusual susceptibility to this product, the drug company was still held liable.[3]

Whether fraudulent or nonfraudulent, the misrepresentation must be of a material fact (a fact concerning the quality, nature, or appropriate use of the product on which a normal buyer may be expected to rely). There must also have been an intent to induce the buyer's reliance on the misrepresentation. Misrepresentation on a label or advertisement is enough to show an intent to induce the reliance of anyone who may use the product. The buyer also

must rely on the misrepresentation. If the buyer is not aware of the misrepresentation or if it does not influence the transaction, there is no liability.

SECTION 3

Strict Product Liability

As explained earlier in Chapter 12, under the doctrine of strict liability people may be liable for the results of their acts regardless of their intentions or their exercise of reasonable care. In several landmark cases involving manufactured goods in the 1960s, courts applied the doctrine of strict liability, and it has since become a common method of holding manufacturers liable. Some states, however, including Massachusetts and Virginia, have refused to recognize strict product liability. Additionally, some courts limit the application of the doctrine only to cases involving personal injuries, not property damage. Until recently, recovery for economic loss was not available in an action based on strict liability; even today, it is rarely available.

STRICT PRODUCT LIABILITY AND PUBLIC POLICY

Strict product liability is imposed by law as a matter of public policy. This public policy rests on the threefold assumption that (1) consumers should be protected against unsafe products; (2) manufacturers and distributors should not escape liability for faulty products simply because they are not in privity of contract with the ultimate user of those products; and (3) manufacturers, sellers, and lessors of products are in a better position to bear the costs associated with injuries caused by their products—costs that they can ultimately pass on to all consumers in the form of higher prices.

California was the first state to impose strict product liability in tort on manufacturers. In the landmark decision that follows, the California Supreme Court sets out the reason for applying tort law rather than contract law (including laws governing warranties—guarantees made by sellers and lessors to those who buy or lease their products) to cases in which consumers are injured by defective products.

---

2. See, for example, *Khan v. Shiley, Inc.*, 217 Cal.App.3d 848, 266 Cal.Rptr. 106 (1990).

3. *Crocker v. Winthrop Laboratories, Division of Sterling Drug, Inc.*, 514 S.W.2d 429 (Tex. 1974).

CASE 13.1   Greenman v. Yuba Power Products, Inc.

Supreme Court of
California, 1962.
59 Cal.2d 57,
377 P.2d 897,
27 Cal.Rptr. 697.
http://mcs.newpaltz.
edu/~zuckerma/cases/
green1.htm[a]

IN THE LANGUAGE
OF THE COURT

BACKGROUND AND FACTS   *The plaintiff, Greenman, wanted a Shopsmith—a combination power tool that could be used as a saw, drill, and wood lathe—after seeing a Shopsmith demonstrated by a retailer and studying a brochure prepared by the manufacturer. The plaintiff's wife bought and gave him one for Christmas. More than a year later, a piece of wood flew out of the lathe attachment of the Shopsmith while the plaintiff was using it, inflicting serious injuries on him. About ten and a half months later, the plaintiff filed suit in a California state court against both the retailer and the manufacturer for breach of warranties and negligence. The trial court jury found for the plaintiff. The case was ultimately appealed to the Supreme Court of California.*

TRAYNOR, Justice.

*   *   *   *

Plaintiff introduced substantial evidence that his injuries were caused by defective design and construction of the Shopsmith. *   *   * The jury could therefore reasonably have concluded that the manufacturer negligently constructed the Shopsmith. The jury could also reasonably have concluded that statements in the manufacturer's brochure were untrue, that they constituted express warranties, and that plaintiff's injuries were caused by their breach.

*   *   *   *

[But] to impose strict liability on the manufacturer under the circumstances of this case, it was not necessary for plaintiff to establish an express warranty *   *   * . *A manufacturer is strictly liable in tort when an article he places on the market, knowing that it is to be used without inspection for defects, proves to have a defect that causes injury to a human being.* *   *   * [Emphasis added.]

*   *   *   *

*   *   * The purpose of such liability is to insure that the costs of injuries resulting from defective products are borne by the manufacturers *   *   * rather than by the injured persons who are powerless to protect themselves.

DECISION
AND REMEDY

The Supreme Court of California upheld the jury verdict for the plaintiff. The manufacturer was held strictly liable in tort for the harm caused by its unsafe product.

a. This case is included within the Web site for an "Introduction to Law" course taught by Paul Zuckerman, a professor with the State University of New York at New Paltz.

THE REQUIREMENTS FOR STRICT PRODUCT LIABILITY

As mentioned in Chapter 1, the courts often look to the *Restatements of the Law* for guidance, even though the *Restatements* are not binding authorities. Section 402A of the *Restatement (Second) of Torts* indicates how it was envisioned that the doctrine of strict product liability should be applied. This *Restatement* was issued in 1964, and during the decade following its

release it became a widely accepted statement of the liabilities of sellers of goods (including manufacturers, processors, assemblers, packagers, bottlers, wholesalers, distributors, retailers, and lessors). Section 402A reads as follows:

(1) One who sells any product in a defective condition unreasonably dangerous to the user or consumer or to his property is subject to liability for physical harm thereby caused to the ultimate user or consumer or to his property, if

(a) the seller is engaged in the business of selling such a product, and

(b) it is expected to and does reach the user or consumer without substantial change in the condition in which it is sold.

(2) The rule stated in Subsection (1) applies although

(a) the seller has exercised all possible care in the preparation and sale of his product, and

(b) the user or consumer has not bought the product from or entered into any contractual relation with the seller.

The bases for an action in strict liability as set forth in Section 402A of the *Restatement (Second) of Torts,* and as the doctrine came to be commonly applied, can be summarized as a series of six requirements, which are listed here. Depending on the jurisdiction, if these requirements were met, a manufacturer's liability to an injured party could be virtually unlimited.[4]

1. The product must be in a defective condition when the defendant sells it.

2. The defendant must normally be engaged in the business of selling (or otherwise distributing) that product.

3. The product must be unreasonably dangerous to the user or consumer because of its defective condition (in most states).

4. The plaintiff must incur physical harm to self or property by use or consumption of the product.

5. The defective condition must be the proximate cause of the injury or damage.

6. The goods must not have been substantially changed from the time the product was sold to the time the injury was sustained.

Thus, under these requirements, in any action against a manufacturer, seller, or lessor, the plaintiff does not have to show why or in what manner the product became defective. To recover damages, however, the plaintiff must show that the product was so "defective" as to be "unreasonably dangerous"; that the product caused the plaintiff's injury; and that at the time the injury was sustained, the condition of the product was essentially the same as when it left the hands of the defendant manufacturer, seller, or lessor.

A court could consider a product so defective as to be an **unreasonably dangerous product** if either (1) the product was dangerous beyond the expectation of the ordinary consumer or (2) a less dangerous alternative was economically feasible for the manufacturer, but the manufacturer failed to produce it. As will be discussed later, a product may be unreasonably dangerous due to a flaw in the manufacturing process, a design defect, or an inadequate warning.

MARKET-SHARE LIABILITY

Generally, in cases involving product liability, a plaintiff must prove that the defective product that caused his or her injury was the product of a specific defendant. In recent decades, however, in cases in which plaintiffs could not prove which of many distributors of a harmful product supplied the particular product that caused their injuries, courts have dropped this requirement.

This has occurred, for example, in several cases involving DES (diethylstilbestrol), a drug administered in the past to prevent miscarriages. DES's harmful character was not realized until, a generation later, daughters of the women who had taken DES developed health problems, including vaginal carcinoma, that were linked to the drug. Partly because of the passage of time, a plaintiff-daughter often could not prove which pharmaceutical company—out of as many as three hundred—had marketed the DES her mother had ingested. In these cases, some courts applied **market-share liability,** holding that all firms that manufactured and distributed DES during the period in question were liable for the plaintiffs' injuries in proportion to the firms' respective shares of the market.[5]

Market-share liability has also been applied in other situations.[6] In one case, the New York Court of Appeals (that state's highest court) held that even if a firm can prove that it did not manufacture the particular product that caused injuries to the plaintiff, the firm can be held liable based on the firm's share of the national market.[7]

---

4. In a number of states, *statutes of repose* (discussed later in this chapter) place a limit on the time period within which product-liability actions may be brought.

5. See, for example, *Martin v. Abbott Laboratories,* 102 Wash.2d 581, 689 P.2d 368 (1984).

6. See, for example, *Smith v. Cutter Biological, Inc.,* 72 Haw. 416, 823 P.2d 717 (1991).

7. *Hymowitz v. Eli Lilly and Co.,* 73 N.Y.2d 487, 539 N.E.2d 1069, 541 N.Y.S.2d 941 (1989).

OTHER APPLICATIONS OF STRICT PRODUCT LIABILITY

Strict product liability also applies to suppliers of component parts. For example, suppose that General Motors buys brake pads from a subcontractor and puts them in Chevrolets without changing their composition. If those pads are defective, both the supplier of the brake pads and General Motors will be held strictly liable for the damages caused by the defects. Under the *Restatement (Third) of Torts: Products Liability*, which will be discussed shortly, a component supplier may be liable if the component is defective "at the time of sale or distribution." A supplier may also be liable if it "substantially participates in the integration of the component into the design of the product," the "integration" causes the product to be defective, and the defect causes harm.[8]

Although the drafters of Section 402A of the *Restatement (Second) of Torts* did not take a position on bystanders, all courts extend the strict liability of manufacturers and other sellers to injured bystanders. For example, in one case, an automobile manufacturer was held liable for injuries caused by the explosion of a car's motor. A cloud of steam that resulted from the explosion caused multiple collisions because other drivers could not see well.[9] In the following classic case, the court indicates some policy reasons for extending the protections of Section 402A to bystanders whose injuries from defective products are reasonably foreseeable.

---

8. *Restatement (Third) of Torts: Products Liability*, Section 5.
9. *Giberson v. Ford Motor Co.*, 504 S.W.2d 8 (Mo. 1974).

CASE 13.2

Embs v. Pepsi-Cola Bottling Co. of Lexington, Kentucky, Inc.

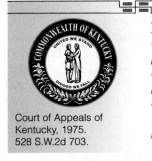

Court of Appeals of Kentucky, 1975.
528 S.W.2d 703.

IN THE LANGUAGE
OF THE COURT

BACKGROUND AND FACTS *Janice Embs was buying some groceries at Stamper's Cash Market. Unnoticed by her, a carton of 7-Up was sitting on the floor at the edge of the produce counter about one foot from where she was standing. Several of the 7-Up bottles exploded. Embs's leg was injured severely enough that Embs had to be taken to the hospital by a managing agent of the store. Embs brought an action in a Kentucky state court against the manufacturer, but the trial court dismissed her claim. Embs appealed.*

JUKOWSKY, Judge.
*   *   *   *

Our expressed public policy will be furthered if we minimize the risk of personal injury and property damage by charging the costs of injuries against the manufacturer who can procure liability insurance and distribute its expense among the public as a cost of doing business; and since the risk of harm from defective products exists for mere bystanders and passersby as well as for the purchaser or user, there is no substantial reason for protecting one class of persons and not the other. The same policy requires us to maximize protection for the injured third party and promote the public interest in discouraging the marketing of products having defects that are a menace to the public by imposing strict liability upon retailers and wholesalers in the distributive chain responsible for marketing the defective product which injures the bystander. *The imposition of strict liability places no unreasonable burden upon sellers because they can adjust the cost of insurance protection among themselves in the course of their continuing business relationship.* [Emphasis added.]

We must not shirk from extending the rule to the manufacturer for fear that the retailer or middleman will be impaled on the sword of liability without regard to fault. Their liability was already established under Section 402A of the *Restatement of Torts 2d.* As a matter of public policy the retailer or middleman as well as the manufacturer should be liable since the loss for injuries resulting from defective products should be placed on those members of the marketing chain best able to pay the loss, who can then distribute such risk among themselves by means of insurance and indemnity agreements. *   *   *

The result which we reach does not give the bystander a "free ride." When products and consumers are considered in the aggregate, bystanders, as a class, purchase most of the same products to which they are exposed as bystanders. Thus, as a class, they indirectly subsidize the liability of the manufacturer, middleman and retailer and in this sense do pay for the insurance policy tied to the product.

Public policy is adequately served if parameters are placed upon the extension of the rule so that it is limited to bystanders whose injury from the defect is reasonably foreseeable.

For the sake of clarity we restate the extension of the rule. The protections of Section 402A of the *Restatement of Torts 2d* extend to bystanders whose injury from the defective product is reasonably foreseeable.

DECISION AND REMEDY   *The appellate court reversed the trial court's dismissal of Embs's claim. The case was remanded to the lower court for a new trial.*

SECTION 4

The *Restatement (Third) of Torts*

Because Section 402A of the *Restatement (Second) of Torts* did not clearly define such terms as "defective" and "unreasonably dangerous," these terms have been subject to different interpretations by different courts. To address these concerns, the American Law Institute (ALI) drafted a new restatement of the principles and policies underlying product-liability law. In particular, the ALI attempted to respond to questions that had not been part of the legal landscape thirty-five years earlier. The result was the *Restatement (Third) of Torts: Products Liability*, which was released in 1997.

Traditionally, the law has categorized product defects into three types: manufacturing defects, design defects, and warning defects—each of which will be discussed shortly. The *Restatement (Third) of Torts: Products Liability* defines the three types of defects and integrates the applicable legal principles into the definitions. By defining defects in this manner, the new *Restatement* does away with some of the hard-to-understand distinctions that developed when different theories of liability were applied to the same defects.

For example, in one case, a court upheld a verdict that found a product "not defective" on a theory of strict liability but its manufacturer liable for harm caused by the product on a theory of breach of warranty.[10] The court based its decision on the various

tests that exist under the different legal theories. The new *Restatement* sets out a single test to be applied for each type of defect regardless of the type of legal claim involved.

MANUFACTURING DEFECTS

According to Section 2(a) of the new *Restatement*, a product "contains a manufacturing defect when the product departs from its intended design even though all possible care was exercised in the preparation and marketing of the product." This statement imposes liability on the manufacturer (and on the wholesaler and retailer) whether or not the manufacturer acted "reasonably." This is strict liability, or liability without fault.

DESIGN DEFECTS

A determination that a product has a design defect (or a warning defect, discussed later in this chapter) can affect all of the units of a product. A product "is defective in design when the foreseeable risks of harm posed by the product could have been reduced or avoided by the adoption of a reasonable alternative design by the seller or other distributor, or a predecessor in the commercial chain of distribution, and the omission of the alternative design renders the product not reasonably safe."[11]

Different states have applied different tests to determine whether a product has a design defect under Section 402A of the *Restatement (Second) of Torts*. There has been much controversy regarding

---

10. *Denny v. Ford Motor Co.*, 87 N.Y.2d 248, 662 N.E.2d 730, 639 N.Y.S.2d 250 (1995). The *Restatement* has not eliminated all of these distinctions, however, because in some cases, they may be necessary.

11. *Restatement (Third) of Torts: Products Liability*, Section 2(b).

the different tests, particularly about one that focused on the "consumer expectations" concerning a product. The test prescribed by the *Restatement (Third) of Torts: Products Liability* focuses on a product's actual design and the reasonableness of that design.

To succeed in a product-liability suit alleging a design defect, a plaintiff has to show that there is a reasonable alternative design. In other words, a manufacturer or other defendant is liable only when the harm was reasonably preventable. According to the Official Comments accompanying the new *Restatement*, factors that a court may consider on this point include

the magnitude and probability of the foreseeable risks of harm, the instructions and warnings accompanying the product, and the nature and strength of consumer expectations regarding the product, including expectations arising from product portrayal and marketing. The relative advantages and disadvantages of the product as designed and as it alternatively could have been designed may also be considered. Thus, the likely effects of the alternative design on production costs; the effects of the alternative design on product longevity, maintenance, repair, and esthetics; and the range of consumer choice among products are factors that may be taken into account.

Note that the "consumer expectations" element, instead of being the whole test, is only one factor taken into consideration. Another factor is the warning that accompanies a product. Can a warning insulate a manufacturer from liability for the harm caused by a design defect? That was the issue in the following case.

Case 13.3   Rogers v. Ingersoll-Rand Co.

United States
Court of Appeals,
District of Columbia
Circuit, 1998.
144 F.3d 841.
**http://laws.findlaw.com
/DC/977131A.html**[a]

COMPANY PROFILE   *Ingersoll-Rand Company (**http://www.ingersoll-rand.com**) is a manufacturer of air compressors, construction and mining equipment, bearings and precision components, tools, locks and architectural hardware, and industrial machinery. The company also makes Bobcat skid-steer loaders, Blaw-Knox pavers, Club Car golf cars and light utility vehicles, and Thermo King transport temperature control systems. In joint ventures with other firms, Ingersoll-Rand is a supplier of pumps and hydrocarbon processing equipment and services. Ingersoll-Rand distributes its products in more than one hundred countries. Forty percent of its sales are outside the United States.*

BACKGROUND AND FACTS   *Among the equipment that Ingersoll-Rand makes is a milling machine. In the maintenance manual that accompanies the machine are warnings that users should stay ten feet away from the rear of the machine when it is operating, verify that the back-up alarm is working, and check the area for the presence of others. There is also a sign on the machine that tells users to stay ten feet away. While using the machine to strip asphalt from a road being repaved, Terrill Wilson backed up the machine. The alarm did not sound, and Cosandra Rogers, who was standing with her back to the machine, was run over and maimed. Rogers filed a suit in a federal district court against Ingersoll-Rand, alleging in part strict liability on the basis of a design defect. The jury awarded Rogers $10.2 million in compensatory damages and $6.5 million in punitive damages. Ingersoll-Rand appealed to the U.S. Court of Appeals for the District of Columbia, emphasizing the adequacy of its warnings.*

IN THE LANGUAGE
OF THE COURT

SENTELLE, Justice.

*   *   *   *

a. This is a page within the Web site of FindLaw, a resource for Internet legal sources.

    *   *   * Under [a risk-utility balancing] test [in a defective design case], a plaintiff must show the risks, costs and benefits of the product in question and alternative designs, and that the magnitude of the danger from the product outweighed the costs of avoiding danger. *   *   *

[Ingersoll-Rand argues that] the adequacy of its warnings [should be] the sole consideration in the risk-utility analysis. As Ingersoll-Rand would have it, once the jury evaluates the milling machine's warnings and finds them adequate, its job is over; it "should find for [the] defendant." *   *   * [T]he "warnings" defense would have instructed the jury that adequate warnings trump all other factors—including the "magnitude of the danger from the product" *   *   * .

    *   *   *   *

We do not mean to dispute that warnings may tip the balance in a manufacturer's favor in individual cases. On the other hand, *warnings need not be the [deciding] factor in every case.* Here, for example, it seems reasonably foreseeable that a worker with her back to a milling machine would be in no position to "heed" a sign on the machine instructing her to keep ten feet away. Under these circumstances, a manufacturer may have a heightened responsibility to incorporate additional safety features to guard against foreseeable harm. [Emphasis added.]

DECISION AND REMEDY   *The U.S. Court of Appeals for the District of Columbia Circuit upheld the jury's award. The court held that an adequate warning cannot immunize a manufacturer from any liability caused by a defectively designed product.*

WARNING DEFECTS

A product may also be deemed defective because of inadequate instructions or warnings. Section 2(c) of the *Restatement (Third) of Torts: Products Liability* states that a product "is defective because of inadequate instructions or warnings when the foreseeable risks of harm posed by the product could have been reduced or avoided by the provision of reasonable instructions or warnings by the seller or other distributor, or a predecessor in the commercial chain of distribution, and the omission of the instructions or warnings renders the product not reasonably safe."[12]

Important factors for a court to consider under the *Restatement (Third) of Torts: Products Liability* include the risks of a product, the "content and comprehensibility" and "intensity of expression" of warnings and instructions, and the "characteristics of expected user groups."[13] For example, children would likely respond readily to bright, bold, simple

warning labels, while educated adults might need more detailed information.

There is no duty to warn about risks that are obvious or commonly known. Warnings about such risks do not add to the safety of a product and could even detract from it by making other warnings seem less significant. The obviousness of a risk and a user's decision to proceed in the face of that risk may be a defense in a product-liability suit based on a warning defect. (Defenses to product liability will be discussed shortly.)

Generally, a seller must warn those who purchase its product of the harm that can result from the foreseeable misuse of the product as well. The key is the foreseeability of the misuse. According to the Official Comments accompanying the new *Restatement,* sellers "are not required to foresee and take precautions against every conceivable mode of use and abuse to which their products might be put."

Is a manufacturer obligated to warn buyers that an alteration to its product (in this case, the removal of the safety guard from a meat grinder) would make the manufacturer's product unsafe? The court addressed this question in the following case.

---

12. *Restatement (Third) of Torts: Products Liability,* Section 2(c).
13. *Restatement (Third) of Torts: Products Liability,* Section 2, Comment h.

CASE 13.4   Liriano v. Hobart Corp.

United States
Court of Appeals,
Second Circuit, 1999.
170 F.3d 264.
http://www.findlaw.com/
casecode/courts/2nd.
html[a]

BACKGROUND AND FACTS   *Hobart Corporation makes and sells commercial food-handling equipment, including meat grinders. In New York, a Super Associated grocery store bought one of the grinders. The grinder did not include a warning indicating that it should be operated only with the safety guard attached. After Super bought the grinder, the guard was removed. Later, Super hired Luis Liriano, who was seventeen years old and a recent immigrant to the United States. During Liriano's first week on the job, although he was not told how to operate the grinder, he used it two or three times. On his next use, his hand became caught in the grinder by a mechanism that anyone operating the appliance was not able to see. He was severely injured—he lost his hand and part of his forearm. He filed a suit in a federal district court against Hobart, claiming, among other things, that the lack of a warning about the safety guard constituted negligence. The jury returned a verdict for Liriano. Hobart appealed, arguing in part that the danger was so obvious that no warning was needed.*

IN THE LANGUAGE
OF THE COURT

CALABRESI, Circuit Judge:

*   *   *   *

*   *   * [A] warning can convey at least two types of messages. One states that a particular place, object, or activity is dangerous. Another explains that people need not risk the danger posed by such a place, object, or activity in order to achieve the purpose for which they might have taken that risk. Thus, a highway sign that says "Danger—Steep Grade" says less than a sign that says "Steep Grade Ahead—Follow Suggested Detour to Avoid Dangerous Areas."

*   *   *   *

One who grinds meat, like one who drives on a steep road, can benefit not only from being told that his activity is dangerous but from being told of a safer way. *   *   * [O]ne can argue about whether the risk involved in grinding meat is sufficiently obvious that a responsible person would fail to warn of that risk, believing reasonably that it would convey no helpful information. But if it is also the case—as it is—that the risk posed by meat grinders can feasibly be reduced by attaching a safety guard, we have a different question. Given that attaching guards is feasible, does reasonable care require that meat workers be informed that they need not accept the risks of using unguarded grinders? Even if most ordinary users may *   *   * know of the risk of using a guardless meat grinder, it does not follow that a sufficient number of them will *   *   * also know that protective guards are available, that using them is a realistic possibility, and that they may ask that such guards be used. It is precisely these last pieces of information that a reasonable manufacturer may have a duty to convey even if the danger of using a grinder were itself deemed obvious.

*   *   * A jury could reasonably find that there exist people who are employed as meat grinders and who do not know (a) that it is feasible to reduce the risk with safety guards, (b) that such guards are made available with the grinders, and (c) that the grinders should be used only with the guards. Moreover, a jury can also reasonably find that there are enough such people, and that warning them is sufficiently inexpensive, that a reasonable manufacturer would inform them that safety guards exist and that the grinder is meant to be used only with such guards.

DECISION
AND REMEDY

The U.S. Court of Appeals for the Second Circuit upheld the verdict in Liriano's favor. The court ruled that a manufacturer could be liable for failing to warn about alterations, such as the removal of a safety guard, that would make its product unsafe.

---

a. This is a page within the Web site of the "Findlaw Internet Legal Resources" database. In the "1999" row, click on "March." On that page, scroll down to the case name and click on it to access the opinion.

SECTION 5

Defenses to Product Liability

Defendants in product-liability suits can raise a number of defenses. One defense, of course, is to show that there is no basis for the plaintiff's claim. For example, in a product-liability case based on negligence, if a defendant can show that the plaintiff has not met the requirements (such as causation) for an action in negligence, the defendant will not be liable. In regard to strict product liability, a defendant can claim that the plaintiff failed to meet one of the requirements for an action in strict liability. For example, if the defendant establishes that the goods have been subsequently altered, the defendant will not be held liable.[14] Defendants may also assert the defenses discussed next.

ASSUMPTION OF RISK

Assumption of risk can sometimes be used as a defense in a product-liability action. To establish such a defense, the defendant must show that (1) the plaintiff knew and appreciated the risk created by the product defect, and (2) the plaintiff voluntarily assumed the risk, even though it was unreasonable to do so. For example, if a buyer failed to heed a seller's product recall, the buyer may be deemed to have assumed the risk of the product defect that the seller offered to cure. (See Chapter 12 for a more detailed discussion of assumption of risk.)

PRODUCT MISUSE

Similar to the defense of voluntary assumption of risk is that of **product misuse.** Here, the injured party *does not know that the product is dangerous for a particular use* (contrast this with assumption of risk), but the use is not the one for which the product was designed. The courts have severely limited this defense, however. Even if the injured party does not know about the inherent danger of using the product in a wrong way, if the misuse is reasonably foreseeable, the seller must take measures to guard against it.

For example, in one case two men were using a crane to retrieve drilling pipe from beneath power lines when the crane cable touched one of the lines. The cable did not have an insulated link and thus conducted electricity from the line to the pipe, electrocuting one of the men. The man's widow sued the crane manufacturer, alleging that the crane—without the insulated link—was defectively designed and unreasonably dangerous. The manufacturer argued that the men had been using the crane to sideload (a practice that causes the crane's cable to extend its slack in unpredictable ways) and that sideloading was an unreasonable misuse of the product. The court held that although sideloading was a misuse, the misuse was reasonably foreseeable. Because the manufacturer had failed to guard against this foreseeable misuse, it was liable to the widow for damages.[15]

CONTRIBUTORY NEGLIGENCE

As discussed in Chapter 12, under the doctrine of contributory negligence, a defendant in a negligence suit may avoid liability in whole or in part if the plaintiff's own negligence contributed to the injury for which the plaintiff seeks damages. Whereas earlier the plaintiff's conduct was not a defense to strict liability, today some jurisdictions consider the negligent or intentional actions of both the plaintiff and the defendant in the apportionment of liability and damages. In other words, in those jurisdictions a comparative negligence standard is applied in strict liability cases.

COMMONLY KNOWN DANGERS

The dangers associated with certain products (such as matches and guns) are so commonly known that manufacturers need not warn users of those dangers. If a defendant succeeds in convincing the court that a plaintiff's injury resulted from a *commonly known danger,* the defendant will not be liable.

A classic case on this issue involved a plaintiff who was injured when an elastic exercise rope she had purchased slipped off her foot and struck her in the eye, causing a detachment of the retina. The plaintiff claimed that the manufacturer should be liable because it had failed to warn users that the exerciser might slip off a foot in such a manner. The court stated that to hold the manufacturer liable in these

---

14. Under some state laws, the failure to properly maintain a product may constitute a subsequent alteration. See, for example, *LaPlante v. American Honda Motor Co.,* 27 F.3d 731 (1st Cir. 1994).

15. *Lutz v. National Crane Corp.,* 884 P.2d 455 (Mont. 1994).

circumstances "would go beyond the reasonable dictates of justice in fixing the liabilities of manufacturers." After all, stated the court, "[a]lmost every physical object can be inherently dangerous or potentially dangerous in a sense. . . . A manufacturer cannot manufacture a knife that will not cut or a hammer that will not mash a thumb or a stove that will not burn a finger. The law does not require [manufacturers] to warn of such common dangers."[16]

A related defense is the *knowledgeable user* defense. If a particular danger is or should be commonly known by particular users of a product, the manufacturer need not warn these users of the danger.

STATUTES OF LIMITATIONS AND REPOSE

As discussed in Chapter 1, *statutes of limitations* restrict the time within which an action may be brought. A typical statute of limitations provides that

---

16. *Jamieson v. Woodward & Lothrop,* 247 F.2d 23 (D.C. 1957).

an action must be brought within a specified period of time after the cause of action accrues. Generally, a cause of action is held to accrue when some damage occurs. Sometimes, the running of the prescribed period is *tolled* (that is, suspended) until the party suffering an injury has discovered it or should have discovered it.

Many states have passed laws placing outer time limits on some claims so that the defendant will not be left vulnerable to lawsuits indefinitely. These **statutes of repose** may limit the time within which a plaintiff can file a product-liability suit. Typically, a statute of repose begins to run at an earlier date and runs for a longer time than a statute of limitations. For example, a statute of repose may require that claims must be brought within twelve years from the date of sale or manufacture of the defective product. It is immaterial that the product is defective or causes an injury if the injury occurs after this statutory period has lapsed. In addition, some of these legislative enactments have limited the application of the doctrine of strict liability to new goods.

TERMS AND CONCEPTS TO REVIEW

bystander 281	product liability 281	unreasonably dangerous product 284
market-share liability 284	product misuse 290	
privity of contract 281	statute of repose 291	

QUESTIONS AND CASE PROBLEMS

13–1. THEORIES OF LIABILITY.   Chen buys a television set manufactured by Quality TV Appliance, Inc. She is going on vacation, so she takes the set to her mother's house for her mother to use. Because the set is defective, it explodes, causing her mother to be seriously injured. Chen's mother sues Quality to obtain compensation for her injury and for the damage to her house. Under what theory or theories discussed in this chapter might Chen's mother recover damages from Quality?

13–2. DEFENSES TO PRODUCT LIABILITY.   A water pipe burst, flooding a company's switchboard and tripping the switchboard circuit breakers. Company employees assigned to reactivate the switchboard included an electrical technician with twelve years of on-the-job training, a licensed electrician, and an electrical engi-

neer with twenty years of experience who had studied power engineering in college. The employees attempted to switch one of the circuit breakers back on without testing for short circuits, which they later admitted they knew how to do and should have done. The circuit breaker failed to engage but ignited an explosive fire. The company sued the supplier of the circuit breakers for damages, alleging that the supplier had failed to give adequate warnings and instructions regarding the circuit breakers. How might the supplier defend against this claim? Discuss.

13–3. LIABILITY IN TORT.   Colt manufactures a new pistol. The firing of the pistol depends on an enclosed high-pressure device. The pistol has been thoroughly tested in two laboratories in the Midwest, and its design and manufacture are in accord with current technology. Wayne purchases one of the new pistols from Hardy's Gun and Rifle Emporium. When he uses the pistol in the high altitude of the Rockies, the difference in pressure causes the pistol to misfire, resulting in serious injury to Wayne. Colt can prove that all due care was used in the manufacturing process, and it refuses to pay for Wayne's injuries. Discuss Colt's liability in tort.

13–4. LIABILITY TO THIRD PARTIES. Baxter manufactures electric hair dryers. Julie purchases a Baxter dryer from her local Ace Drugstore. Cox, a friend and guest in Julie's home, has taken a shower and wants to dry her hair. Julie tells Cox to use the new Baxter hair dryer that she has just purchased. As Cox plugs in the dryer, sparks fly out from the motor, and sparks continue to fly as she operates it. Despite this, Cox begins drying her hair. Suddenly, the entire dryer ignites into flames, severely burning Cox's scalp. Cox sues Baxter on the basis of negligence and strict liability in tort. Baxter admits the dryer was defective but denies liability, particularly because Cox was not the person who purchased the dryer. In other words, Cox had no contractual relationship with Baxter. Discuss the validity of Baxter's defense. Are there any other defenses that Baxter might assert to avoid liability? Discuss fully.

13–5. NEGLIGENCE. A two-year-old child lost his leg when he became entangled in a grain auger on his grandfather's farm. The auger had a safety guard that prevented any item larger than 4⅝ inches from coming into contact with the machine's moving parts. The child's foot was smaller than the openings in the safety guard. Was such an injury reasonably foreseeable? Discuss. [*Richelman v. Kewanee Machinery & Conveyor Co.*, 59 Ill.App.3d 578, 375 N.E.2d 885, 16 Ill.Dec. 778 (1978)]

13–6. DEFENSES TO PRODUCT LIABILITY. The Campbell Soup Co. manufactured, sold, and shipped packages of chicken-flavored Campbell's Ramen Noodle Soup to a distributor. The distributor sold and shipped the packages to Associated Grocers. Associated Grocers shipped the packages to Warehouse Foods, a retail grocer. Six weeks after Campbell first shipped the soup to the distributor, Warehouse Foods sold a package of the soup to Kathy Jo Gates. Gates prepared the soup. Halfway through eating her second bowl, she discovered beetle larvae in the noodles. She filed a product-liability suit against Campbell and others. Gates argued, in effect, that the mere presence of the bugs in the soup was sufficient to hold Campbell strictly liable. How might Campbell defend itself? [*Campbell Soup Co. v. Gates*, 319 Ark. 54, 889 S.W.2d 750 (1994)]

13–7. FAILURE TO WARN. When Mary Bresnahan drove her Chrysler LeBaron, she sat very close to the steering wheel—less than a foot away from the steering-wheel enclosure of the driver's-side air bag. At the time, Chrysler did not provide any warning that a driver should not sit close to the air bag. In an accident with another car, Bresnahan's air bag deployed. The bag caused her elbow to strike the windshield pillar and fracture in three places, resulting in repeated surgery and

physical therapy. Bresnahan filed a suit in a California state court against Chrysler to recover for her injuries, alleging in part that they were caused by Chrysler's failure to warn consumers about sitting near the air bag. At the trial, an expert testified that the air bag was not intended to prevent arm injuries, which were "a predictable, incidental consequence" of the bag's deploying. Should Chrysler pay for Bresnahan's injuries? Why or why not? [*Bresnahan v. Chrysler Corp.*, 76 Cal.Rptr.2d 804, 65 Cal.App.4th 1149 (1998)]

13–8. PRODUCT LIABILITY. New England Ecological Development, Inc. (NEED), a recycling station in Rhode Island, needed a conveyor belt system and gave the specifications to Colmar Belting Co. Colmar did not design or make belts but distributed the component parts. For this system, Emerson Power Transmission Corp. (EPT) manufactured the wing pulley, a component of the nip point (the point at which a belt moves over the stationary part of the system). Kenneth Butler, a welder, assembled the system with assistance from Colmar. Neither Colmar nor EPT recommended the use of a protective shield to guard the nip point, and as finally built, NEED's system did not have a shield. Later, as Americo Buonanno, a NEED employee, was clearing debris from the belt, his arm was pulled into the nip point. The arm was severely crushed and later amputated at the elbow. Buonanno filed a suit in a Rhode Island state court against Colmar and EPT, alleging in part strict liability. The defendants filed a motion for summary judgment, arguing that as sellers of component parts, they had no duty to ensure the proper design of the final product. On what grounds might the court deny the motion? [*Buonanno v. Colmar Belting Co.*, 733 A.2d 712 (R.I. 1999)]

13–9. IN YOUR COURT

Judy Dunne weighed more than 450 pounds. For a birthday present, her children bought her an exercise bike from Wal-Mart Stores, Inc. When Dunne received the bike, she rode it for only a moment. Later, she mounted the bike for a second time and pedaled for three or four rotations. The bike then collapsed, and Dunne fell off, sustaining numerous injuries. The bike was designed for use by people who weigh under 250 pounds (which is 99 percent of the population) and had been tested up to 440 pounds. The manufacturer did not specify any weight limit in marketing the bike, however, and there was no way that Dunne could have known of this weight limit. Assume that you are the judge in this case and answer the following questions:

(a) Was it reasonably foreseeable that a person who weighed over 450 pounds would use the exercise bike?

(b) Why is the question of foreseeability relevant to this case?

(c) Was the bike "unreasonably dangerous" because an adequate warning was not provided?

(d) Suppose that Wal-Mart argues that the risk of the bike collapsing under a weight of more than 450 pounds was "open and obvious." Would you allow Wal-Mart to avoid liability based on this defense?

13–10. A Question of Ethics

William Mackowick, who had worked as an electrician for thirty years, was installing high-voltage capacitors in a switchgear room in a hospital when he noticed that a fellow electrician had removed the cover from an existing capacitor manufactured by Westinghouse Electric Corp. Westinghouse had placed a warning label inside the cover of the metal box containing the capacitor on which users were instructed to ground the electricity before handling. Nothing was said on the label about the propensity of electricity to "arc." (Arcing occurs when electricity grounds itself by "jumping" to a nearby object or instrument.) Mackowick walked over to warn the other electricians opf the danger associated with the exposed capacitor, and, while talking, pointed his screwdriver toward the capacitor box. The electricity flowing through the fuses arced to the screwdriver and sent a high-voltage electric current through Mackowick's body. As a result, he sustained severe burns and was unable to return to work for three months. Discuss. [*Mackowick v. Westinghouse Electric Corp.*, 575 A.2d 100 (Pa. 1990)]

(a) An appellate court held that even though the manufacturer did not include with its capacitor a warning about arcing, the product was not defective for failure to warn of inherent product dangers. The rationale of the court was that the product would only be used by experienced electricians who would be aware of the dangers of arcing. Was this a reasonable assumption?

(b) Is it ethical for a company not to include such a warning if it is even remotely possible that an inexperienced user of the product would not understand its inherent dangers?

LAW ON THE WEB

For updated links to resources available on the Web, as well as a variety of other materials, visit this text's Web site at http://wleb.westbuslaw.com.

For information on the *Restatements of the Law*, including the *Restatement (Second) of Torts* and the *Restatement (Third) of Torts: Products Liability*, go to the Web site of the American Law Institute at

http://www.ali.org

The law firm of Horvitz & Levy offers a review of recent judicial decisions in the area of product liability at

http://www.horvitzlevy.com/yirtoc4b.html

For information on product-liability suits against tobacco companies and recent settlements, go to

http://www.usatoday.com/news/smoke/smoke00.htm

A discussion of the "demise of privity" with respect to product liability in leading cases decided by the New York Court of Appeals can be found at the following Web page within the site offered by the *New York Law Journal*:

http://www.nylj.com/links/150sterk.html

Law Journal EXTRA! has articles on current cases and issues in the area of product liability, as well as proposed legislation, at

www.ljx.com/practice/productliability/index.html

LEGAL RESEARCH EXERCISES ON THE WEB

Go to http://wleb.westbuslaw.com, the Web site that accompanies this text. Select "Internet Applications," and then click on "Chapter 13." There you will find the following Internet research exercise that you can perform to learn more about product-liability litigation.

Activity 13–1: Product-Liability Litigation

CHAPTER 14

Intellectual Property

MOST PEOPLE THINK OF WEALTH in terms of houses, land, cars, stocks, and bonds. Wealth, however, also includes **intellectual property,** which consists of the products that result from intellectual, creative processes. Although it is an abstract term for an abstract concept, intellectual property is nonetheless wholly familiar to virtually everyone. *Trademarks, service marks, copyrights,* and *patents* are all forms of intellectual property. The book you are reading is copyrighted. Undoubtedly, the personal computer you use at home is trademarked. Exhibit 14–1 offers a comprehensive summary of these forms of intellectual property, as well as intellectual property that consists of *trade secrets.* In this chapter, we examine each of these forms in some detail.

The study of intellectual property law is important because intellectual property has taken on increasing significance, not only within the United States but globally as well. Today, ownership rights in intangible intellectual property are more important to the prosperity of many U.S. companies than are their tangible assets. A major challenge to businesspersons today is how to protect these valuable rights in the online world—a topic we treat at some length in Chapter 15. (See also the *Emerging Trends in Technology* feature later in this chapter, which discusses the problem of copyright protection in a digital age.)

The need to protect creative works was voiced by the framers of the U.S. Constitution over two hundred years ago: Article I, Section 8, of the U.S. Constitution authorized Congress "[t]o promote the Progress of Science and useful Arts, by securing for limited Times to Authors and Inventors the exclusive Right to their respective Writings and Discoveries." Laws protecting patents, trademarks, and copyrights are explicitly designed to protect and reward inventive and artistic creativity. Although intellectual property law limits the economic freedom of some individuals, it does so to protect the freedom of others to enjoy the fruits of their labors—in the form of profits.

SECTION 1

Trademarks and Related Property

A **trademark** is a distinctive mark, motto, device, or implement that a manufacturer stamps, prints, or otherwise affixes to the goods it produces so that they may be identified on the market and their origin vouched for. At common law, the person who used a symbol or mark to identify a business or product was protected in the use of that trademark. Clearly, if one used the trademark of another, it would lead consumers to believe that one's goods were made by the

EXHIBIT 14–1   FORMS OF INTELLECTUAL PROPERTY

	PATENT	COPYRIGHT	TRADEMARKS (SERVICE MARKS AND TRADE DRESS)	TRADE SECRETS
Definition	A grant from the government that gives an inventor exclusive rights to an invention.	An intangible property right granted to authors and originators of a literary work or artistic production that falls within specified categories.	Any distinctive word, name, symbol, or device (image or appearance), or combination thereof, that an entity uses to identify and distinguish its goods or services from those of others.	Any information (including formulas, patterns, programs, devices, techniques, and processes) that a business possesses and that gives the business an advantage over competitors who do not know the information or processes.
Requirements	An invention must be: 1. Novel. 2. Not obvious. 3. Useful.	Literary or artistic works must be: 1. Original. 2. Fixed in a durable medium that can be perceived, reproduced, or communicated. 3. Within a copyrightable category.	Trademarks, service marks, and trade dresses must be sufficiently distinctive (or must have acquired a secondary meaning) to enable consumers and others to distinguish the manufacturer's, seller's, or business user's products or services from those of competitors.	Information and processes that have commercial value, that are not known or easily ascertainable by the general public or others, and that are reasonably protected from disclosure.
Types or Categories	1. Utility (general). 2. Design. 3. Plant (flowers, vegetables, and so on).	1. Literary works (including computer programs). 2. Musical works. 3. Dramatic works. 4. Pantomime and choreographic works. 5. Pictorial, graphic, and sculptural works. 6. Films and audiovisual works. 7. Sound recordings.	1. Strong, distinctive marks (such as fanciful, arbitrary, or suggestive marks). 2. Marks that have acquired a secondary meaning by use. 3. Other types of marks, including certification marks and collective marks. 4. Trade dress (such as a distinctive decor, menu, or style or type of service).	1. Customer lists. 2. Research and development. 3. Plans and programs. 4. Pricing information. 5. Production techniques. 6. Marketing techniques. 7. Formulas. 8. Compilations.
How Acquired	By filing a patent application with the U.S. Patent and Trademark Office and receiving that	Automatic (once in tangible form); to recover for infringement, the copyright must be	1. At common law, ownership is created by use of mark. 2. Registration (either with the U.S. Patent and Trademark Office or with the	Through the originality and development of information and processes that are

EXHIBIT 14–1   FORMS OF INTELLECTUAL PROPERTY (CONTINUED)

	PATENT	COPYRIGHT	TRADEMARKS (SERVICE MARKS AND TRADE DRESS)	TRADE SECRETS
How Acquired (continued)	office's approval.	registered with the U.S. Copyright Office.	appropriate state office) gives constructive notice of date of use. 3. Federal registration is permitted if the mark is currently in use *or* if the applicant intends use within six months (period can be extended to three years). 4. Federal registration can be renewed between the fifth and sixth years and, thereafter, every ten years.	unique to a business, that are unknown by others, and that would be valuable to competitors if they knew of the information and processes.
Rights	An inventor has the right to make, use, sell, assign, or license the invention during the duration of the patent's term. The first to invent has patent rights.	The author or originator has the exclusive right to reproduce, distribute, display, license, or transfer a copyrighted work.	The owner has the right to use the mark or trade dress and to exclude others from using it. The right of use can be licensed or sold (assigned) to another.	The owner has the right to sole and exclusive use of the trade secrets and the right to use legal means to protect against misappropriation of the trade secrets by others. The owner can license or assign a trade secret.
Duration	Twenty years from the date of application; for design patents, fourteen years.	1. For authors: the life of the author, plus 70 years. 2. For publishers: 95 years after the date of publication or 120 years after creation.	Unlimited, as long as it is in use. To continue notice by registration, the registration must be renewed by filing.	Unlimited, as long as not revealed to others.
Civil Remedies for Infringement	Monetary damages, which include reasonable royalties and lost profits, *plus* attorneys' fees. (Treble damages are available for intentional infringement.)	Actual damages, plus profits received by the infringer; *or* statutory damages of not less than $500 and not more than $20,000 ($100,000, if infringement is willful); *plus* costs and attorneys' fees.	1. Injunction prohibiting future use of mark. 2. Actual damages, plus profits received by the infringer (can be increased to three times the actual damages under the Lanham Act). 3. Impoundment and destruction of infringing articles. 4. *Plus* costs and attorneys' fees.	Monetary damages for misappropriation (the Uniform Trade Secrets Act permits punitive damages up to twice the amount of actual damages for willful and malicious misappropriation); *plus* costs and attorneys' fees.

other. The law seeks to avoid this kind of confusion. We examine in this section various aspects of the law governing trademarks.

In the following famous case concerning Coca-Cola, the defendants argued that the Coca-Cola trademark was entitled to no protection under the law, because the term did not accurately represent the product.

CASE 14.1   The Coca-Cola Co. v. The Koke Co. of America

Supreme Court of the United States, 1920.
254 U.S. 143,
41 S.Ct. 113,
65 L.Ed. 189.
http://www.findlaw.com/
casecode/supreme.
html[a]

COMPANY PROFILE *John Pemberton, an Atlanta pharmacist, invented a caramel-colored, carbonated soft drink in 1886. His bookkeeper, Frank Robinson, named the beverage Coca-Cola after two of the ingredients, coca leaves and kola nuts. Asa Candler bought the Coca-Cola Company (http://www.cocacolacompany.com) in 1891, and within seven years, he made the soft drink available in all of the United States, as well as in parts of Canada and Mexico. Candler continued to sell Coke aggressively and to open up new markets, reaching Europe before 1910. In doing so, however, he attracted numerous competitors, some of whom tried to capitalize directly on the Coke name.*

BACKGROUND AND FACTS *The Coca-Cola Company sought to enjoin (prevent) the Koke Company of America and other beverage companies from, among other things, using the word Koke for their products. The Koke Company of America and other beverage companies contended that the Coca-Cola trademark was a fraudulent representation and that Coca-Cola was therefore not entitled to any help from the courts. The Koke Company and the other defendants alleged that the Coca-Cola Company, by its use of the Coca-Cola name, represented that the beverage contained cocaine (from coca leaves), which it no longer did. The trial court granted the injunction against the Koke Company, but the appellate court reversed the lower court's ruling. Coca-Cola then appealed to the United States Supreme Court.*

IN THE LANGUAGE OF THE COURT

Mr. Justice *HOLMES* delivered the opinion of the Court.

    *   *   *   *

    *   *   * Before 1900 the beginning of [Coca-Cola's] good will was more or less helped by the presence of cocaine, a drug that, like alcohol or caffeine or opium, may be described as a deadly poison or as a valuable item of the pharmacopoeia according to the rhetorical purposes in view. The amount seems to have been very small,[b] but it may have been enough to begin a bad habit and after the Food and Drug Act of June 30, 1906, if not earlier, long before this suit was brought, it was eliminated from the plaintiff's compound. *   *   *

    *   *   * Since 1900 the sales have increased at a very great rate corresponding to a like increase in advertising. The name now characterizes a beverage to be had at almost any soda fountain. It means a single thing coming from a single source, and well known to the community. It hardly would be too much to say that the drink characterizes the name as much as the name the drink. In other words Coca-Cola probably means to most persons the plaintiff's familiar product to be had everywhere rather than a compound of particular substances. *   *   * [B]efore this suit was brought the plaintiff had advertised to the public that it must not expect and would not find cocaine, and had eliminated everything tending to suggest cocaine effects except the name and the picture of [coca] leaves and nuts, which probably conveyed little or nothing to most who saw it. It appears to us that it would be going too far to deny the plaintiff relief against a palpable fraud

---

a. In the "Citation Search" section, enter "254" in the left box and "143" in the right box, and click "Get It" to access the opinion.

b. In reality, until 1903 the amount of active cocaine in each bottle of Coke was equivalent to one "line" of cocaine.

because possibly here and there an ignorant person might call for the drink with the hope for incipient cocaine intoxication. The plaintiff's position must be judged by the facts as they were when the suit was begun, not by the facts of a different condition and an earlier time.

DECISION AND REMEDY   *The district court's injunction was allowed to stand. The competing beverage companies were enjoined from calling their products* Koke.

STATUTORY PROTECTION OF TRADEMARKS

Statutory protection of trademarks and related property is provided at the federal level by the Lanham Trade-Mark Act of 1946.[1] The Lanham Act was enacted in part to protect manufacturers from losing business to rival companies that used confusingly similar trademarks. The Lanham Act incorporates the common law of trademarks and provides remedies for owners of trademarks who wish to enforce their claims in federal court. Many states also have trademark statutes.

In 1995, Congress amended the Lanham Act by passing the Federal Trademark Dilution Act,[2] which extended the protection available to trademark owners by creating a federal cause of action for trademark **dilution.** Until the passage of this amendment, federal trademark law only prohibited the unauthorized use of the same mark on competing—or on noncompeting but "related"—goods or services when such use would likely confuse consumers as to the origin of those goods and services. Trademark dilution laws, which have also been enacted by about half of the states, protect "distinctive" or "famous" trademarks (such as Jergens, McDonald's, RCA, and Macintosh) from certain unauthorized uses of the marks *regardless* of a showing of competition or a likelihood of confusion.

In one of the first cases to be decided under the 1995 act's provisions, a federal court held that a famous mark may be diluted not only by the use of an *identical* mark but also by the use of a *similar* mark. The lawsuit was brought by Ringling Bros.–Barnum & Bailey, Combined Shows, Inc., against the state of Utah. Ringling Bros. claimed that Utah's use of the slogan "The Greatest Snow on Earth"—to attract visitors to the state's recreational and scenic resorts—diluted the dis-

tinctiveness of the circus's famous trademark, "The Greatest Show on Earth." Utah moved to dismiss the suit, arguing that the 1995 provisions only protect owners of famous trademarks against the unauthorized use of identical marks. The court disagreed and refused to grant Utah's motion to dismiss the case.[3]

TRADEMARK REGISTRATION

Trademarks may be registered with the state or with the federal government. To register for protection under federal trademark law, a person must file an application with the U.S. Patent and Trademark Office in Washington, D.C. Under current law, a mark can be registered (1) if it is currently in commerce or (2) if the applicant intends to put it into commerce within six months.

Under extenuating circumstances, the six-month period can be extended by thirty months, giving the applicant a total of three years from the date of notice of trademark approval to make use of the mark and file the required use statement. Registration is postponed until the mark is actually used. Nonetheless, during this waiting period, any applicant can legally protect his or her trademark against a third party who previously has neither used the mark nor filed an application for it. Registration is renewable between the fifth and sixth years after the initial registration and every ten years thereafter (every twenty years for those trademarks registered before 1990).

Registration of a trademark with the U.S. Patent and Trademark Office gives notice on a nationwide basis that the trademark belongs exclusively to the registrant. The registrant is also allowed to use the symbol ® to indicate that the mark has been registered. Whenever that trademark is copied to a substantial degree or used in its entirety by another, intentionally or

---

1. 15 U.S.C. Sections 1051–1127.
2. 15 U.S.C. Section 1125.

3. *Ringling Bros.–Barnum & Bailey, Combined Shows, Inc. v. Utah Division of Travel Development,* 935 F.Supp. 736 (E.D.Va. 1996).

unintentionally, the trademark has been *infringed* (used without authorization). When a trademark has been infringed, the owner of the mark has a cause of action against the infringer. A person need not have registered a trademark in order to sue for trademark infringement, but registration does furnish proof of the date of inception of the trademark's use.

DISTINCTIVENESS OF MARK

A central objective of the Lanham Act is to reduce the likelihood that consumers will be confused by similar marks. For that reason, only those trademarks that are deemed sufficiently distinctive from all competing trademarks will be protected. A trademark must be sufficiently distinct to enable consumers to identify the manufacturer of the goods easily and to distinguish between those goods and competing products.

Strong Marks. Fanciful, arbitrary, or suggestive trademarks are generally considered to be the most distinctive (strongest) trademarks. This is because these types of marks are normally taken from outside the context of the particular product and thus provide the best means of distinguishing one product from another.

Fanciful trademarks include invented words, such as Xerox for one manufacturer's copiers and Kodak for another company's photographic products. Arbitrary trademarks include actual words used with products that have no literal connection to the words, such as English Leather used as a name for an after-shave lotion (and not for leather processed in England). Suggestive trademarks are those that suggest something about a product without describing the product directly. For example, the trademark Dairy Queen

suggests an association between the products and milk, but it does not directly describe ice cream.

Secondary Meaning. Descriptive terms, geographic terms, and personal names are not inherently distinctive and do not receive protection under the law until they acquire a secondary meaning. A secondary meaning may arise when customers begin to associate a specific term or phrase (such as London Fog) with specific trademarked items (coats with London Fog labels). Whether a secondary meaning becomes attached to a term or name usually depends on how extensively the product is advertised, the market for the product, the number of sales, and other factors. Once a secondary meaning is attached to a term or name, a trademark is considered distinctive and is protected. Even a shade of color can qualify for trademark protection, once customers associate the color with the product.[4]

Generic Terms. Generic terms, such as *bicycle* and *computer*, receive no protection, even if they acquire secondary meanings. A particularly thorny problem arises when a trademark acquires generic use. For example, *aspirin* and *thermos* were originally the names of trademarked products, but today the words are used generically. Other examples are *escalator, trampoline, raisin bran, dry ice, lanolin, linoleum, nylon,* and *corn flakes.* Even so, the courts will not allow another firm to use those marks in such a way as to deceive a potential consumer. In the following case, the issue before the court was whether the phrase "You Have Mail" is a generic term.

---

4. *Qualitex Co. v. Jacobson Products Co.,* 514 U.S. 159, 115 S.Ct. 1300, 131 L.Ed.2d 248 (1995).

CASE 14.2   America Online, Inc. v. AT&T Corp.

United States
District Court,
Eastern District of
Virginia, 1999.
64 F.Supp.2d 549.
**http://zeus.bna.com/
e-law/cases/aolatt.html**[a]

BACKGROUND AND FACTS   *In the late 1960s and early 1970s, AT&T Corporation developed UNIX, a computer operating system facilitating communications over the Internet. When a user connects to UNIX, if the user has e-mail, the system displays a phrase something like "You Have Mail." In the 1980s, America Online, Inc. (AOL), the world's largest Internet service provider, started using "YOU HAVE MAIL" in its e-mail notification service for its members. AT&T provides Internet access to subscribers through its WorldNet Service. Since 1998, when a member visits the WorldNet home page, a "You Have Mail!" notification window pops up. AOL filed a suit in a federal district court against*

---

a. This is a page in the library of documents at the "Electronic Commerce & Law Report" Web site maintained by the Bureau of National Affairs, Inc.

AT&T, alleging in part trademark infringement of the phrase "YOU HAVE MAIL," which AOL claimed to own. AT&T filed a motion for summary judgment, asking the court to rule that the term was generic.

IN THE LANGUAGE OF THE COURT

HILTON, J. [Judge]

*   *   *   *

*   *   * [A] plaintiff who is seeking to establish a valid trademark must show that the primary significance of the term in the minds of the consuming public is not the product but the producer. *   *   * [T]he following evidence [may] be used to determine the primary significance of a mark: (1) competitors' use of the mark, (2) plaintiff's use of the mark, (3) dictionary definitions, (4) media usage, (5) testimony of persons in the trade, and (6) consumer surveys.

*   *   *   *

*   *   * Under the primary significance test, the "mail" component of YOU HAVE MAIL means "e-mail."

First, the Court notes that even AOL uses the words "mail" and "e-mail" interchangeably. For example, in its *   *   * complaint AOL repeatedly uses the word "mail" as referring to "e-mail." *   *   *

Next, it is undisputed that numerous competitors of AOL use "mail" as a synonym for "e-mail." *   *   *

Regarding media usage and testimony of persons involved in the trade, [there are] numerous examples of the books printed to describe the e-mail notification features used by both UNIX and AOL. All of the authors, without fail, use "mail" and "e-mail" interchangeably. *   *   *

Last, the Court would note that *   *   * consumer surveys [are used] as a means of determining whether the primary significance of a mark is generic. However, when determining whether a mark is generic, the Court is not to consider whether the mark has acquired any secondary meaning, because generic marks with secondary meaning are still not entitled to protection. *   *   *

*   *   *   *

The primary significance of the phrase YOU HAVE MAIL indicates to the public-at-large what the service is, not where it came from. *   *   * Further, this holding does not rest on considering solely the "mail" component of the phrase YOU HAVE MAIL. *   *   * The "you" and the "have" of YOU HAVE MAIL (either separately or together) do not carry with them any especial significance which would change the primary significance of the mark as previously stated. Since the "you," "have," and "mail" of YOU HAVE MAIL are all used for their everyday, common meaning, the phrase as a whole is generic *   *   * .

DECISION AND REMEDY

The court granted a summary judgment in favor of AT&T. The court ruled that "You have mail" is a generic expression and therefore cannot be owned by AOL.

TRADE DRESS

The term **trade dress** refers to the image and overall appearance of a product—for example, the distinctive decor, menu, layout, and style of service of a particular restaurant. Basically, trade dress is subject to the same protection as trademarks. In cases involving trade dress infringement, as in trademark infringement cases, a major consideration is whether consumers are likely to be confused by the allegedly infringing use.

SERVICE, CERTIFICATION, AND COLLECTIVE MARKS

A **service mark** is similar to a trademark but is used to distinguish the services of one person or company from those of another. For example, each airline has a particular mark or symbol associated with its name. Titles and character names used in radio and television are frequently registered as service marks.

Other marks protected by law include certification marks and collective marks. A **certification mark** is used by one or more persons other than the owner to certify the region, materials, mode of manufacture, quality, or accuracy of the owner's goods or services. When used by members of a cooperative, association, or other organization, it is referred to as a **collective mark**. Examples of certification marks are the phrases "Good Housekeeping Seal of Approval" and "UL Tested." Collective marks appear at the ends of motion picture credits to indicate the various associations and organizations that participated in the making of the film. The union marks found on the tags of certain products are also collective marks.

TRADE NAMES

Trademarks apply to *products*. The term **trade name** is used to indicate part or all of a business's name, whether the business is a sole proprietorship, a partnership, or a corporation. Generally, a trade name is directly related to a business and its goodwill. A trade name may be protected as a trademark if the trade name is the same as the name of the company's trademarked product—for example, Coca-Cola. Unless also used as a trademark or service mark, a trade name cannot be registered with the federal government. Trade names are protected under the common law, however. As with trademarks, words must be unusual or fancifully used if they are to be protected as trade names. The word *Safeway*, for example, was held by the courts to be sufficiently fanciful to obtain protection as a trade name for a foodstore chain.[5]

SECTION 2

Patents

A **patent** is a grant from the government that gives an inventor the exclusive right to make, use, and sell an invention for a period of twenty years from the date of filing the application for a patent. Patents for a fourteen-year period are given for designs, as opposed to inventions. For either a regular patent or a design patent, the applicant must demonstrate to the satisfaction of the U.S. Patent and Trademark Office that the invention, discovery, process, or design is genuine, novel, useful, and not obvious in light of current technology. A patent holder gives notice to all that an article or design is patented by placing on it the word *Patent* or *Pat.* plus the patent number. In contrast to patent law in other countries, in the United States patent protection is given to the first person to invent a product or process, even though someone else may have been the first to file for a patent on that product or process.

PATENT INFRINGEMENT

If a firm makes, uses, or sells another's patented design, product, or process without the patent owner's permission, the tort of patent infringement occurs. Patent infringement may arise even though the patent owner has not put the patented product in commerce. Patent infringement may also occur even though not all features or parts of an invention are copied. (With respect to a patented process, however, all steps or their equivalents must be copied in order for infringement to occur.)

Often, litigation for patent infringement is so costly that the patent holder will instead offer to sell to the infringer a license to use the patented design, product, or process (licensing will be discussed in Chapter 15). Indeed, in many cases, the costs of detection, prosecution, and monitoring are so high that patents are valueless to their owners, because the owners cannot afford to protect them.

In the past, parties involved in patent litigation also faced another problem: it was often hard to predict the outcome of litigation because jurors found it difficult to understand the issues in dispute. This was particularly true when the claims involved patents on complicated products—such as sophisticated technological or biotechnological products. In a significant case decided in 1996, *Markman v. Westview Instruments, Inc.*,[6] the United States Supreme Court held that it is the responsibility of judges, not juries, to interpret the scope and nature of patent claims. In other words, before a case goes to the jury, the judge must interpret the nature of the claim and give the jury instructions based on that interpretation.

---

5. *Safeway Stores v. Suburban Foods*, 130 F.Supp. 249 (E.D.Va. 1955).

6. 517 U.S. 370, 116 S.Ct. 1384, 134 L.Ed.2d 577 (1996).

EMERGING TRENDS IN TECHNOLOGY

Copyright Protection in a Digital Age

Most intellectual property does not sell for the cost of production plus a normal profit. Rather, intellectual property is sold at a price that reflects heavy research costs for ingenious ideas. Any property that involves high development costs and low production costs is vulnerable to "piracy"—the unauthorized copying and use of the property.

In the past, copying intellectual products was time consuming, and the pirated copies were worse than the originals. In today's online world, however, things have changed. Millions of unauthorized copies can now be reproduced simply by clicking a mouse, and pirated duplicates of copyrighted works obtained via the Internet are exactly the same as the originals—after all, they are digitized.

HOW BIG IS THE PROBLEM?

The Business Software Alliance estimates that half of the global market for software is supplied today by pirated products. The International Federation of the phonographic industry believes that 20 percent of recorded music is pirated. Much of the piracy of intellectual property, especially software and music, is deemed "altruistic." People illegally give intellectual property away not to make any money but because they want to be generous. There is also a problem with respect to copyright law, which makes a distinction between reproduction for public use (which requires the copyright holder's permission) and reproduction for private use (which, within limits, does not require such permission). The difficulty here is distinguishing between private and public use.

Additionally, current copyright law is based on national boundaries. The Internet, however, knows no such limits. Despite attempts to increase protection for intellectual property on a global level (see Chapter 15), countries vary widely in their implementation and enforcement of international agreements.

IS THERE ANY SOLUTION TO THE PROBLEM?

Is there any current solution to the increasing problem of the piracy of intellectual property via the Internet? The simple answer is no. Efforts to find partial solutions are being made, nonetheless. One such attempt is to develop pirate-proof ways of transmitting materials. For example, IBM has developed so-called secure "packaging" for sending digital information over the Internet.

New technologies are also simplifying the task of searching online databases for pirated copies of copyrighted materials. Providers of online "business intelligence," such as Cyveillance, Ewatch, and Cybercheck, help companies detect and combat infringing uses of their software, text, music, or other copyrighted works. These "digital detectives" use special search tools, called "spiders" or "robots," to monitor the Web for sites containing copyrighted works, such as music files.

Once an infringing use is detected, the copyright owner has several options. The owner can send a cease-and-desist (warning) letter to the infringer, take the infringer to court, or issue a license to the infringer. Often, the last option is preferred, simply because the other two may be impractical. For one thing, efforts to shut down infringing Web sites have had limited success. In part, this is because of the ease with which a "mirror" site can be created—at a

PATENTS FOR SOFTWARE

At one time, it was difficult for developers and manufacturers of software to obtain patent protection because many software products simply automate procedures that can be performed manually. In other words, the computer programs do not meet the "novel" and "not obvious" requirements previously mentioned. Also, the basis for software is often a mathematical equation or formula, which is not patentable. In 1981, however, the United States Supreme Court held that it is possible to obtain a patent for a process that incorporates a computer program—providing, of course, that the process itself is

EMERGING TRENDS IN TECHNOLOGY

Copyright Protection in a Digital Age,

continued

new location. Initiating a lawsuit against a Web site or user may also be difficult because of jurisdictional problems (see Chapter 15).

GOVERNMENT EFFORTS TO PROTECT COPYRIGHT HOLDERS

The government has also taken action to protect copyright holders. In 1997, Congress passed the No Electronic Theft (NET) Act, which extended criminal liability for the piracy of copyrighted materials to a broader group. Prior to the act, criminal penalties could be imposed only if unauthorized copies were exchanged for financial gain. To combat "altruistic" piracy, the NET imposes criminal penalties on persons who exchange unauthorized copies of copyrighted works, such as software, even though they realize no profit from the exchange. The act also imposes penalties on

those who make unauthorized electronic copies of books, magazines, movies, or music for *personal* use, thus altering the traditional "fair use" doctrine. The criminal penalties for violating the act are steep; they include fines as high as $250,000 and incarceration for up to five years.

More recently, in 1998, Congress passed the Digital Millennium Copyright Act, which allows civil and criminal penalties to be imposed on persons who circumvent encryption software or other technological antipiracy protection. Global efforts are also under way to protect intellectual property, including copyrights. Some of these efforts are mentioned elsewhere in this chapter. (See also Chapter 9, which treats this topic in greater detail.)

IMPLICATIONS FOR THE BUSINESSPERSON

1. Anybody who has ownership rights in intellectual property should be aware that it is increasingly possible for the property to be pirated via the Internet.
2. Businesspersons must weigh potential benefits against potential costs when deciding how many resources can be devoted to

combating the online piracy of their copyrighted works.

FOR CRITICAL ANALYSIS

1. Can the distribution of copyrighted materials via the Internet ever be effectively regulated by copyright laws? Should it?
2. What argument would you present to convince somebody that stealing intellectual property is no different from stealing tangible property?

RELEVANT WEB SITES

For information on the types of services offered by Cyveillance, go to the company's Web site at http://www.cyveillance.com. For articles containing recent facts and figures on software piracy, as well as a summary of applicable U.S. laws (including the No Electronic Theft Act), go to http://www.nopiracy.com.

---

patentable.[7] Subsequently, many patents have been issued for software-related inventions.

Another obstacle to obtaining patent protection for software is the procedure for obtaining patents. The process can be expensive and slow. The time element

is a particularly important consideration for someone wishing to obtain a patent on software. In light of the rapid changes and improvements in computer technology, the delay could undercut the product's success in the marketplace.

Despite these difficulties, patent protection is used in the computer industry. If a patent is infringed, the patent holder may sue for an injunction, damages,

---

7. *Diamond v. Diehr*, 450 U.S. 175, 101 S.Ct. 1048, 67 L.Ed.2d 155 (1981).

and the destruction of all infringing copies, as well as attorneys' fees and court costs.

SECTION 3

Copyrights

A **copyright** is an intangible property right granted by federal statute to the author or originator of a literary or artistic production of a specified type. Currently, copyrights are governed by the Copyright Act of 1976,[8] as amended. Works created after January 1, 1978, are automatically given statutory copyright protection for the life of the author plus 70 years. For copyrights owned by publishing houses, the copyright expires 95 years from the date of publication or 120 years from the date of creation, whichever is first. For works by more than one author, the copyright expires 70 years after the death of the last surviving author.

Copyrights can be registered with the U.S. Copyright Office in Washington, D.C. A copyright owner no longer needs to place the symbol © or the term *Copr.* or *Copyright* on the work, however, to have the work protected against infringement. Chances are that if somebody created it, somebody owns it.

A major problem facing today's businesspersons is how to protect copyrighted materials, including software, in cyberspace. See this chapter's *Emerging Trends in Technology* feature on pages 302–303 for a discussion of this issue.

WHAT IS PROTECTED EXPRESSION?

Works that are copyrightable include books, records, films, artworks, architectural plans, menus, music videos, product packaging, and computer software. To obtain protection under the Copyright Act, a work must be original and fall into one of the following categories: (1) literary works; (2) musical works; (3) dramatic works; (4) pantomimes and choreographic works; (5) pictorial, graphic, and sculptural works; (6) films and other audiovisual works; and (7) sound recordings. To be protected, a work must be "fixed in a durable medium" from which it can be perceived, reproduced, or communicated. Protection is automatic. Registration is not required.

Section 102 of the Copyright Act specifically excludes copyright protection for any "idea, procedure,

process, system, method of operation, concept, principle, or discovery, regardless of the form in which it is described, explained, illustrated, or embodied." Note that it is not possible to copyright an *idea*. The underlying ideas embodied in a work may be freely used by others. What is copyrightable is the particular way in which an idea is expressed. Whenever an idea and an expression are inseparable, the expression cannot be copyrighted. Generally, anything that is not an original expression will not qualify for copyright protection. Facts widely known to the public are not copyrightable. Page numbers are not copyrightable, because they follow a sequence known to everyone. Mathematical calculations are not copyrightable.

Compilations of facts, however, are copyrightable. Section 103 of the Copyright Act defines a compilation as "a work formed by the collection and assembling of preexisting materials or data that are selected, coordinated, or arranged in such a way that the resulting work as a whole constitutes an original work of authorship." The key requirement in the copyrightability of a compilation is originality. Therefore, the White Pages of a telephone directory do not qualify for copyright protection when the information that makes up the directory (names, addresses, and telephone numbers) is not selected, coordinated, or arranged in an original way.[9] In one case, even the Yellow Pages of a telephone directory did not qualify for copyright protection.[10]

COPYRIGHT INFRINGEMENT

Whenever the form or expression of an idea is copied, an infringement of copyright has occurred. The reproduction does not have to be exactly the same as the original, nor does it have to reproduce the original in its entirety. If a substantial part of the original is reproduced, there is copyright infringement.

Those who infringe copyrights may be liable for damages or criminal penalties. These range from actual damages or statutory damages, imposed at the court's discretion, to criminal proceedings for willful violations. Actual damages are based on the harm caused to the copyright holder by the infringement, while statutory damages, not to exceed $150,000, are provided for under the Copyright Act. Criminal proceedings may result in fines and/or imprisonment.

---

8. 17 U.S.C. Sections 101 *et seq.*

9. *Feist Publications, Inc. v. Rural Telephone Service Co.*, 499 U.S. 340, 111 S.Ct. 1282, 113 L.Ed.2d 358 (1991).

10. *Bellsouth Advertising & Publishing Corp. v. Donnelley Information Publishing, Inc.*, 999 F.2d 1436 (11th Cir. 1993).

An exception to liability for copyright infringement is made under the "fair use" doctrine. In certain circumstances, a person or organization can reproduce copyrighted material without paying royalties (fees paid to the copyright holder for the privilege of reproducing the copyrighted material). Section 107 of the Copyright Act provides as follows:

[T]he fair use of a copyrighted work, including such use by reproduction in copies or phonorecords or by any other means specified by [Section 106 of the Copyright Act], for purposes such as criticism, comment, news reporting, teaching (including multiple copies for classroom use), scholarship, or research, is not an infringement of copyright. In determining whether the use made of a work in any particular case is a fair use the factors to be considered shall include—

(1) the purpose and character of the use, including whether such use is of a commercial nature or is for nonprofit educational purposes;

(2) the nature of the copyrighted work;
(3) the amount and substantiality of the portion used in relation to the copyrighted work as a whole; and
(4) the effect of the use upon the potential market for or value of the copyrighted work.

Because these guidelines are very broad, the courts determine whether a particular use is fair on a case-by-case basis. Thus, anyone reproducing copyrighted material may still be subject to a violation. In determining whether a use is fair, courts have often considered the fourth factor to be the most important.

The following case indicates what must be proved to win a case involving charges of copyright infringement of a musical work.

CASE 14.3   Repp v. Webber

United States
Court of Appeals,
Second Circuit, 1997.
132 F.3d 882.
**http://www.tourolaw.
edu/2ndCircuit/
December97**[a]

HISTORICAL AND CULTURAL SETTING *Musical works fall within the category of works of authorship that can be protected by copyright. A protected musical work can consist of lyrics or music alone, or of both lyrics and music, as in a song. A musical work can exist in a number of different forms, including a tape, a compact disk, and sheet music. To determine whether a copyright of a musical work has been infringed, an expert might dissect the works into musical phrases and compare those phrases to other works by the same, or other, composers. Pitch and rhythm—the elements of a melody—might also be dissected and compared. Harmony—the chordal elements that support the melody—can also be an important element in comparing pop compositions.*

BACKGROUND AND FACTS *Over a period of thirty years, Ray Repp wrote and published more than 120 musical compositions, including the song "Till You," which was registered with the U.S. Copyright Office in 1978. Repp included "Till You" on his album "Benedicamus" and in two books of sheet music, and performed the song in over two hundred concerts. Andrew Lloyd Webber, the composer of such musicals as* Cats *and* Evita, *wrote the musical* Phantom of the Opera *in 1983 and 1984. Claiming that "Phantom Song," one of the songs in* Phantom of the Opera, *infringed on the copyright of "Till You," Repp and others filed a suit in a federal district court against Lloyd Webber and others. Lloyd Webber responded that he never heard of Repp or "Till You" and that "Phantom Song" was an "independent creation." Musical experts offered conflicting testimony about the similarity of the songs' melodies, harmonics, and phrases. Despite this conflict, the court stated that "the two songs do not share a striking similarity" and issued a summary judgment for Lloyd Webber. The court added that Repp failed to show "Phantom Song" was not created independently. Repp appealed to the U.S. Court of Appeals for the Second Circuit.*

a. This is the "Decisions for December 1997" page within the collection of opinions of the U.S. Court of Appeals for the Second Circuit. Scroll down the list of cases to the entry for the *Repp* case. Click on the case name to read the court's opinion.

IN THE LANGUAGE
OF THE COURT

MINER, Circuit Judge:

*   *   *   *

While there was little, if any, evidence demonstrating access, there was considerable evidence that "Phantom Song" is so strikingly similar to "Till You" as to preclude the possibility of independent creation and to allow access to be inferred without direct proof. *   *   * Two highly qualified experts *   *   * gave unequivocal opinions based on musicological analyses. *   *   *

*   *   * The issue of "striking similarity," by virtue of the supported opinions of the experts *   *   * was shown to be a genuine issue of material fact. Access to the music of Repp being an essential element of his case, it cannot be said that there is an absence of evidence to support proof of that element through the inference generated by the striking similarity of the two pieces.

*   *   *   *

*   *   * The plaintiffs here have established a *prima facie* case of access through striking similarity *   *   * . Whether the evidence of independent creation here is sufficient to rebut the *prima facie* case established in this action is a question for the factfinder *   *   * .

DECISION
AND REMEDY

The U.S. Court of Appeals reversed the decision of the lower court and remanded the case. Because the issues of "striking similarity" and "independent creation" were disputed, there was a genuine disagreement about the material facts and summary judgment was not appropriate.

COPYRIGHT PROTECTION FOR SOFTWARE

In 1980, Congress passed the Computer Software Copyright Act, which amended the Copyright Act of 1976 to include computer programs in the list of creative works protected by federal copyright law. The 1980 statute, which classifies computer programs as "literary works," defines a computer program as a "set of statements or instructions to be used directly or indirectly in a computer in order to bring about a certain result."

Because of the unique nature of computer programs, the courts have had many difficulties in applying and interpreting the 1980 act. In a series of cases decided in the 1980s, the courts held that copyright protection extended not only to those parts of a computer program that can be read by humans, such as the "high-level" language of a source code, but also to the binary-language object code of a computer program, which is readable only by the computer.[11] Additionally, such elements as the overall structure, sequence, and organization of a program were deemed copyrightable.[12]

By the early 1990s, the issue had evolved into whether the "look and feel"—the general appearance, command structure, video images, menus, windows, and other screen displays—of computer programs should also be protected by copyright. Although the courts have disagreed on this issue, the tendency has been not to extend copyright protection to look-and-feel aspects of computer programs. For example, in 1995 the Court of Appeals for the First Circuit held that Lotus Development Corporation's menu command hierarchy for its Lotus 1-2-3 spreadsheet was not protectable under the Copyright Act. The court deemed that the menu command hierarchy is a "method of operation," and Section 102 of the Copyright Act specifically excludes methods of operation from copyright protection.[13] The decision was affirmed by the United States Supreme Court in 1996.[14]

---

11. See *Stern Electronics, Inc. v. Kaufman*, 669 F.2d 852 (2d Cir. 1982); and *Apple Computer, Inc. v. Franklin Computer Corp.*, 714 F.2d 1240 (3d Cir. 1983).

12. *Whelan Associates, Inc. v. Jaslow Dental Laboratory, Inc.*, 797 F.2d 1222 (3d Cir. 1986).

13. *Lotus Development Corp. v. Borland International, Inc.*, 49 F.3d 807 (1st Cir. 1995).

14. *Lotus Development Corp. v. Borland International, Inc.*, 517 U.S. 843, 116 S.Ct. 804, 113 L.Ed.2d 610 (1996). This issue may again come before the Supreme Court for a decision, because only eight justices heard the case, and there was a tied vote; the effect of the tie was to affirm the lower court's decision.

SECTION 4

Trade Secrets

Some business processes and information that are not, or cannot be, patented, copyrighted, or trademarked are nevertheless protected against appropriation by competitors as trade secrets. **Trade secrets** consist of customer lists, plans, research and development, pricing information, marketing techniques, production techniques, and generally anything that makes an individual company unique and that would have value to a competitor.

Under Section 757 of the *Restatement of Torts*, "One who discloses or uses another's trade secret, without a privilege to do so, is liable to the other if (1) he discovered the secret by improper means, or (2) his disclosure or use constitutes a breach of confidence reposed in him by the other in disclosing the secret to him." The theft of confidential business data by industrial espionage, as when a business taps into a competitor's computer, is a theft of trade secrets without any contractual violation and is actionable in itself.

One of the problems faced by businesses is that they must share their trade secrets with some persons, particularly key employees. To protect themselves, firms generally have all employees who use the process or information agree in their contracts (in a confidentiality—or nondisclosure—clause) never to divulge it. Thus, if a salesperson tries to solicit the company's customers for noncompany business, or if an employee copies the employer's unique method of manufacture, he or she has appropriated a trade secret and has also broken a contract—two separate wrongs.

Until recently, virtually all law with respect to trade secrets was common law. In an effort to reduce the unpredictability of the common law in this area, a model act, the Uniform Trade Secrets Act, was presented to the states in 1979 for adoption. Parts of the act have been adopted in more than twenty states. Typically, a state that has adopted parts of the act has adopted only those parts that encompass its own existing common law. (In 1996, Congress passed the Economic Espionage Act, which made the theft of trade secrets a federal crime. We examined the provisions and significance of this act in Chapter 7.)

Does a trade secret lose its protection under the Uniform Trade Secrets Act when an employee commits it to memory rather than takes it in written form? That was the question in the following case.

CASE 14.4   Ed Nowogroski Insurance, Inc. v. Rucker

Supreme Court of
Washington, 1999.
137 Wash.2d 427,
971 P.2d 936.

BACKGROUND AND FACTS   *Jerry Kiser, Darwin Rieck, and Michael Rucker worked for Ed Nowogroski Insurance, Inc., an insurance agency, as sales and service representatives. When friction developed between the agency and Kiser, Rieck, and Rucker, the three quit to go to work for Potter, Leonard and Cahan, Inc., a competing insurance firm. During their employment with Potter, the former Nowogroski employees used Nowogroski customer lists to attract business. Kiser and Rucker used written client information that they had copied from their ex-employer's files. Rieck worked chiefly from memory. The Nowogroski agency filed a suit in a Washington state court against its former employees and their new employer, alleging misappropriation of trade secrets. The court concluded that the client information fit the definition of a trade secret under the Uniform Trade Secrets Act and issued a judgment in the plaintiff's favor. The court decided, however, that only the written information was protected and did not award damages for the use of the memorized data. Nowogroski appealed to an intermediate state appellate court, which held that there is no distinction between written and memorized information and ordered a recalculation of the damages. The defendants appealed to the Washington Supreme Court.*

IN THE LANGUAGE OF THE COURT   *HILTON*, J. [Judge]
* * * *

The Uniform Trade Secrets Act does not distinguish between written and memorized information. The Act does not require a plaintiff to prove actual theft or conversion of physical documents embodying the trade secret information to prove misappropriation. The Washington Uniform Trade Secrets Act defines a "trade secret" to include compilations of information which have certain characteristics without regard to the form that such information might take. The definition of "misappropriation" includes unauthorized "disclosure or use." *   *   * [T]wo types of information mentioned in the Uniform Trade Secrets Act as examples of trade secrets include "method" and "technique"; these do not imply the requirement of written documents.

        *   *   *   *

The form of information, whether written or memorized, is immaterial under the trade secrets statute; the Uniform Trade Secrets Act makes no distinction about the form of trade secrets. Whether the information is on a CD, a blueprint, a film, a recording, a hard paper copy or memorized by the employee, the inquiry is whether it meets the definition of a trade secret under the Act and whether it was misappropriated. Absent a contract to the contrary, an employee is free to compete against his or her former employer, and a former employee may use general knowledge, skills and experience acquired during the prior employment in competing with a former employer. However, an employee may not use or disclose trade secrets belonging to the former employer to actively solicit customers from a confidential customer list. In this case, the former employees actively solicited customers from the employer's customer lists, which the trial court found to be of independent value because unknown and subject to reasonable efforts to keep secret. *   *   * [W]e conclude the Court of Appeals was correct in holding that there is no legal distinction between written and memorized information under the Uniform Trade Secrets Act and in remanding for a recalculation of damages.

<table>
<tr>
<td>DECISION
AND REMEDY</td>
<td>*The Washington Supreme Court affirmed the judgment of the state intermediate appellate court. Under the Uniform Trade Secrets Act, there is no legal distinction between written and memorized information.*</td>
</tr>
</table>

SECTION 5

International Protection for Intellectual Property

For many years, the United States has been a party to various international agreements relating to intellectual property rights. For example, the Paris Convention of 1883, to which about ninety countries are signatory, allows parties in one country to file for patent and trademark protection in any of the other member countries. Other international agreements in this area include the Berne Convention and the TRIPS agreement.

THE BERNE CONVENTION

Under the Berne Convention of 1886, an international copyright agreement, if an American writes a book, his or her copyright in the book must be recognized by every country that has signed the convention. Also, if a citizen of a country that has not signed the convention first publishes a book in a country that has signed, all other countries that have signed the convention must recognize that author's copyright. Copyright notice is not needed to gain protection under the Berne Convention for works published after March 1, 1989.

Currently, the laws of many countries as well as international laws are being updated to reflect changes in technology and the expansion of the Internet. Copyright holders and other owners of intellectual property generally agree that changes in the law are needed to stop the increasing international piracy of their property. The World Intellectual Property Organization (WIPO) Copyright Treaty of 1996, a special agreement under the Berne Convention, attempts to update international law governing copyright protection to include more safeguards against copyright infringement via the Internet. The United States, which signed the WIPO treaty in 1996, implemented its terms in the Digital Millennium Copyright Act of 1998. These developments are covered in more detail in Chapter 15, in the context of international protection for intellectual property rights in cyberspace.

The Berne Convention and other international agreements have given some protection to intellectual property on a global level. Another significant worldwide agreement to increase such protection is the Trade-Related Aspects of Intellectual Property Rights agreement—or, more simply, the TRIPS agreement.

The TRIPS Agreement

The TRIPS agreement was signed by representatives from over one hundred nations in 1994. It was one of several documents that were annexed to the agreement that created the World Trade Organization, or WTO, in 1995. The TRIPS agreement established, for the first time, standards for the international protection of intellectual property rights, including patents, trademarks, and copyrights for movies, computer programs, books, and music.

Prior to the TRIPS agreement, one of the difficulties faced by U.S. sellers of intellectual property in the international market was that another country might either lack laws to protect intellectual property rights or fail to enforce what laws it had. To address this problem, the TRIPS agreement provides that each member country must include in its domestic laws broad intellectual property rights and effective remedies (including civil and criminal penalties) for violations of those rights.

Generally, the TRIPS agreement provides that member nations must not discriminate (in terms of the administration, regulation, or adjudication of intellectual property rights) against foreign owners of such rights. In other words, a member nation cannot give its own nationals (citizens) favorable treatment without offering the same treatment to nationals of all member countries. For example, if a U.S. software manufacturer brings a suit for the infringement of intellectual property rights under Japan's national laws, the U.S. manufacturer is entitled to receive the same treatment as a Japanese domestic manufacturer. Each member nation must also ensure that legal procedures are available for parties who wish to bring actions for infringement of intellectual property rights. Additionally, as part of the agreement creating the WTO, a mechanism for settling disputes among member nations was established.

Particular provisions of the TRIPS agreement refer to patent, trademark, and copyright protection for intellectual property. The agreement specifically provides copyright protection for computer programs by stating that compilations of data, databases, and other materials are "intellectual creations" and are to be protected as copyrightable works. Other provisions relate to trade secrets and the rental of computer programs and cinematographic works.

Terms and Concepts to Review

certification mark 301	intellectual property 294	trade name 301
collective mark 301	patent 301	trade secret 307
copyright 304	service mark 300	trademark 294
dilution 298	trade dress 300	

Questions and Case Problems

14–1. Fair Use Doctrine.   Professor Wise is teaching a summer seminar in business torts at State University. Several times during the course, he makes copies of relevant sections from business law texts and distributes them to his students. Wise does not realize that the daughter of one of the textbook authors is a member of his seminar. She tells her father about Wise's copying ac-

tivities, which have taken place without her father's or his publisher's permission. Her father sues Wise for copyright infringement. Wise claims protection under the fair use doctrine. Who will prevail? Explain.

14–2. Copyright Infringement.   In which of the following situations would a court likely hold Ursula liable for copyright infringement?

(a) From a scholarly journal at the library, Ursula photocopies ten pages relating to a topic on which she is writing a term paper.

(b) Ursula makes blouses, dresses, and other clothes and sells them in her small shop. She advertises some of the outfits as Guest items, hoping that customers might mistakenly assume that they were made by Guess, the well-known clothing manufacturer.

(c) Ursula teaches Latin American history at a small university. She has a VCR and frequently tapes television programs relating to Latin America. She then takes the videos to her classroom so that her students can watch them.

14–3. COPYRIGHT PROTECTION.   One day during algebra class, Diedra, an enterprising fourteen-year-old student, began drawing designs on her shoelaces. By the end of the class, Diedra had decorated her shoelaces with the name of the school, Broadson Junior High, written in blue and red (the school colors) and with pictures of bears, the school's mascot. After class, she showed the designs to her teacher, Mrs. Laxton. When Diedra got home that night, she wrote about her idea in her diary, in which she also drew her shoelace design. Mrs. Laxton had been trying to think of how she could build school spirit. She thought about Diedra's shoelaces and decided to go into business for herself. She called her business Spirited Shoelaces and designed shoelaces for each of the local schools, decorating the shoelaces in each case with the school's name, mascot, and colors. The business became tremendously profitable. Even though Diedra never registered her idea with the patent or copyright office, does she nonetheless have intellectual property rights in the shoelace design? Will her diary account be sufficient proof that she created the idea? Discuss.

14–4. TRADEMARK INFRINGEMENT.   In 1987, Quality Inns International, Inc., announced a new chain of economy hotels to be marketed under the name McSleep Inns. McDonald's wrote Quality Inns a letter stating that the use of this name infringed on the McDonald's family of trademarks characterized by the prefix Mc attached to a generic term. Quality Inns claimed that Mc had come into generic use as a prefix and therefore McDonald's had no trademark rights to the prefix itself. Quality Inns filed an action seeking a declaratory judgment from the court that the mark McSleep Inns did not infringe on McDonald's federally registered trademarks or common law rights to its marks and would not constitute an unfair trade practice. What factors must the court consider in deciding this issue? What will be the probable outcome of the case? Explain. [Quality Inns International, Inc. v. McDonald's Corp., 695 F.Supp. 198 (D.Md. 1988)]

14–5. TRADEMARK INFRINGEMENT.   CBS, Inc., owns and operates Television City, a television production facility in Los Angeles that is home to many television series. The name Television City is broadcast each week in connection with each show. CBS sells T-shirts, pins, watches, and so on emblazoned with "CBS Television City." CBS registered the name Television City with the U.S. Patent and Trademark Office as a service mark "for television production services." David and William Liederman wished to open a restaurant in New York City using the name Television City. Besides food, the restaurant would sell television memorabilia such as T-shirts, sweatshirts, and posters. When CBS learned of the Liedermans' plans, it asked a federal district court to order them not to use the name Television City in connection with their restaurant. Does CBS's registration of the Television City mark ensure its exclusive use in all markets and for all products? If not, what factors might the court consider to determine whether the Liedermans can use the name Television City in connection with their restaurant? [CBS, Inc. v. Liederman, 866 F.Supp. 763 (S.D.N.Y. 1994)]

14–6. TRADE SECRETS.   William Redmond, as the general manager for PepsiCo, Inc., in California, had access to the company's inside information and trade secrets. In 1994, Redmond resigned to become chief operating officer for the Gatorade and Snapple Co., which makes and markets Gatorade and Snapple and is a subsidiary of the Quaker Oats Co. PepsiCo brought an action in a federal district court against Redmond and Quaker Oats, seeking to prevent Redmond from disclosing PepsiCo's secrets. The court ordered Redmond not to assume new duties that were likely to trigger disclosure of those secrets. The central issue on appeal was whether a plaintiff can obtain relief for trade secret misappropriation on showing that a former employee's new employment will inevitably lead him or her to rely on the plaintiff's trade secrets. How should the court rule on this issue? Discuss fully. [PepsiCo v. Redmond, 54 F.3d 1262 (7th Cir. 1995)]

14–7. COPYRIGHT INFRINGEMENT.   James Smith, the owner of Michigan Document Services, Inc. (MDS), a commercial copyshop, concluded that it was unnecessary to obtain the copyright owners' permission to reproduce copyrighted materials in coursepacks. Smith publicized his conclusion, claiming that professors would not have to worry about any delay in production at his shop. MDS then compiled, bound, and sold coursepacks to students at the University of Michigan without obtaining the permission of copyright owners. Princeton University Press and two other publishers filed a suit in a federal district court against MDS, alleging copyright infringement. MDS claimed that its coursepacks were covered under the fair use doctrine. Were they? Explain. [Princeton University Press v. Michigan Document Services, Inc., 99 F.3d 1381 (6th Cir. 1996)]

14–8. TRADEMARK INFRINGEMENT.   Elvis Presley Enterprises, Inc. (EPE), owns all of the trademarks of the Elvis Presley estate. None of these marks is registered for use in the restaurant business. Barry Capece registered "The Velvet Elvis" as a service mark for a restaurant and tavern with the U.S. Patent and Trademark Office. Capece opened a nightclub called "The Velvet Elvis" with a menu, décor, advertising, and promotional events that evoked Elvis Presley and his music. EPE filed a suit in a federal district court against Capece and others, claiming, among other things, that "The Velvet Elvis" service mark infringed on EPE's trademarks. During the trial, witnesses testified that they thought the bar was associated with Elvis Presley. Should Capece be ordered to stop using "The Velvet Elvis" mark? Why or why not? [*Elvis Presley Enterprises, Inc. v. Capece,* 141 F.3d 188 (5th Cir. 1998)]

14–9. TRADEMARK INFRINGEMENT. A&H Sportswear Co., a swimsuit maker, obtained a trademark for its MIRACLESUIT in 1992. The MIRACLESUIT design makes the wearer appear slimmer. The MIRACLESUIT, which was widely advertised and discussed in the media, was also sold for a brief time in the Victoria's Secret (VS) catalogue, which is published by Victoria's Secret Catalogue, Inc. In 1993, Victoria's Secret Stores, Inc., began selling a cleavage-enhancing bra, which was named THE MIRACLE BRA and for which a trademark was obtained. The next year, THE MIRACLE BRA swimwear debuted in the VS catalogue and stores. A&H filed a suit in a federal district court against VS Stores and VS Catalogue, alleging in part that THE MIRACLE BRA mark, when applied to swimwear, infringed on the MIRACLESUIT mark. A&H argued that there was a "possibility of confusion" between the marks. The VS entities contended that the appropriate standard was "likelihood of confusion" and that in this case, there was no likelihood of confusion. In whose favor will the court rule, and why? [*A&H Sportswear, Inc. v. Victoria's Secret Stores, Inc.,* 166 F.3d 197 (3d Cir. 1999)]

14–10. IN YOUR COURT

Texaco, Inc., conducts research to develop new products and technology in the petroleum industry. As part of the research, Texaco employees routinely photocopy articles from scientific and medical journals without the permission of the copyright holders. The publishers of the journals brought a copyright infringement action against Texaco in a federal district court. Texaco argued that the copying was a "fair use" of the materials. Assume that you are the judge in the federal court hearing this case and answer the following questions:

(a) Under the "fair use" section of the Copyright Act, what four factors should you consider in determining whether Texaco's actions infringed on the rights of the copyright owners?

(b) How would you characterize the "purpose and character" of Texaco's use of the copyrighted materials? In other words, was the use of a "commercial nature" or was it "for nonprofit educational purposes"? In this respect, is the use of copyrighted materials by Texaco any different from the use of copyrighted materials by the "coursepack" preparer in the case described in Case Problem 14–7?

(c) Generally, what will your opinion be in this case? Will you hold Texaco liable for copyright infringement? Why or why not?

LAW ON THE WEB

For updated links to resources available on the Web, as well as a variety of other materials, visit this text's Web site at http://wleb.westbuslaw.com.

Information on intellectual property law is available at the following site:

http://wbl.legal.net/intellct.htm

You can find answers to frequently asked questions (FAQs) about trademark and patent law—and links to registration forms, statutes, international patent and trademark offices, and numerous other related materials—at the Web site of the U.S. Patent and Trademark Office. Go to

http://www.uspto.gov

To access the federal database of registered trademarks directly, go to

www.uspto.gov/tmdb/index.html

To perform patent searches and to access information on the patenting process, go to

http://www.bustpatents.com

You can also access information on patent law at the following Internet site:

http://www.patents.com

For information on copyrights, go to the U.S. Copyright Office at

lcweb.loc.gov/copyright

You can find extensive information on copyright law—including United States Supreme Court decisions in this area and the texts of the Berne Convention and other international treaties on copyright issues—at the Web site of the Legal Information Institute at Cornell University's School of Law. Go to

http://www.law.cornell.edu/topics/copyright.html

An online magazine that deals, in part, with intellectual property issues is *Law Technology Product News*. The URL for this publication is

http://www.ljextra.com/ltpn

The Cyberspace Law Institute (CLI) offers articles and information on such topics as copyright infringement, privacy, trade secrets, and trademarks. To access the CLI's Web site, go to

http://www.cli.org

LEGAL RESEARCH EXERCISES ON THE WEB

Go to http://wleb.westbuslaw.com, the Web site that accompanies this text. Select "Internet Applications," and then click on "Chapter 14." There you will find the following Internet research exercises that you can perform to learn more about intellectual property rights:

Activity 14–1: The Price of Free Speech

Activity 14–2: Gray-Market Goods

CHAPTER 15

Cyberlaw and E-Commerce

TECHNOLOGY AFFECTS BUSINESS PRACTICES and, for this reason, can affect business law. Cyberspace, the Internet, and the World Wide Web represent the latest in technological developments. In general, the law is attempting to catch up with the changes in business practices caused by these profoundly different capabilities.

There are three aspects to this new technology that are affecting the law. First, the new technology represents mass communication on an unprecedented scale. Geographic limits do not apply—any person or business with a computer has a potentially worldwide audience. Second, this mass communication does not originate from a few central locations. Physical and political limits are immaterial. Third, information on the Internet is highly changeable. A database can be easily downloaded and its data modified and passed on without detection.

These factors challenge the traditional governmental means for controlling the use and communication of information. In fact, they indicate that complete government monitoring and control of cyberspace would be impractical, unrealistic, and probably impossible. Some observers argue that the law does not, or should not, apply in cyberspace. Others think that the law is responding too slowly to technological developments. Still others contend that it is not necessary to change the law to respond to these developments. How the law is currently dealing with these factors is the subject of this chapter.

The Courts

Technological developments, including the Internet, promise to relieve the courts of the burden created by overloaded dockets and record-keeping challenges—providing that the courts, the parties, and their attorneys are willing to use technology. Technology can save judges, lawyers, litigants, and court personnel time and overhead. Technology can reduce storage space, paperwork, and drudgery, and it can speed up legal research.

We have already looked at how electronic filing can reduce the paperwork and storage space required during litigation (see Chapter 2's feature entitled *Emerging Trends in Technology* for details). Here we look at how technology is changing other court practices and procedures as well. We also examine some of the jurisdictional issues posed by Internet transactions.

CHANGES IN PRACTICES AND PROCEDURES

Most courts have sites on the Web. Of course, it is up to each court to decide what to make available at its site. Some courts display only the names of court personnel and office phone numbers. Others add court rules and forms. Some include judicial decisions, although generally the sites do not feature archives of old decisions. Instead, the time period within which decisions are available online is limited. For example, California keeps opinions online for only sixty days.[1] The official opening Web page for the opinions of the California state courts at http://www.courtinfo.ca.gov/opinions is illustrated in Exhibit 15–1.

Someday, we may see the use of **virtual courtrooms,** in which judicial proceedings take place only on the Internet. The parties to a case could meet online to make their arguments and present their evidence. This might be done with e-mail submissions, through video cameras, in designated "chat" rooms, at closed sites, or through the use of any other Internet facility. These courtrooms could be efficient and economical. Will we also see the use of virtual lawyers, judges, or juries—computers or software replacing court personnel? How would this affect the application of the law? Would removing the "human" aspect of justice result in radical changes to the legal system as we know it? These are questions for the future.

---

1. Older judicial opinions are available at other sites. As of this writing, however, except for the decisions of the United States Supreme Court and some opinions in classic cases, there are not many court decisions available online that predate the 1990s.

JURISDICTION IN CYBERSPACE

The Internet's capacity to bypass political and geographic boundaries makes it revolutionary. This ability undercuts the traditional basis for a court to assert personal jurisdiction. This basis includes the contacts a party has with a court's geographic jurisdiction. For a court to compel a defendant to come before the court, there must be at least minimum contacts—the presence of a salesperson within the state, for example. Are there sufficient minimum contacts if the only connection to a jurisdiction is an ad on the Web originating from a remote location?

Consider an example. Adam lives in Florida. Carol, who lives in New York and has never been to Florida or done business with anyone in Florida, advertises her business on the Web. Carol's home page has received hundreds of "hits" by residents of Florida. Adam files a suit against Carol in a Florida state court. Can the court compel Carol to appear?

On the one hand, it could be argued that Carol knows (or should know) that her Web site could be accessed by residents of Florida, and by advertising her business on the Web, she should reasonably expect to be called into court there. If this reasoning is

EXHIBIT 15–1   OPENING WEB PAGE FOR CALIFORNIA COURT OPINIONS

applied, then setting up a Web site could subject the owner to a suit anywhere that the site can be accessed. Some courts have upheld exercises of jurisdiction on the basis of the accessibility of a Web page.[2]

On the other hand, it could be argued that it is not possible for Carol to set up a Web page that excludes residents of Florida (or of any other specific jurisdiction). With this in mind, it would seem unreasonable and unfair to subject Carol to the possible personal jurisdiction of every court in the United States and maybe the world. For this reason, some courts have

concluded that without more, a presence on the Web is not enough to support jurisdiction over nonresident defendants.[3]

Recently, a new standard is becoming generally accepted for evaluating the exercise of jurisdiction based on contacts over the Internet. This standard is a "sliding scale." On this scale, a court's exercise of personal jurisdiction depends on the amount of business that an individual or firm transacts over the Internet. The standard is explained more fully in the following case.

---

2. See, for example, *Minnesota v. Granite Gates Resorts, Inc.*, 568 N.W.2d 715 (Minn.App. 1997), aff'd 576 N.W.2d 747 (Minn. 1998).

3. See, for example, *Weber v. Jolly Hotels*, 977 F.Supp. 327 (D.N.J. 1997).

CASE 15.1   Zippo Manufacturing Co. v. Zippo Dot Com, Inc.

United States
District Court,
Western District of
Pennsylvania, 1997.
952 F.Supp. 1119.
**http://zeus.bna.com/
e-law/cases/zippo.html**[a]

HISTORICAL AND TECHNOLOGICAL SETTING   *In a case decided before 1960, the United States Supreme Court noted that "[a]s technological progress has increased the flow of commerce between States, the need for jurisdiction has undergone a similar increase."*[b] *Twenty-seven years later, the Court observed that jurisdiction could not be avoided "merely because the defendant did not physically enter the forum state.* * * * *[I]t is an inescapable fact of modern commercial life that a substantial amount of commercial business is transacted solely by mail and wire communications across state lines."*[c]

BACKGROUND AND FACTS   *Zippo Manufacturing Company (ZMC) makes, among other things, "Zippo" lighters. Zippo Dot Com, Inc. (ZDC), operates a Web page and an Internet subscription news service. ZDC has the exclusive right to use the domain names "zippo.com," "zippo.net," and "zipponews.com." ZMC is based in Pennsylvania. ZDC is based in California, and its contacts with Pennsylvania have occurred almost exclusively over the Internet. Two percent of its subscribers (3,000 of 140,000) are Pennsylvania residents who contracted over the Internet to receive its service. Also, ZDC has agreements with seven Internet service providers in Pennsylvania to permit their subscribers to access the service. ZMC filed a suit in a federal district court against ZDC, alleging trademark infringement and other claims, based on ZDC's use of the word "Zippo." ZDC filed a motion to dismiss for lack of personal jurisdiction.*

IN THE LANGUAGE OF THE COURT   McLAUGHLIN, District Judge.

*   *   *   *

*   *   * [T]*he likelihood that personal jurisdiction can be constitutionally exercised is directly proportionate to the nature and quality of commercial activity that an entity conducts over the Internet.* *   *   * At one end of the spectrum are situations where a defendant clearly does business over the Internet. If the defendant enters into contracts with residents of a foreign jurisdiction that involve the knowing and repeated transmission of computer files over the Internet, personal jurisdiction is proper. At the opposite end are situations where a defendant has simply posted information on an Internet Web site which is accessible to users in foreign jurisdictions. A passive Web site that does little more than make information available to those who are interested in it is not grounds

---

a. This is a page in the "Electronic Commerce & Law Report" library.
b. *Hanson v. Denckla*, 357 U.S. 235, 78 S.Ct. 1228, 2 L.Ed.2d 1283 (1958).
c. *Burger King Corp. v. Rudzewicz*, 471 U.S. 462, 105 S.Ct. 2174, 85 L.Ed.2d 528 (1985).

for the exercise of personal jurisdiction. The middle ground is occupied by interactive Web sites where a user can exchange information with the host computer. In these cases, the exercise of jurisdiction is determined by examining the level of interactivity and commercial nature of the exchange of information that occurs on the Web site. [Emphasis added.]

*   *   *   *   *

*   *   * We are being asked to determine whether [ZDC's] conducting of electronic commerce with Pennsylvania residents constitutes *   *   * doing business in Pennsylvania. We conclude that it does. [ZDC] has contracted with approximately 3,000 individuals and seven Internet access providers in Pennsylvania. The intended object of these transactions has been the downloading of the electronic messages that form the basis of this suit in Pennsylvania.

DECISION AND REMEDY   *The court held that it has jurisdiction over parties that conduct substantial business in its jurisdiction exclusively over the Internet. The court concluded that ZDC fits this description and denied the motion to dismiss.*

SECTION 2

The Constitution

To date, most of the Internet and new technology issues raised under the Constitution involve regulations of the freedom of speech. Legal challenges to laws that attempt to inhibit speech have generally been most successful when based on the commerce clause or the First Amendment. (For a discussion of the commerce clause, see Chapter 5.)

The problem is related to the unique feature of the Internet—its ability to cross political and geographic borders—and the inability of current technology to effectively filter out what legislators and government regulators might like to block. The issues are not unique to the United States. China and some European countries, among other nations, have attempted, with varying success, to block what their governments believe is bad for their citizens.

One of the basic questions involved in this issue concerns how much freedom of speech we are willing to sacrifice to allow the government to further a particular value, such as shielding children from certain material or preventing terrorism and crime. Phrased another way, how much of any value are we willing to sacrifice to protect our freedom of speech? There is no clear, definite answer to this question. Generally, the courts hold that speech may be restricted to serve a *compelling interest* but only if the restriction is the *least restrictive means* of doing so. (See Chapter 5 for a fuller discussion of freedom of speech.)

ENCRYPTION CODES

Privacy is one of the primary worries of most of those who use the Internet. It is possible to "eavesdrop" on Internet communications. The wrong person might learn your credit-card number when you enter it to make an online purchase. Your Social Security number might be revealed when it is passed through cyberspace. Details of your business transactions or personal specifics of your private life might be revealed to persons to whom you would not otherwise give such information.

Encryption is the process by which a message (plaintext) is transformed into something (ciphertext) that the sender and receiver intend third parties not to understand. Decryption is the process of transforming ciphertext into plaintext. An encryption code is a program used in encryption software to transform plaintext into ciphertext and vice versa. This software includes source codes, object codes, applications software, and system software.

Law enforcement authorities are afraid that the wrong persons, including international terrorists, will take advantage of Internet security to engage in illegal activities. For this reason, the U.S. Department of Commerce has attempted to restrict the export of encryption code. (The export of cryptography is also a violation of a federal criminal statute that is discussed later in this chapter.[4]) These restrictions have been challenged in a few cases on the ground that an

---

4. 15 C.F.R. Part 772.

encryption code is speech and therefore protected by the First Amendment. That would mean that the regulations banning its export are unconstitutional.[5] In a recent case, however, a federal district court held that an encryption code is not speech, because its purpose is to "transfer functions, not to communicate ideas."[6]

THE CONTENTS OF WEB SITES

The Communications Decency Act (CDA) of 1996 sought to protect minors from harmful material on the Internet by taking a broad approach. The CDA made it a crime to make available to minors online any "obscene or indecent" message that "depicts or describes, in terms patently offensive as measured by contemporary community standards, sexual or excretory activities or organs."[7]

The United States Supreme Court disapproved of this approach, and in 1997, in *Reno v. American Civil Liberties Union*,[8] the Court ruled that portions of the act were unconstitutional. The Court said that "[t]he general, undefined terms 'indecent' and 'patently offensive' cover large amounts of nonpornographic material with serious educational or other value. Moreover, the 'community standards' criterion as applied to the Internet means that any communication available to a nationwide audience will be judged by the standards of the community most likely to be offended by the message."

Congress made a further attempt to regulate Internet speech in 1998. Included in the federal budget bill passed in that year was the Child Online Protection Act (COPA). The act imposed criminal penalties on those who distribute material that is "harmful to minors" without using some kind of age-verification system to separate adult and minor users. Like the CDA, the COPA was immediately challenged in court by civil rights groups, Web site operators, and others. In 1999, a federal district court issued an injunction against the COPA's enforcement until the constitutional questions could be decided.[9]

Are there forms of speech that the government can effectively restrict online? On the Internet, extreme hate speech is known as **cyber hate speech.** Racist materials and Holocaust denials on the Web, for example, are cyber hate speech. Can such online speech be restricted?[10] Should it? Are there other forms of speech that the government should limit?[11] Content restrictions generally amount to censorship and can be difficult to enforce. In cyberspace, they are almost impossible to carry out.

Even if it were possible to enforce content restrictions online, U.S. federal law (or the law of any single nation) is only "local" law in cyberspace—less than half of the users of the Internet are in the United States. This highlights one of the criticisms of restricting online content at its source. Such restrictions are out of step with the revolutionary nature of the Internet. Any source of content may be in a different jurisdiction than those who view it. Information may be legal in some jurisdictions and not in others.

ACCESS TO WEB SITES

An alternative to regulating the content of Web sites is to block access to them. An employer may want to limit what his or her employees can do in cyberspace during working hours. A parent may wish to block what his or her child views on the Internet. **Filtering software,** or filters, can prevent certain persons from viewing certain Web sites at certain times by responding to a site's uniform resource locator (URL), or Internet address, or to its **meta tags,** or key words. This technology is at the core of the current debate on the control and regulation of information on the Internet.

There are concerns about this software and whether it effectively does what it claims to do. There are questions about the tags: What should they consist of, and who should decide which sites have which tags? Using filters to control the accessibility of information on the Internet also raises issues about the relationship of technology to law. Because the First Amendment is aimed at curtailing the government's power to censor speech, the fundamental issue is whether the law should apply in cyberspace, and if so, how it should operate.

5. See, for example, *Bernstein v. U.S. Department of Justice*, 176 F.3d 1132 (9th Cir. 1999).

6. *Junger v. Daley*, 8 F.Supp.2d 708 (N.D.Ohio 1998).

7. 47 U.S.C. Section 223(a)(1)(B)(ii).

8. 521 U.S. 844, 117 S.Ct. 2329, 138 L.Ed.2d 874 (1997).

9. *American Civil Liberties Union v. Reno*, 31 F.Supp.2d 473 (E.D.Pa. 1999).

10. In 1999, a jury in Portland, Oregon, ordered antiabortion activists to pay more than $100 million in punitive damages for material posted on a Web site that the jury found violated the federal Racketeer Influenced and Corrupt Organizations Act (RICO). The activists had argued that the material was protected by the First Amendment. For more on RICO, see Chapter 7.

11. The content of some speech is regulated to a certain extent by tort law, copyright law, and other laws. See, for example, the discussions of defamation, cyber fraud, and copyright infringement later in this chapter and in Chapters 12 and 14.

The debate centers on the use of filters by government employers, public schools, and public libraries. In its opinion in the *Reno v. American Civil Liberties Union* case noted above, the United States Supreme Court seemed to approve of the use of filters as a "less restrictive alternative."[12]

SECTION 3

Cyber Crimes

A **cyber crime** is a crime that occurs in the virtual community of the Internet. Some of these crimes are discussed in the following subsections.

The "location" of cyber crime—cyberspace—raises new issues in the investigation of crimes and the prosecution of perpetrators. It is the unique nature of the Internet that causes one of the toughest problems in enforcing laws against cyber crimes: the issue of jurisdiction. A person who commits an act against a business in California, where the act is a cyber crime, might never have set foot in California but instead might reside in New York, or even in Canada, where the act may not be a crime. If the crime were committed via e-mail, would the e-mail constitute sufficient "minimum contacts" for the victim's state to exercise jurisdiction?

Other difficulties include identifying the perpetrators. Cyber criminals do not leave physical traces, such as fingerprints or DNA samples, as evidence of their crimes. Even electronic "footprints" can be hard to find and follow. For example, e-mail may be sent through a remailer, an online service that guarantees that a message cannot be traced to its source.

CYBER STALKING

California enacted the first stalking law in 1990, in response to the contemporary murders of six women—including Rebecca Schaeffer, a television star—by the men who had harassed them. The law made it a crime to harass or follow a person while making a "credible threat" that puts that person in reasonable fear for his or her safety or the safety of the person's immediate family.[13] Most other states have also enacted stalking laws.

Generally speaking, the stalking laws in about half of the states require a physical act (following the victim). **Cyber stalkers**—stalkers who commit their crimes in cyberspace—find their victims through Internet relay chat (or live chat), Usenet newsgroups or other bulletin boards, and e-mail. None of these communications requires that a stalker physically "follow" his or her prey. For this reason, these statutes do not apply in the virtual community. About three-quarters of the stalking laws in the other states *could* apply in cyberspace, because those statutes deem tools of harassment to include written communications (e-mail) or telephones (Internet connections).

As of this writing, seven states have statutes that specifically address stalking by computer, or cyber stalking. It is also a federal crime to harass someone by means of interstate "telecommunications devices."[14] Some of the state statutes are based on California's law and require a "credible threat." Others require only an intention to harass, annoy, or alarm.[15]

CYBER THEFT

In cyberspace, thieves are not subject to the physical limitations of the "real" world. A thief can steal data stored in a networked computer with dial-in access from anywhere on the globe. Only the speed of the connection and the thief's computer equipment limit the quantity of data that can be stolen.

For this reason, laws written to protect physical property are difficult to apply in cyberspace. For example, the federal statute that bans the interstate transportation of stolen property refers to "goods, wares and merchandise."[16] At least one court has held that this does not apply to intangible property such as computer data.[17] Another federal statute makes it illegal to threaten physical violence to property.[18] A threat to delete files may not qualify.

To address abuses that stem from the misuse of new technology, Congress amended the Counterfeit Access Device and Computer Fraud and Abuse Act of

---

12. In 1999, Michigan enacted the Library Privacy Act to permit public libraries to filter their patrons' access to the Internet as long as at least one unfiltered terminal is provided for restricted use by adults and minors accompanied by parents or guardians.

13. Cal. Penal Code Section 646.9.

14. 47 U.S.C. Section 223(1)(A) and (B). See also 18 U.S.C Section 875. Another possibility was indicated in 1998, when a former University of California student was convicted under federal civil rights law for sending hate e-mail to Asian students.

15. See, for example, Conn. General Statutes Sections 53a-182b and 53a-183.

16. 18 U.S.C. Section 2314.

17. *United States v. Brown*, 925 F.2d 1301 (10th Cir. 1991).

18. 18 U.S.C. Section 1951(a).

1984 with the National Information Infrastructure Protection Act of 1996.[19] The 1996 act provides, among other things, that a person who accesses a computer online, without authority, to obtain classified, restricted, or protected data, or attempts to do so, is subject to criminal prosecution. These data could include financial and credit records, medical records, legal files, military and national security files, and other confidential information in government or private computers. The crime has two elements: accessing a computer without authority and taking the data.

This theft is a felony if it is committed for a commercial purpose or for private financial gain, or if the value of the stolen data (or computer time) exceeds $5,000. Penalties include fines and imprisonment for up to twenty years. A victim of computer theft can also bring a civil suit against the violator to obtain damages, an injunction, and other relief.

Persons who use one computer to break into another are sometimes referred to as **hackers**. Hackers who break into computers without authorization commit cyber theft. Often, their principal aim is to prove how smart they are by gaining access to others'

_____

19. 18 U.S.C. Section 1030.

password-protected computers and causing random data errors or making unpaid-for telephone calls.[20] Such crimes should not be taken lightly, but from a larger perspective, they might be considered the equivalent of new-tech car theft.

Cyber Terrorism

Cyber terrorists are hackers who aim not to gain attention but to remain undetected in order to exploit computers for a more serious impact. Just as a "real" terrorist might explode a bomb to shut down an embassy, a cyber terrorist might explode a "logic bomb" to shut down a central computer. Other goals might include a wholesale theft of data, such as a merchant's customer files, or the monitoring of a computer to discover a business firm's plans and transactions. A cyber terrorist might want to insert false codes or data. For example, the processing control system of a food manufacturer could be changed to alter the levels of ingredients so that consumers of the food would become ill.

_____

20. The total cost of crime on the Internet is estimated to be several billion dollars annually, but two-thirds of that total is said to consist of unpaid-for toll calls.

CONCEPT SUMMARY 15.1

CYBER CRIMES

CRIME	DESCRIPTION
Cyber Stalking	Harassing someone by computer.
Cyber Theft	Accessing a computer without authority and taking the data. This is a felony under the National Information Infrastructure Protection Act of 1996.
Cyber Terrorism	Exploiting a computer for a serious impact, such as inserting false codes or data.

SECTION 4

Cyber Torts

In the area of torts, as in other areas of the law affected by the new technology, there are more questions than answers. One of the foremost issues is the question of who should be held liable for a **cyber tort** (a tort committed in cyberspace). For example, who should be held liable when someone in a newsgroup posts a defamatory **flame** (an online message in which one party attacks another in harsh, often personal, terms)?

Should an Internet service provider (ISP) be liable for the remark if the ISP was unaware that it was being made? Who should be held liable for an employee's defamatory remark on a company bulletin board?

Other questions involve issues of proof. How, for example, can it be proved that an online defamatory remark was "published" (which requires that a third party see or hear it)? How can the identity of the person who made the remark be discovered? Can an ISP be forced to reveal the source of an anonymous comment? Answers to some of these questions are explored in the following sections.

DEFAMATION ONLINE

Online forums allow anyone—customers, employees, or crackpots—to complain about a business firm. The complaint could concern the firm's personnel, policies, practices, or products, and it might have an impact on the business of the firm. This is possible regardless of whether the complaint is justified and whether it is true.

If a statement is not true, it may constitute defamation. Defamation is any published or publicly spoken false statement that causes injury to another's good name, reputation, or character. Like other torts, defamation is governed by state law, and the elements of the tort can vary from state to state. As discussed in Chapter 5, generally a plaintiff must show that a statement was false, was not subject to a privilege, was communicated to a third person, and resulted in damage to the plaintiff. A public figure must also show that the statement was made with actual malice.

Newspapers, magazines, and television and radio stations may be held liable for defamatory remarks that they disseminate, even if those remarks are prepared or created by others. Under the Communications Decency Act of 1996, however, Internet service providers (ISPs), or "interactive computer service providers," are not liable with respect to such material.[21] An ISP typically provides access to the Internet through a local phone number and may provide other services, including access to databases available only to the ISP's subscribers.

As of this writing, there is no proved case of an untrue, negative posting on the Internet ruining a business. Defamation suits involving online statements have not yet resulted in decisions in U.S. courts that plaintiffs were defamed and are entitled to a remedy. The courts have focused chiefly on such issues as determining who would be held liable, which was the issue in the following case.

---

21. 47 U.S.C. Section 230.

CASE 15.2   Blumenthal v. Drudge

United States
District Court,
District of Columbia,
1998.
992 F.Supp. 44.
http://www.courttv.com
/legaldocs/cyberlaw/
drudge2.html[a]

COMPANY PROFILE   *Founded in 1985, America Online, Inc. (AOL) (http://www.aol.com), operates two global Internet online services: AOL Interactive Services and CompuServe Interactive Services. This makes AOL the world's largest Internet service provider (ISP). AOL also operates AOL Studios, which develops original and local content for AOL's online and Web-based brands, including AOL, AOL.com, CompuServe, and Digital City. As many as fifty million subscribers or other users use AOL as a conduit to receive and disseminate huge quantities of information over its computer network. In 1998, AOL merged with Netscape. In 2000, AOL bought Time Warner.*

BACKGROUND AND FACTS   *Under a licensing agreement with America Online, Inc. (AOL), the* Drudge Report, *an online political publication, was made available free to all AOL subscribers. According to the agreement, AOL could remove content that it determined was in violation of AOL's "standard terms of service." One issue of the* Drudge Report *contained an article charging that Sidney Blumenthal, an assistant to the president of the United States, "has a spousal abuse past that has been effectively covered up." Blumenthal's spouse, Jacqueline Blumenthal, also worked in the White House as the director of a presidential commission. When the* Report's *editor, Matt Drudge, learned that the article was false, he printed a retraction and publicly apologized to the Blumenthals. The Blumenthals filed a suit in a federal district court against Drudge, AOL, and others, alleging in part that the original remarks were defamatory. AOL filed a motion for summary judgment.*

IN THE LANGUAGE
OF THE COURT

PAUL L. FRIEDMAN, District Judge.
         *   *   *   *
         *   *   * AOL was nothing more than a provider of an interactive computer service on which the *Drudge Report* was carried, and Congress has said quite clearly [in the

---

a. This site is Court TV Online's "Technology and Computers" section within its "Legal Documents" collection.

Communications Decency Act (CDA) of 1996] that such a provider shall not be treated as a "publisher or speaker" and therefore may not be held liable in tort.

*   *   *   *

Plaintiffs make the additional argument, however, that *   *   * Drudge was not just an anonymous person who sent a message over the Internet through AOL. He is a person with whom AOL contracted, whom AOL paid *   *   * and whom AOL promoted to its subscribers and potential subscribers as a reason to subscribe to AOL. *   *   *

*   *   *   *

If it were writing on a clean slate, this Court would agree with plaintiffs. *   *   * But Congress has made a different policy choice by providing immunity even where the interactive service provider has an active, even aggressive role in making available content prepared by others. *   *   * Congress has conferred immunity from tort liability as an incentive to Internet service providers to self-police the Internet for obscenity and other offensive material, even where the self-policing is unsuccessful or not even attempted.

DECISION AND REMEDY   *The court granted AOL's motion for summary judgment. The court held that under the CDA, an Internet service provider is not liable for failing to edit, withhold, or restrict access to defamatory remarks that it disseminates but did not create.*

SPAM

Spam is "junk" e-mail—bulk, unsolicited e-mail—or junk newsgroup postings.[22] Typical spam consists of a product ad sent to all of the users on an e-mailing list or all of the members of a newsgroup.

Because spam can waste user time and network bandwidth (the amount of data that can be transmitted within a certain time), some individuals and organizations are attempting to inhibit its use. The Internet is a public forum, however. Under the First Amendment (see Chapter 5), this limits what can be done to restrict the use of spam.

In California, an unsolicited e-mail ad must state in its subject line that it is an ad ("ADV:"). The ad must also include a toll-free phone number or return e-mail address through which the recipient can contact the sender to request that no more ads be e-mailed.[23] An Internet service provider (ISP) can bring a successful suit in a California state court against a spammer who violates the ISP's policy that prohibits or restricts unsolicited e-mail ads. The court can award damages of up to $25,000 per day.[24]

In the following antispam case, an ISP argued in a federal district court that spamming is trespassing. Would the court accept this argument and block the sending of unsolicited ads to the ISP's subscribers?

---

22. The term *spam* is said to come from a Monty Python song with the lyrics, "Spam spam spam spam, spam spam spam spam, lovely spam, wonderful spam." Like these lyrics, spam online is often considered to be a repetition of worthless text.

23. Ca. Bus. & Prof. Code Section 17538.4.
24. Ca. Bus. & Prof. Code Section 17538.45.

CASE 15.3   CompuServe, Inc. v. Cyber Promotions, Inc.

United States
District Court,
Southern District of
Ohio, 1997.
962 F.Supp. 1015.
**http://www.Loundy.com/
Cases/CompuServe_v_
Cyber_Promo.html[a]**

BACKGROUND AND FACTS   *Through a nationwide computer network, CompuServe, Inc., operates a communication service that includes e-mail for CompuServe subscribers. E-mail sent to the subscribers is processed and stored on CompuServe's equipment. Cyber Promotions, Inc., is in the business of sending unsolicited e-mail ads, or spam, to Internet users. CompuServe subscribers complained to the service about Cyber Promotions's ads, and many canceled their subscriptions. Handling the ads also placed a tremendous burden on CompuServe's equipment. CompuServe told Cyber Promotions to stop using CompuServe's equipment to process and store the ads—in effect, to stop sending the ads to CompuServe subscribers. Ignoring the demand, Cyber Promotions stepped up the volume of its ads. After CompuServe attempted unsuccessfully to block the flow with screening software, it filed a suit against Cyber Promotions in*

---

a. This page is at the E-LAW Web site, "the home page of David J. Loundy, an attorney and author."

a federal district court, seeking an injunction on the ground that the ads constituted trespass to personal property.

IN THE LANGUAGE OF THE COURT

GRAHAM, District Judge.

*   *   *   *

*   *   * [An] actor may commit a trespass by an act which brings him [or her] into an intended physical contact with a chattel [property] in the possession of another[.]

*   *   * It is undisputed that plaintiff has a possessory interest in [a right to possess] its computer systems. Further, defendants' contact with plaintiff's computers is clearly intentional. Although electronic messages may travel through the Internet over various routes, the messages are affirmatively directed to their destination.

*   *   *   *

*   *   * Harm to the personal property or diminution of its quality, condition, or value as a result of defendants' use can also be the predicate for liability. *   *   * To the extent that defendants' multitudinous electronic mailings demand the disk space and drain the processing power of plaintiff's computer equipment, those resources are not available to serve CompuServe subscribers. Therefore, the value of that equipment to CompuServe is diminished even though it is not physically damaged by defendants' conduct.

*   *   *   *

Many subscribers have terminated their accounts specifically because of the unwanted receipt of bulk e-mail messages. Defendants' intrusions into CompuServe's computer systems, insofar as they harm plaintiff's business reputation and goodwill with its customers, are actionable.

DECISION AND REMEDY

The court held that spamming is trespassing. The court issued an injunction, ordering Cyber Promotions to stop distributing its ads to e-mail addresses maintained by CompuServe.

SECTION 5

Virtual Property

The legal issues relating to **virtual property**—property in cyberspace—are essentially legal questions involving intellectual property. As discussed in Chapter 7, intellectual property consists of trademarks, patents, copyrights, and trade secrets. Legal protection for these forms of property makes it possible to market goods and services profitably, which provides an incentive to sell competitive goods and services.

In the context of cyberspace, a fundamental issue has to do with the degree of legal protection that should be given to virtual property. If the protection is inadequate, the incentive to make new works available online will be reduced. If the protection is too strict, the free flow and fair use of data will be impaired.

CYBER MARKS

In cyberspace, trademarks are sometimes referred to as **cyber marks.** An early legal issue relating to cyber

marks concerned the rights of a mark's owner to use it as part of a domain name (an Internet address). The question was whether *cybersquatting* (registering another party's mark as a domain name and offering to forfeit it for a sum of money) constituted a commercial use of the mark so as to violate federal law. Generally, the courts have held that cybersquatting does violate the law.[25]

As the dust settles around this once contentious issue, cyber mark issues that courts are more likely to confront in the future revolve around other uses and abuses of those marks. Some of the questions are not new, but the context of cyberspace requires new answers. Some of the questions, however, are as new as the technological ability to create hypertext links and frames and to embed hidden code called meta tags in Web sites.

Domain Names. The Internet Corporation for Assigned Names and Numbers (ICANN) is a nonprofit corporation that the federal government

---

25. See, for example, *Panavision International, L.P. v. Toeppen,* 141 F.3d 1316 (9th Cir. 1998).

designated to coordinate certain functions of the Internet. Among other responsibilities, ICANN oversees the Internet domain name system and accredits companies to sell domain name registrations in the .com, .net, and .org domains.

In 1999, ICANN approved a draft of a Uniform Domain Name Dispute Resolution Policy. Generally, under this policy, when a registration company receives a complaint concerning the impact of a domain name on a trademark, the company can act only on instructions from the domain-name holder or an order of a court, arbitrator, or other decision maker deciding the parties' dispute. There is an exception for a dispute involving cybersquatting. In that case, a neutral decision maker selected from a panel set up for this purpose may resolve the dispute online, in less than forty-five days. Of course, the parties may still go to court to contest the outcome.

Meta Tags. Search engines compile their results by looking through a Web site's key words field. Meta tags, or key words, may be inserted in this field to increase a site's appearance in search engine results, even though the site has nothing to do with the inserted words. Using this same technique, one site may appropriate the key words of other sites with more frequent hits, so that the appropriating site appears in the same search engine results as the more popular site. One use of meta tags was at issue in the following case.

CASE 15.4 Playboy Enterprises, Inc. v. Welles

United States
District Court,
Southern District of
California, 1998.
7 F.Supp.2d 1098.
http://www.Loundy.com/
CASES/Playboy_v_
Welles.html[a]

COMPANY PROFILE *Playboy Enterprises, Inc. (PEI) (http://www.playboy.com), is an international publishing and entertainment company. Since 1953, PEI has published* Playboy *magazine, a popular magazine with approximately ten million readers each month. PEI also publishes numerous specialty magazines and other publications. In addition, PEI produces television programming for cable and satellite transmission, and sells and licenses other goods and services. PEI bestows on its models, who appear in the magazine, such titles as "Playmate of the Month" and "Playmate of the Year." PEI encourages its models to identify themselves and to use their titles for their self-promotion and the promotion of its magazines and other goods and services.*

BACKGROUND AND FACTS *Playboy Enterprises, Inc. (PEI), maintains Web sites to promote* Playboy *magazine and PEI models. PEI's trademarks include the terms "Playboy," "Playmate," and "Playmate of the Year." Terri Welles is a self-employed model and spokesperson, who was featured as the "Playmate of the Year" in June 1981. Welles maintains a Web site titled "Terri Welles—Playmate of the Year 1981." As meta tags, Welles's site uses the terms "Playboy" and "Playmate," among others. PEI asked Welles to stop using these terms, but she refused. PEI filed a suit in a federal district court against Welles, asking the court to order her to, among other things, stop using those terms as meta tags. PEI argued, in part, that this constituted trademark infringement under the Lanham Act (see Chapter 7). Welles responded in part that her use of the terms is a "fair use," because she was and is the "Playmate of the Year 1981."*

IN THE LANGUAGE OF THE COURT

GRAHAM, District Judge.
* * * *

In a case where the mark is used only to describe the goods or services of [a] party, or their geographic origin, trademark law recognizes a "fair use" defense. * * *
* * * *

It is clear that defendant is selling Terri Welles and only Terri Welles on the website. There is no overt attempt to confuse the websurfer into believing that her site is a Playboy-

---

a. This is a different URL for a page within the E-LAW site described in the footnote to Case 15.3 as "the home page of David J. Loundy, an attorney and author."

related website. In this case, then, defendant's use of the term Playmate of the Year 1981 is descriptive of and used fairly and in good faith only to describe [herself]. * * *

With respect to the meta tags, the court finds there to be no trademark infringement where defendant has used plaintiff's trademarks in good faith to index the content of her website. * * * *Much like the subject index of a card catalog, the meta tags give the websurfer using a search engine a clearer indication of the content of a website.* The use of the term Playboy is not an infringement because it references not only her identity as a "Playboy Playmate of the Year 1981," but it may also reference the legitimate editorial uses of the term Playboy contained in the text of defendant's website. [Emphasis added.]

DECISION AND REMEDY   *The court held that a party can use another's trademarks as meta tags when those marks describe the party who uses them. The court ruled that Welles was entitled to the "fair use" of the "Playboy" and "Playmate" marks as meta tags.*

Dilution. As discussed in Chapter 14, trademark *dilution* occurs when a trademark is used, without authorization, in a way that diminishes the distinctive quality of the mark. Unlike trademark infringement, a dilution cause of action does not require proof that consumers are likely to be confused by a connection between the unauthorized use and the mark. For this reason, the products involved do not have to be similar. In the first case alleging dilution on the Web, a court precluded the use of "candyland.com" as the URL for an adult site. The suit was brought by the maker of the "Candyland" children's game and owner of the "Candyland" mark.[26]

A dilution case does require, however, that a mark be famous when the dilution occurs. Gateway 2000 has been making personal computers since 1985 and owns the mark "Gateway 2000." In 1988, Gateway.com, Inc., an entirely different company, began to use "gateway.com" as part of its URL and registered it as a domain name in 1990. Gateway 2000 later filed a suit to block the use of "gateway" on the ground of dilution. The court refused to grant the request, concluding that Gateway 2000 could not prove that its name was famous at the time Gateway.com chose "gateway" as a domain name.

In another interesting case, a court issued an injunction on the ground that spamming under another's logo is trademark dilution.[27] In that case, Hotmail, Inc., provided e-mail services and worked to dissociate itself from spam. Van$ Money Pie, Inc., and others spammed thousands of e-mail customers,

using the free e-mail Hotmail as a return address. The court ordered the defendants to stop.

Licensing. One of the ways to make use of another's mark (or another's copyright, patent, or trade secret), while avoiding litigation, is to obtain a license to do so. A license in this context is essentially an agreement to permit the use of a mark for certain purposes. A licensee (the party obtaining the license) might be allowed to use the mark of the licensor (the party issuing the license) as part of the name of its company, or as part of its domain name, without otherwise using the mark on any products or services.

A licensee must not break the terms of the license, however, or litigation could ensue and liability may result. In the first case involving a trademark license in cyberspace, the licensee took advantage of its licensor's increasingly famous mark to make its Web site look more like the licensor's. Alleging a violation of the licensing agreement, the licensor sued. The court granted the licensor's motion for a preliminary injunction, holding that the licensee likely breached the license and infringed the mark.[28]

PATENTS ONLINE

There are four noteworthy aspects to patents and the new technology. First is the rapidly increasing number of patents that the U.S. Patent and Trademark Office (USPTO) has granted in recent years. For example, there are now more than ten thousand applications pending. Software technology has progressed

---

26. *Hasbro, Inc. v. Internet Entertainment Group, Ltd.,* 1996 WL 84853 (W.D.Wash. 1996).
27. *Hotmail Corp. v. Van$ Money Pie, Inc.,* 1998 WL 388389 (N.D.Cal. 1998).

28. *Digital Equipment Corp. v. AltaVista Technology, Inc.,* 960 F.Supp. 456 (D.Mass. 1997).

quickly. This points to another important feature of the new technology that relates to patents.

Software developers use combinations of previous software to create new products and processes. This practice has led to uncertainty and controversy about the ownership and the use of patent rights to the hybrid products. One way to prevent legal problems in this regard is for a software developer or maker to obtain licenses for others' products and to issue licenses for its own.

The third aspect of patents as they relate to the new technology concerns one of the most important reasons that a patent is granted. A developer obtains a patent to prevent others from patenting the same product or process. When more than one party is developing the same product or process, the first party to obtain a patent is the party who gets the protection. Even before a patent is obtained, however, the disclosure of a product or process can block others from obtaining a patent for it. For this reason, those who

reveal their inventions to the public are rewarded. It is a practice in the software industry to keep technology secret, but this is risky. A developer could lose all rights to a product by keeping it secret.

Finally, a significant development relating to patents is the availability online of the world's patent databases. The USPTO provides at its Web site searchable databases covering U.S. patents granted since 1976. This page of the USPTO is illustrated in Exhibit 15–2. The European Patent Office (EPO) maintains at its Web site databases covering all patent documents in sixty-five nations and the legal status of patents in twenty-two of those countries.

COPYRIGHTS IN DIGITAL INFORMATION

Copyright law is probably the most important form of intellectual property protection on the Internet. This is because much of the material on the Internet consists of works of authorship (including multimedia

EXHIBIT 15–2   PATENT DATABASES OF THE U.S. PATENT AND TRADEMARK OFFICE

presentations, software, and database information). These works are the traditional focus of copyright law. Copyright law is also important because the nature of the Internet requires that data be "copied" to be transferred online. Copies are a significant part of the traditional controversies arising in this area of the law.

The Copyright Act of 1976.   Remember from the discussion of copyright law in Chapter 14 that copyright law is concerned chiefly with the creation, distribution, and sale of protected works of authorship. When Congress drafted the principal U.S. law governing copyrights, the Copyright Act of 1976, cyberspace did not exist for most of us. The threat to copyright owners was posed not by computer technology but by unauthorized tangible copies of works and the sale of rights to movies, television, and other media.

Some of the issues that were unimagined when the Copyright Act was drafted have posed thorny questions for the courts. For example, to sell a copy of a work, permission of the copyright holder is necessary. Because of the nature of cyberspace, however, one of the early controversies was determining at what point an intangible, electronic "copy" of a work has been made. The courts have held that loading a file or pro-

gram into a computer's random access memory, or RAM, constitutes the making of a "copy" for purposes of copyright law.[29] RAM is a portion of a computer's memory into which a file, for example, is loaded so that it can be accessed (read or written over). Thus, a copyright is infringed when a party downloads software into RAM if that party does not own the software or otherwise have a right to download it.[30] (Technology designed to curb unauthorized copying and other aspects of digital copyright protection are discussed in the *Emerging Trends in Technology* feature in Chapter 14.)

Other rights, including those relating to the revision of "collective works" such as magazines, were acknowledged thirty years ago but were considered to have only limited economic value. Today, technology has made some of those rights vastly more significant. How does the old law apply to these rights? That was one of the questions in the following case.

---

29. *MAI Systems Corp. v. Peak Computer, Inc.*, 991 F.2d 511 (9th Cir. 1993).
30. *DSC Communications Corp. v. Pulse Communications, Inc.*, 170 F.3d 1354 (Fed. Cir. 1999).

CASE 15.5   Tasini v. The New York Times Co.

United States
Court of Appeals,
Second Circuit, 1999.
192 F.3d 356.
http://www.findlaw.com/
casecode/courts/
2nd.html[a]

BACKGROUND AND FACTS   *Magazines and newspapers, including the* New York Times, *buy and publish articles written by freelance writers. Unless the parties agree otherwise, under Section 201(c) of the Copyright Act the writers retain the copyrights in the separate articles, but the publishers obtain copyrights in the "collective work." Besides circulating hard copies of their periodicals, these publishers sell the contents to e-publishers for inclusion in online and other electronic databases. Jonathan Tasini and five other freelance writers filed a suit in a federal district court against the New York Times Company and other publishers, including the e-publishers, contending that the e-publication of the articles violated the Copyright Act. The publishers responded, among other things, that the Copyright Act gave them a right to produce "revisions" of their publications. The writers argued that articles included in e-databases were not "revisions." The publishers filed a motion for summary judgment, which the court granted. The writers appealed to the U.S. Court of Appeals for the Second Circuit.*

IN THE LANGUAGE
OF THE COURT

WINTER, Chief Judge.
    *   *   *   *
    *   *   * [Under Section 201(c) of the Copyright Act] the privilege granted to a collective-work [publisher] to use individually copyrighted contributions is limited to the reproduction and distribution of the individual contribution as part of: (i) "that particular [i.e., the original] collective work"; (ii) "any revision of that collective work"; or

---

a. In the "1999" row, click on "Sept." On that page, scroll down to the case name and click on it to access the opinion.

(iii) "any later collective work in the same series." Because it is undisputed that the electronic databases are neither the original collective work—the particular edition of the periodical—in which the Authors' articles were published nor a later collective work in the same series, appellees [the publishers] rely entirely on the argument that each database constitutes a "revision" of the particular collective work in which each Author's individual contribution first appeared. We reject that argument.

　*　*　*　*

The most natural reading of the "revision" of "that collective work" clause is that the Section 201(c) privilege protects only later editions of a particular issue of a periodical, such as the final edition of a newspaper. Because later editions are not identical to earlier editions, use of the individual contributions in the later editions might not be protected under the preceding clause. Given the context provided by the surrounding clauses, this interpretation makes perfect sense. It protects the use of an individual contribution in a collective work that is somewhat altered from the original in which the copyrighted article was first published, but that is not in any ordinary sense of language a "later" work in the "same series."

　*　*　*　*

Moreover, *　*　* if the contents of an electronic database are merely a "revision" of a particular "collective work," e.g., the August 16, 1999 edition of *The New York Times*, then the third clause of the privilege sentence—permitting the reproduction and distribution of an individually copyrighted work as part of "a later collective work in the same series"—would be superfluous. An electronic database can contain hundreds or thousands of editions of hundreds or thousands of periodicals, including newspapers, magazines, anthologies, and encyclopedias. To view the contents of databases as revisions would eliminate any need for a privilege for "a later collective work in the same series."

DECISION AND REMEDY　*The U.S. Court of Appeals for the Second Circuit held that the publishers, to put the contents of their periodicals into e-databases and onto CD-ROMs, needed the permission of the writers whose articles were included in the periodicals. The court reversed the lower court's summary judgment and remanded the case with instructions to enter a judgment for the writers.*

The World Intellectual Property Organization (WIPO) Copyright Treaty of 1996. Technology, particularly the Internet, offers new outlets for creative products. It also makes them easier to steal—copyrighted works can be pirated and distributed around the world quickly and efficiently. To curb this crime, in 1996 the World Intellectual Property Organization (WIPO) enacted the WIPO Copyright Treaty, a special agreement under the Berne Convention. (The Berne Convention was discussed in Chapter 14.) The purpose was to upgrade global standards of copyright protection, particularly for the Internet.

Special provisions of the WIPO treaty relate to rights in digital data. The treaty strengthens some rights for copyright owners, in terms of their application in cyberspace, but leaves other questions unresolved. For example, the treaty does not make clear what, for purposes of international law, constitutes the making of a "copy" in electronic form. The United States signed the WIPO treaty in 1996 and implemented its terms in the Digital Millennium Copyright Act of 1998, which is discussed next.

The Digital Millennium Copyright Act of 1998. The Digital Millennium Copyright Act of 1998 created civil and criminal penalties for anyone who circumvents encryption software or other technological antipiracy protection. Also prohibited are the manufacture, import, sale, or distribution of devices or services for circumvention.

There are exceptions to fit the needs of libraries, scientists, universities, and others. In general, the new law does not restrict the "fair use" of circumvention for educational and other noncommercial purposes. For example, circumvention is allowed to test computer security, to conduct encryption research, to protect personal privacy, or to allow parents to monitor their children's use of the Internet. The exceptions are to be reconsidered every three years.

An Internet service provider (ISP) is not liable for any copyright infringement by its customer if the ISP is unaware of the subscriber's violation. An ISP may be held liable only after learning of the violation and failing to take action to shut the subscriber down. A copyright holder has to act promptly, however, by pursuing a claim in court, or the subscriber has the right to be restored to online access.

TRADE SECRETS IN CYBERSPACE

The nature of the new technology—the versatility of e-mail in particular—undercuts a business firm's ability to protect its confidential information, including trade secrets (trade secrets were defined and discussed in more detail in Chapter 14).[31] For example, a dishonest employee could transmit trade secrets in a company's computer to anyone via an e-mail connection on the Internet. "Anyone" could be a thief, a

competitor, or a future employer. If e-mail is not an option, the employee might walk out with the information on a computer disk. Even honest employees can make mistakes, sending confidential data to the wrong e-mail address—a competitor, for example, instead of a client—or losing a disk on a business trip.

An illustration of what a departing employee might do is provided by a criminal case that involved two competing software developers, Borland International, Inc., and Symantec. Eugene Wang, a Borland vice president, expressed dissatisfaction with his job and quit. Other Borland officers reviewed Wang's e-mail files and found messages to Gordon Eubanks, Symantec's president and chief executive officer. Believing that the messages contained trade secrets and other confidential information, Borland filed a civil suit to recover damages and also notified the police. After an investigation, criminal charges, including the theft of trade secrets, were filed against both Wang and Eubanks.[32]

---

31. Note that in a recent case, the court indicated that customers' e-mail addresses may constitute trade secrets. See *T-N-T Motorsports, Inc. v. Hennessey Motorsports, Inc.*, 965 S.W.2d 18 (Tex.App.—Hous. [1 Dist.] 1998), rehearing overruled (1998), petition dismissed (1998).

32. *People v. Eubanks*, 14 Cal.4th 580, 14 Cal.4th 1282D, 927 P.2d 310, 59 Cal.Rptr.2d 200 (1996), as modified on denial of rehearing (1997). The charges were dismissed after Borland paid a substantial part of the cost of the criminal investigation. The California Supreme Court felt that Borland's payment made it unlikely that the defendants would receive fair treatment.

CONCEPT SUMMARY 15.2   VIOLATIONS OF VIRTUAL PROPERTY RIGHTS

VIRTUAL PROPERTY	VIOLATION
Cyber Marks	Trademark infringement may occur in cyberspace if (1) another site's key words are used improperly as meta tags; (2) the quality of another's mark is diluted by improper use; (3) another's mark is used without a license; or (4) a licensing agreement is broken. (Trademark infringement can also occur with certain uses of hypertext links and framing technology.)
Patents	Patent infringement of a cyberspace product or process may occur if a user, including a software developer, fails to obtain a license to use the item.
Copyrights	Loading a computer program or data into the RAM of a computer is making a "copy" and may violate U.S. copyright law if it is done without the permission of the copyright holder. (International law does not clearly resolve this issue.) The Digital Millennium Copyright Act of 1998 created civil and criminal penalties for anyone who circumvents encryption software or other technological antipiracy protection.
Trade Secrets	Communicating trade secrets via new technology without authorization may be a violation of criminal and civil laws.

SECTION 6

E-Commerce

The increasing use of the Internet to do business brings to light at least two important concerns for persons who engage in commerce online, or **e-commerce,** and agree to **e-contracts.** There is some question about the ability of current Internet technology to guarantee the security of e-commerce. There is also concern about whether the legal framework can guarantee the enforcement of e-contracts.

In the following sections, we discuss these concerns in the context of the following types of Internet business transactions: contracting in cyberspace, making payments and investing online, and marketing on the Internet.

CONTRACTING IN CYBERSPACE

Over the last ten years, the new technology has transformed society and is defining new ways of doing business. This revolution in technology has even changed the nature of many of the goods and services that are the subjects of e-commerce and e-contracts. The most important legal questions concern how the law should be altered to accommodate these changes.

Cyberspace Agreements. A significant issue is how the law should be adapted to reflect business practices regarding such cyberspace agreements as Web site click-on agreements, software licenses (some types of licensing agreements were discussed earlier in this chapter), e-data interchange, and online sales. Some aspects of these agreements were discussed in the *Emerging Trends in Technology* in Chapter 11. Other facets are discussed in this chapter's *Emerging Trends in Technology* on pages 330–331.

Electronic Transactions. The National Conference of Commissioners (NCC) on Uniform State Laws has also promulgated the Uniform Electronic Transactions Act (UETA). The goal of the UETA is not to create rules for electronic transactions—for example, the act does not require digital signatures—but to support the enforcement of e-contracts.

Under the UETA, contracts entered into online, as well as other electronic documents, are presumed valid. For instance, the UETA defines *record* as "information that is inscribed on a tangible medium or

that is stored in an electronic or other medium and is retrievable in perceivable form."[33] In other words, a contract would not be unenforceable simply because it is in an electronic form.

The act also defines and supports the validity of electronic signatures. An electronic signature is "an electronic sound, symbol, or process attached to or logically associated with an electronic record and executed or adopted by a person with the intent to sign the electronic record."[34] This includes encrypted digital signatures, names (intended as signatures) at the ends of e-mail messages, and the click on a Web page if the click includes the identification of the person.

The UETA does not apply to transactions governed by the Uniform Commercial Code or the Uniform Computer Information Transactions Act, or to wills or testamentary trusts.

E-Contracts. As already indicated, one of the foremost issues in the area of contract law in cyberspace is the enforceability of an e-contract. Does a business deal agreed to online meet the legal requirements for a contract (see Chapter 9)? For example, does an e-contract fulfill the requirement of a "writing"? How can a party to the agreement verify that the other party "signed" this "writing"? These and other issues are discussed in *Emerging Trends in Technology* features in other chapters, including Chapter 11.

A party to a business deal often wants to know that any agreement made online is binding not only in the United States, but in other countries as well. In the United States, as discussed above, the federal government and the National Conference of Commissioners on Uniform State Laws are working on uniform laws to facilitate e-commerce and enforce e-contracts. Internationally, the United Nations Commission on International Trade Law (UNCITRAL) has completed a model law that relates to e-contracts. The International Chamber of Commerce has also issued model e-commerce guidelines.

E-MONEY

The technological revolution is changing the nature of financial services, including banking and investing, in fundamental ways. Traditional concepts of branches, networks, and payment systems do not apply in cyberspace. A bank or an investment broker

---

33. UETA 102(15).
34. UETA 102(8).

EMERGING TRENDS IN TECHNOLOGY

The Uniform Computer Information Transactions Act

To reflect current and future business conditions, the law needs to change to provide a legal framework for e-contracts and contracts related to software, information databases, and other aspects of the new technology.

The National Conference of Commissioners (NCC) on Uniform State Laws is aware of this need. To partially meet it, the NCC promulgated the Uniform Computer Information Transactions Act (UCITA), which governs all contracts for software development, sale, license, maintenance, and support, and contracts for information in digital form. Products, such as computers, that contain software may also be covered.

BEYOND ARTICLE 2 OF THE UCC

UCITA's outline and some of its legal principles parallel those of

Article 2 of the Uniform Commercial Code (UCC) (see Chapter 11). For example, the terms of an Article 2 sales contract and a UCITA licensing agreement include the express terms, as well as the terms arising from the *course of performance,* the *course of dealing,* and the *usage of trade.* Both articles give these concepts the same priority: express terms take precedence over the course of performance, followed by the course of dealing and the usage of trade.[a]

The UCITA goes beyond Article 2, however, to define, among other things, an *electronic transaction* as a contract in which humans may not review the messages. An *electronic agent* is "a computer program, electronic or other automated means used to independently initiate an action or to respond to electronic messages or performances without review by an individual."[b] (For more information on electronic agents, see the *Emerging Trends in Technology* in Chapter 20.)

---

a. UCITA 302.
b. UCITA 102(a)(28).

KEY PROVISIONS OF THE UCITA

The UCITA covers electronically disseminated information. Excluded are other types of licenses of information, such as contracts for motion picture exhibition, and the distribution of information in traditional forms, such as books and magazines.

Under the UCITA, the *licensor* (the party who sells the right to use the software) can control how the *licensee* (the party who buys the right to use the software) uses mass-marketed software. Licensees and other consumers are not entirely without protection, however. The UCITA includes provisions that would do the following:

■ Endorse the shrinkwrap licenses that accompany software.
■ Permit software licensors to electronically disable software after the cancellation of a license.
■ Extend the warranty laws that cover other goods to software licenses.
■ Require a cost-free refund from a software seller to a consumer if the terms of the use of the software are not acceptable to the consumer.

---

with a home office in Kansas, for example, can do business with a customer anywhere in the world. In fact, an online financial institution does not even need a physical office—a Web page is enough.

One of the most important ways in which the new technology is changing the nature of financial services is the method in which payments are made. Electronic money, or **e-money,** includes a number of

alternatives to traditional means of payment. From a consumer's point of view, these alternatives include prepaid funds recorded on the consumer's personal computer or on a card.

Card-Based Money. Card-based e-money is of two types. One type involves recording a balance of funds on a magnetic stripe on a card that is debited by a

EMERGING TRENDS IN TECHNOLOGY

The Uniform Computer Information Transactions Act, continued

SUPPORT AND OPPOSITION

Some observers believe that by providing a legal framework for the emerging technological age, the UCITA may become the most significant law of the new century. Our economy is now centered on information products and services. The UCITA would provide uniform legal rules for some of this commerce, which in turn will encourage its further development.

Others, including consumer groups, law professors, librarians, some software developers, and the Federal Trade Commission's Bureau of Consumer Protection, oppose the enactment of the UCITA. It is claimed that among other things, the UCITA would not make current business practices into law but would instead require modifications to those practices.

Critics charge that under the UCITA, software vendors could disclaim all responsibility for their products, even those that are defective or that damage the buyer's hardware (because, for example, the product is infected by a virus). It is also alleged that software vendors could bury the terms of their licenses or sales in "fine print" or in pamphlets inside their products' boxes. Consumers would have little choice as to whether to accept these terms.

IMPLICATIONS FOR THE BUSINESSPERSON

1. Major software makers and marketers might favor the enactment of the UCITA because of its support for shrinkwrap and clickwrap agreements. If widely enacted, it would make the law governing such agreements consistent throughout the United States.
2. Businesses that need a software program's code to make it compatible with other programs may oppose the enactment of the UCITA. Under the act, a shrinkwrap license may prohibit what is known as "reverse engineering." This would mean that a firm could hire only a

representative of the software maker to fix incompatibilities.

FOR CRITICAL ANALYSIS

1. Should the law treat software and electronic information differently than other products?
2. Is it possible to draft a uniform law that both the proponents and the critics of the UCITA would support?

RELEVANT WEB SITES

To learn more about the UCITA, you can go to the Web site of the National Conference of Commissioners on Uniform State Laws (NCCUSL) at **http://www. nccusl.org**. Click on "Questions & Answers about UCITA." For more background and discussion of the UCITA (which was formerly known as Article 2B of the UCC), see **http://www.2bguide.com**. Click on any link. This site is maintained by Carol Kunze, an attorney who participated in the drafting of the UCITA and the Uniform Electronic Transactions Act.

---

computer terminal on each use. The second type uses a microprocessor chip embedded in a so-called **smart card.** A smart card is safer and more versatile than a magnetic-stripe card. A smart card can be encrypted to protect the value on the card from theft. Also, a smart card can function simultaneously as a credit card, a debit card, a stored value card, and a personal information card, such as a driver's license.

Payment Information. Current technology allows e-money to be used in a variety of ways. E-money can be used like cash, in which no personally identifiable records are created. It can also be used as part of a system that identifies and keeps information about every transaction of every consumer. The use and possible misuse of this information are concerns.

Presently, it is not clear which, if any, laws apply to the security of e-money payment information. The Federal Reserve has decided not to impose Regulation E, which governs certain electronic funds transfers, on e-money transactions. Federal laws prohibiting unauthorized access to electronic communications might apply, however. For example, the Electronic Communications Privacy Act of 1986 prohibits any person from knowingly divulging to any other person the contents of an electronic communication while that communication is in transmission or in electronic storage.

MARKETING ON THE INTERNET

On the Web, advertising is everywhere. It is a source for the funds that pay the Internet servers and others who maintain the connections in cyberspace. It presents opportunities for consumers and merchants around the world. It also presents a challenge for those charged with protecting consumers from dishonest sellers: How can the law be administered without stifling the potential of the Internet?

Fraud, deception, misleading information—despite new advances, some things never change. Here, we point out three situations in which consumers and businesses need to be careful.

Consumer Data. Information about consumers can be used to aim advertising at those persons who might be most interested in what is being sold. It is not illegal to attempt to target only those consumers who might buy what a merchant is selling.

Data about users can also be compiled with their awareness and consent. Nearly all commercial Web sites, for example, collect information about their visitors and members, and most do so with those users' knowledge.[35] Few of these sites have a privacy policy, however, and many do not provide details about what they do with the data.

One commercial site that collects information about its members is GeoCities, a provider of free home pages and e-mail addresses. GeoCities has more than one million members and hosts one of the five most frequently visited sites on the Web. At one time, GeoCities told new members that it would not share the information that it collects with anyone without the permission of the persons from whom it was collected but would "use it to gain a better understanding of who is visiting GeoCities."

In 1998, the Federal Trade Commission (FTC) charged that the contrary was taking place. In the first case involving Internet privacy, the FTC claimed that GeoCities "misrepresent[ed] the purposes for which it collect[ed] personal identifying information from children and adults." On its registration form, GeoCities treated the failure of a member or visitor to click on a box that would let the user opt out of marketing offers as "permission" to share the information. Those who did not click on the box were considered to have opted in. The FTC also claimed that GeoCities sold the data to third parties "who used [the information] to target members solicitations beyond those agreed to by the member." Without admitting any wrongdoing, GeoCities agreed to change its policies on disclosing user information.

Web Site Content. In any market, the prices and the availability of products change quickly. This is as true in cyberspace as it is at your local mall. Even with the global reach of the Internet, what is a glut on a Web market one day can be a scarcity the next. Partly for this reason, one of the most important details to watch for is the date of the content placed on a particular Web site.

It is equally as important for those who host pages on the Web to make sure that their content is current. Merchants should take special care to update their publicized prices to avoid penalties and potential lawsuits. An airline was fined $14,000 for failing to update expired fare information. A bank or other financial institution may be subject to liability if it displays expired interest rate information on its site.

One step to take to guard against liability for outdated information is to include on the site a disclaimer page. Because a visitor may bypass a home page and go directly to an inner page, the disclaimer should be linked to all pages on the site.

Cyber Fraud. No one knows the full extent of cyber fraud (fraud committed on the Internet). Indications are that cyber fraud is increasing with the rising use of the Internet. Scams that were once conducted solely by mail or phone can now be found online, and new technology is contributing to more creative ways to commit fraud.

---

35. Under the Children's Online Privacy Protection Act of 1998 and rules issued by the Federal Trade Commission in 1999, commercial Web sites must normally obtain parents' permission before asking children under the age of thirteen for personal information, and the information cannot be shared with others. See 15 U.S.C. Sections 6501–6506.

Cyber fraud takes many forms. A common form involves the sale of misrepresented or undelivered products and services via the Internet. Cyber fraud also includes bogus bidding in Web auctions, empty promises of huge profits for investing in business "opportunities," schemes in which profits are made from recruiting others instead of from sales of goods or services, and so on.

The unique nature of the Internet makes it easy for cyber wrongdoers to hide their identities and locations. Attractive, impressive Web sites can be set up for a small price. For a similarly low cost, e-mail can be sent to hundreds of thousands of users. Phony tips concerning fraudulent investments can be posted in newsgroups and chat rooms. Return addresses can be falsified or omitted. A wrongdoer can operate from anywhere in the world.

Besides the difficulty of identifying and finding cyber wrongdoers, it can be difficult to bring legal actions against them. When they are located in other states or countries, questions involving jurisdiction may arise (see the discussion of jurisdiction earlier in this chapter). In other places, it can be complicated to obtain search warrants and to seize evidence and the proceeds of criminal activity. Anywhere, it can be expensive to pursue legal proceedings.

Despite these limitations, most state and federal laws that apply to unfair and deceptive acts and practices also apply to cyber fraud. State consumer fraud and false advertising laws are based on Section 5 of the Federal Trade Commission Act, which is discussed in Chapters 24 and 27.

CONCEPT SUMMARY 15.3

LEGAL PROTECTION FOR E-COMMERCE

ASPECT OF E-COMMERCE	LEGAL PROTECTION
Contracts	If the states adopt the Uniform Computer Information Transactions Act and the Uniform Electronic Transactions Act, these model laws may provide the legal framework for an economy centered on the licensing of information products and services.
E-Money	The Electronic Communications Privacy Act, which prohibits a person from revealing the contents of an electronic communication without authority, may protect the security of e-money payment information. Other laws may also cover e-money and e-money transactions.
Marketing	State and federal laws that regulate fraud and deception by other means prohibit those same acts in cyberspace.

TERMS AND CONCEPTS TO REVIEW

cyber crime 318	e-commerce 329	hacker 319
cyber hate speech 317	e-contract 329	meta tags 317
cyber mark 322	e-money 330	smart card 331
cyber stalker 318	encryption 316	spam 321
cyber terrorist 319	filtering software 317	virtual courtroom 314
cyber tort 319	flame 319	virtual property 322

QUESTIONS AND CASE PROBLEMS

15–1. TECHNOLOGY AND THE LAW. Some observers believe that the law should not apply in cyberspace because they think that it inhibits the Internet's development. In what ways is the law facilitating the development of technology in cyberspace?

15–2. FREEDOM OF SPEECH. Jill is a professor who teaches a business law course. Jill maintains a Web site that contains background material for the class sessions. This material includes student research papers, which are submitted in advance of the classes at which they are discussed. In preparation for a class discussion on computers and the law, Mark, one of Jill's students, submits a paper that includes encryption programs he wrote to show how computers work. Jill posts this paper on her Web site. Is this post an "export"? Assuming that it is, what arguments could you make that it is protected by the First Amendment? What arguments could you make that it is not so protected?

15–3. ELECTRONIC FILING. Like other courts, the Washington county courts thoroughly document their proceedings. Even oral proceedings are transcribed so that the written records are complete. The courts make use of copy machines, word processors, and computers (for legal research). The basic functions of filing, storing, locating, updating, searching, and cross-referencing court documents are still done manually, however. What advantages would the Washington county courts realize if they were to switch to an electronic filing system?

15–4. JURISDICTION. Cybersell, Inc., is an Arizona corporation (Cybersell AZ) that provides Internet marketing services. Cybersell AZ applied with the U.S. Patent and Trademark Office (USPTO) to register "Cybersell" as a service mark. Before the application was granted, unrelated parties formed Cybersell, Inc., a Florida corporation (Cybersell FL), to provide consulting services for marketing on the Internet. Cybersell FL put up a Web site using the name "Cybersell," but its interactivity was limited to taking a surfer's name and address. No one in Arizona contacted Cybersell FL, or even hit on its Web page, before the USPTO granted Cybersell AZ's service mark application. Cybersell AZ then told Cybersell FL to stop using "Cybersell" and filed a suit in a federal district court in Arizona against Cybersell FL, alleging, among other things, trademark infringement. Cybersell FL filed a motion to dismiss for lack of jurisdiction. How should the court rule? Why? [*Cybersell, Inc., an Arizona Corporation v. Cybersell, Inc., a Florida Corporation*, 130 F.3d 414 (9th Cir. 1997)]

15–5. FREEDOM OF SPEECH. The Commonwealth (state) of Virginia enacted a statute to restrict the ability of state employees to access sexually explicit material on state-owned or leased computers. Melvin Urofsky and other professors at colleges and universities in Virginia felt that the statute interfered with their teaching. For example, Urofsky was reluctant to have students do certain online research assignments. Urofsky and others filed a suit in a federal district court against Virginia Governor George Allen and others, contending that the statute violated their First Amendment right to free speech. Both sides filed motions for summary judgment. Why would the court grant the professors' motion? Why would the court rule in the Commonwealth's favor? [*Urofsky v. Allen*, 995 F.Supp. 634 (E.D.Va. 1998)]

15–6. DEFAMATION. An unidentified person posted messages on America Online, Inc. (AOL), advertising for sale T-shirts and other items with offensive slogans related to the 1995 bombing of the federal building in Oklahoma City. Buyers were instructed to call the business phone number of Ken Zeran, who knew nothing about the ad. Zeran received a high volume of calls, consisting of derogatory messages and death threats. He called AOL and was assured that the messages would be removed. The postings remained up for five days, however, during which time the angry calls to Zeran intensified. Zeran filed a suit in a federal district court against AOL, arguing in part that AOL was liable for unreasonably delaying the removal of the defamatory messages. Why would the court rule in AOL's favor? [*Zeran v. America Online, Inc.*, 129 F.3d 327 (4th Cir. 1997)]

15–7. CYBER MARKS. Playboy Enterprises, Inc. (PEI), owns the rights to the cyber marks "Playboy," "Playboy magazine," and "Playmate." Without authorization, Calvin Designer Label used the terms as meta tags for its Web sites on the Internet. As tags, the terms were invisible to viewers (in black type on a black background), but they caused the Web sites to be returned at the top of the list of a search engine query for "Playboy" or "Playmate." PEI filed a suit in a federal district court against Calvin Designer Label, alleging, among other things, trademark infringement. Should the court order the defendant to stop using the terms as tags? Why or why not? [*Playboy Enterprises, Inc. v. Calvin Designer Label*, 985 F.Supp. 1220 (N.D.Cal. 1997)]

15–8. COPYRIGHTS. Webbworld operates a Web site called Neptics, Inc. The site accepts downloads of certain images from third parties and makes these images available to any user who accesses the site. Before being allowed to view the images, however, the user must pay a subscription fee of $11.95 per month. Over a period of several months, images were available that were originally created by or for Playboy Enterprises, Inc. (PEI). The images were displayed at Neptics's site without PEI's permission. PEI filed a suit in a federal district court against Webbworld, alleging copyright infringement. Webbworld argued in part that it should not be held liable because, like an Internet service provider that furnishes access to the Internet, it did not create or control the content of the information available to its subscribers. Do you agree with Webbworld? Why or why not? [*Playboy Enterprises, Inc. v. Webbworld*, 968 F.Supp. 1171 (N.D.Tex. 1997)]

15–9. IN YOUR COURT

Storm Impact, Inc., produces software, including the games TaskMaker and MacSki. To market upgraded versions of the games, Storm distributed them as shareware with locks built into the programs. A user could sample the unlocked portions at no charge and then buy a key, in the form of a floppy disk and registration number, to use the whole program. A legend expressly encouraged users to give unaltered copies to others but prohibited users from charging others for the shareware. Software of the Month Club (SOMC) provides collections of new shareware to its members for a $24.95 monthly fee.

When Storm's games were included in one of SOMC's collections, Storm filed a suit against SOMC, alleging, among other things, copyright infringement. Assume that you are the judge in the trial court hearing this case and answer the following questions:

(a) SOMC argued that by endorsing and distributing shareware, it was performing a service for the creators, much like a book reviewer does for a book. Therefore, claimed SOMC, its copying and distribution of the games constituted a "fair use." Was it? (Before you answer this question, you may want to review the "fair use" doctrine discussed in Chapter 14.)

(b) Should the fact that SOMC was charging for something that was otherwise free on the Internet affect your decision in this case? Similarly, should Storm's restriction on charging for its shareware affect your decision?

LAW ON THE WEB

For updated links to resources available on the Web, as well as a variety of other materials, visit this text's Web site at http://wleb.westbuslaw.com.

The Washtenaw County Trial Court in Michigan provides an excellent example of what a court can do at a site on the Web at

http://www.co.washtenaw.mi.us/depts/courts/index.htm

The U.S. Patent and Trademark Office can be accessed at

http://www.uspto.gov

The World Intellectual Property Organization offers information on the background of intellectual property, including copyrights, and its international protection at

http://www.wipo.org/eng/newindex/intellct.htm

The most recent drafts of the Uniform Computer Information Transactions Act and the Uniform Electronic Transactions Act can be found at

http://www.law.upenn.edu/bll/ulc/ulc.htm

LEGAL RESEARCH EXERCISES ON THE WEB

Go to http://wleb.westbuslaw.com, the Web site that accompanies this text. Select "Internet Applications," and then click on "Chapter 15." There you will find the following Internet research exercises that you can perform to learn more about cyber crime and free speech issues in cyberspace:

Activity 15–1: Cyber Crime

Activity 15–2: Cyberspace and Free Speech

CHAPTER 16

Creditor-Debtor Relations and Bankruptcy

N ORMALLY, CREDITORS HAVE NO PROBLEM collecting the debts owed to them. When disputes arise over the amount owed, however, or when the debtor simply cannot or will not pay, what happens? What remedies are available to creditors when debtors default? And what laws assist and protect debtors? The first part of this chapter provides the answers to these questions. It deals with the various rights and remedies available through statutory laws, common law, and contract law to assist the debtor and creditor in resolving their disputes without the debtor's having to resort to bankruptcy. The second part of this chapter discusses bankruptcy as a last resort in resolving debtor-creditor problems.

SECTION 1

Laws Assisting Creditors

Both the common law and statutory laws create various rights and remedies for creditors. We discuss here some of these rights and remedies, including liens, garnishment, creditors' composition agreements,

mortgage foreclosure, and a debtor's assignment of assets for the benefit of creditors.

LIENS

A **lien** is a claim or charge on a debtor's property that must be satisfied before the property (or its proceeds) is available to satisfy the claims of other creditors. As mentioned, liens may arise under the common law or under statutory law. Statutory liens include *mechanic's liens*. Liens created at common law include *artisan's liens* and *innkeeper's liens*. *Judicial liens* include those that represent a creditor's efforts to collect on a debt before or after a judgment is entered by a court.

Generally, a lien creditor has priority over an unperfected secured party but not over a perfected secured party. Thus, a person who becomes a lien creditor before another security interest in the same property is perfected has priority, but one who acquires the lien after perfection does not have priority. Mechanic's and artisan's liens, however, have priority over perfected security interests unless a statute provides otherwise.

Mechanic's Lien. When a person contracts for labor, services, or material to be furnished for the purpose of making improvements on real property but does not immediately pay for the improvements, the creditor can place a **mechanic's lien** on the property. This creates a special type of debtor-creditor relationship in which the real estate itself becomes security for the debt.

For example, a painter agrees to paint a house for a homeowner for an agreed-on price to cover labor and materials. If the homeowner cannot pay or pays only a portion of the charges, a mechanic's lien against the property can be created. The painter is the lienholder, and the real property is encumbered with a mechanic's lien for the amount owed. If the homeowner does not pay the lien, the property can be sold to satisfy the debt. Notice of the *foreclosure* (the enforcement of the lien) must be given to the debtor in advance, however.

The procedures by which a mechanic's lien is created are controlled by state law. Generally, the lienholder must file a written notice of lien against the particular property involved. The notice of lien must be filed within a specific time period, measured from the last date on which materials or labor were provided (usually within 60 to 120 days). Failure to pay the debt entitles the lienholder to foreclose on the real estate on which the improvements were made and to sell it to satisfy the amount of the debt. Of course, as mentioned, the lienholder is required by statute to give notice to the owner of the property prior to foreclosure and sale. The sale proceeds are used to pay the debt and the costs of the legal proceedings; the surplus, if any, is paid to the former owner.

Artisan's Lien. An **artisan's lien** is a security device created at common law through which a creditor can recover payment from a debtor for labor and materials furnished in the repair of personal property. For example, Whitney leaves her diamond ring at the jewelry shop to be repaired and to have her initials engraved on the band. In the absence of an agreement, the jeweler can keep the ring until Whitney pays for the services that the jeweler provides. Should Whitney fail to pay, the jeweler has a lien on Whitney's ring for the amount of the bill and can sell the ring in satisfaction of the lien.

In contrast to a mechanic's lien, an artisan's lien is *possessory*. The lienholder ordinarily must have retained possession of the property and have expressly or impliedly agreed to provide the services on a cash, not a credit, basis. The lien remains in existence as long as the lienholder maintains possession, and the lien is terminated once possession is voluntarily surrendered—unless the surrender is only temporary. With a temporary surrender, there must be an agreement that the property will be returned to the lienholder. Even with such an agreement, if a third party obtains rights in that property while it is out of the possession of the lienholder, the lien is lost.

Modern statutes permit the holder of an artisan's lien to foreclose and sell the property subject to the lien to satisfy payment of the debt. As with the mechanic's lien, the lienholder is required to give notice to the owner of the property prior to foreclosure and sale. In some states, holders of artisan's liens must give notice to title lienholders of automobiles prior to foreclosure. The sale proceeds are used to pay the debt and the costs of the legal proceedings, and the surplus, if any, is paid to the former owner. The artisan's lien has priority over a filed statutory lien (such as a title lien on an automobile or a lien filed under Article 9 of the UCC) as well as priority over a bailee's lien (such as a storage lien).

Judicial Liens. A debt must be past due before a creditor can commence legal action against a debtor. Once legal action is brought, the debtor's property may be seized to satisfy the debt. If the property is seized prior to trial proceedings, the seizure is referred to as an *attachment* of the property. The seizure may also occur following a court judgment in the creditor's favor. In that case, the court's order to seize the property is referred to as a *writ of execution*.

Attachment. **Attachment** refers to a court-ordered seizure and taking into custody of property prior to the securing of a judgment for a past-due debt. Attachment rights are created by state statutes. Normally a *prejudgment* remedy, attachment occurs either at the time of or immediately after the commencement of a lawsuit and before the entry of a final judgment. By statute, the restrictions and requirements for a creditor to attach before judgment are specific and limited. The due process clause of the Fourteenth Amendment to the Constitution limits the courts' power to authorize seizure of a debtor's property without notice to the debtor or a hearing on the facts. In recent years, a number of state attachment laws have been held to be unconstitutional.

To use attachment as a remedy, the creditor must have an enforceable right to payment of the debt under law, and the creditor must follow certain procedures. Otherwise, the creditor can be liable for damages for wrongful attachment. He or she must file with the court an *affidavit* (a written or printed statement, made under oath or sworn to) stating that the debtor is in default and delineating the statutory grounds under which attachment is sought. A bond must be posted by the creditor to cover at least court costs, the value of the loss of use of the good suffered by the debtor, and the value of the property attached. When the court is satisfied that all the requirements have been met, it issues a **writ of attachment,** which is similar to a writ of execution (to be discussed shortly) in that it directs the sheriff or other officer to seize nonexempt property. If the creditor prevails at trial, the seized property can be sold to satisfy the judgment.

Writ of Execution.   If a creditor is successful in a legal action against a debtor, the court awards the creditor a judgment against the debtor (usually for the amount of the debt plus any interest and legal costs incurred in obtaining the judgment). Frequently, the creditor finds it easy to secure a judgment against the debtor but nevertheless fails to collect the awarded amount. If the debtor will not or cannot pay the judgment, the creditor is entitled to go back to the court and obtain a **writ of execution,** which is an order, usually issued by the clerk of the court, directing the sheriff to seize (levy) and sell any of the debtor's nonexempt real or personal property that is within the court's geographic jurisdiction (usually the county in which the courthouse is located). The proceeds of the sale are used to pay off the judgment and the costs of the sale. Any excess is paid to the debtor.

The debtor can pay the judgment and redeem the nonexempt property any time before the sale takes place. Because of exemption laws (which cover the debtor's homestead and designated items of personal property) and bankruptcy laws, however, many judgments are virtually uncollectible.

Garnishment.   An order for **garnishment** permits a creditor to collect a debt by seizing property of the debtor (such as wages or money in a bank account) that is being held by a third party (such as an employer or a bank). Typically, a garnishment judg-

ment is served on a debtor's employer so that part of the debtor's usual paycheck will be paid to the creditor.

The legal proceeding for a garnishment action is governed by state law. As a result of a garnishment proceeding, as noted, a third party (such as the debtor's employer) is ordered by the court to turn over property owned by the debtor (such as wages) to pay the debt. Garnishment can be a prejudgment remedy, requiring a hearing before a court, or a postjudgment remedy. According to the laws in some states, the judgment creditor needs to obtain only one order of garnishment, which will then continuously apply to the judgment debtor's weekly wages until the entire debt is paid. In other states, the judgment creditor must go back to court for a separate order of garnishment for each pay period.

Both federal laws and state laws limit the amount of money that can be taken from a debtor's weekly take-home pay through garnishment proceedings. Federal law provides a minimal framework to protect debtors from losing all their income in order to pay judgment debts.[1] State laws also provide dollar exemptions, and these amounts are often larger than those provided by federal law.[2] State and federal statutes can be applied together to help create a pool of funds sufficient to enable a debtor to continue to provide for family needs while also reducing the amount of the judgment debt in a reasonable way. Under federal law, garnishment of an employee's wages for any one indebtedness cannot be grounds for dismissal of an employee.

One of the questions courts have faced in recent years has to do with whether a debtor's pension fund can be attached by creditors, through garnishment or other proceedings, to satisfy a debt. Under the Employee Retirement Income Security Act (ERISA) of 1974,[3] certain types of pension funds "may not be alienated [transferred]," or attached. The law is less clear, however, on whether pension funds, after they have been received by a retiree, can be subject to attachment by creditors. This issue was before the court in the following case.

---

1. For example, the federal Consumer Credit Protection Act of 1968, 15 U.S.C. Sections 1601–1693r, provides that a debtor can retain either 75 percent of his or her disposable earnings per week or the sum equivalent to thirty hours of work paid at federal minimum wage rates, whichever is greater.
2. A few states (for example, Texas) do not permit garnishment of wages by private parties except under a child-support order.
3. 29 U.S.C. Sections 1001–1461.

CASE 16.1

United States v. Smith

United States
Court of Appeals,
Fourth Circuit, 1995.
47 F.3d 681.
http://www.findlaw.
com/casecode/courts/
4th.html[a]

IN THE LANGUAGE
OF THE COURT

BACKGROUND AND FACTS *For nine years, Charles Smith asked his friends and acquaintances to invest their money in his business schemes. Smith used most of the money—estimated to be more than $350,000—for personal expenses. Smith was indicted for criminal fraud and pleaded guilty to that crime in a federal district court. The court imposed a prison sentence and ordered Smith to repay his victims as much as possible by turning over, each month, the entire amount of his pension benefits. Smith appealed the order, claiming that it violated the "anti-alienation" provision of ERISA.*

ERVIN, Chief Judge:

* * * *

This court has long recognized a strong public policy against the alienability of an ERISA plan participant's benefits. The [United States] Supreme Court, as well, has found that it is not "appropriate to approve any generalized equitable exception * * * to ERISA's prohibition on the assignment or alienation of pension benefits."

* * *

* * * The government's position is that once pension funds have been distributed, the anti-alienability statute no longer applies. * * *

* * * The Supreme Court has noted that the purpose of ERISA is to safeguard a stream of income for pensioners. Where an employee elects to draw on her ERISA plan prior to her retirement, she forfeits the protection provided by the Act. Where, however, the funds are paid pursuant to the terms of the plan as income during retirement years, ERISA prohibits their alienation. * * *

* * * *

In the case at hand, the government attempted to require Smith to draw down his benefits due under the plans as a lump sum and turn it over intact as restitution. Upon discovering that Smith was not eligible for lump sum distribution, the government agreed to the recovery of his benefits as they are paid to him. It is clear that the government would not have been successful in requiring Smith to request a lump sum distribution. * * * *[B]enefits in the hands of the fiduciary are beyond the reach of garnishment.* The government should not be allowed to do indirectly what it cannot do directly; it cannot require Smith to turn over his pension benefits in a lump sum, nor can it require him to turn over his benefits as they are paid to him. Understandably, there may be a natural distaste for the result we reach here. The statute, however, is clear. Congress has made a policy decision to protect the ERISA income of retirees, even if that decision prevents others from securing relief for the wrongs done them. [Emphasis added.]

* * * [There is a] danger in eroding through exception the anti-alienation policy of ERISA. That entire legislation was aimed at guaranteeing the security of retirement income for American workers. * * * We decline to participate in the diminution of these safeguards in circumstances which might seem harmless enough in particular instances but which, in the aggregate, might invite creditors to believe that ERISA funds are not, after all, inviolate.

DECISION
AND REMEDY

The U.S. Court of Appeals for the Fourth Circuit vacated the lower court's order and remanded the case. The appellate court ordered the lower court to redetermine the amount that Smith was to pay to his victims, based on "a balance of the victims' interest in compensation and Smith's other financial resources."

---

a. In the "Browsing" section, in the "1995" row, click on "March." When that page opens, scroll down the list to the *Smith* case name and click on it to access the opinion.

MORTGAGE FORECLOSURE

Mortgage holders have the right to foreclose on mortgaged property in the event of a debtor's default. The usual method of foreclosure is by judicial sale of the property, although the statutory methods of foreclosure vary from state to state. If the proceeds of the foreclosure sale are sufficient to cover both the costs of the foreclosure and the mortgaged debt, any surplus is received by the debtor. If the sale proceeds are insufficient to cover the foreclosure costs and the mortgaged debt, however, the **mortgagee** (the creditor-lender) can seek to recover the difference from the **mortgagor** (the debtor) by obtaining a deficiency judgment representing the difference between the mortgaged debt plus foreclosure costs and the amount actually received from the proceeds of the foreclosure sale. A deficiency judgment is obtained in a separate legal action that is pursued subsequent to the foreclosure action. It entitles the creditor to recover from other property owned by the debtor. Some states do not permit deficiency judgments for some types of real estate interests.

Before the foreclosure sale, a defaulting mortgagor can redeem the property by paying the full amount of the debt, plus any interest and costs that have accrued. This right is known as the **equity of redemption.** In some states, a mortgagor may even redeem the property within a certain period of time—called a **statutory period of redemption**—after the sale. In these states, the deed to the property usually is not delivered to the purchaser until the statutory period has expired.

CONCEPT SUMMARY 16.1

REMEDIES AVAILABLE TO CREDITORS

Liens	1. *Mechanic's lien*—A nonpossessory, filed lien on an owner's real estate for labor, services, or materials furnished to or made on the realty.
	2. *Artisan's lien*—A possessory lien on an owner's personal property for labor performed or value added to the personal property.
	3. *Judicial liens*—
	a. Attachment—A court-ordered seizure of property prior to a court's final determination of the creditor's rights to the property. Attachment is available only on the creditor's posting of a bond and in strict compliance with the applicable state statutes.
	b. Writ of execution—A court order directing the sheriff to seize (levy) and sell a debtor's nonexempt real or personal property to satisfy a court's judgment in the creditor's favor.
Garnishment	A collection remedy that allows the creditor to attach a debtor's money (such as wages owed or bank accounts) and property that are held by a third person.
Mortgage Foreclosure	On the debtor's default, the entire mortgage debt is due and payable, allowing the creditor to foreclose on the realty by selling it to satisfy the debt.

SECTION 2

Suretyship and Guaranty

When a third person promises to pay a debt owed by another in the event the debtor does not pay, either a *suretyship* or a *guaranty* relationship is created. The third person's credit becomes the security for the debt owed.

SURETYSHIP

A contract of strict **suretyship** is a promise made by a third person to be responsible for the debtor's obligation. It is an express contract between the **surety** and the creditor. The surety in the strictest sense is primarily liable for the debt of the principal. The creditor can demand payment from the surety from the moment that the debt is due. A suretyship contract is not a form of indemnity;

that is, it is not merely a promise to make good any loss that a creditor may incur as a result of the debtor's failure to pay. The creditor need not exhaust all legal remedies against the principal debtor before holding the surety responsible for payment. Moreover, a surety agreement does not have to be in writing to be enforceable, although usually such agreements are in writing.

For example, Jason Oller wants to borrow money from the bank to buy a used car. Because Jason is still in college, the bank will not lend him the money unless his father, Stacey Oller, who has dealt with the bank before, will cosign the note (add his signature to the note, thereby becoming jointly liable for payment of the debt). When Mr. Oller cosigns the note, he becomes primarily liable to the bank. On the note's due date, the bank can seek payment from Jason Oller, Stacey Oller, or both jointly.

GUARANTY

A guaranty contract is similar to a suretyship contract in that it includes a promise to answer for the debt or default of another. With a suretyship arrangement, however, the surety is primarily liable for the debtor's obligation. With a guaranty arrangement, the **guarantor**—the third person making the guaranty—is secondarily liable. The guarantor can be required to pay the obligation only after the principal debtor defaults, and usually only after the creditor has made an attempt to collect from the debtor.

For example, a corporation, BX Enterprises, needs to borrow money to meet its payroll. The bank is skeptical about the creditworthiness of BX and requires Dawson, its president, who is a wealthy businessperson and owner of 70 percent of BX Enterprises, to sign an agreement making himself personally liable for payment if BX does not pay off the loan. As a guarantor of the loan, Dawson cannot be held liable until BX Enterprises is in default.

The Statute of Frauds requires that a guaranty contract between the guarantor and the creditor must be in writing to be enforceable unless the *main purpose exception* applies. Briefly, this exception provides that if the main purpose of the guaranty agreement is to benefit the guarantor, then the contract need not be in writing to be enforceable.

The guaranty contract terms determine the extent and time of the guarantor's liability. For example, the guaranty can be *continuing*, designed to cover a series of transactions by the debtor. Also, the guaranty can be *unlimited* or *limited* as to time and amount. In addition, the guaranty can be *absolute*, in which case the guarantor becomes liable immediately on the debtor's default, or *conditional*, in which case the guarantor becomes liable only on the happening of a certain event.

In the following case, the issue was whether a guaranty of a lease signed by the president of a corporation was enforceable against the president personally, although he signed the guaranty as a representative of the corporation.

CASE 16.2 Wilson Court Limited Partnership v. Tony Maroni's, Inc.

Supreme Court of Washington, 1998. 134 Wash.2d 692, 952 P.2d 590.

COMPANY PROFILE *Tony Riviera founded Tony Maroni's, Inc., to sell Tony Maroni's Famous Gourmet Pizza in Seattle, Washington, in the late 1980s. Tony Maroni's began by offering pizzas, salads, calzones, and lasagna for delivery only. By 1995, the firm had begun franchising (licensing its brand to investors to operate Tony Maroni's outlets—franchising is discussed in Chapter 39). Two years later, with eleven locations in the Seattle area, including six franchise outlets, and ten more stores in development, the company announced plans to open five hundred locations nationwide before 2002. Despite these plans, by the end of 1997, Tony Maroni's had yet to turn a profit and was nearly $1 million in debt.*

BACKGROUND AND FACTS *Tony Maroni's, Inc., agreed to lease retail space owned by Wilson Court Limited Partnership. Tony Riviera, Tony Maroni's president, signed the lease for 1,676 square feet of space for a sixty-month term. The lease provided for improvements, estimated to be worth $45,520. Initially, Tony Maroni's contributed $5,000 toward the improvements, and was to pay an additional $7,000 over the life of the lease, at $148.73 per month. Wilson contributed the balance of $33,520. When he signed the* *lease, Riviera also signed a guaranty agreement that was incorporated by reference in the lease. On the signature line of the guaranty, Riviera wrote "President" after his name. The guaranty did not specifically identify who was bound, referring only to "the under-signed" or "Guarantor." Riviera also signed the lease in a representative capacity, but the lease clearly indicated that only Tony Maroni's was bound by its terms. When Tony Maroni's defaulted on the lease, Wilson filed a suit in a Washington state court against Tony Maroni's, Riviera, and others. Riviera asserted in part that he was not personally liable on the guaranty because he signed only in his capacity as a corporate officer. The court issued a summary judgment in favor of Wilson. Riviera appealed to the Washington Supreme Court.*

IN THE LANGUAGE OF THE COURT

TALMADGE, Justice.

* * * *

* * * [The] combination of circumstances [in this case] renders the Guaranty ambiguous.

In construing the Guaranty in light of this ambiguity, we acknowledge contracts to answer for the debt of another must be explicit and are strictly construed, but we must also recognize the commercial context in which this Guaranty was signed. Where two commercial entities sign a commercial agreement, we will give such an agreement a commercially reasonable construction. In this case, such a construction leads us to the conclusion Riviera is personally liable on the Guaranty as a matter of law.

First, any ambiguity in the Guaranty was created by Riviera himself in adding the descriptive language to his signature. *Such ambiguity will be construed against Riviera as the party who drafted this language.* [Emphasis added.]

Second, the language of the Guaranty itself compels the view Riviera is personally liable. We must interpret the Lease and Guaranty as a whole, giving reasonable effect to each of its parts. The plain language of the Guaranty clearly contemplates three separate entities, the Landlord, the Tenant and the Guarantor, and so designates them. It identifies Wilson as the Landlord, Tony Maroni's as the Tenant, and addresses the obligations of a separate third party, referred to interchangeably as the undersigned or Guarantor. * * * The only reasonable interpretation of these provisions is that the Landlord, Tenant and undersigned/Guarantor are three separate and distinct entities. If Riviera signed the Guaranty only in his representative capacity, Tony Maroni's would be both Tenant and Guarantor, rendering the Guaranty provisions absurd. * * *

Moreover, the Guaranty language stands in stark contrast to the language of the Lease where a corporate obligation was unambiguously contemplated. Riviera signed the Lease as president of Tony Maroni's to bind the company. No such intent can be gleaned from the Guaranty. * * *

Third, the very nature of a guaranty is such that Riviera created personal liability by his signature. * * *

* * * *

Riviera is an experienced businessperson with prior experience in commercial leasing who dealt directly with Wilson in securing the Lease. There is no evidence or assertion of any improper conduct by Wilson. Given the commercial sophistication of the parties, the circumstances under which the Guaranty was entered into, and the nature of the Guaranty, a commercially reasonable approach to this case requires us * * * to hold Riviera personally liable under the Guaranty.

DECISION AND REMEDY

The Washington Supreme Court affirmed the judgment of the lower court. The president was personally liable because otherwise the corporation would be the guarantor of its own lease. This would be commercially unreasonable because, as a matter of law, a party cannot be the guarantor of its own contract.

DEFENSES OF THE SURETY AND THE GUARANTOR

The defenses of the surety and the guarantor are basically the same. Therefore, the following discussion applies to both, although it refers only to the surety.

Actions Releasing the Surety. Certain actions will release the surety from the obligation. For example, making any material modification in the terms of the original contract between the principal debtor and the creditor, including the awarding of a binding extension of time for making payment, without first obtaining the consent of the surety will discharge a gratuitous surety (one who receives no consideration in return for acting as a surety) completely and a surety who is compensated to the extent that the surety suffers a loss.

Naturally, if the principal obligation is paid by the debtor or by another person on behalf of the debtor, the surety is discharged from the obligation. Similarly, if valid tender of payment is made, and the creditor for some reason rejects it with knowledge of the surety's existence, then the surety is released from any obligation on the debt.

Defenses of the Principal Debtor. Generally, any defenses available to a principal debtor can be used by the surety to avoid liability on the obligation to the creditor. Defenses available to the principal debtor that the surety *cannot* use include the principal debtor's incapacity or bankruptcy and the statute of limitations. The ability of the surety to assert any defenses the debtor may have against the creditor is the most important concept in suretyship, because most of the defenses available to the surety are also those of the debtor.

Surrender or Impairment of Collateral. In addition, if a creditor surrenders or impairs the debtor's collateral while knowing of the surety and without the surety's consent, the surety is released to the extent of any loss suffered from the creditor's actions. The primary reason for this is to protect the surety who agreed to become obligated only because the debtor's collateral was in the possession of the creditor.

Other Defenses. Obviously, a surety may also have his or her own defenses—for example, incapacity or bankruptcy. If the creditor fraudulently induced the surety to guarantee the debt, the surety can assert fraud as a defense. In most states, the creditor has a legal duty to inform the surety, prior to the formation of the suretyship contract, of material facts known by the creditor that would substantially increase the surety's risk. Failure to so inform is fraud and makes the suretyship obligation voidable.

RIGHTS OF THE SURETY AND THE GUARANTOR

The rights of the surety and the guarantor are basically the same. Therefore, again, the following discussion applies to both.

The Right of Subrogation. When the surety pays the debt owed to the creditor, the surety is entitled to certain rights. First, the surety has the legal **right of subrogation.** Simply stated, this means that any right the creditor had against the debtor now becomes the right of the surety. Included are creditor rights in bankruptcy, rights to collateral possessed by the creditor, and rights to judgments secured by the creditor. In short, the surety now stands in the shoes of the creditor and may pursue any remedies that were available to the creditor against the debtor.

The Right of Reimbursement. Second, the surety has a right to be reimbursed by the debtor. This **right of reimbursement** may stem either from the suretyship contract or from equity. Basically, the surety is entitled to receive from the debtor all outlays made on behalf of the suretyship arrangement. Such outlays can include expenses incurred, as well as the actual amount of the debt paid to the creditor.

The Right of Contribution. Third, in the case of **co-sureties** (two or more sureties on the same obligation owed by the debtor), the **right of contribution** allows a surety who pays more than his or her proportionate share on a debtor's default to recover from the co-sureties the amount paid above the surety's obligation. Generally, a co-surety's liability either is determined by agreement or, in the absence of agreement, is set at the maximum liability under the suretyship contract.

For example, assume that two co-sureties are obligated under a suretyship contract to guarantee the debt of a debtor. Together, the sureties' maximum liability is $25,000. Surety A's maximum liability is $15,000, and surety B's is $10,000. The debtor owes $10,000 and is in default. Surety A pays the creditor the entire $10,000. In the absence of agreement, surety A can recover $4,000 from surety B ($10,000/$25,000 × $10,000 = $4,000, surety B's obligation).

SECTION 3

Protection for Debtors

The law protects debtors, as well as creditors. Certain property of the debtor, for example, is exempt from creditors' actions. Consumer protection statutes also protect debtors' rights. Of course, bankruptcy laws, which will be discussed in the next chapter, are designed specifically to assist debtors in need of help.

EXEMPTIONS

In most states, certain types of real and personal property are exempt from levy of execution or attachment. Probably the most familiar of these exemptions is the **homestead exemption.** Each state permits the debtor to retain the family home, either in its entirety or up to a specified dollar amount, free from the claims of unsecured creditors or trustees in bankruptcy. The purpose is to ensure that the debtor will retain some form of shelter.

Suppose that Beere owes Veltman $40,000. The debt is the subject of a lawsuit, and the court awards Veltman a judgment of $40,000 against Beere. Beere's homestead is valued at $50,000, and the homestead exemption is $25,000. There are no outstanding mortgages or other liens on his homestead. To satisfy the judgment debt, Beere's family home is sold at public auction for $45,000. The proceeds of the sale are distributed as follows:

1. Beere is given $25,000 as his homestead exemption.
2. Veltman is paid $20,000 toward the judgment debt, leaving a $20,000 deficiency judgment (that is, "leftover debt") that can be satisfied from any other nonexempt property (personal or real) that Beere may have, if allowed by state law.

In a few states, statutes permit the homestead exemption only if the judgment debtor has a family. The policy behind this type of statute is to protect the family. If a judgment debtor does not have a family, a creditor may be entitled to collect the full amount realized from the sale of the debtor's home.

State exemption statutes usually include both real and personal property. Personal property that is most often exempt from satisfaction of judgment debts includes the following:

1. Household furniture up to a specified dollar amount.
2. Clothing and certain personal possessions, such as family pictures or a Bible.
3. A vehicle (or vehicles) for transportation (at least up to a specified dollar amount).
4. Certain classified animals, usually livestock but including pets.
5. Equipment that the debtor uses in a business or trade, such as tools or professional instruments, up to a specified dollar amount.

SPECIAL PROTECTION FOR CONSUMER-DEBTORS

There are a number of consumer protection statutes and rules that apply to the debtor-creditor relationship. A brief listing and discussion here of some of the most important of these laws will illustrate their breadth and significance.

Consumer Credit Protection Act. Commonly known as the Truth-in-Lending Act, Title I of the Consumer Credit Protection Act is basically a *disclosure law.* Administered by the Federal Reserve Board, this law requires sellers and lenders to disclose credit terms on loans so that a consumer-debtor can shop around for the best financing arrangements. Essentially, it requires that the creditor clearly indicate to the consumer-debtor what charges are being made for the privilege of paying the debt over a period of time, including the total annual interest percentage rate and finance charges.

Uniform Consumer Credit Code. In an attempt to make consumer credit laws at the state level uniform, the National Conference of Commissioners on Uniform State Laws proposed legislation called the Uniform Consumer Credit Code (UCCC). Its essential points are as follows:

1. To place statutory ceilings on interest rates and other charges.
2. To require disclosure similar to that required by the Truth-in-Lending Act.
3. To limit garnishment actions against take-home wages to a certain amount and to prohibit discharge of an employee solely because of garnishment proceedings.
4. To allow cancellation of a contract solicited by a

seller in the consumer-debtor's home within three business days of the solicitation.

5. To prohibit referral sales, which are sales in which a seller offers a rebate or discount to a buyer for furnishing the names of other prospective purchasers.

6. To provide criminal as well as civil penalties for violations.

Only a handful of states have adopted the UCCC, even though it has undergone numerous drafts. Some other states have passed laws similar to some of the provisions of the UCCC, such as laws concerning home-solicitation sales.

Federal Trade Commission Rule. In many modern consumer transactions buyers make purchases on credit, taking the seller's good and promising to pay the full debt at a later time. The buyer in such transactions often becomes a debtor by executing a *note*—a promise to pay a definite amount within a certain time. Such notes are often transferred to a third party, who purchases the notes from the seller-creditor and is then entitled to payment on the notes when due. If the person holding the note is deemed to be a *holder in due course* (HDC), then he or she is free of all claims to and most defenses against payment on the note—including those of the buyer-debtor who executed the note. The Federal Trade Commission (FTC) promulgated a rule that limits the rights of an HDC when the buyer-debtor executes a note as part of a consumer transaction. The FTC rule provides basically that any defenses the buyer can assert against the seller can also be asserted against an HDC. The seller is also required to disclose this information clearly to the buyer in its sales agreement.

The rule basically eliminates the use of a buyer's waiver-of-defense clause in a consumer transaction. These clauses waive any claim or defense the debtor might have against a third party who, for example, purchases the buyer's note from the seller.

SECTION 4

Bankruptcy and Reorganization

The basic law of bankruptcy in the United States is the federal Bankruptcy Code. The Bankruptcy Code has two goals—to protect a debtor by giving him or her a fresh start, free from creditors' claims, and to ensure equitable treatment to creditors who are competing for a debtor's assets.

The United States Constitution confers on Congress the power to establish uniform laws on bankruptcy.[4] When the Constitution vests power over certain matters in the federal government, as it does with respect to bankruptcy law, the federal law on that subject takes precedence over any state law on the same subject. The Constitution also forbids states from enacting laws that impair contractual obligations, which naturally includes contractual obligations between debtors and creditors. But although the Bankruptcy Code is federal law, the Code incorporates much state law regulating matters important in bankruptcy. State laws on secured transactions, liens, judgments, and exemptions, for example, play a significant role in federal bankruptcy proceedings.

Bankruptcy proceedings are held in specialized federal bankruptcy courts. A bankruptcy court's primary function is to hold *core proceedings*[5] dealing with the procedures required to administer the estate of the debtor in bankruptcy. Bankruptcy courts are under the authority of U.S. district courts, and rulings from bankruptcy courts can be appealed to the district courts. Fundamentally, a bankruptcy court fulfills the role of an administrative court for the district court concerning matters in bankruptcy. Decisions on personal injury, wrongful death, and other civil proceedings affecting the debtor are resolved in other federal or state courts.

The remaining sections in this chapter deal with the most frequently used bankruptcy plans allowed under the various chapters of the Bankruptcy Code: Chapter 7 liquidations, Chapter 11 reorganizations, and Chapter 13 plans. The latter two chapters are sometimes referred to as *rehabilitation chapters*. As you read the following sections on bankruptcy, be sure to keep in mind that references to Chapter 7, Chapter 9, and Chapter 13 are references to chapters contained in the Bankruptcy Code, not references to chapters within this textbook.

Throughout the various chapters of the Bankruptcy Code, a distinction is made between secured and unsecured creditors. A secured creditor is one in whose favor there is a *security interest*—an interest in personal property or fixtures that secures, or serves as collateral for, payment of a debt. Unsecured creditors do not have a security interest in property that serves as collateral to the underlying debt.

---

4. U.S. Constitution, Article I, Section 8. See Appendix B.

5. Core proceedings are procedural functions, such as allowance of claims, decisions on preferences, automatic stay proceedings, confirmation of bankruptcy plans, discharge of debts, and so on.

Even though a creditor may have a security interest in certain personal property, additional steps must be taken to ensure that the creditor's security interest in collateral takes *priority* over claims made on the collateral by third parties, such as other secured or general creditors, trustees in bankruptcy, and later purchasers of the collateral. A secured creditor establishes priority over such third party claims by taking steps to *perfect* the security interest. Although there are other means of perfecting a security interest, the most common one is by filing with an appropriate public office a *financing statement*, signed by the debtor, describing the collateral and giving the names and addresses of the debtor and the creditor.[6]

As will be seen, because bankruptcy generally occurs when the debtor's obligations exceed the debtor's assets, the priority of claims to the available assets is frequently crucial to the outcome of a bankruptcy proceeding.

LIQUIDATION PROCEEDINGS

Liquidation under Chapter 7 of the Bankruptcy Code is generally the most familiar type of bankruptcy proceeding and is often referred to as an *ordinary*, or *straight, bankruptcy*. Put simply, a debtor in a liquidation bankruptcy turns all assets over to a **trustee**. The trustee sells the nonexempt assets and distributes the proceeds to creditors. With certain exceptions, the remaining debts are then **discharged** (extinguished), and the debtors are relieved of their obligation to pay the debts.

Any "person"—defined as including individuals, partnerships, and corporations[7]—may be a debtor in a liquidation proceeding. Railroads, insurance companies, banks, savings and loan associations, investment companies licensed by the Small Business Administration, and credit unions cannot be debtors in a liquidation bankruptcy, however. Rather, other chapters of the Bankruptcy Code or federal or state statutes apply to them.

Filing the Petition. A straight bankruptcy may be commenced by the filing of either a voluntary or an involuntary **petition in bankruptcy**—the document that is filed with a bankruptcy court to initiate bankruptcy proceedings.

Voluntary Bankruptcy. When a voluntary petition in bankruptcy is brought by the debtor, he or she files official forms designated for that purpose in the bankruptcy court. The Code requires a consumer-debtor who has opted for liquidation bankruptcy proceedings to state in the petition, at the time of filing, that he or she understands the relief available under other chapters of the Code and has chosen to proceed under Chapter 7. If the consumer-debtor is represented by an attorney, the attorney must file an affidavit stating that he or she has informed the debtor of the relief available under each chapter. A debtor does not have to be insolvent[8] to file for bankruptcy relief. Anyone liable to a creditor can declare bankruptcy.

The voluntary petition contains the following schedules:

1. A list of both secured and unsecured creditors, their addresses, and the amount of debt owed to each.
2. A statement of the financial affairs of the debtor.
3. A list of all property owned by the debtor, including property claimed by the debtor to be exempt.
4. A listing of current income and expenses. (This schedule provides creditors and the court with relevant information on the debtor's ability to pay creditors a reasonable amount from future income. This information could permit a court, on its own motion, to dismiss a debtor's Chapter 7 petition after a hearing and to encourage the filing of a repayment plan under Chapter 13, when that would substantially improve the chances that creditors would be paid.)

The official forms must be completed accurately, sworn to under oath, and signed by the debtor. To conceal assets or knowingly supply false information on these schedules is a crime under the bankruptcy laws. If the voluntary petition for bankruptcy is found to be proper, the filing of the petition will itself constitute an **order for relief.** (An order for relief is a court's grant of

---

6. There are basically three methods of perfection. First, the debtor may transfer possession of the collateral to the secured creditor. Second, the security interest may be perfected automatically at the time of a credit sale (that is, at the moment the security interest is created under a written security agreement). Third, and most commonly, a security interest may be perfected by the creditor's filing a financing statement.

7. The definition of *corporation* includes unincorporated companies and associations. It also covers labor unions.

8. The inability to pay debts as they become due is known as *equitable* insolvency. A *balance sheet* insolvency, which exists when a debtor's liabilities exceed assets, is not the test. Thus, it is possible for debtors to voluntarily petition for bankruptcy or to be thrown into involuntary bankruptcy even though their assets far exceed their liabilities. This may occur when a debtor's cash flow problems become severe.

assistance to a complainant. In the context of bankruptcy, relief consists of discharging a complainant's debts.) Once a consumer-debtor's voluntary petition has been filed, the clerk of the court or other appointee must give the trustee and creditors mailed notice of the order for relief not more than twenty days after entry of the order. A husband and wife may file jointly for bankruptcy under a single petition.

As mentioned above, debtors do not have to be insolvent to file for voluntary bankruptcy. Debtors do not have unfettered access to bankruptcy proceedings under Chapter 7, however. Section 707(b) of the Bankruptcy Code allows a bankruptcy court to dismiss a petition for relief under Chapter 7 if the granting of relief would constitute "substantial abuse" of Chapter 7. There is no one, uniform standard, or test, for determining what constitutes substantial abuse. In the following case, the court applied the "totality of the circumstances" test to decide whether granting a Chapter 7 discharge to the debtor would constitute substantial abuse.

CASE 16.3   In re Lamanna

United States
Court of Appeals,
First Circuit, 1998.
153 F.3d 1.
http://www.law.emory.
edu/1circuit[a]

BACKGROUND AND FACTS *In 1996, Richard Lamanna was living with his parents. For this reason, his monthly expenses were only $580. His monthly income was $1,350.96, leaving a difference of $770.96, the amount of his disposable income.[b] He had no plans to move out of his parents' house. During four weeks in October and November, he charged $9,994.45 on credit cards. In February 1997, when his total unsecured debt was $15,911.96, he filed a voluntary petition in a federal bankruptcy court to declare bankruptcy under Chapter 7. The court noted that Lamanna was capable of paying all of his debts under a Chapter 13 repayment plan and dismissed the case. The U.S. Bankruptcy Appellate Panel (BAP) for the First Circuit affirmed the dismissal, and Lamanna appealed to the U.S. Court of Appeals for the First Circuit. Lamanna argued in part that if he did not live with his parents, he would not have as much disposable income, and that thus he was being penalized for living with his parents.*

**IN THE LANGUAGE
OF THE COURT**

LYNCH, Circuit Judge.
*   *   *   *

The question of whether allowing Lamanna's bankruptcy petition would constitute "substantial abuse" of Chapter 7 under Section 707(b) contains two components: first, the proper test by which "substantial abuse" is measured; second, whether, applying that test, the BAP correctly decided the issue. *   *   *
*   *   *   *

*   *   * Although tests employed by various courts of appeals do not employ precisely the same language, they share common elements. First and foremost, it is agreed that *a consumer debtor's ability to repay his debts out of future disposable income is strong evidence of "substantial abuse."* *   *   * In determining whether to apply Section 707(b) to an individual debtor, *   *   * a court should ascertain from the totality of the circumstances whether he is merely seeking an advantage over his creditors, or is "honest," *   *   * and whether he is "needy" in the sense that his financial predicament warrants the discharge of his debts in exchange for liquidation of his assets. *   *   * [T]he "totality of the circumstances" test demands a comprehensive review of the debtor's current and potential financial situation. [Emphasis added.]
*   *   *   *

Applying the "totality of the circumstances" test to Lamanna's case results in affirmance of the dismissal of his Chapter 7 petition for "substantial abuse." Lamanna's

---

a. This Web site is maintained by Emory University School of Law. In the "Listing by Month of Decision" section, click on "1998 Decisions." On that page, in the "1998 Decisions" list, click on "August." When the list of cases appears, click on the case name to access the opinion.
b. *Disposable income* is income "not reasonably necessary to be expended for the maintenance or support of the debtor or a dependent of the debtor," according to 11 U.S.C. Section 1325(b)(2).

schedules showed that he has sufficient disposable income to repay his debts under a Chapter 13 repayment plan in three to five years. There is no evidence that Lamanna's living situation was unstable or likely to change in the near future. There is no evidence of other factors that cast doubt on the stability of Lamanna's future income and expenses. Although Lamanna's expenses are particularly low because he lives with his parents, this state of affairs, as the BAP noted, "is not artificial; it is actual." The court properly based its decision on the current and foreseeable facts. If Lamanna's circumstances dramatically change, he is free to seek relief anew.

Lamanna's argument that the court penalized him for living with his parents (and thus having exceptionally low monthly expenses) boils down to the notion that Section 707 requires the bankruptcy court to impute a minimum cost of living to a debtor and then measure the debtor's actual income against the higher of the imputed minimum and the debtor's actual expenses. Section 707 does not contain such an implicit requirement, and this court will not write such a requirement into the statute.

DECISION AND REMEDY	*The U.S. Court of Appeals for the First Circuit affirmed the decision of the lower court and held that granting Lamanna's petition would constitute substantial abuse of Chapter 7. The appellate court looked at the "totality of the circumstances" to reach its conclusion.*

Involuntary Bankruptcy. An involuntary bankruptcy occurs when the debtor's creditors force the debtor into bankruptcy proceedings. An involuntary case cannot be commenced against a farmer[9] or a charitable institution. For an involuntary action to be filed against other debtors, the following requirements must be met: If the debtor has twelve or more creditors, three or more of these creditors having unsecured claims totaling at least $10,775 must join in the petition. If a debtor has fewer than twelve creditors, one or more creditors having a claim of $10,775 may file.

If the debtor challenges the involuntary petition, a hearing will be held, and the bankruptcy court will enter an order for relief if it finds either of the following:

1. The debtor is generally not paying debts as they become due.
2. A general receiver, assignee, or custodian took possession of, or was appointed to take charge of, substantially all of the debtor's property within 120 days before the filing of the petition.

If the court grants an order for relief, the debtor will be required to supply the same information in the bankruptcy schedules as in a voluntary bankruptcy.

An involuntary petition should not be used as an everyday debt-collection device, and the Code provides penalties for the filing of frivolous petitions against debtors. Judgment may be granted against the petitioning creditors for the costs and attorneys' fees incurred by the debtor in defending against an involuntary petition that is dismissed by the court. If the petition is filed in bad faith, damages can be awarded for injury to the debtor's reputation. Punitive damages may also be awarded.

Automatic Stay. The moment a petition, either voluntary or involuntary, is filed, there exists an **automatic stay,** or suspension, of virtually all litigation and other action by creditors against the debtor or the debtor's property. In other words, once a petition has been filed, creditors cannot commence or continue most legal actions, such as foreclosure of liens, execution on judgments, trials, or any action to repossess property in the hands of the debtor. A secured creditor, however, may petition the bankruptcy court for relief from the automatic stay in certain circumstances. Also, the automatic stay does not apply to paternity, alimony, maintenance, and support debts, and to certain other actions, such as criminal

---

9. The definition of *farmer* includes persons who receive more than 80 percent of their gross income from farming operations, such as tilling the soil, dairy farming, ranching, or the production or raising of crops, poultry, or livestock. Corporations and partnerships may qualify under certain conditions.

proceedings, against the debtor. The Code provides that if a creditor knowingly violates the automatic stay (a willful violation), any party injured, including the debtor, is entitled to recover actual damages, costs, and attorneys' fees and may be entitled to recover punitive damages as well.

Underlying the Code's automatic stay provision for a secured creditor is a concept known as *adequate protection.* The **adequate protection doctrine,** among other things, protects secured creditors from losing their security as a result of the automatic stay. The bankruptcy court can provide adequate protection by requiring the debtor or trustee to make periodic cash payments or a one-time cash payment (or to provide additional collateral or replacement liens) to the extent that the stay may actually cause the value of the property to decrease. Or the court may grant other relief that is the "indubitable equivalent" of (that is, equivalent to, without any doubt) the secured party's interest in the property, such as a guaranty by a solvent third party to cover losses suffered by the secured party as a result of the stay.

Property of the Estate. On the commencement of a liquidation proceeding under Chapter 7, an *estate in property* is created. The estate consists of all the debtor's legal and equitable interests in property presently held, wherever located, together with community property, property transferred in a transaction voidable by the trustee, proceeds and profits from the property of the estate, and certain after-acquired property. Interests in certain property—such as gifts, inheritances, property settlements (divorce), and life insurance death proceeds—to which the debtor becomes entitled *within 180 days after filing* may also become part of the estate. Thus, the filing of a bankruptcy petition generally fixes a dividing line: property acquired prior to the filing of the petition becomes property of the estate, and property acquired after the filing of the petition, except as just noted, remains the debtor's.

The issue in the following case was whether payments made under a covenant not to compete should be included in a debtor's estate. The covenant was entered into before the petition was filed, but the payments were due after the filing.

CASE 16.4 In re Andrews

United States
Court of Appeals,
Fourth Circuit, 1996.
80 F.3d 906.
http://www.law.emory.
edu/4circuit/index.
1996.html[a] ·

COMPANY PROFILE *John Andrews worked in the ready-mix concrete business most of his life. In 1974, he and various partners formed a ready-mix concrete company in Herndon, Virginia. The company, which ultimately came to be known as AMAX Corporation, grew to be successful, with annual sales of approximately $30 million. By expanding the customer contacts he developed at AMAX, in 1980 Andrews formed a real estate development company, which participated in joint ventures with builders and developers. In 1989, the owners of AMAX began negotiations with Tarmac Acquisition, Inc. (http://www.tarmac.co.uk), for Tarmac's purchase of AMAX. Experts valued the assets at about $9 million. AMAX's customer list, which represented the goodwill of the company, was valued at an additional $1 million.*

BACKGROUND AND FACTS *Tarmac Acquisition, Inc., bought AMAX Corporation, a ready-mix concrete company. As part of the deal, the AMAX owners, including John Andrews, signed agreements not to compete with Tarmac. Andrews was to receive $1 million, payable in quarterly installments over a five-year period. Three years later, Andrews filed a bankruptcy petition. He asked the federal bankruptcy court not to include, in the property of his estate (which would ultimately be distributed to creditors), any future installments. The court refused, and a federal district court affirmed this decision. Andrews appealed to the U.S. Court of Appeals for the Fourth Circuit.*

a. This Web page, which is part of a Web site maintained by Emory University School of Law, provides access to published opinions of the U.S. Court of Appeals for the Fourth Circuit for 1996. Click on the "April" link. When that page opens, scroll down the list of cases to *Andrews v. Riggs National Bank of Washington.* Click on the case name to access this opinion.

IN THE LANGUAGE
OF THE COURT

ELLIS, District Judge:

*   *   *   *   *

*   *   * Pre-petition assets, like the NCA [noncompetition agreement] payments, are those assets rooted in the debtor's pre-petition activities, including any proceeds that may flow from those assets in the future. These assets belong to the estate and ultimately to the creditors. Post-petition assets are those that result from the debtor's post-petition activities and are his to keep free and clear of the bankruptcy proceeding.

*   *   *   *   *

Seen in this light, the NCA payments due Andrews fall clearly on the pre-bankruptcy or "past" side of the bright line. These payments are plainly rooted in, and grow out of, Andrews's pre-petition activities. *   *   * [B]ut for the [AMAX] sale, there would have been no NCA and no quarterly payments to Andrews. *   *   * Given this close connection between the NCA and the pre-petition sale of the debtor's share in the concrete business, we are persuaded that the payments were well rooted in the pre-bankruptcy past. *   *   * [T]hey should be included in Andrews's estate.

DECISION
AND REMEDY

The U.S. Court of Appeals for the Fourth Circuit affirmed the lower court's decision. Andrews's future installments were to be included in the property of his bankruptcy estate because they were "rooted in the debtor's pre-petition activities."

Creditors' Meeting and Claims. Within a reasonable time after the order for relief has been granted (not less than ten days or more than thirty days), the bankruptcy court must call a meeting of the creditors listed in the schedules filed by the debtor. The bankruptcy judge does not attend this meeting.

The debtor is required to attend the meeting (unless excused by the court) and to submit to examination under oath by the creditors and the trustee. Failing to appear when required or making false statements under oath may result in the debtor's being denied a discharge in bankruptcy. At the meeting, the trustee ensures that the debtor is aware of the potential consequences of bankruptcy and of his or her ability to file for bankruptcy under a different chapter.

To be entitled to receive a portion of the debtor's estate, each creditor must normally file a *proof of claim* with the bankruptcy court clerk within ninety days of the creditors' meeting.[10] The proof of claim lists the creditor's name and address, as well as the amount that the creditor asserts is owed to the creditor by the debtor. If a creditor fails to file a proof of claim, the bankruptcy court or trustee may file the proof of claim on the creditor's behalf but is not obligated to do so.

Generally, any legal obligation of the debtor is a claim. In the case of a disputed, or unliquidated, claim, the bankruptcy court will set the value of the claim. Any creditor holding a debtor's obligation can file a claim against the debtor's estate. These claims are automatically allowed unless contested by the trustee, the debtor, or another creditor. A creditor who files a false claim commits a crime.

The Code, however, does not allow claims for breach of employment contracts or real estate leases for terms longer than one year. Such claims are limited to one year's wages or rent, despite the remaining length of either contract in breach.

Exemptions. The trustee takes control over the debtor's property, but an individual debtor is entitled to exempt certain property from the bankruptcy. The Bankruptcy Code exempts the following property (the dollar amounts stated in the Bankruptcy Code were adjusted automatically on April 1, 1998, and will be adjusted every three years thereafter based on changes in the Consumer Price Index):[11]

1. Up to $16,150 in equity in the debtor's residence and burial plot (the homestead exemption).

---

10. This ninety-day rule applies in Chapter 13 bankruptcies as well.

11. A debtor cannot avoid a judicial lien for paternity, alimony, maintenance, and support debts, however, even if the lien is imposed on exempt property.

2. Interest in a motor vehicle up to $2,575.

3. Interest, up to $425 for a particular item, in household goods and furnishings, wearing apparel, appliances, books, animals, crops, and musical instruments (the aggregate total of all items is limited, however, to $8,625).

4. Interest in jewelry up to $1,750.

5. Interest in any other property up to $850, plus any unused part of the $16,150 homestead exemption up to $8,075.

6. Interest in any tools of the debtor's trade up to $1,625.

7. Any unmatured life insurance contract owned by the debtor.

8. Certain interests in accrued dividends and interest under life insurance contracts owned by the debtor.

9. Professionally prescribed health aids.

10. The right to receive Social Security and certain welfare benefits, alimony and support, and certain pension benefits.

11. The right to receive certain personal injury and other awards up to $16,150.

Individual states have the power to pass legislation precluding debtors from using the federal exemptions within the state; a majority of the states have done this. In those states, debtors may use only state, not federal, exemptions. In the rest of the states, an individual debtor (or a husband and wife filing jointly) may choose either the exemptions provided under state law or the federal exemptions.[12]

The Trustee. Promptly after the order for relief in the liquidation proceeding has been entered, an interim, or provisional, trustee is appointed by the **U.S. Trustee** (a government official who performs appointing and other administrative tasks that a bankruptcy judge would otherwise have to perform). The interim, or provisional, trustee presides over the debtor's property until the first meeting of the creditors. At this first meeting, either a permanent trustee

is elected or the interim trustee becomes the permanent trustee.

The basic duty of the trustee is to collect the debtor's available estate and reduce it to money for distribution, preserving the interests of both the debtor and unsecured creditors. This requires that the trustee be accountable for administering the debtor's estate. To enable the trustee to accomplish this duty, the Code gives the trustee certain powers, stated in both general and specific terms. These powers must be exercised within two years of the order for relief.

Trustee's Powers. The general powers of the trustee are described by the statement that the trustee occupies a position *equivalent* in rights to that of certain other parties. For example, the trustee has the same rights as a *lien creditor* who could have obtained a judicial lien on the debtor's property or who could have levied execution on the debtor's property. This means that a trustee has priority over an unperfected secured party to the debtor's property. This right of a trustee, equivalent to that of a lien creditor, is known as the *strong-arm power.* A trustee also has power equivalent to that of a *bona fide purchaser* of real property from the debtor.

Nevertheless, in most states a creditor with a purchase-money security interest may prevail against a trustee, if the creditor files within ten days (twenty days, in many states) of the debtor's receipt of the collateral, even if the bankruptcy petition is filed before the creditor perfects. For example, Baker loaned Newbury $20,000 on January 1, taking a security interest in the machinery that Newbury purchased with the $20,000 and that was delivered on that same date. On January 27, before Baker had perfected her security interest, Newbury filed for bankruptcy. The trustee can invalidate Baker's security interest, because it was unperfected when Newbury filed the bankruptcy petition. Baker can only assert a claim as an unsecured creditor. But if Newbury had filed for bankruptcy on January 7, and Baker had perfected her security interest on January 8, she would have prevailed, because she would have perfected her purchase-money security interest within ten days of Newbury's receipt of the machinery.

The trustee has the power to require persons holding the debtor's property at the time the petition is filed to deliver the property to the trustee. (A trustee usually does not take actual possession of a debtor's

---

12. State exemptions may or may not be limited with regard to value. Under state exemption laws, a debtor may enjoy an unlimited value exemption on a motor vehicle, for example, even though the federal bankruptcy scheme exempts a vehicle only up to a value of $2,575. A state's law may also define the property coming within an exemption differently than the federal law or may exclude, or except, specific things from an exemption, making it unavailable to a debtor who fits within the exception.

property. Instead, a trustee's possession is constructive. For example, to obtain control of a debtor's business inventory, a trustee might change the locks on the doors to the business and hire a security guard.) The trustee also has specific powers of *avoidance*—that is, the trustee can set aside a sale or other transfer of the debtor's property, taking it back as a part of the debtor's estate. These powers include any voidable rights available to the debtor, preferences, certain statutory liens, and fraudulent transfers by the debtor. Each of these powers is discussed in more detail below.

The debtor shares most of the trustee's avoidance powers. Thus, if the trustee does not take action to enforce one of his or her rights (for example, to recover a preference), the debtor in a liquidation bankruptcy can nevertheless enforce that right.[13]

Voidable Rights.   A trustee steps into the shoes of the debtor. Thus, any reason that a debtor can use to obtain the return of his or her property can be used by the trustee as well. These grounds include fraud, duress, incapacity, and mutual mistake.

For example, Ben sells his boat to Tara. Tara gives Ben a check, knowing that there are insufficient funds in her bank account to cover the check. Tara has committed fraud. Ben has the right to avoid that transfer and recover the boat from Tara. Once an order for relief under Chapter 7 of the Code has been entered for Ben, the trustee can exercise the same right to recover the boat from Tara, and the boat becomes a part of the debtor's estate.

Preferences.   A debtor is not permitted to transfer property or to make a payment that favors—or gives a **preference** to—one creditor over others. The trustee is allowed to recover payments made both voluntarily and involuntarily to one creditor in preference over another.

To have made a preferential payment that can be recovered, an *insolvent* debtor generally must have transferred property, for a *preexisting* debt, within *ninety days* of the filing of the petition in bankruptcy. The transfer must give the creditor more than the creditor would have received as a result of the bankruptcy proceedings. The trustee does not have to prove insolvency, as the Code provides that the debtor

is presumed to be insolvent during this ninety-day period.

Sometimes the creditor receiving the preference is an **insider**—an individual, a partner, a partnership, a corporation, or an officer or a director of a corporation (or a relative of one of these) who has a close relationship with the debtor. If this is the situation, the avoidance power of the trustee is extended to transfers made within *one year* before filing; however, the *presumption* of insolvency is confined to the ninety-day period. Therefore, the trustee must prove that the debtor was insolvent at the time of a transfer that occurred prior to the ninety-day period.

Not all transfers are preferences. To be a preference, the transfer must be made for something other than current consideration. Therefore, it is generally assumed by most courts that payment for services rendered within ten to fifteen days prior to the payment of the current consideration is not a preference. If a creditor receives payment in the ordinary course of business, such as payment of last month's telephone bill, the payment cannot be recovered by the trustee in bankruptcy. To be recoverable, a preference must be a transfer for an antecedent (preexisting) debt, such as a year-old printing bill. In addition, the Code permits a consumer-debtor to transfer any property to a creditor up to a total value of $600, without the transfer's constituting a preference. Also, payment of paternity, alimony, maintenance, and support debts is not a preference.

If a preferred creditor has sold the property to an innocent third party, the trustee cannot recover the property from the innocent party. The creditor, however, generally can be held accountable for the value of the property.

Liens on Debtor's Property.   The trustee has the power to avoid certain statutory liens against the debtor's property, such as a landlord's lien for unpaid rent. The trustee can avoid statutory liens that first became effective against the debtor when the bankruptcy petition was filed or when the debtor became insolvent. The trustee can also avoid any lien against a bona fide purchaser that was not perfected or enforceable on the date of the bankruptcy filing.

Fraudulent Transfers.   The trustee may avoid fraudulent transfers or obligations if they are made within one year of the filing of the petition or if they are made with actual intent to hinder, delay, or defraud a creditor. Transfers made for less than a reasonably equivalent consideration are also vulnerable if by

---

13. Under Chapter 11 (to be discussed later), for which no trustee other than the debtor generally exists, the debtor has the same avoidance powers as a trustee under Chapter 7. Under Chapters 12 and 13 (also to be discussed later), a trustee must be appointed.

making them, the debtor became insolvent, was left engaged in business with an unreasonably small amount of capital, or intended to incur debts that he or she could not pay. When a fraudulent transfer is made outside the Code's one-year limit, creditors may seek alternative relief under state laws. State laws often allow creditors to recover for transfers made up to three years prior to the filing of a petition.

Distribution of Property. The rights of perfected secured creditors were discussed above. The Code provides that a consumer-debtor, either within thirty days of filing a liquidation petition or before the date of the first meeting of the creditors (whichever is first), must file with the clerk a statement of intention with respect to the secured collateral. The statement must indicate whether the debtor will retain the collateral or surrender it to the secured party.[14] The trustee is obligated to enforce the debtor's statement within forty-five days after it is filed.

If the collateral is surrendered to the perfected secured party, the secured creditor can enforce the security interest either by accepting the property in full satisfaction of the debt or by foreclosing on the collateral and using the proceeds to pay off the debt. Thus, the perfected secured party has priority over unsecured parties as to the proceeds from the disposition of the collateral. Indeed, the Code provides that if the value of the collateral exceeds the perfected secured party's claim and if the security agreement so provides, the secured party also has priority as to the proceeds in an amount that will cover reasonable fees and costs incurred because of the debtor's default. Fees include reasonable attorneys' fees. Any excess over this amount is used by the trustee to satisfy the claims of unsecured creditors. Should the collateral be insufficient to cover the secured debt owed, the secured creditor becomes an unsecured creditor for the difference.

Bankruptcy law establishes an order of priority for classes of debts owed to *unsecured* creditors, and they are paid in the order of their priority. Each class must be fully paid before the next class is entitled to any of the remaining proceeds. If there are insufficient proceeds to pay fully all the creditors in a class,

the proceeds are distributed *proportionately* to the creditors in the class, and classes lower in priority receive nothing. The order of priority among classes of unsecured creditors is as follows:

1. Administrative expenses—including court costs, trustee fees, and attorneys' fees.
2. In an involuntary bankruptcy, expenses incurred by the debtor in the ordinary course of business from the date of the filing of the petition up to the appointment of the trustee or the issuance by the court of an order for relief.
3. Unpaid wages, salaries, and commissions earned within ninety days of the filing of the petition, limited to $4,300 per claimant. Any claim in excess of $4,300 or earned before the ninety-day period is treated as a claim of a general creditor (listed as item 9 below).
4. Unsecured claims for contributions to be made to employee benefit plans, limited to services performed during 180 days prior to the filing of the bankruptcy petition and $4,300 per employee.
5. Claims by farmers and fishers, up to $4,300, against debtor operators of grain storage or fish storage or processing facilities.
6. Consumer deposits of up to $1,950 given to the debtor before the petition was filed in connection with the purchase, lease, or rental of property or purchase of services that were not received or provided. Any claim in excess of $1,950 is treated as a claim of a general creditor (listed as item 9 below).
7. Paternity, alimony, maintenance, and support debts.
8. Certain taxes and penalties due to government units, such as income and property taxes.
9. Claims of general creditors.

If any amount remains after the priority classes of creditors have been satisfied, it is turned over to the debtor. Exhibit 16–1 on page 354 illustrates graphically the collection and distribution of property in most voluntary bankruptcies.

In a bankruptcy case in which the debtor has no assets,[15] creditors are notified of the debtor's petition for bankruptcy but are instructed not to file a claim. In such a case, the unsecured creditors will receive no payment, and most, if not all, of these debts will be discharged.

Discharge. From the debtor's point of view, the primary purpose of liquidation is to obtain a fresh start

---

14. Also, if applicable, the debtor must specify whether the collateral will be claimed as exempt property and whether the debtor intends to redeem the property or reaffirm the debt secured by the collateral (the reaffirmation of debts will be discussed shortly).

15. This type of bankruptcy is called a "no asset" case.

EXHIBIT 16–1   COLLECTION AND DISTRIBUTION OF PROPERTY IN MOST VOLUNTARY BANKRUPTCIES

This exhibit illustrates the property that might be collected in a debtor's voluntary bankruptcy and how it might be distributed to creditors. Involuntary bankruptcies and some voluntary bankruptcies could include additional types of property and other creditors.

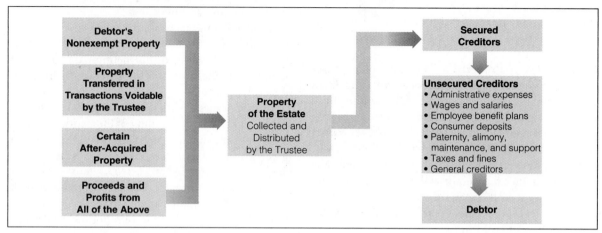

through a discharge of debts.[16] Certain debts, however, are not dischargeable in bankruptcy. Also, certain debtors may not qualify to have all debts discharged in bankruptcy. These situations are discussed below.

Exceptions to Discharge. Discharge of a debt may be denied because of the nature of the claim or the conduct of the debtor. Claims that are not dischargeable in a liquidation bankruptcy include the following:

1. Claims for back taxes accruing within three years prior to bankruptcy.

2. Claims for amounts borrowed by the debtor to pay federal taxes.

3. Claims against property or money obtained by the debtor under false pretenses or by false representations.

4. Claims by creditors who were not notified and did not know of the bankruptcy; these claims did not appear on the schedules the debtor was required to file.

5. Claims based on fraud or misuse of funds by the debtor while he or she was acting in a fiduciary ca-

pacity or claims involving the debtor's embezzlement or larceny.

6. Alimony, child support, and (with certain exceptions) property settlements.

7. Claims based on willful or malicious conduct by the debtor toward another or the property of another.

8. Certain government fines and penalties.

9. Certain student loans, unless payment of the loans imposes an undue hardship on the debtor and the debtor's dependents.

10. Consumer debts of more than $1,075 for luxury goods or services owed to a single creditor incurred within sixty days of the order for relief. This denial of discharge is a rebuttable presumption (that is, the denial may be challenged by the debtor), however, and any debts reasonably incurred to support the debtor or dependents are not classified as luxuries.

11. Cash advances totaling more than $1,075 that are extensions of open-end consumer credit obtained by the debtor within sixty days of the order for relief. A denial of discharge of these debts is also a rebuttable presumption.

12. Judgments or consent decrees against a debtor as a result of the debtor's operation of a motor vehicle while intoxicated.

In the following case, a debtor sought to have his obligation to pay half of the college expenses for his sons discharged in bankruptcy.

---

16. Discharges are granted under Chapter 7 only to individuals, not to corporations or partnerships. The latter may use Chapter 11, or they may terminate their existence under state law.

CASE 16.5 In re Seixas

United States
Bankruptcy Appellate
Panel,
Ninth Circuit, 1999.
239 Bankr. 398.

BACKGROUND AND FACTS *Michael Seixas and Marsha Booth were married in November 1967 and separated in February 1982. At the time of the separation, they had two boys, ages eight and four. As part of the marital settlement, Seixas agreed, in the "College Education Provision," to pay half of the boys' college expenses. Both parties agreed to carry life insurance with the boys as beneficiaries until they graduated from college or turned twenty-three. Seixas failed to pay his share of the college expenses, so Booth paid the entire cost and then filed a suit in a California state court against Seixas for reimbursement of his half. The court ordered Seixas to pay Booth $10,263.01 of the college expenses. Less than a year later, Seixas filed a petition in a federal bankruptcy court to declare bankruptcy under Chapter 7. Booth asked the court to rule that Seixas's college-expense obligation was nondischargeable. The court found that the obligation was "in the nature of [child] support" and granted Booth's request. Seixas appealed to the U.S. Bankruptcy Appellate Panel for the Ninth Circuit, arguing in part that he had no duty to support his children once they reached the age of majority.*

IN THE LANGUAGE OF THE COURT

RYAN, Bankruptcy Judge.

* * * *

[11 U.S.C.] Section 523(a)(5) excepts from discharge any child support obligation resulting from a separation or divorce agreement. * * *

* * * *

* * * [A] parent's obligation to pay a child's college education expenses pursuant to a settlement agreement or court order may be nondischargeable under Section 523(a)(5) even though the parent does not have any legal duty to support a child once that child reaches the age of majority under applicable state law. *Because Congress did not limit the word "child" by prefacing it with the word "minor," Section 523(a)(5) allows for the nondischargeability of certain support obligations owed to children even after they have reached the age of majority.* * * * [Emphasis added.]

* * * *

The intent of the parties and the substance of the obligation are the touchstone of the Section 523(a)(5) analysis * * * . Thus, we look at the surrounding circumstances and all other relevant incidents bearing on the parties' intent to determine whether the parties intended a particular obligation to be in the nature of child support.

* * * *

* * * The plain language of the College Education Provision is unambiguous with respect to the parents' contractual obligation to provide for their children's college education expenses and reflects the parties' intent to equally share those expenses. Also, because no money was set aside for their children and the obligation was of limited duration* * * , this factor supports a finding that the provision was in the nature of support. Indeed, as is evidenced from the College Education Provision, the parties were concerned enough to provide life insurance for their children's college education in the event that either spouse died. Booth testified that she and Debtor "wanted to make sure * * * that there would be money there for their education." This statement is consistent with the plain language of the College Education Provision.

Accordingly, the bankruptcy court's finding that the parties intended the College Education Provision to provide for the educational support of their children was not clearly erroneous. Consequently, the bankruptcy court did not err in determining that Debtor's obligation to pay one half of his children's education expenses was "in the nature of support," and thus, nondischargeable under Section 523(a)(5).

DECISION AND REMEDY *The U.S. Bankruptcy Appellate Panel for the Ninth Circuit affirmed the judgment of the lower court. The debtor's obligation to pay half of his sons' college expenses was nondischargeable. Support obligations owed to children may include educational expenses if, at the time the obligations are agreed to, the parties intend this.*

Objections to Discharge. In addition to the exceptions to discharge previously listed, a bankruptcy court may also deny the discharge of the *debtor* (as opposed to the debt). In the latter situation, the assets of the debtor are still distributed to the creditors, but the debtor remains liable for the unpaid portion of all claims. Some grounds for the denial of discharge of the debtor are the following:

1. The debtor's concealment or destruction of property with the intent to hinder, delay, or defraud a creditor.
2. The debtor's fraudulent concealment or destruction of financial records.
3. The granting of a discharge to the debtor within six years of the filing of the petition.

Effect of Discharge. The primary effect of a discharge is to void any judgment on a discharged debt and enjoin any action to collect a discharged debt. A discharge does not affect the liability of a co-debtor.

Revocation of Discharge. The Code provides that a debtor may lose his or her bankruptcy discharge by revocation on petition by the trustee or a creditor. The bankruptcy court may, within one year, revoke the discharge decree if it is discovered that the debtor acted fraudulently or dishonestly during the bankruptcy proceedings. The revocation renders the discharge void, allowing creditors not satisfied by the distribution of the debtor's estate to proceed with their claims against the debtor.

Reaffirmation of Debt. A debtor may wish to pay a debt—such as, for example, a debt owed to a family member, family doctor, bank, or some other creditor—notwithstanding the fact that the debt could be discharged in bankruptcy. An agreement to pay a debt dischargeable in bankruptcy is called a **reaffirmation agreement.** To be enforceable, reaffirmation agreements must be made before the debtor is granted a discharge. The agreement must be filed with the court. Approval by the court is required unless the debtor's attorney files an affidavit stating that the reaffirmation agreement is voluntarily made, that the debtor understands the consequences of the agreement and of a default under the agreement, and that the agreement will not result in an undue hardship on the debtor or the debtor's family. If court approval is required, a separate hearing will be held.

The agreement must contain a clear and conspicuous statement advising the debtor that reaffirmation is not required. The debtor can rescind, or cancel, the agreement at any time prior to discharge or within sixty days of the filing of the agreement, whichever is *later.* This rescission period must be stated *clearly* and *conspicuously* in the reaffirmation agreement.

REORGANIZATIONS

The type of bankruptcy proceeding used most commonly by corporate debtors is the Chapter 11 *reorganization.* In a reorganization, the creditors and the debtor formulate a plan under which the debtor pays a portion of his or her debts and is discharged of the remainder. The debtor is allowed to continue in business. Although this type of bankruptcy is commonly a corporate reorganization, any debtors (including individuals but excluding stockbrokers and commodities brokers)[17] who are eligible for Chapter 7 relief are eligible for relief under Chapter 11.[18] In 1994, Congress established a "fast track" Chapter 11 for small-business debtors whose liabilities do not exceed $2 million and who do not own or manage real estate. This permits bankruptcy proceedings without the appointment of committees and can save time and costs.

The same principles that govern the filing of a liquidation petition apply to reorganization proceedings. The case may be brought either voluntarily or involuntarily. The same guidelines govern the entry of the order for relief. The automatic stay and adequate protection provisions are applicable in reorganizations as well.

In some instances, creditors may prefer private, negotiated adjustments of creditor-debtor relations, also known as **workouts,** to bankruptcy proceedings. Often, these out-of-court workouts are much more flexible and thus more conducive to a speedy settlement. Speed is critical, because delay is one of the most costly elements in any bankruptcy proceeding. Another advantage of workouts is that they avoid the various administrative costs of bankruptcy proceedings.

Under Section 305(a) of the Bankruptcy Code, a court, after notice and a hearing, may dismiss or suspend all proceedings in a case at any time if dismissal or suspension would better serve the interests of the

---

17. In *Toibb v. Radloff,* 501 U.S. 157, 111 S.Ct. 2197, 115 L.Ed.2d 145 (1991), the United States Supreme Court ruled that a non-business debtor may petition for relief under Chapter 11.
18. In addition, railroads are eligible for Chapter 11 relief.

creditors. Section 1112 also allows a court, after notice and a hearing, to dismiss a case under reorganization "for cause." Cause includes the absence of a reasonable likelihood of rehabilitation, the inability to effect a plan, and an unreasonable delay by the debtor that is prejudicial to (may harm the interests of) creditors.[19]

Debtor in Possession. On entry of the order for relief, the debtor generally continues to operate the business as a **debtor in possession (DIP)**. The court, however, may appoint a trustee (often referred to as a *receiver*) to operate the debtor's business if gross mismanagement of the business is shown or if appointing a trustee is in the best interests of the estate.

Creditors' Committees. As soon as practicable after the entry of the order for relief, a creditors' committee of unsecured creditors is appointed. The committee may consult with the trustee or the DIP concerning the administration of the case or the formulation of the plan. Additional creditors' committees may be appointed to represent special interest creditors. Orders affecting the estate generally will be entered only with either the consent of the committee or after a hearing in which the judge hears the position of the committee.

Businesses with debts of less than $2 million that do not own or manage real estate can avoid creditors' committees. In these cases, orders can be entered without a committee's consent.

The Reorganization Plan. A reorganization plan to rehabilitate the debtor is a plan to conserve and administer the debtor's assets in the hope of an eventual return to successful operation and solvency. The plan must be fair and equitable and must do the following:

1. Designate classes of claims and interests.
2. Specify the treatment to be afforded the classes. (The plan must provide the same treatment for all claims in a particular class.)
3. Provide an adequate means for execution.

Only the debtor may file a plan within the first 120 days after the date of the order for relief. If the debtor does not meet the 120-day deadline, however, or if the debtor fails to obtain the required creditor consent (discussed below) within 180 days, any party may propose a plan. If a small-business debtor chooses to avoid creditors' committees, the time for the debtor's filing is shortened to 100 days, and any other party's plan must be filed within 160 days.

Once the plan has been developed, it is submitted to each class of creditors for acceptance. Each class must accept the plan unless the class is not adversely affected by it. A class has accepted the plan when a majority of the creditors, representing two-thirds of the amount of the total claim, vote to approve it.

Even when all classes of claims accept the plan, the court may refuse to confirm it if it is not "in the best interests of the creditors."[20] A spouse or child of the debtor can block the plan if it does not provide for payment of their claims in cash.

The plan is binding on confirmation. The debtor is given a reorganization discharge from all claims not protected under the plan. This discharge does not apply to any claims that would be denied discharge under liquidation.

Even if only one class of claims has accepted the plan, the court may still confirm the plan under the Code's so-called **cram-down provision.** In other words, the court may confirm the plan over the objections of a class of creditors. Before the court can exercise this right of cram-down confirmation, it must be demonstrated that the plan does not discriminate unfairly against any creditors and that the plan is fair and equitable.

INDIVIDUALS' REPAYMENT PLAN

Chapter 13 of the Bankruptcy Code provides for "Adjustment of Debts of an Individual with Regular Income." Individuals (not partnerships or corporations) with regular income who owe fixed unsecured debts of less than $269,250 or fixed secured debts of less than $807,750 may take advantage of bankruptcy repayment plans. This includes salaried employees; sole proprietors; and individuals who live on welfare, Social Security, fixed pensions, or investment income. Many small-business debtors have a choice of filing a plan for reorganization or for repayment. There are several advantages, however, with repayment plans. One advantage is that they are less expensive and less

---

19. See 11 U.S.C. Section 1112(b). Debtors are not prohibited from filing successive petitions, however. A debtor whose petition is dismissed, for example, can file a new Chapter 11 petition (which may be granted unless it is filed in bad faith).

20. The plan need not provide for full repayment to unsecured creditors. Instead, creditors receive a percentage of each dollar owed to them by the debtor.

complicated than reorganization proceedings or, for that matter, even liquidation proceedings.

Filing the Petition. A repayment plan case can be initiated only by the filing of a voluntary petition by the debtor. Certain liquidation and reorganization cases may be converted to repayment plan cases with the consent of the debtor.[21] A trustee, who will make payments under the plan, must be appointed. On the filing of a repayment plan petition, the automatic stay previously discussed takes effect. Although the stay applies to all or part of a consumer debt, it does not apply to any business debt incurred by the debtor.

The Repayment Plan. A plan of rehabilitation by repayment must provide for the following:

1. The turnover to the trustee of such future earnings or income of the debtor as is necessary for execution of the plan.
2. Full payment in deferred cash payments of all claims entitled to priority.[22]
3. The same treatment of all claims within a particular class. (The Code permits the debtor to list co-debtors, such as guarantors or sureties, as a separate class.)

Filing the Plan. Only the debtor may file for a repayment plan. This plan may provide either for payment of all obligations in full or for payment of a lesser amount. The time for payment under the plan may not exceed three years unless the court approves an extension. The term, with extension, may not exceed five years.

The Code requires the debtor to make "timely" payments, and the trustee is required to ensure that the debtor commences these payments. The debtor must begin making payments under the proposed plan within thirty days after the plan has been *filed*. If the plan has not been confirmed, the trustee is instructed to retain the payments until the plan is confirmed and then distribute them accordingly. If the plan is denied, the trustee will return the payments to the debtor less any costs. Failure of the debtor to make

timely payments or to commence payments within the thirty-day period will allow the court to convert the case to a liquidation bankruptcy or to dismiss the petition.

Confirmation of the Plan. After the plan is filed, the court holds a confirmation hearing, at which interested parties may object to the plan. The court will confirm a plan with respect to each claim of a secured creditor under any of the following circumstances:

1. If the secured creditors have accepted the plan.
2. If the plan provides that creditors retain their liens and if the value of the property to be distributed to them under the plan is not less than the secured portion of their claims.
3. If the debtor surrenders the property securing the claims to the creditors.

Objection to the Plan. Unsecured creditors do not have a vote to confirm a repayment plan, but they can object to it. The court can approve a plan over the objection of the trustee or any unsecured creditor only in either of the following situations:

1. When the value of the property to be distributed under the plan is at least equal to the amount of the claims.
2. When all the debtor's projected disposable income to be received during the three-year plan period will be applied to making payments. Disposable income is all income received less amounts needed to support the debtor and dependents and/or amounts needed to meet ordinary expenses to continue the operation of a business.

Modification of the Plan. Prior to completion of payments, the plan may be modified at the request of the debtor, the trustee, or an unsecured creditor. If there is an objection to the modification by any interested party, the court must hold a hearing to determine approval or disapproval of the modified plan.

Discharge. After completion of all payments, the court grants a discharge of all debts provided for by the repayment plan. Except for allowed claims not provided for by the plan, certain long-term debts provided for by the plan, and claims for alimony and child support, all other debts are dischargeable. A discharge of debts under a Chapter 13 repayment plan is sometimes referred to as a "super-discharge." One of the reasons for this is that the law allows a Chapter 13

---

21. A Chapter 13 case may be converted to a Chapter 7 case either at the request of the debtor or, under certain circumstances, "for cause" by a creditor. A Chapter 13 case may be converted to a Chapter 11 case after a hearing.
22. As with a Chapter 11 reorganization plan, full repayment of all claims is not always required.

discharge to include fraudulently incurred debt and claims resulting from malicious or willful injury. Therefore, a discharge under Chapter 13 may be much more beneficial to some debtors than a liquidation discharge under Chapter 7.

Even if the debtor does not complete the plan, a hardship discharge may be granted if failure to complete the plan was due to circumstances beyond the debtor's control and if the value of the property distributed under the plan was greater than would have been paid in a liquidation. A discharge can be revoked within one year if it was obtained by fraud.

TERMS AND CONCEPTS TO REVIEW

adequate protection doctrine 349

artisan's lien 337

attachment 337

automatic stay 348

co-surety 343

cram-down provision 357

debtor in possession (DIP) 357

discharge 346

equity of redemption 340

garnishment 338

guarantor 341

homestead exemption 344

insider 352

lien 336

liquidation 346

mechanic's lien 337

mortgagee 340

mortgagor 340

order for relief 346

petition in bankruptcy 346

preference 352

reaffirmation agreement 356

right of contribution 343

right of reimbursement 343

right of subrogation 343

statutory period of redemption 340

surety 340

suretyship 340

trustee 346

U.S. Trustee 351

workout 356

writ of attachment 338

writ of execution 338

QUESTIONS AND CASE PROBLEMS

16–1. Liens. Sylvia takes her car to Caleb's Auto Repair Shop. A sign in the window states that all repairs must be paid for in cash unless credit is approved in advance. Sylvia and Caleb agree that Caleb will repair Sylvia's car engine and put in a new transmission. No mention is made of credit. Because Caleb is not sure how much engine repair will be necessary, he refuses to give Sylvia an estimate. He repairs the engine and puts in a new transmission. When Sylvia comes to pick up her car, she learns that the bill is $995. Sylvia is furious, refuses to pay Caleb that amount, and demands possession of her car. Caleb demands payment. Discuss the rights of the parties in this matter.

16–2. Creditors' Remedies. Kanahara is employed by the Cross-Bar Packing Corp. and earns take-home pay of $400 per week. He is $2,000 in debt to the Holiday Department Store for goods purchased on credit over the past eight months. Most of this property is nonexempt and is presently located in Kanahara's apartment. Kanahara is in default on his payments to Holiday. Holiday learns that Kanahara has a girlfriend in another state and that he plans on giving her most of this property for Christmas. Discuss what actions are available and should be taken by Holiday to resolve the debt owed by Kanahara.

16–3. Guaranty. Natalie is a student at Slippery Stone University. In need of funds to pay for tuition and books, she attempts to secure a short-term loan from West Bank. The bank agrees to make a loan if Natalie will have someone financially responsible guarantee the loan payments. Sheila, a well-known businesswoman and a friend of Natalie's family, calls the bank and agrees to pay the loan if Natalie cannot. Because of Sheila's reputation, the loan is made. Natalie is making the payments, but because of illness she is not able to work for one month. She requests that West Bank extend the loan for three months. West Bank agrees, raising the interest rate for the extended period. Sheila is not notified of the extension (and therefore does not consent to it). One month later Natalie drops out of school. All attempts to collect from Natalie fail. West Bank wants to hold Sheila liable. Discuss West Bank's claim against Sheila.

16–4. PRIORITY OF CREDITORS. Sam is a retail seller of television sets. He sells Gracen a $900 set on a retail installment security agreement in which she pays $100 down and agrees to pay the balance in equal installments. Sam retains a security interest in the set, and he perfects that interest by filing a financing statement locally. Two months later, Gracen is in default on her payments to Sam and is involuntarily petitioned into bankruptcy by her creditors. Sam wants to repossess the television set, as provided for in the security agreement, and he wants to have priority over the trustee in bankruptcy as to any proceeds from the disposal of the set. Discuss fully Sam's right to repossess and whether he has priority over the trustee in bankruptcy as to any proceeds from the disposal of the set.

16–5. DISTRIBUTION OF ASSETS. Montoro petitioned himself into voluntary bankruptcy. There were three major claims against his estate. One was made by Carlton, a friend who held Montoro's negotiable promissory note for $2,500; one was made by Elmer, an employee who was owed three months' back wages of $4,500; and one was made by the United Bank of the Rockies on an unsecured loan of $5,000. In addition, Dietrich, an accountant retained by the trustee, was owed $500, and property taxes of $1,000 were owed to Rock County. Montoro's nonexempt property was liquidated, with proceeds of $5,000. Discuss fully what amount each party will receive, and why.

16–6 PREFERENCES. Fred Currey purchased cattle from Itano Farms, Inc. As payment for the cattle, Currey gave Itano Farms worthless checks in the amount of $50,250. Currey was later convicted of passing bad checks, and the state criminal court ordered him to pay Itano Farms restitution in the amount of $50,250. About four months after this court order, Currey and his wife filed for Chapter 7 bankruptcy protection. During the ninety days prior to the filing of the petition, Currey had made three restitution payments to Itano, totaling $14,821. The Curreys sought to recover these payments as preferences. What should the court decide? Explain. [*In re Currey*, 144 Bankr. 490 (D.Ida. 1992)]

16–7. AUTOMATIC STAY. David Sisco had about $600 in an account in Tinker Federal Credit Union. Sisco owed DPW Employees Credit Union a little more than $1,100. To collect on the debt, DPW obtained a garnishment judgment and served it on Tinker. The next day, Sisco filed a bankruptcy petition. Tinker then told DPW that, because of the bankruptcy filing, it could not pay the garnishment. DPW objected, and Tinker asked an Oklahoma state court to resolve the issue. What effect, if any, does Sisco's bankruptcy filing have on DPW's garnishment action? [*DPW Employees Credit Union v. Tinker Federal Credit Union*, 925 P.2d 93 (Okla.App.4th 1996)]

16–8. VOIDABLE PREFERENCE. The Securities and Exchange Commission (SEC) filed a suit in a federal district court against First Jersey Securities, Inc., and others, alleging fraud in First Jersey's sale of securities (stock). The court ordered the defendants to turn over to the SEC $75 million in illegal profits. This order made the SEC the largest unsecured creditor of First Jersey. First Jersey filed a voluntary petition in a federal bankruptcy court to declare bankruptcy under Chapter 11. On the same day, the debtor transferred 200,001 shares of stock to its law firm, Robinson, St. John, & Wayne (RSW), in payment for services in the SEC suit and the bankruptcy petition. The stock represented essentially all of the debtor's assets. RSW did not find a buyer for the stock for more than two months. The SEC objected to the transfer, contending that it was a voidable preference, and asked that RSW be disqualified from representing the debtor. RSW responded that the transfer was made in the ordinary course of business. Also, asserted RSW, the transfer was not in payment of an "antecedent debt," because the firm had not presented First Jersey with a bill for its services and therefore the debt was not yet past due. Was the stock transfer a voidable preference? Should the court disqualify RSW? Why or why not? [*In re First Jersey Securities, Inc.*, 180 F.3d 504 (3d Cir. 1999)]

16–9. IN YOUR COURT

Ellis and Bonnie Jarrell filed a Chapter 7 petition. The reason for the filing was not calamity, sudden illness, disability, or unemployment—both Jarrells were employed. Their petition was full of inaccuracies that understated their income and overstated their obligations. For example, they declared as an expense a monthly contribution to an investment plan. The truth was that they had monthly income of $3,197.45 and expenses of $2,159.44. They were attempting to discharge a total of $15,391.64 in unsecured debts. Most of these were credit-card debts, at least half of which had been taken as cash advances. Assume that you are the judge in the bankruptcy court and answer the following questions:

(a) A key question before you is whether the Jarrells have the ability to pay off their debts in three to five years under a Chapter 13 repayment plan. Can they?

(b) Depending on your answer to the above question, would granting the Jarrells' petition constitute "substantial abuse" of Chapter 7? Explain. (Before making your decision, review the court's opinion in Case 16.3, *In re Lamanna*, on how the courts determine when "substantial abuse" occurs.)

LAW ON THE WEB

For updated links to resources available on the Web, as well as a variety of other materials, visit this text's Web site at http://wleb.westbuslaw.com.

The Legal Information Institute at Cornell University offers a collection of law materials concerning debtor-creditor relationships at

http://www.law.cornell.edu/topics/debtor_creditor.html

For an example of one state's (South Dakota's) laws on garnishment, go to

http://www.state.sd.us/state/legis/lrc/statutes/21/18/211800h.htm

The U.S. Bankruptcy Code is online at

http://www.law.cornell.edu:80/uscode/11

You can find links to an extensive number of bankruptcy resources on the Internet by accessing the Bankruptcy Lawfinder at

http://www.agin.com/lawfind

Another good resource for bankruptcy information is the American Bankruptcy Institute (ABI) at

http://www.abiworld.org

LEGAL RESEARCH EXERCISES ON THE WEB

Go to http://wleb.westbuslaw.com, the Web site that accompanies this text. Select "Internet Applications," and then click on "Chapter 16." There you will find the following Internet research exercises that you can perform to learn more about bankruptcy and its alternatives:

Activity 16–1: Debtor-Creditor Relations

Activity 16–2: Bankruptcy

CHAPTER 17

Sole Proprietorships, Partnerships, and Special Business Organizations

EVERY BUSINESS ACTIVITY INVOLVES—implicitly or explicitly—a form of business organization, whether it be a sole proprietorship, a partnership, a corporation, or some hybrid form. Each form provides different degrees of flexibility and different rights and liabilities, and it is important to be aware of these differences when choosing and structuring one's business organization. In this chapter, we examine the basic features of sole proprietorships, partnerships, joint ventures, syndicates, joint stock companies, business trusts, cooperatives, and private franchises. The corporation will be discussed in detail in Chapter 18. Two relatively new forms of business enterprise—limited liability companies (LLCs) and limited liability partnerships (LLPs)—offer special advantages to businesspersons, particularly with respect to taxation and liability. We will look at these business forms, which are coming into widespread use, in Chapter 18.

Note that there is great variety in the sizes and functions of business organizations even within the same category. For example, businesses conducted as sole proprietorships can range from a small mail order business run out of the owner's home to a multimillion-dollar manufacturing operation occupying acres of an industrial complex. Similarly, partnerships can range from an informal arrangement between two individuals to a formal organization with hundreds of partners. Also, most of the wealthiest U.S. business firms are organized as corporations, but the majority of corporations are small. It has been estimated that over 90 percent of the corporations have ten or fewer shareholders.

The sizes of businesses may differ considerably within a category, but tax liabilities and other obligations faced by the businesses within each category typically are constant. A sole proprietorship doing $22,000 worth of business faces the same federal tax laws as a sole proprietorship doing $10 million worth of business.

SECTION 1

Sole Proprietorships

The simplest form of business is a **sole proprietorship.** In this form, the owner is the business; thus, anyone who does business without creating a separate business organization has a sole proprietorship. Sole proprietorships constitute over two-thirds of all American businesses. They are also usually small enterprises—about 99 percent of the sole proprietorships existing in the United States have revenues of less than $1 million per year. Sole proprietors can own and manage any type of business from an informal, home-office undertaking to a large restaurant or construction firm.

A major advantage of the sole proprietorship is that the proprietor receives all of the profits (because he or she assumes all of the risk). In addition, it is often easier and less costly to start a sole proprietorship than to start any other kind of business, as few legal forms are involved. This type of business organization also provides more flexibility than does a partnership or a corporation. The sole proprietor is free to make any decision he or she wishes to concerning the business—whom to hire, when to take a vacation, what kind of business to pursue, and so on. A sole proprietor pays only personal income taxes on the business's profits, which are reported as personal income on the proprietor's personal income tax return. Sole proprietors are also allowed to establish tax-exempt retirement accounts in the form of Keogh plans.[1]

The major disadvantage of the sole proprietorship is that, as sole owner, the proprietor alone bears the burden of any losses or liabilities incurred by the business enterprise. In other words, the sole proprietor has unlimited liability, or legal responsibility, for all obligations that arise in doing business. This unlimited liability is a major factor to be considered in choosing a business form. The sole proprietorship also has the disadvantage of lacking continuity on the death of the proprietor. When the owner dies, so does the business—it is automatically dissolved. If the business is transferred to family members or other heirs, a new proprietorship is created.

Another disadvantage is that the proprietor's opportunity to raise capital is limited to personal funds and the funds of those who are willing to make loans to him or her. If the owner wishes to expand the business significantly, one way to raise more capital to finance the expansion is to join forces with another entrepreneur and establish a partnership or form a corporation.

---

1. A *Keogh plan* is a retirement program designed for self-employed persons by which a certain percentage of their income can be contributed to the plan, and interest earnings will not be taxed until funds are withdrawn from the plan.

SECTION 2

Partnerships

When two or more persons agree to do business as partners, they enter into a special relationship with one another. To an extent, their relationship is similar to an agency relationship, because each partner is deemed the agent of the other partners and of the partnership. The agency concepts that you will read about in Chapter 20 thus apply—specifically, the imputation of knowledge of, and responsibility for, acts carried out within the scope of the partnership relationship. In their relationship to one another, partners are also bound by the fiduciary ties that bind an agent and principal under agency law.

Partnership law is distinct from agency law in one significant way, however. A partnership is based on a voluntary contract between two or more competent persons who agree to place some or all of their money or other assets, labor, and skills in a business with the understanding that profits and losses will be shared. In a nonpartnership agency relationship, the agent usually does not have an ownership interest in the business, nor is he or she obligated to bear a portion of the ordinary business losses.

The Uniform Partnership Act (UPA) governs the operation of partnerships *in the absence of express agreement* and has done much to reduce controversies in the law relating to partnerships. The UPA has been adopted in all of the states except Louisiana, as well as in the District of Columbia. The entire text of the UPA is presented in Appendix O at the end of this text. A revised version of the UPA, known as the Revised Uniform Partnership Act (RUPA), has been adopted by several states, and others are considering its adoption. Throughout our discussion of partnership law in this chapter, we indicate in footnotes the most significant changes made by the RUPA. Appendix P contains excerpts from the RUPA.

DEFINITION OF PARTNERSHIP

Parties commonly find themselves in conflict over whether their business enterprise is a legal partnership, especially in the absence of a formal, written partnership agreement. The UPA defines the term **partnership** as "an association of two or more persons to carry on as co-owners a business for profit" [UPA 6(1)]. The *intent* to associate is a key element of a partnership, and one cannot join a partnership unless all other partners consent [UPA 18(g)]. In resolving disputes over whether partnership status exists, courts will usually look for the following three essential elements of partnership implicit in the UPA's definition:

1. A sharing of profits or losses.
2. A joint ownership of the business.
3. An equal right in the management of the business.

In the event that the evidence is insufficient to establish all three factors, the UPA provides a set of guidelines to be used. For example, the existence of a partnership will be inferred if profits and losses from a business are shared. No such inference is made, however, if the profits were received as payment of the following:

1. A debt by installments or interest on a loan.
2. Wages of an employee.
3. Rent to a landlord.
4. An annuity to a widow or representative of a deceased partner.
5. A sale of the goodwill of a business or property [UPA 7(4)].

To illustrate: Suppose that a debtor owes a creditor $5,000 on an unsecured debt. To repay the debt, the debtor agrees to pay (and the creditor, to accept) 10 percent of the debtor's monthly business profits until the loan with interest has been paid. Although the creditor is sharing profits from the business, the debtor and creditor are not presumed to be partners.

Joint ownership of property, obviously, does not in and of itself create a partnership. Therefore, the fact that, say, MacPherson and Bunker own real property as joint tenants or as tenants in common (a form of joint ownership) does not establish a partnership. In fact, the sharing of gross returns and even profits from such ownership is usually not enough to create a partnership [UPA 7(2), (3)]. Thus, if MacPherson and Bunker jointly owned a piece of rural property and leased the land to a farmer, the sharing of the profits from the farming operation by the farmer in lieu of set rental payments would ordinarily not make MacPherson, Bunker, and the farmer partners.

In the following case, two brothers and their mother bought a ranch that for many years, the brothers operated together. After the mother disclaimed her interest and one brother stopped participating in ranch activities, a question arose as to whether the brothers were ever partners.

CASE 17.1   Tarnavsky v. Tarnavsky

United States
Court of Appeals,
Eighth Circuit, 1998.
147 F.3d 674.
http://ls.wustl.edu/
cgi-bin/8th_byname.pl[a]

HISTORICAL AND SOCIAL SETTING   *In the 1700s, 90 percent of the U.S. work force was in agriculture. Today, that figure is less than 3 percent, but operating a farm or ranch has become far more of an exact science. To run a successful agribusiness today, a farmer or rancher must have knowledge of computers, economics, financial management, government regulation, human resources, marketing, and risk management. A farmer or rancher must be—or have access to—an accountant, an insurance agent, a lawyer, and a stockbroker and have a connection to his or her representative in Congress. Despite this situation, which would seem to favor agriconglomerates, about 90 percent of U.S. farms are individual or family operations, which account for about two-thirds of total agricultural production.*

BACKGROUND AND FACTS   *In 1967, Mary Tarnavsky and her sons Morris and Thomas (who was called T.R.) bought a ranch known as the Christ place. T.R. and Morris opened a bank account into which they deposited their shares of the ranch's proceeds, which were used to make payments on the property, to pay property taxes, and to buy cattle, equipment, supplies, and services. For the ranch, the brothers took out joint loans and jointly purchased cattle and machinery. They reported their activities on state and federal partnership income tax returns. Morris handled the livestock; T.R. handled the*

a. This database is maintained by Washington University School of Law. From this page, a search can be launched, based on a party's name, for a recent opinion of the U.S. Court of Appeals for the Eighth Circuit. In the "Search String" box, type "Tarnavsky" and then click on "Begin Search." From the search results, click on the appropriate link to access the case.

bookkeeping. In 1980, Mary disclaimed her interest in proceeds from the ranch. Eight years later, T.R. stopped doing the bookkeeping and began spending little time on ranch activities. Morris sent T.R. a "Notice of Dissolution of Partnership." After unsuccessful attempts to arrive at a settlement, T.R. filed a suit in a federal district court, requesting payment for his share of the partnership assets. The court ordered a payment of $220,000. Morris appealed, arguing in part that there was no partnership.

<table>
<tr>
<td>IN THE LANGUAGE
OF THE COURT</td>
<td>

JOHN R. GIBSON, Circuit Judge.

*   *   *   *

*   *   * [C]ertain elements are critical to the existence of a partnership. These elements are: (1) an intention to be partners; (2) co-ownership of the business; and (3) profit motive.

*   *   *   *

*   *   * T.R. and Morris reported their farming activities on state and federal partnership income tax returns *   *   * . Morris and T.R. opened a joint bank account *   *   * . From this account, they made the Christ place property payments, purchased cattle, seed, and related supplies. *   *   * These actions by Morris and T.R. evidence their intent to be partners.

Co-ownership, the second element necessary for a partnership, includes the sharing of profits and losses as well as the power of control in the management of the business. *   *   * [A]fter completing a sale of cattle or grain, the brothers would deposit their share of the income in their joint account. From this account, the brothers jointly paid expenses *   *   * . [J]ointly purchasing land and machinery with profits is a form of profit sharing. *   *   * [A]t the end of each year, Morris and T.R. would allocate the year's profits on the partnership income tax return equally between themselves *   *   * . This sharing of profits is further evidence that Morris and T.R. were partners.

*   *   *   *

*   *   * [B]oth T.R. and Morris handled "marketing the cattle" and performed various administrative functions, such as the discussion of rations. *   *   * Morris was "in charge" of livestock production and "administered" equipment purchases, and *   *   * T.R. was "in charge" of paperwork and finances. This is strong evidence that T.R. and Morris both had the power of control over management of the business. *   *   * Control, when combined with profit sharing, strongly suggests the existence of a partnership.

The final critical element of a partnership is profit motive, and there is no dispute that the farming business was operated with such motive.

</td>
</tr>
<tr>
<td>DECISION
AND REMEDY</td>
<td>

The U.S. Court of Appeals for the Eighth Circuit affirmed the lower court's order. Morris and T.R. were partners.

</td>
</tr>
</table>

THE NATURE OF PARTNERSHIPS

A partnership is sometimes called a *company* or a *firm*, terms that suggest that the partnership is an entity separate and apart from its aggregate members. Sometimes the law of partnership recognizes the independent entity for some purposes but may treat the partnership as a composite of individual partners for other purposes.

At common law, a partnership was never treated as a separate legal entity. Thus, a common law suit could never be brought by or against the firm in its own name; each individual partner had to sue or be sued. Many states today provide specifically that the partnership can be treated as an entity for certain purposes. These usually include the capacity to sue or be sued, to collect judgments, and to have all accounting procedures in the name of the partnership. In addition, the UPA recognizes that partnership property may be held in the name of the partnership rather than in the names of the individual partners. Finally, federal procedural laws frequently permit the partnership to be treated as an entity in such matters as lawsuits in federal courts, bankruptcy proceedings, and the filing of federal information tax returns.

When the partnership is not regarded as a separate legal entity, it is treated as an *aggregate* of the individual partners. For example, for federal income tax purposes, a partnership is not a tax-paying entity. The profits or losses incurred by a partnership are "passed through" the partnership framework and attributed to the partners on their individual tax returns. The partnership as an entity has no tax liability. It is an entity only for the filing of an **information return** with the Internal Revenue Service, indicating the profit or loss that each partner will report on his or her individual tax return.

PARTNERSHIP FORMATION

As a general rule, agreements to form a partnership can be *oral, written,* or *implied by conduct.* Some partnership agreements, however, must be in writing to be legally enforceable within the Statute of Frauds (see Chapter 9 for details). For example, a partnership agreement that, by its terms, is to continue for more than one year or a partnership agreement that authorizes the partners to deal in transfers of real property must be evidenced by a sufficient writing. Generally, a partnership agreement, called **articles of partnership,** can include virtually any terms that the partners wish, unless they are illegal or contrary to public policy. Practically speaking, it is better if the provisions of any partnership agreement are in writing.[2]

Duration of the Partnership. The partnership agreement can specify the duration of the partnership by designating a date or the completion of a particular project. This is called a *partnership for a term.* A dissolution of the partnership (how dissolution may occur will be discussed later in the chapter) without the consent of all the partners prior to the expiration of the partnership term constitutes a breach of the agreement, and the partner responsible for the breach can be liable for any losses resulting from it.

If no fixed duration is specified, the partnership is a *partnership at will.* Any partner can dissolve this type of partnership at any time without violating the agreement and without incurring liability for losses to other partners that result from the termination.

The Corporation as Partner. The UPA specifically permits a corporation to be a partner. By definition, "a partnership is an association of two or more persons," and the UPA defines a person as including corporations [UPA 2].

Although some states restrict the ability of corporations to become partners, such restrictions have become less common over the years. Many decisions in jurisdictions that do not permit corporate partners nevertheless validate the arrangements by characterizing them as joint ventures (discussed later in this chapter) rather than as partnerships.

Partnership by Estoppel. Parties who are not partners can hold themselves out as partners and make representations that third persons rely on in dealing with them. In such a situation, a court may conclude that a **partnership by estoppel** exists, in which case liability is imposed on the alleged partner or partners (although partnership *rights* are not conferred on these persons).

When a real partnership exists and a partner represents that a nonpartner is a member of the firm, the nonpartner is regarded as an agent whose acts are binding on the partner (but normally not on the partnership). For example, Middle Earth Movers has three partners—Jansen, Mathews, and Harran. Mathews represents to the business community that Tully is also a partner. If Tully negotiates a contract in the name of Middle Earth Movers, the contract will be binding on Mathews but normally not on Jansen and Harran (unless, of course, Jansen and Harran knew about, and consented to, Mathews's representation about Tully). Again, partnership by estoppel requires that a third person reasonably and detrimentally rely on the representation that a person was part of the partnership.

PARTNERSHIP OPERATION

The rights and duties of partners are governed largely by the specific terms of their partnership agreement. In the absence of provisions to the contrary in the partnership agreement, the law imposes the rights and duties discussed in the following subsections. The character and nature of the partnership business generally influence the application of these rights and duties.

---

2. The RUPA provides for the voluntary filing of a partnership statement, containing such information as the agency authority of the partners, with the secretary of state. The statement must be executed by at least two partners, a copy must be sent to all partners, and a certified copy must be filed in the office in which transfers of real property are recorded (in most states, in the county in which the property is located).

Rights among Partners. The rights held by partners in a partnership relate to the following areas: management, interest in the partnership, compensation, inspection of books, accounting, and property.

Management. In a general partnership, "All partners have equal rights in the management and conduct of partnership business" [UPA 18(e)]. Unless the partners agree otherwise, each partner has one vote in management matters *regardless of the proportional size of his or her interest in the firm.* Often, in a large partnership partners will agree to delegate daily management responsibilities to a management committee made up of one or more of the partners.

The majority rule controls decisions in ordinary matters connected with partnership business, unless otherwise specified in the agreement. Unanimous consent of the partners is required, however, to bind the firm in any of the following actions, which significantly affect the nature of the partnership:

1. To alter the essential nature of the firm's business as expressed in the partnership agreement or to alter the capital structure of the partnership.
2. To admit new partners or to enter a wholly new business [UPA 18(g), (h)].
3. To assign partnership property into a trust for the benefit of creditors [UPA 9(3)(a)].
4. To dispose of the partnership's goodwill [UPA 9(3)(b)].
5. To confess judgment against the partnership or submit partnership claims to arbitration [UPA 9(3)(d), (e)]. (A *confession of judgment* is the act of a debtor in permitting a judgment to be entered against him or her by a creditor, for an agreed sum, without the institution of legal proceedings.)
6. To undertake any act that would make further conduct of partnership business impossible [UPA 9(3)(c)].
7. To amend the articles of the partnership.

Interest in the Partnership. Each partner is entitled to the proportion of business profits and losses that is designated in the partnership agreement. If the agreement does not apportion profits or losses, the UPA provides that profits are to be shared equally and losses are to be shared in the same ratio as profits [UPA 18(a)].

Compensation. Devoting time, skill, and energy to partnership business is a partner's duty and generally not a compensable service. Partners can, of course, agree otherwise. For example, the managing partner of a law firm often receives a salary in addition to his or her share of profits for performing special administrative duties in office and personnel management. UPA 18(f) provides that on the death of a partner, a surviving partner is entitled to compensation for services in winding up partnership affairs (and reimbursement for expenses incurred in the process) above and apart from his or her share in the partnership profits.

Inspection of Books. Partnership books and records must be kept accessible to all partners. Each partner has the right to receive (and the corresponding duty to produce) full and complete information concerning the conduct of all aspects of partnership business [UPA 20]. Each firm retains books in which to record and secure such information. Partners contribute the information, and a bookkeeper typically has the duty to preserve it. The books must be kept at the firm's principal business office unless the partners agree otherwise [UPA 19]. Every partner, whether active or inactive, is entitled to inspect all books and records on demand and can make copies of the materials. The personal representative of a deceased partner's estate has the same right of access to partnership books and records that the decedent would have had.

Accounting. An accounting of partnership assets or profits is done to determine the value of each partner's proportionate share in the partnership. An accounting can be called for voluntarily, or it can be compelled by the order of a court. Formal accounting occurs by right in connection with dissolution proceedings, but under UPA 22, a partner also has the right to a formal accounting in the following situations:

1. When the partnership agreement provides for a formal accounting.
2. When a partner is wrongfully excluded from the business, from access to the books, or from both.
3. When any partner is withholding profits or benefits belonging to the partnership in breach of the partner's fiduciary duty.
4. When circumstances render a formal accounting "just and reasonable."

Property Rights. A partner's interest in the firm is a personal asset consisting of a proportionate share of the profits earned [UPA 26] and a return of capital on the partnership's termination.

Also, a partner is co-owner with his or her partners of specific partnership property, holding the property as a tenant in partnership. A specific asset may constitute partnership property even when title to it is in an individual partner's name. UPA 8(1) provides that "all property originally brought into the partnership's stock or subsequently acquired, by purchase or otherwise, *on account of the partnership*, is partnership property" (emphasis added). Evidence that an asset was acquired with the intention that it be a partnership asset is at the heart of the phrase *on account of the partnership*. Thus, the more closely an asset is associated with the business operations of the partnership, the more likely it is to be a partnership asset.[3]

Tenancy in partnership has several important effects. If a partner dies, the surviving partners, not the heirs of the deceased partner, have the right of survivorship to the specific property. Although surviving partners are entitled to possession, they have a duty to account to the decedent's estate for the value of the deceased partner's interest in that property [UPA 25(2)(d), (e)].

A partner has no right to sell, assign, or in any way deal with a particular item of partnership property other than for partnership purposes [UPA 25(2)(a), (b)]. Nor is a partner's personal credit related to partnership property; his or her creditors cannot use partnership property to satisfy the personal debts of the partner. Partnership property is available only to satisfy partnership debts, to enhance the firm's credit, or to achieve other business purposes.

Every partner is a co-owner with all other partners of specific partnership property, such as office equipment, office supplies, and vehicles. Each partner has an equal right to possess partnership property for business purposes or in satisfaction of firm debts, but not for any other purpose without the consent of all the other partners.

Duties, Powers, and Liabilities of Partners. The duties and powers of partners consist of a fiduciary duty of each partner to the others and general agency powers.

Fiduciary Duties. Partners stand in a fiduciary relationship to one another just as principals and agents do (see Chapter 20). It is a relationship of extraordinary trust and loyalty. This fiduciary duty imposes a responsibility on each partner to act in utmost good faith for the benefit of the partnership. It requires that each partner subordinate his or her personal interests to the mutual welfare of the partners.[4] Thus, a partner cannot engage in any independent competitive activities without the other partners' consent.

This fiduciary duty underlies the entire body of law pertaining to partnership and to agency. From it, certain other duties are commonly implied. Thus, a partner must account to the partnership for any personal profits or benefits derived without the consent of all the partners in any partnership transactions.[5] These include transactions among partners; transactions with third parties connected with the formation, conduct, or liquidation of the partnership; and transactions involving any use of partnership property [UPA 21].

General Agency Powers. Each partner is an *agent* of every other partner and acts as both a principal and an agent in any business transaction within the scope of the partnership agreement. Each partner is a general agent of the partnership in carrying out the usual business of the firm.[6] Thus, every act of a partner concerning partnership business and every contract signed in the partnership name bind the firm [UPA 9(1)].

In an ordinary partnership, firm members can exercise all implied powers reasonably necessary and customary to carry on that particular business. Some

---

3. Under the RUPA, property that is not acquired in the name of the partnership is nonetheless partnership property if the instrument transferring title refers to (1) the person taking title as a partner or (2) the existence of the partnership [RUPA 204(a)(2)]. If the instrument refers to neither of these, the property is still presumed to be partnership property if it is acquired with partnership funds [RUPA 204(c)]. In all other circumstances, the property is presumed to be the property of an individual partner or partners, even if it is used in the partnership business [RUPA 204(d)].

4. The RUPA states that partners may pursue their own interests without automatically violating their fiduciary duties [RUPA 404(e)].
5. In this sense, to account to the partnership means not only to divulge the information but also to determine the value of any benefits or profits derived and to hold that money or property in trust on behalf of the partnership.
6. The RUPA adds "or business of the kind carried on by the partnership" [RUPA 301(1)]. Basically, this addition gives added protection to third parties that deal with a partnership that is not familiar to them.

customarily implied powers include the authority to make warranties on goods in the sales business, the power to convey real property in the firm name when such conveyances are part of the ordinary course of partnership business, the power to enter into contracts consistent with the firm's regular course of business, and the power to make admissions and representations concerning partnership affairs [UPA 11].

If a partner acts within the scope of authority, the partnership is bound to third parties. For example, a partner's authority to sell partnership products carries with it the implied authority to transfer title and to make usual warranties. Hence, in a partnership that operates a retail tire store, any partner negotiating a contract with a customer for the sale of a set of tires can warrant that "each tire will be warranted for normal wear for 40,000 miles."

This same partner, however, does not have the authority to sell office equipment, fixtures, or the partnership office building without the consent of all the other partners. In addition, because partnerships are formed for profit, a partner does not generally have the authority to make charitable contributions without the consent of the other partners. No such action is binding on the partnership unless it is ratified by all of the other partners.

Joint Liability.   In most states, partners are subject to joint liability on partnership debts and contracts [UPA 15(b)]. **Joint liability** means that if a third party sues a partner on, for example, a partnership debt, the partner has the right to insist that the other partners be sued with him or her. In fact, if the third party does not sue all of the partners, those partners sued cannot be required to pay a judgment, and the assets of the partnership cannot be used to satisfy the judgment. (Similarly, the third party's release of one partner releases all partners.) In other words, to bring a successful claim against the partnership on a debt or contract, a plaintiff must name all the partners as defendants. To simplify this rule, some states have enacted statutes providing that a partnership may be sued in its own name, and a judgment will be binding on the partnership and the individual partners even though not all the partners are named in the complaint.[7]

If the third party is successful, he or she may collect on the judgment against the assets of one or more of the partners. In other words, each partner is liable and may be required to pay the entire amount of the judgment. When one partner pays the entire amount, the partnership is required to indemnify (reimburse) that partner [UPA 18(b)]. If the partnership cannot do so, the obligation falls on the other partners.

Joint and Several Liability.   In a few states, partners are jointly and severally liable for partnership debts and contracts. In all states, partners are jointly and severally liable for torts and breaches of trust [UPA 15(a)].[8]

Joint and several liability means a third party may sue one or more of the partners separately (severally) or all of them together (jointly), at his or her option.[9] This is true even when a partner did not participate in, ratify, or know about whatever it was that gave rise to the cause of action.[10]

A judgment against one partner on his or her several (separate) liability does not extinguish the others' liability. (Similarly, a release of one partner discharges the partners' joint, but not several, liability.) Thus, those not sued in the first action may be sued subsequently. The first action, however, may have been conclusive on the question of liability. If, for example, in an action against one partner, the court held that the partnership was in no way liable, the third party cannot bring an action against another partner and succeed on the issue of the partnership's liability.

If the third party is successful, he or she may collect on the judgment only against the assets of those partners named as defendants. The partner who committed the tort, though, is required to indemnify the partnership for any damages it pays.

Liability of Incoming Partner.   A partner newly admitted to an existing partnership has limited liability

---

7. California is such a state.

8. Under the RUPA, partners' liability is joint and several for all debts [RUPA 306].

9. The term *several* stems from the medieval English term *severall*, which meant "separately," or "severed from" one another. As used here, *several* liability means *separate* liability.

10. The RUPA prevents creditors from bringing an action to collect debts from the partners of a nonbankrupt partnership without first having attempted unsuccessfully to collect from the partnership (or having convinced a court that the attempt would be unsuccessful) [RUPA 307(d)].

for whatever debts and obligations the partnership incurred *prior* to the new partner's admission. UPA 17 provides that the new partner's liability can be satisfied only from partnership assets. This means that the new partner has no personal liability for these debts and obligations, but the new partner's capital contribution may be used to satisfy the debts and obligations.

PARTNERSHIP TERMINATION

Generally, any change in the relations of the partners that demonstrates unwillingness or inability to carry on partnership business dissolves the partnership, resulting in termination [UPA 29]. If any partner wishes to continue the business, he or she is free to reorganize into a new partnership with the remaining partners.

The termination of a partnership has two stages—dissolution and winding up. Both stages must take place before termination is complete. **Dissolution** occurs when any partner ceases to be associated with the carrying on of partnership business. **Winding up** is the actual process of collecting and distributing the partnership's assets. Dissolution terminates the right of a partnership to endure as an ongoing concern, but the partnership continues to exist long enough to wind up its affairs. When winding up is complete, the partnership's *legal* existence is terminated.

Dissolution.   Dissolution, the first stage in the termination of a partnership, can be brought about by acts of the partners, by operation of law, or by judicial decree.

Dissolution by Acts of the Partners.   The following acts of the partners can bring about dissolution: agreement, the withdrawal of a partner,[11] the addition of a partner, and the transfer of a partner's interest. For example, when a partnership agreement expresses a fixed time or a particular business objective to be accomplished, the passing of the date or the accomplishment of the project dissolves the partnership.

Although a partner always has the *power* to withdraw from the partnership, he or she may not always have the *right* to do so. In a partnership for a specified term or for a specified purpose, a partner does not have the right to withdraw until the term has lapsed or the purpose has been fulfilled. If a partner withdraws in violation of the partnership agreement, he or she will be liable to the other partners for damages resulting from wrongful dissolution of the partnership.

A change in the composition of the partnership due to the admission of a new partner (without the consent of the other partners) results in dissolution. The new partnership carries the debts of the dissolved partnership. Creditors of the prior partnership become creditors of the partnership that is continuing the business [UPA 41].

The UPA provides that neither a voluntary transfer of a partner's interest[12] nor an involuntary sale of a partner's interest for the benefit of creditors [UPA 28] by itself dissolves the partnership. Either occurrence, however, can ultimately lead to judicial dissolution of the partnership, as will be discussed.

Dissolution by Operation of Law.   A partnership is dissolved on the death of any partner, even if the partnership agreement provides for carrying on the business with the executor of the decedent's estate.[13] Any change in the composition of the partnership results in a new partnership.

The bankruptcy of a partner will dissolve a partnership. Insolvency alone will not result in dissolution. Naturally, bankruptcy of the firm itself will result in dissolution of the partnership.

Any event that makes it unlawful for the partnership to continue its business or for any partner to carry on in the partnership will result in dissolution. If the illegality of the partnership business is a cause for dissolution, however, the partners can decide to change the nature of their business and continue in the partnership. When the illegality applies to an

---

11. The RUPA distinguishes the withdrawal of a partner that causes a breakup of a partnership from a withdrawal that causes only the end of a partner's participation in the business (and results in a buyout of that partner's interest) [RUPA 601, 701, 801]. Dissolution results only if the partnership must be liquidated [RUPA 801].

12. A single partner cannot make another person a partner in a partnership merely by transferring his or her interest to that person [UPA 27].

13. Under the RUPA, the death of a partner represents that partner's "dissociation" from the partnership, but it is not an automatic ground for the partnership's dissolution [RUPA 601].

individual partner, the dissolution must occur. For example, suppose that the state legislature passes a law making it illegal for magistrates to engage in the practice of law. If an attorney in a law firm is appointed a magistrate, the partnership must be dissolved.

Dissolution by Judicial Decree. Under UPA 32, a court can dissolve a partnership for the reasons discussed here or whenever circumstances render it equitable to do so.

A partnership can obtain a judicial declaration of dissolution when a partner is adjudicated insane or is shown to be of unsound mind. When it otherwise appears that a partner has become incapable of performing his or her duties under the partnership agreement, a decree of dissolution may be required. It must appear that the incapacity is permanent and will substantially affect the partner's ability to discharge his or her duties to the firm.

When it becomes obvious that the firm's business can be operated only at a loss, judicial dissolution may be ordered. Also, a partner's impropriety involving partnership business (for example, fraud perpetrated on the other partners) or improper behavior reflecting unfavorably on the firm (for instance, habitual drunkenness resulting in gross neglect of the partnership's business) will provide grounds for a judicial decree of dissolution.

Notice of Dissolution. A partner must communicate his or her intent to dissolve or to withdraw from a firm to each of the other partners. This notice of intent can come from the words of the partner (actual notice) or from the actions of the partner (constructive notice). All partners will share liability for the acts of any partner who continues to conduct business for the firm without knowing that the partnership has been dissolved.

To avoid liability for obligations a partner incurs after dissolution of a partnership, the firm must give notice to all affected third persons. The manner of giving notice depends on the third person's relationship to the firm. Any third person who has extended credit to the partnership must receive actual notice. For all others, a newspaper announcement or similar public notice is sufficient.

Winding Up. Once dissolution has occurred and partners have been notified, they cannot create new obligations on behalf of the partnership. Their only authority is to complete transactions begun but not finished at the time of dissolution and to wind up the business of the partnership. Winding up includes collecting and preserving partnership assets, discharging liabilities (paying debts), and accounting to each partner for the value of his or her interest in the partnership.

Creditors of the partnership, as well as creditors of the individual partners, can make claims on the partnership's assets when the partnership is terminated. Creditors of the partnership have priority over creditors of individual partners in the distribution of partnership assets; the converse priority is followed in the distribution of individual partner assets—except under bankruptcy law, which provides that a partner's individual assets may be utilized to pay claims against a partnership involved in bankruptcy proceedings. (Bankruptcy law in general was discussed in Chapter 16.)

The priorities in the distribution of a partnership's assets are as follows [UPA 40(b)]:[14]

1. Payment of third party debts.
2. Refund of advances (loans) made to or for the firm by a partner.
3. Return of capital contribution to a partner.
4. Distribution of the balance, if any, to partners in accordance with the relative proportions of their respective shares in the profits.

Does winding up require that all of the assets of a partnership be liquidated? Or is it enough if, on the death of a partner, the surviving partners take an inventory, provide an accounting to the dead partner's estate for the value of the business as of the date of dissolution, and pay the estate its proportionate share of the value of the partnership? Can the surviving partners then continue in business as a new partnership? Those were the questions in the following case.

---

14. Under the RUPA, partner creditors are included among creditors who take first priority [RUPA 808]. Capital contributions and profits or losses are then calculated together to determine the amounts that the partners receive or the amounts that they pay.

CASE 17.2   Creel v. Lilly

Court of Appeals of
Maryland, 1999.
354 Md. 77,
725 A.2d 385.

BACKGROUND AND FACTS   *Joseph Creel, Arnold Lilly, and Roy Altizer formed a general partnership called "Joe's Racing" to sell NASCAR racing memorabilia. Their written agreement stated, in paragraph 7(a), that "at the termination of this partnership a full and accurate inventory shall be prepared, and the assets, liabilities, and income * * * shall be ascertained." Paragraph 7(d) added, "Upon the death or illness of a partner, his share will go to his estate. If his estate wishes to sell his interest, they must offer it to the remaining partners first." Nine months later, Creel died, and Joe's Racing dissolved. Creel's spouse, Anne Creel, was appointed personal representative of his estate.[a] Lilly and Altizer asked Mrs. Creel to release funds in a partnership account to which only Creel had had access. When she refused, Lilly and Altizer filed a suit in a Maryland state court against her. Meanwhile, Lilly and Altizer took an inventory of the merchandise, had an accountant compute the value of the business, and offered Mrs. Creel payment for Creel's share. Lilly and Altizer then ceased doing business as Joe's Racing and used the assets to begin doing business as "Good Ole Boys Racing." The court held, among other things, that Lilly and Altizer did not breach any fiduciary duty to Creel's estate. Mrs. Creel appealed, arguing in part that they should have liquidated the assets of Joe's Racing. The state intermediate appellate court affirmed the lower court's judgment. Mrs. Creel appealed to the Maryland Court of Appeals, the state's highest court.*

IN THE LANGUAGE
OF THE COURT

CHASANOW, Judge.
*   *   *   *

Even though the [Joe's Racing] partnership agreement uses the word "termination," paragraph 7(a) is really discussing the dissolution of the partnership and the attendant winding-up process that ultimately led to termination. Paragraph 7(a) requires that the assets, liabilities, and income be "ascertained," but it in no way mandates that this must be accomplished by a forced sale of the partnership assets. Indeed, a liquidation or sale of assets is not mentioned anywhere in 7(a).

In this case, the winding-up method outlined in 7(a) was followed exactly by the surviving partners: a full and accurate inventory was prepared * * * ; this information was given to an accountant, who ascertained the assets, liabilities, and income of the partnership; and finally, the remaining debt or profit was distributed * * * .

Mrs. Creel argues that the partnership agreement does not address the winding-up process and that we should look to UPA's default rules to fill in this gap. Her contention is incorrect. We only turn to UPA and its liquidation rule if there is no other option, and such is clearly not the case here. * * *
*   *   *   *

Assuming *arguendo* [for the sake of argument] that the Joe's Racing partnership agreement cannot be interpreted as outlining an alternative to liquidation in winding up the partnership in the event of a dissolution caused by a partner's death, we still find that a sale of all partnership assets is not required under either UPA or RUPA in order to ascertain the true value of the business. Support for this is found in Maryland's recent adoption of RUPA, which encourages businesses to continue in either their original or successor form, and also the holdings of out-of-state cases where other options besides a "fire sale" have been chosen when a partnership is dissolved under UPA.
*   *   *   *

We find it is sound public policy to permit a partnership to continue either under the same name or as a successor partnership without all of the assets being liquidated. Liquidation can be a harmful and destructive measure, especially to a small business like Joe's Racing, and is often unnecessary to determining the true value of the partnership.

---

a. A *personal representative* administers a deceased person's estate. This administration includes taking an inventory of the deceased's assets and managing them to preserve their value.

<table>
<tr>
<td>DECISION
AND REMEDY</td>
<td>*The Maryland Court of Appeals affirmed the decision of the lower court. Winding up does not require a forced sale of all partnership assets to determine the value of the business. On the death of a partner, it is acceptable to pay the deceased partner's estate its proportionate share of the value of the partnership, derived from an accurate accounting, without having to fully liquidate the business.*</td>
</tr>
</table>

SECTION 3

Special Business Forms

For the most part, these special business forms are hybrid organizations—that is, they have characteristics similar to those of partnerships or corporations, or combine features of both.

JOINT VENTURE

A **joint venture,** which is sometimes referred to as a joint adventure, is a relationship in which two or more persons or business entities combine their efforts or their property for a single transaction or project or a related series of transactions or projects. Unless otherwise agreed, joint venturers share profits and losses equally. For example, when several contractors combine their resources to build and sell houses in a single development, their relationship is a joint venture.

Joint ventures range in size from very small activities to huge, multimillion-dollar joint actions undertaken by some of the world's largest corporations. Large organizations often investigate new markets or new ideas by forming joint ventures with other enterprises. For instance, General Motors Corporation and Volvo Truck Corporation were involved in a joint venture—Volvo GM—to manufacture heavy-duty trucks and market them in the United States.

Characteristics of Joint Ventures. A joint venture resembles a partnership and is taxed like a partnership. The essential difference is that a joint venture typically involves the pursuit of a single project or series of transactions, and a partnership usually concerns an ongoing business. Of course, a partnership may be created to conduct a single transaction. For this reason, most courts apply the same principles to joint ventures as they apply to partnerships. Exceptions include the following:

1. The members of a joint venture have less implied and apparent authority than the partners in a partnership (under partnership law, each partner is an agent of the other partners), because the activities of a joint venture are more limited than the business of a partnership.
2. Although the death of a partner terminates a partnership, the death of a joint venturer ordinarily does not terminate a joint venture.

Duration. The members of a joint venture can specify its duration. If the members do not stipulate a duration, a joint venture normally terminates when the project or the transaction for which it was formed has been completed. Thus, the joint venture to build and sell houses in a single development would terminate once all the houses had been built and sold. If the members of a joint venture do not specify a particular duration and the joint venture does not clearly relate to the achievement of a certain goal, the joint venture is terminable at the will of any of its members.

Duties, Rights, and Liabilities among Joint Venturers. The duties that joint venturers owe to each other are the same as the duties that partners owe to each other. Thus, joint venturers owe each other fiduciary duties, including a duty of loyalty. If one of the venturers secretly buys land that was to be acquired by the joint venture, the other joint venturers may be awarded damages for the breach of loyalty.

When the members of a joint venture are separately engaged in business operations that are similar to the activity of the joint venture, conflicts may develop in two areas of the law. First, when the members of a joint venture are competitors, each member may face a choice between disclosing trade secrets to a competitor and breaching the duty to disclose. Second, in those circumstances, there is also a potential for a violation of the antitrust laws (see Chapters 27 and 28). For both reasons, joint venturers should specify exactly the information that each will be required to disclose.

The joint venturers have equal rights to manage the activities of the enterprise. Control of the operation may be given to one of the members, however, without affecting the status of the relationship. Each joint venturer is liable to third parties for the actions of the other members of the joint venture in pursuit of the enterprise's goal.

At issue in the following case was the use that a joint venturer could make of the joint venture's property. The "property" consisted of what one party had learned in fulfilling its part of the deal. Although the joint venturers were not competitors, they had agreed to keep confidential what they disclosed to each other as part of the joint venture. The dispute, however, concerned knowledge that had been developed by one party alone.

CASE 17.3   Ultralite Container Corp. v. American President Lines, Ltd.

United States
Court of Appeals,
Seventh Circuit, 1999.
170 F.3d 784.
http://www.ca7.
uscourts.gov[a]

BACKGROUND AND FACTS   *American President Lines, Limited (APL), and Stoughton Composites, Limited Liability Company, formed a joint venture, Ultralite Container Corporation, to manufacture intermodal shipping containers with thin walls.[b] APL contributed its knowledge of shipping requirements, plus about $4 million. Stoughton contributed its expertise in the design and manufacture of containers, plus manufacturing facilities. Stoughton was to design and make the containers. APL was to buy and sell some of them. The parties signed confidentiality agreements that prohibited each from using in its own business, or transferring to others, information disclosed by the other party as part of the joint venture. Ultralite produced and delivered the first containers, but APL believed that they were prone to delamination (separation of the foam insulation from the wall) and refused to pay. Meanwhile, Stoughton began using what it had learned in developing the intermodal containers to make and market over-the-road containers for its own business. Stoughton and Ultralite filed a suit in a federal district court against APL, alleging breach of contract. APL counterclaimed, asking the court to order Stoughton not to use what APL argued was confidential information—the know-how to produce thin-walled shipping containers. The court ordered APL to pay damages to Stoughton and Stoughton to stop making thin-walled over-the-road containers. Stoughton appealed to the U.S. Court of Appeals for the Seventh Circuit, arguing that it could use information, in its own business, that it had developed. APL asserted that any information generated by either party as part of the joint venture could not be used for any other purpose.*

IN THE LANGUAGE
OF THE COURT

EASTERBROOK, Circuit Judge.

*   *   *   *

*   *   * Having put up development capital, APL wants to control (or profit from) all uses of the technology. Why would it finance Stoughton's engineering for a separate business, APL asks? But things are not so simple *   *   * . Stoughton invested too, contributing its personnel and manufacturing facilities. Stoughton's total outlay exceeded APL's. Ultralite was more likely to make progress if Stoughton committed the engineers most familiar with [the] technology. If the contracts mean what APL says they mean, however, by putting its staff to work on the Ultralite project even for a day Stoughton disabled everyone, perhaps forever, from working on the over-the-road part of its business. It would have had to erect a Chinese Wall to separate the knowledge, and the only practical way to do this would have been to have separate staffs for intermodal containers and over-the-road containers. That would have forfeited any economies of scope from

---

a. This Web site is maintained by the U.S. Court of Appeals for the Seventh Circuit. In the left-hand column, click on "Judicial Opinions." On that page, in the "Last Name or Corporation" section, click on "Begins," enter "Ultralite" in the box, and click on "Search for Person." When the result appears, click on the docket number to access the opinion.

b. Intermodal containers can be hauled by ship, rail, or truck, and commonly use a combination of these to reach their destinations.

investigating [the] technology that has applications to different kinds of containers—in other words, it would have required Stoughton to perform the same work twice, perhaps by sending Ultralite a cadre of inexperienced engineers, so that it would not poison the well for its core business.

Sometimes partners to a joint venture agree to a Chinese Wall around the information. Such agreements are most common when the parties otherwise are competitors, for neither wants to give the other a leg up, but APL and Stoughton are not rivals. Their businesses are complementary. (APL has conceded that Stoughton's over-the-road containers do not compete with it, and that it had no lost profits.) This joint venture was designed to jump off from intellectual property Stoughton already possessed; that could not be achieved if Stoughton had to segregate the bodies of knowledge rigidly, on pain of forfeiting the opportunity to make any technical advances in its original product base. Nothing in the [confidentiality] agreements demonstrates that the parties were this self-destructive. *   *   * Thus we conclude that the contracts permit Stoughton to use information from the Ultralite project in Stoughton's original business.

DECISION AND REMEDY   *The U.S. Court of Appeals for the Seventh Circuit reversed the lower court's order. The parties' confidentiality agreements did not prevent Stoughton from using the joint venture's intellectual property, which it had developed from knowledge and expertise that it already possessed.*

SYNDICATE

A group of individuals getting together to finance a particular project, such as the building of a shopping center or the purchase of a professional basketball franchise, is called a **syndicate,** or an *investment group*. The form of such groups varies considerably. A syndicate may exist as a corporation or as a general or limited partnership. In some cases, the members merely own property jointly and have no legally recognized business arrangement.

JOINT STOCK COMPANY

A **joint stock company** is a true hybrid of a partnership and a corporation. It has many characteristics of a corporation in that (1) its ownership is represented by transferable shares of stock, (2) it is usually managed by directors and officers of the company or association, and (3) it can have a perpetual existence. Most of its other features, however, are more characteristic of a partnership, and it is usually treated like a partnership. As with a partnership, it is formed by agreement (not statute), property is usually held in the names of the members, shareholders have personal liability, and generally the company is not treated as a legal entity for purposes of a lawsuit. In a joint stock company, however, shareholders are not considered to be agents of each other, as would be the case if the company were a true partnership.

BUSINESS TRUST

A **business trust** is created by a written trust agreement that sets forth the interests of the beneficiaries and the obligations and powers of the trustees. With a business trust, legal ownership and management of the property of the business stay with one or more of the trustees, and the profits are distributed to the beneficiaries.

The business trust was started in Massachusetts in an attempt to obtain the limited liability advantage of corporate status while avoiding certain restrictions on a corporation's ownership and development of real property. The business trust resembles a corporation in many respects. Beneficiaries of the trust, for example, are not personally responsible for the trust's debts or obligations. In fact, in a number of states, business trusts must pay corporate taxes.

COOPERATIVE

A **cooperative** is an association, either incorporated or not, that is organized to provide an economic service, without profit, to its members (or shareholders). An incorporated cooperative is subject to state laws governing nonprofit corporations. It makes distributions of dividends, or profits, to its owners on the basis of their transactions with the cooperative rather than on the basis of the amount of capital they contribute. Cooperatives that are unincorporated are often treated like partnerships. The members have joint liability for the cooperative's acts.

The cooperative form of business is generally adopted by groups of individuals who wish to pool their resources to gain some advantage in the marketplace. Consumer purchasing co-ops are formed to obtain lower prices through quantity discounts. Seller marketing co-ops are formed to control the market and thereby obtain higher sales prices from consumers. Often, because of their special status, cooperatives are exempt from certain federal laws, such as antitrust laws (laws prohibiting anticompetitive practices—see Chapters 27 and 28).

SECTION 4

Private Franchises

A **franchise** is defined as any arrangement in which the owner of a trademark, a trade name, or a copyright licenses others to use the trademark, trade name, or copyright in the selling of goods or services. A **franchisee** (a purchaser of a franchise) is generally legally independent of the **franchisor** (the seller of the franchise). At the same time, the franchise is economically dependent on the franchisor's integrated business system. In other words, a franchisee can operate as an independent businessperson but still obtain the advantages of a regional or national organization. Well-known franchises include McDonald's, KFC, and Burger King.

TYPES OF FRANCHISES

Because the franchising industry is so extensive and so many different types of businesses sell franchises, it is difficult to summarize the many types of franchises that now exist. Generally, though, franchises fall into one of the following three classifications: distributorships, chain-style business operations, and manufacturing or processing-plant arrangements.

Distributorship. A *distributorship* arises when a manufacturing concern (franchisor) licenses a dealer (franchisee) to sell its product. Often, a distributorship covers an exclusive territory. An example is an automobile dealership.

Chain-Style Business Operation. A *chain-style business operation* exists when a franchise operates under a franchisor's trade name and is identified as a member of a select group of dealers that engage in the franchisor's business. The franchisee is generally required to follow standardized or prescribed methods of operation. Often, the franchisor demands that the franchisee maintain certain standards of operation. In addition, sometimes the franchisee is obligated to deal exclusively with the franchisor to obtain materials and supplies. Examples of this type of franchise are McDonald's and most other fast-food chains.

Manufacturing or Processing-Plant Arrangement. A *manufacturing* or *processing-plant arrangement* exists when the franchisor transmits to the franchisee the essential ingredients or formula to make a particular product. The franchisee then markets it either at wholesale or at retail in accordance with the franchisor's standards. Examples of this type of franchise are Coca-Cola and other soft-drink bottling companies.

LAWS GOVERNING FRANCHISING

Because a franchise relationship is primarily a contractual relationship, it is governed by contract law. If the franchise exists primarily for the sale of products manufactured by the franchisor, the law governing sales contracts as expressed in Article 2 of the Uniform Commercial Code applies (see Chapter 11). Additionally, the federal government and most states have enacted laws governing certain aspects of franchising. Generally, these laws are designed to protect prospective franchisees from dishonest franchisors and to prohibit franchisors from terminating franchises without good cause.

Federal Protection for Franchisees. Automobile dealership franchisees are protected from automobile manufacturers' bad faith termination of their franchises by the Automobile Dealers' Franchise Act[15]— also known as the Automobile Dealers' Day in Court Act—of 1965. If a manufacturer-franchisor terminates a franchise because of a dealer-franchisee's failure to comply with unreasonable demands (for example, failure to attain an unrealistically high sales quota), the manufacturer may be liable for damages.

---

15. 15 U.S.C. Sections 1221 *et seq.*

Another federal statute is the Petroleum Marketing Practices Act (PMPA)[16] of 1979, which prescribes the grounds and conditions under which a franchisor may terminate or decline to renew a gasoline station franchise. Federal antitrust laws (discussed in Chapter 45), which prohibit certain types of anticompetitive agreements, may also apply in certain circumstances.

Additionally, the Federal Trade Commission (FTC) has issued regulations that require franchisors to disclose material facts necessary to a prospective franchisee's making an informed decision concerning the purchase of a franchise.

State Protection for Franchisees. State legislation tends to be similar to federal statutes and the FTC regulations. For example, to protect franchisees, a state law might require the disclosure of information that is material to making an informed decision regarding the purchase of a franchise. This could include such information as the actual costs of operation, recurring expenses, and profits earned, along with facts substantiating these figures. State deceptive trade practices acts may also prohibit certain types of actions on the part of franchisors.

In response to the need for a uniform franchise law, the National Conference of Commissioners on Uniform State Laws drafted a model law that standardizes the various state franchise regulations. Because the uniform law represents a compromise of so many diverse interests, it has met with little success in being adopted as law by the various states.

THE FRANCHISE CONTRACT

The franchise relationship is defined by a contract between the franchisor and the franchisee. The franchise contract specifies the terms and conditions of the franchise and spells out the rights and duties of the franchisor and the franchisee. If either party fails to perform its contractual duties, that party may be subject to a lawsuit for breach of contract. Furthermore, if a franchisee is induced to enter into a franchise contract by the franchisor's fraudulent misrepresentation, the franchisor may be liable for damages. Generally, the statutory and case law governing franchising tend to emphasize the importance of good faith and fair dealing in franchise relationships.

Because each type of franchise relationship has its own characteristics, it is difficult to describe the broad

---

16. 15 U.S.C. Sections 2801 *et seq.*

range of details a franchising contract may include. In the remaining pages of this chapter, we look at some of the major issues that typically are addressed in a franchise contract.

Payment for the Franchise. The franchisee ordinarily pays an initial fee or lump-sum price for the franchise license (the privilege of being granted a franchise). This fee is separate from the various products that the franchisee purchases from or through the franchisor. In some industries, the franchisor relies heavily on the initial sale of the franchise for realizing a profit. In other industries, the continued dealing between the parties brings profit to both. In most situations, the franchisor will receive a stated percentage of the annual sales or annual volume of business done by the franchisee. The franchise agreement may also require the franchisee to pay a percentage of the franchisor's advertising costs and certain administrative expenses.

Business Premises. The franchise agreement may specify whether the premises for the business must be leased or purchased outright. In some cases, construction of a building is necessary to meet the terms of the agreement. Certainly, the agreement will specify whether the franchisor supplies equipment and furnishings for the premises or whether this is the responsibility of the franchisee.

Location of the Franchise. Typically, the franchisor will determine the territory to be served. Some franchise contracts will give the franchisee exclusive rights, or "territorial rights," to a certain geographic area. Other franchise contracts, while they define the territory allotted to a particular franchise, either specifically state that the franchise is nonexclusive or are silent on the issue of territorial rights.

Many franchise lawsuits involve disputes over territorial rights, and this is one area of franchising in which the implied covenant of good faith and fair dealing often comes into play. For example, suppose that a franchisee is not given exclusive territorial rights in the franchise contract, or the contract is silent on the issue. If the franchisor allows a competing franchise to be established nearby, the franchisee may suffer a significant loss in profits. In this situation, a court may hold that the franchisor's actions breached an implied covenant of good faith and fair dealing. At issue in the following case was whether a franchisor had breached this implied covenant.

CASE 17.4

Camp Creek Hospitality Inns, Inc. v. Sheraton Franchise Corp.

United States
Court of Appeals,
Eleventh Circuit, 1998.
139 F.3d 1396.
http://www.findlaw.
com/casecode/courts/
11th.html[a]

BACKGROUND AND FACTS   *In 1990, Camp Creek Hospitality Inns, Inc., entered into a contract with Sheraton Franchise Corporation (a subsidiary of ITT Sheraton Corporation) to operate a Sheraton Inn franchise west of the Atlanta airport. Because another franchisee, the Sheraton Hotel Atlanta Airport, already served that market, Sheraton named Camp Creek's facility "Sheraton Inn Hartsfield-West, Atlanta Airport." Three years later, ITT Sheraton bought a Hyatt hotel in the vicinity of the Atlanta airport and gave it the name "Sheraton Gateway Hotel, Atlanta Airport." The presence of three Sheraton properties in the same market caused some customer confusion. Also, the Inn and the Gateway competed for the same customers, which caused the Inn to suffer a decrease in the growth of its business. Camp Creek filed a suit in a federal district court against Sheraton and others, alleging in part that by establishing the Gateway, ITT Sheraton denied Camp Creek the fruits of its contract in breach of the implied covenant of good faith and fair dealing. The court issued a summary judgment in favor of the defendants. Camp Creek appealed to the U.S. Court of Appeals for the Eleventh Circuit.*

IN THE LANGUAGE
OF THE COURT

BIRCH, Circuit Judge:

*   *   *   *

*   *   * [T]he contract, as executed, says nothing about whether or where Sheraton could establish a competing hotel. *   *   * Camp Creek had no contractual right to expect the Sheraton Franchise to refrain from licensing the Sheraton name to additional franchises beyond the site of the Inn. By the express terms of the contract, therefore, Sheraton could have authorized a competing franchise directly across the street from the Inn, and Camp Creek would have little recourse.

Sheraton, however, did not establish such a franchise in this case; instead, it purchased and operated the Gateway on its own behalf. *   *   *

As a result, we must determine whether the implied covenant of good faith and fair dealing permits the Sheraton to establish its own hotel in the same vicinity as the Inn. *   *   *

*   *   * Sheraton emphasizes that the Inn has been more profitable every year since the Gateway opened. Camp Creek, however, *   *   * describe[d] a number of trends present in the market for hotel rooms in the Atlanta area, both before and after Sheraton began operating the Gateway, and present[ed] credible theories and measures of damages attributable to the additional intra-brand competition associated with the Gateway's entry to the market. We hold that Camp Creek's evidence is sufficient to withstand Sheraton's motion for summary judgment on this claim.

DECISION
AND REMEDY

The U.S. Court of Appeals for the Eleventh Circuit held that unless a franchise contract expressly provides otherwise, it could violate the implied covenant of good faith and fair dealing for a franchisor to compete against a franchisee in the same market for the same customers. The court reversed the judgment of the lower court and remanded the case for trial.

---

a. This page contains links to recent opinions of the U.S. Court of Appeals for the Eleventh Circuit. In the "1998" row, click on the "April" link. When the results appear, click on the *Camp Creek* case name to access the opinion. This Web site is maintained by FindLaw.

Business Organization.   The business organization of the franchisee is of great concern to the franchisor. Depending on the terms of the franchise agreement, the franchisor may specify particular requirements for the form and capital structure of the business. The franchise agreement may also provide that standards of operation—relating to such aspects of the business as sales quotas, quality, and record keeping—be met by the franchisee. Furthermore, a franchisor may wish to retain stringent control over the training of personnel involved in the operation and over administrative aspects of the business.

Quality Control. Although the day-to-day operation of the franchise business is normally left up to the franchisee, the franchise agreement may provide for the amount of supervision and control agreed on by the parties. When the franchise is a service operation, such as a motel, the contract often provides that the franchisor will establish certain standards for the facility in order to protect the franchise's name and reputation. Typically, the contract will state that the franchisor is permitted to make periodic inspections to ensure that the standards are being maintained.

As a general rule, the validity of a provision permitting the franchisor to establish and enforce certain

quality standards is unquestioned. Because the franchisor has a legitimate interest in maintaining the quality of the product or service to protect its name and reputation, it can exercise greater control in this area than would otherwise be tolerated. Increasingly, however, franchisors are finding that if they exercise too much control over the operations of their franchisees, they may incur liability under agency theory for the acts of their franchisees' employees—as the following case illustrates. (A court may also find that a franchisee is, in fact, an employee, if the franchisor exercises a significant degree of control over the franchisee's work schedule and activities.)[17]

---

17. See, for example, *West Sanitation Services, Inc. v. Francis*, 1998 WL 11023 (N.Y.Sup.Ct.App.Div. 1998).

CASE 17.5   Miller v. D. F. Zee's, Inc.

United States
District Court,
District of Oregon, 1998.
31 F.Supp.2d 792.

COMPANY PROFILE   *Based in South Carolina, Flagstar Corporation franchised or owned Denny's restaurants, as well as the Carrows, Coco's, El Pollo Loco, Hardee's, and Quincy's Family Steakhouse chains. In the early 1990s, Denny's was the defendant in two civil rights class-action suits brought by African American customers who claimed that some restaurants refused to seat or serve them. Denny's paid more than $54 million to settle those suits and responded "quickly, decisively, and sincerely" to, among other things, hire and promote more minorities.[a] In the mid-1990s, Flagstar declared bankruptcy, sold the Hardee's and Quincy's chains, and renamed itself Advantica Restaurant Group, Inc. (**http://www.advantica-dine.com**). By the late 1990s, Advantica's annual sales approached $3 billion, with about 2 percent annual growth.*

BACKGROUND AND FACTS   *D. F. Zee's, Inc., owns a Denny's restaurant in Tualatin, Oregon. Under the franchise agreement, Zee's agreed to train and supervise employees in accordance with Denny's Operations and Food Service Standards Manuals. Denny's regularly sent inspectors to assess compliance and reserved the right to terminate the franchise for noncompliance. Denny's logo was displayed throughout the restaurant, and there was no indication that its owners were other than "Denny's." Christine Miller worked as a server at the restaurant. After several incidents of sexually inappropriate comments and conduct, Miller complained to Stanley Templeton, the manager. When her complaints were unavailing, Miller contacted the manager of another Denny's restaurant, who referred her to the district franchise manager for Denny's, who referred the complaint to Zee's. Templeton resigned, but the harassment continued. Finally, Miller and three other employees filed a suit in a federal district court against Zee's, Denny's, and others. Denny's filed a motion for summary judgment, contending in part that a franchisor cannot be held liable for harassment by franchise employees.*

IN THE LANGUAGE   AIKEN, J.
OF THE COURT   *   *   *   *

---

a. Anne Faircloth, "Guess Who's Coming to Denny's," *Fortune*, August 3, 1998.

Here, Denny's is responsible for acts of harassment by employees at the Tualatin Denny's because employees of the Tualatin Denny's are agents of [Denny's].

* * * [A]n agency results from the manifestation of consent by one person to another so that the other will act on his or her behalf and "subject" to his or her control, and consent by the other to so act. An agency relationship may be evidenced by an express agreement between the parties, or it may be implied from the circumstances and conduct of the parties. The principal's consent and "right to control" are the essential elements of an agency relationship. * * *

* * * * *

Here, *. * * the franchise agreement requires adherence to comprehensive, detailed [Franchise Operations and Food Service Standards] manuals for the operation of the restaurant. * * *

Here, * * * defendants enforce the use of these methods by regularly sending inspectors into the restaurant to assess compliance and by its retained power to cancel the agreement.

Further, the Franchise Operations Manual provides that the defendants had the right to control their franchisees in the precise parts of the franchisee's business that allegedly resulted in plaintiffs' injuries—training and discipline of employees.

DECISION AND REMEDY   *The court denied Denny's motion for summary judgment. The court held that a franchisor may be held vicariously liable under an agency theory for the intentional acts of discrimination by the employees of a franchisee.*

Pricing Arrangements. Franchises provide the franchisor with an outlet for the firm's goods and services. Depending on the nature of the business, the franchisor may require the franchisee to purchase certain supplies from the franchisor at an established price.[18] A franchisor who sets the prices at which the franchisee will resell the goods may violate state or federal antitrust laws, or both, however. A franchisor can suggest retail prices without violating the law.

Termination of the Franchise. The duration of the franchise is a matter to be determined between the parties. Generally, a franchise relationship starts with a short trial period, such as a year, so that the franchisee and the franchisor can determine whether they want to stay in business with one another. Usually, the franchise agreement specifies that termination must

be "for cause," such as death or disability of the franchisee, insolvency of the franchisee, breach of the franchise agreement, or failure to meet specified sales quotas. Most franchise contracts provide that notice of termination must be given. If no set time for termination is specified, then a reasonable time, with notice, is implied. A franchisee must be given reasonable time to wind up the business—that is, to do the accounting and return the copyright or trademark or any other property of the franchisor.

Because a franchisor's termination of a franchise often has adverse consequences for the franchisee, much franchise litigation involves claims of wrongful termination. Generally, the termination provisions of contracts are more favorable to the franchisor than the franchisee. This means that the franchisee, who normally invests a substantial amount of time and money in the franchise operation to make it successful, may receive little or nothing for the business on termination. The franchisor owns the trademark and hence the business.

It is in this area that statutory and case law become important. The federal and state laws discussed earlier attempt, among other things, to protect franchisees from the arbitrary or unfair termination of their franchises by the franchisors. Generally, both

---

18. Although a franchisor can require franchisees to purchase supplies from it, requiring a franchisee to purchase exclusively from the franchisor may violate federal antitrust laws (see Chapters 27 and 28). For two landmark cases in these areas, see *United States v. Arnold, Schwinn & Co.,* 388 U.S. 365, 87 S.Ct. 1956, 18 L.Ed.2d 1249 (1967), and *Fortner Enterprises, Inc. v. U.S. Steel Corp.,* 394 U.S. 495, 89 S.Ct. 1252, 22 L.Ed.2d 495 (1969).

statutory and case law emphasize the importance of good faith and fair dealing in terminating a franchise relationship.

In determining whether a franchisor has acted in good faith when terminating a franchise agreement, the courts generally try to balance the rights of both parties. If a court perceives that a franchisor has arbitrarily or unfairly terminated a franchise, the franchisee will be provided with a remedy for wrongful termination. If a franchisor's decision to terminate a franchise was made in the normal course of the franchisor's business operations, however, and reasonable notice of termination was given to the franchisee, normally a court would not consider the termination wrongful.

TERMS AND CONCEPTS TO REVIEW

articles of partnership 366	franchisor 376	partnership 363
business trust 375	information return 366	partnership by estoppel 366
cooperative 375	joint and several liability 369	sole proprietorship 362
dissolution 370	joint liability 369	syndicate 375
franchise 376	joint stock company 375	winding up 370
franchisee 376	joint venture 373	

QUESTIONS AND CASE PROBLEMS

17–1. BUSINESS ORGANIZATIONS. Alan, Jane, and Kyle organize a nonprofit business—AJK Markets, Inc.—to buy groceries from wholesalers and sell them to consumers who buy a membership in AJK. Because the firm is a nonprofit entity, it is able to sell the groceries for less than a commercial grocer could. What form of business organization is AJK Markets? Is it significant that AJK is incorporated?

17–2. INDICATIONS OF PARTNERSHIP. Daniel is the owner of a chain of shoe stores. He hires Rubya as the manager of a new store, which is to open in Grand Rapids, Michigan. Daniel, by written contract, agrees to pay Rubya a monthly salary. Also, Daniel agrees to pay Rubya 20 percent of the profits. Without Daniel's knowledge, Rubya represents himself to Classen as Daniel's partner, showing Classen the agreement to share profits. Classen extends credit to Rubya. Rubya defaults. Discuss whether Classen can hold Daniel liable as a partner.

17–3. RIGHTS OF PARTNERS. Meyer, Knapp, and Cavanna establish a partnership to operate a window-washing service. Meyer contributes $10,000 to the partnership, and Knapp and Cavanna contribute $1,000 each. The partnership agreement is silent on how profits and losses will be shared. One month after the partnership has begun operation, Knapp and Cavanna vote, over Meyer's objection, to purchase another truck for the firm's operation. Meyer believes that because he contributed $10,000, no major commitment to purchase by the partnership can be made over his objection. In addition, Meyer claims that, in the absence of agreement, profits must be divided in the same ratio as capital contributions. Discuss Meyer's contentions.

17–4. BUSINESS FORMS AND LIABILITY. Assume that Bateson Corp. is considering entering into two contracts—one with a joint stock company that distributes home products east of the Mississippi River and the other with a business trust formed by a number of sole proprietors who are sellers of home products on the West Coast. Both contracts involve large capital outlays for Bateson to supply the businesses with restaurant equipment. In both business organizations, at least two shareholders or beneficiaries are personally wealthy, but both business organizations have limited financial resources. The owner-managers of Bateson are not familiar with either form of business organization. Because each form resembles a corporation, they are concerned with potential limits on liability in the event that either business organization breaches the contract by failing to pay for the equipment. Discuss fully Bateson's concern.

17–5. FRANCHISE AGREEMENTS. Otmar has been interested in securing a particular high-quality ice cream franchise. The franchisor is willing to give him a franchise. A franchise agreement is made that calls for Otmar to sell the ice cream only at a specific location; to buy all the ice cream from the franchisor; to order and sell all the flavors produced by the franchisor; and to refrain from selling any ice cream stored for more than two weeks after delivery by the franchisor, as this ice cream decreases in quality after that period. After two months of operation, Otmar believes that he can increase his profits by moving the store to another part of the city. He refuses to order even a limited quantity of the "fruit delight" flavor because of its higher cost, and he has sold ice cream that has been stored longer than two weeks without customer complaint. Otmar claims that the franchisor has no right to restrict him in these practices. Discuss his claims.

17–6. LIABILITY OF PARTNERS. Frank Kolk was the manager of Triples American Grill, a sports bar and restaurant. Kolk and John Baines opened bank accounts in the name of the bar, each signing the account signature cards as "owner." Baines was often at the bar and had free access to its office. Baines told others that he was "an owner" and "a partner." Kolk told Steve Mager, the president of Cheesecake Factory, Inc., that Baines was a member of a partnership that owned Triples. On this basis, Cheesecake delivered its goods to Triples on credit. In fact, the bar was owned by a corporation. When the unpaid account totaled more than $20,000, Cheesecake filed a suit in a New Mexico state court against Baines to collect. On what basis might Baines be liable to Cheesecake? What does Cheesecake have to show to win its case? [*Cheesecake Factory, Inc. v. Baines,* 964 P.2d 183 (N.M.App. 1998)]

17–7. INDICATIONS OF PARTNERSHIP. Sandra Lerner was one of the original founders of Cisco Systems. When she sold her interest in Cisco, she received a substantial amount of money, which she invested, and she became extremely wealthy. Patricia Holmes met Lerner at Holmes's horse training facility, and they became friends. One evening in Lerner's mansion, while applying nail polish, Holmes layered a raspberry color over black to produce a new color, which Lerner liked. Later, the two created other colors with names like "Bruise," "Smog," and "Oil Slick," and titled their concept "Urban Decay." Lerner and Holmes started a firm to produce and market the polishes but never discussed the sharing of profits and losses. They agreed to build the business and then sell it. Together, they did market research, experimented with colors, worked on a logo and advertising, obtained capital from an investment firm, and hired employees. Then Lerner began working to edge Holmes out of the firm. Several months later, when Holmes was told not to attend meetings of the firm's officers, she filed a suit in a California state court against Lerner, claiming, among other things, a breach of their partnership agreement. Lerner responded in part that there was no partnership agreement because there was no agreement to divide profits. Was Lerner right? Why or why not? How should the court rule? [*Holmes v. Lerner,* 74 Cal.App.4th 442, 88 Cal.Rptr.2d 130 (1 Dist. 1999)]

17–8. JOINT VENTURES. Frank Hartman, Jr., and Robert Wiesner visited the site of a derailment of a Burlington Northern (BN) train to bid on lumber carried on the train. Hartman was to provide the salvage expertise, and Wiesner was to provide the expertise to sell the lumber. They submitted a bid of $113,663, which BN accepted. To make the payment, Hartman and Wiesner contacted Dave Anderson, who contacted Doug Feller, the managing partner of BBD Partnership. Hartman, Wiesner, Anderson, and Feller agreed to share profits from the sale of the lumber. BBD then borrowed the money to pay BN. BBD, through Feller, had promised to get involved only if it could own the lumber, however. Thus, on the bill of sale, BN entered the names "Hartman Construction" and "Feller Associates," a sole proprietorship owned by Feller. BBD later sold its interest in the deal to another party. Two years later, Hartman, Wiesner, BBD, and Feller became involved in a lawsuit over the funds that BBD had borrowed. Was the deal between the parties a joint venture or simply a loan from BBD to Hartman and the others? Discuss fully. [*Wiesner v. BBD Partnership,* 845 P.2d 120 (Mont. 1993)]

17–9. FRANCHISE TERMINATION. Heating and Air Specialists, Inc., doing business as A/C Service Co., marketed heating and air conditioning products. A/C contracted with Lennox Industries, Inc., to be a franchised dealer of Lennox products. The parties signed a standard franchise contract drafted by Lennox. The contract provided that either party could terminate the agreement with or without cause on thirty days' notice and that the agreement would terminate immediately if A/C opened another facility at a different location. At the time, A/C operated only one location in Arkansas. A few months later, A/C opened a second location in Tulsa, Oklahoma. Lennox's district sales manager gave A/C oral authorization to sell Lennox products in Tulsa, at least on a temporary basis, but nothing was put in writing. Several of Lennox's other dealers in Tulsa complained to Lennox about A/C's presence. Lennox gave A/C notice that it was terminating A/C's Tulsa franchise. Meanwhile, A/C had failed to keep its Lennox account current and owed the franchisor more than $200,000. Citing this delinquency, Lennox notified A/C that unless it paid its account within ten days, Lennox would terminate both franchises. A/C did not pay. Lennox terminated the franchises. A/C filed a suit in a federal district court against Lennox, alleging in part breach of the franchise agreement for terminating the Tulsa franchise. Is A/C right? Explain. [*Heating & Air Specialists, Inc. v. Jones,* 180 F.3d 923 (8th Cir. 1999)]

17–10. IN YOUR COURT

 As a franchise, Entre Computer Associates sold, among other products, computer systems marketed by Kruger Systems, Inc. Entre's agreement with Kruger included a forum-selection clause that provided that any suit between the parties had to be filed in a California court. When Kruger terminated its relationship with Entre, Entre brought a suit against Kruger in a New Jersey state court. Kruger argued that the suit should be dismissed on the basis of the forum-selection clause. Entre argued that the clause violated California state franchise law, which invalidated forum-selection clauses in auto dealership franchises. Assume that you are the judge in the New Jersey court hearing this case and answer the following questions:

(a) The first issue you need to address in this case is whether a forum-selection clause in a franchise contract is fundamentally unfair to the franchisee.

(b) If you conclude that such a clause is unfair to the franchisee, what legal reasoning would you use to justify a decision to extend the California law governing auto dealership franchises to cover other types of franchises?

LAW ON THE WEB

For updated links to resources available on the Web, as well as a variety of other materials, visit this text's Web site at http://wleb.westbuslaw.com.

The Web site of the law firm of Reinhart et al. provides extensive information about business organizations. The URL for this site is

http://www.rbvdnr.com

To learn how the U.S. Small Business Administration assists in forming, financing, and operating businesses, go to

http://www.sbaonline.sba.gov

For information on the FTC regulations on franchising, as well as state laws regulating franchising, go to

http://www.ftc.gov/bcp/franchise/netfran.htm

A good source of information on the purchase and sale of franchises is Franchising.org, which is online at

http://www.franchising.org

LEGAL RESEARCH EXERCISES ON THE WEB

Go to http://wleb.westbuslaw.com, the Web site that accompanies this text. Select "Internet Applications," and then click on "Chapter 17." There you will find the following Internet research exercises that you can perform to learn more about franchising:

Activity 17–1: Partnerships

Activity 17–2: Franchises

CHAPTER 18

Limited Liability Companies and Limited Partnerships

THE TWO MOST COMMON FORMS of business organization selected by two or more persons entering into business together are the partnership and the corporation. As explained in previous chapters, each form has distinct advantages and disadvantages. For partnerships, the advantage is that partnership income is taxed only once (all income is "passed through" the partnership entity to the partners themselves, who are taxed only as individuals); the disadvantage is the personal liability of the partners. For corporations, the advantage is the limited liability of shareholders; the disadvantage is the double taxation of corporate income. For many entrepreneurs and investors, the ideal business form would combine the tax advantages of the partnership form of business with the limited liability of the corporate enterprise.

A relatively new form of business organization called the **limited liability company (LLC)** is a hybrid form of business enterprise that meets these needs by offering the limited liability of the corporation and the tax advantages of a partnership. Increasingly, LLCs are becoming an organizational form of choice among businesspersons, a trend encouraged by state statutes permitting their use.

In this chapter, we begin by examining the LLC. We then look at a similar type of entity that is also rel-atively new—the limited liability partnership (LLP). The chapter concludes with a discussion of the limited partnership, a special type of partnership in which some of the partners have limited liability, and the limited liability limited partnership (LLLP).

SECTION 1

Limited Liability Companies

In 1977, Wyoming became the first state to pass legislation authorizing the creation of a limited liability company (LLC). Although LLCs emerged in the United States only in 1977, they have been in existence for over a century in other areas, including several European and South American nations. For example, the South American *limitada* is a form of business organization that operates more or less as a partnership but provides limited liability for the owners.

In the United States, after Wyoming's adoption of an LLC statute, it still was not known how the Internal Revenue Service (IRS) would treat the LLC for tax purposes. In 1988, however, the IRS ruled that Wyoming LLCs would be taxed as partnerships instead of as corporations, providing that certain requirements were met. Prior to this ruling, only one other state—Florida, in 1982—had authorized LLCs. The 1988 ruling encouraged other states to enact LLC statutes, and in less than a decade, all states had done so.

IRS rules that went into effect on January 1, 1997, encouraged even more widespread use of LLCs in the business world. These rules provide that any unincorporated business will automatically be taxed as a partnership unless it indicates otherwise on the tax form. The exceptions involve publicly traded companies, companies formed under a state incorporation statute, and certain foreign-owned companies. If a business chooses to be taxed as a corporation, it can indicate this choice by checking a box on the IRS form.

Part of the impetus behind creating LLCs in this country is that foreign investors are allowed to become LLC members. Generally, in an era increasingly characterized by global business efforts and investments, the LLC offers U.S. firms and potential investors from other countries flexibility and opportunities greater than those available through partnerships or corporations.

LLC FORMATION

Like the corporation, an LLC must be formed and operated in compliance with state law. About one-fourth of the states specifically require LLCs to have at least two owners, called **members.** In the rest of the states, although some LLC statutes are silent on this issue, one-member LLCs are usually permitted.

To form an LLC, **articles of organization** must be filed with a central state agency—usually the secretary of state's office. Typically, the articles are required to set forth such information as the name of the business, its principal address, the name and address of a registered agent, the names of the owners, and information on how the LLC will be managed. The business's name must include the words "Limited Liability Company" or the initials "LLC." In addition to filing the articles of organization, a few states require that a notice of the intention to form an LLC be published in a local newspaper.

Note that although the LLC, like the corporation, is a legal entity apart from its owners, for federal jurisdictional purposes an LLC is treated differently than a corporation. The federal jurisdiction statute provides that a corporation is deemed to be a citizen of the state in which it is incorporated and in which it maintains its principal place of business. The statute does not mention the citizenship of partnerships and other unincorporated associations, but courts have tended to regard these entities as citizens of every state in which their members are citizens.

The citizenship of LLCs may come into play when a party sues an LLC based on diversity of citizenship. Remember from Chapter 2 that in some circumstances, such as when parties to a lawsuit are from different states, a federal court can exercise diversity jurisdiction in cases in which the amount in controversy exceeds $75,000. *Complete* diversity of citizenship must exist, however. For example, a citizen of New York will not be able to bring a suit in federal court—on the basis of diversity jurisdiction—against multiple defendants if one of the defendants is also a citizen of New York.

One of the issues in the following case concerned the state citizenship of a limited liability company. Was there diversity of citizenship between the parties so that a federal court could exercise jurisdiction?

CASE 18.1   Cosgrove v. Bartolotta

United States
Court of Appeals,
Seventh Circuit, 1998.
150 F.3d 729.
**http://www.findlaw.
com/casecode/courts/
7th.html**[a]

BACKGROUND AND FACTS   *Joseph Bartolotta wanted to open a restaurant. He asked Barry Cosgrove, his friend and an experienced corporate attorney, for a $100,000 loan, plus Cosgrove's business and legal advice. Bartolotta promised, among other things, to give Cosgrove a 19 percent ownership interest in the restaurant. In reliance on this promise, Cosgrove helped Bartolotta negotiate a lease for the restaurant premises and advised Bartolotta to organize the venture as a limited liability company (LLC). Bartolotta formed Mary-Bart, LLC, and with Cosgrove's help, obtained other financing. Then, before Cosgrove made his loan, Bartolotta cut him out of the deal. The restaurant,*

a. This is a page, within the FindLaw Web site, that provides access to recent opinions of the U.S. Court of Appeals for the Seventh Circuit. In the "1998" row, click on the "July" link. When that page opens, scroll down the list of cases to the *Cosgrove* case. Click on the case name to access the opinion.

"Bartolotta's Lake Park Bistro," proved to be a success. Cosgrove filed a suit in a federal district court against Bartolotta and Mary-Bart, based in part on diversity of citizenship (Cosgrove and Bartolotta were residents of different states). The jury awarded Cosgrove $135,000, but the judge reduced the award, and both sides appealed.

IN THE LANGUAGE OF THE COURT

POSNER, Chief Judge.
    * * * *

The principal defendant is Joseph Bartolotta, but his company—Mary-Bart, LLC—is also named as a defendant; and in a diversity case, whenever there is an unconventional party (that is, someone or something other than either a natural person suing in his own rather than a representative capacity, or a business corporation) a jurisdictional warning flag should go up. In the case of a regular corporation, the owners' state of citizenship is irrelevant to whether there is the required complete diversity; but in the case of a partnership, it is crucial. *The citizenship of a partnership is the citizenship of the partners, even if they are limited partners,* so that if even one of the partners (general or limited) is a citizen of the same state as the plaintiff, the suit cannot be maintained as a diversity suit. [Emphasis added.]

Mary-Bart is neither a partnership nor a corporation, but a "limited liability company." This animal is like a limited partnership;[b] the principal difference is that it need have no equivalent to a general partner, that is, an owner who has unlimited personal liability for the debts of the firm. Given the resemblance between an LLC and a limited partnership, and what seems to have crystallized as a principle that members of associations are citizens for diversity purposes unless Congress provides otherwise (as it has with respect to corporations), we conclude that the citizenship of an LLC for purposes of the diversity jurisdiction is the citizenship of its members. That does not defeat jurisdiction in this case, however, because Mary-Bart, LLC has only one member—Mr. Bartolotta, who is not a citizen of the same state as the plaintiff.

DECISION AND REMEDY

The U.S. Court of Appeals for the Seventh Circuit ruled that a federal court could exercise jurisdiction in this case. For purposes of federal court jurisdiction, the citizenship of an LLC is the citizenship of its members. The court also remanded the case with orders to reinstate the award to Cosgrove.

---

b. As will be discussed later in this chapter, the limited partnership is a special form of partnership in which some partners (called *limited partners*) have limited liability and some partners (called *general partners*) assume personal liability for the firm's debts and obligations. There must be at least one general partner in a limited partnership.

ADVANTAGES AND DISADVANTAGES OF LLCs

A key advantage of the LLC is that the liability of members is limited to the amount of their investments. Another significant advantage is that an LLC with two or more members can choose whether to be taxed as a partnership or a corporation.

LLCs that want to distribute profits to the members may prefer to be taxed as a partnership, to avoid the "double taxation" characteristic of the corporate entity. Remember that in the corporate form of business, the corporation as an entity pays income taxes on its profits, and the shareholders pay personal income taxes on profits distributed as dividends. Unless the LLC indicates that it wishes to be taxed as a corporation, it is automatically taxed as a partnership by the IRS. This means that the LLC as an entity pays no taxes; rather, as in a partnership, profits are "passed through" the LLC and paid personally by the members. If LLC members want to reinvest profits in the business, however, rather than distribute the profits to members, they may prefer to be taxed as a corporation if corporate income tax rates are lower than personal tax rates. Part of the attractiveness of the LLC for businesspersons is this flexibility with respect to taxation options.

For federal income tax purposes, one-member LLCs are automatically taxed as sole proprietorships unless they indicate that they wish to be taxed as corporations. With respect to state taxes, most states follow the IRS rules. Still another advantage of the LLC for businesspersons is the flexibility it offers in terms of business operations and management—as will be discussed shortly.

The disadvantages of the LLC are relatively few. Some of the initial disadvantages with respect to uncertainties over how LLCs would be taxed no longer exist. The only remaining disadvantage of the LLC is that state statutes are not yet uniform. In an attempt to promote some uniformity among the states in respect to LLC statutes, the National Conference of Commissioners on Uniform State Laws drafted a Uniform Limited Liability Company Act for submission to the states to consider for adoption. Until all of the states have adopted the uniform law, however, an LLC in one state will have to check the rules in the other states in which the firm does business to ensure that it retains its limited liability.

THE LLC OPERATING AGREEMENT

In an LLC, the members themselves can decide how to operate the various aspects of the business by forming an **operating agreement.** Operating agreements typically contain provisions relating to management, how profits will be divided, the transfer of member-

ship interests, whether the LLC will be dissolved on the death or departure of a member, and other important issues.

Operating agreements need not be in writing, and indeed they need not even be formed for an LLC to exist. Generally, though, LLC members should protect their interests by forming a written operating agreement.[1] As with any business arrangement, disputes may arise over any number of issues. If there is no agreement covering the topic being disputed, such as how profits will be divided, the state LLC statute will govern the outcome. For example, most LLC statutes provide that if the members have not specified how profits will be divided among the members, they will be divided equally.

Generally, with respect to issues not covered by an operating agreement or by an LLC statute, the principles of partnership law are applied. At issue in the following case was whether partnership law should apply to a dispute between LLC members as to how business receipts were to be divided on the firm's dissolution.

---

1. Some experts suggest that even a one-member LLC should have an operating agreement. An operating agreement provides evidence that the LLC is a separate entity and thus strengthens the member-owner's protection against being held personally liable for a business obligation.

CASE 18.2   Hurwitz v. Padden

Court of Appeals of
Minnesota, 1998.
581 N.W.2d 359.
http://www.courts.
state.mn.us/library/
archive/capgi.html[a]

BACKGROUND AND FACTS   *Thomas Hurwitz and Michael Padden formed a two-person law firm as a partnership without a written agreement. They shared all proceeds on a fifty-fifty basis and reported all income as partnership income. Less than eighteen months later, Hurwitz filed articles of organization with the state of Minnesota to establish the firm as an LLC. More than three years later, Padden told Hurwitz that he wanted to dissolve their professional relationship. They resolved all business issues between them, except for a division of fees from several of the firm's cases. Hurwitz filed a suit in a Minnesota state court against Padden, seeking, among other things, a distribution of the fees on a fifty-fifty basis. The court applied the principles of partnership law, ruled that the fees should be divided equally, and entered a judgment in favor of Hurwitz for $101,750. Padden appealed, arguing in part that these principles of partnership law should not apply to an LLC.*

IN THE LANGUAGE   *SHORT*, Judge.
OF THE COURT   *   *   *   *

---

a. This page includes a partial list of Minnesota Court of Appeals opinions available in the Minnesota State Law Library online database. The last name of the parties in these cases begins with the letter G, H, or I. Scroll down the list to the *Hurwitz* name and click on the link to read the case.

*   *   * [T]he Minnesota Limited Liability Company Act specifically incorporates the definition and use of the term "dissolution" from the Uniform Partnership Act [UPA]. Under both statutes, the entity is not terminated upon dissolution, but continues until all business issues are resolved. Thus, the UPA provides guidance when examining the end stages of either entity's life. *   *   *

It is undisputed: (1) the firm had no written or oral agreement regarding the division of *   *   * fees upon dissolution; (2) the firm existed for approximately five-and-a-half years before Padden requested dissolution; (3) a little over five months elapsed between the date of dissolution and the date the parties [filed a suit] to settle the firm's remaining issues; (4) the firm's [disputed] fee cases were acquired before the firm's dissolution; (5) prior to its dissolution, the firm divided fees equally between the parties; and (6) at the time the parties filed suit, the firm was in a winding-up phase. Under these circumstances, partnership principles *   *   * govern the division of fees obtained from pre-dissolution *   *   * files. Thus, the *   *   * fees obtained from pre-dissolution case files must be divided equally between the parties, which is consistent with the pre-dissolution method of allocation.

DECISION AND REMEDY   *The state intermediate appellate court affirmed the decision of the lower court. The state intermediate appellate court concluded that the disputed fees should be divided equally, as the receipts were divided before the dissolution.*

LLC MANAGEMENT

Basically, there are two options with respect to the management of an LLC. The members may decide in their operating agreement to be either a "member-managed" or a "manager-managed" LLC.

In a *member-managed* LLC, all of the members participate in management. In a *manager-managed* LLC, the members designate a group of persons to manage the firm. The management group may consist of only members, both members and nonmembers, or only nonmembers. Most LLC statutes provide that unless the members agree otherwise, all members of the LLC will participate in management.

The members of an LLC can also set forth in their operating agreement provisions governing decision-making procedures. For example, the agreement can indicate what procedures are to be followed for choosing or removing managers, an issue on which most LLC statutes are silent. The members are also free to include in the agreement provisions designating when and for what purposes formal members' meetings will be held. In contrast to state laws governing corporations, LLC statutes in most states have no provisions regarding members' meetings. Members may also specify in their agreement how voting rights will be apportioned. If they do not, LLC statutes in most states provide that voting rights are apportioned according to the capital contributions made by each member. Some states provide that, in the absence of an agreement to the contrary, each member has one vote.

SECTION 2

Limited Liability Partnerships

The **limited liability partnership (LLP)** is similar to the LLC. The difference between an LLP and an LLC is that the LLP is designed more for professionals who normally do business as partners in a partnership. The major advantage of the LLP is that it allows a partnership to continue as a pass-through entity for tax purposes but limits the personal liability of the partners.

The first state to enact an LLP statute was Texas, in 1991. Other states quickly followed suit, and by 1997, virtually all of the states had enacted LLP statutes. Like LLCs, LLPs must be formed and operated in compliance with state statutes. The appropriate form must be filed with a central state agency, usually the secretary of state's office, and the business's name must include either "Limited Liability Partnership" or "LLP."

In most states, it is relatively easy to convert a traditional partnership into an LLP because the firm's basic organizational structure remains the same. Additionally, all of the statutory and common law rules governing partnerships still apply (apart from those modified by the LLP statute). Normally, LLP statutes are simply amendments to a state's already existing partnership law.

The LLP is especially attractive for two categories of businesses: professional services and family businesses. Professional service companies include law firms and accounting firms. Family limited liability partnerships are basically business organizations in which all of the partners are related (see the discussion later in this chapter).

LIABILITY IN AN LLP

Many professionals, such as attorneys and accountants, work together using the business form of the partnership. Remember from Chapter 17 that a major disadvantage of the partnership is the unlimited personal liability of its owner-partners. Partners are also subject to joint and several (individual) liability for partnership obligations. For example, suppose that a group of lawyers is operating as a partnership. A client sues one of the attorneys for malpractice and wins a large judgment, and the firm's malpractice insurance is insufficient to cover the obligation. When the attorney's personal assets are exhausted, the personal assets of the other, innocent partners can be used to satisfy the judgment.

The LLP allows professionals to avoid personal liability for the malpractice of other partners. Although LLP statutes vary from state to state, generally each state statute limits in some way the liability of partners. For example, Delaware law protects each innocent partner from the "debts and obligations of the partnership arising from negligence, wrongful acts, or misconduct." In North Carolina, Texas, and Washington, D.C., the statutes protect innocent partners from obligations arising from "errors, omissions, negligence, incompetence, or malfeasance." Although the language of these statutes may seem to apply specifically to attorneys, virtually any group of professionals can use the LLP.

Questions remain, however, regarding the exact limits of this exemption from liability. One question concerns limits on liability outside the state in which the LLP was formed. Another question involves whether liability should be imposed to some extent on a negligent partner's supervising partner.

Liability outside the State of Formation. Because state LLP statutes are not uniform, a question arises when an LLP formed in one state does business in another state. If the LLP statutes in the two states provide different liability protection, which law applies? Most states apply the law of the state in which the LLP was formed, even when the firm does business in another state. Some states, though, do not expressly recognize foreign LLPs (that is, LLPs formed in another state), and others do not require foreign LLPs to register before doing business.[2] In these states, there have been no cases to date, but disputes will likely arise over which law to apply.

Supervising Partner's Liability. A partner who commits a wrongful act, such as negligence, is liable for the results of the act. Also liable is the partner who supervises the party who commits a wrongful act. This is generally true for all types of partners and partnerships, including LLPs.

When the partners are members of an LLP and more than one member is negligent, there is a question as to how liability is to be shared. Is each partner jointly and severally liable for the entire result, as a general partner would be in most states? Some states provide for proportionate liability—that is, for separate determinations of the negligence of the partners.[3]

For example, suppose that accountants Don and Jane are partners in an LLP, with Don supervising Jane. Jane negligently fails to file tax returns for their client, Centaur Tools. Centaur files a suit against Don and Jane. In a state that does not allow for proportionate liability, Don can be held liable for the entire loss. Under a proportionate liability statute, Don will be liable for no more than his portion of the responsibility for the missed tax deadline. (Even if Jane settles the case quickly, Don will still be liable for his portion.)

FAMILY LIMITED LIABILITY PARTNERSHIPS

A **family limited liability partnership (FLLP)** is a limited liability partnership in which the majority of the partners are persons related to each other, essentially as spouses, parents, grandparents, siblings, cousins, nephews, or nieces. A person acting in a fiduciary capacity for persons so related can also be a partner. All of the partners must be natural persons or persons acting in a fiduciary capacity for the benefit of natural persons.

Probably the most significant use of the FLLP form of business organization is in agriculture. Family-owned farms sometimes find this form to their benefit. The FLLP has the same advantages as other LLPs with some additional advantages, such as, in Iowa, an exemption from real estate transfer taxes when partnership real estate is transferred among partners.[4]

---

2. For example, Delaware and Texas do not expressly recognize foreign LLPs, and Utah does not require the registration of foreign LLPs.

3. See, for example, Colorado Revised Statutes Annotated Section 13-21-111.5(1) and Utah Code Annotated Section 78-27-39. The American Institute of Certified Public Accountants also supports the enactment of proportionate liability statutes.

4. Iowa Statutes Section 428A.

Section 3

Limited Partnerships

To this point, we have been discussing relatively new forms of limited liability business organizations. We now look at a far older business organizational form that limits the liability of some of its owners—the **limited partnership.** Limited partnerships originated in medieval Europe and have been existence in the United States since the early 1800s. In many ways, limited partnerships are like the general partnerships discussed in Chapter 17, but they also differ from general partnerships in several ways. Because of this, they are sometimes referred to as *special partnerships.*

Limited partnerships consist of at least one **general partner** and one or more **limited partners.** A general partner assumes management responsibility for the partnership and so has full responsibility for the partnership and for all debts of the partnership. A limited partner contributes cash or other property and owns an interest in the firm but does not undertake any management duties and is not personally liable for partnership debts beyond the amount of his or her investment.

A limited partner can forfeit limited liability by taking part in the management of the business. A comparison of the basic characteristics of general partnerships and limited partnerships appears in Exhibit 18–1.[5]

Until 1976, the law governing limited partnerships in all states except Louisiana was the Uniform Limited Partnership Act (ULPA). Since 1976, most states and the District of Columbia have adopted the revised version of the ULPA, known as the Revised Uniform Limited Partnership Act (RULPA). Because the RULPA is the dominant law governing limited partnerships in the United States, we will refer to the RULPA in the following discussion of limited partnerships.

FORMATION OF A LIMITED PARTNERSHIP

Compared with the informal, private, and voluntary agreement that usually suffices for a general partnership

---

5. Under the Revised Uniform Partnership Act (RUPA), which was discussed in Chapter 17, a general partnership can be converted into a limited partnership and vice versa [RUPA 902, 903]. The RUPA also provides for the merger of a general partnership with one or more general or limited partnerships under rules that are similar to those governing corporate mergers [RUPA 905].

EXHIBIT 18–1   A COMPARISON OF GENERAL PARTNERSHIPS AND LIMITED PARTNERSHIPS

CHARACTERISTIC	GENERAL PARTNERSHIP (UPA)	LIMITED PARTNERSHIP (RULPA)
Creation	By agreement of two or more persons to carry on a business as co-owners for profit.	By agreement of two or more persons to carry on a business as co-owners for profit. Must include one or more general partners and one or more limited partners. Filing of a certificate with the secretary of state is required.
Sharing of Profits and Losses	By agreement; or, in the absence of agreement, profits are shared equally by the partners, and losses are shared in the same ratio as profits.	Profits are shared as required in the certificate agreement, and losses are shared likewise, up to the amount of the limited partners' capital contributions. In the absence of a provision in the certificate agreement, profits and losses are shared on the basis of percentages of capital contributions.
Liability	Unlimited personal liability of all partners.	Unlimited personal liability of all general partners; limited partners liable only to the extent of their capital contributions.
Capital Contribution	No minimum or mandatory amount; set by agreement.	Set by agreement.
Management	By agreement, or in the absence of agreement, all partners have an equal voice.	General partners by agreement, or else each has an equal voice. Limited partners have no voice or else are subject to liability as general partners (but *only* if a third party has reason to believe that the limited partner is a general partner). A limited partner may act as an agent or employee

EXHIBIT 18–1 A COMPARISON OF GENERAL PARTNERSHIPS AND LIMITED PARTNERSHIPS (CONTINUED)

CHARACTERISTIC	GENERAL PARTNERSHIP (UPA)	LIMITED PARTNERSHIP (RULPA)
Management (continued)		of the partnership and vote on amending the certificate or on the sale or dissolution of the partnership.
Duration	By agreement, or can be dissolved by action of the partners (withdrawal), operation of law (death or bankruptcy), or court decree.	By agreement in the certificate or by withdrawal, death, or mental incompetence of a general partner in the absence of the right of the other general partners to continue the partnership. Death of a limited partner, unless he or she is the only remaining limited partner, does not terminate the partnership.
Distribution of Assets on Liquidation— Order of Priorities	1. Outside creditors. 2. Partner creditors. 3. Partners, according to capital contributions. 4. Partners, according to profits.	1. Outside creditors and partner creditors. 2. Partners and former partners entitled to distributions before withdrawal under the agreement or the RULPA. 3. Partners, according to capital contributions. 4. Partners, according to profits.

(see Chapter 17), the formation of a limited partnership is a public and formal proceeding that must follow statutory requirements. A limited partnership must have at least one general partner and one limited partner, as mentioned previously. Additionally, the partners must sign a **certificate of limited partnership,** which requires information similar to that found in a corporate charter (see Chapter 19). The certificate must be filed with the designated state official—under the RULPA, the secretary of state. The certificate is usually open to public inspection.

The following case illustrates the importance of complying carefully with the formal statutory requirements imposed on limited partnerships.

CASE 18.3   Miller v. Department of Revenue, State of Oregon

Supreme Court of Oregon, 1998.
327 Or. 129,
958 P.2d 833.
http://www.ejsimmons.com/advanced.html[a]

HISTORICAL AND ECONOMIC SETTING *Oregon statutes provide that "[i]t is the intent of the [Oregon] Legislative Assembly * * * to make the Oregon personal income tax law identical in effect to the provisions of the federal Internal Revenue Code relating to the measurement of taxable income of individuals." Oregon applies federal tax laws and federal court interpretations of those laws in resolving the issues raised by taxpayers. Under federal law, taxes are to be based on the "objective economic realities of a transaction rather than * * * the particular form [that] the parties employed."[b] Under state law, a taxpayer has the burden of proving by a preponderance of the evidence that a claimed deduction is allowable.[c]*

BACKGROUND AND FACTS *Robert Loverin and Paul Miller bought a low-income housing project and retained Rockwood Development Corporation to manage it. For the project, Loverin and Miller formed a limited partnership. The certificate and articles of limited partnership identified Loverin and Miller as general partners and Rockwood as the only limited partner. It allocated 2 percent of the profits and losses to the general partners and 98 percent to the limited partner. Eventually, twenty-one investors became limited*

a. This page provides access to opinions of the Oregon Supreme Court decided between July 1997 and December 3, 1998. In the "Query" box, type "Loverin" and click on "Submit Query." When the results appear, click on the "full" link to access the opinion. This site is maintained by attorney E. J. Simmons.
b. *Frank Lyon Co. v. United States,* 435 U.S. 561, 98 S.Ct. 1291, 55 L.Ed.2d 550 (1978).
c. *Reed v. Department of Revenue,* 310 Or. 260, 798 P.2d 235 (1990).

partners, but none of them signed the articles or the certificate. When American Properties Corporation (APC) replaced Rockwood as a limited partner, Loverin, Miller, and the president of APC signed a document that purported to amend the articles. The document provided in part that the partners could reallocate profits and losses as they "may agree." On their income tax returns, Loverin and Miller allocated 99.9 percent of the losses to themselves. The Oregon Department of Revenue reallocated the losses according to the provisions in the original articles—2 percent to general partners and 98 percent to limited partners. Miller and others appealed to the Oregon state tax court. The court upheld the assessment, and the plaintiffs appealed to the Oregon Supreme Court.

IN THE LANGUAGE OF THE COURT

LEESON, Justice.
* * * *

* * * [Oregon Revised Statute (ORS)] 69.180(1) describes the procedure required for forming a limited partnership * * * . It provides, in part, that when two or more persons desire to form a limited partnership they shall "[s]ign and verify a certificate" and shall "[f]ile one copy of such certificate in the office of the Corporation Commissioner." Taxpayers followed that procedure with respect to the [original] articles * * * . ORS 69.410(1) describes the procedure required to amend a certificate of limited partnership to change a limited partnership's composition. That statute provides that the writing to amend a certificate of limited partnership shall: "Be signed and verified by all partners. * * * "

The only evidence regarding the amended articles that taxpayers submitted to the Tax Court was a document signed by taxpayers and the president of APC. There is no evidence in this record that the amended articles were signed by the 21 [other] limited partners * * * . Thus, the amended articles were not properly executed. Consequently, taxpayers were not entitled to rely on * * * the amended articles for the purposes of allocating profits and losses * * * . The only document that conforms to the statutory requirements and that is binding is the [original] articles. * * * [Those] articles unambiguously allocate 2 percent of the losses to the general partners and 98 percent of the losses to the limited partners.

DECISION AND REMEDY

The Oregon Supreme Court affirmed the lower court's decision, concluding that Loverin and Miller were not entitled to allocate 99.9 percent of the losses to themselves. The fact that none of the investing limited partners signed the purported amendments rendered them invalid.

RIGHTS AND LIABILITIES OF PARTNERS

General partners, unlike limited partners, are personally liable to the partnership's creditors; thus, at least one general partner is necessary in a limited partnership so that someone has personal liability. This policy can be circumvented in states that allow a corporation to be the general partner in a partnership. Because the corporation has limited liability by virtue of corporate laws, if a corporation is the general partner, no one in the limited partnership has personal liability.

Rights of Limited Partners.   Subject to the limitations that will be discussed here, limited partners have essentially the same rights as general partners, including the right of access to partnership books and the

right to other information regarding partnership business. On dissolution of the partnership, limited partners are entitled to a return of their contributions in accordance with the partnership certificate. They can also assign their interests subject to the certificate.

The RULPA provides a limited partner with the right to sue an outside party on behalf of the firm if the general partners with authority to do so have refused to file suit. In addition, investor protection legislation, such as securities laws (discussed in Chapter 29), may give some protection to limited partners.

Liabilities of Limited Partners.   In contrast to the personal liability of general partners, the liability of a limited partner is limited to the capital that he or she contributes or agrees to contribute to the partnership.

A limited partnership is formed by good faith compliance with the requirements for signing and filing the certificate, even if it is incomplete or defective. When a limited partner discovers a defect in the formation of the limited partnership, he or she can avoid future liability by causing an appropriate amendment or certificate to be filed or by renouncing an interest in the profits of the partnership. If the limited partner takes neither of these actions on the discovery of the defect, however, the partner can be held personally liable by the firm's creditors. Liability for false statements in a partnership certificate runs in favor of persons relying on the false statements and against members who know of the falsity but still sign the certificate.

Limited Partners and Management. Limited partners enjoy limited liability so long as they do not participate in management. A limited partner who participates in management will be just as liable as a general partner to any creditor who transacts business

with the limited partnership and believes, based on a limited partner's conduct, that the limited partner is a general partner. How much actual review and advisement a limited partner can engage in before being exposed to liability is an unsettled question.[6] A limited partner who knowingly permits his or her name to be used in the name of the limited partnership is liable to creditors who extend credit to the limited partnership without knowledge that the limited partner is not a general partner.

Although limited partners cannot participate in management, this does not mean that the general partners are totally free of restrictions in running the business. The general partners in a limited partnership have fiduciary obligations to the partnership and to the limited partners, as the following case illustrates.

---

6. It is an unsettled question partly because there are differences among the laws in different states.

CASE 18.4

BT-I v. Equitable Life Assurance Society of the United States

California Court
of Appeal,
Fourth District, 1999.
75 Cal.App.4th 1406,
76 Cal.App.4th 684E,
89 Cal.Rptr.2d 811.

BACKGROUND AND FACTS *BT-I, a general partnership, entered into a general partnership with Equitable Life Assurance Society of the United States to develop and operate an office building and retail complex in California. Banque Paribas lent the firm $62.5 million for the project. Six years later, BT-I and Equitable dissolved their general partnership and entered into a limited partnership, with Equitable as general partner and BT-I as limited partner. Equitable was given title to the retail complex and the sole right to manage the partnership. Paragraph 5.1(c) of the limited partnership agreement gave Equitable broad powers, "provided, however, . . . that in no event shall the General Partner be required to take any action . . . to prevent Banque Paribas or any other lender from exercising any remedies in connection with any loan made to the Partnership." Later, when Banque Paribas solicited bids to "sell" its loan, Equitable (in its capacity as a corporate entity) bought it for $38.5 million. On the due date, Equitable demanded full payment from the partnership, but none was made. A month later, Equitable offered to sell the loan to the partnership, but the offer was not accepted. Equitable scheduled a foreclosure sale. Three days before the sale, BT-I offered $39 million for the project but Equitable turned it down. At the sale, Equitable bought the partnership's office building. BT-I filed a suit in a California state court against Equitable, alleging in part breach of fiduciary duty. Equitable argued that the partnership agreement allowed it to buy the loans and foreclose the same as any other lender. The court entered a judgment in Equitable's favor. BT-I appealed to a state intermediate appellate court.*

IN THE LANGUAGE OF THE COURT

BEDSWORTH, J. [Judge]

* * * * *

In general, under the California Revised Limited Partnership Act, partners may determine by agreement many aspects of their relationship. But there are limitations. A general partner of a limited partnership is subject to the same restrictions, and has the same liabilities to the partnership and other partners, as in a general partnership. * * *

*   *   *   *

We do not believe the partnership agreement can be read as permitting Equitable to purchase the loans for its own account and foreclose. Certainly, it does not expressly allow such conduct. Even if the language were broad enough to justify such an interpretation, we hold *a partnership agreement cannot relieve a general partner of its fiduciary duties to a limited partner and the partnership where the purchase and foreclosure of partnership debt is involved.* [Emphasis added.]

Paragraph 5.1(c) provides Equitable did not have to contribute any more money to the partnership or otherwise take any action to prevent foreclosure by any lender. Fairly read, this absolves Equitable of the duty to act affirmatively to bail out the partnership from the consequences of default. But Equitable's conduct in buying and foreclosing the loans went far beyond whatever safe harbor might be found in the partnership agreement. It is one thing simply to do nothing and suffer the consequences equally with all other partners. It is another to step out of the role of partner and into that of an aggressive (and apparently greedy) lender in the marketplace. *   *   * Equitable was BT-I's partner, not its lender, and it lost sight of this most basic distinction in its haste to pounce upon the loan.

Nor can we agree with Equitable that the Revised Uniform Limited Partnership Act *   *   * [justifies] what it did. It is true the act permits the parties to vary its effect *   *   * . But the fact that the act allows the parties to structure many aspects of their relationship is not a license to freely engage in self-dealing—it remains our responsibility to delimit the outer boundaries of permissible conduct by a fiduciary. In view of the rule against waiving fundamental fiduciary duties, we cannot stretch these general provisions to include giving Equitable a free hand to act for its own self-interest. Equitable was still a fiduciary, and its conduct must be measured by fiduciary standards.

DECISION AND REMEDY   *The state intermediate appellate court reversed the judgment of the lower court. A general partner in a limited partnership has the same fiduciary obligation as a general partner in a general partnership, and this duty cannot be contracted away.*

DISSOLUTION OF THE LIMITED PARTNERSHIP

A limited partnership is dissolved in much the same way as an ordinary partnership (see Chapter 17). The retirement, death, or mental incompetence of a general partner can dissolve the partnership, but not if the business can be continued by one or more of the other general partners in accordance with their certificate or by the consent of all of the members. The death or assignment of interest of a limited partner does not dissolve the limited partnership. A limited partnership can be dissolved by court decree.

Bankruptcy or the withdrawal of a general partner dissolves a limited partnership. Bankruptcy of a limited partner, however, does not dissolve the partnership unless it causes the bankruptcy of the limited partnership. The retirement of a general partner causes a dissolution unless the members consent to a continuation by the remaining general partners or unless this contingency is provided for in the certificate.

On dissolution, creditors' rights, including those of partners who are creditors, take first priority. Then partners and former partners receive unpaid distributions of partnership assets and, except as otherwise agreed, amounts representing returns on their contributions and amounts proportionate to their shares of the distributions.

SECTION 4

Limited Liability Limited Partnerships

A **limited liability limited partnership (LLLP)** is a type of limited partnership. The difference between a limited partnership and an LLLP is that the liability of a general partner in an LLLP is the same as the liability of a limited partner. That is, the liability of all partners is limited to the amount of their investments in the firm.

EXHIBIT 18–2   MAJOR FORMS OF BUSINESS COMPARED

CHARACTERISTIC	SOLE PROPRIETORSHIP	PARTNERSHIP	CORPORATION
Method of Creation	Created at will by owner.	Created by agreement of the parties.	Charter issued by state—created by statutory authorization.
Legal Position	Not a separate entity; owner is the business.	Not a separate legal entity in many states.	Always a legal entity separate and distinct from its owners—a legal fiction for the purposes of owning property and being a party to litigation.
Liability	Unlimited liability.	Unlimited liability.	Limited liability of shareholders—shareholders are not liable for the debts of the corporation.
Duration	Determined by owner; automatically dissolved on owner's death.	Terminated by agreement of the partners, by the death of one or more of the partners, by withdrawal of a partner, by bankruptcy, and so on.	Can have perpetual existence.
Transferability of Interest	Interest can be transferred, but individual's proprietorship then ends.	Although partnership interest can be assigned, assignee does not have full rights of a partner.	Shares of stock can be transferred.
Management	Completely at owner's discretion.	Each general partner has a direct and equal voice in management unless expressly agreed otherwise in the partnership agreement.	Shareholders elect directors, who set policy and appoint officers.
Taxation	Owner pays personal taxes on business income.	Each partner pays pro rata share of income taxes on net profits, whether or not they are distributed.	Double taxation—corporation pays income tax on net profits, with no deduction for dividends, and shareholders pay income tax on disbursed dividends they receive.
Organizational Fees, Annual License Fees, and Annual Reports	None.	None.	All required.
Transaction of Business in Other States	Generally no limitation.	Generally no limitation.[a]	Normally must qualify to do business and obtain certificate of authority.

a. A few states have enacted statutes requiring that foreign partnerships qualify to do business there.

EXHIBIT 18–2   MAJOR FORMS OF BUSINESS COMPARED (CONTINUED)

CHARACTERISTIC	LIMITED PARTNERSHIP	LIMITED LIABILITY COMPANY	LIMITED LIABILITY PARTNERSHIP
Method of Creation	Created by agreement to carry on a business for a profit. At least one party must be a general partner and the other(s) limited partner(s). Certificate of limited partnership is filed. Charter must be issued by the state.	Created by an agreement of the owner-members of the company. Articles of organization are filed. Charter must be issued by the state.	Created by agreement of the partners. Certificate of a limited liability partnership is filed. Charter must be issued by state.
Legal Position	Treated as a legal entity.	Treated as a legal entity.	Generally, treated same as a general partnership.
Liability	Unlimited liability of all general partners; limited partners are liable only to the extent of capital contributions.	Member-owners' liability is limited to the amount of capital contributions or investments.	Varies from state to state but usually limits liability of a partner for certain acts committed by other partners.
Duration	By agreement in certificate, or by termination of the last general partner (withdrawal, death, and so on) or last limited partner.	Unless a single-member LLC, can have perpetual existence (same as a corporation).	Terminated by agreement of partners, by death or withdrawal of a partner, or by law (such as bankruptcy).
Transferability of Interest	Interest can be assigned (same as general partnership), but if assignee becomes a member with consent of other partners, certificate must be amended.	Member interests are freely transferable.	Interest can be assigned same as in a general partnership.
Management	General partners have equal voice or by agreement. Limited partners may not retain limited liability if they actively participate in management.	Member-owners can fully participate in management, or member-owners can select managers to manage the firm on behalf of the members.	Same as a general partnership.
Taxation	Generally taxed as a partnership.	LLC is not taxed, and members are taxed personally on profits "passed through" the LLC.	Same as a general partnership.
Organizational Fees, Annual License Fees, and Annual Reports	Organizational fee required; usually not others.	Organizational fee required; others vary with states.	Organizational fee required (such as a set amount per partner); usually not others.
Transaction of Business in Other States	Generally, no limitation.	Generally, no limitation but may vary depending on state.	Generally, no limitation, but state laws vary as to formation and limitation of liability.

A few states provide expressly for LLLLPs.[7] In states that do not provide for LLLPs but do allow for limited partnerships and limited liability partnerships, a limited partnership should probably still be able to register with the state as an LLLP.

SECTION 5

Major Business Forms Compared

When deciding which form of business organization would be most appropriate, businesspersons normally take several factors into consideration. As mentioned earlier, these factors include ease of creation, the liability of the owners, tax considerations, and the need for capital. Each major form of business organization offers distinct advantages and disadvantages with respect to these and other factors.

---

7. See, for example, Colorado Revised Statutes Annotated Section 7-62-109. Other states that provide expressly for limited liability limited partnerships include Delaware, Florida, Missouri, Pennsylvania, Texas, and Virginia.

For example, the sole proprietorship has the advantage of being easily and inexpensively established, but the owner faces personal liability for business obligations as well as restrictions on obtaining capital for additional financing. The partnership is relatively easy to establish and provides a way for the business to obtain capital (from partners' contributions). It enjoys tax benefits as well. The partnership also has a major disadvantage: the personal liability of the partners. One of the advantages of the corporate form (which will be discussed in more detail in Chapter 19) is that capital for expansion can be obtained by the issuance of shares of stock. Another advantage is the limited liability of the shareholder-owners. The limited liability company and the limited liability partnership increasingly are becoming forms of choice because of the many advantages they offer with respect to both the liability of the owners and taxation.

Exhibit 18–2 on pages 395 and 396 summarizes the essential advantages and disadvantages of each of the forms of business organization discussed in Chapters 17 through 19.

TERMS AND CONCEPTS TO REVIEW

articles of organization 385
certificate of limited partnership 391
family limited liability partnership (FLLP) 389
general partner 390

limited liability company (LLC) 384
limited liability limited partnership (LLLP) 394
limited liability partnership (LLP) 388

limited partner 390
limited partnership 390
member 385
operating agreement 387

QUESTIONS AND CASE PROBLEMS

18–1. LIMITED LIABILITY COMPANIES. John, Lesa, and Trevor form an LLC. John contributes 60 percent of the capital, and Lesa and Trevor each contribute 20 percent. Nothing is decided about how profits will be divided. John assumes that he will be entitled to 60 percent of the profits, in accordance with his contribution. Lesa and Trevor, however, assume that the profits will be divided equally. A dispute over the issue arises,

and ultimately a court has to decide the issue. What law will the court apply? In most states, what will result? How could this dispute have been avoided in the first place? Discuss fully.

18–2. LIABILITY OF LIMITED PARTNERS. Asher and Breem form a limited partnership with Asher as the general partner and Breem as the limited partner. Breem puts up $15,000, and Asher contributes some office equipment that he owns. A certificate of limited partnership is properly filed, and business is begun. One month later, Asher becomes ill. Instead of hiring someone to manage the business, Breem takes over complete management himself. While Breem is in control, he makes a contract with Thaler involving a large sum of money. Asher returns to work. Because of other commitments, Asher and Breem breach the Thaler contract. Thaler contends that Asher and Breem will be personally liable for damages caused by the breach if the damages cannot be satisfied out of the assets of the limited partnership. Discuss this contention.

18–3. LIMITED PARTNERSHIPS. Dorinda, Lois, and Elizabeth form a limited partnership. Dorinda is a general partner, and Lois and Elizabeth are limited partners. Consider each of the separate events below, and discuss fully which event(s) constitute(s) a dissolution of the limited partnership.

   (a) Lois assigns her partnership interest to Ashley.
   (b) Elizabeth is petitioned into involuntary bankruptcy.
   (c) Dorinda dies.

18–4. LIABILITY OF LIMITED PARTNERS. Combat Associates was formed as a limited partnership to promote an exhibition boxing match between Lyle Alzado (a professional football player) and Muhammad Ali. Alzado and others had formed Combat Promotions; this organization was to be the general partner and Blinder, Robinson & Co. (Blinder), the limited partner in Combat Associates. The general partner's contribution consisted of assigning all contracts pertaining to the match, and the limited partner's contribution was a $250,000 letter of credit to ensure Ali's compensation. Alzado personally guaranteed to repay Blinder for any amount of loss if the proceeds of the match were less than $250,000. In preparation for the match, at Alzado's request, Blinder's president participated in interviews and a promotional rally, and the company sponsored parties and allowed its local office to be used as a ticket sales outlet. The proceeds of the match were insufficient, and Blinder sued Alzado on his guaranty. Alzado counterclaimed by asserting that Blinder had taken an active role in the control and management of Combat Associates and should be held liable as a general partner. How did the court rule on Alzado's counterclaim? Discuss. [Blinder, Robinson & Co. v. Alzado, 713 P.2d 1314 (Colo.App. 1985)]

18–5. LIABILITY OF GENERAL PARTNERS. Val Somers, Pat McGowan, and Brent Roberson were general partners in Vermont Place, a limited partnership formed to construct duplexes on a tract of land in Fort Smith, Arkansas. In 1984, the partnership mortgaged the property so that it could build there. McGowan owned a separate company, Advance Development Corp., which was hired by the partnership to develop the project. On September 3, 1984, Somers and Roberson discovered that McGowan had not been paying the suppliers to the project, including National Lumber Co., and had not been making the mortgage payments. The suppliers and

the bank sued the partnership and the general partners individually. Discuss whether Somers and Roberson could be held individually liable for the debts incurred by McGowan. [National Lumber Co. v. Advance Development Corp., 293 Ark. 1, 732 S.W.2d 840 (1987)]

18–6. FOREIGN LIMITED LIABILITY COMPANIES. Page, Scrantom, Sprouse, Tucker & Ford, a Georgia law firm, entered into a lease of office equipment in Georgia. The lessor assigned the lease to Danka Funding Co. (DFC), a New York limited liability company (LLC) with its principal place of business in New Jersey. DFC was registered as a foreign LLC in New Jersey for almost two years before the registration lapsed or was withdrawn. Under the applicable statute, a foreign LLC "may not maintain any action . . . in this State until it has registered." When Page defaulted on the lease, DFC filed a complaint in a New Jersey state court against Page for more than $100,000. In its response, Page pointed out that DFC was not registered as a foreign LLC. DFC reregistered. Asserting that DFC had not been registered when it filed its suit, Page asked a federal district court to dismiss it. Should the court grant this request? Why or why not? [Danka Funding, L.L.C. v. Page, Scrantom, Sprouse, Tucker & Ford, P.C., 21 F.Supp.2d 465 (D.N.J. 1998)]

18–7. LIMITED LIABILITY PARTNERSHIPS. Mudge Rose Guthrie Alexander & Ferdon, a law firm, was organized as a general partnership but converted into a limited liability partnership (LLP). Mudge's principal place of business was New York, where it was organized, but some of its members were citizens of Maryland. The firm filed a suit in a federal district court to recover unpaid legal fees from Robert Pickett and other citizens of Maryland. The defendants filed a motion to dismiss on the ground that there was not complete diversity of citizenship, because some of the LLC members were Maryland citizens also. Mudge argued that an LLP was like a corporation, and therefore the citizenship of the firm's members was irrelevant. How should the court rule? Explain. [Mudge Rose Guthrie Alexander & Ferdon v. Pickett, 11 F.Supp.2d 449 (S.D.N.Y. 1998)]

18–8. LIMITED LIABILITY COMPANIES. Gloria Duchin, a Rhode Island resident, was the sole shareholder and chief executive officer of Gloria Duchin, Inc. (Duchin, Inc.), which manufactured metallic Christmas ornaments and other novelty items. The firm was incorporated in Rhode Island. Duchin Realty, Inc., also incorporated in Rhode Island, leased real estate to Duchin, Inc. The Duchin entities hired Gottesman Co. to sell Duchin, Inc., and to sign with the buyer a consulting agreement for Gloria Duchin and a lease for Duchin Realty's property. Gottesman negotiated a sale, a consulting agreement, and a lease with Somerset Capital Corp. James Mitchell, a resident of Massachusetts, was the chairman and president of Somerset, and Mary Mitchell, also a resident of Massachusetts, was the senior vice president. The parties agreed that to buy Duchin, Inc., Somerset would create a new limited liability company, JMTR Enterprises, L.L.C., in Rhode Island, with the Mitchells as its members. When the deal fell apart, JMTR filed a suit in a Massachusetts state court against the Duchin entities, alleging, among other things, breach of contract. When the defendants tried to remove the case to a federal district court, JMTR argued that the court did not have jurisdiction because there was no diversity of citizenship between the parties: all of the plaintiffs and defendants were citizens of Rhode Island. Is JMTR correct? Why or why not? [*JMTR Enterprises, L.L.C. v. Duchin,* 42 F.Supp.2d 87 (D.Mass. 1999)]

18–9. IN YOUR COURT

Caton Avenue Associates was a limited partnership that owned rental property. Caton paid Theodore Dalmazio, one of the general partners, a management fee to manage the property. Dalmazio paid his employees with Caton's money. Dalmazio billed Caton for services that are normally performed by other property management firms at no cost and also billed Caton at an hourly rate for work that is normally billed to the rental unit. Alfred Friedman and the other limited partners filed a suit on Caton's behalf against Dalmazio and the other general partner to recover the improper billings as damages. Assume that you are the judge in the trial court hearing this case and answer the following questions:

    (a) What is the basic issue in this case? Is it similar to the issue involved in Case 18.4 (*BT-I v. Equitable Life Assurance Society of the United States*)?

    (b) On what basis might you rule in favor of the limited partners? What reasoning would you use to justify your decision?

LAW ON THE WEB

For updated links to resources available on the Web, as well as a variety of other materials, visit this text's Web site at http://wleb.westbuslaw.com.

    You can find information on how to form an LLC, including the fees charged in each state for filing LLC articles of organization, at the Web site of BIZCORP International, Inc. Go to

http://www.bizcorp.com

Nolo Press provides information on LLCs and how they are operated at

http://www.nolo.com/chapter/RUNS/RUNS_toc.html

For an example of a state law (that of Florida) governing LLPs, go to the Internet Legal Resource Guide's Web page at

http://www.ilrg.com/whatsnews/statute.html

and scroll down the page to "Registered Limited Liability Partnerships."

    The law firm of Wordes, Wilshin, Goren & Conner offers a comparison of the advantages and disadvantages of major business forms with respect to various factors, including ease of formation, management, and ability to raise capital. The firm's Web site can be accessed at

http://www.wwgc.com/wwgc-be1.htm

LEGAL RESEARCH EXERCISES ON THE WEB

Go to http://wleb.westbuslaw.com, the Web site that accompanies this text. Select "Internet Applications," and then click on "Chapter 18." There you will find the following Internet research exercise that you can perform to learn more about limited liability companies:

Activity 18–1: Limited Liability Companies

CHAPTER 19

Corporations

THE **CORPORATION** IS A CREATURE OF STATUTE. A corporation is an artificial being, existing in law only and neither tangible nor visible. Its existence depends generally on state law, although some corporations, especially public organizations, can be created under federal law. Each state has its own body of corporate law, and these laws are not entirely uniform.

The Model Business Corporation Act (MBCA) is a codification of modern corporation law that has been influential in the codification of state corporation statutes. Today, the majority of state statutes are guided by the most recent version of the MBCA, often referred to as the Revised Model Business Corporation Act (RMBCA). You should keep in mind, however, that there is considerable variation among the regulations of the states that have used the MBCA or the RMBCA as a basis for their statutes, and several states do not follow either act. Because of this, individual state corporation laws should be relied on to determine corporate law rather than the MBCA or RMBCA.

In this chapter, we examine the corporate form of business enterprise. Under modern law, except as limited by charters, statutes, or constitutions, *a corporation can engage in any act and enter into any contract available to a natural person in order to accomplish the purposes for which it was created.* When a corporation is created, the express and implied powers necessary to achieve its purpose also come into existence.

The Nature of the Corporation

A corporation can consist of one or more *natural* persons (as opposed to the artificial "person" of the corporation) identified under a common name. The corporation substitutes itself for its shareholders in conducting corporate business and in incurring liability, yet its authority to act and the liability for its actions are separate and apart from the individuals who own it. (In certain limited situations, the "corporate veil" can be pierced; that is, liability for the corporation's obligations can be extended to shareholders, a topic to be discussed later in this chapter.)

CORPORATE PERSONNEL

Responsibility for the overall management of the corporation is entrusted to a board of directors, which is elected by the shareholders. The board of directors hires corporate officers and other employees to run the daily business operations of the corporation.

When an individual purchases a share of stock in a corporation, that person becomes a shareholder and an owner of the corporation. Unlike the members in a partnership, the body of shareholders can change constantly without affecting the continued existence of the corporation. A shareholder can sue the corporation, and the corporation can sue a shareholder. Additionally, under certain circumstances, a shareholder can sue on behalf of a corporation. The rights and duties of all corporate personnel will be examined later in this chapter.

CORPORATE TAXATION

Corporate profits are taxed by state and federal governments. Corporations can do one of two things with corporate profits—retain them or pass them on to shareholders in the form of dividends. The corporation receives no tax deduction for dividends distributed to shareholders. Dividends are again taxable (except when they represent distributions of capital) as ordinary income to the shareholder receiving them. This double-taxation feature of the corporation is one of its major disadvantages.

Profits that are not distributed are retained by the corporation. These **retained earnings,** if invested properly, will yield higher corporate profits in the future and thus cause the price of the company's stock to rise. Individual shareholders can then reap the benefits of the retained earnings in the capital gains they receive when they sell their shares.

SECTION 2

Classification of Corporations

The classification of a corporation normally depends on its location, purpose, and ownership characteristics.

DOMESTIC, FOREIGN, AND ALIEN CORPORATIONS

A corporation is known as a *domestic corporation* in its home state (the state in which it incorporates). A corporation that is formed in one state but is doing business in another is referred to in that other state as a *foreign corporation.* A corporation formed in another country (say, Mexico) but doing business in the United States is referred to in the United States as an *alien corporation.*

A corporation does not have an automatic right to do business in a state other than its state of incorporation. A corporation normally is required to obtain a *certificate of authority* in any state in which it plans to do business. Once the certificate has been issued, the powers conferred on the corporation by its home state generally can be exercised in the other state. Should a foreign corporation do business without obtaining a certificate of authority, the state can fine the corporation; deny it the privilege of using state courts; and even hold its officers, directors, or agents personally liable for corporate obligations, including contractual obligations, incurred in that state.[1]

PUBLIC AND PRIVATE CORPORATIONS

A public corporation is one formed by the government to meet some political or governmental purpose. Cities and towns that incorporate are common examples. In addition, many federal government organizations, such as the U.S. Postal Service, the Tennessee Valley Authority, and AMTRAK, are public corporations.

Private corporations, in contrast, are created either wholly or in part for private benefit. Most corporations are private. Although they may serve a public purpose, as a public utility does, they are owned by private persons rather than by the government.

NONPROFIT CORPORATIONS

Corporations formed for purposes other than making a profit are called *nonprofit* or *not-for-profit* corporations. Nonprofit corporations are usually (although not necessarily) private corporations. Private hospitals, educational institutions, charities, religious organizations, and the like are frequently organized as nonprofit corporations. The nonprofit corporation is a convenient form of organization that allows various groups to own property and to form contracts without the individual members' being personally exposed to liability.

CLOSE CORPORATIONS

A **close corporation** is one whose shares are held by members of a family or by relatively few persons. Close corporations are also referred to as *closely held, family,* or *privately held* corporations. Usually, the members of the small group constituting a close corporation are personally known to one another. Because the number of shareholders is so small, there is no trading market for the shares. In practice, a close corporation is often operated like a partnership. Some states recognize this similarity and have enacted special statutory provisions that cover close corporations. These provisions expressly permit close corporations to depart significantly from certain formalities required by traditional corporation law.[2]

---

1. *Robertson v. Levy,* 197 A.2d 443 (D.C.App. 1964).
2. For example, in some states (such as Maryland), the close corporation need not have a board of directors.

Additionally, Section 7.32 of the RMBCA—a provision added to the RMBCA in 1991 and adopted in several states—gives close corporations a substantial amount of flexibility in determining the rules by which they will operate. Under Section 7.32, if all of the shareholders of a corporation agree in writing, the corporation can operate without directors, bylaws, annual or special shareholders' or directors' meetings, stock certificates, or formal records of shareholders' or directors' decisions.[3]

Management of Close Corporations.   The close corporation has a single shareholder or a closely knit group of shareholders, who usually hold the positions of directors and officers. Management of a close corporation resembles that of a sole proprietorship or a partnership. As a corporation, however, the firm must meet whatever specific legal requirements are set forth in state statutes.

To prevent a majority shareholder from dominating a close corporation, the corporation may specify that action can be taken by the board only on approval of more than a simple majority of the directors. Typically, this would not be required for ordinary business decisions but only for extraordinary actions, such as changing the amount of dividends or dismissing an employee-shareholder. Additionally, in some cases, courts have held that majority shareholders owe a fiduciary duty to minority shareholders (discussed later in this chapter).

Transfer of Shares in Close Corporations.   By definition, a close corporation has a small number of

shareholders. The transfer of one shareholder's shares to someone else can thus cause serious management problems. The other shareholders may find themselves required to share control with someone they do not know or like.

Consider an example. Three brothers, Terry, Damon, and Henry Johnson, are the only shareholders of Johnson's Car Wash, Inc. Henry wants to sell his shares to an unknown third person. Terry and Damon object to Henry's idea, and a dispute ensues. What could they have done to avoid this situation? The articles of incorporation could have restricted the transferability of shares to outside persons by stipulating that shareholders offer their shares to the corporation or other shareholders before selling them to an outside purchaser. In fact, a few states have statutes under which close corporation shares cannot be transferred unless certain persons—including shareholders, family members, and the corporation—are first given the opportunity to purchase the shares for the same price.

Another way that control of a close corporation can be stabilized is through the use of a shareholder agreement. A shareholder agreement can provide that when one of the original shareholders dies, his or her shares of stock in the corporation will be divided in such a way that the proportionate holdings of the survivors, and thus their proportionate control, will be maintained.

Key employees may be among those who are allowed to buy shares in the close corporation for which they work. A shareholder agreement may provide that if a key employee is discharged, the employee must offer to sell his or her shares to the corporation, which may be required to buy them. In such circumstances, a question may arise as to whether the corporation discharged its employees merely to buy their shares. That was one of the questions raised in the following case.

---

3. Shareholders cannot agree, however, to eliminate certain rights of shareholders, such as the right to inspect corporate books and records or the right to bring derivative actions (lawsuits on behalf of the corporation, discussed later in this chapter).

CASE 19.1   **Crowder Construction Co. v. Kiser**

Court of Appeals of North Carolina, 1999.
517 S.E.2d 178.
http://www.aoc.state.nc.us/www/public/html/opinions.htm[a]

BACKGROUND AND FACTS   *Crowder Construction Company allowed only members of the Crowder family and key employees to buy company stock. Under a shareholders' agreement, if a key employee was terminated, the employee was obligated to sell his or her shares to the company. Under a "buyout" provision, the company was required to buy the shares at a price based on their book value.[b] If those shares had been held for less than seven years, the price was less. In 1981, the firm hired Eugene Kiser, a certified pub-*

---

a. This Web site is maintained by the North Carolina Administrative Office of the Courts. In the "Court of Appeals Opinions" section, click on the "1999" box. When that page opens, scroll to "20 July 99" and click on the case name to access the opinion.
b. The *book value* of a corporation is generally understood to mean the value of the corporation's total assets less its total liabilities.

lic accountant who became the firm's chief financial officer. As a key employee, he bought Crowder stock at a substantial discount. By the end of 1994, Kiser had begun to openly question the competence of Otis Crowder, the firm's president, to make decisions. In January 1995, Kiser was discharged and told to sell his stock to the company. Had Kiser worked until August, he would have held all of his shares for more than seven years, which would have entitled him to an extra $180,000. When he refused to sell the shares that he had held for less than seven years, the firm filed a suit in a North Carolina state court against him to enforce the shareholders' agreement. Kiser argued, among other things, that the shareholders' agreement was unconscionable. In support of this argument, he claimed in part that he had been discharged so the company would not have to pay the full price for his stock. The court granted a summary judgment in favor of Crowder, and Kiser appealed to a state intermediate appellate court.

IN THE LANGUAGE OF THE COURT

HORTON, Judge.

* * * *

* * * In family owned corporations, or other corporations in which all shares of stock are held by a relatively small number of shareholders, it is not unusual for all shareholders to agree that the corporation, or the other shareholders, will be given the first opportunity to purchase the shares of a terminated or retiring shareholder. This agreement is valid under the North Carolina Corporations Act provided it is "reasonable" and is not "unconscionable under the circumstances." * * *

Since such restrictions make it even more difficult to dispose of minority stock interests in a closely held corporation, *these agreements often contain some version of mandatory "buy-out" provisions to ensure shareholders a ready market for their shares where there otherwise might not be one.* * * * [Emphasis added.]

* * * *

* * * Defendant [Kiser] contends that by prematurely terminating him, plaintiff saved $180,000.00 which defendant would have been due, and that defendant's termination * * * raises a reasonable inference * * * that the termination was motivated by plaintiff's desire to avoid paying defendant full value for his shares of stock. We disagree.

* * * Plaintiff's evidence tends to show that defendant was discharged for openly questioning the ability and competence of Company management to guide the affairs of the Company, resulting in an adversarial relationship between Kiser and other members of management. * * *

* * * *

* * * Even assuming, for the sake of argument, that enforcement of the stock purchase agreement would be inequitable if plaintiff had terminated defendant's employment solely to prevent his stock options from fully vesting, defendant comes forward with no evidence to support his bare assertion that he was discharged for an improper purpose. * * * Other than defendant's argument that an inference of wrongful purpose arises from his termination, defendant does not offer any evidence * * * . Plaintiff having offered competent evidence of a justifiable business purpose motivating defendant's termination, and defendant having failed to offer evidence on this issue in opposition to the motion for summary judgment, the trial court properly entered summary judgment on this issue.

DECISION AND REMEDY

The state intermediate appellate court affirmed the judgment of the lower court. There was no evidence that Kiser had been discharged so that Crowder could avoid paying him a higher price for his shares in the company. In the absence of such proof, neither the shareholder agreement nor Kiser's termination was unreasonable.

S CORPORATIONS

A close corporation that meets the qualifying requirements specified in Subchapter S of the Internal Revenue Code can operate as an **S corporation.** If a corporation has S corporation status, it can avoid the imposition of income taxes at the corporate level while retaining many of the advantages of a corporation, particularly limited liability.

Qualification Requirements for S Corporations. Among the numerous requirements for S corporation status, the following are the most important:

1. The corporation must be a domestic corporation.
2. The corporation must not be a member of an affiliated group of corporations.
3. The shareholders of the corporation must be individuals, estates, or certain trusts. Nonqualifying trusts and partnerships cannot be shareholders. Corporations can be shareholders under certain circumstances.
4. The corporation must have seventy-five or fewer shareholders.
5. The corporation must have only one class of stock, although not all shareholders need have the same voting rights.
6. No shareholder of the corporation may be a nonresident alien.

Benefits of S Corporations. At times, it is beneficial for a regular corporation to elect S corporation status. Benefits include the following:

1. When the corporation has losses, the S election allows the shareholders to use the losses to offset other income.
2. When the stockholder's tax bracket is lower than the tax bracket for regular corporations, the S election causes the corporation's entire income to be taxed in the shareholder's bracket (because it is taxed as personal income), whether or not it is distributed. This is particularly attractive when the corporation wants to accumulate earnings for some future business purpose.

Because of these tax benefits, many close corporations opted for S corporation status in the past. Today, however, the S corporation is losing some of its significance—because the limited liability company and the limited liability partnership (discussed in Chapter 18) offer similar advantages plus additional benefits, including more flexibility in forming and operating the business.

SECTION 3

Corporate Formation

Corporations generally come into existence through two steps: (1) preliminary organizational and promotional undertakings (particularly, obtaining capital for the future corporation) and (2) the legal process of incorporation.

PROMOTIONAL ACTIVITIES

Before a corporation becomes a reality, people invest in the proposed corporation as subscribers, and contracts are frequently made by promoters on behalf of the future corporation. *Promoters* are those who, for themselves or others, take the preliminary steps in organizing a corporation. One of the tasks of the promoter is to issue a *prospectus*, which is a document required by federal or state securities laws (see Chapter 29) that describes the financial operations of the corporation, thus allowing an investor to make an informed decision. The promoter also secures the corporate charter.

Promoter's Liability. A promoter may purchase or lease property with a view toward selling it to the corporation when the corporation is formed. In addition, a promoter may enter into contracts with attorneys, accountants, architects, and other professionals whose services will be needed in planning for the proposed corporation. Finally, a promoter induces people to purchase stock in the corporation.

As a general rule, a promoter is held personally liable on preincorporation contracts. Courts simply hold that promoters are not agents when a corporation has yet to come into existence. If, however, the promoter secures the contracting party's agreement to hold only the corporation (not the promoter) liable on the contract, the promoter will not be liable in the event of any breach of contract.

Once the corporation is formed (the charter issued), the promoter remains personally liable until the corporation assumes the preincorporation contract by *novation*. Novation releases the promoter and makes the corporation liable for performing the contractual obligations. In some cases, the corporation adopts the promoter's contract by undertaking to perform it. Most courts hold that adoption in and of itself does not discharge the promoter from contractual liability. A corporation normally cannot ratify a preincorporation contract, as no principal was in existence at the time the contract was made.

Subscribers and Subscriptions. Prior to the actual formation of the corporation, the promoter can contact potential individual investors, and they can agree to purchase capital stock in the future corporation. This agreement is often referred to as a *subscription agreement,* and the potential investor is called a *subscriber.* Depending on state law, subscribers become shareholders as soon as the corporation is formed or as soon as the corporation accepts the agreement. This way, if corporation X becomes insolvent, the trustee in bankruptcy (see Chapter 16) can collect the consideration for any unpaid stock from a preincorporation subscriber.

Most courts view preincorporation subscriptions as continuing offers to purchase corporate stock. On or after its formation, the corporation can choose to accept the offer to purchase stock. Many courts also treat a subscription as a contract between the subscribers, making it irrevocable except with the consent of all of the subscribers. Under the RMBCA, a subscription is irrevocable for a period of six months unless otherwise provided in the subscription agreement or unless all the subscribers agree to the revocation of the subscription. In other jurisdictions, the preincorporation subscriber can revoke the offer to purchase before acceptance without liability, however.

INCORPORATION PROCEDURES

Exact procedures for incorporation differ among the states, but the basic requirements are similar.

State Chartering. The first step in the incorporation procedure is to select a state in which to incorporate. Because state incorporation laws differ, individuals have found some advantage in looking for the states that offer the most advantageous tax or incorporation provisions. Delaware has historically had the least restrictive laws. Consequently, many corporations, including a number of the largest, have incorporated there. Delaware's statutes permit firms to incorporate in Delaware and carry out business and locate operating headquarters elsewhere. (Most other states now permit this as well.) Closely held corporations, however, particularly those of a professional nature, generally incorporate in the state in which their principal stockholders live and work.

Articles of Incorporation. The primary document needed to begin the incorporation process is called the *articles of incorporation.* The articles include basic information about the corporation and serve as a primary source of authority for its future organization and business functions. The person or persons who execute the articles are called *incorporators* and will be discussed shortly. Generally, the information indicated below should be included in the articles of incorporation.

Corporate Name. The choice of a corporate name is subject to state approval to ensure against duplication or deception. State statutes usually require that the secretary of state run a check on the proposed name in the state of incorporation. Some states require that the incorporators, at their own expense, run a check on the proposed name for the newly formed corporation. Once cleared, a name can be reserved for a short time, for a fee, pending the completion of the articles of incorporation. All corporate statutes require the corporation name to include the word *Corporation, Incorporated, Company,* or *Limited* or an abbreviation of one of these terms.

The new corporation's name may not be the same as, or deceptively similar to, the name of an existing corporation doing business within the state. For example, if an existing corporation is named General Dynamics, Inc., the state will not allow another corporation to be called General Dynamic, Inc., because that name is deceptively similar to the first, and it would impliedly transfer a part of the goodwill established by the first corporate user to the second corporation. (See Chapter 14 for a fuller discussion of trade names.)

Nature and Purpose. The intended business activities of the corporation must be specified in the articles, and naturally, they must be lawful. Stating a general corporate purpose is usually sufficient to give rise to all of the powers necessary or convenient to the purpose of the organization. The corporate charter can state, for example, that the corporation is organized "to engage in the production and sale of agricultural products." There is a trend toward allowing corporate charters to state that the corporation is organized for "any legal business." A broadly stated purpose creates greater flexibility and avoids unnecessary future amendments to the corporate charter should the corporation change or modify its line of business.

Duration. A corporation can have perpetual existence under the corporate statutes of most states. A few states, however, prescribe a maximum duration, after which the corporation must formally renew its existence.

Capital Structure. The capital structure of the corporation is generally set forth in the articles. A few state statutes require a very small capital investment for ordinary business corporations but a greater capital investment for those engaged in insurance or banking. The articles must also indicate the number of shares of stock the corporation is authorized to issue and may include other information, such as the valuation of the shares and the types or classes of stock authorized for issuance.

Internal Organization. The articles should describe the internal management structure of the corporation, although this can be included in bylaws adopted after the corporation is formed. The articles of incorporation commence the corporation; the bylaws are formed after commencement by the board of directors. Bylaws are subject to, and cannot conflict with, the incorporation statute or the corporation's charter.

Under the RMBCA, shareholders may amend or repeal bylaws. The board of directors may also amend or repeal bylaws unless the articles of incorporation or provisions of the incorporation statute reserve that power to shareholders exclusively. Typical bylaw provisions describe voting procedures and requirements for shareholders, the election of the board of directors, the methods of replacing directors, and the manner and time of scheduling shareholders' meetings and board meetings.

Registered Office and Agent. The corporation must indicate the location and address of its registered office within the state. Usually, the registered office is also the principal office of the corporation. The corporation must give the name and address of a specific person who has been designated as an agent and who can receive legal documents on behalf of the corporation. These legal documents include service of process (the delivery of a court order requiring an appearance in court).

Incorporators. Each incorporator must be listed by name and must also indicate an address. An incorporator is a person—often, the corporate promoter—who applies to the state on behalf of the corporation to obtain its corporate charter. The incorporator need not be a subscriber and need not have any interest at all in the corporation. Many states do not impose residency or age requirements for incorporators. States vary as to the required number of incorporators; it can be as few as one or as many as three. Incorporators are

required to sign the articles of incorporation when they are submitted to the state; often, this is their only duty. In some states, they participate at the first organizational meeting of the corporation.

Certificate of Incorporation. Once the articles of incorporation have been prepared, signed, and authenticated by the incorporators, they are sent to the appropriate state official, usually the secretary of state, along with the appropriate filing fee. In many states, the secretary of state will then issue a *certificate of incorporation* representing the state's authorization for the corporation to conduct business. (This may be called the *corporate charter.*) The certificate and a copy of the articles are returned to the incorporators. The incorporators then hold the initial organizational meeting, which completes the details of incorporation.

Today, it is possible to incorporate—and receive a certificate of incorporation—via online incorporation services. For further information on this topic, see this chapter's *Emerging Trends in Technology.*

SECTION 4

Improper Incorporation

The procedures for incorporation are very specific. If they are not followed precisely, others may be able to challenge the existence of the corporation.

Errors in incorporation procedures can become important when, for example, a third person who is attempting to enforce a contract or bring suit for a tort injury fortuitously learns of them. On the basis of improper incorporation, the plaintiff could seek to make the would-be shareholders personally liable. Also, when the corporation attempts to enforce a contract against a defaulting party, if the defaulting party learns of a defect in the incorporation procedures, he or she may be able to avoid liability on that ground.

To prevent injustice, courts will sometimes attribute corporate existence to an improperly formed corporation by holding it to be a *de jure* corporation or a *de facto* corporation, as discussed below. In some cases, corporation by estoppel may also occur.

DE JURE AND DE FACTO CORPORATIONS

In the event of substantial compliance with all conditions precedent to incorporation, a corporation is said

EMERGING TRENDS IN TECHNOLOGY

Online Incorporation

Today, just about anybody can form a corporation for any lawful purpose in any state. The requirements differ from state to state. You do not have to form your corporation in the state in which you live or the state in which you are doing business, however. In fact, many individuals obtain their corporate charters from the state of Delaware, because it has the fewest legal restrictions on corporate formation and operation. Traditionally, Delaware has also been the state most often chosen for "mail-order incorporation." Today, instead of incorporating by mail, entrepreneurs have the option of incorporating in the states of their choice via online companies that offer incorporation services.

FINDING INFORMATION ON INCORPORATION REQUIREMENTS

Most of the over one hundred companies that offer incorporation services are now online, and you can obtain information about incorporation at their Web sites. For example, at the Web site of The Company Corporation (TCC) of Delaware (at **http://www. incorporate.com**), you can read about the advantages and disadvantages of incorporating your business, the cost of

incorporating in your state (or in any other state), and the pros and cons of the various types of corporate entities that are available.

You can find similar information at other sites, including the Web site of Harvard Business Services, Inc. (at **http://www.delawareinc. com**). Here you can find guidelines that will help you choose the type of corporation that best suits your needs, a list of frequently asked questions about incorporation, telephone numbers for each state's corporations division, the annual legal costs of maintaining a corporation, and so on.

INCORPORATING ONLINE

If you wish to incorporate via an online incorporation service, all you need to do is fill out a form. For example, if you fill out the incorporation forms at the TCC Web site, TCC will then file the forms with the appropriate state office and obtain a certificate of incorporation (corporate charter) for you. Optional TCC services include making arrangements for a registered agent for your corporation, mail-forwarding services, obtaining a tax ID number, and obtaining a domain name registration for your business.

IMPLICATIONS FOR THE BUSINESSPERSON

1. "Do-it-yourself" incorporation via online incorporation services

may be sufficient for those who are interested in starting small businesses but who have no serious aspirations that their companies will grow much larger. **2.** If you believe that the business in which you are going to engage has growth potential and may require significant financing in the future, you are best advised to contact a local lawyer to take you through the necessary steps in incorporating your business.

FOR CRITICAL ANALYSIS

1. Before incorporating (online or otherwise), what factors should you consider when deciding which form of business organization best suits your needs? **2.** How can you determine whether an online incorporation service is accurately representing the law governing corporations in the state in which you wish to incorporate?

RELEVANT WEB SITES

For further information on incorporation, as well as how you can incorporate online, visit the Web sites of NCCF, Inc. (at **http://www.nccf.com**) and American Incorporators, Ltd. (at **www.ailcorp.com**). (You can also find providers of online incorporation services simply by searching the term *incorporation* using a search engine such as Yahoo.)

to have *de jure* existence in law. In most states and under the RMBCA, the certificate of incorporation is viewed as evidence that all mandatory statutory provi- sions have been met. This means that the corporation is properly formed, and neither the state nor a third party can attack its existence. If, for example, an incorporator's address was incorrectly listed, this would mean that the corporation was improperly formed. The law, however, does not regard such inconsequential procedural defects as detracting from substantial compliance, and courts will uphold the *de jure* status of the corporate entity.

Sometimes there is a defect in complying with statutory mandates—for example, the corporation charter may have expired. Under these circumstances, the corporation may have *de facto* status, meaning that its existence cannot be challenged by third parties except the state. The following elements are required for *de facto* status:

1. There must be a state statute under which the corporation can be validly incorporated.
2. The parties must have made a good faith attempt to comply with the statute.
3. The enterprise must already have undertaken to do business as a corporation.

CORPORATION BY ESTOPPEL

If an association that is neither an actual corporation nor a *de facto* or *de jure* corporation holds itself out as being a corporation, it will be estopped from denying corporate status in a lawsuit by a third party. This usually occurs when a third party contracts with an association that claims to be a corporation but does not hold a certificate of incorporation. When the third party brings suit naming the so-called corporation as the defendant, the association may not escape from liability on the ground that no corporation exists. When justice requires, the courts treat an alleged corporation as if it were an actual corporation for the purpose of determining the rights and liabilities involved in a particular situation. Corporation by estoppel is thus determined by the circumstances. It does not extend recognition of corporate status beyond the resolution of the problem at hand.

SECTION 5

Disregarding the Corporate Entity

In some unusual situations, a corporate entity is used by its owners to perpetrate a fraud, circumvent the law, or in some other way accomplish an illegitimate objective. In these cases, the court will ignore the corporate structure by "piercing the corporate veil," exposing the shareholders to personal liability.

The following are some of the factors that may cause the courts to pierce the corporate veil:

1. A party is tricked or misled into dealing with the corporation rather than the individual.
2. The corporation is set up never to make a profit or always to be insolvent, or it is too "thinly" capitalized—that is, it has insufficient capital at the time it is formed to meet its prospective debts or potential liabilities.
3. Statutory corporate formalities, such as holding required corporation meetings, are not followed.
4. Personal and corporate interests are mixed together, or *commingled*, to the extent that the corporation has no separate identity.

To elaborate on the fourth factor in the preceding list, consider a close corporation that is formed according to law by a single person or by a few family members. In such a situation, the corporate entity and the sole stockholder (or family-member stockholders) must carefully preserve the separate status of the corporation and its owners. Certain practices invite trouble for the one-person or family-owned corporation: the commingling of corporate and personal funds; the failure to remit taxes, including payroll and sales taxes; and the shareholders' continuous personal use of corporate property (for example, vehicles).

Corporation laws usually do not specifically prohibit a stockholder from lawfully lending money to his or her corporation. When an officer, director, or majority shareholder lends the corporation money and takes back security in the form of corporate assets, however, the courts will scrutinize the transaction closely. Any such transaction must be made in good faith and for fair value.

When the corporate privilege is abused for personal benefit and the corporate business is treated in such a careless manner that the corporation and the shareholder in control are no longer separate entities, the court usually will require the shareholder to assume personal liability to creditors for the corporation's debts. In short, when the facts show that great injustice would result from the use of a corporation to avoid individual responsibility, a court of equity will look behind the corporate structure to the individual stockholder.

The following case illustrates a situation in which a corporation did business under an assumed name that was not registered with the state. At issue in the case was whether the president of the corporation could be held personally liable for corporate debts incurred under the assumed name.

CASE 19.2   Hoskins Chevrolet, Inc. v. Hochberg

Appellate Court of
Illinois, First District,
First Division, 1998.
294 Ill.App.3d 550,
691 N.E.2d 28,
229 Ill.Dec. 92.
http://www.state.il.us/
court/ap1_98ix.html[a]

BACKGROUND AND FACTS   *Ronald Hochberg is the president of Diamond Auto Body & Repair, Inc. Under the name "Diamond Auto Construction," Hochberg ordered and received auto parts from Hoskins Chevrolet, Inc. Hoskins Chevrolet sent invoices to "Diamond Auto Construction." Hochberg paid some of the invoices with checks drawn on the bank account of "Diamond Auto Construction." When the unpaid invoices totaled more than $40,000, Hoskins Chevrolet filed a suit in an Illinois state court to collect from Hochberg individually. Hochberg asserted that he did business with Hoskins Chevrolet only as the president of a corporation. Hoskins Chevrolet responded that "Diamond Auto Construction" was not registered with the state as the name of a corporation. The court granted a summary judgment in favor of Hoskins Chevrolet. Hochberg appealed.*

IN THE LANGUAGE OF THE COURT

Presiding Justice BUCKLEY delivered the opinion of the court:

*   *   *   *

The [Illinois] Business Corporations Act (the Act) permits a corporation to elect to adopt an assumed name provided that certain procedures are followed. Where those procedures are not followed, the corporation is required to conduct business under its corporate name. *   *   *

*   *   * Diamond Auto Body & Repair, Inc., used the assumed name of Diamond Auto Construction without complying with *   *   * the Act. Further, the record contains no evidence that while using the assumed name in his dealings with plaintiff, defendant also disclosed the corporate name *   *   * . Accordingly, we find no error in the trial court's determination that under the Act, Diamond Auto Construction was neither a corporation nor the assumed name of a corporation for purposes of establishing contract liability in anyone other than defendant.

DECISION AND REMEDY

The state intermediate appellate court affirmed the lower court's judgment. A person who incurs corporate debts under an unregistered corporate name is personally liable for those debts.

a. This Web site is maintained by the state of Illinois. In the "Appellate Court" section, in the "First District Opinions" row, click on "1998." When that page opens, scroll down the list to the name of the case and click on it to read the opinion.

SECTION 6

Directors, Officers, and Shareholders

Corporate directors, officers, and shareholders all play different roles within the corporate entity. Sometimes, actions that may benefit the corporation as a whole do not coincide with the separate interests of the individuals making up the corporation. In such situations, it is important to know the rights and duties of all participants in the corporate enterprise. The following sections focus on these rights and duties and the ways in which conflicts among corporate participants are resolved.

ROLE OF DIRECTORS

Every corporation is governed by a board of directors. A director occupies a position of responsibility unlike that of other corporate personnel. Directors are sometimes inappropriately characterized as *agents* because they act on behalf of the corporation. No individual director, however, can act as an agent to bind the corporation; and as a group, directors collectively control the corporation in a way that no agent is able to control a principal. Directors are sometimes incorrectly characterized as *trustees* because they occupy positions of trust and control over the corporation. Unlike trustees, however, they do not own or hold title to property for the use and benefit of others.

Few legal requirements exist concerning directors' qualifications. Only a handful of states impose minimum age and residency requirements. A director is sometimes a shareholder, but this is not a necessary qualification—unless, of course, statutory provisions or corporate articles or bylaws require ownership.

Election of Directors.   Subject to statutory limitations, the number of directors is set forth in the corporation's articles or bylaws. Historically, the minimum number of directors has been three, but today many states permit fewer. Indeed, the RMBCA permits corporations with fewer than fifty shareholders to eliminate the board of directors.

The first board of directors is normally appointed by the incorporators on the creation of the corporation, or directors are named by the corporation itself in the articles. The initial board serves until the first annual shareholders' meeting. Subsequent directors are elected by a majority vote of the shareholders.

The term of office for a director is usually one year—from annual meeting to annual meeting. Longer and staggered terms are permissible under most state statutes. A common practice is to elect one-third of the board members each year for a three-year term. In this way, there is greater management continuity.

A director can be removed *for cause* (that is, for failing to perform a required duty), either as specified in the articles or bylaws or by shareholder action. Even the board of directors itself may be given power to remove a director for cause, subject to shareholder review. In most states, unless the shareholders have reserved the right at the time of election, a director cannot be removed without cause.

Vacancies can occur on the board of directors because of death or resignation or when a new position is created through amendment of the articles or bylaws. In these situations, either the shareholders or the board itself can fill the position, depending on state law or on the provisions of the bylaws.

Board of Directors' Meetings.   The board of directors conducts business by holding formal meetings with recorded minutes. The date on which regular meetings are held is usually established in the articles or bylaws or by board resolution, and no further notice is customarily required. Special meetings can be called, with notice sent to all directors.

Quorum requirements can vary among jurisdictions. (A **quorum** is the minimum number of members of a body of officials or other group that must be present in order for business to be validly transacted.) Many states leave the decision as to quorum requirements to the corporate articles or bylaws. In the absence of specific state statutes, most states provide that a quorum is a majority of the number of directors authorized in the articles or bylaws. Voting is done in person (unlike voting at shareholders' meetings, which can be done by proxy, as discussed later in this chapter).[4] The rule is one vote per director. Ordinary matters generally require a simple majority vote; certain extraordinary issues may require a greater-than-majority vote.

Rights of Directors.   A director of a corporation has a number of rights, including the rights of participation, inspection, compensation, and indemnification.

Participation and Inspection.   A corporate director must have certain rights to function properly in that position. The main right is one of participation—meaning that the director must be notified of board of directors' meetings so as to participate in them. As pointed out earlier in this chapter, regular board meetings are usually established by the bylaws or by board resolution, and no notice of these meetings is required. If special meetings are called, however, notice is required unless waived by the director.

A director must have access to all of the corporate books and records to make decisions and to exercise the necessary supervision over corporate officers and employees. This right of inspection is virtually absolute and cannot be restricted.

Compensation and Indemnification.   Nominal sums are often paid as honorariums to directors. In many corporations, directors are also chief corporate officers (president or chief executive officer, for example) and receive compensation in their managerial positions. Most directors also gain through indirect benefits, such as business contacts, prestige, and other rewards. There is a trend toward providing more than nominal compensation for directors, especially in large corporations in which directorships can be burdensome in terms of time, work, effort, and risk.

---

4. Except in Louisiana, which allows a director to vote by proxy under certain circumstances. Most states, including California, Delaware, and New York, expressly permit companies to hold board meetings by conference call or similar means, as long as all participants can hear one another. To date, only one state—California—permits a board of directors to conduct meetings via electronic video screens.

Many states permit the corporate articles or bylaws to authorize compensation for directors, and in some cases the board can set its own compensation unless the articles or bylaws provide otherwise.

Corporate directors may become involved in lawsuits by virtue of their positions and their actions as directors. Most states permit a corporation to indemnify (guarantee reimbursement to) a director for legal costs, fees, and judgments involved in defending corporation-related suits. Many states specifically permit a corporation to purchase liability insurance for the directors and officers to cover indemnification. When the statutes are silent on this matter, the authority to purchase such insurance is usually considered to be part of the corporation's implied power.

Directors' Management Responsibilities.   Directors have responsibility for all policymaking decisions necessary to the management of all corporate affairs. Just as shareholders cannot act individually to bind the corporation, the directors must act as a body in carrying out routine corporate business. One director has one vote, and customarily the majority rules. The general areas of responsibility of the board of directors include the following:

1. Authorization for major corporate policy decisions—for example, the initiation of proceedings for the sale or lease of corporate assets outside the regular course of business, the determination of new product lines, and the overseeing of major contract negotiations and major management-labor negotiations.
2. Appointment, supervision, and removal of corporate officers and other managerial employees and determination of their compensation.
3. Financial decisions, such as the declaration and payment of dividends to shareholders and the issuance of authorized shares and bonds.

Most states permit the board of directors to elect an executive committee from among the directors to handle the interim management decisions between board of directors' meetings, as provided in the bylaws. The executive committee is limited to making management decisions about ordinary business matters.

The board of directors can delegate some of its functions to an executive committee or to corporate officers. In doing so, the board is not relieved of its overall responsibility for directing the affairs of the corporation, but corporate officers and managerial personnel are empowered to make decisions relating to ordinary, daily corporate affairs within well-defined guidelines.

ROLE OF CORPORATE OFFICERS AND EXECUTIVES

Officers and other executive employees are hired by the board of directors or, in rare instances, by the shareholders. In addition to carrying out the duties articulated in the bylaws, corporate and managerial officers act as agents of the corporation, and the ordinary rules of agency (discussed in Chapter 20) normally apply to their employment. The qualifications required of officers and executive employees are determined at the discretion of the corporation and are included in the articles or bylaws. In most states, a person can hold more than one office and can be both an officer and a director of the corporation.

The rights of corporate officers and other high-level managers are defined by employment contracts, because these persons are employees of the company. Corporate officers, though, can normally be removed by the board of directors at any time with or without cause and regardless of the terms of the employment contracts—although in so doing, the corporation may be liable for breach of contract. The duties of corporate officers are the same as those of directors, because both groups are involved in decision making and are in similar positions of control. Hence, officers and directors are viewed as having the same fiduciary duties of care and loyalty in their conduct of corporate affairs, a subject to which we now turn.

FIDUCIARY DUTIES OF DIRECTORS AND OFFICERS

Directors and officers are deemed fiduciaries of the corporation, because their relationship with the corporation and its shareholders is one of trust and confidence. As fiduciaries, directors and officers owe ethical—and legal—duties to the corporation and the shareholders. These fiduciary duties include the duty of care and the duty of loyalty.

Duty of Care.   Directors and officers must exercise due care in performing their duties. The standard of *due care* has been variously described in judicial decisions and codified in many corporation codes. Generally, a director or officer is expected to act in good faith, to exercise the care that an ordinarily prudent person would exercise in similar circumstances, and to act in what he or she considers to be the best interests of the corporation. Directors and officers who have not exercised the required duty of care can be held liable for the harms suffered by the corporation as a result of their negligence.

Duty to Make Informed and Reasonable Decisions. Directors and officers are expected to be informed on corporate matters. To be informed, a director or officer must do what is necessary to become informed: attend presentations, ask for information from those who have it, read reports, review other written materials such as contracts—in other words, carefully study a situation and its alternatives. Depending on the nature of the business, directors and officers are often expected to act in accordance with their own knowledge and training. Most states and the RMBCA, however, allow a director to make decisions in reliance on information furnished by competent officers or employees, professionals such as attorneys and accountants, or even an executive committee of the board without being accused of acting in bad faith or failing to exercise due care if such information turns out to be faulty.

Directors are also expected to make reasonable decisions. For example, a director should not accept a tender offer (an offer to purchase shares in the company that is made by another company directly to the shareholders) with only a moment's consideration based solely on the market price of the corporation's shares.

Duty to Exercise Reasonable Supervision. Directors are also expected to exercise a reasonable amount of supervision when they delegate work to corporate officers and employees. For example, suppose that a corporate bank director fails to attend any board of directors' meetings for five years, never inspects any of the corporate books or records, and generally neglects to supervise the efforts of the bank president and the loan committee. Meanwhile, a corporate officer, the bank president, makes various improper loans and permits large overdrafts. In this situation, the corporate director may be held liable to the corporation for losses resulting from the unsupervised actions of the bank president and the loan committee.

Dissenting Directors. Directors are expected to attend board of directors' meetings, and their votes should be entered into the minutes of corporate meetings. Unless a dissent is entered, the director is presumed to have assented. Directors who dissent are rarely held individually liable for mismanagement of the corporation. For this reason, a director who is absent from a given meeting sometimes registers with the secretary of the board a dissent to actions taken at the meeting.

Duty of Loyalty. *Loyalty* can be defined as faithfulness to one's obligations and duties. In the corporate context, the duty of loyalty requires directors and officers to subordinate their personal interests to the welfare of the corporation.

For example, directors may not use corporate funds or confidential corporate information for personal advantage. Similarly, they must refrain from putting their personal interests above those of the corporation. For instance, a director should not oppose a transaction that is in the corporation's best interest simply because its acceptance may cost the director her or his position. Cases dealing with fiduciary duty typically involve one or more of the following:

1. Competing with the corporation.
2. Usurping (taking personal advantage of) a corporate opportunity.
3. Having an interest that conflicts with the interest of the corporation.
4. Engaging in insider trading (using information that is not public to make a profit trading securities, as discussed in Chapter 29).
5. Authorizing a corporate transaction that is detrimental to minority shareholders.
6. Selling control over the corporation.

Conflicts of Interest. Corporate directors often have many business affiliations, and a director can sit on the board of more than one corporation. Of course, directors are precluded from entering into or supporting businesses that operate in direct competition with corporations on whose boards they serve. Their fiduciary duty requires them to make a full disclosure of any potential conflicts of interest that might arise in any corporate transaction.

Sometimes a corporation enters into a contract or engages in a transaction in which an officer or director has a personal interest. The director or officer must make a *full disclosure* of that interest and must abstain from voting on the proposed transaction. For example, Ballo Corporation needs office space. Stephan Colson, one of its five directors, owns the building adjoining the corporation's headquarters. He negotiates a lease with Ballo for the space, making a full disclosure to Ballo and the other four board directors. The lease arrangement is fair and reasonable, and it is unanimously approved by the other members of the corporation's board of directors. In such a case, the contract is valid. The rule is one of reason; otherwise, directors would be prevented from ever giving financial assistance to the corporations they serve.

State statutes contain different standards, but a contract will generally not be voidable if it was fair and reasonable to the corporation at the time it was made, if there was a full disclosure of the interest of the officers or directors involved in the transaction, and if the contract was approved by a majority of the disinterested directors or shareholders.

Often, contracts are negotiated between corporations having one or more directors who are members of both boards. Such transactions require great care, as they are closely scrutinized by the courts. (As will be discussed in Chapter 28, in certain circumstances—if two large corporations are competing with each other, for example—it may constitute a violation of antitrust laws for a director to sit on the boards of both companies.)

LIABILITY OF DIRECTORS AND OFFICERS

Directors and officers are exposed to liability on many fronts. Corporate directors and officers may be held liable for the crimes and torts committed by themselves or by corporate employees under their supervision. Additionally, shareholders may perceive that the corporate directors are not acting in the best interests of the corporation and may sue the directors, in what is called a *shareholder's derivative suit*, on behalf of the corporation. (This type of action is discussed later in this chapter, in the context of shareholders' rights.) Directors and officers are expected to exercise due care and to use their best judgment in guiding corporate management; if they do not, they may be held liable to the corporation for any resulting damages.

Under the so-called **business judgment rule,** however, a corporate director or officer may be able to avoid liability to the corporation or to its shareholders for exercising poor business judgment. After all, directors and officers are not insurers of business success, and honest mistakes of judgment and poor business decisions on their part do not automatically make them liable to the corporation. The business judgment rule generally immunizes directors and officers from liability for the consequences of a decision that is within managerial authority, as long as the decision complies with management's fiduciary duties and as long as acting on the decision is within the powers of the corporation. Consequently, if there is a reasonable basis for a business decision, it is unlikely that the court will interfere with that decision, even if the corporation suffers as a result.

To benefit from the rule, directors and officers must act in good faith, in what they consider to be the best interests of the corporation, and with the care that an ordinarily prudent person in a similar position would exercise in like circumstances. This requires an informed decision, with a rational basis, and with no conflict between the decision maker's personal interest and the interest of the corporation.

At issue in the following case was whether the business judgment rule immunizes directors from liability for purely negligent acts.

CASE 19.3   Federal Deposit Insurance Corp. v. Castetter

United States
Court of Appeals,
Ninth Circuit, 1999.
184 F.3d 1040.
http://www.ce9.
uscourts.gov[a]

BACKGROUND AND FACTS   *Edward Peterson, a banker with twenty-six years of experience, opened Balboa National Bank in California in February 1983. Peterson was president, chief executive officer, and a member of the board of directors. None of the other directors, including Robert Castetter, had any significant banking experience. Peterson decided that the bank would focus on lending money to auto buyers. Frances Cragen, an experienced, high-level employee in Bank of America's auto loan department, came to work for Balboa. Peterson died unexpectedly in May 1984. The federal Office of the Comptroller of the Currency (OCC) examined the bank and found many problems. The board hired a new president and told him to implement better procedures for lending and collecting. The board also hired outside consultants for advice. In December, the directors fired Cragen and hired a national accounting firm to look more closely at the bank's lending practices. Problems continued, however, and the accounting firm's*

---

a. In the "Info Links" column, click on the "Appeals Court Decisions" icon. On that page, click on "1999" to open the menu. Click on "July" and scroll down the list to the name of the case (released "07/21/99") and click on it to access the opinion.

reports were found to be invalid. In 1987, the OCC found the board's supervision to be "inexcusable" and the bank's condition to be critical. Meanwhile, directors personally contributed over $2.8 million to the bank in an attempt to save it. In 1988, the OCC ordered the bank to close. The Federal Deposit Insurance Corporation (FDIC)[b] filed a suit in a federal district court against Castetter and the other directors, contending that they were negligent and personally liable for the bank's losses. The court applied California's business judgment rule in favor of the directors. The FDIC appealed to the U.S. Court of Appeals for the Ninth Circuit.

IN THE LANGUAGE OF THE COURT

THOMAS, Circuit Judge.

*   *   *   *

*   *   * The California business judgment rule is intended to protect a director from liability for a mistake in business judgment which is made in good faith and in what he or she believes to be the best interest of the corporation, where no conflict of interest exists. It requires directors to act in good faith and with the prudence that an ordinary person would under like circumstances. However, it also entitles a director to rely on information supplied by others. *If directors meet the requirements of the business judgment rule, they are entitled to immunity from personal liability for acts of ordinary negligence* under California law. [Emphasis added.]

*   *   *   *

*   *   * Under California law, a *prima facie* showing of good faith and reasonable investigation is established when a majority of the board is comprised of outside directors and the board has received the advice of independent consultants.

*   *   *   *

Here, the defendant directors established a *prima facie* showing of a reasonable investigation. A majority of the board consisted of outside directors and it is undisputed that the board sought and obtained the advice of a number of outside expert consultants.

*   *   *   *

This is not to say that directors of California corporations may immunize themselves simply by acquiring information. It is clear that the rule does not protect a director in certain situations, such as where there is a conflict of interest, fraud, oppression, or corruption. Neither does the business judgment rule protect a director who has wholly abdicated his corporate responsibility, closing his or her eyes to corporate affairs. But the rule does protect well-meaning directors who are misinformed, misguided, and honestly mistaken. *   *   *

*   *   *   *

In this case, there is no dispute that the directors acted in good faith and with the belief that their actions were in the best interests of the corporation. The directors were initially misguided by the analysis of former President Peterson, who had over a quarter century of experience as a bank regulator. They were further misguided by an analysis of a national accounting firm. They attempted to follow the advice of several consultants, and invested—and lost—substantial sums of their own money. Despite these efforts, they were unable to avert the bank's collapse. The undisputed record indicates that the directors were entitled to the protection of the business judgment rule.

DECISION AND REMEDY

The U.S. Court of Appeals for the Ninth Circuit affirmed the judgment of the lower court. The business judgment rule insulated the bank's directors from individual liability for the bank's losses.

---

b. The Federal Deposit Insurance Corporation is a federal agency that insures, up to $100,000, the deposits in banks and savings associations.

THE ROLE OF SHAREHOLDERS

The acquisition of a share of stock makes a person an owner and shareholder in a corporation. Shareholders thus own the corporation. Although they have no legal title to corporate property vested in the corporation, such as buildings and equipment, they do have an *equitable* (ownership) interest in the firm.

As a general rule, shareholders have no responsibility for the daily management of the corporation, although they are ultimately responsible for choosing the board of directors, which does have such control. Ordinarily, corporate officers and other employees owe no direct duty to individual stockholders. Their duty is to the corporation as a whole. A director, however, is in a fiduciary relationship to the corporation and therefore serves the interests of the shareholders in general. Ordinarily, there is no legal relationship between shareholders and creditors of the corporation. Shareholders can, in fact, be creditors of the corporation and have the same rights of recovery against the corporation as any other creditor.

In this section, we look at the powers, rights, and liabilities of shareholders, which may be established in the articles of incorporation and under the state's general incorporation law.

Shareholders' Powers. Shareholders must approve fundamental changes affecting the corporation before the changes can be implemented. Hence, shareholders are empowered to amend the articles of incorporation (charter) and bylaws, approve a merger or the dissolution of the corporation, and approve the sale of all or substantially all of the corporation's assets. Some of these powers are subject to prior board approval.

Election and removal of the board of directors are accomplished by a vote of the shareholders. The first board of directors is either named in the articles of incorporation or chosen by the incorporators to serve until the first shareholders' meeting. From that time on, selection and retention of directors are exclusively shareholder functions.

Directors usually serve their full terms; if they are not satisfactory, they are simply not reelected. Shareholders have the inherent power, however, to remove a director from office *for cause* (breach of duty or misconduct) by a majority vote.[5] Some state statutes even permit removal of directors without

cause by the vote of a majority of the holders of outstanding shares entitled to vote.[6] Some corporate charters also expressly provide that shareholders, by majority vote, can remove a director at any time without cause.

Shareholders' Meetings. Shareholders' meetings must occur at least annually, and in addition, special meetings can be called to take care of urgent matters. Shareholders are notified of the date and hour of a shareholders' meeting in a written announcement that is sent a reasonable length of time prior to the date of the meeting.[7] Notices of special meetings must include a statement of the purpose of the meeting; business transacted at a special meeting is limited to that purpose.

Shareholder Voting. Shareholders exercise ownership control through the power of their votes.

Quorum Requirements. For shareholders to act during a meeting, a quorum must be present. Generally, this condition is met when shareholders holding more than 50 percent of the outstanding shares are present. Corporate business matters are presented in the form of resolutions, which shareholders vote to approve or disapprove. If a state statute sets forth specific voting requirements, the corporation's articles or bylaws must be consistent with these statutory limitations. Some states provide that obtaining the unanimous written consent of shareholders is a permissible alternative to holding a shareholders' meeting.

Once a quorum is present, voting can proceed. A majority vote of the shares represented at the meeting is usually required to pass resolutions. Assume that Novo Pictures, Inc., has 10,000 outstanding shares of voting stock. Its articles of incorporation set the quorum at more than 50 percent of outstanding shares

---

5. A director can often demand court review of removal for cause.

6. Most states allow *cumulative voting* (which will be discussed shortly) for directors. If cumulative voting is authorized, a director may not be removed if the number of votes sufficient to elect him or her under cumulative voting is voted against his or her removal. See, for example, California Corporate Code Section 303A.

7. The shareholder can waive the requirement of written notice by signing a waiver form. A shareholder who does not receive written notice but who learns of the meeting and attends without protesting the lack of notice is said to have waived notice by such conduct. State statutes and corporate bylaws typically set forth the time within which notice must be sent, what methods can be used, and what the notice must contain.

and provide that a majority vote of the shares present is necessary to pass on ordinary matters. Therefore, for this firm, at the shareholders' meeting, a quorum of stockholders representing 5,000 outstanding shares must be present to conduct business, and a vote of at least 2,501 of those shares is needed to pass ordinary resolutions. If 6,000 shares are represented, a vote of 3,001 will be necessary, and so on.

At times, more than a simple majority vote will be required either by statute or by corporate charter. Extraordinary corporate matters, such as a merger, a consolidation, or the dissolution of the corporation, require approval by a higher percentage of the representatives of all corporate shares entitled to vote, not just a majority of those present at that particular meeting.

Voting Lists. A voting list is prepared by the corporation prior to each shareholders' meeting. Persons whose names appear on the corporation's stockholder records as owners are the ones ordinarily entitled to vote.[8] The voting list contains the name and address of each shareholder as shown on the corporate records on a given cutoff date, or record date. (The record date may be as much as seventy days before the meeting.) The voting list also includes the number of voting shares held by each owner. The list is usually kept at the corporate headquarters and is available for shareholder inspection.

Cumulative Voting. Most states permit or require shareholders to elect directors by *cumulative voting,* a method of voting designed to allow minority shareholders representation on the board of directors.[9] When cumulative voting is allowed or required, the number of members of the board to be elected is multiplied by the total number of voting shares. The result equals the number of votes a shareholder has, and this total can be cast for one or more nominees for director. All nominees stand for election at the same time. When cumulative voting is not required either by statute or under the articles, the entire board can be elected by a majority of shares at a shareholders' meeting.

Suppose, for example, that a corporation has 10,000 shares issued and outstanding. The minority shareholders hold only 3,000 shares, and the majority shareholders hold the other 7,000 shares. Three members of the board are to be elected. The majority shareholders' nominees are Alomon, Beasley, and Caravel. The minority shareholders' nominee is Dovrik. Can Dovrik be elected to the board by the minority shareholders?

If cumulative voting is allowed, the answer is yes. The minority shareholders have 9,000 votes among them (the number of directors to be elected times the number of shares equals 3 times 3,000, which equals 9,000 votes). All of these votes can be cast to elect Dovrik. The majority shareholders have 21,000 votes (3 times 7,000 equals 21,000 votes), but these votes have to be distributed among their three nominees. The principle of cumulative voting is that no matter how the majority shareholders cast their 21,000 votes, they will not be able to elect all three directors if the minority shareholders cast all of their 9,000 votes for Dovrik, as illustrated in Exhibit 19–1.

Other Voting Techniques. A group of shareholders can agree in writing prior to a shareholders' meeting, in a *shareholder voting agreement,* to vote their shares together in a specified manner. Such agreements usually are held to be valid and enforceable. A shareholder can also appoint a voting agent and vote by proxy. A **proxy** is a written authorization to cast the shareholder's vote, and a person can solicit proxies from a number of shareholders in an attempt to concentrate voting power.

Another technique is for shareholders to enter into a **voting trust,** which is an agreement (a trust contract) under which legal title (recorded ownership on the corporate books) is transferred to a trustee who is responsible for voting the shares. The agreement can specify how the trustee is to vote, or it can allow the trustee to use his or her discretion. The trustee takes physical possession of the stock certificate and in return gives the shareholder a *voting trust certificate.* The shareholder retains all of the rights of ownership (for example, the right to receive dividend payments) except for the power to vote the shares.

RIGHTS OF SHAREHOLDERS

Shareholders possess numerous rights. A significant right—the right to vote their shares—has already been discussed. In addition to voting rights, a share-

---

8. When the legal owner is deceased, bankrupt, incompetent, or in some other way under a legal disability, his or her vote can be cast by a person designated by law to control and manage the owner's property.

9. See, for example, California Corporate Code Section 708. Under the RMBCA, however, no cumulative voting rights exist unless the articles of incorporation so provide.

EXHIBIT 19–1   RESULTS OF CUMULATIVE VOTING

BALLOT	MAJORITY SHAREHOLDER VOTES			MINORITY SHAREHOLDER VOTES	DIRECTORS ELECTED
	Alomon	*Beasley*	*Caravel*	*Dovrik*	
1	10,000	10,000	1,000	9,000	Alomon, Beasley, Dovrik
2	9,001	9,000	2,999	9,000	Alomon, Beasley, Dovrik
3	6,000	7,000	8,000	9,000	Beasley, Caravel, Dovrik

holder has the rights, based on ownership of stock, to receive stock certificates (depending on the jurisdiction), to purchase newly issued stock, to receive dividends, to inspect corporate records, to transfer shares (with some exceptions), to receive a proportionate share of corporate assets on corporate dissolution, and to file suit on behalf of the corporation. These rights are discussed in the following subsections.

Stock Certificates.   A **stock certificate** is a certificate issued by a corporation that evidences ownership of a specified number of shares in the corporation. In jurisdictions that require the issuance of stock certificates, shareholders have the right to demand that the corporation issue certificates and record their names and addresses in the corporate stock record books. In most states, boards of directors may provide that shares of stock be uncertificated (that is, that no actual, physical stock certificates need be issued). In that circumstance, the corporation may be required to send the holders of uncertificated shares letters or some other form of notice containing the same information required to be included on the face of stock certificates.

Stock is intangible personal property, and the ownership right exists independently of the certificate itself. A stock certificate may be lost or destroyed, but ownership is not destroyed with it. A new certificate can be issued to replace one that has been lost or destroyed.[10] Notice of shareholders' meetings, dividends, and operational and financial reports are all distributed according to the recorded ownership listed in the corporation's books, not on the basis of possession of the certificate.

Preemptive Rights.   A **preemptive right** is a common law concept under which a preference is given to a shareholder over all other purchasers to subscribe to or purchase a prorated share of a new issue of stock. This right does not apply to **treasury shares**—shares that are authorized but that have not been issued. This allows the shareholder to maintain his or her portion of control, voting power, or financial interest in the corporation. Most statutes either (1) grant preemptive rights but allow them to be negated in the corporation's articles or (2) deny preemptive rights except to the extent that they are granted in the articles. The result is that the articles of incorporation determine the existence and scope of preemptive rights. Generally, preemptive rights apply only to additional, newly issued stock sold for cash and must be exercised within a specified time period (such as thirty days).

For example, Tron Corporation authorizes and issues 1,000 shares of stock, and Omar Loren purchases 100 shares, making him the owner of 10 percent of the company's stock. Subsequently, Tron, by vote of its shareholders, authorizes the issuance of another 1,000 shares (amending the articles of incorporation). This increases its capital stock to a total of 2,000 shares. If preemptive rights have been provided, Loren can purchase one additional share of the new stock being issued for each share currently owned—or 100 additional shares. Thus, he can own 200 of the 2,000 shares outstanding, and his relative position as a shareholder will be maintained. If preemptive rights are not reserved, his proportionate control and voting power will be diluted from that of a 10 percent shareholder to that of a 5 percent shareholder because of the issuance of the additional 1,000 shares.

Preemptive rights can be very important for shareholders in close corporations. This is because of the relatively small number of shares and the substantial interest that each shareholder controls in a close corporation. Without preemptive rights, it would be pos-

---

10. For a lost or destroyed certificate to be reissued, a shareholder normally must furnish an indemnity bond (a guaranty of payment) to protect the corporation against potential loss should the original certificate reappear at some future time in the hands of a bona fide purchaser [UCC 8–302, 8–405(2)].

sible for a shareholder to lose his or her proportionate control over the firm.

Stock Warrants. Usually, when preemptive rights exist and a corporation is issuing additional shares, each shareholder is given **stock warrants,** which are transferable options to acquire a given number of shares from the corporation at a stated price. Warrants are often publicly traded on securities exchanges. When the warrant option is for a short period of time, the stock warrants are usually referred to as *rights.*

Dividends. A **dividend** is a distribution of corporate profits or income *ordered by the directors* and paid to the shareholders in proportion to their respective shares in the corporation. Dividends can be paid in cash, property, stock of the corporation that is paying the dividends, or stock of other corporations.[11]

State laws vary, but every state determines the general circumstances and legal requirements under which dividends are paid. State laws also control the sources of revenue to be used; only certain funds are legally available for paying dividends. Once declared, a cash dividend becomes a corporate debt enforceable at law like any other debt. Depending on state law, dividends may be paid from the following sources:

1. *Retained earnings.* All state statutes allow dividends to be paid from the undistributed net profits earned by the corporation, including capital gains from the sale of fixed assets. The undistributed net profits are called retained earnings.
2. *Net profits.* A few state statutes allow dividends to be issued from current net profits without regard to deficits in prior years.
3. *Surplus.* A number of state statutes allow dividends to be paid out of any kind of surplus.

Illegal Dividends. Sometimes dividends are improperly paid from an unauthorized account, or their payment causes the corporation to become insolvent. Generally, in such cases, shareholders must return illegal dividends only if they knew that the dividends were illegal when they received them. A dividend paid while the corporation is insolvent is automatically an illegal dividend, and shareholders may be liable for returning the payment to the corporation or its creditors. In all cases of illegal and improper dividends, the board of directors can be held personally liable for the amount of the payment. When directors can show that a shareholder knew a dividend was illegal when it was received, however, the directors are entitled to reimbursement from the shareholder.

Directors' Failure to Declare a Dividend. When directors fail to declare a dividend, shareholders can ask a court of equity for an injunction to compel the directors to meet and to declare a dividend. For the injunction to be granted, it must be shown that the directors have acted so unreasonably in withholding the dividend that their conduct is an abuse of their discretion.

Often, large money reserves are accumulated for a bona fide purpose, such as expansion, research, or some other legitimate corporate use. The mere fact that sufficient corporate earnings or surplus is available to pay a dividend is not enough to compel directors to distribute funds that, in the board's opinion, should not be distributed.[12] The courts are hesitant to interfere with corporate operations and will not compel directors to declare dividends unless abuse of discretion is clearly shown.

Inspection Rights. Shareholders in a corporation enjoy both common law and statutory inspection rights. The shareholder's right of inspection is limited, however, to the inspection and copying of corporate books and records for a *proper purpose,* provided the request is made in advance. Either the shareholder can inspect in person, or an attorney, accountant, or other type of assistant can do so as the shareholder's agent. The RMBCA requires the corporation to maintain an alphabetical voting list of shareholders with addresses and number of shares owned; this list must be kept open at the annual meeting for inspection by any shareholder of record.

The power of inspection is fraught with potential abuses, and the corporation is allowed to protect itself from them. For example, a shareholder can properly be denied access to corporate records to prevent harassment or to protect trade secrets or other confidential corporate information. Some states require

---

11. Technically, dividends paid in stock are not dividends. They maintain each shareholder's proportional interest in the corporation. On one occasion, a distillery declared and paid a "dividend" in bonded whiskey.

12. A striking exception to this rule was made in *Dodge v. Ford Motor Co.,* 204 Mich. 459, 170 N.W. 668 (1919), when Henry Ford, the president and major stockholder of Ford Motor Company, refused to declare a dividend notwithstanding the firm's large capital surplus. The court, holding that Ford had abused his discretion, ordered the company to declare a dividend.

that a shareholder must have held his or her shares for a minimum period of time immediately preceding the demand to inspect or must hold a minimum number of outstanding shares. The RMBCA provides that every shareholder is entitled to examine specified corporate records. A shareholder who is denied the right of inspection can seek a court order to compel the inspection.

Transfer of Shares. Corporate stock represents an ownership right in intangible personal property. The law generally recognizes the right of an owner to transfer property to another person unless there are valid restrictions on its transferability. Although stock certificates are negotiable and freely transferable by indorsement and delivery, transfer of stock in closely held corporations is generally restricted by the bylaws, by a restriction stamped on the stock certificate, or by a shareholder agreement. The existence of any restrictions on transferability must always be noted on the face of the stock certificate, and these restrictions must be reasonable.

Sometimes, corporations or their shareholders restrict transferability by reserving the option to purchase any shares offered for resale by a shareholder. This **right of first refusal** remains with the corporation or the shareholders for only a specified time or a reasonable period of time. Variations on the purchase option are possible. For example, a shareholder might be required to offer the shares to other shareholders or to the corporation first.

When shares are transferred, a new entry is made in the corporate stock book to indicate the new owner. Until the corporation is notified and the entry is complete, voting rights, notice of shareholders' meetings, dividend distribution, and so forth are all held by the current record owner.

Rights on Dissolution. When a corporation is dissolved and its outstanding debts and the claims of its creditors have been satisfied, the remaining assets are distributed on a pro rata basis among the shareholders. If no preferences in distribution of assets on liquidation are given to any class of stock, then all of the stockholders share the remaining assets.

Shareholders also have the right to petition the court to dissolve the corporation. Suppose that a minority shareholder knows that the board of directors is mishandling corporate assets or is permitting a deadlock to threaten or irreparably injure the corporation's finances. The minority shareholder is not powerless

to intervene. He or she can petition a court to appoint a receiver and to liquidate the business assets of the corporation.

The RMBCA permits any shareholder to initiate such an action in any of the following circumstances:

1. The directors are deadlocked in the management of corporate affairs, shareholders are unable to break that deadlock, and irreparable injury to the corporation is being suffered or threatened.
2. The acts of the directors or those in control of the corporation are illegal, oppressive, or fraudulent.
3. Corporate assets are being misapplied or wasted.
4. The shareholders are deadlocked in voting power and have failed, for a specified period (usually two annual meetings), to elect successors to directors whose terms have expired or would have expired with the election of successors.

Shareholder's Derivative Suits. When those in control of a corporation—the corporate directors—fail to sue in the corporate name to redress a wrong suffered by the corporation, shareholders are permitted to do so "derivatively" in what is known as a shareholder's derivative suit. Some wrong must have been done to the corporation, and before a derivative suit can be brought, the shareholders must first state their complaint to the board of directors. Only if the directors fail to solve the problem or to take appropriate action can the derivative suit go forward.

The right of shareholders to bring a derivative action is especially important when the wrong suffered by the corporation results from the actions of corporate directors. This is because the directors and officers would probably be unwilling to take any action against themselves.

The shareholder's derivative suit is singular in that those suing are not pursuing rights or benefits for themselves personally but are acting as guardians of the corporate entity. Therefore, any damages recovered by the suit normally go into the corporation's treasury, not to the shareholders personally.

LIABILITY OF SHAREHOLDERS

One of the hallmarks of the corporate organization is that shareholders are not personally liable for the debts of the corporation. If the corporation fails, shareholders can lose their investments, but that is generally the limit of their liability. In certain instances of fraud, undercapitalization, or careless observance of corporate formalities, a court will pierce the corporate veil (disregard the corporate entity) and hold the shareholders individually liable. But these situations are the exception, not the rule.

Although rare, there are certain other instances in which a shareholder can be personally liable. One relates to illegal dividends, which were discussed previously. Two others relate to *stock subscriptions* and *watered stock.*

Stock-Subscription Agreements.   Sometimes, stock-subscription agreements—written contracts by which one agrees to buy capital stock of a corporation—exist prior to incorporation. Normally, these agreements are treated as continuing offers and are irrevocable (for up to six months under the RMBCA). Once the corporation has been formed, it can sell shares to investors. In either case, once the subscription agreement or stock offer is accepted, a binding contract is formed. Any refusal to pay constitutes a breach resulting in the personal liability of the shareholder.

Watered Stock.   Shares of stock can be paid for with property or services rendered instead of cash. (Shares cannot be purchased with promissory notes, however.) The general rule is that for **par-value shares** (that is, shares that have a specific face value, or formal cash-in value, written on them, such as one penny or one dollar), the corporation must receive a value at least equal to the par-value amount. For **no-par shares** (that is, shares without a par value), the corporation must receive the value of the shares as determined by the board or the shareholders.

For either par-value or no-par shares, the setting of the value is based on the same factors: tax rates, whether the corporation needs capital surplus, and what the corporation will receive for the shares (money, property, or services). When shares are issued by the corporation for less than these stated values, the shares are referred to as **watered stock.**[13] In most cases, the shareholder who receives watered stock must pay the difference to the corporation (the shareholder is personally liable). In some states, the shareholder who receives watered stock may be liable to creditors of the corporation for unpaid corporate debts.

To illustrate the concept of watered stock: Suppose that during the formation of a corporation, Gomez, as one of the incorporators, transfers his property, Sunset Beach, to the corporation for 10,000 shares of stock at a par value of $100 per share for a total price of $1 million. After the property is transferred and the shares are issued, Sunset Beach is carried on the corporate books at a value of $1 million. On appraisal, it is discovered that the market value of the property at the time of transfer was only $500,000. The shares issued to Gomez are therefore watered stock, and he is liable to the corporation for the difference between the value of the shares and the value of the property.

DUTIES OF MAJORITY SHAREHOLDERS

In some cases, a majority shareholder is regarded as having a fiduciary duty to the corporation and to the minority shareholders. This occurs when a single shareholder (or a few shareholders acting in concert) owns a sufficient number of shares to exercise *de facto* (actual) control over the corporation. In these situations, majority shareholders owe a fiduciary duty to minority shareholders.

Consider an example. Three brothers, Alfred, Carl, and Eugene, each own a one-third interest in a corporation and had worked for the corporation for most of their adult lives. When a dispute arose concerning discrepancies in the corporation's accounting records, Carl and Eugene fired Alfred and told the company's employees that Alfred had had a nervous breakdown, which was not true. Alfred sued Carl and Eugene, alleging, among other things, that they had breached their fiduciary duties. The brothers argued that because there was no diminution in the value of the corporation or the value of Alfred's shares in the company, they had not breached their fiduciary duties. The court, however, held that the brothers' conduct, which was unfairly prejudicial toward Alfred, supported a finding of breach of fiduciary duty.[14]

---

13. The phrase *watered stock* was originally used to describe cattle that—kept thirsty during a long drive—were allowed to drink large quantities of water just prior to their sale. The increased weight of the "watered stock" allowed the seller to reap a higher profit.

14. *Pedro v. Pedro*, 489 N.W.2d 798 (Minn.App. 1992).

TERMS AND CONCEPTS TO REVIEW

business judgment rule 413	preemptive rights 417	stock certificate 417
close corporation 401	proxy 416	stock warrant 418
corporation 400	quorum 410	treasury share 417
dividend 418	retained earnings 401	voting trust 416
no-par share 420	right of first refusal 419	watered stock 420
par-value share 420	S corporation 403	

QUESTIONS AND CASE PROBLEMS

19–1. NATURE OF CORPORATIONS. Jonathan, Gary, and Rob are active members of a partnership called Swim City. The partnership manufactures, sells, and installs outdoor swimming pools in the states of Texas and Arkansas. The partners want to continue to be active in management and to expand the business into other states as well. They are concerned about rather large recent judgments entered against swimming pool companies throughout the United States. Based on these facts only, discuss whether the partnership should incorporate.

19–2. CORPORATE STATUS. Three brothers inherited a small paper-supply business from their father, who had operated the business as a sole proprietorship. The brothers decided to incorporate under the name of Miwa Corp. and retained an attorney to draw up the necessary documents. The attorney drew up the papers and had the brothers sign them but neglected to send the application for a corporate charter to the secretary of state's office. The brothers assumed that all necessary legal work had been taken care of, and they proceeded to do business as Miwa Corp. One day, a Miwa Corp. employee was delivering a carton of paper supplies to one of Miwa's customers. On the way to the customer's office, the employee negligently ran a red light and caused a car accident. Harman, the driver of the other vehicle, was injured as a result and sued Miwa Corp. for damages. Harman then learned that no state charter had ever been issued to Miwa Corp., so he sued each of the brothers personally for damages. Can the brothers avoid personal liability for the tort of their employee? Explain.

19–3. DUTIES OF DIRECTORS. Otts Corp. is negotiating with the Wick Construction Co. for the renovation of the Otts corporate headquarters. Wick, owner of the Wick Construction Co., is also one of the five members of the board of directors of Otts. The contract terms are standard for this type of contract. Wick has previously informed two of the other directors of his interest in the construction company. The contract is approved by Otts's board on a three-to-two vote, with Wick voting with the majority. Discuss whether this contract is binding on the corporation.

19–4. RIGHTS OF SHAREHOLDERS. Lucia has acquired one share of common stock of a multimillion-dollar corporation with over 500,000 shareholders. Lucia wants to know whether this one share entitles her to (1) attend and vote at shareholders' meetings, (2) inspect the corporate books, and (3) receive yearly dividends. Discuss Lucia's rights in these three matters.

19–5. LIABILITY OF SHAREHOLDERS. Moseley Group Management Co. (MGM) provided management services to apartment complexes. MGM's only assets were equipment worth $500 and a bank account with an average balance of $1,500. Richard Moseley ran the company and owned half of the stock. MGM contracted with Property Tax Research Co. (PTR) to obtain a lower property tax assessment on one of its complexes. PTR performed, but MGM refused to pay and transferred its assets and employees to Terrace Management, Inc., a corporation controlled by Moseley. PTR filed a suit in a Missouri state court against Moseley and others to recover the unpaid fees. Should the court pierce the corporate veil and hold Moseley personally liable for the debt? If so, on what basis? [*Sansone v. Moseley,* 912 S.W.2d 666 (Mo.App.W.D. 1995)]

19–6. DUTY OF LOYALTY. Mackinac Cellular Corp. offered to sell Robert Broz a license to operate a cellular phone system in Michigan. Broz was a director of Cellular Information Systems, Inc. (CIS). CIS, as a result of bankruptcy proceedings, was in the process of selling its cellular holdings. Broz did not formally present the opportunity to the CIS board, but he told some of the firm's officers and directors, who replied that CIS was not interested. At the time, PriCellular, Inc., a firm that wanted the Michigan license, was attempting to buy CIS. Without telling PriCellular, Broz bought the license himself. After PriCellular took over CIS, the company sued Broz, alleging that he had usurped a corporate opportunity. Has Broz done anything wrong? Discuss. [*Broz v. Cellular Information Systems, Inc.*, 673 A.2d 148 (Del. 1996)]

19–7. CORPORATE STATUS. Cecil Hill was in the construction trade. He did business as "C&M Builders, Inc.," although there was no such corporation. County Concrete Co. supplied "C&M Builders, Inc." with over $50,000 worth of concrete for which it was not paid. The supplier filed a suit in a Maryland state court against Hill personally. Hill argued that because the supplier thought it was doing business with a corporate entity, C&M was a *de facto* corporation, and thus Hill was not personally liable. Should Hill be allowed to avoid liability on this basis? Why or why not? [*Hill v. County Concrete Co.*, 108 Md.App. 527, 672 A.2d 667 (1996)]

19–8. S CORPORATIONS. James, Randolph, and Judith Agley, and Michael and Nancy Timmis were shareholders in F & M Distributors, Inc., Venture Packaging, Inc., and Diamond Automations, Inc. James Agley was also a shareholder in Middletown Aerospace. All of the firms were S corporations organized and located in Michigan and doing business in Ohio. None of the shareholders was a resident of Ohio, and none of them personally did business in Ohio. Between 1988 and 1992, the Agleys and the Timmises included their prorated share of the S corporations' income on Ohio personal income tax returns. They believed, however, that an out-of-state shareholder should not be taxed in Ohio on the income that he or she receives from an S corporation doing business in Ohio. They contended it is the S corporation that earns the income, not the shareholder. They also emphasized that none of them personally did business in the state. Finally, they asked the Ohio Tax Commissioner for refunds for those years. Should the state grant their request? Why or why not? [*Agley v. Tracy*, 87 Ohio St.3d 265, 719 N.E.2d 951 (1999)]

19–9. BUSINESS JUDGMENT RULE. Charles Pace and Maria Fuentez were shareholders of Houston Industries, Inc. (HII), and employees of Houston Lighting & Power, a subsidiary of HII, when they lost their jobs because of a company-wide reduction in its work force. Pace, as a shareholder, three times wrote to HII, demanding that the board of directors terminate certain HII directors and officers, and file a suit to recover damages for breach of fiduciary duty. Three times, the directors referred the charges to board committees and an outside law firm, which found that the facts did not support the charges. The board also received input from federal regulatory authorities about the facts behind some of the charges. The board notified Pace that it would refuse his demands. In response, Pace and Fuentez filed a shareholder's derivative suit against Don Jordan and the other HII directors, contending that the board's investigation was inadequate. The defendants moved for summary judgment, arguing that the suit was barred by the business judgment rule. How should the court rule? Why? [*Pace v. Jordan*, 999 S.W.2d 615 (Tex.App.—Houston [1 Dist.] 1999)]

19–10. IN YOUR COURT

 Jim Halter, the sole shareholder of J-Mart Jewelry Outlets, Inc., knew that as a result of financial difficulties, J-Mart would soon go out of business. Eight days before the firm stopped doing business, it paid the balance due on Halter's personal credit card. At the same time, Halter paid J-Mart $1 for a Cadillac that the firm had bought new for his personal use and on which it had made three payments. Four of J-Mart's creditors, including Standard Design, sued Halter to recover for J-Mart's unpaid debts. Assume that you are the judge in the trial court hearing this case and answer the following questions:

(a) Should you "pierce the corporate veil" and hold Halter personally liable to J-Mart's creditors in this case? Explain your reasoning.

(b) Compare this case to Case 19.2 (*Hoskins Chevrolet, Inc. v. Hochberg*). Why did the court in that case hold Hochberg personally liable for ostensibly corporate obligations? Does the court's ruling in that case shed any light on the issue in the case before your court? Why or why not?

LAW ON THE WEB

For updated links to resources available on the Web, as well as a variety of other materials, visit this text's Web site at http://wleb.westbuslaw.com.

One of the best sources on the Web for information on corporations, including their directors, is the EDGAR database of the Securities and Exchange Commission (SEC) at

http://www.sec.gov/edgarhp.htm

Cornell University's Legal Information Institute has links to state corporation statutes at

http://fatty.law.cornell.edu/topics/state_statutes.html

LEGAL RESEARCH EXERCISES ON THE WEB

Go to http://wleb.westbuslaw.com, the Web site that accompanies this text. Select "Internet Applications," and then click on "Chapter 19." There you will find the following Internet research exercise that you can perform to learn more about the liability of corporate directors and officers:

Activity 19–1: Corporate Law

Activity 19–2: Liability of Directors and Officers

UNIT THREE—CUMULATIVE HYPOTHETICAL PROBLEM

Samuel Polson has an idea for a new software application. Polson hires an assistant and invests a considerable amount of his own time and money developing the application. To develop other software, and to manufacture and market his applications, Polson needs capital.

1. Polson borrows $5,000 from his friend, Michael Brant. Polson promises to repay Brant the $5,000 in three weeks. Brant, in urgent need of money, borrows $5,000 from his friend Mary Viva and assigns his rights to the $5,000 Polson owes him to Viva in return for the loan. Viva notifies Polson of the assignment. Polson pays Brant the $5,000 on the date stipulated in their contract. Brant refuses to give the money to Viva, and Viva sues Polson. Is Polson obligated to pay Viva $5,000 also? Discuss.

2. Polson learns that a competitor, Trivan, Inc., has already filed for a patent on a nearly identical program and has manufactured and sold the software to some customers. Polson learns from a reliable source that Trivan paid Polson's assistant a substantial sum of money to obtain a copy of the program. What legal recourse does Polson have against Trivan? Discuss fully.

3. While Polson is developing his idea and founding his business, he has no income. He continues to have living expenses, however, as well as payments due on his mortgage, various credit-card debts, and some loans that he took out to pay for his son's college tuition. As his business begins to make money, Polson files for Chapter 7 liquidation to be rid of his personal debts entirely, even though he believes that he could probably pay them off over a four-year period if he scrimped and used every cent available to pay his creditors. Are all of Polson's personal debts dischargeable under Chapter 7, including the debts incurred for his son's education? Given the fact that Polson could foreseeably pay off his debts over a four-year period, will the court allow Polson to obtain relief under Chapter 7? Why or why not?

4. Polson is the sole owner of the business and pays no business income taxes. What is the form of Polson's business organization? What other options, in terms of business organizational forms, does Polson have? What are the advantages and disadvantages of each option? If Polson decides to incorporate the business under the name Polson Software, Inc., what steps will he need to take to do so?

FOCUS ON LEGAL REASONING
Demasse v. ITT Corp.

INTRODUCTION

In Chapter 9, we discussed the contract law requirement of consideration. In this *Focus on Legal Reasoning*, we examine *Demasse v. ITT Corp.*,[1] a decision involving the application of the elements of consideration in the context of an employment contract and the newest edition of an employee handbook.

CASE BACKGROUND

ITT Cannon (a division of ITT Industries, Inc.) is based in Phoenix, Arizona. ITT issued five editions of its employee handbook, the most recent in 1989. All of the editions stated that layoffs would be made according to

<hr>

1. 984 P.2d 1138 (Ariz. 1999).

seniority. The 1989 handbook added two new provisions. First, a disclaimer provided that "ITT Cannon does not guarantee continued employment to employees and retains the right to terminate or lay off employees." Second, a new provision read that "ITT Cannon reserves the right to amend, modify or cancel this handbook, as well as any or all of the various policies, rules, procedures and programs outlined in it" through methods other than by issuing a new handbook.

Four years later, ITT notified Roger Demasse and its other hourly employees that effective April 19, 1993, its layoff guidelines would not be based on seniority but on each employee's "abilities and documentation of performance." On April 29, Demasse was laid off, and

over the next nine months, other hourly employees suffered the same fate. All were laid off before less senior employees.

Demasse and the others filed a suit in a federal district court against ITT, alleging the breach of an implied contract created by the pre-1989 handbooks. The court ruled in favor of ITT, and the employees appealed to the U.S. Court of Appeals for the Ninth Circuit. That court asked the Arizona Supreme Court to answer two questions. Most important was whether continued employment alone is sufficient consideration to modify contract terms so that when employees continue to work after a new handbook is distributed, the new edition supersedes prior editions.

MAJORITY OPINION

FELDMAN, Justice.

* * * *

* * * [A]n implied-in-fact employment term [is] governed by the same traditional contract law that governs express promises and must be modified accordingly. See *McIlravy v. Kerr-McGee Corp.,* 119 F.3d 876 (10th Cir.1997) * * * . As a result, to effectively modify a contract, whether implied-in-fact or express, there must be: (1) an offer to modify the contract, (2) assent to or acceptance of that offer, and (3) consideration.

The 1989 handbook, published with terms that purportedly modified or permitted modification of pre-existing contractual provisions, was therefore no more than an offer to modify the existing contract. * * *

* * * *

* * * [C]onsideration necessary to modify an existing contract is any detriment to promisee, or benefit to promisor that supports the new promise. Moreover, legal consideration, like every other part of a contract, must be the result of agreement. The parties must understand

and be influenced to the particular action by something of value * * * that is recognized by all parties * * * as the moving cause. Consideration will be found when an employer and its employees have made a bargained for exchange to support the employees' * * * relinquishment of the protections they are entitled to under the existing contract.

* * * *

The Tenth Circuit Court of Appeals recently dealt with this issue in *McIlravy*. Kerr-McGee issued five handbooks over a twelve-year span. The early handbooks contained a seniority layoff provision. Later handbooks contained disclaimer provisions expressly stating that employment with Kerr-McGee was at will. * * * [T]he Tenth Circuit held that Kerr-McGee failed to show that the disclaimer successfully modified the pre-existing implied-in-fact contract created by the earlier handbooks. * * * [W]e, too, hold that continued employment alone is not sufficient consideration to support a modification to an implied-in-fact contract. Any other result brings us to an absurdity: the employer's threat to breach its promise of job security provides consideration for its rescission of that promise.

* * * *

Continued employment after issuance of a new handbook does not constitute acceptance, otherwise the illusion (and the irony) is apparent: to preserve their right under the existing contract * * * plaintiffs would be forced to quit. It is too much to require an employee to preserve his or her rights under the original employment contract by quitting working. Thus, the employee does not manifest consent to an offer modifying an existing contract without taking affirmative steps, beyond continued performance, to accept. [Emphasis added.]

DISSENTING OPINION

MARTONE, Justice, dissenting * * * .

I disagree with the majority's answer to [the] question [in this case]. The handbook promise here cannot reasonably be construed as a promise that runs in favor of the employee for as long as the employee is employed or else the unilateral promise turns out to be a better deal than a collective bargaining agreement. * * * That the employer could avoid this result by simply laying everyone off (and thus not violate the seniority provision) shows just how untenable the majority approach is. Instead, I believe that the Michigan Supreme Court was correct in concluding that the promise is enforceable against the employer by an individual employee, unless and until the

employer changes the promise as to all employees by changing the handbook. See *In re Certified Question (Bankey),* 432 Mich.438, 443 N.W.2d 112 (1989).

This does not make the promise illusory. An employer would have to think long and hard about changing a valuable benefit for 10,000 employees just to disadvantage a single employee. And, unless the employer is willing to pay that price, the employee can enforce the promise against the employer * * * . [T]he promise here was not to provide seniority rights to Demasse for as long as he decided to work for ITT, but was instead a promise to provide seniority rights to him as an individual employee so long as all other ITT employees were also receiving this benefit under the handbook. Demasse's power of acceptance by performance existed only as long as the offer was made.

* * * Both employers and employees will suffer from [the majority's decision in this case]. It will create havoc with employer-employee relations. For example, employers will be subject to different obligations to their many employees depending on the handbook in existence at the time of employment. And, one employee's contract rights may be derived from several different editions of the handbook. Worse, the contract rights of some employees created by one edition of the handbook may conflict with rights provided other employees in other editions. This spells the demise of all such handbooks. No employer will ever issue one for fear of endless obligation * * * .

LEGAL REASONING AND ANALYSIS

1. Legal Analysis. Find the *McIlravy v. Kerr-McGee Corp.* case and the *In re Certified Question (Bankey)* case (see the *Law on the Web* feature at the end of Chapter 2 for instructions on how to access federal court opinions). Compare the facts and issues in those cases to the facts and issues of the *Demasse* case. Do you think that the courts' decisions in the *McIlravy* and *Bankey* cases affected the justices' opinions in this case, or did the justices simply cite those cases to support their opinions? Explain your answer.

2. Legal Reasoning. Contrast the conclusions of the majority and the dissent. What reasons did the dissent give to support its assertion that the majority's conclusion was incorrect? What reasons did the dissent cite to justify its position?

3. Legal Application. An at-will employment agreement is for an indefinite term and can be terminated at any time for good cause or no cause at the will of either party. An at-will employment contract is unilateral and typically starts with an employer's offer of a wage in exchange for work performed. The

employee's subsequent performance provides the consideration to create the contract. What is different about the employment contract in the *Demasse* case? Why?

4. Implications for the Employer. Does the decision in this case mean that all employee handbooks create contractual promises? How might an employer avoid creating such promises when issuing a handbook?

5. Case Briefing Assignment. Using the guidelines for briefing cases given in Appendix A of this text, brief the *Demasse* case.

GOING ONLINE

This text's Web site, at http://wleb.westbuslaw.com, offers links to court cases, as well as to other online research sources. You can also locate court cases at the Web sites listed in the *Law on the Web* section at the end of Chapter 2.

The Private Environment

Many aspects of the private environment lend themselves to ethical analysis. Businesspersons certainly face ethical questions when they deal with the application of black-letter law to contracts. (*Black-letter law* is an informal term for the principles of law that courts generally accept or that are embodied in statutes.) Courts, for example, generally will not inquire into the adequacy of the consideration given in a contract. In other words, a court will not reevaluate a contract to determine whether what each party gave is equivalent to what each party received.

Ethical questions are also at the core of many principles of the law of sales. Many of the UCC provisions such as good faith and commercial reasonableness, though designed to meet the practical needs of business dealings, express ethical standards as well. Product liability also involves ethics. Many of the principles of product liability are based on principles designed to aid individuals injured, without extensive inquiry into issues of fault.

Ethical issues are not only prevalent in dealings between the firm and others outside the firm, they also are fundamental to relations within the firm. Ethical considerations, for example, underlie the fiduciary duties owed by corporate directors and managers to shareholders. The fiduciary duties are central to the relationship between the owners of a corporation and those charged with managing its affairs. In this *Focus on Ethics,* we examine selected areas in which ethical problems relate to the private

environment of business.

ETHICS AND FREEDOM OF CONTRACT

In Chapter 4, we pointed out that generally a responsible business manager will evaluate a business transaction on the basis of three criteria—legality, profitability, and ethics. But what does acting ethically mean in the area of contracts? If an individual with whom you enter into a contract fails to look after his or her own interests, is that your fault, and should you therefore be doing something about it? If the contract happens to be to your advantage and therefore to the other party's detriment, do you have a responsibility to correct the situation?

For example, assume that a neighbor whom you rarely see places a "for sale" sign on her car, offering to sell it for $3,000. You learn that she is moving to another state and needs the extra cash to help finance the move. You know that she could easily get $6,000 for the car, and you congratulate yourself on your good fortune. Even if you do not need a car, you can purchase it and then sell it at a profit. But you also learn that your neighbor has failed to do the preliminary research—checking *Blue Book* prices on the Web and so on—that most reasonable individuals would undertake when selling a car, and therefore she is unaware that the car is underpriced.

Are you obligated to tell her that she is essentially giving away $3,000 if she sells you the car for

only $3,000? Do you have an ethical responsibility toward this woman—whom you will probably never see again—simply because she failed to look after her own interests? This kind of situation, transplanted into the world of commercial transactions, raises an obvious question: At what point should the savvy businessperson cease looking after his own economic welfare and become "his brother's keeper," so to speak?

The answer to this question is not simple. On the one hand, a common ethical assumption in our society is that individuals should be held responsible for the consequences of their own actions, including their contractual promises. This principle is expressed in the legal concept of freedom of contract. Applying this ethical precept to the above example, you could justify not saying anything about the true value of the car to your neighbor by stating that you were upholding the principle of freedom of contract.

On the other hand, another common assumption in our society is that individuals should not harm one another by their actions. This is the basis of both tort law and criminal law. If you applied this ethical yardstick to the example, would you be obligated not to harm your neighbor's interests by taking advantage of her offer? How would you balance these two ethical principles?

In the area of contract law, ethical behavior often involves just such a "balancing act." In the example, if you purchased the car and the neighbor later learned its true value and sued you for the difference, very likely no court of law would agree that the contract should be rescinded. In other words, the law would not "answer" your ethical question in this case. The court probably would not come to the aid of the neighbor, because she could easily have prevented the injustice by learning, as a "reasonable person" would have, the market value of the car. There are times, however, when courts will hold that the principle of freedom *of* contract should give way to the principle of freedom *from* contract, a principle based on the assumption that people should not be harmed by the actions of others. We look below at some examples of how parties to contracts may be excused from performance under their contracts if that is the only way injustice can be prevented.

Unconscionability

The doctrine of unconscionability represents a good example of how the law attempts to enforce ethical behavior. Under this doctrine, a contract may be deemed to be so unfair to one party as to be unenforceable—even though that party voluntarily agreed to the contract's terms. Unconscionable action, like unethical action, is incapable of precise definition. Information about the particular facts and specific circumstances surrounding the contract is essential. For example, a contract with a marginally literate consumer might be seen as unfair and unenforceable, whereas the same contract with a major business firm would be upheld by the courts.

Section 2–302 of the Uniform Commercial Code, which incorporates the common law concept of unconscionability, similarly does not define the concept with any precision. Rather, it leaves it to the courts to determine when a contract is so

one sided and unfair to one party as to be unconscionable and thus unenforceable.

Usually, courts will do all they can to save contracts rather than render them unenforceable. Thus, only in extreme situations, as when a contract or clause is so one sided as to "shock the conscience" of the court, will a court hold a contract or contractual clause unconscionable.

Covenants Not to Compete

In today's complicated, technological business world, knowledge learned on the job, including trade secrets, has become a valuable commodity. To prevent this knowledge from falling into the hands of competitors, more and more employers are requiring their employees to sign covenants not to compete. The increasing number of lawsuits over noncompete clauses in employment contracts has caused numerous courts to reconsider the reasonableness of these covenants.

Noncompete covenants in employment contracts for Web-based work pose some unique issues with respect to fairness and reasonability. For example, in one case Mark Schlack, who worked as a Web site manager for EarthWeb, Inc., signed a covenant stating that, on termination of his employment, he would not work for any competing company for one year. When the employee later accepted an offer from another company to design a Web site, EarthWeb sued to enforce the covenant not to compete. The court pointed out that the covenant, in effect, prohibited Schlack from working for a competing company located anywhere in the world for one year—because the Internet lacks physical borders. For this reason, and because of the "dynamic nature of this industry," the court held that the one-year time period

was excessive in duration and refused to enforce the covenant.[1]

ETHICS AND SALES: GOOD FAITH AND COMMERCIAL REASONABLENESS

Good faith and commercial reasonableness are two key concepts that permeate the UCC and help to prevent unethical behavior by businesspersons. These two concepts are read into every contract and impose certain duties on all parties. Section 2–311(1) of the UCC indicates that when parties leave the particulars of performance to be specified by one of the parties, "[a]ny such specification must be made in good faith and within limits set by commercial reasonableness."

The requirement of commercial reasonableness means that the term subsequently supplied by one party should not come as a surprise to the other. The party filling in the missing term may not take advantage of the opportunity to add a contractual term that will be beneficial to himself or herself (and detrimental to the other party) and then demand contractual performance of the other party that was totally unanticipated. Under the UCC, the party filling in the missing term may not deviate from what is commercially reasonable in the context of the transaction. Courts frequently look to course of dealing, usage of trade, and the surrounding circumstances in determining what is commercially reasonable in a given situation.

The obligation of good faith is particularly important in so-called output and requirements contracts. UCC 2–306 states that "quantity" in these contracts "means such actual output or requirements as may occur in good faith." In many situations, parties may find it

---

1. *EarthWeb, Inc. v. Schlack,* 71 F.Supp.2d 299 (S.D.N.Y. 1999).

advantageous (profitable) to avoid a legal obligation. Without the counterobligation of good faith, there exists potential for abuse in the area of sales and lease contracts.

Suppose, for example, that the market price of the goods subject to a requirements contract rises rapidly and dramatically because of a shortage of materials necessary to their production. The buyer could claim that his or her needs are equivalent to the entire output of the seller. Then, after buying all of the seller's output at the contract price, which is substantially below the market price, the buyer could turn around and sell the goods that he or she does not need at the higher market price. Under the UCC, this type of unethical behavior is prohibited—even though the buyer in this instance has not technically breached the contract.

THE ETHICAL CONSIDERATIONS OF DEBT

We are certainly many years away from that period in our history when debtors' prisons existed. Today, debtors are in a much more favorable position—they can file for protection under bankruptcy law. Indeed, some now say that we have proceeded too far in the direction of protecting debtors and have made it too easy for debtors to avoid paying what they legally owe. Clearly, it is difficult to ensure the rights of both debtors and creditors at the same time, and laws governing debtor-creditor relationships are frequently perceived, by one group or another, as being unfair.

Creditors are given numerous remedies under both the common law and statutory law to protect their legitimate interests. When these rights and remedies are invoked, however, the creditor is often considered by the general public to be employing unfair

tactics. For many, the question of fairness revolves around the purpose for which the debt was incurred. If the debt was incurred for a needed item, such as a refrigerator, then common opinion seems to be that the debtor should be dealt with leniently. If, however, the debt was incurred for a trip to the Bahamas, the issue appears to be significantly different.

There is obviously no way in which the law can protect both debtors and creditors at all times under all circumstances. Attempts to balance the rights of both groups necessarily raise questions of fairness and justice.

ETHICS AND BANKRUPTCY

The first goal of bankruptcy law is to provide relief and protection to debtors who have "gotten in over their heads." Society has generally concluded that everyone should be given the chance to start over again. But how far should society go in letting debtors avoid obligations that they voluntarily incurred?

Consider the concept of bankruptcy from the point of view of the creditor. The creditor has extended a transfer of purchasing power from himself or herself to the debtor. That transfer of purchasing power represents a transfer of an asset for an asset. The debtor obtains the asset of money, goods, or services, and the creditor obtains the asset called a *secured* or *unsecured* legal obligation to pay. Once the debtor is in bankruptcy, voluntarily or involuntarily, the asset that the creditor owns most often has a diminished value. Indeed, in many circumstances, that asset has no value. Yet the easier it becomes for debtors to hide behind bankruptcy laws, the greater will be the incentive for debtors to use such laws to avoid payment of legally owed sums of money.

Clearly, bankruptcy law is a balancing act between providing a

second chance and ensuring that creditors are given "a fair shake." Understandably, ethical issues arise in the process.

Is Bankruptcy Too Easy?

The total number of bankruptcies has increased dramatically since the Bankruptcy Code was revised in 1978 to make it easier to petition for bankruptcy relief. In 1976, for example, 193,000 debtors petitioned for bankruptcy. By 1999, bankruptcy filings were about 1.4 million per year. Most of those filings (an estimated 97 percent in 1999) were personal bankruptcies. To be sure, bankruptcy filings dropped by 2.6 percent in 1999 over what they had been the year before. But still, overall there has been a staggering rise in bankruptcy filings in the last two decades. In fact, more than half of the 20 million Americans who have filed for personal bankruptcy since the federal bankruptcy laws were created a century ago have done so just since 1985.

Some claim that the law has gone too far in providing relief for debtors and should be changed. Indeed, Congress has been considering proposed legislation that would amend the Bankruptcy Code to make it more difficult for some debtors to obtain relief. One proposal, for example, would prevent those earning over $50,000 a year from obtaining relief under Chapter 7; rather, such debtors would have to resort to a Chapter 13 repayment plan, so that creditors would be repaid to the fullest extent possible. Another proposal would make *all* credit-card debt incurred within ninety days of filing for Chapter 7 nondischargeable. The idea behind this proposal is to discourage spending sprees by people who know they will never be able to pay back those debts. (Under current law, credit-card bills up to $1,075 incurred within sixty days of filing for luxury items or cash are nondischargeable.)

Others criticize the credit-card industry for making credit too readily available to consumers. This group would like to see stiffer disclosure requirements imposed on credit-card companies—so that a consumer does not have to rely on the fine print to learn that, say, a "come-on" APR (annual percentage rate) of 2.9 percent will rise to 18 percent four months later. How Congress will ultimately attempt to balance the various interests involved in the bankruptcy reform debate is yet to be seen.

Bankruptcy and Economics

Among other things, the increasing number of bankruptcies means that creditors incur higher risks in making loans, because bankruptcy shifts the cost of the debt from the debtor to the creditor. To compensate for these higher risks, creditors will do one or more of the following: increase the interest rates charged to everyone, require more security (collateral), or be more selective in the granting of credit. Thus, the more lenient bankruptcy laws are, the better off will be those debtors who find themselves in bankruptcy; but those debtors who will never be in bankruptcy will be worse off. Ethical concerns here must be matched with the economic concerns of other groups of individuals affected by the law.

Consequences for Debtors

Some contend that debtors take unfair advantage of bankruptcy law and see bankruptcy as an easy solution to their financing problems. While it is true that there is less of a stigma attached to bankruptcy today than there once was, bankruptcy is never easy for debtors. Many debtors feel a sense of shame and failure when they petition for bankruptcy. After all, bankruptcy is a matter of public

record, and there is no way to avoid this fact. In one case, for example, a couple who filed for Chapter 7 bankruptcy wanted to use their attorney's mailing address in another town on their bankruptcy schedules so that it would be less likely that an elderly parent and one of their employers would learn about the bankruptcy. The court, however, held that debtors are not entitled to be protected from publicity surrounding the filing of their cases.[2]

There are other consequences of bankruptcy for debtors—blemished credit ratings for up to ten years, higher interest charges for new debts, such as those incurred through the purchase of cars or homes, and so on. They may even find it difficult to get jobs. Although a private employer may not fire an employee who has filed for bankruptcy protection, the employer may refuse to hire a job applicant who has done so. The courts provide little relief for job applicants who encounter such an experience.[3]

Clearly, balancing the rights of debtors and creditors is not easy. Because of the consequences of bankruptcy, debtors do not always get the "fresh start" promised by bankruptcy law. At the same time, creditors rarely are able to recover all of the money owed them once a debtor petitions for bankruptcy.

Reaffirmation Agreements

Another ethically problematic aspect of bankruptcy law has to do with reaffirmation agreements. As discussed in Chapter 16, the Bankruptcy Code allows debtors undergoing bankruptcy proceedings to reaffirm certain debts. In other words, a debtor may agree with a particular creditor to go ahead and pay the

debt, even though it could have been discharged in bankruptcy. In a sense, reaffirmation agreements conflict with the basic purpose of bankruptcy law, which is to give debtors a fresh start, free from debt. Because of this, the Code imposes special requirements with respect to such agreements—a reaffirmation agreement must be made *before* the debtor is granted a discharge, and the agreement *must* be filed with the court.

Notwithstanding these requirements, some debtors who have had their debts discharged in bankruptcy have fallen victim to creditors through reaffirmations of debt. One of the most notorious examples occurred in the late 1990s, when it was discovered that Sears, Roebuck and Co. had convinced thousands of debtors to reaffirm their credit-card debts to Sears, even though the debts had already been discharged in bankruptcy.

It took years for these practices to come to light because the reaffirmations had not been filed with the court, as required by the Bankruptcy Code. Debtors were enticed to sign the agreements by promises of low monthly payments in return for Sears's promise not to repossess goods purchased on credit. In 1999, following an investigation by the Federal Bureau of Investigation, Sears agreed to plead guilty to a charge of criminal bankruptcy fraud and to pay the government a fine of some $60 million. It also agreed to settle a nationwide class-action suit against the company for $36 million in cash and $118 million in store coupons.[4]

BUSINESS AND FIDUCIARY DUTIES REVISITED

An important duty that arises in the law of agency, and that applies to

---

2. *In the Matter of Laws,* 223 Bankr. 714 (D.Neb. 1998).

3. See, for example, *Pastore v. Medford Savings Bank,* 186 Bankr. 553 (D. Mass. 1995).

4. Laurel-Ann Dooley, "Come See the Legal Side of Sears," *The National Law Journal,* October 18, 1999, p. B3.

all partners and corporate directors, officers, and management personnel, is the duty of loyalty. As caretakers of the shareholders' wealth, corporate directors and officers also have a fiduciary duty to exercise care when making decisions affecting the corporate enterprise.

The Duty of Loyalty

Every individual has his or her own personal interests, which may at times conflict with the interests of the partnership or corporation with which he or she is affiliated. In particular, a partner or a corporate director may face a conflict between personal interests and the interests of the business entity. Corporate officers may find themselves in a position to acquire assets that would also benefit the corporation if acquired in the corporation's name.

In one landmark case, *Guth v. Loft, Inc.,*[5] Charles G. Guth, the president and a director of Loft, Inc., a soft-drink bottling company, negotiated with the Coca-Cola Company for a discount on its syrups. When negotiations with Coca-Cola failed to result in a discount for Loft, Guth decided to see what Pepsi Cola could offer. During his investigation of this possibility, Guth set up a new corporation to acquire the secret formula and trademark for the manufacture of Pepsi Cola. He did so without offering the opportunity to Loft. A shareholder brought a suit against Guth, arguing that the shares of the new corporation should belong to Loft, and not to Guth personally. The shareholder prevailed. The court ruled that Guth had *usurped* a corporate opportunity in violation of his duty of loyalty to the corporation.

The Duty of Care

In addition to the duty of loyalty, every corporate director or officer

has a duty of care, which involves a duty to be informed and to make informed decisions. Traditionally, though, the duty of care did not include a duty to monitor the behavior of corporate employees to detect and prevent wrongdoing unless the directors had some reason to suspect that wrongful acts were in fact occurring. For example, in a leading case on the issue, the Delaware Supreme Court held in 1963 that corporate directors did not have a duty "to install and operate a corporate system of espionage to ferret out wrongdoing which they have no reason to suspect exists."[6]

Enter the corporate sentencing guidelines in 1991. Under these guidelines, the courts may impose—and have been imposing fairly regularly—substantial penalties on corporations and corporate directors for criminal wrongdoing. The guidelines, though, allow these penalties to be mitigated if a company can show that it has a compliance program in place—an effective program to detect and prevent wrongdoing by corporate personnel. The question here is, do the guidelines imply that directors have a *duty* to have such a program in place?

In 1996, a Delaware chancery (trial) court suggested that corporate directors do have such a duty. The case involved criminal behavior on the part of a company's middle-level and lower-level employees, and the question was whether the directors, who were apparently unaware of the actions, had breached their oversight duties. Under the traditional rule, as mentioned, directors had no duty to detect and "ferret out" wrongdoing. According to the court in this case, though, the corporate sentencing guidelines have changed this

standard. The court stated that "a director's obligation includes a duty to attempt in good faith to assure that a corporation information and reporting system, which the board concludes is adequate, exists." The court also noted that in view of the potential impact of the sentencing guidelines on any business organization, "[a]ny rational person attempting in good faith to meet an organizational governance responsibility would be bound to take into account this development and the enhanced penalties and the opportunities for reduced sanctions that it offers."[7]

Clearly, the corporate sentencing guidelines are altering the business and legal environment in which directors operate. In the case just discussed, the directors were able to avoid liability because there was a compliance program in place—which the company agreed to modify so that it would be more effective in the future.

DISCUSSION QUESTIONS

1. Suppose that you contract to purchase steel at a fixed price per ton. A lengthy steelworkers' strike causes the price of steel to triple from the price specified in the contract. If you demand that the supplier fulfill the contract, the supplier will go out of business. What are your ethical obligations in this situation? What are your legal rights?

2. Employers often include covenants not to compete in employment contracts to protect their trade secrets. What effect, if any, will the growth in e-commerce have on the reasonability of covenants not to compete?

---

5. 5 A.2d 503 (Del. 1939).

6. *Graham v. Allis-Chalmers Manufacturing Co.,* 188 A.2d 125 (Del. 1963).

7. *In re Caremark International, Inc. Derivative Litigation* (Del.Ch. 1996) [1996 WL 549894]. This decision, which has not yet been published in a reporter, can be accessed by use of the WESTLAW (WL) citation.

3. How can a court objectively measure good faith and commercial reasonableness?

4. Merchants may "huff and puff" their wares as they traditionally have and still—in most instances—not violate their duty of dealing honestly and in good faith with the buyers of their products. Do you think that the commonplace custom of puffing is a fundamentally dishonest practice that should be abandoned? Is there anything the law can or should do to ensure that buyers and lessees will not be taken in by sellers' and lessors' statements of opinion?

5. Do you think that the law favors debtors at the expense of creditors, or vice versa? Is there any way a better balance between creditors' and debtors' interests could be achieved?

6. Three decades ago, prosecution of corporations and corporate directors for crimes was a rare event, and penalties for corporate crime were relatively light. Today, this is no longer true. According to the U.S. Sentencing Commission, companies are being sentenced under the corporate sentencing guidelines at a rate of more than two a week, and corporate fines reaching hundreds of millions of dollars are not especially uncommon. Does this development mean that corporations are committing more crimes today than in the past? Or is the government just getting tougher on corporate crime? How can a company avoid liability for crimes committed by its employees?

UNIT FOUR

The Employment
Environment

CONTENTS

CHAPTER 20

Agency

O NE OF THE MOST COMMON, important, and pervasive legal relationships is that of **agency**. In an agency relationship between two parties, one of the parties, called the *agent*, agrees to represent or act for the other, called the *principal*. The principal has the right to control the agent's conduct in matters entrusted to the agent. By using agents, a principal can conduct multiple business operations simultaneously in various locations. Thus, for example, contracts that bind the principal can be made at different places with different persons at the same time.

A familiar example of an agent is a corporate officer who serves in a representative capacity for the owners of the corporation. In this capacity, the officer has the authority to bind the principal (the corporation) to a contract. Indeed, agency law is essential to the existence and operation of a corporate entity, because only through its agents can a corporation function and enter into contracts. Because agency relationships permeate the business world, an understanding of the law of agency is crucial to understanding business law.

SECTION 1

Agency Relationships

Section 1(1) of the *Restatement (Second) of Agency*[1] defines *agency* as "the fiduciary relation which results from the manifestation of consent by one person to another that the other shall act in his behalf and subject to his control, and consent by the other so to act." The term **fiduciary** is at the heart of agency law. The term can be used both as a noun and as an adjective. When used as a noun, it refers to a person having a duty created by his or her undertaking to act primarily for another's benefit in matters connected with the undertaking. When used as an adjective, as in the phrase "fiduciary relationship," it means that the relationship involves trust and confidence.

Agency relationships commonly exist between employers and employees. Agency relationships may

---

1. The *Restatement (Second) of Agency* is an authoritative summary of the law of agency and is often referred to by jurists in their decisions and opinions.

sometimes also exist between employers and independent contractors who are hired to perform special tasks or services.

EMPLOYER-EMPLOYEE RELATIONSHIPS

Normally, all employees who deal with third parties are deemed to be agents. All employment laws (state and federal) apply only to the employer-employee relationship. Statutes governing Social Security, withholding taxes, workers' compensation, unemployment compensation, workplace safety laws, employment discrimination, and the like (see Chapters 21 and 22) are applicable only when an employer-employee relationship exists. *These laws do not apply to the independent contractor.*

Because employees may be deemed agents of their employers, agency law and employment law overlap considerably. Agency relationships, though, as will become apparent, can exist outside an employer-employee relationship and thus have a broader reach than employment laws do.

EMPLOYER–INDEPENDENT CONTRACTOR RELATIONSHIPS

Independent contractors are not employees, because by definition, those who hire them have no control over the details of their work performance. Section 2 of the *Restatement (Second) of Agency* defines an **independent contractor** as follows:

> [An independent contractor is] a person who contracts with another to do something for him but who is not controlled by the other nor subject to the other's right to control with respect to his physical conduct in the performance of the undertaking. He may or may not be an agent.

Building contractors and subcontractors are independent contractors, and a property owner does not control the acts of either of these professionals. Truck drivers who own their equipment and hire out on a per-job basis are independent contractors, but truck drivers who drive company trucks on a regular basis are usually employees.

The relationship between a principal and an independent contractor may or may not involve an agency relationship. To illustrate: An owner of real estate who hires a real estate broker to negotiate a sale of his or her property not only has contracted with an independent contractor (the real estate broker) but also

has established an agency relationship for the specific purpose of assisting in the sale of the property. Another example is an insurance agent, who is both an independent contractor and an agent of the insurance company for which he or she sells policies.

CRITERIA FOR ESTABLISHING EMPLOYEE STATUS

A question that frequently comes before the courts is whether a worker should be deemed an employee or an independent contractor. How a court decides this issue can have a significant effect on the rights and liabilities of the parties.

For example, employers normally are held liable as principals for the actions of their employee-agents if those actions are carried out within the scope of employment. Additionally, federal and state statutory laws governing employment discrimination, workplace safety, and compensation for on-the-job injuries normally apply only to employees—not to independent contractors. The tax liability of employers is also affected by the determination of worker status. Whereas employers are responsible for certain taxes, such as Social Security and unemployment taxes, with respect to employees, they are not responsible for these taxes if their workers are classified as independent contractors. (For further discussion of these various topics in the context of the relationship between employers and employees, see Chapters 21 and 22.)

In deciding whether a worker is categorized as an employee or an independent contractor, courts often consider the following questions:

1. How much control can the employer exercise over the details of the work? (If an employer can exercise considerable control over the details of the work and the day-to-day activities of the worker, this indicates employee status. This is perhaps the most important factor weighed by the courts in determining employee status.)
2. Is the worker engaged in an occupation or business distinct from that of the employer? (If so, this points to independent-contractor status, not employee status.)
3. Is the work usually done under the employer's direction or by a specialist without supervision? (If the work is usually done under the employer's direction, this indicates employee status.)
4. Does the employer supply the tools at the place of work? (If so, this indicates employee status.)

5. For how long is the person employed? (If the person is employed for a long period of time, this indicates employee status.)

6. What is the method of payment—by time period or at the completion of the job? (Payment by time period, such as once every two weeks or once a month, indicates employee status.)

7. What degree of skill is required of the worker? (If a great degree of skill is required, this may indicate that the person is an independent contractor hired for a specialized job and not an employee.)

Often, the criteria for determining employee status are established by a statute or administrative agency regulation. The Internal Revenue Service (IRS), for example, has guidelines for its auditors to follow in determining whether a worker is an independent contractor or an employee. In the past, auditors were to consider twenty factors in making such a decision. New guidelines effective in 1997, however, encourage IRS examiners to look closely at just one of those factors—the degree of control the business exercises over the worker.

The IRS tends to scrutinize closely a firm's classification of a worker as an independent contractor rather than an employee, because employers can avoid certain tax liabilities by hiring independent contractors instead of employees. Regardless of the firm's classification of a worker's status as an independent contractor, if the IRS decides that the worker should be classified as an employee, then the employer will be responsible for paying any applicable Social Security, withholding, and unemployment taxes.

Sometimes, it is advantageous to have employee status—to take advantage of laws protecting employees, for example. At other times, it may be advantageous to have independent-contractor status—for instance, for tax purposes.

The following case involved a dispute over ownership rights in a computer program. Under the Copyright Act of 1976, any copyrighted work created by an employee within the scope of his or her employment at the request of the employer is a "work for hire," and the employer owns the copyright to the work. When an employer hires an independent contractor, however, normally the contractor owns the copyright unless the parties agree in writing that the work is a "work for hire." The outcome of the case thus hinged on whether the creator of the program, at the time it was created, was an employee or an independent contractor.

CASE 20.1   Graham v. James

United States
Court of Appeals,
Second Circuit, 1998.
144 F.3d 229.
http://www.findlaw.
com/casecode/courts/
2nd.html[a]

BACKGROUND AND FACTS   *Richard Graham marketed CD-ROM disks containing compilations of shareware, freeware, and public domain software.[b] With five to ten thousand programs per disk, Graham needed a file-retrieval program to allow users to access the software on the disks. Larry James agreed to create the program in exchange for, among other things, credit on the final product. James built into the final version of the program a notice attributing authorship and copyright to himself. Graham removed the notice, claiming that the program was a work for hire and the copyright was his. Graham used the program on several subsequent releases. James sold the program to another CD-ROM publisher. Graham filed a suit in a federal district court against James, alleging, among other things, copyright infringement. The court ruled that James was an independent contractor and that he owned the copyright. Graham appealed the ruling.*

**IN THE LANGUAGE
OF THE COURT**

JACOBS, Circuit Judge.

*   *   *   *

The Copyright Act provides, *inter alia* [among other things], that "a work prepared by an employee within the scope of his or her employment" is a work for hire. "[T]he

---

a. This is a page, part of the Findlaw Web site, with links to some of the opinions of the U.S. Court of Appeals for the Second Circuit. In the "1998" row, click on "May." When that page opens, scroll down the list of cases to the *Graham* case and click on the link to access it.

b. *Shareware* is software released to the public to sample, with the understanding that anyone using it will register with the author and pay a fee. *Freeware* is software available for use at no charge. *Public domain software* is software unprotected by copyright.

employer or other person for whom the work [for hire] was prepared is considered the author" and the employer owns the copyright *   *   * .

*   *   *   *

*   *   * [In determining whether a hired party is an employee, the important factors are:] (i) the hiring party's right to control the manner and means of creation; (ii) the skill required; (iii) the provision of employee benefits; (iv) the tax treatment of the hired party; and (v) whether the hiring party had the right to assign additional projects to the hired party. *   *   *

We are persuaded by the district court's conclusion that James was an independent contractor. Almost all of the *   *   * factors line up in favor of that conclusion: James is a skilled computer programmer, he was paid no benefits, no payroll taxes were withheld, and his engagement by Graham was project-by-project. The only *   *   * factor arguably favoring Graham is his general control over the work; but the district court has found, plausibly, that Graham's participation in the development of the [file-retrieval program] was minimal and that his instructions to James were very general.

· **DECISION AND REMEDY**   *The U.S. Court of Appeals for the Second Circuit affirmed the lower court's judgment on this issue. The court agreed that James owned the copyright because he was an independent contractor when he developed the program.*

SECTION 2

Formation of the Agency Relationship

Agency relationships are *consensual*; that is to say, they come about by voluntary consent and agreement between the parties. Generally, the agreement need not be in writing, and consideration is not required.

A principal must have contractual capacity. A person who cannot legally enter into contracts directly should not be allowed to do so indirectly through an agent. Because an agent derives the authority to enter into contracts from the principal and because a contract made by an agent is legally viewed as a contract of the principal, it is immaterial whether the agent personally has the legal capacity to make that contract. Thus, a minor can be an agent but in some states cannot be a principal appointing an agent.[2] (When a minor is permitted to be a principal, however, any resulting contracts will be voidable by the minor principal but not by the adult third party.) In sum, any person can be an agent, regardless of whether he or she has the capacity to contract. Even a person who is legally incompetent can be appointed an agent.

An agency relationship can be created for any legal purpose. An agency relationship created for a purpose that is illegal or contrary to public policy is unenforceable. If LaSalle (as principal) contracts with Burke (as agent) to sell illegal narcotics, the agency relationship is unenforceable, because selling illegal narcotics is a felony and is contrary to public policy. It is also illegal for medical doctors and other licensed professionals to employ unlicensed agents to perform professional actions.

Generally, an agency relationship can arise in four ways: by agreement of the parties, by ratification, by estoppel, and by operation of law. We look here at each of these possibilities.

AGENCY BY AGREEMENT

Because an agency relationship is, by definition, consensual, normally it must be based on an express or implied agreement that the agent will act for the principal and the principal agrees to have the agent so act. An agency agreement can take the form of an express written contract. For example, Arnstein enters into a written agreement with Vogel, a real estate agent, to sell Arnstein's house. An agency relationship exists between Arnstein and Vogel for the sale of the house and is detailed in a document that both parties sign.

Many express agency relationships are created by oral agreement and not based on a contract. If Arnstein asks Grace, a gardener, to contract with others for the

---

2. Some courts have granted exceptions to allow a minor to appoint an agent for the limited purpose of contracting for the minor's necessities of life. See *Casey v. Kastel*, 237 N.Y. 305, 142 N.E. 671 (1924).

care of his lawn on a regular basis, and Grace agrees, an agency relationship exists between Arnstein and Grace for the lawn care.

An agency relationship can also be implied by conduct. For example, a hotel expressly allows only Hans Cooper to park cars, but Hans has no employment contract there. The hotel's manager tells Hans when to work, as well as where and how to park the cars. The hotel's conduct amounts to a manifestation of its willingness to have Hans park its customers' cars, and Hans can infer from the hotel's conduct that he has authority to act as a parking valet. It can be inferred that Hans is an agent for the hotel, his purpose being to provide valet parking services for hotel guests.

AGENCY BY RATIFICATION

On occasion, a person who is in fact not an agent may make a contract on behalf of another (a principal). If the principal approves or affirms that contract by word or by action, an agency relationship is created by ratification. Ratification involves a question of intent, and intent can be expressed by either words or conduct.

AGENCY BY ESTOPPEL

When a principal causes a third person to believe that another person is the principal's agent, and the third person acts to his or her detriment in reasonable reliance on that belief, the principal is "estopped to deny" the agency relationship. In such a situation, the principal's actions have created the *appearance* of an agency that does not in fact exist. The third person

must prove that he or she *reasonably* believed that an agency relationship existed, however.[3]

Suppose that Jerry accompanies Grant, a seed sales representative, to call on a customer, Palko, the proprietor of the Neighborhood Seed Store. Jerry has performed independent sales work but has never signed an employment agreement with Grant. Grant boasts to Palko that he wishes he had three more assistants "just like Jerry." Palko has reason to believe from Grant's statements that Jerry is an agent for Grant, because Grant's representation to Palko created the impression that Jerry was Grant's agent and had authority to solicit orders. Palko then places seed orders with Jerry.

If Grant does not correct the impression that Jerry is an agent, Grant will be bound to fill the orders just as if Jerry were really Grant's agent. The acts or declarations of a purported agent in and of themselves do not create an agency by estoppel. Rather, it is the deeds or statements of the principal that create an agency by estoppel. If Jerry walked into Palko's store and claimed to be Grant's agent, when in fact he was not, and Grant had no knowledge of Jerry's representations, Grant would not be bound to any deal struck by Jerry and Palko.

The court in the following case considered whether an agency existed by estoppel between the owner of a jewelry cart in a mall and the seller of "The Only Completely Safe, Sterile Ear Piercing Method."

---

3. These concepts also apply when a person who is in fact an agent undertakes an action that is beyond the scope of his or her authority, as will be discussed later in this chapter.

CASE 20.2   Williams v. Inverness Corp.

Supreme Judicial Court of Maine, 1995. 664 A.2d 1244.

COMPANY PROFILE   *Inverness Corporation is the world's largest maker of body-piercing equipment. Sam Mann founded Inverness in 1975 with a design for piercing equipment that was more sterile and less threatening than the products then in use. The first year, sales totaled more than $750,000. Today, the company makes disposable ear-piercing kits, skin-care products, hair-removal waxes, electrolysis kits, and jewelry dips. Based in Fair Lawn, New Jersey, Inverness sells its products in fifty-two countries. In 1998, Inverness sold the assets of its jewelry components division for more than $38.7 million to Cookson Group (**http://www.cooksongroup.co.uk**), an international industrial materials group based in the United Kingdom.*

BACKGROUND AND FACTS   *Inverness Corporation markets the Inverness Ear Piercing System, which includes a training course, an "eye-catching assortment of selling aids" such as counter displays, and release forms that tout the system as "The Only*

Completely Safe, Sterile Ear Piercing Method." Margaret Barrera, the owner of a jewelry cart in a mall, bought the system, took the course, and set up the displays. Seventeen-year-old Angela Williams paid Barrera to pierce Williams's ear. The ear became infected, which led to complications. Williams's mother filed a suit on Angela's behalf in a Maine state court against Inverness and Barrera, claiming in part that Inverness was liable on a theory of agency by estoppel. The court issued a judgment in Williams's favor. Inverness appealed to Maine's highest state court.

IN THE LANGUAGE OF THE COURT

DANA, Justice.

* * * *

* * * There are critical pieces of evidence in the record that can fairly be interpreted as leading to an inference that Inverness did hold Barrera out as its agent. Most important, a jury reasonably could infer that Inverness knew, or should have known, that Barrera distributed Inverness's release forms * * *.

* * * A jury reasonably could infer * * * that Inverness knew, or should have known, that Barrera was using the Inverness Ear Piercing System, that she displayed Inverness's "eye-catching assortment of selling aids," and that she used Inverness's training program.

Finally, there was evidence that Angela believed that Barrera was Inverness's agent, that Angela relied on Inverness's manifestations of agency, and that Angela's reliance on Barrera's care and skill was justifiable. * * * The release form and display promote the Inverness Ear Piercing System as "The Only Completely Safe, Sterile Ear Piercing Method."

DECISION AND REMEDY

The Supreme Judicial Court of Maine affirmed the lower court's judgment. Inverness was liable for Williams's injury because Inverness's actions created the appearance of an agency between it and Barrera.

AGENCY BY OPERATION OF LAW

There are also other situations in which the courts will find an agency relationship in the absence of a formal agreement. This may occur in family relationships. For example, suppose one spouse purchases certain basic necessaries (such as food or clothing) and charges them to the other spouse's charge account. The courts will often rule that the latter is liable for

CONCEPT SUMMARY 20.1

FORMATION OF PRINCIPAL-AGENT RELATIONSHIP

METHOD OF FORMATION	DESCRIPTION
By Agreement	Agency relationship is formed through express consent (oral or written) or implied by conduct.
By Ratification	Principal either by act or by agreement ratifies conduct of a person who is not in fact an agent.
By Estoppel	Principal causes a third person to believe that another person is the principal's agent, and the third person acts to his or her detriment in reasonable reliance on that belief.
By Operation of Law	Agency relationship is based on a social duty (such as the need to support family members) or formed in emergency situations when the agent is unable to contact the principal.

payment of the necessaries, either because of a social policy of promoting the general welfare of the spouse or because of a legal duty to supply necessaries to family members.

Agency by operation of law may also occur in emergency situations, when the agent's failure to act outside the scope of his or her authority would cause the principal substantial loss. If the agent is unable to contact the principal, the courts will often grant this emergency power. For example, a railroad engineer may contract on behalf of his or her employer for medical care for an injured motorist hit by the train.

Section 3

Duties of Agents and Principals

Once the principal-agent relationship has been created, both parties have duties that govern their conduct. As discussed previously, the principal-agent relationship is *fiduciary*—one of trust. In a fiduciary relationship, each party owes the other the duty to act with the utmost good faith. In this section, we examine the various duties of agents and principals.

AGENT'S DUTIES TO THE PRINCIPAL

Generally, the agent owes the principal five duties—performance, notification, loyalty, obedience, and accounting.

Performance. An implied condition in every agency contract is the agent's agreement to use reasonable diligence and skill in performing the work. When an agent fails to perform his or her duties, liability for breach of contract may result. The degree of skill or care required of an agent is usually that expected of a reasonable person under similar circumstances. Generally, this is interpreted to mean ordinary care. An agent may, however, have represented himself or herself as possessing special skills or, by virtue of his or her profession, be expected to exercise certain skills (such as those that an accountant or attorney possesses). Similarly, a corporate director, as an agent of the corporation, is expected to exercise a reasonable degree of diligence and oversight in the performance of his or her duties (see Chapter 19). In these situations, the agent is expected to exercise the skill or skills claimed. Failure to do so constitutes a breach of the agent's duty.

Not all agency relationships are based on contract. In some situations, an agent acts gratuitously—that is, without payment. A gratuitous agent cannot be liable for breach of contract, as there is no contract; he or she is subject only to tort liability. Once a gratuitous agent has begun to act in an agency capacity, he or she has the duty to continue to perform in that capacity in an acceptable manner and is subject to the same standards of care and duty to perform as other agents. For example, Bower's friend Alcott is a real estate broker. Alcott offers to sell Bower's farm at no charge. If Alcott never attempts to sell the farm, Bower has no legal cause of action to force Alcott to do so. If Alcott does find a buyer, however, but fails to provide a sales contract within a reasonable period of time, thus causing the buyer to seek other property, then Bower has a cause of action in tort against Alcott for negligence.

Notification. An agent is required to notify the principal of all matters that come to his or her attention concerning the subject matter of the agency. This is the duty of notification, or the duty to inform. For example, suppose that Lang, an artist, is about to negotiate a contract to sell a series of paintings to Barber's Art Gallery for $15,000. Lang's agent learns that Barber is insolvent and will be unable to pay for the paintings. Lang's agent has a duty to inform Lang of this knowledge because it is relevant to the subject matter of the agency—the sale of Lang's paintings. Generally, the law assumes that the principal knows of any information acquired by the agent that is relevant to the agency—regardless of whether the agent actually passes on this information to the principal.

Loyalty. Loyalty is one of the most fundamental duties in a fiduciary relationship. Basically stated, the agent has the duty to act solely for the benefit of his or her principal and not in the interest of the agent or a third party. For example, an agent cannot represent two principals in the same transaction unless both know of the dual capacity and consent to it. The duty of loyalty also means that any information or knowledge acquired through the agency relationship is confidential. It would be a breach of loyalty to disclose such information either during the agency relationship or after its termination. Typical examples of confidential information are trade secrets and customer lists compiled by the principal.

In short, the agent's loyalty must be undivided. The agent's actions must be strictly for the benefit of the principal and must not result in any secret profit for the agent. For example, suppose that Remington contracts with Averly, a real estate agent, to sell Remington's property. Averly knows that he can find a buyer who will pay substantially more for the property than Remington is asking. If Averly secretly purchased Remington's property, however, and then sold it at a profit to another buyer, Averly would breach his duty of loyalty as Remington's agent. Averly has a duty to act in Remington's best interests and can only become the purchaser in this situation with Remington's knowledge and approval.

Does an agent breach the duty of loyalty if, while working for a principal, the agent solicits the principal's customers for a new competing business? That was an issue in the following case.

CASE 20.3 American Express Financial Advisors, Inc. v. Topel

United States
District Court,
District of Colorado,
1999.
38 F.Supp.2d 1233.

BACKGROUND AND FACTS *Stephen Topel worked as a financial planner for American Express Financial Advisors, Inc. (AMEX), beginning in April 1992. More than four years later, Topel decided to resign to work for Multi-Financial Securities Corporation, an AMEX competitor. Before resigning, Topel encouraged his customers to liquidate their AMEX holdings and sent them new account forms for Multi-Financial. He ignored the request of customers James and Nancy Hemming to keep their investments with AMEX. In a letter on AMEX letterhead, Topel told Chris and Teresa Mammel to liquidate their AMEX holdings and invest in Multi-Financial's products. Another couple, Mr. and Ms. Rogers, changed their investments on Topel's advice. Before leaving AMEX, Topel sent a letter to all of his clients in which he wrote that he was ending his relationship with AMEX and that their accounts would be assigned to another AMEX adviser. After Topel resigned in May 1997, he solicited the business of Theodore Benavidez, another AMEX customer. AMEX filed a suit in a federal district court against Topel, alleging, among other things, breach of fiduciary duty (duty of loyalty) and seeking damages. AMEX filed a motion for summary judgment on this issue.*

IN THE LANGUAGE
OF THE COURT

BABCOCK, District Judge.

*   *   *   *

[The] law provides that unless otherwise agreed, an agent is subject to a duty to his principal to act solely for the benefit of the principal in all matters connected with the agency. While an agent is entitled to make some preparations to compete with his principal after the termination of their relationship, an agent violates his duty of loyalty if he engages in pre-termination solicitation of customers for a new competing business.

As the undisputed facts make clear, Mr. Topel solicited customers for his new venture while he was still affiliated with AMEX. In some instances, there is evidence that Mr. Topel ignored his AMEX customers' requests to keep their investments with AMEX. He also sent correspondence to his AMEX customers to solicit them for his new venture while he was still employed by AMEX and, in at least one instance, on AMEX letterhead. *   *   *

Mr. Topel has not challenged AMEX's statement of the law on this issue; nor has he successfully challenged the facts upon which AMEX relies. *   *   *

*   *   *   *

Nor does Mr. Topel create a genuine issue of material fact by offering the testimony of one customer, Theodore Benavidez, whose unrebutted testimony is that Mr. Topel did not solicit his business until after he left AMEX. Mr. Benavidez' testimony does not negate the testimony of other customers who testified that Mr. Topel solicited their business for Multi-Financial while he was still affiliated with AMEX. Furthermore, even if Mr. Topel sent a neutral letter regarding his resignation to the AMEX clients he serviced on its behalf, it does not follow that no solicitation occurred prior to that letter. In fact, many customers had already signed new account forms with Multi-Financial by the time this neutral letter was purportedly sent. Thus, that it is genuinely disputed whether Mr. Topel solicited improperly some of his customers is irrelevant when [it] is undisputed that he improperly solicited the [Hemmings], [Mr. and] Ms. Rogers, and [the Mammels] before he terminated his employment with AMEX. *   *   * Therefore, I grant AMEX's summary judgment motion on its claim *   *   * for breach of fiduciary duty.

DECISION AND REMEDY   *The court granted AMEX's motion for summary judgment on its claim against Topel for breach of fiduciary duty. Topel breached his duty of loyalty, while working for his principal, by soliciting his principal's customers for his new, competing business.*

Obedience.   When an agent is acting on behalf of the principal, a duty is imposed on that agent to follow all lawful and clearly stated instructions of the principal. Any deviation from such instructions is a violation of this duty. During emergency situations, however, when the principal cannot be consulted, the agent may deviate from the instructions without violating this duty. Whenever instructions are not clearly stated, the agent can fulfill the duty of obedience by acting in good faith and in a manner reasonable under the circumstances.

Accounting.   Unless an agent and a principal agree otherwise, the agent has the duty to keep and make available to the principal an account of all property and money received and paid out on behalf of the principal. The agent has a duty to maintain separate accounts for the principal's funds and the agent's personal funds, and no intermingling of these accounts is allowed. Whenever a licensed professional (such as an attorney) violates this duty to account, he or she may be subject to disciplinary proceedings carried out by the appropriate regulatory institution (such as the state bar association) in addition to being liable to the principal (the professional's client) for failure to account.

PRINCIPAL'S DUTIES TO THE AGENT

The principal also has certain duties to the agent. These duties relate to compensation, reimbursement and indemnification, cooperation, and safe working conditions.

Compensation.   In general, when a principal requests certain services from an agent, the agent reasonably expects payment. The principal therefore has a duty to pay the agent for services rendered. For example, when an accountant or an attorney is asked to act as an agent, an agreement to compensate the agent for this service is implied. The principal also has a duty to

pay that compensation in a timely manner. Except in a gratuitous agency relationship, in which the agent does not act for money, the principal must pay the agreed-on value for the agent's services. If no amount has been expressly agreed on, then the principal owes the agent the customary compensation for such services.

Reimbursement and Indemnification.   Whenever an agent disburses sums of money to fulfill the request of the principal or to pay for necessary expenses in the course of a reasonable performance of his or her agency duties, the principal has the duty to reimburse the agent for these payments.[4] Agents cannot recover for expenses incurred by their own misconduct or negligence, however.

Subject to the terms of the agency agreement, the principal has the duty to *indemnify* (compensate) an agent for liabilities incurred because of authorized and lawful acts and transactions. For example, if the agent, on the principal's behalf, forms a contract with a third party, and the principal fails to perform the contract, the third party may sue the agent for damages. In this situation, the principal is obligated to compensate the agent for any costs incurred by the agent as a result of the principal's failure to perform the contract. Additionally, the principal must indemnify (pay) the agent for the value of benefits that the agent confers on the principal. The amount of indemnification is usually specified in the agency contract. If it is not, the courts will look to the nature of the business and the type of loss to determine the amount.

Cooperation.   A principal has a duty to cooperate with the agent and to assist the agent in performing his or her duties. The principal must do nothing to

---

4. This principle applies to acts by gratuitous agents as well. If a finder of a dog that becomes sick takes the dog to a veterinarian and pays the required fees for the veterinarian's services, the agent is entitled to be reimbursed by the owner of the dog for those fees.

prevent such performance. For example, when a principal grants an agent an exclusive territory, creating an exclusive agency, the principal cannot compete with the agent or appoint or allow another agent to so compete in violation of the *exclusive agency*. If the principal did so, he or she would be exposed to liability for the agent's lost sales or profits.

Safe Working Conditions.   The common law requires the principal to provide safe working premises, equipment, and conditions for all agents and employees. The principal has a duty to inspect working areas and to warn agents and employees about any unsafe situations. When the agency is one of employment, the employer's liability is frequently covered by state workers' compensation insurance, which is the primary remedy for an employee's injury on the job (see Chapter 21).

SECTION 4

Remedies and Rights of Agents and Principals

It is said that every wrong has its remedy. In business situations, disputes between agents and principals may arise out of either contract or tort laws and carry corresponding remedies. These remedies include monetary damages, termination of the agency relationship, injunction, and required accountings.

AGENT'S RIGHTS AND REMEDIES AGAINST PRINCIPAL

For every duty of the principal, the agent has a corresponding right. Therefore, the agent has the right to be compensated, reimbursed, and indemnified and to work in a safe environment. An agent also has the right to perform agency duties without interference by the principal.

Remedies of the agent for breach of duty by the principal follow normal contract and tort remedies. For example, suppose that Aaron Hart, a builder who has just completed construction on a new house, contracts with a real estate agent, Fran Boller, to sell the house. The contract calls for the agent to have an exclusive, ninety-day listing and to receive 6 percent of the selling price when the home is sold. Boller holds several open houses and shows the property to a number of potential buyers. One month before the ninety-

day listing terminates, Hart agrees to sell the house to another buyer—not one to whom Boller has shown the house—after the ninety-day listing expires. Hart and the buyer agree that Hart will reduce the price of the house by 3 percent, because he will sell it directly and thus will not have to pay Boller's commission. In this situation, if Boller learns of Hart's actions, she can terminate the agency relationship and sue Hart for damages—including the 6 percent commission she should have earned on the sale of the house.

An agent can also withhold further performance and demand that the principal give an accounting. For example, a sales agent may demand an accounting if the agent and principal disagree on the amount of commissions the agent should have received for sales made during a specific period of time.

When the principal-agent relationship is not contractual, an agent has no right to specific performance. An agent can recover for past services and future damages but cannot force the principal to allow him or her to continue acting as an agent.

PRINCIPAL'S RIGHTS AND REMEDIES AGAINST AGENT

In general, a principal has contract remedies for an agent's breach of fiduciary duties. The principal also has tort remedies for misrepresentation, negligence, fraud, deceit, libel, slander, and trespass committed by the agent. In addition, any breach of a fiduciary duty by an agent may justify the principal's termination of the agency. The main actions available to the principal are constructive trust, avoidance, and indemnification.

Constructive Trust.   Anything an agent obtains by virtue of the employment or agency relationship belongs to the principal. It is a breach of an agent's fiduciary duty to retain secretly benefits or profits that, by right, belong to the principal. For example, Andrews, a purchasing agent, gets cash rebates from a customer. If Andrews keeps the rebates, he violates his fiduciary duty to his principal, Metcalf. On finding out about the cash rebates, Metcalf can sue Andrews and recover them.

An agent is also prohibited from taking advantage of the agency relationship to obtain goods or property that the principal wants to purchase. For example, Peterson (the principal) wants to purchase property in the suburbs. Cox, Peterson's agent, learns that a valuable tract of land has just become available. Cox cannot buy the land for herself. Peterson gets the right of first refusal. If Cox purchases the land for her own benefit, the courts will impose a constructive trust on the land; that is, the land will be held for, and on behalf of, the principal despite the fact that the agent attempted to buy it in her own name.

Avoidance. When an agent breaches the agency agreement or agency duties under a contract, the principal has a right to avoid any contract entered into with the agent. This right of avoidance is at the election of the principal.

Indemnification. In certain situations, when a principal is sued by a third party for an agent's negligent conduct, the principal can sue the agent for an equal amount of damages. This is called *indemnification*. The same holds true if the agent violates the principal's instructions. For example, Lewis (the principal) tells his agent Moore, who is a used-car salesperson, to make no warranties for the used cars. Moore is eager to make a sale to Walters, a third party, and makes a warranty for the car's engine. Lewis is not absolved from liability to Walters for engine failure, but if Walters sues Lewis, Lewis normally can then sue Moore for indemnification for violating his instructions.

Sometimes it is difficult to distinguish between instructions of the principal that limit an agent's authority and those that are merely advice. For example, Willis (the principal) owns an office supply company; Jones (the agent) is the manager. Willis tells Jones, "Don't order any more inventory this month." Willis goes on vacation. A large order comes in from a local business, and the present inventory is insufficient to meet it. What is Jones to do? In this situation, Jones probably has the inherent authority to order more inventory despite Willis's command. It is unlikely that Jones would be required to indemnify Willis in the event that the local business subsequently canceled the order.

SECTION 5

Scope of Agent's Authority

Once the principal-agent relationship is created, attention focuses on the rights of third persons who deal with the agent. A principal's liability in a contract with a third party arises from the authority given the agent to enter legally binding contracts on the principal's behalf. An agent's authority can be either *actual* (express or implied) or *apparent*.

ACTUAL AUTHORITY— EXPRESS AND IMPLIED

Express authority is embodied in that which the principal has engaged the agent to do. Express authority can be given orally or in writing. The **equal dignity rule** in most states requires that if the contract being executed is or must be in writing, then the agent's authority must also be in writing. Failure to comply with the equal dignity rule can make a contract voidable *at the option of the principal.* The law regards the contract at that point as a mere offer. If the principal decides to accept the offer, acceptance must be ratified, or affirmed, in writing. Assume that Pattberg (the principal) orally asks Austin (the agent) to sell a ranch that Pattberg owns. Austin finds a buyer and signs a sales contract (a contract for an interest in realty must be in writing) on behalf of Pattberg to sell the ranch. The buyer cannot enforce the contract unless Pattberg subsequently ratifies Austin's agency status in writing. Once the contract is ratified, either party can enforce rights under the contract.

Implied authority is conferred by custom, can be inferred from the position the agent occupies, or is implied by virtue of being reasonably necessary to carry out express authority. For example, Carlson is employed by Packard Grocery to manage one of its stores. Packard has not specified (expressly stated) Carlson's authority to contract with third persons. In this situation, though, authority to manage a business implies authority to do what is reasonably required (as is customary or can be inferred from a manager's position) to operate the business. This includes making contracts for obtaining employee help, for buying merchandise and equipment, and even for advertising the products sold in the store.

Because implied authority is conferred on the basis of custom, it is important for third persons to be familiar with the custom of the trade. The list of rules that have developed to determine what authority is implied based on custom or on the agent's position is extensive. In general, implied authority is authority customarily associated with the position occupied by the agent or authority that can be inferred from the express authority given to the agent to perform fully his or her duties.

For example, an agent who has authority to solicit orders for goods sold by the principal has no authority to collect payments for the goods unless the agent possesses the goods. The test is whether it was reasonable for the agent to believe that he or she had the authority to enter into the contract in question.

APPARENT AUTHORITY AND ESTOPPEL

Actual authority (express or implied) arises from what the principal manifests *to the agent*. An agent has **apparent authority** when the principal, by either word or action, causes a *third party* reasonably to believe that the agent has authority to act, even though the agent has no express or implied authority. If the third party changes his or her position in reliance on the principal's representations, the principal may be *estopped* from denying that the agent had authority.

For example, assume that Adam is a traveling sales agent for a pesticide company. Adam neither possesses the goods ordered nor delivers them, and he has no express or implied authority to collect payments from customers. Now assume that a customer, Ling, pays Adam for a solicited order. Adam then takes the payment to the principal's accounting department. An accountant accepts payment and sends Ling a receipt. This procedure is thereafter followed for other orders solicited by Adam and paid for by Ling. Later, Adam solicits an order, and Ling pays Adam as before. This time, however, Adam absconds with the money.

Can Ling claim that the payment to Adam was authorized and thus, in effect, a payment to the principal? The answer is yes, because the principal's *repeated* acts of accepting Ling's payments through Adam led Ling reasonably to believe that Adam had authority to receive payments for goods solicited.

Although Adam did not have express or implied authority, the principal's conduct gave Adam apparent authority to collect.

There are other ways in which agency by estoppel may arise based on apparent authority. If, for example, the principal has "clothed the agent" with both possession and apparent ownership of the principal's property, the agent has very broad powers and can deal with the property as if he or she were the true owner. For example, to deceive certain creditors, Sikora (the principal) and Hunter (the agent) agree verbally that Hunter will hold certain stock certificates for Sikora. Because the certificates are bearer paper (that is, they do not require indorsement to be transferred), Hunter's possession and apparent ownership of the stock certificates are such strong indications of ownership that a reasonable person would conclude that Hunter was the actual owner. If Hunter negotiates the stock certificates to a third person, Sikora will be estopped from denying Hunter's authority to transfer the stock.

When land is involved, courts have held that possession alone is not a sufficient indication of ownership. If, however, the agent also possesses the deed to the property and sells the property against the principal's wishes to an unsuspecting buyer, the principal normally cannot cancel the sale or assert the claim to title.

The following case illustrates a situation dealing with apparent authority.

CASE 20.4   Cargill, Inc. v. Mountain Cement Co.

Supreme Court of
Wyoming, 1995.
891 P.2d 57.

**IN THE LANGUAGE
OF THE COURT**

BACKGROUND AND FACTS   *Cargill, Inc., hired Charlie Mandry to work as a sales representative. Cargill provided Mandry with an office, a telephone, and an expense account. Through Mandry, Salt Creek Welding ordered steel from Cargill to build a silo for Mountain Cement Company. Mandry arranged to have some of the steel supplied by another company. The other firm's product was defective, which caused the silo to collapse. Mountain Cement filed a suit in a Wyoming state court against Cargill and others. The court ruled in favor of Mountain Cement. On appeal, one of the issues was whether Mandry acted as Cargill's agent in arranging the sale of the defective steel to Salt Creek.*

TAYLOR, Justice.

 *   *   *   *

Apparent authority is created when the principal holds the agent out as possessing the authority to bind the principal or when the principal allows the agent to claim such authority. *   *   * To recover on this theory [apparent authority] the third party must establish two facts: (1) the principal was responsible for the appearance of authority in the agent to conduct the transaction in question, and (2) the third party reasonably relied on the representations of the agent. *   *   *

*   *   *   *

*   *   * Cargill provided Mandry with a telephone, an expense account and office space. These facts indicate that Cargill intended to hold Mandry out as an agent who possessed the authority to bind Cargill. Further, Salt Creek reasonably relied on that apparent authority when it ordered steel from Cargill. Thus, both prongs of the apparent authority test are satisfied.

<table>
<tr><td>DECISION
AND REMEDY</td><td>The Supreme Court of Wyoming affirmed the lower court's decision on this issue and up-held the ruling in favor of Mountain Cement. Cargill held Mandry out as its agent, and Salt Creek reasonably relied on that apparent authority.</td></tr>
</table>

EMERGENCY POWERS

When an unforeseen emergency demands action by the agent to protect or preserve the property and rights of the principal, but the agent is unable to communicate with the principal, the agent has emergency power.

For example, Fulsom is an engineer for Pacific Railroad. While Fulsom is acting within the scope of his employment, he falls under the train many miles from home and is severely injured. Dusky, the conductor, directs Thompson, a doctor, to give medical aid to Fulsom and to charge Pacific for the medical services. Dusky, an agent, has no express or implied authority to bind the principal, Pacific Railroad, for the services of Thompson. Because of the emergency situation, however, the law recognizes Dusky as having authority to act appropriately under the circumstances.

RATIFICATION

Ratification occurs when the principal affirms an agent's unauthorized act. Ratification binds the principal to the agent's act and creates a situation in which the act is treated as if it had been authorized by the principal *from the outset.* Ratification can be either express or implied.

With respect to a contract, if the principal does not ratify, the principal is not bound, and the third party's agreement with the agent is merely an unaccepted offer. Because the third party's agreement is an unaccepted offer, the third party can revoke it any time before the principal ratifies, without liability. The agent, however, may be liable to the third party for misrepresenting his or her authority.

To be effective, a ratification must meet certain requirements. These include the following:

1. The agent must act on behalf of an identified principal who subsequently ratifies the action.
2. The principal must affirm the agent's act in its entirety.
3. The principal's affirmance must occur before the third party withdraws from the transaction.
4. The principal must have the legal capacity to authorize the transaction at the time the agent engages in the act and at the time the principal ratifies. The third party must also have the legal capacity to engage in the transaction.
5. The principal must know all of the material facts involved in the transaction.

Regarding this last requirement, if a principal ratifies a contract *without knowing* all of the facts, the principal can rescind (cancel) the ratification. If the third party has changed his or her position in reliance on the apparent contract, however, the principal can rescind but must reimburse the third party for his or her costs.

For example, suppose that an agent, without authority, contracts with a third person on behalf of a principal for repair work to the principal's office building. The principal learns of the contract and agrees to "some repair work," thinking that it will involve only patching and painting the exterior of the building. In fact, the contract includes resurfacing the parking lot, which the principal does not want done. On learning of the additional provision, the principal rescinds the contract. If the third party has made preparations to do the work (such as purchasing materials, hiring additional workers, or renting equipment), in reliance on the principal's apparent ratification, the principal must reimburse the third party for the cost of those preparations.

Section 6

Liability for Contracts

Liability for contracts formed by an agent depends on how the principal is classified and on whether the actions of the agent were authorized or unauthorized.

Principals are classified as disclosed, partially disclosed, or undisclosed.[5] A **disclosed principal** is a principal whose identity is known by the third party at the time the contract is made by the agent. A **partially disclosed principal** is a principal whose identity is not known by the third party, but the third party knows that the agent is or may be acting for a principal at the time that the contract is made. An **undisclosed principal** is a principal whose identity is totally unknown by the third party, and the third party has no knowledge that the agent is acting in an agency capacity at the time the contract is made.

AUTHORIZED ACTS

If an agent acts within the scope of his or her authority, a disclosed or partially disclosed principal is liable to a third party for a contract made by the agent. If the principal is disclosed, an agent has no contractual liability for the nonperformance of the principal or the third party. If the principal is partially disclosed, in most states the agent is also treated as a party to the contract, and the third party can hold the agent liable for contractual nonperformance.[6]

When neither the fact of agency nor the identity of the principal is disclosed, the undisclosed principal is fully bound to perform just as if the principal had been fully disclosed at the time the contract was made. Exceptions to this rule are made in the following circumstances:

1. The undisclosed principal was expressly excluded as a party in the contract. For example, an agent contracts with a landlord for the lease of a building. The landlord does not know of the agency, and the lease specifically lists the agent as tenant, with no right of assignment without the landlord's consent. The undisclosed principal cannot enforce the lease.

2. The contract is a negotiable instrument, such as a check or a promissory note. Here, the UCC provides that only the agent is liable if the instrument neither names the principal nor shows that the agent signed in a representative capacity.
3. The performance of the agent is personal to the contract, allowing the third party to refuse the principal's performance. Typical examples involve extensions of credit and highly personal services, such as surgery.
4. The third party would not have entered into a contract with the principal had the third party known the principal's identity, the agent or the principal knew this, and the third party rescinds the contract.

When a principal's identity is undisclosed and the agent is forced to pay the third party, the agent is entitled to indemnification by the principal. It was the principal's duty to perform, even though his or her identity was undisclosed,[7] and failure to do so will make the principal ultimately liable. Once the undisclosed principal's identity is revealed, the third party generally can elect to hold either the principal or the agent liable on the contract.

UNAUTHORIZED ACTS

If an agent has no authority but nevertheless contracts with a third party, the principal cannot be held liable to the contract. It does not matter whether the principal was disclosed, partially disclosed, or undisclosed. The agent is liable, however. For example, Scammon signs a contract for the purchase of a truck, purportedly acting as an agent under authority granted by Johnson. In fact, Johnson has not given Scammon any such authority. Johnson refuses to pay for the truck, claiming that Scammon had no authority to purchase it. The seller of the truck is entitled to hold Scammon liable for payment.

If the principal is disclosed or partially disclosed, the agent's liability to the third party is based on the theory of breach of implied warranty of authority, not on breach of the contract itself.[8] The agent's implied warranty of authority can be breached intentionally or by a good faith mistake.[9] The agent is liable, as long

---

5. *Restatement (Second) of Agency*, Section 4.
6. *Restatement (Second) of Agency*, Section 321.

7. If the agent is a gratuitous agent, and the principal accepts the benefits of the agent's contract with a third party, then the principal will be liable to the agent on the theory of quasi contract (see Chapter 9).
8. The agent is not liable on the contract because the agent was never intended personally to be a party to the contract.
9. If the agent intentionally misrepresents his or her authority, then the agent can also be liable in tort for fraud.

as the third party relied on the agency status. Conversely, if the third party knows at the time the contract is made that the agent is mistaken about the extent of his or her authority, or the agent indicates to the third party *uncertainty* about the extent of authority, the agent is not personally liable for breach of warranty.

SECTION 7

Liability for Agent's Torts

Obviously, an agent is liable for his or her own torts. A principal may also be liable for an agent's torts if they result from one of the following:

1. The principal's own tortious conduct.
2. The principal's authorization of a tortious act.
3. The agent's unauthorized but tortious misrepresentation made within the scope of the agency.

If the agent is an employee, whose conduct the principal-employer controls, the employer may also be liable for torts committed by the employee in the course of employment under the doctrine of *respondeat superior*, as discussed below.

PRINCIPAL'S TORTIOUS CONDUCT

A principal conducting an activity through an agent may be liable for harm resulting from the principal's own negligence or recklessness, which may include giving improper instructions; authorizing the use of improper materials, tools, or the like; establishing improper rules; or failing to prevent others' tortious conduct while they are on the principal's property or using the principal's equipment, materials, or tools. For instance, if Jack knows that Kathy cannot drive but nevertheless authorizes her to use the company truck to deliver some equipment to a customer, he will be liable for his own negligence to anyone injured by her negligent driving.

PRINCIPAL'S AUTHORIZATION OF AGENT'S TORTIOUS CONDUCT

Similarly, a principal who authorizes an agent to commit a tortious act may be liable to persons or property injured thereby, because the act is considered to be the principal's. For example, Selkow directs Warren—an agent Selkow retained to oversee the

harvest of crops he bought—to cut the corn on specific acreage, which neither of them has the right to do. The harvest is therefore a trespass, and Selkow is liable to whoever owns the corn.

In the same vein, assume that Victoria instructs Guthrie, her real estate agent, to tell prospective purchasers that there is oil beneath her property, when she knows there is not. Victoria will be liable to anyone who buys the property in reliance on the statements.

MISREPRESENTATION

A principal is exposed to tort liability whenever a third person sustains a loss due to the agent's misrepresentation. The principal's liability depends on whether the agent was actually or apparently authorized to make representations and whether such representations were made within the scope of the agency.

Fraudulent Misrepresentation. Assume that Bassett is a demonstrator for Moore's products. Moore sends Bassett to a home show to demonstrate the products and to answer questions from consumers. Moore has given Bassett authority to make statements about the products. If Bassett makes only true representations, all is fine; but if he makes false claims, Moore will be liable for any injuries or damages sustained by third parties in reliance on Bassett's false representations.

An interesting series of cases has arisen on the theory that when a principal has placed an agent in a position to defraud a third party, the principal is liable for the agent's fraudulent acts. For example, Frendak is a loan officer at First Security Bank. In the ordinary course of the job, Frendak approves and services loans and has access to the credit records of all customers. Frendak falsely represents to a borrower, McMillan, that the bank feels insecure about McMillan's loan and intends to call it in unless McMillan provides additional collateral, such as stocks and bonds. McMillan gives Frendak numerous stock certificates, which Frendak keeps in her own possession and later uses to make personal investments. The bank is liable to McMillan for losses sustained on the stocks even though the bank had no direct role in or knowledge of the fraudulent scheme.

The legal theory used here is that the agent's position conveys to third persons the impression that the agent has the authority to make statements and perform acts consistent with the ordinary duties that are within the scope of the position. When an agent appears to be acting within the scope of the authority that the position of agency confers but is actually taking advantage of a third party, the principal who placed the agent in that position is liable. In the example above, if a bank teller had told McMillan that the bank required additional security for the loan, McMillan would not have been justified in relying on the person's authority to make that representation. McMillan, however, could reasonably expect that the loan officer was telling the truth.

Innocent Misrepresentation. Tort liability based on fraud requires proof that a material misstatement was made knowingly and with the intent to deceive. An agent's innocent mistakes occurring in a contract transaction or involving a warranty contained in the contract can provide grounds for the third party's rescission of the contract and the award of damages. Moreover, justice dictates that when a principal knows that an agent is not accurately advised of facts but does not correct either the agent's or the third party's impressions, the principal is directly responsible to the third party for resulting damages. The point is that the principal is always directly responsible for an agent's misrepresentation made within the scope of authority.

The Doctrine of *Respondeat Superior*

Under the doctrine of **respondeat superior,**[10] the principal-employer is liable for any harm caused to a third party by an agent-employee within the scope of employment. This doctrine imposes **vicarious liability** on the employer—that is, liability without regard to the personal fault of the employer for torts committed by an employee in the course or scope of employment.[11] Third persons injured through the negligence of an employee can sue either the employee who was negligent or the employer, if the employee's negligent conduct occurred while the employee was acting within the scope of employment.

At early common law, a servant (employee) was viewed as the master's (employer's) property. The master was deemed to have absolute control over the servant's acts and was held strictly liable for them no matter how carefully the master supervised the servant. The rationale for the doctrine of *respondeat superior* is based on the principle of social duty that requires every person to manage his or her affairs, whether accomplished by the person or through agents, so as not to injure another. Liability is imposed on employers because they are deemed to be in a better financial position to bear the loss. The superior financial position carries with it the duty to be responsible for damages.

Today the doctrine continues, but employers carry liability insurance and spread the cost of risk over the entire business enterprise. Public policy requires that an injured person be afforded effective relief, and recovery from a business enterprise provides far more effective relief than recovery from an individual employee. Liability rights exist under law because of public-policy protections of third parties. Thus, a master (employer) cannot contract with a servant (employee) to disclaim responsibilities for injuries resulting from the servant's acts, because such disclaimers are against public policy.

Liability for Employee's Negligence. For the employer to be liable for an employee's negligence, the employee's injury-causing act must have occurred within the course and scope of the employee's employment.

Scope of Employment. The *Restatement (Second) of Agency*, Section 229, indicates the following general factors that courts will consider in determining whether or not a particular act occurred within the course and scope of employment:

1. Whether the employee's act was authorized by the employer.
2. The time, place, and purpose of the act.
3. Whether the act was one commonly performed by employees on behalf of their employers.
4. The extent to which the employer's interest was advanced by the act.
5. The extent to which the private interests of the employee were involved.
6. Whether the employer furnished the means or instrumentality (for example, a truck or a machine) by which an injury was inflicted.
7. Whether the employer had reason to know that the employee would perform the act in question and whether the employee had done it before.
8. Whether the act involved the commission of a serious crime.

---

10. Pronounced ree-*spahn*-dee-uht soo-*peer*-ee-your. The doctrine of *respondeat superior* applies not only to employer-employee relationships but also to other principal-agent relationships in which the principal has the right of control over the agent.
11. The theory of *respondeat superior* is similar to the theory of strict liability covered in Chapter 12.

EMERGING TRENDS IN TECHNOLOGY

The Use of Intelligent Agents

"Intelligent agents," or electronic agents, are semiautonomous Internet computer programs that are capable of executing specific tasks. For example, intelligent agents on the World Wide Web can search through many databases and retrieve only relevant information for the user. Some intelligent agents are used to make purchases on the Internet. A user might use BargainFinder (PriceScan), for example, to search the many Internet Web sites that offer compact discs (CDs) and seek out the lowest price for a particular album. Once the lowest price is found, the intelligent agent usually offers links to the appropriate Web sites. Different shopping agents locate other specific products in online catalogues and actually negotiate product acquisition, as well as delivery.

WHAT AGENCY LAW APPLIES?

Intelligent agents may be just that, but standard agency principles have applied only to *human* agents, who have express or implied authority to enter into specific contracts. Many questions in agency law revolve around whether the human agent acted within the scope of his or her authority. What does this concept mean when dealing with an electronic intelligent agent?

Consider a not-unusual example. Software that an intelligent agent might find for its user will undoubtedly involve a "click-on" agreement (see the discussion of electronic sales contracts in the *Emerging Trends in Technology* presented in Chapter 11).

Intelligent agents searching the Internet may run into a wide variety of such "click-on" agreements, which by necessity, contain many different terms and conditions. If the intelligent agent ignores the terms and conditions of a licensing agreement outlined in the "click-on" setting, is the user of the agent nonetheless bound by the agreement? Conversely, many "click-on" agreements exempt third parties from any liability resulting from the underlying product or service. Is the user of the intelligent agent bound by this particular term? With respect to human agents, the courts occasionally have found that an agent could not agree to such a term without explicit authority.[a]

To avoid problems created by the use of intelligent agents, some online stores have blocked intelligent agents from accessing

---

a. *Bernstein v. Seacliff Beach Club, Inc.,* 35 Misc.2d 153, 228 N.Y.S.2d 567 (1962).

Consider an example. Mandel (the employee) is a delivery driver for Schwartz (the employer). Schwartz provides Mandel with a vehicle and instructs him to use it for making company deliveries. One day, while he is making deliveries, Mandel negligently runs into Chan, a pedestrian, causing Chan to be seriously injured. Because the negligence occurred as part of Mandel's regular duties of employment (making deliveries), Schwartz is liable to Chan for the injuries caused by Mandel's negligence.

An employee going to and from work or to and from meals is usually considered outside the scope of employment. All travel time of traveling salespersons or others whose jobs require them to travel is normally considered within the scope of employment for the duration of the business trip, including the return trip home, unless there is a significant departure from the employer's business.

Departures from the Employer's Business. When an employee goes off on his or her own—that is, departs from the employer's business to take care of personal affairs—is the employer liable? The answer depends on whether the employee's activity is a minor departure from the employer's business or a substan-

EMERGING TRENDS IN TECHNOLOGY

The Use of Intelligent Agents, continued

pricing information. Other online stores are developing click-on agreements that can be understood by a computer and that are therefore more conspicuous for intelligent agents.

THE UNIFORM COMPUTER INFORMATION TRANSACTIONS ACT

The Uniform Computer Information Transactions Act (UCITA), which was proposed for adoption by the states in 1999, specifically addresses the issue of intelligent agents. Section 107(d) of the act provides that any individual or company that uses an electronic agent "is bound by the operations of the electronic agent, even if no

individual was aware of or reviewed the agent's operations or the results of the operations." The liability of individuals and companies for the acts of electronic agents, however, is qualified by Section 206(a) of the UCITA, which states that "a court may grant appropriate relief if the operations resulted from fraud, electronic mistake, or the like." As discussed in Chapter 15, the UCITA's provisions have generated substantial controversy, and it is not yet clear whether the act will be adopted by the states or, if it is, how it may be modified on adoption.

IMPLICATIONS FOR THE BUSINESSPERSON

1. Any businessperson who is contemplating the use of an electronic agent must proceed with caution. Time may be saved, but users of such agents must consider the possibility that they might be bound to contract terms

of which they are unaware.
2. Although intelligent agents are becoming increasingly sophisticated, there is still the possibility that they may have more contracting authority than any businessperson wants them to have. The message for businesspersons is "user beware."

FOR CRITICAL ANALYSIS

1. What are the costs and benefits of using an intelligent shopping agent?
2. How might online shopping-site owners develop standardized click-on agreements that can be understood by electronic agents?

RELEVANT WEB SITES

For information on PriceScan, go to http://www.pricescan.com. Go to SelectSurf at http://www.selectsurf.com/shopping/compare, where you will find hot links to many intelligent shopping agents.

---

tial departure akin to an utter abandonment of the employer's business. For example, a traveling salesperson, while driving the employer's vehicle to call on a customer, decides to stop at the post office—which is one block off his route—to mail a personal letter. As the employee approaches the post office, he negligently runs into a parked vehicle owned by Inga. In this situation, because the employee's detour from the employer's business is not substantial, the employee is still within the scope of employment, and the employer is liable.

The result would be different if the employee had decided to pick up a few friends for cocktails in an-

other city and in the process had negligently run his vehicle into Inga's. In this situation, the departure from the employer's business would be substantial, to the point of abandoning the employer's business, and the employer normally would not be liable to Inga for damages. The employee would be considered to be on a "frolic" of his own, and only the employee could be held liable to Inga.

Courts often refer to the "detour-frolic" distinction when deciding whether a given action was within the course and scope of employment. The distinction was first drawn in the following classic case on "master-servant" (employer-employee) law.

CASE 20.5   Joel v. Morison

Court of Exchequer,
England, 1834.
172 Eng.Rep. 1338.

BACKGROUND AND FACTS   *The plaintiff was walking across Bishopsgate Street when he was knocked down by a cart driven negligently by a servant of the defendant. The plaintiff suffered a fractured leg and multiple injuries. The plaintiff took the position that the defendant was liable for his injuries because the defendant's servant was driving the cart that caused the injuries. The defendant argued that his cart was never driven in the neighborhood in which the plaintiff was injured. Moreover, it was suggested that the defendant's servant had gone out of his way for his own purposes and might have taken the cart at a time when it was not wanted for business purposes to pay a visit to some friends.*

IN THE LANGUAGE OF THE COURT   *PARKE*, Judge.

*   *   *   *

*   *   * This is an action to recover damages for an injury sustained by the plaintiff, in consequence of the negligence of the defendant's servant. *   *   * If the servants, being on their master's business, took a detour to call upon a friend, the master will be responsible. If *   *   * the servants lent the cart to a person who was driving without the defendant's knowledge, he will not be responsible. Or, if *   *   * the young man who was driving took the cart surreptitiously, and was not at the time employed on his master's business, the defendant will not be liable. The master is only liable where the servant is acting in the course of his employment. If he was going out of his way, against his master's implied commands, when driving on his master's business, he will make his master liable; *but if he was going on a frolic of his own, without being at all on his master's business, the master will not be liable.* As to the damages, the master *   *   * [although not himself] guilty of any offence, *   *   * is only responsible in law, therefore the amount should be reasonable. [Emphasis added.]

DECISION AND REMEDY   *The verdict was for the plaintiff, and he was awarded damages of £30. In this case, the master was held liable for the acts of his servant.*

INTERNATIONAL CONSIDERATIONS   **Respondeat Superior *in Islamic Countries***   *The doctrine of respondeat superior is well established in the legal systems of the United States and most Western countries. Middle Eastern countries, however, do not employ the principle. Islamic law holds to a strict principle that responsibility for human actions lies with the individual and cannot be vicariously extended to others.*

Notice of Dangerous Conditions.   The employer is charged with knowledge of any dangerous conditions discovered by an employee and pertinent to the employment situation. To illustrate: A maintenance employee in Martin's apartment building notices a lead pipe protruding from the ground in the building's courtyard. The employee neglects either to fix it or to inform the employer of the danger. John falls on the pipe and is injured. The employer is charged with knowledge of the dangerous condition regardless of whether or not the employee actually informed the employer. That knowledge is imputed to the employer by virtue of the employment relationship.

Liability for Employee's Intentional Torts.   Most intentional torts that employees commit have no relation to their employment; thus, their employers will not be held liable. Under the doctrine of *respondeat superior*, however, the employer is liable for intentional torts of the employee that are committed within the course and scope of employment, just as the employer is liable for negligence. For example, an employer is liable when an employee (such as a "bouncer" at a nightclub or a security guard at a department store) commits assault and battery or false imprisonment while acting within the scope of employment.

An employee acting at the employer's direction can be liable as a *tortfeasor* (one who commits a wrong, or tort), along with the employer, for committing the tortious act even if the employee was unaware of the wrongfulness of the act. For example, an employer directs an employee to burn out a field of crops. The employee does so, assuming that the field belongs to the employer, which it does not. Both can be found liable to the owner of the field for damages.

An employer who knows or should know that an employee has a propensity for committing tortious acts is liable for the employee's acts even if they would not ordinarily be considered within the scope of employment. For example, the Blue Moon employs Arnold Munn as a bouncer, knowing that he has a history of arrests for assault and battery. While he is working one night, and within the scope of his employment, he viciously attacks a patron who "looks at him funny." The Blue Moon will bear the responsibility for Munn's misdeeds, because it knew that he had a propensity for committing tortious acts.

An employer is also liable for permitting an employee to engage in reckless actions that can injure others. For example, an employer observes an employee smoking while filling containerized trucks with highly flammable liquids. Failure to stop the employee will cause the employer to be liable for any injuries that result if a truck explodes.

To reduce the likelihood of liability losses, employers set up stringent work rules. For example, employees who drive company vehicles may be prohibited from giving rides to other passengers. Employees who violate these rules by being careless or committing unlawful or tortious acts may be subject to discipline, including discharge. Almost without exception, employers purchase liability insurance to cover the actions of certain employees.

SECTION 8

Liability for Independent Contractor's Torts

The general rule concerning liability for the acts of independent contractors is that the employer is not liable for physical harm caused to a third person by the negligent act of an independent contractor in the performance of the contract. An employer who has no legal power to control the details of the physical performance of a contract cannot be held liable. Here again, the test is the *right to control*. Because an employer bargains with an independent contractor only for results and retains no control over the manner in which those results are achieved, the employer is generally not expected to bear the responsibility for torts committed by an independent contractor. A collection agency is a typical example of an independent contractor. The creditor is generally not liable for the acts of the collection agency, because collection is a distinct business occupation.

Generally, an exception to this doctrine prevails when unusually hazardous activities are involved. Typical examples of such activities include blasting operations, the transportation of highly volatile chemicals, and the use of poisonous gases. In these cases, an employer cannot be shielded from liability merely by using an independent contractor. Strict liability is imposed on the employer-principal as a matter of law. Also, in some states, strict liability may be imposed by statute.

In the following case, one of the issues before the court was whether the negligence of an independent contractor, who was acting as an agent, could be imputed to the principal.

CASE 20.6   **Haag v. Bongers**

Supreme Court of
Nebraska, 1999.
256 Neb. 170,
589 N.W.2d 318.
http://www.findlaw.
com/11stategov/ne/
neca.html[a]

BACKGROUND AND FACTS   *When Leo Bongers died, his nephew, Alfred Bongers, was appointed one of the personal representatives of his estate, which included more than 120 antique cars, trucks, and motorcycles. The estate hired Bauer-Moravec Auctioneers and Clerks, and Dolan Realty and Auction Company to jointly conduct an auction of the vehicles. The auctioneers suggested that the auction be held in the summer, with the vehicles lined up outside, but the estate insisted on holding the auction as soon as possible, in the winter. The auction was heavily advertised at the estate's insistence, and was held on a farm owned by the estate, in a building open at both ends. With the estate's agree-*

---

a. In the "Supreme Court Opinions" section, click on "1999." In that row, click on "February." On that page, scroll down the list of cases to the name of the case (the decision was issued on "02/12/1999") and click on the docket number to access the opinion.

ment, tents were set up at either end to enlarge the "bid barn," and each attendee was charged $25. Bongers was there. Assistants paid by the estate moved the vehicles through the members of the crowd, who were standing shoulder to shoulder in the barn. The estate had failed in its responsibility to put all of the vehicles in running order, so many of the vehicles were towed into the building using tractors, which the estate had approved, with hitch balls. As the assistants attempted to tow an antique Studebaker truck out of the barn, the hitch ball became detached, flew off the tractor, and hit Joseph Haag, who suffered serious head injuries. Haag filed a suit in a Nebraska state court against the estate and others, alleging, among other things, negligence on the part of the auctioneers. Haag argued that as agents for the estate, the auctioneers' negligence should be imputed to the estate. The estate responded in part that it was not liable for the acts of the auctioneers because they were independent contractors. The court entered a judgment in favor of Haag. The estate appealed to the Nebraska Supreme Court.

IN THE LANGUAGE OF THE COURT

MILLER-LEHRMAN, J. [Justice]

*   *   *   *

Generally, the employer of an independent contractor is not liable for physical harm caused to another by the acts or omissions of the contractor or his servants. *   *   * *The employer of an independent contractor may be vicariously liable to a third party* *   *   * *if the employer retains control over the contractor's work* *   *   * . [Emphasis added.]

*   *   *   *

Based on the facts of this case, we conclude that the auctioneers served as independent contractors. However, the Estate exercised sufficient control over the auction to subject it to liability, notwithstanding the participation of the auctioneers as independent contractors. The factors which demonstrate the Estate's control include, but are not limited to, the following facts: The auction was held on the Estate's property, and the Estate insisted that the auction be conducted in winter rather than in summer in a more expansive setting. The Estate was responsible for putting the vehicles in running order but failed to do so, resulting in the necessity of towing the vehicles at the auction. The Estate approved the use of tractors to tow the vehicles at the auction. The Estate approved the use of assistants. The Estate paid the assistants. The Estate insisted that the auction be heavily advertised, resulting in a shoulder-to-shoulder crowd through which the vehicles were to be towed. The Estate and the auctioneers decided to extend the bid barn and charge a $25 fee. Bongers was present at the auction at the time of the accident.

Although actual performance of the task of towing the vehicles was to be performed by the independent contractor auctioneers, the facts in this case as to the Estate's active and considerable control over the activities that led to the accident are sufficient to subject the Estate to liability. In this regard, we note that the *Restatement (Second) of Torts,* Section 414 provides:

> One who entrusts work to an independent contractor, but who retains the control of any part of the work, is subject to liability for physical harm to others for whose safety the employer owes a duty to exercise reasonable care, which is caused by his failure to exercise his control with reasonable care.

We conclude that because the Estate retained considerable control over the relevant work, it is therefore liable for a failure to exercise reasonable care in the use of that control. Accordingly, imputing the negligence of the assistants to the Estate was justified by the facts *   *   * .

DECISION AND REMEDY

The Nebraska Supreme Court affirmed the judgment of the trial court. The negligence of the assistants, who worked for the independent contractors (who acted as the agents of the estate and were paid by the estate) could be imputed to the estate because of the control exercised by the principal over the independent contractors.

Section 9

Liability for Agent's Crimes

Obviously, an agent is liable for his or her own crimes. A principal or employer is not liable for an agent's or employee's crime simply because the agent or employee committed the crime while otherwise acting within the scope of authority or employment, unless the principal or employer participated by conspiracy or other action. In some jurisdictions, under specific statutes, a principal may be liable for an agent's violating, in the course and scope of employment, such regulations as those governing sanitation, prices, weights, and the sale of liquor.

Section 10

Termination of an Agency

Agency law is similar to contract law in that both an agency and a contract may be terminated by an act of the parties or by operation of law. Once the relationship between the principal and the agent has ended, the agent no longer has *actual* authority to bind the principal—that is, he or she lacks the principal's consent to act in the principal's behalf. Generally, if the agency is terminated by an act of the parties, the principal can still be bound by the agent's acts if the agent has acted within the scope of his or her *apparent* authority, however. To terminate the agent's apparent authority, third parties must be notified of the agency termination—as will be discussed later.

Termination by Act of the Parties

An agency relationship may be terminated by act of the parties in a number of ways, including those discussed here.

Lapse of Time. An agency agreement may specify the time period during which the agency relationship will exist. If so, the agency ends when that time expires. For example, Akers signs an agreement of agency with Jefferson "beginning January 1, 1998, and ending December 31, 1999." The agency is automatically terminated on December 31, 1999. Of course, the parties can agree to continue the relationship, in which case the same terms will apply.

If no definite time is stated, then the agency continues for a reasonable time and can be terminated at will by either party. What constitutes a reasonable time depends on the circumstances and the nature of the agency relationship. For example, Jefferson asks Akers to sell her car. If after two years Akers has not sold Jefferson's car and there has been no communication between Jefferson and Akers, it is safe to assume that the agency relationship has terminated. Akers no longer has the authority to sell Jefferson's car.

Purpose Achieved. An agent can be employed to accomplish a particular objective, such as the purchase of stock for a cattle rancher. In that situation, the agency automatically ends after the cattle have been purchased. If more than one agent is employed to accomplish the same purpose, such as the sale of real estate, the first agent to complete the sale automatically terminates the agency relationship for all the others.

Occurrence of a Specific Event. An agency can be created to terminate on the happening of a certain event. For example, Jefferson appoints Akers to handle her business affairs while she is away. When Jefferson returns, the agency automatically terminates.

Sometimes one aspect of the agent's authority terminates on the occurrence of a particular event, but the agency relationship itself does not terminate. For example, Jefferson, a banker, permits Akers, the credit manager, to grant a credit line of $5,000 to certain depositors who maintain a balance of $5,000 in a savings account. If any customer's savings account balance falls below $5,000, Akers can no longer make the credit line available to that customer. Akers, however, continues to have the right to extend credit to the other customers maintaining the minimum balance.

Mutual Agreement. Recall from basic contract law that parties can rescind (cancel) a contract by mutually agreeing to terminate the contractual relationship. The same holds true in agency law regardless of whether the agency contract is in writing or whether it is for a specific duration. For example, Jefferson no longer wishes Akers to be her agent, and Akers does not want to work for Jefferson anymore. Either party can communicate to the other the intent to terminate the relationship. Agreement to terminate effectively relieves each of the rights, duties, and powers inherent in the relationship.

Termination by One Party. As a *general* rule, either party can terminate the agency relationship. The agent's act is said to be a renunciation of authority. The principal's act is a revocation of authority. Although both parties may have the *power* to terminate—because agency is a consensual relationship, and thus neither party can be compelled to continue in the relationship—they may not possess the *right* to terminate and may therefore be liable for breach of contract. Wrongful termination can subject the canceling party to a suit for damages. For example, Akers has a one-year employment contract with Jefferson to act as Jefferson's agent for $25,000. Jefferson can discharge Akers before the contract period expires (Jefferson has the *power* to breach the contract); however, Jefferson will be liable to Akers for money damages, because Jefferson has no *right* to breach the contract.

Even in an agency at will (that is, an agency that either party may terminate at any time), the principal who wishes to terminate must give the agent a reasonable notice—that is, at least sufficient notice to allow the agent to recoup his or her expenses and, in some cases, to make a normal profit.

A special rule applies in an *agency coupled with an interest*. This type of agency is not an agency in the usual sense, because it is created for the agent's benefit instead of for the principal's benefit. For example, suppose that Julie borrows $5,000 from Rob, giving Rob some of her jewelry and signing a letter authorizing Rob to sell the jewelry as her agent if she fails to repay the loan. Julie, after she has received the $5,000 from Rob, then attempts to revoke Rob's authority to sell the jewelry. Julie will not succeed in this attempt, because a principal cannot revoke an agency created for the agent's benefit.

An agency coupled with an interest should not be confused with a situation in which the agent merely derives proceeds or profits from the sale of the subject matter. For example, an agent who merely receives a commission from the sale of real property does not have a beneficial interest in the property itself. Likewise, an attorney whose fee is a percentage of the recovery (a *contingency fee*—see Chapter 2) merely has an interest in the proceeds. These agency relationships are revocable by the principal, subject to any express contractual arrangements between the principal and the agent.

Notice of Termination. When an agency has been terminated by act of the parties, it is the principal's duty to inform any third parties who know of the existence of the agency that it has been terminated (although notice of the termination may be given by others).

An agent's authority continues until the agent receives some notice of termination. As previously mentioned, notice to third parties follows the general rule

that an agent's *apparent authority* continues until the third person receives notice (from any source of information) that the authority has been terminated. The principal is expected to notify *directly* any third person who the principal knows has dealt with the agent. For third persons who have heard about the agency but have not dealt with the agent, *constructive notice* is sufficient.[12]

No particular form is required for notice of termination of the principal-agent relationship to be effective. The principal can actually notify the agent, or the agent can learn of the termination through some other means. For example, Manning bids on a shipment of steel, and Stone is hired as an agent to arrange transportation of the shipment. When Stone learns that Manning has lost the bid, Stone's authority to make the transportation arrangement terminates.

If the agent's authority is written, it must be revoked in writing, and the writing must be shown to all people who saw the original writing that established the agency relationship. Sometimes, a written authorization (such as a power of attorney) contains an expiration date. The passage of the expiration date is sufficient notice of termination.

TERMINATION BY OPERATION OF LAW

Certain events will terminate agency authority automatically, because their occurrence makes it impossible for the agent to perform or improbable that the principal would continue to want performance. These events include death or insanity of either the principal or the agent, loss of the agency's subject matter (impossibility) or a change in circumstances that has an unusual effect on the subject matter, bankruptcy of either the principal or the agent, and war between the respective countries. Note that when an agency terminates by operation of law, there is no duty to notify third persons—unless the agent's authority is coupled with an interest.[13]

---

12. With *constructive notice* of a fact, knowledge of the fact is imputed by law to a person if he or she could have discovered the fact by proper diligence. Constructive notice is often accomplished by publication in a newspaper.

13. There is an exception to this rule in banking. The UCC provides that the bank, as agent, can continue to exercise specific types of authority even after the customer's death or insanity unless it has knowledge of the death or insanity. When the bank has knowledge of the customer's death, it has authority for ten days after the death to pay checks (but not notes or drafts) drawn by the customer unless it receives a stop-payment order from someone who has an interest in the account, such as an heir.

TERMS AND CONCEPTS TO REVIEW

agency 434

apparent authority 445

disclosed principal 447

equal dignity rule 444

express authority 444

fiduciary 434

independent contractor 435

implied authority 444

partially disclosed
   principal 447

ratification 446

respondeat superior 449

undisclosed principal 447

vicarious liability 449

QUESTIONS AND CASE PROBLEMS

20–1. AGENT'S DUTY TO PRINCIPAL. Peter hires Alice as an agent to sell a piece of property he owns. The price is to be at least $30,000. Alice discovers that because a shopping mall is planned for the area in which Peter's property is located, the fair market value of the property will be at least $45,000 and could be higher. Alice forms a real estate partnership with her cousin Carl, and she prepares for Peter's signature a contract for sale of the property to Carl for $32,000. Peter signs the contract. Just before closing and passage of title, Peter learns about the shopping mall and the increased fair market value of his property. Peter refuses to deed the property to Carl. Carl claims that Alice, as agent, solicited a price above that agreed on in the creation of the agency and that the contract is therefore binding and enforceable. Discuss fully whether Peter is bound to this contract.

20–2. AGENCY FORMATION. John Paul Corp. made the following contracts:

(a) A contract with Able Construction to build an addition to the corporate office building.

(b) A contract with a certified public accountant (CPA), a recent college graduate, to head the cost accounting section.

(c) A contract with a salesperson to travel a designated area to solicit orders (contracts) for the corporation.

Able contracts with Apex for materials for the addition; the CPA hires an experienced accountant to advise her on certain accounting procedures; and the salesperson contracts to sell a large order to Green, agreeing to deliver the goods in person within twenty days. Later, Able refuses to pick up the materials, the CPA is in default in paying the hired consultant, and the salesperson does not deliver on time. Apex, the accountant, and Green claim John Paul Corp. is liable under agency law. Discuss fully whether an agency relationship was created by John Paul with Able, the CPA, or the salesperson.

20–3. AGENT'S DUTIES TO PRINCIPAL. Ankir is hired by Peters as a traveling salesperson. Ankir not only solicits orders but also delivers the goods and collects payments from his customers. Ankir places all payments in his private checking account and at the end of each month draws sufficient cash from his bank to cover the payments made. Peters is totally unaware of this procedure. Because of a slowdown in the economy, Peters tells all his salespeople to offer 20 percent discounts on orders. Ankir solicits orders, but he offers only 15 percent discounts, pocketing the extra 5 percent paid by customers. Ankir has not lost any orders by this practice, and he is rated one of Peters's top salespersons. Peters learns of Ankir's actions. Discuss fully Peters's rights in this matter.

20–4. LIABILITY FOR AGENT'S CONTRACTS. Alice Adams is a purchasing agent-employee for the A & B Coal Supply partnership. Adams has authority to purchase the coal needed by A & B to satisfy the needs of its customers. While Adams is leaving a coal mine from which she has just purchased a large quantity of coal, her car breaks down. She walks into a small roadside grocery store for help. While there, she runs into Will Wilson. Wilson owns 360 acres back in the mountains with all mineral rights. Wilson, in need of money, offers to sell Adams the property at $1,500 per acre. On inspection of the property, Adams forms the opinion that the subsurface contains valuable coal deposits. Adams contracts to purchase the property for A & B Coal Supply, signing the contract "A & B Coal Supply, Alice Adams, agent." The closing date is August 1. Adams takes the contract to the partnership. The managing partner is furious, as A & B is not in the property business. Later, just before closing, both Wilson and the partnership learn that the value of the land is at least $15,000 per acre. Discuss the rights of A & B and Wilson concerning the land contract.

20–5. UNDISCLOSED PRINCIPAL. Paula Enterprises hires Able to act as its agent to purchase a one-thousand-acre tract of land from Thompson for $1,000 per acre. Paula Enterprises does not wish Thompson to know that it is the principal or that Able is its agent. Paula wants the land for a new country housing development, and Thompson may not sell the land for that purpose or may demand a premium price. Able makes the contract for the purchase, signing only his name as purchaser and not disclosing to Thompson the agency relationship. The closing and transfer of deed are to take place on September 1.

   (a) If Thompson learns of Paula's identity on August 1, can Thompson legally refuse to deed the property on September 1? Explain.

   (b) Paula gives Able the money for the closing, but Able absconds with the money, causing a breach of Able's contract at the date of closing. Thompson then learns of Paula's identity and wants to enforce the contract. Discuss fully Thompson's rights under these circumstances.

20–6. Principal's Liability for Agent's Torts. Able is hired as a traveling salesperson for the ABC Tire Corp. Able has a designated geographic area and time schedule within which to solicit orders and service customers. Able is given a company car to use in covering the territory. One day, Able decides to take his personal car to cover part of his territory. It is 11:00 A.M., and Able has just finished calling on all customers in the city of Tarrytown. Able's next appointment is in the city of Austex, twenty miles down the road, at 2:00 P.M. Able starts out for Austex, but halfway there he decides to visit a former college roommate who runs a farm ten miles off the main highway. Able is enjoying his visit with his former roommate when he realizes that it is 1:45 P.M. and that he will be late for the appointment in Austex. Driving at a high speed down the country road to reach the main highway, Able crashes his car into Thomas's tractor, severely injuring Thomas, a farmer. Thomas claims he can hold the ABC Tire Corp. liable for his injuries. Discuss fully ABC's liability in this situation.

20–7. Employee versus Independent Contractor. Stephen Hemmerling was a driver for the Happy Cab Co. Hemmerling paid certain fixed expenses and abided by a variety of rules relating to the use of the cab, the hours that could be worked, the solicitation of fares, and so on. Rates were set by the state. Happy Cab did not withhold taxes from Hemmerling's pay. While driving a cab, Hemmerling was injured in an accident and filed a claim against Happy Cab in a Nebraska state court for workers' compensation benefits. Such benefits are not available to independent contractors. On what basis might the court hold that Hemmerling is an employee? Explain. [*Hemmerling v. Happy Cab Co.*, 247 Neb. 919, 530 N.W.2d 916 (1995)]

20–8. Agent's Duties to Principal. Ana Barreto and Flavia Gugliuzzi asked Ruth Bennett, a real estate salesperson who worked for Smith Bell Real Estate, to list for sale their house in the Pleasant Valley area of Underhill, Vermont. Diana Carter, a California resident, visited the house as a potential buyer. Bennett

worked under the supervision of David Crane, an officer of Smith Bell. Crane knew, but did not disclose to Bennett or Carter, that the house was subject to frequent and severe winds, that a window had blown in years earlier, and that other houses in the area had suffered wind damage. Crane knew of this because he lived in the Pleasant Valley area, had sold a number of nearby properties, and had been Underhill's zoning officer. Many valley residents, including Crane, had wind gauges on their homes to measure and compare wind speeds with their neighbors. Carter bought the house, and several months later, high winds blew in a number of windows and otherwise damaged the property. Carter filed a suit in a Vermont state court against Smith Bell and others, alleging fraud. She argued in part that Crane's knowledge of the winds was imputable to Smith Bell. Smith Bell responded that Crane's knowledge was obtained outside the scope of employment. What is the rule regarding how much of an agent's knowledge a principal is assumed to know? How should the court rule in this case? Why? [*Carter v. Gugliuzzi*, 716 A.2d 17 (Vt. 1998)]

20–9. Liability for Employee's Acts. Federated Financial Reserve Corp. leases consumer and business equipment. As part of its credit approval and debt-collection practices, Federated hires credit collectors, whom it authorizes to obtain credit reports on its customers. Janice Caylor, a Federated collector, used this authority to obtain a report on Karen Jones, who was not a Federated customer but who was the former wife of Caylor's roommate, Randy Lind. When Jones discovered that Lind had her address and how he had obtained it, she filed a suit in a federal district court against Federated and the others. Jones claimed in part that they had violated the Fair Credit Reporting Act, the goal of which is to protect consumers from the improper use of credit reports. Under what theory might an employer be held liable for an employee's violation of a statute? Does that theory apply in this case? Explain. [*Jones v. Federated Financial Reserve Corp.*, 144 F.3d 961 (6th Cir. 1998)]

20–10. In Your Court

Richard Lanno worked for the Thermal Equipment Corp. as a project engineer. Lanno was allowed to keep a company van and tools at his home because he routinely drove to work sites directly from his home and because he was often needed for unanticipated trips during his off-hours. The arrangement had been made for the convenience of Thermal Equipment, even though Lanno's managers permitted him to make personal use of the van. Lanno was involved in a collision with Adams while driving the van home from work. At the time of the accident, Lanno had taken a detour to stop at a store—he had intended to purchase a few items and then go home. Adams sued Thermal Equipment, claiming that Lanno had acted within the scope of his employment. Assume that you are the judge in the trial court hearing this case and answer the following questions:

(a) How does the principle of law enunciated in Case 20.5 (*Joel v. Morison*) relate to the case now before your court?

(b) What will your ruling be with respect to Adams's claim? How will you justify your decision?

LAW ON THE WEB

For updated links to resources available on the Web, as well as a variety of other materials, visit this text's Web site at http://wleb.westbuslaw.com.

An excellent source for information on agency law, including court cases involving agency concepts, is the Legal Information Institute (LII) at Cornell University. You can access the LII's Web page on this topic at

http://www.law.cornell.edu/topics/agency.html

The 'Lectric Law Library's Lawcopedia contains a summary of agency laws at

http://www.lectlaw.com/d-a.htm

Scroll down through the A's and select the link to Agent for useful information on this area of the law.

LEGAL RESEARCH EXERCISES ON THE WEB

Go to http://wleb.westbuslaw.com, the Web site that accompanies this text. Select "Internet Applications," and then click on "Chapter 20." There you will find the following Internet research exercise that you can perform to learn more about agency law:

Activity 20–1: Employees or Independent Contractors?

Activity 20–2: Liability in Agency Relationships

CHAPTER 21

Employment Relationships

A T ONE TIME IN THE UNITED STATES, employment relationships were governed primarily by the common law. Under the common law doctrine of **employment at will**, normally either party can terminate the employment relationship at any time and for any reason, unless an employment contract provides to the contrary. Other common law concepts governing employment relationships include those of contract, agency, and tort law.

Today, in contrast, the workplace is regulated extensively by federal and state statutes. Recall from Chapter 1 that common law doctrines only apply to areas *not* covered by statutory law. The common law employment-at-will doctrine has thus been displaced to a significant extent by statutory law. Additionally, even when the at-will doctrine is applicable, courts make a number of exceptions to the doctrine—as you will read later in this chapter.

In this chapter, we look at the most significant laws regulating employment relationships. We examine other important laws regulating the workplace—those concerning labor unions and employment discrimination—in Chapter 22 and Chapter 23.

SECTION 1

Wage-Hour Laws

In the 1930s, to protect employees against some of the adverse effects of the employment-at-will doctrine, Congress enacted several laws regulating the wages and working hours of employees. In 1931, Congress passed the Davis-Bacon Act,[1] which requires the payment of "prevailing wages" to employees of contractors and subcontractors working on government construction projects. In 1936, the Walsh-Healey Act[2] was passed. This act requires that a minimum wage, as well as overtime pay of time and a half, be paid to employees of manufacturers or suppliers entering into contracts with agencies of the federal government.

In 1938, with the passage of the Fair Labor Standards Act[3] (FLSA), Congress extended wage-hour requirements to cover all employers engaged in interstate commerce or engaged in the production of goods for interstate commerce. We examine here the FLSA's provisions in regard to child labor, maximum hours, and minimum wages.

CHILD LABOR

The FLSA prohibits oppressive child labor. Children under fourteen years of age are allowed to do certain types of work, such as deliver newspapers, work for their parents, and be employed in the entertainment and (with some exceptions) agricultural areas. Children who are fourteen or fifteen years of age are allowed to work, but not in hazardous occupations. There are also numerous restrictions on how many hours per day and per week they can work. For example, they cannot work

---

1. 40 U.S.C. Sections 276a–276a-5.
2. 41 U.S.C. Sections 35–45.
3. 29 U.S.C. Sections 201–260.

during school hours, for more than three hours on a school day (or eight hours on a nonschool day), for more than eighteen hours during a school week (or forty hours during a nonschool week), or before 7 A.M. or after 7 P.M. (9 P.M. during the summer). Most states require persons under sixteen years of age to obtain work permits.

Persons between the ages of sixteen and eighteen do not face such restrictions on working times and hours, but they cannot be employed in hazardous jobs or in jobs detrimental to their health and well-being. Persons over the age of eighteen are not affected by any of the above-mentioned restrictions.

HOURS AND WAGES

Under the FLSA, any employee who agrees to work more than forty hours per week must be paid no less than one and a half times his or her regular pay for all hours over forty. Certain employees are exempt from the overtime provisions of the act. Exempt employees fall into four categories: executives, administrative employees, professional employees, and outside salespersons. Generally, to fall into one of these categories, an employee must earn more than a specified amount of income per week and devote a certain percentage of work time to the performance of specific types of duties, as determined by the FLSA. To qualify as an outside salesperson, the employee must regularly engage in sales work away from the office and spend no more than 20 percent of work time per week performing duties other than sales.

The FLSA provides that a **minimum wage** of a specified amount (currently, $5.15 per hour) must be paid to employees in covered industries. Congress periodically revises the amount of the minimum wage. Under the FLSA, the term *wages* includes the reasonable costs of the employer in furnishing employees with board, lodging, and other facilities if they are customarily furnished by that employer.

SECTION 2

Worker Health and Safety

Under the common law, employees injured on the job had to rely on tort law or contract law theories in suits they brought against their employers. Additionally, workers had some recourse under the common law governing agency relationships (discussed in Chapter 20), which imposes a duty on a principal-employer to provide a safe workplace for his or her agent-employee. Today, numerous state and federal statutes protect employees from the risk of accidental injury, death, or disease resulting from their employment. This section discusses the primary federal statute governing health and safety in the workplace, along with state workers' compensation acts.

THE OCCUPATIONAL SAFETY AND HEALTH ACT

At the federal level, the primary legislation for employee health and safety protection is the Occupational Safety and Health Act of 1970.[4] Congress passed this act in an attempt to ensure safe and healthful working conditions for practically every employee in the country. The act provides for specific standards that employers must meet, plus a general duty to keep workplaces safe.

Enforcement Agencies. Three federal agencies develop and enforce the standards set by the Occupational Safety and Health Act. The Occupational Safety and Health Administration (OSHA) is part of the Department of Labor and has the authority to promulgate standards, make inspections, and enforce the act. OSHA has safety standards governing many workplace details, such as the structural stability of ladders and the requirements for railings. OSHA also establishes standards that protect employees against exposure to substances that may be harmful to their health.

The National Institute for Occupational Safety and Health is part of the Department of Health and Human Services. Its main duty is to conduct research on safety and health problems and to recommend standards for OSHA to adopt. Finally, the Occupational Safety and Health Review Commission is an independent agency set up to handle appeals from actions taken by OSHA administrators.

Procedures and Violations. OSHA compliance officers may enter and inspect facilities of any establishment covered by the Occupational Safety and Health Act.[5] Employees may also file complaints of violations. Under the act, an employer cannot discharge an employee who files a complaint or who, in good faith, refuses to work in a high-risk area if bodily harm or death might result.

---

4. 29 U.S.C. Sections 553, 651–678.
5. In the past, warrantless inspections were conducted. In 1978, however, the United States Supreme Court held that warrantless inspections violated the warrant clause of the Fourth Amendment to the Constitution. See *Marshall v. Barlow's, Inc.*, 436 U.S. 307, 98 S.Ct. 1816, 56 L.Ed.2d 305 (1978).

Employers with eleven or more employees are required to keep occupational injury and illness records for each employee. Each record must be made available for inspection when requested by an OSHA inspector. Whenever a work-related injury or disease occurs, employers must make reports directly to OSHA. Whenever an employee is killed in a work-related accident or when five or more employees are hospitalized in one accident, the employer must notify the Department of Labor within forty-eight hours. If the company fails to do so, it will be fined. Following the accident, a complete inspection of the premises is mandatory.

Criminal penalties for willful violation of the Occupational Safety and Health Act are limited. Employers may be prosecuted under state laws, however. In other words, the act does not preempt state and local criminal laws.[6]

STATE WORKERS' COMPENSATION LAWS

State **workers' compensation laws** establish an administrative procedure for compensating workers injured on the job. Instead of suing, an injured worker files a claim with the administrative agency or board that administers the local workers' compensation claims.

Most workers' compensation statutes are similar. No state covers all employees. Typically excluded are domestic workers, agricultural workers, temporary employees, and employees of common carriers (companies that provide transportation services to the public). Generally, the statutes cover minors. Usually, the statutes allow employers to purchase insurance from a private insurer or a

state fund to pay workers' compensation benefits in the event of a claim. Most states also allow employers to be *self-insured*—that is, employers who show an ability to pay claims do not need to buy insurance.

In general, the right to recover benefits is predicated wholly on the existence of an employment relationship and the fact that the worker's injury was *accidental* and *occurred on the job or in the course of employment*, regardless of fault. Intentionally inflicted self-injury, for example, would not be considered accidental and hence would not be covered. If an injury occurred while an employee was commuting to or from work, it usually would not be considered to have occurred on the job or in the course of employment and hence would not be covered.

An employee must notify his or her employer of an injury promptly (usually within thirty days of the injury's occurrence). Generally, an employee also must file a workers' compensation claim with the appropriate state agency or board within a certain period (sixty days to two years) from the time the injury is first noticed, rather than from the time of the accident.

An employee's acceptance of workers' compensation benefits bars the employee from suing for injuries caused by the employer's negligence. By barring lawsuits for negligence, workers' compensation laws also bar employers from raising common law defenses to negligence, such as contributory negligence. For example, an employer can no longer raise such defenses as contributory negligence or assumption of risk to avoid liability for negligence. A worker may sue an employer who *intentionally* injures the worker, however.

The court in the following case considered whether an employee's injury in an automobile accident arose out of and in the course of employment for purposes of workers' compensation.

---

6. *Pedraza v. Shell Oil Co.*, 942 F.2d 48 (1st Cir. 1991); cert. denied, *Shell Oil Co. v. Pedraza*, 502 U.S. 1082, 112 S.Ct. 993, 117 L.Ed.2d 154 (1992).

CASE 21.1   Rogers v. Pacesetter Corp.

Missouri Court of
Appeals,
Eastern District,
Division 4, 1998.
972 S.W.2d 540.
http://www.osca.state.
mo.us/courts/
pubopinions.nsf[a]

COMPANY PROFILE   Pacesetter Corporation (**http://www.pacesettercorp.com**), which has been in the home improvement business since 1962, calls itself "America's Leading Home Improvement Company!" Pacesetter sells a range of building supplies, including cabinet refacing, doors, siding, windows, and patio awnings and covers. The company designs, manufactures, finances the purchase of, installs, guarantees, and services its products, which are advertised as durable and energy efficient.

BACKGROUND AND FACTS   Sean Rogers was a manager for Pacesetter Corporation. He worked at the Pacesetter offices from 9:00 A.M. to 9:00 P.M. Mondays through Fridays

---

a. This page contains links to some of the opinions of the Missouri state courts. Click on "Eastern District." Click on "Eastern Appellate District." When that page opens, in the "Search for the following word(s)" box, type "Pacesetter" and click on "Search."

and 10:00 A.M. to 4:00 P.M. Saturdays. He also worked at home, drafting ads and conducting performance reviews, because he did not have enough time to do all of his work at the office. At the invitation of Rogers's supervisor, Rogers and the supervisor met at the River Port Club, a bar, to discuss a promotion. It was a Monday, when Rogers normally conducted performance reviews at home, which he planned to do after leaving the bar. While driving home, Rogers was injured in an automobile accident. He filed a claim for workers' compensation with the Missouri Division of Workers' Compensation. After a hearing, the administrative law judge awarded Rogers temporary compensation for a permanent partial disability. Pacesetter appealed to the Missouri Labor and Industrial Relations Commission, which reversed the award. Rogers appealed to a Missouri state court.

IN THE LANGUAGE OF THE COURT

ROBERT G. DOWD, JR., Presiding Judge.

* * * *

An employee's injuries arise out of his employment if they are a natural and reasonable incident thereof, and they are in the course of employment if the accident occurs within the period of employment at a place where the employee may reasonably be fulfilling the duties of employment. * * *

* * * *

* * * *[C]ompensation for injuries while traveling home may be proper* * * * *when it can genuinely* * * * *be said that the home has become part of the employment premises.* * * * [A]n employee demonstrates this by showing a clear business use of the home at the end of the specific journey during which the accident occurred. [Emphasis added.]

* * * *

* * * Here, Claimant [Rogers] regularly worked twelve hours, Monday through Friday, and six hours each Saturday. Claimant also regularly did work for his employer at home * * * . The night of the accident was a Monday and it was Claimant's practice to do performance reviews * * * on Monday evenings in order that on Tuesday mornings he could discuss [the employees'] performance with them. Claimant testified it was necessary to conduct these performance reviews at home because * * * "there was insufficient time to perform [his duties] during regular office hours." Moreover, * * * the work performed at home by Claimant was an integral part of the conduct of his employer's business, and not only a convenience to Claimant. Clearly a benefit accrued to employer by Claimant conducting these performance reviews at home. We conclude that * * * Claimant demonstrated that the demands of his employment created the expectation that work needed to be done at home for the benefit of his employer.

DECISION AND REMEDY

The court reversed the decision of the commission and remanded the case for the entry of an award of compensation. The court held that Rogers's injury arose out of and in the course of employment for purposes of workers' compensation.

SECTION 3

Income Security

Federal and state governments participate in insurance programs designed to protect employees and their families by covering the financial impact of retirement, disability, death, hospitalization, and unemployment. The key federal law on this subject is the Social Security Act of 1935.[7]

SOCIAL SECURITY AND MEDICARE

The Social Security Act of 1935 provides for old age (retirement), survivors, and disability insurance. The act is therefore often referred to as OASDI. Both employers and employees must "contribute" under the Federal Insurance Contributions Act (FICA)[8] to help pay for the employees' loss of income on retirement. The basis for the employee's and the employer's contribution is the employee's annual wage base—the

7. 42 U.S.C. Sections 301–1397e.

8. 26 U.S.C. Sections 3101–3125.

maximum amount of the employee's wages that are subject to the tax. The employer withholds the employee's FICA contribution from the employee's wages and then matches this contribution. (In 2000, employers were required to withhold 6.2 percent of each employee's wages, up to a maximum amount of $76,200, and to match this contribution.)

Retired workers are eligible to receive monthly payments from the Social Security Administration, which administers the Social Security Act. Social Security benefits are fixed by statute but increase automatically with increases in the cost of living.

Medicare, a health-insurance program, is administered by the Social Security Administration for people sixty-five years of age and older and for some under age sixty-five who are disabled. It has two parts, one pertaining to hospital costs and the other to nonhospital medical costs, such as visits to doctors' offices. People who have Medicare hospital insurance can obtain additional federal medical insurance if they pay small monthly premiums, which increase as the cost of medical care increases. As with Social Security contributions, both the employer and the employee contribute to Medicare. Currently, 1.45 percent of the amount of all wages and salaries paid to employees, plus a matching amount paid by the employer, go toward financing Medicare. There is no cap on the amount of wages subject to the Medicare tax.

Private Pension Plans

There has been significant legislation to regulate employee retirement plans set up by employers to supplement Social Security benefits. The major federal act covering these retirement plans is the Employee Retirement Income Security Act (ERISA) of 1974.[9] This statute empowers the Labor Management Services Administration of the Department of Labor to enforce its provisions governing employers who have private pension funds for their employees. ERISA does not require an employer to establish a pension plan. When a plan exists, however, ERISA establishes standards for its management.

A key provision of ERISA concerns vesting. **Vesting** gives an employee a legal right to receive pension benefits at some future date when he or she stops working. Before ERISA was enacted, some employees who had worked for companies for as long as thirty years received no pension benefits when their

employment terminated, because those benefits had not vested. ERISA establishes complex vesting rules. Generally, however, all employee contributions to pension plans vest immediately, and employee rights to employer pension-plan contributions vest after five years of employment.

In an attempt to prevent mismanagement of pension funds, ERISA has established rules on how they must be invested. Pension managers must be cautious in their investments and refrain from investing more than 10 percent of the fund in securities of the employer. ERISA also contains detailed record-keeping and reporting requirements.

Unemployment Compensation

The United States has a system of unemployment insurance in which employers pay into a fund, the proceeds of which are paid out to qualified unemployed workers. The Federal Unemployment Tax Act of 1935[10] created a state-administered system that provides unemployment compensation to eligible individuals. The FUTA and state laws require employers that fall under the provisions of the act to pay unemployment taxes at regular intervals.

Section 4

COBRA

Federal legislation also addresses the issue of health insurance for workers whose jobs have been terminated and who are thus no longer eligible for group health-insurance plans. The Consolidated Omnibus Budget Reconciliation Act (COBRA) of 1985[11] prohibits the elimination of a worker's medical, optical, or dental insurance coverage on the voluntary or involuntary termination of the worker's employment. The act applies to most workers who have either lost their jobs or had their hours decreased so that they are no longer eligible for coverage under the employer's health plan. Only workers fired for gross misconduct are excluded from protection.

Application of COBRA

The worker has sixty days (beginning with the date that the group coverage would stop) to decide

---

9. 29 U.S.C. Sections 1001 *et seq.*

10. 26 U.S.C. Sections 3301–3310.
11. 29 U.S.C. Sections 1161–1169.

whether to continue with the employer's group insurance plan or not. If the worker chooses to discontinue the coverage, then the employer has no further obligation. If the worker chooses to continue coverage, however, the employer is obligated to keep the policy active for up to eighteen months. If the worker is disabled, the employer must extend coverage up to twenty-nine months. The coverage provided must be the same as that enjoyed by the worker prior to the termination or reduction of employment. If family members were originally included, for example, COBRA would prohibit their exclusion. This is not a free ride for the worker, however. To receive continued benefits, he or she may be required to pay all of the premium, as well as a 2 percent administrative charge.

EMPLOYERS' OBLIGATIONS UNDER COBRA

Employers, with some exceptions, must comply with COBRA if they employ twenty or more workers and provide a benefit plan to those workers. An employer must inform an employee of COBRA's provisions when that worker faces termination or a reduction of hours that would affect his or her eligibility for coverage under the plan.

An employer is relieved of the responsibility to provide benefit coverage if it completely eliminates its group benefit plan. An employer is also relieved of responsibility when the worker becomes eligible for Medicare, falls under a spouse's health plan, becomes insured under a different plan (with a new employer, for example), or fails to pay the premium.

An employer that fails to comply with COBRA risks substantial penalties. These penalties include a tax of up to 10 percent of the annual cost of the group plan or $500,000, whichever is less.

SECTION 5

Family and Medical Leave

In 1993, Congress passed the Family and Medical Leave Act (FMLA)[12] to protect employees who need time off work for family or medical reasons. A majority of the states also have legislation allowing for a leave from employment for family or medical reasons,

and many employers maintain private family-leave plans for their workers.

COVERAGE AND APPLICATION OF THE FMLA

The FMLA requires employers who have fifty or more employees to provide employees with up to twelve weeks of family or medical leave during any twelve-month period. During the employee's leave, the employer must continue the worker's health-care coverage and guarantee employment in the same or a comparable position when the employee returns to work. An important exception to the FMLA, however, allows the employer to avoid reinstatement of a *key employee*—defined as an employee whose pay falls within the top 10 percent of the firm's work force. Additionally, the act does not apply to employees who have worked less than one year or less than twenty-five hours a week during the previous twelve months.

Generally, an employee may take family leave when he or she wishes to care for a newborn baby, a newly adopted child, or a foster child just placed in the employee's care.[13] An employee may take medical leave when the employee or the employee's spouse, child, or parent has a "serious health condition" requiring care. For most absences, the employee must demonstrate that the health condition requires continued treatment by a health-care provider and includes a period of incapacity of more than three days.

Under regulations issued by the Department of Labor (DOL) in 1995, employees suffering from certain chronic health conditions may take FMLA leave for their own incapacities that require absences of less than three days. For example, an employee who has asthma or diabetes may have periodic occurrences of illness, rather than episodes continuing over an extended period of time. Similarly, pregnancy may involve periodic visits to a health-care provider and bouts of morning sickness. According to the DOL's regulations, employees with such conditions are covered by the FMLA.

REMEDIES FOR VIOLATIONS OF THE FMLA

Remedies for violations of the FMLA include (1) damages for unpaid wages (or salary), lost benefits, denied

---

12. 29 U.S.C. Sections 2601, 2611–2619, 2651–2654.

13. The foster care must be state sanctioned for such an arrangement to fall within the coverage of the FMLA.

compensation, and actual monetary losses (such as the cost of providing for care) up to an amount equivalent to the employee's wages for twelve weeks; (2) job reinstatement; and (3) promotion. The successful plaintiff is entitled to court costs, attorneys' fees, and—in cases involving bad faith on the part of the employer—double damages.

SECTION 6

Employee Privacy Rights

Recall from Chapter 5 that there is no provision in the U.S. Constitution that guarantees a right to privacy. A personal right to privacy, however, has been inferred from other constitutional guarantees provided by the First, Third, Fourth, Fifth, and Ninth Amendments to the Constitution. Additionally, state laws providing for privacy rights may apply in the employment context. Finally, remember from Chapter 12 that the invasion of another's privacy may constitute a tort.

In the last two decades, concerns about the privacy rights of employees have arisen in response to the sometimes invasive tactics used by employers in their efforts to monitor and screen workers. Lie-detector tests, drug tests, and other practices have increasingly been subject to challenge as violations of employee privacy rights. A particularly troublesome issue today has to do with electronic monitoring in the workplace. For a discussion of this issue, see this chapter's *Emerging Trends in Technology* (pages 468–469).

LIE-DETECTOR TESTS

At one time, many employers required employees or job applicants to take polygraph examinations (lie-detector tests) in connection with their employment. To protect the privacy interests of employees and job applicants, in 1988 Congress passed the Employee Polygraph Protection Act.[14] The statute prohibits employers from (1) requiring or causing employees or job applicants to take lie-detector tests or suggesting or requesting that they do so; (2) using, accepting, referring to, or asking about the results of lie-detector tests taken by employees or applicants; and (3) taking or threatening negative employment-related action against employees or applicants based on results of lie-detector tests or on their refusal to take the tests.

Employers excepted from these prohibitions include federal, state, and local government employers; certain security service firms; and companies manufacturing and distributing controlled substances. Other employers may use polygraph tests when investigating losses attributable to theft, including embezzlement and the theft of trade secrets.

DRUG TESTING

In the interests of public safety and to reduce unnecessary costs, many of today's employers, including the government, require their employees to submit to drug testing. Laws relating to the privacy rights of private-sector employees vary from state to state. Some state constitutions prohibit private employers from testing for drugs, and state statutes may restrict drug testing by private employers in any number of ways. A collective bargaining agreement may also provide protection against drug testing. In some instances, employees have brought actions against their employers for the tort of invasion of privacy.

Constitutional limitations apply to the testing of government employees. The Fourth Amendment provides that individuals have the right to be "secure in their persons" against "unreasonable searches and seizures" conducted by government agents. Drug tests have been held to be constitutional, however, when there was a reasonable basis for suspecting government employees of using drugs. Additionally, when drug use in a particular government job could threaten public safety, testing has been upheld. For example, a U.S. Department of Transportation rule that requires employees engaged in oil and gas pipeline operations to submit to random drug testing was upheld, even though the rule did not require that before being tested the individual must have been suspected of drug use.[15] The court held that the government's interest in promoting public safety in the pipeline industry outweighed the employees' privacy interests.

An ongoing problem with respect to drug testing is that such tests are not foolproof. Suppose that a job applicant is not hired because of a positive drug test. If the results of the test are false, does the applicant have any legal recourse? In one case, for example, after a drug-testing laboratory mistakenly reported to an employer that a job applicant had failed a drug test, the applicant filed a suit against the laboratory. The court

---

14. 29 U.S.C. Sections 2001 *et seq.*

15. *Electrical Workers Local 1245 v. Skinner*, 913 F.2d 1454 (9th Cir. 1990).

granted the employer's request for summary judgment, holding—as have a number of other courts—that while a laboratory may owe a duty of care to the employer for whom it conducts the drug tests, it owes no such duty to the employee being tested.[16]

In another case, a worker who had been fired because of a positive drug test sued the employer, alleging that the real reason he had been fired was racial animus. The fired employee claimed that his job had been classified as a "safety-sensitive position" even though it should not have been and that he had not ingested any drugs that would account for the positive drug-testing results. In short, claimed the worker, he had been "set up" by the employer. The court, however, granted summary judgment for the employer, largely because the employee did not follow the proper procedures for contesting drug-test results. (The procedures require the employee to mail a request in writing, along with $125, to the laboratory that performed the test. Moreover, the request had to arrive within twenty-four hours, and the laboratory would only re-test the same sample, not a new one.)[17]

AIDS TESTING

An increasing number of employers are testing their workers for acquired immune deficiency syndrome (AIDS). Few public issues involve more controversy than this practice. Some state laws restrict AIDS testing, and federal statutes offer some protection to employees and job applicants who have AIDS or have tested positive for the AIDS virus. The federal Americans with Disabilities Act of 1990[18] (discussed in Chapter 22), for example, prohibits discrimination against individuals with disabilities, and the term *disability* has been broadly defined to include those individuals with diseases such as AIDS. The law also requires employers to reasonably accommodate the needs of persons with disabilities. Generally, although the law may not prohibit AIDS testing, it may prohibit the discharge of employees based on the results of those tests.

SCREENING PROCEDURES

An area of concern to potential employees has to do with preemployment screening procedures. What kinds of questions on an employment application or a preemployment test are permissible? What kinds of questions go too far in terms of invading the potential employee's privacy? Is it an invasion of the potential employee's privacy, for example, to ask questions about his or her sexual orientation or religious convictions? Although an employer may believe that such information is relevant to the job for which the individual has applied, the applicant may feel differently about the matter. Generally, questions on an employment application must have a reasonable nexus, or connection, with the job for which an applicant is applying.[19]

SECTION 7

Employment-Related Immigration Laws

The most important immigration laws governing employment relationships are the Immigration Reform and Control Act (IRCA) of 1986[20] and the Immigration Act of 1990.[21] The IRCA, which is administered by the U.S. Immigration and Naturalization Service (INS), prohibits employers from hiring illegal immigrants. Employers must complete a special form—called INS Form I-9—for each employee and indicate on it that the employer has verified that the employee is either a U.S. citizen or is otherwise entitled to work in this country.

The Immigration Act of 1990 limits the number of legal immigrants entering the United States by capping the number of visas (entry permits) that are issued each year. Under the act, employers recruiting employees from other countries must complete a certification process and satisfy the Department of Labor that there is a shortage of qualified U.S. workers capable of performing the work. The employer must also establish that bringing immigrants into this country will not adversely affect the existing labor market in that particular area. In this way, the act attempts to serve two purposes: encouraging skilled workers to enter this country and at the same time restricting competition for American jobs.

16. *Ney v. Axelrod*, 723 A.2d 719 (Pa.Super. 1999).

17. *Brown v. Allied Printing Ink Co.*, 241 Ga.App. 310, ___S.E.2d___ (1999).

18. 42 U.S.C. Sections 12102–12118.

19. See, for example, *Soroka v. Dayton Hudson Corp.*, 7 Cal.App.4th 203, 1 Cal.Rptr.2d 77 (1991).

20. 29 U.S.C. Section 1802.

21. This act amended various provisions of the Immigration and Nationality Act of 1952, 8 U.S.C. Sections 1101 *et seq.*

EMERGING TRENDS IN TECHNOLOGY

Electronic Monitoring in the Workplace

In today's workplace, employees' use of electronic communications systems may subject employers to liability on many fronts. One risk is that e-mail could be used to harass employees. Another risk is that employees could reproduce, without authorization, copyright-protected materials on the Internet. Still another risk is that confidential information contained in e-mail or voice mail messages could fall into the hands of an outside party. Finally, personal use of the Internet by employees cuts into their work time. In an attempt to shield themselves from liability and to increase worker productivity, some companies monitor their employees' electronic communications.

ELECTRONIC MONITORING PRACTICES

According to the American Management Association, more than 45 percent of U.S. corporations engage in some intrusive employee monitoring practices. These practices may include monitoring employees'

e-mail, voice mail, and telephone exchanges; recording employees' computer keystrokes; tracking employees' Internet use; and video-recording employees' job performance.[a]

Tracking employees' Internet use is made easier by a variety of specially designed software products. For example, software such as SurfWatch Professional Edition and LittleBrother allows employers to track virtually every move made by a worker using the Internet, including the specific Web sites visited by the worker and the time spent surfing the Internet. Other software, such as that created by Content Technologies, matches taboo key words in employees' e-mail messages against a stored list. Once alerted, the message is examined to see if it violates company policy. AT&T Corporation has gone even further: it has developed software that will "understand" taboo phrases, not just words, in e-mail messages.

Clearly, employers need to protect themselves from liability for their employees' online activities. At the same time, employees expect to have a certain zone of privacy in the workplace, and some claim that employers have gone too far in their monitoring practices.

a. "Don't Expect Privacy in the Workplace," *International Herald Tribune*, January 16–17, 1999, p. 4.

LAWS GOVERNING ELECTRONIC MONITORING

Generally, there is little specific government regulation of monitoring activities, although electronic monitoring by employers may violate the Electronic Communications Privacy Act (ECPA) of 1986.[b] This act amended existing federal wiretapping law to cover electronic forms of communications, such as communications via cellular telephones or e-mail. The ECPA prohibits the intentional interception of any wire or electronic communication or the intentional disclosure or use of the information obtained by the interception.

The act excludes from coverage, however, any electronic communications through devices that are "furnished to the subscriber or user by a provider of wire or electronic communication service" and that are being used by the subscriber or user, or by the provider of the service, "in the ordinary course of its business." Another exception to the ECPA allows employers to avoid liability under the act if employees *consent* to having their electronic communications intercepted by the employer. Thus, an employer may be able to avoid what laws do exist by simply informing employees that

b. 18 U.S.C. Sections 2510–2521.

SECTION 8

Wrongful Discharge

Whenever an employer discharges an employee in violation of an employment contract or a statutory law protecting employees, the employee may bring an action for **wrongful discharge.** If an employer's actions

do not violate any express employment contract or statute, then the question is whether the employer has violated a common law doctrine. Because of the harsh effects of the employment-at-will doctrine for employees, courts have carved out various exceptions to the doctrine. These exceptions are based on contract theory, tort theory, and public policy.

EMERGING TRENDS IN TECHNOLOGY

Electronic Monitoring in the Workplace,

continued

they are subject to monitoring. Then, if employees challenge the monitoring practice, the employer can raise the defense of consent by claiming that the employees consented to the monitoring.[c] Generally, in cases challenging employee monitoring practices, the courts have sided with the employers, concluding that the employers' actions are based on legitimate concerns.

ALTERNATIVE APPROACHES

Many companies are finding that the benefits of electronic monitoring may not be worth the costs—a major cost being employee resentment of monitoring practices. An alternative being pursued by a growing number of

c. In some cases, even a verbal an-nouncement to employees that their electronic communications would be monitored was sufficient to justify the use of the consent defense. See, for example, *Griffin v. City of Milwaukee,* 74 F.3d 824 (7th Cir. 1996).

companies, particularly in the high-tech industry, is to allow their employees to use their own discretion with respect to Internet use. Hewlett-Packard, for example, does not monitor employees' Internet use or block access to any Web sites.

Some observers claim that this "hands-off" approach with respect to employee use of the Internet is a sensible one. For one thing, some highly qualified job candidates may not want to work for a company that monitors their Internet use. For another, there is no evidence that Internet monitoring has increased worker productivity. Finally, how can an employer monitor Internet use while its employees are traveling or working at home—as more and more employees are doing?

Another alternative adopted by some companies is to use filtering software (discussed in Chapter 15). Instead of monitoring Internet use, these companies utilize filtering software to block access to certain Web sites, such as pornographic sites.

IMPLICATIONS FOR THE BUSINESSPERSON

1. Employers should carefully weigh the pros and cons of elec-tronic monitoring in their work-places to make sure that the monitoring practices are, in fact,

effective in increasing worker pro-ductivity and decreasing certain risks—of theft, for example, or lia-bility for employee actions.
2. Employers who want to hire "the brightest and the best" employees may find it difficult to do so if they engage in overly intrusive monitor-ing practices.

FOR CRITICAL ANALYSIS

1. Why might an employer allow employees to make personal tele-phone calls using office telephones but prohibit them from using the Internet for personal reasons?
2. Should an employee have a reasonable expectation of privacy when using his or her employer's computer system to send personal e-mail messages? Why or why not?

RELEVANT WEB SITES

You can find a summary of the monitoring capabilities of LittleBrother at **http://www. kansmen.com/products/lb/index. htm**. To view the results of the latest American Management Association survey on electronic monitoring in the workplace, go to **http://www.amanet.org/research/ specials/monit.htm**.

EXCEPTIONS BASED ON CONTRACT THEORY

Some courts have held that an *implied* employment contract exists between the employer and the em-ployee. If the employee is fired outside the terms of the implied contract, he or she may succeed in an ac-

tion for breach of contract even though no written employment contract exists.

For example, an employer's manual or personnel bulletin may state that, as a matter of policy, work-ers will be dismissed only for good cause. If the em-ployee is aware of this policy and continues to work for the employer, a court may find that there is an implied contract based on the terms stated in the manual or bulletin. Promises that an employer makes to employees regarding discharge policy may also be considered part of an implied contract. If the employer fires a worker in a manner contrary to the procedure promised, a court may hold that the employer has violated the implied contract and is liable for damages. Most state courts will consider this claim and judge it by traditional contract standards.

A few states have gone further and held that all employment contracts contain an implied covenant of good faith. This means that both sides promise to abide by the contract in good faith. If an employer fires an employee for an arbitrary or unjustified reason, the employee can claim that the covenant of good faith was breached and the contract violated.

EXCEPTIONS BASED ON TORT THEORY

In a few cases, the discharge of an employee may give rise to an action for wrongful discharge under tort theories. Abusive discharge procedures may result in intentional infliction of emotional distress or defamation. In one case, a restaurant had suffered some thefts of supplies, and the manager announced that he would start firing waitresses alphabetically until the thief was identified. The first waitress fired said that she suffered great emotional distress as a result. The state's highest court upheld her claim as stating a valid cause of action.[22]

Some courts have permitted workers to sue their employers under the tort theory of fraud. Under this theory, an employer may be held liable for making false promises to a prospective employee if the employee detrimentally relies on the employer's representations by taking the job. For example, suppose that an employer induces a prospective employee to leave a lucrative job and move to another state by offering "a long-term job with a thriving business." In fact, the employer is having significant financial problems. Furthermore, the employer is planning a merger that will involve the elimination of the position offered to the prospective employee. If the employee takes the job in reliance on the employer's representations and is fired shortly thereafter, the

employee may be able to bring an action against the employer for fraud.[23]

EXCEPTIONS BASED ON PUBLIC POLICY

The most widespread common law exception to the employment-at-will doctrine is an exception made on the basis of public policy. Courts may apply this exception when an employer fires a worker for reasons that violate a fundamental public policy of the jurisdiction.

Generally, the courts require that the public policy involved must be expressed clearly in the statutory law governing the jurisdiction. The public policy against employment discrimination, for example, is expressed clearly in federal and state statutes. Thus, if a worker is fired for discriminatory reasons but has no cause of action under statutory law (for example, if the workplace has too few employees to be covered by the statute), that worker may succeed in a suit against the employer for wrongful discharge in violation of public policy.[24]

Sometimes, an employer will direct an employee to perform an illegal act. If the employee refuses to perform the act, the employer may decide to fire the worker. Similarly, employees who "blow the whistle" on the wrongdoing of their employers often find themselves disciplined or even out of a job. **Whistleblowing** occurs when an employee tells a government official, upper-management authorities, or the press that his or her employer is engaged in some unsafe or illegal activity. Whistleblowers on occasion have been protected from wrongful discharge for reasons of public policy. For example, a bank was held to have wrongfully discharged an employee who pressured the employer to comply with state and federal consumer credit laws.[25]

The following case involved an employee who was discharged for refusing to perform an illegal act. The employee sued the company, alleging that her discharge violated public policy.

---

22. *Agis v. Howard Johnson Co.*, 371 Mass. 140, 355 N.E.2d 315 (1976).

23. See, for example, *Lazar v. Superior Court of Los Angeles Co.*, 12 Cal.4th 631, 909 P.2d 981, 49 Cal.Rptr.2d 377 (1996).
24. See, for example, *Molesworth v. Brandon*, 341 Md. 621, 672 A.2d 608 (1996).
25. *Harless v. First National Bank in Fairmont*, 162 W.Va. 116, 246 S.E.2d 270 (1978).

CASE 21.2   Lins v. Children's Discovery Centers of America, Inc.

Court of Appeals of
Washington,
Division 2, 1999.
95 Wash.App. 486,
976 P.2d 168.
http://www.findlaw.
com/11stategov/wa/
waca.html[a]

BACKGROUND AND FACTS   *Children's Discovery Centers of America, Inc. (CDC), operates child-care centers. Diane Lins was a regional director in charge of six centers in the Pacific Northwest, including the state of Washington. During her tenure, CDC promoted her and gave her good performance ratings. In March 1995, Pam French was hired to be CDC's West Coast operations director, Lins's supervisor. Less than ten days later, Lins and five of her subordinates were injured in an auto accident that occurred within the course and scope of their employment. Each employee filed a workers' compensation claim. Within two weeks of the accident, French ordered Lins to fire the other five employees. French had heard that two of them were consulting attorneys and she "didn't trust either of them not to sue the company, and she was not going to allow that to happen." She harbored similar feelings about the remaining three, even though they had not seen attorneys. A Washington state statute provides that "no employer may discharge or in any manner discriminate against any employee because such employee has filed or communicated to the employer an intent to file a claim for compensation or exercise any [related] rights." Realizing that she could not lawfully perform French's order, Lins refused to do so. On May 5, French gave Lins a poor performance rating and put her on probation. On June 22, French fired Lins for "Neglect of Duties/Poor Performance." Lins filed a suit in a Washingon state court against CDC, alleging that she had been wrongfully discharged in violation of the state's public policy. CDC filed a motion for summary judgment, which the court granted. Lins appealed to a state intermediate appellate court.*

MORGAN, J. [Judge]

*   *   *   *

Public policy *   *   * prohibits an employer from considering certain activities when deciding whether to discharge an employee. *   *   * [This principle is] often summarized by saying that *it is unlawful for an employer to retaliate against an employee for protected activity.* [Emphasis added.]

The problem, of course, is defining the "activity" that public policy "protects." Either the legislature or the judiciary may address that problem, the legislature through statutes and the judiciary through decisional law. When the judiciary addresses the problem, it inquires (1) whether a clear public policy exists; (2) whether that policy will be jeopardized unless the activity in issue is protected; (3) whether employers in general have overriding justification for wanting to use the activity in issue as a factor affecting the decision to discharge; and (4) whether the particular employee's activity in the case at bar was a substantial factor in (i.e., a cause of) the particular employer's decision to discharge. *   *   *

Turning to the first of the four elements *   *   * , we hold that Washington has a clear public policy against firing an employee because he or she has filed a worker's compensation claim. *   *   * [T]he legislature declared that "no employer may discharge or in any manner discriminate against any employee because such employee has filed or communicated to the employer an intent to file a claim for compensation or exercises any [related] rights *   *   * ."

Turning to the second element, we hold that the policy just described will be jeopardized if, without incurring liability, an employer can fire an employee for refusing to carry out a clearly unlawful order. If the employee's refusal is not protected from retaliation, the employee will likely perform the order to save his or her job; the employer will have a readily available means by which to implement its unlawful order; and the policy *   *   * will be impaired or destroyed. But if the employee's refusal is protected, the

---

a. In the "Court of Appeals: Published" section, click on "1999." When the list appears, in the group of decisions released on "May 07, 1999," find the case name (it begins "IIDiane Lins") and click on the docket number ("22424-1") to access the opinion.

employee will be likely to refuse the order; the employer will be denied a readily available means by which to implement the order; and the policy * * * will be served.

Turning to the third element, we hold that employers do not have any overriding justification for wanting to consider an employee's refusal to perform an unlawful order when deciding whether to fire the employee. By virtue of the order being unlawful in the first instance, the employer should not have given it, and the employer has no legitimate interest in having it carried out.

Finally, on the fourth element, a jury could reasonably infer from the evidence in this record that Lins' refusal to carry out French's unlawful order was a substantial factor in Lins' being fired.

DECISION AND REMEDY *The Court of Appeals of Washington concluded that Lins's refusal to carry out French's order was conduct protected by public policy and that French's retaliation was thus unlawful. Public policy prevents an employer from discharging an employee in retaliation for the employee's refusal to carry out the employer's unlawful order. The court reversed the decision of the lower court and remanded the case for trial.*

SECTION 9

Statutory Protection for Whistleblowers

To encourage workers to report employers' wrongdoing, such as fraud, most states have enacted so-called whistleblower statutes. These statutes protect whistleblowers from subsequent retaliation on the part of employers. On the federal level, the Whistleblower Protection Act of 1989[26] protects federal employees

who blow the whistle on their employers from their employers' retaliatory actions. Whistleblower statutes may also provide an incentive to disclose information by providing the whistleblower with a monetary reward. For example, the federal False Claims Reform Act of 1986[27] requires that a whistleblower who has disclosed information relating to a fraud perpetrated against the U.S. government receive between 15 and 25 percent of the proceeds if the government brings suit against the wrongdoer.

---

26. 5 U.S.C. Section 1201.

27. 31 U.S.C. Sections 3729–3733. This act amended the False Claims Act of 1863.

TERMS AND CONCEPTS TO REVIEW

employment at will 460	whistleblowing 470	wrongful discharge 468
minimum wage 461	workers' compensation	
vesting 464	laws 462	

QUESTIONS AND CASE PROBLEMS

21–1. LABOR LAWS. Calzoni Boating Co. is an interstate business engaged in manufacturing and selling boats. The company has five hundred nonunion employees. Representatives of these employees are requesting a four-day, ten-hours-per-day workweek, and Calzoni is concerned that this would require paying time and a half after eight hours per day. Which federal act is Calzoni thinking of that might require this? Will the act in fact require paying time and a half for all hours worked over eight hours per day if the employees' proposal is accepted? Explain.

21–2. HEALTH AND SAFETY REGULATIONS. Denton and Carlo were employed at an appliance plant. Their job required them to do occasional maintenance work while standing on a wire mesh twenty feet above the plant floor. Other employees had fallen through the mesh, and one of them had been killed by the fall. When Denton and Carlo were asked by their supervisor to do work that would likely require them to walk on the mesh, they refused because of their fear of bodily harm or death. Because of their refusal to do the requested work, the two employees were fired from their jobs. Was their discharge wrongful? If so, under what federal employment law? To what federal agency or department should they turn for assistance?

21–3. UNFAIR LABOR PRACTICES. Suppose that Consolidated Stores is undergoing a unionization campaign. Prior to the union election, management says that the union is unnecessary to protect workers. Management also provides bonuses and wage increases to the workers during this period. The employees reject the union. Union organizers protest that the wage increases during the election campaign unfairly prejudiced the vote. Should these wage increases be regarded as an unfair labor practice? Discuss.

21–4. WORKERS' COMPENSATION. Galvin Strang worked for a tractor company in one of its factories. Near his work station was a conveyor belt that ran through a large industrial oven. Sometimes, the workers would use the oven to heat their meals. Thirty-inch-high flasks containing molds were fixed at regular intervals on the conveyor and were transported into the oven. Strang had to walk between the flasks to get to his work station. One day, the conveyor was not moving, and Strang used the oven to cook a frozen pot pie. As he was removing the pot pie from the oven, the conveyor came on. One of the flasks struck Strang and seriously injured him. Strang sought recovery under the state workers' compensation law. Should he recover? Why or why not?

21–5. EMPLOYMENT AT WILL. Robert Adams worked as a delivery truck driver for George W. Cochran & Co. Adams persistently refused to drive a truck that lacked a required inspection sticker and was subsequently fired as a result of his refusal. Adams was an at-will employee, and Cochran contended that because there was no written employment contract stating otherwise, Cochran was entitled to discharge Adams at will—that is, for cause or no cause. Adams sought to recover $7,094 in lost wages and $200,000 in damages for the "humiliation, mental anguish and emotional distress" that he had suffered as a result of being fired from his job. Under what legal doctrines discussed in this chapter—or exceptions to those doctrines—might Adams be able to recover damages from Cochran? Discuss fully. [*Adams v. George W. Cochran & Co.*, 597 A.2d 28 (D.C.App. 1991)]

21–6. WORKERS' COMPENSATION. Linda Burnett Kidwell, employed as a state traffic officer by the California Highway Patrol (CHP), suffered an injury at home, off duty, while practicing the standing long jump. The jump is a required component of the CHP's annual physical performance program fitness test. Kidwell filed a claim for workers' compensation benefits. The CHP and the California workers' compensation appeals board denied her claim. Kidwell appealed to a state appellate court. What is the requirement for granting a workers' compensation claim? Should Kidwell's claim be granted? [*Kidwell v. Workers' Compensation Appeals Board*, 33 Cal.App.4th 1130, 39 Cal.Rptr.2d 540 (1995)]

21–7. WHISTLEBLOWING. Gabor Nagy was a car salesperson for Whittlesey Automotive Group. Whittlesey asked Nagy to allow some of his phone conversations with "customers" to be recorded. The "customers" were actually employees of a company Whittlesey had hired to conduct a sales training program. Nagy refused to consent. He was eventually fired for his "negative attitude." Nagy filed a suit in a California state court against Whittlesey. He cited a state statute that makes eavesdropping a crime and alleged in part that he was wrongfully terminated in violation of public policy. Will the court agree? Discuss fully. [*Nagy v. Whittlesey Automotive Group*, 40 Cal.App.4th 1328, 47 Cal.Rptr.2d 395 (1995)]

21–8. WRONGFUL DISCHARGE. Stephen Fredrick, a pilot for Simmons Airlines, Inc., criticized the safety of the aircraft that Simmons used on many of its flights and warned the airline about possible safety problems. Simmons took no action. After one of the planes crashed, Fredrick appeared on the television program *Good Morning America* to discuss his safety concerns. The same day, Fredrick refused to allow employees of Simmons to search his personal bags before a flight that he was scheduled to work. Claiming insubordination, the airline terminated Fredrick. Fredrick filed a suit in a federal district court against Simmons, claiming, among other things, retaliatory discharge for his public criticism of the safety of Simmons's aircraft and that this discharge violated the public policy of providing for safe air travel. Simmons responded that an employee who "goes public" with his or her concerns should not be protected by the law. Will the court agree with Simmons? Explain. [*Fredrick v. Simmons Airlines Corp.*, 144 F.3d 500 (7th Cir. 1998)]

21–9. HOURS AND WAGES. Richard Ackerman was an advance sales representative and account manager for Coca-Cola Enterprises, Inc. His primary responsibility was to sell Coca-Cola products to grocery stores, convenience stores, and other sales outlets. Coca-Cola also employed merchandisers, who did not sell Coca-Cola products but performed tasks associated with their distribution and promotion, including restocking shelves, filling vending machines, and setting up displays. The account managers, who serviced the smaller accounts themselves, regularly worked between fifty-five and seventy-two hours each week. Coca-Cola paid them a salary, bonuses, and commissions, but it did not pay them—unlike the merchandisers—additional compensation for the overtime. Ackerman and the other account managers filed a suit in a federal district court against Coca-Cola, alleging that they were entitled to overtime compensation. Coca-Cola responded that because of an exemption under the Fair Labor Standards Act, it was not required to pay them overtime. Is Coca-Cola correct? Explain. [*Ackerman v. Coca-Cola Enterprises, Inc.*, 179 F.3d 1260 (10th Cir. 1999)]

21–10. IN YOUR COURT

Loomis Armored, Inc., has a company rule forbidding its armored truck drivers from leaving their trucks unattended. The employee handbook states, "Violations of this rule will be grounds for termination." Kevin Gardner worked for Loomis as a driver. During a scheduled stop at a bank, Gardner left the truck to aid a woman who was being threatened by a man with a knife. Gardner was discharged for violating Loomis's rule. Gardner subsequently sued Loomis, claiming that his employment termination in these circumstances violated public policy. Assume that you are the judge in the trial court hearing this case and answer the following questions:

(a) The court opinion in Case 41.3 (*Lins v. Children's Discovery Centers of America, Inc.*) lists four factors that courts consider when determining whether a certain type of activity is "protected." How would you apply each of these factors to the case now before your court?

(b) What public policy, if any, has Loomis violated? How will you rule on this issue, and why?

21–11. A QUESTION OF ETHICS

Keith Cline worked for Wal-Mart Stores, Inc., as a night maintenance supervisor. When he suffered a recurrence of a brain tumor, he took a leave from work, which was covered by the Family Medical and Leave Act of 1993 and authorized by his employer. When he returned to work, his employer refused to allow him to continue his supervisory job and demoted him to the status of a regular maintenance worker. A few weeks later, the company fired him, ostensibly because he "stole" company time by clocking in thirteen minutes early for a company meeting. Cline sued Wal-Mart, alleging, among other things, that Wal-Mart had violated the FMLA by refusing to return him to his prior position when he returned to work. In view of these facts, answer the following questions. [*Cline v. Wal-Mart Stores, Inc.*, 144 F.3d 294 (4th Cir. 1998)]

(a) Did Wal-Mart violate the FMLA by refusing to return Cline to his prior position when he returned to work?

(b) From an ethical perspective, the FMLA has been viewed as a choice on the part of society to shift to the employer family burdens caused by changing economic and social needs. What "changing" needs does the act meet? In other words, why did Congress feel that workers should have the right to family and medical leave in 1993, but not in 1983, or 1973, or earlier?

(c) "Congress should amend the FMLA, which currently applies to employers with fifty or more employees, so that it applies to employers with twenty-five or more employees." Do you agree with this statement? Why or why not?

LAW ON THE WEB

For updated links to resources available on the Web, as well as a variety of other materials, visit this text's Web site at http://wleb.westbuslaw.com.

An excellent Web site for information on employee benefits, including the full text of the FMLA, COBRA, other relevant statutes and case law, and current articles, is BenefitsLink. Go to

http://www.benefitslink.com/columns.shtml

The American Federation of Labor–Congress of Industrial Organizations (AFL–CIO) provides links to a broad variety of labor-related resources at

http://www.aflcio.org

The Occupational Safety and Health Administration (OSHA) offers information related to workplace health and safety at

http://www.osha.gov

The Bureau of Labor Statistics provides a wide variety of data on employment, including data on employment compensation, working conditions, and productivity. Go to

http://stats.bls.gov/blshome.html

The National Labor Relations Board is online at the following URL:

http://www.nlrb.gov

LEGAL RESEARCH EXERCISES ON THE WEB

Go to http://wleb.westbuslaw.com, the Web site that accompanies this text. Select "Internet Applications," and then click on "Chapter 21." There you will find the following Internet research exercises that you can perform to learn more about employment laws and issues:

Activity 21–1: Workers' Compensation

Activity 21–2: Workplace Monitoring and Surveillance

CHAPTER 22

Employment Discrimination

OUT OF THE 1960S CIVIL RIGHTS movement to end racial and other forms of discrimination grew a body of law protecting employees against discrimination in the workplace. This protective legislation further eroded the employment-at-will doctrine, which was discussed in Chapter 21. In the past several decades, judicial decisions, administrative agency actions, and legislation have restricted the ability of employers, as well as unions, to discriminate against workers on the basis of race, color, religion, national origin, gender, age, or disability. A class of persons defined by one or more of these criteria is known as a **protected class.**

Several federal statutes prohibit **employment discrimination** against members of protected classes. The most important statute is Title VII of the Civil Rights Act of 1964.[1] Title VII prohibits employment discrimination on the basis of race, color, religion, national origin, and gender. Discrimination on the basis of age and disability are prohibited by the Age Discrimination in Employment Act of 1967[2] and the Americans with Disabilities Act of 1990,[3] respectively. The protections afforded under these laws extend to U.S. citizens who are working abroad for U.S. firms or for companies that are controlled by U.S. firms— *unless* to do so would violate the laws of the countries

in which their workplaces are located. This "foreign laws exception" allows employers to avoid being subjected to conflicting laws.

This chapter focuses on the kinds of discrimination prohibited by these federal statutes. Note, however, that discrimination against employees on the basis of any of the above-mentioned criteria may also violate state human rights statutes or other state laws prohibiting discrimination.

SECTION 1

Title VII of the Civil Rights Act of 1964

Title VII of the Civil Rights Act of 1964 and its amendments prohibit job discrimination against employees, applicants, and union members on the basis of race, color, national origin, religion, and gender at any stage of employment. Title VII applies to employers affecting interstate commerce with fifteen or more employees, labor unions with fifteen or more members, labor unions that operate hiring halls (to which members go regularly to be rationed jobs as they become available), employment agencies, and state and local governing units or agencies. A special section of the act prohibits discrimination in most federal government employment.

---

1. 42 U.S.C. Sections 2000e–2000e-17.
2. 29 U.S.C. Sections 621–634.
3. 42 U.S.C. Sections 12102–12118.

Title VII applies to any employer that "has fifteen or more employees for each working day in each of twenty or more calendar weeks in the current or preceding calendar year." One of the problems that courts have faced in applying Title VII is how to interpret the phrase "has fifteen or more employees." Does an employer "have" an employee on any working day on which the employer maintains an employment relationship with the employee, or only on working days on which the employee is actually receiving compensation from the employer?

In 1997, the United States Supreme Court resolved this issue by holding that the test for when an employer "has" an employee is whether the employer has an employment relationship with the individual on the day in question. This test is generally called the "payroll method," because the employment relationship is most readily demonstrated by the individual's appearance on the employer's payroll as a full-time or part-time worker.[4]

PROCEDURES UNDER TITLE VII

Compliance with Title VII is monitored by the Equal Employment Opportunity Commission (EEOC). A victim of alleged discrimination, before bringing a suit against the employer, must first file a claim with the EEOC. The EEOC may investigate the dispute and attempt to obtain the parties' voluntary consent to an out-of-court settlement. If voluntary agreement cannot be reached, the EEOC may then file a suit against the employer on the employee's behalf. If the EEOC decides not to investigate the claim, the victim may bring his or her own lawsuit against the employer.

The EEOC does not investigate every claim of employment discrimination; rather, it investigates only "priority cases." Generally, priority cases are cases that affect many workers, cases involving retaliatory discharge (firing an employee in retaliation for submitting a claim with the EEOC), and cases involving types of discrimination that are of particular concern to the EEOC.

INTENTIONAL AND UNINTENTIONAL DISCRIMINATION

Title VII of the Civil Rights Act of 1964 prohibits both intentional and unintentional discrimination.

---

4. *Walters v. Metropolitan Educational Enterprises, Inc.,* 519 U.S. 202, 117 S.Ct. 660, 136 L.Ed.2d 644 (1997).

Intentional Discrimination. Intentional discrimination by an employer against an employee is known as **disparate-treatment discrimination.** Because intent may sometimes be difficult to prove, courts have established certain procedures for resolving disparate-treatment cases. Suppose that a woman applies for employment with a construction firm and is rejected. If she sues on the basis of disparate-treatment discrimination in hiring, she must show that (1) she is a member of a protected class, (2) she applied and was qualified for the job in question, (3) she was rejected by the employer, and (4) the employer continued to seek applicants for the position or filled the position with a person not in a protected class.

If the woman can meet these relatively easy requirements, she makes out a ***prima facie* case** of illegal discrimination. Making out a *prima facie* case of discrimination means that the plaintiff has met her initial burden of proof and will win in the absence of a legally acceptable employer defense (defenses to claims of employment discrimination will be discussed later in this chapter). The burden then shifts to the employer-defendant, who must articulate a legal reason for not hiring the plaintiff. For example, the employer might say that the plaintiff was not hired because she lacked sufficient experience or training. To prevail, the plaintiff must then show that the employer's reason is a *pretext* (not the true reason) and that discriminatory intent actually motivated the employer's decision.

Disparate-Impact Discrimination. Employers often find it necessary to use interviews and testing procedures to choose from among a large number of applicants for job openings. Minimum educational requirements are also common. Employer practices, such as those involving educational requirements, may have an unintended discriminatory impact on a protected class. **Disparate-impact discrimination** occurs when, as a result of educational or other job requirements or hiring procedures, an employer's work force does not reflect the percentage of nonwhites, women, or members of other protected classes that characterizes the pool of qualified individuals in the local labor market. If a person challenging an employment practice having a discriminatory effect can show a connection between the practice and the disparity, he or she makes out a *prima facie* case, and no evidence of discriminatory intent needs to be shown.

Disparate-impact discrimination can also occur when an educational or other job requirement or hiring procedure excludes members of a protected class from an employer's work force at a substantially higher rate than nonmembers, regardless of the racial balance in the employer's work force. The EEOC has devised a test, called the "four-fifths rule," to determine whether an employment examination is discriminatory on its face. Under this rule, a selection rate for protected classes that is less than four-fifths, or 80 percent, of the rate for the group with the highest rate will generally be regarded as evidence of disparate impact. To illustrate: One hundred majority applicants take an employment test, and fifty pass the test and are hired. One hundred minority applicants take the test, and twenty pass the test and are hired. Because twenty is less than four-fifths (80 percent) of fifty, the test would be considered discriminatory under the EEOC guidelines.

DISCRIMINATION BASED ON RACE, COLOR, AND NATIONAL ORIGIN

Title VII prohibits employers from discriminating against employees or job applicants on the basis of race, color, or national origin. This prohibition extends to both intentional (disparate-treatment) and unintentional (disparate-impact) discrimination. If a company's standards or policies for selecting or promoting employees have the effect of discriminating

against employees or job applicants on the basis of race, color, or national origin, they are illegal—unless (except for race) they have a substantial, demonstrable relationship to realistic qualifications for the job in question. Discrimination against these protected classes in regard to employment conditions and benefits is also illegal.

Note that victims of racial or ethnic discrimination also may have a cause of action under 42 U.S.C. Section 1981. This section, which was enacted as part of the Civil Rights Act of 1866, prohibits discrimination on the basis of race or ethnicity in the formation or enforcement of contracts. Although Section 1981 remained a "dead letter" on the books for over a century, since the 1970s many plaintiffs have succeeded in Section 1981 cases against their employers. Unlike Title VII, Section 1981 does not place a cap on damages (see the discussion of Title VII remedies later in this chapter). Thus, if an employee can prove that he or she was discriminated against in the formation or enforcement of a contract, the employee may be able to obtain a greater amount in damages under Section 1981 than under Title VII.

In the following case, the court had to decide whether an employer's decision to promote one employee over another constituted discrimination based on race.

CASE 22.1   McCullough v. Real Foods, Inc.

United States
Court of Appeals,
Eighth Circuit, 1998.
140 F.3d 1123.
http://ls.wustl.edu/8th.
cir/opinions.html[a]

BACKGROUND AND FACTS   *In 1992, Cynthia McCullough, an African American woman with a college degree in urban affairs, began working at a deli in Chubb's Finer Foods (Real Foods, Inc.), a grocery store owned and managed by Ron Meredith. More than a year later, Meredith hired Kathy Craven, a white woman, to work at the deli. Craven had no prior deli experience, only a sixth-grade education, and poor reading and math skills. For example, Craven could not calculate prices or read recipes. McCullough and Craven were the only deli employees. Three months after Craven's arrival, Meredith appointed her "deli manager." Meredith later said that he did not promote McCullough because he "understood" that she would not work past 3:00 P.M., that she felt she was overeducated for the position, that she spoke of quitting, and that she would not accept a managerial job for the salary he was willing to pay. Denying all of what Meredith "understood," McCullough filed a suit in a federal district court against Real Foods, alleging discrimination on the basis of race. The court granted a summary judgment in*

---

a. This page contains links to opinions of the U.S. Court of Appeals for the Eighth Circuit. Click on the "Party Name" link. In the "Search string" box, type "Real Foods" and click "Begin Search." When the results appear, click on the case number to access the opinion. This Web site is maintained by Washington University School of Law in St. Louis, Missouri.

favor of Real Foods, and McCullough appealed to the U.S. Court of Appeals for the Eighth Circuit.

IN THE LANGUAGE OF THE COURT

HANSEN, Circuit Judge.

* * * *

* * * McCullough had 15 months more hands-on experience working in the deli than did Craven, * * * [and] McCullough's objective educational qualifications greatly exceeded those of Craven. * * * [W]hen McCullough's education and experience are contrasted with Craven's poor reading, writing, and math skills—as evidenced by her inability to read recipes or calculate prices—a reasonable inference arises that Meredith promoted a substantially less qualified white woman over a substantially better qualified black woman. *We believe it is common business practice to pick the best qualified candidate for promotion. When that is not done, a reasonable inference arises that the employment decision was based on something other than the relative qualifications of the applicants.* [Emphasis added.]

Critical to our analysis in this case is the extremely subjective nature of the employer's stated promotion criteria. * * * [S]ubjective criteria for promotions are particularly easy for an employer to invent in an effort to sabotage a plaintiff's *prima facie* case and mask discrimination. * * *

* * * [W]hen the employer's asserted nondiscriminatory reasons are essentially checkmated by McCullough's denials that she ever made the statements the employer advances as its nondiscriminatory reasons, the failure to promote the objectively better qualified black woman raises a reasonable, nonspeculative inference that the decision to promote the less qualified white woman was based on an impermissible consideration—in this case race.

DECISION AND REMEDY

The U.S. Court of Appeals for the Eighth Circuit reversed the lower court's judgment and remanded the case for trial. The court held that McCullough raised an inference that Real Foods's articulated reasons for promoting Craven were a pretext and that the real reason was illegal discriminatory intent.

DISCRIMINATION BASED ON RELIGION

Title VII of the Civil Rights Act of 1964 also prohibits government employers, private employers, and unions from discriminating against persons because of their religion. An employer must "reasonably accommodate" the religious practices of its employees, unless to do so would cause undue hardship to the employer's business. For example, if an employee's religion prohibits him or her from working on a certain day of the week or at a certain type of job, the employer must make a reasonable attempt to accommodate these religious requirements. Employers must reasonably accommodate an employee's religious belief even if the belief is not based on the tenets or dogma of a particular church, sect, or denomination. The only requirement is that the belief be sincerely held by the employee.[5]

DISCRIMINATION BASED ON GENDER

Under Title VII, as well as other federal acts, employers are forbidden to discriminate against employees on the basis of gender. Employers are prohibited from classifying jobs as male or female and from advertising in help-wanted columns that are designated male or female unless the employer can prove that the gender of the applicant is essential to the job. Furthermore, employers cannot have separate male and female seniority lists. Generally, to succeed in a suit for gender discrimination, a plaintiff must demonstrate that gender was a determining factor in the employer's decision to hire, fire, or promote him or her. Typically, this involves looking at all of the surrounding circumstances.

The Pregnancy Discrimination Act of 1978,[6] which amended Title VII, expanded the definition of

---

5. *Frazee v. Illinois Department of Employment Security*, 489 U.S. 829, 109 S.Ct. 1514, 103 L.Ed.2d 914 (1989).

6. 42 U.S.C. Section 2000e(k).

gender discrimination to include discrimination based on pregnancy. Women affected by pregnancy, child-birth, or related medical conditions must be treated—for all employment-related purposes, including the conferring of benefits under employee benefit pro-grams—the same as other persons not so affected but similar in ability to work.

In the following case, the plaintiff (a male) charged the defendant (a female) with gender discrimination. The plaintiff made out a *prima facie* case, and the defendant presented a nondiscriminatory reason as a defense. Was the defendant's reason a pretext covering a discriminatory motive? That was the question before the court.

CASE 22.2   ## Carey v. Mount Desert Island Hospital

United States
Court of Appeals,
First Circuit, 1998.
156 F.3d 31.
http://www.law.emory.
edu/1circuit/aug98[a]

COMPANY PROFILE   *Mount Desert Island Hospital (MDI) (http://www.mdihospital.org) is a forty-nine-bed facility in Bar Harbor, Maine, with a medical staff that specializes in family practice, general surgery, internal medicine, ophthalmology, pathology, and radiology. A consulting staff includes practitioners of other medical specialties. MDI also operates an occupational health service, community health education, and affiliated health centers: Community Health Center in Southwest Harbor; Family Health Center, Women's Health Center, Breast Center, and High Street Health Center in Bar Harbor; and Northeast Harbor Clinic, open seasonally in Northeast Harbor. MDI is licensed by the state of Maine and fully accredited by the Joint Commission on Accreditation of Healthcare Organizations.*

BACKGROUND AND FACTS   *Michael Carey was a vice president in charge of the finance department for Mount Desert Island Hospital (MDI). When the position of chief executive officer (CEO) opened up, Carey applied, and his application was endorsed by Dan Hobbs, the acting CEO. At the time, an audit of the finance department revealed some deficiencies, but the auditor concluded that the department was "already attacking the problem." MDI's board offered the CEO post to Leslie Hawkins, a woman, who accepted. Less than a year later, Hawkins terminated Carey, giving as reasons the problems cited in the audit and "lack of confidence" in Carey. Carey filed a suit in a federal district court against MDI for gender discrimination in violation of Title VII and other laws. Evidence introduced during the trial included a statement by one female executive that "we have different standards for men and women," with regard to discipline and termination; and a statement by another female executive that "it's about time that we get a woman for this [CEO] position." The court awarded Carey more than $300,000 in damages. MDI appealed to the U.S. Court of Appeals for the First Circuit.*

IN THE LANGUAGE
OF THE COURT

COFFIN, Senior Circuit Judge.
  *   *   *   *

  *   *   * [T]his was a case with much to say on either side, involving the always difficult question of probing the wellsprings of human motivation. *   *   *
  *   *   *   *

In a case such as this, where a plaintiff must rely on circumstantial as opposed to direct evidence of gender discrimination, the evidence will necessarily be composed of bits and pieces, which may or may not point to an atmosphere of gender discrimination. While an employer should not find itself in jeopardy by reason of occasional stray remarks by ordinary employees, *circumstantial evidence of a discriminatory atmosphere at a plaintiff's place of employment is relevant to the question of motive in considering a discrimination claim *   *   * .* [Emphasis added.]

---

a. This page contains links to opinions of the U.S. Court of Appeals for the First Circuit decided in August 1998. Click on the *Carey* case name to access the opinion. This Web site is maintained by Emory University School of Law in Atlanta, Georgia.

* * * *

* * * [Based on the record, we] hold that there was sufficient evidence to support a finding that deficiencies in Carey's handling of financial controls were not the real reason for his discharge but instead covered an action stemming from gender discrimination.

DECISION
AND REMEDY

The U.S. Court of Appeals for the First Circuit affirmed the lower court's judgment. The court held that that there was sufficient evidence to support a finding that the reason for Carey's discharge was gender discrimination.

SEXUAL HARASSMENT

Title VII also protects employees against **sexual harassment** in the workplace. Sexual harassment can take two forms: *quid pro quo* harassment and hostile-environment harassment. *Quid pro quo* is a Latin phrase that is often translated to mean "something in exchange for something else." *Quid pro quo* harassment occurs when job opportunities, promotions, salary increases, and so on are given in return for sexual favors. According to the United States Supreme Court, hostile-environment harassment occurs when "the workplace is permeated with discriminatory intimidation, ridicule, and insult, that is sufficiently severe or pervasive to alter the conditions of the victim's employment and create an abusive working environment."[7]

Generally, the courts apply this Supreme Court guideline on a case-by-case basis. Some courts have held that just one incident of sexually offensive conduct—such as a sexist remark by a co-worker or a photo on an employer's desk of his bikini-clad wife—can create a hostile environment.[8] At least one court has held that a worker may recover damages under Title VII because *other* persons were harassed sexually in the workplace.[9] According to some employment specialists, employers should assume that hostile-environment harassment has occurred if an employee claims that it has.

Harassment by Supervisors. What if an employee is harassed by a manager or supervisor of a large firm,

and the firm itself (the "employer") is not aware of the harassment? Should the employer be held liable for the harassment nonetheless? For some time, the courts were in disagreement on this issue. Typically, employers were held liable for Title VII violations by the firm's managerial or supervisory personnel in *quid pro quo* harassment cases regardless of whether the employer knew about the harassment. In hostile-environment cases, in contrast, the majority of courts tended to hold employers liable only if the employer knew or should have known of the harassment and failed to take prompt remedial action.

In 1998, in two separate cases, the United States Supreme Court issued some significant guidelines relating to the liability of employers for their supervisors' harassment of employees in the workplace. In *Faragher v. City of Boca Raton*,[10] the Court held that an employer (a city) could be held liable for a supervisor's harassment of employees even though the employer was unaware of the behavior. The Court reached this conclusion primarily because, although the city had a written policy against sexual harassment, the policy had not been distributed to city employees. Additionally, the city had not established any procedures that could be followed by employees who felt that they were victims of sexual harassment. In *Burlington Industries, Inc. v. Ellerth*,[11] the Court ruled that a company could be held liable for the harassment of an employee by one of its vice presidents even though the employee suffered no adverse job consequences.

In these two cases, the Court set forth some common-sense guidelines on liability for harassment in the workplace that will be helpful to employers and employees alike. On the one hand, employees benefit

---

7. *Harris v. Forklift Systems*, 510 U.S. 17, 114 S.Ct. 367, 126 L.Ed.2d 295 (1993).
8. For other examples, see *Radtke v. Everett*, 442 Mich. 368, 501 N.W.2d 155 (1993); and *Nadeau v. Rainbow Rugs, Inc.*, 675 A.2d 973 (Me. 1996).
9. *Leibovitz v. New York City Transit Authority*, 4 F.Supp.2d 144 (E.D.N.Y. 1998).

10. 524 U.S. 725, 118 S.Ct. 2275, 141 L.Ed.2d 662 (1998).
11. 524 U.S. 742, 118 S.Ct. 2257, 141 L.Ed.2d 633 (1998).

by the ruling that employers may be held liable for their supervisors' harassment even though they were unaware of the actions and even though the employees suffered no adverse job consequences. On the other hand, the Court made it clear in both decisions that employers have an affirmative defense against liability for their supervisors' harassment of employees if they can show that (1) they have taken "reasonable care to prevent and correct promptly any sexually harassing behavior" (by establishing effective harassment policies and complaint procedures, for example), and (2) the employee suing for harassment failed to follow these policies and procedures.

Harassment by Co-Workers and Nonemployees. Often, employees alleging harassment complain that the actions of co-workers, not supervisors, are responsible for creating a hostile working environment. In such cases, the employee still has a cause of action against the employer. Generally, though, the employer will be held liable only if it knew or should have known about the harassment and failed to take immediate remedial action.

Employers may also be liable for harassment by *nonemployees* under certain conditions. For example, if a restaurant owner or manager knows that a certain customer repeatedly harasses a waitress and permits the harassment to continue, the restaurant owner may be liable under Title VII even though the customer is not an employee of the restaurant. The issue turns on the control that the employer exerts over a nonemployee. In one case, the owner of a Pizza Hut franchise was held liable for the harassment of a waitress by two male customers because no steps were taken to prevent the harassment.[12]

Same-Gender Harassment. The courts have also had to address the issue of whether men who are harassed by other men, or women who are harassed by other women, are also protected by laws that prohibit gender-based discrimination in the workplace. For example, what if the male president of a firm demands sexual favors from a male employee? Does this action qualify as sexual harassment? For some time, the courts were widely split on this question. In 1998, in *Oncale v. Sundowner Offshore Services, Inc.,*[13] the Supreme

Court resolved the issue by holding that Title VII protection extends to situations in which individuals are harassed by members of the same gender.

REMEDIES UNDER TITLE VII

Employer liability under Title VII may be extensive. If the plaintiff successfully proves that unlawful discrimination occurred, he or she may be awarded reinstatement, back pay, retroactive promotions, and damages.[14] Compensatory damages are available only in cases of intentional discrimination. Punitive damages may be recovered against a private employer only if the employer acted with malice or reckless indifference to an individual's rights. The sum of the amount of compensatory and punitive damages is limited by the statute to specific amounts against specific employers—ranging from $50,000 against employers with one hundred or fewer employees to $300,000 against employers with more than five hundred employees.

SECTION 2

Equal Pay Act of 1963

The Equal Pay Act of 1963 was enacted as an amendment to the Fair Labor Standards Act of 1938. Basically, the act prohibits gender-based discrimination in the wages paid for similar work. For the equal pay requirements to apply, the male and female employees must be employed at the same establishment.

A person alleging wage discrimination in violation of the Equal Pay Act may sue his or her employer. To determine whether the act has been violated, a court will look to the primary duties of the two jobs—it is job content rather than job description that controls in all cases. The jobs of a barber and a beautician, for example, are considered essentially equal. So, too, are those of a tailor and a seamstress. Small differences in job content do not justify higher pay for one gender. An employer will not be found liable for violating the act if it can be shown that the wage differential for equal work was based on (1) a seniority system, (2) a merit system, (3) a system that pays according to

---

12. *Lockard v. Pizza Hut, Inc.,* 162 F.3d 1062 (10th Cir. 1998).
13. 523 U.S. 75, 118 S.Ct. 998, 140 L.Ed.2d 207 (1998).

---

14. Damages were not available under Title VII until 1991. The Civil Rights Act of that year amended Title VII to provide for both compensatory and punitive damages, as well as jury trials.

quality or quantity of production, or (4) any factor other than gender.

SECTION 3

Discrimination Based on Age

Age discrimination is potentially the most widespread form of discrimination, because anyone—regardless of race, color, national origin, or gender—could be a victim at some point in life. The Age Discrimination in Employment Act (ADEA) of 1967, as amended, prohibits employment discrimination on the basis of age against individuals forty years of age or older. The act also prohibits mandatory retirement for nonmanagerial workers. For the act to apply, an employer must have twenty or more employees, and the employer's business activities must affect interstate commerce. The EEOC administers the ADEA, but the act also permits private causes of action against employers for age discrimination.

PROCEDURES UNDER THE ADEA

The burden-shifting procedure under the ADEA is similar to that under Title VII. If a plaintiff can establish that he or she (1) was a member of the protected age group, (2) was qualified for the position from which he or she was discharged, and (3) was discharged under circumstances that give rise to an inference of discrimination, the plaintiff has established a *prima facie* case of unlawful age discrimination. The burden then shifts to the employer, who must articulate a legitimate reason for the discrimination. If the plaintiff can prove that the employer's reason is only a pretext and that the plaintiff's age was a determining factor in the employer's decision, the employer will be held liable under the ADEA.

Numerous cases of alleged age discrimination have been brought against employers who, to cut costs, replaced older, higher-salaried employees with younger, lower-salaried workers. Whether a firing is discriminatory or simply part of a rational business decision to prune the company's ranks is not always clear. Companies generally defend a decision to discharge a worker by asserting that the worker could no longer perform his or her duties or that the worker's skills were no longer needed. The employee must prove that the discharge was motivated, at least in part, by age bias. Proof that qualified older employees are generally discharged before employees who are younger or that co-workers continually made unflattering age-related comments about the discharged worker may be enough.

In the past, courts sometimes held that to establish a *prima facie* case of age discrimination, the plaintiff had to prove that he or she had been replaced by a person outside the protected class—that is, by a person under the age of forty years. In 1996, however, in *O'Connor v. Consolidated Coin Caterers Corp.*,[15] the United States Supreme Court held that a cause of action for age discrimination under the ADEA does not require the replacement worker to be outside the protected class. Rather, the issue in all ADEA cases turns on whether age discrimination has in fact occurred, regardless of the age of the replacement worker.

A SPECIAL CASE—STATE EMPLOYEES

Under the Eleventh Amendment to the Constitution, as that amendment has been interpreted by the Supreme Court, states are immune from lawsuits brought by private individuals in federal court, unless a state consents to the suit. In a number of age-discrimination cases brought in the late 1990s, state agencies that were sued by state employees for age discrimination sought to have the suits dismissed on this ground.

For example, in two Florida cases, professors and librarians contended that their employers—two Florida state universities—denied them salary increases and other benefits because they were getting old and their successors could be hired at lower cost. The universities claimed that as agencies of a sovereign state, they could not be sued without the state's consent. Because the courts were rendering conflicting opinions in these cases, the United States Supreme Court agreed to address the issue. In *Kimel v. Florida Board of Regents*,[16] decided in early 2000, the Court held that the sovereign immunity granted the states by the Eleventh Amendment precluded suits against them by private parties alleging violations of the ADEA. According to the Court, Congress had exceeded its constitutional authority

---

15. 517 U.S. 308, 116 S.Ct. 1307, 134 L.Ed.2d 433 (1996).
16. ___U.S.___, 120 S.Ct. 631, 145 L.Ed.2d 522 (2000).

when it included in the ADEA a provision stating that "all employers," including state employers, were subject to the act.

Understandably, the *Kimel* decision has been controversial, and it may become more so as state employees face the consequences of this decision. Even the Court was strongly divided on the issue (the vote was five to four). Shortly after the Court rendered its decision in *Kimel*, it agreed to decide another question with serious implications for state employees—whether a state employer can be sued for disability discrimination under the Americans with Disabilities Act.[17]

SECTION 4

Discrimination Based on Disability

The Americans with Disabilities Act (ADA) of 1990 is designed to eliminate discriminatory employment practices that prevent otherwise qualified workers with disabilities from fully participating in the national labor force. Prior to 1990, the major federal law providing protection to those with disabilities was the Rehabilitation Act of 1973. That act covered only federal government employees and those employed under federally funded programs. The ADA extends federal protection against disability-based discrimination to all workplaces with fifteen or more workers. Basically, the ADA requires that employers "reasonably accommodate" the needs of persons with disabilities unless to do so would cause the employer to suffer an "undue hardship."

To prevail on a claim under the ADA, a plaintiff must show that he or she (1) has a disability, (2) is otherwise qualified for the employment in question, and (3) was excluded from the employment solely because of the disability. As in Title VII cases, a claim alleging violation of the ADA may be commenced only after the plaintiff has pursued the claim through the EEOC, which administers the provisions of the act relating to disability-based discrimination in the employment context. Plaintiffs may sue for many of the same remedies available under Title VII. They may seek reinstatement, back pay, a limited amount of compensatory and punitive damages (for intentional discrimination), and

certain other forms of relief. Repeat violators may be ordered to pay fines of up to $100,000.

WHAT IS A DISABILITY?

The ADA is broadly drafted to define persons with disabilities as persons with physical or mental impairments that "substantially limit" their everyday activities. More specifically, the ADA defines *disability* as "(1) a physical or mental impairment that substantially limits one or more of the major life activities of such individuals; (2) a record of such impairment; or (3) being regarded as having such an impairment."

Generally, the determination of whether an individual has a disability as defined by the ADA is made on a case-by-case basis. Unlike plaintiffs in cases brought under Title VII or the ADEA, who clearly are or are not members of the classes protected by those acts, a plaintiff suing under the ADA must *prove* that he or she has a disability and thus falls under the protection of the ADA. Meeting this first requirement for a case of disability-based discrimination may be difficult.

Health conditions that have been considered disabilities under federal law include blindness, alcoholism, heart disease, cancer, muscular dystrophy, cerebral palsy, paraplegia, diabetes, acquired immune deficiency syndrome (AIDS), and morbid obesity (defined as existing when an individual's weight is two times that of a normal person).[18] The ADA excludes from coverage certain conditions, such as kleptomania.

For some time, the courts were divided on the issue of whether a person who is infected with the human immunodeficiency virus (HIV) but who has no symptoms of AIDS should come under the protection of the ADA as a person with a disability. In 1998, the Supreme Court resolved this issue by holding that an HIV infection is a disability even if the infection has not yet progressed to the symptomatic phase.[19]

One issue that frequently arises in ADA cases is whether a person whose impairment is mitigated by medication or a corrective device qualifies for protection under the ADA. That issue arose in the following case, which was appealed to the United States Supreme Court by two pilots whose severe myopia could be corrected with glasses or contact lenses.

---

17. The Court will review a decision by the Court of Appeals for the Eleventh Circuit in which that court held that a state can be sued for disability discrimination. See *Florida Department of Corrections v. Dickson*, 139 F.3d 1326 (11th Cir. 1998).

18. *Cook v. Rhode Island Department of Mental Health*, 10 F.3d 17 (1st Cir. 1993).

19. *Bragdon v. Abbott*, 524 U.S. 624, 118 S.Ct. 2196, 141 L.Ed.2d 540 (1998).

CASE 22.3   Sutton v. United Airlines, Inc.

Supreme Court of the
United States, 1999.
527 U.S. 471,
119 S.Ct. 2139,
144 L.Ed.2d 450.
http://supct.law.
cornell.edu/supct/
supct.1999a.html[a]

BACKGROUND AND FACTS   *Karen and Kimberly Sutton are twin sisters, both of whom have severe myopia. Each woman's uncorrected visual acuity is 20/200 or worse in her right eye and 20/400 or worse in her left eye, but with the use of corrective lenses, such as glasses or contact lenses, each has vision that is 20/20 or better. In other words, without corrective lenses, neither individual can see well enough to do such things as drive a vehicle, watch television, or shop, but with corrective measures, each functions identically to individuals without a similar impairment. In 1992, the Suttons applied to United Airlines, Inc. (UA), for employment as commercial airline pilots. They met UA's age, education, experience, and Federal Aviation Administration certification qualifications, and were invited to flight simulator tests and interviews. Because the Suttons did not meet UA's minimum vision requirement, which was uncorrected visual acuity of 20/100 or better, the interviews were terminated, and neither pilot was offered a position. The Suttons filed a suit in a federal district court against UA, alleging discrimination under the Americans with Disabilities Act (ADA). The Suttons asserted in part that due to their severe myopia, they have a substantially limiting impairment and are thus disabled. The court disagreed and dismissed their complaint, and the U.S. Court of Appeals for the Tenth Circuit affirmed this judgment. The Suttons appealed to the United States Supreme Court.*

IN THE LANGUAGE
OF THE COURT

Justice O'CONNOR delivered the opinion of the Court.

*   *   *   *

*   *   * The Act defines a "disability" as "a physical or mental impairment that substantially limits one or more of the major life activities" of an individual. Because the phrase "substantially limits" appears in the Act in the present indicative verb form, we think the language is properly read as requiring that a person be presently—not potentially or hypothetically—substantially limited in order to demonstrate a disability. A "disability" exists only where an impairment "substantially limits" a major life activity, not where it "might," "could," or "would" be substantially limiting if mitigating measures were not taken. A person whose physical or mental impairment is corrected by medication or other measures does not have an impairment that presently "substantially limits" a major life activity. To be sure, a *person whose physical or mental impairment is corrected by mitigating measures still has an impairment, but if the impairment is corrected it does not "substantially limi[t]" a major life activity.* [Emphasis added.]

*   *   *   *

*   *   * The use of a corrective device does not, by itself, relieve one's disability. Rather, one has a disability under [the Act] if, notwithstanding the use of a corrective device, that individual is substantially limited in a major life activity. For example, individuals who use prosthetic limbs or wheelchairs may be mobile and capable of functioning in society but still be disabled because of a substantial limitation on their ability to walk or run. The same may be true of individuals who take medicine to lessen the symptoms of an impairment so that they can function but nevertheless remain substantially limited. *   *   * The use or nonuse of a corrective device does not determine whether an individual is disabled; that determination depends on whether the limitations an individual with an impairment actually faces are in fact substantially limiting.

Applying this reading of the Act to the case at hand, we conclude that the Court of Appeals correctly resolved the issue of disability in respondent's favor. *   *   * [P]etitioners allege that with corrective measures, their visual acuity is 20/20, and that they "function identically to individuals without a similar impairment." In addition, petitioners concede that they "do not argue that the use of corrective lenses in itself demonstrates a substantially limiting impairment." Accordingly, because we decide that

---

a. This page includes an alphabetical list of the 1999 decisions of the United States Supreme Court. Scroll down the list of cases to the *Sutton* case, and click on the name to access the opinion.

disability under the Act is to be determined with reference to corrective measures, we agree with the courts below that petitioners have not stated a claim that they are substantially limited in any major life activity. [Emphasis added.]

DECISION AND REMEDY   *The United States Supreme Court affirmed the decision of the lower court. The Supreme Court held that a person is not disabled (substantially limited in any major life activity) under the ADA if he or she has a condition that can be corrected with medication, or one, such as poor vision, that can be rectified with corrective devices, such as glasses.*

REASONABLE ACCOMMODATION

If a job applicant or an employee with a disability can perform essential job functions with reasonable accommodation, the employer must make the accommodation. Required modifications may include installing ramps for a wheelchair, establishing flexible working hours, creating or modifying job assignments, and creating or improving training materials and procedures.

Generally, employers should give primary consideration to employees' preferences in deciding what accommodations should be made. If an applicant or employee fails to let the employer know how his or her disability can be accommodated, the employer may avoid liability for failing to hire or retain the individual on the ground that the individual has failed to meet the "otherwise qualified" requirement.[20] Employers should be cautious in making this assumption in cases involving mental illness, though. For example, in one case, an employee was held to have a cause of action against his employer under the ADA even though the employee never explicitly told the employer how his disability could be accommodated.[21]

Employers who do not accommodate the needs of persons with disabilities must demonstrate that the accommodations would cause *undue hardship*. Generally, the law offers no uniform standards for identifying what is an undue hardship other than the imposition of a "significant difficulty or expense" on the employer.

Usually, the courts decide whether an accommodation constitutes an undue hardship on a case-by-case basis. In one case, the court decided that paying for a parking space near the office for an employee with a disability was not an undue hardship.[22] In another case, the court held that accommodating the request of an employee with diabetes for indefinite leave until his disease was under control would create an undue hardship for the employer, because the employer would not know when the employee was returning to work. The court stated that reasonable accommodation under the ADA means accommodation so that the employee can perform the job now or "in the immediate future" rather than at some unspecified distant time.[23]

Job Applications and Preemployment Physical Exams. Employers must modify their job-application process so that those with disabilities can compete for jobs with those who do not have disabilities. A job announcement that has only a phone number, for example, would discriminate against potential job applicants with hearing impairments. Thus, the job announcement must also provide an address.

Employers are restricted in the kinds of questions they may ask on job-application forms and during preemployment interviews. Furthermore, employers cannot require persons with disabilities to submit to preemployment physicals unless such exams are required of all other applicants. Employers can condition an offer of employment on the employee's successfully passing a medical examination, but disqualifications must result from the discovery of problems that render the applicant unable to perform the job for which he or she is to be hired.

Dangerous Workers. Employers are not required to hire or retain workers who, because of their disabili-

---

20. See, for example, *Beck v. University of Wisconsin Board of Regents*, 75 F.3d 1130 (7th Cir. 1996); and *White v. York International Corp.*, 45 F.3d 357 (10th Cir. 1995).

21. *Bultemeyer v. Fort Wayne Community Schools*, 100 F.3d 1281 (7th Cir. 1996).

22. See *Lyons v. Legal Aid Society*, 68 F.3d 1512 (2d Cir. 1995).

23. *Myers v. Hase*, 50 F.3d 278 (4th Cir. 1995).

ties, pose a "direct threat to the health or safety" of their co-workers. In the wake of the AIDS epidemic, many employers are concerned about hiring or continuing to employ a worker who has AIDS under the assumption that he or she might pose a direct threat to the health or safety of others in the workplace. Courts have generally held, however, that AIDS is not so contagious as to disqualify employees from most jobs. Therefore, employers must reasonably accommodate job applicants or employees who have AIDS or who test positive for HIV, the virus that causes AIDS.

The ADA prohibits employers from refusing to hire or retain persons with disabilities who are otherwise qualified for a particular position. The ADA does not require that *unqualified* disabled applicants be hired or retained, however.

Substance Abusers. Drug addiction is a disability under the ADA, because drug addiction is a substantially limiting impairment. Those who are currently using illegal drugs are not protected by the act. The ADA only protects persons with *former* drug addictions—those who have completed a supervised drug-rehabilitation program or who are currently in a supervised rehabilitation program. Individuals who have used drugs casually in the past are not protected under the act. They are not considered addicts and therefore do not have a disability (addiction).

People suffering from alcoholism are protected by the ADA. Employers cannot legally discriminate against employees simply because they are living with alcoholism and must treat them in the same way as they treat other employees. For example, an employee with alcoholism who comes to work late because he or she was drinking the night before cannot be disciplined any differently than an employee who comes to work late for another reason. Of course, employers have the right to prohibit the use of alcohol in the workplace and can require that employees not be under the influence of alcohol while working. Employers can also fire or refuse to hire a person with alcoholism if he or she poses a substantial risk of harm either to himself or herself or to others and the risk cannot be reduced by reasonable accommodation.

Health-Insurance Plans. Workers with disabilities must be given equal access to any health insurance provided to other employees. Employers can exclude from coverage preexisting health conditions and certain types of diagnostic or surgical procedures, however. An employer can also put a limit, or cap, on health-care payments in its particular group-health policy—as long as such caps are "applied equally to all insured employees" and do not "discriminate on the basis of disability." Whenever a group health-care plan makes a disability-based distinction in its benefits, the plan violates the ADA. The employer must then be able to justify the distinction by proving one of the following:

1. That limiting coverage of certain ailments is required to keep the plan financially sound.
2. That coverage of certain ailments would cause a significant increase in premium payments or their equivalent, making the plan unappealing to a significant number of employees.
3. That the disparate treatment is justified by the risks and costs associated with a particular disability.

SECTION 5

Defenses to Employment Discrimination

The first line of defense for an employer charged with employment discrimination is, of course, to assert that the plaintiff has failed to meet his or her initial burden of proof—proving that discrimination in fact occurred. As noted, plaintiffs bringing cases under the ADA may find it difficult to meet this initial burden, because they must prove that their alleged disabilities are disabilities covered by the ADA. Furthermore, plaintiffs in ADA cases must prove that they were otherwise qualified for the job.

Once a plaintiff succeeds in proving that discrimination occurred, then the burden shifts to the employer to justify the discriminatory practice. Often, employers attempt to justify the discrimination by claiming that it was the result of a business necessity, a bona fide occupational qualification, a seniority system, or employee misconduct.

BUSINESS NECESSITY

An employer may defend against a claim of discrimination by asserting that a practice that has a discriminatory effect is a **business necessity**. If requiring a high school diploma, for example, is shown to have a discriminatory effect, an employer might argue that a high school education is required for workers to perform the job at a required level of competence. If the employer can demonstrate to the court's satisfaction that a definite connection exists between a high school education and job performance, then the employer will succeed in this business necessity defense.

Bona Fide Occupational Qualification

Another defense applies when discrimination against a protected class is essential to a job—that is, when a particular trait is a **bona fide occupational qualification (BFOQ)**. For example, a women's clothing boutique might legitimately hire only female attendants if part of an attendant's job involves assisting clients in the boutique's dressing rooms. Similarly, the Federal Aviation Administration can legitimately impose age limits for airline pilots. Race, however, can never be a BFOQ. Generally, courts have restricted the BFOQ defense to instances in which the employee's gender or religion is essential to the job.

Seniority Systems

An employer with a history of discrimination may have no members of protected classes in upper-level positions. Even if the employer now seeks to be unbiased, it may face a lawsuit seeking an order that minorities be promoted ahead of schedule to compensate for past discrimination. If no present intent to discriminate is shown, however, and if promotions or other job benefits are distributed according to a fair **seniority system** (in which workers with more years of service are promoted first or laid off last), the employer has a good defense against the suit.

After-Acquired Evidence of Employee Misconduct

In some situations, employers have attempted to avoid liability for employment discrimination on the basis of "after-acquired evidence" of an employee's misconduct. For example, suppose that an employer fires a worker, and the employee sues the employer for employment discrimination. During pretrial investigation, the employer learns that the employee made material misrepresentations on his or her employment application—misrepresentations that, had the employer known about them, would have served

as a ground to fire the individual. Can this after-acquired evidence be used as a defense?

According to the United States Supreme Court, after-acquired evidence of wrongdoing should not operate, "in every instance, to bar all relief for an earlier violation" of a federal law prohibiting discrimination.[24] Since this decision, the courts have generally held that after-acquired evidence, at best, can only serve to limit liability. While such evidence cannot be used to shield an employer entirely from liability for employment discrimination, it may be used to limit the amount of damages for which the employer is liable.

Section 6

Affirmative Action

Federal statutes and regulations providing for equal opportunity in the workplace were designed to reduce or eliminate discriminatory practices with respect to hiring, retaining, and promoting employees. **Affirmative action** programs go a step further and attempt to "make up" for past patterns of discrimination by giving members of protected classes preferential treatment in hiring or promotion.

Affirmative action programs have caused much controversy, particularly when they result in what is frequently called "reverse discrimination"—discrimination against "majority" workers, such as white males (or discrimination against other minority groups that are not given preferential treatment under a particular affirmative action program). At issue is whether affirmative action programs, because of their inherently discriminatory nature, violate the equal protection clause of the Fourteenth Amendment to the Constitution.

The Bakke Case

An early nonemployment-related case addressing this issue, *Regents of the University of California v. Bakke*,[25] involved an affirmative action program implemented by the University of California at Davis. Allan Bakke, who had been turned down for medical school at the Davis campus, sued the university for reverse discrimi-

---

24. *McKennon v. Nashville Banner Publishing Co.*, 513 U.S. 352, 115 S.Ct. 879, 130 L.Ed.2d 852 (1995).
25. 438 U.S. 265, 98 S.Ct. 2733, 57 L.Ed.2d 750 (1978).

nation after he discovered that his academic record was better than those of some of the minority applicants who had been admitted to the program.

The United States Supreme Court held that affirmative action programs were subject to intermediate scrutiny. Recall from the discussion of the equal protection clause in Chapter 5 that any law or action evaluated under a standard of intermediate scrutiny, to be constitutionally valid, must be substantially related to important government objectives. Applying this standard, the Court held that the university could give favorable weight to minority applicants as part of a plan to increase minority enrollment so as to achieve a more culturally diverse student body. The Court stated, however, that the use of a quota system, in which a certain number of places are explicitly reserved for minority applicants, violated the equal protection clause of the Fourteenth Amendment.

THE *ADARAND* CASE AND SUBSEQUENT DEVELOPMENTS

Although the *Bakke* case and later court decisions alleviated the harshness of the quota system, today's courts are going even further in questioning the constitutional validity of affirmative action programs. In 1995, in its landmark decision in *Adarand Constructors, Inc. v. Peña*,[26] the United States Supreme Court held that any federal, state, or local affirmative action program that uses racial or ethnic classifications as the basis for making decisions is subject to strict scrutiny by the courts.

In effect, the Court's opinion in *Adarand* means that an affirmative action program is constitutional only if it attempts to remedy past discrimination and does not make use of quotas or preferences. Furthermore, once such a program has succeeded in the goal of remedying past discrimination, it must be changed or dropped. Since then, other federal courts have followed the Supreme Court's lead by declaring affirmative action programs invalid unless they attempt to remedy past or current discrimination.[27]

The Court of Appeals for the Fifth Circuit went even further than the Supreme Court in its 1996 decision in *Hopwood v. State of Texas*.[28] In that case, two white law school applicants sued the University of Texas School of Law in Austin, alleging that they were denied admission because of the school's affirmative action program. The program allowed admitting officials to take racial and other factors into consideration when determining which students would be admitted. The Court of Appeals for the Fifth Circuit held that the program violated the equal protection clause because it discriminated in favor of minority applicants. In its decision, the court directly challenged the *Bakke* decision by stating that the use of race even as a means of achieving diversity on college campuses "undercuts the Fourteenth Amendment." The United States Supreme Court declined to hear the case, thus letting the lower court's decision stand.

Additionally, California and Washington, by voter initiatives in 1996 and 1998, respectively, ended state-sponsored affirmative action in those states. Similar movements are currently under way in other states as well, such as Florida.

SECTION 7

State Laws Prohibiting Discrimination

Although the focus of this chapter is on federal legislation, most states also have statutes that prohibit employment discrimination. Generally, the kinds of discrimination prohibited under federal legislation are also prohibited by state laws. In addition, state statutes often provide protection for certain individuals who are not protected under federal laws. For example, a New Jersey appellate court has held that anyone over the age of eighteen was entitled to sue for age discrimination under the state law, which specified no threshold age limit.[29] Furthermore, state laws prohibiting discrimination may apply to firms with fewer employees than the threshold number required under federal statutes, thus offering protection to a greater number of workers. Finally, state laws may provide for additional damages, such as damages for emotional distress, that are not provided for under federal statutes.

---

26. 575 U.S. 200, 115 S.Ct. 2097, 132 L.Ed.2d 158 (1995).
27. See, for example, *Taxman v. Board of Education of the Township of Piscataway*, 91 F.3d 1547 (3d Cir. 1996); and *Schurr v. Resorts International Hotel, Inc.*, 196 F.3d 486 (3d Cir. 1999).

28. 84 F.3d 720 (5th Cir. 1996).
29. *Bergen Commercial Bank v. Sisler*, 307 N.J.Super. 333, 704 A.2d 1017 (1998).

TERMS AND CONCEPTS TO REVIEW

affirmative action 488

bona fide occupational
    qualification (BFOQ) 488

business necessity 487

disparate-impact
    discrimination 477

disparate-treatment
    discrimination 477

employment discrimination 476

prima facie case 477

protected class 476

seniority system 488

sexual harassment 481

QUESTIONS AND CASE PROBLEMS

22–1. TITLE VII VIOLATIONS. Discuss fully whether any of the following actions would constitute a violation of Title VII of the 1964 Civil Rights Act, as amended.

(a) Tennington, Inc., is a consulting firm and has ten employees. These employees travel on consulting jobs in seven states. Tennington has an employment record of hiring only white males.

(b) Novo Films is making a movie about Africa and needs to employ approximately one hundred extras for this picture. Novo advertises in all major newspapers in southern California for the hiring of these extras. The ad states that only African Americans need apply.

22–2. DISCRIMINATION BASED ON AGE. Tavo Jones had worked since 1974 for Westshore Resort, where he maintained golf carts. During the first decade, he received positive job evaluations and numerous merit pay raises. He was promoted to the position of supervisor of golf-cart maintenance at three courses. Then a new employee, Ben Olery, was placed in charge of the golf courses. He demoted Jones, who was over the age of forty, to running one of the three cart facilities, and he froze Jones's salary indefinitely. Olery also demoted five other men over the age of forty. Another cart facility was placed under the supervision of Blake Blair. Later, the cart facilities for the three courses were again consolidated, but Blair—not Jones—was put in charge. At the time, Blair was in his twenties. Jones overheard Blair say that "we are going to have to do away with these . . . old and senile" men. Jones quit and sued Westshore for employment discrimination. Should he prevail? Explain.

22–3. DISCRIMINATION BASED ON DISABILITY. Ananda is a hearing-impaired repairperson currently employed with the Southwestern Telephone Co. Her job requires her to drive the company truck to remote rural areas in all kinds of weather, to climb telephone poles, to make general repairs to telephone lines, and so on. She has held this position for five years, a full year longer than any other employee, and she is quite competent. Ananda recently applied for a promotion to the position of repair crew coordinator, a position that would require her to be in constant communication with all repairpersons in the field. Southwestern rejected Ananda's application, stating that the company "needs someone in this critical position who can speak and hear clearly, someone who does not suffer from any hearing disability." Ananda says she could easily perform the essentials of the job if Southwestern would provide her with a sign interpreter. Although Southwestern agrees that Ananda is otherwise qualified for the coordinator position, the company has concluded that the cost of hiring an interpreter would be prohibitive, and therefore it should not be required to accommodate her disability under the Americans with Disabilities Act. Who is correct? Discuss.

22–4. DEFENSES TO EMPLOYMENT DISCRIMINATION. Dorothea O'Driscoll had worked as a quality control inspector for Hercules, Inc., for six years when her employment was terminated in 1986. O'Driscoll, who was over forty years of age, sued Hercules for age discrimination in violation of the Age Discrimination in Employment Act of 1967. While preparing for trial, Hercules learned that O'Driscoll had made several misrepresentations when she applied for the job. Among other things, she misrepresented her age, did not disclose a previous employer, falsely represented that she had never applied for work with Hercules before, and untruthfully stated that she had completed two quarters of study at a technical college. Additionally, on her application for group insurance coverage, she misrepresented the age of her son, who would otherwise have been ineligible for coverage as her dependent. Hercules defended against O'Driscoll's claim of age discrimination by stating that had it known of this misconduct, it would have terminated her employment anyway. What should the court decide? Discuss fully. [*O'Driscoll v. Hercules, Inc.*, 12 F.3d 176 (10th Cir. 1994)]

22–5. DISCRIMINATION BASED ON NATIONAL ORIGIN. Phanna Xieng was sent by the Cambodian government to the United States in 1974 for "advanced military training." When the Cambodian government fell in 1975, Xieng remained in the United States and in 1979 was employed by Peoples National Bank of Washington. In performance appraisals from 1980 through 1985, Xieng was rated by his supervisors as "capable of dealing effectively with customers" and qualified for promotion, although in each appraisal it was noted that Xieng might improve his communication skills to maximize his possibilities for future advancement. Xieng sought job promotions on numerous occasions but was never promoted. In 1986, he filed a complaint against the bank, alleging employment discrimination based on national origin. The employer argued that its refusal to promote Xieng because of his accent or communication skills did not amount to discrimination based on national origin. Is it possible to separate discrimination based on an employee's accent and communication skills from discrimination based on national origin? How should the court rule on this issue? [*Xieng v. Peoples National Bank of Washington*, 120 Wash.2d 512, 844 P.2d 389 (1993)]

22–6. DISCRIMINATION BASED ON DISABILITY. When the University of Maryland Medical System Corp. learned that one of its surgeons was HIV positive, the university offered him transfers to positions that did not involve surgery. The surgeon refused, and the university terminated him. The surgeon filed a suit in a federal district court against the university, alleging in part a violation of the Americans with Disabilities Act. The surgeon claimed that he was "otherwise qualified" for his former position. What does he have to prove to win his case? Should he be reinstated? [*Doe v. University of Maryland Medical System Corp.*, 50 F.3d 1261 (4th Cir. 1995)]

22–7. DISCRIMINATION BASED ON RACE. Theodore Rosenblatt, a white attorney, worked for the law firm of Bivona & Cohen, P.C. When Bivona & Cohen terminated Rosenblatt's employment, he filed a suit in a federal district court against the firm. Rosenblatt claimed that he had been discharged because he was married to an African American and that a discharge for such a reason violated Title VII and other laws. The firm filed a motion for summary judgment, arguing that he was alleging discrimination against his wife, not himself, and thus did not have standing to sue under Title VII for racial discrimination. Should the court grant or deny the motion? Explain. [*Rosenblatt v. Bivona & Cohen, P.C.*, 946 F.Supp. 298 (S.D.N.Y. 1996)]

22–8. RELIGIOUS DISCRIMINATION. Mary Tiano, a devout Roman Catholic, worked for Dillard Department Stores, Inc. (Dillard's), in Phoenix, Arizona. Dillard's considered Tiano a productive employee because her sales exceeded $200,000 a year. At the time, the store gave its managers the discretion to grant unpaid leave to employees but prohibited vacations or leave during the holiday season—October through December. Tiano felt that she had a "calling" to go on a "pilgrimage" in October 1988 to Medjugorje, Yugoslavia, where some persons claimed to have had visions of the Virgin Mary. The Catholic Church had not designated the site an official pilgrimage site, the visions were not expected to be stronger in October, and tours were available at other times. The store managers denied Tiano's request for leave, but she had a nonrefundable ticket and left anyway. Dillard's terminated her employment. For a year, Tiano searched for a new job and did not attain the level of her Dillard's salary for four years. She filed a suit in a federal district court against Dillard's, alleging religious discrimination in violation of Title VII. Can Tiano establish a *prima facie* case of religious discrimination? Explain. [*Tiano v. Dillard Department Stores, Inc.*, 139 F.3d 679 (9th Cir. 1998)]

22–9. DISCRIMINATION BASED ON DISABILITY. Vaughn Murphy was first diagnosed with hypertension (high blood pressure) when he was ten years old. Unmedicated, his blood pressure is approximately 250/160. With medication, however, he can function normally and engage in the same activities as anyone else. In 1994, United Parcel Service, Inc. (UPS), hired Murphy to be a mechanic, a position that required him to drive commercial motor vehicles. To get the job, Murphy had to meet a U.S. Department of Transportation (DOT) regulation that a driver have "no current clinical diagnosis of high blood pressure likely to interfere with his/her ability to operate a commercial vehicle safely." At the time, Murphy's blood pressure was measured at 186/124, but he was erroneously certified and started work. Within a month, the error was discovered and he was fired. Murphy obtained another mechanic's job—one that did not require DOT certification—and filed a suit in a federal district court against UPS, claiming discrimination under the Americans with Disabilities Act. UPS filed a motion for summary judgment. Should the court grant UPS's motion? Explain. [*Murphy v. United Parcel Service, Inc.*, 527 U.S. 516, 119 S.Ct. 2133, 144 L.Ed.2d 484 (1999)]

22–10. IN YOUR COURT

Calvin Rhodes sold oil-field equipment for Anson Oil Tools. When he was discharged in 1986 at age fifty-six, he was told that the discharge was part of a reduction in the work force (RIF), and that he would be considered for reemployment. Within six weeks, Anson hired a forty-two-year-old person to do the same job. Rhodes brought a suit against Anson in a federal district court, claiming that the real reason he was discharged was age discrimination. At the trial, Anson offered as a defense Rhodes's "poor work performance" but did not present any company sales records or goals. Rhodes countered with customers' testimony about his expertise and diligence. The jury found that Rhodes was discharged because of his age. Anson appealed the decision. Assume that you are a judge on the federal appellate court reviewing this case and answer the following questions:

(a) Remember that as an appellate court judge, you should defer to the trial court's findings of fact—unless you conclude that there is no justification for the trial court's findings. The question you need to decide is therefore whether a reasonable

jury could have found that Rhodes was a victim of age discrimination in violation of the ADEA. How will you answer this question? Why?

(b) Does it matter that Rhodes's replacement was also a member of the class of persons protected by the ADEA? Will your answer to this question affect your answer to question (a) above?

LAW ON THE WEB

For updated links to resources available on the Web, as well as a variety of other materials, visit this text's Web site at http://wleb.westbuslaw.com.

The law firm of Arent Fox posts articles on current issues in the area of employment law, including sexual harassment, on its Web site at

http://www.arentfox.com

An abundance of helpful information on disability-based discrimination, including the text of the Americans with Disabilities Act of 1990, can be found at the following Web site:

http://janweb.icdi.wvu.edu/kinder

An excellent source for information on various forms of employment discrimination is the Equal Employment Opportunity Commission's Web site at

http://www.eeoc.gov

LEGAL RESEARCH EXERCISES ON THE WEB

Go to http://wleb.westbuslaw.com, the Web site that accompanies this text. Select "Internet Applications," and then click on "Chapter 22." There you will find the following Internet research exercises that you can perform to learn more about laws prohibiting employment discrimination:

Activity 22–1: Americans with Disabilities

Activity 22–2: Equal Employment Opportunity

CHAPTER 23

Labor Law

THROUGH THE FIRST HALF OF THE nineteenth century, most Americans were self-employed, often in
agriculture. For those who were employed by others,
the employers generally set the terms of employment.
The nature of employment changed with the growth of
the Industrial Revolution, which had begun about
1760. Fewer Americans were self-employed. Terms of
employment were sometimes set through bargaining
between employees and employers. Most industrial enterprises were in their infancies, however, and to encourage their development, the government gave
employers considerable freedom to hire, fire, and determine other employment conditions in response to
changing conditions in the marketplace.

With increasing industrialization, the size of workplaces and the number of workplace hazards increased. Workers came to believe that to counter the
power and freedom of their employers and to protect
themselves, they needed to organize into unions.
Employers discouraged—sometimes forcibly—collective activities such as unions. In support of unionization, Congress enacted such legislation as the Railway
Labor Act of 1926.[1] These laws were often restricted to
particular industries. Beginning in 1932, Congress enacted a number of statutes that increased employees'

rights generally. At the heart of these rights is the right
to join unions and engage in *collective bargaining* with
management to negotiate working conditions, salaries,
and benefits for a group of workers.

This chapter describes the development of labor
law and legal recognition of the right to form unions.
The laws that govern the management-union relationship are set forth in historical perspective. Then
the chapter describes the process of unionizing a
company, the collective bargaining required of a
unionized employer, the "industrial war" of strikes
and lockouts that may result if bargaining fails, and
the labor practices that are considered unfair under
federal law.

SECTION 1

Federal Labor Law

Federal labor laws governing union-employer relations have developed considerably since the first law
was enacted in 1932. Initially, the laws were concerned with protecting the rights and interests of
workers. Subsequent legislation placed some restraints on unions and granted rights to employers.
This section summarizes the four major federal labor
law statutes.

---

1. 45 U.S.C. Sections 151–188.

NORRIS-LAGUARDIA ACT

Congress protected peaceful strikes, picketing, and boycotts in 1932 in the Norris-LaGuardia Act.[2] The statute restricted federal courts in their power to issue injunctions against unions engaged in peaceful strikes. The act also provided that contracts limiting an employee's right to join a union are unlawful.

---

2. 29 U.S.C. Sections 101–115.

Such contracts are known as **yellow dog contracts.** (In the early part of the twentieth century, "yellow dog" meant "coward.") In effect, this act declared a national policy permitting employees to organize.

In the following case, a union threatened to picket an employer unless the employer agreed to subcontract work only to subcontractors who employed the union's members. The court had to decide whether, under the Norris-LaGuardia Act, it could issue an injunction to restrain the union from picketing.

CASE 23.1

Burlington Northern Santa Fe Railway Co. v. International Brotherhood of Teamsters Local 174

United States
Court of Appeals,
Ninth Circuit, 2000.
203 F.3d 703.
http://www.ce9.
uscourts.gov[a]

BACKGROUND AND FACTS   *Burlington Northern and Santa Fe Railway Company operates a hub in Seattle, Washington. Burlington terminated a subcontract with Eagle Systems, Inc., for loading and unloading services at the Seattle hub and transferred the work to another subcontractor, Parsec, Inc. As a consequence, fifty-three Eagle employees lost their jobs. International Brotherhood of Teamsters Local 174 represented the Eagle employees who lost their jobs, as well as the employees of other subcontractors who worked under subcontracts with Burlington. Local 174 did not represent the Parsec employees, however. The union was afraid that Burlington's use of other subcontractors who did not employ Local 174's members would cause "substantial economic costs and personal hardship." The union asked Burlington to persuade Parsec to hire the former Eagle employees. Burlington refused. Local 174 asked Burlington to agree not to subcontract in the future any loading and unloading services to any subcontractor whose employees were not represented by Local 174. The union threatened to picket in support of this demand. Burlington filed a suit in a federal district court against Local 174, alleging violations of federal labor law, among other things, and seeking an injunction. The court granted the injunction, restraining Local 174 from "[c]alling, ordering, authorizing, encouraging, inducing, approving, continuing, starting, suffering, permitting or carrying out any strike, picket or work stoppage" at Burlington's facilities. The union appealed to the U.S. Court of Appeals for the Ninth Circuit.*

IN THE LANGUAGE OF THE COURT

PREGERSON, Circuit Judge.
*   *   *   *

The Norris-LaGuardia Act deprives federal courts of jurisdiction to issue an injunction to restrain peaceful picketing in "any case involving or growing out of any labor dispute." Norris-LaGuardia defines the term "labor dispute" as

> any controversy concerning terms or conditions of employment, or concerning the association or representation of persons in negotiating, fixing, maintaining, changing, or seeking to arrange terms or conditions of employment, regardless of whether or not the disputants stand in the proximate relation of employer and employee.

We hold that a dispute between a union and a client company (here, Burlington Northern) over whether the client company's subcontractors must employ that union's members is a Norris-LaGuardia labor dispute. Thus, *   *   * the district court had no power to enjoin Local 174 from picketing Burlington Northern.

---

a. In the right column, click on "Appeals Court Decisions". On the page, click on "2000". In the expanded list, click on "February". In that list, scroll to the name of the case ("BURLINGTON NORTHERN V IBET") and click on it to access the opinion.

*   *   *   *

*   *   * *The [United States] Supreme Court has consistently characterized Norris-LaGuardia's definition of "labor dispute" as "broad."* Equally expansive is the test that the Supreme Court fashioned for determining whether a particular controversy is a labor dispute. Simply, "the employer-employee relationship [must be at] the matrix of the controversy." [Emphasis added.]

It is clear that "the matrix" of Local 174's dispute with Burlington Northern is "the employer-employee relationship." Members of Local 174 lost their jobs because Burlington Northern transferred their work to a subcontractor who did not rehire them and who signed a collective bargaining agreement with a different union. Local 174 feared that Burlington Northern would terminate other subcontracts under which its members worked, leading to more job losses and causing wages and working conditions to deteriorate. Local 174 asked Burlington Northern to guarantee that this process would not occur, but Burlington Northern refused. In short, this dispute is about who will perform work at Burlington Northern's Seattle hub, which union will represent the employees of Burlington Northern's subcontractors, and what will be the terms of their employment.

<table>
<tr><td>DECISION
AND REMEDY</td><td>*The U.S. Court of Appeals for the Ninth Circuit vacated the lower court's order and remanded with instructions to dismiss the case. The court could not issue an injunction to block Local 174's picketing because the disagreement between Burlington and Local 174 was a "labor dispute" within the meaning of the Norris-LaGuardia Act. Under that act, a federal court cannot issue an injunction to block peaceful picketing that is part of a labor dispute.*</td></tr>
</table>

NATIONAL LABOR RELATIONS ACT

The National Labor Relations Act of 1935 (NLRA),[3] also called the Wagner Act, established the right of employees to form unions, the right of those unions to engage in collective bargaining (negotiate contracts for their members), and the right to strike. The act also created the National Labor Relations Board (NLRB) to oversee union elections and to prevent employers from engaging in unfair labor union activities and unfair labor practices.

The purpose of the NLRA was to secure for employees the rights to organize, to bargain collectively through representatives of their own choosing, and to engage in concerted activities for that and other purposes. Section 8(a) of the act specifically defined a number of employer practices as unfair to labor. These unfair labor practices are central to labor law and are discussed throughout the remainder of the chapter.

Another purpose of the act was to promote fair and just settlements of disputes by peaceful processes. The NLRB was granted investigatory powers and was authorized to issue complaints against employers in response to employee charges of unfair labor practices. The NLRB was further empowered to issue cease-and-desist or-

ders—which could be enforced by a federal court of appeals if necessary—when violations were found.

Employers viewed the NLRA as a drastic piece of legislation. Those who opposed the act claimed that the Constitution's commerce clause (Article I, Section 8, Clause 3) did not grant Congress the power to regulate labor relations. They argued that labor was subject to state, not federal, law. Those who were willing to admit that the NLRA did fall under the commerce clause claimed that the NLRA created an undue burden, which rendered it unconstitutional. The constitutionality of the act was tested in 1937 in *NLRB v. Jones & Laughlin Steel Corp.*[4] In its decision, the United States Supreme Court held that the act and its application were constitutionally valid.

To be protected under the NLRA, an individual must be an "employee," as that term is defined in the statute. Courts have long held that job applicants fall within the definition (otherwise, the NLRA's ban on discrimination in regard to hiring would mean nothing). In the following case, the United States Supreme Court considered whether an individual can be a company's "employee" if, at the same time, a union pays the individual to organize the company.

---

3. 29 U.S.C. Sections 151–169.

4. 301 U.S. 1, 57 S.Ct. 615, 81 L.Ed. 893 (1937).

CASE 23.2   NLRB v. Town & Country Electric, Inc.

Supreme Court of the
United States, 1995.
516 U.S. 85,
116 S.Ct. 450,
133 L.Ed.2d 371.
http://www.findlaw.
com/casecode/
supreme.html[a]

BACKGROUND AND FACTS   *Town & Country Electric, Inc., advertised for job applicants but refused to interview ten of eleven applicants who were members of a union, the International Brotherhood of Electrical Workers. The applicants were union "salts"—persons paid by the union to apply for a job with a company and then, when hired, to unionize the company (in this case, Town & Country's work force). The applicants filed a complaint with the National Labor Relations Board (NLRB), alleging that the company had committed an unfair labor practice by discriminating against the applicants on the basis of union membership. The issue turned on whether job applicants paid by a union to organize a company could be considered employees under the National Labor Relations Act (NLRA). The NLRB determined that the applicants were employees and ruled in their favor. Town & Country appealed, and the U.S. Court of Appeals for the Eighth Circuit reversed. The applicants appealed to the United States Supreme Court.*

**IN THE LANGUAGE
OF THE COURT**

Justice *BREYER* delivered the opinion of the Court.

*   *   *   *

*   *   * [T]he Board's decision is consistent with the broad language of the [NLRA] *   *   *. *The ordinary dictionary definition of "employee" includes any "person who works for another in return for financial or other compensation."* The phrasing of the [NLRA] seems to reiterate the breadth of the ordinary dictionary definition, for it says "[t]he term 'employee' shall include any employee." *   *   * [Emphasis added.]

For another thing, the Board's broad, literal interpretation of the word "employee" is consistent with several of the [NLRA's] purposes, such as protecting "the right of employees to organize for mutual aid without employer interference" *   *   *.

**DECISION
AND REMEDY**

The United States Supreme Court reversed the decision of the appellate court and remanded the case. The Court held that the applicants were employees and thus could not be discriminated against.

---

a. In the "Party Name Search" box, type "Town & Country Electric" and click "Search." When the results appear, click on the case name to access the opinion.

LABOR-MANAGEMENT RELATIONS ACT

The Labor-Management Relations Act of 1947 (LMRA, or the Taft-Hartley Act)[5] was passed to proscribe certain union practices. The Taft-Hartley Act contained provisions protecting employers as well as employees. The act was bitterly opposed by organized labor groups. It provided a detailed list of unfair labor activities that unions as well as management were now forbidden to practice. In addition, the law gave the president the authority to intervene in labor disputes and delay strikes that would "imperil the national health or safety."

An important provision of the LMRA concerned the **closed shop**—a firm that requires union membership of its workers as a condition of obtaining employment. Closed shops were made illegal under the

Taft-Hartley Act. The act preserved the legality of the **union shop,** which does not require membership as a prerequisite for employment but can, and usually does, require that workers join the recognized union after a specified amount of time on the job. The act also allowed individual states to pass their own **right-to-work laws**—laws making it illegal for union membership to be required for *continued* employment in any establishment. Thus, union shops are technically illegal in states with right-to-work laws.

LABOR-MANAGEMENT REPORTING AND DISCLOSURE ACT

The Labor-Management Reporting and Disclosure Act of 1959 (the Landrum-Griffin Act)[6] established

---

5. 29 U.S.C. Sections 141, 504.

6. 29 U.S.C. Sections 153, 1111.

an employee bill of rights, as well as reporting requirements for union activities to prevent corruption. The Landrum-Griffin Act strictly regulated internal union business procedures.

Union elections, for example, are regulated by the Landrum-Griffin Act, which requires that regularly scheduled elections of officers occur and that secret ballots be used. Ex-convicts and Communists are prohibited from holding union office. Moreover, union officials are made accountable for union property and funds. Members have the right to attend and to participate in union meetings, to nominate officers, and to vote in most union proceedings.

COVERAGE AND PROCEDURES

Coverage of the federal labor laws is broad and extends to all employers whose business activity either involves or affects interstate commerce. Some workers are specifically excluded from these laws. Railroads and airlines are not covered by the NLRA but are covered by a separate act, the Railway Labor Act, which closely parallels the NLRA. Other types of workers, such as agricultural workers and domestic servants, are excluded from the NLRA and have no coverage under separate legislation.

When a union or employee believes that the employer has violated federal labor law (or vice versa), the union or employee files a charge with a regional office of the NLRB. The form for an employee to use to file an unfair labor practice charge against an employer is shown in Exhibit 23–1 on page 498. The charge is investigated, and if it is found worthy, the regional director files a complaint. An administrative law judge (ALJ) initially hears the complaint and rules on it (see Chapter 6). The board reviews the ALJ's findings and decision. If the NLRB finds a violation, it may issue remedial orders (including requiring rehiring of discharged workers). The NLRB decision may be appealed to a U.S. court of appeals.

SECTION 2

The Decision to Form or Select a Union

The key starting point for labor relations law is the decision by a company's employees to form a union, which is usually referred to in the law as their bargaining representative. Many workplaces have no union, and workers bargain individually with the employer. If the workers decide that they want the added power of collective union representation, they must follow certain steps to have a union certified. Usually, the employer will fight these efforts to unionize.

PRELIMINARY ORGANIZING

Suppose that a national union, such as the American Federation of Labor and Congress of Industrial Organizations (AFL-CIO), wants to organize workers who produce semiconductor chips. The union would visit a manufacturing plant of a company—SemiCo in this example. If some SemiCo workers are interested in joining the union, they must begin organizing. An essential part of the process is to decide exactly which workers will be covered in the planned union. Will all manufacturing workers be covered or just those engaged in a single step in the manufacturing process?

The first step in forming a union is to get the relevant workers to sign **authorization cards.** These cards usually state that the worker desires to have a certain union, such as the AFL-CIO, represent the work force. If those in favor of the union can obtain authorization cards from a majority of workers, they may present the cards to the employer and ask the employer, SemiCo, to recognize the union formally. SemiCo is not required to do so, however.

More frequently, authorization cards are obtained to justify an election among workers for unionization. If SemiCo refuses to recognize the union based on authorization cards, an election is necessary to determine whether unionization has majority support among the workers. After the unionizers obtain authorization cards from at least 30 percent of the workers to be represented, the unionizers present these cards to the NLRB regional office with a petition for an election.

This 30 percent support is generally considered a sufficient showing of interest to justify an election on union representation. Union backers are not required to employ authorization cards but generally must have some evidence that at least 30 percent of the relevant work force supports a union or an election on unionization.

APPROPRIATE BARGAINING UNIT

The NLRB considers the employees' petition as a basis for calling an election. In addition to a sufficient

EXHIBIT 23–1 UNFAIR LABOR PRACTICE COMPLAINT FORM

FORM EXEMPT UNDER 44 U.S.C. 3512

FORM NLRB-501
(8-83)

UNITED STATES OF AMERICA
NATIONAL LABOR RELATIONS BOARD
CHARGE AGAINST EMPLOYER

DO NOT WRITE IN THIS SPACE

Case	Date Filed

INSTRUCTIONS: File an original and 4 copies of this charge with NLRB Regional Director for the region in which the alleged unfair labor practice occurred or is occurring.

1. EMPLOYER AGAINST WHOM CHARGE IS BROUGHT

a. Name of Employer

b. Number of workers employed

c. Address (street, city, state, ZIP code)

d. Employer Representative

e. Telephone No.

f. Type of Establishment (factory, mine, wholesaler, etc.)

g. Identify principal product or service

h. The above-named employer has engaged in and is engaging in unfair labor practices within the meaning of section 8(a). subsections (1) and (list subsections) _____ of the National Labor Relations Act. and these unfair labor practices are unfair practices affecting commerce within the meaning of the Act.

2. Basis of the Charge (be specific as to facts, names, addresses, plants involved, dates, places, etc.)

By the above and other acts, the above-named employer has interfered with, restrained, and coerced employees in the exercise of the rights guaranteed in Section 7 of the Act

3. Full name of party filing charge (if labor organization, give full name, including local name and number)

4a. Address (street and number, city, state, and ZIP code)

4b. Telephone No.

5. Full name of national or international labor organization of which it is an affiliate or constituent unit (to be filled in when charge is filed by a labor organization)

6. DECLARATION

I declare that I have read the above charge and that the statements are true to the best of my knowledge and belief.

By _____ (signature of representative or person making charge)

_____ (title if any)

Address _____

(Telephone No.)   (date)

WILLFUL FALSE STATEMENTS ON THIS CHARGE CAN BE PUNISHED BY FINE AND IMPRISONMENT (U.S. CODE, TITLE 18, SECTION 1001)

showing of interest in unionization, the proposed union must represent an **appropriate bargaining unit.**

Not every group of workers can form together into a single union. One key requirement of an appropriate bargaining unit is a *mutuality of interest* among all the workers to be represented. Groups of workers with significantly conflicting interests may not be represented in a single union.

Job Similarity. One factor in determining the mutuality of interest is the *similarity of the jobs* of all the workers to be unionized. The NLRB considers factors such as similar levels of skill and qualifications, similar levels of wages and benefits, and similar working conditions. If represented workers have vastly different working conditions, they are unlikely to have the mutuality of interest necessary to bargain as a single unit with their employer.

One issue of job similarity has involved companies that employ both general industrial workers and craft workers (those with specialized skills, such as electricians). On many occasions, the NLRB has found that industrial and craft workers should be represented by different unions, although this is not an absolute rule.

Work-Site Proximity. A second factor in determining the appropriate bargaining unit is *geographical.* If workers at only a single manufacturing plant are to be unionized, the geographical factor is not a problem. Even if the workers desire to join a national union, such as the AFL-CIO, they can join together in a single "local" division of that union. Geographical disparity may become a problem if a union is attempting to join workers at many different manufacturing sites together into a single union.

Nonmanagement Employees. A third factor to be considered is the rule against unionization of *management* employees. The labor laws differentiate between labor and management and preclude members of management from being part of a union. There is no clear-cut definition of management, but supervisors are considered management and may not be included in worker unions. A supervisor is an individual who has the discretionary authority, as a representative of the employer, to make decisions such as hiring, suspending, promoting, firing, or disciplining other workers.[7] Professional employees, including legal and medical personnel, may be considered labor rather than management.

MOVING TOWARD CERTIFICATION

A union, then, becomes certified through a procedure that begins with petitioning the NLRB. The proposed union must present authorization cards or other evidence showing an employee interest level of at least 30 percent. The organization must also show that the proposed union represents an appropriate bargaining unit. If the workers are under the NLRA's jurisdiction and if no other union has been certified within the past twelve months for these workers, the NLRB will schedule an election.

SECTION 3

Union Election

Labor law provides for an election to determine whether employees choose to be represented by a union and, if so, which union. The NLRB supervises this election, ensuring secret voting and voter eligibility. The election is usually held about a month after the NLRB orders the vote (although it may be much longer, if management disputes the composition of an appropriate bargaining unit). If the election is a fair one, and if the proposed union receives majority support, the board certifies the union as the bargaining representative. Otherwise, the board will not certify the union.

Sometimes, a plant with an existing union may attempt to *decertify* the union (de-unionize). Although this action may be encouraged by management, it must be conducted by the employees. This action also requires a petition to the NLRB, with a showing of 30 percent employee support and no certification within the past year. The NLRB may grant this petition and call for a decertification election.

UNION ELECTION CAMPAIGN

Union organizers may campaign among workers to solicit votes for unionization. Considerable litigation has arisen over the rights of workers and outside union supporters to conduct such campaigns.

The employer retains great control over any activities, including unionization campaigns, that take place on company property and company time. Employers

---

7. *Waldau v. Merit Systems Protection Board,* 19 F.3d 1395 (Fed.Cir. 1994).

may lawfully use this authority to limit the campaign activities of union supporters. For example, management may prohibit all solicitations and distribution of pamphlets on company property as long as it has a legitimate business reason for doing so (such as to ensure safety or to prevent interference with business). The employer may also reasonably limit the places where solicitation occurs (for example, limit it to the lunchroom), limit the times during which solicitation can take place, and prohibit all outsiders from access to the workplace. All these actions are lawful.

Suppose that a union seeks to organize clerks at a department store. Courts have found that an employer can prohibit all solicitation in areas of the store open to the public. Union campaign activities in these circumstances could seriously interfere with the store's business.

There are some legal restrictions on management regulation of union solicitation. The key restriction is the *nondiscrimination* rule. An employer may prohibit all solicitation during work time or in certain places but may not selectively prohibit union solicitation during work time. If the employer permits political candidates to campaign on the employer's premises, for example, it also must permit union solicitation.[8]

Workers have a right to some reasonable opportunity to campaign. For example, the Supreme Court held that employees have a right to distribute a pro-union newsletter in nonworking areas on the employer's property during nonworking time. In this case, management had the burden to show some material harm from this action and could not do so.[9]

MANAGEMENT ELECTION CAMPAIGN

Management may also campaign among its workers against the union (or for decertification of an existing union). Campaign tactics, however, are carefully monitored and regulated by the NLRB. Otherwise, the economic power of management might allow coercion of the workers.

Management still has many advantages in the campaign. For example, management is allowed to call all workers together during work time and make a speech against unionization. Management need not give the union supporters an equal opportunity for rebuttal. The NLRB does restrict what management may say in such a speech, however.

No Threats.   In campaigning against the union, the employer may not make threats of reprisals if employees vote to unionize. A supervisor may not state, "If the union wins, you'll all be fired." This would be a threat. Employers must be very careful on this issue. For example, suppose an employer says, "Our competitor's plant in town unionized, and half the workers lost their jobs." The NLRB might consider this to be a veiled threat and therefore unfair.

An interesting controversy arose over a film that employers showed during union campaigns, *And Women Must Weep*. This film was prepared to help employers fight unionization efforts. The film dramatizes union misconduct during a strike, including vandalism, bomb threats, and attacks on neutral individuals such as a minister and an infant, who is shot and killed. Although this film is arguably inaccurate, courts have found it legal. One court wrote that "the film is a one-sided brief against unionism, devoid of significant rational content perhaps, but nevertheless not reasonably to be construed as threatening retaliation or force."[10]

"Laboratory Conditions."   Obviously, union election campaigns are not like national political campaigns, when a political party can make almost any claim. The NLRB tries to maintain "laboratory conditions" for a fair election that is unaffected by pressure. In establishing such conditions, the board considers the totality of circumstances in the campaign. The NLRB is especially strict about promises (or threats) made by the employer at the last minute, immediately before the election, because the union lacks an opportunity to respond effectively to these last-minute statements.

There is even a specific rule that prohibits an employer from making any election speech on company time, to massed assemblies of workers, within twenty-four hours of the time for voting. Such last-minute speeches are permitted only if employees attend voluntarily and on their own time.[11]

The employer is also prohibited from taking actions that might intimidate its workers. Employers

---

8. *Nonemployee* union organizers do not have the right to trespass on an employer's property to organize employees, however. See *Lechmere, Inc. v. NLRB*, 502 U.S. 527, 507, 112 S.Ct. 841, 117 L.Ed.2d 79 (1992).

9. *Eastex, Inc. v. NLRB*, 437 U.S. 556, 98 S.Ct. 2505, 57 L.Ed.2d 428 (1978).

10. *Luxray of New York v. NLRB*, 447 F.2d 112 (2d Cir. 1971).

11. Political party-like electioneering on behalf of a union, on the day of a union election, however, has been held acceptable and does not invalidate the election. See *Overnite Transportation Co. v. NLRB*, 104 F.3d 109 (7th Cir. 1997).

may not undertake certain types of surveillance of workers or even create the impression of observing workers to identify union sympathizers. Management also is limited in its ability to question individual workers about their positions on unionization. These actions are deemed to contain implicit threats.

NLRB Options. If the employer issues threats or engages in other unfair labor practices and then wins the election, the NLRB may invalidate the results. The NLRB may certify the union, even though it lost the election, and direct the employer to recognize the union as the employees' exclusive bargaining representative. Or the NLRB may ask a court to order a new election.

SECTION 4

Collective Bargaining

If a fair election is held and the union wins, the NLRB will certify the union as the *exclusive bargaining representative* of the workers polled. Unions may provide a variety of services to their members, but the central legal right of a union is to serve as the sole representative of the group of workers in bargaining with the employer over the workers' rights.

The concept of bargaining is at the heart of the federal labor laws. When a union is officially recognized, it may make a demand to bargain with the employer. The union then sits at the table opposite the representatives of management to negotiate contracts for its workers. The terms of employment that result from the negotiations apply to all workers in the bargaining unit, even those who do not choose to belong to the union. This process is known as **collective bargaining.** Such bargaining is like most other business negotiations, and each side uses its economic power to pressure or persuade the other side to grant concessions.

Bargaining is a somewhat vague term. Bargaining does not mean that either side must give in on demands or even that the sides must always compromise. It does mean that a demand must be taken seriously and considered as part of a package to be negotiated. Importantly, both sides must bargain in "good faith."

SUBJECTS OF BARGAINING

A common issue in collective bargaining concerns the subjects over which the parties can bargain. The law makes certain subjects mandatory for collective bargaining. These topics cannot be "taken off the table" unilaterally but must be discussed and bargained over.

Terms and Conditions of Employment. The NLRA provides that employers may bargain with workers over wages, hours of work, and other terms and conditions of employment. These are broad terms that cover many employment issues. Suppose that a union wants a contract provision granting all workers four weeks of paid vacation. The company need not give in to this demand but must at least consider it and bargain over it.

Many other employment issues are also considered appropriate subjects for collective bargaining. These include safety rules, insurance coverage, pension and other employee benefits plans, procedures for employee discipline, and procedures for employee grievances against the company. The Supreme Court has held that an employer must bargain even over the price of food sold in the company cafeteria.[12]

A few subjects are illegal in collective bargaining. Management need not bargain over a provision that would be illegal if included in a contract. Thus, if a union presents a demand for **featherbedding** (the hiring of unnecessary excess workers) or for an unlawful closed shop, management need not respond to these demands.

Closing or Relocating a Plant. Management need not bargain with a union over the decision to close a particular facility. Similarly, management need not bargain over a decision to relocate a plant if the move involves a basic change in the nature of the employer's operation.[13] Management may choose to bargain over such decisions, however, to obtain concessions on other bargaining subjects.

Management must bargain over the economic consequences of such decisions. Thus, issues such as **severance pay** (compensation for the termination of employment) in the event of a plant shut-down are appropriate for collective bargaining. Also, if a relocation does *not* involve a basic change in the nature of an operation, management must bargain over the decision unless it can show (1) that the work performed at the new location varies significantly from the work performed at the former plant; (2) that the work

---

12. *Ford Motor Co. v. NLRB,* 441 U.S. 488, 99 S.Ct. 1842, 60 L.Ed.2d 420 (1979).
13. *Dubuque Packing Co.,* 303 N.L.R.B. No. 386 (1991).

performed at the former plant is to be discontinued entirely and not moved to the new location; (3) that the move involves a change in the scope and direction of the enterprise; (4) that labor costs were not a factor in the decision; or (5) that even if labor costs were a factor, the union could not have offered concessions that would have changed the decision to relocate.

GOOD FAITH BARGAINING

Parties engaged in collective bargaining often claim that the other side is not bargaining in good faith, as required by labor law. Although good faith is a matter of subjective intent, a party's actions are used to evaluate the finding of good or bad faith in bargaining.

Obviously, the employer must be willing to meet with union representatives. Excessive delaying tactics may be proof of bad faith, as is insistence on obviously unreasonable contract terms. Suppose that a company makes a single overall contract offer on a "take-it-or-leave-it" basis and refuses to consider modifications of individual terms. This also is considered bad faith in bargaining.

While bargaining is going on, management may not make unilateral changes in important working conditions, such as wages or hours of employment. These changes must be bargained over. Once bargaining reaches an impasse, management may make such unilateral changes. The law also includes an exception permitting unilateral changes in cases of business necessity.

A series of decisions have found other actions to constitute bad faith in bargaining, including the following:

1. Engaging in a campaign among workers to undermine the union.
2. Constantly shifting positions on disputed contract terms.
3. Sending bargainers who lack authority to commit the company to a contract.

If an employer (or a union) refuses to bargain in good faith without justification, it has committed an unfair labor practice, and the other party may petition the NLRB for an order requiring good faith bargaining. Except in extreme cases, the NLRB does not have authority to require a party to accede to any specific contract terms. The NLRB may require a party to reimburse the other side for its litigation expenses.

A party to collective bargaining may be excused from bargaining when the other party refuses to bargain. The following case illustrates this situation.

CASE 23.3   Stroehmann Bakeries, Inc. v. NLRB

United States
Court of Appeals,
Second Circuit, 1996.
95 F.3d 218.
http://www.findlaw.
com/casecode/courts/
2nd.html[a]

BACKGROUND AND FACTS   *Stroehmann Bakeries, Inc., operated a distribution center for its baked goods in Syracuse, New York, where employees—known as shippers—loaded the goods onto local delivery trucks. The shippers were represented by a union. When their collective bargaining agreement expired, Stroehmann proposed eliminating their positions. In subsequent negotiations, the company admitted that it could obtain the capital to keep the Syracuse center open and proposed cutting only half of the positions. The union asked Stroehmann for extensive financial information, including lists of customers and sales accounts, accounts payable journals, supplier invoices, production reports, employee compensation, and employee pension plans. The company refused to comply with the request and, when the union did not return to the negotiations, declared that bargaining was at an impasse. Ten days later, Stroehmann eliminated the shippers' jobs. The National Labor Relations Board ordered the company to reinstate the shippers. Stroehmann asked the U.S. Court of Appeals for the Second Circuit to deny enforcement of the order.*

IN THE LANGUAGE OF THE COURT   WINTER, Circuit Judge:

*   *   *   *

---

a. This page contains links to opinions of the U.S. Court of Appeals for the Second Circuit. In the "Browsing" section, in the "1996" row, click on "Sept". When that page opens, scroll down the list of cases to the *Stroehmann* case and click on the case name to access the opinion.

Once Stroehmann conceded that it had access to capital sufficient to continue the Syracuse shipping unit, the Union's need for financial information to bargain intelligently was virtually non-existent. *   *   * Stroehmann did not enter the negotiations with a closed mind but rather offered proposals in response to the Union's request for ways to save jobs. It was the Union that refused to bargain after it made a request for financial information [that was denied].

The comprehensive and detailed information requested by the Union had virtually no relevance to the issues at stake in bargaining *   *   *. We conclude, therefore, that Stroehmann was under no obligation to respond to the voluminous requests for information submitted by the Union.

Because Stroehmann's refusal to furnish the information was permissible, it was entitled to declare an impasse when the Union refused to return to the bargaining table. The unilateral decision to close the shipping unit was, therefore, lawful.

DECISION AND REMEDY   *The U.S. Court of Appeals for the Second Circuit denied enforcement of the NLRB's order. The company acted within its rights in eliminating the shippers' jobs.*

INTERNATIONAL CONSIDERATIONS   **Union Rights in Great Britain**   *In Great Britain, a union that has been recognized by an employer for collective bargaining purposes has certain rights. These rights include the right to receive information related to collective bargaining issues, the right to time off, the right to appoint a representative to handle safety matters, and the right to be consulted before an employer relocates its place of business.*

SECTION 5

Strikes

The law does not require parties to reach a contract agreement in collective bargaining. Even when parties have bargained in good faith, they may be unable to reach a final agreement. When extensive collective bargaining has been conducted and the parties still cannot agree, an impasse has been reached.

When bargaining has reached an impasse, the union may call a strike against the employer to pressure it into making concessions. A strike occurs when the unionized workers leave their jobs and refuse to work. The workers also typically picket the plant, standing outside the facility with signs that complain of management's unfairness.

A strike is an extreme action. Striking workers lose their right to be paid. Management loses production and may lose customers, whose orders cannot be filled. Labor law regulates the circumstances and conduct of strikes. Most strikes are "economic strikes," which are initiated because the union wants a better contract. A union may also strike when the employer has engaged in unfair labor practices.

The right to strike is guaranteed by the NLRA, within limits, and strike activities, such as picketing, are protected by the free speech guarantee of the First Amendment to the Constitution. Nonworkers have a right to participate in picketing an employer. The NLRA also gives workers the right to refuse to cross a picket line of fellow workers who are engaged in a lawful strike. Not all strikes are lawful, however.

ILLEGAL STRIKES

An otherwise lawful strike may become illegal because of the conduct of the strikers. Violent strikes (including the threat of violence) are illegal. The use of violence against management employees or substitute workers is illegal. Certain forms of "massed picketing" are also illegal. If the strikers form a barrier and deny management or other nonunion workers access to the plant, the strike is illegal. Similarly, "sit-down" strikes, in which employees simply stay in the plant without working, are illegal.

Secondary Boycotts.   A strike directed against someone other than the strikers' employer, such as the companies that sell materials to the employer, is a **secondary boycott.** Suppose that the unionized workers of SemiCo (our hypothetical semiconductor company) go out on strike. To increase their economic leverage, the workers picket the leading suppliers and customers of SemiCo in an attempt to hurt the company's business. SemiCo is considered the primary employer, and its suppliers and customers are considered secondary employers. Picketing of the suppliers or customers is a secondary boycott, which was made illegal by the Taft-Hartley Act.

Common Situs Picketing. A controversy may arise in a strike when both the primary employer and a secondary employer occupy the same job site. In this case, it may be difficult to distinguish between lawful picketing of the primary employer and an unlawful strike against a secondary employer. The law permits a union to picket a site occupied by both primary and secondary employers, an act called **common situs picketing.** If evidence indicates that the strike is directed against the secondary employer, however, it may become illegal. For example, if a union sends a threatening letter to the secondary employer about the strike, that fact may show that the picketing includes an illegal secondary boycott.

Hot-Cargo Agreements. In a **hot-cargo agreement,** employers voluntarily agree with unions not to handle, use, or deal in non-union-produced goods of other employers. This particular type of secondary boycott was *not* made illegal by the Taft-Hartley Act, because that act only prevented unions from inducing *employees* to strike or otherwise act to force employers not to handle these goods. The Landrum-Griffin Act addressed this problem:

> It shall be [an] unfair labor practice for any labor organization and any employer to enter into any contract or any agreement . . . whereby such employer . . . agrees to refrain from handling, using, selling, transporting or otherwise dealing in any of the products of any other employer, or to cease doing business with any other person.

Hot-cargo agreements are therefore illegal. Parties injured by an illegal hot-cargo agreement or other secondary boycott may sue the union for damages.

A union may legally urge consumer boycotts of the primary employer, even at the site of a secondary employer. Suppose that a union is on strike against SemiCo, which manufactures semiconductors that are bought by Intellect, Inc., a distributor of electronic components. Intellect sells SemiCo's semiconductors to computer manufacturers. The striking workers can urge the manufacturers not to buy SemiCo's products. The workers cannot urge a total boycott of Intellect, as that would constitute a secondary boycott.

Wildcat Strikes. A **wildcat strike** occurs when a minority group of workers, perhaps dissatisfied with a union's representation, calls its own strike. The union is the exclusive bargaining representative of a group of workers, and only the union can call a strike. A wildcat strike, unauthorized by the certified union, is illegal.

In one case, several concrete workers left their jobs because it was raining and went on "strike." The court found the strike illegal because it was not preceded by a demand on the employer for action and because the employer had made shelter available for the workers and paid them for waiting time.

Strikes That Threaten National Health or Safety. The law also places some restrictions on strikes that threaten national health or safety. The law does not prohibit such strikes, nor does it require the settlement of labor disputes that threaten the national welfare. The Taft-Hartley Act simply provides time to encourage the settlement of these disputes, called the "cooling-off period."

One of the most controversial aspects of the Taft-Hartley Act was the establishment of this **eighty-day cooling-off period**—a provision allowing federal courts to issue injunctions against strikes that would create a national emergency. The president of the United States can obtain a court injunction that will last for eighty days, and presidents have occasionally used this provision. During these eighty days, the president and other government officials can work with the employer and the union to produce a settlement and avoid a strike that may cause a national emergency.

Strikes That Contravene No-Strike Clauses. A strike may also be illegal if it contravenes a **no-strike clause.** The previous collective bargaining agreement between a union and an employer may have contained a clause in which the union agreed not to strike (a no-strike clause). The law permits the employer to enforce this no-strike clause and obtain an injunction against the strike in some circumstances.

The Supreme Court held that a no-strike clause could be enforced with an injunction if the contract contained a clause providing for arbitration of unresolved disputes.[14] The Court held that the arbitration clause was an effective substitute for the right to strike. In the absence of an applicable arbitration pro-

---

14. *Boys Markets, Inc. v. Retail Clerks Local 770,* 398 U.S. 235, 90 S.Ct. 1583, 26 L.Ed.2d 199 (1970).

vision, however, an employer cannot enjoin (forbid) a strike, even if the contract contains a no-strike clause.

REPLACEMENT WORKERS

Suppose that SemiCo's workers go out on strike. SemiCo is not required to shut down its operations but may find substitute workers to replace the strikers, if possible. These substitute workers are often called "scabs" by union supporters. An employer may even give the replacement workers permanent positions with the company.

In the 1930s and 1940s, strikes were powerful in part because employers often had difficulty finding trained replacements to keep their businesses running during strikes. Since the illegal air traffic controller strike in 1981, when President Ronald Reagan successfully hired replacement workers, employers have increasingly used this strategy, with considerable success. Even the National Football League (NFL), when struck by the players in 1987, found replacements to play for the NFL teams. Although some scoffed at the ability of the replacement players, the tactic was largely successful for management, as the strike was called off after only three weeks. An employer can even use an employment agency to recruit replacement workers.[15]

RIGHTS OF STRIKERS AFTER THE STRIKE

An important issue concerns the rights of strikers after the strike ends. In a typical economic strike over working conditions, the strikers have no right to return to their jobs. If satisfactory replacement workers have been found, the strikers may find themselves out of work. The law does prohibit the employer from discriminating against former strikers. Even if the employer fires all the strikers and retains all the replacement workers, former strikers must be rehired to fill any new vacancies. Former strikers who are rehired retain their seniority rights.

Different rules apply when a union strikes because the employer has engaged in unfair labor practices. If an employer is discriminating against a union's workers, they may go out on an unfair labor practice strike. Furthermore, an economic strike may become an unfair labor practice strike if the employer refuses to bargain in good faith. In the case of an unfair labor practice strike, the employer may still hire replacements but must give the strikers back their jobs once the strike is over. An employer may, however, refuse to rehire unfair labor practice strikers if the strike was deemed unlawful or if there is simply no longer any work for them to do.

SECTION 6

Lockouts

Lockouts are the employer's counterpart to the worker's right to strike. A **lockout** occurs when the employer shuts down to prevent employees from working. Lockouts are usually used when the employer believes that a strike is imminent.

Lockouts may be a legal employer response. In the leading Supreme Court case, a union and an employer had reached a stalemate in collective bargaining. The employer feared that the union would delay a strike until the busy season and thereby cause the employer to suffer more greatly from the strike. The employer called a lockout before the busy season to deny the union this leverage, and the Supreme Court held that this action was legal.[16]

Some lockouts are illegal, however. An employer may not use its lockout weapon as a tool to break the union and pressure employees into decertification. Consequently, an employer must show some economic justification for instituting a lockout.

SECTION 7

Unfair Labor Practices

The preceding sections have discussed unfair labor practices in the significant acts of union elections, collective bargaining, and strikes. Many unfair labor practices may occur within the normal working relationship as well. The most significant of these practices are discussed below. Exhibit 23–2 on the next page lists the basic unfair labor practices.

---

15. *Professional Staff Nurses Association v. Dimensions Health Corp.*, 110 Md.App. 270, 677 A.2d 87 (1996).

16. *American Ship Building Co. v. NLRB*, 380 U.S. 300, 85 S.Ct. 955, 13 L.Ed.2d 855 (1965).

EXHIBIT 23–2   BASIC UNFAIR LABOR PRACTICES

EMPLOYERS	UNIONS
1. Refuse to recognize a union and to bargain in good faith.	1. Refuse to bargain in good faith.
2. Interfere with, restrain, or coerce employees in their efforts to form a union and bargain collectively.	2. Picket to coerce unionization without the majority support of the employees.
3. Dominate a union.	3. Demand the hiring of unnecessary excess workers.
4. Discriminate against union workers.	4. Discriminate against nonunion workers.
5. Agree to participate in a secondary boycott.	5. Agree to participate in a secondary boycott.
6. Punish employees for engaging in concerted activity.	6. Engage in an illegal strike.
	7. Charge excessive membership fees.

EMPLOYER'S REFUSAL TO RECOGNIZE UNION AND NEGOTIATE

As noted above, once a union has been certified as the exclusive representative of a bargaining unit, an employer must recognize and bargain in good faith with the union over issues affecting all employees who are within the bargaining unit. Failure to do so is an unfair labor practice. Because the National Labor Relations Act embraces a policy of majority rule, certification of the union as the bargaining unit's representative binds *all* of the employees in that bargaining unit. Thus, the union must fairly represent all the members of the bargaining unit.[17]

Presumption of Employee Support. Certification does not mean that a union will continue indefinitely as the exclusive representative of the bargaining unit. If the union loses the majority support of those it represents, an employer is not obligated to continue recognition of, or negotiation with, the union. As a practical matter, a newly elected representative needs time to establish itself among the workers and to begin to formulate and implement its programs. Therefore, as a matter of labor policy, a union is immune from attack by employers and from repudiation by the employees for a period of one year after certification. During this period, it is *presumed* that the union enjoys majority support among the employees;

the employer cannot refuse to deal with the union as the employees' exclusive representative, even if the employees prefer not to be represented by that union.

Beyond the one-year period, the presumption of majority support continues, but it is *rebuttable*. An employer may rebut (refute) the presumption with objective evidence that a majority of employees do not wish to be represented by the union. If the evidence is sufficient to support a *good faith* belief that the union no longer enjoys majority support among the employees, the employer may refuse to continue to recognize and negotiate with the union.[18]

Questions of Majority Support. A delicate question arises during a strike in which an employer hires replacement workers. Specifically, should it be *assumed* that the replacement workers do not support the union? If they do not, and if as a result the union no longer has majority support, the employer need not continue negotiating with the union.

Another question arises when two companies merge or consolidate, when one company buys the assets or stock of another, or when, under any other circumstances, one employer steps into the shoes of another. Is a collective bargaining agreement between a union and a predecessor employer binding on the union and the successor employer? This is the issue in the following case.

---

17. Thus, when an employee has a grievance against the employer, the union cannot arbitrarily ignore it or handle it perfunctorily, although a union does not have to pursue all employee grievances to arbitration. See *Vaca v. Sipes*, 386 U.S. 171, 87 S.Ct. 903, 17 L.Ed.2d 842 (1967).

18. An employer cannot agree to a collective bargaining agreement and later refuse to abide by it, however, on the ground of a good faith belief that the union did not have majority support when the agreement was negotiated. See *Auciello Iron Works, Inc. v. NLRB*, 517 U.S. 781, 116 S.Ct. 1754, 135 L.Ed.2d 64 (1996).

CASE 23.4   Canteen Corp. v. NLRB

United States
Court of Appeals,
Seventh Circuit, 1997.
103 F.3d 1355.
http://www.ca7.
uscourts.gov[a]

BACKGROUND AND FACTS *The food service employees at the Medical College of Wisconsin were represented by the Hotel Employees and Restaurant Employees Union. When Canteen Corporation took over the food service, it agreed to negotiate a new contract with the union. Meanwhile, without informing the union, Canteen told the employees that their wages would be cut 20 to 25 percent. The employees resigned. Canteen then recruited employees from other sources and refused to negotiate with the union on the ground that it no longer represented the employees. The union filed an unfair labor practice charge with the National Labor Relations Board (NLRB). The NLRB ordered Canteen to reinstate the employees at their previous wage rates until a new contract could be negotiated. Canteen asked the U.S. Court of Appeals for the Seventh Circuit to review the order.*

IN THE LANGUAGE
OF THE COURT

RIPPLE, Circuit Judge.

*   *   *   *

*   *   *A new employer must consult with the union when it is clear that the employer intends to hire the employees of its predecessor as the initial workforce. *   *   *

*   *   *   *

*   *   * The totality of Canteen's conduct demonstrated that it was perfectly clear that Canteen planned to retain the predecessor employees. *   *   *

*   *   * Canteen's intention to retain the *   *   * employees was backed by an expectation so strong that it neglected to take serious steps to recruit from other sources until it was informed that [the employees] had rejected job offers. *   *   * Canteen intended from the outset to hire all of the predecessor employees and did not mention in [its] discussions [with the union] the possibility of any other changes in its initial terms and conditions of employment.

DECISION
AND REMEDY

The U.S. Court of Appeals for the Seventh Circuit mandated that the NLRB's order be enforced. The employer was required to reinstate the employees at their previous wage rates until a new contract could be negotiated.

---

a. This page provides access to some of the opinions of the U.S. Court of Appeals for the Seventh Circuit, which maintains this Web site. In the left column, in the "Judicial Opinions" frame, in the "Last Name or Corporation" box, enter "Canteen", select "Begins", and click "Search for Person". From the results, click on docket number "95-2736" next to the case name to access the opinion.

EMPLOYER'S INTERFERENCE IN UNION ACTIVITIES

The NLRA declares it to be an unfair labor practice for an employer to interfere with, restrain, or coerce employees in the exercise of their rights to form a union and bargain collectively. Unlawful employer interference may take a variety of forms.

Courts have found it an unfair labor practice for an employer to make threats that may interfere with an employee's decision to join a union. Even asking employees about their views on the union may be considered coercive. Employees responding to such questioning must be able to remain anonymous and must receive assurances against employer reprisals. Employers also may not prohibit certain forms of union activity in the workplace. If an employee has a grievance with the company, the employer cannot prevent the union's participation in support of the employee, for example.

If an employer has unlawfully interfered with the operation of a union, the NLRB or a reviewing court may issue a cease-and-desist order halting the practice. The company typically is required to post the order on a bulletin board and renounce its past unlawful conduct.

EMPLOYER'S DOMINATION OF UNION

In the early days of unionization, employers fought back by forming employer-sponsored unions to represent employees. These "company unions" were seldom more than the puppets of management. The NLRA outlawed company unions and any other form of employer domination of workers' unions.

A number of acts are considered unfair labor practices under the law against employer domination. For example, an employer can have no say in which employees belong to the union or which employees serve as union officers. Nor may supervisors or other management personnel participate in union meetings.

Company actions that support a union may be considered improper potential domination. For this reason, a company cannot give union workers pay for time spent on union activities, because this is considered undue support for the union. The company may not provide financial aid to a union and may not solicit workers to join a union.

EMPLOYER'S DISCRIMINATION AGAINST UNION EMPLOYEES

The NLRA prohibits employers from discriminating against workers because they are union officers or are otherwise associated with a union. When workers must be laid off, the company cannot consider union participation as a criterion for deciding whom to fire.

The antidiscrimination provisions also apply to hiring decisions. Suppose that certain employees of SemiCo are represented by a union, but the company is attempting to weaken the union's strength. The company cannot require potential new hires to guarantee that they will not join the union.

Discriminatory punishment of union members or officers can be difficult to prove. The company will claim to have good reasons for its action. The NLRB has specified a series of factors to be considered in determining whether an action had an unlawful, discriminatory motivation. These include giving inconsistent reasons for the action, applying rules inconsistently and more strictly against union members, failing to give an expected warning prior to discharge or other discipline, and acting contrary to worker seniority.

In one case, an employer, Wright Line, fired an employee, Bernard Lamoureux, for knowingly altering time reports and payroll records. Lamoureux conceded that he had not worked the precise hours he reported on his time card but claimed that he had worked an equivalent number of hours at other times. Lamoureux had been a leading union advocate. The NLRB found that the company had shown particular dislike for Lamoureux because it considered him to be the "union kingpin" in the company. In addition, the company had never before discharged a worker for this type of violation. The NLRB found that this was sufficient evidence of discrimination to shift the burden of proof to the company to demonstrate that it had not had a discriminatory motive. The company could not meet this burden, and the discharge was held unlawful.[19]

The decision to close a facility cannot be made with a discriminatory motive. If a company has several facilities and only one is unionized, the company cannot shut down the union plant simply because of the union. The company could shut down the union plant if it were demonstrably less efficient than the other facilities, however.

UNION'S UNFAIR LABOR PRACTICES

Certain union activities are declared to be unfair labor practices by the Taft-Hartley Act. Secondary boycotts, discussed above, are one such union unfair labor practice.

Coercion. Another significant union unfair labor practice is coercion or restraint on an employee's decision to participate in or refrain from participating in union activities. Obviously, it is unlawful for a union to threaten an employee or a family with violence for failure to join the union. The law's prohibition includes economic coercion as well. Suppose that a union official declares, "We have a lot of power here; you had better join the union, or you may lose your job." This threat is an unfair labor practice.

The NLRA provides unions with the authority to regulate their own internal affairs, which includes disciplining union members. This discipline cannot be used in an improperly coercive fashion, however. Suppose a disaffected union member feels that the union is no longer providing proper representation for employees and starts a campaign to decertify the union. The union may expel the employee from

---

19. *Wright Line, a Division of Wright Line, Inc.,* 251 N.L.R.B. No. 150 (1980).

membership but may not fine or otherwise discipline the worker.

Discrimination. Another significant union unfair labor practice is discrimination. A union may not discriminate against workers because they refuse to join. This provision also prohibits a union from using its influence to cause an employer to discriminate against workers who refuse to join the union. A union cannot force an employer to deny promotions to workers who fail to join the union.

Other Unfair Practices. Other union unfair labor practices include featherbedding, participation in picketing to coerce unionization without majority employee support, and refusal to engage in good faith bargaining with employer representatives.

Unions are allowed to bargain for certain "union security clauses" in contracts. Although closed shops are illegal, a union can bargain for a provision that requires workers to contribute to the union within thirty days after they are hired. This is typically called an agency shop, or union shop, clause.

The union shop clause can compel workers to begin paying dues to the certified union but cannot require the worker to "join" the union. Dues payment can be required to prevent workers from taking the benefits of union bargaining without contributing to the union's efforts. The clause cannot require workers to contribute their efforts to the union, however, or to go out on strike.

Even a requirement of dues payment has its limits. Excessive initiation fees or dues may be illegal. Unions often use their revenues to contribute to causes or to lobby politicians. A nonunion employee subject to a union shop clause who must pay dues cannot be required to contribute to this sort of union expenditure.[20]

Section 8(a)(3) of the NLRA sets out the right of a union to bargain for a union security clause. The United States Supreme Court has interpreted this statute in several cases and imposed the limits discussed above. In the following case, the Supreme Court was asked to consider whether a union breached its duty of fair representation by negotiating a clause that was phrased in the language of the statute without explaining the Court's interpretation of that language.

---

20. *Communication Workers of America v. Beck*, 487 U.S. 735, 108 S.Ct. 2641, 101 L.Ed.2d 634 (1988).

CASE 23.5   Marquez v. Screen Actors Guild, Inc.

Supreme Court of the
United States, 1998.
525 U.S. 33,
119 S.Ct. 292,
142 L.Ed.2d 242.
http://supct.law.
cornell.edu:8080/supct[a]

BACKGROUND AND FACTS *The Screen Actors Guild (SAG) is a union that represents performers in the entertainment industry. In 1994, Lakeside Productions signed a collective bargaining agreement with SAG, making SAG the exclusive bargaining agent for the performers that Lakeside hired for its productions. The agreement contained a union security clause, providing that to work under the agreement, any performer who had worked more than thirty days in the industry must be "a member of the Union in good standing." This clause tracked the language of Section 8(a)(3) of the NLRA without explaining that to be a "member," a worker only had to pay certain dues. Naomi Marquez, a part-time actress, was offered a one-line role in an episode of the television series "Medicine Ball," which was produced by Lakeside. Because she had previously worked in the motion picture industry for more than thirty days, she was told to pay about $500 in union fees before she could begin work for Lakeside. Marquez delayed until SAG agreed to allow her to pay the fees after Lakeside paid her for her work. By this time, however, Lakeside had hired a different actress. Marquez filed a suit in a federal district court against SAG and Lakeside, arguing, among other things, that SAG breached its duty of fair representation by negotiating a union security clause written in the language of the NLRA. She claimed that this was arbitrary and in bad faith. The court granted the defendants' motion for summary judgment, which the U.S. Court of Appeals for the Ninth Circuit affirmed. Marquez appealed to the United States Supreme Court.*

---

a. In the right column, in the "Arrayed by party name" section, in the "1998" row, click on "1st party". On that page, scroll to the case name ("Marquez v. Screen Actors") and click on it to access a syllabus of the case. From that page, click on the link to the version of the opinion that you want to read.

IN THE LANGUAGE
OF THE COURT

Justice O'CONNOR delivered the opinion of the Court.

*   *   *   *

*   *   * SAG's negotiation of a union security clause with language derived from the NLRA section authorizing such a clause is far from arbitrary. *   *   *[B]y tracking the statutory language, the clause incorporates all of the refinements that have become associated with that language. *   *   *[T]he relevant provisions of [Section] 8(a)(3) have become terms of art; the words and phrasing of the section now encompass the rights that we announced in [our decisions]. After we stated that the statutory language incorporates an employee's right not to "join" the union (except by paying fees and dues) and an employee's right to pay for only representational activities, we cannot fault SAG for using this very language to convey these very concepts.

Petitioner [Marquez] also invites us to conclude that the union's conduct in negotiating the union security clause breached the duty of fair representation because it was done in bad faith. *   *   * . According to petitioner, *   *   * it is bad faith for a union to use the statutory language in the collective bargaining agreement because such use can only mislead employees. Petitioner's argument fails because it is so broad. It is difficult to conclude that a union acts in bad faith by notifying workers of their rights through more effective means of communication and by using a term of art to describe those rights in a contract workers are unlikely to read. *   *   *

The second part of petitioner's bad faith argument—that there was no other reason for the union's choice of the statutory language—also fails. *The statutory language, which we have said incorporates all of the refinements associated with the language, is a shorthand description of workers' legal rights.* A union might choose to use this shorthand precisely because it incorporates all of the refinements. Petitioner argues that this reason for failing to explain all of the intricate rights and duties associated with a legal term of art is bad faith. The logic of petitioner's argument has no stopping point; it would require unions (and all other contract drafters) to spell out all the intricacies of every term used in a contract. Contracts would become massive and unwieldy treatises, yet there would be no discernible benefit from the increased mass. *   *   * Contrary to petitioner's claim, we conclude that it may be perfectly reasonable for a union to use terms of art in a contract. [Emphasis added.]

DECISION
AND REMEDY

The Supreme Court affirmed the decision of the lower court. The union's conduct in negotiating a union security clause that tracked the statutory language was not arbitrary or in bad faith. By negotiating this clause, the union did not breach its duty of fair representation.

SECTION 8

Rights of Nonunion Employees

Most of labor law involves the formation of unions and associated rights. Even nonunion employees have some similar rights, however. Most workers do not belong to unions, so this issue is significant. The NLRA protects concerted employee action, for example, and does not limit its protection to certified unions.

CONCERTED ACTIVITY

Data from the NLRB indicate that a growing number of nonunion employees are challenging employer barriers to their **concerted action.** Protected concerted action is that taken by employees for their mutual benefit regarding wages, hours, or terms and conditions of employment.

Even an action by a single employee may be protected concerted activity, if that action is taken for the benefit of other employees and if the employee has at least discussed the action with other approving workers. If only a single worker engages in a protest or walkout, the employer will not be liable for an unfair labor practice if it fires the worker unless the employer is aware that this protest or walkout is concerted activity taken with the assent of other workers. Sometimes the mutual interest of other workers should be obvious to the employer, however.

SAFETY

A common circumstance for nonunion activity is concern over workplace safety. The Labor-Management Relations Act authorizes an employee to walk off the job if he or she has a good faith belief that the working conditions are abnormally dangerous. The employer cannot lawfully discharge the employee under these conditions.

Suppose that Knight Company operates a plant building mobile homes. A large ventilation fan at the plant blows dust and abrasive materials into the faces of workers. The workers have complained, but Knight Company has done nothing. The workers finally refuse to work until the fan is modified, and Knight fires them. The NLRB will find that the walkout is a protected activity and can command Knight to rehire the workers with back pay.

To be protected under federal labor law, a safety walkout must be *concerted* activity. If a single worker walks out over a safety complaint, other workers must be affected by the safety issue for the walkout to be protected under the LMRA.

EMPLOYEE COMMITTEES

Personnel specialists note that worker problems are often attributable to a lack of communication between labor and management. In a nonunion work force, a company may wish to create some institution to communicate with workers and act together with them to improve workplace conditions.

This institution, generally called an **employee committee,** is composed of representatives from both management and labor. The committee meets periodically and has some authority to create rules. The committee gives employees a forum to voice their dissatisfaction with certain conditions and gives management a conduit to inform workers fully of policy decisions.

The creation of an employee committee may be entirely well motivated on the company's part and may serve the interests of workers as well as management. Nevertheless, employee committees are fraught with potential problems under federal labor laws, and management must be aware of these problems.

The central problem with employee committees is that they may become the functional equivalent of unions dominated by management, in violation of the NLRA. Thus, these committees cannot perform union functions. For example, the employee representatives on such a committee should not present a package of proposals on wages and terms of employment, because this is the role of a union negotiating committee.

In the following case, a union complained that an employer had committed an unfair labor practice by maintaining an employee committee.

CASE 23.6   In re Simmons Industries, Inc.

National Labor Relations Board, 1996.
321 N.L.R.B. No. 32.
http://www.nlrb.gov/
decision.html[a]

HISTORICAL AND SOCIAL SETTING   *In the 1930s and 1940s, after Congress enacted the first laws protecting unions, union membership as a percentage of the work force grew rapidly, until about a third of all workers belonged to unions. As the size of the work force continued to grow, however, the number of workers belonging to unions did not increase proportionately. By the mid-1990s, union members made up only about 15 percent of the work force. Unions, which have sometimes been frustrated by employees' reluctance to organize, often blame unsuccessful attempts to unionize a particular employer's work force on the employer.*

BACKGROUND AND FACTS   *Simmons Industries, Inc., operated chicken processing plants. One of Simmons's customers was Kentucky Fried Chicken (KFC). To satisfy KFC's concerns with quality, Simmons formed at each plant a total quality management (TQM) committee. Simmons appointed managers and employees from a cross-section of the plants to serve on the committees and set the committees' agendas, which*

---

a. In the "Bound Volumes" row, click on "321". On that page, scroll to the case name ("Simmons Industries") and click on "TEXT" to read the opinion.

included such topics as employee bonuses and absences. Later, the United Food and Commercial Workers Union attempted unsuccessfully to organize the employees. The union filed a complaint with the National Labor Relations Board (NLRB), alleging that Simmons had committed unfair labor practices by, among other things, maintaining a TQM committee at its plant in Jay, Oklahoma. The union argued that the committee was a "labor organization" dominated by management in violation of the National Labor Relations Act (NLRA).

IN THE LANGUAGE OF THE COURT

DECISION AND ORDER

* * * *

* * * [T]he concept of "labor organization" * * * includes very loose, informal, unstructured, and irregular meeting groups. Such a loose organization will meet the [NLRA] definition if: (1) employees participate, (2) the organization exists, at least in part, for the purpose of dealing with employers, and (3) these dealings concern conditions of work or concern other statutory subjects such as grievances, labor disputes, wages, rates of pay, or hours of employment.

* * * * *

* * * [E]mployee members were representative of each * * * grouping of employees. * * * [T]he committee discussed and made proposals solicited by [Simmons] with respect to the formulation and implementation of an incentive bonus pay program, clearly a mandatory bargaining subject. [Simmons] accepted some of the committee's proposal and guided itself by others in formulating the bonus plan. * * * Furthermore, the * * * Committee continued * * * to discuss and make proposals with respect to employee discipline, attendance and punctuality problems and employee courtesy breaks. On recommendations based in large part on employee member complaints, the plant manager issued a set of rules that clearly affected these conditions of employment and mandatory bargaining subjects. Thus the * * * Committee * * * effectively constituted a representational employee committee, in effect a labor organization, which was unlawfully dominated, interfered with in operation and administration, and rendered unlawful assistance to by [Simmons] in violation of [the NLRA].

DECISION AND REMEDY

The NLRB ordered Simmons to, among other things, "[i]mmediately disestablish and cease giving assistance or any other support" to its TQM committees.[b]

---

b. This decision was an application of the principle declared in the leading case in this area, *Electromation, Inc.,* 309 N.L.R.B. 990 (1992).

TERMS AND CONCEPTS TO REVIEW

appropriate bargaining unit 499

authorization card 497

closed shop 496

collective bargaining 501

common situs picketing 504

concerted action 510

eighty-day cooling-off period 504

employee committee 511

featherbedding 501

hot-cargo agreement 504

lockout 505

no-strike clause 504

right-to-work law 496

secondary boycott 503

severance pay 501

union shop 496

wildcat strike 504

yellow dog contract 494

QUESTIONS AND CASE PROBLEMS

23–1. PRELIMINARY ORGANIZING. A group of employees at the Briarwood Furniture Company's manufacturing plant were interested in joining a union. A representative of the American Federation of Labor and Congress of Industrial Organizations (AFL-CIO) told the group that her union was prepared to represent the workers and suggested that the group begin organizing by obtaining authorization cards from their fellow employees. After obtaining 252 authorization cards from among Briarwood's 500 nonmanagement employees, the organizers requested that the company recognize the AFL-CIO as the official representative of the employees. The company refused. Has the company violated federal labor laws? What should the organizers do?

23–2. APPROPRIATE BARGAINING UNIT. The Briarwood Furniture Company, discussed in the preceding problem, employs 400 unskilled workers and 100 skilled workers in its plant. The unskilled workers operate the industrial machinery used in processing Briarwood's line of standardized plastic office furniture. The skilled workers, who work in an entirely separate part of the plant, are experienced artisans who craft Briarwood's line of expensive wood furniture products. Do you see any problems with a single union's representing all the workers at the Briarwood plant? Explain. Would your answers to Problem 23–1 change if you knew that 51 of the authorization cards had been signed by the skilled workers, with the remainder signed by the unskilled workers?

23–3. UNFAIR LABOR PRACTICES. Suppose that Consolidated Stores is undergoing a unionization campaign. Prior to the election, management says that the union is unnecessary to protect workers. Management also provides bonuses and wage increases to the workers during this period. The employees reject the union. Union organizers protest that the wage increases during the election campaign unfairly prejudiced the vote. Should these wage increases be regarded as an unfair labor practice? Discuss.

23–4. UNFAIR LABOR PRACTICES. SimpCo was engaged in ongoing negotiations over a new labor contract with the union representing the company's employees. As the deadline for expiration of the old labor contract drew near, several employees who were active in union activities were disciplined for being late to work. The union claimed that other employees had not been dealt with as harshly and that the company was discriminating on the basis of union activity. When the negotiations failed to prove fruitful and the old contract expired, the union called a strike. The company claimed the action was an economic strike to press the union's demands for higher wages. The union contended the action was an unfair labor practice strike because of the alleged discrimination. What importance does the distinction have for the striking workers and the company?

23–5. SECONDARY BOYCOTTS. For many years, grapefruit was shipped to Japan from Fort Pierce and Port Canaveral, Florida. In 1990, Coastal Stevedoring Co. in Fort Pierce and Port Canaveral Stevedoring Ltd. in Port Canaveral—nonunion firms—were engaged in a labor dispute with the International Longshoremen's Association (ILA). The ILA asked the National Council of Dockworkers' Unions of Japan to prevent Japanese shippers from using nonunion stevedores in Florida, and the council warned Japanese firms that their workers would not unload fruit loaded in the United States by nonunion labor. The threat caused all citrus shipments from Florida to Japan to go through Tampa, where they were loaded by stevedores represented by the ILA. Coastal, Canaveral, and others complained to the National Labor Relations Board (NLRB), alleging that the ILA's request of the Japanese unions was an illegal secondary boycott. How should the NLRB rule? [*International Longshoremen's Association, AFL-CIO,* 313 N.L.R.B. No. 53 (1993)]

23–6. UNFAIR LABOR PRACTICES. The Teamsters Union represented twenty-seven employees of Curtin Matheson Scientific, Inc. When a collective bargaining agreement between the union and the company expired, the company made an offer for a new agreement, which the union rejected. The company locked out the twenty-seven employees, and the union began an economic strike. The company hired replacement workers. When the union ended its strike and offered to accept the company's earlier offer, the company refused. The company also refused to bargain further, asserting doubt that the union was supported by a majority of the employees. The union sought help from the National Labor Relations Board (NLRB), which refused to presume that the replacement workers did not support the union. On the company's appeal, a court overturned the NLRB's ruling. The union appealed to the United States Supreme Court. How should the Court rule? [*NLRB v. Curtin Matheson Scientific, Inc.,* 494 U.S. 775, 110 S.Ct. 1542, 108 L.Ed.2d 801 (1990)]

23–7. GOOD FAITH BARGAINING. American Commercial Barge Line Co. was an affiliation made up of a number of barge and towing companies. The Seafarers International Union of North America (SIU) represented workers for Inland Tugs (IT), a separate corporate division of American Commercial Barge Line. When SIU and IT began negotiating a new collective bargaining agreement, SIU demanded that the bargaining unit include all the employees of American Commercial Barge Line. SIU also demanded that any contract include a pledge by other American Commercial Barge Line companies to continue their contributions to SIU funds, which provided for union activities. Unable to agree on these issues, the parties continued to meet for several years. Meanwhile, on the basis of an employee poll, IT changed its system of calculating wages. SIU filed a complaint with the NLRB, claiming that these changes were an unfair labor practice. IT responded that SIU was not bargaining in good faith. What should the NLRB rule? Explain. [*Inland Tugs, A Division of American Commercial Barge Line Co. v. NLRB*, 918 F.2d 1299 (7th Cir. 1990)]

23–8. EMPLOYEE COMMITTEES. Electromation, Inc., a manufacturer of electrical components and related products, cut wages, bonuses, and incentive pay and tightened attendance and leave policies. When the employees complained, Electromation set up "action committees," each consisting of employees and management representatives. No employee was involved in drafting the goals of the committees. The committees were told to suggest solutions, which would be implemented if management "believed they were within budget concerns" and "would be acceptable to the employees." Employee committee members were expected to discuss suggestions with their co-workers. The Teamsters Union, which had been seeking to organize the employees, challenged the establishment of the committees as an unfair labor practice and asked the NLRB to order that they be dissolved. On what basis might the NLRB grant the union's request? [*Electromation, Inc.*, 309 N.L.R.B. 990 (1992)]

23–9. UNION RECOGNITION. The International Association of Machinists and Aerospace Workers was certified as the exclusive representative of a unit of employees of F & A Food Sales, Inc. The employees were associated with F & A's trucking operations. The parties negotiated a collective bargaining agreement (CBA) that recognized the union as the employees' representative and reserved F & A's right to subcontract work as the company deemed necessary. Five months after negotiating the CBA, F & A subcontracted the services performed by the unit to Ryder Dedicated Logistics, Inc. Ryder operated from the same facility, used the same trucks, and employed substantially the same employees as had F & A. The union did not represent the workers while Ryder employed them. Seventeen months later, Ryder terminated the subcontract, and F & A resumed its own trucking operations with the same facility, the

same trucks, and many of the same employees. The union asserted its right to represent the employees under the CBA. F & A refused to recognize the union. The union filed a charge of unfair labor practice with the NLRB. Is the CBA still in effect? Is the union still the representative of this unit of employees? Explain. [*National Labor Relations Board. v. F & A Food Sales, Inc.*, 202 F.3d 1258 (10th Cir. 2000)]

23–10. IN YOUR COURT

Salvatore Monte was president of Kenrich Petrochemicals, Inc. Helen Chizmar had been Kenrich's office manager since 1963. Among the staff that Chizmar supervised were her sister, daughter, and daughter-in-law. In 1987, Chizmar's relatives and four other staff members designated the Oil, Chemical and Atomic Workers International Union as their bargaining representative. Chizmar was not involved, but when Monte was notified that his office was unionizing, he told Chizmar that someone else could do her job for "$20,000 less" and fired her. He told another employee that one of his reasons for firing Chizmar was that he "was not going to put up with any union bullsh—." During negotiations with the union, Monte said that he planned to "get rid of the whole family." Chizmar's family complained to the National Labor Relations Board (NLRB) that the firing was an unfair labor practice. The NLRB agreed and ordered that Chizmar be reinstated with back pay. Kenrich appealed. Assume that you are the judge hearing this case and answer the following questions:

(a) The National Labor Relations Act does not protect supervisors who engage in union activities. Should you affirm the NLRB's order nonetheless? If you do not affirm the NLRB's order, what message will you be sending to the supervisors and employees of Kenrich?

(b) Is there anything Kenrich could (legally) do to avoid the unionization of its employees? Would it be ethical to counter the wishes of the employees to unionize?

LAW ON THE WEB

For updated links to resources available on the Web, as well as a variety of other materials, visit this text's Web site at <u>http://wleb.westbuslaw.com</u>. Here we list selected Web sites that offer information relevant to the topics covered in this chapter.

The American Federation of Labor–Congress of Industrial Organizations (AFL–CIO) provides links to a broad variety of labor-related resources at

<u>http://www.aflcio.org</u>

The National Labor Relations Board is online at the following URL:

<u>http://www.doc.gov/nlrb/homepg.html</u>

LEGAL RESEARCH EXERCISES ON THE WEB

Go to http://wleb.westbuslaw.com, the Web site that accompanies this text. Select "Internet Applications," and then click on "Chapter 23." There you will find the following Internet research exercise that you can perform to learn more about consumer and environmental law:

Activity 23–1: The National Labor Relations Board

UNIT FOUR—CUMULATIVE BUSINESS HYPOTHETICAL

Falwell Motors, Inc., is a large corporation that manufactures automobile batteries.

1. One of Falwell's salespersons, Loren, puts in long hours every week. He spends most of his time away from the office generating sales. Less than 10 percent of his work time is devoted to other duties. Usually, he receives a substantial bonus at the end of each year from his employer, and Loren has come to rely on this supplement to his annual salary and commissions. One year, the employer does not give any of its employees year-end bonuses. Loren calculates the amount of hours he had worked during the year beyond the required forty hours a week. Then he tells Falwell's president that if he is not paid for these overtime hours, he will sue the company for the overtime pay he has "earned." Falwell's president tells Loren that Falwell is not obligated to pay Loren overtime because Loren is a salesperson. What federal statute governs this dispute? Under this statute, is Falwell required to pay Loren for the "overtime hours"? Why or why not?

2. One day Barry, one of the salespersons, anxious to make a sale, intentionally quotes a price to a customer that is $500 lower than Falwell has authorized for that particular product. The customer purchases the product at the quoted price. When Falwell learns of the deal, it claims that it is not legally bound to the sales contract because it did not authorize Barry to sell the product at that price. Is Falwell bound by the contract? Discuss fully.

3. One day Gina, a Falwell employee, suffered a serious burn when she accidentally spilled some acid on her hand. The accident occurred because another employee, who was suspected of using illegal drugs, carelessly bumped into her. The hand required a series of skin-grafting operations before it healed sufficiently to allow Gina to return to work. Gina wants to obtain compensation for her lost wages and medical expenses. Can she do so? If so, how?

4. After Gina's injury, Falwell decides to conduct random drug tests on all of its employees. Several employees claim that the testing violates their privacy rights. If the dispute is litigated, what factors will the court consider in deciding whether the random drug testing is legally permissible?

5. Aretha, a Falwell employee, is disgusted by the sexually offensive behavior of several male employees. She has complained to her supervisor on several occasions about the offensive behavior, but the supervisor merely laughs at her concerns. Aretha decides to bring a legal action against the company for sexual harassment. Does Aretha's complaint concern *quid pro quo* harassment or hostile-environment harassment? What federal statute protects employees from sexual harassment? What remedies are available under that statute? What procedures must Aretha follow in pursuing her legal action?

FOCUS ON LEGAL REASONING
Babick v. Oregon Arena Corp.

INTRODUCTION

Wrongful discharge and the legal bases supporting it are discussed in Chapter 21. In this *Focus on Legal Reasoning,* we examine *Babick v. Oregon Arena Corp.,*[1] a decision in a suit focused on that topic. Under the employment-at-will doctrine, an employer may discharge an employee at any time for any reason without consequences. Courts have created some exceptions to this doctrine, however. The opinion in the *Babick* case centered on the most common exception: the discharge of a worker for reasons that violate a public policy of the jurisdiction.

CASE BACKGROUND

Oregon Arena Corporation (OAC)

1. 160 Or.App. 140, 980 P.2d 1147 (1999).

owns the Memorial Coliseum, a large entertainment forum in Portland, Oregon. OAC hired Kenneth Babick and others to provide security and medical assistance at music concerts and other entertainment events held there. As part of their employment, Babick and the others received training from OAC to carry out their functions as security officers. That training included instruction on defensive tactics, the use of force, actions to be taken in cases of suspected drug possession and the possession of alcohol by minors, and arrest procedures.

One night, at a Phish concert, some of the security officers attempted to arrest some members of the audience for assaulting others and illegal drug and alcohol possession. The officers' actions were consistent with the training that they

had received from OAC and were otherwise lawful under Oregon state law. Other members of the audience, as well as some Phish employees, attacked the officers. OAC representatives publicly berated the officers and then forced them to release the audience members who had been arrested.

After the concert, OAC fired its entire security staff, including those who were not involved in the arrests, in retaliation for those enforcement actions. Babick and others filed a suit in an Oregon state court against OAC, claiming, among other things, wrongful discharge. When the court dismissed their claim, they appealed to an intermediate state appellate court, arguing that although they had been at-will employees, their discharge fell within the public-policy exception to the at-will employment rule.

MAJORITY OPINION

DE MUNIZ, P.J. [Presiding Judge].

* * * * *

* * * Peace officers are statutorily authorized to enforce the criminal laws, and generally are the persons who make arrests. However, the [Oregon] legislature also has extended explicit arrest authority to private citizens, including authority for the use of justifiable force. *In empowering private citizens to make arrests, the public has tacitly recognized that peace officers may not be present in every situation where criminal laws are broken and has demonstrated a common concern for law enforcement in such situations.* [Emphasis added.]

Other statutes, as they relate to the circumstances here, further define the public policy involved. As pleaded by plaintiffs, defendant hired and trained plaintiffs solely to maintain order at a large, public music concert and, if necessary, to make arrests to effectuate that purpose. In such large public gatherings, the

potential for public disorder is increased. Further, it is reasonable to infer from defendant's hiring of plaintiffs that [peace] officers would not be present or not be present in sufficient numbers at the concert to ensure the preservation of public order. In those circumstances, Oregonians have expressed a common concern for reliable and effective private law enforcement, as demonstrated by ORS [Oregon Revised Statute] 181.870 through ORS 181.991, which regulate the licensing and training of persons who provide security services at such "public activities."

It is apparent from the above laws that Oregonians value an orderly and safe community. * * * Thus, we hold that, because plaintiffs were discharged for taking steps to maintain order at a large, public event, plaintiffs' discharge thwarted the important public policy of preserving order at such an event, where social disorder might occur and where police officers might not be present or not be present in sufficient numbers to ensure public order on their own.

Notwithstanding, defendant * * * [relies] on the substance of this employment relationship—i.e., that plaintiffs were hired as security officers—in arguing that the "public duty" exception to the employment-at-will doctrine does not apply here. Defendant argues that, at its core, this case turns on whether "an employer may decide against having its own employees perform [law enforcement] services on its property" * * *.

Underlying those arguments is the premise that defendant's discharge decision was based on plaintiffs' unsatisfactory job performance, not on the exercise of a public duty, and therefore was within the at-will employment rule. We disagree with that premise for the following [reason].

* * * There is no fact pleaded, nor is there any favorable inference that reasonably may be drawn from those facts, to suggest that plaintiffs performed their job duties unsatisfactorily. * * * Defendant fired plaintiffs solely in retaliation for preserving public safety and order at a large, public music concert where police officers might not be present or not be present in sufficient numbers to maintain public order. That factual assertion squarely implicates the public policy identified above.

DISSENTING OPINION

LINDER, J. [Judge], * * * dissenting * * *.
* * * *

* * * [P]laintiffs are not the police. They were people who were hired to perform services for defendant that, in some particulars, might resemble the law enforcement and public safety functions that the police provide. Significantly, the only authority that plaintiffs had at defendant's premises and over the persons on the premises stemmed from the fact that defendant hired them to be there. That is, plaintiffs were there, doing what they were doing, pursuant to their private contract of employment. Defendant terminated plaintiffs' employment, in effect, because plaintiffs were providing more "law enforcement" than defendant or defendant's patrons wanted. In other words, defendant regarded plaintiffs' performance of the parties' private agreement to be unsatisfactory.

* * * *

The majority's holding creates a significant dilemma for private employers. An employer is liable for the torts of its employees committed in the course and scope of the employment relationship. Law enforcement-type activities can be a source of substantial tort exposure, involving, as they do, an often delicate balance between maintaining public order and respecting individual civil liberties. An employee who overzealously or otherwise crosses the line between permissible law enforcement and an infringement of civil rights can create significant liability—even punitive in nature—for an employer. See, e.g., *Blume v. Fred Meyer, Inc.,* 155 Or.App. 102, 963 P.2d 700 (1998). For that and other legitimate reasons, an employer may decide to limit the authorization for employees to respond to suspected violations of the law (which can encompass potential acts of theft, trespass, harassment, and underage alcohol use, to identify only a few).

LEGAL REASONING AND ANALYSIS

1. **Legal Analysis.** The dissent cites, in its opinion, *Blume v. Fred Meyer, Inc.,* 155 Or.App. 102, 963 P.2d 700 (1998) (see the *Law on the Web* feature at the end of Chapter 2 for instructions on how to access state court opinions). Do the facts and issues in that case compare to the facts and issues of the *Babick* case? How do the holdings in the two cases compare? Is the dissent correct in its use of the *Blume* case, or is it unrelated to the circumstances in the *Babick* case?

2. **Legal Reasoning.** What reasons does the majority provide to justify its conclusion? How do those reasons contrast with the dissent's reasoning? With whom do you agree? Why?

3. **Social Considerations.** Do employees owe to the customers of their employers any obligations besides a public duty to obey the law? If so, what is the nature of those obligations? Do employers owe to their employees any obligations that go beyond the satisfaction of the employers' customers? If so, what is the nature of those obligations?

4. **Implications for Employers.** What do the reasoning and the outcome in this case indicate to those employers who expect their employees to obey the law?

5. **Case Briefing Assignment.** Using the guidelines for briefing cases given in Appendix A of this text, brief the *Blume* case.

GOING ONLINE

The Legal Information Institute (LII) offers links to federal, state, and private employment law resources at <u>http://www.law.cornell.edu/topics/employment.html</u>, a page within the LII Web site. LII is affiliated with Cornell Law School in Ithaca, New York.

FOCUS ON ETHICS
The Employment Environment

The employment environment is one in which individuals come together for the purpose of achieving a common purpose. In this sense, the employment environment is like most others we have examined thus far. Yet in spite of the similarities, the employment environment remains unique.

Part of the uniqueness of the employment environment stems from the close nature of the relationship between employers and employees, a relationship that, as seen in this unit, often involves intricate duties of agency. In earlier times, most individuals were self-employed, usually on the family farm. The farm was the center of the family unit. At any given time, several generations might have their entire social and financial security invested in the family farm.

With the onset of the industrial revolution, this structure gave way to another—one in which individuals worked with and depended on those individuals that did not share the special bonds of family relationship. Yet because employment relationships typically exist for an extended period, there was inevitably a tendency to incorporate aspects of the family into the employment environment. The result has been that there is sometimes a conflict between the impersonal nature of the market—labor is, after all, a factor of production—and the family-like aspect of the close, long-term relation between an employer and employee. Moreover, the aspects that account for the uniqueness of the employment environment generate numerous ethical issues. In this unit's *Focus on Ethics* we

examine two such issues. First, we examine the ethical problems surrounding the high degree of loyalty demanded in an agency relationship. Second, we examine the degree to which society should rely on business to utilize affirmative action programs in eliminating the lingering social problem of discrimination against minorities.

THE DUTIES OF AGENTS AND PRINCIPALS

When one person agrees to act on behalf of another, as an agent does in an agency relationship, that person assumes certain ethical responsibilities. An agent acting *on behalf of* a principal implicitly promises to place the principal's interests above his or her own interests. Similarly, a principal in an agency relationship assumes certain ethical duties. If an agent incurs expenses or liability while acting on the principal's behalf, for example, it is only fair that the principal should assume responsibility for those expenses or that liability. In essence, agency law gives legal force to the ethical duties arising in an agency relationship. Although agency law also focuses on the rights of agents and principals, those rights are framed by the concept of duty—that is, an agent's duty becomes a right for the principal and vice versa.

Significantly, most of the duties of the principal and agent described below are negotiable at law. In forming a contract, the principal and the agent can extend or abridge many of the ordinary

duties owed in such a relationship. Legal rules generally come into play when the contract is silent or ambiguous on an issue. Allowing the parties to negotiate their relative duties seems ethically fair, as long as the parties are able to understand their rights and make informed decisions.

DISABILITY-BASED DISCRIMINATION

In providing protection for disabled persons in the employment context through the Americans with Disabilities Act (ADA), Congress expressed society's concern that persons with disabilities should be given a fair opportunity to compete in the workplace. Yet who should decide when a person with disabilities is "otherwise qualified" for a particular job? This is a thorny issue in the employment context, and the decisions of employers in this respect are often at odds with the law.

Consider an example: Should a freight company or airline be required to hire job candidates with monocular vision—persons who are blind in one eye? According to some federal courts, the answer to this question is yes. For instance, in one case, a federal appellate court held that a truck driver who was blind in one eye was "disabled" and thus could sue an employer who refused to hire him under the ADA.[1]

Another challenging problem for employers has to do with employees who have a history of

---

1. *Kirkingburg v. Albertson's, Inc.,* 143 F.3d 1228 (9th Cir. 1998).

alcohol abuse. Consider, for example, the problem faced by Exxon Corporation. When its supertanker, the *Exxon Valdez,* hit a reef in Prince William Sound, Alaska, in 1989, it caused one of the worst oil spills in history. Because it was widely believed that the captain of the tanker was intoxicated at the time of the accident, Exxon established a policy of not allowing anyone with a history of alcohol abuse to be a tanker captain or to work in certain other safety-sensitive positions.

It turned out that Exxon's policy, designed to minimize accidents and shield the company from liability under environmental laws, violated the ADA. In a suit against Exxon, the Equal Employment Opportunity Commission (EEOC) claimed that Exxon had violated the ADA by discriminating against some fifty employeees who were "rehabilitated substance abusers." The federal court agreed and held that Exxon could not discriminate against such employees unless it could show that they posed a direct threat to the health or safety of others.[2]

English-Only Policies

As the U.S. population becomes more and more multilingual, so does the work force. In response to this development, many employers have instituted English-only policies in their workplaces. Are such policies fair to workers who do not speak English? Do they violate Title VII of the Civil Rights Act of 1964, which, among other things, prohibits discrimination on the basis of race and national origin?

Employers seem to be caught between the proverbial "rock and a hard place" with respect to this issue. In one case, for example, an employee sued her employer, claiming that the employer's *failure*

to institute an English-only policy violated her rights under Title VII. The federal court declined to dismiss the suit.[3] In several other cases, however, employers who have adopted English-only policies have been sued for violating Title VII's prohibition against discrimination based on national origin.

For example, when a Texas communications company prohibited employees from speaking any language but English at work except to customers who did not speak English, a number of workers complained about the policy and were fired as a result. The Equal Employment Opportunity Commission, on behalf of the fired workers, brought an action against the company, alleging that the work rule violated Title VII. The employer argued that the rule had a legitimate business basis— improvement of customer service and better employee oversight. Nonetheless, the court refused to dismiss the case, in part because the rule applied to employees even while they were on breaks.[4]

Generally, though, the courts have shown a fair degree of tolerance with respect to English-only rules. In *Garcia v. Spun Steak Co.,*[5] for example, several African American and Chinese American employees complained that the company's Spanish-speaking employees were making racist comments about them. Hoping to resolve the problem, the employer adopted an English-only policy— only to be faced with a lawsuit brought by the Spanish-speaking employees. They claimed that they had been denied their "right" to express their cultural heritage on the job. Additionally, they contended that they had been

denied a privilege held by English-speaking employees: the opportunity to speak their native language in the workplace. They also argued that the policy intimidated them and made them feel isolated and inferior.

The Court of Appeals for the Ninth Circuit held for the defendant company, however. The court concluded that Title VII does not protect an employee's right to express his or her cultural heritage on the job. Furthermore, in the court's eyes, the employees had not been denied any privilege enjoyed by the English-speaking employees, because, as bilingual persons, they could elect to speak in English and therefore had the capability to converse in the workplace. Finally, in regard to the claim of "intimidation," which the court regarded as a type of hostile-environment claim, the court stated that it was unwilling to adopt a blanket rule that English-only policies create a hostile work environment.

Labor Law and Quality Control

One of the ways in which today's corporations have increased their productivity and product quality— and hence their ability to compete effectively—is by using some type of employee-participation program. Such programs are established not only to promote labor-management cooperation but also to incorporate employee input into the decision-making process in order to improve the quality of the firm's products or services.

While employee-participation programs appear to be an effective approach to the problems of productivity and product quality, they have recently come under attack as violating labor laws. To illustrate: Electromation, Inc., an electrical-components manufacturer, set up a series of committees involving employee

---

2. *EEOC v. Exxon Corp.,* 1 F.Supp.2d 635 (N.D.Tex. 1998).

3. *McNeil v. Aguilos,* 831 F.Supp. 1079 (S.D.N.Y. 1993).
4. *EEOC v. Premier Operator Services, Inc.,* 75 F.Supp.2d 550 (N.D.Tex 1999).
5. 998 F.2d 1480 (9th Cir. 1993).

and management participation. The committees were initially established to counter employee dissatisfaction with new employment policies that related to absenteeism, nonsmoking rules, and so on.

The workers who participated in these committees involved themselves in developing solutions to these and various other problems, including worker benefits. The Teamsters Union, which was attempting to unionize Electromation's work force, successfully argued to the National Labor Relations Board (NLRB) that the committees violated the National Labor Relations Act (NLRA) because, in essence, the committees were labor organizations that were unlawfully "dominated" by the employer. [6]

Because numerous companies throughout the United States use similar action committees, the corporate community felt that it had been dealt a severe blow by the NLRB's decision. Almost any type

of employee-participation program, regardless of how beneficial for employer and employee alike, could possibly be characterized as a labor organization as defined under the NLRA. As a result, employers will be wary of employee-participation programs, regardless of how beneficial they are.

The U.S. Constitution is premised on the belief that we benefit as a society by the free exchange of ideas and political beliefs. Should labor laws function to restrict the expression of ideas? Can a balance be struck between the goals of free speech and assembly and the prevention of an employer-dominated workplace in which the employee is underrepresented?

DISCUSSION QUESTIONS

1. How much obedience and loyalty does an agent-employee owe an employer? What if the employer engages in an activity—or requests the employee to engage in an activity—that violates the employee's ethical standards but does not necessarily violate any public policy or law? In such a

situation, does an employee's duty to abide by his or her own ethical standards override the employee's duty of loyalty to the employer?

2. If an agent injures a third party during the course of employment, under the doctrine of *respondeat superior,* the employer may be held liable for the agent's actions even though the employer did not authorize the action and was not even aware of it. Do you think that it is fair to hold employers liable in such situations? Do you think that it would be fairer to hold that the employee alone should bear responsibility for his or her tortious actions to third parties, even when the actions are committed within the scope of employment?

3. Do you think that the Americans with Disabilities Act goes too far in protecting the rights of employees with disabilities (or perceived disabilities)? Does it go far enough?

4. Do you see any need for English-only policies in the workplace? Can such policies ever reduce tensions between different ethnic groups, some of which are caused by the use of different languages?

---

6. *Electromation, Inc.,* 309 N.L.R.B. No. 163 (1992).

UNIT FIVE

The Regulatory Environment

CONTENTS

CHAPTER 24

Consumer Protection

ALL STATUTES, AGENCY RULES, AND COMMON law judicial decisions that serve to protect the interests of consumers are classified as **consumer law.** Traditionally, in disputes involving consumers, it was assumed that the freedom to contract carried with it the obligation to live by the deal made. Over time, this attitude has changed considerably. Today, myriad federal and state laws protect consumers from unfair trade practices, unsafe products, discriminatory or unreasonable credit requirements, and other problems related to consumer transactions. Nearly every agency and department of the federal government has an office of consumer affairs, and most states have one or more such offices to help consumers. Also, typically the attorney general's office assists consumers at the state level.

Consumer transactions take a variety of forms, but they generally include those that involve an exchange of value for the purpose of acquiring goods, services, land, or credit for personal or family use. Because of the wide variation among state consumer protection laws, our primary focus in this chapter is on federal legislation. Exhibit 24–1 indicates some of the types of consumer transactions that are regulated by federal laws.

SECTION 1

Deceptive Advertising

One of the earliest federal consumer protection laws—and still one of the most important—was the Federal Trade Commission Act of 1914.[1] As mentioned in the preceding chapter, the act created the Federal Trade Commission (FTC) to carry out the broadly stated goal of preventing unfair and deceptive trade practices, including deceptive advertising.[2]

DECEPTIVE ADVERTISING DEFINED

Advertising will be deemed deceptive if a consumer would be misled by the advertising claim. Vague generalities and obvious exaggerations are permissible. These claims are known as *puffing*. When a claim takes on the appearance of literal authenticity, however, it may create problems. Advertising that *appears* to be based on factual evidence but that in fact is not will be deemed deceptive. A classic example is

---

1. 15 U.S.C. Sections 41–58.
2. 15 U.S.C. Section 45.

EXHIBIT 24–1   AREAS OF CONSUMER LAW REGULATED BY STATUTES

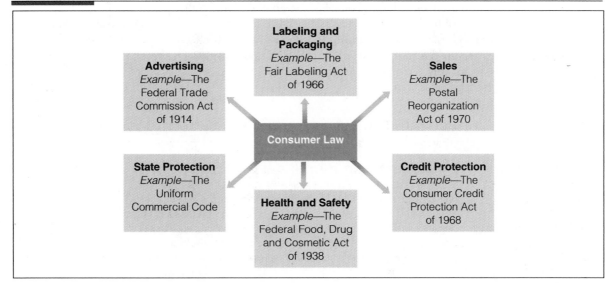

provided by a 1944 case in which the claim that a skin cream would restore youthful qualities to aged skin was deemed deceptive.[3]

Some advertisements contain "half-truths," meaning that the presented information is true but incomplete, and it leads consumers to a false conclusion. For example, the makers of Campbell's soups advertised that "most" Campbell's soups were low in fat and cholesterol and thus were helpful in fighting heart disease. What the ad did not say was that Campbell's soups are high in sodium, and high-sodium diets may increase the risk of heart disease. The FTC ruled that Campbell's claims were thus deceptive. Advertising that contains an endorsement by a celebrity may be deemed deceptive if the celebrity actually makes no use of the product.

BAIT-AND-SWITCH ADVERTISING

The FTC has promulgated specific rules to govern advertising techniques. One of the most important rules is contained in the FTC's "Guides Against Bait Advertising,"[4] issued in 1968. The rule seeks to prevent **bait-and-switch advertising**—that is, advertising a very low price for a particular item that will likely be unavailable to the consumer, who will then be encour-

aged to purchase a more expensive item. The low price is the "bait" to lure the consumer into the store. The salesperson is instructed to "switch" the consumer to a different, more expensive item. Under the FTC guidelines, bait-and-switch advertising occurs if the seller refuses to show the advertised item, fails to have in stock a reasonable quantity of the item, fails to promise to deliver the advertised item within a reasonable time, or discourages employees from selling the item.

FTC ACTIONS AGAINST DECEPTIVE ADVERTISING

The FTC receives complaints from many sources, including competitors of alleged violators, consumers, consumer organizations, trade associations, Better Business Bureaus, government organizations, and state and local officials. If enough consumers complain and the complaints are widespread, the FTC will investigate the problem. If the FTC concludes that a given advertisement is unfair or deceptive, it drafts a formal complaint, which is sent to the alleged offender. The company may agree to settle the complaint without further proceedings, or the FTC can conduct a hearing in which the company can present its defense (see Chapter 6).

If the FTC succeeds in proving that an advertisement is unfair or deceptive, it usually issues a **cease-and-desist order** requiring that the challenged advertising be stopped. It might also impose a sanction

---

3. *Charles of the Ritz Distributing Corp. v. Federal Trade Commission*, 143 F.2d 676 (2d Cir. 1944).
4. 16 C.F.R. Part 238.

known as **counteradvertising** by requiring the company to advertise anew—in print, on radio, and on television—to inform the public about the earlier misinformation. The FTC may institute **multiple product orders,** which require a firm to cease and desist from false advertising not only in regard to the product that was the subject of the action but also in regard to all of the firm's other products.

Is it false or misleading to advertise a product as effective when its effectiveness results only from users' belief that it works? The court addressed this issue in the following case.

CASE 24.1 — Federal Trade Commission v. Pantron I Corp.

United States
Court of Appeals,
Ninth Circuit, 1994.
33 F.3d 1088.

IN THE LANGUAGE
OF THE COURT

BACKGROUND AND FACTS   *Pantron I Corporation sold the Helsinki Formula as a "cure" for baldness. Pantron claimed that the product reduced hair loss and promoted hair growth. The Federal Trade Commission filed a suit in a federal district court against Pantron and its owner, Hal Lederman, alleging that these claims constituted an unfair or deceptive trade practice. The court concluded in part that the product had a "placebo effect"—that is, that it worked when its users believed it would. The court issued an order that, among other things, allowed Pantron to continue claiming its product "works some of the time for a lot of people." The FTC appealed this order.*

REINHARDT, Circuit Judge:
　　*   *   *   *

*   *   *   Where, as here, a product's effectiveness arises solely as a result of the placebo effect, a representation that the product is effective constitutes a false advertisement even though some consumers may experience positive results. In such circumstances, the efficacy claim is misleading because the [product] is not inherently effective, its results being attributable to the psychosomatic effect produced by *   *   * advertising *   *   * .

*   *   *   Under the evidence in the record before us, it appears that massaging vegetable oil on one's head would likely produce the same positive results as using the Helsinki Formula. *   *   *   [A] court should not allow a seller to rely on such a placebo effect in supporting a claim of effectiveness *   *   * . [W]ere we to hold otherwise, advertisers would be encouraged to foist unsubstantiated claims on an unsuspecting public in the hope that consumers would believe the ads and the claims would be self-fulfilling.

DECISION
AND REMEDY

The U.S. Court of Appeals for the Ninth Circuit reversed this part of the lower court's order and remanded the case. Pantron could not continue to claim that its product "works some of the time for a lot of people."

TELEMARKETING AND ELECTRONIC ADVERTISING

The pervasive use of the telephone to market goods and services to homes and businesses led to the passage in 1991 of the Telephone Consumer Protection Act (TCPA).[5] The act prohibits telephone solicitation

using an automatic telephone dialing system or a prerecorded voice. Most states also have laws regulating telephone solicitation. The TCPA also makes it illegal to transmit ads via fax without first obtaining the recipient's permission. (Similar issues have arisen with respect to junk e-mail, called "spam"—see Chapter 15 for a discussion of this topic.)

The act is enforced by the Federal Communications Commission and also provides for a private right of ac-

_____
5. 47 U.S.C. Sections 227 *et seq.*

tion. Consumers can recover any actual monetary loss resulting from a violation of the act or receive $500 in damages for each violation, whichever is greater. If a court finds that a defendant willfully or knowingly violated the act, the court has the discretion to treble the damages awarded.

The Telemarketing and Consumer Fraud and Abuse Prevention Act[6] of 1994 directed the FTC to establish rules governing telemarketing and to bring actions against fraudulent telemarketers. The FTC's Telemarketing Sales Rule[7] of 1995 requires a telemarketer, before making a sales pitch, to inform the recipient that the call is a sales call and to identify the seller's name and the product being sold. The rule makes it illegal for telemarketers to misrepresent information (including facts about their goods or services, earnings potential, profitability, the risk attending an investment, or the nature of a prize). Additionally, telemarketers must inform the people they call of the total cost of the goods being sold, any restrictions on obtaining or using the goods, and whether a sale will be considered to be final and nonrefundable. A telemarketer must also remove a consumer's name from its list of potential contacts if the customer so requests.

A major challenge in today's legal environment has to do with the advertising of products and services via the Internet. See this chapter's *Emerging Trends in Technology* on page 526 for a discussion of this issue.

SECTION 2

Labeling and Packaging Laws

A number of federal and state laws deal specifically with the information given on labels and packages. In general, labels must be accurate, and they must use words that are easily understood by the ordinary consumer. For example, a box of cereal cannot be labeled "giant" if that would exaggerate the amount of cereal contained in the box. In some instances, labels must specify the raw materials used in the product, such as the percentage of cotton, nylon, or other fiber used in a garment. In other instances, the product must carry a warning. Cigarette packages and advertising, for example, must include one of several warnings about the health hazards associated with smoking.[8]

Federal laws regulating the labeling and packaging of products include the Wool Products Labeling Act of 1939,[9] the Fur Products Labeling Act of 1951,[10] the Flammable Fabrics Act of 1953,[11] the Fair Packaging and Labeling Act of 1966,[12] the Smokeless Tobacco Health Education Act of 1986,[13] and the Nutrition Labeling and Education Act of 1990.[14] The Smokeless Tobacco Health Education Act, for example, requires that producers, packagers, and importers of smokeless tobacco label their product with one of several warnings about the health hazards associated with the use of smokeless tobacco; the warnings are similar to those contained on other tobacco product packages.

The Fair Packaging and Labeling Act requires that products carry labels that identify the product; the net quantity of the contents, as well as the quantity of servings, if the number of servings is stated; the manufacturer; and the packager or distributor. The act also authorizes requirements concerning words used to describe packages, terms that are associated with savings claims, information disclosures for ingredients in nonfood products, and standards for the partial filling of packages. Food products must bear labels detailing nutritional content, including how much fat the food contains and what kind of fat it is. These restrictions are enforced by the Department of Health and Human Services, as well as the FTC. The Nutrition Labeling and Education Act of 1990 requires standard nutrition facts (including fat content) on food labels; regulates the use of such terms as *fresh* and *low fat*; and, subject to the federal Food and Drug Administration's approval, authorizes certain health claims.

SECTION 3

Sales

Many of the laws that protect consumers concern the disclosure of certain terms in sales transactions and provide rules governing the various forms of sales, such as door-to-door sales, mail-order sales, referral sales, and the unsolicited receipt of merchandise. Much of the federal regulation of sales is conducted by the FTC

---

6. 15 U.S.C. Sections 6101–6108.
7. 16 C.F.R. Sections 310.1–310.8.
8. 15 U.S.C. Sections 1331–1341.

9. 15 U.S.C. Section 68.
10. 15 U.S.C. Section 69.
11. 15 U.S.C. Section 1191.
12. 15 U.S.C. Sections 1451 *et seq.*
13. 15 U.S.C. Sections 4401–4408.
14. 21 U.S.C. Section 343-1.

EMERGING TRENDS IN TECHNOLOGY

Protection against Internet Fraud

For years, the Federal Trade Commission (FTC) has fought deceptive advertising in printed materials and in radio and television broadcasts. Since the 1990s, it has spent a considerable portion of its resources on fighting deceptive advertising on the Internet. The FTC has moved particularly quickly on commercial Internet fraud schemes. It has even provided "hot links" on Web sites that it has targeted. A hot link takes the user to the FTC's own Web site, on which the complaint, restraining order, and other documents in the case can be read and downloaded.

Other agencies are also fighting online fraud and false advertising. For example, the Securities and Exchange Commission (SEC) has initiated actions against dozens of entities that have perpetrated online investment scams. One fraudulent scheme involved twenty thousand investors, who lost in all more than $3 million. Some cases have involved false claims about the earnings potential of home-

business programs, such as the claim that one could "earn $4,000 or more each month." Others have concerned claims for "guaranteed credit repair."

The Department of Transportation (DOT) has also brought actions against purported online violators of advertising and disclosure laws. In one case, the DOT fined Virgin Airlines for failing to disclose the true price of a flight that it advertised on the Web. Also, the Consumer Product Safety Commission (CPSC) has created what it calls a one-stop Web site at which it provides information that allows consumers to avoid the most obvious fraud problems on the Web and elsewhere.

Consumers themselves have also taken action to curb online fraud. For example, the National Consumers League has developed Web pages to help consumers learn about the most common types of Internet fraud. Various states are also setting up information sites to help consumers protect themselves.

IMPLICATIONS FOR THE BUSINESSPERSON

1. All business entities must be aware that the laws and government regulations controlling standard "paper" commerce and

advertising apply equally to the Internet.
2. Businesspersons should realize that even though Internet sites are seemingly infinite in number, the vastness of this number will not prevent federal and state agency "watchdogs" from discovering fraud and false advertising. An increasing number of government regulatory dollars are going into policing the Internet.

FOR CRITICAL ANALYSIS

1. Can there be more consumer fraud on the Internet than there has been with the use of mail-order catalogues? Explain.
2. How can a set of guidelines for online advertising be developed, given that the technology is changing so rapidly?

RELEVANT WEB SITES

For a list of the ten most common scams perpetrated online, go to the National Consumers League Web site at **http://www.fraud. org/ifw.htm.** You can access the CPSC's consumer law Web site at **http://www.consumer.gov.** For an example of a well-designed state Web site to help consumers, go to **http://www.state.nh.us/nhdoj/ Consumer/cpb.html.**

---

under its regulatory authority to curb unfair trade practices. Other federal agencies, however, are involved to various degrees. For example, the Federal Reserve Board of Governors has issued **Regulation Z,**[15] which governs credit provisions associated with sales contracts. Many states have also enacted laws governing consumer sales transactions. Moreover, states have pro-

vided a number of consumer protection provisions through the adoption of the Uniform Commercial Code and, in those states that have adopted it, the Uniform Consumer Credit Code.

DOOR-TO-DOOR SALES

Door-to-door sales are singled out for special treatment in the laws of most states, in part because of the

---

15. 12 C.F.R. Sections 226.1–226.30.

nature of the sales transaction. Repeat purchases are not as likely as they are in stores, and thus the seller has less incentive to cultivate the goodwill of the purchaser. Furthermore, the seller is unlikely to present alternative products and their prices. Thus, a number of states have passed "cooling-off" laws that permit the buyers of goods sold door-to-door to cancel their contracts within a specified period of time, usually two to three days after the sale.

An FTC regulation also requires sellers to give consumers three days to cancel any door-to-door sale. Because this rule applies in addition to the relevant state statutes, consumers are given the most favorable benefits of the FTC rule and their own state statutes. In addition, the FTC rule requires that consumers be notified in Spanish of this right if the oral negotiations for the sale were in that language.

TELEPHONE AND MAIL-ORDER SALES

Sales made by either telephone or mail order are the greatest source of complaints to the nation's Better Business Bureaus. Many mail-order firms are far removed from most of their buyers, thus making it burdensome for buyers to bring complaints against them. To a certain extent, consumers are protected under federal laws prohibiting mail fraud, which were discussed in Chapter 7, and under state consumer protection laws that parallel and supplement the federal laws.

The FTC Mail or Telephone Order Merchandise Rule of 1993, which amended the FTC Mail-Order Rule of 1975,[16] provides specific protections for consumers who purchase goods via phone lines or through the mails. The 1993 rule extended the 1975 rule to include sales in which orders are transmitted by computer, fax machine, or some similar means involving telephone lines. Among other things, the rule requires mail-order merchants to ship orders within the time promised in their catalogues or advertisements, to notify consumers when orders cannot be shipped on time, and to issue a refund within a specified period of time when a consumer cancels an order.

In addition, the Postal Reorganization Act of 1970[17] provides that *unsolicited* merchandise sent by U.S. mail may be retained, used, discarded, or disposed of in any manner deemed appropriate, without the recipient's incurring any obligation to the sender.

FTC REGULATION OF SPECIFIC INDUSTRIES

Over the last decade, the FTC has begun to target certain sales practices on an industry-wide basis. Two examples involve the used-car business and the funeral-home trade. In 1984, the FTC enacted the Used Motor Vehicle Regulation Rule,[18] which is more commonly known as the used-car rule. This rule requires used-car dealers to affix a buyer's guide label to all cars sold on their lots. The label must disclose the following information: (1) the car's warranty or a statement that the car is being sold "as is," (2) information regarding any service contract or promises being made by the dealer, and (3) a suggestion that the purchaser obtain both an inspection of the car and a written statement of any promises made by the dealer.

In 1984, the FTC also enacted rules requiring that funeral homes provide customers with itemized prices of all charges incurred for a funeral.[19] In addition, the regulations prohibit funeral homes from requiring specific embalming procedures or specific types of caskets for bodies that are to be cremated.

REAL ESTATE SALES

Various federal and state laws apply to consumer transactions involving real estate. These laws are designed to prevent fraud and to provide buyers with certain types of information. In some cases, these protections mirror those provided in non–real estate sales. The disclosure requirements of the Truth-in-Lending Act apply to a number of real estate transactions, as will be discussed shortly.

Interstate Land Sales Full Disclosure Act. The Interstate Land Sales Full Disclosure Act[20] was passed by Congress in 1968, and it is administered by the Department of Housing and Urban Development (HUD). The purpose of the act is to ensure disclosure of certain information to consumers so that they can make reasoned decisions about land purchases. The act is similar to the Securities Act of 1933 in both purpose and design. The act requires anyone proposing to sell or lease one hundred or more lots of unimproved land, if the sale or lease is to be part of a common promotional plan, to file an

16. 16 C.F.R. Sections 435.1–435.2.
17. 39 U.S.C. Section 3009.

18. 16 C.F.R. Sections 455.1–455.5.
19. 16 C.F.R. Section 453.2.21. 15 U.S.C. Sections 1601–1693r.
20. 15 U.S.C. Sections 1701–1720.

initial statement of record with HUD's Office of Interstate Land Sales Registration.

The act only applies if the promotional plan can be deemed part of interstate commerce. As in cases involving securities, this is generally an easy requirement to meet. For example, even strictly local sales might be considered interstate commerce if transacted in part over the phone; although the calls might be local, the phone lines traverse state boundaries. For the same reason, use of the mail system is likely to ensure that a promotional plan is in the stream of interstate commerce.

Once the initial statement is filed, it must be approved by HUD before the developer can begin to offer the land for sale or lease. The act also provides purchasers with a private right of action for the land promoter's fraud, misrepresentation, or noncompliance with pertinent provisions of the act. Criminal penalties are provided under the act, and HUD is given certain rights with regard to inspections, injunctions, and prosecution of offenses. Three provisions of the act give purchasers rights of rescission (cancellation).

Real Estate Settlement Procedures Act.   For many individuals, purchasing a home involves a bewildering array of procedures and requirements. Settlement (finalizing a real estate transaction) may require title insurance, attorneys' fees, appraisal fees, taxes, insurance, and brokers' fees. To aid home buyers, federal legislation requires specific disclosures regarding settlement procedures. The 1976 revisions of the Real Estate Settlement Procedures Act of 1974 make the following stipulations:

1. Within three business days after a person applies for a mortgage loan, the lender must send a booklet prepared by HUD that explains the settlement procedures, describes the costs to the potential buyer, and outlines the applicant's legal rights.
2. Within the three-day period, the lender must give an estimate of most of the settlement costs.
3. The lender must clearly identify individuals or firms that the applicant is required to use for legal or other services, including title search and insurance.
4. If the loan is approved, the lender must provide a truth-in-lending statement that shows the annual percentage rate on the mortgage loan.
5. Lenders, title insurers, and others involved in the transaction cannot pay kickbacks for business referred to them.

SECTION 4

Credit Protection

Because of the extensive use of credit by American consumers, credit protection has become an especially important area regulated by consumer protection legislation. One of the most significant statutes regulating the credit and credit-card industry is Title I of the Consumer Credit Protection Act (CCPA),[21] which was passed by Congress in 1968 and is commonly referred to as the Truth-in-Lending Act (TILA).

THE TRUTH-IN-LENDING ACT

The TILA is basically a *disclosure law*. It is administered by the Federal Reserve Board and requires sellers and lenders to disclose credit terms or loan terms so that individuals can shop around for the best financing arrangements. TILA requirements apply only to persons who, in the ordinary course of business, lend money, sell on credit, or arrange for the extension of credit. Thus, sales or loans made between two consumers do not come under the protection of the act. Additionally, only debtors who are natural persons (as opposed to the artificial "person" of the corporation) are protected by this law; other legal entities are not.

The disclosure requirements are contained in Regulation Z, which, as mentioned earlier in this chapter, was promulgated by the Federal Reserve Board. If the contracting parties are subject to the TILA, the requirements of Regulation Z apply to any transaction involving an installment sales contract in which payment is to be made in more than four installments. Transactions subject to Regulation Z typically include installment loans, retail and installment sales, car loans, home-improvement loans, and certain real estate loans if the amount of financing is less than $25,000.

Under the provisions of the TILA, all of the terms of a credit instrument must be clearly and conspicuously disclosed. The TILA provides for contract rescission (cancellation) if a creditor fails to follow *exactly* the procedures required by the act.[22] TILA requirements are strictly enforced.

---

21. 12 U.S.C. Sections 2601–2617.
22. Note, however, that amendments to the TILA enacted in 1995 prevent borrowers from rescinding loans for minor clerical errors in closing documents [15 U.S.C. Sections 1605, 1631, 1635, 1640, and 1641].

In the following case, a consumer sued a lender, alleging TILA violations. The lender claimed that the consumer was not entitled to relief because she had lied on her credit application.

CASE 24.2   Purtle v. Eldridge Auto Sales, Inc.

United States
Court of Appeals,
Sixth Circuit, 1996.
91 F.3d 797.

BACKGROUND AND FACTS *Renee Purtle bought a 1986 Chevrolet Blazer from Eldridge Auto Sales, Inc. To finance the purchase through Eldridge, Purtle filled out a credit application on which she misrepresented her employment status. Based on the misrepresentation, Eldridge extended credit. In the credit contract, Eldridge did not disclose the finance charge, the annual percentage rate, or the total sales price or use the term "amount financed," as the TILA and its regulations require. Purtle defaulted on the loan, and Eldridge repossesed the vehicle. Purtle filed a suit in a federal district court against Eldridge, alleging violations of the TILA. The court awarded Purtle $1,000 in damages, plus attorneys' fees and costs. Eldridge appealed, arguing in part that Purtle was not entitled to damages because she had committed fraud on her credit application.*

**IN THE LANGUAGE
OF THE COURT**

FORESTER, District Judge.

*   *   *   *

*   *   * [T]he TILA imposes mandatory disclosure requirements on those who extend credit to consumers. *   *   * In the event that a creditor fails to disclose any of the credit terms required under the TILA and its regulations, a consumer may bring a civil action against the creditor. If a violation is proven, the consumer may recover twice the amount of the finance charge (but not less than $100.00 nor more than $1,000.00). The purpose of the statutory recovery is "to encourage lawsuits by individual consumers as a means of enforcing creditor compliance with the Act." The TILA also permits recovery of reasonable attorney's fees and costs. *   *   *

*   *   * [O]nce a court finds a violation of the TILA, no matter how technical, the court has no discretion as to the imposition of civil liability. *   *   * Based on the unambiguous statutory language, it is clear that *   *   * the district court appropriately awarded Purtle the statutory penalty set out above.

**DECISION
AND REMEDY**

The U.S. Court of Appeals for the Sixth Circuit affirmed the lower court's award. The lender was required to pay damages based on its violation of the TILA, despite the borrower's fraud.

Equal Credit Opportunity. In 1974, the Equal Credit Opportunity Act (ECOA)[23] was enacted as an amendment to the TILA. The ECOA prohibits the denial of credit solely on the basis of race, religion, national origin, color, gender, marital status, or age. The act also prohibits credit discrimination on the basis of whether an individual receives certain forms of income, such as public-assistance benefits. Under the ECOA, a creditor may not require the signature of an applicant's spouse, other than as a joint applicant, on a credit instrument if the applicant qualifies under the creditor's standards of creditworthiness for the amount and terms of the credit request. Creditors are permitted to ask for any information from a credit applicant except that which could be used for the type of discrimination covered in the act or its amendments. In the following case, the issue concerns whether a creditor violated the ECOA by requiring the signature of an applicant's spouse on a loan guaranty.

---

23. 15 U.S.C. Sections 1691–1691f.

CASE 24.3   Federal Deposit Insurance Corp. v. Medmark, Inc.

United States
 District Court,
District of Kansas, 1995.
897 F.Supp. 511.

BACKGROUND AND FACTS   *Bruce Shalberg was a director of Medmark, Inc., a small medical equipment supply company. As a condition of a loan to Medmark, the Merchants Bank asked Shalberg—whom the bank found to be independently creditworthy—to sign a guaranty of repayment. Later, for another loan, the bank required Shalberg's wife, Mary— who had nothing to do with Medmark—to sign the guaranty. When the bank failed, the Federal Deposit Insurance Corporation (FDIC) took over its assets. The FDIC filed a suit in a federal district court against Medmark and the Shalbergs to recover the amount of the loans. Mary Shalberg filed a motion for summary judgment, contending that the bank, in re- quiring her to sign the guaranty, had violated the Equal Credit Opportunity Act (ECOA).*

IN THE LANGUAGE
OF THE COURT

VRATIL, District Judge.
      *   *   *   *

[A regulation issued under the ECOA] specifically provides that a creditor may not require the signature of an applicant's spouse if the applicant qualifies under the credi- tor's standards of creditworthiness for the amount and terms of the credit requested. The FDIC argues that the Bank "obviously" did not believe Mr. Shalberg to be independ- ently creditworthy   *   *   * . [But the] record contains no evidence that Mr. Shalberg was not creditworthy, in his own right, in the Bank's eyes. Summary judgment in favor of Mrs. Shalberg is therefore appropriate.

DECISION
AND REMEDY

The federal district court issued a summary judgment in favor of Mary Shalberg, re- lieving her from any obligation on the loans. The creditor violated the ECOA by requiring Shalberg's signature on the loan guaranty.

Credit-Card Rules.   The TILA also contains provi- sions regarding credit cards. One provision limits the liability of a cardholder to $50 per card for unauthor- ized charges made before the creditor is notified that the card has been lost. Another provision prohibits a credit-card company from billing a consumer for any unauthorized charges if the credit card was improp- erly issued by the company; for example, if a con- sumer receives an unsolicited credit card in the mail and the card is later stolen and used by the thief to make purchases, the consumer to whom the card was sent will not be liable for the unauthorized charges.

Further provisions of the act concern billing dis- putes related to credit-card purchases. If a debtor thinks that an error has occurred in billing or wishes to withhold payment for a faulty product purchased by credit card, the act outlines specific procedures for both the consumer and the credit-card company to follow in settling the dispute.

Consumer Leases.   The Consumer Leasing Act (CLA) of 1988[24] amended the TILA to provide pro-

tection for consumers who lease automobiles and other goods. The CLA applies to those who lease or arrange to lease consumer goods in the ordinary course of their business. The act applies only if the goods are priced at $25,000 or less and if the lease term exceeds four months. The CLA and its implementing regulation, Regulation M,[25] require lessors to disclose in writing all of the material terms of the lease.

THE FAIR CREDIT REPORTING ACT

In 1970, to protect consumers against inaccurate credit reporting, Congress enacted the Fair Credit Reporting Act (FCRA).[26] The act provides that consumer credit reporting agencies may issue credit reports to users only for specified purposes, including the extension of credit, the issuance of insurance policies, compliance with a court order, and in re- sponse to a consumer's request for a copy of his or her own credit report. The act further provides that any time a consumer is denied credit or insurance on the

---

24. 15 U.S.C. Sections 1667–1667e.

25. 12 C.F.R. Part 213.
26. 15 U.S.C. Sections 1681–1681t.

basis of the consumer's credit report, or is charged more than others ordinarily would be for credit or insurance, the consumer must be notified of that fact and of the name and address of the credit reporting agency that issued the credit report.

Under the act, consumers may request the source of any information being given out by a credit agency, as well as the identity of anyone who has received an agency's report. Consumers are also permitted to have access to the information contained about them in a credit reporting agency's files. If a consumer discovers that a credit reporting agency's files contain inaccurate information about the consumer's credit standing, the agency, on the consumer's written request, must investigate the matter and delete any unverifiable or erroneous information within a reasonable period of time.

An agency that fails to comply with the act is liable for actual damages, plus additional damages not to exceed $1,000 and attorneys' fees.[27] Damages are also available against anyone who uses a credit report for an improper purpose, as well as banks, credit-card companies, and other businesses that report information to credit agencies and do not respond adequately to customer complaints.

The following case illustrates the liability exposure of companies that maintain credit reports and ratings.

_____
27. 15 U.S.C. Section 1681n.

CASE 24.4 Guimond v. Trans Union Credit Information Co.

United States
Court of Appeals,
Ninth Circuit, 1995.
45 F.3d 1329.

HISTORICAL AND ECONOMIC SETTING *A credit report reflects a consumer's bill-paying history. It lists the consumer's creditors and whether he or she has made payments on time. Inaccurate information can keep an individual from obtaining credit, because lenders rely on credit reports when deciding whether to extend credit. The major credit reporting agencies include the Trans Union Credit Information Company.*

BACKGROUND AND FACTS *Renie Guimond learned of inaccuracies that Trans Union Credit Information Company had in its file on her. She notified Trans Union, which told her the file would be corrected; however, it was not corrected for a year. Guimond filed a suit in a federal district court against Trans Union, in part to recover damages under the Fair Credit Reporting Act (FCRA) for the company's failure to correct the information more quickly. Trans Union countered that Guimond had no claim, because she had not been denied credit before the information was corrected. The court ruled in favor of Trans Union, and Guimond appealed.*

IN THE LANGUAGE
OF THE COURT

FONG, District Judge:
*   *   *   *

[The FCRA] states: Whenever a consumer reporting agency prepares a consumer report it shall follow reasonable procedures to assure maximum possible accuracy of the information *   *   * .
*   *   *   *

Liability *   *   * is predicated on the reasonableness of the credit reporting agency's procedures *   *   * .

*   *   * [T]he focus should not have been on Guimond's damage claims. Rather the inquiry should have centered on whether Trans Union's procedures for preparing Guimond's file contained reasonable procedures to prevent inaccuracies. Guimond has made out a *prima facie* case under [the FCRA] by showing that there were inaccuracies in her credit report. The district court was then required to consider whether Trans Union was liable under [the FCRA] before it determined that Guimond had suffered no recoverable damages.

The U.S. Court of Appeals for the Ninth Circuit reversed this part of the lower court's ruling and remanded the case for trial. The agency could be held liable if its procedures to assure the accuracy of its information were not reasonable.

THE FAIR DEBT COLLECTION PRACTICES ACT

In 1977, Congress enacted the Fair Debt Collection Practices Act (FDCPA)[28] in an attempt to curb what were perceived to be abuses by collection agencies. The act applies only to specialized debt-collection agencies that regularly attempt to collect debts on behalf of someone else, usually for a percentage of the amount owed. Creditors attempting to collect debts are not covered by the act unless, by misrepresenting themselves, they cause debtors to believe they are collection agencies. The act explicitly prohibits a collection agency from using any of the following tactics:

1. Contacting the debtor at the debtor's place of employment if the debtor's employer objects.
2. Contacting the debtor during inconvenient or unusual times (for example, calling the debtor at three o'clock in the morning) or at any time if the debtor is being represented by an attorney.
3. Contacting third parties other than the debtor's parents, spouse, or financial adviser about payment of a debt unless a court authorizes such action.
4. Using harassment or intimidation (for example, using abusive language or threatening violence) or employing false or misleading information (for example, posing as a police officer).
5. Communicating with the debtor at any time after receiving notice that the debtor is refusing to pay the debt, except to advise the debtor of further action to be taken by the collection agency.

---

28. 15 U.S.C. Section 1692.

The FDCPA also requires a collection agency to include a **validation notice** whenever it initially contacts a debtor for payment of a debt or within five days of that initial contact. The notice must state that the debtor has thirty days within which to dispute the debt and to request a written verification of the debt from the collection agency. The debtor's request for debt validation must be in writing.

The enforcement of the FDCPA is primarily the responsibility of the Federal Trade Commission. The act provides that a debt collector that fails to comply with the act is liable for actual damages, plus additional damages not to exceed $1,000[29] and attorneys' fees.

Cases brought under the FDCPA often raise questions as to who qualifies as a debt collector or debt-collection agency subject to the act. For example, for several years it was not clear whether attorneys who attempted to collect debts owed to their clients were subject to the FDCPA's provisions. In 1995, the United States Supreme Court addressed this issue to resolve conflicting opinions in the lower courts. The Court held that an attorney who regularly tries to obtain payment of consumer debts through legal proceedings meets the FDCPA's definition of "debt collector."[30]

Another question that sometimes arises in the context of FDCPA litigation has to do with what, exactly, constitutes a "debt." In the following case, the court considered whether a dishonored check constituted a "debt" within the meaning of the FDCPA.

---

29. According to the U.S. Court of Appeals for the Sixth Circuit, the $1,000 limit on damages applies to each lawsuit, not to each violation. See *Wright v. Finance Service of Norwalk, Inc.*, 22 F.3d 647 (6th Cir. 1994).
30. *Heintz v. Jenkins*, 514 U.S. 291, 115 S.Ct. 1489, 131 L.Ed.2d 395 (1995).

CASE 24.5   Snow v. Jesse L. Riddle, P.C.

United States
Court of Appeals,
Tenth Circuit, 1998.
143 F.3d 1350.
**http://www.kscourts.
org/ca10**[a]

HISTORICAL AND SOCIAL SETTING   *The FDCPA defines debt as "any obligatory or alleged obligation of a consumer to pay money arising out of a transaction in which the money, property, insurance, or services which are the subject of the transaction are primarily for personal, family, or household purposes, whether or not such obligation has been reduced to judgment."*[b] *At one time, it was generally held that the type of transaction giving rise to a debt, within this definition, is the same type of transaction that is dealt with in all other parts of the Consumer Credit Protection Act: a transaction that involves*

---

a. Washburn University School of Law maintains this Web site. Click on "Finding lists by plaintiff/defendant case name." After the page loads, scroll to the case name and click on it to access the opinion.
b. 15 U.S.C. Section 1692a(5).

an offer or extension of credit to a consumer. By the time the U.S. Court of Appeals for the Tenth Circuit decided this case, however, this view had changed.

BACKGROUND AND FACTS   *At a Circle-K store, Alan Snow paid for merchandise with his personal check in the amount of $23.12. Circle-K deposited the check at its bank, but the check was dishonored because of insufficient funds. Circle-K sent the returned check to its attorney, Jesse L. Riddle, P.C., for collection. In a letter to Snow, Riddle wrote that "the check amount, along with a service fee of $15, must be paid within seven (7) days of this notice. If it is not paid, * * * [a] suit [will] be filed." Snow paid the check and then filed a suit in a federal district court against Riddle. Snow alleged in part that Riddle's letter violated the FDCPA because it did not contain a "validation notice." Riddle filed a motion to dismiss on the ground that the FDCPA does not cover a dishonored check because it is not an "offer or extension of credit." The court granted the motion, and Snow appealed to the U.S. Court of Appeals for the Tenth Circuit.*

IN THE LANGUAGE OF THE COURT

McWILLIAMS, Senior Circuit Judge.

*   *   *   *

[The FDCPA] provides as follows:

*   *   * Abusive debt collection practices contribute to the number of personal bankruptcies, to marital instability, to the loss of jobs, and to invasions of individual privacy. *   *   * It is the purpose of [the FDCPA] to eliminate abusive debt collection practices by debt collectors *   *   * .

*   *   *   *

*   *   * [A] payment obligation arising from a dishonored check create[s] a "debt" triggering the protections of the [FDCPA]. *   *   * [A]n offer or extension of credit is not required for a payment obligation to constitute a "debt" under the [FDCPA]. *   *   *

*   *   *   *

*   *   * Under the "plain meaning" test, it would seem to us that a "debt" is created where one obtains goods and gives a dishonored check in return therefor.

DECISION AND REMEDY   *The U.S. Court of Appeals for the Tenth Circuit reversed the decision of the lower court and remanded the case. The appellate court held that a dishonored check constitutes a debt within the meaning of the FDCPA.*

GARNISHMENT OF WAGES

Despite the increasing number of protections afforded debtors, creditors are not without means of securing payment on debts. One of these is the right to garnish a debtor's wages after the debt has gone uncollected for a prolonged period. Recall from Chapter 16 that *garnishment* is the legal procedure by which a creditor may collect on a debt by directly attaching, or seizing, a portion of the debtor's assets (such as wages) that are in the possession of a third party (such as an employer).

State law provides the basis for a process of garnishment, but the law varies among the states as to how easily garnishment can be obtained. Indeed, a few states, such as Texas, prohibit garnishment of wages altogether except for child support. In addition, constitutional due process and federal legislation

under the TILA provide further protections against abuse.[31] In general, the debtor is entitled to notice and an opportunity to be heard in a process of garnishment. Moreover, wages cannot be garnished beyond 25 percent of the debtor's after-tax earnings, and the garnishment must leave the debtor with at least a specified minimum income.

SECTION 5

Consumer Health and Safety

Laws discussed earlier regarding the labeling and packaging of products go a long way toward promoting consumer health and safety. There is a significant

---

31. 15 U.S.C. Sections 1671–1677.

distinction between regulating the information dispensed about a product and regulating the content of the product, however. The classic example is tobacco products. Tobacco products have not been altered by regulation or banned outright despite their obvious hazards. What has been regulated are the warnings that producers are required to give consumers about the hazards of tobacco.[32] This section focuses on laws that regulate the actual products made available to consumers.

THE FEDERAL FOOD, DRUG AND COSMETIC ACT

The first federal legislation regulating food and drugs was enacted in 1906 as the Pure Food and Drugs Act. That law, as amended in 1938, exists presently as the Federal Food, Drug and Cosmetic Act (FFDCA).[33] The act protects consumers against adulterated and misbranded foods and drugs. More recent amendments have added substantive and procedural requirements to the act. In its present form, the act establishes food standards, specifies safe levels of potentially hazardous food additives, and sets classifications of food and food advertising.

Most of these statutory requirements are monitored and enforced by the Food and Drug Administration (FDA). Under an extensive set of procedures established by the FDA, drugs must be shown to be effective as well as safe before they may be marketed to the public, and the use of some food additives suspected of being carcinogenic is prohibited. A 1976 amendment to the FFDCA[34] authorizes the FDA to regulate medical devices, such as pacemakers and other health devices and equipment, and to withdraw from the market any such device that is mislabeled.

THE CONSUMER PRODUCT SAFETY ACT

Consumer product-safety legislation began in 1953 with the passage of the Flammable Fabrics Act, which prohibits the sale of highly flammable clothing or materials. Over the next two decades, Congress enacted legislation regarding the design or composition of specific classes of products. Then, in 1972, Congress, by enacting the Consumer Product Safety Act,[35] created a comprehensive scheme of regulation over matters of consumer safety. The act also established far-reaching authority over consumer safety under the Consumer Product Safety Commission (CPSC).

The CPSC conducts research on the safety of individual products, and it maintains a clearinghouse of information on the risks associated with various consumer products. The Consumer Product Safety Act authorizes the CPSC to set standards for consumer products and to ban the manufacture and sale of any product that it deems to be potentially hazardous to consumers. The CPSC also has authority to remove from the market any products it believes to be imminently hazardous and to require manufacturers to report on any products already sold or intended for sale if the products have proved to be dangerous. The CPSC also has authority to administer other product-safety legislation, such as the Child Protection and Toy Safety Act of 1969[36] and the Federal Hazardous Substances Act of 1960.[37]

The CPSC's authority is sufficiently broad to allow it to ban any product that it believes poses an "unreasonable risk" to consumers. Some of the products that the CPSC has banned include various types of fireworks, cribs, and toys, as well as many products containing asbestos or vinyl chloride.

SECTION 6

State Consumer Protection Laws

Thus far, our primary focus has been on federal legislation. State laws, however, often provide more sweeping and significant protections for the consumer than do federal laws. The warranty and unconscionability provisions of the Uniform Commercial Code (discussed in Chapter 11) offer important protections for consumers against unfair practices on the part of sellers and lessors. The Magnuson-Moss Warranty Act of 1975[38] supplements the UCC provisions in cases involving both a

---

32. We are ignoring recent civil litigation concerning the liability of tobacco product manufacturers for injuries that arise from the use of tobacco.
33. 21 U.S.C. Sections 301–393.
34. 21 U.S.C. Sections 352(o), 360(j), 360(k), and 360c–360k.

35. 15 U.S.C. Sections 2051–2083.
36. This act consists of amendments to 15 U.S.C. Sections 1261, 1262, and 1274.
37. 15 U.S.C. Sections 1261–1277.
38. 15 U.S.C. Sections 2301–2312.

consumer transaction of at least $10 and an express written warranty.

Far less widely adopted than the UCC is the Uniform Consumer Credit Code (UCCC). The UCCC has provisions concerning truth in lending, maximum credit ceilings, door-to-door sales, fine-print clauses, and other practices affecting consumer transactions.

Virtually all states have specific consumer protection acts, often titled "deceptive trade practices acts."

Although state consumer protection statutes vary widely in their provisions, a common thread runs through most of them. Typically, state consumer protection laws are directed at deceptive trade practices, such as a seller's providing false or misleading information to consumers. As just mentioned, some of the legislation provides broad protection for consumers. A prime example is the Texas Deceptive Trade Practices Act of 1973, which forbids a seller from selling to a buyer anything that the buyer does not need or cannot afford.

TERMS AND CONCEPTS TO REVIEW

bait-and-switch advertising 523

cease-and-desist order 523

consumer law 522

counteradvertising 524

multiple product orders 524

Regulation Z 526

validation notice 532

QUESTIONS AND CASE PROBLEMS

24–1. UNSOLICITED MERCHANDISE. Andrew, a resident of California, received a flyer in the U.S. mail announcing a new line of regional cookbooks distributed by the Every-Kind Cookbook Co. Andrew was not interested and threw the flyer away. Two days later, Andrew received in the mail an introductory cookbook entitled *Lower Mongolian Regional Cookbook,* as announced in the flyer, on a "trial basis" from Every-Kind. Andrew was not interested but did not go to the trouble to return the cookbook. Every-Kind demanded payment of $20.95 for the *Lower Mongolian Regional Cookbook.* Discuss whether Andrew can be required to pay for the cookbook.

24–2. CONSUMER PROTECTION. Fireside Rocking Chair Co. advertised in the newspaper a special sale price of $159 on machine-caned rocking chairs. In the advertisement was a drawing of a natural-wood rocking chair with a caned back and seat. The average person would not be able to tell from the drawing whether the rocking chair was machine caned or hand caned. Hand-caned rocking chairs sold for $259. Lowell and Celia Gudmundson went to Fireside because they had seen the ad for the machine-caned rocking chair and were very interested in purchasing one. The Gudmundsons arrived on the morning the sale began. Fireside's agent said the only machine-caned rocking chairs he had were painted lime green and were priced at $159. He imme-

diately turned the Gudmundsons' attention to the hand-caned rocking chairs, praising their quality and pointing out that for the extra $100, the hand-caned chairs were surely a good value. The Gudmundsons, preferring the natural-wood machine-caned rocking chair for $159 as pictured in the advertisement, said they would like to order one. The Fireside agent said he could not order a natural-wood, machine-caned rocking chair. Discuss fully whether Fireside has violated any consumer protection laws.

24–3. DOOR-TO-DOOR SALES. On June 28, a sales representative for Renowned Books called on the Gonchars at their home. After a very persuasive sales pitch on the part of the sales agent, the Gonchars agreed in writing to purchase a twenty-volume set of historical encyclopedias from Renowned Books for a total of $299. An initial down payment of $35 was required, with the remainder of the price to be paid in monthly payments over a one-year period. Two days later the Gonchars, having second thoughts, contacted the book company and stated that they had decided to rescind the contract. Renowned Books said this would be impossible. Has Renowned Books violated any consumer law by not allowing the Gonchars to rescind their contract? Explain.

24–4. TRUTH IN LENDING. Michael and Patricia Jensen purchased a new 1989 Ford Tempo from Ray

Kim Ford, Inc. The Jensens signed a retail installment contract that provided for an estimated trade-in value of $800 for their old car. When the traded-in car turned out to be worth $1,388.08, Ray Kim prepared a second retail installment contract without the Jensens' knowledge. The second contract, although it credited the increased trade-in value of the car, compensated for this credit by increasing the interest rate, increasing the sales price of the car, and making other adjustments so that the second contract basically called for future cash payments by the Jensens of about the same amount as the first contract. In effect, the second contract gave the Jensens almost no benefit for the increased value of their traded-in car. The Jensens made payments under the contract until they noticed the minor difference in monthly payments, asked for a copy of the contract, and realized that it was not the contract that they had signed. The Jensens sued Ray Kim, alleging that the second contract was a forgery and that Ray Kim had violated the Truth-in-Lending Act (TILA) by not disclosing to them the credit terms of the second contract. Has Ray Kim violated the TILA? If the Jensens choose to adopt the terms of the second contract, despite the forgery, has the act been violated? Discuss fully. [*Jensen v. Ray Kim Ford, Inc.*, 920 F.2d 3 (7th Cir. 1990)]

24–5. DECEPTIVE ADVERTISING. Thompson Medical Co. marketed a new cream called Aspercreme that was supposed to help arthritis victims and others suffering from minor aches. Aspercreme contained no aspirin. Thompson's television advertisements stated that the product provided "the strong relief of aspirin right where you hurt" and showed the announcer holding up aspirin tablets as well as a tube of Aspercreme. The Federal Trade Commission held that the advertisements were misleading, because they led consumers to believe that Aspercreme contained aspirin. Thompson Medical Co. appealed this decision and argued that the advertisements never actually stated that the product contained aspirin. How should the court rule? Discuss. [*Thompson Medical Co. v. Federal Trade Commission*, 791 F.2d 189 (D.C.Cir. 1986)]

24–6. DECEPTIVE ADVERTISING. Dennis and Janice Geiger saw an advertisement in a newspaper for a Kimball Whitney spinet piano on sale for $699 at the McCormick Piano & Organ Co. Because the style of the piano drawn in the advertisement matched their furniture, the Geigers were particularly interested in the Kimball. When they went to McCormick Piano & Organ, however, they learned that the drawing closely resembled another, more expensive Crest piano and that the Kimball spinet looked quite different from the piano sketched in the drawing. The salesperson told the Geigers that she was unable to order a spinet piano of the style they requested. When the Geigers asked for the names of other customers who had purchased the advertised pianos, the salesperson became extremely upset and said she would not, under any circumstances, sell the Geigers a piano. The Geigers then brought suit against the piano store, alleging that the store had engaged in deceptive advertising in violation of Indiana law. Was the McCormick Piano & Organ Co. guilty of deceptive advertising? Explain. [*McCormick Piano & Organ Co. v. Geiger*, 412 N.E.2d 842 (Ind.App. 1980)]

24–7. EQUAL CREDIT OPPORTUNITY. The Riggs National Bank of Washington, D.C., lent more than $11 million to Samuel Linch and Albert Randolph. To obtain the loan, Linch and Randolph provided personal financial statements. Linch's statement included substantial assets that he owned jointly with his wife, Marcia. As a condition of the loan, Riggs required that Marcia, as well as Samuel and Albert, sign a personal guaranty for repayment. When the borrowers defaulted, Riggs filed a suit in a federal district court to recover its money, based on the personal guaranties. The court ruled against the borrowers, who appealed. On what basis might the borrowers argue that Riggs violated the Equal Credit Opportunity Act? [*Riggs National Bank of Washington, D.C. v. Linch*, 36 F.3d 370 (4th Cir. 1994)]

24–8. FAIR DEBT COLLECTION. A condominium association, Rancho Santa Margarita Recreation and Landscape Corp., attempted unsuccessfully to collect an assessment fee from Andrew Ladick. The association referred the matter to the Law Offices of Gerald J. Van Gemert. Van Gemert sent Ladick a letter demanding payment of the fee. The letter did not include a "validation notice," as required by the Fair Debt Collection Practices Act (FDCPA), nor did it disclose that Van Gemert was attempting to collect a debt and that any information obtained would be used for that purpose. Ladick filed a suit in a federal district court against Van Gemert and his office, alleging violations of the FDCPA. Van Gemert filed a motion for summary judgment on the ground that the assessment was not a "debt," as defined by the FDCPA, in part because there was no "transaction," as required by the FDCPA definition, out of which Ladick's obligation arose. Will the court agree with Van Gemert? Why or why not? [*Ladick v. Van Gemert*, 146 F.3d 1205 (10th Cir. 1998)]

24–9. FAIR DEBT COLLECTION. Gloria Mahon incurred a bill of $279.70 for medical services rendered by Dr. Larry Bowen. For more than two years, Bowen sent monthly billing statements to the Mahons at their home address (where they had lived for forty-five years). Getting no response, Bowen assigned the collection of their account to Credit Bureau of Placer County, Inc. Credit Bureau uses computerized collection tracking and filing software, known as Columbia Ultimate Business Systems (CUBS). CUBS automatically generates standardized collection notices and acts as an electronic filing system for each account, recording all collection activities, including which notices are sent to whom and on what date. Credit Bureau employees monitor the activity, routinely noting whether an envelope is returned undelivered. Credit Bureau mailed three CUBS—generated notices to the Mahons. According to Credit Bureau's records, the notices were not returned and the Mahons did not respond. Credit Bureau reported the Mahons' account as delinquent. The Mahons filed a suit in a federal district court against Credit Bureau, alleging in part that the agency had failed to send a validation notice, as required by the Fair Debt Collection Practices Act. Credit Bureau filed a motion for summary judgment. Should a notice be considered sent only if a debtor acknowledges its receipt? Why or why not? [*Mahon v. Credit Bureau of Placer County, Inc.*, 171 F.3d 1197 (9th Cir. 1999)]

24–10. IN YOUR COURT

Kimberly Sage saw an advertisement in a newspaper for a Kimball spinet piano on sale for $899 at a local piano store. Because the style of the piano drawn in the advertisement matched her furniture, Sage was particularly interested in the Kimball. When she went to the piano store, however, she learned that the drawing closely resembled·

another, more expensive Crest piano and that the Kimball spinet looked quite different from the piano sketched in the drawing. The salesperson told Sage that he was unable to order a spinet piano of the style Sage requested. When Sage asked for the names of other customers who had purchased the advertised piano, the salesperson became extremely upset and said that he would not, under any circumstances, sell Sage a piano. Sage then brought suit against the piano store in a state court, alleging that the store had engaged in deceptive advertising in violation of state law. Assume that you are the judge in the trial court hearing this case and answer the following questions:

(a) Assume that bait-and-switch advertising is illegal under your state's deceptive practices act. Did the piano store's actions constitute bait-and-switch advertising? Why or why not?

LAW ON THE WEB

For updated links to resources available on the Web, as well as a variety of other materials, visit this text's Web site at http://wleb.westbuslaw.com.

For current articles concerning consumer issues, go to the Alexander Law Firm's "Consumer Law Page," which is online at

http://consumerlawpage.com/intro.html

The law firm of Arent Fox offers extensive information relating to advertising law at

http://www.advertisinglaw.com

LEGAL RESEARCH EXERCISES ON THE WEB

Go to http://wleb.westbuslaw.com, the Web site that accompanies this text. Select "Internet Applications," and then click on "Chapter 24." There you will find the following Internet research exercise that you can perform to learn more about consumer and environmental law:

Activity 24–1: Consumer Law

CHAPTER 25

Environmental Law

We now turn to a discussion of the various ways in which businesses are regulated by the government in the interest of protecting the environment. Concern over the degradation of the environment has increased over time in response to the environmental effects of population growth, urbanization, and industrialization. Environmental protection is not without a price, however. For many businesses, the costs of complying with environmental regulations are high, and for some they are too high. There is constant tension between the desirability of increasing profits and productivity and the need to attain higher quality in the environment.

Environmental law—all law pertaining to environmental protection—is not new. Indeed, the federal government began to regulate some activities, such as those involving the pollution of navigable waterways, in the late 1800s. In the last few decades, however, the body of environmental law has expanded substantially as government has attempted to control industrial waste and to protect certain natural resources and endangered species.

In this chapter, we first discuss the common law actions that can be brought against business firms and individuals for damages caused by polluting activities. The remainder of the chapter examines the various statutes and regulations that have been created to protect the environment.

SECTION 1

Common Law Actions

Common law remedies against environmental pollution originated centuries ago in England. Those responsible for operations that created dirt, smoke, noxious odors, noise, or toxic substances were sometimes held liable under common law theories of nuisance or negligence. Today, injured individuals continue to rely on the common law to obtain damages and injunctions against business polluters. (Statutory remedies are also available, a topic that we treat later.)

NUISANCE

Under the common law doctrine of **nuisance**, persons may be held liable if they use their property in a manner that unreasonably interferes with others' rights to use or enjoy their own property. In these situations, it is common for courts to balance the equities between the harm caused by the pollution and the costs of stopping it.

Courts have often denied injunctive relief on the ground that the hardships to be imposed on the polluter and on the community are greater than the hardships to be suffered by the plaintiff. For example, a factory that causes neighboring landowners to suffer from smoke, dirt, and vibrations may be left in operation if it is the core of a local economy. The injured parties may be awarded only money damages. These damages may include compensation for the decreased value of their property that results from the factory's operation.

A property owner may be given relief from pollution in situations in which he or she can identify a distinct harm separate from that affecting the general public. This harm is referred to as a "private" nuisance. Under the common law, citizens were denied standing (access to the courts—see Chapter 2) unless they suffered a harm distinct from the harm suffered by the public at large. Some states still require this. Therefore, a group of citizens who wished to stop a new development that would cause significant water pollution was denied access to the courts on the ground that the harm to them did not differ from the harm to the general public.[1] A public authority (such as a state's attorney general) can sue to abate a "public" nuisance.

In the following case, landowners sued their neighbor under the doctrine of nuisance.

1. *Save the Bay Committee, Inc. v. Mayor of City of Savannah*, 227 Ga. 436, 181 S.E.2d 351 (1971).

CASE 25.1   Maddocks v. Giles

Supreme Judicial Court
of Maine, 1996.
686 A.2d 1069.

BACKGROUND AND FACTS *Sewall and Janice Maddocks owned property next to a gravel pit owned and operated by Elbridge Giles, doing business as E. A. Giles & Son. Below the surface of the Maddockses' property was a subterranean spring that produced large quantities of high-quality water. Giles's excavation in the gravel pit caused the spring to dry up. The Maddockses filed a suit against Giles in a Maine state court, seeking damages on the ground that the excavation was a nuisance because the excavation caused a disruption of the flow of the spring. The court dismissed the complaint, and the Maddockses appealed to the state's highest court, the Supreme Judicial Court of Maine.*

IN THE LANGUAGE
OF THE COURT

GLASSMAN, Justice.

*   *   *   *

Although we recognize the general principle that a property owner may use his land as he pleases for all lawful purposes, there is a long standing limitation of this rule preventing a landowner from drastically altering the flow of a watercourse. *   *   * A watercourse cannot be stopped up or diverted to the injury of other[s]. There is a public or natural [right] in such a stream, belonging to all persons whose lands are benefitted by it. *   *   * Application of these principles to the facts of this case leads us to conclude that the trial court erred when it dismissed the Maddockses' complaint.

The complaint alleges that Giles' excavation activities created a nuisance that caused a disruption of the flow of a subterranean spring from aquifers [subsurface water] beneath Giles' property into the Maddockses' property. *   *   * [W]e conclude that the complaint sufficiently alleges a nuisance by the disruption of a watercourse *   *   * .

DECISION
AND REMEDY

The Supreme Judicial Court of Maine vacated (set aside) the lower court's dismissal of the Maddockses' complaint. Disruption of the flow of a subterranean spring may constitute a nuisance. The case could proceed to trial.

NEGLIGENCE AND STRICT LIABILITY

An injured party may sue a business polluter in tort under the negligence and strict liability theories discussed in Chapter 12. The basis for a negligence action is a business's alleged failure to use reasonable care toward a party whose injury was foreseeable and, of course, caused by the lack of reasonable care. For example, employees might sue an employer whose failure to use proper pollution controls contaminated the air, causing the employees to suffer respiratory illnesses. A developing area of tort law involves **toxic torts**—actions against toxic polluters.

Businesses that engage in ultrahazardous activities—such as the transportation of radioactive materials—are strictly liable for whatever injuries the activities cause. In a strict liability action, the injured party does not need to prove that the business failed to exercise reasonable care.

SECTION 2

State and Local Regulation

Many states regulate the degree to which the environment may be polluted. Thus, for example, even when state zoning laws permit a business's proposed development, the proposal may have to be altered to change the development's impact on the environment. State laws may restrict a business's discharge of chemicals into the air or water or regulate its disposal of toxic wastes. States may also regulate the disposal or recycling of other wastes, including glass, metal, and plastic containers and paper. Additionally, states may restrict the emissions from motor vehicles.

City, county, and other local governments control some aspects of the environment. For instance, local zoning laws control some land use. These laws may be designed to inhibit or direct the growth of cities and suburbs or to protect the natural environment. Other aspects of the environment may be subject to local regulation for other reasons. Methods of waste and garbage removal and disposal, for example, can have a substantial impact on a community. The appearance of buildings and other structures, including advertising signs and billboards, may affect traffic safety, property values, or local aesthetics. Noise generated by a business or its customers may be annoying, disruptive, or damaging to its neighbors. The location and condition of parks, streets, and other public uses of land subject to local control affect the environment and can also affect business.

SECTION 3

Federal Regulation

Congress has passed a number of statutes to control the impact of human activities on the environment. Exhibit 25–1 on the next page lists and summarizes the major federal environmental statutes discussed in

this chapter. Some of these statutes were passed in an attempt to improve air and water quality. Others specifically regulate toxic chemicals—including pesticides, herbicides, and hazardous wastes. Some are concerned with radiation.

ENVIRONMENTAL REGULATORY AGENCIES

Much of the body of federal law governing business activities consists of the regulations issued and enforced by administrative agencies.

The most well known of the agencies regulating environmental law is the Environmental Protection Agency (EPA), which was created in 1970 to coordinate federal environmental responsibilities. Other federal agencies with authority for regulating specific environmental matters include the Department of the Interior, the Department of Defense, the Department of Labor, the Food and Drug Administration, and the Nuclear Regulatory Commission. These regulatory agencies—and all other agencies of the federal government—must take environmental factors into consideration when making significant decisions.

ASSESSMENT OF THE IMPACT OF AGENCY ACTIONS ON THE ENVIRONMENT

The National Environmental Policy Act (NEPA) of 1969[2] requires that for every major federal action that significantly affects the quality of the environment, an **environmental impact statement (EIS)** must be prepared. An action qualifies as "major" if it involves a substantial commitment of resources (monetary or otherwise). An action is "federal" if a federal agency has the power to control it. Construction by a private developer of a ski resort on federal land, for example, may require an EIS.[3] Building or operating a nuclear plant, which requires a federal permit,[4] or constructing a dam as part of a federal project would require an EIS.[5] If an agency decides that an EIS is unnecessary, it must issue a statement supporting this conclusion.

---

2. 42 U.S.C. Sections 4321–4370d.
3. *Robertson v. Methow Valley Citizens' Council*, 490 U.S. 332, 109 S.Ct. 1835, 104 L.Ed.2d 351 (1989).
4. *Calvert Cliffs Coordinating Committee v. Atomic Energy Commission*, 449 F.2d 1109 (D.C. Cir. 1971).
5. *Marsh v. Oregon Natural Resources Council*, 490 U.S. 360, 109 S.Ct. 1851, 104 L.Ed.2d 377 (1989).

EXHIBIT 25–1 FEDERAL ENVIRONMENTAL STATUTES

POPULAR NAME	PURPOSE	STATUTE REFERENCE
Rivers and Harbors Appropriations Act (1899)	To prohibit ships and manufacturers from discharging and depositing refuse in navigable waterways.	33 U.S.C. Sections 401–418.
Federal Insecticide, Fungicide, and Rodenticide Act (FIFRA) (1947)	To control the use of pesticides and herbicides.	7 U.S.C. Sections 136–136y.
Federal Water Pollution Control Act (FWPCA) (1948)	To eliminate the discharge of pollutants from major sources into navigable waters.	33 U.S.C. Sections 1251–1387.
Atomic Energy Act (1954)	To limit environmental harm from the private nuclear industry.	42 U.S.C. Sections 2011 to 2297g-4.
Clean Air Act (1963)	To control air pollution from mobile and stationary sources.	42 U.S.C. Sections 7401–7671q.
National Environmental Policy Act (NEPA) (1969)	To limit environmental harm from federal government activities.	42 U.S.C. Sections 4321–4370d.
Marine Protection, Research, and Sanctuaries Act (Ocean Dumping Act) of 1972	To regulate the transporting and dumping of material into ocean waters.	16 U.S.C. Sections 1401–1445.
Noise Control Act (1972)	To regulate noise pollution from transportation and nontransportation sources.	42 U.S.C. Sections 4901–4918.
Endangered Species Act (1973)	To protect species that are threatened with extinction.	16 U.S.C. Sections 1531–1544.
Safe Drinking Water Act (1974)	To regulate pollutants in public drinking water systems.	42 U.S.C. Sections 300f to 300j-25.
Resource Conservation and Recovery Act (RCRA) (1976)	To establish standards for hazardous waste disposal.	42 U.S.C. Sections 6901–6986.
Toxic Substances Control Act (1976)	To regulate toxic chemicals and chemical compounds.	15 U.S.C. Sections 2601–2692.
Comprehensive Environmental Response, Compensation, and Liability Act (CERCLA) (Superfund) (1980)	To regulate the clean-up of hazardous waste-disposal sites.	42 U.S.C. Sections 9601–9675.
Low Level Radioactive Waste Policy Act (1980)	To assign to the states responsibility for nuclear power plants' low-level radioactive waste.	42 U.S.C. Sections 2021b–2021j.
Nuclear Waste Policy Act (1982)	To provide for the designation of a permanent radioactive waste-disposal site.	42 U.S.C. Sections 10101–10270.
Oil Pollution Act (1990)	To establish liability for the clean-up of navigable waters after oil-spill disasters.	33 U.S.C. Sections 2701–2761.

An EIS must analyze (1) the impact on the environment that the action will have, (2) any adverse effects on the environment and alternative actions that might be taken, and (3) irreversible effects the action might generate. EISs have become instruments for private citizens, consumer interest groups, businesses, and others to challenge federal agency actions on the basis that the actions improperly threaten the environment.

Other federal laws also require that environmental values be considered in agency decision making. Among the most important of these laws are those that have been enacted to protect fish and wildlife. Under the Fish and Wildlife Coordination Act of 1958,[6] federal agencies proposing to approve the impounding or diversion of a stream's waters must consult with the Fish and Wildlife Service with a view to preventing the loss of fish and wildlife resources. Also important is the Endangered Species Act of 1973.[7] Under this act, all federal agencies are required to take steps to ensure that their actions "do not jeopardize the continued existence of endangered species" or the habitat of an endangered species. An action may jeopardize the continued existence of a species if it sets in motion a chain of events that reduces the chances that the species will survive.

Section 4

Air Pollution

Federal involvement with air pollution goes back to the 1950s, when Congress authorized funds for air-pollution research. In 1963, the federal government passed the Clean Air Act,[8] which focused on multi-state air pollution and provided assistance to states. Various amendments, particularly in 1970, 1977, and 1990, strengthened the government's authority to regulate air quality. These laws provide the basis for issuing regulations to control pollution coming primarily from mobile sources (such as automobiles) and stationary sources (such as electric utilities and industrial plants).

MOBILE SOURCES

Regulations governing air pollution from automobiles and other mobile sources specify pollution standards and time schedules for meeting these standards. For example, under the 1990 amendments to the Clean Air Act, automobile manufacturers must cut new automobiles' exhaust emission of nitrogen oxide by 60 percent and emission of other pollutants by 35 percent. By 1998, all new automobiles had to meet this

standard. Regulations that will go into effect beginning with 2004 model cars call for cutting nitrogen oxide tailpipe emissions by nearly 10 percent by 2007. For the first time, sport utility vehicles and light trucks were also required to meet the same emission standards as automobiles.

Service stations are also subject to environmental regulations. The 1990 amendments require service stations to sell gasoline with a higher oxygen content in forty-one cities that experience carbon monoxide pollution in the winter. Service stations are required to sell even cleaner burning gasoline in Los Angeles and another eight of the most polluted urban areas.

The EPA attempts to update pollution-control standards when new scientific information becomes available. In light of evidence that very small particles (2.5 microns, or millionths of a meter) of soot affect our health as significantly as larger particles, the EPA issued new particulate standards for motor vehicle exhaust systems and other sources of pollution. The EPA also increased the acceptable standard for ozone, which is formed when sunlight combines with pollutants from cars and other sources. Ozone is the basic ingredient of smog. The EPA's particulate standards and the acceptable standard for ozone are being challenged in the courts.[9] Meanwhile, the old standards are in force.

STATIONARY SOURCES

The Clean Air Act authorizes the EPA to establish air-quality standards for stationary sources (such as manufacturing plants) but recognizes that the primary responsibility for preventing and controlling air pollution rests with state and local governments. The EPA sets primary and secondary levels of ambient standards—that is, the maximum levels of certain pollutants—and the states formulate plans to achieve those standards. The plans are to provide for the attainment of primary standards within three years and secondary standards within a reasonable time. For economic, political, and technological reasons, however, the deadlines are often subject to change.

Different standards apply to sources of pollution in clean areas and those in polluted areas. Different standards also apply to existing sources of pollution

---

6. 16 U.S.C. Sections 661–666c.

7. 16 U.S.C. Sections 1531–1544.

8. 42 U.S.C. Sections 7401–7671q.

9. See, for example, *American Trucking Associations v. Environmental Protection Agency*, 175 F.3d 1027 (D.C.Cir. 1999), modified on rehearing, 195 F.3d 4 (D.C.Cir. 1999); and *American Petroleum Institute v. U.S. Environmental Protection Agency*, 198 F.3d 275 (D.C.Cir. 2000).

and major new sources. Major new sources include existing sources modified by a change in a method of operation that increases emissions. Performance standards for major sources require use of the *maximum achievable control technology,* or MACT, to reduce emissions from the combustion of fossil fuels (coal and oil). As mentioned, the EPA issues guidelines as to what equipment meets this standard.

Under the 1990 amendments to the Clean Air Act, 110 of the oldest coal-burning power plants in the United States must cut their emissions by 40 percent by the year 2001 to reduce acid rain. Utilities were granted "credits" to emit certain amounts of sulfur dioxide, and those that emit less than the allowed amounts can sell their credits to other polluters. Controls on other factories and businesses are intended to reduce ground-level ozone pollution in ninety-six cities to healthful levels by 2005 (except Los Angeles, which has until 2010). Industrial emissions of 189 hazardous air pollutants must be reduced by 90 percent by 2000. By 2002, the production of chlorofluorocarbons (such as Freon), carbon tetrachloride, and methyl chloroform—used in air conditioning, refrigeration, and insulation and linked to depletion of the ozone layer—must stop.

Hazardous Air Pollutants

Hazardous air pollutants are those likely to cause an increase in mortality or in serious irreversible or incapacitating illness. As noted, there are 189 of these pollutants, including asbestos, benzene, beryllium, cadmium, mercury, and vinyl chloride. These pollutants may cause cancer as well as neurological and reproductive damage. They are emitted from stationary sources by a variety of business activities, including smelting, dry cleaning, house painting, and commercial baking. Instead of establishing specific emissions standards for each hazardous air pollutant, the 1990 amendments to the Clean Air Act require industry to use pollution-control equipment that represents the maximum achievable control technology, or MACT, to limit emissions. As mentioned, the EPA issues guidelines as to what equipment meets this standard.

In 1996, the EPA issued a rule to regulate hazardous air pollutants emitted by landfills. The rule requires landfills constructed after May 30, 1991, that emit more than a specified amount of pollutants to install landfill gas collection and control systems. The rule also requires the states to impose the same requirements on landfills constructed before May 30, 1991, if they accepted waste after November 8, 1987.[10]

Violations of the Clean Air Act

For violations of emission limits under the Clean Air Act, the EPA can assess civil penalties of up to $25,000 per day. Additional fines of up to $5,000 per day can be assessed for other violations, such as failing to maintain the required records. To penalize those for whom it is more cost effective to violate the act than to comply with it, the EPA is authorized to obtain a penalty equal to the violator's economic benefits from noncompliance. Persons who provide information about violators may be paid up to $10,000. Private citizens can also sue violators.

Those who knowingly violate the act may be subject to criminal penalties, including fines of up to $1 million and imprisonment for up to two years (for false statements or failures to report violations). Corporate officers are among those who may be subject to these penalties.

Section 5

Water Pollution

Federal regulations governing water pollution can be traced back to the Rivers and Harbors Appropriations Act of 1899.[11] These regulations prohibited ships and manufacturers from discharging or depositing refuse in navigable waterways.

Navigable Waters

Once limited to waters actually used for navigation, the term *navigable waters* is today interpreted to include intrastate lakes and streams used by interstate travelers and industries, as well as coastal and freshwater wetlands. (The EPA defines wetlands as "those areas that are inundated or saturated by surface or ground water at a frequency and duration sufficient to support, and that under normal circumstances do support, a prevalence of vegetation typically adapted for life in saturated soil conditions.") In 1948, Congress passed the Federal Water Pollution Control Act (FWPCA),[12] but its regulatory system and enforcement proved inadequate. In

---

10. 40 C.F.R. Sections 60.750–759.
11. 33 U.S.C. Sections 401–418.
12. 33 U.S.C. Sections 1251–1387.

1972, amendments to the FWPCA—known as the Clean Water Act—established the following goals: (1) make waters safe for swimming, (2) protect fish and wildlife, and (3) eliminate the discharge of pollutants into the water. The amendments required that municipal and industrial polluters apply for permits before discharging wastes into navigable waters.

They also set forth specific time schedules, which were extended by amendment in 1977 and by the Water Quality Act of 1987.[13] Under these schedules, the EPA establishes limitations for discharges of types of pollutants based on the technology available for controlling them. Regulations, for the most part, specify that the *best available control technology*, or BACT, be installed. The EPA issues guidelines as to what equipment meets this standard, which essentially requires the most effective pollution-control equipment available. New sources must install BACT

equipment before beginning operations. Existing sources are subject to timetables for installation of BACT equipment. These sources must immediately install equipment that utilizes the *best practical control technology*, or BPCT. The EPA also issues guidelines as to what equipment meets this standard.

Wetlands. The Clean Water Act prohibits the filling or dredging of wetlands unless a permit is obtained from the Army Corps of Engineers. The EPA defines **wetlands** as "those areas that are inundated or saturated by surface or ground water at a frequency and duration sufficient to support, and that under normal circumstances do support, a prevalence of vegetation typically adapted for life in saturated soil conditions." In recent years, federal regulatory policy in regard to wetlands has elicited substantial controversy because of the broad interpretation of what constitutes a wetland subject to the regulatory authority of the federal government. The following case is illustrative.

---

13. This act amended 33 U.S.C. Section 1251.

CASE 25.2

Hoffman Homes, Inc. v. Administrator, United States Environmental Protection Agency

United States
Court of Appeals,
Seventh Circuit, 1993.
999 F.2d 256.

COMPANY PROFILE   *Sam and Jack Hoffman started F&S Construction in 1947. Over the next few years, the company—renamed the Hoffman Group—built thousands of low-priced houses throughout the United States, becoming the nation's third largest builder by 1955. Norman Hassinger, a residential marketing expert, became president of the Hoffman Group in 1982 and gradually took over the firm. In 1987, the Hoffman Group became the Hassinger Companies. Hassinger created Hoffman Homes, Inc., as a home-building subsidiary.*

BACKGROUND AND FACTS   *Hoffman Homes, Inc., in preparation for the construction of a housing subdivision, filled and graded a 0.8-acre, bowl-shaped depression ("Area A"). Before Hoffman filled Area A, rainwater periodically collected there. The EPA issued an order stating that Hoffman had filled wetlands without a permit in violation of the Clean Water Act and ordered Hoffman to, among other things, cease its filling activities and pay a fine of $50,000 for violating the act. Hoffman protested that the EPA had no regulatory authority over Area A because the area in no way affected interstate commerce. The EPA stated that it had authority to regulate discharges of fill materials into intrastate wetlands that have a "minimal, potential effect" on interstate commerce and that Area A had such an effect because migratory birds could potentially use the area. Hoffman appealed the decision to the Seventh Circuit Court of Appeals.*

IN THE LANGUAGE OF THE COURT

HARLINGTON WOOD, Senior Circuit Judge.
    *   *   *   *
    *   *   * It is true, of course, that migratory birds can alight most anywhere. As [a witness] testified, he has seen mallards in parking lot puddles. The ALJ [administrative law judge of the EPA], however, was in the unique position to view the evidence, to hear the

testimony, and to judge the credibility of the witnesses. He concluded that the evidence did not support the conclusion that Area A had characteristics whose use by and value to migratory birds is well established. We agree. The migratory birds are better judges of what is suitable for their welfare than are we [or anyone at the EPA]. Having avoided Area A the migratory birds have thus spoken and submitted their own evidence. We see no need to argue with them. No justification whatsoever is seen from the evidence to interfere with private ownership based on what appears to be no more than a well intentioned effort in these particular factual circumstances to expand government control beyond reasonable or practical limits. After April showers not every temporary wet spot necessarily becomes subject to government control.

DECISION AND REMEDY   *The court, holding that Area A was not subject to regulation under the Clean Water Act, vacated the EPA's order requiring Hoffman Homes to pay a $50,000 administrative penalty for the filling of Area A.*

Violations of the Clean Water Act.   Under the Clean Water Act, violators are subject to a variety of civil and criminal penalties. Depending on the violation, civil penalties range from a maximum of $10,000 per day, and not more than $25,000 per violation, to as much as $25,000 per day. Criminal penalties range from a fine of $2,500 per day and imprisonment for up to one year to a fine of $1 million and fifteen years' imprisonment. Injunctive relief and damages can also be imposed. The polluting party can be required to clean up the pollution or pay for the cost of doing so. Criminal penalties apply only if a violation was intentional.

DRINKING WATER

Another statute governing water pollution is the Safe Drinking Water Act.[14] Passed in 1974, this act requires the EPA to set maximum levels for pollutants in public water systems. Operators of public water supply systems must come as close as possible to meeting the EPA's standards by using the best available technology that is economically and technologically feasible. The EPA is particularly concerned with contamination from underground sources. Pesticides and wastes leaked from landfills or disposed of in underground injection wells are among the more than two hundred pollutants known to exist in groundwater used for drinking in at least thirty-four states. Many of these substances are associated with cancer and damage to the central nervous system, liver, and kidneys.

The act was amended in 1996 to give the EPA greater flexibility in setting regulatory standards governing drinking water. Prior to the 1996 amendments, the EPA had to set standards for twenty-five different drinking water contaminants every three years, which it had largely failed to do. Under the 1996 amendments, the EPA can move at whatever rate it deems necessary to control contaminants that are of greatest concern to the public health. The 1996 amendments also imposed new requirements on suppliers of drinking water. Each supplier must send to every household it supplies with water an annual statement describing the source of its water, the level of any contaminants contained in the water, and any possible health concerns associated with the contaminants.

OCEAN DUMPING

The Marine Protection, Research, and Sanctuaries Act of 1972[15] (known popularly as the Ocean Dumping Act) regulates the transportation and dumping of material into ocean waters. (The term *material* is synonymous with the term *pollutant* as used in the Federal Water Pollution Control Act.) The Ocean Dumping Act prohibits entirely the ocean-dumping of radiological, chemical, and biological warfare agents and high-level radioactive waste. The act establishes a permit program for transporting and dumping other materials. There are specific exemptions—materials subject to the permit provisions of other pollution legislation, wastes from structures regulated by other laws (for example, offshore oil exploration and drilling platforms), sewage, and other wastes. The Ocean Dumping Act also authorizes the designation of marine sanctuaries for

---

14. 42 U.S.C. Sections 300f to 300j-25.

15. 16 U.S.C. Sections 1401–1445.

"preserving or restoring such areas for their conservation, recreational, ecological, or esthetic values."

Each violation of any provision or permit may result in a civil penalty of not more than $50,000 or revocation or suspension of the permit. A knowing violation is a criminal offense that may result in a $50,000 fine, imprisonment for not more than a year, or both. An injunction may also be imposed.

OIL POLLUTION

The Oil Pollution Act of 1990[16] provides that any onshore or offshore oil facility, oil shipper, vessel owner, or vessel operator that discharges oil into navigable waters or onto an adjoining shore may be liable for clean-up costs, as well as damages. The act created a $1 billion oil clean-up and economic compensation fund and decreed that by the year 2011, oil tankers using U.S. ports must be double hulled to limit the severity of accidental spills.

Under the act, damage to natural resources, private property, and the local economy, including the increased cost of providing public services, is compensable. The act provides for civil penalties of $1,000 per barrel spilled or $25,000 for each day of the violation. The party held responsible for the clean-up costs can bring a civil suit for contribution from other potentially liable parties.

SECTION 6

Noise Pollution

Regulations concerning noise pollution include the Noise Control Act of 1972.[17] This act requires the EPA to establish noise emission standards (maximum noise levels below which no harmful effects occur from interference with speech or other activity)—for example, for railroad noise emissions. The standards must be achievable by the best available technology, and they must be economically within reason.

The act prohibits, among other things, distributing products manufactured in violation of the noise emission standards and tampering with noise control devices. Either of these activities can result in an injunction or whatever other remedy "is necessary to protect the public health and welfare." Illegal product distribution can also result in a fine and imprisonment.

Violations of provisions of the Noise Control Act can result in penalties of not more than $50,000 per day and imprisonment for not more than two years.

SECTION 7

Toxic Chemicals

Originally, most environmental clean-up efforts were directed toward reducing smog and making water safe for fishing and swimming. Over time, however, control of toxic chemicals has become an important part of environmental law.

PESTICIDES AND HERBICIDES

The first toxic chemical problem to receive widespread public attention was that posed by pesticides and herbicides. Using these chemicals to kill insects and weeds has increased agricultural productivity, but their residue remains in the environment. In some instances, accumulations of this residue have killed animals, and scientists have identified potential long-term effects that are detrimental to people.

Federal Insecticide, Fungicide, and Rodenticide Act (FIFRA). The federal statute regulating pesticides and herbicides is the Federal Insecticide, Fungicide, and Rodenticide Act (FIFRA) of 1947.[18] Under FIFRA, pesticides and herbicides must be (1) registered before they can be sold, (2) certified and used only for approved applications, and (3) used in limited quantities when applied to food crops. If a substance is identified as harmful, the EPA can cancel its registration after a hearing. If the harm is imminent, the EPA can suspend registration pending the hearing. The EPA, or state officers or employees, may also inspect factories in which these chemicals are manufactured.

Under 1996 amendments to the Federal Food, Drug and Cosmetic Act, for a pesticide to remain on the market, there must be a "reasonable certainty of no harm" to people from exposure to the pesticide.[19] This means that there must be no more than a one-in-a-million risk to people of developing cancer from exposure in any way, including eating food that contains residues from the pesticide. Pesticide residues are in nearly all fruits and vegetables and processed foods. Under the 1996 amendments, the EPA must distribute

---

16. 33 U.S.C. Sections 2701–2761.
17. 42 U.S.C. Sections 4901–4918.

18. 7 U.S.C. Sections 136–136y.
19. 21 U.S.C. Section 346a.

to grocery stores brochures on high-risk pesticides that are in food, and the stores must display these brochures for consumers.

Violations of FIFRA. It is a violation of FIFRA to sell a pesticide or herbicide that is unregistered, a pesticide or herbicide with a registration that has been canceled or suspended, or a pesticide or herbicide with a false or misleading label. For example, it is an offense to sell a substance that is adulterated (that has a chemical strength different from the concentration declared on the label). It is also an offense to destroy or deface any labeling required under the act. The act's labeling requirements include directions for the use of the pesticide or herbicide, warnings to protect human health and the environment, a statement of treatment in the case of poisoning, and a list of the ingredients.

A private party can petition the EPA to suspend or cancel the registration of a pesticide or herbicide. If the EPA fails to act, the private party can petition a federal court to review the EPA's failure. Penalties for registrants and producers for violating FIFRA include imprisonment for up to one year and a fine of no more than $50,000. Penalties for commercial dealers include imprisonment for up to one year and a fine of no more than $25,000. Farmers and other private users of pesticides or herbicides who violate the act are subject to a $1,000 fine and imprisonment for up to thirty days.

TOXIC SUBSTANCES

The first comprehensive law covering toxic substances was the Toxic Substances Control Act of 1976.[20] The act was passed to regulate chemicals and chemical compounds that are known to be toxic—such as asbestos and polychlorinated biphenyls, popularly known as PCBs—and to institute investigation of any possible harmful effects from new chemical compounds. The regulations authorize the EPA to require that manufacturers, processors, and other organizations planning to use chemicals first determine their effects on human health and the environment. The EPA can regulate substances that may pose an imminent hazard or an unreasonable risk of injury to health or the environment. The EPA may require special labeling, limit the use of a substance, set production quotas, or prohibit the use of a substance altogether.

HAZARDOUS WASTES

Some industrial, agricultural, and household wastes pose more serious threats than others. If not properly disposed of, these toxic chemicals may present a substantial danger to human health and the environment. If released into the environment, they may contaminate public drinking water resources.

Resource Conservation and Recovery Act. In 1976, Congress passed the Resource Conservation and Recovery Act (RCRA)[21] in reaction to an ever-increasing concern with the effects of hazardous waste materials on the environment. The RCRA required the EPA to establish regulations to monitor and control hazardous waste disposal and to determine which forms of solid waste should be considered hazardous and thus subject to regulation. The act authorized the EPA to promulgate various technical requirements for some types of facilities for storage and treatment of hazardous waste. The act also requires all producers of hazardous waste materials to label and package properly any hazardous waste to be transported.

The RCRA was amended in 1984 and 1986 to decrease the use of land containment in the disposal of hazardous waste and to require compliance with the act by some generators of hazardous waste—such as those generating less than 1,000 kilograms (2,200 pounds) a month—that had previously been excluded from regulation under the RCRA.

Under the RCRA, a company may be assessed a civil penalty based on the seriousness of the violation, the probability of harm, and the extent to which the violation deviates from RCRA requirements. The assessment may be up to $25,000 for each violation. Criminal penalties include fines up to $50,000 for each day of violation, imprisonment for up to two years (in most instances), or both. Criminal fines and the time of imprisonment can be doubled for certain repeat offenders.

Superfund. In 1980, the U.S. Congress passed the Comprehensive Environmental Response, Compensation, and Liability Act (CERCLA),[22] commonly known as Superfund. The basic purpose of Superfund is to regulate the clean-up of disposal sites in which hazardous waste is leaking into the environment. A special federal fund was created for that purpose.

---

20. 15 U.S.C. Sections 2601–2692.

21. 42 U.S.C. Sections 6901–6986.
22. 42 U.S.C. Sections 9601–9675.

Potentially Responsible Parties. Superfund provides that when a release or a threatened release of hazardous chemicals from a site occurs, the EPA can clean up the site and recover the cost of the clean-up from the following persons: (1) the person who generated the wastes disposed of at the site, (2) the person who transported the wastes to the site, (3) the person who owned or operated the site at the time of the disposal, or (4) the current owner or operator. A person falling within one of these categories is referred to as a **potentially responsible party (PRP)**.

Liability under Superfund is usually joint and several—that is, a PRP who generated only a fraction of the hazardous waste disposed of at the site may nevertheless be liable for all of the clean-up costs. CERCLA authorizes a party who has incurred clean-up costs to bring a "contribution action" against any other person who is liable or potentially liable for a percentage of the costs. The following case involved a challenge to a court's allocation of clean-up costs among PRPs.

CASE 25.3   Browning-Ferris Industries of Illinois, Inc. v. Ter Maat

United States
Court of Appeals,
Seventh Circuit, 1999.
195 F.3d 953.
http://www.ca7.
uscourts.gov[a]

BACKGROUND AND FACTS   *In 1971, the owners of a landfill leased it to a company that later became Browning-Ferris Industries of Illinois, Inc., which operated it until the fall of 1975. During that time, the operator illegally dumped at the site a large quantity of particularly toxic wastes from an auto plant run by Chrysler Corporation. Between the fall of 1975 and 1988, M.I.G. Investments, Inc., and AAA Disposal Systems, Inc., operated the landfill. Richard Ter Maat was the president and principal shareholder of M.I.G. and AAA. In June 1988, after AAA was sold and Ter Maat moved to Florida, M.I.G. abandoned the landfill without covering it properly. Two years later, the EPA ordered that the site be cleaned up. Browning-Ferris, and other companies that shared responsibility for the pollution at the site, agreed to clean it up. Browning-Ferris and the others then filed a suit in a federal district court against Ter Maat, M.I.G., and AAA under CERCLA to recover the costs. The court ruled, among other things, that 45 percent of the costs was allocable to the owners of the landfill and the generators of the toxic wastes dumped in it, 22 percent was the responsibility of Browning-Ferris, and the other 33 percent was the responsibility of M.I.G. and AAA. The plaintiffs appealed to the U.S. Court of Appeals for the Seventh Circuit. Browning-Ferris claimed in part that too much of the liability for the pollution at the site had been allocated to it relative to M.I.G. and AAA. Browning-Ferris argued that the costs should be allocated according to the volume of wastes for which each party was responsible.*

IN THE LANGUAGE
OF THE COURT

POSNER, Chief Judge.
         *   *   *   *
    The   *   *   *   question   *   *   *   is whether the court must find a causal relation between a party's pollution and the actual cost of cleaning up the site. To answer this question we have to distinguish between a necessary condition (or "but-for cause") and a sufficient condition. If event A is a necessary condition of event B, this means that, without A, B will not occur. If A is a sufficient condition of B, this means that, if A occurs, B will occur. If A is that the murder weapon was loaded and B is the murder, then A is a necessary condition. If A is shooting a person through the heart and B is the death of the shooting victim, then A is a sufficient condition of B but not a necessary condition, because a wound to another part of the victim's body might have been fatal as well.
    This distinction may sometimes be important in the pollution context. It is easy to imagine a case in which, had X not polluted a site, no clean-up costs would have been incurred; X's pollution would be a necessary condition of those costs and it would be

---

a. In the left-hand column, click on "Judicial Opinions." On that page, in the "Last Name or Corporation" section, click on "Begins," enter "Browning-Ferris" in the box, and click on "Search for Person." When the result appears, click on the docket number for the case to access the opinion.

natural to think that he should pay at least a part of them. But suppose that even if X had not polluted the site, it would have to be cleaned up—and at the same cost—because of the amount of pollution by Y. *   *   * Then X's pollution would not be a necessary condition of the clean up, or of any of the costs incurred in the clean up. But that should not necessarily let X off the hook. For suppose that though if X had not polluted the site at all there still would have been enough pollution from Y to require a clean up, if Y had not polluted the site X's pollution would have been sufficient to require the clean up. In that case, the conduct of X and the conduct of Y would each be a sufficient but not a necessary condition of the clean up, and it would be entirely arbitrary to let either (or, even worse, both) off the hook on this basis. So far as appears, this is such a case; Browning-Ferris's pollution was serious enough (if indeed it dumped a large quantity of Chrysler's particularly toxic wastes) to require that the site be cleaned up, but the other pollution at the site was also enough. If Browning-Ferris's conduct was thus a sufficient though not a necessary condition of the clean up, it is not inequitable to make it contribute substantially to the cost.

*   *   * [N]o principle of law, logic, or common sense required the court to allocate [the] total costs among the polluters on the basis of the volume of wastes alone. Not only do wastes differ in their toxicity, harm to the environment, and costs of cleaning up, and so relative volume is not a reliable guide to the marginal costs imposed by each polluter; but polluters differ in the blameworthiness of the decisions or omissions that led to the pollution, and blameworthiness is relevant to an equitable allocation of joint costs.

DECISION AND REMEDY *The U.S. Court of Appeals for the Seventh Circuit held that the allocation of 22 percent of the clean-up costs to Browning-Ferris had been fair. There were a number of factors to consider, and the lower court had not abused its discretion in deciding that those factors warranted this allocation. The court remanded the case for the determination of other issues.*

Liability of Lending Institutions and Fiduciaries. Courts wrestled with the question of whether lending institutions can be held liable for toxic waste on property they hold as collateral for their loans. Some courts followed the lead of the U.S. Court of Appeals for the Eleventh Circuit, which held in 1990 that a bank can be held liable as a PRP if the bank has the "capacity to influence" a borrower's decisions about toxic waste.[23] Other courts held to the contrary. In one case, the court held that to impose liability on a bank for involving itself in the debtor's affairs would be to "punish the Bank for engaging in its normal course of business."[24] To clarify this issue, Congress amended CERCLA in 1996 to provide that banks and other lenders can be held liable under CERCLA for property they hold as collateral only if they actually participate in the management or operational affairs of the borrower.[25]

Another issue on which the courts disagreed was whether certain fiduciaries, such as trustees and executors of estates, could be held liable as PRPs. In at least one case, a federal court held that a trustee could be personally liable for those costs of cleaning up a hazardous waste site that exceeded the value of the trust's assets.[26] The 1996 amendments also addressed this issue by stating that a fiduciary can only be held personally liable as a PRP in limited circumstances—such as when the hazardous waste pollution is caused by the fiduciary's own negligence.[27]

SECTION 7

Radiation

Nuclear power plants are built and operated by private industry. The nuclear industry is regulated

---

23. *United States v. Fleet Factors Corp.*, 901 F.2d 1550 (11th Cir. 1990).

24. *Z & Z Leasing, Inc. v. Graying Reel, Inc.*, 873 F.Supp. 51 (E.D.Mich. 1995).

25. 42 U.S.C. Section 9601.

26. *Phoenix v. Garbage Services Co.*, 816 F.Supp. 564 (D.Ariz. 1993).

27. 42 U.S.C. Section 9607.

almost exclusively by the federal government under the Atomic Energy Act of 1954.[28] The Nuclear Regulatory Commission (NRC) is the federal agency responsible for regulating the private nuclear industry. The NRC reviews the plans for each proposed nuclear plant and issues a construction permit only after preparing an environmental impact statement that considers the impact of an accidental release of radiation. After construction, the NRC licenses the plant's operation.

The Environmental Protection Agency sets standards for radioactivity in the overall environment and for the disposal of some radioactive waste. Low-level radioactive waste generated by private facilities is the responsibility of each state under the Low Level Radioactive Waste Policy Act of 1980.[29] The NRC regulates the use and disposal of other nuclear materials and radioactive waste. Some radioactive waste is

buried, burned, or dumped in the ocean. Currently, however, most of it is stored at the plants in which it is produced. Under the Nuclear Waste Policy Act of 1982,[30] the government is looking for a permanent disposal site.

A common law theory may serve as the basis for liability for harms caused by radiation. For example, in one case, the court held that the party creating a radiation hazard is strictly liable in tort for its clean-up and any damages.[31] Liability for injury resulting from radiation may also arise under one of the statutes discussed elsewhere in this chapter. For example, the release of radioactive materials into the environment may violate the Clean Water Act, the RCRA, or the CERCLA.[32]

---

28. 42 U.S.C. Sections 2011 to 2297g-4.
29. 42 U.S.C. Sections 2021b–2021j.

30. 42 U.S.C. Sections 10101–10270.
31. *T&E Industries, Inc. v. Safety Light Corp.*, 123 N.J. 371, 587 A.2d 1249 (1991).
32. See, for example, *Ohio v. Department of Energy*, 904 F.2d 1058 (6th Cir. 1990).

Terms and Concepts to Review

environmental impact statement (EIS) 540	nuisance 538	toxic tort 540
environmental law 538	potentially responsible party (PRP) 548	wetland 544

Questions and Case Problems

25–1. CLEAN AIR ACT. The Environmental Protection Agency (EPA) has set ambient standards for several pollutants, including sulfur dioxide, specifying the maximum concentration allowable in the outdoor air. One way to meet these standards is to reduce emissions. Companies discovered, however, that they could also meet the standards at less cost by building very high smokestacks. When emitted from such high stacks, pollutants were more widely dispersed and remained below the concentration level specified by the ambient standards. Environmental groups claimed that the Clean Air Act was designed to reduce pollution, not to disperse it, and argued that industry should not be allowed to rely

on tall stacks. Are the environmental groups correct, or should industry be allowed to use the less expensive dispersal method? Discuss.

25–2. CLEAN AIR ACT. Some scientific knowledge indicates that there is no safe level of exposure to a cancer-causing agent. In theory, even one molecule of such a substance has the potential for causing cancer. Section 112 of the Clean Air Act requires that all cancer-causing substances be regulated to ensure a margin of safety. Some environmental groups have argued that all emissions of such substances must be eliminated in order for such a margin of safety to be reached. A total elimination would likely shut down many major U.S. industries.

Should the Environmental Protection Agency totally eliminate all emissions of cancer-causing chemicals? Discuss.

25–3. ENVIRONMENTAL LAWS. Moonbay is a real estate development corporation that primarily develops retirement communities. Farmtex owns a number of feedlots in Sunny Valley. Moonbay purchased twenty thousand acres of farmland in the same area and began building and selling retirement homes on this acreage. In the meantime, Farmtex continued to expand its feedlot business, and eventually only five hundred feet separated the two operations. Because of the odor and flies from the feedlots, Moonbay found it difficult to sell the homes in its development. Moonbay wants to enjoin Farmtex from operating its feedlots in the vicinity of the retirement home development. Discuss under what theory Moonbay would file this action. Discuss fully whether Farmtex has violated any federal environmental laws.

25–4. ENVIRONMENTAL LAWS. Fruitade, Inc., is a processor of a soft drink called Freshen Up. Fruitade uses returnable bottles, as well as a special acid to clean its bottles for further beverage processing. The acid is diluted by water and then allowed to pass into a navigable stream. Fruitade crushes its broken bottles and throws the crushed glass into the stream. Discuss fully any environmental laws that Fruitade has violated.

25–5. PESTICIDE REGULATION. The Environmental Protection Agency (EPA) canceled the registration of the pesticide Diazinon for use on golf courses and sod farms because of concern about the effects of Diazinon on birds. The Federal Insecticide, Fungicide, and Rodenticide Act authorizes cancellation of the registration of products that "generally cause unreasonable adverse effects on the environment." The statute further defines "unreasonable adverse effects on the environment" to mean "any unreasonable risk to man or the environment, taking into account the . . . costs and benefits." Thus, in determining whether a pesticide should continue to be used, one must balance the risks and benefits of the use of the pesticide. Does this mean that the pesticide must be found to kill birds more often than not before its use can be prohibited? [CIBA-Geigy Corp. v. Environmental Protection Agency, 874 F.2d 277 (5th Cir. 1989)]

25–6. COMMON LAW NUISANCE. Taylor Bay Protective Association is a nonprofit corporation established for the purpose of restoring and improving the water quality of Taylor Bay. Local water districts began operating a flood control project in the area. As part of the project, a pumping station was developed. Testimony at trial revealed that the pumps were operated contrary to the instructions provided in the operation and maintenance manual. The pumps acted as vacuums, sucking up increased amounts of silt and depositing the silt in Taylor Bay. Thus, the project resulted in sedimentation and turbidity problems in the downstream watercourse of Taylor Bay. The association sued the local water districts, alleging that the pumping operations

created a nuisance. Do the pumping operations qualify as a common law nuisance? Who should be responsible for the clean-up costs? Discuss both questions fully. [Taylor Bay Protective Association v. Environmental Protection Agency, 884 F.2d 1073 (8th Cir. 1989)]

25–7. WATER POLLUTION. The Environmental Protection Agency (EPA) promulgated water-pollution discharge limits for several mining industries. These standards authorized variances exempting mining operations from coverage by the standards if the operations could show that they used special processes or facilities that made the standards inapplicable. Cost was not a consideration in granting the variances. An industry trade association sued, claiming that the EPA should consider costs in granting variances, and the Fourth Circuit Court of Appeals agreed. Discuss whether the United States Supreme Court should overturn this decision or affirm it and let costs be considered in the granting of variances under the Clean Water Act. [Environmental Protection Agency v. National Crushed Stone Association, 449 U.S. 64, 101 S.Ct. 295, 66 L.Ed.2d 268 (1980)]

25–8. SUPERFUND. During the 1970s, a number of chemical companies disposed of their wastes at a facility maintained by South Carolina Recycling and Disposal, Inc. Hazardous chemical wastes were stored rather haphazardly; some leaked into the ground, and fires occurred on several occasions. Eventually, the Environmental Protection Agency (EPA) conducted clean-up operations under Superfund and sued companies that had used the site for the costs of the clean-up. Five of the defendant companies claimed that they should not be liable for the clean-up costs because there was no evidence that their waste materials had contributed in any way to the leakage problem or to any other hazard posed by the site. The EPA asserted that causation was not required for the companies' liability, only evidence that the companies had sent waste to the site. Will the EPA succeed in its claim? Discuss. [United States v. South Carolina Recycling and Disposal, Inc., 653 F.Supp. 984 (D.S.C. 1986)]

25–9. COMMON LAW NUISANCE. In 1987, John and Jean Zarlenga purchased a new home in Bloomingdale, Illinois. Bloomingdale Partners (BP) then built an eight-story apartment complex across the street from the Zarlenga home. Each of the 168 apartments had an air conditioner weighing about nine hundred pounds. Over sixty air conditioners were on the side of the complex that faced the Zarlenga home. The Zarlengas testified that the noise from these air conditioners during the summer was a "loud rumbling sound" that was "continuous and monotonous." The machines disrupted their sleep. Jean Zarlenga suffered from headaches and irritability. In her testimony, she stated, "It's made my life miserable. I cannot use my deck. I cannot have company over . . . I can't open my windows in my bedroom. I toss and turn all night." The Zarlengas sued BP for creating a nuisance, claiming that the apartment complex substantially interfered with the use and enjoyment of their home. The Zarlengas sought damages from BP for the devaluation of their home caused by the noise and for their suffering. How should the court decide this case? Discuss fully. [*In re Bloomingdale Partners*, 160 Bankr. 101 (N.D.Ill. 1993)]

25–10. CLEAN WATER ACT. Attique Ahmad owned the Spin-N-Market, a convenience store and gas station. The gas pumps were fed by underground tanks, one of which had a leak at its top that allowed water to enter. Ahmad emptied the tank by pumping its contents into a storm drain and a sewer system. Through the storm drain, gasoline flowed into a creek, forcing the city to clean the water. Through the sewer system, gasoline flowed into a sewage treatment plant, forcing the city to evacuate the plant and two nearby schools. Ahmad was charged with discharging a pollutant without a permit, which is a criminal violation of the Clean Water Act. The act provides that a person who "knowingly violates" the act commits a felony. Ahmad claimed that he had believed he was discharging only water. Did Ahmad commit a felony? Why or why not? Discuss fully. [*U.S. v. Ahmad*, 101 F.3d 386 (5th Cir. 1996)]

25–11. IN YOUR COURT

The Endangered Species Act of 1973 makes it unlawful for any person to "take" endangered or threatened species. The act defines *take* to mean to "harass, harm, pursue," "wound," or "kill." The secretary of the interior (Bruce Babbitt) issued a regulation that further defined harm to include "significant habitat modification or degradation where it actually kills or injures wildlife." A group of businesses and individuals involved in the timber industry brought an action against the secretary of the interior and others. The group complained that the application of the "harm" regulation to the red-cockaded woodpecker and the northern spotted owl had injured the group economically, because it prevented logging operations (habitat modification) in Pacific Northwest forests containing these species. The group challenged the regulation's validity, contending that Congress did not intend the word *take* to include habitat modification. Assume that you are the judge in the court hearing this case and answer the following questions:

(a) Traditionally, the term take has been used to refer to the capture or killing of wildlife, usually for private gain. Is the secretary's regulation prohibiting habitat modification consistent with this definition?

(b) Generally, should the economic welfare of private parties be taken into consideration when environmental statutes and regulations are created and applied?

LAW ON THE WEB

For updated links to resources available on the Web, as well as a variety of other materials, visit this text's Web site at http://wleb.westbuslaw.com.

The Virtual Law Library of the Indiana University School of Law provides numerous links to online environmental law sources. Go to

http://www.law.indiana.edu

For information on the standards, guidelines, and regulations of the Environmental Protection Agency, go to

http://www.epa.gov

LEGAL RESEARCH EXERCISES ON THE WEB

Go to http://wleb.westbuslaw.com, the Web site that accompanies this text. Select "Internet Applications," and then click on "Chapter 25." There you will find the following Internet research exercise that you can perform to learn more about consumer and environmental law:

Activity 25–1: Nuisance Law

Land-Use Control and Real Property

P ROPERTY OWNERSHIP CONFERS certain rights. An owner generally has the right to possess the property; the right either to use the property or to derive profits from another's use of the property; and the right to *alienate*[1] the property—that is, to sell, bequeath (pass on through a will), or give to others the same rights of ownership. Not all forms of ownership provide such a complete bundle of rights, but one or more of these attributes are normally included when we say that property is "owned."

Even for one who possesses the entire bundle of rights we have delineated, however, ownership is not absolute. The law places restrictions on how property may be used. It also imposes duties on the owners regarding how the land is to be maintained. In addition, individual owners may agree with others to restrict or limit the use of their property. Thus, property owners cannot always do with their property whatever they wish. Nuisance and environmental laws, for example, restrict how people carry out certain types of activities on their own land.

Briefly stated, the rights of every property owner are subject to certain conditions and limitations.

In this chapter, we first look at the nature of real property and of ownership rights in real property. We then focus on restrictions on ownership in real property. **Real property** (sometimes called *realty* or *real estate*) means the land and everything permanently attached to the land. When structures are *permanently* attached to the land, then everything attached permanently to the structures is also realty. Everything else is **personal property** (or *personalty*). Although real property includes more than land, it is generally referred to simply as "land." Hence, the control over ownership and use that we examine in this chapter is commonly referred to as **land-use control.**

S E C T I O N   1

The Nature of Real Property

Real property consists of land and the buildings, plants, and trees that it contains. Whereas personal property is movable, real property is immovable. Real property usually means land, but it also includes air

---

1. *Alienate* derives from the Latin word *alienus* (alien), which is from the Latin *alus* (other). In legal terms, alienate means to transfer the title to property.

and subsurface rights, plant life and vegetation, and *fixtures* (which are explained below).

LAND

Land includes the soil on the surface of the earth and the natural products or artificial structures that are attached to it. It further includes all the waters contained on or under the earth's surface and the air space above it. In other words, absent a contrary statute or case law, a landowner has the right to everything existing permanently below the surface of his or her property to the center of the earth and above it to the heavens (subject to certain qualifications).

AIR SPACE AND SUBSURFACE RIGHTS

The owner of real property has relatively exclusive rights to the air space above the land, as well as to the soil and minerals underneath it. When no limitations on air rights or subsurface rights are indicated on the document transferring title at the time of purchase, a purchaser can generally expect to have an unrestricted right to possession of the property (subject to the limits on ownership rights examined in detail later in this chapter).

Cases involving air rights present questions such as the right of commercial and private planes to fly over property and the right of individuals and governments to seed clouds and produce artificial rain. Flights over private land do not normally violate the property owners' rights unless the flights are low and frequent, causing a direct interference with the enjoyment and use of the land.[2]

Ownership of the surface of land can be separated from ownership of its subsurface. Subsurface rights can be extremely valuable when minerals, oil, or natural gas is located beneath the surface. A subsurface owner's rights would be of little value if he or she could not use the surface to exercise those rights. Hence, a subsurface owner will have a right (called a *profit*—discussed below) to use the surface of the land to, for example, find and remove minerals. If

the owners of the subsurface rights excavate and their excavation causes the surface to subside, however, they may be liable to the owner of the surface rights.

PLANT LIFE AND VEGETATION

Plant life, both natural and cultivated, is also considered to be real property. In many instances, natural vegetation, such as trees, adds greatly to the value of realty. When a parcel of land is sold and the land has growing crops on it, the sale includes the crops, unless otherwise specified in the sales contract. When crops are sold by themselves, however, they are considered to be personal property or goods. Consequently, the sale of crops is a sale of goods, and it is governed by the Uniform Commercial Code (see Chapter 11) rather than by real property law.

FIXTURES

Certain personal property can become so closely associated with the real property to which it is attached that the law views it as real property. Such property is known as a **fixture**—a thing *affixed* to realty. A thing is affixed to realty when it is attached to it by roots; embedded in it; or permanently attached by means of cement, plaster, bolts, nails, or screws. The fixture can be physically attached to real property, can be attached to another fixture, or can even be without any actual physical attachment to the land, as long as the owner *intends* the property to be a fixture.

Fixtures are included in the sale of land if the sales contract does not provide otherwise. The sale of a house includes the land and the house and garage on it, as well as the cabinets, plumbing, and windows. Because these are permanently affixed to the property, they are considered to be a part of it. Unless otherwise agreed, however, the curtains and throw rugs are not included. Items such as drapes and window-unit air conditioners are difficult to classify. Thus, a contract for the sale of a house or commercial realty should indicate which items of this sort are included in the sale. At issue in the following case was whether telephone poles, wires, and other communications equipment qualified as fixtures.

---

2. *United States v. Causby*, 328 U.S. 256, 66 S.Ct. 1062, 90 L.Ed. 1206 (1946).

CASE 26.1

New England Telephone and Telegraph Co. v. City of Franklin

Supreme Court of
New Hampshire, 1996.
685 A.2d 913.
http://www.state.nh.us/
courts/supreme/
opinions/9611.htm[a]

HISTORICAL AND TECHNOLOGICAL SETTING   *Although telephone poles, wires, and underground conduits often have an expected life of at least forty years, the equipment is installed with its removal and relocation in mind. As a result, removal is normally not complicated or time-consuming, and does not harm the underlying real property or change its usefulness. In obtaining a state license, a property owner's consent, or an easement to install telecommunications equipment, the installer typically insists on maintaining ownership of it and refuses any requests to make it a permanent part of the real property. In fact, telecommunications office equipment is also usually portable and designed to permit easy removal and relocation. Technology changes quickly, and telecommunications companies want to be able to adapt.*

BACKGROUND AND FACTS   *To obtain revenue, cities and towns tax the owners of real property within the municipalities' jurisdiction. The tax is based on an assessment of the value of the property. New England Telephone and Telegraph Company (NETT) and other telephone companies filed a lawsuit in a New Hampshire state court against the City of Franklin and other municipalities challenging the cities' property assessments. NETT and the other plaintiffs objected to the inclusion in their assessments of communications equipment, including telephone poles, wires, and central office equipment. They argued that the equipment was personal property and therefore should not have been taxed. The court granted the telephone companies' motion for summary judgment, and the cities appealed.*

IN THE LANGUAGE OF THE COURT

HORTON, Justice.
  *   *   *   *
  *   *   * [W]hether an item of property is properly classified as either personalty [personal property] or a fixture turns on several factors, including: the item's nature and use; the intent of the party making the annexation; the degree and extent to which the item is specially adapted to the realty; the degree and extent of the item's annexation to the realty; and the relationship between the realty's owner and the person claiming the item. *The central factors are the nature of the article and its use, as connected with the use of the underlying land, because these factors provide the basis for ascertaining the intent of the party who affixes or annexes the item in question.* [Emphasis added.]
  In this case, the items of communications equipment did not constitute fixtures. *   *   * The poles, wires, and central office equipment, though placed in the ground or bolted to the buildings, were readily removable and transportable without affecting the utility of the underlying land, the buildings, or the equipment itself. *   *   * In addition, the very nature of telephone poles and wires, as well as their use by the [telephone companies] in connection with integrated telecommunications systems, belies the proposition that the equipment became a permanent and essential part of the underlying realty so as to pass by conveyance [transfer of the title to property] with it.

DECISION AND REMEDY   *The Supreme Court of New Hampshire affirmed the trial court's decision. The telephone poles, wires, and central office equipment were not fixtures and thus not subject to taxation by the cities as real property.*

a. Click on the name of the case to access the opinion. This Web site is maintained by the New Hampshire state library for the New Hampshire state government.

SECTION 2

Ownership Interests in Real Property

Ownership of property is an abstract concept that cannot exist independently of the legal system. No one actually possesses or *holds* a piece of land, along with the air above, the earth below, and all the water contained on it. One can only possess *rights* in real property. Numerous rights are involved in real property ownership. One who holds the entire bundle of rights owns in *fee simple absolute*. We look first at the fee simple absolute and then at the various types of limited property interests that exist when an owner in fee simple absolute parts with some, but not all, of his or her rights in real property.

FEE SIMPLE

In a **fee simple absolute,** the owner has the greatest aggregation of rights, privileges, and power possible. The owner can give the property away, sell the property for a price, or transfer the property by will to another. The fee simple absolute is limited absolutely to a person and his or her heirs and is assigned forever without limitation or condition. The rights that accompany a fee simple absolute include the right to use the land for whatever purpose the owner sees fit, subject to laws that prevent the owner from unreasonably interfering with another person's land and subject to applicable zoning laws. Furthermore, the owner has the right of *exclusive* possession of the property. A fee simple absolute is potentially infinite in duration and can be disposed of by deed or by will (by selling or by giving away). When there is no will, the fee simple absolute passes to the owner's legal heirs.

Ownership in fee simple may become limited when the property is transferred to another *conditionally*. When this occurs, the fee simple is known as a **fee simple defeasible** (the word *defeasible* means capable of being terminated, or annulled). For example, a **conveyance,** or transfer of real property, "to A and his heirs as long as the land is used for charitable purposes" creates a fee simple defeasible, because ownership of the property is conditioned on the land's being used for charitable purposes. The original owner retains a *partial* ownership interest, because if

the specified condition does not occur (if the land ceases to be used for charitable purposes), then the land reverts, or returns, to the original owner. If the original owner is not living at the time, the land passes to his or her heirs. The conveyance of a fee simple defeasible usually includes the words as *long as, until, while,* or *during.*

LIFE ESTATES

A **life estate** is an estate that lasts for the life of some specified individual. A conveyance "to A for his life" creates a life estate.[3] In a life estate, the life tenant (the party who holds the estate) has fewer rights of ownership than the holder of a fee simple defeasible, because the rights necessarily cease to exist on the life tenant's death. The life tenant has the right to use the land, provided no *waste* (injury to the land) is committed. In other words, the life tenant cannot injure the land in a manner that would adversely affect its value to the owner of the future interest in it. The life tenant can use the land to harvest crops or, if mines and oil wells are already on the land, can extract minerals and oil from it, but the life tenant cannot exploit the land by creating new wells or mines.

With few exceptions, the owner of a life estate has an exclusive right to possession during his or her lifetime. In addition, the life tenant has the right to mortgage the life estate and create other interests in the land, but none can extend beyond the life of the tenant.

Along with these rights, the life tenant also has some duties—to keep the property in repair and to pay property taxes. In short, the owner of the life estate has the same rights as a fee simple owner except that he or she must maintain the value of the property during his or her tenancy, less the decrease in value resulting from the normal use of the property allowed by the life tenancy.

At issue in the following case was whether the removal of timber, under a right to do so specifically granted in a deed to a life tenant, constituted waste.

---

3. A less common type of life estate is created by the conveyance "to A for the life of B." This is known as an estate *pur autre vie,* or an estate for the duration of the life of another.

CASE 26.2   Meadows v. Belknap

Supreme Court of
Appeals of West
Virginia, 1997.
483 S.E.2d 826.
http://www.state.wv.us/
wvsca/spring97.htm[a]

BACKGROUND AND FACTS   *Carma and Derstine Perrine were married in 1942. During their marriage, Mr. Perrine bought, in his name alone, land in West Virginia. In 1989, Mr. Perrine signed a deed that transferred the land to the Perrines' married daughters, Roberta Meadows and Tara Sue Morgan, but reserved, to the Perrines, a life estate and the right to sell the timber on the land. In 1991, Mr. Perrine died. Three years later, Mrs. Perrine sold the timber to Wade Belknap. The daughters filed a suit in a West Virginia state court against Belknap, Mrs. Perrine, and others to stop the timber's removal, which the daughters argued was committing waste. The court ruled that Mrs. Perrine could not remove timber without the daughters' consent. Mrs. Perrine appealed.*

IN THE LANGUAGE OF THE COURT

DAVIS, Justice.

*   *   *   *

*   *   * [In the deed] Mr. Perrine stated in plain language that he was "retain[ing] the free lifetime usage of all said tracts or parcels of land for and during the lifetime" of himself and Mrs. Perrine. *   *   * Mr. Perrine specifically set out in the deed that during his lifetime and the lifetime of Mrs. Perrine, each of them retained "the right to use any timber thereon for farm purposes and with the specific right to sell any timber on said tracts[.]" The clarity of the latter passage denudes the argument raised by the daughters. The daughters had no right to interfere with Mrs. Perrine's sale of any or all of the timber on the property. The very words of the deed foreclosed such interference.

DECISION AND REMEDY   *The Supreme Court of Appeals reversed the decision of the lower court. The life tenant (Mrs. Perrine) could remove the timber from the land because the deed provided specifically for it.*

---

a. Scroll down the list of cases to the name of the case (no. "23534") and click on it to access the opinion. This Web site is maintained by the state of West Virginia.

FUTURE INTERESTS

When an owner in fee simple absolute conveys the estate conditionally to another (such as with a fee simple defeasible) or for a limited period of time (such as with a life estate), the original owner still retains an interest in the land. The owner retains the right to repossess ownership of the land if the conditions of the fee simple defeasible are not met or when the life of the life-estate holder ends. The residuary (or leftover) interest in the property that the owner retains is called a **future interest,** because if it arises, it will only arise in the future.

If the owner retains ownership of the future interest, then the future interest is a **reversionary interest,** because the property will *revert* to the original owner if the condition specified in the fee sim-

ple defeasible fails or when the life tenant dies. If, however, the owner of the future interest transfers ownership rights in that future interest to another, the future interest is a **remainder.** For example, a conveyance "to A for life, then to B" creates a life estate for A and a remainder (future interest) for B. An **executory interest** is a type of future interest very similar to a remainder, but an executory interest does not take effect immediately on the expiration of another interest, such as a life estate. For example, a conveyance "to A for life and one year after A's death to B" creates an executory interest for B.

LEASEHOLD ESTATES

A **leasehold estate** is created when a real property owner or lessor (landlord) agrees to convey the right to possess and use the property to a lessee (tenant) for a certain period of time. The tenant has a *qualified* right to exclusive possession (qualified by the right of the landlord to enter upon the premises to assure that waste is not being committed). The tenant can use the land—for example, by harvesting crops—but cannot injure it by such activities as cutting down timber for sale or extracting oil. Here we look at the types of leasehold estates, or tenancies, that can be created when real property is leased.

Tenancy for Years.   A **tenancy for years** is created by an express contract (which can sometimes be oral) by which property is leased for a specified period of time, such as a month, a year, or a period of years. For example, signing a one-year lease to occupy an apartment creates a tenancy for years. At the end of the period specified in the lease, the lease ends (without notice), and possession of the apartment returns to the lessor. The lease may provide for renewal or extension.

Periodic Tenancy.   A **periodic tenancy** is created by a lease that does not specify how long it is to last but does specify that rent is to be paid at certain intervals. This type of tenancy is automatically renewed for another rental period unless properly terminated. For example, a periodic tenancy is created by a lease that states, "Rent is due on the tenth day of every month." This provision creates a tenancy from month to month. This type of tenancy can also be from week to week or from year to year. A periodic tenancy sometimes arises when a landlord allows a tenant under a tenancy for years to remain in possession after the lease expires and continue paying monthly or weekly rent. At common law, to terminate a periodic tenancy, the landlord or tenant must give one period's notice to the other party. If the tenancy is month to month, for example, one month's notice must be given. State statutes often require a different period for notice of termination in a periodic tenancy, however.

Tenancy at Will.   Suppose a landlord rents an apartment to a tenant "for as long as both agree." In such a case, the tenant receives a **tenancy at will**. At common law, either party can terminate the tenancy without notice (that is, "at will"). This type of tenancy usually arises when a tenant who has been under a tenancy for years retains possession after the termination date of that tenancy with the landlord's consent.

Before the tenancy has been converted into a periodic tenancy (by the periodic payment of rent), it is a tenancy at will, terminable by either party without notice. The death of either party or the voluntary commission of waste by the tenant will terminate a tenancy at will.

Tenancy at Sufferance.   The mere possession of land without right is called a **tenancy at sufferance.** It is not a true tenancy. A tenancy at sufferance is not an estate, because it is created by a tenant's *wrongfully* retaining possession of property. Whenever a life estate, tenancy for years, periodic tenancy, or tenancy at will ends and the tenant continues to retain possession of the premises without the owner's permission, a tenancy at sufferance is created.

CONCURRENT OWNERSHIP

Persons who share ownership rights simultaneously in particular property are said to be *concurrent owners.* There are two principal types of **concurrent ownership:** *tenancy in common* and *joint tenancy.* Concurrent ownership rights can also be held in a *tenancy by the entirety* or as *community property*, although these latter two types of concurrent ownership are less common.

Tenancy in Common.   A form of co-ownership in which each of two or more persons owns an undivided portion of the property is a **tenancy in common.** The portions need not be equal. When a tenant in common dies, the property interest passes to the heirs. For example, suppose Henri and Luis own equal interests in a rare coin collection as tenants in common. If Henri dies before Luis, one-half of the coin collection will become the property of Henri's heirs. If instead Henri sells his interest to Stella, Stella and Luis will become co-owners as tenants in common. If Stella dies, her interest in the personal property will pass to her heirs, and they in turn will own the property with Luis as tenants in common.

Joint Tenancy.   In a **joint tenancy,** each of two or more persons owns an undivided interest in the whole (personal property), and a deceased joint tenant's interest *passes to the surviving joint tenant or tenants.* Joint tenancy can be terminated at any time before the joint tenant's death by gift or by sale. If no termination occurs, then upon the death of a joint tenant, his or her interest transfers to the remaining joint tenants, not to the heirs of the deceased joint tenant. To illustrate: If Henri and Luis from the preceding example are joint tenants and if Henri dies before Luis, the entire collection will become the property of Luis. Henri's heirs will receive absolutely no interest in the collection. If Henri sells his interest to Stella, Stella and Luis will become co-owners. Henri's sale, however, will have terminated the joint tenancy, and Stella and Luis will become owners as tenants in common.

Exhibit 26–1 illustrates the concepts of tenancy in common and joint tenancy.

Tenancy by the Entirety.   **A tenancy by the entirety** is created by a *conveyance* (transfer) of real property to a husband and wife. It is distinguished from a joint tenancy by the inability of either spouse to transfer separately his or her interest during his or her lifetime. In states in which statutes give the wife the right to convey her property, tenancy by the entirety has been effectively abolished. A divorce, either spouse's death, or mutual agreement will terminate a tenancy by the entirety.

Community Property.   A limited number of states[4] allow property to be owned as **community property.** If property is held as community property, each spouse technically owns an *undivided* one-half interest in it. This type of ownership generally does not apply to property acquired prior to the marriage or to property acquired by gift or inheritance during the marriage.

---

4. These states include Alaska, Arizona, California, Idaho, Louisiana, Nevada, New Mexico, Texas, Washington, and Wisconsin, as well as Puerto Rico.

EXHIBIT 26–1   TENANCY IN COMMON AND JOINT TENANCY

If Henri and Luis own equal interests in a coin collection as tenants in common, and Henri dies, one-half of the coin collection will become the property of Henri's heirs. If instead Henri sells his interest to Stella, Stella and Luis will become co-owners as tenants in common. If Henri and Luis own the coin collection as joint tenants, however, and Henri dies, the entire collection will become the property of Luis. If instead Henri sells his interest to Stella, Luis and Stella will become co-owners as tenants in common.

CONCEPT
SUMMARY 26.1   OWNERSHIP INTERESTS IN REAL PROPERTY

TYPE OF INTEREST	DESCRIPTION
Fee Simple	1. *Fee simple absolute*—The most complete form of ownership. 2. *Fee simple defeasible*—Ownership in fee simple that can end if a specified event or condition occurs.
Life Estate	An estate that lasts for the life of a specified individual; ownership rights in a life estate are subject to the rights of the future-interest holder.
Future Interest	A residuary interest not granted by the grantor in conveying an estate to another for life, for a specified period of time, or on the condition that a specific event does or does not occur. These include the following: 1. *Reversionary interest*—The grantor retains the residuary interest. 2. *Remainder*—The grantor transfers ownership rights in the future interest to another who will take possession immediately on the expiration another interest. 3. *Executory interest*—Like a remainder, but it does not take effect immediately on the expiration of another interest.
Leasehold Estate	A leasehold interest, or estate, is an interest in real property that is held only for a limited period of time, as specified in the lease agreement. Types of tenancies relating to leased property include the following: 1. *Tenancy for years*—Tenancy for a period of time stated by express contract. 2. *Periodic tenancy*—Tenancy for a period determined by the frequency of rent payments; automatically renewed unless proper notice is given. 3. *Tenancy at will*—Tenancy for as long as both parties agree; no notice of termination is required. 4. *Tenancy at sufferance*—Possession of land without legal right.
Concurrent Ownership	Exists when title to property is held by two or more persons. Co-ownership can take the following forms: 1. *Tenancy in common*—Two or more persons own an undivided interest in property; on one tenant's death, the property interest passes to his or her heirs. 2. *Joint tenancy*—Two or more persons own an undivided interest in property; on the death of a joint tenant, the property interest transfers to the remaining tenant(s), not to the heirs of the deceased. 3. *Tenancy by the entirety*—Between a husband and wife, and similar to a joint tenancy, except that a spouse cannot transfer separately his or her interest during his or her lifetime. 4. *Community property*—Between a husband and wife, and each spouse technically owns an undivided one-half interest in property acquired during the marriage. This type of ownership occurs in only a few states.

SECTION 3

Private Control of Land Use

One source of land-use control is voluntary agreements between private individuals. A landowner's use of his or her property may be limited by another individual's right to, for example, cross the property. Such interests do not depend on the individual's possession of the property but still limit the use of the property. These interests may be created in a deed. Other promises included in a deed, or in an assignment, lease, mortgage, or other instrument relating to real property, may limit a landowner's use of his or her property in other ways. Here, we examine the ways in which private agreements serve as mechanisms for control of land use.

NONPOSSESSORY INTERESTS

Some interests in land do not include any rights of possession. These interests, known as nonpossessory interests, include *easements*, *profits*, and *licenses*. Because easements and profits are similar, and the same rules apply to both, they will be discussed together.

Easements and Profits. An **easement** is the right of a person to make limited use of another person's real property without taking anything from the property. Suppose Sara, the owner of Whiteacres, has a right to drive her car across Ken's land, Greenacres, which is adjacent to Whiteacres. This right-of-way over Greenacres is an easement. In contrast, a **profit** is the right to go onto land in possession of another and take away some part of the land itself or some product of the land. For example, Chen, the owner of Sea View, gives Loretta the right to go there and remove all the sand and gravel that she needs for her cement business. Loretta has a profit.[5]

Creation of an Easement or Profit. Profits and easements can be created by *deed* or *will* or by *implication*, *necessity*, or *prescription*. Creation by deed or will involves simply the delivery of a *deed* or a transfer by a *will*, by the owner of an easement, stating that the grantee (the person receiving the profit or easement) is granted the rights in the easement or profit that the grantor had. An easement or profit is created by *implication* when the circumstances surrounding the division of a parcel of property imply its creation. If Adrian divides a parcel of land that has only one well for drinking water and conveys the half without a well to Victor, a profit by implication arises, because Victor needs drinking water.

An easement may also be created by *necessity*. An easement by necessity does not require division of property for its existence. A person who rents an apartment, for example, has an easement by necessity in the private road leading up to it. An easement or profit arises by *prescription* when one person exercises an easement, such as a right-of-way, on another person's land without the landowner's consent, and the use is apparent and continues for a period of time equal to the applicable statute of limitations.

Effect of a Sale of Property. When a parcel of land that is *benefited* by an easement or profit on adjacent land is sold, the property carries the easement or profit along with it. Thus, if Sara sells Whiteacres to MacDonald and includes the right-of-way across her neighbor Ken's land, Greenacres, in the deed to MacDonald, MacDonald will own both the property and the easement that benefits it.

When a parcel of land that has the *burden* of an easement or profit benefiting adjacent land is sold, the new owner must recognize its existence only if he or she knew or should have known of it or if it was recorded in the appropriate office of the county. Thus, if Sara records her easement across Greenacres in the appropriate county office before Ken conveys his land, the new owner of Greenacres will have to allow Sara, or any subsequent owner of Whiteacres, to continue to use the right-of-way across Greenacres.

Termination of an Easement or Profit. An easement or profit can be terminated or extinguished in several ways. The simplest way is to deed it back to the owner of the land that is burdened by it. Also, if the owner of an easement or profit becomes the owner of the property burdened by it, then it is merged into the property. Another way is to abandon the easement with the intent to relinquish the right to use it. In the following case, one of the questions was whether ceasing to use an easement for the purpose for which it was granted constitutes abandonment.

---

5. Easements and profits may be *appurtenant* or *in gross*. An easement or profit appurtenant arises when the owner of one piece of land has a right to go onto (or remove things from) an adjacent piece of land owned by another. An easement or profit in gross simply gives the owner of the easement or profit the right to go onto (or remove something from) land owned by another; there is no requirement that the owner of the easement or profit also own land.

CASE 26.3   Preseault v. United States

United States
Court of Appeals,
Federal Circuit, 1996.
100 F.3d 1525.
**http://www.ll.
georgetown.edu/
Fed-Ct/cafed.html[a]**

BACKGROUND AND FACTS   *In 1899, Rutland-Canadian Railroad Company acquired an easement over land in Burlington, Vermont, on which it laid rails and operated a railroad. Over the years, ownership of the railroad passed through the hands of several different companies. At the same time, the land burdened by the easement also passed to different owners, until J. Paul and Patricia Preseault built a home on it. In 1970, the current owner of the railroad stopped using the line and, in 1975, removed the rails. Eleven years later, the state of Vermont asked the Interstate Commerce Commission (ICC)[b] to authorize a lease of the easement to the city of Burlington for use as a hiking and biking trail. The ICC granted the request, and the trail became popular—on warm weekends, up to two hundred people per hour passed any given spot. The Preseaults filed a suit in the Court of Federal Claims against the federal government, claiming in part that the easement had been abandoned and thus, by authorizing the trail, the government had taken their property and they should be paid for it. The United States filed a motion for summary judgment, which the court granted. The Preseaults appealed.*

**IN THE LANGUAGE
OF THE COURT**

PLAGER, Circuit Judge.

＊   ＊   ＊   ＊

＊   ＊   ＊ [I]n 1986 when the ICC issued its Order authorizing the City to establish a public recreational biking and pedestrian trail on [the Preseaults' land], there was as a matter of state law no railroad easement in existence on [the land], nor had there been for more than ten years. The easement had been abandoned in 1975, and the properties were held by the Preseaults in fee simple, unencumbered by any former property rights of the Railroad. When the City, pursuant to federal authorization, took possession of [the land] and opened [it] to public use, that was a physical taking of the right of exclusive possession that belonged to the Preseaults as an incident of their ownership of the land.

**DECISION
AND REMEDY**

The U.S. Court of Appeals for the Federal Circuit reversed the judgment of the lower court. When the railroad stopped using the line and removed the rails, it abandoned the easement. The court remanded the case for a determination of how much the Preseaults should be paid.

---

a. Click on "1996 Decisions". In the list that opens, click on "November". From that results, click on the name of the case to access the opinion. This Web site is maintained by the Edward Bennett Williams Library at the Georgetown University Law Center in Washington, D.C.
b. The Interstate Commerce Commission was a federal agency with jurisdiction over railroad operations. It was abolished in 1996.

Licenses.   A **license** is the revocable right of a person to come onto another person's land. It is a personal privilege that arises from the consent of the owner of the land and that can be revoked by the owner. A ticket to attend a movie at a theater is an example of a license. The ticket is only a revocable license, not a conveyance of an interest in property.

RESTRICTIVE COVENANTS

A private restriction on the use of land is known as a **restrictive covenant.** If the restriction is binding on

the party who purchases the property originally as well as on subsequent purchasers—in other words, if its benefit or obligation passes with the land's ownership—it is said to "run with the land."

Covenants Running with the Land.   A restrictive covenant that runs with the land goes with the land and cannot be separated from it. Consider an example. Owen is the owner of Grasslands, a twenty-acre estate whose northern half contains a small reservoir. Owen wishes to convey the northern half to Arid City, but before he does, he digs an irrigation ditch connecting the reservoir with the lower ten acres, which he uses as farmland. When Owen conveys the northern ten acres to Arid City, he enters into an agreement with the city. The agreement, which is contained in the deed, states, "Arid City, its heirs and assigns, promises not to remove more than five thousand gallons of water per day from the Grasslands reservoir." Owen has created a restrictive covenant running with the land under which Arid City and all future owners of the northern ten acres of Grasslands are limited as to the amount of water they can draw from its reservoir.

Four requirements must be met for a covenant running with the land to be enforceable. If they are not met, the covenant will apply to the two original parties to a contract only and will not run with the land to future owners. The requirements are as follows:

1. The covenant running with the land must be created in a written agreement (covenant). It is usually contained in the document that conveys the land.
2. The parties must intend that the covenant run with the land. In other words, the instrument that contains the covenant must state not only that the promisor is bound by the terms of the covenant but that all the promisor's "successors, heirs, or assigns" will be bound.
3. The covenant must touch and concern the land. That is, the limitations on the activities of the owner of the burdened land must have some connection with the land. For example, a purchaser of land cannot be bound by a covenant requiring him or her to drive only Ford pickups, because such a restriction has no relation to the land purchased.
4. The successors to the original parties to the covenant must have notice of the covenant.

To satisfy the last requirement, the notice may be actual or constructive. For example, in the course of developing a fifty-lot suburban subdivision, Levitt records a declaration of restrictions that effectively limits construction on each lot to one single-family house. In each lot's deed is a reference to the declaration with a provision that the purchaser and his or her successors are bound to those restrictions. Thus, each purchaser assumes ownership with notice of the restrictions. If an owner attempts to build a duplex (or any structure that does not comply with the restrictions) on a lot, the other owners may obtain a court order enjoining the construction.

In fact, Levitt might simply have included the restrictions on the subdivision's map, filed the map in the appropriate public office, and included a reference to the map in each deed. In this way, each owner would have been held to have constructive notice of the restrictions.

Illegal Restrictive Covenants. Restrictive covenants have sometimes been used to perpetuate neighborhood segregation, and in these cases they have been invalidated by the courts. In the United States Supreme Court case of *Shelley v. Kraemer*,[6] restrictive covenants proscribing resale to minority groups were declared unconstitutional and could no longer be enforced in courts of law. In addition, the Civil Rights Act of 1968 (also known as the Fair Housing Act) prohibits all discrimination based on race, color, religion, or national origin in the sale and leasing of housing.

SECTION 4

Public Control of Land Use

Land use is subject to regulation by the state within whose political boundaries the land is located. Most states authorize control over land use through various planning boards and zoning authorities at a city or county level. The federal government does not engage in land-use control under normal circumstances, except with respect to federally owned land.[7] The federal government does influence state and local regulation, however, through the allocation of federal funds. Stipulations on land use may be a condition to the states' receiving such funds.

SOURCES OF PUBLIC CONTROL

The states' power to control the use of land through legislation is derived from their *police power* and the doctrine of *eminent domain*. Under their police power, state governments enact legislation that promotes the health, safety, and welfare of their citizens. This legislation includes land-use controls. The power of **eminent domain** is the government's authority to take private property for public use or purpose without the owner's consent. Typically, this is accomplished through a judicial proceeding to obtain title to the land.

---

6. 334 U.S. 1, 68 S.Ct. 836, 92 L.Ed. 1161 (1948).
7. Federal (and state) laws concerning environmental matters such as air and water quality, the protection of endangered species, and the preservation of natural wetlands are also a source of land-use control.

POLICE POWER

As an exercise of its police power,[8] a state can regulate the use of land within its jurisdiction. A few states control land use at the state level. Hawaii, for instance, employs a statewide land-use classification scheme. Some states have a land-permit process that operates in conjunction with local control. Florida, for example, uses such a scheme in certain areas of "critical environmental concern" to permit or prohibit development on the basis of available roads, sewers, and so on. Vermont also utilizes a statewide land-permit scheme.

Usually, however, a state authorizes its city or county governments to regulate the use of land within their local jurisdictions. A state confers this power through *enabling legislation*. Enabling legislation normally requires local governments to devise *general plans* before imposing other land-use controls. Enabling acts also typically authorize local bodies to enact *zoning laws* to regulate the use of land and the types of and specifications for structures. Local planning boards may regulate the development of subdivisions, in which private developers subdivide large tracts of land and construct commercial or residential units for resale to others. Local governments may also enact growth-management ordinances to control development in their jurisdictions.

Government Plans.   Most states require that land-use laws follow a local government's general plan. A **general plan** is a comprehensive, long-term scheme dealing with the physical development, and in some cases redevelopment, of a city or community. It addresses such concerns as types of housing, protection of natural resources, provision of public facilities and transportation, and other issues related to land use. A plan indicates the direction of growth in a community and the contributions that private developers must make toward providing such public facilities as roads. If a proposed use is not authorized by the general plan, the plan may be amended to permit the use. (A plan may also be amended to preclude a proposed use.)

Even when a proposed use complies with a general plan, it may not be allowed. Most jurisdictions have requirements in addition to those in the general plan. These requirements are included in specific plans—also called special, area, or community plans.

Specific plans typically pertain to only a portion of a jurisdiction's area. For example, a specific plan may concern a downtown area subject to redevelopment efforts, an area with special environmental concerns, or an area with increased public transportation needs arising from population growth.

Zoning Laws.   In addition to complying with a general plan and any specific plans, a particular land use must comply with zoning laws. The term **zoning** refers to the dividing of an area into districts to which specific land-use regulations apply. A typical zoning law consists of a zoning map and a zoning ordinance. The zoning map indicates the characteristics of each parcel of land within an area and divides that area into districts. The zoning ordinance specifies the restrictions on land use within those districts.

Zoning ordinances generally include two types of restrictions. One type pertains to the kind of land use—such as commercial versus residential—to which property within a particular district may be put. The second type dictates the engineering features and architectural design of structures built within that district.

Use Restrictions.   Districts are typically zoned for residential, commercial, industrial, or agricultural use. Each district may be further subdivided for degree or intensity of use. For example, a residential district may be subdivided to permit a certain number of apartment buildings and a certain number of units in each building. Commercial and industrial districts are often zoned to permit heavy or *light* activity. Heavy activity might include the operation of large factories. Light activity might include the operation of professional office buildings or small retail shops. Zoning that specifies the use to which property may be put is referred to as **use zoning.**

Structural Restrictions.   Restrictions known as *bulk regulations* cover such details as minimum floor-space requirements and minimum lot-size restrictions. For example, a particular district's minimum floor-space requirements might specify that a one-story building contain a minimum of 1,240 square feet of floor space, and minimum lot-size restrictions might specify that each single-family dwelling be built on a lot that is at least one acre in size. Referred to collectively as **bulk zoning,** these regulations also dictate *setback* (the distance between a building and a street, sidewalk, or other boundary) and the height of buildings, with different requirements for buildings in different areas.

---

8. As pointed out in Chapter 5, the police power of a state encompasses the right to regulate private activities to protect or promote the public order, health, safety, morals, and general welfare.

Restrictions related to structure may also be concerned with such matters as architectural control, the overall appearance of a community, and the preservation of historic buildings. An ordinance may require that all proposed construction be approved by a design review board composed of local architects. A community may restrict the size and placement of outdoor advertising, such as billboards and business signs. A property owner may be prohibited from tearing down or remodeling a historic landmark or building. In challenges against these types of restrictions, the courts have generally upheld the regulations.[9]

Variances.　A **zoning variance** allows property to be used or structures to be built in some way that varies from the restrictions of a zoning ordinance. A variance may exempt property from a use restriction to allow, for example, a bakery shop in a residential area. Or a variance may exempt a building from a height

restriction so that, for example, a two-story house can be built in a district in which houses are otherwise limited to one floor. Some jurisdictions do not permit variances from use restrictions.

Variances are normally granted by local adjustment boards. In general, a property owner must meet three criteria to obtain a variance:

1. The owner must find it impossible to realize a reasonable return on the land as currently zoned.
2. The adverse effect of the zoning ordinance must be particular to the party seeking the variance and not have a similar effect on other owners in the same zone.
3. Granting the variance must not substantially alter the essential character of the zoned area.

Perhaps the most important of these criteria is whether the variance would substantially alter the character of the area. Courts are more lenient about the other requirements when reviewing decisions of adjustment boards. As the following case illustrates, courts also tend to defer to the discretion of such boards unless there has been a clear abuse of authority.

9. See, for example, *Penn Central Transportation Co. v. New York City*, 438 U.S. 104, 98 S.Ct. 2646, 57 L.Ed.2d 631 (1978).

CASE 26.4

Allegheny West Civic Council, Inc. v. Zoning Board of Adjustment of the City of Pittsburgh

Supreme Court of
Pennsylvania, 1997.
689 A.2d 225.

BACKGROUND AND FACTS　*Irwin Associates, Inc., contracted to sell, for $431,500, a vacant lot in an area in Pittsburgh, Pennsylvania, zoned for residential use. The deal collapsed when it was learned that the lot was contaminated with petroleum hydrocarbon and benzene in excess of state and federal guidelines. Estimated clean-up costs were substantial. Irwin asked the Pittsburgh Zoning Board of Adjustment for a variance to use the property as a parking lot. Allegheny West Civic Council wanted residential housing in the area and opposed Irwin's request. The board concluded that Irwin's proposed use would not be detrimental to the neighborhood and granted the variance. Allegheny West appealed to a Pennsylvania state court, which affirmed the board's decision. Ultimately, the case was appealed to the state supreme court.*

IN THE LANGUAGE
OF THE COURT

NIGRO, Justice.
* 　* 　* 　*

Irwin Associates' environmental consultant testified that the contamination exceeded state and federal guidelines and that a building on the property may be a health hazard because vapors could accumulate inside. Its real estate financing expert testified that it was unlikely that a financial institution would lend money for a construction project on the property because it would expose itself to potential liability for [clean-up] costs. Irwin Associates' president testified that the relatively small size of the lot precluded other permitted uses not involving improvements. The environmental consultant estimated that the [clean-up] cost would be $2.5 [million] to $3 million and annual monitoring costs would be $10,000 to $20,000. There is thus substantial evidence that

Irwin Associates cannot use the property for a permitted purpose or can only conform it for a permitted purpose at a prohibitive cost. Furthermore, *   *   * there is evidence that the property is now without value as zoned. The local property assessment board assigned the property a fair market value of zero.

The Zoning Board did not abuse its discretion *   *   * in granting the variance.

DECISION AND REMEDY *The Supreme Court of Pennsylvania affirmed the board's decision to grant the variance. The variant use would not harm the character of the neighborhood, and denying the variance would create unnecessary hardship for the property owner.*

Subdivision Regulations. When subdividing a parcel of land into smaller plots, a private developer must comply not only with local zoning ordinances but also with local subdivision regulations. Subdivision regulations are different from zoning ordinances, although they may be administered by the same local agencies that oversee the zoning process. In the design of a subdivision, the local authorities may demand, for example, the allocation of space for a public park or school or may require a developer to construct streets to accommodate a specific level of traffic.

Growth-Management Ordinances. To prevent population growth from racing ahead of the community's ability to provide necessary public services, local authorities may enact a growth-management ordinance to limit, for example, the number of residential building permits. A property owner may thus be precluded from constructing a residential building on his or her property even if the area is zoned for the use and the proposed structure complies with all other requirements. A growth-management ordinance may prohibit the issuance of residential building permits for a specific period of time, until the occurrence of a specific event (such as a decline in the total number of residents in the community), or on the basis of the availability of necessary public services (such as the capacity for drainage in the area or the proximity of hospitals and police stations).

Limitations on the Exercise of Police Power. The government's exercise of its police power to regulate the use of land is limited in at least three ways. Two of these limitations arise under the Fourteenth Amendment to the Constitution. The third limitation arises under the Fifth Amendment and requires that, under certain circumstances, the government must compensate an owner who is deprived of the use of his or her property.

Due Process and Equal Protection. A government cannot regulate the use of land in a way that violates either the due process clause or the equal protection clause of the Fourteenth Amendment. A government may be deemed to violate the due process clause if it acts arbitrarily or unreasonably. Thus, there must be a *rational basis* for classifications that are imposed on property. Any classification that is reasonably related to the health or general welfare of the public is deemed to have a rational basis.

Under the equal protection clause, land-use controls cannot be discriminatory. A zoning ordinance is discriminatory if it affects one parcel of land in a way in which it does not affect surrounding parcels and if there is no rational basis for the difference. For example, classifying a single parcel in a way that does not accord with a general plan is discriminatory. Similarly, a zoning ordinance cannot be racially discriminatory. For example, a community may not zone itself to exclude all low-income housing if the intention is to exclude minorities.

The following case involved a challenge to a zoning ordinance on the ground that it did not relate to any legitimate governmental health, safety, or welfare concerns.

CASE 26.5   Shemo v. Mayfield Heights

Supreme Court
of Ohio, 2000.
88 Ohio St.3d 7,
722 N.E.2d 1018.
http://www.
lawyersweekly.com/
ohsc.htm[a]

BACKGROUND AND FACTS   *Michael Shemo and Larry Goldberg owned an undeveloped 22.6-acre parcel of land in Mayfield Heights, Ohio. Residential properties were to the west of the parcel. Commercial properties, including a Best Buy store, a Budgetel Motel, and a Bob Evans restaurant, bordered the property to the south. High-tension power lines and Interstate 271, with high-intensity lighting, ran along the eastern edge of the property. A shopping center was on the other side of the highway. The property was zoned "U-1" for single-family homes when the Mayfield Heights City Council enacted an ordinance to rezone the property "U-2-A" for cluster single-family homes. Shemo and Goldberg filed a suit in an Ohio state court against the city to invalidate the ordinance and have the property rezoned "U-4" to permit retail and warehouse use. They proposed to widen and replace the commercial driveway and install a traffic light to improve the traffic flow. They also proposed to limit access from their property to the residential streets to emergency vehicles. The court declared the ordinance unconstitutional, in part on the ground that it did not substantially advance a legitimate health, safety, or welfare concern of the city. The city appealed to a state intermediate appellate court, which remanded the case for reconsideration. Shemo and Goldberg appealed to the Ohio Supreme Court.*

**IN THE LANGUAGE
OF THE COURT**

FRANCIS E. SWEENEY, SR., J. [Judge]
     *   *   *   *

     The city argued that the zoning ordinance advances three legitimate governmental health, safety, and welfare concerns: (1) it will maintain the residential character of the neighborhood, (2) it will maintain a balanced mix of uses in the city, and (3) it will not exacerbate traffic congestion *   *   * .
     *   *   * [T]he city presented the testimony of some current residents who are opposed to the commercial development of the property because there will likely be increased traffic in their neighborhood. While we do not mean to minimize the concerns of these residents and, in fact, sympathize with their plight, we cannot ignore the fact that their homes are adjacent to high-density commercial property, which carries with it a heavy volume of traffic. *   *   * We reject the city's argument that the U-2-A zoning is necessary to maintain the residential character of the neighborhood.
     We also reject the city's argument that the U-2-A zoning classification is necessary to advance the legitimate governmental interests of maintaining a balanced mix of uses in the city *   *   * . Since the area contains both residential and commercial properties, there already exists a balanced mix of uses in the city. *   *   *
     Nor did the trial court err in rejecting the city's argument that decreasing traffic congestion is a legitimate governmental concern. Although the U-4 zoning classification would increase traffic in the area, one of appellants' expert witnesses testified that the impact of the increased traffic would not be severe. *   *   * [A]ppellants have proposed to widen and replace the current driveway at their expense and to have a traffic light installed to improve the flow of traffic in the area and to alleviate current safety concerns. Appellants have also proposed to limit direct access from their property to the residential streets to cases of emergency only. *   *   *
     *   *   *   *

---

a. In the "2000 Opinions" section, click on "February". When the page opens, scroll to the name of the case and click on it to access the opinion. This Web site is maintained by Lawyers Weekly, Inc., a publisher of legal newspapers for practicing attorneys.

Since appellants have shown that the city lacks any legitimate governmental health, safety, and welfare concerns in support of the U-2-A zoning classification, we find that the trial court was correct in declaring the U-2-A zoning ordinance unconstitutional.

DECISION AND REMEDY   *The Ohio Supreme Court reversed the judgment of the state intermediate appellate court and reinstated the trial court's judgment declaring the zoning ordinance unconstitutional. Shemo and Goldberg showed that the city did not have any legitimate governmental health, safety, or welfare concerns to support the ordinance.*

Just Compensation.   Under the Fifth Amendment, private property may not be taken for a public purpose without the payment of just compensation.[10] If government restrictions on a landowner's property rights are overly burdensome, the regulation may be deemed a **taking.** A taking occurs when a regulation denies an owner the ability to use his or her property for any reasonable income-producing or private purpose for which it is suited. This requires the government to pay the owner.

Suppose Perez purchases a large tract of land with the intent to subdivide and develop it into residential properties. At the time of the purchase, there are no zoning laws restricting use of the land. After Perez has taken significant steps to develop the property, the county attempts to zone the tract "public parkland only." If this prohibits Perez from developing any of the land, it will be deemed a taking. If the county does not fairly compensate Perez, the regulation will be held unconstitutional and void.

The distinction between an ordinance that merely restricts land use and an outright taking is crucial. A restriction is simply an exercise of the state's police power; even though it limits a property owner's land use, the owner generally need not be compensated for the limitation. An ordinance that completely deprives an owner of use or benefit of property, or an outright governmental taking of property, however, must be compensated.

The United States Supreme Court has held that restrictions do not constitute a taking of an owner's property if they "substantially advance legitimate state interests" and do not "den[y] an owner economically viable use of his land."[11] It is not clear, however, exactly what constitutes a "legitimate state interest" or when particular restrictions "substantially advance" that interest. Furthermore, the term "economically viable use" has not yet been clearly defined.

State constitutions also contain provisions that prohibit the taking of private property for a public purpose without the payment of just compensation. The following case involved a challenge to a state statute on this basis.

---

10. Although the Fifth Amendment pertains to actions taken by the federal government, the Fourteenth Amendment has been interpreted as extending this limitation to state actions.

11. *Agins v. Tiburon,* 447 U.S. 255, 100 S.Ct. 2138, 65 L.Ed. 2d 106 (1980).

CASE 26.6   Purdie v. Attorney General

Supreme Court of
New Hampshire, 1999.
732 A.2d 442.
http://www.state.nh.us/
courts/supreme/
opinions/9906.html[a]

BACKGROUND AND FACTS   *In 1995, the New Hampshire state legislature enacted a statute that recognized the state's public trust rights[b] in "all shorelands subject to the ebb and flow of the tide to the high water mark and subject to those littoral rights recognized at common law." (Littoral rights concern property that abuts an ocean, a sea, or a lake, rather than a river or a stream.) The statute defined "high water mark" in part as "the furthest landward limit reached by the highest tidal flow" over the nineteen-year tidal cycle, excluding "abnormal" storms. William Purdie and forty other beach-front property owners*

---

a. The "Judicial Branch of the New Hampshire State Government" maintains this Web site. In the "June 24, 1999" section, click on the case name to access the opinion.

b. *Public trust rights* are the public's rights to the use of land under water for navigation, fishing, and recreation. A state has a responsibility to act as the public's trustee to protect and preserve those rights.

filed a suit in a New Hampshire state court against the state, asserting that the statute effected a taking of their property without just compensation in violation of the state constitution and the Fifth Amendment of the U.S. Constitution. The state filed a motion for summary judgment. In ruling for the plaintiffs, the court concluded that common law defines the phrase "high water mark" as the "mean high tide line," and therefore, the legislature's action in setting the boundary line at the highest elevation of tidal action was an unconstitutional extension of public property rights and a taking of the plaintiffs' property. The state appealed to the New Hampshire Supreme Court.

IN THE LANGUAGE OF THE COURT

BRODERICK, J. [Justice]

* * * *

After an extensive review, we conclude that New Hampshire common law establishes the high water mark at the level of mean high tide. In 1862, this court referred to the public-private shoreland boundary line as the "ordinary high water mark." Over one hundred years later [in 1969, in *Sibson v. State*] we held that public "[t]idewaters are those in which the tide ordinarily ebbs and flows."

The context of the *Sibson* case makes clear that the common law public-private boundary line or "ordinary high water mark" was at the level of mean high tide. * * * [T]he United States Supreme Court [has] held that the shoreland boundary for purposes of federal grants was the "ordinary high water mark," which it defined as the "mean high tide line," that is, "the average height of all the high waters" over a complete tidal cycle.

* * *

* * * *

Finally, New Hampshire common law regarding other public waters indicates that the mean high tide mark was intended as the public-private shoreland boundary. [In other cases, we] have held that large ponds are owned by the State in trust for public use up to their "natural mean high water mark." Moreover, we have noted that "[t]he law of public waters is presumably uniform, and on many questions it is not material whether an authority relates to tide-water or to large ponds." Accordingly, we conclude that the mean high tide is the high water mark or common law coastal boundary between public and private shorelands.

* * * *

Having determined that New Hampshire common law limits public ownership of the shorelands to the mean high water mark, we conclude that the legislature went beyond these common law limits by extending public trust rights to the highest high water mark. Although the legislature has the power to change or redefine the common law to conform to current standards and public needs, *property rights created by the common law may not be taken away legislatively without due process of law.* Because [the statute in question] unilaterally authorizes the taking of private shoreland for public use and provides no compensation for landowners whose property has been appropriated, it violates the prohibition in the State Constitution and the Fifth Amendment of the Federal Constitution against the taking of property for public use without just compensation. Although it may be desirable for the State to expand public beaches to cope with increasing crowds, the State may not do so without compensating the affected landowners. [Emphasis added.]

DECISION AND REMEDY

The New Hampshire Supreme Court affirmed the ruling of the lower court and remanded the case for a decision regarding the actual location of the mean high water mark and a determination as to which, if any, of the plaintiffs were entitled to damages. The statute was unconstitutional because it constituted a taking of private property without just compensation.

EMINENT DOMAIN

As noted above, governments have an inherent power to take property for public use or purpose without the consent of the owner. This is the power of eminent domain, and it is very important in the public control of land use.

Every property owner holds his or her interest in land subject to a superior interest. Just as in medieval England the king was the ultimate landowner, so in the United States the government retains an ultimate ownership right in all land. This right, known as eminent domain, is sometimes referred to as the *condemnation power* of the government to take land for public use. It gives to the government a right to acquire possession of real property in the manner directed by the Constitution and the laws of the state whenever the public interest requires it. Property may not be taken for private benefit, but only for public use.

For example, when a new public highway is to be built, the government must decide where to build it and how much land to condemn. After the government determines that a particular parcel of land is necessary for public use, it brings a judicial proceeding to obtain title to the land. A property owner whose land is being condemned may oppose the condemnation. Arguing that the government does not need

the land is not usually enough, however. The owner must show fraud or some other illegality, such as that the taking is for a private purpose.

Under the Fifth Amendment, although the government may take land for public use, it must pay fair and just compensation for it. Thus, in the previous highway example, after the proceeding to obtain title to the land, there is a second proceeding in which the court determines the *fair value* of the land. Fair value is usually approximately equal to market value.

Sometimes, as might occur in the highway example, only part of an owner's property is taken. The impact of the public use of this part on the owner's remaining land may be considered in determining just compensation, if this impact includes benefits that are "special" to that owner's property. Any special benefits, however, must be different than the "general" benefits that accrue to the rest of the neighborhood from, for example, having a new highway. Just compensation and a consideration of special benefits were at the heart of the following case.

CASE 26.7 **City of Branson v. Estate of LaFavre**

Missouri Court of Appeals,
Southern District, 2000.
9 S.W.3d 755.
http://www.osca.state.
mo.us/courts/
pubopinions.nsf[a]

BACKGROUND AND FACTS *Shepherd of the Hills Expressway in Branson, Missouri, was a two-lane road without curbs, streetlights, or sidewalks. The City of Branson and Taney County, in which Branson is located, wanted to widen the expressway to five lanes, including a center turn lane, and add curbs, gutters, sidewalks, and streetlights. Andrew Gugar, Jr, owned property next to the expressway.[b] The city and the county filed a condemnation suit against Gugar to obtain the land and the easements to widen the road. Through the suit, the city and the county obtained title to 0.26 acres for the right of way, 0.21 acres for a utility easement, 0.39 acres for a drainage easement, and a temporary construction easement covering 1.08 acres. When it came to determining how much compensation to pay Gugar, the plaintiffs argued that they owed him nothing. They claimed that the widening of the road, and the other improvements, specially benefited his remaining property. Their witnesses testified that Gugar's property increased in value between $17,000 and $19,000 beyond any loss caused by the taking. Gugar's witnesses valued his land at $60,000 to $68,000 less than before the "improvements." The court awarded Gugar $68,000. The city and the county appealed to a state intermediate appellate court.*

IN THE LANGUAGE
OF THE COURT

KENNETH W. SHRUM, Judge.

*   *   *   *

In Missouri, special benefits to a condemnee's remaining real estate may be set off against an award of compensation for the real estate that is taken, but general benefits may not be set off. *   *   *

---

a Click on "Southern Appellate District." When that page opens, click on "Collapse." From that list, click on the triangle next to "01/27/2000". When the date expands, click on the case name to access the opinion. This Web site is maintained by the Missouri Office of State Courts Administrator.
b The full title of this case includes, as the defendant, "The Estate of Grace K. LaFavre (Exceptions of Andrew Gugar, Jr.)." Gugar's property was a part of LaFavre's estate that had been withheld and did not otherwise pass with the title to the rest of the estate property.

* * * *

Here, Plaintiffs assert that the trial court ruled as a matter of law that sidewalks and street lights were general benefits, not special benefits. This premise is contradicted by the record. The trial judge expressly stated that his findings regarding whether the sidewalks and street lights were special benefits was based, at least in part, on a review of the evidence. By characterizing the trial court's finding regarding the nature of the sidewalk and street light benefits as an erroneous declaration or misapplication of law—rather than what it was, i.e., a resolution of relevant but conflicting evidence concerning whether Defendant's adjacent land was, in fact, specially benefited—Plaintiffs are essentially asking us to convict the trial court of an error it did not commit. This we will not do. * * *

* * * *

In discussing special benefits, Missouri courts have said that "[a] prime example of a special benefit * * * is when highway construction changes available use of land to a higher and better use." Here, all expert witnesses, both for Plaintiffs and Defendant, agreed that this project did not change the available use of this land to a higher and better use. On this subject, the trial court found: "After reviewing the evidence * * * [b]ecause the highest and best use of the property has not changed * * *, this Court concludes that the property is not specially benefitted by this project." * * *

* * * *

Contrary to Plaintiffs' assertion, the trial court did not declare as a matter of law that a change in the highest and best use is required before special benefits can be found. * * * [T]he trial court's "highest and best use" finding is merely a summary of the testimony of the expert witnesses, all of whom testified that the project did not change the available use of the remaining land to a higher and better use. This finding is followed by the trial court's conclusion that Defendant's remaining land was not specially benefited on that basis. Any other reading of the judgment is tortured and illogical. Once again, Plaintiffs have mischaracterized the trial court's finding in an apparent effort to have us convict the trial court of an error it never made. As stated before, this we will not do.

DECISION AND REMEDY *The Missouri Court of Appeals affirmed the decision of the lower court. Gugar was entitled to compensation. The improvements to the expressway provided general, not special, benefits to Gugar's remaining property, and the improvements did not change the use of this remaining property to a higher and better use.*

TERMS AND CONCEPTS TO REVIEW

bulk zoning 564	fixture 554	personal property 553
community property 559	future interest 557	profit 561
concurrent ownership 558	general plan 564	real property 553
conveyance 556	joint tenancy 558	remainder 557
easement 561	land-use control 553	restrictive covenant 562
eminent domain 563	leasehold estate 557	reversionary interest 557
executory interest 557	license 562	taking 568
fee simple absolute 556	life estate 556	tenancy at sufferance 558
fee simple defeasible 556	periodic tenancy 558	tenancy at will 558

| tenancy by the entirety 559 | tenancy in common 558 | zoning 564 |
| tenancy for years 558 | use zoning 564 | zoning variance 565 |

QUESTIONS AND CASE PROBLEMS

26–1. OWNERSHIP OF REAL PROPERTY. Glenn is the owner of a lakeside house and lot. He deeds the house and lot to "my wife, Livia, for life, then to my daughter, Sarina." Given these facts, answer the following questions:

(a) Does Glenn have any ownership interest in the lakeside house after making these transfers? Explain.

(b) What is Livia's interest called? Is there any limitation on her rights to use the property as she wishes? Discuss.

(c) What is Sarina's interest called? Explain.

26–2. EASEMENTS AND PROFITS. Murray owns 640 acres of rural land. A new highway is being built nearby by Ajax Corporation, Inc. Ajax purchases from Murray the rights to build and use a road across Murray's land for construction vehicles to pass over and to remove sand and gravel required to build the highway. A deed is prepared and filed in the county by Ajax. Later, a dispute arises between Murray and Ajax, and Murray refuses Ajax the right to use the road or to remove sand and gravel. Ajax claims its property rights cannot be revoked by Murray. Discuss fully what property rights Ajax has in this matter.

26–3. LIMITATIONS ON POLICE POWER. The county intends to rezone an area from industrial use to residential use. Land within the affected area is largely undeveloped, but nonetheless it is expected that the proposed action will reduce the market value of the affected land by as much as 50 percent. Will landowners be successful in suing to have the action declared a taking of their property, entitling them to just compensation?

26–4. SUBDIVISION REGULATIONS. Suppose that as a condition of a developer's receiving approval for constructing a new residential community, the local authorities insist that the developer dedicate, or set aside, land for a new hospital. The hospital would serve not only the proposed residential community but also the rest of the city. If the developer challenges the condition in court, under what standard might the court invalidate the condition?

26–5. GROWTH-MANAGEMENT ORDINANCES. To prevent population growth from racing ahead of the local government's ability to provide adequate police and fire protection, as well as road development for the increase in traffic, the local planning board imposes an ordinance limiting the issuance of residential building permits to one thousand per year for the next three years. A property developer who owns several tracts zoned for residential housing and whose development plans comply with all other existing ordinances challenges the ban in court. Will she succeed? Discuss all the relevant issues.

What difference would it make if the developer had already expended considerable resources and taken the last step toward approval of the development project?

26–6. EASEMENTS. Merton Peterson owned a golf course, a supper club, and the parking lot between them. Both golfers and club patrons always parked in the lot. Peterson sold the club and the lot to the American Legion, which sold them to VBC, Inc. (owned by Richard Beck and others). When VBC demanded rent from Peterson for use of the lot, Peterson filed a suit in a South Dakota state court to determine title. On what basis might the court hold that Peterson has an easement for the use of the lot? Does Peterson have an easement? [*Peterson v. Beck*, 537 N.W.2d 375 (S.Dak. 1995)]

26–7. TAKING. Richard and Jaquelyn Jackson owned property in a residential subdivision near an airport operated by the Metropolitan Knoxville Airport Authority in Blount County, Tennessee. The Airport Authority considered extending a runway near the subdivision and undertook a study that found that the noise, vibration, and pollution from aircraft using the extension would render the Jacksons' property incompatible with residential use. The airport built the extension, bringing about the predicted results, and the Jacksons filed a suit against the Airport Authority, alleging a taking of their property. The Airport Authority responded that there was no taking because there were no direct flights over the Jacksons' property. In whose favor will the court rule, and why? [*Jackson v. Metropolitan Knoxville Airport Authority*, 922 S.W.2d 860 (Tenn. 1996)]

26–8. LIMITATIONS ON POLICE POWER. John and Florence Dolan owned the A-Boy West Hardware store in downtown Tigard, Oregon. Wanting to expand the store and its parking lot, the Dolans applied to the city for a permit. Under the local zoning regulations, the city could attach conditions to downtown development to provide for projected public needs. The city told the Dolans that they could expand if they would dedicate a portion of their property for the improvement of a storm drainage system and dedicate an additional strip of land as a pedestrian and bicycle path. The dedication would involve about 10 percent of the Dolans' property. The Dolans sought a variance, which the city denied, and the Dolans appealed. The city claimed that there was a sufficient connection between the expansion of the store and the dedication requirements, because the expansion would increase traffic to the area and would also increase storm runoff. The Dolans conceded that there would be increases but contended that the increases would not be enough to justify taking 10 percent of their property. The Dolans claimed that the city's condition was an uncompensated taking of their property in violation of the Fifth Amendment. How should the court rule? Discuss fully. [*Dolan v. City of Tigard*, 512 U.S. 374, 114 S.Ct. 2309, 129 L.Ed.2d 304 (1994)]

26–9. EMINENT DOMAIN. The state of Indiana, through its department of transportation, planned to improve U.S. Highway 41 in Parke County, Indiana. To accomplish the improvement, Indiana sought to obtain from Thomas Collom approximately half an acre of his property abutting the east side of the highway and offered him $4,495 for it. When Collom refused to sell, the state filed a suit in an Indiana state court against Collom to obtain the property. Collom denied that his half acre was necessary for the improvement that the state wanted to make to the highway. He asserted that the state did not need his land because the highway would curve west, away from his property, and no drainage ditch was necessary given the existing water flow in the area. The state argued that this was not an appropriate response because a determination of the need for a taking was the responsibility of the state, not the owner of the property that the state was trying to take. In whose favor should the court rule, and why? [*State of Indiana. v. Collom*, 720 N.E.2d 737 (Ind.App. 1999)]

26–10. IN YOUR COURT

Lorenz and his wife purchased a home. Although the title to the property did not indicate it, the home had been designated as a landmark building. Lorenz later sought a vari-ance that would have allowed him to make certain building changes, such as the installation of vinyl siding on the home. The local council denied the request. Lorenz later learned that the Weslings, an elderly couple whose home was also designated as a landmark building, had been granted a variance similar to the one Lorenz had sought. Lorenz filed a suit against the council, arguing that the discrepancy demonstrated that its decision had been arbitrary and capricious. The council members contended that they were within their discretion in allowing the Weslings' variance because of the Weslings' advanced age and because the Weslings had apparently been unaware of the ordinance at the time they made their modifications. Assume that you are the judge hearing this case and answer the following questions:

(a) Were the Weslings and Lorenz "similarly situated," as Lorenz argued? Suppose Lorenz offers evidence that like the Weslings, he suffers from physical hardship, but that evidence is contradicted by other evidence. Should the council have limited its inquiry and based its decision solely on property-related issues?

(b) Given that the underlying rationale of all zoning and other forms of land-use control is the well-being of the community, did the council act properly by allowing special consideration for the Weslings? Or was Lorenz forced to bear a disproportionate share of the burden by being denied an identical variance?

LAW ON THE WEB

For updated links to resources available on the Web, as well as a variety of other materials, visit this text's Web site at http://wleb.westbuslaw.com.

Homes and Communities is a Web site offered by the U.S. Department of Housing and Urban Development. Information of interest to both consumers and businesses is available at this site, which can be accessed at

http://www.hud.gov

Information on the buying and financing of homes, as well as the full text of the Real Estate Settlement Procedures Act, is online at

http://www.hud.gov/fha/fhahome.html

LEGAL RESEARCH EXERCISES ON THE WEB

Go to http://wleb.westbuslaw.com, the Web site that accompanies this text. Select "Internet Applications," and then click on "Chapter 26." There you will find the following Internet research exercise that you can perform to learn more about laws governing real property:

Activity 26–1: Real Estate Law

CHAPTER 27

Antitrust and Monopoly

T HE ENVIRONMENT OF BUSINESS IS generally one of competition among rival firms. In free and open competition, businesses attempt to develop and sell products that are more appealing to customers than are the products of rival firms. Competition among sellers therefore promotes the development of appealing products. When products sold by different firms are similar, firms compete by trying to sell at the lowest price possible while still earning enough after costs to make it worthwhile to remain in that particular endeavor. For example, if Acme, Inc., develops a new digital video disc (DVD) drive that has broad appeal among consumers, it will begin to earn profits greater than those of its rivals—profits commensurate with the appeal of its new product. All else being equal, the greater the appeal of Acme's DVD drive, the greater its profits.

The legal environment of business is premised on encouraging innovative, competitive business behavior. The law attempts to prevent and correct conduct that interferes with free and open competition. The law is concerned with two broad categories of behavior: conduct that leads to or tends to produce *monopoly power* and conduct that is an unreasonable *restraint of trade*. In this chapter, we consider the federal laws that deal with individual firms' behavior leading to or tending to create monopolies. In Chapter 28, we discuss in detail the

federal laws that regulate activities that restrain competition.

SECTION 1

Market Power

To encourage innovative behavior, we might feel justified in allowing Acme to have a *monopoly* over the sale of the DVD drive, at least for a while—say twenty years, which is the duration of a patent. The term **monopoly** is generally used to describe a market in which there is a single seller. In that respect, Acme would be a monopolist, albeit for a limited time, in the DVD drive market. In legal terms, *monopolist* may also describe a firm that, although not the sole seller in the market, can nonetheless substantially ignore rival firms in setting a selling price for its product or can in some way limit rivals from competing in the market (possibly by preventing rivals from entering the market altogether). Acme's monopoly would give it **market power** (the power of a firm to control the market for its product). Acme would have the power during the term of its monopoly to prevent other firms from selling the DVD drive. Acme would be free to charge whatever price it chose to, and it would choose a price that made its profits as large as possible.

COMPETITIVE BEHAVIOR

Another firm might seek to develop a different type of DVD drive, one with appeal equal to or greater than Acme's DVD drive. If it succeeded, it would draw customers away from Acme. It too might seek a legal monopoly over its product. There would then be two monopolies rather than one, but society would have the benefit of two unique and valued products. Moreover, Acme would be concerned that if it charged too high a price for its DVD drive, it would lose customers to its rival. Acme's rival would have the same concern over the price of its product.

Eventually, after the legal monopolies expired, numerous firms would be allowed to market identical products. Each firm would seek to attract customers by charging the lowest price. The only thing that would prevent prices from falling ever lower is that at some point the price of a DVD drive would be so low that new firms would quit trying to enter the market to compete for DVD drive consumers. They would instead devote their efforts and resources to alternative, more profitable ventures. Ultimately, the DVD drive would sell for a competitive price—one that would, of course, cover the costs of production, as well as earn a return equal to that which could be earned by employing the same resources in an alternative industry.

THE GOALS OF ANTITRUST LAW

The scenario described above highlights the benefits to society of having firms develop, produce, and sell goods and services, even though obtaining those benefits may involve conferring a limited monopoly such as that given to Acme. Our scenario should make clear an often overlooked point: market power is not inherently bad. Market power can correlate to high profits, which are the reward for innovation, foresight, and good management. Market power is the prize that motivates firms to benefit society with innovative products and competitive prices.

What is at issue is not market power *per se* but how firms go about acquiring market power and what firms do with that power once they acquire it. **Antitrust law** is the body of statutes and principles that regulate business conduct so as to promote the forms of competition that benefit society while simultaneously seeking to rein in the exercise of market power that often is the fruit of such competition.

The Common Law and the Restraint of Trade

Socially beneficial commercial activity involves cooperation, as well as competition. A business firm, for example, may compete with certain firms in some markets but cooperate with other firms in other markets. A firm that sells finished goods directly to the public may itself act as a consumer by purchasing intermediate products from a second firm. In this sense, the two firms act cooperatively rather than competitively, at least vis-à-vis one another. Similarly, two firms may cooperate to develop or market a new product.

PUBLIC POLICY AND CONTRACTS

Any mutual effort that calls for more than a brief period of sustained cooperation requires commitment from all the parties. The principal means of ensuring such a sustained commitment is through a contract between the parties. Most cooperative efforts among business firms, in fact, are embodied in some form of contract. But a principle of the common law of contracts is that no contract is enforceable if it is against public policy.

Economic Efficiency. Many contracts between business firms promote competition. Because competition, as noted above, is beneficial to society, such contracts are not against public policy. A contract may provide assurances that one firm will be able to obtain necessary inputs from another on a long-term basis. Similarly, a contract may provide assurances to two firms entering into a joint venture that each will continue fulfilling its obligation on the project beyond the initial investment stage. In both these instances, the rights and remedies afforded by contract law promote economic efficiency. Such agreements are not against public policy.

Restraints of Trade. Some agreements between business firms, however, may reduce competition. An agreement between two bakers to coordinate their production of bread so as to limit output and charge a uniform, higher price in the market might entirely eliminate competition in the affected market. If the two bakers were the only suppliers in the market, their combining together would in effect create a joint monopoly under which they would share exclusive control over the market. Such an agreement would be condemned under the common law as an *unreasonable restraint of trade.*

Consider, though, a restaurant owner who decides to sell her restaurant to the manager. The manager might demand that, as a condition to the sale, the owner refrain from opening another restaurant across the street. Should such an agreement be condemned as against public policy? At first glance, it is a restraint of trade: it prevents the local community from benefiting from the restauranting skills of the owner. If the agreement were not enforced, however, the manager, who was willing to pay a price commensurate with the current earnings of the restaurant, would not recover the price; customers would probably follow the owner with the established reputation to her new restaurant across the street from the old one.

If the manager knew beforehand that the agreement would not be enforced, it would be the owner who would suffer, because the manager would not be willing to pay a price reflecting the expectation that the earnings of the restaurant would continue at the current level. Society might consider enforcing such agreements in spite of the restraint of trade so that entrepreneurs who contemplate opening new businesses will be ensured of later being able to sell those businesses at full value. If others know that sellers will be held to the promise not to compete, the sellers can sell their businesses for more than they could if such promises were condemned as being against public policy.

INTERFERENCE WITH FREE TRADE

Compare the two agreements just discussed. Both interfere with free trade. The first involves outright collusion between two competitors (the bakers) to completely eliminate competition between themselves. Their agreement calls for artificially driving prices higher by restricting output. The second agreement (the one between the restaurant owner and the manager) also restrains trade, but the restraint is not the primary purpose of the agreement. The restraint is really the only means of ensuring that both parties to the sale of an established restaurant can reap the full benefit of their bargain: the sale of the restaurant for its highest value. The second agreement thus can be viewed as reasonable given that it is the only means of achieving a legitimate end. It also has offsetting benefits in that it encourages entrepreneur-

ship by allowing the owner to sell her business for its highest value.

SECTION 3

The Origins of Federal Antitrust Legislation

Despite condemning anticompetitive agreements on the basis of public policy, the common law proved to be an ineffective means of protecting free competition. There are temptations for business firms to agree to limit competition or to harm other rivals. Such agreements, to be sure, are unenforceable, because they are held to be against public policy. But the problem under the common law is that such agreements are left unchallenged unless one of the parties to an agreement refuses to abide by its terms. *Unenforceable* means only that a court will not sanction a party that reneges on its promise; it does not mean that a forum will be provided in which anticompetitive agreements can be challenged by others who are not parties to the agreements. These shortcomings became acutely obvious in the United States during the latter half of the 1800s as a concentrated group of powerful individuals began to acquire unrivaled market power by combining competing firms under singular control.

THE TREND TOWARD MONOPOLY

After the Civil War ended, the nation renewed its drive westward. With the movement westward came the expansion of the railroads—which soon developed into monopolies—and the further integration of the economy. The growth of national markets also witnessed the efforts of a number of small companies to combine into large business organizations, many of which gained considerable market power. These large organizations became known as **trusts**, the most famous—or infamous—being John D. Rockefeller's Standard Oil Trust. In general, a trust is an arrangement in which some party, referred to as a trustee, holds legal title to property for the benefit of another. As used by Standard Oil and others around the turn of the century, trusts were a device used to amass market power. The participants transferred their stock to a trustee and in return received trust certificates. The trustee then made decisions fixing prices, controlling output, and allocating geographical markets in which specified members could operate without competition from other members.

In some cases, an entire industry was dominated by a single organization. The public perception was that the trusts used their market power to drive small competitors out of business, leaving the trusts free to raise prices virtually at will.[1]

THE FEDERAL RESPONSE

Congress initially dealt with the railroad monopolies, attempting regulation rather than an outright assault on monopoly power. The result was the Interstate Commerce Act of 1887.[2]

Congress next attempted to deal with trusts in a direct, unified way by passing the Sherman Act in 1890.[3] The Sherman Act is a broadly worded pronouncement that prohibits competitors from making agreements that unreasonably restrain trade and condemns conduct leading to or tending to produce monopoly power. Violations of the Sherman Act are criminal offenses, as well as civil ones.

The Sherman Act, however, failed to end public concerns over monopolies. The United States Supreme Court initially construed the statute too narrowly to give it much effect and subsequently applied it so rigorously as to make the act unworkable. Lackluster enforcement also contributed to the public's dissatisfaction. Concern over the trust problem dominated the 1912 presidential election and eventually, in 1914, led to enactment of the Clayton Act[4] and the Federal Trade Commission Act.[5] This legislation sought to deal with the monopoly problem by proscribing specific acts and providing for more aggressive means of enforcement.

The Clayton Act (as amended by the Robinson-Patman Act in 1936 and the Celler-Kefauver Act of 1950) addresses specific acts that are considered to be anticompetitive. The Federal Trade Commission Act created the Federal Trade Commission and invested it with broad enforcement powers to *prevent*, as well as correct, business behavior broadly defined as *unfair trade practices*.

---

1. There is now a considerable amount of literature that questions whether predatory tactics are economically viable and whether they in fact characterize the activities of Rockefeller and the other "robber barons" of the late nineteenth century.
2. 49 U.S.C. Sections 1–22.
3. 15 U.S.C. Sections 1–7.
4. 15 U.S.C. Sections 12–27.
5. 15 U.S.C. Sections 41–58.

In the remainder of this chapter, we consider the federal legislation in more detail and examine the means of enforcement. We also examine the narrower area of antitrust law that deals with individual firms' behavior leading to or tending to create monopolies. We reserve for Chapter 28 the broader area of antitrust law that deals with all forms of joint activities that restrain competition.

SECTION 4

Overview of the Major Federal Antitrust Laws

The major pieces of federal antitrust legislation—the Sherman Act, the Clayton Act, and the Federal Trade Commission Act—are briefly outlined below and discussed in more detail later in this chapter and in Chapter 28.

THE SHERMAN ACT

The main provisions of the Sherman Act are contained in Sections 1 and 2 of the act. Both sections describe illegal conduct in very broad terms. Section 1 prohibits a concerted activity on the part of two or more persons to restrain trade:

> Section 1: Every contract, combination in the form of trust or otherwise, or conspiracy, in restraint of trade or commerce among the several States, or with foreign nations, is hereby declared to be illegal [and is a felony punishable by fine or imprisonment].

Section 2 applies to both unilateral and concerted actions:

> Section 2: Every person who shall monopolize, or attempt to monopolize, or combine or conspire with any other person or persons, to monopolize any part of the trade or commerce among the several States, or with foreign nations, shall be deemed guilty of a felony [and is similarly punishable].

Section 1 of the act prohibits concerted activity that unreasonably restrains trade. Section 2 condemns individual anticompetitive behavior that produces, or is intended to produce, monopoly power. Both restraint of trade and monopoly power are fundamental concepts in antitrust law.

A **restraint of trade** is any agreement between firms that has the effect of reducing competition in the marketplace. Some restraints of trade are so blatantly anticompetitive—such as agreements to restrict output or fix prices—that they are condemned without inquiry into any business justification that may be advanced in defense of the agreements. These are known as *per se* violations. Other agreements judge the restraints under a rule of reason (discussed later in this chapter) similar to the common law analysis of the reasonableness of the restraint discussed earlier. Restraints of trade are discussed more completely in the next chapter.

Monopoly power is an extreme amount of market power. Recall our initial discussion of Acme's market power in the hypothetical scenario in which Acme was given, for a time, exclusive control over the DVD drive market; specifically, Acme could ignore the effect of raising its product price on the ability of competitors to enter the DVD drive market. Such extreme market power is an example of monopoly power. Any firm, even if it is not the sole supplier of its product, that is not completely constrained by the potential response of a rival in deciding what price to charge for its product has some degree of market power. Deciding whether such power is great enough to be classified as monopoly power is one of the most difficult tasks encountered in the application of antitrust law.

THE CLAYTON ACT

In contrast to the Sherman Act's broad proscriptions, the Clayton Act's provisions deal with *specific* practices that are not expressly covered by the Sherman Act but that are considered to reduce competition or lead to monopoly power. These practices are divided into four categories—price discrimination, exclusionary practices, corporate mergers, and interlocking directorates. These behaviors violate the Clayton Act only if they substantially tend to lessen competition or create monopoly power. Violations of the Clayton Act are civil, not criminal, violations.

Price Discrimination. *Price discrimination* occurs when sellers charge different buyers different prices for identical goods. Section 2 of the Clayton Act prohibits certain classes of price discrimination for reasons other than differences in production or transportation costs. The Clayton Act was amended in 1936 by the Robinson-Patman Act as Congress sought to make it more difficult for businesses to evade the terms of Section 2. To violate Section 2, the seller must be engaged in interstate commerce, and the effect of the price discrimination must be to lessen competition

substantially. Under the Robinson-Patman Act, sellers are prohibited from reducing prices to levels substantially below those charged by their competitors unless they can justify the reduction by demonstrating that the lower price was charged "in good faith to meet an equally low price of a competitor."[6]

Exclusionary Practices. Section 3 of the Clayton Act prohibits sellers and lessors from selling or leasing "on the condition, agreement or understanding that the . . . purchaser or lessee thereof shall not use or deal in the goods . . . of a competitor or competitors of the seller." Section 3 in effect prohibits two types of vertical arrangements involving exclusionary tactics: exclusive-dealing contracts and tie-in sales agreements.

An *exclusive-dealing contract* is one in which a seller forbids the buyer from purchasing products from the seller's competitors. For example, imagine that most soft drinks are produced by one firm, that most soft drinks are marketed by one other firm, and that the producer signs an exclusive-dealing contract with the retail seller. Because the retail seller has committed itself to the established producer, any other soft-drink producer that wants to enter the soft-drink market may find it difficult to do so. Such contracts are prohibited under Section 3 if the effect of the contract will "substantially lessen competition or tend to create a monopoly."

In a *tying arrangement*, or *tie-in sales agreement*, the seller conditions the sale of a product (the tying product) on the buyer's agreeing to purchase another product (the tied product) produced or distributed by the same seller. The legality of such agreements depends on many factors, especially on consideration of the purpose of the arrangement and its likely effect on competition in the relevant markets (consider that there are two markets, because the agreement involves both the tying and the tied product). In the next chapter, we deal in depth with both exclusive dealing contracts and tying arrangements as part of our analysis of restraints of trade.

Corporate Mergers. Under Section 7 of the Clayton Act, a person or business organization is forbidden to hold stock or assets in another business if "the effect . . . may be to substantially lessen competition." This section provides the statutory authorization for the government's challenging corporate mergers that

6. *United States v. United States Gypsum Co.*, 438 U.S. 422, 98 S.Ct. 2864, 5 L.Ed.2d 854 (1978).

could have an anticompetitive effect. Two crucial considerations are the market shares among firms in the relevant market and barriers to a firm's entry into the market.

Interlocking Directorates.   Section 8 of the Clayton Act deals with *interlocking directorates*, which result when individuals serve as directors on the boards of two or more competing companies simultaneously. No person may be a director in two or more corporations at the same time if either of the corporations has capital, surplus, or undivided profits aggregating more than $16,732,000 or competitive sales of $1,673,200. The threshold amounts are adjusted upward each year by the Federal Trade Commission (FTC). (The amounts given here are those announced by the FTC in 2000.)

The Federal Trade Commission Act

The Federal Trade Commission Act's sole substantive provision is Section 5. It provides, in part, as follows:

> Unfair methods of competition in or affecting commerce, and unfair or deceptive acts or practices in or affecting commerce are hereby declared illegal.

Notice that whereas the Clayton Act prohibits specific forms of anticompetitive behavior, the FTC Act is a "catchall." Section 5 condemns all forms of anticompetitive behavior that are not covered under other federal antitrust laws.

The FTC Act also created the Federal Trade Commission, an administrative agency with functions that include antitrust enforcement, as well as other duties concerning consumer protection.

Section 5

Enforcement of the Antitrust Laws

Government agencies enforce the federal antitrust laws. In some circumstances, a private party can sue violators for damages. Before the government can prosecute successfully or a private party can win a lawsuit, however, certain jurisdictional requirements must be met.

Jurisdictional Requirements

The Sherman Act applies only to conduct that has a significant impact on commerce. Because Congress can regulate only interstate commerce, in principle only interstate commerce is affected by this act.[7] Courts have generally held that any activity that substantially affects interstate commerce falls under the Sherman Act. Courts have construed the meaning of *interstate commerce* more and more broadly each year, bringing even local activities within the regulatory power of the national government. Whether a seemingly local activity touched sufficiently on interstate commerce to come under the purview of the Sherman Act was at issue in the following case.

---

7. See the discussion of the commerce clause in Chapter 5.

Case 27.1   Summit Health, Ltd. v. Pinhas

Supreme Court of the
United States, 1991.
500 U.S. 322,
111 S.Ct. 1842,
114 L.Ed.2d 366.
http://supct.law.
cornell.edu/supct[a]

HISTORICAL AND POLITICAL SETTING   *The record of the congressional debates on the Sherman Act reveals, in Senator John Sherman's words, an intent to "[go] as far as the Constitution permits Congress to go,*[b] *Congress intended to deal comprehensively and effectively with "the evils resulting from contracts, combinations and conspiracies in restraint of trade, and to that end to exercise all the power it possessed.*[c] *Since the passage of the Sherman Act more than a century ago, the U.S. economy has grown, and the federal power over commerce has experienced similar expansion. The United States Supreme Court has long allowed the reach of the Sherman Act to expand with the expanding notions of congressional power.*

---

a. In the right column, in the "Arrayed by party name" section, in the "1991" row, click on "1st party". On that page, scroll to the case name and click on it to access a syllabus of the case. From that page, click on the link to the version of the opinion that you want to read.
b. 20 Congressional Record 1167 (1889).
c. *Atlantic Cleaners & Dyers, Inc. v. United States,* 286 U.S. 427, 52 S.Ct. 607, 76 L.Ed. 1204 (1932).

BACKGROUND AND FACTS   *Dr. Simon Pinhas was an ophthalmologist on the staff of Midway Hospital Medical Center (a subsidiary of Summit Health, Ltd.) in Los Angeles. In February 1986, the administrators of the Medicare program announced that they would no longer reimburse physicians for the services of assistants, and most hospitals in the area abolished their requirements that assistant surgeons be used. Midway refused to do so. For Pinhas, who performed numerous surgeries at Midway, this meant that it would cost him $60,000 a year to pay for assistant surgeons that he did not need. He told Midway that if the requirement was not eliminated, he would leave. In response, the medical staff initiated peer-review proceedings against Pinhas, terminated his staff privileges, and began preparing an adverse report about Pinhas to distribute to all hospitals in the area. Pinhas filed a complaint alleging that the Midway medical staff had entered into a conspiracy to drive him out of business so that other ophthalmologists would obtain a greater share of the market for ophthalmologic services in Los Angeles. The trial court dismissed his complaint on the ground that interstate commerce was not affected by Pinhas's removal from the Midway medical staff, and therefore the Sherman Act did not apply. Pinhas appealed, and ultimately the case was reviewed by the United States Supreme Court.*

IN THE LANGUAGE OF THE COURT

Justice STEVENS delivered the opinion of the Court.
*   *   *   *

*   *   * [T]his case involves the provision of ophthalmological services. It seems clear *   *   * that these services are regularly performed for out-of-state patients and generate revenues from out-of-state sources; their importance as part of the entire operation of the hospital is evident from the allegations of the complaint. A conspiracy to eliminate the entire ophthalmological department of the hospital, like a conspiracy to destroy the hospital itself, would unquestionably affect interstate commerce. *   *   * Petitioners [the Midway medical staff] argue that respondent's [Pinhas's] complaint is insufficient because there is no factual nexus [connection] between the restraint on this one surgeon's practice and interstate commerce.

There are two flaws in petitioners' argument. First, *   *   * proper analysis focuses, not upon actual consequences, but rather upon the potential harm that would ensue if the conspiracy were successful. *   *   * Second, if the conspiracy alleged in the complaint is successful, "as a matter of practical economics" there will be a reduction in the provision of ophthalmological services in the Los Angeles market. *   *   *

DECISION AND REMEDY

The United States Supreme Court held that the medical staff's peer-review proceedings affected interstate commerce and thus their actions against Pinhas fell within the jurisdiction of the Sherman Act.

ETHICAL CONSIDERATIONS

The substantial disagreement on whether essentially local activities—such as the medical staff's actions against Pinhas—should be subject to the "long arm of federal law" is reflected in the Court's five-to-four decision in this case. Justice Scalia, who wrote the dissenting opinion, stated, "As I understand the Court's opinion, the test of Sherman Act jurisdiction is whether the entire line of commerce from which Dr. Pinhas has been excluded affects interstate commerce . . . , which of course it does. This analysis tells us nothing about the substantiality of the impact on interstate commerce generated by the particular conduct at issue here."

FEDERAL ENFORCEMENT

The federal agencies that enforce the federal antitrust laws are the Department of Justice (DOJ) and the Federal Trade Commission (FTC). The DOJ can prosecute violations of the Sherman Act as either criminal or civil violations. Violations of the Clayton Act are not crimes, and the DOJ can enforce that statute only through civil proceedings. The various remedies that the DOJ has asked the courts to impose include **divestiture** (making a company give up one or more of its operating functions) and **dissolution** (making a company end its operating functions). A group of meat packers, for example, can be forced to divest itself of control or ownership of butcher shops.

The FTC enforces the Clayton Act and has sole authority to enforce the only substantive provision of the Federal Trade Commission Act, Section 5. FTC actions are effected through administrative cease-and-desist proceedings, but the FTC can seek court sanctions for violations of its administrative orders. As part of its enforcement of the Clayton Act, the FTC requires certain persons involved in a merger, consolidation, or other acquisition to notify the agency.[8] The first page of the notification form is shown in Exhibit 27–1 on page 583. Antitrust law as it applies to mergers is discussed in detail in Chapter 28.

PRIVATE ACTIONS

A private party can sue for **treble damages** (three times what he or she has suffered) and attorneys' fees under Section 4 of the Clayton Act if the party is injured as a result of a violation of any of the federal antitrust laws (except Section 5 of the Federal Trade Commission Act). In some instances, private parties

may also seek injunctive relief to prevent antitrust violations. The courts have determined that the ability to sue depends on the directness of the injury suffered by the would-be plaintiff. Thus, a person wishing to sue under the Sherman Act must prove (1) that the antitrust violation either directly caused, or was at least a substantial factor in causing, the injury that was suffered and (2) that the unlawful actions of the accused party affected business activities of the plaintiff that were protected by the antitrust laws.

In recent years, more than 90 percent of all antitrust actions have been brought by private plaintiffs. One reason for this is, of course, that successful plaintiffs recover treble damages as a result of the defendants' antitrust law violations. Such recoveries by private plaintiffs for antitrust violations have been rationalized as encouraging "private attorneys general" who will vigorously pursue antitrust violators on their own initiative. This policy consideration has also prompted the courts to ask, in assessing whether a litigant has standing to sue for an alleged antitrust violation, whether the particular plaintiff is properly suited to fulfill the role of a private attorney general.

The court in the following case was asked to decide whether the defendants' alleged antitrust violations were a sufficiently direct cause of injury to the plaintiffs to give the plaintiffs standing (that is, a sufficient stake in the controversy to bring the lawsuit—see Chapter 2).

---

8. See 15 U.S.C. Section 18a.

CASE 27.2   **Amarel v. Connell**

United States
Court of Appeals,
Ninth Circuit, 1997.
102 F.3d 1494.
http://www.findlaw.
com/casecode/courts/
9th.html[a]

BACKGROUND AND FACTS   *William Amarel and other rice farmers signed contracts to sell their paddy rice (raw rice harvested in the field) to Pacific International Rice Mills, Inc. (PIRMI), for a share of the profits from the sale of the milled rice (rice refined and processed for consumption). PIRMI contracted to sell to the Republic of Korea (South Korea) 200,000 tons of milled Southern rice. Unable to obtain enough Southern rice, PIRMI offered to substitute California rice. Within three days of this offer, Connell Rice & Sugar Company offered Korea more than seven times as much California rice for a considerably lower per-unit price. In order to match this competitive offer, PIRMI then accepted a reduced price for its rice and lost $12 million on the sale. The farmers filed a lawsuit in a federal district court against Connell's president, Grover Connell, and others. They alleged that the defendants had violated the antitrust laws by, among other things, engaging in predatory pricing in the deal with Korea. The farmers claimed, as their injury, the reduced return they earned on the rice they sold to PIRMI for export to Korea. The defendants argued, among other things, that the farmers' alleged injury was indirect and that thus they lacked standing. On most of the allegations, the court ruled against the plaintiffs, who appealed.*

---

a. In the "Browsing" section, in the "1997" row, click on "Jan". When that page opens, scroll down to the name of the case and click on it to access the opinion.

<table>
<tr><td>IN THE LANGUAGE
OF THE COURT</td><td>

MICHAEL DALY HAWKINS, Circuit Judge:

*   *   *   *

Defendants *   *   * assert that plaintiffs' alleged harm is merely "derivative and in-direct" because it "derived from the lower prices supposedly obtained for milled rice as a result of defendants' acts." We disagree. *   *   * Among the particular injuries, plain-tiffs allege, are depressed earnings caused by predatorily low prices *   *   * .

*   *   *   *

*   *   * Given the close ties between the paddy rice market and the milled rice mar-ket, and given that plaintiffs' profits were, in part, a function of profits in the milled rice market, defendants' alleged predatory pricing in the market for milled rice predictably would have impacted the price of paddy rice.

</td></tr>
<tr><td>DECISION
AND REMEDY</td><td>

The U.S. Court of Appeals for the Ninth Circuit concluded that the plaintiffs were suffi-ciently direct victims of the defendants' alleged anticompetitive activities to have stand-ing. The court reversed the judgment in the defendants' favor and remanded the case for a new trial.

</td></tr>
<tr><td>INTERNATIONAL
CONSIDERATIONS</td><td>

Regulation of Purely Foreign Trade *Although U.S. courts have not always been con-sistent in applying antitrust laws to firms doing business in the United States, they have consistently expressed concern about the anticompetitive practices of firms doing busi-ness in other countries. Foreign subsidiaries of U.S. companies often benefit from a lack of enforcement of antitrust laws in other countries. In the mid-1990s, the U.S. Department of Justice expanded its antitrust efforts against foreign firms.[b] Sanctions included fines of $10 million and $15 million against two international firms accused of fixing dynamite prices and a total of $170 million in a food-commodities case involving four Asian com-panies, a U.S. subsidiary of Bayer AG of Germany, and U.S.-based Archer Daniels Midland Company.*

</td></tr>
</table>

b. See, for example, *United States v. Nippon Paper Industries Co.*, 109 F.3d 1 (1st Cir. 1997).

SECTION 6

U.S. Antitrust Laws in the Global Context

U.S. antitrust laws have a broad application. They may subject persons in foreign nations to their provi-sions as well as protect foreign consumers and com-petitors from violations committed by U.S. business firms. Consequently, *foreign persons*, a term that by definition includes foreign governments, may sue under U.S. antitrust laws in U.S. courts.

Section 1 of the Sherman Act of 1890 provides for the extraterritorial effect of the U.S. antitrust laws. The United States is a major proponent of free competition in the global economy, and thus any conspiracy that has a substantial effect on U.S. commerce is within the reach of the Sherman Act. The violation may even occur outside the United States, and foreign govern-

ments as well as persons can be sued for violation of U.S. antitrust laws. Before U.S. courts will exercise ju-risdiction and apply antitrust laws, it must be shown that the alleged violation had a *substantial effect on U.S. commerce*. U.S. jurisdiction is automatically in-voked, however, when a *per se* violation occurs.

If a domestic firm, for example, joins a foreign car-tel to control the production, price, or distribution of goods, and this cartel has a *substantial effect* on U.S. commerce, a *per se* violation may exist. Hence, both the domestic firm and the foreign cartel could be sued for violation of the U.S. antitrust laws. Likewise, if foreign firms doing business in the United States enter into a price-fixing or other anticompetitive agreement to control a portion of U.S. markets, a *per se* violation may exist.

In 1982, Congress amended the Sherman Act and the Federal Trade Commission Act of 1914 to limit their application when unfair methods of competition

EXHIBIT 27–1 FTC NOTIFICATION FORM

16 C.F.R. Part 803 - Appendix	Approved by OMB
NOTIFICATION AND REPORT FORM FOR CERTAIN MERGERS AND ACQUISITIONS	3084-0006 Expires 8-31-97

THE INFORMATION REQUIRED TO BE SUPPLIED ON THESE ANSWER SHEETS IS SPECIFIED IN THE INSTRUCTIONS	FOR OFFICE USE ONLY TRANSACTION NUMBER

➤ Attach the Affidavit required by § 803.5 to this page.

IS THIS ACQUISITION A CASH TENDER OFFER?
☐ YES   ☐ NO

☐ CTO   ☐ ETR

DO YOU REQUEST EARLY TERMINATION OF THE WAITING PERIOD? *(Grants of early termination are published in the Federal Register.)*
☐ YES   ☐ NO

ITEM 1

(a) NAME AND HEADQUARTERS ADDRESS OF PERSON FILING NOTIFICATION

(b) PERSON FILING NOTIFICATION IS

☐ an acquiring person   ☐ an acquired person   ☐ both

(c) LIST NAMES OF ULTIMATE PARENT ENTITIES OF ALL ACQUIRING PERSONS

LIST NAMES OF ULTIMATE PARENT ENTITIES OF ALL ACQUIRED PERSONS

(d) THIS ACQUISITION IS *(put an X in all the boxes that apply)*

☐ an acquisition of assets
☐ a merger (see § 801.2)
☐ an acquisition subject to § 802.2(e)
☐ a formation of a joint venture of other corporation (see § 801.40)
☐ an acquisition subject to § 801.30 *(specify type)* _____
☐ other *(specify)* _____

☐ a consolidation (see § 801.2)
☐ an acquisition of voting securities
☐ a secondary acquisition
☐ an acquisition subject to § 801.31

(e) INDICATE HIGHEST NOTIFICATION THRESHOLD IN § 801.1(h) FOR WHICH THIS FORM IS BEING FILED *(acquiring person only)*

☐ $15 million   ☐ 15%   ☐ 25%   ☐ 50%

(f) VALUE OF VOTING SECURITIES TO BE HELD AS A RESULT OF THE ACQUISITION

VALUE OF ASSETS

(g) PUT AN "X" IN THE APPROPRIATE BOX TO DESCRIBE PERSON FILING NOTIFICATION

☐ Corporation   ☐ Partnership   ☐ Other *(specify)* _____

(h) DATA FURNISHED BY

☐ calendar year   ☐ fiscal year *(specify period)* _____ *(month/year)* to _____ *(month/year)*

THIS FORM IS REQUIRED BY LAW and must be filed separately by each person which, by reason of a merger, consolidation or acquisition, is subject to § 7A of the Clayton Act, 15 U.S.C. § 18a, as added by Section 201 of the Hart-Scott-Rodino Antitrust Improvements Act of 1976. Pub. L. No. 94-435, 90 Stat. 1390, and rules promulgated thereunder (hereinafter referred to as "the rules" or by section number). The statute and rules are set forth in the *Federal Register* at 43 FR 33450; the rules may also be found at 18 CFR parts 801-03. Failure to file this **Notification and Report Form,** and to observe the required waiting period before consummating the acquisition, in accordance with the applicable provisions of 15 U.S.C. § 18a and the rules, subjects any "person," as defined in the rules, or any individuals responsible for noncompliance, to liability for a penalty of not more than $10,000 for each day during which such person is in violation of 15 U.S.C. § 18a.

All information and documentary material filed in or with this Form is confidential. It is exempt from disclosure under the Freedom of Information Act, and may be made public only in an administrative or judicial proceeding, or disclosed to Congress or to a duly authorized committee or subcommittee of Congress.

Complete and return *two* notarized copies (with *one* set of documentary attachments) of this **Notification and Report Form** to Premerger Notification Office, Bureau of Competition, Room 303, Federal Trade Commission, Washington, DC 20580, and *three* notarized copies (with *one set* of documentary attachments) to Director of Operations, Antitrust Division, Room 3218, Department of Justice, Washington, D.C. 20530. The central office for information and assistance with respect to matters in connection with this *Notification and Report Form* is Room 303, Federal Trade Commission, Washington, DC 20580, phone (202) 326-3100.

DISCLOSURE NOTICE - Public reporting burden for this report is estimated to vary from 8 to 160 hours per response, with an average of 39 hours per response, including time for reviewing instructions, searching existing data sources, gathering and maintaining the data needed, and completing and reviewing the collection of information. Send comments regarding the burden estimate or any other aspect of

this report, including suggestions for reducing this burden to:

Premerger Notification Office, H-303
Federal Trade Commission
Washington, DC 20580

Office of Information and Regulatory Affairs,
Office of Management and Budget
Washington, DC 20503

are involved in U.S. export trade or commerce with foreign nations. The acts are not limited, however, when there is a "direct, substantial, and reasonably foreseeable effect" on U.S. domestic commerce that results in a claim for damages.

SECTION 7

Exemptions

There are many legislative and constitutional limitations on antitrust enforcement. Most are statutory and judicially created exemptions that apply in such areas as labor, insurance, and foreign trade. These exemptions are listed and explained in Exhibit 27–2.

One of the most significant of these exemptions covers joint efforts by businesspersons to obtain legislative, judicial, or executive action. This is often referred to as the *Noerr-Pennington* doctrine.[9] For example, video producers might jointly lobby Congress to change the copyright laws, or some video-rental companies might sue another video-rental firm, without being held liable for attempting to restrain trade. Although selfish rather than purely public-minded conduct is permitted, there is an exception: an action will not be protected if it is clear that the action is "objectively baseless in the sense that no reasonable [person] could reasonably expect success on the merits" and it is an attempt to make anticompetitive use of government processes.[10]

SECTION 8

Monopolies

As noted above, the impetus for the initial federal antitrust legislation was concern over monopolies—specifically, concern that in particular markets a single, dominant firm could acquire and use market power to dictate or influence prices and output. Section 2 of the Sherman Act deals broadly with such cases. Section 2 condemns "every person who shall monopolize or attempt to monopolize." (Note that Section 2 applies to activities in the restraint of trade on the part of a single firm or individual. In contrast, Section 1, as de-

scribed in the next chapter, applies to certain activities in the restraint of trade on the part of more than one individual or firm.) The essence of a single entity's violation of Section 2 is the entity's willful acquisition or maintenance of monopoly power, or its specifically intended *attempt* to do so, provided the attempt has a reasonable chance of success.

In the remainder of this chapter, we focus on single-firm behavior that is intended either to create or to preserve a monopoly within a particular market. Notice that two distinct types of behavior are subject to sanction under Section 2. First, conduct pursued by a firm that is already a monopolist is condemned as *monopolization* if the conduct interferes with free trade and is intended to preserve the firm's monopoly. Second, conduct intended to capture monopoly power is condemned as an *attempt to monopolize*.

Another Section 2 offense is the act of **predatory pricing**. Predatory pricing involves an attempt by one firm to drive its competitors from the market by selling its product substantially *below* normal costs of production. Once the competitors are eliminated, the firm will attempt to recapture its losses and go on to earn very high profits by driving prices up far above their competitive levels.

MONOPOLIZATION

In *United States v. Grinnell Corp.*,[11] the United States Supreme Court defined the offense of **monopolization** as involving the following two elements: "(1) the possession of monopoly power in the relevant market and (2) the willful acquisition or maintenance of the power as distinguished from growth or development as a consequence of a superior product, business acumen, or historic accident." A violation of Section 2 requires that both these elements be established.

Monopoly Power. The Sherman Act does not define *monopoly*. In economic parlance, monopoly refers to control by a single entity of an entire market. It is well established in antitrust law, however, that a firm may be a monopolist even though it is not the sole seller in a market. Nor is monopoly a function of size alone (for example, a "mom and pop" grocery located in an isolated desert town is a geographic monopolist if it is the only grocery serving that particular market). In theory, size in relation to the market is what matters, because monopoly involves power to affect prices and output.

---

9. See *Eastern Railroad Presidents Conference v. Noerr Motor Freight, Inc.*, 365 U.S. 127, 81 S.Ct. 523, 5 L.Ed.2d 464 (1961), and *United Mine Workers of America v. Pennington*, 381 U.S. 657, 89 S.Ct. 1585, 14 L.Ed.2d 626 (1965).

10. *Professional Real Estate Investors Inc. v. Columbia Pictures Industries Inc.*, 508 U.S. 49, 113 S.Ct. 1920, 123 L.Ed.2d 611 (1993).

11. 384 U.S. 563, 86 S.Ct. 1698, 16 L.Ed.2d 778 (1966).

EXHIBIT 27–2 EXEMPTIONS TO ANTITRUST ENFORCEMENT

EXEMPTION	SOURCE AND SCOPE
Labor	Clayton Act—Permits unions to organize and bargain without violating antitrust laws and specifies that strikes and other labor activities do not normally violate any federal law.
Agricultural Associations	Clayton Act and Capper-Volstead Act of 1992—Allow agricultural cooperatives to set prices.
Fisheries	Fisheries Cooperative Marketing Act of 1976—Allows the fishing industry to set prices.
Insurance Companies	McCarran-Ferguson Act of 1945—Exempts the insurance business in states in which the industry is regulated.
Exporters	Webb-Pomerene Act of 1918—Allows U.S. exporters to engage in cooperative activity to compete with similar foreign associations; Export Trading Company Act of 1982—Permits the Department of Justice to exempt certain exporters.
Professional Baseball	The United States Supreme Court has held that professional baseball is exempt because it is not "interstate commerce."[a]
Oil Marketing	Interstate Oil Compact of 1935—Allows states to set quotas on oil to be marketed in interstate commerce.
Defense Activities	Defense Production Act of 1950—Allows the president to approve, and thereby exempt, certain activities to further the military defense of the United States.
Small Businesses' Cooperative Research	Small Business Administration Act of 1958—Allows small firms to undertake cooperative research.
Joint Ventures' Research or Production	National Cooperative Research Act of 1984 and National Cooperative Production Amendments of 1993—Permit research or production of a product, process, or service by joint ventures consisting of competitors.
State Actions	The United States Supreme Court has held that actions by a state are exempt if the state clearly articulates and actively supervises the policy behind its action.[b]
Regulated Industries	Industries (such as airlines) are exempt when a federal administrative agency (such as the Federal Aviation Administration) has primary regulatory authority.
Businesspersons' Joint Efforts to Seek Government Action	Cooperative efforts by businesspersons to obtain legislative, judicial, or executive action are exempt unless it is clear that an effort is "objectively baseless" and is an attempt to make anticompetitive use of government processes.[c]

a. *Federal Baseball Club of Baltimore, Inc. v. National League of Professional Baseball Clubs,* 259 U.S. 200, 42 S.Ct. 465, 66 L. Ed. 898 (1922). A federal district court has held that this exemption applies only to the game's reserve system. (Under the reserve system, teams hold players' contracts for the players' entire careers. The reserve system is generally being replaced by the free agency system.) See *Piazza v. Major League Baseball,* 831 F.Supp. 420 (E.D.Pa. 1993).
b. See *Parker v. Brown,* 317 U.S. 341, 63 S.Ct. 307, 87 L.Ed. 315 (1943).
c. *Eastern Railroad Presidents Conference v. Noerr Motor Freight, Inc.,* 365 U.S. 127, 81 S.Ct. 523, 5 L.Ed.2d 464 (1961), and *United Mine Workers of America v. Pennington,* 381 U.S. 657, 89 S.Ct. 1585, 14 L.Ed.2d 626 (1965).

The United States Supreme Court has defined monopoly power as "the power to control prices or exclude competition." This definition is of limited help, though, and most scholars generally consider monopoly power to be simply a *considerable* degree of market power or, otherwise stated, a *significant* degree of freedom from competitive pressure regarding output and pricing decisions. This generally is the way in which the Supreme Court has applied the concept.

As difficult as it is to define market power precisely, it is even more difficult to measure it. As a workable proxy, courts often look to the firm's percentage share of the "relevant market." This is the so-called **market-share test**.[12] The relevant market consists of two elements: (1) a relevant product market and (2) a relevant geographical market. A firm generally is considered to have monopoly power if its share of the relevant market is 70 percent or more. This is not an absolute, however. It is only a loose rule of thumb; in some cases, a smaller share may be held to constitute monopoly power.[13] We discuss below examples of the two elements of the market-share test.

Product Market. No doubt the relevant product market should include all products that, although produced by different firms, nonetheless have identical attributes. But in determining the relevant market, it must be remembered that products that are not identical may be substituted for one another. Coffee may substitute for tea, cellophane may substitute for waxed paper, and so on. In defining the relevant product market, the key issue is the degree of interchangeability between products. If one product is a sufficient substitute for another, the two are considered to be part of the same product market.

In *United States v. E. I. du Pont de Nemours & Co.*,[14] du Pont was sued for monopolizing the cello-

phane market. Du Pont controlled about 75 percent of cellophane production but contended that it had no monopoly power, because the relevant market included not only cellophane but also all other flexible packaging materials. The United States Supreme Court found that there was indeed a sufficient degree of interchangeability between cellophane and alternatives such as waxed paper and aluminum foil. The Court noted, for example, that although 35 percent of the snack-food industry used cellophane, an even larger percentage used some other packaging material. Consequently, the Court concluded that du Pont did not control a share of the relevant market sufficient to constitute monopoly power.

Many times, decisions concerning relevant product markets can be interpreted as arbitrary. For example, the FTC blocked a merger between Staples, Inc., and Office Depot, Inc., on the ground that, in the office supply business, they had only one other competitor, OfficeMax, Inc. To eliminate any of the three, the FTC claimed, would violate antitrust laws. Staples contended, however, that, combined with Office Depot, it would control less than 6 percent of a market that included such giant retailers as Wal-Mart Stores, Inc., warehouse clubs, and national catalogue dealers. In other words, the FTC was looking at the way office supplies are sold, while Staples was arguing that the agency should look at office supplies as a product. Even after Office Depot agreed to sell sixty-three of its stores to OfficeMax, the FTC still refused to approve the merger and asked a federal district court to block it.

The following case demonstrates a court's efforts to determine the relevant product market for replacement parts for machinery manufactured by Caterpillar, Inc.

---

12. Other measures have been devised, but the market-share test is the most widely used.

13. This standard was first articulated by Judge Learned Hand in the famous *Aluminum Co. of America* case discussed below. A 90 percent share was held to be clear evidence of monopoly power. Anything less than 64 percent, said Judge Hand, made monopoly power doubtful, and anything less than 30 percent was clearly not monopoly power. This is merely a rule of thumb, however; it is not a binding principle of law.

14. 351 U.S. 377, 76 S.Ct. 994, 100 L.Ed.2d 1264 (1956).

CASE 27.3   Godix Equipment Export Corp. v. Caterpillar, Inc.

United States
District Court,
Southern District of
Florida, Miami Division,
1996.
948 F.Supp. 1570.

COMPANY PROFILE *Caterpillar, Inc., (**http://www.caterpillar.com**) manufactures and sells construction machinery, agricultural machinery, engines, and parts for those machines to customers worldwide. Caterpillar is one of the world's largest companies in this field, with sales exceeding $10 billion annually. As part of its operations, Caterpillar authorizes certain dealers to sell Caterpillar-made replacement parts and provides service and support for those who buy genuine Caterpillar parts through the authorized dealers.*

BACKGROUND AND FACTS *Replacement parts for Caterpillar products are either genuine parts, made by Caterpillar, or "will-fit" parts, made by others to operate in Caterpillar machines. Godix Equipment Export Corporation and Universal Service Company negotiated with some of Caterpillar's authorized dealers to buy genuine*

Caterpillar parts at a discount and then resold them for export. Because Godix and Universal obtained the parts at a discount and did not provide service or other support, they could charge less than the authorized dealers and still profit. To gain control of the sales of its parts, Caterpillar created Caterpillar Export Services (CES). CES compiled a list of "resellers," including Godix and Universal, to whom it refused to sell parts. Godix and Universal filed a lawsuit in a federal district court against Caterpillar, alleging, among other things, that Caterpillar was attempting to monopolize the replacement parts market. Caterpillar filed a motion for judgment as a matter of law.[a]

IN THE LANGUAGE OF THE COURT

NESBITT, District Judge.

* * * *

In the instant case, Plaintiffs * * * define the relevant product market as comprising replacement parts for Caterpillar equipment. [The plaintiffs' representatives] testified that as buyers in the market place, they choose between genuine and non-genuine Caterpillar replacement parts to resell * * * . [Universal] is currently still in business selling non-genuine "will-fit" parts for Caterpillar machines to customers to whom [it] previously sold the interchangeable genuine Caterpillar parts. * * *

Caterpillar has also presented evidence which would define the relevant product market as the market for replacement Caterpillar parts, either genuine or will-fit. Caterpillar presented [customers] who testified that they choose from either genuine Caterpillar parts or other will-fit parts depending on pricing, quality and service * * * . [S]uppliers of will-fit parts produce interchangeable parts for over ninety percent of the 500,000 genuine Caterpillar replacement parts. That percentage becomes higher when parts that are in low demand are eliminated from the equation. Thus, for purposes of the Motion for Judgment as a Matter of Law, the relevant product market is defined as replacement parts for Caterpillar machines, either genuine or non-genuine will-fit parts.

DECISION AND REMEDY

The court defined the relevant product market as including both genuine and will-fit replacement parts. The court concluded that although Caterpillar could control which dealers sold genuine Caterpillar parts, it could not control who sold will-fit parts. The court granted Caterpillar's motion for judgment as a matter of law on this issue.

---

a. With this motion, Caterpillar asked the judge to direct a verdict for it on the ground that the plaintiffs had presented no evidence to support their claim. State courts generally use the term *motion for a directed verdict*. See Chapter 2.

Geographical Market. The second component of the relevant market is the geographical boundaries of the market. For products that are sold nationwide, the geographical boundaries encompass the entire United States. If transportation costs are significant or if a producer and its competitors sell in only a limited area—one in which customers have no access to other sources of the product—then the geographical market is limited to that area. In this sense, a national firm may compete in several distinct areas, having monopoly power in one but not another. Generally, the geographical market is that section of the country within which a firm can increase its price a bit without attracting new sellers or without losing many customers to alternative suppliers outside that area.

The advent of e-commerce and the Internet is likely to dramatically change the notion of the size and limits of a geographical market. It may become difficult to perceive any geographical market as local, except for such products as concrete.

Anticompetitive Behavior. Monopoly power is not, in and of itself, illegal. Recall that the monopolization offense has two elements. In addition to monopoly power, there is the requirement of "willful acquisition or maintenance of that power." A dominant market share may be the result of business acumen or the development of a superior product, or it may simply be the result of historical accident. None of these situations should give rise to antitrust concerns. Indeed, it would be counter to society's interest to condemn a firm that had acquired its position on the basis of the first two reasons.

If, however, a firm possesses monopoly power as a result of engaging in some purposeful act to acquire or to maintain that power through anticompetitive means, then the firm is in violation of Section 2. The United States Supreme Court has interpreted this second element as requiring some conduct intended to diminish competition.

Conduct that diminishes competition may not necessarily be anticompetitive. Devising new, low-cost production methods and developing and producing better products all hurt competitors. But they do not injure competition; they are the result of competition. In our initial hypothetical scenario, even if Acme had not received an exclusive monopoly, its DVD drive breakthrough would have given it monopoly power for a period of time until rival firms had had sufficient time to develop and market products that could effectively compete. But ultimately, Acme's innovation would have led to increased competition. Thus, only certain acts are condemned under Section 2, even if the acting firm possesses monopoly power. The hallmark of an action that does violate Section 2 is that, without providing better production or products, action makes competing in the relevant market more difficult for the acting firm's rivals.

Anticompetitive Intent. The qualifier that the sanctioned action have been "willful" is said to require intent, but the intent requirement is difficult to formulate. In most monopolization cases, intent may be inferred from evidence that the firm had monopoly power and engaged in anticompetitive behavior.

For example, in *United States v. Aluminum Co. of America*,[15] the seemingly innocent act of expanding the demand for its products ran Alcoa afoul of Section 2. The court found that Alcoa had intentionally and artificially stimulated demand and then increased its own capacity to meet that increased demand.

The Court of Appeals for the Second Circuit[16] relied on the fact that Alcoa clearly possessed a market share sufficient to give it monopoly power (90 percent of what the court determined to be the relevant market) and that the only apparent reason for its expansion was to prevent competitors from entering the aluminum market. This factual conclusion is often criticized, but the principle set out is now well established. Market domination that results from legitimate competitive behavior—such as foresight, innovation, skill, and good management—will not be condemned unless that domination is abused or acquired through behavior that harms, rather than flows from, competition.

A firm's unilateral refusal to deal with another individual or organization is generally permissible.[17] In the following case, however, the refusal to deal was made by a firm possessing monopoly power, and its apparent intent was to injure competition in the relevant market.

---

15. 148 F.2d 416 (2d Cir. 1945).

16. The Second Circuit acted as the court of final appeal in place of the United States Supreme Court because the latter could not muster a quorum of six qualified justices to hear the case. The case was referred to the court of appeals of the circuit from which it had come under a specially drawn statute (28 U.S.C. Section 2109).

17. Antitrust law does not forbid America Online, Inc., for example, from refusing to deal with advertisers who will not adhere to its rules. See *Cyber Promotions, Inc. v. America Online, Inc.*, 948 F.Supp. 456 (E.D.Pa. 1996).

CASE 27.4   Aspen Skiing Co. v. Aspen Highlands Skiing Corp.

Supreme Court of the United States, 1985.
472 U.S. 585,
105 S.Ct. 2847,
86 L.Ed.2d 467.
http://www.findlaw.
com/casecode/
supreme.html[a]

BACKGROUND AND FACTS   *Aspen, Colorado, is a leading ski resort, and private investors developed four major facilities there for downhill skiing: Ajax, Aspen Highlands, Buttermilk, and Snowmass. The facilities were owned by independent investors, and they jointly offered an "all-Aspen ticket," which could be used for skiing at any of the facilities. Receipts from the tickets were paid to the various facilities according to their use, based on surveys of skiers. By 1977, Aspen Skiing Company (Ski Co.) had acquired ownership of Ajax, Buttermilk, and Snowmass, and Aspen Highlands was owned by the Aspen Highlands Skiing Corporation. At that time, the two companies were engaged in a dispute over the proper distribution of receipts from the all-Aspen ticket. Ski Co. discontinued the all-Aspen ticket and replaced it with a three-area ticket that covered only its own facilities.*

---

a. In the "Citation Search" section, in the left box enter "472", in the right box enter "585", and click "Get It" to access the opinion.

The Aspen Highlands share of the local downhill skiing market declined from over 20 percent in 1976–1977 to 11 percent in 1980–1981. Aspen Highlands filed an antitrust complaint against Ski Co., alleging that Ski Co. had monopolized the market for downhill skiing services at Aspen, in violation of Section 2 of the Sherman Act. Aspen Highlands argued that the discontinuation of the all-Aspen ticket was a purposeful act with intent to monopolize the market. The court issued a judgment in favor of Aspen Highlands, and the Tenth Circuit Court of Appeals affirmed in all respects. Ski Co. appealed to the United States Supreme Court.

IN THE LANGUAGE OF THE COURT

Justice *STEVENS* delivered the opinion of the Court.

*   *   *   *

In this Court, Ski Co. contends that even a firm with monopoly power has no duty to engage in joint marketing with a competitor, that *a violation of [Section] 2 cannot be established without evidence of substantial exclusionary conduct*, and that none of its activities can be characterized as exclusionary. *   *   * [Emphasis added.]

*   *   *   *

*   *   * In the actual case that we must decide, the monopolist did not merely reject a novel offer to participate in a cooperative venture that had been proposed by a competitor. Rather, the monopolist elected to make an important change in a pattern of distribution that had originated in a competitive market and had persisted for several years. The all-Aspen, 6-day ticket with revenues allocated on the basis of usage was first developed when three independent companies operated three different ski mountains in the Aspen area. It continued to provide a desirable option for skiers when the market was enlarged to include four mountains, and when the character of the market was changed by Ski Co.'s acquisition of monopoly power. Moreover, since the record discloses that interchangeable tickets are used in other multimountain areas which apparently are competitive, it seems appropriate to infer that such tickets satisfy consumer demand in free competitive markets.

*   *   *   *

Perhaps most significant, however, is the evidence relating to Ski Co. itself, for Ski Co. did not persuade the jury that its conduct was justified by any normal business purpose. Ski Co. was apparently willing to forgo daily ticket sales both to skiers who sought to exchange the coupons contained in Highlands' Adventure Pack, and to those who would have purchased Ski Co. daily lift tickets from Highlands if Highlands had been permitted to purchase them in bulk. The jury may well have concluded that Ski Co. elected to forgo these short-run benefits because it was more interested in reducing competition in the Aspen market over the long run by harming its smaller competitor.

DECISION AND REMEDY

The United States Supreme Court affirmed the decision of the lower federal courts. The original jury had found that Aspen Highlands had suffered $2.5 million in actual damages, which were trebled under the Sherman Act to an award of $7.5 million. This award was affirmed by the United States Supreme Court.

PREDATORY PRICING

In monopolization cases, predatory pricing—selling below cost—is one form of conduct that continues to receive considerable attention. One reason for this is that a dominant theme in antitrust cases is the promotion of consumer welfare. But consumers benefit from low prices. If a firm sells a valuable product for a price below cost, then it is the firm that loses, not the consumer.

Despite the fact that consumers benefit from the low price, predatory pricing is still condemned.

Condemnation of predatory pricing is based on the fear that although it may benefit consumers in the short term, in the longer term, it will harm competition. The harm feared is that a rich rival, by pricing below its competitors' costs, could drive the competitors out of the market by outlasting them during the phase in which prices were below cost. In the subsequent phase, the rich rival would still be in the market but would no longer face any competitors. The firm would then be free to reap large profits by raising the price far above what it had been when the firm faced market competition.

In any event, there are procompetitive reasons not only for low prices but even for prices below cost. Such pricing may be, for example, the only way in which a new firm can gain a "toehold" in a market populated by established firms, especially if the latter have established brand-name recognition in the market. To prevent the entry of new competitors into a market by forbidding them from using low prices, perhaps even prices below cost, would hinder rather than promote competition.

Faced with such uncertainty as to the purpose and effect of firms' pricing decisions, courts have struggled to invent a workable standard for judging predatory pricing. Some courts look at market structure in deciding predatory pricing cases. Under this approach, a court looks at the potential for harm to consumers created by a firm's below-cost pricing. If it appears that a firm pricing below cost will be unable to capture

monopoly profits at a later time, the court rejects any attempt to discern intent. The essence of the market approach is that if the firm is unlikely to capture monopoly profits through high prices in the future, intent does not matter.[18] Consumers benefit from the low prices regardless. Moreover, if the firm is pursuing a legitimate objective of trying to gain access to an established market, the efforts should not be hampered by rivals crying foul simply because they lose business to a competitor selling at a lower price.

In an action alleging predatory pricing, a plaintiff must prove that the allegedly predatory prices are below an appropriate measure of its competitor's costs and that the competitor has a reasonable prospect of recouping the difference. This requirement is illustrated in the following case.

---

18. See, for example, *Brooke Group, Ltd. v. Brown & Williamson Tobacco Corp.*, 509 U.S. 209, 113 S.Ct. 2578, 125 L.Ed.2d 168 (1993), in which the Supreme Court held that a seller's price-cutting policies could not be predatory "[g]iven the market's realities"—the size of the seller's market share, the expanding output by other sellers, and other factors.

CASE 27.5   C.B. Trucking, Inc. v. Waste Management, Inc.

United States District Court, District of Massachusetts, 1996. 944 F.Supp. 66.

IN THE LANGUAGE OF THE COURT

BACKGROUND AND FACTS   *Every three years, the towns of Franklin and Medway, Massachusetts, publicly solicit bids from private firms to collect residential waste. In 1990, C.B. Trucking, Inc., was the low bidder and was awarded the contracts. On the next round of bidding, Waste Management of Massachusetts, Inc., submitted the low bid. C.B. Trucking filed a lawsuit in a federal district court against Waste Management and others, alleging, among other things, that Waste Management had violated the Sherman Act by attempting to monopolize the residential solid waste business through the practice of predatory pricing. Waste Management filed a motion to dismiss the complaint, in part on the ground that the claims of predatory pricing were "inherently implausible."*

LASKER, District Judge.

*   *   *   *

In support of its motion, Waste Management has submitted the affidavit of Rory J. Fallon, the officer responsible for preparing, submitting and overseeing the preparation and submission of the municipal bids at issue. Fallon's affidavit *   *   * explains that Waste Management was able to bid as low as it did because it did not need to make any capital expenditures to perform the *   *   * contracts.

*   *   *   *

Fallon's affidavit, based as it is on personal knowledge, lowers the boom on C.B. Trucking's case. *   *   *

Moreover, assuming *arguendo* [for the sale of argument] (in direct contradiction of Fallon's sworn statement) that Waste Management's bid prices were set below its own

<table>
<tr><td>DECISION AND REMEDY</td><td>costs, it is nevertheless economically implausible to conclude that Waste Management had a [reasonable prospect] of recouping its investment in below-cost prices when its contracts * * * were subject to public bidding; limited in duration to three years; and set a fixed price for the services rendered.</td></tr>
</table>

The court granted Waste Management's motion and dismissed C.B. Trucking's complaint. Waste Management showed that its prices were not predatory because they were not below its costs. The court reasoned that, even if the prices had been below cost, Waste Management had no reasonable prospect of recouping the difference.

ATTEMPTS TO MONOPOLIZE

Section 2 also prohibits an **attempt to monopolize** a market. Any action challenged as an attempt to monopolize must have been specifically intended to exclude competitors and garner monopoly power. In addition, the attempt must have had a "dangerous" probability of success; that is, the attempt need not have succeeded but must have posed a *serious* threat of monopolization. A probability cannot be dangerous unless the alleged offender possesses at least some degree of market power. (See this chapter's *Emerging*

Trends in Technology on page 593 for a discussion of the widely publicized case brought by the U.S. Department of Justice and twenty states' attorneys general against Microsoft Corporation for alleged violations of antitrust laws, including monopolization and attempted monopolization.)

In the following case, another antitrust suit brought against Microsoft Corporation, the court considered whether, from the facts, it could be concluded that an attempt to monopolize a certain market had been made.

CASE 27.6   Caldera, Inc. v. Microsoft Corp.

United States District Court; District of Utah, 1999. 72 F.Supp.2d 1295.

HISTORICAL AND TECHNOLOGICAL SETTING *Critical to the evolution of the personal computer (PC) was the development of the computer operating system (OS). An OS controls a computer's interaction with peripheral hardware, such as modems and printers, and also serves as the support for other software. Independent developers write software applications, such as games and word processing programs, to operate on general functions written into an OS. The dominant OS in the late 1970s and early 1980s was developed and marketed by Digital Research, Inc. (DRI). Seattle Computer Products, a small computer equipment maker, developed a "clone" of DRI's OS, known as QDOS ("Quick and Dirty Operating System"). A new start-up partnership called Microsoft Corporation bought QDOS from Seattle Computer Products for $50,000.*

BACKGROUND AND FACTS *Microsoft licensed its new OS to International Business Machines (IBM) to be installed on each IBM PC. Microsoft sold the OS as MS-DOS to other manufacturers, who made IBM PC clones. In 1985, Microsoft launched Windows, graphical user interface (GUI) software through which users execute commands with point-and-click technology. By 1988, Microsoft had a monopoly position in the OS market. Meanwhile, DRI developed DR DOS to compete directly with MS-DOS and be compatible with software, such as Windows, written for use with MS-DOS. When*

Microsoft developed Windows 3.1, it allowed other software manufacturers to "beta" test Windows 3.1 to work out incompatibilities between their products, but refused DRI's request for a beta copy. Although DR DOS was, with minor adjustments, compatible with Windows, Microsoft told customers that using a system other than MS-DOS put users at risk. Phil Barrett, a Microsoft executive, e-mailed other Microsoft officers that "[t]he approach we will take is [for Windows] to detect [DR DOS] and refuse to load. The error message should be something like 'Invalid device driver interface.' " Barrett also proposed to have DR DOS's running blocked by Bambi (Microsoft's code name for a utility that, among other things, could detect a computer's OS). Microsoft also added programming that made it impossible for Windows to be installed on a DR DOS system. DRI withdrew DR DOS from the market. Caldera, Inc., acquired DRI and filed a suit in a federal district court against Microsoft. Caldera charged, among other things, that in violation of Section 2 of the Sherman Act, Microsoft used its monopoly in the GUI market to illegally maintain its monopoly in the OS market. Microsoft filed a motion for summary judgment.

IN THE LANGUAGE
OF THE COURT

BENSON, District Judge.

*   *   *   *

*   *   * Caldera's claim of unlawful predatory conduct is based on the aggregate effect of all of Microsoft's anticompetitive behavior. While each separate fact used to support Caldera's [Section] 2 claim may not by itself legally support the claim, the overall effect may be prohibited anticompetitive conduct.

Accordingly, it would be inappropriate to view these alleged incompatibilities in isolation and out of the context in which they occurred. *   *   *

*   *   *   *

Perhaps the most direct evidence offered by plaintiff that suggests the incompatibilities were intentionally placed by Microsoft for the purpose of eliminating DR DOS as a competitor, and not for procompetitive purposes, comes from a series of e-mails sent between [Microsoft executives] Charles Stevens, Phil Barrett, and Brad Silverberg *   *   * relating to the Bambi incompatibility. *   *   * Barrett [writes to Stevens:] "The approach we will take is to detect [DR DOS] and refuse to load. The error message should be something like 'Invalid device driver interface.' *   *   * Do you have a reliable [DR DOS] detection mechanism?" That same day Barrett also sent an e-mail to Brad Silverberg which read: "heh, heh, heh *   *   * My proposal is to have Bambi refuse to run on this alien OS. Comments?"

Each of these incompatibilities arose at a time when Microsoft had excluded DRI from beta testing DR DOS with the new Windows version 3.1 before its public release. Consequently, any incompatibility which arose, intentionally placed there by Microsoft or not, could not be detected or remedied before Windows' public release. Moreover, it is alleged Microsoft was aware of *   *   * the *   *   * incompatibilities and knew that [DR DOS] could be altered and made to work with Windows 3.1 with relatively minor modifications. However, Caldera asserts that Microsoft continued to create the illusion that DR DOS was incompatible with Windows by inserting error messages conveying to the user that either DR DOS was incompatible with Windows or that MS-DOS was the only environment in which Windows could properly function. While technically this may not be false, a fact finder [jury] could reasonably conclude that laid against this backdrop there existed an anticompetitive campaign to eliminate competition in the DOS market in violation of [Section] 2.

DECISION
AND REMEDY

The court denied Microsoft's motion for summary judgment on Caldera's claims. The court ruled that if Caldera's allegations were proved, a jury could reasonably conclude that Microsoft had intended to eliminate competition in the OS market in violation of Section 2 of the Sherman Act.

EMERGING TRENDS IN TECHNOLOGY

Protecting Competition in Cyberspace

In the United States, competition between businesses is seen as a primary factor for the success of our economy. It is believed that those who violate laws protecting competition—antitrust laws—cause us to pay higher prices for products of lesser quality. Violations of antitrust laws can also block new advances in technology.

To date, there are very few cases involving the application of antitrust law in cyberspace. One court has held that it likely was not a violation of antitrust law for an Internet service provider, America Online, Inc. (AOL), to refuse to transmit e-mail ads to its subscribers for free.[a]

THE CASE AGAINST MICROSOFT

Currently, the most well-known instance involving cyberspace technology and antitrust law is the case brought by the U.S. Department of Justice and twenty states' attorneys general against Microsoft Corporation. The plaintiffs charged, in part, that Microsoft committed such violations of antitrust law as the following.

■ Unreasonably restrained competition by "tying" its Internet browser to Windows 98, by entering into "exclusive-dealing" arrangements with various Internet providers, and by

imposing start-up screen restrictions on computer manufacturers. (The elements of these and other violations of antitrust law are discussed in more detail in Chapter 28.)
■ Illegally maintained a monopoly in its operating system software.
■ Attempted to monopolize the market for Internet browsers.
■ Unlawfully used its operating system monopoly to obtain a competitive advantage in the browser market.

In "findings of fact" issued in late 1999, U.S. district court judge Thomas Jackson declared that Microsoft held monopoly power in the relevant market and that it has used its dominant position in the operating-system and browser markets to thwart competition from other companies. The judge added that some innovations "that would truly benefits consumers never occur for the sole reason that they do not coincide with Microsoft's self interest." Harm to consumers, according to the judge, was "immediate and easily discernible."[b]

AFTER THE FINDINGS, THEN WHAT?

In April 2000, the judge issued the court's opinion, in which he concluded that "Microsoft maintained its monopoly power by anticompetitive means and attempted to monopolize the Web browser market, both in violation of [Section 2 of the Sherman Act]. Microsoft also violated [Section] 1 of the Sherman Act by tying its

Web browser to its operating system."[c]

It was expected that the penalty would be a break up of Microsoft into two companies—one to produce the operating software and the other to handle other software applications, including the browser. It was also expected that this would be postponed during what could be years of appeals.

IMPLICATIONS FOR THE BUSINESSPERSON

1. Companies that provide Internet-related software should think twice about asking the government to intervene. The end result may include government regulation where it never existed before.

FOR CRITICAL ANALYSIS

1. How is it possible to define the relevant market with respect to Internet products?
2. Some argue that breaking up Microsoft into component parts would generate so much confusion in the marketplace that consumers would inevitably suffer as a result. Do you agree?

RELEVANT WEB SITES

Judge Jackson's conclusions of law, and other trial documents, are posted on the U.S. Department of Justice's Web site at **http://www.usdoj.gov/atr/cases/ms_index.htm.** For Microsoft's response, go to **http://www.mercurycenter.com/business/microsoft/trial/content.html**.

---

a. *Cyber Promotions, Inc. v. America Online, Inc.,* 948 F.Supp. 456 (E.D.Pa. 1996).

b. *United States v. Microsoft Corp.,* 84 F.Supp.2d 9 (D.D.C. 1999).

c. *United States v. Microsoft Corp.,* 87 F.Supp.2d 30 (D.D.C. 2000).

TERMS AND CONCEPTS TO REVIEW

antitrust law 575	market-share test 586	predatory pricing 584
attempt to monopolize 591	monopolization 584	restraint of trade 577
dissolution 581	monopoly 574	treble damages 581
divestiture 581	monopoly power 578	trust 576
market power 574	Noerr-Pennington doctrine 584	

QUESTIONS AND CASE PROBLEMS

27–1. EXEMPTIONS. The Southern Motor Carriers Rate Conference is a private organization that lobbies regulatory commissions in various southern states on behalf of national and regional private commercial carriers. A new carrier claims that the organization is really in the business of setting rates and controlling the issuance of licenses through its influence over the members of the various regulatory boards. How might the organization violate antitrust laws? If the organization does no more than lobby the various agencies, does it run afoul of the antitrust laws in light of the Supreme Court's enunciation of the Noerr-Pennington doctrine?

27–2. PREDATORY PRICING. A car rental firm specializes in renting automobiles to insurance company customers who need temporary replacements while their cars are being repaired. Several other car rental agencies serve the same geographical area. The specialty agency substantially reduces the daily rental fee on its cars. Other firms in the area contend that the reductions amount to predatory pricing. If an antitrust action is brought against the specialty agency, how should the case be decided? Discuss all factors that must be considered.

27–3. MONOPOLIES. Super-Tech Industries presently controls 55 percent of the market in the manufacture and sale of computers. The balance of the market is controlled by five other manufacturers, with Alcan Corp. having 25 percent of the market. Alcan has an innovative research staff, but every time Alcan introduces a faster, more powerful, and more efficient computer in the market, Super-Tech immediately informs its customers of the upcoming development of a competing computer that it will sell at 30 percent below the Alcan price. Alcan claims that these activities on the part of Super-Tech are an antitrust violation. Discuss fully whether this unilateral action by Super-Tech violates antitrust law.

27–4. PUBLIC POLICY AND CONTRACTS. Goodfellows, Inc., is a close corporation with only two shareholders. Goodfellows is engaged in the pizza delivery business. Two other such firms serve the same market, but Goodfellows controls a 75 percent share. The two shareholders agree that one will purchase all of the shares that belong to the other. As a condition of the transaction, the shareholder selling the shares agrees not to open a competing pizza delivery business within a seventy-mile radius or become employed by any rival firm within the same designated area. The covenant is to last five years. Is it an unreasonable restraint of trade? Would a court likely declare unenforceable the promise not to compete?

27–5. ANTICOMPETITIVE BEHAVIOR. Syufy, a movie theater operator, opened a lavish six-screen theater in Las Vegas. All theater owners in Las Vegas obtained films from distributors by submitting bids on first-run movie releases. Successful bidders obtained an exhibition license specifying that the distributor would receive a percentage of the theaters' weekly receipts. Syufy's uniquely opulent theater generated considerable patronage, and soon a price war was under way between Syufy and the other Las Vegas theater owners. Eventually, the competition was reduced to just Syufy and Roberts, a small exhibitor of predominantly second-run films, with the former controlling nearly 100 percent of the Las Vegas theater market. After a major film distributor stopped doing business with Syufy and began to deal exclusively with Roberts, Syufy suffered a reversal of fortunes. Soon thereafter, Roberts became the dominant force in the market. Ultimately, Roberts sold out to a national theater chain. The government sued Syufy, alleging a violation of Section 2 of the Sherman Act. The government argued that Syufy had acquired monopoly power by buying out his competition. Syufy defended by arguing that he could not have violated Section 2 because there were no barriers preventing other firms from entering the Las Vegas theater market. Which side is likely to prevail? [*United States v. Syufy Enterprises*, 903 F.2d 659 (9th Cir. 1990)]

27–6. MONOPOLIES. American Academic Suppliers, Inc., and Beckley-Cardy, Inc., were wholesalers engaged in the sale of school supplies. American's major markets were largely concentrated in the Midwest; Beckley's markets were on a more national scale. American had been started by Beckley's former president on a small initial investment of less than $500,000. American had also hired a number of salespersons away from Beckley. Initially, American had experienced fairly rapid expansion in the markets in which it competed with Beckley. Beckley had responded by giving steep discounts in the prices of some of its products and, according to American, by making disparaging remarks and starting rumors about American's business operations. American sued Beckley, alleging, among other things, that Beckley had violated Section 2 of the Sherman Act by attempting to monopolize the school-supply market. Did Beckley's actions constitute an attempt to monopolize the school-supply market in violation of Section 2 of the Sherman Act? Discuss fully. [*American Academic Suppliers, Inc. v. Beckley-Cardy, Inc.*, 922 F.2d 1317 (7th Cir. 1991)]

27–7. MONOPOLIES. BTR, Inc., owns the patent rights to sorbothane (an elastic polymer with characteristics that make it useful in a variety of products). In 1980, BTR granted Shirley and Larry McQuillan all distribution rights to sorbothane and exclusive rights to buy sorbothane for use in equestrian products. In 1981, BTR split the distribution rights between the McQuillans and Spectrum Sports, Inc. The next year, BTR asked the McQuillans to relinquish more of their distribution rights, but they refused. A few months later, BTR appointed another company as national distributor for sorbothane equestrian products. In August 1983, BTR refused to accept the McQuillans' orders, and Spectrum replaced them as national distributor of some sorbothane products. The McQuillans' business failed. They sued BTR and Spectrum. Did the defendants violate Section 2 of the Sherman Act? [*Spectrum Sports, Inc. v. McQuillan*, 506 U.S. 884, 113 S.Ct. 884, 122 L.Ed.2d 247 (1993)]

27–8. ANTITRUST LAWS. Great Western Directories, Inc. (GW), is an independent publisher of telephone directory Yellow Pages. GW buys information for its listings from Southwestern Bell Telephone Co. (SBT). Southwestern Bell Corp. owns SBT and Southwestern Bell Yellow Pages (SBYP), which publishes a directory in competition with GW. In June 1988, in some markets, SBT raised the price for its listing information, and SBYP lowered the price for advertising in its Yellow Pages. GW feared that these companies would do the same thing in other local markets, and it would then be too expensive to compete in those markets. Because of this fear, GW left one market and declined to compete in another. Consequently, SBYP had a monopoly in those markets. GW and another independent publisher filed a suit in a federal district court against Southwestern Bell Corp. What antitrust law, if any, did Southwestern Bell Corp. violate? Should the independent companies be entitled to damages? [*Great Western Directories, Inc. v. Southwestern Bell*

Telephone Co., 74 F.3d 613 (5th Cir. 1996)]

27–9. MONOPOLIES. At one time, all advertisers and advertising agencies sent their ads to newspapers by mail, courier, or some other form of physical delivery. By the mid–1980s, electronic delivery emerged as an alternative. In 1986, AD/SAT, a division of Skylight, Inc., began to deliver ads from New York and Los Angeles to newspapers through AD/SAT's high-speed facsimile system over a satellite network owned and operated by the Associated Press (AP). The AP, a cooperative association whose members include more than 1,500 U.S. newspapers, collects and distributes news and photographs to newspapers. AD/SAT's competitors included DigiFlex, Ad eXpress, AdStar, AdLink, and Business Link. By 1994, forty-eight of the fifty largest papers in the United States were AD/SAT customers, but 80 percent of all ads delivered to newspapers were sent by overnight couriers, such as Federal Express. That year, the AP launched AdSEND to compete in the delivery of ads to newspapers via the AP's satellite network. Unlike AD/SAT, AdSEND handled the delivery of ads using computers and charged only advertisers for the delivery. AD/SAT filed a suit in a federal district court against the AP and others. Did the AP's entry into the ad delivery business violate Section 2 of the Sherman Act? Why or why not? [*AD/SAT, a Division of Skylight, Inc. v. Associated Press*, 181 F.3d 216 (2d.Cir. 1999)]

27–10. IN YOUR COURT

Mr. Furniture Warehouse, Inc., was a company engaged in the wholesale and retail furniture business. Like many other companies in its line of business, Mr. Furniture frequently obtained its furniture products from manufacturers by making purchases on credit. Credit usually was not provided by the manufacturers themselves but rather by institutions engaged in "commercial factoring." Such institutions typically purchase manufacturers' accounts receivable at a discount and assume direct responsibility for collecting the outstanding debts. Moreover, factored-credit institutions often purchase debt on a nonrecourse basis, meaning that they assume the entire risk of a debtor's failure to repay. The institutions rely on credit ratings and similar criteria in deciding which purchasers should be extended credit. Barclays American/Commercial, Inc., was almost certainly the dominant factored credit institution in the market in which Mr. Furniture operated. Barclays refused to extend credit for Mr. Furniture's inventory purchases from furniture manufacturers. Mr. Furniture's president, Howard Cassett, asserted that the refusal was based on two elements: (1) Barclays's attempt to monopolize the factored-credit market and (2) the personal animosity that Barclays's manager, Jim Stenhouse, harbored toward Cassett. Mr. Furniture sued Barclays, alleging, among other things, violations of the Sherman Act. Assume that you are the judge hearing this case and answer the following questions:

(a) Should Mr. Furniture be allowed to complain that because, as a "consumer" of factored-credit services, it was harmed by the alleged monopoly over credit extension acquired by Barclays? Or should only Barclays's rivals be allowed to bring the suit?

(b) If monopoly power—assuming Barclays had such power—is used for personal motives, would it be reasonable to allow standing on that basis?

LAW ON THE WEB

For updated links to resources available on the Web, as well as a variety of other materials, visit this text's Web site at http://wleb.westbuslaw.com.

You can access the Antitrust Division of the U.S. Department of Justice online at

http://www.usdoj.gov

To see the American Bar Association's Web page on antitrust law, go to

http://www.abanet.org/antitrust

LEGAL RESEARCH EXERCISES ON THE WEB

Go to http://wleb.westbuslaw.com, the Web site that accompanies this text. Select "Internet Applications," and then click on "Chapter 27." There you will find the following Internet research exercise that you can perform to learn more about the application of antitrust laws to vertical restraints:

Activity 27–1: Microsoft and Monopolization

CHAPTER 28

Antitrust and Restraints of Trade

THE MAJOR THRUST OF FEDERAL antitrust legislation has been directed at anticompetitive agreements between rival firms. Agreements to fix prices, restrict output, divide markets, exclude other competitors, and otherwise impede the dynamics of a free market have all been condemned as violations of federal antitrust laws. Such joint actions have been prosecuted as impermissible restraints of trade under Section 1 of the Sherman Act and, if the firms possess substantial market power, as conspiracies to monopolize under Section 2 of the same act.

Some agreements may be forced on an unwilling firm by another firm possessing substantial market power. Typical of such agreements are exclusive-dealing contracts and tying arrangements, described in the preceding chapter. Recall that an exclusive-dealing contract conditions one firm's willingness to deal with another on the latter's continued refusal to deal with the former's rivals. Tying arrangements normally require that the purchaser of one product also purchase a second product. Also recall that such agreements violate provisions of the Clayton Act if the contracts or arrangements harm the competitive process or interfere with free trade.

In this chapter, we continue our study of antitrust law by examining in detail the various forms of *concerted behavior* that are condemned as harmful to competition. In particular, we examine how courts attempt to distinguish between those types of trade restrictions that are necessary—perhaps even beneficial—to the competitive process and those that impede competition. We also examine the legal standards for determining whether mergers between firms should be declared illegal on the ground that the result would be to lessen competition.

SECTION 1

Restraints of Trade: Overview

The underlying assumption of Section 1 of the Sherman Act is that society's welfare is harmed if rival firms are permitted to join in an agreement that consolidates their market power or otherwise restrains competition. Not all agreements between rivals, however, result in enhanced market power or *unreasonably* restrain trade. It is virtually inconceivable that an agreement to fix prices or restrict output could be designed for any purpose other than to diminish interfirm competition. Yet there are numerous instances in which agreements among rivals might actually increase social welfare by making firms more efficient, by making information more readily available, or by creating joint

597

incentives to undertake risky research and development projects.

PER SE Violations

Some agreements are considered so blatantly and substantially anticompetitive that they are deemed **per se violations** of Section 1. For example, if two competitors in a concentrated industry agree to set the prices for their products at the same level, their agreement is considered so anticompetitive that it is deemed a *per se* violation. If an agreement is found to be a *per se* violation, a court is precluded from inquiring whether the agreement should be upheld on the ground that it provides benefits that outweigh its anticompetitive effects. If an agreement is not found to be a *per se* violation of Section 1, then the court proceeds to analyze its legality under what is referred to as a **rule of reason,** according to which the court balances the reasons for the agreement against its potentially anticompetitive effects.

THE RULE OF REASON

In determining whether a specific agreement that is not a *per se* violation should nonetheless be condemned as a Section 1 offense, a court will consider several factors. The court must evaluate the parties' purposes in effecting the agreement, determine whether the parties have power to implement the agreement's purposes, and assess what the effect or potential effect of the agreement is. Some antitrust scholars maintain that case law suggests that courts will also consider a fourth element: whether the parties could have relied on less restrictive means to achieve their goals.

THE SOFT PER SE Rule, or Narrow Rule of Reason

Sometimes, it is not clear whether a restraint of trade is being judged under the *per se* rule or is being subjected to a rule-of-reason analysis. In some cases, for example, the United States Supreme Court has stated, or at least implied, that it is applying a *per se* rule, and yet a careful reading of its analysis suggests that it is weighing benefits against harms under a rule of reason.[1] Some have

termed this a "soft," or "limited," *per se* rule. Others have termed it a "narrow" rule of reason. Perhaps the most that can be said with certainty is that although the distinction between the two rules seems clear in theory, in the actual application of antitrust laws, the distinction has not always been so clear.

SECTION 2

Horizontal Restraints

The term **horizontal restraint** is encountered frequently in antitrust law. A horizontal restraint is any agreement that in some way restrains competition between rival firms competing in the same market. Whenever firms at the same level of operation and in direct competition with one another (for example, retailers of a similar product located in the same geographical market) agree to operate in a way that restricts their market activities, they are said to have imposed a horizontal restraint on trade. Some horizontal restraints are *per se* violations of Section 1, but others may be permissible; those that are not *per se* violations are tested under the rule of reason.

PRICE FIXING

Consider the scenario presented in Chapter 27 involving the introduction of a new digital video disc (DVD) drive. Suppose our hypothetical firm, Acme, had instead sought large profits by some means other than arduous and financially risky research into innovative DVD drive technology. Assume that advanced DVD drive technology does not yet exist. Acme's managers decide to make life easy for themselves. They go to other DVD drive producers and say, "Let's not work to one another's disadvantage. There's enough demand for DVD drives for all of us to charge higher prices if we don't undercut one another's prices." Acme's plan calls for each producer to charge a price higher than an established minimum. The minimum price is set as the total cost of the least productive producer plus a 10 percent profit margin. More efficient firms (that is, firms that can produce at lower cost) will, of course, enjoy higher profits.

Although not all such schemes are as simple or as blatant as our hypothetical example suggests, they all involve some means of eliminating competition between rivals to sell at the lowest price while still earning a normal profit (that is, one commensurate with the profit that could be earned in some alternative en-

---

1. See, for example, *Fashion Originator's Guild of America, Inc. v. Federal Trade Commission,* 312 U.S. 457, 61 S.Ct. 703, 85 L.Ed. 949 (1941); *Klor's, Inc. v. Broadway-Hale Stores, Inc.,* 359 U.S. 207, 79 S.Ct. 705, 3 L.Ed.2d 741 (1959); and *Silver v. New York Stock Exchange,* 373 U.S. 341, 83 S.Ct. 1246, 10 L.Ed.2d 389 (1963).

deavor using the same resources). By eliminating price competition in which firms seek to sell more by charging less than their rivals, firms restrict output. This is the essence of **price fixing.**

Per Se Violation.   Perhaps the definitive case regarding price-fixing agreements remains the 1940 case of *United States v. Socony-Vacuum Oil Co.,* also known as the *Madison Oil* case.[2] In this case, a group of independent oil producers in Texas and Louisiana were caught between falling demand due to the Great Depression and increasing supply from newly discovered oil fields in the region. In response, a group of the major refining companies agreed to buy "distress" gasoline (excess supplies) from the independents so as to dispose of it in an "orderly manner." Although there was no explicit agreement as to price, it was clear that the purpose of the agreement was to limit the supply of gasoline on the market, thereby raising prices.

There may have been good reasons for such an agreement. The refiners may simply have wanted to

avoid a temporary situation that would have driven the independent suppliers out of business, thus making it difficult to secure crude oil supplies later, after the economic climate had improved. Nonetheless, the threats posed by such agreements to open and free competition were deemed significant. The United States Supreme Court recognized these dangers in the *Socony-Vacuum* case. The Court held that the asserted reasonableness of a price-fixing agreement is never a defense; any agreement that restricts output or artificially fixes price is a *per se* violation of Section 1. The rationale of the *per se* rule was best stated in what is now the most famous portion of the Court's decision: footnote 59 of Justice William O. Douglas's opinion. In it, he compared a freely functioning price system to a body's central nervous system, condemning price-fixing agreements as threats to "the central nervous system of the economy."

Identifying a Price-fixing Arrangement.   Price-fixing arrangements are not always easy to identify. An otherwise legitimate arrangement may unintentionally result in price fixing. Price fixing also may be difficult to detect because the parties wish to conceal their scheme. The following case provides an illustration.

2. 310 U.S. 150, 60 S.Ct. 811, 84 L.Ed.2d 1129 (1940).

CASE 28.1 | In re Medical X-Ray Film Antitrust Litigation

United States District Court, Eastern District of New York, 1996. 946 F.Supp. 209.

BACKGROUND AND FACTS   *Eastman Kodak Company; E. I. du Pont de Nemours & Company; Miles, Inc.; Fuji Medical Systems, U.S.A., Inc.; and other companies sell medical X-ray film. During the late 1980s and early 1990s, Kodak, Du Pont, Miles, and Fuji increased the prices of their film every year. The increases, which were generally close in time and amount, were announced late each year. Before the announcements, supervisors with the various companies would tell their employees that their competitors were going to raise prices. Sometimes they distributed copies of competitors' intracompany memos concerning the increases. At meetings of the American Association of Radiological Technicians, some of the competitors' sales representatives exchanged pricing information, including copies of their respective companies' internal memos regarding proposed increases. Victoria Orthopedic Associates and other buyers of the film filed a suit in a federal district court against Kodak and the others, alleging price fixing in violation of the Sherman Act. In response to the plaintiffs' evidence of exchange of information among competitors, the defendants argued in part that prices were set before any of the information was exchanged, that none of the individuals involved had any authority to set prices, and that the contacts were random, unplanned encounters. The defendants filed a motion for summary judgment.*

IN THE LANGUAGE OF THE COURT

SIFTON, Chief Judge.

*   *   *   *

*   *   * [P]laintiffs have presented a basis upon which the existence of a price-fixing agreement or conspiracy among defendants can reasonably be inferred. Despite the plausibility of defendants' innocent explanations for the circumstantial evidence plaintiffs have presented * * * , this evidence * * * tends to exclude the possibility that defendants acted independently in setting their prices for medical x-ray film each year. * * * [T]here is sufficient evidence in this case to infer that the market of medical x-ray film dealers and customers, in conjunction with the ease of interfirm communications, served as a kind of clearinghouse from which competitors could gather information regarding current prices and impending price increases in order to coordinate their pricing activities.

DECISION AND REMEDY   *The court denied the defendants' motion for summary judgment. There was a reasonable basis from which to infer a price-fixing agreement. The case could proceed to trial.*

HORIZONTAL MARKET DIVISIONS

Prices can be controlled indirectly through agreements to restrict output, as well as explicitly through agreements to fix prices. Because the former type of agreement operates to decrease the supplies available to consumers, it has the same effect as a direct agreement to raise prices. Efforts to control prices are often effected by **horizontal market divisions**—that is, agreements to divide the market up among rival firms. The allocation may be geographical (for example, letting one firm serve the Midwest, another the East Coast, and so on), or it may be functional, by class of customer (for example, having one firm deal exclusively with retailers and a second firm deal solely with wholesalers).

In some respects, market divisions may have an even greater impact on competition than do price-fixing agreements. Each firm has a monopoly over its allocated share of the market for that particular brand—it is the sole supplier. The sole supplier is free not only from price competition for that brand but also from competition for that brand regarding quality, customer service, and all other dimensions of competition.

Applying the *Per Se* Rule. Consider once again our hypothetical scenario involving Acme and its rival DVD drive producers. Suppose that, flush with the initial success of their price-fixing agreement, the producers agree that each firm that begins selling DVD drives to dealers in remote communities in which DVD drives have not been available will thereafter have an exclusive right to sell retail or through dealers in that area. Initially, there is intense competition to find such virgin markets. After all the profitable markets have been taken, however, conditions in the exclusive markets may change. Suppliers may begin to limit the warranties they offer. Prices may begin to rise despite the lack of warranties. And service may diminish. Because of such potential effects, agreements like that made by the DVD drive producers are generally treated as *per se* violations of Section 1.

The following case considers whether an allocation of customers is a horizontal restraint that should be treated as a *per se* violation of Section 1 of the Sherman Act. The case also shows the procedural effects of characterizing conduct as a *per se* violation.

CASE 28.2   ## United States v. Suntar Roofing, Inc.

United States Circuit
Court of Appeals,
Tenth Circuit, 1990.
897 F.2d 469.

BACKGROUND AND FACTS   *Suntar Roofing, Inc., and Ronan's Roofing, Inc., built roofs on new homes in and around Kansas City, Kansas. Some of Suntar's and Ronan's officers and owners agreed to a customer allocation plan that would divide roofing customers in the area between the two corporations. The U.S. government brought criminal charges against some of the officers and owners. During the trial, the judge ruled that all customer allocation schemes are* per se *violations of Section 1 of the Sherman Act. This ruling prevented the defendants from introducing evidence to show the reasonableness of their agreement. The defendants were found guilty of violating federal antitrust laws, and they appealed.*

IN THE LANGUAGE
OF THE COURT

BRORBY, Circuit Judge.

*   *   *   *

*   *   * [S]ince the passage of the Sherman Act, the courts have formulated and applied a *per se* rule of illegality for certain restrictive practices that are deemed to be manifestly anticompetitive. As the Supreme Court explained *   *   * , "there are certain agreements or practices which because of their pernicious [harmful] effect on competition and lack of any redeeming virtue are conclusively presumed to be unreasonable and therefore illegal without elaborate inquiry as to the precise harm they have caused or the business excuse for their use." Here, appellants [Suntar and Ronan's] argue that the indictment in this case did not justify the trial court's application of *per se* analysis *   *   * .

*   *   * [T]he government argued that the conduct charged in the indictment, a "horizontal" customer allocation agreement, represented conduct which is illegal *per se*. Prior to trial, the trial court ruled that the indictment did in fact allege a *per se* violation of the Sherman Act, and that, assuming the government could present evidence establishing the violation charged in the indictment, the defendants would therefore be precluded from introducing evidence of reasonableness or justification at trial. At trial, the court concluded that the government had established the violation charged and therefore precluded defendants' additional evidence. Consistent with the analysis of the Supreme Court and previous holdings of this court and of other circuits, we concur with the determination of the trial court and hold that the activity alleged in the indictment in this case, an agreement to allocate or divide customers between competitors within the same horizontal market, constitutes a *per se* violation of Section 1 of the Sherman Act.

DECISION
AND REMEDY

The appellate court sustained the trial judge's ruling that a customer allocation scheme is a per se *violation of Section 1 of the Sherman Act. Therefore, the trial judge's exclusion of evidence regarding the reasonableness of, or business justification for, the scheme was not an error.*

Criticisms of Applying the *Per Se* Rule. The *per se* rule regarding market divisions has been criticized in certain circumstances, and its future status is uncertain. Some actual cases have involved circumstances very dissimilar to those presented in our hypothetical scenario involving DVD drive production and sales. In one instance, a group of small- and medium-sized groceries agreed to market a common brand of grocery products by allocating regional territories to members of the group so that individual members could focus their marketing efforts on a single territory. The group accounted for only about 6 percent of sales in its market and directly competed with such large chain stores as A&P and Safeway, which carried their own brand-name products.[3] A similar venture using territorial restrictions involved a group of small firms attempting to market mattresses under the trademark Sealy.[4]

In both these cases, the individual firms did not have sufficient resources to create their own brands individually and joined together so as to compete with larger, established firms selling their own brand-name products. Nonetheless, both cases were treated as *per se* violations of Section 1. It is possible that the United States Supreme Court will ultimately adopt a rule of reason for judging such horizontal restraints. As shown by some cases considered later in this chapter, the Court has been more willing in recent years to consider economic factors rather than relying solely on mechanical characterizations in judging concerted business conduct.

TRADE ASSOCIATIONS

The common interests of firms or individuals within an industry or profession are frequently promoted by trade associations or professional organizations. These organizations may provide for the exchange of information among the members, the enhancement of the public image of the trade or profession, the setting of industry or professional standards, or the pooling of

---

3. See *United States v. Topco Associates, Inc.*, 405 U.S. 596, 92 S.Ct. 1126, 31 L.Ed.2d 515 (1972).
4. See *United States v. Sealy, Inc.*, 388 U.S. 350, 87 S.Ct. 1847, 18 L.Ed.2d 1238 (1967).

resources to represent the members' interests to various governmental bodies. Some of these activities benefit society, as well as the individual members. Even those activities that benefit the members' general economic well-being may not necessarily be anticompetitive.

For example, lumber producers might be concerned about whether or not they are cutting more trees than expected future demand would warrant given the cutting levels of rival firms. The market for lumber might be widely dispersed over the whole nation, making it especially difficult for small firms to gauge overall demand conditions in the lumber market. Lumber firms might thus decide to form a trade association that could amass data on the output and price levels of its members in various markets.[5] The association would be of economic benefit to lumber firms by reducing the costs of projecting market demand. Such knowledge could also benefit society by making the lumber market function more smoothly, dampening cycles of oversupply and undersupply of lumber output. Even if it did not make the industry function more smoothly, such knowledge would be unlikely to harm competition in the industry unless the industry was *concentrated*.

A **concentrated industry** is one in which either a single firm or a small number of firms control a large percentage of market sales. In concentrated industries, trade associations can be, and have been, used as a means to facilitate anticompetitive actions, such as fixing prices, allocating markets, or, as discussed in the next section, conducting boycotts—all with the clear objective of lessening competition. For example, consider again the lumber association. Such an association would provide information that members could use to determine whether a secret agreement to fix prices was being adhered to by the conspirators. Thus, such associations offer possibilities of both great benefit and substantial harm.

In most instances, the rule of reason is applied in evaluating such practices and agreements. If a court finds that a particular practice or agreement that restrains trade involves no apparent intent to fix prices or limit output, and that it benefits the public as well as the association, then the court will weigh those benefits against the harms to competition under the rule of reason. As in other cases, however, if the harm to competition is substantial, a trade association's activities will be condemned as a Section 1 violation. As shown in the following case, not even action undertaken by a health-care professional organization allegedly for the sole purpose of protecting the public will escape scrutiny if it is likely to harm market competition.

---

5. See, for example, *American Column & Lumber Co. v. United States*, 257 U.S. 377, 42 S.Ct. 114, 66 L.Ed.2d 284 (1921).

CASE 28.3   Wilk v. American Medical Association

United States
Court of Appeals,
Seventh Circuit, 1990.
895 F.2d 352.

BACKGROUND AND FACTS   *In 1966, the American Medical Association (AMA) passed a resolution labeling chiropractic an unscientific cult. (Chiropractors attempt to cure or relieve bodily ailments by making skeletal adjustments.) In effect, this label prevented physicians from associating with chiropractors, because Principle 3 of the Principles of Medical Ethics—the AMA's code of ethical conduct—provided that a "physician should practice a method of healing founded on a scientific basis; and he should not voluntarily associate with anyone who violates this principle." Medical doctors used Principle 3 to justify their refusal to have anything to do with chiropractors or to allow chiropractors to use hospital diagnostic services or become members of hospital medical staffs. Despite the AMA's efforts, chiropractic became licensed in all fifty states; and in a 1980 revision of the AMA's ethical code, Principle 3 was eliminated. Chester Wilk and four other chiropractors brought an action against the AMA, claiming that the boycott had violated Section 1 of the Sherman Act and seeking injunctive relief from the boycott's "lingering effects" on chiropractors. The trial court, holding that the AMA had violated Section 1 of the Sherman Act by conducting an illegal boycott in restraint of trade, granted an injunction that, among other things, required the AMA to publish widely the trial court's order. The AMA appealed.*

IN THE LANGUAGE   MANION, Circuit Judge.
   OF THE COURT   *   *   *   *

Despite the fact that * * * the conspiracy ended in 1980, * * * the illegal boycott's "lingering effects" still threatened plaintiffs with current injury * * * . [T]he boycott caused injury to chiropractors' reputations which had not been repaired, and current economic injury to chiropractors. Further, the AMA never affirmatively acknowledged that there are no impediments to professional association and cooperation between chiropractors and medical physicians * * * .

* * * Essentially, the AMA argues that * * * health care consumers almost invariably lack sufficient information needed to evaluate the quality of medical services. This increases the risk of fraud and deception on consumers by unscrupulous health care providers * * * . The AMA's conduct, the theory goes on, * * * allowed consumers to be assured that physicians would use only scientifically valid treatments. This in effect * * * provided consumers with essential information * * * .

Getting information to the market is a fine goal, but * * * the AMA was not motivated solely by such altruistic concerns. Indeed, * * * the AMA intended to "destroy a competitor," namely, chiropractors. It is not enough to carry the day to argue that competition should be eliminated in the name of public safety.

DECISION AND REMEDY *The appellate court affirmed both the trial court's ruling that the AMA had violated Section 1 of the Sherman Act by conducting an illegal boycott of chiropractors and the trial court's decision to grant an injunction against the AMA.*

GROUP BOYCOTTS

A **group boycott**, or concerted refusal to deal, is any agreement by which two or more buyers or sellers refuse to engage in any transactions with a particular person or organization, the object of the boycott. An obvious, and indeed frequent, purpose of a boycott is to eliminate or discipline a competitor of the boycotting group. Boycotts are thus a powerful tool for enforcing anticompetitive arrangements among firms.

Anticompetitive Intent. Refer again to the DVD drive producers and their hypothetical attempts to fix prices and allocate market territories. After their initial success in obtaining greater profits for the industry, they face at least two problems. The first is how to discipline errant firms that attempt to increase their profits by selling for less than the agreed price or by encroaching on another firm's exclusive territory. The second is how to prevent new firms attracted by the large profits in the DVD drive industry from entering the market and reducing each member's share of profits.

Observe the actions of the group members further. They have now formed the High-Quality DVD Drive Association. The function of the association, at least as stated in its charter, is to "promote the interests of the consumer above all other considerations by ensuring that DVD drives are always manufactured according to the highest possible standards." To facilitate its

goals, the association has decided to confer its "seal of approval" on all DVD drive products deemed of worthy quality. In fact, the association has never denied an original producer-member's request for approval except in those instances when the producer happens to have failed to abide by the original price and market-allocation terms the group has set.

Things are not so easy, however, for subsequent arrivals into the DVD drive industry. Alleging that the new firms are able to enter the market and compete only by use of "substandard components," the association refuses to bestow any new seals of approval. Moreover, the association urges dealers, some of whom have been invited to become members of the association, not to carry or service any products that do not have the association's seal of approval. In concert, the group refuses to have any dealings with any retailers, wholesalers, or other manufacturers who do not exclusively use products carrying the association's seal of approval. This is a group boycott.

Procompetitive Intent. Sometimes, however, group boycotts are intended to promote economic efficiency, moral or social causes, or the general well-being of the group, without intending to injure competition. For example, a professional organization or a trade association might seek to promote its public image by sponsoring a program to prevent its members from engaging in deceptive advertising or employing high-pressure sales tactics. A member's failure to abide by the program guidelines could be punished by expulsion from the organization or association or by denial of the group's endorsement, such as withholding of the association's "seal of approval."

Despite the possibility of a procompetitive intent or some other socially valuable objective, concerted refusals to deal—group boycotts—are generally said to be *per se* violations of Section 1. A more accurate statement is that a court will treat a group boycott as a *per se* violation of Section 1 in cases in which the group possesses market power and the boycott is intended to restrict or exclude a competitor. If, however, these elements are missing, the court may be inclined to weigh the benefits of the group's efforts against the harm inflicted by the boycott. The court in the following case emphasizes these principles.

CASE 28.4   NYNEX Corp. v. Discon, Inc.

Supreme Court of the United States, 1998.
525 U.S. 128,
119 S.Ct. 493,
142 L.Ed.2d 510.
http://supct.law.
cornell.edu/supct[a]

BACKGROUND AND FACTS   *NYNEX Corporation owns New York Telephone Company (NYTel), which provides telephone service to most of New York. NYTel has a monopoly on phone service in the areas that it serves. NYNEX also owns NYNEX Material Enterprises. Material Enterprises obtains removal services for NYTel. These services consist salvaging and disposing of obsolete equipment. Material Enterprises, which had been using the services of Discon, Inc., switched its business to AT&T Technologies, Inc., which supplied the removal services at inflated prices. Material Enterprises charged the inflated prices to NYTel, which passed the charges onto its customers. Material Enterprises later received secret rebates of the excessive charges from AT&T. (Essentially, Material Enterprises and NYNEX used NYTel's monopoly to obtain increased revenues.) When the scheme was uncovered, NYTel agreed to refund over $35 million to its customers. Discon, Inc., filed a suit in a federal district court against NYNEX and others, alleging, among other things, that as part of their scheme, the defendants had conspired to eliminate Discon from the market, in favor of AT&T because Discon had refused to participate in the rebate scheme. Discon contended that this was an illegal group boycott. The defendants filed a motion to dismiss, which the court granted. Discon appealed to the U.S. Court of Appeals for the Second Circuit, which reversed the lower court's judgment and held that the treatment of Discon could be an illegal group boycott. The defendants appealed to the United States Supreme Court.*

IN THE LANGUAGE
OF THE COURT

Justice *BREYER* delivered the opinion of the Court.
　*　*　*　*

*　*　* [T]he specific legal question before us is whether an antitrust court considering an agreement by a buyer to purchase goods or services from one supplier rather than another should (after examining the buyer's reasons or justifications) apply the *per se* rule if it finds no legitimate business reason for that purchasing decision. We conclude no boycott-related *per se* rule applies and that the plaintiff here must allege and prove harm, not just to a single competitor, but to the competitive process, i.e., to competition itself.

Our conclusion rests in large part upon precedent, for *precedent limits the* per se *rule* in the boycott context to cases involving horizontal agreements among direct competitors. *　*　* [Emphasis added.]

*　*　* [In a previous case] this Court *　*　* held that a "vertical restraint is not illegal *per se* unless it includes some agreement on price or price levels." This precedent makes the *per se* rule inapplicable, for the case before us concerns only a vertical agree-

---

a. In the right column, in the "Arrayed by party name:" section, in the "1998" row, click "1st party". On the page that opens, scroll to the case name and click on it. When that page opens, choose the format in which you want to view the opinion and click on its link to access it.

ment and a vertical restraint, a restraint that takes the form of depriving a supplier of a potential customer.

Nor have we found any special feature of this case that could distinguish it from the precedent *   *   * . We concede Discon's claim that the petitioners' behavior hurt consumers by raising telephone service rates. But that consumer injury naturally flowed not so much from a less competitive market for removal services, as from the exercise of market power that is lawfully in the hands of a monopolist, namely, New York Telephone, combined with a deception worked upon the regulatory agency that prevented the agency from controlling New York Telephone's exercise of its monopoly power.

To apply the *per se* rule here—where the buyer's decision, though not made for competitive reasons, composes part of a regulatory fraud—would transform cases involving business behavior that is improper for various reasons, say, cases involving nepotism or personal pique, into treble-damages antitrust cases. And that *per se* rule would discourage firms from changing suppliers—even where the competitive process itself does not suffer harm.

The freedom to switch suppliers lies close to the heart of the competitive process that the antitrust laws seek to encourage. At the same time, other laws, for example, "unfair competition" laws, business tort laws, or regulatory laws, provide remedies for various competitive practices thought to be offensive to proper standards of business morality. Thus, this Court has refused to apply *per se* reasoning in cases involving that kind of activity. [Emphasis added.]

DECISION AND REMEDY *The Supreme Court vacated the decision of the U.S. Court of Appeals for the Second Circuit and remanded the case for further proceedings. A choice by a single buyer to buy from one supplier rather than another is not subject to the* per se *group boycott rule, even if there is no legitimate business reason for that buyer's purchasing decision.*

JOINT VENTURES

A **joint venture** is any undertaking by two or more firms or individuals that, while maintaining their distinct identities, come together for the limited purpose of achieving a specific goal. Antitrust analysis of joint ventures involves two issues: first, whether the joining together is itself a violation of antitrust laws; and second, whether the purpose or means of the joint venture is impermissible. The first issue is covered by Section 7 of the Clayton Act, as well as Section 1 of the Sherman Act. An important consideration is the joint venture's percentage market share. Here we limit our focus to the legality of the joint venture's purpose and actions.

Permissible Purposes.   Unlike price-fixing agreements and market divisions, joint ventures are not necessarily anticompetitive. Indeed, many are likely to provide economic efficiencies. For example, it may be beneficial to society, as well as to the individual firms involved, if firms engaging in substantial research and development (R&D) efforts pool their resources. Pooling R&D resources prevents firms from duplicating one another's efforts. Once the R&D phase has been completed, the firms will compete along other dimensions, such as price, quality, and consumer services. Pooling resources also allows the firms to share the risk that the initial efforts may be fruitless. In some cases, a venture that is desirable from society's point of view involves risks so substantial that no single firm would want to undertake the venture alone. When the risk is spread among many firms, individual risk is reduced, and the venture is more appealing.

No Less Restrictive Means.   Investment bankers often form underwriting syndicates to bring issues of new securities to the market. During the initial offering, it is common for the underwriters to "make a market" by agreeing to buy back enough of the securities to keep the price above a predetermined minimum if demand is less than was anticipated initially. Such an arrangement has all the earmarks of price fixing. In *United States v. Morgan*,[6] however, the court held that the arrangement was not an unreasonable restraint of trade.

---

6. 118 F.Supp. 621 (S.D.N.Y. 1953).

Sometimes, the *Morgan* case is cited as an exception to the rule that price fixing is a *per se* violation of Section 1. The decision cannot be taken to mean that price fixing is ever reasonable; distinct features of the case make it clear that the court did not view this as ordinary price fixing, which remains a *per se* violation of Section 1.[7] The court took into consideration several unique aspects of the arrangement: the duration of the syndicate was extremely short; new syndicates involving different investment houses were continually being formed for new offerings; there was a competitive process by which investment houses sought to form and join the new syndicates; and competitive pressures were sufficient to ensure that those seeking to raise investment capital were provided a relatively low-cost, efficient vehicle for doing so. What is perhaps most significant in the *Morgan* case is that the government, in challenging the practice, was unable to point to any less restrictive means of raising capital as efficiently.

If a joint venture does not involve price fixing or market divisions, the agreement will be analyzed under the rule of reason. Whether the venture will then be upheld under Section 1 depends on an overall assessment of the purposes of the venture, a strict analysis of the potential benefits relative to the likely harms, and in some cases an assessment of whether there are less restrictive alternatives for achieving the same goals.

SECTION 3

Vertical Restraints

Another distinct set of restraints of trade comprises those imposed by the seller on the buyer (or vice

versa), as distinct from those imposed *among* sellers or buyers. The latter restraints involve what is termed a vertical relationship. Horizontal relationships occur at the same level of operations. Vertical relationships, by comparison, encompass the entire chain of production: the purchase of inputs, basic manufacturing, distribution to wholesalers, and eventual sale of a product at the retail level. For some products, these distinct phases are carried on by different firms. In other instances, a single firm may carry out two or more of the functional phases. Firms such as the latter are considered to be **vertically integrated firms.**

There are two kinds of vertical integration—backward and forward. A firm that is integrated backward moves down the chain of production toward a supplier. A firm that is integrated forward moves up the chain of production toward the consumer market. For example, if the Red Ball Shoe Manufacturing Company, a shoe manufacturer, owns its source of leather, it is integrated backward; if Red Ball owns its retail outlets, it is integrated forward (see Exhibit 28–1).

Even though firms operating at different functional levels do not directly compete with one another, each does compete with other firms operating at its own level of operation. Thus, agreements between firms standing in a vertical relationship may affect competition. For example, suppose that a contractual agreement between tire manufacturer Firestone and Billy Ray's Automotive Supplies, an independent retailer, conditions Billy Ray's future supply of Firestone tires on its willingness to resell only at a price set by Firestone. This agreement is a form of **vertical restraint**—an anticompetitive agreement between entities operating at different levels of the market structure. Other types of vertical restraints are often encountered, but not all of them necessarily harm competition. Indeed, many are procompetitive.

Marketing decisions within a vertically integrated firm are not subject to attack under Section 1. The

---

7. The case is more often cited as a classic example of how to judge joint ventures under the rule of reason.

EXHIBIT 28–1   BACKWARD AND FORWARD INTEGRATION

A firm that is integrated backward moves up the chain of production. A firm that is integrated forward moves down the chain of production.

legality of certain other classes of vertical restraints is judged under a rule of reason. Still others are deemed *per se* violations of Section 1.

TERRITORIAL OR CUSTOMER RESTRICTIONS

In arranging for the distribution of its product, a manufacturing firm may seek to insulate its dealers or retailers from direct competition with one another. There may be legitimate, procompetitive reasons for doing so. One such reason is to prevent a dealer from cutting costs and undercutting same-brand rivals by providing the product without promotion or customer service, while relying on a nearby same-brand dealer to provide these services. The cost-cutting same-brand dealer could thus enjoy the benefits of the promotional and customer service costs expended by his or her rivals without incurring the associated costs. This

is an example of the "free rider" problem.[8] One way of addressing the problem is to restrict same-brand dealers to selling in specific markets or to certain classes of customers. These restrictions are judged under a rule of reason.

The following case, *Continental T.V., Inc. v. GTE Sylvania, Inc.*, overturned the United States Supreme Court's earlier stance, which had been set out in *United States v. Arnold, Schwinn & Co.*[9] In *Schwinn*, the Court had held territorial or customer restrictions to be *per se* violations. The *Continental* case has been heralded as one of the most important antitrust cases since the 1940s. It represents a definite shift away from rigid characterization to a more flexible approach emphasizing economics and efficiency.

---

8. For a discussion of the free rider problem in the context of sports telecasting, see *Chicago Professional Sports Limited Partnership v. National Basketball Association*, 961 F.2d 667 (7th Cir. 1993).
9. 388 U.S. 365, 87 S.Ct. 1856, 18 L.Ed.2d 1249 (1967).

CASE 28.5   # Continental T.V., Inc. v. GTE Sylvania, Inc.

Supreme Court of the United States, 1977.
433 U.S. 36,
97 S.Ct. 2549,
53 L.Ed.2d 568.
http://www.findlaw.
com/casecode/
supreme.html[a]

HISTORICAL AND ECONOMIC SETTING   *In determining what is or is not permitted under the antitrust laws, the trend has been to establish a flexible standard, rather than a rigid one, particularly in regard to conduct that is considered to have procompetitive benefits. Under a flexible standard, a business practice that is considered a criminal offense in one decade may be judged a corporate virtue in the next. In the mid-1970s, for example, the United States Supreme Court began to qualify or overrule many of its previous decisions that prohibited certain business practices as per se violations of the antitrust laws. The Court appeared to be focusing on economic considerations, such as consumer welfare,[b] economic efficiency,[c] and intrabrand competition.*

BACKGROUND AND FACTS   *GTE Sylvania, Inc., a manufacturer of television sets, adopted a franchise plan that limited the number of franchises granted in any given geographical area and that required each franchise to sell only Sylvania products from the location or locations at which it was franchised. A franchise did not constitute an exclusive territory, and Sylvania retained sole discretion to increase the number of retailers in an area, depending on the success or failure of existing retailers in developing their market. Continental T.V., Inc., was a retailer under Sylvania's franchise plan. Shortly after Sylvania proposed a new franchise that would compete with Continental, Sylvania terminated Continental's franchise, and a suit was brought in a federal district court for money owed. Continental claimed that Sylvania's vertically restrictive franchise system violated Section 1 of the Sherman Act. The district court ruled in favor of Continental, and Sylvania appealed. The appellate court reversed the trial court's decision. Continental appealed to the United States Supreme Court.*

---

a. In the "Citation Search" section, type "433" in the first box, type "36" in the second box, and click "Get It" to access the case.
b. *Reiter v. Sonotone Corp.*, 442 U.S. 330, 99 S.Ct. 2326, 60 L.Ed.2d 931 (1979).
c. *Broadcast Music, Inc. v. Columbia Broadcasting System, Inc.*, 441 U.S. 1, 99 S.Ct. 1551, 60 L.Ed.2d 1 (1979).

IN THE LANGUAGE OF THE COURT

Mr. Justice *POWELL* delivered the opinion of the Court.

*   *   *   *

Vertical restrictions reduce intrabrand competition by limiting the number of sellers of a particular product competing for the business of a given group of buyers. *   *   *

Vertical restrictions promote interbrand competition by allowing the manufacturer to achieve certain efficiencies in the distribution of his products. *   *   * Established manufacturers can use them to induce retailers to engage in promotional activities or to provide service and repair facilities necessary to the efficient marketing of their products. *   *   * The availability and quality of such services affect a manufacturer's goodwill and the competitiveness of his product. *   *   *

*   *   *   *

*   *   * When anticompetitive effects are shown to result from particular vertical restrictions they can be adequately policed under the rule of reason *   *   * .

DECISION AND REMEDY

The United States Supreme Court upheld the appellate court's reversal of the district court's decision. Sylvania's vertical system, which was not price restrictive, did not constitute a per se *violation of Section 1 of the Sherman Act.*

RESALE PRICE MAINTENANCE AGREEMENTS

Resale price maintenance agreements, also referred to as *fair trade agreements,* occur when a manufacturer seeks to establish a minimum price that a retailer or wholesaler may charge for the manufacturer's product. Under these agreements, the manufacturer conditions sales to the retailer or wholesaler on the latter's reselling only at a price allowed by the manufacturer.

For many years, such agreements were authorized in some states under so-called *fair trade laws.* Federal law eliminated these provisions in 1975. Subsequently, resale price maintenance agreements were usually condemned as *per se* violations of Section 1 of the Sherman Act. During the Reagan administration (1981–1989), there was considerable criticism on the part of some representatives of government enforcement agencies and in some lower-court decisions of the application of the *per se* rule to resale price maintenance agreements. In a 1968 case, *Albrecht v. Herald Co.,*[10] the United States Supreme Court had held that these vertical price-fixing agreements constituted *per se* violations of Section 1 of the Sherman Act, however, so the courts applied the *per se* standard.

In the following case, which involved an agreement that set a maximum price for the resale of products supplied by a wholesaler to a dealer, the Supreme Court reevaluated its approach in *Albrecht.* At issue is whether such price-fixing arrangements should continue to be deemed *per se* violations of Section 1 of the Sherman Act or whether the rule of reason should be applied.

---

10. 390 U.S. 145, 88 S.Ct. 869, 19 L.Ed.2d 998 (1968).

CASE 28.6   State Oil Co. v. Khan

Supreme Court of the United States, 1997.
522 U.S. 3,
118 S.Ct. 275
139 L.Ed.2d 199.
http://www.findlaw.
com/casecode/
supreme.html[a]

BACKGROUND AND FACTS   *Barkat Khan leased a gas station under a contract with State Oil Company, which also agreed to supply gas to Khan for resale. Under the contract, State Oil would set a suggested retail price and sell gas to Khan for 3.25 cents per gallon less than that price. Khan could sell the gas at a higher price, but he would then be required to pay State Oil the difference (which would equal the entire profit Khan realized from raising the price). Khan failed to pay some of the rent due under the lease, and State Oil terminated the contract. Khan filed a suit in a federal district court against State Oil, alleging, among other things, price fixing in violation of the Sherman Act. The court granted summary judgment for State Oil. Khan appealed. The U.S. Court of*

---

a. This page, which is part of a Web site maintained by FindLaw, contains links to opinions of the United States Supreme Court. In the "Party Name Search" box, type "Khan" and click "Search." When the results appear, click on the case name to access the opinion.

Appeals for the Seventh Circuit reversed this judgment, and State Oil appealed to the United States Supreme Court.

IN THE LANGUAGE OF THE COURT

Justice O'CONNOR delivered the opinion of the Court.

* * * *

* * * Our analysis is * * * guided by our general view that the primary purpose of the antitrust laws is to protect interbrand competition. * * * [C]ondemnation of practices resulting in lower prices to consumers is especially costly because cutting prices in order to increase business often is the very essence of competition.

* * * [W]e find it difficult to maintain that vertically-imposed maximum prices could harm consumers or competition to the extent necessary to justify their *per se* invalidation. * * *

* * * *

* * * [T]he *per se* rule * * * could in fact exacerbate problems related to the unrestrained exercise of market power by monopolist-dealers. Indeed, *both courts and antitrust scholars have noted that [the* per se*] rule may actually harm consumers and manufacturers.* * * * [Emphasis added.]

* * * *

* * *[V]ertical maximum price fixing, like the majority of commercial arrangements subject to the antitrust laws, should be evaluated under the rule of reason. In our view, rule-of-reason analysis can effectively identify those situations in which vertical maximum price fixing amounts to anticompetitive conduct.

DECISION AND REMEDY

The United States Supreme Court vacated the decision of the appellate court and remanded the case. The Supreme Court held that vertical price-fixing is not a per se *violation of the Sherman Act but should be evaluated under the rule of reason.*

INTERNATIONAL CONSIDERATIONS

Regulation in Other Countries *Other countries have begun to adopt their own versions of U.S. antitrust laws. For example, the Japan Fair Trade Commission has adopted a set of guidelines to reduce anticompetitive practices by Japanese companies. Under the guidelines, manufacturers are prohibited from terminating dealers who sell their products for prices below those suggested by the manufacturers. The European Court of Justice has upheld a fine levied against a Dutch company for threatening to engage in below-cost pricing to force a British competitor out of a particular market.[b] And newly independent republics that were once part of the Soviet Union have sought the assistance of U.S. economic and technical experts in revamping their centrally planned economies.*

b. *AKZO Chemie BV v. Commission of the European Community,* E.C.Ct.Jus., No. C-62/86, July 3, 1991. (The European Community is now called the European Union, or EU.)

REFUSALS TO DEAL

Group boycotts, as mentioned, are subject to sharp scrutiny under Section 1. In contrast, basic freedom of contract has been held to support the rule that manufacturers, acting unilaterally rather than in concert, as in a group boycott, are free to deal—or not to deal—with whomever they choose. For example, assume that in our hypothetical example, Acme acts alone to set the price for the resale of its DVD drives by refusing to deal with any wholesaler that resells them at a different price. Acme has not violated the Sherman Act; it has only exercised its right to deal with whomever it chooses.

In some instances, however, a refusal to deal will violate antitrust laws. These instances involve offenses proscribed under Section 2 of the Sherman Act and occur only if (1) the firm refusing to deal has, or is likely to acquire, monopoly power and (2) the refusal is likely to have an anticompetitive effect on a particular market.[11]

---

11. A good example is provided by the *Aspen Skiing* case discussed in the preceding chapter (Case 27.4) in relation to the Section 2 offense of monopolization.

PRICE DISCRIMINATION

Whenever a seller charges different buyers different prices for identical goods, the seller is engaging in **price discrimination.** Recall from the preceding chapter that such behavior may violate the Robinson-Patman Act, which was enacted in 1936 and amended Section 2 of the Clayton Act. A violation of Section 2 occurs if a seller discriminates in the prices it charges different customers for commodities of like quality and grade in interstate commerce and the practice results in injury to competition. The act prohibits indirect discrimination, such as variations in the terms of delivery and differences in sales returns, cash discounts, and the like, as well as direct price discrimination.

Customer Preferences.   Although the act appears to embrace the goals of fairness and equality in the marketplace, it has often been criticized as being economically unrealistic. For instance, a difference in packaging, labeling, or product quality normally does not exempt the pricing of the differing products from scrutiny under the act if the difference is deemed to be *negligible.* Thus, orange juice containers that differ by one-eighth inch are considered to be of like grade and quality, because they are *functionally* identical in terms of performance. Despite functional equivalence, however, customer perceptions may favor one type of container over another.

In the same vein, identical products sold under different labels are deemed to be of like quality, though some experts note that many customers exhibit strong preferences for better-known brand names even though the products are physically identical. In *Federal Trade Commission v. Borden Co.,*[12] the United States Supreme Court addressed the issue of a milk producer's charging different prices for milk sold under different labels. Borden sold evaporated milk under the Borden label, a well-known brand, and at the same time, it packed and marketed evaporated milk under private labels owned by its customers. Although the milk was physically indistinguishable, Borden charged a higher price for its brand-labeled milk. In spite of obvious customer preference for the Borden brand of milk, the Court concluded that the act applied to the

pricing difference because the milk was of like quality and grade in terms of physical attributes. The Court held that preferences due to brand-name recognition created through national advertising should not be considered in resolving whether goods are of like grade and quality.

Time and Cost Considerations.   Despite these examples, some economic aspects are taken into account in judging the legality of pricing practices under the Robinson-Patman Act. For example, as noted in the preceding chapter, Section 2 is not violated even though the goods sold are identical if the seller can justify the price differential on the basis of differences in cost, such as the cost of transporting the goods to buyers in disparate locations. Similarly, consideration is given to the fact that prices are not static but fluctuate as market conditions change. Thus, price discrimination occurs only if sales at different price levels are made reasonably close together in time.

Closeness in time is determined by the economic circumstances of the sales. For example, sales of products that are not frequently sold and that involve considerable production costs may be considered close in time even if they occur years apart. Conversely, sales of low-cost products sold in high volume may be considered close in time when they occur a day or even a few hours apart. Jet aircraft typify high-cost, low-volume products. Closeness in time for sales of aircraft could be two years or more. In contrast, sales of bakery goods occur on an almost continuous basis. Closeness in time for sales of such products could be several hours or, at most, a day.

EXCLUSIONARY PRACTICES

Recall also from the preceding chapter that Section 3 of the Clayton Act prohibits sellers and lessors from selling or leasing goods, machinery, supplies, and the like "on the condition, agreement or understanding that the . . . purchaser or lessee thereof shall not use or deal in the goods . . . of a competitor or competitors of the seller." Two types of vertical arrangements involving exclusionary tactics—exclusive-dealing contracts and tying arrangements—are within the reach of Section 3 of the Clayton Act.

---

12. 383 U.S. 637, 86 S.Ct. 1092, 16 L.Ed.2d 153 (1966).

Exclusive-Dealing Contracts. Contracts under which a seller forbids the buyer from purchasing products from the seller's competitors are called **exclusive-dealing contracts.** Such contracts are prohibited under Section 3 if the effect of the contract will "substantially lessen competition or tend to create a monopoly."

The leading decision on exclusive-dealing contracts remains the 1949 case of *Standard Oil Co. of California v. United States,*[13] in which the then-largest gasoline seller in the United States was challenged by the government under Section 3 for making exclusive-dealing contracts with independent stations in seven western states. The United States Supreme Court, in assessing the impact of the exclusive-dealing agreement on competition in the retail market, noted that the "independents" covered under the arrangement constituted 16 percent of all retail outlets and 7 percent of all retail gas sales in the area. The Court also noted that the market was substantially concentrated because the seven largest suppliers all used exclusive-dealing contracts with their independent retailers and together controlled 65 percent of the market. Looking at market conditions after the arrangements were instituted, the Court noted that market shares were extremely stable and entry into the market was apparently restricted. Thus, the Court found that Section 3 had been violated, because competition was "foreclosed in a substantial share" of the relevant market.

Tying Arrangements. A seller may condition the sale of a product (the tying product) on the buyer's agreeing to purchase another product (the tied product) produced or distributed by the same seller. As noted in the preceding chapter, the legality of such **tying arrangements** depends on factors such as the purpose of the arrangement and its likely effect on competition in the relevant markets. There are two relevant markets, because the agreement involves two distinct products, the tying and the tied product. In 1936, the United States Supreme Court held that International Business Machines and Remington Rand, by requiring purchase of their own machine cards as a condition of leasing their tabulation machines, had violated Section 3 of the Clayton Act. The

two firms were the only ones in the market with completely automated tabulation machines, and the Court concluded that each possessed market power sufficient to "substantially lessen competition" through their respective tying arrangements.[14]

Standards of Application. The Clayton Act provisions in Section 3 have been held to apply only to commodities, not to services. But tying arrangements also can be considered agreements that restrain trade in violation of Section 1 of the Sherman Act. Cases involving tying arrangements for services have been brought under Section 1 of the Sherman Act. Although the Court continues to state that many tying arrangements are illegal *per se*, it nonetheless has shown a willingness to look at factors that are important in a rule-of-reason analysis. This is another example of the so-called soft *per se* rule referred to in regard to group boycotts.

Practical Results. The United States Supreme Court held that U.S. Steel Corporation's practice of tying its attractive credit services for home builders to the builders' purchase of U.S. Steel's prefabricated houses did not violate antitrust laws, because U.S. Steel did not possess market power in either the credit market or the prefabricated housing market.[15] A similar result was reached in *Jefferson Parish Hospital District No. 2 v. Hyde.*[16] Most courts today generally judge the legality of tying arrangements involving services or commodities by looking at both the firm's market power in the tying product market and the amount of commerce affected in the tied product market. The firm must have sufficient market power in the tying product to coerce the purchase of the tied product, and the tying arrangement must affect a substantial amount of commerce in the market for the tied product.

What if a tying arrangement affects only one customer? Can the arrangement nonetheless violate Section 1 of the Sherman Act? The following case addresses this issue.

---

13. 337 U.S. 293, 69 S.Ct. 1051, 93 L.Ed. 1371 (1949).

14. *International Business Machines Corp. v. United States,* 298 U.S. 131, 56 S.Ct. 701, 80 L.Ed.2d 1085 (1936).
15. *U.S. Steel Corp. v. Fortner Enterprises, Inc.,* 429 U.S. 610, 97 S.Ct. 861, 51 L.Ed.2d 80 (1977).
16. 466 U.S. 2, 104 S.Ct. 1551, 80 L.Ed.2d 2 (1984).

CASE 28.7   Datagate, Inc. v. Hewlett-Packard Co.

United States
Court of Appeals,
Ninth Circuit, 1995.
60 F.3d 1421.
http://www.findlaw.
com/casecode/courts/
9th.html[a]

HISTORICAL AND TECHNOLOGICAL SETTING *Military investment in the 1940s fueled the growth of the electronics industry. Computers made at this time weighed several tons and required the space of a warehouse to store operating components. With the advent of smaller components in the 1960s, computers and other technological equipment became more compact. Hewlett-Packard Company (HP) produced the first hand-held scientific calculator in 1972. In the decades since then, the growth of the electronics and computer industries has seemed unstoppable. Today, HP makes a variety of electronic products, including computer hardware and software.*

BACKGROUND AND FACTS *Datagate, Inc., provided repair service for computer hardware made by HP. HP offered the same service. HP also offered support for those who used its software, but the company refused to provide software support to those who did not buy its hardware service. Datagate filed a suit in a federal district court against HP, claiming in part that HP's practice constituted an illegal tying arrangement. The arrangement had been imposed on only one HP customer, Rockwell International, but the Rockwell hardware service contract was worth $100,000 per year. The court held that one customer was not enough and entered a judgment in favor of HP. Datagate appealed.*

IN THE LANGUAGE OF THE COURT

BEEZER, Circuit Judge:

    *   *   *   *

[One of the] elements [that] must be satisfied to establish that a tying arrangement is illegal *per se* [is that] the tying arrangement affects a not insubstantial volume of commerce. *   *   *

    *   *   *   *

*   *   * The *   *   * requirement can be satisfied by the foreclosure of a single purchaser, so long as the purchaser represents a "not insubstantial" dollar-volume of sales.

    *   *   *   *

*   *   * [T]he Rockwell hardware service contract at issue was worth approximately $100,000 per year. *   *   *

This amount is sufficient.

DECISION AND REMEDY *The U.S. Court of Appeals for the Ninth Circuit reversed the decision of the lower court and remanded the case for trial.*

---

a. In the "Browsing" section, click on the "1995" link. When that page opens, scroll down the list of cases to the *Datagate* case and click on the case name to access the opinion.

MERGERS

Under Section 7 of the Clayton Act, a person or business organization cannot hold stock or assets in another business "where the effect . . . may be to substantially lessen competition." This section is the statutory authority for preventing mergers that could result in monopoly power or a substantial lessening of competition in the marketplace.

A crucial consideration in most merger cases is **market concentration.** Market concentration roughly translates into the allocation of percentage market shares among the various firms in the relevant product market. For example, if the four largest grocery stores in Chicago accounted for 80 percent of all retail food sales, the market clearly would be concentrated in those four firms. Competition, however, is not necessarily diminished solely as a result of market concentration, and other factors will be considered, including whether the merger will make it more difficult for potential competitors to enter the relevant market.

Horizontal Mergers. Mergers between firms that compete with each other in the same market are called **horizontal mergers.** If a horizontal merger creates an entity with anything other than a small percentage market share, the merger will be presumed illegal. This is because of the United States Supreme Court's interpretation that Congress, in amending Section 7 of the Clayton Act in 1950, intended to prevent mergers that increase market concentration.[17] Three other factors are also considered: overall concentration of the relevant market, the relevant market's history of tending toward concentration, and whether the apparent design of the merger is to establish market power or restrict competition.

Market Share and Market Concentration. The Court's intense focus on market share in horizontal merger decisions has made the definition of relevant markets especially critical in most Section 7 cases. As a result, the Federal Trade Commission (FTC) and the Department of Justice (DOJ) have established guidelines indicating which mergers will be challenged.

Under the guidelines, the first factor to be considered in determining whether a merger will be challenged is the degree of concentration in the relevant market. In determining market concentration, the FTC and the DOJ employ what is known as the **Herfindahl-Hirschman index (HHI).** The HHI is computed by summing the squares of the percentage market shares of the firms in the relevant market. For example, if there are four firms with shares of 30 percent, 30 percent, 20 percent, and 20 percent, respectively, then the HHI equals 2,600 (900 + 900 + 400 + 400 = 2,600). If the pre-merger HHI is less than 1,000, then the market is unconcentrated, and the merger will not likely be challenged. If the pre-merger HHI is between 1,000 and 1,800, the industry is moderately concentrated, and the merger will be challenged only if it increases the HHI by 100 points or more.[18] If the HHI is greater than 1,800, the market is highly concentrated. In a highly concentrated market, a merger that produces an increase in the HHI between 50 and 100 points raises significant competitive concerns. Mergers that produce an increase in the HHI of more than 100 points in a highly concentrated market are deemed likely to enhance market power.[19]

Other Factors. The guidelines stress that determining market share and market concentration is only the starting point in analyzing the potential anticompetitive effects of a merger. Before deciding to challenge a merger, the FTC and the DOJ will look at a number of other factors, including the ease of entry into the relevant market, economic efficiency, the financial condition of the merging firms, the nature and price of the product or products involved, and so on. If a firm is a leading one—having at least a 35 percent share and twice that of the next leading firm—any merger with a firm having as little as a 1 percent share will be challenged.

Political Considerations in Defining the Relevant Market. Not considered in the above discussion are the sometimes unfathomable definitions of the relevant market determined by the federal government. To take an example, reconsider the proposed Office Depot–Staples merger that the Federal Trade Commission (FTC) refused to approve in 1997. Had the two merged as originally planned, they would have accounted for 6 percent of the market for office supplies. When the FTC initially indicated its disapproval, Office Depot agreed to sell sixty-three of its stores to OfficeMax, thereby bringing the proposed merger to only 4 percent of the office supplies market. The FTC decided that the relevant product market was not office supplies, but rather office supplies sold at large specialty discount stores! It then concluded that the proposed merger would seriously weaken competition in the newly defined market. In other words, the decision was evidently political rather than based on any theory of the economics of antitrust law. After all, office supplies are also sold at Costco, Wal-Mart, Sam's Club, Kmart, and elsewhere. To exclude these obvious competitors from the FTC's analysis was indeed baffling.[20]

Vertical Mergers. A **vertical merger** occurs when a company at one stage of production acquires a

---

17. *Brown Shoe v. United States,* 370 U.S. 294, 82 S.Ct. 1502, 8 L.Ed.2d 510 (1962).
18. Compute the change in the index by doubling the product of the merging firms' pre-merger market shares. For example, a merger between a firm with a 5 percent share and one with a 6 percent share will increase the HHI by 2 × (5 × 6) = 60. For an analysis of the HHI concentration of companies in the credit-card market, see *SCFC ILC, Inc. v. Visa U.S.A. Inc.,* 819 F.Supp. 956 (D.Utah 1993).

19. See, for example, *United States v. United Tote, Inc.,* 768 F.Supp. 1064 (D.Del. 1991), in which the court ordered the divestiture of a firm whose HHI was 3,940 before a merger and 4,640 after the merger.
20. At the FTC's request, a court blocked the merger on antitrust grounds.

company at a higher or lower stage of production. Courts in the past have almost exclusively focused on "foreclosure" in assessing vertical mergers. Foreclosure occurs because competitors of the merging firms lose opportunities either to sell or to buy products from the merging firms. For example, in *United States v. E. I. du Pont de Nemours & Co.,*[21] du Pont was challenged for acquiring a considerable amount of General Motors (GM) stock. In holding that the transaction was illegal, the United States Supreme Court noted that stock acquisition would enable du Pont to prevent other sellers of fabrics and finishes from selling to GM, which then accounted for 50 percent of all auto fabric and finish purchases.

More recently, whether a vertical merger has been deemed illegal has depended on several factors, including market concentration, barriers to entry into the market, and the apparent intent of the merging parties. Mergers that do not prevent competitors of either of the merging firms from competing in a segment of the

market will not be condemned as "foreclosing" competition and are legal.

Conglomerate Mergers. There are three general types of **conglomerate mergers:** market-extension, product-extension, and diversification mergers. Conglomerate mergers are mergers between firms that do not compete with each other because they are in different markets. A market-extension merger occurs when a firm seeks to sell its product in a new market by merging with a firm already established in that market. A product-extension merger occurs when a firm seeks to add a closely related product to its existing line by merging with a firm already producing that product. For example, a manufacturer might seek to extend its product line of household products to include floor wax by acquiring a leading manufacturer of floor wax. Diversification occurs when a firm merges with another firm that offers a product or service wholly unrelated to the first firm's existing activities. An example of a diversification merger would be Chrysler Corporation's acquisition of Holiday Inns.

---

21. 353 U.S. 586, 77 S.Ct. 872, 1 L.Ed.2d 1057 (1957).

CONCEPT SUMMARY 28.1

RESTRAINTS OF TRADE AND THEIR LAWFULNESS

PER SE ILLEGAL	SUBJECT TO RULE-OF-REASON ANALYSIS[a]	SUBJECT TO "SOFT" PER SE RULE/NARROW RULE-OF-REASON ANALYSIS
Price Fixing Market Division	**Trade Association Activity**—Illegal if undertaken in a concentrated industry to facilitate anticompetitive effect. Not illegal if there is no intent to fix prices or limit output and the activity benefits the public. **Joint Venture**—Illegal if undertaken to facilitate anticompetitive effect. Not illegal if there is no intent to fix prices or limit output, the activity benefits the public, and there are no acceptable alternatives to achieve the same goal. **Territorial or Customer Restriction**—Illegal if undertaken to facilitate anticompetitive effect. **Refusal to Deal**—Illegal if the firm that refuses to deal has monopoly power and the refusal has an anticompetitive effect.	**Group Boycott**—Illegal if the group possesses market power and the boycott is intended to restrict or exclude a competitor. **Tying Arrangement**—Illegal if undertaken to facilitate anticompetitive effect in the tying product market and the tied product market. **Horizontal Merger**—Illegal if undertaken to facilitate anticompetitive effect or if the percentage of the firm's market share after the merger is large in light of the market's concentration and its history of tending toward concentration. **Vertical Merger**—Illegal if undertaken to facilitate anticompetitive effect or actually has such effect in light of the

CONCEPT
SUMMARY 28.1

RESTRAINTS OF TRADE
AND THEIR LAWFULNESS (CONTINUED)

PER SE ILLEGAL	SUBJECT TO RULE-OF-REASON ANALYSIS[a]	SUBJECT TO "SOFT" PER SE RULE/NARROW RULE-OF-REASON ANALYSIS
	Price Discrimination—Illegal if undertaken to facilitate anticompetitive effect. **Exclusive Dealing Contract**—Illegal if the effect is to substantially lessen competition or to create a monopoly. **Resale Price Maintenance Agreement**—Illegal if amounts to anticompetitive conduct.	market's concentration and barriers to entry. **Conglomerate Merger**—Illegal if undertaken to facilitate anticompetitive effect or actually has such effect in light of the market's concentration, barriers to entry, whether the firm's entry would have been possible without the merger, and whether other firms are "waiting in the wings."

a. A rule-of-reason analysis generally requires an evaluation of (1) the intent of the parties in practicing the restraint of trade, (2) whether the parties have the power to accomplish that intent, and (3) the practice's actual and potential effect, which includes any benefit to the public. Sometimes, a court will consider whether the parties could have achieved the same result in a less restrictive way.

TERMS AND CONCEPTS TO REVIEW

QUESTIONS AND CASE PROBLEMS

28–1. HORIZONTAL RESTRAINTS. Most of the egg wholesalers supplying eggs to grocery stores in a particular area sell eggs to the retailers under various credit terms. The credit terms vary among the different buyers and sellers, but all of the wholesalers follow a common practice of reducing by 10 percent the price charged to a retailer if the retailer pays the wholesaler within three days of delivery. The various wholesalers agree that henceforth the 10 percent discount will be discontinued. If the agreement is indeed carried out by the wholesalers and the discount policy is discontinued, have the wholesalers violated any antitrust laws? Explain. If suit is brought against the wholesalers, what—if any—justification could they offer for the agreement?

28–2. HORIZONTAL RESTRAINTS. Suppose that the wholesale egg suppliers in the preceding problem agree that the three largest suppliers should sell exclusively to the area's large chain-store groceries, leaving the remaining suppliers to sell solely to local individual "mom and pop" stores. Does the agreement violate any antitrust laws? Is it a defense that the larger suppliers, because of their scale of operations, enjoy a cost advantage that allows them to supply the large chain buyers more efficiently?

28–3. VERTICAL RESTRAINTS. Discuss *fully* whether each of the following situations violates the Sherman Act.

(a) Trujillo Foods, Inc., is the leading seller of frozen Mexican foods in three southwestern states. The various retail outlets that sell Trujillo products are in close competition, and customers are very price conscious. Trujillo has conditioned its sales to retailers with the agreement that the retailers will not sell below a minimum price nor above a maximum price. The retailers are allowed to set any price within these limits.

(b) Franklin, Inc., Green, Inc., and Fill-It, Inc., are competitors in the manufacture and sale of microwave ovens sold primarily east of the Mississippi River. As a patriotic gesture and to assist the unemployed, the three competitors agree to lower their prices on all microwave models by 20 percent for a three-month period that includes the Fourth of July and Labor Day.

(c) Foam Beer, Inc., sells its beer to distributors all over the United States. Foam sends each of its distributors a recommended price list, explaining that past records indicate that selling beer at those prices should ensure the distributor a reasonable rate of return. The price list clearly states that the sale of beer by Foam to the distributor is not conditioned on the distributor's reselling the beer at the recommended price and that the distributor is free to set the price.

28–4. HORIZONTAL RESTRAINTS. Mickey's Appliance Store was a new retail seller of appliances in Sunwest City. Mickey's innovative sales techniques and financing caused the appliance department of Luckluster Department Store to lose a great many sales. Luckluster was a large department store and part of a large chain with substantial buying power. Luckluster told a number of appliance manufacturers that if they continued to sell to Mickey's, Luckluster would stop purchasing from them. The manufacturers immediately stopped selling appliances to Mickey's. Mickey's filed suit against Luckluster and the manufacturers, claiming their actions constituted an antitrust violation. Luckluster and the manufacturers could prove that Mickey's was a small retailer with a small portion of the market. Because the relevant market was not substantially affected, they claimed they were not guilty of restraint of trade. Discuss *fully* whether there was an antitrust violation.

28–5. HORIZONTAL RESTRAINTS. Thomas Blackburn, Raymond Green, Charles Sweeney, and Daniel Pfeiffer practiced law together as partners, relying on advertising to attract clients. When they came to a disagreement over the use of partnership funds, they split into separate partnerships—one formed by Blackburn and Green and the other by Sweeney and Pfeiffer. After the split, they negotiated and signed an agreement that included a term restricting, for an indefinite time, the geographical area within which each could advertise. Less than a year later, the Blackburn firm filed a suit in a federal district court against the Sweeney firm, alleging in part that the

restriction on advertising was a *per se* violation of the Sherman Act. On what basis might the court hold that the agreement to restrict advertising was a horizontal agreement to divide markets among competitors? [*Blackburn v. Sweeney*, 53 F.3d 825 (7th Cir. 1995)]

28–6. ROBINSON-PATMAN ACT. The Stelwagon Manufacturing Co. agreed with Tarmac Roofing Systems, Inc., to promote and develop a market for Tarmac's products in the Philadelphia area. In return, Tarmac promised not to sell its products to other area distributors. In 1991, Stelwagon learned that Tarmac had been selling its products to Stelwagon's competitors—the Standard Roofing Co. and the Celotex Corp.—at substantially lower prices. Stelwagon filed a suit against Tarmac in a federal district court. What is the principal factor in determining whether Tarmac violated the Robinson-Patman Act? Did Tarmac violate the act? [*Stelwagon Manufacturing Co. v. Tarmac Roofing Systems, Inc.*, 63 F.3d 1267 (3d Cir. 1995)]

28–7. VERTICAL RESTRAINTS. Eastman Kodak Co. has about a 20 percent share of the highly competitive market for high-volume photocopiers and microfilm equipment and controls nearly the entire market for replacement parts for its equipment (which are not interchangeable with parts for other manufacturers' equipment). Prior to 1985, Kodak sold replacement parts for its equipment without significant restrictions. As a result, a number of independent service organizations (ISOs) purchased Kodak parts to use when repairing and servicing Kodak copiers. In 1985, Kodak changed its policy to prevent the ISOs from competing with Kodak's own service organizations. It ceased selling parts to ISOs and refused to sell replacement parts to its customers unless they agreed *not* to have their equipment serviced by ISOs. In 1987, Image Technical Services, Inc., and seventeen other ISOs sued Kodak, alleging that Kodak's policy was a tying arrangement in violation of Section 1 of the Sherman Act. Kodak claimed that its policy was not an illegal tying arrangement because it had no market power with respect to its equipment. Therefore, it did not have market power with respect to replacement parts—it could not raise the price of replacement parts and service beyond competitive rates, because if it did, it would lose customers, who would purchase other manufacturers' equipment. Assuming that Kodak does not have market power in the market for photocopying and microfilm equipment, does Kodak's restrictive policy constitute an illegal tying arrangement? Does it violate antitrust laws in any way? Discuss fully. [*Eastman Kodak Co. v. Image Technical Services, Inc.*, 504 U.S. 451, 112 S.Ct. 2072, 119 L.Ed.2d 265 (1992)]

28–8. RESTRAINT OF TRADE. The National Collegiate Athletic Association (NCAA) coordinates the intercollegiate athletic programs of its members by issuing rules and setting standards governing, among other things, the coaching staffs. The NCAA set up a "Cost Reduction Committee" to consider ways to cut the costs of intercollegiate athletics while maintaining competition. The committee included financial aid personnel, intercollegiate athletic administrators, college presidents, university faculty members, and a university chancellor. It was felt that "only a collaborative effort could reduce costs while maintaining a level playing field." The committee proposed a rule to restrict the annual compensation of certain coaches to $16,000. The NCAA adopted the rule. Basketball coaches affected by the rule filed a suit in a federal district court against the NCAA, alleging a violation of Section 1 of the Sherman Antitrust Act. Is the rule a *per se* violation of the Sherman Act or should it be evaluated under the rule of reason? If it is subject to the rule of reason, is it an illegal restraint of trade? Explain fully. [*Law v. National Collegiate Athletic Association*, 134 F.3d 1010 (10th Cir. 1998)]

28–9. TYING ARRANGEMENT. Public Interest Corp. (PIC) owned and operated television station WTMV-TV in Lakeland, Florida. MCA Television, Ltd., owns and licenses syndicated television programs. The parties entered into a licensing contract with respect to several television shows. MCA conditioned the license on PIC's agreeing to take another show, "Harry and the Hendersons." PIC agreed to this arrangement, although it would not have chosen to license "Harry" if it did not have to do so to secure the licenses for the other shows. More than two years into the contract, a dispute arose over PIC's payments, and negotiations failed to resolve the dispute. In a letter, MCA suspended PIC's broadcast rights for all of its shows and stated that "[a]ny telecasts of MCA programming by WTMV-TV . . . will be deemed unauthorized and shall constitute an infringement of MCA's copyrights." PIC nonetheless continued broadcasting MCA's programs, with the exception of "Harry." MCA filed a suit in a federal district court against PIC, alleging breach of contract and copyright infringement. PIC filed a counterclaim, contending in part that MCA's deal was an illegal tying arrangement. Is PIC correct? Explain. [*MCA Television, Ltd. v. Public Interest Corp.*, 171 F.3d 1265 (11th Cir. 1999)]

28–10. IN YOUR COURT

Timothy Lane purchased feed from Fur Breeders Agricultural Cooperative (the co-op) for use in his fur-breeding business. All members of the co-op, including Lane, were charged the same price for the feed. The co-op, however, offered free delivery services to all of its members except Lane, who had to pick up the feed. Lane sued the co-op, alleging that the co-op's actions constituted price discrimination in violation of Section 2 of the Clayton Act, as amended. Lane argued that the added cost he had to incur in picking up the feed (about $16,000 per year) effectively raised the "price" he paid for the feed relative to the other members. As a result, contended Lane, it was difficult for him to make significant profits in this highly competitive industry. The co-op moved to dismiss the case on the ground that all members were charged the same "price," and therefore there could be no "price" discrimination. Assume that you are the judge in the trial court hearing this case and answer the following questions:

(a) Should the cost of picking up the feed should be included in the "price" Lane paid for the feed? How will you answer this question?

(a) Generally, what factors should you consider in determining whether to grant a motion to dismiss a case? In the case now before your court, should you grant the defendant's motion to dismiss? Why or why not?

LAW ON THE WEB

For updated links to resources available on the Web, as well as a variety of other materials, visit this text's Web site at http://wleb.westbuslaw.com.

The Federal Trade Commission offers an abundance of information on antitrust law, including "A Plain English Guide to Antitrust Laws," at

http://www.ftc.gov/ftc/antitrust.htm

The Tech Law Journal presents "news, records, and analysis of legislation, litigation, and regulation affecting the computer and Internet industry" in the area of antitrust law at

http://www.techlawjournalcom/atr/default.htm

LEGAL RESEARCH EXERCISES ON THE WEB

Go to http://wleb.westbuslaw.com, the Web site that accompanies this text. Select "Internet Applications," and then click on "Chapter 28." There you will find the following Internet research exercise that you can perform to learn more about the application of antitrust laws to vertical restraints:

Activity 28–1: Vertical Restraints and the Rule of Reason

CHAPTER 29

Securities Regulation and Investor Protection

THE STOCK MARKET CRASH OF OCTOBER 29, 1929, and the ensuing economic depression caused the public to focus on the importance of securities markets for the economic well-being of the nation. Congress was pressured to regulate securities trading, and the result was the Securities Act of 1933[1] and the Securities Exchange Act of 1934.[2] Both acts were designed to provide investors with more information to help them make buying and selling decisions about *securities*—generally defined as any documents evidencing corporate ownership (stock) or debts (bonds)—and to prohibit deceptive, unfair, and manipulative practices in the purchase and sale of securities. Basically, the 1933 act regulates the initial sales of corporate securities by businesses, and the 1934 act regulates subsequent purchases and sales of securities once they have been issued.

This chapter discusses the nature of federal securities regulation and its effect on the business world.

---

1. 15 U.S.C. Sections 77a–77aa.
2. 15 U.S.C. Sections 78a–78mm.

SECTION 1

Corporate Financing

Corporations are financed by the issuance and sale of corporate securities—that is, bonds and stock. **Securities** evidence the obligation to pay money or the right to participate in earnings and the distribution of corporate assets. **Stocks,** or *equity securities*, represent the purchase of ownership in the business firm. **Bonds** (debentures), or *debt securities*, represent the borrowing of money by firms (and governments). Of course, not all debt is in the form of debt securities. For example, some debt is in the form of accounts payable and notes payable. Accounts and notes payable are typically short-term debts. Bonds are simply a way for a corporation to split up its long-term debt so that it can market the debt more easily.

BONDS

Bonds are issued by business firms and by governments at all levels as evidence of the funds they are borrowing from investors. Bonds almost always have a designated *maturity date*—the date when the principal, or face amount, of the bond (or loan) is returned to the investor—and are sometimes referred to as *fixed-income securities*, because their owners receive fixed-dollar interest payments during the period of time prior to maturity.

The characteristics of corporate bonds vary widely, in part because corporations differ in their ability to generate the earnings and cash flow necessary to make interest payments and to repay the principal amount of the bonds at maturity. Furthermore, corporate bonds are only a part of the total debt and the overall financial structure of corporate business. The various types of corporate bonds are described in Exhibit 29–1.

STOCKS

Issuing stocks is another way for corporations to obtain financing [RMBCA 6.01]. The ways in which stocks differ from bonds are summarized in Exhibit 29–2 on page 620. Basically, stocks represent ownership in a business firm, whereas bonds represent borrowing by the firm.

EXHIBIT 29–1 TYPES OF CORPORATE BONDS

TYPE	DEFINITION
Debenture Bonds	Bonds for which no specific assets of the corporation are pledged as backing. Rather, they are backed by the general credit rating of the corporation, plus any assets that can be seized if the corporation allows the debentures to go into default.
Mortgage Bonds	Bonds that pledge specific property. If the corporation defaults on the bonds, the bondholders can foreclose on the property.
Convertible Bonds	Bonds that can be exchanged for a specified number of shares of stock under certain conditions.
Callable Bonds	Bonds that may be called in and the principal repaid at specified times or under conditions stipulated in the bond when it is issued.

Exhibit 29–3 on page 620 offers a summary of the types of stocks issued by corporations. The two major types are *common stock* and *preferred stock*.

Common Stock. **Common stock** represents the true ownership of a corporation. It provides a proportionate interest in the corporation with regard to (1) control, (2) earnings, and (3) net assets. A shareholder's interest is generally in proportion to the number of shares owned out of the total number of shares issued.

Any person who purchases shares acquires voting rights—one vote per share held. Voting rights in a corporation apply to the election of the firm's board of directors and to any proposed changes in the ownership structure of the firm.[3] For example, a holder of common stock generally has the right to vote in a decision on a proposed merger, as mergers can change the proportion of ownership.

Holders of common stock are a group of investors who assume a *residual* position in the overall financial structure of a business. In terms of receiving returns on their investments, they are last in line. Their earnings depend on the corporation's paying all the other groups—suppliers, employees, managers, bankers, governments, bondholders, and holders of preferred stock—what is due them first. Once those groups are paid, the owners of common stock may be entitled to *all* the remaining earnings. But the board of directors normally is not under any duty to declare the remaining earnings as dividends.

Preferred Stock. **Preferred stock** is stock with *preferences.* Usually, this means that holders of preferred stock have priority over holders of common stock as to dividends and to payment on dissolution of the corporation. Preferred stockholders may or may not have the right to vote (the trend is toward giving preferred stockholders the right to vote).

From an investment standpoint, preferred stock is more similar to bonds than to common stock. Preferred shareholders receive periodic dividend payments, usually established as a fixed percentage of the face amount of each preferred share. A share of 6 percent preferred stock with a face amount of $100 per share would pay its owner a $6 dividend each year. Payment of these dividends is not a legal obligation

---

3. State corporation law specifies the types of actions for which shareholder approval must be obtained.

EXHIBIT 29–2   HOW DO STOCKS AND BONDS DIFFER?

STOCKS	BONDS
1. Stocks represent ownership.	1. Bonds represent debt.
2. Stocks (common) do not have a fixed dividend rate.	2. Interest on bonds must always be paid, whether or not any profit is earned.
3. Stockholders can elect a board of directors, which controls the corporation.	3. Bondholders usually have no voice in or control over management of the corporation.
4. Stocks do not have a maturity date; the corporation does not usually repay the stockholder.	4. Bonds have a maturity date, when the corporation is to repay the bondholder the face value of the bond.
5. All corporations issue or offer to sell stocks. This is the usual definition of a corporation.	5. Corporations do not necessarily issue bonds.
6. Stockholders have a claim against the property and income of a corporation after all creditors' claims have been met.	6. Bondholders have a claim against the property and income of a corporation that must be met before the claims of stockholders.

on the part of the firm. Preferred stock is not included among the liabilities of a business, because it is technically equity. Like other equity securities, preferred shares have no fixed maturity date on which they must be retired by the firm. Although occasionally firms retire preferred stock, they are not legally obligated to do so. A sample cumulative convertible preferred-stock certificate is shown in Exhibit 29–4.

SECTION 2

The Securities and Exchange Commission

The 1934 act created the Securities and Exchange Commission (SEC) as an independent regulatory

EXHIBIT 29–3   TYPES OF STOCKS

TYPE	DEFINITION
Common Stock	Voting shares that represent ownership interest in a corporation. Common stock has the lowest priority with respect to payment of dividends and distribution of assets on the corporation's dissolution.
Preferred Stock	Shares of stock that have priority over common-stock shares as to payment of dividends and distribution of assets on dissolution. Dividend payments are usually a fixed percentage of the face value of the share. Preferred shares may or may not be nonvoting shares.
Cumulative Preferred Stock	Preferred shares for which required dividends not paid in a given year must be paid in a subsequent year before any common-stock dividends can be paid.
Participating Preferred Stock	Preferred shares entitling the owner to receive (1) the preferred-stock dividend and (2) additional dividends after the corporation has paid dividends on common stock.
Convertible Preferred Stock	Preferred shares entitling the owner to convert his or her shares into a specified number of common shares either in the issuing corporation or, sometimes, in another corporation.
Redeemable, or Callable, Preferred Stock	Preferred shares issued with the express condition that the issuing corporation has the right to repurchase the shares as specified.

EXHIBIT 29-4 CUMULATIVE CONVERTIBLE PREFERRED-STOCK CERTIFICATE

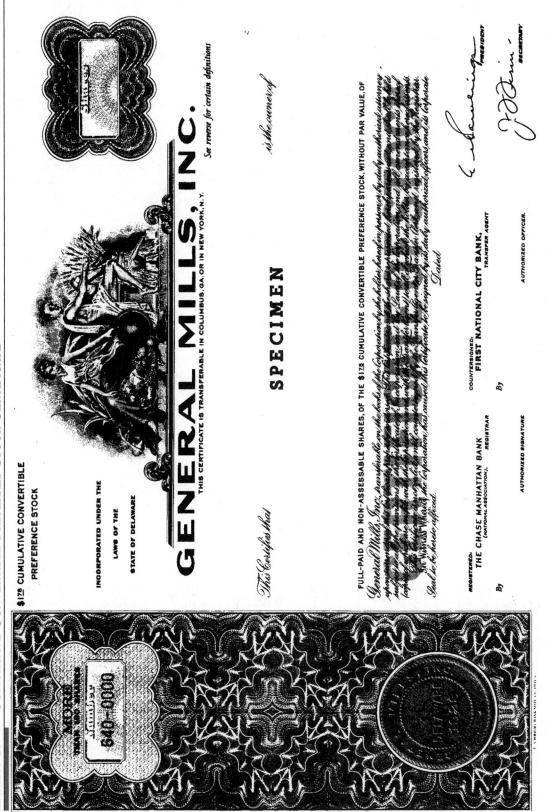

agency whose function was to administer the 1933 and 1934 acts. The SEC plays a key role in interpreting the provisions of these acts (and their amendments) and in creating regulations governing the purchase and sale of securities.

THE BASIC FUNCTIONS OF THE SEC

The SEC regulates the securities industry by undertaking the following activities:

1. Requiring disclosure of facts concerning offerings of securities listed on national securities exchanges and offerings of certain securities traded over the counter (OTC).
2. Regulating the trade in securities on the national and regional securities exchanges and in the OTC markets.
3. Investigating securities fraud.
4. Requiring the registration of securities brokers, dealers, and investment advisers and regulating their activities.
5. Supervising activities conducted by mutual funds companies.
6. Recommending administrative sanctions, injunctive remedies, and criminal prosecution in cases involving violations of securities laws. (The Fraud Section of the Criminal Division of the Department of Justice prosecutes violations of federal securities laws.)

THE REGULATORY POWERS OF THE SEC

From the time of its creation until the present, the SEC's regulatory functions have gradually been increased by legislation granting it authority in different areas. During the 1990s, for example, Congress passed several acts that have significantly expanded the SEC's powers.

To further curb securities fraud, the Securities Enforcement Remedies and Penny Stock Reform Act of 1990[4] amended existing securities laws to expand greatly the types of securities violation cases that SEC administrative law judges can hear and the SEC's enforcement options. The act also provides that courts can bar persons who have engaged in securities fraud from serving as officers and directors of publicly held corporations.

The Securities Acts Amendments of 1990[5] authorized the SEC to seek sanctions against those who violate foreign securities laws. These amendments increase the ability of the SEC to cooperate in international enforcement of securities laws. Under the Market Reform Act of 1990, the SEC can suspend trading in securities in the event that prices rise and fall excessively in a short period of time.[6]

The National Securities Markets Improvement Act of 1996 expanded the power of the SEC to exempt persons, securities, and transactions from the requirements of the securities laws.[7] (This part of the act is also known as the Capital Markets Efficiency Act.) The act also limited the authority of the states to regulate certain securities transactions, as well as particular investment advisory firms.[8]

Over the years, as more and more SEC rules were issued, the body of regulations governing securities transactions became increasingly cumbersome and complex. Congress and the SEC are now in the process of eliminating some rules, revising others, and generally attempting to streamline the regulatory process to make it more efficient and more relevant to today's securities trading practices.

SECTION 3

The Securities Act of 1933

As mentioned, the Securities Act of 1933 governs initial sales of stock by businesses. The act was designed to prohibit various forms of fraud and to stabilize the securities industry by requiring that all essential information concerning the issuance of securities be made available to the investing public.

Basically, the courts have interpreted the act's definition of what constitutes a security[9] to mean that a security exists in any transaction in which a person (1) invests (2) in a common enterprise (3) reasonably expecting profits (4) derived *primarily* or *substantially* from others' managerial or entrepreneurial efforts.[10]

For our purposes, it is probably most convenient to think of securities in their most common form—

---

4. 15 U.S.C. Section 77g.

5. See, for example, 15 U.S.C. Section 78o(b)(4)(B).
6. 15 U.S.C. Section 78i(h).
7. 15 U.S.C. Sections 77z-3, 78mm.
8. 15 U.S.C. Section 80b-3a.
9. See 15 U.S.C. Section 77b(a)(1).
10. *SEC v. W. J. Howey Co.*, 328 U.S. 293, 66 S.Ct. 1100, 90 L.Ed. 1244 (1946).

stocks and bonds issued by corporations. Bear in mind, though, that securities can take many forms and have been held to include whiskey, cosmetics, worms, beavers, boats, vacuum cleaners, muskrats, and cemetery lots, as well as investment contracts in condominiums, franchises, limited partnerships, oil or gas or other mineral rights, and farm animals accompanied by care agreements.

REGISTRATION STATEMENT

Section 5 of the Securities Act of 1933 broadly provides that if a security does not qualify for an exemption, that security must be *registered* before it is offered to the public either through the mails or through any facility of interstate commerce, including securities exchanges. Issuing corporations must file a *registration statement* with the SEC. Investors must be provided with a prospectus that describes the security being sold, the issuing corporation, and the risk attaching to the security. In principle, the registration statement and the prospectus supply sufficient information to enable unsophisticated investors to evaluate the financial risk involved.

Contents of the Registration Statement. The registration statement must include the following:

1. A description of the significant provisions of the security offered for sale, including the relationship between that security and the other capital securities of the registrant. Also, the corporation must disclose how it intends to use the proceeds of the sale.
2. A description of the registrant's properties and business.
3. A description of the management of the registrant; its security holdings; and its remuneration and other benefits, including pensions and stock options. Any interests of directors or officers in any material transactions with the corporation must be disclosed.
4. A financial statement certified by an independent public accounting firm.
5. A description of pending lawsuits.

Other Requirements. Before filing the registration statement and the prospectus with the SEC, the corporation is allowed to obtain an underwriter who will monitor the distribution of the new issue. There is a twenty-day waiting period (which can be accelerated by the SEC) after registration before the sale can take place. During this period, oral offers between interested investors and the issuing corporation concerning the purchase and sale of the proposed securities may take place, and very limited written advertising is allowed. At this time, what is known as a **red herring** prospectus may be distributed. It gets its name from the red legend printed across it stating that the registration has been filed but has not yet become effective.

After the waiting period, the registered securities can be legally bought and sold. Written advertising is allowed in the form of a so-called **tombstone ad,** so named because historically the format resembled a tombstone. Such ads simply tell the investor where and how to obtain a prospectus. Normally, any other type of advertising is prohibited.

EXEMPT SECURITIES

A number of specific securities are exempt from the registration requirements of the Securities Act of 1933. These securities—which can also generally be resold without being registered—include the following:[11]

1. All bank securities sold prior to July 27, 1933.
2. Commercial paper, if the maturity date does not exceed nine months.
3. Securities of charitable organizations.
4. Securities resulting from a corporate reorganization issued for exchange with the issuer's existing security holders and certificates issued by trustees, receivers, or debtors in possession under the bankruptcy laws (bankruptcy was discussed in Chapter 16).
5. Securities issued exclusively for exchange with the issuer's existing security holders, provided no commission is paid (for example, stock dividends and stock splits).
6. Securities issued to finance the acquisition of railroad equipment.
7. Any insurance, endowment, or annuity contract issued by a state-regulated insurance company.
8. Government-issued securities.
9. Securities issued by banks, savings and loan associations, farmers' cooperatives, and similar institutions subject to supervision by governmental authorities.
10. In consideration of the "small amount involved,"[12] an issuer's offer of up to $5 million in securities in any twelve-month period.

For the last exemption, under Regulation A,[13] the issuer must file with the SEC a notice of the issue and

---

11. 15 U.S.C. Section 77c.
12. 15 U.S.C. Section 77c(b).
13. 17 C.F.R. Sections 230.251–230.263.

an offering circular, which must also be provided to investors before the sale. This is a much simpler and less expensive process than the procedures associated with full registration. Companies are allowed to "test the waters" for potential interest before preparing the offering circular. (To *test the waters* means to determine potential interest without actually selling any securities or requiring any commitment on the part of those who are interested.) Small-business issuers (companies with less than $25 million in annual revenues and less than $25 million in outstanding voting stock) can also utilize an integrated registration and reporting system that uses simpler forms than the full registration system.

Exhibit 29–5 summarizes the securities and transactions (discussed next) that are exempt from the registration requirements under the Securities Act of 1933 and SEC regulations.

EXEMPT TRANSACTIONS

An issuer of securities that are not exempt under any of the categories listed above can avoid the high cost and complicated procedures associated with registration by taking advantage of certain *exempt transactions*. These exemptions are very broad, and thus many sales occur without registration. Because there is some overlap in the coverage of the exemptions, an offering may qualify for more than one.

Small Offerings—Regulation D. The SEC's Regulation D contains four separate exemptions from registration requirements for limited offers (offers that either involve a small amount of money or are made in a limited manner). Regulation D provides that any of these offerings made during any twelve-month period are exempt from the registration requirements.

EXHIBIT 29–5   EXEMPTIONS UNDER THE 1933 ACT FOR SECURITIES OFFERINGS BY BUSINESSES

Rule 504. Noninvestment company offerings up to $1 million in any twelve-month period are exempt.[14] In contrast to investment companies (discussed later in this chapter), noninvestment companies are firms that are not engaged primarily in the business of investing or trading in securities.

Rule 504a. Offerings up to $500,000 in any one year by so-called blank check companies—companies with no specific business plans except to locate and acquire presently unknown businesses or opportunities—are exempt if no general solicitation or advertising is used; the SEC is notified of the sales; and precaution is taken against nonexempt, unregistered resales.[15] The limits on advertising and unregistered resales do not apply if the offering is made solely in states that provide for registration and disclosure and the securities are sold in compliance with those provisions.[16]

Rule 505. Private, noninvestment company offerings up to $5 million in any twelve-month period are exempt, regardless of the number of **accredited investors** (banks, insurance companies, investment companies, the issuer's executive officers and directors, and persons whose income or net worth exceeds certain limits), so long as there are no more than thirty-five unaccredited investors; no general solicitation or advertising is used; the SEC is notified of the sales; and precaution is taken against nonexempt, unregistered resales. If the sale involves *any* unaccredited investors, *all* investors must be given material information about the offering company, its business, and the securities before the sale. Unlike Rule 506 (discussed next), Rule 505 includes no requirement that the issuer believe each unaccredited investor "has such knowledge and experience in financial and business matters that he is capable of evaluating the merits and the risks of the prospective investment."[17]

Rule 506. Private offerings in unlimited amounts that are not generally solicited or advertised are exempt if the SEC is notified of the sales; precaution is taken against nonexempt, unregistered resales; and the issuer believes that each unaccredited investor has sufficient knowledge or experience in financial matters to be capable of evaluating the investment's merits and risks. There may be no more than thirty-five unaccredited investors, although there may be an unlimited number of accredited investors. If there are any unaccredited investors, the issuer must provide to all purchasers material information about itself, its business, and the securities before the sale.[18]

This exemption is perhaps most important to those firms that want to raise funds through the sale of securities without registering them. It is often referred to as the *private placement* exemption, because it exempts "transactions not involving any public offering."[19] This provision applies to private offerings to a limited number of persons who are sufficiently sophisticated and in a sufficiently strong bargaining position to be able to assume the risk of the investment (and who thus have no need for federal registration protection), as well as to private offerings to similarly situated institutional investors.

Small Offerings—Section 4(6). Under Section 4(6) of the Securities Act of 1933, an offer made *solely* to accredited investors is exempt if its amount is not more than $5 million. Any number of accredited investors may participate, but no unaccredited investors may do so. No general solicitation or advertising may be used; the SEC must be notified of all sales; and precaution must be taken against nonexempt, unregistered resales. Precaution is necessary because these are *restricted* securities and may be resold only by registration or in an exempt transaction.[20] (The securities purchased and sold by most people who deal in stock are called, in contrast, *unrestricted* securities.)

Intrastate Issues—Rule 147. Also exempt are intrastate transactions involving purely local offerings.[21] This exemption applies to most offerings that are restricted to residents of the state in which the issuing company is organized and doing business. For nine months after the last sale, virtually no resales may be

---

14. 17 C.F.R. Section 230.504. Rule 504 is the exemption used by most small businesses, but that could change under new SEC Rule 1001. This rule permits, under certain circumstances, "testing the waters" for offerings of up to $5 million *per transaction*. These offerings, however, can be made only to "qualified purchasers" (knowledgeable, sophisticated investors).

15. Precautions to be taken against nonexempt, unregistered resales include asking the investor whether he or she is buying the securities for others; before the sale, disclosing to each purchaser in writing that the securities are unregistered and thus cannot be resold, except in an exempt transaction, without first being registered; and indicating on the certificates that the securities are unregistered and restricted.

16. 17 C.F.R. Section 230.504a.

17. 17 C.F.R. Section 230.505.

18. 17 C.F.R. Section 230.506.

19. 15 U.S.C. Section 77d(2).

20. 15 U.S.C. Section 77d(6).

21. 15 U.S.C. Section 77c(a)(11); 17 C.F.R. Section 230.147.

made to nonresidents, and precautions must be taken against this possibility. These offerings remain subject to applicable laws in the state of issue.

Resales. Most securities can be resold without registration (although some resales may be subject to restrictions, which are discussed above in connection with specific exemptions). The Securities Act of 1933 provides exemptions for resales by most persons other than issuers or underwriters. The average investor who sells shares of stock does not have to file a registration statement with the SEC. Resales of restricted securities acquired under Rule 504a, Rule 505, Rule 506, or Section 4(6), however, trigger the registration requirements unless the party selling them complies with Rule 144 or Rule 144A. These rules are sometimes referred to as "safe harbors."

Rule 144. Rule 144 exempts restricted securities from registration on resale if there is adequate current public information about the issuer, the person selling the securities has owned them for at least one year, they are sold in certain limited amounts in unsolicited brokers' transactions, and the SEC is given notice of the resale.[22] "Adequate current public information" consists of the reports that certain companies are required to file under the Securities Exchange Act of 1934. A person who has owned the securities for at least two years is subject to none of these requirements, unless the person is an affiliate. An *affiliate* is one who controls, is controlled by, or is in common control with the issuer. Sales of *nonrestricted* securities by an affiliate are also subject to the requirements for an exemption under Rule 144 (except that the affiliate need not have owned the securities for at least two years).

Rule 144A. Securities that at the time of issue are not of the same class as securities listed on a national securities exchange or quoted in a U.S. automated interdealer quotation system may be resold under Rule 144A.[23] They may be sold only to a qualified institutional buyer (an institution, such as an insurance company, an investment company, or a bank, that owns and invests at least $100 million in securities). The seller must take reasonable steps to ensure that the buyer knows that the seller is relying on the ex-

---

22. 17 C.F.R. Section 230.144.
23. 17 C.F.R. Section 230.144A.

emption under Rule 144A. A sample restricted stock certificate is shown in Exhibit 29–6 on page 627.

VIOLATIONS OF THE 1933 ACT

It is a violation of the Securities Act of 1933 to intentionally defraud investors by misrepresenting or omitting facts in a registration statement or prospectus. Liability is also imposed on those who are negligent for not discovering the fraud. Selling securities before the effective date of the registration statement or under an exemption for which the securities do not qualify results in liability.

Defenses. There are three basic defenses to charges of violations under the 1933 act. A defendant can avoid liability if he or she can prove that, even if a statement was not true or a fact was left out, the statement or omission was not material. A defendant can also avoid liability by proving that the plaintiff knew about the misrepresentation and bought the stock anyway.

Any defendant, except the issuer of the stock, can also assert what is called the *due diligence* defense. To make this defense, a person must prove that he or she reasonably believed, at the time the registration statement became effective, that the statements in it were true and there were no omissions of material facts. (This defense is discussed in further detail in Chapter 51, in the context of the liability of accountants.)

Criminal Penalties. The U.S. Department of Justice brings criminal actions against those who willfully violate the 1933 act. Violators may be penalized by fines up to $10,000, imprisonment up to five years, or both.

Civil Sanctions. The SEC is authorized to seek, against those who willfully violate the 1933 act, an injunction against further sales of the securities involved. The SEC can also ask the court to grant other relief, such as an order to a violator to refund profits.

Those who purchase the securities and suffer harm as a result of the false or omitted statements, or other violation, may bring a suit in a federal court to recover their losses and other damages. If a registration statement or a prospectus contains material false statements or material omissions, for example, damages may be imposed on those who signed the statement or those who provided information used in preparing the statement (such as accountants and other experts).

EXHIBIT 29–6 A SAMPLE RESTRICTED STOCK CERTIFICATE

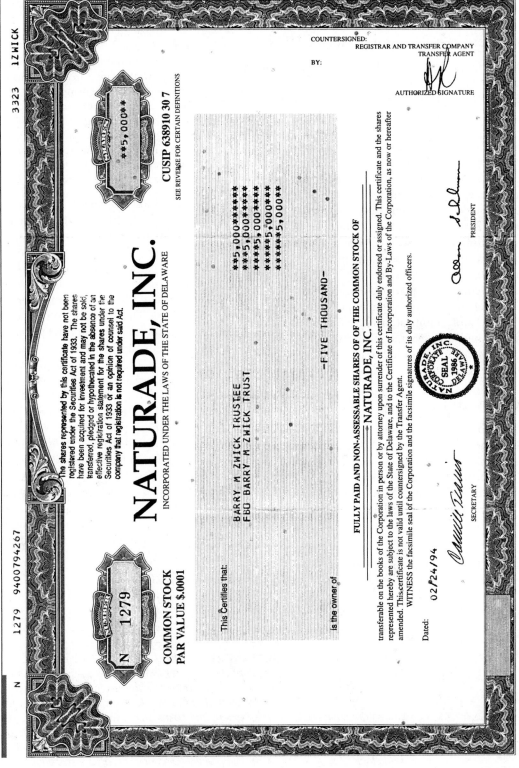

SECTION 4

The Securities Exchange Act of 1934

The Securities Exchange Act of 1934 provides for the regulation and registration of securities exchanges, brokers, dealers, and national securities associations, such as the National Association of Securities Dealers (NASD). The SEC regulates the markets in which securities are traded by maintaining a continuous disclosure system for all corporations with securities on the securities exchanges and for those companies that have assets in excess of $10 million and five hundred or more shareholders. These corporations are referred to as Section 12 companies, as they are required to register their securities under Section 12 of the 1934 act.

The act regulates proxy solicitation for voting (see Chapter 19), and it allows the SEC to engage in market surveillance to regulate undesirable market practices such as fraud, market manipulation, misrepresentation, and stabilization. (*Stabilization* is a market-manipulating technique by which securities underwriters bid for securities to stabilize their prices during their issuance.)

SECTION 10(b) AND SEC RULE 10b-5

Section 10(b) is one of the most important sections of the Securities Exchange Act of 1934. This section prohibits the use of any manipulative or deceptive device in violation of SEC rules and regulations. Among the rules that the SEC has prescribed is **SEC Rule 10b-5,** which prohibits the commission of fraud in connection with the purchase or sale of any security. Rule 10b-5 states as follows:

It shall be unlawful for any person, directly or indirectly, by the use of any means or instrumentality of interstate commerce, or of the mails or of any facility of any national securities exchange,

(a) To employ any device, scheme, or artifice to defraud,

(b) To make any untrue statement of a material fact or to omit to state a material fact necessary in order to make the statements made, in the light of the circumstances under which they were made, not misleading, or

(c) To engage in any act, practice, or course of business which operates or would operate as a fraud or deceit upon any person, in connection with the purchase or sale of any security.[24]

One of the most important purposes of Section 10(b) and SEC Rule 10b-5 relates to what is called **insider trading.** Because of their positions, corporate directors and officers often obtain advance inside information that can affect the future market value of the corporate stock. Obviously, their positions can give them a trading advantage over the general public and shareholders. The 1934 Securities Exchange Act defines inside information and extends liability to officers and directors in their personal transactions for taking advantage of such information when they know that it is unavailable to the person with whom they are dealing.

Section 10(b) of the 1934 act and SEC Rule 10b-5 cover not only corporate officers, directors, and majority shareholders but also any persons having access to or receiving information of a nonpublic nature on which trading is based.

In the following classic case, a shareholder alleged that a corporate officer and a corporate director had breached their fiduciary duties by trading corporate shares on the basis of nonpublic information.

---

24. 17 C.F.R. Section 240.10b-5.

CASE 29.1   Diamond v. Oreamuno

Court of Appeals of New York, 1969.
24 N.Y.2d 494,
248 N.E.2d 910,
301 N.Y.S.2d 78.

BACKGROUND AND FACTS   *The defendants in this case were the chairman of the board (Oreamuno) and president (Gonzalez) of Management Assistance, Inc. (MAI), a corporation that bought and leased computers, with maintenance services being provided by IBM. The defendants learned that IBM was going to increase its maintenance prices dramatically, to such an extent that MAI's profits would be cut by 75 percent per month. Just before the IBM maintenance price increase was announced, the defendants sold their MAI stock for $28 per share. After IBM publicly announced its price increase, MAI stock fell to $11 per share. The plaintiff (Diamond) brought a shareholder's derivative lawsuit on behalf of MAI to recover the profits the defendants had made by selling their shares at the higher price. The trial court granted the defendants' motion to dismiss, and the plaintiff appealed.*

FULD, Chief Judge.

*   *   *   *

Accepting the truth of the complaint's allegations, there is no question but that the defendants were guilty of withholding material information from the purchasers of the shares and, indeed, the defendants acknowledge that the facts asserted constitute a violation of rule 10b-5. *   *   * Of course, any individual purchaser who could prove an injury as a result of a rule 10b-5 violation can bring his own action for rescission but we have not been referred to a single case in which such an action has been successfully prosecuted where the public sale of securities is involved. The reason for this is that sales of securities, whether through a stock exchange or over-the-counter, are characteristically anonymous transactions, usually handled through brokers, and the matching of the ultimate buyer with the ultimate seller presents virtually insurmountable obstacles.

*   *   *

*   *   * There is ample room in a situation such as is here presented for a "private Attorney General" to come forward and enforce proper behavior on the part of corporate officials through the medium of the derivative action brought in the name of the corporation. Only by sanctioning such a cause of action will there be any effective method to prevent the type of abuse of corporate office complained of in this case.

The court of appeals held that when corporate fiduciaries have breached their duty to the corporation by the use of nonpublic information, a shareholder may bring a derivative action for any profit resulting from the breach of duty.

Disclosure Requirements under SEC Rule 10b-5. Any material omission or misrepresentation of material facts in connection with the purchase or sale of a security may violate Section 10(b) and SEC Rule 10b-5. The key to liability (which can be civil or criminal) under this rule is whether the insider's information is *material*. The following are some examples of material facts calling for disclosure under the rule:

1. Fraudulent trading in the company stock by a broker-dealer.
2. A dividend change (whether up or down).
3. A contract for the sale of corporate assets.
4. A new discovery, a new process, or a new product.
5. A significant change in the financial condition of the firm.
6. Potential litigation against the company.

Ironically, one of the effects of SEC Rule 10b-5 was to deter disclosure. To understand why, consider an example. A company announces that its projected earnings in a certain time period will be X amount. It turns out that the forecast is wrong. The earnings are in fact much lower, and the price of the company's stock is affected—negatively. The shareholders then bring a class-action suit against the company, alleging that the directors violated SEC Rule 10b-5 by disclosing misleading financial information.

In an attempt to rectify this problem and promote disclosure, Congress passed the Private Securities Litigation Reform Act of 1995. Among other things, the act provides a "safe harbor" for publicly held companies that make forward-looking statements, such as financial forecasts. Those who make such statements are protected against federal liability for securities fraud as long as the statements are accompanied by "meaningful cautionary statements identifying important factors that could cause actual results to differ materially from those in the forward-looking statement."[25]

The following is a landmark case interpreting SEC Rule 10b-5. The SEC sued several of Texas Gulf Sulphur Company's directors, officers, and employees under SEC Rule 10b-5 after these persons had purchased large amounts of the corporate stock prior to the announcement of a rich ore discovery by the corporation. At issue was whether the ore discovery was a material fact that had to be disclosed under Rule 10b-5.

---

25. 15 U.S.C. Sections 77z-2, 78u-5.

CASE 29.2   SEC v. Texas Gulf Sulphur Co.

United States
Court of Appeals,
Second Circuit, 1968.
401 F.2d 833.

BACKGROUND AND FACTS *Texas Gulf Sulphur Company (TGS) conducted aerial geophysical surveys over more than 15,000 square miles of eastern Canada. The operations indicated concentrations of commercially exploitable minerals. At one site near Timmins, Ontario, TGS drilled a hole that appeared to yield a core with an exceedingly high mineral content. TGS kept secret the results of the core sample. Officers and employees of the company made substantial purchases of TGS's stock or accepted stock options after learning of the ore discovery, even though further drilling was necessary to establish whether there was enough ore to be mined commercially. Several months later, TGS announced that the strike was expected to yield at least 25 million tons of ore, substantially driving up the price of TGS stock. The SEC brought suit against the officers and employees of TGS for violating SEC Rule 10b-5. The officers and employees argued that the information on which they had traded had not been material at the time of their trades because the mine had not then been commercially proved. The trial court held that most of the defendants had not violated SEC Rule 10b-5, and the SEC appealed.*

IN THE LANGUAGE OF THE COURT

WATERMAN, Circuit Judge.

    *   *   *   *

  *   *   * [W]hether facts are material within Rule 10b-5 when the facts relate to a particular event and are undisclosed by those persons who are knowledgeable thereof will depend at any given time upon a balancing of both the indicated probability that the event will occur and the anticipated magnitude of the event in light of the totality of the company activity. Here, *   *   * knowledge of the possibility, which surely was more than marginal, of the existence of a mine of the vast magnitude indicated by the remarkably rich drill core located rather close to the surface (suggesting mineability by the less expensive openpit method) within the confines of a large anomaly (suggesting an extensive region of mineralization) might well have affected the price of TGS stock and would certainly have been an important fact to a reasonable, if speculative, investor in deciding whether he should buy, sell, or hold.

    *   *   *   *

  *   *   * [A] major factor in determining whether the *   *   * discovery was a material fact is the importance attached to the drilling results by those who knew about it. *   *   * [T]he timing by those who knew of it of their stock purchases *   *   *—purchases in some cases by individuals who had never before purchased *   *   * TGS stock—virtually compels the inference that the insiders were influenced by the drilling results.

DECISION AND REMEDY

The appellate court ruled in favor of the SEC. All of the trading by insiders who knew of the mineral find before its true extent had been publicly announced violated SEC Rule 10b-5.

Applicability of SEC Rule 10b-5. SEC Rule 10b-5 applies in virtually all cases concerning the trading of securities, whether on organized exchanges, in over-the-counter markets, or in private transactions. The rule covers notes, bonds, certificates of interest and participation in any profit-sharing agreement, agreements to form a corporation, and joint-venture agreements; in short, the rule covers just about any form of security. It is immaterial whether a firm has securities registered under the 1933 act for the 1934 act to apply.

    SEC Rule 10b-5 is applicable only when the requisites of federal jurisdiction (such as the use of the mails, of stock exchange facilities, or of any instrumentality of interstate commerce) are present. Virtually no commercial transaction, however, can be completed without such contact. In addition, the states have corporate securities laws, many of which include provisions similar to SEC Rule 10b-5.

    SEC Rule 10b-5 and state securities laws also apply to online securities offerings and disclosures. See this chapter's *Emerging Trends in Technology* on pages 636–637 for a further discussion of this topic.

Outsiders and SEC Rule 10b-5. The traditional insider-trading case involves true insiders—corporate officers, directors, and majority shareholders who have access to (and trade on) inside information. Increasingly, liability under Section 10(b) of the 1934 act and SEC Rule 10b-5 has been extended to include certain "outsiders"—those who trade on inside information acquired indirectly. Two theories have been developed under which outsiders may be held liable for insider trading: the *tipper/tippee theory* and the *misappropriation theory*.

Tipper/Tippee Theory. Anyone who acquires inside information as a result of a corporate insider's breach of his or her fiduciary duty can be liable under SEC Rule 10b-5. This liability extends to **tippees** (those who receive "tips" from insiders) and even remote tippees (tippees of tippees).

The key to liability under this theory is that the inside information be obtained as a result of someone's breach of a fiduciary duty to the corporation whose shares are involved in the trading. Unless there is a breach of a duty not to disclose inside information, the disclosure is made in exchange for personal benefit, and the tippee knows of this breach (or should know of it) and benefits from it, there is no liability under this theory.[26] Is the offering of a tip as a gift of profits to someone with whom the insider has a close relationship enough to infer that the insider realized a personal benefit? That was at issue in the following case.

---

26. See, for example, *Chiarella v. United States,* 445 U.S. 222, 100 S.Ct. 1108, 63 L.Ed.2d 348 (1980); and *Dirks v. SEC,* 463 U.S. 646, 103 S.Ct. 3255, 77 L.Ed.2d 911 (1983).

CASE 29.3   SEC v. Warde

United States
Court of Appeals,
Second Circuit, 1998.
151 F.3d 42.
**http://www.tourolaw.
edu/2ndcircuit/July98**[a]

BACKGROUND AND FACTS *Edward Downe was a close friend of Fred Sullivan, chairman of Kidde, Inc. At Sullivan's request, Downe became a director of Kidde. Thomas Warde was a good friend of Downe. In June 1987, Sullivan learned that Kidde was the target of a takeover attempt by Hanson Trust PLC, a British firm. After negotiations, the Kidde board announced in August that it would merge with Hanson. The price of Kidde stock increased, and warrants for the shares, which had been priced at $1 in June, went to $26.50.[b] Between learning about the takeover attempt in June and the merger in August, Downe and Warde bought and sold warrants several times, earning very large profits. The SEC filed a suit in a federal district court against Warde and others, alleging insider trading in violation, in part, of Section 10(b). Warde contended that his purchases were based on market savvy, rumor, and public information. The jury found him liable. The court ordered him to pay more than $3 million in penalties and interest. Warde appealed to the U.S. Court of Appeals for the Second Circuit.*

IN THE LANGUAGE OF THE COURT

LEVAL, Circuit Judge:

*   *   *   *

To affirm Warde's liability as a tippee *   *   * , we must find sufficient evidence to permit a reasonable finding that *   *   * Downe benefitted by the disclosure to Warde.

*   *   *

     *   *   *   *

*   *   * [In *Dirks v. SEC,* 463 U.S. 646, 103 S.Ct. 3255, 77 L.Ed.2d 911 (1983), the United States] Supreme Court *   *   * made plain that to prove a Section 10(b) violation, the SEC need not show that the tipper expected or received a specific or tangible benefit in exchange for the tip. Rather, the "benefit" element of Section 10(b) is satisfied when the tipper "intend[s] to benefit the *   *   * recipient" or "makes a gift of confidential information to a trading relative or friend."

     Under this standard, Downe clearly benefitted from Warde's inside trades. Warde's trades "resemble[d] trading by the insider himself followed by a gift of the profits to the recipient." The close friendship between Downe and Warde suggests that Downe's tip was

---

a. This page provides access to opinions of the U.S. Court of Appeals for the Second Circuit decided in July 1998. Scroll down the list of cases to the *Warde* case and click on the link to access the opinion.

b. A warrant is an agreement to buy stock at a certain price before a certain date. If, before the warrant is exercised, the price goes up, the buyer profits. If the price never exceeds the level in the warrant, the warrant is worthless.

"inten[ded] to benefit" Warde, and therefore allows a jury finding that Downe's tip breached a duty under Section 10(b).

DECISION AND REMEDY   *The U.S. Court of Appeals for the Second Circuit affirmed the lower court's decision, concluding that the SEC presented sufficient evidence to support every element necessary to hold Warde liable. Warde was ordered to pay the fines, with interest.*

Misappropriation Theory.   Liability for insider trading may also be established under the misappropriation theory. This theory holds that if an individual wrongfully obtains (misappropriates) inside information and trades on it for his or her personal gain, then the individual should be held liable because, in essence, the individual stole information rightfully belonging to another.

The misappropriation theory has been controversial because it significantly extends the reach of SEC Rule 10b-5 to outsiders who would not ordinarily be deemed fiduciaries of the corporations in whose stock they trade. At issue in the following case was whether the misappropriation theory can be applied under Rule 10b-5.

CASE 29.4   United States v. O'Hagan

Supreme Court of the
United States, 1997.
521 U.S. 642,
117 S.Ct. 2199,
138 L.Ed.2d 724.
**http://supct.law.
cornell.edu/supct**[a]

COMPANY PROFILE   *The law firm of Dorsey & Whitney LLP (Limited Liability Partnership) (**http://www.dorseylaw.com**) was founded in 1912. Today, Dorsey & Whitney is one of the forty largest law firms in the United States, with more than five hundred lawyers and seven hundred support staff. The firm is based in Minneapolis, Minnesota, with offices in a dozen other U.S. cities and in London, Brussels, and Hong Kong. The firm's attorneys have included the late Harry Blackmun, a former United States Supreme Court justice, and Walter Mondale, a former vice president of the United States and ambassador to Japan. The firm is organized into two large groups, each of which is broken down into smaller "practice" groups. These smaller groups include "Mergers & Acquisitions," the members of which, according to the firm's Web site, "have extensive experience in all types of mergers and acquisitions work."*

BACKGROUND AND FACTS   *James O'Hagan was a partner in the law firm of Dorsey & Whitney. Grand Metropolitan PLC (Grand Met) hired Dorsey & Whitney to assist in a takeover of the Pillsbury Company. Before Grand Met made its tender offer, O'Hagan bought shares of Pillsbury stock. When the tender offer was announced, the price of Pillsbury stock increased more than 35 percent. O'Hagan sold his shares for a profit of more than $4 million. The Securities and Exchange Commission (SEC) prosecuted O'Hagan for, among other things, securities fraud in violation of Rule 10b-5 under the misappropriation theory. The SEC contended that O'Hagan breached fiduciary duties he owed to his law firm and Grand Met. When O'Hagan was convicted, he appealed to the U.S. Court of Appeals for the Eighth Circuit, which reversed the convictions. The SEC appealed to the United States Supreme Court.*

IN THE LANGUAGE OF THE COURT   Justice *GINSBURG* delivered the opinion of the Court.
*   *   *   *

---

a. This page provides access to some of the published opinions of the United States Supreme Court. In the right-hand column, in the "Arrayed by party name" section, in the "1997" row, click on "2nd party." When that page opens, find the *O'Hagan* case name and click on the link. From that page, click on the appropriate link to access the Court's opinion.

> * * * [M]isappropriation * * * satisfies [Section] 10(b)'s requirement that chargeable conduct involve a "deceptive device or contrivance" used "in connection with" the purchase or sale of securities. * * * [M]isappropriators * * * deal in deception. A fiduciary who pretends loyalty to the principal while secretly converting the principal's information for personal gain dupes or defrauds the principal.
>
> * * * *
>
> * * * [T]he fiduciary's fraud is consummated * * * when, without disclosure to his principal, he uses the information to purchase or sell securities. * * *
>
> * * * *
>
> * * * An investor's informational disadvantage vis-à-vis a misappropriator with material, nonpublic information stems from contrivance, not luck; it is a disadvantage that cannot be overcome with research or skill.

DECISION AND REMEDY   *The United States Supreme Court held that liability under Rule 10b-5 can be based on the misappropriation theory, reversed the judgment, and remanded the case.*

INSIDER REPORTING AND TRADING—SECTION 16(b)

Officers, directors, and certain large stockholders[27] of Section 12 corporations are required to file reports with the SEC concerning their ownership and trading of the corporation's securities.[28] To discourage such insiders from using nonpublic information about their companies to their personal benefit in the stock market, Section 16(b) of the 1934 act provides for the recapture by the corporation of all profits realized by the insider on any purchase and sale or sale and purchase of the corporation's stock within any six-month period. It is irrelevant whether the insider actually uses inside information; *all such short-swing profits must be returned to the corporation.*

Section 16(b) applies not only to stock but to warrants, options, and securities convertible into stock. In addition, the courts have fashioned complex rules for determining profits. The SEC exempts a number of transactions under Rule 16b-3.[29] For all of these reasons, corporate insiders are wise to seek competent counsel prior to trading in the corporation's stock. Exhibit 29–7 on page 635 compares the effects of SEC Rule 10b-5 and Section 16(b).

Shareholders owning 10 percent or more of the stock of a Section 12 corporation may be held liable under Section 16(b). Determining whether a shareholder owns 10 percent is not always easy, however, as illustrated by the following case.

---

27. Those stockholders owning 10 percent of the class of equity securities registered under Section 12 of the 1934 act.
28. 15 U.S.C. Section 78l.

29. 17 C.F.R. Section 240.16b-3.

CASE 29.5   ## Medtox Scientific, Inc. v. Morgan Capital, L.L.C.[a]

United States District Court, District of Minnesota, 1999.
50 F.Supp.2d 896.

BACKGROUND AND FACTS   *On February 1, 1996, Editek, Inc.,[b] issued shares of convertible preferred stock.[c] Each share could be converted to Editek common stock at a price equal to the average price of the common stock for the five days preceding the date that a notice of conversion was given to Editek. In other words, the number of shares of common stock that the preferred stock would buy depended on the average price of*

---

a. L.L.C. is an abbreviation for "limited liability company." An LLC is a hybrid form of business enterprise that offers the limited liability of the corporation and the tax advantages of a partnership. See Chapter 18.
b. Editek later changed its name to Medtox Scientific, Inc.
c. *Convertible preferred stock* is preferred stock entitling the owner to convert the preferred shares into a specified number of common shares. See Exhibits 29–4 and 29–5.

the common shares. If this price declined, the number of shares that the preferred stock would buy increased, and vice versa. Morgan Capital, L.L.C., bought some of the preferred stock. At the time, the number of common shares that Morgan Capital could have received on conversion would have been less than 10 percent of the outstanding stock. The price of Editek's common shares decreased, however, and at any time after April 9, Morgan Capital could have converted its preferred shares for more than 10 percent of the common stock. On May 1, Morgan Capital converted all of its preferred stock and received more than 18 percent of the common stock. Before the end of June, Morgan Capital sold some of the common stock, realizing a profit of $551,456.84. Editek filed a suit in a federal district court against Morgan Capital, alleging that the firm had violated Section 16(b). Morgan Capital responded in part that before it converted its preferred shares, it could not have been a 10 percent owner of Editek stock, as required to violate Section 16(b), because the amount of common stock that it could acquire changed every day. Editek filed a motion for summary judgment.

IN THE LANGUAGE OF THE COURT

MONTGOMERY, District Judge.

*   *   *   *

*   *   * [I]f Morgan Capital could have converted its Preferred Stock into more than ten percent of the outstanding shares of Editek's Common Stock on any given day, then the presumption arises under Section 16(b) that Morgan Capital's holdings afforded it the potential for access to corporate information not available to a smaller shareholder on that day. At the same time, however, due to the floating conversion rate of the Preferred Stock, Morgan Capital's standing as a "ten percent beneficial owner" was potentially subject to change daily. Thus, to establish liability under Section 16(b), Plaintiff [would] not simply have to show that Morgan Capital could have obtained more than ten percent of Editek's Common Stock on any given day prior to May 1, 1996, but that Morgan Capital could have obtained more than ten percent of Editek's Common Stock on the day before it actually made the illicit purchase—April 30, 1996. Otherwise, Morgan Capital presumably would not have had access to inside information when it actually purchased Editek Common Stock and, therefore, would not be subject to the strictures of Section 16(b).

*   *   *   *

The price of Editek's Common Stock steadily declined throughout March and April 1996. As a result, on any day between April 9 and April 30, 1996, the price was sufficiently low that had Morgan Capital elected to convert its Preferred Stock, it would have received more than ten percent of the outstanding shares of Editek's Common Stock. *   *   *

*   *   *   *

Morgan Capital became a "ten percent beneficial owner" of Editek Common Stock on April 9, 1996 *   *   * . By exercising the option to convert its Preferred Stock into Common Stock on May 1, 1996, Morgan Capital fixed the conversion price and thereby engaged in a matchable purchase of Editek's Common Stock for Section 16(b) liability purposes. Over the next two months, Morgan Capital sold a portion of the stock it purchased on May 1, 1996, for a total profit of $551,456.84. Because these transactions constitute "short-swing" insider trading in violation of Section 16(b), Editek is entitled to recover the full profit realized by Morgan Capital. Plaintiff's motion is therefore granted.

DECISION AND REMEDY

The court granted Editek's motion for summary judgment. Morgan Capital was a 10 percent shareholder of Editek for purposes of Section 16(b) liability, because for at least one day before Morgan Capital converted its preferred shares, those shares could have been converted to obtain more than 10 percent of the common stock.

PROXY STATEMENTS

Section 14(a) of the Securities Exchange Act of 1934 regulates the solicitation of proxies from shareholders of Section 12 companies. The SEC regulates the content of proxy statements, which are statements sent to shareholders by corporate managers who are requesting authority to vote on behalf of the shareholders in a

EXHIBIT 29–7 COMPARISON OF COVERAGE, APPLICATION, AND LIABILITY UNDER SEC RULE 10b-5 AND SECTION 16(b)

	RULE 10b-5	SECTION 16(b)
Subject matter of transaction	Any security (does not have to be registered).	Any security (does not have to be registered).
Transactions covered	Purchase or sale.	Short-swing purchase and sale or short-swing sale and purchase.
Who is subject to liability?	Virtually anyone with inside information under a duty to disclose—including officers, directors, controlling stockholders, and tippees.	Officers, directors, and certain holders of large amounts of stock.
Is omission or misrepresentation necessary for liability?	Yes.	No.
Any exempt transactions?	No.	Yes, a variety of exemptions.
Is direct dealing with the party necessary?	No.	No.
Who may bring an action?	A person transacting with an insider, the SEC, or a purchaser or seller damaged by a wrongful act.	Corporation and shareholder by derivative action.

particular election on specified issues. Whoever solicits a proxy must fully and accurately disclose in the proxy statement all of the facts that are pertinent to the matter on which the shareholders are to vote. SEC Rule 14a-9 is similar to the antifraud provisions of SEC Rule 10b-5. Remedies for violations are extensive, ranging from injunctions to prevent a vote from being taken to monetary damages.

VIOLATIONS OF THE 1934 ACT

Violations of Section 10(b) and Rule 10b-5 of the Securities Exchange Act of 1934 include insider trading. This is a criminal offense, with criminal penalties. Violators of these laws may also be subject to civil liability. For any sanctions to be imposed, however, there must be *scienter*—the violator must have had an intent to defraud or knowledge of his or her misconduct (see Chapter 9). *Scienter* can be proved by showing a defendant made false statements or wrongfully failed to disclose material facts.

Violations of Section 16(b) include the sale by insiders of stock acquired less than six months before the sale. These violations are subject to civil sanctions. Liability under Section 16(b) is strict liability. *Scienter* is not required.

Criminal Penalties. For violations of Section 10(b) and Rule 10b-5, an individual may be fined up to $1 million, imprisoned up to ten years, or both. A partnership or a corporation may be fined up to $2.5 million.

Civil Sanctions. Both the SEC and private parties can bring actions to seek civil sanctions against violators of the 1934 act.

The Insider Trading Sanctions Act of 1984 permits the SEC to bring suit in a federal district court against anyone violating or aiding in a violation of the 1934 act or SEC rules by purchasing or selling a security while in the possession of material nonpublic information.[30] The violation must occur on or through the facilities of a national securities exchange or from or through a broker or dealer. Transactions pursuant to a public offering by an issuer of securities are excepted. The court may assess as a penalty as much as triple the profits gained or the loss avoided by the guilty party. Profit or loss is defined as "the difference between the purchase or sale price of the security and the value of that security as measured by the trading price of the

---

30. 15 U.S.C. Section 78u(d)(2)(A).

EMERGING TRENDS IN TECHNOLOGY

Online Securities Offerings and Disclosures

We have emphasized elsewhere how technological advances have affected business practices, as well as the law governing those practices. Not surprisingly, technology is also affecting practices in the securities industry—and securities law. Corporations are using the Internet to communicate information to the Securities and Exchange Commission (SEC), shareholders, potential investors, and others. Indeed, the SEC has changed or modified a number of its rules to encourage online filings of securities documents, including prospectuses.

Investors, in turn, can now use the Internet to access information that can help them make informed decisions. At the SEC's Web site (at **http://www.sec.gov**), for example, investors and others can view new SEC rules, recent announcements, enforcement actions, and the EDGAR (Electronic Data Gathering, Analysis, and Retrieval) database. This database includes initial public offerings, proxy statements, annual corporate reports, registration statements, and other

documents that have been filed with the SEC. EDGAR also provides public access to information regarding securities trading suspensions and current class-action suits for securities fraud.

These developments have brought about, according to one scholar, a "near-revolution" in the way in which securities are issued and traded.[a] Of course, the Internet has also been used to commit fraud, and the SEC has stepped up its monitoring of the Internet to detect fraudulent securities offerings and other activities.

SECURITIES OFFERINGS

In 1996, when the SEC allowed Spring Street Brewing Company to trade its shares via its Web site without registering as a broker-dealer, many people looked to the Internet as the stock market of tomorrow. It appears, however, that we are going to have to wait a few more years for that to take place. Although many other companies have taken advantage of the SEC's "green light" and offered stock directly to the public over the Internet, there have been no great success stories so far. No doubt, this will soon change as more and more established firms begin to

a. Robert A. Prentice, "The Future of Corporate Disclosure: The Internet, Securities Fraud, and Rule 10b-5," *Emory Law Journal*, Vol. 47, No. 1 (Winter 1998), p. 1.

use the Internet to publish prospectuses.

To date, offerings by small, nonpublic companies have been limited in scope, mainly because of regulatory restraints. To a large extent, any company wishing to make an initial public offering (IPO) of securities over the Internet has to comply with filing requirements dictated by federal and state law. Such filings are costly and time consuming. Typically, only those companies that are exempt from registration requirements have gone to the Internet to raise capital. Another problem relates to the lack of secondary markets for IPO shares sold directly on the Internet.

One of the questions raised by Internet transactions has to do with securities offerings by foreign companies. Today, anybody in the world can offer shares of stock worldwide via the Web without any additional cost. Traditionally, foreign companies have not been able to offer new shares to the U.S. public without first registering them with the SEC. How can these requirements be enforced for offerings made using the Internet?

In 1998, the SEC issued an interpretive release to address this question and similar concerns. The SEC stated that foreign issuers must implement measures to avoid targeting U.S. investors. For example, a foreign company offering shares of stock on the Internet must add a disclaimer on its Web site stating that it has not gone through the registration

security at a reasonable period of time after public dissemination of the nonpublic information."[31]

The Insider Trading and Securities Fraud Enforcement Act of 1988 enlarged the class of persons who may be subject to civil liability for insider-trading violations. This act also gave the SEC authority to award **bounty payments** (rewards given

31. 15 U.S.C. Section 78u(d)(2)(C).

EMERGING TRENDS IN TECHNOLOGY

Online Securities Offerings and Disclosures,

continued

procedure in the United States. If the SEC believes that a Web site's offering of foreign securities has been targeted at U.S. residents, it will pursue that company in an attempt to require it to register in the United States.[b] Given that some Web site prospectuses for new security offerings have full audio and downloadable video, the investing public will probably become more interested in such Web sites. This means that the SEC's job of policing these Web sites will become increasingly difficult.

ONLINE DISCLOSURES

Virtually all major companies today have Web sites on which they post a variety of information, including forward-looking statements, press releases, and the like. If any of this information is misleading, a firm may face liability under securities

b. International Series Release #1125, March 23, 1998.

laws for violating the SEC's disclosure requirements.

For example, suppose that a company posts a press release on its Web site stating that its earnings for 2000 were $300 million and that the company expects to double those earnings in 2001. In June of 2001, the company learns that its 2000 earnings were, in fact, only $200 million and that the earnings could not possibly climb to $600 million in 2001. Further suppose that the company does not remove the former statement, which is now misleading, from its Web site. In this situation, the company would face potential liability for violating the disclosure requirements of the Securities Exchange Act of 1934.

A company also may face potential liability for misleading reports by securities analysts and magazine articles that are hyperlinked to the company's Web site. Even though the information may have been accurate when it was published, a viewer might reasonably rely on the information after it becomes outdated—and the company, by hyperlinking the materials to its Web page, could be held liable for violating SEC disclosure requirements.

IMPLICATIONS FOR THE BUSINESSPERSON

1. The message for businesspersons is clear. All forward-looking statements and other documents that investors

could reasonably rely on should be removed from Web sites after a reasonable time, such as three months.
2. Hyperlinked materials should also be examined frequently; if they become dated, the link should be deleted from the Web site.
3. Businesspersons should consider including disclaimers on their Web sites, indicating that certain information may be outdated.

FOR CRITICAL ANALYSIS

1. The SEC has initiated enforcement actions against issuers of securities, holding them responsible for false or misleading information disseminated online through third party analyst reports, even though the issuer did not participate in preparing the information. Is this fair?
2. Can fraudulent securities offerings via the Internet be policed effectively by the SEC?

RELEVANT WEB SITES

The SEC has issued an alert to help investors evaluate investments on the Internet at **http://www.sec.gov/consumer/cyberfr.htm**. A Web interface called EdgarScan allows users to locate key financial information on the SEC's EDGAR database and compare the information across companies. Go to **http://edgarscan.tc.pw.com**.

---

by government officials for acts beneficial to the state) to persons providing information leading to the prosecution of insider-trading violations.[32]

32. 15 U.S.C. Section 78u-1.

Private parties may also sue violators of Section 10(b) and Rule 10b-5. A private party may obtain rescission of a contract to buy securities or damages to the extent of the violator's illegal profits. Those found liable have a right to seek contribution from those who share responsibility for the violations, including accountants, attorneys, and corporations.[33] For violations of Section 16(b), a corporation can bring an action to recover the short-swing profits.

SECTION 5

Regulation of Investment Companies

Investment companies, and mutual funds in particular, grew rapidly after World War II. **Investment companies** act on behalf of many smaller shareholders/owners by buying a large portfolio of securities and managing that portfolio professionally. A **mutual fund** is a specific type of investment company that continually buys or sells to investors shares of ownership in a portfolio. Such companies are regulated by the Investment Company Act of 1940,[34] which provides for SEC regulation of their activities. The 1940 act was expanded by the Investment Company Act Amendments of 1970. Further minor changes were made in the Securities Acts Amendments of 1975. The National Securities Markets Improvement Act of 1996 increased the SEC's authority to regulate investment companies by limiting virtually all of the authority of the states to regulate these enterprises.

The 1940 act requires that every investment company register with the SEC and imposes restrictions on the activities of such companies and persons connected with them. For the purposes of the act, an investment company is defined as any entity that (1) "is . . . engaged primarily . . . in the business of investing, reinvesting, or trading in securities" or (2) is engaged in such business and more than 40 percent of the company's assets consist of investment securities. Excluded from coverage by the act are banks, insurance companies, savings and loan associations, finance companies, oil and gas drilling firms, charitable foundations, tax-exempt pension funds, and other special types of institutions, such as closely held corporations.

All investment companies must register with the SEC by filing a notification of registration. Each year, registered investment companies must file reports with the SEC. To safeguard company assets, all securities must be held in the custody of a bank or stock exchange member, and that bank or stock exchange member must follow strict procedures established by the SEC.

No dividends may be paid from any source other than accumulated, undistributed net income. Furthermore, there are some restrictions on investment activities. For example, investment companies are not allowed to purchase securities on the margin (pay only part of the total price, borrowing the rest), sell short (sell shares not yet owned), or participate in joint trading accounts.

SECTION 6

State Securities Laws

Today, all states have their own corporate securities laws, or **blue sky laws,** that regulate the offer and sale of securities within individual state borders. (The phrase *blue sky laws* dates to a 1917 United States Supreme Court decision in which the Court declared that the purpose of such laws was to prevent "speculative schemes which have no more basis than so many feet of 'blue sky.'"[35]) Article 8 of the Uniform Commercial Code, which has been adopted by all of the states, also imposes various requirements relating to the purchase and sale of securities. State securities laws apply only to intrastate transactions. Since the adoption of the 1933 and 1934 federal securities acts, the state and federal governments have regulated securities concurrently. Issuers must comply with both federal and state securities laws, and exemptions from federal law are not exemptions from state laws.

There are differences in philosophy among state statutes, but certain features are common to all state blue sky laws. Typically, state laws have disclosure requirements and antifraud provisions, many of which are patterned after Section 10(b) of the Securities Exchange Act of 1934 and SEC Rule 10b-5. State laws also provide for the registration or qualification of securities offered or issued for sale within the state and impose disclosure requirements. Unless an applicable exemption from registration is found, issuers must register or qualify their stock with the appropriate state official, often called a *corporations commissioner.* Additionally, most state securities laws regulate securities brokers and dealers. The Uniform Securities Act, which has been adopted in part by several states, was

---

33. Note that a private cause of action under Section 10(b) and SEC Rule 10b-5 cannot be brought against accountants, attorneys, and others who "aid and abet" violations of the act. Only the SEC can bring actions against so-called aiders and abettors. See *SEC v. Fehn*, 97 F.3d 1276 (9th Cir. 1996).

34. 15 U.S.C. Sections 80a-1 to 80a-64.

35. *Hall v. Geiger-Jones Co.*, 242 U.S. 539, 37 S.Ct. 217, 61 L.Ed. 480 (1917).

drafted to be acceptable to states with differing regulatory philosophies.

The dual federal and state system has not always worked well, particularly during the early 1990s, when there was considerable expansion of the securities markets. The National Securities Markets Improvement Act of 1996 eliminated some of the duplicate regulations. While the states still regulate local and regional matters, the SEC exclusively regulates most of the national securities activities.

TERMS AND CONCEPTS TO REVIEW

accredited investor 625	insider trading 628	SEC Rule 10b-5 628
blue sky law 638	investment company 638	securities 618
bond 618	mutual fund 638	stock 618
bounty payment 636	preferred stock 619	tippee 631
common stock 619	red herring 623	tombstone ad 623

QUESTIONS AND CASE PROBLEMS

29–1. REGISTRATION REQUIREMENTS. A corporation incorporated and doing business in Florida, Estrada Hermanos, Inc., decides to sell $1 million worth of its no-par-value common stock to the public. The stock will be sold only within the state of Florida. Jose Estrada, the chairman of the board, says the offering need not be registered with the Securities and Exchange Commission. His brother, Gustavo, disagrees. Who is right? Explain.

29–2. REGISTRATION REQUIREMENTS. Huron Corp. has 300,000 common shares outstanding. The owners of these outstanding shares live in several different states. Huron has decided to split the 300,000 shares two for one. Will Huron Corp. have to file a registration statement and prospectus on the 300,000 new shares to be issued as a result of the split? Explain.

29–3. SEC RULE 10b-5. Danny Cherif was employed by the First National Bank of Chicago in its International Financial Institutions Department from 1979 until 1987, when Cherif's position was eliminated because of an internal reorganization. Cherif, using a forged memo to the bank's security department, caused his magnetic identification (ID) card—which he had received as an employee to allow him to enter the bank building—to remain activated after his employment was terminated. Cherif used his ID card to enter the building at night to obtain confidential financial information from the bank's Specialized Finance Department regarding extraordinary business transactions, such as tender offers. During 1988 and 1989, Cherif made substantial profits through securities trading based on this information. Eventually, Cherif's activities were investigated by the Securities and Exchange Commission (SEC), and Cherif was charged with violating Section 10(b) and SEC Rule 10b-5 by misappropriating and trading on inside information in violation of his fiduciary duties to his former employer. Cherif argued that the SEC had wrongfully applied the misappropriation theory to his activities, because as a former employee, he no longer had a fiduciary duty to the bank. Explain whether Cherif is liable under SEC Rule 10b-5. [*SEC v. Cherif*, 933 F.2d 403 (7th Cir. 1991)]

29–4. SEC RULE 10b-5. Susan Waldbaum was a niece of the president and controlling shareholder of Waldbaum, Inc. Susan's mother (the president's sister) told Susan that the company was going to be sold at a favorable price and that a tender offer was soon to be made. She told Susan not to tell anyone except her husband, Keith Loeb, about the sale. The next day, Susan told her husband of the sale and cautioned him not to tell anyone, because "it could possibly ruin the sale." The day after he learned of the sale, Loeb called Robert Chestman, his broker, and told him that he "had some accurate information" that the company was about to be sold at a price "substantially higher" than the market value of its stock. That day, Chestman purchased shares of the company for himself, as well as for Loeb. Chestman was later convicted by a jury of, among other things, trading on misappropriated inside information in violation of SEC Rule 10b-5. On appeal, the central question in regard to liability under the misappropriation theory was whether Chestman had acquired the inside information about the Waldbaum company as a result of an insider's breach of a fiduciary duty. Essentially, the inquiry focused on whether Loeb owed a fiduciary duty to his wife's family or to his wife to keep the information confidential. How should the court rule? [*United States v. Chestman*, 947 F.2d 551 (2d Cir. 1991)]

29–5. INVESTOR PROTECTION. U.S. News & World Report, Inc., set up a profit-sharing plan in 1962 that allotted to certain employees specially issued stock known as bonus or anniversary stock. The stock was given to the employees for past services and could not be traded or sold to anyone other than the corporate issuer, U.S. News. This special stock was issued only to employees and for no other purpose than as bonuses. Because there was no market for the stock, U.S. News hired an independent appraiser to estimate the fair value of the stock so that the employees could redeem the shares. Charles Foltz and several other employees held stock through this plan and sought to redeem the shares with U.S. News, but Foltz disputed the value set by the appraisers. Foltz sued U.S. News for violation of securities regulations. What defense would allow U.S. News to resist Foltz's claim successfully? [*Foltz v. U.S. News & World Report, Inc.*, 627 F.Supp. 1143 (D.D.C. 1986)]

29–6. SEC RULE 10b-5. Louis Ferraro was the chairman and president of Anacomp, Inc. In June 1988, Ferraro told his good friend Michael Maio that Anacomp was negotiating a tender offer for stock in Xidex Corp. Maio passed on the information to Patricia Ladavac, a friend of both Ferraro and Maio. Maio and Ladavac immediately purchased shares in Xidex stock. On the day that the tender offer was announced—an announcement that caused the price of Xidex shares to increase—Maio and Ladavac sold their Xidex stock and made substantial profits (Maio made $211,000 from the transactions, and Ladavac gained $78,750). The SEC brought an action against the three individuals, alleging that they had violated, among other laws, SEC Rule 10b-5. Maio and Ladavac claimed that they had done nothing illegal. They argued that they had no fiduciary duty either to Anacomp or to Xidex, and therefore they had no duty to disclose or abstain from trading in the stock of those corporations. Had Maio and Ladavac violated SEC Rule 10b-5? Discuss fully. [*SEC v. Maio*, 51 F.3d 623 (7th Cir. 1995)]

29–7. SECTION 10(b). Joseph Jett worked for Kidder, Peabody & Co., a financial services firm owned by General Electric Co. (GE). Over a three-year period, Jett allegedly engaged in a scheme to generate false profits at Kidder, Peabody to increase his performance-based bonuses. When the scheme was discovered, Daniel Chill and other GE shareholders who had bought stock in the previous year filed a suit in a federal district court against GE. The shareholders alleged that GE had engaged in securities fraud in violation of Section 10(b). They claimed that GE's interest in justifying its investment in Kidder, Peabody gave GE "a motive to willfully blind itself to facts casting doubt on Kidder's purported profitability." On what basis might the court dismiss the shareholders' complaint? Discuss fully. [*Chill v. General Electric Co.*, 101 F.3d 263 (2d Cir. 1996)]

29–8. SEC RULE 10b-5. Grand Metropolitan PLC (Grand Met) planned to make a tender offer as part of an attempted takeover of the Pillsbury Company. Grand Met hired Robert Falbo, an independent contractor, to complete electrical work as part of security renovations to its offices to prevent leaks of information concerning the planned tender offer. Falbo was given a master key to access the executive offices. When an executive secretary told Falbo that a takeover was brewing, he used his key to access the offices and eavesdrop on conversations to learn that Pillsbury was the target. Falbo bought thousands of shares of Pillsbury stock for less than $40 per share. Within two months, Grand Met made an offer for all outstanding Pillsbury stock at $60 per share and ultimately paid up to $66 per share. Falbo made over $165,000 in profit. The Securities and Exchange Commission (SEC) filed a suit in a federal district court against Falbo and others for alleged violations of, among other things, SEC Rule 10b-5. Under what theory might Falbo be liable? Do the circumstances of this case meet all of the requirements for liability under that theory? Explain. [*SEC v. Falbo*, 14 F.Supp.2d 508 (S.D.N.Y. 1998)]

29–9. DEFINITION OF A SECURITY. In 1997, Scott and Sabrina Levine formed Friendly Power Co. (FPC) and Friendly Power Franchise Co. (FPC-Franchise). FPC obtained a license to operate as a utility company in California. FPC granted FPC-Franchise the right to pay commissions to "operators" who converted residential customers to FPC. Each operator paid for a "franchise"—a geographic area, determined by such factors as the number of households and competition from other utilities. In exchange for 50 percent of FPC's net profits on sales to residential customers in its territory, each franchise was required to maintain a 5 percent market share of power customers in that territory. Franchises were sold to telemarketing firms, which solicited customers. The telemarketers sold interests in each franchise to between fifty and ninety-four "partners," each of whom invested money. FPC began supplying electricity to its customers in May 1998. Less than three months later, the Securities and Exchange Commission (SEC) filed a suit in a federal district court against the Levines and others, alleging that the "franchises" were unregistered securities offered for sale to the public in violation of the Securities Act of 1933. What is the definition of a security? Should the court rule in favor of the SEC? Why or why not? [*SEC v. Friendly Power Co., LLC*, 49 F.Supp.2d 1363 (S.D.Fla. 1999)]

29–10. IN YOUR COURT

Emerson Electric Co. purchased 13.2 percent of Dodge Manufacturing Co.'s stock. Less than six months later, when Dodge merged with Reliance Electric Co., Emerson decided to sell its shares. To avoid being subject to the short-swing profit restrictions of Section 16(b) of the Securities Exchange Act of 1934, which pertain to any purchase and sale by any owner of 10 percent or more of a corporation's stock, Emerson decided on a two-step selling plan. First, it sold off sufficient shares to reduce its holdings to 9.96 percent, and then it sold the remaining stock—all within a six-month period. Reliance demanded that Emerson return the profits made on both sales. Emerson sought a declaratory judgment from the court that it was not liable, arguing that because at the time of the second sale it had not owned 10 percent of Dodge stock, Section 16 did not apply. Assume that you are the judge in the trial court hearing this case and answer the following questions:

    (a) Does Section 16(b) of the Securities Exchange Act of 1934 apply to Emerson's transactions? Is Emerson liable to Reliance for its profits? How will you rule on these issues? Why?

    (b) Does the court's opinion in Case 29.5 (*Medtox Scientific, Inc. v. Morgan Capital, L.L.C.*), which also involved an alleged violation of Section 16(b), shed any light on the issues now before your court? If so, in what way?

    (c) Should Emerson's deliberate attempt to avoid the restrictions of Section 16(b) influence your decision? Why or why not?

LAW ON THE WEB

For updated links to resources available on the Web, as well as a variety of other materials, visit this text's Web site at http://wleb.westbuslaw.com.

To access the SEC's EDGAR database, go to

http://www.sec.gov/edgarhp.htm

The Center for Corporate Law at the University of Cincinnati College of Law examines all of the acts discussed in this chapter. Go to

http://www.law.uc.edu/CCL

To find the Securities Act of 1933, go to

http://www.law.uc.edu/CCL/33Act/index.html

To examine the Securities Exchange Act of 1934, go to

http://www.law.uc.edu/CCL/34Act/index.html

For information on investor protection and securities fraud, including answers to frequently asked questions on the topic of securities fraud, go to

http://www.securitieslaw.com

LEGAL RESEARCH EXERCISES ON THE WEB

Go to http://wleb.westbuslaw.com, the Web site that accompanies this text. Select "Internet Applications," and then click on "Chapter 29." There you will find the following Internet research exercise that you can perform to learn more about the SEC:

Activity 29–1: The SEC's Role

UNIT FIVE—CUMULATIVE BUSINESS HYPOTHETICAL

Falwell Motors, Inc., is a large corporation that manufactures automobile batteries.

1. The Occupational Safety and Health Administration (OSHA) has proposed a new safety rule governing the handling of certain acids in the workplace, including those used by Falwell in its manufacturing operations. Falwell concludes that the rule, which will involve substantial compliance costs, will not significantly increase workplace safety. Falwell sends a letter to OSHA indicating its objections to the proposed rule and enclosing research reports and other data supporting those objections. Does OSHA have any obligation to consider these objections? What procedures must OSHA follow when it makes new rules, such as this one?

2. The Federal Trade Commission (FTC) learns that one of the retail stores that sells Falwell's batteries engages in deceptive advertising practices. What actions can the FTC take against the retailer?

3. For years, Falwell has shipped the toxic waste created by its manufacturing process to a waste-disposal site in the next county. The waste site has become contaminated by leakage from toxic waste containers delivered to the site by other manufacturers. Can Falwell be held liable for clean-up costs, even though its containers were not the ones that leaked? If so, what is the extent of its liability?

4. Falwell faces stiff competition from Alchem, Inc., another battery manufacturer. To acquire control over Alchem, Falwell makes a tender offer to Alchem's shareholders. If Falwell succeeds in its attempt and Alchem is merged into Falwell, will the merger violate any antitrust laws? Suppose the merger falls through. The vice president of Falwell's battery division and the president of Alchem agree to divide up the market between them, so they will not have to compete for customers. Is this agreement legal? Explain.

FOCUS ON LEGAL REASONING
California Dental Association
v. Federal Trade Commission

INTRODUCTION

The application of Section 5 of the Federal Trade Commission Act in the context of antitrust law is discussed in Chapter 27. In this *Focus on Legal Reasoning*, we examine *California Dental Association v. Federal Trade Commission*,[1] a decision by the United States Supreme Court concerning that statute. The case involved a trade association. Generally, the rule of reason is applied to assess the anticompetitive or procompetitive nature of such an association's activities when those activities are challenged under the antitrust laws, including sections of the Federal Trade Commision Act.

1. 526 U.S. 756, 119 S.Ct. 1604, 143 L.Ed.2d 935 (1999).

CASE BACKGROUND

The California Dental Association (CDA) is a nonprofit association of local dentists' organizations to which about 75 percent of California's dentists belong. The CDA provides preferential insurance arrangements and other benefits for its members, and engages in lobbying, litigation, marketing, and public relations on the members' behalf.

The CDA's members agree to abide by the association's Code of Ethics, which, among other things, prohibits false or misleading advertising. The CDA has issued interpretive advisory opinions and guidelines relating to advertising. These guidelines included restrictions on two types of truthful, nondeceptive advertising: price

advertising, particularly discounted fees, and advertising relating to the quality of dental services.

The Federal Trade Commission (FTC) filed a complaint with an administrative law judge (ALJ), alleging that the CDA violated Section 5 of the Federal Trade Commission Act in applying its guidelines to restrict the price and quality advertising. The ALJ found that the CDA violated Section 5. On appeal, the FTC upheld this finding, as did the U.S. Court of Appeals for the Ninth Circuit. The CDA appealed to the United States Supreme Court. One issue was the "sufficiency of the analysis of the anticompetitive effects" by the lower court.

MAJORITY OPINION

Justice *SOUTER* delivered the opinion of the Court.
* * * *

The case before us * * * fails to present a situation in which the likelihood of anticompetitive effects is * * * obvious. Even on [the] view that bars [prohibitions] on truthful and verifiable price and quality advertising are *prima facie* anticompetitive and place the burden of procompetitive justification on those who agree to adopt them, the very issue at the threshold of this case is whether professional price and quality advertising is sufficiently verifiable in theory and in fact to fall within such a general rule. * * * [I]t seems to us that the CDA's advertising restrictions might plausibly be thought to have a net procompetitive effect, or possibly no effect at all on competition. The restrictions on * * * advertising are, at least on their face, designed to avoid false or deceptive advertising in a market characterized by striking disparities between

the information available to the professional and the patient. In a market for professional services, in which advertising is relatively rare and the comparability of service packages not easily established, the difficulty for customers or potential competitors to get and verify information about the price and availability of services magnifies the dangers to competition associated with misleading advertising. What is more, the quality of professional services tends to resist either calibration or monitoring by individual patients or clients, partly because of the specialized knowledge required to evaluate the services, and partly because of the difficulty in determining whether, and the degree to which, an outcome is attributable to the quality of services (like a poor job of tooth-filling) or to something else (like a very tough walnut). Patients' attachments to particular professionals, the rationality of which is difficult to assess, complicate the picture even further. The existence of such significant challenges to informed decisionmaking by the customer for professional services immediately suggests that advertising restrictions arguably protecting patients from misleading or irrelevant advertising call for more than cursory treatment as obviously comparable to classic horizontal agreements to limit output or price competition.

* * * *

* * * Because the Court of Appeals did not scrutinize the assumption of relative anticompetitive tendencies, we vacate the judgment and remand the case for a fuller consideration of the issue.

DISSENTING OPINION

Justice *BREYER,* * * * dissenting * * * .

* * * *

In the Court's view, the legal analysis conducted by the Court of Appeals was insufficient, and the Court remands the case for a more thorough application of the rule of reason. But in what way did the Court of Appeals fail? * * *

* * * *

The upshot, in my view, is that the Court of Appeals, applying ordinary antitrust principles, reached an unexceptional conclusion. It is the same legal conclusion that this Court itself reached in *FTC v. Indiana Federation of Dentists,* 476 U.S. 447, 106 S.Ct. 2009, 90 L.Ed.2d 445 (1986)—a much closer case than this one. There the Court found that an agreement by dentists not to submit dental X rays to insurers violated the rule of reason. The anticompetitive tendency of that agreement was to reduce competition among dentists in respect to their willingness to submit X rays to insurers—a matter in respect to which consumers are relatively indifferent, as compared to advertising of price discounts and service quality, the matters at issue here. The redeeming virtue in *Indiana Federation* was the alleged undesirability of having insurers consider a range of matters when deciding whether treatment was justified—a virtue no less plausible, and no less proved, than the virtue offered here. The "power" of the dentists to enforce their agreement was no greater than that at issue here (control of 75% to 90% of the relevant markets). It is difficult to see how the two cases can be reconciled.

LEGAL REASONING AND ANALYSIS

1. Legal Reasoning. What reasons does the majority provide to justify its conclusion? How do those reasons contrast with the dissent's analysis? What seems to be the issue of contention in this case? With whom do you agree? Why?

2. Legal Analysis. The dissent cites, in its opinion, *Federal Trade Commission v. Indiana Federation of Dentists,* 476 U.S. 447, 106 S.Ct. 2009, 90 L.Ed.2d 445 (1986) (see the *Law on the Web* feature at the end of Chapter 2 for instructions on how to access federal court opinions). Do the facts and issues in that case compare to the facts and issues of the *California Dental* case? How do the holdings in the cases compare? Do the reasoning and the law of the *Indiana Federation* case support the position of the majority or the dissent in the *California Dental* case?

3. Economic Considerations. Under what circumstances might a court conclude that a trade association's restraint of trade is reasonable?

4. Implications for Associations. What do the reasoning and the outcome in this case suggest to those nonprofit associations that expect their members to follow the associations' marketing guidelines?

5. Case Briefing Assignment. Using the guidelines for briefing cases given in Appendix A of this text, brief the *Indiana Federation* case.

GOING ONLINE

Within the Web site of the Federal Trade Commission (FTC), the page at http://www.ftc.gov/ftc/antitrust.htm includes links to complaints, orders, and final actions by the FTC in the area of antitrust law.

The Regulatory Environment

If this text had been written a hundred years ago, it would have had little to say about federal government regulation. To be sure, by the 1890s, the beginnings of federal antitrust law had been manifested in the form of the Interstate Commerce Act and the Sherman Act, but there was little or no legislation designed to protect consumers or the environment. Today, in contrast, virtually every area of economic activity is regulated by the government.

From a very broad perspective, ethical issues in government regulation arise because regulation, by its very nature, means that some traditional rights and freedoms have to be given up to ensure that other rights and freedoms are protected. Essentially, government regulation brings two ethical principles into conflict. On the one hand, deeply embedded in American culture is the idea that the government should play a limited role in directing our lives. Indeed, this nation was founded so that Americans could be free from the "heavy hand of government" experienced by the colonists under English rule. On the other hand, one of the basic functions of government is to protect the welfare of individuals and the environment in which they live.

Ultimately, virtually every law or rule regulating business represents a decision to give up certain rights in order to protect other perceived rights. In this *Focus on Ethics,* we look at some of the ethical aspects of government regulation.

ENVIRONMENTAL LAW

Questions of fairness inevitably arise in regard to environmental law. Has the government gone too far in regulating businesses in the interest of protecting the environment? Has the government gone far enough? At what point do the costs of environmental regulations become too burdensome for society to bear? These are broad questions, but they are ethical in nature, because they ultimately relate to society's notions of what is right, just, or good.

If manufacturers ceased all production and Americans returned to the rural life of earlier times, the environment would certainly benefit. Obviously, Americans do not want to pay that high a cost. Certainly, we want to enjoy the fruits of our advanced economy, and economic productivity has always been a policy goal of the American government. But environmental protection means that some sacrifices will have to be made. How much are we willing to sacrifice today to ensure that future generations will continue to have a healthful world in which to live?

Economic Productivity versus Environmental Protection

This tension between the two goals of economic productivity and environmental protection was highlighted in a case brought by two Oregon ranchers—Brad Bennett and Mario Giordano—and two Oregon irrigation districts (collectively, the Bennett group) against the Fish and Wildlife Service (FWS) and the secretary of

the Department of the Interior. The case originated after the FWS proposed that the minimum water levels in two reservoirs be increased to protect two endangered species of fish. If the proposal were implemented, less water could be drawn from the reservoirs for irrigation and other purposes, which would have a serious economic impact on the ranchers' businesses.

In a citizens' suit against the FWS, the Bennett group claimed that the agency neglected to use the best available scientific and commercial data in making its decision, as required under the Endangered Species Act (ESA) of 1973; nor did the FWS take into account the economic impact of its water-level recommendations. At issue in the case, which ultimately reached the United States Supreme Court, was whether the ranchers had standing to sue under the ESA. The question was significant because the Bennett group was not seeking to protect the environment but to safeguard their economic interests.

Both a federal district court and a federal appellate court held that the group did not have standing to sue because its claim did not fall within the "zone of interests" watched over by the ESA, which was to protect species. The zone-of-interests test has long been applied by the federal courts in determining whether a party has standing to sue under a specific law. Basically, to have standing under this test, a plaintiff must show that the interest that he or she seeks to protect is the kind of interest protected by that specific law.

The Supreme Court, however, unanimously reversed the appellate court's decision. In applying the zone-of-interests test, the Court looked to the citizen-suit language of the ESA, which gives "any person" the right to sue. According to the Court, this language was expansive enough to include the economic interests of the Bennett group.

Moreover, the Court held that in determining whether a party has standing, the courts must look not to the overall purpose of an act but to the particular provision of an act on which the party based his or her complaint. In this case, the Bennett group alleged that the FWS failed to abide by a specific ESA provision that requires an agency to use the "best scientific and commercial data available." The Court noted that while this provision "no doubt serves to advance the ESA's overall goal of species preservation, we think it readily apparent that another objective (if not indeed the primary one) is to avoid needless economic dislocation produced by agency officials zealously but unintelligently pursuing their environmental objectives."[1]

Superfund and Toxic Waste

Although everybody is in favor of cleaning up America's toxic waste dumps, nobody has the slightest idea what this task will ultimately cost. Much of the problem in determining the eventual costs of the Superfund program (CERCLA—see Chapter 25) stems from the difficulty of estimating the costs of cleaning up a site. Until the clean-up is actually undertaken, it is often difficult to assess the extent of contamination. Moreover, there is no agreed-on standard as to how clean these sites need to be before they no

longer pose any threat of harm to life. Do you have to remove *all* of the contamination, or would removal of some lesser amount achieve a reasonable degree of environmental quality? On the cost side of the picture, another question exists: If, say, 90 percent of the waste at a given site could be removed for $50,000, but the removal of the other 10 percent would cost $2 million, is it reasonable to remove that remaining 10 percent?

Another aspect of Superfund that raises questions of fairness is the joint and several liability imposed by the act. This means that a party may be liable for the total costs of cleaning up a hazardous waste site, even though that party was responsible for only a small fraction of the toxic waste dumped at the site.

For some time, Congress has been under pressure to overhaul the Superfund legislation for these and other reasons. Proposed changes to the law would, among other things, allow the Environmental Protection Agency to consider what the land is likely to be used for in the future when determining how clean a site has to be. Another proposed change would eliminate joint and several liability at most sites and exempt certain small businesses from liability.

FAIR DEBT COLLECTION

By passing the Fair Debt Collection Practices Act (FDCPA), Congress expressed society's concern with unfair debt-collection practices. The act prohibits those that collect debts for other parties, such as collection agencies, from engaging in certain abusive tactics, as discussed in Chapter 24. Some have argued that the act did not go far enough in the direction of protecting consumer-debtors, because the act does not cover creditors that collect their own

debts rather than have a third party, such as a collection agency, do so.

Consider, for example, the situation in *Sterling Mirror of Maryland, Inc. v. Gordon.*[2] Sterling Mirror of Maryland, Inc., had installed mirrors in the home of John and Daisy Gordon. Only John signed the contract. Because one of the mirrors was chipped while it was being installed, John Gordon refused to pay the balance due to Sterling Mirror. Sterling Mirror tried to pressure the Gordons into paying for the mirrors by making numerous calls to Daisy at her place of employment. When Sterling Mirror sued the Gordons for the balance due, Daisy counterclaimed for damages under the FDCPA, asserting, among other things, that Sterling Mirror had violated the provisions of that act by contacting her at work. Had Sterling Mirror violated the FDCPA? No, it had not, because Sterling Mirror was not a collection agency, and thus the FDCPA did not apply. Had it been a collection agency, however, it would have violated the FDCPA, because under the act, collection agencies are allowed to contact only the debtor (not the debtor's spouse) at the debtor's place of employment, and then only if the employer does not object.

ANTITRUST LAW AND CONSUMER PROTECTION

From its beginnings in the nineteenth century, antitrust law has sought to maintain a freely competitive business environment so that consumers would not be victimized by monopoly pricing tactics. Consumer welfare has thus from the outset been a touchstone issue in antitrust cases. Sometimes, though, this aspect of antitrust law, which is rooted in ethical notions of fairness, becomes lost in the thicket

1. *Bennett v. Spear,* 520 U.S. 154, 117 S.Ct. 1154, 137 L.Ed.2d 281 (1997).

2. 619 A.2d 64 (D.C.App. 1993).

of antitrust lawsuits among competitors.

The Court of Appeals for the Eighth Circuit emphasized the importance of the consumer perspective in antitrust law in a case involving alleged predatory pricing. The case was brought by Gilbert Bathke and other gasoline retailers (the plaintiffs) located in small Iowa communities against Casey's General Stores, Inc. During the 1980s, Casey's, a multistate retailer of gasoline and other goods, had begun to lose profits to its competitors. In an attempt to increase its sales, Casey's had directed its stores that were losing sales to reduce gas prices. The plaintiffs claimed that Casey's price reductions amounted to predatory pricing in violation of, among other laws, Section 2 of the Sherman Act.

One of the central issues in the case concerned Casey's share of the relevant geographic market. The plaintiffs contended that the relevant geographic market consisted of the small towns in which Casey's operated its stores. After all, contended the plaintiffs, consumers preferred to buy their gasoline in the towns in which they lived, and gasoline retailers' trade came mostly from in-town customers. The court, however, stated that a geographic market is determined not by where consumers actually go for their gasoline but where they *could* go. Evidence of consumers' actual habits is not enough, said the court, to establish the relevant geographic market. To demonstrate the "logic and necessity of applying such a requirement in this case," the court illustrated the difference between a "trade area" and a "relevant market."

"Consider the following illustration," stated the court. "Fifteen miles outside of City A is a small town, Town B, which contains a single shoe store, Smith's Clothing. The only people who ever shop in Smith's Clothing are residents of Town B. When Smith's is accused of monopolization, the plaintiffs argue that Town B defines the relevant geographic market, since all of the store's customers come from there. In that case, Smith's market share is 100%. But further inquiry shows the following. Last year 800 residents of Town B purchased shoes. 400 of them purchased from Smith's Clothing, and the other 400 purchased from the numerous shoe stores in City A. Note that this conclusion is absolutely consistent with the proposition that Smith's 'trade area' is Town B. . . . In sum, 'trade area' considers the extent to which customers will travel in order to do business at Smith's. 'Relevant market' considers the extent to which customers will travel in order to avoid doing business at Smith's."

The court concluded that the plaintiffs' evidence, at best, demonstrated only the "trade area" of Casey's stores. The plaintiffs looked at the issue "only from the perspective of Casey's rivals, not from the perspective of the consumer. This is not the correct approach to use in antitrust cases."[3]

INSIDER TRADING

Only in the last few years have Americans seen rich, successful financiers end up in jail because of some violation of securities laws. One law prohibits the use of inside information to profit in the trading of shares of stock in the corporation from which the information was gleaned. Even a *tippee* (an outsider) can be liable for insider trading under securities law if the tippee's acquisition of inside information followed from an officer's or director's breach of his or her fiduciary duties. Tippees of tippees (remote tippees) can also be held liable if they knew, or should have known, that they were trading on improperly obtained insider information.

For example, in *SEC v. Musella,*[4] a manager of a law firm passed inside information about corporate mergers and acquisitions planned by the firm's clients to a friend and the friend's stockbroker. The stockbroker passed the information on to a third party. That third party then shared the information with his brother, a police officer. The police officer then recommended to two other police officers that they purchase certain securities. All parties involved, including the latter two police officers, profited substantially from their investments, and other tips and investments followed. Could the two police officers, who never were told (and never inquired about) the source of the information, be held liable for insider trading as remote tippees? Yes, according to the court. Their liability was founded not on the fact that they *knew* that they were trading on improperly acquired inside information but on the fact that they *should have known* that such was the case. The court held that the two police officers "did not ask because they did not want to know." The fact that they had consciously avoided knowledge about the source of the information did not mean that they were not guilty under laws prohibiting insider trading.

Outsiders trading on inside information are normally held liable for violating securities laws only if the trading is related to a breach of some duty. In *Chiarella v. United States,*[5] Chiarella was not held liable for trading on information obtained in the course of his work as a printer because the court held that no fiduciary duty had been breached. Yet, had the jury been

---

3. *Bathke v. Casey's General Stores, Inc.,* 64 F.3d 340 (8th Cir. 1995).

4. 678 F.Supp. 1060 (S.D.N.Y. 1988).
5. 445 U.S. 222, 100 S.Ct. 1108, 63 L.Ed.2d 348 (1980).

instructed to find liability under the misappropriation theory, Chiarella might well have been held liable for violating insider trading laws on the basis that he had violated a duty of loyalty to his employer. In a sense, the development of the misappropriation theory of liability has allowed courts to address more directly the simple ethical question: "Is such behavior right?"

EMINENT DOMAIN: PUBLIC GOOD VERSUS INDIVIDUAL RIGHTS

All law-abiding citizens accept government regulation, though sometimes begrudgingly. Usually we accept regulation because it is to our benefit to do so. For example, we willingly comply with the restriction that cars are to be driven on the right side of the road, and we expect the government to ensure that everyone else does as well. The benefit is that we have at least some assurance that a car will not be careening into us head-on just over the bend or around the next corner.

Other forms of regulation are not as uniformly beneficial, however. Most of us are glad that the government imposes some form of control over the quality of the food we eat. Food processors, though, confront higher costs because of it. Depending on supply and demand conditions in the food market, some or all of the additional costs may be passed on to consumers. In general, we accept these burdens because we believe that the greater good of the public is served by such regulation. But when the burdens of regulation are not distributed evenly over the population, how far does the sentiment for the greater public good carry us? The question is particularly difficult with regard to the "taking" of land through the government's power of eminent domain.

All cultures exhibit an attitude approaching reverence toward "the land." Not surprisingly, ownership of land is one of the most important issues governments face. Where, as in the United States, private ownership and reverence for land go hand in hand, the very idea of "taking" land is controversial. The aversion most feel toward such acts is mitigated by the requirement that the government justly compensate those who must forfeit land for the "public use." But the sentimental attachment often felt toward particular pieces of land—land on which stands the home to several generations of a family, for example—is seldom compensable. All such takings are made more acceptable by the condition that they be for the public good. But ethically, is it right to have a single individual incur the lion's share of the burden by having to give up his or her parcel of land for the greater good of all? Moreover, who can say without question precisely what the public's interests are and which are so important as to justify the taking of an individual's land?

Some years ago the United States Supreme Court confronted this issue in *Berman v. Parker.*[6] The District of Columbia condemned certain properties for the purpose of urban renewal in the affected area. Controversy arose because the land was subsequently reconveyed to private developers. How could private development of the land be a "public use" as required by the Constitution? The Court held that "use" meant purpose, not who would *physically* use or occupy the land. Moreover, the clearing of slums to make an area more attractive is a legitimate exercise of governmental police powers. Thus it is considered appropriate to take property

through eminent domain to carry out those powers and achieve the governmental purpose.

Under the Court's broad interpretation of the doctrine of eminent domain, land may be taken for purely commercial and industrial development and use. In the same vein, the Supreme Court of Michigan upheld the taking of property not in fact "blighted" by urban decay so that the land could be resold to General Motors which planned to erect a manufacturing plant on the land.[7] The purpose that sustained the taking was the creation of new jobs and creation of a tax base for the local government. It is in the nature of government that select individuals must define for the many what the public good is, what purposes should be pursued, and how they should be achieved. But given the wide latitude for discretion in exercising the power of eminent domain, the best safeguard against abuse in taking private property is that governments strive to act ethically even if they do not face strict legal constraints.

DISCUSSION QUESTIONS

1. In the discussion of Superfund in this *Focus on Ethics,* the following question was raised: "If, say, 90 percent of the waste at a given site could be removed for $50,000, but the removal of the other 10 percent would cost $2 million, is it reasonable to remove that remaining 10 percent?" How would you answer this question?
2. Both environmental and occupational safety laws strive to protect the public health from hazardous substances. Should standards in these two contexts be the same? Or should employees be allowed to voluntarily accept

---

6. 348 U.S. 26, 75 S.Ct. 98, 99 L.Ed. 57 (1954).

7. *Poletown Neighborhood Council v. City of Detroit,* 410 Mich. 617, 304 N.W.2d 455 (1981).

some greater risk in return for a higher wage scale?

3. Assume that removing all asbestos from all public buildings in the nation would save perhaps ten lives per year. If the cost of the asbestos removal were $250 billion, in effect, Americans would be paying $250 million per life saved. Is this too high a price to pay? Should cost ever be a consideration when human lives are at stake?

4. Creditors must comply strictly with the requirements of such consumer protection laws as the Truth-in-Lending Act, the Equal Credit Opportunity Act, and the Fair Debt Collection Practices Act. Even a minor, unintended violation may permit a consumer to sue a creditor for damages. In some cases, consumers have sought damages for violations when the creditor has abided by the "spirit" of the law but not the "letter." Should courts make exceptions when consumers are clearly abusing these protective laws for their own gain? Or should the courts hold creditors liable even when the result is unfair to the creditor?

APPENDICES

CONTENTS

APPENDIX A

Briefing Cases and Analyzing Case Problems

HOW TO BRIEF CASES

To fully understand the law with respect to business, you need to be able to read and understand court decisions. To make this task easier, you can use a method of case analysis that is called *briefing*. There is a fairly standard procedure that you can follow when you "brief" any court case. You must first read the case opinion carefully. When you feel you understand the case, you can prepare a brief of it.

Although the format of the brief may vary, typically it will present the essentials of the case under headings such as those listed below.

1. Citation. Give the full citation for the case, including the name of the case, the date it was decided, and the court that decided it.

2. Facts. Briefly indicate (a) the reasons for the lawsuit; (b) the identity and arguments of the plaintiff(s) and defendant(s), respectively; and (c) the lower court's decision—if appropriate.

3. Issue. Concisely phrase, in the form of a question, the essential issue before the court. (If more than one issue is involved, you may have two—or even more—questions here.)

4. Decision. Indicate here—with a "yes" or "no," if possible—the court's answer to the question (or questions) in the *Issue* section above.

5. Reason. Summarize as briefly as possible the reasons given by the court for its decision (or decisions) and the case

or statutory law relied on by the court in arriving at its decision.

BRIEFED SAMPLE COURT CASE

As an example of the format used in briefing cases, we present here a briefed version of the sample court case that was presented in the Appendix to Chapter 1 in Exhibit 1A–3.

FEDERAL EXPRESS CORP. v. FEDERAL ESPRESSO, INC.
United States Court of Appeals,
Second Circuit, 2000.
201 F.3d 168.

FACTS In 1997, Federal Express sued a small company called Federal Espresso and its owners, John Dobbs, Anna Dobbs, and David J. Ruston (collectively, the defendants). The defendants operated two coffee shops called Federal Espresso in Syracuse, New York. Federal Express asserted that the defendants, by using the name Federal Espresso, had infringed on its trademark and diluted the distinctive quality of its famous mark. Federal Express sought a preliminary injunction against the defendants' continued use of the Federal Espresso name for their business. The district court denied the motion, concluding that Federal Express had failed to demonstrate any likelihood of confusion between the two products and hence did not show that it was likely to succeed on the merits of those claims. Federal Express appealed.

ISSUE Was there a likelihood of confusion sufficient to allow Federal Express to succeed on the merits of its trademark claims, thus warranting a preliminary injunction?

DECISION No. The appellate court affirmed the lower court's decision.

REASON The appellate court stated that because coffee and overnight delivery service were dissimilar products, there would be little likelihood of confusion. The court also emphasized that while Federal Express is "a vast organization, operating in 210 countries, employing 140,000 persons, and grossing more than $11 billion annually," the defendants were merely three individuals who operated two stores in Syracuse, New York. Given the dissimilar products and the small extent of overlap among customers of Federal Express and Federal Espresso, Federal Express was unlikely to succeed on the merits of its trademark claims, and thus a preliminary injunction against Federal Espresso was not warranted.

REVIEW OF SAMPLE COURT CASE

Here we provide a review of the briefed version to indicate the kind of information that is contained in each section.

CITATION The name of the case is *Federal Express Corp. v. Federal Espresso, Inc.* The plaintiff is Federal Express Corp., and the defendant is Federal Espresso, Inc. The case was decided by the United States Court of Appeals for the Second Circuit in 2000. The citation indicates that the case can be found in Volume 201 of West's *Federal Reporter, Third Series,* on page 168.

FACTS The *Facts* section identifies the parties to the lawsuit—the plaintiff and the defendants—and describes the events leading up to the lawsuit and its appeal. Because this is an appeal to a federal appellate court—the United States Court of Appeals for the Second Circuit—the lower (district) court's opinion is included as part of the history of the case.

ISSUE The *Issue* section presents the central issue (or issues) to be decided by the court. In this case, the issue before the United States Court of Appeals for the Second Circuit is whether the trial court erred in refusing to grant Federal Express's motion for a preliminary injunction against Federal Espresso's continued use of its business name. Because this question turns on whether Federal Express had a cause of action for trademark infringement, including dilution, the real question on appeal was whether there was a likelihood of confusion between the products of the two companies sufficient to allow Federal Express to succeed on the merits of its trademark claims, thus warranting a preliminary injunction.

DECISION The *Decision* section, as the term indicates, contains the court's decision on the issue or issues before it. The decision reflects the opinion of the majority of the judges or justices hearing the case. Decisions by appellate courts are frequently phrased in reference to the lower court's decision. That is, the appellate court may "affirm" the lower court's decision or "reverse" it. In this particular case, the federal appellate court affirmed the lower (district) court's decision.

REASON The *Reason* section indicates what relevant laws and judicial principles were applied in forming the particular conclusion arrived at in the case at bar (before the court). In this case, the relevant law consisted of judicial principles that have been established over time to indicate when a "likelihood of confusion" between trademarks may exist.

HOW TO ANALYZE CASE PROBLEMS

In addition to learning how to brief cases, students of business law also find it helpful to know how to analyze case problems. Part of the study of business law usually involves analyzing case problems, such as those included in this text at the end of each chapter.

For each case problem in this book, we provide the relevant background and facts of the lawsuit and the issue before the court. When you are assigned one of these problems, your job will be to determine how the court should decide the issue and why. In other words, you will need to engage in legal analysis and reasoning. Here we offer some suggestions on how to make this task less daunting. We begin by presenting a sample problem:

> While Janet Lawson, a famous pianist, was shopping in Quality Market, she slipped and fell on a wet floor in one of the aisles. The floor had recently been mopped by one of the store's employees, but there were no signs warning customers that the floor in that area was wet. As a result of the fall, Lawson injured her right arm and was unable to perform piano concerts for the next six months. Had she been able to perform the scheduled concerts, she would have earned approximately $60,000 over that period of time. Lawson sued Quality Market for this amount, plus another $10,000 in medical expenses. She claimed that the store's failure to warn customers of the wet floor constituted negligence and therefore the market was liable for her injuries. Will the court agree with Lawson? Discuss.

UNDERSTAND THE FACTS

This may sound obvious, but before you can analyze or apply the relevant law to a specific set of facts, you must clearly understand those facts. In other words, you should read through the case problem carefully and more than once, if necessary, to make sure you understand the identity of the plaintiff(s) and defendant(s) in the case and the progression of events that led to the lawsuit.

In the sample case just given, the identity of the parties is fairly obvious. Janet Lawson is the one bringing the suit; therefore, she is the plaintiff. Quality Market, against whom she is bringing the suit, is the defendant. Some of the case problems you work on may have multiple plaintiffs or defendants. Often, it is helpful to use abbreviations for the parties. To indicate a reference to a plaintiff, for example, the pi symbol—π—is often used, and a defendant is denoted by a delta—Δ—a triangle.

The events leading to the lawsuit are also fairly straightforward. Lawson slipped and fell on a wet floor, and she contends that Quality Market should be liable for her injuries because it was negligent in not posting a sign warning customers of the wet floor.

When you are working on case problems, realize that the facts should be accepted as they are given. For example, in our sample problem, it should be accepted that the floor was wet and that there was no sign. In other words, avoid making conjectures, such as "Maybe the floor wasn't too wet," or "Maybe an employee was getting a sign to put up," or "Maybe someone stole the sign." Questioning the facts as they are presented only adds confusion to your analysis.

LEGAL ANALYSIS AND REASONING

Once you understand the facts given in the case problem, you can begin to analyze the case. Recall from Chapter 1 that the IRAC method is a helpful tool to use in the legal analysis and reasoning process. IRAC is an acronym for Issue, Rule, Application, Conclusion. Applying this method to our sample problem would involve the following steps:

1. First, you need to decide what legal **issue** is involved in the case. In our sample case, the basic issue is whether Quality Market's failure to warn customers of the wet floor constituted negligence. As discussed in Chapter 12, negligence is a *tort*—a civil wrong. In a tort lawsuit, the plaintiff seeks to be compensated for another's wrongful act. A defendant will be deemed negligent if he or she breached a duty of care owed to the plaintiff and the breach of that duty caused the plaintiff to suffer harm.

2. Once you have identified the issue, the next step is to determine what **rule of law** applies to the issue. To make this determination, you will want to review carefully the text of the chapter in which the problem appears to find the relevant rule of law. Our sample case involves the tort of negligence, covered in Chapter 12. The applicable rule of law is the tort law principle that business owners owe a duty to exercise reasonable care to protect their customers ("business invitees"). Reasonable care, in this context, includes either removing—or warning customers of—*foreseeable* risks about which the owner *knew* or *should have known*. Business owners need not warn customers of "open and obvious" risks, however. If a business owner breaches this duty of care (fails to exercise the appropriate degree of care toward customers), and the breach of duty causes a customer to be injured, the business owner will be liable to the customer for the customer's injuries.

3. The next—and usually the most difficult—step in analyzing case problems is the **application** of the relevant rule of law to the specific facts of the case you are studying. In our sample problem, applying the tort law principle just discussed presents few difficulties. An employee of the store had mopped the floor in the aisle where Lawson slipped and fell, but no sign was present indicating that the floor was wet. That a customer might fall on a wet floor is clearly a foreseeable risk. Therefore, the failure to warn customers about the wet floor was a breach of the duty of care owed by the business owner to the store's customers.

4. Once you have completed step 3 in the IRAC method, you should be ready to draw your **conclusion**. In our sample case, Quality Market is liable to Lawson for her injuries, because the market's breach of its duty of care caused Lawson's injuries.

The fact patterns in the case problems presented in this text are not always as simple as those presented in our sample problem. Often, for example, there may be more than one plaintiff or defendant. There also may be more than one issue involved in a case and more than one applicable rule of law. Furthermore, in some case problems the facts may indicate that the general rule of law should not apply. For example, suppose a store employee advised Lawson not to walk on the floor in the aisle because it was wet, but Lawson decided to walk on it anyway. This fact could alter the outcome of the case because the store could then raise the defense of assumption of risk (see Chapter 12). Nonetheless, a careful review of the chapter should always provide you with the knowledge you need to analyze the problem thoroughly and arrive at accurate conclusions.

The Constitution of the United States

PREAMBLE

We the People of the United States, in Order to form a more perfect Union, establish Justice, insure domestic Tranquility, provide for the common defence, promote the general Welfare, and secure the Blessings of Liberty to ourselves and our Posterity, do ordain and establish this Constitution for the United States of America.

ARTICLE I

Section 1. All legislative Powers herein granted shall be vested in a Congress of the United States, which shall consist of a Senate and House of Representatives.

Section 2. The House of Representatives shall be composed of Members chosen every second Year by the People of the several States, and the Electors in each State shall have the Qualifications requisite for Electors of the most numerous Branch of the State Legislature.

No Person shall be a Representative who shall not have attained to the Age of twenty five Years, and been seven Years a Citizen of the United States, and who shall not, when elected, be an Inhabitant of that State in which he shall be chosen.

Representatives and direct Taxes shall be apportioned among the several States which may be included within this Union, according to their respective Numbers, which shall be determined by adding to the whole Number of free Persons, including those bound to Service for a Term of Years, and excluding Indians not taxed, three fifths of all other Persons. The actual Enumeration shall be made within three Years after the first Meeting of the Congress of the United States, and within every subsequent Term of ten Years, in such Manner as they shall by Law direct. The Number of Representatives shall not exceed one for every thirty Thousand, but each State shall have at Least one Representative; and until such enumeration shall be made, the State of New Hampshire shall be entitled to chuse three, Massachusetts eight, Rhode Island and Providence Plantations one, Connecticut five, New York six, New Jersey four, Pennsylvania eight, Delaware one, Maryland six, Virginia ten, North Carolina five, South Carolina five, and Georgia three.

When vacancies happen in the Representation from any State, the Executive Authority thereof shall issue Writs of Election to fill such Vacancies.

The House of Representatives shall chuse their Speaker and other Officers; and shall have the sole Power of Impeachment.

Section 3. The Senate of the United States shall be composed of two Senators from each State, chosen by the Legislature thereof, for six Years; and each Senator shall have one Vote.

Immediately after they shall be assembled in Consequence of the first Election, they shall be divided as equally as may be into three Classes. The Seats of the Senators of the first Class shall be vacated at the Expiration of the second Year, of the second Class at the

Expiration of the fourth Year, and of the third Class at the Expiration of the sixth Year, so that one third may be chosen every second Year; and if Vacancies happen by Resignation, or otherwise, during the Recess of the Legislature of any State, the Executive thereof may make temporary Appointments until the next Meeting of the Legislature, which shall then fill such Vacancies.

No Person shall be a Senator who shall not have attained to the Age of thirty Years, and been nine Years a Citizen of the United States, and who shall not, when elected, be an Inhabitant of that State for which he shall be chosen.

The Vice President of the United States shall be President of the Senate, but shall have no Vote, unless they be equally divided.

The Senate shall chuse their other Officers, and also a President pro tempore, in the Absence of the Vice President, or when he shall exercise the Office of President of the United States.

The Senate shall have the sole Power to try all Impeachments. When sitting for that Purpose, they shall be on Oath or Affirmation. When the President of the United States is tried, the Chief Justice shall preside: And no Person shall be convicted without the Concurrence of two thirds of the Members present.

Judgment in Cases of Impeachment shall not extend further than to removal from Office, and disqualification to hold and enjoy any Office of honor, Trust, or Profit under the United States: but the Party convicted shall nevertheless be liable and subject to Indictment, Trial, Judgment, and Punishment, according to Law.

Section 4. The Times, Places and Manner of holding Elections for Senators and Representatives, shall be prescribed in each State by the Legislature thereof; but the Congress may at any time by Law make or alter such Regulations, except as to the Places of chusing Senators.

The Congress shall assemble at least once in every Year, and such Meeting shall be on the first Monday in December, unless they shall by Law appoint a different Day.

Section 5. Each House shall be the Judge of the Elections, Returns, and Qualifications of its own Members, and a Majority of each shall constitute a Quorum to do Business; but a smaller Number may adjourn from day to day, and may be authorized to compel the Attendance of absent Members, in such Manner, and under such Penalties as each House may provide.

Each House may determine the Rules of its Proceedings, punish its Members for disorderly Behavior, and, with the Concurrence of two thirds, expel a Member.

Each House shall keep a Journal of its Proceedings, and from time to time publish the same, excepting such Parts as may in their Judgment require Secrecy; and the Yeas and Nays of the Members of either House on any question shall, at the Desire of one fifth of those Present, be entered on the Journal.

Neither House, during the Session of Congress, shall, without the Consent of the other, adjourn for more than three days, nor to any other Place than that in which the two Houses shall be sitting.

Section 6. The Senators and Representatives shall receive a Compensation for their Services, to be ascertained by Law, and paid out of the Treasury of the United States. They shall in all Cases, except Treason, Felony and Breach of the Peace, be privileged from Arrest during their Attendance at the Session of their respective Houses, and in going to and returning from the same; and for any Speech or Debate in either House, they shall not be questioned in any other Place.

No Senator or Representative shall, during the Time for which he was elected, be appointed to any civil Office under the Authority of the United States, which shall have been created, or the Emoluments whereof shall have been increased during such time; and no Person holding any Office under the United States, shall be a Member of either House during his Continuance in Office.

Section 7. All Bills for raising Revenue shall originate in the House of Representatives; but the Senate may propose or concur with Amendments as on other Bills.

Every Bill which shall have passed the House of Representatives and the Senate, shall, before it become a Law, be presented to the President of the United States; If he approve he shall sign it, but if not he shall return it, with his Objections to the House in which it shall have originated, who shall enter the Objections at large on their Journal, and proceed to reconsider it. If after such Reconsideration two thirds of that House shall agree to pass the Bill, it shall be sent together with the Objections, to the other House, by which it shall likewise be reconsidered, and if approved by two thirds of that House, it shall become a Law. But in all such Cases the Votes of both Houses shall be determined by Yeas and Nays, and the Names of the Persons voting for and against the Bill shall be entered on the Journal of each House respectively. If any Bill shall not be returned by the President within ten Days (Sundays excepted) after it shall have been presented to him, the Same shall be a Law, in like Manner as if he had signed it, unless the Congress by their Adjournment prevent its Return in which Case it shall not be a Law.

Every Order, Resolution, or Vote, to which the Concurrence of the Senate and House of Representatives may be necessary (except on a question of Adjournment) shall be presented to the President of the United States; and before the Same shall take Effect, shall be approved by him, or being disapproved by him, shall be repassed by two thirds of the Senate and House of Representatives, according to the Rules and Limitations prescribed in the Case of a Bill.

Section 8. The Congress shall have Power To lay and collect Taxes, Duties, Imposts and Excises, to pay the Debts and provide for the common Defence and general Welfare of the United States; but all Duties, Imposts and Excises shall be uniform throughout the United States;

To borrow Money on the credit of the United States;

To regulate Commerce with foreign Nations, and among the several States, and with the Indian Tribes;

To establish an uniform Rule of Naturalization, and uniform Laws on the subject of Bankruptcies throughout the United States;

To coin Money, regulate the Value thereof, and of foreign Coin, and fix the Standard of Weights and Measures;

To provide for the Punishment of counterfeiting the Securities and current Coin of the United States;

To establish Post Offices and post Roads;

To promote the Progress of Science and useful Arts, by securing for limited Times to Authors and Inventors the exclusive Right to their respective Writings and Discoveries;

To constitute Tribunals inferior to the supreme Court;

To define and punish Piracies and Felonies committed on the high Seas, and Offenses against the Law of Nations;

To declare War, grant Letters of Marque and Reprisal, and make Rules concerning Captures on Land and Water;

To raise and support Armies, but no Appropriation of Money to that Use shall be for a longer Term than two Years;

To provide and maintain a Navy;

To make Rules for the Government and Regulation of the land and naval Forces;

To provide for calling forth the Militia to execute the Laws of the Union, suppress Insurrections and repel Invasions;

To provide for organizing, arming, and disciplining, the Militia, and for governing such Part of them as may be employed in the Service of the United States, reserving to the States respectively, the Appointment of the Officers, and the Authority of training the Militia according to the discipline prescribed by Congress;

To exercise exclusive Legislation in all Cases whatsoever, over such District (not exceeding ten Miles square) as may, by Cession of particular States, and the Acceptance of Congress, become the Seat of the Government of the United States, and to exercise like Authority over all Places purchased by the Consent of the Legislature of the State in which the Same shall be, for the Erection of Forts, Magazines, Arsenals, dock-Yards, and other needful Buildings;—And

To make all Laws which shall be necessary and proper for carrying into Execution the foregoing Powers, and all other Powers vested by this Constitution in the Government of the United States, or in any Department or Officer thereof.

Section 9. The Migration or Importation of such Persons as any of the States now existing shall think proper to admit, shall not be prohibited by the Congress prior to the Year one thousand eight hundred and eight, but a Tax or duty may be imposed on such Importation, not exceeding ten dollars for each Person.

The privilege of the Writ of Habeas Corpus shall not be suspended, unless when in Cases of Rebellion or Invasion the public Safety may require it.

No Bill of Attainder or ex post facto Law shall be passed.

No Capitation, or other direct, Tax shall be laid, unless in Proportion to the Census or Enumeration herein before directed to be taken.

No Tax or Duty shall be laid on Articles exported from any State.

No Preference shall be given by any Regulation of Commerce or Revenue to the Ports of one State over those of another: nor shall Vessels bound to, or from, one State be obliged to enter, clear, or pay Duties in another.

No Money shall be drawn from the Treasury, but in Consequence of Appropriations made by Law; and a regular Statement and Account of the Receipts and Expenditures of all public Money shall be published from time to time.

No Title of Nobility shall be granted by the United States: And no Person holding any Office of Profit or Trust under them, shall, without the Consent of the Congress, accept of any present, Emolument, Office, or Title, of any kind whatever, from any King, Prince, or foreign State.

Section 10. No State shall enter into any Treaty, Alliance, or Confederation; grant Letters of Marque and Reprisal; coin Money; emit Bills of Credit; make any Thing but gold and silver Coin a Tender in Payment of Debts; pass any Bill of Attainder, ex post facto Law, or Law impairing the Obligation of Contracts, or grant any Title of Nobility.

No State shall, without the Consent of the Congress, lay any Imposts or Duties on Imports or Exports, except what may be absolutely necessary for executing its inspection Laws: and the net Produce of all Duties and Imposts, laid by any State on Imports or Exports, shall be for the Use of the Treasury of the United States; and all such Laws shall be subject to the Revision and Controul of the Congress.

No State shall, without the Consent of Congress, lay any Duty of Tonnage, keep Troops, or Ships of War in time of Peace, enter into any Agreement or Compact with another State, or with a foreign Power, or engage in War, unless actually invaded, or in such imminent Danger as will not admit of delay.

ARTICLE II

Section 1. The executive Power shall be vested in a President of the United States of America. He shall hold his Office during the Term of four Years, and, together with the Vice President, chosen for the same Term, be elected, as follows:

Each State shall appoint, in such Manner as the Legislature thereof may direct, a Number of Electors, equal to the whole Number of Senators and Representatives to which the State may be entitled in the Congress; but no Senator or Representative, or Person holding an Office of Trust or Profit under the United States, shall be appointed an Elector.

The Electors shall meet in their respective States, and vote by Ballot for two Persons, of whom one at least shall not be an Inhabitant of the same State with themselves. And they shall make a List of all the Persons voted for, and of the Number of Votes for each; which List they shall sign and certify, and transmit sealed to the Seat of the Government of the United States, directed to the President of the Senate. The President of the Senate shall, in the Presence of the Senate and House of Representatives, open all the Certificates, and the Votes shall then be counted. The Person having the greatest Number of Votes shall be the President, if such Number be a Majority of the whole Number of Electors appointed; and if there be more than one who have such Majority, and have an equal Number of Votes, then the House of Representatives shall immediately chuse by Ballot one of them for President; and if no Person have a Majority, then from the five highest on the List the said House shall in like Manner chuse the President. But in chusing the President, the Votes shall be taken by States, the Representation from each State having one Vote; A quorum for this Purpose shall consist of a Member or Members from two thirds of the States, and a Majority of all the States shall be necessary to a Choice. In every Case, after the Choice of the President, the Person having the greater Number of Votes of the Electors shall be the Vice President. But if there should remain two or more who have equal Votes, the Senate shall chuse from them by Ballot the Vice President.

The Congress may determine the Time of chusing the Electors, and the Day on which they shall give their Votes; which Day shall be the same throughout the United States.

No person except a natural born Citizen, or a Citizen of the United States, at the time of the Adoption of this Constitution, shall be eligible to the Office of President; neither shall any Person be eligible to that Office who shall not have attained to the Age of thirty five Years, and been fourteen Years a Resident within the United States.

In Case of the Removal of the President from Office, or of his Death, Resignation or Inability to discharge the Powers and Duties of the said Office, the same shall devolve on the Vice President, and the Congress may by Law provide for the Case of Removal, Death, Resignation or Inability, both of the President and Vice President, declaring what Officer shall then act as President, and such Officer shall act accordingly, until the Disability be removed, or a President shall be elected.

The President shall, at stated Times, receive for his Services, a Compensation, which shall neither be increased nor diminished during the Period for which he shall have been elected, and he shall not receive within that Period any other Emolument from the United States, or any of them.

Before he enter on the Execution of his Office, he shall take the following Oath or Affirmation: "I do solemnly swear (or affirm) that I will faithfully execute the Office of President of the United States, and will to the best of my Ability, preserve, protect and defend the Constitution of the United States."

Section 2. The President shall be Commander in Chief of the Army and Navy of the United States, and of the Militia of the several States, when called into the actual Service of the United States; he may require the Opinion, in writing, of the principal Officer in each of the executive Departments, upon any Subject relating to the Duties of their respective Offices, and he shall have Power to grant Reprieves and Pardons for Offenses against the United States, except in Cases of Impeachment.

He shall have Power, by and with the Advice and Consent of the Senate to make Treaties, provided two thirds of the Senators present concur; and he shall nominate, and by and with the Advice and Consent of the Senate, shall appoint Ambassadors, other public Ministers and Consuls, Judges of the supreme Court, and all other Officers of the United States, whose Appointments are not herein otherwise provided for, and which shall be established by Law; but the Congress may by Law vest the Appointment of such inferior Officers, as they think proper, in the President alone, in the Courts of Law, or in the Heads of Departments.

The President shall have Power to fill up all Vacancies that may happen during the Recess of the Senate, by granting Commissions which shall expire at the End of their next Session.

Section 3. He shall from time to time give to the Congress Information of the State of the Union, and recommend to their Consideration such Measures as he shall judge necessary and expedient; he may, on extraordinary Occasions, convene both Houses, or either of them, and in Case of Disagreement between them, with Respect to the Time of Adjournment, he may adjourn them to such Time as he shall think proper; he shall receive Ambassadors and other public Ministers; he shall take Care that the Laws be faithfully executed, and shall Commission all the Officers of the United States.

Section 4. The President, Vice President and all civil Officers of the United States, shall be removed from Office on Impeachment for, and Conviction of, Treason, Bribery, or other high Crimes and Misdemeanors.

ARTICLE III

Section 1. The judicial Power of the United States, shall be vested in one supreme Court, and in such inferior Courts as the Congress may from time to time ordain and establish. The Judges, both of the supreme and inferior Courts, shall hold their Offices during good Behaviour, and shall, at stated Times, receive for their Services a Compensation, which shall not be diminished during their Continuance in Office.

Section 2. The judicial Power shall extend to all Cases, in Law and Equity, arising under this Constitution, the Laws of the United States, and Treaties made, or which shall be made, under their Authority;—to all Cases affecting Ambassadors, other public Ministers and Consuls;—to all Cases of admiralty and maritime Jurisdiction;—to Controversies to which the United States shall be a Party;—to Controversies between two or more States;—between a State and Citizens of another State;—between Citizens of different States;—between Citizens of the same State claiming Lands under Grants of different States, and between a State, or the Citizens thereof, and foreign States, Citizens or Subjects.

In all Cases affecting Ambassadors, other public Ministers and Consuls, and those in which a State shall be a Party, the supreme Court shall have original Jurisdiction. In all the other Cases before mentioned, the supreme Court shall have appellate Jurisdiction, both as to Law and Fact, with such Exceptions, and under such Regulations as the Congress shall make.

The Trial of all Crimes, except in Cases of Impeachment, shall be by Jury; and such Trial shall be held in the State where the said Crimes shall have been committed; but when not committed within any State, the Trial shall be at such Place or Places as the Congress may by Law have directed.

Section 3. Treason against the United States, shall consist only in levying War against them, or, in adhering to their Enemies, giving them Aid and Comfort. No Person shall be convicted of Treason unless on the Testimony of two Witnesses to the same overt Act, or on Confession in open Court.

The Congress shall have Power to declare the Punishment of Treason, but no Attainder of Treason shall work Corruption of Blood, or Forfeiture except during the Life of the Person attainted.

ARTICLE IV

Section 1. Full Faith and Credit shall be given in each State to the public Acts, Records, and judicial Proceedings of every other State. And the Congress may by general Laws prescribe the Manner in which such Acts, Records and Proceedings shall be proved, and the Effect thereof.

Section 2. The Citizens of each State shall be entitled to all Privileges and Immunities of Citizens in the several States.

A Person charged in any State with Treason, Felony, or other Crime, who shall flee from Justice, and be found in another State, shall on Demand of the executive Authority of the State from which he fled, be delivered up, to be removed to the State having Jurisdiction of the Crime.

No Person held to Service or Labour in one State, under the Laws thereof, escaping into another, shall, in Consequence of any Law or Regulation therein, be discharged from such Service or Labour, but shall be delivered up on Claim of the Party to whom such Service or Labour may be due.

Section 3. New States may be admitted by the Congress into this Union; but no new State shall be formed or erected within the Jurisdiction of any other State; nor any State be formed by the Junction of two or more States, or Parts of States, without the Consent of the Legislatures of the States concerned as well as of the Congress.

The Congress shall have Power to dispose of and make all needful Rules and Regulations respecting the Territory or other Property belonging to the United States; and nothing in this Constitution shall be so construed as to Prejudice any Claims of the United States, or of any particular State.

Section 4. The United States shall guarantee to every State in this Union a Republican Form of Government, and shall protect each of them against Invasion; and on Application of the Legislature, or of the Executive (when the Legislature cannot be convened) against domestic Violence.

ARTICLE V

The Congress, whenever two thirds of both Houses shall deem it necessary, shall propose Amendments to this Constitution, or, on the Application of the Legislatures of two thirds of the several States, shall call a Convention for proposing Amendments, which, in either Case, shall be valid to all Intents and Purposes, as part of this Constitution, when ratified by the Legislatures of three fourths of the several States, or by Conventions in three fourths thereof, as the one or the other Mode of Ratification may be proposed by the Congress; Provided that no Amendment which may be made prior to the Year One thousand eight hundred and eight shall in any Manner affect the first and fourth Clauses in the Ninth Section of the first Article; and that no State, without its Consent, shall be deprived of its equal Suffrage in the Senate.

ARTICLE VI

All Debts contracted and Engagements entered into, before the Adoption of this Constitution shall be as valid against the United States under this Constitution, as under the Confederation.

This Constitution, and the Laws of the United States which shall be made in Pursuance thereof; and all Treaties made, or which shall be made, under the Authority of the United States, shall be the supreme Law of the Land; and the Judges in every State shall be bound thereby, any Thing in the Constitution or Laws of any State to the Contrary notwithstanding.

The Senators and Representatives before mentioned, and the Members of the several State Legislatures, and all executive and judicial Officers, both of the United States and of the several States, shall be bound by Oath or Affirmation, to support this Constitution; but no religious Test shall ever be required as a Qualification to any Office or public Trust under the United States.

ARTICLE VII

The Ratification of the Conventions of nine States shall be sufficient for the Establishment of this Constitution between the States so ratifying the Same.

AMENDMENT I [1791]

Congress shall make no law respecting an establishment of religion, or prohibiting the free exercise thereof; or abridging the freedom of speech, or of the press; or the right of the people peaceably to assembly, and to petition the Government for a redress of grievances.

AMENDMENT II [1791]

A well regulated Militia, being necessary to the security of a free State, the right of the people to keep and bear Arms, shall not be infringed.

AMENDMENT III [1791]

No Soldier shall, in time of peace be quartered in any house, without the consent of the Owner, nor in time of war, but in a manner to be prescribed by law.

AMENDMENT IV [1791]

The right of the people to be secure in their persons, houses, papers, and effects, against unreasonable searches and seizures, shall not be violated, and no Warrants shall issue, but upon probable cause, supported by Oath or affirmation, and particularly describing the place to be searched, and the persons or things to be seized.

AMENDMENT V [1791]

No person shall be held to answer for a capital, or otherwise infamous crime, unless on a presentment or indictment of a Grand Jury, except in cases arising in the land or naval forces, or in the Militia, when in actual service in time of War or public danger; nor shall any person be subject for the same offence to be twice put in jeopardy of life or limb; nor shall be compelled in any criminal case to be a witness against himself, nor be deprived of life, liberty, or property, without due process of law; nor shall private property be taken for public use, without just compensation.

AMENDMENT VI [1791]

In all criminal prosecutions, the accused shall enjoy the right to a speedy and public trial, by an impartial jury of the State and district wherein the crime shall have been committed, which district shall have been previously ascertained by law, and to be informed of the nature and cause of the accusation; to be confronted with the witnesses against him; to have compulsory process for obtaining witnesses in his favor, and to have the Assistance of Counsel for his defence.

AMENDMENT VII [1791]

In Suits at common law, where the value in controversy shall exceed twenty dollars, the right of trial by jury shall be preserved, and no fact tried by jury, shall be otherwise re-examined in any Court of the United States, than according to the rules of the common law.

AMENDMENT VIII [1791]

Excessive bail shall not be required, nor excessive fines imposed, nor cruel and unusual punishments inflicted.

AMENDMENT IX [1791]

The enumeration in the Constitution, of certain rights, shall not be construed to deny or disparage others retained by the people.

AMENDMENT X [1791]

The powers not delegated to the United States by the Constitution, nor prohibited by it to the States, are reserved to the States respectively, or to the people.

AMENDMENT XI [1798]

The Judicial power of the United States shall not be construed to extend to any suit in law or equity, commenced or prosecuted against one of the United States by Citizens of another State, or by Citizens or Subjects of any Foreign State.

AMENDMENT XII [1804]

The Electors shall meet in their respective states, and vote by ballot for President and Vice-President, one of whom, at least, shall not be an inhabitant of the same state with themselves; they shall name in their ballots the person voted for as President, and in distinct ballots the person voted for as Vice-President, and they shall make distinct lists of all persons voted for as President, and of all persons voted for as Vice-President, and of the number of votes for each, which lists they shall sign and certify, and transmit sealed to the seat of the government of the United States, directed to the President of the Senate;—The President of the Senate shall, in the presence of the Senate and House of Representatives, open all the certificates and the votes shall then be counted;—The person having the greatest number of votes for President, shall be the President, if such number be a majority of the whole number of Electors appointed; and if no person have such majority, then from the persons having the highest numbers not exceeding three on the list of those voted for as President, the House of Representatives shall choose immediately, by ballot, the President. But in choosing the President, the votes shall be taken by states, the representation from each state having one vote; a quorum for this purpose shall consist of a member or members from two-thirds of the states, and a majority of all states shall be necessary to a choice. And if the House of Representatives shall not choose a President whenever the right of choice shall devolve upon them, before the fourth day of March next following, then the Vice-President shall act as President, as in the case of the death or other constitutional disability of the President.—The person having the greatest number of votes as Vice-President, shall be the Vice-President, if such number be a majority of the whole number of Electors appointed, and if no person have a majority, then from the two highest numbers on the list, the Senate shall choose the Vice-President; a quorum for the purpose shall consist of two-thirds of the whole number of Senators, and a majority of the whole number shall be necessary to a choice. But no person constitutionally ineligible to the office of President shall be eligible to that of Vice-President of the United States.

AMENDMENT XIII [1865]

Section 1. Neither slavery nor involuntary servitude, except as a punishment for crime whereof the party shall have been duly convicted, shall exist within the United States, or any place subject to their jurisdiction.

Section 2. Congress shall have power to enforce this article by appropriate legislation.

AMENDMENT XIV [1868]

Section 1. All persons born or naturalized in the United States, and subject to the jurisdiction thereof, are citizens of the United States and of the State wherein they reside. No State shall make or enforce any law which shall abridge the privileges or immunities of citizens of the United States; nor shall any State deprive any person of life, liberty, or property, without due process of law; nor deny to any person within its jurisdiction the equal protection of the laws.

Section 2. Representatives shall be apportioned among the several States according to their respective numbers, counting the whole number of persons in each State, excluding Indians not taxed. But when the right to vote at any election for the choice of electors for President and Vice President of the United States, Representatives in Congress, the Executive and Judicial officers of a State, or the members of the Legislature thereof, is denied to any of the male inhabitants of such State, being twenty-one years of age, and citizens of the United States, or in any way abridged, except for participation in rebellion, or other crime, the basis of representation therein shall be reduced in the proportion which the number of such male citizens shall bear to the whole number of male citizens twenty-one years of age in such State.

Section 3. No person shall be a Senator or Representative in Congress, or elector of President and Vice President, or hold any office, civil or military, under the United States, or under any State, who having previously taken an oath, as a member of Congress, or as an officer of the United States, or as a member of any State legislature, or as an executive or judicial officer of any State, to support the Constitution of the United States, shall have engaged in insurrection or rebellion against the same, or given aid or comfort to the enemies thereof. But Congress may by a vote of two-thirds of each House, remove such disability.

Section 4. The validity of the public debt of the United States, authorized by law, including debts incurred for payment of pensions and bounties for services in suppressing insurrection or rebellion, shall not be questioned. But neither the United States nor any State shall assume or pay any debt or obligation incurred in aid of insurrection or rebellion against the United States, or any claim for the loss or emancipation of any slave; but all such debts, obligations and claims shall be held illegal and void.

Section 5. The Congress shall have power to enforce, by appropriate legislation, the provisions of this article.

AMENDMENT XV [1870]

Section 1. The right of citizens of the United States to vote shall not be denied or abridged by the United States or by any State on account of race, color, or previous condition of servitude.

Section 2. The Congress shall have power to enforce this article by appropriate legislation.

AMENDMENT XVI [1913]

The Congress shall have power to lay and collect taxes on incomes, from whatever source derived, without apportionment among the several States, and without regard to any census or enumeration.

AMENDMENT XVII [1913]

Section 1. The Senate of the United States shall be composed of two Senators from each State, elected by the people thereof, for six years; and each Senator shall have one vote. The electors in each State shall have the qualifications requisite for electors of the most numerous branch of the State legislatures.

Section 2. When vacancies happen in the representation of any State in the Senate, the executive authority of such State shall issue writs of election to fill such vacancies: *Provided,* That the legislature of any State may empower the executive thereof to make temporary appointments until the people fill the vacancies by election as the legislature may direct.

Section 3. This amendment shall not be so construed as to affect the election or term of any Senator chosen before it becomes valid as part of the Constitution.

AMENDMENT XVIII [1919]

Section 1. After one year from the ratification of this article the manufacture, sale, or transportation of intoxicating liquors within, the importation thereof into, or the exportation thereof from the United States and all territory subject to the jurisdiction thereof for beverage purposes is hereby prohibited.

Section 2. The Congress and the several States shall have concurrent power to enforce this article by appropriate legislation.

Section 3. This article shall be inoperative unless it shall have been ratified as an amendment to the Constitution by the legislatures of the several States, as provided in the Constitution, within seven years from the date of the submission hereof to the States by the Congress.

AMENDMENT XIX [1920]

Section 1. The right of citizens of the United States to vote shall not be denied or abridged by the United States or by any State on account of sex.

Section 2. Congress shall have power to enforce this article by appropriate legislation.

AMENDMENT XX [1933]

Section 1. The terms of the President and Vice President shall end at noon on the 20th day of January, and the terms of Senators and Representatives at noon on the 3d day of January, of the years in which such terms would have ended if this article had not been ratified; and the terms of their successors shall then begin.

Section 2. The Congress shall assemble at least once in every year, and such meeting shall begin at noon on the 3d day of January, unless they shall by law appoint a different day.

Section 3. If, at the time fixed for the beginning of the term of the President, the President elect shall have died, the Vice President elect shall become President. If the President shall not have been chosen before the time fixed for the beginning of his term, or if the President elect shall have failed to qualify, then the Vice President elect shall act as President until a President shall have qualified; and the Congress may by law provide for the case wherein neither a President elect nor a Vice President elect shall have qualified, declaring who shall then act as President, or the manner in which one who is to act shall be selected, and such person shall act accordingly until a President or Vice President shall have qualified.

Section 4. The Congress may by law provide for the case of the death of any of the persons from whom the House of Representatives may choose a President whenever the right of choice shall have devolved upon them, and for the case of the death of any of the persons from whom the Senate may choose a Vice President whenever the right of choice shall have devolved upon them.

Section 5. Sections 1 and 2 shall take effect on the 15th day of October following the ratification of this article.

Section 6. This article shall be inoperative unless it shall have been ratified as an amendment to the Constitution by the legislatures of three-fourths of the several States within seven years from the date of its submission.

AMENDMENT XXI [1933]

Section 1. The eighteenth article of amendment to the Constitution of the United States is hereby repealed.

Section 2. The transportation or importation into any State, Territory, or possession of the United States for delivery or use therein of intoxicating liquors, in violation of the laws thereof, is hereby prohibited.

Section 3. This article shall be inoperative unless it shall have been ratified as an amendment to the Constitution by conventions in the several States, as provided in the Constitution, within seven years from the date of the submission hereof to the States by the Congress.

AMENDMENT XXII [1951]

Section 1. No person shall be elected to the office of the President more than twice, and no person who has held the office of President, or acted as President, for more than two years of a term to which some other person was elected President shall be elected to the office of President more than once. But this Article shall not apply to any person holding the office of President when this Article was proposed by the Congress, and shall not prevent any person who may be holding the office of President, or acting as President, during the term within which this Article becomes operative from holding the office of President or acting as President during the remainder of such term.

Section 2. This article shall be inoperative unless it shall have been ratified as an amendment to the Constitution by the legislatures of three-fourths of the several States within seven years from the date of its submission to the States by the Congress.

AMENDMENT XXIII [1961]

Section 1. The District constituting the seat of Government of the United States shall appoint in such manner as the Congress may direct:

A number of electors of President and Vice President equal to the whole number of Senators and Representatives in Congress to which the District would be entitled if it were a State, but in no event more than the least populous state; they shall be in addition to those appointed by the states, but they shall be considered, for the purposes of the election of President and Vice President, to be electors appointed by a state; and they shall meet in the District and perform such duties as provided by the twelfth article of amendment.

Section 2. The Congress shall have power to enforce this article by appropriate legislation.

AMENDMENT XXIV [1964]

Section 1. The right of citizens of the United States to vote in any primary or other election for President or Vice President, for electors for President or Vice President, or for Senator or Representative in Congress, shall not be denied or abridged by the United States, or any State by reason of failure to pay any poll tax or other tax.

Section 2. The Congress shall have power to enforce this article by appropriate legislation.

AMENDMENT XXV [1967]

Section 1. In case of the removal of the President from office or of his death or resignation, the Vice President shall become President.

Section 2. Whenever there is a vacancy in the office of the Vice President, the President shall nominate a Vice President who shall take office upon confirmation by a majority vote of both Houses of Congress.

Section 3. Whenever the President transmits to the President pro tempore of the Senate and the

Speaker of the House of Representatives his written declaration that he is unable to discharge the powers and duties of his office, and until he transmits to them a written declaration to the contrary, such powers and duties shall be discharged by the Vice President as Acting President.

Section 4. Whenever the Vice President and a majority of either the principal officers of the executive departments or of such other body as Congress may by law provide, transmit to the President pro tempore of the Senate and the Speaker of the House of Representatives their written declaration that the President is unable to discharge the powers and duties of his office, the Vice President shall immediately assume the powers and duties of the office as Acting President.

Thereafter, when the President transmits to the President pro tempore of the Senate and the Speaker of the House of Representatives his written declaration that no inability exists, he shall resume the powers and duties of his office unless the Vice President and a majority of either the principal officers of the executive department or of such other body as Congress may by law provide, transmit within four days to the President pro tempore of the Senate and the Speaker of the House of Representatives their written declaration that the President is unable to discharge the powers and duties of his office. Thereupon Congress shall decide the issue, assembling within forty-eight hours for that purpose if not in session. If the Congress, within twenty-one days after receipt of the latter written declaration, or, if Congress is not in session, within twenty-one days after Congress is required to assemble, determines by two-thirds vote of both Houses that the President is unable to discharge the powers and duties of his office, the Vice President shall continue to discharge the same as Acting President; otherwise, the President shall resume the powers and duties of his office.

AMENDMENT XXVI [1971]

Section 1. The right of citizens of the United States, who are eighteen years of age or older, to vote shall not be denied or abridged by the United States or by any State on account of age.

Section 2. The Congress shall have power to enforce this article by appropriate legislation.

AMENDMENT XXVII [1992]

No law, varying the compensation for the services of the Senators and Representatives, shall take effect, until an election of Representatives shall have intervened.

The Administrative Procedure Act of 1946 (Excerpts)

Section 551. Definitions

For the purpose of this subchapter—

*   *   *   *

(4) "rule" means the whole or a part of an agency statement of general or particular applicability and future effect designed to implement, interpret, or prescribe law or policy or describing the organization, procedure, or practice requirements of an agency and includes the approval or prescription for the future of rates, wages, corporate or financial structures or reorganizations thereof, prices, facilities, appliances, services or allowances therefor or of valuations, costs, or accounting, or practices bearing on any of the foregoing[.]

*   *   *   *

Section 552. Public Information; Agency Rules, Opinions, Orders, Records, and Proceedings

(a) Each agency shall make available to the public information as follows:

(1) Each agency shall separately state and currently publish in the Federal Register for the guidance of the public—

(A) descriptions of its central and field organization and the established places at which, the employees *   *   * from whom, and the methods whereby, the public may obtain information, make submittals or requests, or obtain decisions;

*   *   *   *

(C) rules of procedure, descriptions of forms available or the places at which forms may be obtained, and instructions as to the scope and contents of all papers, reports, or examinations;

(D) substantive rules of general applicability adopted as authorized by law, and statements of general policy or interpretations of general applicability formulated and adopted by the agency[.]

*   *   *

*   *   *   *

Section 552b. Open Meetings

*   *   *   *

(j) Each agency subject to the requirements of this section shall annually report to Congress regarding its compliance with such requirements, including a tabulation of the total number of agency meetings open to the public, the total number of meetings closed to the public, the reasons for closing such meetings, and a description of any litigation brought against the agency under this section, including any costs assessed against the agency in such litigation * * *.

* * * *

Section 553. Rule Making

* * * *

(b) General notice of proposed rule making shall be published in the Federal Register, unless persons subject thereto are named and either personally served or otherwise have actual notice thereof in accordance with law. * * *

(c) After notice required by this section, the agency shall give interested persons an opportunity to participate in the rule making through submission of written data, views, or arguments with or without opportunity for oral presentation. * * *

* * * *

Section 554. Adjudications

* * * *

(b) Persons entitled to notice of an agency hearing shall be timely informed of—

(1) the time, place, and nature of the hearing;

(2) the legal authority and jurisdiction under which the hearing is to be held; and

(3) the matters of fact and law asserted.

* * * *

(c) The agency shall give all interested parties opportunity for—

(1) the submission and consideration of facts, arguments, offers of settlement, or proposals of adjustment when time, the nature of the proceeding, and the public interest permit; and

(2) to the extent that the parties are unable so to determine a controversy by consent, hearing and decision on notice * * *.

* * * *

Section 555. Ancillary Matters

* * * *

(c) Process, requirement of a report, inspection, or other investigative act or demand may not be issued, made, or enforced except as authorized by law. A person compelled to submit data or evidence is entitled to retain or, on payment of lawfully prescribed costs, procure a copy or transcript thereof, except that in a nonpublic investigatory proceeding the witness may for good cause be limited to inspection of the official transcript of his testimony.

* * * *

(e) Prompt notice shall be given of the denial in whole or in part of a written application, petition, or other request of an interested person made in connection with any agency proceeding. * * *

Section 556. Hearings; Presiding Employees; Powers and Duties; Burden of Proof; Evidence; Record as Basis of Decision

* * * *

(b) There shall preside at the taking of evidence—

(1) the agency;

(2) one or more members of the body which comprises the agency; or

(3) one or more administrative law judges * * *.

* * * *

(c) Subject to published rules of the agency and within its powers, employees presiding at hearings may—

(1) administer oaths and affirmations;

(2) issue subpoenas authorized by law;

(3) rule on offers of proof and receive relevant evidence;

(4) take depositions or have depositions taken when the ends of justice would be served;

(5) regulate the course of the hearing;

(6) hold conferences for the settlement or simplification of the issues by consent of the parties or by the use of alternative means of dispute resolution as provided in subchapter IV of this chapter;

(7) inform the parties as to the availability of one or more alternative means of dispute resolution, and encourage use of such methods;

* * * *

(9) dispose of procedural requests or similar matters;

(10) make or recommend decisions in accordance with * * * this title; and

(11) take other action authorized by agency rule consistent with this subchapter.

* * * *

Section 702. Right of Review

A person suffering legal wrong because of agency action * * * is entitled to judicial review thereof. An action in a court of the United States seeking relief other than money damages and stating a claim that an agency or an officer or employee thereof acted or failed to act in an official capacity or under color of legal authority shall not be dismissed nor relief therein be denied on the ground that it is against the United States or that the United States is an indispensable party. The United States may be named as a defendant in any such action, and a judgment or decree may be entered against the United States: Provided, [t]hat any mandatory or injunctive decree shall specify the [f]ederal officer or officers (by name or by title), and their successors in office, personally responsible for compliance. *   *   *

     *   *   *   *

Section 704. Actions Reviewable

Agency action made reviewable by statute and final agency action for which there is no other adequate remedy in a court are subject to judicial review. A preliminary, procedural, or intermediate agency action or ruling not directly reviewable is subject to review on the review of the final agency action.

A P P E N D I X D

The Uniform
Commercial Code (Excerpts)

Article 2
SALES

Part 1 Short Title, General Construction and Subject Matter

§ 2—101. Short Title.

This Article shall be known and may be cited as Uniform Commercial Code—Sales.

§ 2—102. Scope; Certain Security and Other Transactions Excluded From This Article.

Unless the context otherwise requires, this Article applies to transactions in goods; it does not apply to any transaction which although in the form of an unconditional contract to sell or present sale is intended to operate only as a security transaction nor does this Article impair or repeal any statute regulating sales to consumers, farmers or other specified classes of buyers.

§ 2—103. Definitions and Index of Definitions.

(1) In this Article unless the context otherwise requires

(a) "Buyer" means a person who buys or contracts to buy goods.

(b) "Good faith" in the case of a merchant means honesty in fact and the observance of reasonable commercial standards of fair dealing in the trade.

(c) "Receipt" of goods means taking physical possession of them.

(d) "Seller" means a person who sells or contracts to sell goods.

(2) Other definitions applying to this Article or to specified Parts thereof, and the sections in which they appear are:

"Acceptance". Section 2—606.
"Banker's credit". Section 2—325.
"Between merchants". Section 2—104.
"Cancellation". Section 2—106(4).
"Commercial unit". Section 2—105.
"Confirmed credit". Section 2—325.
"Conforming to contract". Section 2—106.
"Contract for sale". Section 2—106.
"Cover". Section 2—712.
"Entrusting". Section 2—403.
"Financing agency". Section 2—104.
"Future goods". Section 2—105.
"Goods". Section 2—105.
"Identification". Section 2—501.
"Installment contract". Section 2—612.
"Letter of Credit". Section 2—325.
"Lot". Section 2—105.
"Merchant". Section 2—104.
"Overseas". Section 2—323.
"Person in position of seller". Section 2—707.
"Present sale". Section 2—106.

"Sale". Section 2—106.
"Sale on approval". Section 2—326.
"Sale or return". Section 2—326.
"Termination". Section 2—106.

(3) The following definitions in other Articles apply to this Article:

"Check". Section 3—104.
"Consignee". Section 7—102.
"Consignor". Section 7—102.
"Consumer goods". Section 9—109.
"Dishonor". Section 3—507.
"Draft". Section 3—104.

(4) In addition Article 1 contains general definitions and principles of construction and interpretation applicable throughout this Article.

§ 2—104. Definitions: "Merchant"; "Between Merchants"; "Financing Agency".

(1) "Merchant" means a person who deals in goods of the kind or otherwise by his occupation holds himself out as having knowledge or skill peculiar to the practices or goods involved in the transaction or to whom such knowledge or skill may be attributed by his employment of an agent or broker or other intermediary who by his occupation holds himself out as having such knowledge or skill.

(2) "Financing agency" means a bank, finance company or other person who in the ordinary course of business makes advances against goods or documents of title or who by arrangement with either the seller or the buyer intervenes in ordinary course to make or collect payment due or claimed under the contract for sale, as by purchasing or paying the seller's draft or making advances against it or by merely taking it for collection whether or not documents of title accompany the draft. "Financing agency" includes also a bank or other person who similarly intervenes between persons who are in the position of seller and buyer in respect to the goods (Section 2—707).

(3) "Between merchants" means in any transaction with respect to which both parties are chargeable with the knowledge or skill of merchants.

§ 2—105. Definitions: Transferability; "Goods"; "Future" Goods; "Lot"; "Commercial Unit".

(1) "Goods" means all things (including specially manufactured goods) which are movable at the time of identification to the contract for sale other than the money in which the price is to be paid, investment securities (Article 8) and things in action. "Goods" also includes the unborn young of animals and growing crops and other identified things attached to realty as described in the section on goods to be severed from realty (Section 2—107).

(2) Goods must be both existing and identified before any interest in them can pass. Goods which are not both existing and identified are "future" goods. A purported present sale of future goods or of any interest therein operates as a contract to sell.

(3) There may be a sale of a part interest in existing identified goods.

(4) An undivided share in an identified bulk of fungible goods is sufficiently identified to be sold although the quantity of the bulk is not determined. Any agreed proportion of such a bulk or any quantity thereof agreed upon by number, weight or other measure may to the extent of the seller's interest in the bulk be sold to the buyer who then becomes an owner in common.

(5) "Lot" means a parcel or a single article which is the subject matter of a separate sale or delivery, whether or not it is sufficient to perform the contract.

(6) "Commercial unit" means such a unit of goods as by commercial usage is a single whole for purposes of sale and division of which materially impairs its character or value on the market or in use. A commercial unit may be a single article (as a machine) or a set of articles (as a suite of furniture or an assortment of sizes) or a quantity (as a bale, gross, or carload) or any other unit treated in use or in the relevant market as a single whole.

§ 2—106. Definitions: "Contract"; "Agreement"; "Contract for Sale"; "Sale"; "Present Sale"; "Conforming" to Contract; "Termination"; "Cancellation".

(1) In this Article unless the context otherwise requires "contract" and "agreement" are limited to those relating to the present or future sale of goods. "Contract for sale" includes both a present sale of goods and a contract to sell goods at a future time. A "sale" consists in the passing of title from the seller to the buyer for a price (Section 2—401). A "present sale" means a sale which is accomplished by the making of the contract.

(2) Goods or conduct including any part of a performance are "conforming" or conform to the contract when they are in accordance with the obligations under the contract.

(3) "Termination" occurs when either party pursuant to a power created by agreement or law puts an end to the contract otherwise than for its breach. On "termination" all obligations which are still executory on both sides are discharged but any right based on prior breach or performance survives.

(4) "Cancellation" occurs when either party puts an end to the contract for breach by the other and its effect is the same as that of "termination" except that the cancelling party also retains any remedy for breach of the whole contract or any unperformed balance.

§ 2—107. Goods to Be Severed From Realty: Recording.

(1) A contract for the sale of minerals or the like (including oil and gas) or a structure or its materials to be removed from realty is a contract for the sale of goods within this Article if

they are to be severed by the seller but until severance a purported present sale thereof which is not effective as a transfer of an interest in land is effective only as a contract to sell.

(2) A contract for the sale apart from the land of growing crops or other things attached to realty and capable of severance without material harm thereto but not described in subsection (1) or of timber to be cut is a contract for the sale of goods within this Article whether the subject matter is to be severed by the buyer or by the seller even though it forms part of the realty at the time of contracting, and the parties can by identification effect a present sale before severance.

(3) The provisions of this section are subject to any third party rights provided by the law relating to realty records, and the contract for sale may be executed and recorded as a document transferring an interest in land and shall then constitute notice to third parties of the buyer's rights under the contract for sale.

Part 2 Form, Formation and Readjustment of Contract

§ 2—201. Formal Requirements; Statute of Frauds.

(1) Except as otherwise provided in this section a contract for the sale of goods for the price of $500 or more is not enforceable by way of action or defense unless there is some writing sufficient to indicate that a contract for sale has been made between the parties and signed by the party against whom enforcement is sought or by his authorized agent or broker. A writing is not insufficient because it omits or incorrectly states a term agreed upon but the contract is not enforceable under this paragraph beyond the quantity of goods shown in such writing.

(2) Between merchants if within a reasonable time a writing in confirmation of the contract and sufficient against the sender is received and the party receiving it has reason to know its contents, its satisfies the requirements of subsection (1) against such party unless written notice of objection to its contents is given within ten days after it is received.

(3) A contract which does not satisfy the requirements of subsection (1) but which is valid in other respects is enforceable

(a) if the goods are to be specially manufactured for the buyer and are not suitable for sale to others in the ordinary course of the seller's business and the seller, before notice of repudiation is received and under circumstances which reasonably indicate that the goods are for the buyer, has made either a substantial beginning of their manufacture or commitments for their procurement; or

(b) if the party against whom enforcement is sought admits in his pleading, testimony or otherwise in court that a contract for sale was made, but the contract is not enforceable under this provision beyond the quantity of goods admitted; or

(c) with respect to goods for which payment has been made and accepted or which have been received and accepted (Sec. 2—606).

§ 2—202. Final Written Expression: Parol or Extrinsic Evidence.

Terms with respect to which the confirmatory memoranda of the parties agree or which are otherwise set forth in a writing intended by the parties as a final expression of their agreement with respect to such terms as are included therein may not be contradicted by evidence of any prior agreement or of a contemporaneous oral agreement but may be explained or supplemented

(a) by course of dealing or usage of trade (Section 1—205) or by course of performance (Section 2—208); and

(b) by evidence of consistent additional terms unless the court finds the writing to have been intended also as a complete and exclusive statement of the terms of the agreement.

§ 2—203. Seals Inoperative.

The affixing of a seal to a writing evidencing a contract for sale or an offer to buy or sell goods does not constitute the writing a sealed instrument and the law with respect to sealed instruments does not apply to such a contract or offer.

§ 2—204. Formation in General.

(1) A contract for sale of goods may be made in any manner sufficient to show agreement, including conduct by both parties which recognizes the existence of such a contract.

(2) An agreement sufficient to constitute a contract for sale may be found even though the moment of its making is undetermined.

(3) Even though one or more terms are left open a contract for sale does not fail for indefiniteness if the parties have intended to make a contract and there is a reasonably certain basis for giving an appropriate remedy.

§ 2—205. Firm Offers.

An offer by a merchant to buy or sell goods in a signed writing which by its terms gives assurance that it will be held open is not revocable, for lack of consideration, during the time stated or if no time is stated for a reasonable time, but in no event may such period of irrevocability exceed three months; but any such term of assurance on a form supplied by the offeree must be separately signed by the offeror.

§ 2—206. Offer and Acceptance in Formation of Contract.

(1) Unless other unambiguously indicated by the language or circumstances

(a) an offer to make a contract shall be construed as inviting acceptance in any manner and by any medium reasonable in the circumstances;

(b) an order or other offer to buy goods for prompt or current shipment shall be construed as inviting acceptance either by a prompt promise to ship or by the prompt or current shipment of conforming or non-conforming goods, but such a shipment of non-conforming goods does not constitute an acceptance if the seller seasonably notifies the buyer that the shipment is offered only as an accommodation to the buyer.

(2) Where the beginning of a requested performance is a reasonable mode of acceptance an offeror who is not notified of acceptance within a reasonable time may treat the offer as having lapsed before acceptance.

§ 2—207. Additional Terms in Acceptance or Confirmation.

(1) A definite and seasonable expression of acceptance or a written confirmation which is sent within a reasonable time operates as an acceptance even though it states terms additional to or different from those offered or agreed upon, unless acceptance is expressly made conditional on assent to the additional or different terms.

(2) The additional terms are to be construed as proposals for addition to the contract. Between merchants such terms become part of the contract unless:

(a) the offer expressly limits acceptance to the terms of the offer;

(b) they materially alter it; or

(c) notification of objection to them has already been given or is given within a reasonable time after notice of them is received.

(3) Conduct by both parties which recognizes the existence of a contract is sufficient to establish a contract for sale although the writings of the parties do not otherwise establish a contract. In such case the terms of the particular contract consist of those terms on which the writings of the parties agree, together with any supplementary terms incorporated under any other provisions of this Act.

§ 2—208. Course of Performance or Practical Construction.

(1) Where the contract for sale involves repeated occasions for performance by either party with knowledge of the nature of the performance and opportunity for objection to it by the other, any course of performance accepted or acquiesced in without objection shall be relevant to determine the meaning of the agreement.

(2) The express terms of the agreement and any such course of performance, as well as any course of dealing and usage of trade, shall be construed whenever reasonable as consistent with each other; but when such construction is unreasonable, express terms shall control course of performance and course of performance shall control both course of dealing and usage of trade (Section 1—205).

(3) Subject to the provisions of the next section on modification and waiver, such course of performance shall be relevant to show a waiver or modification of any term inconsistent with such course of performance.

§ 2—209. Modification, Rescission and Waiver.

(1) An agreement modifying a contract within this Article needs no consideration to be binding.

(2) A signed agreement which excludes modification or rescission except by a signed writing cannot be otherwise modified or rescinded, but except as between merchants such a requirement on a form supplied by the merchant must be separately signed by the other party.

(3) The requirements of the statute of frauds section of this Article (Section 2—201) must be satisfied if the contract as modified is within its provisions.

(4) Although an attempt at modification or rescission does not satisfy the requirements of subsection (2) or (3) it can operate as a waiver.

(5) A party who has made a waiver affecting an executory portion of the contract may retract the waiver by reasonable notification received by the other party that strict performance will be required of any term waived, unless the retraction would be unjust in view of a material change of position in reliance on the waiver.

§ 2—210. Delegation of Performance; Assignment of Rights.

(1) A party may perform his duty through a delegate unless otherwise agreed or unless the other party has a substantial interest in having his original promisor perform or control the acts required by the contract. No delegation of performance relieves the party delegating of any duty to perform or any liability for breach.

(2) Unless otherwise agreed all rights of either seller or buyer can be assigned except where the assignment would materially change the duty of the other party, or increase materially the burden or risk imposed on him by his contract, or impair materially his chance of obtaining return performance. A right to damages for breach of the whole contract or a right arising out of the assignor's due performance of his entire obligation can be assigned despite agreement otherwise.

(3) Unless the circumstances indicate the contrary a prohibition of assignment of "the contract" is to be construed as barring only the delegation to the assignee of the assignor's performance.

(4) An assignment of "the contract" or of "all my rights under the contract" or an assignment in similar general terms is an assignment of rights and unless the language or the circumstances (as in an assignment for security) indi-

cate the contrary, it is a delegation of performance of the duties of the assignor and its acceptance by the assignee constitutes a promise by him to perform those duties. This promise is enforceable by either the assignor or the other party to the original contract.

(5) The other party may treat any assignment which delegates performance as creating reasonable grounds for insecurity and may without prejudice to his rights against the assignor demand assurances from the assignee (Section 2—609).

Part 3 General Obligation and Construction of Contract

§ 2—301. General Obligations of Parties.

The obligation of the seller is to transfer and deliver and that of the buyer is to accept and pay in accordance with the contract.

§ 2—302. Unconscionable Contract or Clause.

(1) If the court as a matter of law finds the contract or any clause of the contract to have been unconscionable at the time it was made the court may refuse to enforce the contract, or it may enforce the remainder of the contract without the unconscionable clause, or it may so limit the application of any unconscionable clause as to avoid any unconscionable result.

(2) When it is claimed or appears to the court that the contract or any clause thereof may be unconscionable the parties shall be afforded a reasonable opportunity to present evidence as to its commercial setting, purpose and effect to aid the court in making the determination.

§ 2—303. Allocations or Division of Risks.

Where this Article allocates a risk or a burden as between the parties "unless otherwise agreed", the agreement may not only shift the allocation but may also divide the risk or burden.

§ 2—304. Price Payable in Money, Goods, Realty, or Otherwise.

(1) The price can be made payable in money or otherwise. If it is payable in whole or in part in goods each party is a seller of the goods which he is to transfer.

(2) Even though all or part of the price is payable in an interest in realty the transfer of the goods and the seller's obligations with reference to them are subject to this Article, but not the transfer of the interest in realty or the transferor's obligations in connection therewith.

§ 2—305. Open Price Term.

(1) The parties if they so intend can conclude a contract for sale even though the price is not settled. In such a case the price is a reasonable price at the time for delivery if

(a) nothing is said as to price; or

(b) the price is left to be agreed by the parties and they fail to agree; or

(c) the price is to be fixed in terms of some agreed market or other standard as set or recorded by a third person or agency and it is not so set or recorded.

(2) A price to be fixed by the seller or by the buyer means a price for him to fix in good faith.

(3) When a price left to be fixed otherwise than by agreement of the parties fails to be fixed through fault of one party the other may at his option treat the contract as cancelled or himself fix a reasonable price.

(4) Where, however, the parties intend not to be bound unless the price be fixed or agreed and it is not fixed or agreed there is no contract. In such a case the buyer must return any goods already received or if unable so to do must pay their reasonable value at the time of delivery and the seller must return any portion of the price paid on account.

§ 2—306. Output, Requirements and Exclusive Dealings.

(1) A term which measures the quantity by the output of the seller or the requirements of the buyer means such actual output or requirements as may occur in good faith, except that no quantity unreasonably disproportionate to any stated estimate or in the absence of a stated estimate to any normal or otherwise comparable prior output or requirements may be tendered or demanded.

(2) A lawful agreement by either the seller or the buyer for exclusive dealing in the kind of goods concerned imposes unless otherwise agreed an obligation by the seller to use best efforts to supply the goods and by the buyer to use best efforts to promote their sale.

§ 2—307. Delivery in Single Lot or Several Lots.

Unless otherwise agreed all goods called for by a contract for sale must be tendered in a single delivery and payment is due only on such tender but where the circumstances give either party the right to make or demand delivery in lots the price if it can be apportioned may be demanded for each lot.

§ 2—308. Absence of Specified Place for Delivery.

Unless otherwise agreed

(a) the place for delivery of goods is the seller's place of business or if he has none his residence; but

(b) in a contract for sale of identified goods which to the knowledge of the parties at the time of contracting are in some other place, that place is the place for their delivery; and

(c) documents of title may be delivered through customary banking channels.

§ 2—309. Absence of Specific Time Provisions; Notice of Termination.

(1) The time for shipment or delivery or any other action under a contract if not provided in this Article or agreed upon shall be a reasonable time.

(2) Where the contract provides for successive performances but is indefinite in duration it is valid for a reasonable time but unless otherwise agreed may be terminated at any time by either party.

(3) Termination of a contract by one party except on the happening of an agreed event requires that reasonable notification be received by the other party and an agreement dispensing with notification is invalid if its operation would be unconscionable.

§ 2—310. Open Time for Payment or Running of Credit; Authority to Ship Under Reservation.

Unless otherwise agreed

(a) payment is due at the time and place at which the buyer is to receive the goods even though the place of shipment is the place of delivery; and

(b) if the seller is authorized to send the goods he may ship them under reservation, and may tender the documents of title, but the buyer may inspect the goods after their arrival before payment is due unless such inspection is inconsistent with the terms of the contract (Section 2—513); and

(c) if delivery is authorized and made by way of documents of title otherwise than by subsection (b) then payment is due at the time and place at which the buyer is to receive the documents regardless of where the goods are to be received; and

(d) where the seller is required or authorized to ship the goods on credit the credit period runs from the time of shipment but post-dating the invoice or delaying its dispatch will correspondingly delay the starting of the credit period.

§ 2—311. Options and Cooperation Respecting Performance.

(1) An agreement for sale which is otherwise sufficiently definite (subsection (3) of Section 2—204) to be a contract is not made invalid by the fact that it leaves particulars of performance to be specified by one of the parties. Any such specification must be made in good faith and within limits set by commercial reasonableness.

(2) Unless otherwise agreed specifications relating to assortment of the goods are at the buyer's option and except as otherwise provided in subsections (1)(c) and (3) of Section 2—319 specifications or arrangements relating to shipment are at the seller's option.

(3) Where such specification would materially affect the other party's performance but is not seasonably made or where one party's cooperation is necessary to the agreed performance of the other but is not seasonably forthcoming, the other party in addition to all other remedies

(a) is excused for any resulting delay in his own performance; and

(b) may also either proceed to perform in any reasonable manner or after the time for a material part of his own performance treat the failure to specify or to cooperate as a breach by failure to deliver or accept the goods.

§ 2—312. Warranty of Title and Against Infringement; Buyer's Obligation Against Infringement.

(1) Subject to subsection (2) there is in a contract for sale a warranty by the seller that

(a) the title conveyed shall be good, and its transfer rightful; and

(b) the goods shall be delivered free from any security interest or other lien or encumbrance of which the buyer at the time of contracting has no knowledge.

(2) A warranty under subsection (1) will be excluded or modified only by specific language or by circumstances which give the buyer reason to know that the person selling does not claim title in himself or that he is purporting to sell only such right or title as he or a third person may have.

(3) Unless otherwise agreed a seller who is a merchant regularly dealing in goods of the kind warrants that the goods shall be delivered free of the rightful claim of any third person by way of infringement or the like but a buyer who furnishes specifications to the seller must hold the seller harmless against any such claim which arises out of compliance with the specifications.

§ 2—313. Express Warranties by Affirmation, Promise, Description, Sample.

(1) Express warranties by the seller are created as follows:

(a) Any affirmation of fact or promise made by the seller to the buyer which relates to the goods and becomes part of the basis of the bargain creates an express warranty that the goods shall conform to the affirmation or promise.

(b) Any description of the goods which is made part of the basis of the bargain creates an express warranty that the goods shall conform to the description.

(c) Any sample or model which is made part of the basis of the bargain creates an express warranty that the whole of the goods shall conform to the sample or model.

(2) It is not necessary to the creation of an express warranty that the seller use formal words such as "warrant" or "guarantee" or that he have a specific intention to make a warranty, but an affirmation merely of the value of the goods or a statement purporting to be merely the seller's opinion or commendation of the goods does not create a warranty.

§ 2—314. Implied Warranty: Merchantability; Usage of Trade.

(1) Unless excluded or modified (Section 2—316), a warranty that the goods shall be merchantable is implied in a contract for their sale if the seller is a merchant with respect to goods of that kind. Under this section the serving for value of food or drink to be consumed either on the premises or elsewhere is a sale.

(2) Goods to be merchantable must be at least such as

(a) pass without objection in the trade under the contract description; and

(b) in the case of fungible goods, are of fair average quality within the description; and

(c) are fit for the ordinary purposes for which such goods are used; and

(d) run, within the variations permitted by the agreement, of even kind, quality and quantity within each unit and among all units involved; and

(e) are adequately contained, packaged, and labeled as the agreement may require; and

(f) conform to the promises or affirmations of fact made on the container or label if any.

(3) Unless excluded or modified (Section 2—316) other implied warranties may arise from course of dealing or usage of trade.

§ 2—315. Implied Warranty: Fitness for Particular Purpose.

Where the seller at the time of contracting has reason to know any particular purpose for which the goods are required and that the buyer is relying on the seller's skill or judgment to select or furnish suitable goods, there is unless excluded or modified under the next section an implied warranty that the goods shall be fit for such purpose.

§ 2—316. Exclusion or Modification of Warranties.

(1) Words or conduct relevant to the creation of an express warranty and words or conduct tending to negate or limit warranty shall be construed wherever reasonable as consistent with each other; but subject to the provisions of this Article on parol or extrinsic evidence (Section 2—202) negation or limitation is inoperative to the extent that such construction is unreasonable.

(2) Subject to subsection (3), to exclude or modify the implied warranty of merchantability or any part of it the language must mention merchantability and in case of a writing must be conspicuous, and to exclude or modify any implied warranty of fitness the exclusion must be by a writing and conspicuous. Language to exclude all implied warranties of fitness is sufficient if it states, for example, that "There are no warranties which extend beyond the description on the face hereof."

(3) Notwithstanding subsection (2)

(a) unless the circumstances indicate otherwise, all implied warranties are excluded by expressions like "as is", "with all faults" or other language which in common understanding calls the buyer's attention to the exclusion of warranties and makes plain that there is no implied warranty; and

(b) when the buyer before entering into the contract has examined the goods or the sample or model as fully as he desired or has refused to examine the goods there is no implied warranty with regard to defects which an examination ought in the circumstances to have revealed to him; and

(c) an implied warranty can also be excluded or modified by course of dealing or course of performance or usage of trade.

(4) Remedies for breach of warranty can be limited in accordance with the provisions of this Article on liquidation or limitation of damages and on contractual modification of remedy (Sections 2—718 and 2—719).

§ 2—317. Cumulation and Conflict of Warranties Express or Implied.

Warranties whether express or implied shall be construed as consistent with each other and as cumulative, but if such construction is unreasonable the intention of the parties shall determine which warranty is dominant. In ascertaining that intention the following rules apply:

(a) Exact or technical specifications displace an inconsistent sample or model or general language of description.

(b) A sample from an existing bulk displaces inconsistent general language of description.

(c) Express warranties displace inconsistent implied warranties other than an implied warranty of fitness for a particular purpose.

§ 2—318. Third Party Beneficiaries of Warranties Express or Implied.

Note: If this Act is introduced in the Congress of the United States this section should be omitted. (States to select one alternative.)

Alternative A

A seller's warranty whether express or implied extends to any natural person who is in the family or household of his buyer or who is a guest in his home if it is reasonable to expect that such person may use, consume or be affected by the goods and who is injured in person by breach of the warranty. A seller may not exclude or limit the operation of this section.

Alternative B

A seller's warranty whether express or implied extends to any natural person who may reasonably be expected to use, consume or be affected by the goods and who is injured in person by breach of the warranty. A seller may not exclude or limit the operation of this section.

Alternative C

A seller's warranty whether express or implied extends to any person who may reasonably be expected to use, consume or be affected by the goods and who is injured by breach of the warranty. A seller may not exclude or limit the operation of this section with respect to injury to the person of an individual to whom the warranty extends. As amended 1966.

§ 2—319. F.O.B. and F.A.S. Terms.

(1) Unless otherwise agreed the term F.O.B. (which means "free on board") at a named place, even though used only in connection with the stated price, is a delivery term under which

(a) when the term is F.O.B. the place of shipment, the seller must at that place ship the goods in the manner provided in this Article (Section 2—504) and bear the expense and risk of putting them into the possession of the carrier; or

(b) when the term is F.O.B. the place of destination, the seller must at his own expense and risk transport the goods to that place and there tender delivery of them in the manner provided in this Article (Section 2—503);

(c) when under either (a) or (b) the term is also F.O.B. vessel, car or other vehicle, the seller must in addition at his own expense and risk load the goods on board. If the term is F.O.B. vessel the buyer must name the vessel and in an appropriate case the seller must comply with the provisions of this Article on the form of bill of lading (Section 2—323).

(2) Unless otherwise agreed the term F.A.S. vessel (which means "free alongside") at a named port, even though used only in connection with the stated price, is a delivery term under which the seller must

(a) at his own expense and risk deliver the goods alongside the vessel in the manner usual in that port or on a dock designated and provided by the buyer; and

(b) obtain and tender a receipt for the goods in exchange for which the carrier is under a duty to issue a bill of lading.

(3) Unless otherwise agreed in any case falling within subsection (1)(a) or (c) or subsection (2) the buyer must seasonably give any needed instructions for making delivery, including when the term is F.A.S. or F.O.B. the loading berth of the vessel and in an appropriate case its name and sailing date. The seller may treat the failure of needed instructions as a failure of cooperation under this Article (Section 2—311). He may also at his option move the goods in any reasonable manner preparatory to delivery or shipment.

(4) Under the term F.O.B. vessel or F.A.S. unless otherwise agreed the buyer must make payment against tender of the required documents and the seller may not tender nor the buyer demand delivery of the goods in substitution for the documents.

§ 2—320. C.I.F. and C. & F. Terms.

(1) The term C.I.F. means that the price includes in a lump sum the cost of the goods and the insurance and freight to the named destination. The term C. & F. or C.F. means that the price so includes cost and freight to the named destination.

(2) Unless otherwise agreed and even though used only in connection with the stated price and destination, the term C.I.F. destination or its equivalent requires the seller at his own expense and risk to

(a) put the goods into the possession of a carrier at the port for shipment and obtain a negotiable bill or bills of lading covering the entire transportation to the named destination; and

(b) load the goods and obtain a receipt from the carrier (which may be contained in the bill of lading) showing that the freight has been paid or provided for; and

(c) obtain a policy or certificate of insurance, including any war risk insurance, of a kind and on terms then current at the port of shipment in the usual amount, in the currency of the contract, shown to cover the same goods covered by the bill of lading and providing for payment of loss to the order of the buyer or for the account of whom it may concern; but the seller may add to the price the amount of the premium for any such war risk insurance; and

(d) prepare an invoice of the goods and procure any other documents required to effect shipment or to comply with the contract; and

(e) forward and tender with commercial promptness all the documents in due form and with any indorsement necessary to perfect the buyer's rights.

(3) Unless otherwise agreed the term C. & F. or its equivalent has the same effect and imposes upon the seller the same obligations and risks as a C.I.F. term except the obligation as to insurance.

(4) Under the term C.I.F. or C. & F. unless otherwise agreed the buyer must make payment against tender of the required documents and the seller may not tender nor the buyer demand delivery of the goods in substitution for the documents.

§ 2—321. C.I.F. or C. & F.: "Net Landed Weights"; "Payment on Arrival"; Warranty of Condition on Arrival.

Under a contract containing a term C.I.F. or C. & F.

(1) Where the price is based on or is to be adjusted according to "net landed weights", "delivered weights", "out turn"

quantity or quality or the like, unless otherwise agreed the seller must reasonably estimate the price. The payment due on tender of the documents called for by the contract is the amount so estimated, but after final adjustment of the price a settlement must be made with commercial promptness.

(2) An agreement described in subsection (1) or any warranty of quality or condition of the goods on arrival places upon the seller the risk of ordinary deterioration, shrinkage and the like in transportation but has no effect on the place or time of identification to the contract for sale or delivery or on the passing of the risk of loss.

(3) Unless otherwise agreed where the contract provides for payment on or after arrival of the goods the seller must before payment allow such preliminary inspection as is feasible; but if the goods are lost delivery of the documents and payment are due when the goods should have arrived.

§ 2—322. Delivery "Ex-Ship".

(1) Unless otherwise agreed a term for delivery of goods "ex-ship" (which means from the carrying vessel) or in equivalent language is not restricted to a particular ship and requires delivery from a ship which has reached a place at the named port of destination where goods of the kind are usually discharged.

(2) Under such a term unless otherwise agreed

(a) the seller must discharge all liens arising out of the carriage and furnish the buyer with a direction which puts the carrier under a duty to deliver the goods; and

(b) the risk of loss does not pass to the buyer until the goods leave the ship's tackle or are otherwise properly unloaded.

§ 2—323. Form of Bill of Lading Required in Overseas Shipment; "Overseas".

(1) Where the contract contemplates overseas shipment and contains a term C.I.F. or C. & F. or F.O.B. vessel, the seller unless otherwise agreed must obtain a negotiable bill of lading stating that the goods have been loaded on board or, in the case of a term C.I.F. or C. & F., received for shipment.

(2) Where in a case within subsection (1) a bill of lading has been issued in a set of parts, unless otherwise agreed if the documents are not to be sent from abroad the buyer may demand tender of the full set; otherwise only one part of the bill of lading need be tendered. Even if the agreement expressly requires a full set

(a) due tender of a single part is acceptable within the provisions of this Article on cure of improper delivery (subsection (1) of Section 2—508); and

(b) even though the full set is demanded, if the documents are sent from abroad the person tendering an incomplete set may nevertheless require payment upon furnishing an indemnity which the buyer in good faith deems adequate.

(3) A shipment by water or by air or a contract contemplating such shipment is "overseas" insofar as by usage of trade or agreement it is subject to the commercial, financing or shipping practices characteristic of international deep water commerce.

§ 2—324. "No Arrival, No Sale" Term.

Under a term "no arrival, no sale" or terms of like meaning, unless otherwise agreed,

(a) the seller must properly ship conforming goods and if they arrive by any means he must tender them on arrival but he assumes no obligation that the goods will arrive unless he has caused the non-arrival; and

(b) where without fault of the seller the goods are in part lost or have so deteriorated as no longer to conform to the contract or arrive after the contract time, the buyer may proceed as if there had been casualty to identified goods (Section 2—613).

§ 2—325. "Letter of Credit" Term; "Confirmed Credit".

(1) Failure of the buyer seasonably to furnish an agreed letter of credit is a breach of the contract for sale.

(2) The delivery to seller of a proper letter of credit suspends the buyer's obligation to pay. If the letter of credit is dishonored, the seller may on seasonable notification to the buyer require payment directly from him.

(3) Unless otherwise agreed the term "letter of credit" or "banker's credit" in a contract for sale means an irrevocable credit issued by a financing agency of good repute and, where the shipment is overseas, of good international repute. The term "confirmed credit" means that the credit must also carry the direct obligation of such an agency which does business in the seller's financial market.

§ 2—326. Sale on Approval and Sale or Return; Consignment Sales and Rights of Creditors.

(1) Unless otherwise agreed, if delivered goods may be returned by the buyer even though they conform to the contract, the transaction is

(a) a "sale on approval" if the goods are delivered primarily for use, and

(b) a "sale or return" if the goods are delivered primarily for resale.

(2) Except as provided in subsection (3), goods held on approval are not subject to the claims of the buyer's creditors until acceptance; goods held on sale or return are subject to such claims while in the buyer's possession.

(3) Where goods are delivered to a person for sale and such person maintains a place of business at which he deals in goods of the kind involved, under a name other than the name of the person making delivery, then with respect to claims of creditors of the person conducting the

business the goods are deemed to be on sale or return. The provisions of this subsection are applicable even though an agreement purports to reserve title to the person making delivery until payment or resale or uses such words as "on consignment" or "on memorandum". However, this subsection is not applicable if the person making delivery

    (a) complies with an applicable law providing for a consignor's interest or the like to be evidenced by a sign, or

    (b) establishes that the person conducting the business is generally known by his creditors to be substantially engaged in selling the goods of others, or

    (c) complies with the filing provisions of the Article on Secured Transactions (Article 9).

(4) Any "or return" term of a contract for sale is to be treated as a separate contract for sale within the statute of frauds section of this Article (Section 2—201) and as contradicting the sale aspect of the contract within the provisions of this Article on parol or extrinsic evidence (Section 2—202).

§ 2—327. Special Incidents of Sale on Approval and Sale or Return.

(1) Under a sale on approval unless otherwise agreed

    (a) although the goods are identified to the contract the risk of loss and the title do not pass to the buyer until acceptance; and

    (b) use of the goods consistent with the purpose of trial is not acceptance but failure seasonably to notify the seller of election to return the goods is acceptance, and if the goods conform to the contract acceptance of any part is acceptance of the whole; and

    (c) after due notification of election to return, the return is at the seller's risk and expense but a merchant buyer must follow any reasonable instructions.

(2) Under a sale or return unless otherwise agreed

    (a) the option to return extends to the whole or any commercial unit of the goods while in substantially their original condition, but must be exercised seasonably; and

    (b) the return is at the buyer's risk and expense.

§ 2—328. Sale by Auction.

(1) In a sale by auction if goods are put up in lots each lot is the subject of a separate sale.

(2) A sale by auction is complete when the auctioneer so announces by the fall of the hammer or in other customary manner. Where a bid is made while the hammer is falling in acceptance of a prior bid the auctioneer may in his discretion reopen the bidding or declare the goods sold under the bid on which the hammer was falling.

(3) Such a sale is with reserve unless the goods are in explicit terms put up without reserve. In an auction with reserve the auctioneer may withdraw the goods at any time until he announces completion of the sale. In an auction without reserve, after the auctioneer calls for bids on an article or lot, that article or lot cannot be withdrawn unless no bid is made within a reasonable time. In either case a bidder may retract his bid until the auctioneer's announcement of completion of the sale, but a bidder's retraction does not revive any previous bid.

(4) If the auctioneer knowingly receives a bid on the seller's behalf or the seller makes or procures such as bid, and notice has not been given that liberty for such bidding is reserved, the buyer may at his option avoid the sale or take the goods at the price of the last good faith bid prior to the completion of the sale. This subsection shall not apply to any bid at a forced sale.

Part 4 Title, Creditors and Good Faith Purchasers

§ 2—401. Passing of Title; Reservation for Security; Limited Application of This Section.

Each provision of this Article with regard to the rights, obligations and remedies of the seller, the buyer, purchasers or other third parties applies irrespective of title to the goods except where the provision refers to such title. Insofar as situations are not covered by the other provisions of this Article and matters concerning title became material the following rules apply:

(1) Title to goods cannot pass under a contract for sale prior to their identification to the contract (Section 2—501), and unless otherwise explicitly agreed the buyer acquires by their identification a special property as limited by this Act. Any retention or reservation by the seller of the title (property) in goods shipped or delivered to the buyer is limited in effect to a reservation of a security interest. Subject to these provisions and to the provisions of the Article on Secured Transactions (Article 9), title to goods passes from the seller to the buyer in any manner and on any conditions explicitly agreed on by the parties.

(2) Unless otherwise explicitly agreed title passes to the buyer at the time and place at which the seller completes his performance with reference to the physical delivery of the goods, despite any reservation of a security interest and even though a document of title is to be delivered at a different time or place; and in particular and despite any reservation of a security interest by the bill of lading

    (a) if the contract requires or authorizes the seller to send the goods to the buyer but does not require him to deliver them at destination, title passes to the buyer at the time and place of shipment; but

    (b) if the contract requires delivery at destination, title passes on tender there.

(3) Unless otherwise explicitly agreed where delivery is to be made without moving the goods,

(a) if the seller is to deliver a document of title, title passes at the time when and the place where he delivers such documents; or

(b) if the goods are at the time of contracting already identified and no documents are to be delivered, title passes at the time and place of contracting.

(4) A rejection or other refusal by the buyer to receive or retain the goods, whether or not justified, or a justified revocation of acceptance revests title to the goods in the seller. Such revesting occurs by operation of law and is not a "sale".

§ 2—402. Rights of Seller's Creditors Against Sold Goods.

(1) Except as provided in subsections (2) and (3), rights of unsecured creditors of the seller with respect to goods which have been identified to a contract for sale are subject to the buyer's rights to recover the goods under this Article (Sections 2—502 and 2—716).

(2) A creditor of the seller may treat a sale or an identification of goods to a contract for sale as void if as against him a retention of possession by the seller is fraudulent under any rule of law of the state where the goods are situated, except that retention of possession in good faith and current course of trade by a merchant-seller for a commercially reasonable time after a sale or identification is not fraudulent.

(3) Nothing in this Article shall be deemed to impair the rights of creditors of the seller

(a) under the provisions of the Article on Secured Transactions (Article 9); or

(b) where identification to the contract or delivery is made not in current course of trade but in satisfaction of or as security for a pre-existing claim for money, security or the like and is made under circumstances which under any rule of law of the state where the goods are situated would apart from this Article constitute the transaction a fraudulent transfer or voidable preference.

§ 2—403. Power to Transfer; Good Faith Purchase of Goods; "Entrusting".

(1) A purchaser of goods acquires all title which his transferor had or had power to transfer except that a purchaser of a limited interest acquires rights only to the extent of the interest purchased. A person with voidable title has power to transfer a good title to a good faith purchaser for value. When goods have been delivered under a transaction of purchase the purchaser has such power even though

(a) the transferor was deceived as to the identity of the purchaser, or

(b) the delivery was in exchange for a check which is later dishonored, or

(c) it was agreed that the transaction was to be a "cash sale", or

(d) the delivery was procured through fraud punishable as larcenous under the criminal law.

(2) Any entrusting of possession of goods to a merchant who deals in goods of that kind gives him power to transfer all rights of the entruster to a buyer in ordinary course of business.

(3) "Entrusting" includes any delivery and any acquiescence in retention of possession regardless of any condition expressed between the parties to the delivery or acquiescence and regardless of whether the procurement of the entrusting or the possessor's disposition of the goods have been such as to be larcenous under the criminal law.

(4) The rights of other purchasers of goods and of lien creditors are governed by the Articles on Secured Transactions (Article 9), Bulk Transfers (Article 6) and Documents of Title (Article 7).

Part 5 Performance

§ 2—501. Insurable Interest in Goods; Manner of Identification of Goods.

(1) The buyer obtains a special property and an insurable interest in goods by identification of existing goods as goods to which the contract refers even though the goods so identified are non-conforming and he has an option to return or reject them. Such identification can be made at any time and in any manner explicitly agreed to by the parties. In the absence of explicit agreement identification occurs

(a) when the contract is made if it is for the sale of goods already existing and identified;

(b) if the contract is for the sale of future goods other than those described in paragraph (c), when goods are shipped, marked or otherwise designated by the seller as goods to which the contract refers;

(c) when the crops are planted or otherwise become growing crops or the young are conceived if the contract is for the sale of unborn young to be born within twelve months after contracting or for the sale of crops to be harvested within twelve months or the next normal harvest season after contracting whichever is longer.

(2) The seller retains an insurable interest in goods so long as title to or any security interest in the goods remains in him and where the identification is by the seller alone he may until default or insolvency or notification to the buyer that the identification is final substitute other goods for those identified.

(3) Nothing in this section impairs any insurable interest recognized under any other statute or rule of law.

§ 2—502. Buyer's Right to Goods on Seller's Insolvency.

(1) Subject to subsection (2) and even though the goods have not been shipped a buyer who has paid a part or all of the price of goods in which he has a special property under

the provisions of the immediately preceding section may on making and keeping good a tender of any unpaid portion of their price recover them from the seller if the seller becomes insolvent within ten days after receipt of the first installment on their price.

(2) If the identification creating his special property has been made by the buyer he acquires the right to recover the goods only if they conform to the contract for sale.

§ 2—503. Manner of Seller's Tender of Delivery.

(1) Tender of delivery requires that the seller put and hold conforming goods at the buyer's disposition and give the buyer any notification reasonably necessary to enable him to take delivery. The manner, time and place for tender are determined by the agreement and this Article, and in particular

(a) tender must be at a reasonable hour, and if it is of goods they must be kept available for the period reasonably necessary to enable the buyer to take possession; but

(b) unless otherwise agreed the buyer must furnish facilities reasonably suited to the receipt of the goods.

(2) Where the case is within the next section respecting shipment tender requires that the seller comply with its provisions.

(3) Where the seller is required to deliver at a particular destination tender requires that he comply with subsection (1) and also in any appropriate case tender documents as described in subsections (4) and (5) of this section.

(4) Where goods are in the possession of a bailee and are to be delivered without being moved

(a) tender requires that the seller either tender a negotiable document of title covering such goods or procure acknowledgment by the bailee of the buyer's right to possession of the goods; but

(b) tender to the buyer of a non-negotiable document of title or of a written direction to the bailee to deliver is sufficient tender unless the buyer seasonably objects, and receipt by the bailee of notification of the buyer's rights fixes those rights as against the bailee and all third persons; but risk of loss of the goods and of any failure by the bailee to honor the non-negotiable document of title or to obey the direction remains on the seller until the buyer has had a reasonable time to present the document or direction, and a refusal by the bailee to honor the document or to obey the direction defeats the tender.

(5) Where the contract requires the seller to deliver documents

(a) he must tender all such documents in correct form, except as provided in this Article with respect to bills of lading in a set (subsection (2) of Section 2—323); and

(b) tender through customary banking channels is sufficient and dishonor of a draft accompanying the documents constitutes non-acceptance or rejection.

§ 2—504. Shipment by Seller.

Where the seller is required or authorized to send the goods to the buyer and the contract does not require him to deliver them at a particular destination, then unless otherwise agreed he must

(a) put the goods in the possession of such a carrier and make such a contract for their transportation as may be reasonable having regard to the nature of the goods and other circumstances of the case; and

(b) obtain and promptly deliver or tender in due form any document necessary to enable the buyer to obtain possession of the goods or otherwise required by the agreement or by usage of trade; and

(c) promptly notify the buyer of the shipment.

Failure to notify the buyer under paragraph (c) or to make a proper contract under paragraph (a) is a ground for rejection only if material delay or loss ensues.

§ 2—505. Seller's Shipment under Reservation.

(1) Where the seller has identified goods to the contract by or before shipment:

(a) his procurement of a negotiable bill of lading to his own order or otherwise reserves in him a security interest in the goods. His procurement of the bill to the order of a financing agency or of the buyer indicates in addition only the seller's expectation of transferring that interest to the person named.

(b) a non-negotiable bill of lading to himself or his nominee reserves possession of the goods as security but except in a case of conditional delivery (subsection (2) of Section 2—507) a non-negotiable bill of lading naming the buyer as consignee reserves no security interest even though the seller retains possession of the bill of lading.

(2) When shipment by the seller with reservation of a security interest is in violation of the contract for sale it constitutes an improper contract for transportation within the preceding section but impairs neither the rights given to the buyer by shipment and identification of the goods to the contract nor the seller's powers as a holder of a negotiable document.

§ 2—506. Rights of Financing Agency.

(1) A financing agency by paying or purchasing for value a draft which relates to a shipment of goods acquires to the extent of the payment or purchase and in addition to its own rights under the draft and any document of title securing it any rights of the shipper in the goods including the right to stop delivery and the shipper's right to have the draft honored by the buyer.

(2) The right to reimbursement of a financing agency which has in good faith honored or purchased the draft under commitment to or authority from the buyer is not impaired by subsequent discovery of defects with reference to any relevant document which was apparently regular on its face.

§ 2—507. Effect of Seller's Tender; Delivery on Condition.

(1) Tender of delivery is a condition to the buyer's duty to accept the goods and, unless otherwise agreed, to his duty to pay for them. Tender entitles the seller to acceptance of the goods and to payment according to the contract.

(2) Where payment is due and demanded on the delivery to the buyer of goods or documents of title, his right as against the seller to retain or dispose of them is conditional upon his making the payment due.

§ 2—508. Cure by Seller of Improper Tender or Delivery; Replacement.

(1) Where any tender or delivery by the seller is rejected because non-conforming and the time for performance has not yet expired, the seller may seasonably notify the buyer of his intention to cure and may then within the contract time make a conforming delivery.

(2) Where the buyer rejects a non-conforming tender which the seller had reasonable grounds to believe would be acceptable with or without money allowance the seller may if he seasonably notifies the buyer have a further reasonable time to substitute a conforming tender.

§ 2—509. Risk of Loss in the Absence of Breach.

(1) Where the contract requires or authorizes the seller to ship the goods by carrier

(a) if it does not require him to deliver them at a particular destination, the risk of loss passes to the buyer when the goods are duly delivered to the carrier even though the shipment is under reservation (Section 2—505); but

(b) if it does require him to deliver them at a particular destination and the goods are there duly tendered while in the possession of the carrier, the risk of loss passes to the buyer when the goods are there duly so tendered as to enable the buyer to take delivery.

(2) Where the goods are held by a bailee to be delivered without being moved, the risk of loss passes to the buyer

(a) on his receipt of a negotiable document of title covering the goods; or

(b) on acknowledgment by the bailee of the buyer's right to possession of the goods; or

(c) after his receipt of a non-negotiable document of title or other written direction to deliver, as provided in subsection (4)(b) of Section 2—503.

(3) In any case not within subsection (1) or (2), the risk of loss passes to the buyer on his receipt of the goods if the seller is a merchant; otherwise the risk passes to the buyer on tender of delivery.

(4) The provisions of this section are subject to contrary agreement of the parties and to the provisions of this Article on sale on approval (Section 2—327) and on effect of breach on risk of loss (Section 2—510).

§ 2—510. Effect of Breach on Risk of Loss.

(1) Where a tender or delivery of goods so fails to conform to the contract as to give a right of rejection the risk of their loss remains on the seller until cure or acceptance.

(2) Where the buyer rightfully revokes acceptance he may to the extent of any deficiency in his effective insurance coverage treat the risk of loss as having rested on the seller from the beginning.

(3) Where the buyer as to conforming goods already identified to the contract for sale repudiates or is otherwise in breach before risk of their loss has passed to him, the seller may to the extent of any deficiency in his effective insurance coverage treat the risk of loss as resting on the buyer for a commercially reasonable time.

§ 2—511. Tender of Payment by Buyer; Payment by Check.

(1) Unless otherwise agreed tender of payment is a condition to the seller's duty to tender and complete any delivery.

(2) Tender of payment is sufficient when made by any means or in any manner current in the ordinary course of business unless the seller demands payment in legal tender and gives any extension of time reasonably necessary to procure it.

(3) Subject to the provisions of this Act on the effect of an instrument on an obligation (Section 3—310), payment by check is conditional and is defeated as between the parties by dishonor of the check on due presentment.

§ 2—512. Payment by Buyer Before Inspection.

(1) Where the contract requires payment before inspection non-conformity of the goods does not excuse the buyer from so making payment unless

(a) the non-conformity appears without inspection; or

(b) despite tender of the required documents the circumstances would justify injunction against honor under the provisions of this Act (Section 5—114).

(2) Payment pursuant to subsection (1) does not constitute an acceptance of goods or impair the buyer's right to inspect or any of his remedies.

§ 2—513. Buyer's Right to Inspection of Goods.

(1) Unless otherwise agreed and subject to subsection (3), where goods are tendered or delivered or identified to the contract for sale, the buyer has a right before payment or acceptance to inspect them at any reasonable place and time and in any reasonable manner. When the seller is required or authorized to send the goods to the buyer, the inspection may be after their arrival.

(2) Expenses of inspection must be borne by the buyer but may be recovered from the seller if the goods do not conform and are rejected.

(3) Unless otherwise agreed and subject to the provisions of this Article on C.I.F. contracts (subsection (3) of Section 2—321), the buyer is not entitled to inspect the goods before payment of the price when the contract provides

    (a) for delivery "C.O.D." or on other like terms; or

    (b) for payment against documents of title, except where such payment is due only after the goods are to become available for inspection.

(4) A place or method of inspection fixed by the parties is presumed to be exclusive but unless otherwise expressly agreed it does not postpone identification or shift the place for delivery or for passing the risk of loss. If compliance becomes impossible, inspection shall be as provided in this section unless the place or method fixed was clearly intended as an indispensable condition failure of which avoids the contract.

§ 2—514. When Documents Deliverable on Acceptance; When on Payment.

Unless otherwise agreed documents against which a draft is drawn are to be delivered to the drawee on acceptance of the draft if it is payable more than three days after presentment; otherwise, only on payment.

§ 2—515. Preserving Evidence of Goods in Dispute.

In furtherance of the adjustment of any claim or dispute

    (a) either party on reasonable notification to the other and for the purpose of ascertaining the facts and preserving evidence has the right to inspect, test and sample the goods including such of them as may be in the possession or control of the other; and

    (b) the parties may agree to a third party inspection or survey to determine the conformity or condition of the goods and may agree that the findings shall be binding upon them in any subsequent litigation or adjustment.

Part 6 Breach, Repudiation and Excuse

§ 2—601. Buyer's Rights on Improper Delivery.

Subject to the provisions of this Article on breach in installment contracts (Section 2—612) and unless otherwise agreed under the sections on contractual limitations of remedy (Sections 2—718 and 2—719), if the goods or the tender of delivery fail in any respect to conform to the contract, the buyer may

    (a) reject the whole; or

    (b) accept the whole; or

    (c) accept any commercial unit or units and reject the rest.

§ 2—602. Manner and Effect of Rightful Rejection.

(1) Rejection of goods must be within a reasonable time after their delivery or tender. It is ineffective unless the buyer seasonably notifies the seller.

(2) Subject to the provisions of the two following sections on rejected goods (Sections 2—603 and 2—604),

    (a) after rejection any exercise of ownership by the buyer with respect to any commercial unit is wrongful as against the seller; and

    (b) if the buyer has before rejection taken physical possession of goods in which he does not have a security interest under the provisions of this Article (subsection (3) of Section 2—711), he is under a duty after rejection to hold them with reasonable care at the seller's disposition for a time sufficient to permit the seller to remove them; but

    (c) the buyer has no further obligations with regard to goods rightfully rejected.

(3) The seller's rights with respect to goods wrongfully rejected are governed by the provisions of this Article on Seller's remedies in general (Section 2—703).

§ 2—603. Merchant Buyer's Duties as to Rightfully Rejected Goods.

(1) Subject to any security interest in the buyer (subsection (3) of Section 2—711), when the seller has no agent or place of business at the market of rejection a merchant buyer is under a duty after rejection of goods in his possession or control to follow any reasonable instructions received from the seller with respect to the goods and in the absence of such instructions to make reasonable efforts to sell them for the seller's account if they are perishable or threaten to decline in value speedily. Instructions are not reasonable if on demand indemnity for expenses is not forthcoming.

(2) When the buyer sells goods under subsection (1), he is entitled to reimbursement from the seller or out of the proceeds for reasonable expenses of caring for and selling them, and if the expenses include no selling commission then to such commission as is usual in the trade or if there is none to a reasonable sum not exceeding ten per cent on the gross proceeds.

(3) In complying with this section the buyer is held only to good faith and good faith conduct hereunder is neither acceptance nor conversion nor the basis of an action for damages.

§ 2—604. Buyer's Options as to Salvage of Rightfully Rejected Goods.

Subject to the provisions of the immediately preceding section on perishables if the seller gives no instructions within a reasonable time after notification of rejection the buyer may store the rejected goods for the seller's account or reship them to him or resell them for the seller's account with reimbursement as provided in the preceding section. Such action is not acceptance or conversion.

§ 2—605. Waiver of Buyer's Objections by Failure to Particularize.

(1) The buyer's failure to state in connection with rejection a particular defect which is ascertainable by reasonable inspection precludes him from relying on the unstated defect to justify rejection or to establish breach

(a) where the seller could have cured it if stated seasonably; or

(b) between merchants when the seller has after rejection made a request in writing for a full and final written statement of all defects on which the buyer proposes to rely.

(2) Payment against documents made without reservation of rights precludes recovery of the payment for defects apparent on the face of the documents.

§ 2—606. What Constitutes Acceptance of Goods.

(1) Acceptance of goods occurs when the buyer

(a) after a reasonable opportunity to inspect the goods signifies to the seller that the goods are conforming or that he will take or retain them in spite of their non-conformity; or

(b) fails to make an effective rejection (subsection (1) of Section 2—602), but such acceptance does not occur until the buyer has had a reasonable opportunity to inspect them; or

(c) does any act inconsistent with the seller's ownership; but if such act is wrongful as against the seller it is an acceptance only if ratified by him.

(2) Acceptance of a part of any commercial unit is acceptance of that entire unit.

§ 2—607. Effect of Acceptance; Notice of Breach; Burden of Establishing Breach After Acceptance; Notice of Claim or Litigation to Person Answerable Over.

(1) The buyer must pay at the contract rate for any goods accepted.

(2) Acceptance of goods by the buyer precludes rejection of the goods accepted and if made with knowledge of a non-conformity cannot be revoked because of it unless the acceptance was on the reasonable assumption that the non-conformity would be seasonably cured but acceptance does not of itself impair any other remedy provided by this Article for non-conformity.

(3) Where a tender has been accepted

(a) the buyer must within a reasonable time after he discovers or should have discovered any breach notify the seller of breach or be barred from any remedy; and

(b) if the claim is one for infringement or the like (subsection (3) of Section 2—312) and the buyer is sued as a result of such a breach he must so notify the seller within a reasonable time after he receives notice of the litigation or be barred from any remedy over for liability established by the litigation.

(4) The burden is on the buyer to establish any breach with respect to the goods accepted.

(5) Where the buyer is sued for breach of a warranty or other obligation for which his seller is answerable over

(a) he may give his seller written notice of the litigation. If the notice states that the seller may come in and defend and that if the seller does not do so he will be bound in any action against him by his buyer by any determination of fact common to the two litigations, then unless the seller after seasonable receipt of the notice does come in and defend he is so bound.

(b) if the claim is one for infringement or the like (subsection (3) of Section 2—312) the original seller may demand in writing that his buyer turn over to him control of the litigation including settlement or else be barred from any remedy over and if he also agrees to bear all expense and to satisfy any adverse judgment, then unless the buyer after seasonable receipt of the demand does turn over control the buyer is so barred.

(6) The provisions of subsections (3), (4) and (5) apply to any obligation of a buyer to hold the seller harmless against infringement or the like (subsection (3) of Section 2—312).

§ 2—608. Revocation of Acceptance in Whole or in Part.

(1) The buyer may revoke his acceptance of a lot or commercial unit whose non-conformity substantially impairs its value to him if he has accepted it

(a) on the reasonable assumption that its nonconformity would be cured and it has not been seasonably cured; or

(b) without discovery of such non-conformity if his acceptance was reasonably induced either by the difficulty of discovery before acceptance or by the seller's assurances.

(2) Revocation of acceptance must occur within a reasonable time after the buyer discovers or should have discovered the ground for it and before any substantial change in condition of the goods which is not caused by their own defects. It is not effective until the buyer notifies the seller of it.

(3) A buyer who so revokes has the same rights and duties with regard to the goods involved as if he had rejected them.

§ 2—609. Right to Adequate Assurance of Performance.

(1) A contract for sale imposes an obligation on each party that the other's expectation of receiving due performance will not be impaired. When reasonable grounds for insecurity arise with respect to the performance of either party

the other may in writing demand adequate assurance of due performance and until he receives such assurance may if commercially reasonable suspend any performance for which he has not already received the agreed return.

(2) Between merchants the reasonableness of grounds for insecurity and the adequacy of any assurance offered shall be determined according to commercial standards.

(3) Acceptance of any improper delivery or payment does not prejudice the party's right to demand adequate assurance of future performance.

(4) After receipt of a justified demand failure to provide within a reasonable time not exceeding thirty days such assurance of due performance as is adequate under the circumstances of the particular case is a repudiation of the contract.

§ 2—610. Anticipatory Repudiation.

When either party repudiates the contract with respect to a performance not yet due the loss of which will substantially impair the value of the contract to the other, the aggrieved party may

(a) for a commercially reasonable time await performance by the repudiating party; or

(b) resort to any remedy for breach (Section 2—703 or Section 2—711), even though he has notified the repudiating party that he would await the latter's performance and has urged retraction; and

(c) in either case suspend his own performance or proceed in accordance with the provisions of this Article on the seller's right to identify goods to the contract notwithstanding breach or to salvage unfinished goods (Section 2—704).

§ 2—611. Retraction of Anticipatory Repudiation.

(1) Until the repudiating party's next performance is due he can retract his repudiation unless the aggrieved party has since the repudiation cancelled or materially changed his position or otherwise indicated that he considers the repudiation final.

(2) Retraction may be by any method which clearly indicates to the aggrieved party that the repudiating party intends to perform, but must include any assurance justifiably demanded under the provisions of this Article (Section 2—609).

(3) Retraction reinstates the repudiating party's rights under the contract with due excuse and allowance to the aggrieved party for any delay occasioned by the repudiation.

§ 2—612. "Installment Contract"; Breach.

(1) An "installment contract" is one which requires or authorizes the delivery of goods in separate lots to be separately accepted, even though the contract contains a clause "each delivery is a separate contract" or its equivalent.

(2) The buyer may reject any installment which is non-conforming if the non-conformity substantially impairs the

value of that installment and cannot be cured or if the non-conformity is a defect in the required documents; but if the non-conformity does not fall within subsection (3) and the seller gives adequate assurance of its cure the buyer must accept that installment.

(3) Whenever non-conformity or default with respect to one or more installments substantially impairs the value of the whole contract there is a breach of the whole. But the aggrieved party reinstates the contract if he accepts a non-conforming installment without seasonably notifying of cancellation or if he brings an action with respect only to past installments or demands performance as to future installments.

§ 2—613. Casualty to Identified Goods.

Where the contract requires for its performance goods identified when the contract is made, and the goods suffer casualty without fault of either party before the risk of loss passes to the buyer, or in a proper case under a "no arrival, no sale" term (Section 2—324) then

(a) if the loss is total the contract is avoided; and

(b) if the loss is partial or the goods have so deteriorated as no longer to conform to the contract the buyer may nevertheless demand inspection and at his option either treat the contract as voided or accept the goods with due allowance from the contract price for the deterioration or the deficiency in quantity but without further right against the seller.

§ 2—614. Substituted Performance.

(1) Where without fault of either party the agreed berthing, loading, or unloading facilities fail or an agreed type of carrier becomes unavailable or the agreed manner of delivery otherwise becomes commercially impracticable but a commercially reasonable substitute is available, such substitute performance must be tendered and accepted.

(2) If the agreed means or manner of payment fails because of domestic or foreign governmental regulation, the seller may withhold or stop delivery unless the buyer provides a means or manner of payment which is commercially a substantial equivalent. If delivery has already been taken, payment by the means or in the manner provided by the regulation discharges the buyer's obligation unless the regulation is discriminatory, oppressive or predatory.

§ 2—615. Excuse by Failure of Presupposed Conditions.

Except so far as a seller may have assumed a greater obligation and subject to the preceding section on substituted performance:

(a) Delay in delivery or non-delivery in whole or in part by a seller who complies with paragraphs (b) and (c) is not a breach of his duty under a contract for sale if performance as agreed has been made impracticable by the occurrence of a contingency the nonoccurrence of which was a basic assumption on which the contract was made or by compliance in good faith with any applicable foreign or domestic governmental regulation or order whether or not it later proves to be invalid.

(b) Where the causes mentioned in paragraph (a) affect only a part of the seller's capacity to perform, he must allocate production and deliveries among his customers but may at his option include regular customers not then under contract as well as his own requirements for further manufacture. He may so allocate in any manner which is fair and reasonable.

(c) The seller must notify the buyer seasonably that there will be delay or non-delivery and, when allocation is required under paragraph (b), of the estimated quota thus made available for the buyer.

§ 2—616. Procedure on Notice Claiming Excuse.

(1) Where the buyer receives notification of a material or indefinite delay or an allocation justified under the preceding section he may by written notification to the seller as to any delivery concerned, and where the prospective deficiency substantially impairs the value of the whole contract under the provisions of this Article relating to breach of installment contracts (Section 2—612), then also as to the whole,

(a) terminate and thereby discharge any unexecuted portion of the contract; or

(b) modify the contract by agreeing to take his available quota in substitution.

(2) If after receipt of such notification from the seller the buyer fails so to modify the contract within a reasonable time not exceeding thirty days the contract lapses with respect to any deliveries affected.

(3) The provisions of this section may not be negated by agreement except in so far as the seller has assumed a greater obligation under the preceding section.

Part 7 Remedies

§ 2—701. Remedies for Breach of Collateral Contracts Not Impaired.

Remedies for breach of any obligation or promise collateral or ancillary to a contract for sale are not impaired by the provisions of this Article.

§ 2—702. Seller's Remedies on Discovery of Buyer's Insolvency.

(1) Where the seller discovers the buyer to be insolvent he may refuse delivery except for cash including payment for all goods theretofore delivered under the contract, and stop delivery under this Article (Section 2—705).

(2) Where the seller discovers that the buyer has received goods on credit while insolvent he may reclaim the goods upon demand made within ten days after the receipt, but if misrepresentation of solvency has been made to the par-

ticular seller in writing within three months before delivery the ten day limitation does not apply. Except as provided in this subsection the seller may not base a right to reclaim goods on the buyer's fraudulent or innocent misrepresentation of solvency or of intent to pay.

(3) The seller's right to reclaim under subsection (2) is subject to the rights of a buyer in ordinary course or other good faith purchaser under this Article (Section 2—403). Successful reclamation of goods excludes all other remedies with respect to them.

§ 2—703. Seller's Remedies in General.

Where the buyer wrongfully rejects or revokes acceptance of goods or fails to make a payment due on or before delivery or repudiates with respect to a part or the whole, then with respect to any goods directly affected and, if the breach is of the whole contract (Section 2—612), then also with respect to the whole undelivered balance, the aggrieved seller may

(a) withhold delivery of such goods;

(b) stop delivery by any bailee as hereafter provided (Section 2—705);

(c) proceed under the next section respecting goods still unidentified to the contract;

(d) resell and recover damages as hereafter provided (Section 2—706);

(e) recover damages for non-acceptance (Section 2—708) or in a proper case the price (Section 2—709);

(f) cancel.

§ 2—704. Seller's Right to Identify Goods to the Contract Notwithstanding Breach or to Salvage Unfinished Goods.

(1) An aggrieved seller under the preceding section may

(a) identify to the contract conforming goods not already identified if at the time he learned of the breach they are in his possession or control;

(b) treat as the subject of resale goods which have demonstrably been intended for the particular contract even though those goods are unfinished.

(2) Where the goods are unfinished an aggrieved seller may in the exercise of reasonable commercial judgment for the purposes of avoiding loss and of effective realization either complete the manufacture and wholly identify the goods to the contract or cease manufacture and resell for scrap or salvage value or proceed in any other reasonable manner.

§ 2—705. Seller's Stoppage of Delivery in Transit or Otherwise.

(1) The seller may stop delivery of goods in the possession of a carrier or other bailee when he discovers the buyer to be insolvent (Section 2—702) and may stop delivery of carload, truckload, planeload or larger shipments of express or

freight when the buyer repudiates or fails to make a payment due before delivery or if for any other reason the seller has a right to withhold or reclaim the goods.

(2) As against such buyer the seller may stop delivery until

(a) receipt of the goods by the buyer; or

(b) acknowledgment to the buyer by any bailee of the goods except a carrier that the bailee holds the goods for the buyer; or

(c) such acknowledgment to the buyer by a carrier by reshipment or as warehouseman; or

(d) negotiation to the buyer of any negotiable document of title covering the goods.

(3) (a) To stop delivery the seller must so notify as to enable the bailee by reasonable diligence to prevent delivery of the goods.

(b) After such notification the bailee must hold and deliver the goods according to the directions of the seller but the seller is liable to the bailee for any ensuing charges or damages.

(c) If a negotiable document of title has been issued for goods the bailee is not obliged to obey a notification to stop until surrender of the document.

(d) A carrier who has issued a non-negotiable bill of lading is not obliged to obey a notification to stop received from a person other than the consignor.

§ 2—706. Seller's Resale Including Contract for Resale.

(1) Under the conditions stated in Section 2—703 on seller's remedies, the seller may resell the goods concerned or the undelivered balance thereof. Where the resale is made in good faith and in a commercially reasonable manner the seller may recover the difference between the resale price and the contract price together with any incidental damages allowed under the provisions of this Article (Section 2—710), but less expenses saved in consequence of the buyer's breach.

(2) Except as otherwise provided in subsection (3) or unless otherwise agreed resale may be at public or private sale including sale by way of one or more contracts to sell or of identification to an existing contract of the seller. Sale may be as a unit or in parcels and at any time and place and on any terms but every aspect of the sale including the method, manner, time, place and terms must be commercially reasonable. The resale must be reasonably identified as referring to the broken contract, but it is not necessary that the goods be in existence or that any or all of them have been identified to the contract before the breach.

(3) Where the resale is at private sale the seller must give the buyer reasonable notification of his intention to resell.

(4) Where the resale is at public sale

(a) only identified goods can be sold except where there is a recognized market for a public sale of futures in goods of the kind; and

(b) it must be made at a usual place or market for public sale if one is reasonably available and except in the case of goods which are perishable or threaten to decline in value speedily the seller must give the buyer reasonable notice of the time and place of the resale; and

(c) if the goods are not to be within the view of those attending the sale the notification of sale must state the place where the goods are located and provide for their reasonable inspection by prospective bidders; and

(d) the seller may buy.

(5) A purchaser who buys in good faith at a resale takes the goods free of any rights of the original buyer even though the seller fails to comply with one or more of the requirements of this section.

(6) The seller is not accountable to the buyer for any profit made on any resale. A person in the position of a seller (Section 2—707) or a buyer who has rightfully rejected or justifiably revoked acceptance must account for any excess over the amount of his security interest, as hereinafter defined (subsection (3) of Section 2—711).

§ 2—707. "Person in the Position of a Seller".

(1) A "person in the position of a seller" includes as against a principal an agent who has paid or become responsible for the price of goods on behalf of his principal or anyone who otherwise holds a security interest or other right in goods similar to that of a seller.

(2) A person in the position of a seller may as provided in this Article withhold or stop delivery (Section 2—705) and resell (Section 2—706) and recover incidental damages (Section 2—710).

§ 2—708. Seller's Damages for Non-Acceptance or Repudiation.

(1) Subject to subsection (2) and to the provisions of this Article with respect to proof of market price (Section 2—723), the measure of damages for non-acceptance or repudiation by the buyer is the difference between the market price at the time and place for tender and the unpaid contract price together with any incidental damages provided in this Article (Section 2—710), but less expenses saved in consequence of the buyer's breach.

(2) If the measure of damages provided in subsection (1) is inadequate to put the seller in as good a position as performance would have done then the measure of damages is the profit (including reasonable overhead) which the seller would have made from full performance by the buyer, together with any incidental damages provided in this Article (Section 2—710), due allowance for costs reasonably incurred and due credit for payments or proceeds of resale.

§ 2—709. Action for the Price.

(1) When the buyer fails to pay the price as it becomes due the seller may recover, together with any incidental damages under the next section, the price

    (a) of goods accepted or of conforming goods lost or damaged within a commercially reasonable time after risk of their loss has passed to the buyer; and

    (b) of goods identified to the contract if the seller is unable after reasonable effort to resell them at a reasonable price or the circumstances reasonably indicate that such effort will be unavailing.

(2) Where the seller sues for the price he must hold for the buyer any goods which have been identified to the contract and are still in his control except that if resale becomes possible he may resell them at any time prior to the collection of the judgment. The net proceeds of any such resale must be credited to the buyer and payment of the judgment entitles him to any goods not resold.

(3) After the buyer has wrongfully rejected or revoked acceptance of the goods or has failed to make a payment due or has repudiated (Section 2—610), a seller who is held not entitled to the price under this section shall nevertheless be awarded damages for non-acceptance under the preceding section.

§ 2—710. Seller's Incidental Damages.

Incidental damages to an aggrieved seller include any commercially reasonable charges, expenses or commissions incurred in stopping delivery, in the transportation, care and custody of goods after the buyer's breach, in connection with return or resale of the goods or otherwise resulting from the breach.

§ 2—711. Buyer's Remedies in General; Buyer's Security Interest in Rejected Goods.

(1) Where the seller fails to make delivery or repudiates or the buyer rightfully rejects or justifiably revokes acceptance then with respect to any goods involved, and with respect to the whole if the breach goes to the whole contract (Section 2—612), the buyer may cancel and whether or not he has done so may in addition to recovering so much of the price as has been paid

    (a) "cover" and have damages under the next section as to all the goods affected whether or not they have been identified to the contract; or

    (b) recover damages for non-delivery as provided in this Article (Section 2—713).

(2) Where the seller fails to deliver or repudiates the buyer may also

    (a) if the goods have been identified recover them as provided in this Article (Section 2—502); or

    (b) in a proper case obtain specific performance or replevy the goods as provided in this Article (Section 2—716).

(3) On rightful rejection or justifiable revocation of acceptance a buyer has a security interest in goods in his possession or control for any payments made on their price and any expenses reasonably incurred in their inspection, receipt, transportation, care and custody and may hold such goods and resell them in like manner as an aggrieved seller (Section 2—706).

§ 2—712. "Cover"; Buyer's Procurement of Substitute Goods.

(1) After a breach within the preceding section the buyer may "cover" by making in good faith and without unreasonable delay any reasonable purchase of or contract to purchase goods in substitution for those due from the seller.

(2) The buyer may recover from the seller as damages the difference between the cost of cover and the contract price together with any incidental or consequential damages as hereinafter defined (Section 2—715), but less expenses saved in consequence of the seller's breach.

(3) Failure of the buyer to effect cover within this section does not bar him from any other remedy.

§ 2—713. Buyer's Damages for Non-Delivery or Repudiation.

(1) Subject to the provisions of this Article with respect to proof of market price (Section 2—723), the measure of damages for non-delivery or repudiation by the seller is the difference between the market price at the time when the buyer learned of the breach and the contract price together with any incidental and consequential damages provided in this Article (Section 2—715), but less expenses saved in consequence of the seller's breach.

(2) Market price is to be determined as of the place for tender or, in cases of rejection after arrival or revocation of acceptance, as of the place of arrival.

§ 2—714. Buyer's Damages for Breach in Regard to Accepted Goods.

(1) Where the buyer has accepted goods and given notification (subsection (3) of Section 2—607) he may recover as damages for any non-conformity of tender the loss resulting in the ordinary course of events from the seller's breach as determined in any manner which is reasonable.

(2) The measure of damages for breach of warranty is the difference at the time and place of acceptance between the value of the goods accepted and the value they would have had if they had been as warranted, unless special circumstances show proximate damages of a different amount.

(3) In a proper case any incidental and consequential damages under the next section may also be recovered.

§ 2—715. Buyer's Incidental and Consequential Damages.

(1) Incidental damages resulting from the seller's breach include expenses reasonably incurred in inspection, receipt, transportation and care and custody of goods rightfully rejected, any commercially reasonable charges, expenses or commissions in connection with effecting cover and any other reasonable expense incident to the delay or other breach.

(2) Consequential damages resulting from the seller's breach include

(a) any loss resulting from general or particular requirements and needs of which the seller at the time of contracting had reason to know and which could not reasonably be prevented by cover or otherwise; and

(b) injury to person or property proximately resulting from any breach of warranty.

§ 2—716. Buyer's Right to Specific Performance or Replevin.

(1) Specific performance may be decreed where the goods are unique or in other proper circumstances.

(2) The decree for specific performance may include such terms and conditions as to payment of the price, damages, or other relief as the court may deem just.

(3) The buyer has a right of replevin for goods identified to the contract if after reasonable effort he is unable to effect cover for such goods or the circumstances reasonably indicate that such effort will be unavailing or if the goods have been shipped under reservation and satisfaction of the security interest in them has been made or tendered.

§ 2—717. Deduction of Damages From the Price.

The buyer on notifying the seller of his intention to do so may deduct all or any part of the damages resulting from any breach of the contract from any part of the price still due under the same contract.

§ 2—718. Liquidation or Limitation of Damages; Deposits.

(1) Damages for breach by either party may be liquidated in the agreement but only at an amount which is reasonable in the light of the anticipated or actual harm caused by the breach, the difficulties of proof of loss, and the inconvenience or nonfeasibility of otherwise obtaining an adequate remedy. A term fixing unreasonably large liquidated damages is void as a penalty.

(2) Where the seller justifiably withholds delivery of goods because of the buyer's breach, the buyer is entitled to restitution of any amount by which the sum of his payments exceeds

(a) the amount to which the seller is entitled by virtue of terms liquidating the seller's damages in accordance with subsection (1), or

(b) in the absence of such terms, twenty per cent of the value of the total performance for which the buyer is obligated under the contract or $500, whichever is smaller.

(3) The buyer's right to restitution under subsection (2) is subject to offset to the extent that the seller establishes

(a) a right to recover damages under the provisions of this Article other than subsection (1), and

(b) the amount or value of any benefits received by the buyer directly or indirectly by reason of the contract.

(4) Where a seller has received payment in goods their reasonable value or the proceeds of their resale shall be treated as payments for the purposes of subsection (2); but if the seller has notice of the buyer's breach before reselling goods received in part performance, his resale is subject to the conditions laid down in this Article on resale by an aggrieved seller (Section 2—706).

§ 2—719. Contractual Modification or Limitation of Remedy.

(1) Subject to the provisions of subsections (2) and (3) of this section and of the preceding section on liquidation and limitation of damages,

(a) the agreement may provide for remedies in addition to or in substitution for those provided in this Article and may limit or alter the measure of damages recoverable under this Article, as by limiting the buyer's remedies to return of the goods and repayment of the price or to repair and replacement of nonconforming goods or parts; and

(b) resort to a remedy as provided is optional unless the remedy is expressly agreed to be exclusive, in which case it is the sole remedy.

(2) Where circumstances cause an exclusive or limited remedy to fail of its essential purpose, remedy may be had as provided in this Act.

(3) Consequential damages may be limited or excluded unless the limitation or exclusion is unconscionable. Limitation of consequential damages for injury to the person in the case of consumer goods is prima facie unconscionable but limitation of damages where the loss is commercial is not.

§ 2—720. Effect of "Cancellation" or "Rescission" on Claims for Antecedent Breach.

Unless the contrary intention clearly appears, expressions of "cancellation" or "rescission" of the contract or the like shall not be construed as a renunciation or discharge of any claim in damages for an antecedent breach.

§ 2—721. Remedies for Fraud.

Remedies for material misrepresentation or fraud include all remedies available under this Article for non-fraudulent breach. Neither rescission or a claim for rescission of the contract for sale nor rejection or return of the goods shall bar or be deemed inconsistent with a claim for damages or other remedy.

§ 2—722. Who Can Sue Third Parties for Injury to Goods.

Where a third party so deals with goods which have been identified to a contract for sale as to cause actionable injury to a party to that contract

(a) a right of action against the third party is in either party to the contract for sale who has title to or a security interest or a special property or an insurable interest in the goods; and if the goods have been destroyed or converted a right of action is also in the party who either bore the risk of loss under the contract for sale or has since the injury assumed that risk as against the other;

(b) if at the time of the injury the party plaintiff did not bear the risk of loss as against the other party to the contract for sale and there is no arrangement between them for disposition of the recovery, his suit or settlement is, subject to his own interest, as a fiduciary for the other party to the contract;

(c) either party may with the consent of the other sue for the benefit of whom it may concern.

§ 2—723. Proof of Market Price: Time and Place.

(1) If an action based on anticipatory repudiation comes to trial before the time for performance with respect to some or all of the goods, any damages based on market price (Section 2—708 or Section 2—713) shall be determined according to the price of such goods prevailing at the time when the aggrieved party learned of the repudiation.

(2) If evidence of a price prevailing at the times or places described in this Article is not readily available the price prevailing within any reasonable time before or after the time described or at any other place which in commercial judgment or under usage of trade would serve as a reasonable substitute for the one described may be used, making any proper allowance for the cost of transporting the goods to or from such other place.

(3) Evidence of a relevant price prevailing at a time or place other than the one described in this Article offered by one party is not admissible unless and until he has given the other party such notice as the court finds sufficient to prevent unfair surprise.

§ 2—724. Admissibility of Market Quotations.

Whenever the prevailing price or value of any goods regularly bought and sold in any established commodity market is in issue, reports in official publications or trade journals or in newspapers or periodicals of general circulation published as the reports of such market shall be admissible in evidence. The circumstances of the preparation of such a report may be shown to affect its weight but not its admissibility.

§ 2—725. Statute of Limitations in Contracts for Sale.

(1) An action for breach of any contract for sale must be commenced within four years after the cause of action has accrued. By the original agreement the parties may reduce the period of limitation to not less than one year but may not extend it.

(2) A cause of action accrues when the breach occurs, regardless of the aggrieved party's lack of knowledge of the breach. A breach of warranty occurs when tender of delivery is made, except that where a warranty explicitly extends to future performance of the goods and discovery of the breach must await the time of such performance the cause of action accrues when the breach is or should have been discovered.

(3) Where an action commenced within the time limited by subsection (1) is so terminated as to leave available a remedy by another action for the same breach such other action may be commenced after the expiration of the time limited and within six months after the termination of the first action unless the termination resulted from voluntary discontinuance or from dismissal for failure or neglect to prosecute.

(4) This section does not alter the law on tolling of the statute of limitations nor does it apply to causes of action which have accrued before this Act becomes effective.

The National Labor Relations Act of 1935 (Excerpts)

* * * *

§ 157. Right of Employees as to Organization, Collective Bargaining, etc.

Employees shall have the right to self-organization, to form, join, or assist labor organizations, to bargain collectively through representatives of their own choosing, and to engage in other concerted activities for the purpose of collective bargaining or other mutual aid or protection, and shall also have the right to refrain from any or all of such activities except to the extent that such right may be affected by an agreement requiring membership in a labor organization as a condition of employment as authorized in section 158(a)(3) of this title.

§ 158. Unfair Labor Practices

(a) Unfair labor practices for an employer

It shall be an unfair labor practice for an employer—

(1) to interfere with, restrain, or coerce employees in the exercise of the rights guaranteed in section 157 of this title;

(2) to dominate or interfere with the formation or administration of any labor organization or contribute financial or other support to it: Provided, [t]hat subject to rules and regulations made and published by the Board pursuant to section 156 of this title, an employer shall not be prohibited from permitting employees to confer with him during working hours without loss of time or pay;

(3) by discrimination in regard to hire or tenure of employment or any term or condition of employment to encourage or discourage membership in any labor organization: Provided, [t]hat nothing in this subchapter, or in any other statute of the United States, shall preclude an employer from making an agreement with a labor organization (not established, maintained, or assisted by any action defined in this subsection as an unfair labor practice) to require as a condition of employment membership therein on or after the thirtieth day following the beginning of such employment or the effective date of such agreement, whichever is the later, (i) if such labor organization is the representative of the employees as provided in section 159(a) of this title, in the appropriate collective-bargaining unit covered by such agreement when made, and (ii) unless following an election held as provided in section 159(e) of this title within one year preceding the effective date of such agreement, the Board shall have certified that at least a majority of the employees eligible to vote in such election have voted to rescind the authority of such labor organization to make such an agreement: Provided further, [t]hat no employer shall justify any discrimination against an employee for nonmembership in a labor organization (A) if he has reasonable grounds for believing that such membership was not available to the employee on the same terms and conditions generally applicable to other members, or (B) if he has reasonable grounds for believing that membership was denied or terminated for reasons

other than the failure of the employee to tender the periodic dues and the initiation fees uniformly required as a condition of acquiring or retaining membership;

(4) to discharge or otherwise discriminate against an employee because he has filed charges or given testimony under this subchapter;

(5) to refuse to bargain collectively with the representatives of his employees, subject to the provisions of section 159(a) of this title.

(b) Unfair labor practices by labor organization

It shall be an unfair labor practice for a labor organization or its agents—

(1) to restrain or coerce (A) employees in the exercise of the rights guaranteed in section 157 of this title: Provided, [t]hat this paragraph shall not impair the right of a labor organization to prescribe its own rules with respect to the acquisition or retention of membership therein; or (B) an employer in the selection of his representatives for the purposes of collective bargaining or the adjustment of grievances;

(2) to cause or attempt to cause an employer to discriminate against an employee in violation of subsection (a)(3) of this section or to discriminate against an employee with respect to whom membership in such organization has been denied or terminated on some ground other than his failure to tender the periodic dues and the initiation fees uniformly required as a condition of acquiring or retaining membership;

(3) to refuse to bargain collectively with an employer, provided it is the representative of his employees subject to the provisions of section 159(a) of this title;

(4) (i) to engage in, or to induce or encourage any individual employed by any person engaged in commerce or in an industry affecting commerce to engage in, a strike or a refusal in the course of his employment to use, manufacture, process, transport, or otherwise handle or work on any goods, articles, materials, or commodities or to perform any services; or (ii) to threaten, coerce, or restrain any person engaged in commerce or in an industry affecting commerce[.] * * *

(5) to require of employees covered by an agreement authorized under subsection (a)(3) of this section the payment, as a condition precedent to becoming a member of such organization, of a fee in an amount which the Board finds excessive or discriminatory under all the circumstances. In making such a finding, the Board shall consider, among other relevant factors, the practices and customs of labor organizations in the particular industry, and the wages currently paid to the employees affected;

(6) to cause or attempt to cause an employer to pay or deliver or agree to pay or deliver any money or other thing of value, in the nature of an exaction, for services which are not performed or not to be performed; and

(7) to picket or cause to be picketed, or threaten to picket or cause to be picketed, any employer where an object thereof is forcing or requiring an employer to recognize or bargain with a labor organization as the representative of his employees, or forcing or requiring the employees of an employer to accept or select such labor organization as their collective bargaining representative[.] * * *

(c) Expression of views without threat of reprisal or force or promise of benefit

The expressing of any views, argument, or opinion, or the dissemination thereof, whether in written, printed, graphic, or visual form, shall not constitute or be evidence of an unfair labor practice under any of the provisions of this subchapter, if such expression contains no threat of reprisal or force or promise of benefit.

(d) Obligation to bargain collectively

For the purposes of this section, to bargain collectively is the performance of the mutual obligation of the employer and the representative of the employees to meet at reasonable times and confer in good faith with respect to wages, hours, and other terms and conditions of employment, or the negotiation of an agreement, or any question arising thereunder, and the execution of a written contract incorporating any agreement reached if requested by either party, but such obligation does not compel either party to agree to a proposal or require the making of a concession: Provided, [t]hat where there is in effect a collective-bargaining contract covering employees in an industry affecting commerce, the duty to bargain collectively shall also mean that no party to such contract shall terminate or modify such contract, unless the party desiring such termination or modification—

(1) serves a written notice upon the other party to the contract of the proposed termination or modification sixty days prior to the expiration date thereof, or in the event such contract contains no expiration date, sixty days prior to the time it is proposed to make such termination or modification;

(2) offers to meet and confer with the other party for the purpose of negotiating a new contract or a contract containing the proposed modifications;

(3) notifies the Federal Mediation and Conciliation Service within thirty days after such notice of the existence of a dispute, and simultaneously therewith notifies any State or Territorial agency established to mediate and conciliate disputes within the State or Territory where the dispute occurred, provided no agreement has been reached by that time; and

(4) continues in full force and effect, without resorting to strike or lock-out, all the terms and conditions of the existing contract for a period of sixty days after such notice is given or until the expiration date of such contract, whichever occurs later[.] * * *

The Sherman Act of 1890 (Excerpts)

Section 1. Every contract, combination in the form of trust or otherwise, or conspiracy, in restraint of trade or commerce among the several States, or with foreign nations, is declared to be illegal. Every person who shall make any contract or engage in any combination or conspiracy hereby declared to be illegal shall be deemed guilty of a felony, and, on conviction thereof, shall be punished by fine not exceeding $10,000,000 if a corporation, or, if any other person, $350,000, or by imprisonment not exceeding three years, or by both said punishments, in the discretion of the court.

Section 2. Every person who shall monopolize, or attempt to monopolize, or combine or conspire with any other person or persons, to monopolize any part of the trade or commerce among the several States, or with foreign nations, shall be deemed guilty of a felony, and, on conviction thereof, shall be punished by fine not exceeding $10,000,000 if a corporation, or, if any other person, $350,000, or by imprisonment not exceeding three years, or by both said punishments, in the discretion of the court.

Section 3. Every contract, combination in form of trust or otherwise, or conspiracy, in restraint of trade or commerce in any Territory of the United States or of the District of Columbia, or in restraint of trade or commerce between any such Territory and another, or between any such Territory or Territories and any State or States or the District of Columbia, or with foreign nations, or between the District of Columbia and any State or States or foreign nations, is declared illegal. Every person who shall make any such contract or engage in any such combination or conspiracy, shall be deemed guilty of a felony, and, on conviction thereof, shall be punished by fine not exceeding $10,000,000 if a corporation, or, if any other person, $350,000, or by imprisonment not exceeding three years, or by both said punishments, in the discretion of the court.

* * * *

Section 7. Every combination, conspiracy, trust, agreement, or contract is declared to be contrary to public policy, illegal, and void when the same is made by or between two or more persons or corporations, either of whom, as agent or principal, is engaged in importing any article from any foreign country into the United States, and when such combination, conspiracy, trust, agreement, or contract is intended to operate in restraint of lawful trade, or free competition in lawful trade or commerce, or to increase the market price in any part of the United States of any article or articles imported or intended to be imported into the United States, or of any manufacture into which such imported article enters or is intended to enter. Every person who shall be engaged in the importation of goods or any commodity from any foreign country in violation of this section, or who shall combine or conspire with another to violate the same, is guilty of a misdemeanor, and on conviction thereof in any court of the United States such person shall be fined in a sum not less than $100 and not exceeding $5,000, and shall be further punished by imprisonment, in the discretion of the court, for a term not less than three months nor exceeding twelve months.

Section 8. The word "person", or "persons", wherever used in sections 1 to 7 of this title shall be deemed to include corporations and associations existing under or authorized by the laws of either the United States, the laws of any of the Territories, the laws of any State, or the laws of any foreign country.

APPENDIX G

The Clayton Act of 1914 (Excerpts)

Section 3. That it shall be unlawful for any person engaged in commerce, in the course of such commerce, to lease or make a sale or contract for sale of goods, wares, merchandise, machinery, supplies, or other commodities, whether patented or unpatented, for use, consumption, or resale within the United States or * * * other place under the jurisdiction of the United States, or fix a price charged therefor, or discount from, or rebate upon, such price, on the condition, agreement, or understanding that the lessee or purchaser thereof shall not use or deal in the goods, wares, merchandise, machinery, supplies, or other commodities of a competitor or competitors of the lessor or seller, where the effect of such lease, sale, or contract for sale or such condition, agreement, or understanding may be to substantially lessen competition to tend to create a monopoly in any line of commerce.

Section 4. That any person who shall be injured in his business or property by reason of anything forbidden in the antitrust laws may sue therefor in any district court of the United States in the district in which the defendant resides or is found, or has an agent, without respect to the amount in controversy, and shall recover threefold the damages by him sustained, and the cost of suit, including a reasonable attorney's fee.

Section 4A. Whenever the United States is hereafter injured in its business or property by reason of anything forbidden in the antitrust laws it may sue therefor in the United States district court for the district in which the defendant resides or is found or has an agent, without respect to the amount in controversy, and shall recover actual damages by it sustained and the cost of suit.

Section 4B. Any action to enforce any cause of action under sections 4 or 4A shall be forever barred unless commenced within four years after the cause of action accrued. No cause of action barred under existing law on the effective date of this act shall be revived by this Act.

* * * *

Section 6. That the labor of a human being is not a commodity or article of commerce. Nothing contained in the antitrust laws shall be construed to forbid the existence and operation of labor, agricultural or horticultural organizations, instituted for the purposes of mutual help, and not having capital stock or conducted for profit, or to forbid or restrain individual members of such organizations from lawfully carrying out the legitimate objects thereof; nor shall such organizations or the members thereof, be held or construed to be illegal combinations or conspiracies in restraint of trade, under the antitrust laws.

Section 7. That no person engaged in commerce shall acquire, directly or indirectly, the whole or any part of the stock or other share capital and no corporation subject to the jurisdiction of the Federal Trade Commission shall acquire the whole or any part of the assets of another corporation engaged also in commerce, where in any line of commerce in any section of the country, the effect of such acquisition may be substantially to lessen competition, or to tend to create a monopoly.

No person shall acquire, directly or indirectly, the whole or any part of the stock or other share capital and no corporation subject to the jurisdiction of the Federal Trade Commission shall acquire the whole or any part of the assets of one or more corporations engaged in commerce, where in any line of commerce in any section of the country, the effect of such acquisition, of such stocks or assets, or of the use of such stock by the voting or granting of proxies or otherwise, may be substantially to lessen competition, or to tend to create a monopoly.

This section shall not apply to persons purchasing such stock solely for investment and not using the same by voting or otherwise to bring about, or in attempting to bring about, the substantial lessening of competition * * * .

Section 8. * * * No person at the same time shall be a director in any two or more corporations any one of which has capital, surplus, and undivided profits aggregating more than $1,000,000 engaged in whole or in part in commerce, * * * if such corporations are or shall have been theretofore, by virtue of their business and location of operation, competitors, so that the elimination of competition by agreement between them would constitute a violation of any of the provisions of the antitrust laws. * * *

The Federal Trade Commission Act of 1914 (Excerpts)

Section 5. (a)(1) Unfair methods of competition in or affecting commerce, and unfair or deceptive acts or practices in or affecting commerce, are hereby declared unlawful.

(2) The Commission is hereby empowered and directed to prevent persons, partnerships, or corporations from using unfair methods of competition in or affecting commerce and unfair or deceptive acts or practices in or affecting commerce.

(1) Any person, partnership, or corporation who violates an order of the Commission after it has become final, and while such order is in effect, shall forfeit and pay to the United States a civil penalty of not more than $10,000 for each violation, which shall accrue to the United States and may be recovered in a civil action brought by the Attorney General of the United States. Each separate violation of such an order shall be a separate offense, except that in the case of a violation through continuing failure to obey or neglect to obey a final order of the Commission, each day of continuance of such failure or neglect shall be deemed a separate offense. In such actions, the United States district courts are empowered to grant mandatory injunctions and such other and further equitable relief as they deem appropriate in the enforcement of such final orders of the Commission.

The Robinson-Patman Act of 1936 (Excerpts)

Section 2. Discrimination in Price, Services, or Facilities—Price; Selection of Customers

(a) It shall be unlawful for any person engaged in commerce, in the course of such commerce, either directly or indirectly, to discriminate in price between different purchasers of commodities of like grade and quality, where either or any of the purchases involved in such discrimination are in commerce, where such commodities are sold for use, consumption, or resale within the United States or any Territory thereof or the District of Columbia or any insular possession or other place under the jurisdiction of the United States, and where the effect of such discrimination may be substantially to lessen competition or tend to create a monopoly in any line of commerce, or to injure, destroy, or prevent competition with any person who either grants or knowingly receives the benefit of such discrimination, or with customers of either of them; *Provided,* That nothing herein contained shall prevent differentials which make only due allowance for differences in the cost of manufacture, sale, or delivery resulting from the differing methods or quantities in which such commodities are to such purchasers sold or delivered: *Provided, however,* That the Federal Trade Commission may, after due investigation and hearing to all interested parties, fix and establish quantity limits, and revise the same as it finds necessary, as to particular commodities or classes of commodities, where it finds that available purchasers in greater quantities are so few as to render differentials on account thereof unjustly discriminatory or promotive of monopoly in any line of commerce; and the foregoing shall then not be construed to permit differentials based on differences in quantities greater than those so fixed and established: *And provided further,* That nothing herein contained shall prevent persons engaged in selling goods, wares, or merchandise in commerce from selecting their own customers in bona fide transactions and not in restraint of trade: *And provided further,* That nothing herein contained shall prevent price changes from time to time where in response to changing conditions affecting the market for or the marketability of the goods concerned, such as but not limited to actual or imminent deterioration of perishable goods, obsolescence of seasonal goods, distress sales under court process, or sales in good faith in discontinuance of business in the goods concerned.

Burden of Rebutting Prima-Facie Case of Discrimination

(b) Upon proof being made, at any hearing on a complaint under this section, that there has been discrimination in price or services or facilities furnished, the burden of rebutting the prima-facie case thus made by showing justification shall be upon the person charged with a violation of this section, and unless justification shall be affirmatively shown, the Commission is authorized to issue an order terminating the discrimination: *Provided, however,* That nothing herein contained shall prevent a seller rebutting the prima-facie case thus made by showing that his [or her] lower price or the furnishing of services or facilities to any purchaser or purchasers was made in good faith to meet an equally low price of a competitor, or the services or facilities furnished by a competitor.

Payment or Acceptance of Commission, Brokerage, or Other Compensation

(c) It shall be unlawful for any person engaged in commerce, in the course of such commerce, to pay or grant, or to receive or accept, anything of value as a commission, brokerage, or other compensation, or any allowance or discount in lieu thereof, except for services rendered in connection with the sale or purchase of goods, wares, or merchandise, either to the other party to such transaction or to an agent, representative, or other intermediary therein where such intermediary is acting in fact for or in behalf, or is subject to the direct or indirect control, of any party to such transaction other than the person by whom such compensation is so granted or paid.

Payment for Services or Facilities for Processing or Sale

(d) It shall be unlawful for any person engaged in commerce to pay or contract for the payment of anything of value to or for the benefit of a customer of such person in the course of such commerce as compensation or in consideration for any services or facilities furnished by or through such customer in connection with the processing, handling, sale or offering for sale of any products or commodities manufactured, sold, or offered for sale by such person, unless such payment or consideration is available on proportionally equal terms to all other customers competing in the distribution of such products or commodities.

Furnishing Services or Facilities for Processing, Handling, etc.

(e) It shall be unlawful for any person to discriminate in favor of one purchaser against another purchaser or purchasers of a commodity bought for resale, with or without processing, by contracting to furnish or furnishing, or by contributing to the furnishing of, any services or facilities connected with the processing, handling, sale, or offering for sale of such commodity so purchased upon terms not accorded to all purchasers on proportionally equal terms.

Knowingly Inducing or Receiving Discriminatory Price

(f) It shall be unlawful for any person engaged in commerce, in the course of such commerce, knowingly to induce or receive a discrimination in price which is prohibited by this section.

Section 3. Discrimination in Rebates, Discounts, or Advertising Service Charges; Underselling in Particular Localities; Penalties

It shall be unlawful for any person engaged in commerce, in the course of such commerce, to be a party to, or assist in, any transaction of sale, or contract to sell, which discriminates to his [or her] knowledge against competitors of the purchaser, in that, any discount, rebate, allowance, or advertising service charge is granted to the purchaser over and above any discount, rebate, allowance, or advertising service charge available at the time of such transaction to said competitors in respect of a sale of goods of like grade, quality, and quantity; to sell, or contract to sell, goods in any part of the United States at prices lower than those exacted by said person elsewhere in the United States for the purpose of destroying competition, or eliminating a competitor in such part of the United States; or, to sell, or contract to sell, goods at unreasonably low prices for the purpose of destroying competition or eliminating a competitor.

Any person violating any of the provisions of this section shall, upon conviction thereof, be fined not more than $5,000 or imprisoned not more than one year, or both.

The Securities Act of 1933 (Excerpts)

Definitions

Section 2. When used in this title, unless the context requires—

(1) The term "security" means any note, stock, treasury stock, bond, debenture, evidence of indebtedness, certificate of interest or participation in any profit-sharing agreement, collateral-trust certificate, preorganization certificate or subscription, transferable share, investment contract, voting-trust certificate, certificate of deposit for a security, fractional undivided interest in oil, gas, or other mineral rights, any put, call, straddle, option, or privilege on any security, certificate of deposit, or group or index of securities (including any interest therein or based on the value thereof), or any put, call, straddle, option, or privilege entered into on a national securities exchange relating to foreign currency, or, in general, any interest or participation in, temporary or interim certificate for, receipt for, guarantee of, or warrant or right to subscribe to or purchase, any of the foregoing.

Exempted Securities

Section 3. (a) Except as hereinafter expressly provided the provisions of this title shall not apply to any of the following classes of securities:

*   *   *   *

(2) Any security issued or guaranteed by the United States or any territory thereof, or by the District of Columbia, or by any State of the United States, or by any political subdivision of a State or Territory, or by any public instrumentality of one or more States or Territories, or by any person controlled or supervised by and acting as an instrumentality of the Government of the United States pursuant to authority granted by the Congress of the United States; or any certificate of deposit for any of the foregoing; or any security issued or guaranteed by any bank; or any security issued by or representing an interest in or a direct obligation of a Federal Reserve Bank. *   *   *

(3) Any note, draft, bill of exchange, or banker's acceptance which arises out of a current transaction or the proceeds of which have been or are to be used for current transactions, and which has a maturity at the time of issuance of not exceeding nine months, exclusive of days of grace, or any renewal thereof the maturity of which is likewise limited;

(4) Any security issued by a person organized and operated exclusively for religious, educational, benevolent, fraternal, charitable, or reformatory purposes and not for pecuniary profit, and no part of the net earnings of which inures to the benefit of any person, private stockholder, or individual;

*   *   *   *

(11) Any security which is a part of an issue offered and sold only to persons resident within a single State or Territory, where the issuer of such security is a person resident and doing business within, or, if a corporation,

incorporated by and doing business within, such State or Territory.

(b) The Commission may from time to time by its rules and regulations and subject to such terms and conditions as may be described therein, add any class of securities to the securities exempted as provided in this section, if it finds that the enforcement of this title with respect to such securities is not necessary in the public interest and for the protection of investors by reason of the small amount involved or the limited character of the public offering; but no issue of securities shall be exempted under this subsection where the aggregate amount at which such issue is offered to the public exceeds $5,000,000.

Exempted Transactions

Section 4. The provisions of section 5 shall not apply to—

(1) transactions by any person other than an issuer, underwriter, or dealer.

(2) transactions by an issuer not involving any public offering.

(3) transactions by a dealer (including an underwriter no longer acting as an underwriter in respect of the security involved in such transactions), except—

(A)   transactions taking place prior to the expiration of forty days after the first date upon which the security was bona fide offered to the public by the issuer or by or through an underwriter.

(B)   transactions in a security as to which a registration statement has been filed taking place prior to the expiration of forty days after the effective date of such registration statement or prior to the expiration of forty days after the first date upon which the security was bona fide offered to the public by the issuer or by or through an underwriter after such effective date, whichever is later (excluding in the computation of such forty days any time during which a stop order issued under section 8 is in effect as to the security), or such shorter period as the Commission may specify by rules and regulations or order, and

(C)   transactions as to the securities constituting the whole or a part of an unsold allotment to or subscription by such dealer as a participant in the distribution of such securities by the issuer or by or through an underwriter.

With respect to transactions referred to in clause (B), if securities of the issuer have not previously been sold pursuant to an earlier effective registration statement the applicable period, instead of forty days, shall be ninety days, or such shorter period as the Commission may specify by rules and regulations or order.

(4) brokers' transactions, executed upon customers' orders on any exchange or in the over-the-counter market but not the solicitation of such orders.

*   *   *   *

(6) transactions involving offers or sales by an issuer solely to one or more accredited investors, if the aggregate offering price of an issue of securities offered in reliance on this paragraph does not exceed the amount allowed under Section 3(b) of this title, if there is no advertising or public solicitation in connection with the transaction by the issuer or anyone acting on the issuer's behalf, and if the issuer files such notice with the Commission as the Commission shall prescribe.

Prohibitions Relating to Interstate Commerce and the Mails

Section 5. (a) Unless a registration statement is in effect as to a security, it shall be unlawful for any person, directly or indirectly—

(1) to make use of any means or instruments of transportation or communication in interstate commerce or of the mails to sell such security through the use or medium of any prospectus or otherwise; or

(2) to carry or cause to be carried through the mails or in interstate commerce, by any means or instruments of transportation, any such security for the purpose of sale or for delivery after sale.

(b) It shall be unlawful for any person, directly or indirectly—

(1) to make use of any means or instruments of transportation or communication in interstate commerce or of the mails to carry or transmit any prospectus relating to any security with respect to which a registration statement has been filed under this title, unless such prospectus meets the requirements of section 10, or

(2) to carry or to cause to be carried through the mails or in interstate commerce any such security for the purpose of sale or for delivery after sale, unless accompanied or preceded by a prospectus that meets the requirements of subsection (a) of section 10.

(c) It shall be unlawful for any person, directly, or indirectly, to make use of any means or instruments of transportation or communication in interstate commerce or of the mails to offer to sell or offer to buy through the use or medium of any prospectus or otherwise any security, unless a registration statement has been filed as to such security, or while the registration statement is the subject of a refusal order or stop order or (prior to the effective date of the registration statement) any public proceeding of examination under section 8.

The Securities Exchange Act of 1934 (Excerpts)

Definitions and Application of Title

Section 3. (a) When used in this title, unless the context otherwise requires—

*   *   *   *

(4) The term "broker" means any person engaged in the business of effecting transactions in securities for the account of others, but does not include a bank.

(5) The term "dealer" means any person engaged in the business of buying and selling securities for his own account, through a broker or otherwise, but does not include a bank, or any person insofar as he buys or sells securities for his own account, either individually or in some fiduciary capacity, but not as part of a regular business.

*   *   *   *

(7) The term "director" means any director of a corporation or any person performing similar functions with respect to any organization, whether incorporated or unincorporated.

(8) The term "issuer" means any person who issues or proposes to issue any security; except that with respect to certificates of deposit for securities, voting-trust certificates, or collateral-trust certificates, or with respect to certificates of interest or shares in an unincorporated investment trust not having a board of directors or the fixed, restricted management, or unit type, the term "issuer" means the person or persons performing the acts and assuming the duties of depositor or manager pursuant to the provisions of the trust or other agreement or instrument under which such securities are issued; and except that with respect to equipment-trust certificates or like securities, the term "issuer" means the person by whom the equipment or property is, or is to be, used.

(9) The term "person" means a natural person, company, government, or political subdivision, agency, or instrumentality of a government.

Regulation of the Use of Manipulative and Deceptive Devices

Section 10. It shall be unlawful for any person, directly or indirectly, by the use of any means or instrumentality of interstate commerce or of the mails, or of any facility of any national securities exchange—

(a) To effect a short sale, or to use or employ any stop-loss order in connection with the purchase or sale, of any security registered on a national securities exchange, in contravention of such rules and regulations as the Commission may prescribe as necessary or appropriate in the public interest or for the protection of investors.

(b) To use or employ, in connection with the purchase or sale of any security registered on a national securities exchange or any security not so registered, any manipulative or deceptive device or contrivance in contravention of such rules and regulations as the Commission may prescribe as necessary or appropriate in the public interest or for the protection of investors.

APPENDIX L

Title VII of the Civil Rights Act of 1964 (Excerpts)

Section 703. Unlawful Employment Practices. (a) It shall be an unlawful employment practice for an employer—

(1) to fail or refuse to hire or to discharge any individual, or otherwise to discriminate against any individual with respect to his compensation, terms, conditions, or privileges of employment, because of such individual's race, color, religion, sex, or national origin; or

(2) to limit, segregate, or classify his employees or applicants for employment in any way which would deprive or tend to deprive any individual of employment opportunities or otherwise adversely affect his status as an employee, because of such individual's race, color, religion, sex, or national origin.

(b) It shall be an unlawful employment practice for an employment agency to fail or refuse to refer for employment, or otherwise to discriminate against, any individual because of his race, color, religion, sex, or national origin, or to classify or refer for employment any individual on the basis or his race, color, religion, sex, or national origin.

(c) It shall be an unlawful employment practice for a labor organization—

(1) to exclude or to expel from its membership, or otherwise to discriminate against, any individual because of his race, color, religion, sex, or national origin;

(2) to limit, segregate, or classify its membership or applicants for membership, or to classify or fail or refuse to refer

for employment any individual, in any way which would deprive or tend to deprive any individual of employment opportunities, or would limit such employment opportunities or otherwise adversely affect his status as an employee or as an applicant for employment, because of such individual's race, color, religion, sex, or national origin; or

(3) to cause or attempt to cause an employer to discriminate against an individual in violation of this section.

(d) It shall be an unlawful employment practice for any employer, labor organization, or joint labor-management committee controlling apprenticeship or other training or retraining, including on-the-job training programs to discriminate against any individual because of his race, color, religion, sex, or national origin in admission to, or employment in, any program established to provide apprenticeship or other training.

(e) Notwithstanding any other provision of this subchapter—

(1) it shall not be an unlawful employment practice for an employer to hire and employ employees, for an employment agency to classify, or refer for employment any individual, for a labor organization to classify its membership or to classify or refer for employment any individual, or for an employer, labor organization, or joint labor-management committee controlling apprenticeship or other training or retraining programs to admit or employ any individual in any such program, on the basis of his religion, sex, or

A-50

national origin in those certain instances where religion, sex, or national origin is a bona fide occupational qualification reasonably necessary to the normal operation of that particular business or enterprise, and

(2) it shall not be an unlawful employment practice for a school, college, university, or other educational institution or institution of learning to hire and employ employees of a particular religion if such school, college, university, or other educational institution or institution of learning is, in whole or in substantial part, owned, supported, controlled, or managed by a particular religion or by a particular religious corporation, association, or society, or if the curriculum of such school, college, university, or other educational institution or institution of learning is directed toward the propagation of a particular religion.

(f) As used in this subchapter, the phrase "unlawful employment practice" shall not be deemed to include any action or measure taken by an employer, labor organization, joint labor-management committee, or employment agency with respect to an individual who is a member of the Communist Party of the United States or of any other organization required to register as a Communist-action or Communist-front organization. * * *

(g) Notwithstanding any other provision of this subchapter, it shall not be an unlawful employment practice for an employer to fail or refuse to hire and employ any individual for any position, for an employer to discharge any individual from any position, or for an employment agency to fail or refuse to refer any individual for employment in any position, or for a labor organization to fail or refuse to refer any individual for employment in any position, if—

(1) the occupancy of such position, or access to the premises in or upon which any part of the duties of such position is performed or is to be performed, is subject to any requirement imposed in the interest of the national security of the United States * * * and

(2) such individual has not fulfilled or has ceased to fulfill that requirement.

(h) Notwithstanding any other provision of this subchapter, it shall not be an unlawful employment practice for an employer to apply different standards of compensation, or different terms, conditions, or privileges of employment pursuant to a bona fide seniority or merit system, or a system which measures earnings by quantity or quality of production or to employees who work in different locations, provided that such differences are not the result of an intention to discriminate because of race, color, religion, sex, or national origin, nor shall it be an unlawful employment practice for an employer to give and act upon the results of any professionally developed ability test provided that such test, its administration or action upon the results is not designed, intended or used to discriminate because of race, color, religion, sex, or national origin. * * *

(j) Nothing contained in this subchapter shall be interpreted to require any employer, employment agency, labor organization, or joint labor-management committee subject to this subchapter to grant preferential treatment to any individual or to any group because of the race, color, religion, sex, or national origin of such individual or group on account of an imbalance which may exist with respect to the total number or percentage of persons of any race, color, religion, sex, or national origin employed by any employer, referred or classified for employment by any employment agency or labor organization, or admitted to, or employed in, any apprenticeship or other training program, in comparison with the total number or percentage of persons of such race, color, religion, sex, or national origin in any community, State, section, or other area, or in the available work force in any community, State, section, or other area.

* * * *

Section 704. **Other Unlawful Employment Practices.** (a) It shall be an unlawful employment practice for an employer to discriminate against any of his employees or applicants for employment, for an employment agency, or joint labor-management committee controlling apprenticeship or other training or retraining, including on-the-job training programs, to discriminate against any individual, or for a labor organization to discriminate against any member thereof or applicant for membership, because he has opposed any practice made an unlawful employment practice by this subchapter, or because he has made a charge, testified, assisted, or participated in any manner in an investigation, proceeding, or hearing under this subchapter.

(b) It shall be an unlawful employment practice for an employer, labor organization, employment agency, or joint labor-management committee controlling apprenticeship or other training or retraining, including on-the-job training programs, to print or publish or cause to be printed or published any notice or advertisement relating to employment by such an employer or membership or any classification or referral for employment by such a labor organization, or relating to any classification or referral for employment by such an employment agency, or relating to admission to, or employment in, any program established to provide apprenticeship or other training by such a joint-labor-management committee, indicating any preference, limitation, specification, or discrimination, based on race, color, religion, sex, or national origin, except that such a notice or advertisement may indicate a preference, limitation, specification, or discrimination based on religion, sex or national origin when religion, sex, or national origin is a bona fide occupational qualification for employment.

APPENDIX M

The Civil Rights Act of 1991 (Excerpts)

Section 3. Purposes.

The purposes of this Act are—

(1) to provide appropriate remedies for intentional discrimination and unlawful harassment in the workplace;

(2) to codify the concepts of "business necessity" and "job related" enunciated by the Supreme Court in *Griggs v. Duke Power Co.,* 401 U.S. 424 (1971), and in the other Supreme Court decisions prior to *Wards Cove Packing Co. v. Atonio,* 490 U.S. 642 (1989);

(3) to confirm statutory authority and provide statutory guidelines for the adjudication of disparate impact suits under title VII of the Civil Rights Act of 1964 (42 U.S.C. 2000e *et seq.*); and

(4) to respond to recent decisions of the Supreme Court by expanding the scope of relevant civil rights statutes in order to provide adequate protection to victims of discrimination.

Section 101. Prohibition against All Racial Discrimination in the Making and Enforcement of Contracts.

Section 1977 of the Revised Statutes (42 U.S.C. 1981) is amended * * * by adding at the end the following new subsections:

(b) For purposes of this section, the term "make and enforce contracts" includes the making, performance, modification, and termination of contracts, and the enjoyment of all benefits, privileges, terms, and conditions of the contractual relationship.

(c) The rights protected by this section are protected against impairment by nongovernmental discrimination and impairment under color of State law.

Section 102. Damages in Cases of Intentional Discrimination.

The Revised Statutes are amended by inserting after section 1977 (42 U.S.C.1981) the following new section:

Section 1977A. Damages in Cases of Intentional Discrimination in Employment.

(a) Right of Recovery.—

(1) Civil Rights.—In an action brought by a complaining party under section 706 or 717 of the Civil Rights Act of 1964 (42 U.S.C. 2000e-5) against a respondent who engaged in unlawful intentional discrimination (not an employment practice that is unlawful because of its disparate impact) prohibited under section 703, 704, or 717 of the Act (42 U.S.C. 2000e-2 or 2000e-3), and provided that the complaining party cannot recover under section 1977 of the Revised Statutes (42 U.S.C.1981), the complaining party may recover compensatory and punitive damages as allowed in subsection (b), in addition to any relief authorized by section 706(g) of the Civil Rights Act of 1964, from the respondent.

* * * *

(b) Compensatory and Punitive Damages.—

(1) Determination of Punitive Damages. — A complaining party may recover punitive damages under this section against a respondent (other than a government, government agency or political subdivision) if the complaining party demonstrates that the respondent engaged in a discriminatory practice or discriminatory practices with malice or with reckless indifference to the federally protected rights of an aggrieved individual.

(2) Exclusions from Compensatory Damages. — Compensatory damages awarded under this section shall not include backpay, interest on backpay, or any other type of relief authorized under section 706(g) of the Civil Rights Act of 1964.

(3) Limitations. — The sum of the amount of compensatory damages awarded under this section for future pecuniary losses, emotional pain, suffering, inconvenience, mental anguish, loss of enjoyment of life, and other nonpecuniary losses, and the amount of punitive damages awarded under this section, shall not exceed, for each complaining party —

(A) in the case of a respondent who has more than 14 and fewer than 101 employees in each of 20 or more calendar weeks in the current or preceding calendar year, $50,000;

(B) in the case of a respondent who has more than 100 and fewer than 201 employees in each of 20 or more calendar weeks in the current or preceding calendar year, $100,000; and

(C) in the case of a respondent who has more than 200 and fewer than 501 employees in each of 20 or more calendar weeks in the current or preceding calendar year, $200,000; and

(D) in the case of a respondent who has more than 500 employees in each of 20 or more calendar weeks in the current or preceding calendar year, $300,000.

*   *   *   *

Section 105. Burden of Proof in Disparate Impact Cases.

(a) Section 703 of the Civil Rights Act of 1964 (42 U.S.C. 2000e-2) is amended by adding at the end the following new [subsections to 703(k)(1)] —

(A) An unlawful employment practice based on disparate impact is established under this title only if —

(i) a complaining party demonstrates that a respondent uses a particular employment practice that causes a disparate impact on the basis of race, color, religion, sex, or national origin and the respondent fails to demonstrate that the challenged practice is job related for the position in question and consistent with business necessity; or

(ii) the complaining party makes the demonstration described in subparagraph (C) with respect to an alternative employment practice and the respondent refuses to adopt such alternative employment practice.

*   *   *   *

(C) The demonstration referred to by subparagraph (A)(ii) shall be in accordance with the law as it existed on June 4, 1989, with respect to the concept of "alternative employment practice."

*   *   *   *

Section 107. Clarifying Prohibition against Impermissible Consideration of Race, Color, Religion, Sex, or National Origin in Employment Practices.

(a) In General. — Section 703 of the Civil Rights Act of 1964 (42 U.S.C. 2000e-2) (as amended by sections 105 and 106) is further amended by adding at the end the following new subsection:

(m) Except as otherwise provided in this title, an unlawful employment practice is established when the complaining party demonstrates that race, color, religion, sex, or national origin was a motivating factor for any employment practice, even though other factors also motivated the practice.

*   *   *   *

Section 109. Protection of Extraterritorial Employment.

(a) Definition of Employee. — Section 701(f) of the Civil Rights Act of 1964 (42 U.S.C. 2000e(f)) and section 101(4) of the Americans with Disabilities Act of 1990 (42 U.S.C. 12111(4)) are each amended by adding at the end the following: "With respect to employment in a foreign country, such term includes an individual who is a citizen of the United States."

The Americans with Disabilities Act of 1990 (Excerpts)

Title I—EMPLOYMENT

Sec. 101. Definitions.

As used in this title: *   *   *

(8) **Qualified individual with a disability.**—The term "qualified individual with a disability" means an individual with a disability who, with or without reasonable accommodation, can perform the essential functions of the employment position that such individual holds or desires. For the purposes of this title, consideration shall be given to the employer's judgment as to what functions of a job are essential, and if an employer has prepared a written description before advertising or interviewing applicants for the job, this description shall be considered evidence of the essential functions of the job.

(9) **Reasonable accommodation.**—The term "reasonable accommodation" may include—

(A) making existing facilities used by employees readily accessible to and usable by individuals with disabilities; and

(B) job restructuring, part-time or modified work schedules, reassignment to a vacant position, acquisition or modification of equipment or devices, appropriate adjustment or modifications of examinations, training materials or policies, the provision of qualified readers or interpreters, and other similar accommodations for individuals with disabilities.

(10) **Undue Hardship.**—

(A) **In general.**—The term "undue hardship" means an action requiring significant difficulty or expense, when con-

sidered in light of the factors set forth in subparagraph (B).

(B) **Factors to be considered.**—In determining whether an accommodation would impose an undue hardship on a covered entity, factors to be considered include—

(i) the nature and cost of accommodation needed under this Act;

(ii) the overall financial resources of the facility or facilities involved in the provision of the reasonable accommodation; the number of persons employed at such facility; the effect on expenses and resources, or the impact otherwise of such accommodation upon the operation of the facility;

(iii) the overall financial resources of the covered entity; the overall size of the business of a covered entity with respect to the number of its employees; the number, type, and location of its facilities; and

(iv) the type of operation or operations of the covered entity, including the composition, structure, and functions of the workforce of such entity; the geographic separateness, administrative, or fiscal relationship of the facility or facilities in question to the covered entity.

Sec. 102. Discrimination.

(a) **General Rule.**—No covered entity shall discriminate against a qualified individual with a disability because of the disability of such individual in regard to job application procedures, the hiring, advancement, or discharge of employees, employee compensation, job training, and other terms, conditions, and privileges of employment.

(b) **Construction.**—As used in subsection (a), the term "discriminate" includes—

(1) limiting, segregating, or classifying a job applicant or employee in a way that adversely affects the opportunities or status of such applicant or employee because of the disability of such applicant or employee;

(2) participating in a contractual or other arrangement or relationship that has the effect of subjecting a covered entity's qualified applicant or employee with a disability to the discrimination prohibited by this title (such relationship includes a relationship with an employment or referral agency, labor union, an organization providing fringe benefits to an employee of the covered entity, or an organization providing training and apprenticeship programs);

(3) utilizing standards, criteria, or methods of administration—

(A) that have the effect of discrimination on the basis of disability; or

(B) that perpetuate the discrimination of others who are subject to common administrative control;

(4) excluding or otherwise denying equal jobs or benefits to a qualified individual because of the known disability of an individual with whom the qualified individual is known to have a relationship or association;

(5)

(A) not making reasonable accommodations to the known physical or mental limitations of an otherwise qualified individual with a disability who is an applicant or employee, unless such covered entity can demonstrate that the accommodation would impose an undue hardship on the operation of the business of such covered entity; or

(B) denying employment opportunities to a job applicant or employee who is an otherwise qualified individual with a disability, if such denial is based on the need of such covered entity to make reasonable accommodation to the physical or mental impairments of the employee or applicant;

(6) using qualification standards, employment tests or other selection criteria that screen out or tend to screen out an individual with a disability or a class of individuals with disabilities unless the standard, test or other selection criteria, as used by the covered entity, is shown to be job-related for the position in question and is consistent with business necessity; and

(7) failing to select and administer tests concerning employment in the most effective manner to ensure that, when such test is administered to a job applicant or employee who has a disability that impairs sensory, manual, or speaking skills, such test results accurately reflect the skills, aptitude, or whatever other factor of such applicant or employee that such test purports to measure, rather than reflecting the impaired sensory, manual, or speaking skills of such employee or applicant (except where such skills are the factors that the test purports to measure). * * *

Sec. 104. Illegal Use of Drugs and Alcohol. * * *

(b) **Rules of Construction.**—Nothing in subsection (a) shall be construed to exclude as a qualified individual with a disability an individual who—

(1) has successfully completed a supervised drug rehabilitation program and is no longer engaging in the illegal use of drugs, or has otherwise been rehabilitated successfully and is no longer engaging in such use;

(2) is participating in a supervised rehabilitation program and is no longer engaging in such use; or

(3) is erroneously regarded as engaging in such use, but is not engaging in such use; except that it shall not be a violation of this Act for a covered entity to adopt or administer reasonable policies or procedures, including but not limited to drug testing, designed to ensure that an individual described in paragraph (1) or (2) is no longer engaging in the illegal use of drugs. * * *

Sec. 107. Enforcement.

(a) **Powers, Remedies, and Procedures.**—The powers, remedies, and procedures set forth in sections 705, 706, 707, 709, and 710 of the Civil Rights Act of 1964 (42 U.S.C. 2000e-4, 2000e-5, 2000e-6, 2000e-8, and 2000e-9) shall be the powers, remedies, and procedures this title provides to the Commission, to the Attorney General, or to any person alleging discrimination on the basis of disability in violation of any provision of this Act, or regulations promulgated under section 106, concerning employment.

(b) **Coordination.**—The agencies with enforcement authority for actions which allege employment discrimination under this title and under the Rehabilitation Act of 1973 shall develop procedures to ensure that administrative complaints filed under this title and under the Rehabilitation Act of 1973 are dealt with in a manner that avoids duplication of effort and prevents imposition of inconsistent or conflicting standards for the same requirements under this title and the Rehabilitation Act of 1973. The Commission, the Attorney General, and the Office of Federal Contract Compliance Programs shall establish such coordinating mechanisms (similar to provisions contained in the joint regulations promulgated by the Commission and the Attorney General at part 42 of title 28 and part 1691 of title 29, Code of Federal Regulations, and the Memorandum of Understanding between the Commission and the Office of Federal Contract Compliance Programs dated January 16, 1981 (46 Fed. Reg. 7435, January 23, 1981)) in regulations implementing this title and Rehabilitation Act of 1973 not later than 18 months after the date of enactment of this Act.

Sec. 108. Effective Date.

This title shall become effective 24 months after the date of enactment.

The Uniform Partnership Act

(Adopted in forty-nine states [all of the states except Louisiana], the District of Columbia, the Virgin Islands, and Guam. The adoptions by Alabama and Nebraska do not follow the official text in every respect, but are substantially similar, with local variations.)

The Act consists of 7 Parts as follows:

I.   Preliminary Provisions

II. Nature of Partnership

III. Relations of Partners to Persons Dealing with the Partnership

IV. Relations of Partners to One Another

V.   Property Rights of a Partner

VI. Dissolution and Winding Up

VII. Miscellaneous Provisions

An Act to make uniform the Law of Partnerships

Be it enacted, etc.:

Part I   Preliminary Provisions

Sec. 1. Name of Act

This act may be cited as Uniform Partnership Act.

Sec. 2. Definition of Terms

In this act, "Court" includes every court and judge having jurisdiction in the case.

"Business" includes every trade, occupation, or profession.

"Person" includes individuals, partnerships, corporations, and other associations.

"Bankrupt" includes bankrupt under the Federal Bankruptcy Act or insolvent under any state insolvent act.

"Conveyance" includes every assignment, lease, mortgage, or encumbrance.

"Real property" includes land and any interest or estate in land.

Sec. 3. Interpretation of Knowledge and Notice

(1) A person has "knowledge" of a fact within the meaning of this act not only when he has actual knowledge thereof, but also when he has knowledge of such other facts as in the circumstances shows bad faith.

(2) A person has "notice" of a fact within the meaning of this act when the person who claims the benefit of the notice:

(a) States the fact to such person, or

(b) Delivers through the mail, or by other means of communication, a written statement of the fact to such person or to a proper person at his place of business or residence.

Sec. 4. Rules of Construction

(1) The rule that statutes in derogation of the common law are to be strictly construed shall have no application to this act.

(2) The law of estoppel shall apply under this act.

(3) The law of agency shall apply under this act.

(4) This act shall be so interpreted and construed as to effect its general purpose to make uniform the law of those states which enact it.

(5) This act shall not be construed so as to impair the obligations of any contract existing when the act goes into effect, nor to affect any action or proceedings begun or right accrued before this act takes effect.

Sec. 5. Rules for Cases Not Provided for in This Act.

In any case not provided for in this act the rules of law and equity, including the law merchant, shall govern.

Part II   Nature of Partnership

Sec. 6. Partnership Defined

(1) A partnership is an association of two or more persons to carry on as co-owners a business for profit.

(2) But any association formed under any other statute of this state, or any statute adopted by authority, other than the authority of this state, is not a partnership under this act, unless such association would have been a partnership in this state prior to the adoption of this act; but this act shall apply to limited partnerships except in so far as the statutes relating to such partnerships are inconsistent herewith.

Sec. 7. Rules for Determining the Existence of a Partnership

In determining whether a partnership exists, these rules shall apply:

(1) Except as provided by Section 16 persons who are not partners as to each other are not partners as to third persons.

(2) Joint tenancy, tenancy in common, tenancy by the entireties, joint property, common property, or part ownership does not of itself establish a partnership, whether such co-owners do or do not share any profits made by the use of the property.

(3) The sharing of gross returns does not of itself establish a partnership, whether or not the persons sharing them have a joint or common right or interest in any property from which the returns are derived.

(4) The receipt by a person of a share of the profits of a business is prima facie evidence that he is a partner in the business, but no such inference shall be drawn if such profits were received in payment:

(a) As a debt by installments or otherwise,

(b) As wages of an employee or rent to a landlord,

(c) As an annuity to a widow or representative of a deceased partner,

(d) As interest on a loan, though the amount of payment vary with the profits of the business,

(e) As the consideration for the sale of a good-will of a business or other property by installments or otherwise.

Sec. 8. Partnership Property

(1) All property originally brought into the partnership stock or subsequently acquired by purchase or otherwise, on account of the partnership, is partnership property.

(2) Unless the contrary intention appears, property acquired with partnership funds is partnership property.

(3) Any estate in real property may be acquired in the partnership name. Title so acquired can be conveyed only in the partnership name.

(4) A conveyance to a partnership in the partnership name, though without words of inheritance, passes the entire estate of the grantor unless a contrary intent appears.

Part III   Relations of Partners to Persons Dealing with the Partnership

Sec. 9. Partner Agent of Partnership as to Partnership Business

(1) Every partner is an agent of the partnership for the purpose of its business, and the act of every partner, including the execution in the partnership name of any instrument, for apparently carrying on in the usual way the business of the partnership of which he is a member binds the partnership, unless the partner so acting has in fact no authority to act for the partnership in the particular matter, and the person with whom he is dealing has knowledge of the fact that he has no such authority.

(2) An act of a partner which is not apparently for the carrying on of the business of the partnership in the usual way does not bind the partnership unless authorized by the other partners.

(3) Unless authorized by the other partners or unless they have abandoned the business, one or more but less than all the partners have no authority to:

(a) Assign the partnership property in trust for creditors or on the assignee's promise to pay the debts of the partnership,

(b) Dispose of the good-will of the business,

(c) Do any other act which would make it impossible to carry on the ordinary business of a partnership,

(d) Confess a judgment,

(e) Submit a partnership claim or liability to arbitration or reference.

(4) No act of a partner in contravention of a restriction on authority shall bind the partnership to persons having knowledge of the restriction.

Sec. 10. Conveyance of Real Property of the Partnership

(1) Where title to real property is in the partnership name, any partner may convey title to such property by a conveyance executed in the partnership name; but the partnership may recover such property unless the partner's act binds the partnership under the provisions of paragraph (1) of section 9, or unless such property has been conveyed by the grantee or a person claiming through such grantee to a holder for value without knowledge that the partner, in making the conveyance, has exceeded his authority.

(2) Where title to real property is in the name of the partnership, a conveyance executed by a partner, in his own name, passes the equitable interest of the partnership, provided the act is one within the authority of the partner under the provisions of paragraph (1) of section 9.

(3) Where title to real property is in the name of one or more but not all the partners, and the record does not disclose the right of the partnership, the partners in whose name the title stands may convey title to such property, but the partnership may recover such property if the partners' act does not bind the partnership under the provisions of paragraph (1) of section 9, unless the purchaser or his assignee, is a holder for value, without knowledge.

(4) Where the title to real property is in the name of one or more or all the partners, or in a third person in trust for the partnership, a conveyance executed by a partner in the partnership name, or in his own name, passes the equitable interest of the partnership, provided the act is one within the authority of the partner under the provisions of paragraph (1) of section 9.

(5) Where the title to real property is in the names of all the partners a conveyance executed by all the partners passes all their rights in such property.

Sec. 11. Partnership Bound by Admission of Partner

An admission or representation made by any partner concerning partnership affairs within the scope of his authority as conferred by this act is evidence against the partnership.

Sec. 12. Partnership Charged with Knowledge of or Notice to Partner

Notice to any partner of any matter relating to partnership affairs, and the knowledge of the partner acting in the particular matter, acquired while a partner or then present to his mind, and the knowledge of any other partner who reasonably could and should have communicated it to the acting partner, operate as notice to or knowledge of the partnership, except in the case of a fraud on the partnership committed by or with the consent of that partner.

Sec. 13. Partnership Bound by Partner's Wrongful Act

Where, by any wrongful act or omission of any partner acting in the ordinary course of the business of the partnership or with the authority of his co-partners, loss or injury is caused to any person, not being a partner in the partnership, or any penalty is incurred, the partnership is liable therefor to the same extent as the partner so acting or omitting to act.

Sec. 14. Partnership Bound by Partner's Breach of Trust

The partnership is bound to make good the loss:

(a) Where one partner acting within the scope of his apparent authority receives money or property of a third person and misapplies it; and

(b) Where the partnership in the course of its business receives money or property of a third person and the money or property so received is misapplied by any partner while it is in the custody of the partnership.

Sec. 15. Nature of Partner's Liability

All partners are liable

(a) Jointly and severally for everything chargeable to the partnership under sections 13 and 14.

(b) Jointly for all other debts and obligations of the partnership; but any partner may enter into a separate obligation to perform a partnership contract.

Sec. 16. Partner by Estoppel

(1) When a person, by words spoken or written or by conduct, represents himself, or consents to another representing him to any one, as a partner in an existing partnership or with one or more persons not actual partners, he is liable to any such person to whom such representation has been made, who has, on the faith of such representation, given credit to the actual or apparent partnership, and if he has made such representation or consented to its being made in a public manner he is liable to such person, whether the representation has or has not been made or communicated to such person so giving credit by or with the knowledge of the apparent partner making the representation or consenting to its being made.

(a) When a partnership liability results, he is liable as though he were an actual member of the partnership.

(b) When no partnership liability results, he is liable jointly with the other persons, if any, so consenting to the contract or representation as to incur liability, otherwise separately.

(2) When a person has been thus represented to be a partner in an existing partnership, or with one or more persons not actual partners, he is an agent of the persons consenting to such representation to bind them to the same extent and in the same manner as though he were a partner in fact, with respect to persons who rely upon the representation. Where all the members of the existing partnership consent to the representation, a partnership act or obligation results; but in all other cases it is the joint act or

obligation of the person acting and the persons consenting to the representation.

Sec. 17. Liability of Incoming Partner

A person admitted as a partner into an existing partnership is liable for all the obligations of the partnership arising before his admission as though he had been a partner when such obligations were incurred, except that this liability shall be satisfied only out of partnership property.

Part IV Relations of Partners to One Another

Sec. 18. Rules Determining Rights and Duties of Partners

The rights and duties of the partners in relation to the partnership shall be determined, subject to any agreement between them, by the following rules:

(a) Each partner shall be repaid his contributions, whether by way of capital or advances to the partnership property and share equally in the profits and surplus remaining after all liabilities, including those to partners, are satisfied; and must contribute towards the losses, whether of capital or otherwise, sustained by the partnership according to his share in the profits.

(b) The partnership must indemnify every partner in respect of payments made and personal liabilities reasonably incurred by him in the ordinary and proper conduct of its business, or for the preservation of its business or property.

(c) A partner, who in aid of the partnership makes any payment or advance beyond the amount of capital which he agreed to contribute, shall be paid interest from the date of the payment or advance.

(d) A partner shall receive interest on the capital contributed by him only from the date when repayment should be made.

(e) All partners have equal rights in the management and conduct of the partnership business.

(f) No partner is entitled to remuneration for acting in the partnership business, except that a surviving partner is entitled to reasonable compensation for his services in winding up the partnership affairs.

(g) No person can become a member of a partnership without the consent of all the partners.

(h) Any difference arising as to ordinary matters connected with the partnership business may be decided by a majority of the partners; but no act in contravention of any agreement between the partners may be done rightfully without the consent of all the partners.

Sec. 19. Partnership Books

The partnership books shall be kept, subject to any agreement between the partners, at the principal place of business of the partnership, and every partner shall at all times have access to and may inspect and copy any of them.

Sec. 20. Duty of Partners to Render Information

Partners shall render on demand true and full information of all things affecting the partnership to any partner or the legal representative of any deceased partner or partner under legal disability.

Sec. 21. Partner Accountable as a Fiduciary

(1) Every partner must account to the partnership for any benefit, and hold as trustee for it any profits derived by him without the consent of the other partners from any transaction connected with the formation, conduct, or liquidation of the partnership or from any use by him of its property.

(2) This section applies also to the representatives of a deceased partner engaged in the liquidation of the affairs of the partnership as the personal representatives of the last surviving partner.

Sec. 22. Right to an Account

Any partner shall have the right to a formal account as to partnership affairs:

(a) If he is wrongfully excluded from the partnership business or possession of its property by his co-partners,

(b) If the right exists under the terms of any agreement,

(c) As provided by section 21,

(d) Whenever other circumstances render it just and reasonable.

Sec. 23. Continuation of Partnership beyond Fixed Term

(1) When a partnership for a fixed term or particular undertaking is continued after the termination of such term or particular undertaking without any express agreement, the rights and duties of the partners remain the same as they were at such termination, so far as is consistent with a partnership at will.

(2) A continuation of the business by the partners or such of them as habitually acted therein during the term, without any settlement or liquidation of the partnership affairs, is prima facie evidence of a continuation of the partnership.

Part V Property Rights of a Partner

Sec. 24. Extent of Property Rights of a Partner

The property rights of a partner are (1) his rights in specific partnership property, (2) his interest in the partnership, and (3) his right to participate in the management.

Sec. 25. Nature of a Partner's Right in Specific Partnership Property

(1) A partner is co-owner with his partners of specific partnership property holding as a tenant in partnership.

(2) The incidents of this tenancy are such that:

(a) A partner, subject to the provisions of this act and to any agreement between the partners, has an equal right with his partners to possess specific partnership property for partnership purposes; but he has no right to possess such property for any other purpose without the consent of his partners.

(b) A partner's right in specific partnership property is not assignable except in connection with the assignment of rights of all the partners in the same property.

(c) A partner's right in specific partnership property is not subject to attachment or execution, except on a claim against the partnership. When partnership property is attached for a partnership debt the partners, or any of them, or the representatives of a deceased partner, cannot claim any right under the homestead or exemption laws.

(d) On the death of a partner his right in specific partnership property vests in the surviving partner or partners, except where the deceased was the last surviving partner, when his right in such property vests in his legal representative. Such surviving partner or partners, or the legal representative of the last surviving partner, has no right to possess the partnership property for any but a partnership purpose.

(e) A partner's right in specific partnership property is not subject to dower, curtesy, or allowances to widows, heirs, or next of kin.

Sec. 26. Nature of Partner's Interest in the Partnership

A partner's interest in the partnership is his share of the profits and surplus, and the same is personal property.

Sec. 27. Assignment of Partner's Interest

(1) A conveyance by a partner of his interest in the partnership does not of itself dissolve the partnership, nor, as against the other partners in the absence of agreement, entitle the assignee, during the continuance of the partnership, to interfere in the management or administration of the partnership business or affairs, or to require any information or account of partnership transactions, or to inspect the partnership books; but it merely entitles the assignee to receive in accordance with his contract the profits to which the assigning partner would otherwise be entitled.

(2) In case of a dissolution of the partnership, the assignee is entitled to receive his assignor's interest and may require an account from the date only of the last account agreed to by all the partners.

Sec. 28. Partner's Interest Subject to Charging Order

(1) On due application to a competent court by any judgment creditor of a partner, the court which entered the judgment, order, or decree, or any other court, may charge the interest of the debtor partner with payment of the unsatisfied amount of such judgment debt with interest thereon; and may then or later appoint a receiver of his share of the profits, and of any other money due or to fall due to him in respect of the partnership, and make all other orders, directions, accounts and inquiries which the debtor partner might have made, or which the circumstances of the case may require.

(2) The interest charged may be redeemed at any time before foreclosure, or in case of a sale being directed by the court may be purchased without thereby causing a dissolution:

(a) With separate property, by any one or more of the partners, or

(b) With partnership property, by any one or more of the partners with the consent of all the partners whose interests are not so charged or sold.

(3) Nothing in this act shall be held to deprive a partner of his right, if any, under the exemption laws, as regards his interest in the partnership.

Part VI   Dissolution and Winding up

Sec. 29. Dissolution Defined

The dissolution of a partnership is the change in the relation of the partners caused by any partner ceasing to be associated in the carrying on as distinguished from the winding up of the business.

Sec. 30. Partnership not Terminated by Dissolution

On dissolution the partnership is not terminated, but continues until the winding up of partnership affairs is completed.

Sec. 31. Causes of Dissolution

Dissolution is caused:

(1) Without violation of the agreement between the partners,

(a) By the termination of the definite term or particular undertaking specified in the agreement,

(b) By the express will of any partner when no definite term or particular undertaking is specified,

(c) By the express will of all the partners who have not assigned their interests or suffered them to be charged for their separate debts, either before or after the termination of any specified term or particular undertaking,

(d) By the expulsion of any partner from the business bona fide in accordance with such a power conferred by the agreement between the partners;

(2) In contravention of the agreement between the partners, where the circumstances do not permit a dissolution under any other provision of this section, by the express will of any partner at any time;

(3) By any event which makes it unlawful for the business

of the partnership to be carried on or for the members to carry it on in partnership;

(4) By the death of any partner;

(5) By the bankruptcy of any partner or the partnership;

(6) By decree of court under section 32.

Sec. 32. Dissolution by Decree of Court

(1) On application by or for a partner the court shall decree a dissolution whenever:

(a) A partner has been declared a lunatic in any judicial proceeding or is shown to be of unsound mind,

(b) A partner becomes in any other way incapable of performing his part of the partnership contract,

(c) A partner has been guilty of such conduct as tends to affect prejudicially the carrying on of the business,

(d) A partner wilfully or persistently commits a breach of the partnership agreement, or otherwise so conducts himself in matters relating to the partnership business that it is not reasonably practicable to carry on the business in partnership with him,

(e) The business of the partnership can only be carried on at a loss,

(f) Other circumstances render a dissolution equitable.

(2) On the application of the purchaser of a partner's interest under sections 28 or 29 [should read 27 or 28];

(a) After the termination of the specified term or particular undertaking,

(b) At any time if the partnership was a partnership at will when the interest was assigned or when the charging order was issued.

Sec. 33. General Effect of Dissolution on Authority of Partner

Except so far as may be necessary to wind up partnership affairs or to complete transactions begun but not then finished, dissolution terminates all authority of any partner to act for the partnership,

(1) With respect to the partners,

(a) When the dissolution is not by the act, bankruptcy or death of a partner; or

(b) When the dissolution is by such act, bankruptcy or death of a partner, in cases where section 34 so requires.

(2) With respect to persons not partners, as declared in section 35.

Sec. 34. Rights of Partner to Contribution from Copartners after Dissolution

Where the dissolution is caused by the act, death or bankruptcy of a partner, each partner is liable to his copartners for his share of any liability created by any partner acting for the partnership as if the partnership had not been dissolved unless

(a) The dissolution being by act of any partner, the partner acting for the partnership had knowledge of the dissolution, or

(b) The dissolution being by the death or bankruptcy of a partner, the partner acting for the partnership had knowledge or notice of the death or bankruptcy.

Sec. 35. Power of Partner to Bind Partnership to Third Persons after Dissolution

(1) After dissolution a partner can bind the partnership except as provided in Paragraph (3).

(a) By any act appropriate for winding up partnership affairs or completing transactions unfinished at dissolution;

(b) By any transaction which would bind the partnership if dissolution had not taken place, provided the other party to the transaction

(I) Had extended credit to the partnership prior to dissolution and had no knowledge or notice of the dissolution; or

(II) Though he had not so extended credit, had nevertheless known of the partnership prior to dissolution, and, having no knowledge or notice of dissolution, the fact of dissolution had not been advertised in a newspaper of general circulation in the place (or in each place if more than one) at which the partnership business was regularly carried on.

(2) The liability of a partner under paragraph (1b) shall be satisfied out of partnership assets alone when such partner had been prior to dissolution

(a) Unknown as a partner to the person with whom the contract is made; and

(b) So far unknown and inactive in partnership affairs that the business reputation of the partnership could not be said to have been in any degree due to his connection with it.

(3) The partnership is in no case bound by any act of a partner after dissolution

(a) Where the partnership is dissolved because it is unlawful to carry on the business, unless the act is appropriate for winding up partnership affairs; or

(b) Where the partner has become bankrupt; or

(c) Where the partner has no authority to wind up partnership affairs; except by a transaction with one who

(I) Had extended credit to the partnership prior to dissolution and had no knowledge or notice of his want of authority; or

(II) Had not extended credit to the partnership prior to dissolution, and, having no knowledge or notice of his want of authority, the fact of his want of authority has not been advertised in the manner provided for advertising the fact of dissolution in paragraph (1bII).

(4) Nothing in this section shall affect the liability under Section 16 of any person who after dissolution represents himself or consents to another representing him as a partner in a partnership engaged in carrying on business.

Sec. 36. Effect of Dissolution on Partner's Existing Liability

(1) The dissolution of the partnership does not of itself discharge the existing liability of any partner.

(2) A partner is discharged from any existing liability upon dissolution of the partnership by an agreement to that effect between himself, the partnership creditor and the person or partnership continuing the business; and such agreement may be inferred from the course of dealing between the creditor having knowledge of the dissolution and the person or partnership continuing the business.

(3) Where a person agrees to assume the existing obligations of a dissolved partnership, the partners whose obligations have been assumed shall be discharged from any liability to any creditor of the partnership who, knowing of the agreement, consents to a material alteration in the nature or time of payment of such obligations.

(4) The individual property of a deceased partner shall be liable for all obligations of the partnership incurred while he was a partner but subject to the prior payment of his separate debts.

Sec. 37. Right to Wind Up

Unless otherwise agreed the partners who have not wrongfully dissolved the partnership or the legal representative of the last surviving partner, not bankrupt, has the right to wind up the partnership affairs; provided, however, that any partner, his legal representative or his assignee, upon cause shown, may obtain winding up by the court.

Sec. 38. Rights of Partners to Application of Partnership Property

(1) When dissolution is caused in any way, except in contravention of the partnership agreement, each partner, as against his co-partners and all persons claiming through them in respect of their interests in the partnership, unless otherwise agreed, may have the partnership property applied to discharge its liabilities, and the surplus applied to pay in cash the net amount owing to the respective partners. But if dissolution is caused by expulsion of a partner, bona fide under the partnership agreement and if the expelled partner is discharged from all partnership liabilities, either by payment or agreement under section 36(2), he shall receive in cash only the net amount due him from the partnership.

(2) When dissolution is caused in contravention of the partnership agreement the rights of the partners shall be as follows:

(a) Each partner who has not caused dissolution wrongfully shall have,

(I) All the rights specified in paragraph (1) of this section, and

(II) The right, as against each partner who has caused the dissolution wrongfully, to damages for breach of the agreement.

(b) The partners who have not caused the dissolution wrongfully, if they all desire to continue the business in the same name, either by themselves or jointly with others, may do so, during the agreed term for the partnership and for that purpose may possess the partnership property, provided they secure the payment by bond approved by the court, or pay to any partner who has caused the dissolution wrongfully, the value of his interest in the partnership at the dissolution, less any damages recoverable under clause (2a II) of the section, and in like manner indemnify him against all present or future partnership liabilities.

(c) A partner who has caused the dissolution wrongfully shall have:

(I) If the business is not continued under the provisions of paragraph (2b) all the rights of a partner under paragraph (1), subject to clause (2a II), of this section,

(II) If the business is continued under paragraph (2b) of this section the right as against his co-partners and all claiming through them in respect of their interests in the partnership, to have the value of his interest in the partnership, less any damages caused to his co-partners by the dissolution, ascertained and paid to him in cash, or the payment secured by bond approved by the court, and to be released from all existing liabilities of the partnership; but in ascertaining the value of the partner's interest the value of the good-will of the business shall not be considered.

Sec. 39. Rights Where Partnership Is Dissolved for Fraud or Misrepresentation

Where a partnership contract is rescinded on the ground of the fraud or misrepresentation of one of the parties thereto, the party entitled to rescind is, without prejudice to any other right, entitled,

(a) To a lien on, or right of retention of, the surplus of the partnership property after satisfying the partnership liabilities to third persons for any sum of money paid by him for the purchase of an interest in the partnership and for any capital or advances contributed by him; and

(b) To stand, after all liabilities to third persons have been satisfied, in the place of the creditors of the partnership for any payments made by him in respect of the partnership liabilities; and

(c) To be indemnified by the person guilty of the fraud or making the representation against all debts and liabilities of the partnership.

Sec. 40. Rules for Distribution

In settling accounts between the partners after dissolution, the following rules shall be observed, subject to any agreement to the contrary:

(a) The assets of the partnership are:

(I) The partnership property,

(II) The contributions of the partners necessary for the payment of all the liabilities specified in clause (b) of this paragraph.

(b) The liabilities of the partnership shall rank in order of payment, as follows:

(I) Those owing to creditors other than partners,

(II) Those owing to partners other than for capital and profits,

(III) Those owing to partners in respect of capital,

(IV) Those owing to partners in respect of profits.

(c) The assets shall be applied in the order of their declaration in clause (a) of this paragraph to the satisfaction of the liabilities.

(d) The partners shall contribute, as provided by section 18(a) the amount necessary to satisfy the liabilities; but if any, but not all, of the partners are insolvent, or, not being subject to process, refuse to contribute, the other partners shall contribute their share of the liabilities, and, in the relative proportions in which they share the profits, the additional amount necessary to pay the liabilities.

(e) An assignee for the benefit of creditors or any person appointed by the court shall have the right to enforce the contributions specified in clause (d) of this paragraph.

(f) Any partner or his legal representative shall have the right to enforce the contributions specified in clause (d) of this paragraph, to the extent of the amount which he has paid in excess of his share of the liability.

(g) The individual property of a deceased partner shall be liable for the contributions specified in clause (d) of this paragraph.

(h) When partnership property and the individual properties of the partners are in possession of a court for distribution, partnership creditors shall have priority on partnership property and separate creditors on individual property, saving the rights of lien or secured creditors as heretofore.

(i) Where a partner has become bankrupt or his estate is insolvent the claims against his separate property shall rank in the following order:

(I) Those owing to separate creditors,

(II) Those owing to partnership creditors,

(III) Those owing to partners by way of contribution.

Sec. 41. Liability of Persons Continuing the Business in Certain Cases

(1) When any new partner is admitted into an existing partnership, or when any partner retires and assigns (or the representative of the deceased partner assigns) his rights in partnership property to two or more of the partners, or to one or more of the partners and one or more third persons, if the business is continued without liquidation of the partnership affairs, creditors of the first or dissolved partnership are also creditors of the partnership so continuing the business.

(2) When all but one partner retire and assign (or the representative of a deceased partner assigns) their rights in partnership property to the remaining partner, who continues the business without liquidation of partnership affairs, either alone or with others, creditors of the dissolved partnership are also creditors of the person or partnership so continuing the business.

(3) When any partner retires or dies and the business of the dissolved partnership is continued as set forth in paragraphs (1) and (2) of this section, with the consent of the retired partners or the representative of the deceased partner, but without any assignment of his right in partnership property, rights of creditors of the dissolved partnership and of the creditors of the person or partnership continuing the business shall be as if such assignment had been made.

(4) When all the partners or their representatives assign their rights in partnership property to one or more third persons who promise to pay the debts and who continue the business of the dissolved partnership, creditors of the dissolved partnership are also creditors of the person or partnership continuing the business.

(5) When any partner wrongfully causes a dissolution and the remaining partners continue the business under the provisions of section 38(2b), either alone or with others, and without liquidation of the partnership affairs, creditors of the dissolved partnership are also creditors of the person or partnership continuing the business.

(6) When a partner is expelled and the remaining partners continue the business either alone or with others, without liquidation of the partnership affairs, creditors of the dissolved partnership are also creditors of the person or partnership continuing the business.

(7) The liability of a third person becoming a partner in the partnership continuing the business, under this section, to the creditors of the dissolved partnership shall be satisfied out of partnership property only.

(8) When the business of a partnership after dissolution is continued under any conditions set forth in this section the creditors of the dissolved partnership, as against the separate creditors of the retiring or deceased partner or the representative of the deceased partner, have a prior right to any claim of the retired partner or the representative of the

deceased partner against the person or partnership continuing the business, on account of the retired or deceased partner's interest in the dissolved partnership or on account of any consideration promised for such interest or for his right in partnership property.

(9) Nothing in this section shall be held to modify any right of creditors to set aside any assignment on the ground of fraud.

(10) The use by the person or partnership continuing the business of the partnership name, or the name of a deceased partner as part thereof, shall not of itself make the individual property of the deceased partner liable for any debts contracted by such person or partnership.

Sec. 42. Rights of Retiring or Estate of Deceased Partner When the Business Is Continued

When any partner retires or dies, and the business is continued under any of the conditions set forth in section 41 (1, 2, 3, 5, 6), or section 38(2b) without any settlement of accounts as between him or his estate and the person or partnership continuing the business, unless otherwise agreed, he or his legal representative as against such persons or partnership may have the value of his interest at the date of dissolution ascertained, and shall receive as an ordinary creditor an amount equal to the value of his interest in the dissolved partnership with interest, or, at his option

or at the option of his legal representative, in lieu of interest, the profits attributable to the use of his right in the property of the dissolved partnership; provided that the creditors of the dissolved partnership as against the separate creditors, or the representative of the retired or deceased partner, shall have priority on any claim arising under this section, as provided by section 41(8) of this act.

Sec. 43. Accrual of Actions

The right to an account of his interest shall accrue to any partner, or his legal representative, as against the winding up partners or the surviving partners or the person or partnership continuing the business, at the date of dissolution, in the absence of any agreement to the contrary.

Part VII   Miscellaneous Provisions

Sec. 44. When Act Takes Effect

This act shall take effect on the ___ day of ___ one thousand nine hundred and ___ .

Sec. 45. Legislation Repealed

All acts or parts of acts inconsistent with this act are hereby repealed.

The Revised Uniform Partnership Act (Excerpts)

Article 2.
GENERAL PROVISIONS

* * * *

§ 201. Partnership as Entity.

A partnership is an entity.

* * * *

§ 203. Partnership Property.

Property transferred to or otherwise acquired by a partnership is property of the partnership and not of the partners individually.

§ 204. When Property is Partnership Property.

(a) Property is partnership property if acquired in the name of:

(1) the partnership; or

(2) one or more partners with an indication in the instrument transferring title to the property of the person's capacity as a partner or of the existence of a partnership but without an indication of the name of the partnership.

(b) Property is acquired in the name of the partnership by a transfer to:

(1) the partnership in its name; or

(2) one or more partners in their capacity as partners

in the partnership, if the name of the partnership is indicated in the instrument transferring title to the property.

(c) Property is presumed to be partnership property if purchased with partnership assets, even if not acquired in the name of the partnership or of one or more partners with an indication in the instrument transferring title to the property of the person's capacity as a partner or of the existence of a partnership.

(d) Property acquired in the name of one or more of the partners, without an indication in the instrument transferring title to the property of the person's capacity as a partner or of the existence of a partnership and without use of partnership assets, is presumed to be separate property, even if used for partnership purposes.

Article 3.
RELATIONS OF PARTNERS TO PERSONS DEALING WITH PARTNERSHIP

* * * *

§ 302. Transfer of Partnership Property.

(a) Subject to the effect of a statement of partnership authority under Section 303:

(1) Partnership property held in the name of the partnership may be transferred by an instrument of transfer executed by a partner in the partnership name.

(2) Partnership property held in the name of one or more partners with an indication in the instrument transferring the property to them of their capacity as partners or of the existence of a partnership, but without an indication of the name of the partnership, may be transferred by an instrument of transfer executed by the persons in whose name the property is held.

(3) A partnership may recover property transferred under this subsection if it proves that execution of the instrument of transfer did not bind the partnership under Section 301, unless the property was transferred by the initial transferee or a person claiming through the initial transferee to a subsequent transferee who gave value without having notice that the person who executed the instrument of initial transfer lacked authority to bind the partnership.

(b) Partnership property held in the name of one or more persons other than the partnership, without an indication in the instrument transferring the property to them of their capacity as partners or of the existence of a partnership, may be transferred free of claims of the partnership or the partners by the persons in whose name the property is held to a transferee who gives value without having notice that it is partnership property.

(c) If a person holds all of the partners' interests in the partnership, all of the partnership property vests in that person. The person may execute a document in the name of the partnership to evidence vesting of the property in that person and may file or record the document.

*   *   *   *

§ 306. Partner's Liability.

All partners are liable jointly and severally for all obligations of the partnership unless otherwise agreed by the claimant or provided by law.

§ 307. Actions by and Against Partnership and Partners.

(a) A partnership may sue and be sued in the name of the partnership.

(b) An action may be brought against the partnership and any or all of the partners in the same action or in separate actions.

(c) A judgment against a partnership is not by itself a judgment against a partner. A judgment against a partnership may not be satisfied from a partner's assets unless there is also a judgment against the partner.

(d) A judgment creditor of a partner may not levy execution against the assets of the partner to satisfy a judgment based on a claim against the partnership unless:

(1) a judgment based on the same claim has been obtained against the partnership and a writ of execution on the judgment has been returned unsatisfied in whole or in part;

(2) an involuntary case under Title 11 of the United States Code has been commenced against the partnership and has not been dismissed within 60 days after commencement, or the partnership has commenced a voluntary case under Title 11 of the United States Code and the case has not been dismissed;

(3) the partner has agreed that the creditor need not exhaust partnership assets;

(4) a court grants permission to the judgment creditor to levy execution against the assets of a partner based on a finding that partnership assets subject to execution are clearly insufficient to satisfy the judgment, that exhaustion of partnership assets is excessively burdensome, or that the grant of permission is an appropriate exercise of the court's equitable powers; or

(5) liability is imposed on the partner by law or contract independent of the existence of the partnership.

(e) This section applies to any partnership liability or obligation resulting from a representation by a partner or purported partner under Section 308.

*   *   *   *

Article 5.
TRANSFEREES AND CREDITORS OF PARTNER

§ 501. Partner's Interest in Partnership Property not Transferable.

A partner is not a co-owner of partnership property and has no interest in partnership property which can be transferred, either voluntarily or involuntarily.

*   *   *   *

Article 6.
PARTNER'S DISSOCIATION

§ 601. Events Causing Partner's Dissociation.

A partner is dissociated from a partnership upon:

(1) receipt by the partnership of notice of the partner's express will to withdraw as a partner or upon any later date specified in the notice;

(2) an event agreed to in the partnership agreement as causing the partner's dissociation;

(3) the partner's expulsion pursuant to the partnership agreement;

(4) the partner's expulsion by the unanimous vote of the other partners if:

(i) it is unlawful to carry on the partnership business with that partner;

(ii) there has been a transfer of all or substantially all of that partner's transferable interest in the partnership, other than a transfer for security purposes, or a court order charging the partner's interest, which has not been foreclosed;

(iii) within 90 days after the partnership notifies a corporate partner that it will be expelled because it has filed a certificate of dissolution or the equivalent, its charter has been revoked, or its right to conduct business has been suspended by the jurisdiction of its incorporation, there is no revocation of the certificate of dissolution or no reinstatement of its charter or its right to conduct business; or

(iv) a partnership that is a partner has been dissolved and its business is being wound up;

(5) on application by the partnership or another partner, the partner's expulsion by judicial determination because:

(i) the partner engaged in wrongful conduct that adversely and materially affected the partnership business;

(ii) the partner willfully or persistently committed a material breach of the partnership agreement or of a duty owed to the partnership or the other partners under Section 404; or

(iii) the partner engaged in conduct relating to the partnership business which makes it not reasonably practicable to carry on the business in partnership with the partner;

(6) the partner's:

(i) becoming a debtor in bankruptcy;

(ii) executing an assignment for the benefit of creditors;

(iii) seeking, consenting to, or acquiescing in the appointment of a trustee, receiver, or liquidator of that partner or of all or substantially all of that partner's property; or

(iv) failing, within 90 days after the appointment, to have vacated or stayed the appointment of a trustee, receiver, or liquidator of the partner or of all or substantially all of the partner's property obtained without the partner's consent or acquiescence, or failing within 90 days after the expiration of a stay to have the appointment vacated;

(7) in the case of a partner who is an individual:

(i) the partner's death;

(ii) the appointment of a guardian or general conservator for the partner; or

(iii) a judicial determination that the partner has otherwise become incapable of performing the partner's duties under the partnership agreement;

(8) in the case of a partner that is a trust or is acting as a partner by virtue of being a trustee of a trust, distribution of the trust's entire transferable interest in the partnership, but not merely by reason of the substitution of a successor trustee;

(9) in the case of a partner that is an estate or is acting as a partner by virtue of being a personal representative of an estate, distribution of the estate's entire transferable interest in the partnership, but not merely by reason of the substitution of a successor personal representative; or

(10) termination of a partner who is not an individual, partnership, corporation, trust, or estate.

*   *   *   *

Article 7.
PARTNER'S DISSOCIATION WHEN BUSINESS NOT WOUND UP

§ 701. Purchase of Dissociated Partner's Interest.

(a) If a partner is dissociated from a partnership without resulting in a dissolution and winding up of the partnership business under Section 801, the partnership shall cause the dissociated partner's interest in the partnership to be purchased for a buyout price determined pursuant to subsection (b).

(b) The buyout price of a dissociated partner's interest is the amount that would have been distributable to the dissociating partner under Section 808(b) if, on the date of dissociation, the assets of the partnership were sold at a price equal to the greater of the liquidation value or the value based on a sale of the entire business as a going concern without the dissociated partner and the partnership were wound up as of that date. In either case, the selling price of the partnership assets must be determined on the basis of the amount that would be paid by a willing buyer to a willing seller, neither being under any compulsion to buy or sell, and with knowledge of all relevant facts. Interest must be paid from the date of dissociation to the date of payment.

(c) Damages for wrongful dissociation under Section 602(b), and all other amounts owing, whether or not presently due, from the dissociated partner to the partnership, must be offset against the buyout price. Interest must be paid from the date the amount owed becomes due to the date of payment.

(d) A partnership shall indemnify a dissociated partner against all partnership liabilities incurred before the dissociation, except liabilities then unknown to the partnership, and against all partnership liabilities incurred after the dissociation, except liabilities incurred by an act of the dissociated partner under Section 702. For purposes of this subsection, a liability not known to a partner other than the dissociated partner is not known to the partnership.

(e) If no agreement for the purchase of a dissociated partner's interest is reached within 120 days after a written demand for payment, the partnership shall pay, or cause to be paid, in cash to the dissociated partner the amount the partnership estimates to be the buyout price and accrued interest, reduced by any offsets and accrued interest under subsection (c).

(f) If a deferred payment is authorized under subsection (h), the partnership may tender a written offer to pay the amount it estimates to be the buyout price and accrued interest, reduced by any offsets under subsection (c), stating the time of payment, the amount and type of security for payment, and the other terms and conditions of the obligation.

(g) The payment or tender required by subsection (e) or (f) must be accompanied by the following:

(1) a statement of partnership assets and liabilities as of the date of dissociation;

(2) the latest available partnership balance sheet and income statement, if any;

(3) an explanation of how the estimated amount of the payment was calculated; and

(4) written notice that the payment is in full satisfaction of the obligation to purchase unless, within 120 days after the written notice, the dissociated partner commences an action to determine the buyout price, any offsets under subsection (c), or other terms of the obligation to purchase.

(h) A partner who wrongfully dissociates before the expiration of a definite term or the completion of a particular undertaking is not entitled to payment of any portion of the buyout price until the expiration of the term or completion of the undertaking, unless the partner establishes to the satisfaction of the court that earlier payment will not cause undue hardship to the business of the partnership. A deferred payment must be adequately secured and bear interest.

(i) A dissociated partner may maintain an action against the partnership, pursuant to Section 406(b)(2)(ii), to determine the buyout price of that partner's interest, any offsets under subsection (c), or other terms of the obligation to purchase. The action must be commenced within 120 days after the partnership has tendered payment or an offer to pay or within one year after written demand for payment if no payment or offer to pay is tendered. The court shall determine the buyout price of the dissociated partner's interest, any offset due under subsection (c), and accrued interest, and enter judgment for any additional payment or refund. If deferred payment is authorized under subsection (h), the court shall also determine the security for payment and other terms of the obligation to purchase. The court may assess reasonable attorney's fees and the fees and expenses of appraisers or other experts for a party to the action, in amounts the court finds equitable, against a party that the court finds acted arbitrarily, vexatiously, or not in good faith. The finding may be based on the partnership's failure to tender payment or an offer to pay or to comply with subsection (g).

The Uniform Limited Liability Company Act (Excerpts)

[ARTICLE] 2.
ORGANIZATION

Section 201. Limited liability company as legal entity.

A limited liability company is a legal entity distinct from its members.

Section 202. Organization.

(a) One or more persons may organize a limited liability company, consisting of one or more members, by delivering articles of organization to the office of the [Secretary of State] for filing.

(b) Unless a delayed effective date is specified, the existence of a limited liability company begins when the articles of organization are filed.

(c) The filing of the articles of organization by the [Secretary of State] is conclusive proof that the organizers satisfied all conditions precedent to the creation of a limited liability company.

Section 203. Articles of organization.

(a) Articles of organization of a limited liability company must set forth:

    (1) the name of the company;

    (2) the address of the initial designated office;

    (3) the name and street address of the initial agent for service of process;

    (4) the name and address of each organizer;

    (5) whether the company is to be a term company and, if so, the term specified;

    (6) whether the company is to be manager-managed, and, if so, the name and address of each initial manager; and

    (7) whether one or more of the members of the company are to be liable for its debts and obligations under Section 303(c).

(b) Articles of organization of a limited liability company may set forth:

    (1) provisions permitted to be set forth in an operating agreement; or

    (2) other matters not inconsistent with law.

(c) Articles of organization of a limited liability company may not vary the nonwaivable provisions of Section 103(b). As to all other matters, if any provision of an operating agreement is inconsistent with the articles of organization:

    (1) the operating agreement controls as to managers, members, and members' transferees; and

(2) the articles of organization control as to persons, other than managers, members and their transferees, who reasonably rely on the articles to their detriment.

*　　*　　*　　*

Section 208. Certificate of existence or authorization.

(a) A person may request the [Secretary of State] to furnish a certificate of existence for a limited liability company or a certificate of authorization for a foreign limited liability company.

(b) A certificate of existence for a limited liability company must set forth:

(1) the company's name;

(2) that it is duly organized under the laws of this State, the date of organization, whether its duration is at-will or for a specified term, and, if the latter, the period specified;

(3) if payment is reflected in the records of the [Secretary of State] and if nonpayment affects the existence of the company, that all fees, taxes, and penalties owed to this State have been paid;

(4) whether its most recent annual report required by Section 211 has been filed with the [Secretary of State];

(5) that articles of termination have not been filed; and

(6) other facts of record in the office of the [Secretary of State] which may be requested by the applicant.

(c) A certificate of authorization for a foreign limited liability company must set forth:

(1) the company's name used in this State;

(2) that it is authorized to transact business in this State;

(3) if payment is reflected in the records of the [Secretary of State] and if nonpayment affects the authorization of the company, that all fees, taxes, and penalties owed to this State have been paid;

(4) whether its most recent annual report required by Section 211 has been filed with the [Secretary of State];

(5) that a certificate of cancellation has not been filed; and

(6) other facts of record in the office of the [Secretary of State] which may be requested by the applicant.

(d) Subject to any qualification stated in the certificate, a certificate of existence or authorization issued by the [Secretary of State] may be relied upon as conclusive evidence that the domestic or foreign limited liability company is in existence or is authorized to transact business in this State.

*　　*　　*　　*

[ARTICLE] 3.
RELATIONS OF MEMBERS AND MANAGERS TO PERSONS DEALING WITH LIMITED LIABILITY COMPANY

*　　*　　*　　*

Section 303. Liability of members and managers.

(a) Except as otherwise provided in subsection (c), the debts, obligations, and liabilities of a limited liability company, whether arising in contract, tort, or otherwise, are solely the debts, obligations, and liabilities of the company. A member or manager is not personally liable for a debt, obligation, or liability of the company solely by reason of being or acting as a member or manager.

(b) The failure of a limited liability company to observe the usual company formalities or requirements relating to the exercise of its company powers or management of its business is not a ground for imposing personal liability on the members or managers for liabilities of the company.

(c) All or specified members of a limited liability company are liable in their capacity as members for all or specified debts, obligations, or liabilities of the company if:

(1) a provision to that effect is contained in the articles of organization; and

(2) a member so liable has consented in writing to the adoption of the provision or to be bound by the provision.

*　　*　　*　　*

[ARTICLE] 4.
RELATIONS OF MEMBERS TO EACH OTHER AND TO LIMITED LIABILITY COMPANY

*　　*　　*　　*

Section 404. Management of limited liability company.

(a) In a member-managed company:

(1) each member has equal rights in the management and conduct of the company's business; and

(2) except as otherwise provided in subsection (c) or in Section 801(b)(3)(i), any matter relating to the business of the company may be decided by a majority of the members.

(b) In a manager-managed company:

(1) each manager has equal rights in the management and conduct of the company's business;

(2) except as otherwise provided in subsection (c) or in Section 801(b)(3)(i), any matter relating to the

business of the company may be exclusively decided by the manager or, if there is more than one manager, by a majority of the managers; and

(3) a manager:

(i) must be designated, appointed, elected, removed, or replaced by a vote, approval, or consent of a majority of the members; and

(ii) holds office until a successor has been elected and qualified, unless the manager sooner resigns or is removed.

(c) The only matters of a member or manager-managed company's business requiring the consent of all of the members are:

(1) the amendment of the operating agreement under Section 103;

(2) the authorization or ratification of acts or transactions under Section 103(b)(2)(ii) which would otherwise violate the duty of loyalty;

(3) an amendment to the articles of organization under Section 204;

(4) the compromise of an obligation to make a contribution under Section 402(b);

(5) the compromise, as among members, of an obligation of a member to make a contribution or return money or other property paid or distributed in violation of this [Act];

(6) the making of interim distributions under Section 405(a), including the redemption of an interest;

(7) the admission of a new member;

(8) the use of the company's property to redeem an interest subject to a charging order;

(9) the consent to dissolve the company under Section 801(b)(2);

(10) a waiver of the right to have the company's business wound up and the company terminated under Section 802(b);

(11) the consent of members to merge with another entity under Section 904(c)(1); and

(12) the sale, lease, exchange, or other disposal of all, or substantially all, of the company's property with or without goodwill.

(d) Action requiring the consent of members or managers under this [Act] may be taken without a meeting.

(e) A member or manager may appoint a proxy to vote or otherwise act for the member or manager by signing an appointment instrument, either personally or by the member's or manager's attorney-in-fact.

*   *   *   *

The General Agreement on Tariffs and Trade of 1994 (Excerpts)

Part I
FINAL ACT EMBODYING THE RESULTS OF THE URUGUAY ROUND OF MULTILATERAL TRADE NEGOTIATIONS

1. Having met in order to conclude the Uruguay Round of Multilateral Trade Negotiations, the representatives of the Governments and of the European Communities, members of the Trade Negotiations Committee * * *, *agree* that the Agreement Establishing the Multilateral Trade Organization and the Ministerial Decisions and Declarations * * * embody the results of their negotiations and form an integral part of this Final Act.

*   *   *   *

Part II
AGREEMENT ESTABLISHING THE MULTILATERAL TRADE ORGANIZATION

The *Parties* to this Agreement,

Recognizing that their relations in the field of trade and economic endeavour should be conducted with a view to raising standards of living, ensuring full employment and a large and steadily growing volume of real income and effective demand, and expanding the production and trade in good and services, while allowing for the optimal use of the world's resources in accordance with the objective of sustainable development, seeking both to protect and preserve the environment and enhance the means for doing so in a manner consistent with their respective needs and concerns at different levels of economic development,

Recognizing further that there is need for positive efforts designed to ensure that developing countries * * * secure a share in the growth in international trade commensurate with the needs of their economic development,

Being desirous of contributing to these objectives by entering into reciprocal and mutually advantageous arrangements directed to the substantial reduction of tariffs and other barriers to trade and to the elimination of discriminatory treatment in international trade relations,

Resolved, therefore, to develop an integrated, more viable and durable multilateral trading system encompassing the General Agreement on Tariffs and Trade, the results of the past trade liberalization efforts, and all of the results of the Uruguay Round of multilateral trade negotiations,

Determined to preserve the basic principles and to further the objectives underlying this multilateral trading system,

Agree as follows:

* * * *

The Multilateral Trade Organization [MTO] * * * is hereby established.

* * * *

[The] MTO shall facilitate the implementation, administration, operation, and further the objectives, of this Agreement and of the Multilateral Trade Agreements, and shall also provide the framework for the implementation, administration and operation of the Plurilateral Trade Agreements.

* * * *

[Except] as otherwise provided for under this Agreement or the Multilateral Trade Agreements, the MTO shall be guided by the decisions, procedures and customary practices followed by the contracting parties of the GATT 1947 and the bodies established in the framework of the GATT 1947.

* * * *

AGREEMENT ON AGRICULTURE

* * * *

2. In accordance with the Mid-Term Review Agreement that government measures of assistance, whether direct or indirect, to encourage agricultural and rural development are an integral part of the development programmes of developing countries, investment subsidies which are generally available to agriculture in developing country Members and agricultural input subsidies generally available to low-income or resource poor producers in developing country Members shall be exempt from domestic support reduction commitments that would otherwise be applicable to such measures, as shall domestic support to producers in developing country Members to encourage diversification from growing illicit narcotic crops. * * *

* * * *

AGREEMENT ON TEXTILES AND CLOTHING

* * * *

1. Members agree that circumvention by transshipment, rerouting, false declaration concerning country or place of origin, and falsification of official documents, frustrates the implementation of this Agreement to integrate the textiles and clothing sector into the GATT 1994. Accordingly, Members should establish the necessary legal provisions and/or administrative procedures to address and take action against such circumvention. Members further agree that, consistent with their domestic laws and procedures,

they will cooperate fully to address problems arising from circumvention.

* * * *

2. Safeguard action may be taken * * * when, on the basis of a determination by a Member, it is demonstrated that a particular product is being imported into its territory in such increased quantities as to cause serious damage, or actual threat thereof, to the domestic industry producing like and/or directly competitive products. Serious damage or actual threat thereof must demonstrably be caused by such increased quantities in total imports of that product and not by such other factors as technological changes or changes in consumer preference.

* * * *

AGREEMENT ON TECHNICAL BARRIERS TO TRADE

* * * *

2.2 Members shall ensure that technical regulations are not prepared, adopted or applied with a view to or with the effect of creating unnecessary obstacles to international trade. For this purpose, technical regulations shall not be more trade-restrictive than necessary to fulfil a legitimate objective, taking account of the risks non-fulfilment would create. Such legitimate objectives [include] national security requirements; the prevention of deceptive practices; protection of human health or safety, animal or plant life or health, or the environment. In assessing such risks, relevant elements of consideration [include] * * * available scientific and technical information, related processing technology or intended end uses of products.

* * * *

AGREEMENT ON IMPLEMENTATION OF ARTICLE VI OF GATT 1994

* * * *

2.1 For the purpose of this Agreement a product is to be considered as being dumped, i.e., introduced into the commerce of another country at less than its normal value, if the export price of the product exported from one country to another is less than the comparable price, in the ordinary course of trade, for the like product when destined for consumption in the exporting country.

* * * *

3.5 It must be demonstrated that the dumped imports are * * * causing injury within the meaning of this Agreement. The demonstration of a causal relationship between the dumped imports and the injury to the domestic industry shall be based on an examination of all relevant evidence before the authorities. The authorities shall also examine any known factors other than the dumped imports which at the same time are injuring the domestic industry, and the injuries caused by these other factors must not be attributed to the dumped imports. Factors which may be relevant in this respect include *　*　* the volume and prices of imports not sold at dumping prices, contraction in demand or changes in the patterns of consumption, trade restrictive practices of and competition between the foreign and domestic producers, developments in technology and the export performance and productivity of the domestic industry.

*　*　*　*

9.2 When an anti-dumping duty is imposed in respect of any product, such anti-dumping duty shall be collected in the appropriate amounts in each case, on a non-discriminatory basis on imports of such product from all sources found to be dumped and causing injury, except as to imports from those sources from which price undertakings under the terms of this Agreement have been accepted. The authorities shall name the supplier or suppliers of the product concerned. If, however, several suppliers from the same country are involved, and it is impracticable to name all of these suppliers, the authorities may name the supplying country concerned. If several suppliers from more than one country are involved, the authorities may name either all the suppliers involved, or, if this is impracticable, all the supplying countries involved.

*　*　*　*

AGREEMENT ON PRESHIPMENT INSPECTION

*　*　*　*

12. User Members shall ensure that preshipment inspection entities do not request exporters to provide information regarding:

(a) manufacturing data related to patented, licensed or undisclosed processes, or to processes for which a patent is pending;

(b) unpublished technical data other than necessary to demonstrate compliance with technical regulations or standards;

(c) internal pricing, including manufacturing costs;

(d) profit levels;

(e) the terms of contracts between exporters and their suppliers unless it is not otherwise possible for the entity to conduct the inspection in question. In such cases, the entity shall only request the information necessary for this purpose.

*　*　*　*

AGREEMENT ON SUBSIDIES AND COUNTERVAILING MEASURES

*　*　*　*

3.1 Except as provided in the Agreement on Agriculture, the following subsidies *　*　* shall be prohibited:

(a) subsidies contingent, in law or in fact, whether solely or as one of several other conditions, upon export performance *　*　* ;

(b) subsidies contingent, whether solely or as one of several other conditions, upon the use of domestic over imported goods.

*　*　*　*

AGREEMENT ON SAFEGUARDS

*　*　*　*

2. A Member may apply a safeguard measure to a product only if that Member has determined *　*　* that such product is being imported into its territory in such increased quantities, absolute or relative to domestic production, and under such conditions as to cause or threaten to cause serious injury to the domestic industry that produces like or directly competitive products.

*　*　*　*

8. Safeguard measures shall be applied only to the extent as may be necessary to prevent or remedy serious injury and to facilitate adjustment. *　*　*

*　*　*　*

12. The total period of application of a safeguard measure including the period of application of any provisional measure, the period of initial application and any extension thereof, shall not exceed eight years.

*　*　*　*

19. Safeguard measures shall not be applied against a product originating in a developing country Member as long as its share of imports of the product concerned in the importing Member does not exceed 3 [percent], provided that, developing country Members with less than 3 [percent] import share collectively account for not more than 9 [percent] of total imports of the product concerned.

*　*　*　*

GENERAL AGREEMENT ON TRADE IN SERVICES

*　*　*　*

1. With respect to any measure covered by this Agreement, each Member shall accord immediately and unconditionally to services and service suppliers of any other Member, treatment no less favourable than that it accords to like services and service suppliers of any other country.

*   *   *   *

AGREEMENT ON TRADE-RELATED ASPECTS OF INTELLECTUAL PROPERTY RIGHTS, INCLUDING TRADE IN COUNTERFEIT GOODS

*   *   *   *

1. Members shall ensure that enforcement procedures *   *   * are available under their national laws so as to permit effective action against any act of infringement of intellectual property rights covered by this Agreement, including expeditious remedies to prevent infringements and remedies which constitute a deterrent to further infringements. These procedures shall be applied in such a manner as to avoid the creation of barriers to legitimate trade and to provide for safeguards against their abuse.

2. Procedures concerning the enforcement of intellectual property rights shall be fair and equitable. They shall not be unnecessarily complicated or costly, or entail unreasonable time-limits or unwarranted delays.

*   *   *   *

UNDERSTANDING ON RULES AND PROCEDURES GOVERNING THE SETTLEMENT OF DISPUTES

*   *   *   *

2.1 The Dispute Settlement Body (DSB) *   *   * shall administer these rules and procedures and *   *   * the consultation and dispute settlement provisions of the covered agreements. *   *   *

The North American Free Trade Agreement of 1993 (Excerpts)

Part One: GENERAL PART

Chapter One: Objectives

Article 101: Establishment of the Free Trade Area

The Parties to this Agreement * * * hereby establish a free trade area.

Article 102: Objectives

1. The objectives of this Agreement * * * are to: (a) eliminate barriers to trade in, and facilitate the cross-border movement of, goods and services between the territories of the Parties; (b) promote conditions of fair competition in the free trade area; (c) increase substantially investment opportunities in the territories of the Parties; (d) provide adequate and effective protection and enforcement of intellectual property rights in each Party's territory; (e) create effective procedures for the implementation and application of this Agreement, for its joint administration and for the resolution of disputes; and (f) establish a framework for further trilateral, regional and multilateral cooperation to expand and enhance the benefits of this Agreement.

     * * * *

Part Two: TRADE IN GOODS

Chapter Three: National Treatment and Market Access for Goods

     * * * *

Article 301: National Treatment

1. Each Party shall accord national treatment to the goods of another Party in accordance with Article III of the General Agreement on Tariffs and Trade (GATT) * * * .

2. [N]ational treatment shall mean, with respect to a state or province, treatment no less favorable than the most favorable treatment accorded by such state or province to any like, directly competitive or substitutable goods, as the case may be, of the Party of which it forms a part.

     * * * *

Article 302: Tariff Elimination

1. Except as otherwise provided in this Agreement, no Party may increase any existing customs duty, or adopt any customs duty, on an originating good.

2. [E]ach Party shall progressively eliminate its customs duties on originating goods in accordance with its Schedule * * * .

*   *   *   *

Article 316: Consultations and Committee on Trade in Goods

1. The Parties hereby establish a Committee on Trade in Goods, comprising representatives of each Party.

*   *   *   *

3. The Parties shall convene at least once each year a meeting of their officials responsible for customs, immigration, inspection of food and agricultural products, border inspection facilities, and regulation of transportation for the purpose of addressing issues related to movement of goods through the Parties' ports of entry.

*   *   *   *

Part Three: TECHNICAL BARRIERS TO TRADE
Chapter Nine: Standards-Related Measures

*   *   *   *

Article 904: Basic Rights and Obligations

Right to Take Standards-Related Measures

1. Each Party may *   *   * adopt, maintain or apply any standards-related measure, including any such measure relating to safety, the protection of human, animal or plant life or health, the environment or consumers, and any measure to ensure its enforcement or implementation. Such measures include those to prohibit the importation of a good of another Party or the provision of a service by a service provider of another Party that fails to comply with the applicable requirements of those measures or to complete the Party's approval procedures.

*   *   *   *

Unnecessary Obstacles

4. No Party may prepare, adopt, maintain or apply any standards-related measure with a view to or with the effect of creating an unnecessary obstacle to trade between the Parties. An unnecessary obstacle to trade shall not be deemed to be created where: (a) the demonstrable purpose of the measure is to achieve a legitimate objective; and (b) the measure does not operate to exclude goods of another Party that meet that legitimate objective.

*   *   *   *

Article 913: Committee on Standards-Related Measures

1. The Parties hereby establish a Committee on Standards-Related Measures, comprising representatives of each Party.

2. The Committee's functions shall include: (a) monitoring the implementation and administration of this Chapter

*   *   * ; (b) facilitating the process by which the Parties make compatible their standards-related measures; (c) providing a forum for the Parties to consult on issues relating to standards-related measures *   *   * ; (d) enhancing cooperation on the development, application and enforcement of standards-related measures; and (e) considering non-governmental, regional and multilateral developments regarding standards-related measures, including under the GATT.

*   *   *   *

Part Five: INVESTMENT, SERVICES AND RELATED MATTERS
Chapter Eleven: Investment
SECTION A—INVESTMENT

*   *   *   *

Article 1102: National Treatment

*   *   *   *

2. Each Party shall accord to investments of investors of another Party treatment no less favorable than that it accords, in like circumstances, to investments of its own investors with respect to the establishment, acquisition, expansion, management, conduct, operation, and sale or other disposition of investments.

*   *   *   *

4. For greater certainty, no Party may: (a) impose on an investor of another Party a requirement that a minimum level of equity in an enterprise in the territory of the Party be held by its nationals, other than nominal qualifying shares for directors or incorporators of corporations; or (b) require an investor of another Party, by reason of its nationality, to sell or otherwise dispose of an investment in the territory of the Party.

*   *   *   *

Part Six: INTELLECTUAL PROPERTY
Chapter Seventeen: Intellectual Property
Article 1701: Nature and Scope of Obligations

1. Each Party shall provide in its territory to the nationals of another Party adequate and effective protection and enforcement of intellectual property rights, while ensuring that measures to enforce intellectual property rights do not themselves become barriers to legitimate trade.

*   *   *   *

Article 1705: Copyright

*   *   *   *

2. Each Party shall provide to authors and their successors

in interest those rights enumerated in the Berne Convention in respect of works covered by paragraph 1, including the right to authorize or prohibit: (a) the importation into the Party's territory of copies of the work made without the right holder's authorization; (b) the first public distribution of the original and each copy of the work by sale, rental or otherwise; (c) the communication of a work to the public; and (d) the commercial rental of the original or a copy of a computer program. Subparagraph (d) shall not apply where the copy of the computer program is not itself an essential object of the rental. Each Party shall provide that putting the original or a copy of a computer program on the market with the right holder's consent shall not exhaust the rental right.

*　*　*　*

4. Each Party shall provide that, where the term of protection of a work, other than a photographic work or a work of applied art, is to be calculated on a basis other than the life of a natural person, the term shall be not less than 50 years from the end of the calendar year of the first authorized publication of the work or, failing such authorized publication within 50 years from the making of the work, 50 years from the end of the calendar year of making.

5. Each Party shall confine limitations or exceptions to the rights provided for in this Article to certain special cases that do not conflict with a normal exploitation of the work and do not unreasonably prejudice the legitimate interests of the right holder.

*　*　*　*

Article 1706: Sound Recordings

1. Each Party shall provide to the producer of a sound recording the right to authorize or prohibit: (a) the direct or indirect reproduction of the sound recording; (b) the importation into the Party's territory of copies of the sound recording made without the producer's authorization; (c) the first public distribution of the original and each copy of the sound recording by sale, rental or otherwise; and (d) the commercial rental of the original or a copy of the sound recording, except where expressly otherwise provided in a contract between the producer of the sound recording and the authors of the works fixed therein. Each Party shall provide that putting the original or a copy of a sound recording on the market with the right holder's consent shall not exhaust the rental right.

*　*　*　*

Article 1708: Trademarks

*　*　*　*

4. Each Party shall provide a system for the registration of trademarks, which shall include: (a) examination of applications; (b) notice to be given to an applicant of the reasons for the refusal to register a trademark; (c) a reasonable

opportunity for the applicant to respond to the notice; (d) publication of each trademark either before or promptly after it is registered; and (e) a reasonable opportunity for interested persons to petition to cancel the registration of a trademark. A Party may provide for a reasonable opportunity for interested persons to oppose the registration of a trademark.

*　*　*　*

7. Each Party shall provide that the initial registration of a trademark be for a term of at least 10 years and that the registration be indefinitely renewable for terms of not less than 10 years when conditions for renewal have been met.

*　*　*　*

Article 1709: Patents

1. Subject to paragraphs 2 and 3, each Party shall make patents available for any inventions, whether products or processes, in all fields of technology, provided that such inventions are new, result from an inventive step and are capable of industrial application. For purposes of this Article, a Party may deem the terms "inventive step" and "capable of industrial application" to be synonymous with the terms "non-obvious" and "useful," respectively.

*　*　*　*

Article 1711: Trade Secrets

1. Each Party shall provide the legal means for any person to prevent trade secrets from being disclosed to, acquired by, or used by others without the consent of the person lawfully in control of the information in a manner contrary to honest commercial practices, in so far as: (a) the information is secret in the sense that it is not, as a body or in the precise configuration and assembly of its components, generally known among or readily accessible to persons that normally deal with the kind of information in question; (b) the information has actual or potential commercial value because it is secret; and (c) the person lawfully in control of the information has taken reasonable steps under the circumstances to keep it secret.

*　*　*　*

Article 1714: Enforcement of Intellectual Property Rights: General Provisions

*　*　*　*

3. Each Party shall provide that decisions on the merits of a case in judicial and administrative enforcement proceedings shall: (a) preferably be in writing and preferably state the reasons on which the decisions are based; (b) be made available at least to the parties in a proceeding without undue delay; and (c) be based only on evidence in respect of which such parties were offered the opportunity to be heard.

4. Each Party shall ensure that parties in a proceeding have an opportunity to have final administrative decisions

reviewed by a judicial authority of that Party and, subject to jurisdictional provisions in its domestic laws concerning the importance of a case, to have reviewed at least the legal aspects of initial judicial decisions on the merits of a case. Notwithstanding the above, no Party shall be required to provide for judicial review of acquittals in criminal cases.

*   *   *   *

Article 1717: Criminal Procedures and Penalties

1. Each Party shall provide criminal procedures and penalties to be applied at least in cases of willful trademark counterfeiting or copyright piracy on a commercial scale. Each Party shall provide that penalties available include imprisonment or monetary fines, or both, sufficient to provide a deterrent, consistent with the level of penalties applied for crimes of a corresponding gravity.

2. Each Party shall provide that, in appropriate cases, its judicial authorities may order the seizure, forfeiture and destruction of infringing goods and of any materials and implements the predominant use of which has been in the commission of the offense.

The Small Business Regulatory Enforcement Fairness Act of 1966 (Excerpts)

Section 801. **Congressional review**

(a)(1)(A) Before a rule can take effect, the Federal agency promulgating such rule shall submit to each House of the Congress * * * a report containing—(i) a copy of the rule; (ii) a concise general statement relating to the rule, including whether it is a major rule; and (iii) the proposed effective date of the rule.

*   *   *   *

(C) Upon receipt of a report submitted under subparagraph (A), each House shall provide copies of the report to the chairman and ranking member of each standing committee with jurisdiction under the rules of the House of Representatives or the Senate to report a bill to amend the provision of law under which the rule is issued.

*   *   *   *

(3) A major rule relating to a report submitted under paragraph (1) shall take effect on the latest of—

(A) the later of the date occurring 60 days after the date on which—(i) the Congress receives the report submitted under paragraph (1); or (ii) the rule is published in the *Federal Register*, if so published;

(B) if the Congress passes a joint resolution of disapproval * * * relating to the rule, and the President signs a veto of such resolution, the earlier date—(i) on which either House of Congress votes and fails to override the veto of the President; or (ii) occurring 30 session days after the date on which the Congress received the veto and objections of the President; or

(C) the date the rule would have otherwise taken effect, if not for this section (unless a joint resolution of disapproval * * * is enacted).

*   *   *   *

(b)(1) A rule shall not take effect (or continue), if the Congress enacts a joint resolution of disapproval * * * .

*   *   *   *

Section 657. **Oversight of regulatory enforcement**

*   *   *   *

(b) (2) The [SBA Enforcement] Ombudsman shall—

(A) work with each agency with regulatory authority over small businesses to ensure that small business concerns that receive or are subject to an audit, on-site inspection, compliance assistance effort, or other enforcement related communication or contact by agency personnel are provided with a means to comment on the enforcement activity conducted by such personnel;

(B) establish means to receive comments from small business concerns regarding actions by agency employees conducting compliance or enforcement activities with respect to the small business concern * * * on a confidential basis * * * ;

(C) based on substantiated comments received from small business concerns and the [Regional Small Business Regulatory Fairness] Boards, annually report to Congress and affected agencies evaluating the enforcement activities of agency personnel including a rating of the responsive-ness to small business of the various regional and program offices of each agency; [and]

(D) coordinate and report annually on the activities, findings and recommendations of the [Regional Small Business Regulatory Fairness] Boards to the Administrator [of the Small Business Adminstration] and to the heads of affected agencies[.]

* * * *

(c)(2) Each [Regional Small Business Regulatory Fairness] Board * * * shall—

(A) meet at least annually to advise the Ombudsman on matters of concern to small businesses relating to the enforcement activities of agencies[.]

Spanish Equivalents for Important Legal Terms in English

Abandoned property: bienes abandonados

Acceptance: aceptación; consentimiento; acuerdo

Acceptor: aceptante

Accession: toma de posesión; aumento; accesión

Accommodation indorser: avalista de favor

Accommodation party: firmante de favor

Accord: acuerdo; convenio; arregio

Accord and satisfaction: transacción ejecutada

Act of state doctrine: doctrina de acto de gobierno

Administrative law: derecho administrativo

Administrative process: procedimiento o metódo administrativo

Administrator: administrador (-a)

Adverse possession: posesión de hecho susceptible de proscripción adquisitiva

Affirmative action: acción afirmativa

Affirmative defense: defensa afirmativa

After-acquired property: bienes adquiridos con posterioridad a un hecho dado

Agency: mandato; agencia

Agent: mandatorio; agente; representante

Agreement: convenio; acuerdo; contrato

Alien corporation: empresa extranjera

Allonge: hojas adicionales de endosos

Answer: contestación de la demande; alegato

Anticipatory repudiation: anuncio previo de las partes de su imposibilidad de cumplir con el contrato

Appeal: apelación; recurso de apelación

Appellate jurisdiction: jurisdicción de apelaciones

Appraisal right: derecho de valuación

Arbitration: arbitraje

Arson: incendio intencional

Articles of partnership: contrato social

Artisan's lien: derecho de retención que ejerce al artesano

Assault: asalto; ataque; agresión

Assignment of rights: transmisión; transferencia; cesión

Assumption of risk: no resarcimiento por exposición voluntaria al peligro

Attachment: auto judicial que autoriza el embargo; embargo

Bailee: depositario

Bailment: depósito; constitución en depósito

Bailor: depositante

Bankruptcy trustee: síndico de la quiebra

Battery: agresión; física

Bearer: portador; tenedor

Bearer instrument: documento al portador

Bequest or legacy: legado (de bienes

muebles)

Bilateral contract: contrato bilateral

Bill of lading: conocimiento de embarque; carta de porte

Bill of Rights: declaración de derechos

Binder: póliza de seguro provisoria; recibo de pago a cuenta del precio

Blank indorsement: endoso en blanco

Blue sky laws: leyes reguladoras del comercio bursátil

Bond: título de crédito; garantía; caución

Bond indenture: contrato de emisión de bonos; contrato del ampréstito

Breach of contract: incumplimiento de contrato

Brief: escrito; resumen; informe

Burglary: violación de domicilio

Business judgment rule: regla de juicio comercial

Business tort: agravio comercial

Case law: ley de casos; derecho casuístico

Cashier's check: cheque de caja

Causation in fact: causalidad en realidad

Cease-and-desist order: orden para cesar y desistir

Certificate of deposit: certificado de depósito

Certified check: cheque certificado

Charitable trust: fideicomiso para fines benéficos

Chattel: bien mueble

Check: cheque

Chose in action: derecho inmaterial; derecho de acción

Civil law: derecho civil

Close corporation: sociedad de un solo accionista o de un grupo restringido de accionistas

Closed shop: taller agremiado (emplea solamente a miembros de un gremio)

Closing argument: argumento al final

Codicil: codicilo

Collateral: garantía; bien objeto de la guarantía real

Comity: cortesía; cortesía entre naciones

Commercial paper: instrumentos negociables; documentos a valores commerciales

Common law: derecho consuetudinario; derecho común; ley común

Common stock: acción ordinaria

Comparative negligence: negligencia comparada

Compensatory damages: daños y perjuicios reales o compensatorios

Concurrent conditions: condiciones concurrentes

Concurrent jurisdiction: competencia concurrente de varios tribunales para entender en una misma causa

Concurring opinion: opinión concurrente

Condition: condición

Condition precedent: condición suspensiva

Condition subsequent: condición resolutoria

Confiscation: confiscación

Confusion: confusión; fusión

Conglomerate merger: fusión de firmas que operan en distintos mercados

Consent decree: acuerdo entre las partes aprobado por un tribunal

Consequential damages: daños y perjuicios indirectos

Consideration: consideración; motivo; contraprestación

Consolidation: consolidación

Constructive delivery: entrega simbólica

Constructive trust: fideicomiso creado por aplicación de la ley

Consumer protection law: ley para proteger el consumidor

Contract: contrato

Contract under seal: contrato formal o sellado

Contributory negligence: negligencia de la parte actora

Conversion: usurpación; conversión de valores

Copyright: derecho de autor

Corporation: sociedad anónima; corporación; persona juridica

Co-sureties: cogarantes

Counterclaim: reconvención; contrademanda

Counteroffer: contraoferta

Course of dealing: curso de transacciones

Course of performance: curso de cumplimiento

Covenant: pacto; garantía; contrato

Covenant not to sue: pacto or contrato a no demandar

Covenant of quiet enjoyment: garantía del uso y goce pacífico del inmueble

Creditors' composition agreement: concordato preventivo

Crime: crimen; delito; contravención

Criminal law: derecho penal

Cross-examination: contrainterrogatorio

Cure: cura; cuidado; derecho de remediar un vicio contractual

Customs receipts: recibos de derechos aduaneros

Damages: daños; indemnización por daños y perjuicios

Debit card: tarjeta de dé bito

Debtor: deudor

Debt securities: seguridades de deuda

Deceptive advertising: publicidad engañosa

Deed: escritura; título; acta translativa de domino

Defamation: difamación

Delegation of duties: delegación de obligaciones

Demand deposit: depósito a la vista

Depositions: declaración de un testigo fuera del tribunal

Devise: legado; deposición testamentaria (bienes inmuebles)

Directed verdict: veredicto según orden del juez y sin participación activa del jurado

Direct examination: interrogatorio directo; primer interrogatorio

Disaffirmance: repudiación; renuncia; anulación

Discharge: descargo; liberación; cumplimiento

Disclosed principal: mandante revelado

Discovery: descubrimiento; producción de la prueba

Dissenting opinion: opinión disidente

Dissolution: disolución; terminación

Diversity of citizenship: competencia de los tribunales federales para entender en causas cuyas partes intervinientes son cuidadanos de distintos estados

Divestiture: extinción premature de derechos reales

Dividend: dividendo

Docket: orden del día; lista de causas pendientes

Domestic corporation: sociedad local

Draft: orden de pago; letrade cambio

Drawee: girado; beneficiario

Drawer: librador

Duress: coacción; violencia

Easement: servidumbre

Embezzlement: desfalco; malversación

Eminent domain: poder de expropiación

Employment discrimination: discriminación en el empleo

Entrepreneur: empresario

Environmental law: ley ambiental

Equal dignity rule: regla de dignidad egual

Equity security: tipo de participación en una sociedad

Estate: propiedad; patrimonio; derecho

Estop: impedir; prevenir

Ethical issue: cuestión ética

Exclusive jurisdiction: competencia exclusiva

Exculpatory clause: cláusula eximente

Executed contract: contrato ejecutado

Execution: ejecución; cumplimiento

Executor: albacea

Executory contract: contrato aún no completamente consumado

Executory interest: derecho futuro

Express contract: contrato expreso

Expropriation: expropriación

Federal question: caso federal

Fee simple: pleno dominio; dominio absoluto

Fee simple absolute: dominio absoluto

Fee simple defeasible: dominio sujeta a una condición resolutoria

Felony: crimen; delito grave

Fictitious payee: beneficiario ficticio

Fiduciary: fiduciaro

Firm offer: oferta en firme

Fixture: inmueble por destino, incorporación a anexación

Floating lien: gravamen continuado

Foreign corporation: sociedad extranjera; U.S. sociedad constituída en otro estado

Forgery: falso; falsificación

Formal contract: contrato formal

Franchise: privilegio; franquicia; concesión

Franchisee: persona que recibe una concesión

Franchisor: persona que vende una concesión

Fraud: fraude; dolo; engaño

Future interest: bien futuro

Garnishment: embargo de derechos

General partner: socio comanditario

General warranty deed: escritura translativa de domino con garantía de título

Gift: donación

Gift *causa mortis*: donación por causa de muerte

Gift *inter vivos*: donación entre vivos

Good faith: buena fe

Good faith purchaser: comprador de buena fe

Holder: tenedor por contraprestación

Holder in due course: tenedor legítimo

Holographic will: testamento ológrafico

Homestead exemption laws: leyes que exceptúan las casas de familia de ejecución por duedas generales

Horizontal merger: fusión horizontal

Identification: identificación

Implied-in-fact contract: contrato implícito en realidad

Implied warranty: guarantía implícita

Implied warranty of merchantability: garantía implícita de vendibilidad

Impossibility of performance: imposibilidad de cumplir un contrato

Imposter: imposter

Incidental beneficiary: beneficiario incidental; beneficiario secundario

Incidental damages: daños incidentales

Indictment: auto de acusación; acusación

Indorsee: endorsatario

Indorsement: endoso

Indorser: endosante

Informal contract: contrato no formal; contrato verbal

Information: acusación hecha por el ministerio público

Injunction: mandamiento; orden de no innovar

Innkeeper's lien: derecho de retención que ejerce el posadero

Installment contract: contrato de pago en cuotas

Insurable interest: interés asegurable

Intended beneficiary: beneficiario destinado

Intentional tort: agravio; cuasi-delito intención

International law: derecho internación

Interrogatories: preguntas escritas sometidas por una parte a la otra o a un testigo

Inter vivos trust: fideicomiso entre vivos

Intestacy laws: leyes de la condición de morir intestado

Intestate: intestado

Investment company: compañia de inversiones

Issue: emisión

Joint tenancy: derechos conjuntos en un bien inmueble en favor del beneficiario sobreviviente

Judgment *n.o.v.*: juicio no obstante veredicto

Judgment rate of interest: interés de juicio

Judicial process: acto de procedimiento; proceso jurídico

Judicial review: revisión judicial

Jurisdiction: jurisdicción

Larceny: robo; hurto

Law: derecho; ley; jurisprudencia

Lease: contrato de locación; contrato de alquiler

Leasehold estate: bienes forales

Legal rate of interest: interés legal
Legatee: legatario
Letter of credit: carta de crédito
Levy: embargo; comiso
Libel: libelo; difamación escrita
Life estate: usufructo
Limited partner: comanditario
Limited partnership: sociedad en comandita
Liquidation: liquidación; realización
Lost property: objetos perdidos

Majority opinion: opinión de la mayoría
Maker: persona que realiza u ordena; librador
Mechanic's lien: gravamen de constructor
Mediation: mediación; intervención
Merger: fusión
Mirror image rule: fallo de reflejo
Misdemeanor: infracción; contravención
Mislaid property: bienes extraviados
Mitigation of damages: reducción de daños
Mortgage: hypoteca
Motion to dismiss: excepción parentoria
Mutual fund: fondo mutual

Negotiable instrument: instrumento negociable
Negotiation: negociación
Nominal damages: daños y perjuicios nominales
Novation: novación
Nuncupative will: testamento nuncupativo

Objective theory of contracts: teoria objetiva de contratos
Offer: oferta
Offeree: persona que recibe una oferta
Offeror: oferente
Order instrument: instrumento o documento a la orden
Original jurisdiction: jurisdicción de primera instancia
Output contract: contrato de producción

Parol evidence rule: regla relativa a la prueba oral

Partially disclosed principal: mandante revelado en parte
Partnership: sociedad colectiva; asociación; asociación de participación
Past consideration: causa o contraprestación anterior
Patent: patente; privilegio
Pattern or practice: muestra o práctica
Payee: beneficiario de un pago
Penalty: pena; penalidad
Per capita: por cabeza
Perfection: perfeción
Performance: cumplimiento; ejecución
Personal defenses: excepciones personales
Personal property: bienes muebles
Per stirpes: por estirpe
Plea bargaining: regateo por un alegato
Pleadings: alegatos
Pledge: prenda
Police powers: poders de policia y de prevención del crimen
Policy: póliza
Positive law: derecho positivo; ley positiva
Possibility of reverter: posibilidad de reversión
Precedent: precedente
Preemptive right: derecho de prelación
Preferred stock: acciones preferidas
Premium: recompensa; prima
Presentment warranty: garantía de presentación
Price discrimination: discriminación en los precios
Principal: mandante; principal
Privity: nexo jurídico
Privity of contract: relación contractual
Probable cause: causa probable
Probate: verificación; verificación del testamento
Probate court: tribunal de sucesiones y tutelas
Proceeds: resultados; ingresos
Profit: beneficio; utilidad; lucro
Promise: promesa
Promisee: beneficiario de una promesa
Promisor: promtente
Promissory estoppel: impedimento

promisorio
Promissory note: pagaré; nota de pago
Promoter: promotor; fundador
Proximate cause: causa inmediata o próxima
Proxy: apoderado; poder
Punitive, or exemplary, damages: daños y perjuicios punitivos o ejemplares

Qualified indorsement: endoso con reservas
Quasi contract: contrato tácito o implícito
Quitclaim deed: acto de transferencia de una propiedad por finiquito, pero sin ninguna garantía sobre la validez del título transferido

Ratification: ratificación
Real property: bienes inmuebles
Reasonable doubt: duda razonable
Rebuttal: refutación
Recognizance: promesa; compromiso; reconocimiento
Recording statutes: leyes estatales sobre registros oficiales
Redress: reporacíon
Reformation: rectificación; reforma; corrección
Rejoinder: dúplica; contrarréplica
Release: liberación; renuncia a un derecho
Remainder: substitución; reversión
Remedy: recurso; remedio; reparación
Replevin: acción reivindicatoria; reivindicación
Reply: réplica
Requirements contract: contrato de suministro
Rescission: rescisión
Res judicata: cosa juzgada; res judicata
Respondeat superior: responsabilidad del mandante o del maestro
Restitution: restitución
Restrictive indorsement: endoso restrictivo
Resulting trust: fideicomiso implícito
Reversion: reversión; sustitución
Revocation: revocación; derogación
Right of contribution: derecho de contribución

Right of reimbursement: derecho de reembolso

Right of subrogation: derecho de subrogación

Right-to-work law: ley de libertad de trabajo

Robbery: robo

Rule 10b-5: Regla 10b-5

Sale: venta; contrato de compreventa

Sale on approval: venta a ensayo; venta sujeta a la aprobación del comprador

Sale or return: venta con derecho de devolución

Sales contract: contrato de compraventa; boleto de compraventa

Satisfaction: satisfacción; pago

Scienter: a sabiendas

S corporation: S corporación

Secured party: acreedor garantizado

Secured transaction: transacción garantizada

Securities: volares; titulos; seguridades

Security agreement: convenio de seguridad

Security interest: interés en un bien dado en garantía que permite a quien lo detenta venderlo en caso de incumplimiento

Service mark: marca de identificación de servicios

Shareholder's derivative suit: acción judicial entablada por un accionista en nombre de la sociedad

Signature: firma; rúbrica

Slander: difamación oral; calumnia

Sovereign immunity: immunidad soberana

Special indorsement: endoso especial; endoso a la orden de una person en particular

Specific performance: ejecución precisa, según los términos del contrato

Spendthrift trust: fideicomiso para pródigos

Stale check: cheque vencido

Stare decisis: acatar las decisiones, observar los precedentes

Statutory law: derecho estatutario; derecho legislado; derecho escrito

Stock: acciones

Stock warrant: certificado para la compra de acciones

Stop-payment order: orden de suspensión del pago de un cheque dada por el librador del mismo

Strict liability: responsabilidad uncondicional

Summary judgment: fallo sumario

Tangible property: bienes corpóreos

Tenancy at will: inguilino por tiempo indeterminado (según la voluntad del propietario)

Tenancy by sufferance: posesión por tolerancia

Tenancy by the entirety: locación conyugal conjunta

Tenancy for years: inguilino por un término fijo

Tenancy in common: specie de copropiedad indivisa

Tender: oferta de pago; oferta de ejecución

Testamentary trust: fideicomiso testamentario

Testator: testador (-a)

Third party beneficiary contract: contrato para el beneficio del tercero-beneficiario

Tort: agravio; cuasi-delito

Totten trust: fideicomiso creado por un depósito bancario

Trade acceptance: letra de cambio aceptada

Trademark: marca registrada

Trade name: nombre comercial; razón social

Traveler's check: cheque del viajero

Trespass to land: ingreso no authorizado a las tierras de otro

Trespass to personal property: violación de los derechos posesorios de un tercero con respecto a bienes muebles

Trust: fideicomiso; trust

Ultra vires: ultra vires; fuera de la facultad (de una sociedad anónima)

Unanimous opinion: opinión unámine

Unconscionable contract or clause: contrato leonino; cláusula leonino

Underwriter: subscriptor; asegurador

Unenforceable contract: contrato que no se puede hacer cumplir

Unilateral contract: contrato unilateral

Union shop: taller agremiado; empresa en la que todos los empleados son miembros del gremio o sindicato

Universal defenses: defensas legitimas o legales

Usage of trade: uso comercial

Usury: usura

Valid contract: contrato válido

Venue: lugar; sede del proceso

Vertical merger: fusión vertical de empresas

Voidable contract: contrato anulable

Void contract: contrato nulo; contrato inválido, sin fuerza legal

Voir dire: examen preliminar de un testigo a jurado por el tribunal para determinar su competencia

Voting trust: fideicomiso para ejercer el derecho de voto

Waiver: renuncia; abandono

Warranty of habitability: garantía de habitabilidad

Watered stock: acciones diluídos; capital inflado

White-collar crime: crimen administrativo

Writ of attachment: mandamiento de ejecución; mandamiento de embargo

Writ of *certiorari*: auto de avocación; auto de certiorari

Writ of execution: auto ejecutivo; mandamiento de ejecutión

Writ of mandamus: auto de mandamus; mandamiento; orden judicial

GLOSSARY

A

Abandoned property Property with which the owner has voluntarily parted, with no intention of recovering it.

Abandonment In landlord-tenant law, a tenant's departure from leased premises completely, with no intention of returning before the end of the lease term.

Abus de droit A doctrine developed in the French courts. The doctrine modified employment at will and protected workers exercising their rights from wrongful discharge and other employer abuses.

Acceptance In contract law, the offeree's notification to the offeror that the offeree agrees to be bound by the terms of the offeror's proposal. Although historically the terms of acceptance had to be the mirror image of the terms of the offer, the Uniform Commercial Code provides that even modified terms of the offer in a definite expression of acceptance constitute a contract.

Accord and satisfaction An agreement for payment (or other performance) between two parties, one of whom has a right of action against the other. After the payment has been accepted or other performance has been made, the "accord and satisfaction" is complete and the obligation is discharged.

Accredited investors In the context of securities offerings, "sophisticated" investors, such as banks, insurance companies, investment companies, the issuer's executive officers and directors, and persons whose income or net worth exceeds certain limits.

Acquittal A certification or declaration following a trial that the individual accused of a crime is innocent, or free from guilt, and is thus absolved of the charges.

Act of state doctrine A doctrine that provides that the judicial branch of one country will not examine the validity of public acts committed by a recognized foreign government within its own territory.

Actionable Capable of serving as the basis of a lawsuit.

Actual authority Authority of an agent that is express or implied.

Actual malice Real and demonstrable evil intent. In a defamation suit, a statement made about a public figure normally must be made with actual malice (with either knowledge of its falsity or a reckless disregard of the truth) for liability to be incurred.

Actus reus (pronounced *ak*-tus *ray*-uhs) A guilty (prohibited) act. The commission of a prohibited act is one of the two essential elements required for criminal liability, the other element being the intent to commit a crime.

Adequate protection doctrine In bankruptcy law, a doctrine that protects secured creditors from losing their security as a result of an automatic stay on legal proceedings by creditors against the debtor once the debtor petitions for bankruptcy relief. In certain circumstances, the bankruptcy court may provide adequate protection by requiring the debtor or trustee to pay the creditor or provide additional guaranties to protect the creditor against the losses suffered by the creditor as a result of the stay.

Adhesion contract A "standard-form" contract, such as that between a large retailer and a consumer, in which the stronger party dictates the terms.

Adjudicate To render a judicial decision. In the administrative process, the proceeding in which an administrative law judge hears and decides on issues that arise when an administrative agency charges a person or a firm with violating a law or regulation enforced by the agency.

Adjudication The process of adjudicating. *See* Adjudicate

Administrative agency A federal or state government agency established to perform a specific function. Administrative agencies are authorized by legislative acts to make and enforce rules to administer and enforce the acts.

Administrative law The body of law created by administrative agencies (in the form of rules, regulations, orders, and decisions) in order to carry out their duties and responsibilities.

Administrative law judge (ALJ) One who presides over an administrative agency hearing and who has the power to administer oaths, take testimony, rule on questions of evidence, and make determinations of fact.

Administrative process The procedure used by administrative agencies in the administration of law.

Administrator One who is appointed by a court to handle the probate (disposition) of a person's estate if that person dies intestate (without a valid will) or if the executor named in the will cannot serve.

Adverse possession The acquisition of title to real property by occupying it openly, without the consent of the owner, for a period of time specified by a state statute. The occupation must be actual, open, notorious, exclusive, and in opposition to all others, including the owner.

Affidavit A written or printed voluntary statement of facts, confirmed by the oath or affirmation of the party making it and made before a person having the authority to administer the oath or affirmation.

Affirm To validate; to give legal force to. *See also* Ratification

Affirmative action Job-hiring policies that give special consideration to members of protected classes in an effort to overcome present effects of past discrimination.

Affirmative defense A response to a plaintiff's claim that does not deny the plaintiff's facts but attacks the plaintiff's legal right to bring an action. An example is the running of the statute of limitations.

After-acquired evidence A type of evidence submitted in support of an affirmative defense in employment discrimination cases. Evidence that, prior to the employer's discriminatory act, the employee engaged in misconduct sufficient to warrant dismissal had the employer known of it earlier.

After-acquired property Property of the debtor that is acquired after the execution of a security agreement.

Age of majority The age at which an individual is considered legally capable of conducting himself or herself responsibly. A person of this age is entitled to the full rights of citizenship, including the right to vote in elections. In contract law, one who is no longer an infant and can no longer disaffirm a contract.

Agency A relationship between two parties in which one party (the agent) agrees to represent or act for the other (the principal).

Agency by estoppel Arises when a principal negligently allows an agent to exercise powers not granted to the agent, thus justifying others in believing that the agent possesses the requisite agency authority. *See also* Promissory estoppel

Agent A person who agrees to represent or act for another, called the principal.

Agreement A meeting of two or more minds in regard to the terms of a contract; usually broken down into two events—an offer by one party to form a contract, and an acceptance of the offer by the person to whom the offer is made.

Alien corporation   A designation in the United States for a corporation formed in another country but doing business in the United States.

Allegation   A statement, claim, or assertion.

Allege   To state, recite, assert, or charge.

Alteration   In the context of leaseholds, an improvement or change made that materially affects the condition of the property. Thus, for example, erecting an additional structure probably would (and painting interior walls would not) be considered making an alteration.

Alternative dispute resolution (ADR)   The resolution of disputes in ways other than those involved in the traditional judicial process. Negotiation, mediation, and arbitration are forms of ADR.

Amend   To change and improve through a formal procedure.

American Arbitration Association (AAA)   The major organization offering arbitration services in the United States.

Analogy   In logical reasoning, an assumption that if two things are similar in some respects, they will be similar in other respects also. Often used in legal reasoning to infer the appropriate application of legal principles in a case being decided by referring to previous cases involving different facts but considered to come within the policy underlying the rule.

Annul   To cancel; to make void.

Answer   Procedurally, a defendant's response to the plaintiff's complaint.

Anticipatory repudiation   An assertion or action by a party indicating that he or she will not perform an obligation that the party is contractually obligated to perform at a future time.

Antitrust law   The body of federal and state laws and statutes protecting trade and commerce from unlawful restraints, price discrimination, price fixing, and monopolies. The principal federal antitrust statues are the Sherman Act of 1890, the Clayton Act of 1914, and the Federal Trade Commission Act of 1914.

Apparent authority   Authority that is only apparent, not real. In agency law, a person may be deemed to have had the power to act as an agent for another party if the other party's manifestations to a third party led the third party to believe that an agency existed when, in fact, it did not.

Appeal   Resort to a superior court, such as an appellate court, to review the decision of an inferior court, such as a trial court or an administrative agency.

Appellant   The party who takes an appeal from one court to another.

Appellate court   A court having appellate jurisdiction. Each state court system has at least one level of appellate courts. In the federal court system, the appellate courts are the circuit courts of appeals (intermediate appellate courts) and the United States Supreme Court (the highest appellate court in the federal system).

Appellate jurisdiction   Courts having appellate jurisdiction act as reviewing courts, or appellate courts. Generally, cases can be brought before appellate courts only on appeal from an order or a judgment of a trial court or other lower court.

Appellee   The party against whom an appeal is taken—that is, the party who opposes setting aside or reversing the judgment.

Appraisal right   The right of a dissenting shareholder, if he or she objects to an extraordinary transaction of the corporation (such as a merger or consolidation), to have his or her shares appraised and to be paid the fair value of his or her shares by the corporation.

Appropriation   In tort law, the use by one person of another person's name, likeness, or other identifying characteristic without permission and for the benefit of the user.

Arbitrary and capricious test   The court reviewing an informal administrative agency action applies this test to determine whether or not that action was in clear error. The court gives wide discretion to the expertise of the agency and decides if the agency had sufficient factual information on which to base its action. If no clear error was made, then the agency's action stands.

Arbitration   The settling of a dispute by submitting it to a disinterested third party (other than a court), who renders a decision.

The decision may or may not be legally binding.

Arbitration clause   A clause in a contract that provides that, in the event of a dispute, the parties will submit the dispute to arbitration rather than litigate the dispute in court.

Arraignment   A procedure in which an accused person is brought before the court to plead to the criminal charge in the indictment or information. The charge is read to the person, and he or she is asked to enter a plea—such as "guilty" or "not guilty."

Arson   The malicious burning of another's dwelling. Some statutes have expanded this to include any real property regardless of ownership and the destruction of property by other means—for example, by explosion.

Articles of incorporation   The document filed with the appropriate governmental agency, usually the secretary of state, when a business is incorporated; state statutes usually prescribe what kind of information must be contained in the articles of incorporation.

Articles of organization   The document filed with a designated state official by which a limited liability company is formed.

Articles of partnership   A written agreement that sets forth each partner's rights and obligations with respect to the partnership.

Artisan's lien   A possessory lien given to a person who has made improvements and added value to another person's personal property as security for payment for services performed.

Assault   Any word or action intended to make another person fearful of immediate physical harm; a reasonably believable threat.

Assignee   The person to whom contract rights are assigned.

Assignment   The act of transferring to another all or part of one's rights arising under a contract.

Assignor   The person who assigns contract rights.

Assumption of risk   A defense against negligence that can be used when the plaintiff is aware of a danger and voluntarily assumes the risk of injury from that danger.

Attachment   In the context of judicial liens, a court-ordered seizure and taking into custody of property prior to the securing of a judgment for a past-due debt.

Attempted monopolization   Any actions by a firm to eliminate competition and gain monopoly power.

Authority   In agency law, the agent's permission to act on behalf of the principal. An agent's authority may be actual (express or implied) or apparent. *See also* Actual authority; Apparent authority

Authorized means   In contract law, the means of acceptance authorized by the offeror.

Automatic stay   In bankruptcy proceedings, the suspension of virtually all litigation and other action by creditors against the debtor or the debtor's property; the stay is effective the moment the debtor files a petition in bankruptcy.

Award   In the context of litigation, the amount of money awarded to a plaintiff in a civil lawsuit as damages. In the context of arbitration, the arbitrator's decision.

B

Bail   An amount of money set by the court that must be paid by a criminal defendant to the court before the defendant will be released from custody. Bail is set to assure that an individual accused of a crime will appear for further criminal proceedings. If the accused provides bail, whether in cash or in a surety bond, then he or she is released from jail.

Bailee   One to whom goods are entrusted by a bailor. Under the Uniform Commercial Code, a party who, by a bill of lading, warehouse receipt, or other document of title, acknowledges possession of goods and contracts.

Bailee's lien   A possessory lien, or claim, that a bailee entitled to compensation can place on the bailed property to ensure that he or she will be paid for the services provided. The lien is effective as long as the bailee retains possession of the bailed goods and has not agreed to extend credit to the bailor. Sometimes referred to as an artisan's lien.

Bailment A situation in which the personal property of one person (a bailor) is entrusted to another (a bailee), who is obligated to return the bailed property to the bailor or dispose of it as directed.

Bailor One who entrusts goods to a bailee.

Bait-and-switch advertising Advertising a product at a very attractive price (the "bait") and then informing the consumer, once he or she is in the store, that the advertised product is either not available or is of poor quality; the customer is then urged to purchase ("switched" to) a more expensive item.

Bankruptcy court A federal court of limited jurisdiction that handles only bankruptcy proceedings. Bankruptcy proceedings are governed by federal bankruptcy law.

Bargain A mutual undertaking, contract, or agreement between two parties; to negotiate over the terms of a purchase or contract.

Basis of the bargain In contract law, the affirmation of fact or promise on which the sale of goods is predicated, creating an express warranty.

Battery The unprivileged, intentional touching of another.

Beyond a reasonable doubt The standard used to determine the guilt or innocence of a person criminally charged. To be guilty of a crime, one must be proved guilty "beyond and to the exclusion of every reasonable doubt." A reasonable doubt is one that would cause a prudent person to hesitate before acting in matters important to him or her.

Bilateral contract A type of contract that arises when a promise is given in exchange for a return promise.

Bill of lading A document that serves both as evidence of the receipt of goods for shipment and as documentary evidence of title to the goods.

Bill of Rights The first ten amendments to the U.S. Constitution.

Binding authority Any source of law that a court must follow when deciding a case. Binding authorities include constitutions, statutes, and regulations that govern the issue being decided, as well as court decisions that are controlling precedents within the jurisdiction.

Blue laws State or local laws that prohibit the performance of certain types of commercial activities on Sunday.

Blue sky laws State laws that regulate the offer and sale of securities.

Bona fide Good faith. A bona fide obligation is one made in good faith—that is, sincerely and honestly.

Bona fide occupational qualification (BFOQ) Identifiable characteristics reasonably necessary to the normal operation of a particular business. These characteristics can include gender, national origin, and religion, but not race.

Bond A certificate that evidences a corporate (or government) debt. It is a security that involves no ownership interest in the issuing entity.

Bond indenture A contract between the issuer of a bond and the bondholder.

Bounty payment A reward (payment) given to a person or persons who perform a certain service—such as informing legal authorities of illegal actions.

Boycott A concerted refusal to do business with a particular person or entity in order to obtain concessions or to express displeasure with certain acts or practices of that person or business. *See also* Secondary boycott

Breach To violate a law, by an act or an omission, or to break a legal obligation that one owes to another person or to society.

Breach of contract The failure, without legal excuse, of a promisor to perform the obligations of a contract.

Bribery The offering, giving, receiving, or soliciting of anything of value with the aim of influencing an official action or an official's discharge of a legal or public duty or (with respect to commercial bribery) a business decision.

Brief A formal legal document submitted by the attorney for the appellant—or the appellee (in answer to the appellant's brief)—to an appellate court when a case is appealed. The appellant's brief outlines the facts and issues of the case, the judge's rulings or jury's findings that should be reversed or modified, the applicable law, and the arguments on the client's behalf.

Bulk transfer A bulk sale or transfer, not made in the ordinary course of business, of a major part of the materials, supplies, merchandise, or other inventory of an enterprise.

Bureaucracy A large organization that is structured hierarchically to carry out specific functions.

Burglary The unlawful entry into a building with the intent to commit a felony. (Some state statutes expand this to include the intent to commit any crime.)

Business ethics Ethics in a business context; a consensus of what constitutes right or wrong behavior in the world of business and the application of moral principles to situations that arise in a business setting.

Business invitees Those people, such as customers or clients, who are invited onto business premises by the owner of those premises for business purposes.

Business judgment rule A rule that immunizes corporate management from liability for actions that result in corporate losses or damages if the actions are undertaken in good faith and are within both the power of the corporation and the authority of management to make.

Business necessity A defense to allegations of employment discrimination in which the employer demonstrates that an employment practice that discriminates against members of a protected class is related to job performance.

Business plan A document describing a company, its products, and its anticipated future performance. Creating a business plan is normally the first step in obtaining loans or venture-capital funds for a new business enterprise.

Business tort The wrongful interference with the business rights of another.

Business trust A voluntary form of business organization in which investors (trust beneficiaries) transfer cash or property to trustees in exchange for trust certificates that represent their investment shares. Management of the business and trust property is handled by the trustees for the use and benefit of the investors. The certificate holders have limited liability (are not responsible for the debts and obligations incurred by the trust) and share in the trust's profits.

Buyer in the ordinary course of business A buyer who, in good faith and without knowledge that the sale to him or her is in violation of the ownership rights or security interest of a third party in the goods, purchases goods in the ordinary course of business from a person in the business of selling goods of that kind.

Buy-sell agreement In the context of partnerships, an express agreement made at the time of partnership formation for one or more of the partners to buy out the other or others should the situation warrant—and thus provide for the smooth dissolution of the partnership.

Bylaws A set of governing rules adopted by a corporation or other association.

Bystander A spectator, witness, or person standing nearby when an event occurred and who did not engage in the business or act leading to the event.

C

C.I.F. or C.&F. Cost, insurance, and freight—or just cost and freight. A pricing term in a contract for the sale of goods requiring, among other things, that the seller place the goods in the possession of a carrier before risk passes to the buyer.

C.O.D. Cash on delivery. In sales transactions, a term meaning that the buyer will pay for the goods on delivery and before inspecting the goods.

Callable bond A bond that may be called in and the principal repaid at specified times or under conditions specified in the bond when it is issued.

Cancellation The act of nullifying, or making void. *See also* Rescission

Capital Accumulated goods, possessions, and assets used for the production of profits and wealth; the equity of owners in a business.

Carrier An individual or organization engaged in transporting passengers or goods for hire. *See also* Common carrier

Case law The rules of law announced in court decisions. Case law includes the aggregate of reported cases that interpret judicial precedents, statutes, regulations, and constitutional provisions.

Case on point A previous case involving factual circumstances and issues that are similar to the case before the court.

Categorical imperative A concept developed by the philosopher Immanuel Kant as an ethical guideline for behavior. In deciding whether an action is right or wrong, or desirable or undesirable, a person should evaluate the action in terms of what would happen if everybody else in the same situation, or category, acted the same way.

Causation in fact An act or omission without ("but for") which an event would not have occurred.

Cause of action A situation or state of facts that would entitle a party to sustain a legal action and give the party a right to seek a judicial remedy.

Cease-and-desist order An administrative or judicial order prohibiting a person or business firm from conducting activities that an agency or court has deemed illegal.

Certificate of incorporation The primary document that evidences corporate existence (referred to as articles of incorporation in some states).

Certificate of limited partnership The basic document filed with a designated state official by which a limited partnership is formed.

Certification mark A mark used by one or more persons, other than the owner, to certify the region, materials, mode of manufacture, quality, or accuracy of the owner's goods or services. When used by members of a cooperative, association, or other organization, such a mark is referred to as a collective mark. Examples of certification marks include the "Good Housekeeping Seal of Approval" and "UL Tested."

Certiorari *See* Writ of *certiorari*

Chain-style business franchise A franchise that operates under a franchisor's trade name and that is identified as a member of a select group of dealers that engage in the franchisor's business. The franchisee is generally required to follow standardized or prescribed methods of operation. Examples of this type of franchise are McDonald's and most other fast-food chains.

Chancellor An adviser to the king at the time of the early king's courts of England. Individuals petitioned the king for relief when they could not obtain an adequate remedy in a court of law, and these petitions were decided by the chancellor.

Charging order In partnership law, an order granted by a court to a judgment creditor that entitles the creditor to attach profits or assets of a partner on dissolution of the partnership.

Charter *See* Corporate charter

Chattel All forms of personal property.

Chattel paper Any writing or writings that show both a debt and the fact that the debt is secured by personal property. In many instances, chattel paper consists of a negotiable instrument coupled with a security agreement.

Checks and balances The national government is composed of three separate branches: the executive, the legislative, and the judicial branches. Each branch of the government exercises a check on the actions of the others.

Citation A reference to a publication in which a legal authority—such as a statute or a court decision—or other source can be found.

Civil law The branch of law dealing with the definition and enforcement of all private or public rights, as opposed to criminal matters.

Civil law system A system of law derived from that of the Roman Empire and based on a code rather than case law; the predominant system of law in the nations of continental Europe and the nations that were once their colonies. In the United States, Louisiana is the only state that has a civil law system.

Claim As a verb, to assert or demand. As a noun, a right to payment.

Close corporation A corporation whose shareholders are limited to a small group of persons, often including only family members. The rights of shareholders of a close corporation usually are restricted regarding the transfer of shares to others.

Closed shop A firm that requires union membership by its workers as a condition of employment. The closed shop was made illegal by the Labor-Management Relations Act of 1947.

Closing argument An argument made after the plaintiff and defendant have rested their cases. Closing arguments are made prior to the jury charges.

Collateral promise A secondary promise that is ancillary (subsidiary) to a principal transaction or primary contractual relationship, such as a promise made by one person to pay the debts of another if the latter fails to perform. A collateral promise normally must be in writing to be enforceable.

Collective bargaining The process by which labor and management negotiate the terms and conditions of employment, including working hours and workplace conditions.

Collective mark A mark used by members of a cooperative, association, or other organization to certify the region, materials, mode of manufacture, quality, or accuracy of the specific goods or services. Examples of collective marks include the labor union marks found on tags of certain products and the credits of movies, which indicate the various associations and organizations that participated in the making of the movies.

Comity A deference by which one nation gives effect to the laws and judicial decrees of another nation. This recognition is based primarily on respect.

Comment period A period of time following an administrative agency's publication or a notice of a proposed rule during which private parties may comment in writing on the agency proposal in an effort to influence agency policy. The agency takes any comments received into consideration when drafting the final version of the regulation.

Commerce clause The provision in Article I, Section 8, of the U.S. Constitution that gives Congress the power to regulate interstate commerce.

Commercial impracticability A doctrine under which a seller may be excused from performing a contract when (1) a contingency occurs, (2) the contingency's occurrence makes performance impracticable, and (3) the nonoccurrence of the contingency was a basic assumption on which the contract was made. Despite the fact that UCC 2–615 expressly frees only sellers under this doctrine, courts have not distinguished between buyers and sellers in applying it.

Commingle To mix together. To put funds or goods together into one mass so that the funds or goods are so mixed that they no longer have separate identities. In corporate law, if personal and corporate interests are commingled to the extent that the corporation has no separate identity, a court may "pierce the corporate veil" and expose the shareholders to personal liability.

Common carrier A carrier that holds itself out or undertakes to carry persons or goods of all persons indifferently, or of all who choose to employ it.

Common law That body of law developed from custom or judicial decisions in English and U.S. courts, not attributable to a legislature.

Common stock Shares of ownership in a corporation that give the owner of the stock a proportionate interest in the corporation with regard to control, earnings, and net assets; shares of common stock are lowest in priority with respect to payment of dividends and distribution of the corporation's assets on dissolution.

Community property A form of concurrent ownership of property in which each spouse technically owns an undivided one-half interest in property acquired during the marriage. This form of joint ownership occurs in only nine states and Puerto Rico.

Comparative law The study and comparison of legal systems and laws across nations.

Comparative negligence A theory in tort law under which the liability for injuries resulting from negligent acts is shared by all parties who were negligent (including the injured party), on the basis of each person's proportionate negligence.

Compensatory damages A money award equivalent to the actual value of injuries or damages sustained by the aggrieved party.

Complaint The pleading made by a plaintiff alleging wrongdoing on the part of the defendant; the document that, when filed with a court, initiates a lawsuit.

Complete performance Performance of a contract strictly in accordance with the contract's terms.

Composition agreement *See* Creditors' composition agreement

Computer crime Any wrongful act that is directed against computers and computer parties, or wrongful use or abuse of computers or software.

Concentrated industry An industry in which a large percentage of market sales is controlled by either a single firm or a small number of firms.

Conciliation A form of alternative dispute resolution in which the parties reach an agreement themselves with the help of a neutral third party, called a conciliator, who facilitates the negotiations.

Concurrent jurisdiction Jurisdiction that exists when two different courts have the power to hear a case. For example, some cases can be heard in either a federal or a state court.

Concurrent ownership Joint ownership.

Concurring opinion A written opinion outlining the views of a judge or justice to make or emphasize a point that was not made or emphasized in the majority opinion.

Condition A qualification, provision, or clause in a contractual agreement, the occurrence of which creates, suspends, or terminates the obligations of the contracting parties.

Confession of judgment The act of a debtor in permitting a judgment to be entered against him or her by a creditor, for an agreed sum, without the institution of legal proceedings.

Confiscation A government's taking of privately owned business or personal property without a proper public purpose or an award of just compensation.

Conforming goods Goods that conform to contract specifications.

Confusion The mixing together of goods belonging to two or more owners so that the separately owned goods cannot be identified.

Conglomerate merger A merger between firms that do not compete with each other because they are in different markets (as opposed to horizontal and vertical mergers).

Consent Voluntary agreement to a proposition or an act of another. A concurrence of wills.

Consequential damages Special damages that compensate for a loss that is not direct or immediate (for example, lost profits). The special damages must have been reasonably foreseeable at the time the breach or injury occurred in order for the plaintiff to collect them.

Consideration Generally, the value given in return for a promise. The consideration, which must be present to make the contract legally binding, must be something of legally sufficient value and bargained for and must result in a detriment to the promisee or a benefit to the promisor.

Consignee One to whom goods are delivered on consignment. *See also* Consignment

Consignment A transaction in which an owner of goods (the consignor) delivers the goods to another (the consignee) for the consignee to sell. The consignee pays the consignor for the goods when they are sold by the consignee.

Consignor One who consigns goods to another. *See also* Consignment

Consolidation A contractual and statutory process in which two or more corporations join to become a completely new corporation. The original corporations cease to exist, and the new corporation acquires all their assets and liabilities.

Constitutional law Law that is based on the U.S. Constitution and the constitutions of the various states.

Constructive delivery An act equivalent to the actual, physical delivery of property that cannot be physically delivered because of difficulty or impossibility; for example, the transfer of a key to a safe constructively delivers the contents of the safe.

Constructive eviction A form of eviction that occurs when a landlord fails to perform adequately any of the undertakings (such as providing heat in the winter) required by the lease, thereby making the tenant's further use and enjoyment of the property exceedingly difficult or impossible.

Consumer credit Credit extended primarily for personal or household use.

Consumer goods Goods that are primarily for personal or household use.

Consumer law The body of statutes, agency rules, and judicial decisions protecting consumers of goods and services from dangerous manufacturing techniques, mislabeling, unfair credit practices, deceptive advertising, and so on. Consumer laws provide remedies and protections that are not ordinarily available to merchants or to businesses.

Contingency fee An attorney's fee that is based on a percentage of the final award received by his or her client as a result of litigation.

Contract An agreement that can be enforced in court; formed by two or more parties, each of whom agrees to perform or to refrain from performing some act now or in the future.

Contract implied in law *See* Quasi contract

Contract under seal A formal agreement in which the seal is a substitute for consideration. A court will not invalidate a contract under seal for lack of consideration.

Contractual agreement *See* Contract

Contractual capacity The threshold mental capacity required by the law for a party who enters into a contract to be bound by that contract.

Contribution *See* Right of contribution

Contributory negligence A theory in tort law under which a complaining party's own negligence contributed to or caused his or her injuries. Contributory negligence is an absolute bar to recovery in a minority of jurisdictions.

Conversion The wrongful taking, using, or retaining possession of personal property that belongs to another.

Convertible bond A bond that can be exchanged for a specified number of shares of common stock under certain conditions.

Conveyance The transfer of a title to land from one person to another by deed; a document (such as a deed) by which an interest in land is transferred from one person to another.

Conviction The outcome of a criminal trial in which the defendant has been found guilty of the crime with which he or she was charged and on which sentencing, or punishment, is based.

Cooperative An association that is organized to provide an economic service to its members (or shareholders). An incorporated cooperative is a nonprofit corporation. It will make distributions of dividends, or profits, to its owners on the basis of their transactions with the cooperative rather than on the basis of the amount of capital they contributed. Examples of cooperatives are consumer purchasing cooperatives, credit cooperatives, and farmers' cooperatives.

Co-ownership Joint ownership.

Copyright The exclusive right of authors to publish, print, or sell an intellectual production for a statutory period of time. A copyright has the same monopolistic nature as a patent or trademark, but it differs in that it applies exclusively to works of art, literature, and other works of authorship, including computer programs.

Corporate charter The document issued by a state agency or authority (usually the secretary of state) that grants a corporation legal existence and the right to function.

Corporation A legal entity formed in compliance with statutory requirements. The entity is distinct from its shareholders-owners.

Cosign The act of signing a document (such as a note promising to pay another in return for a loan or other benefit) jointly with another person and thereby assuming liability for performing what was promised in the document.

Cost-benefit analysis A decision-making technique that involves weighing the costs of a given action against the benefits of the action.

Co-surety A joint surety. One who assumes liability jointly with another surety for the payment of an obligation.

Counteradvertising New advertising that is undertaken pursuant to a Federal Trade Commission order for the purpose of correcting earlier false claims that were made about a product.

Counterclaim A claim made by a defendant in a civil lawsuit that in effect sues the plaintiff.

Counteroffer An offeree's response to an offer in which the offeree rejects the original offer and at the same time makes a new offer.

Course of dealing Prior conduct between parties to a contract that establishes a common basis for their understanding.

Course of performance The conduct that occurs under the terms of a particular agreement; such conduct indicates what the parties to an agreement intended it to mean.

Court of equity A court that decides controversies and administers justice according to the rules, principles, and precedents of equity.

Court of law A court in which the only remedies that could be granted were things of value, such as money damages. In the early English king's courts, courts of law were distinct from courts of equity.

Covenant not to compete A contractual promise to refrain from competing with another party for a certain period of time (not excessive in duration) and within a reasonable geographic area. Although covenants not to compete restrain trade, they are commonly found in partnership agreements, business sale agreements, and employment contracts. If they are ancillary to such agreements, covenants not to compete will normally be enforced by the courts unless the time period or geographic area is deemed unreasonable.

Covenant not to sue An agreement to substitute a contractual obligation for some other type of legal action based on a valid claim.

Covenant of quiet enjoyment A promise by a grantor (or landlord) that the grantee (or tenant) will not be evicted or disturbed by the grantor or a person having a lien or superior title.

Covenant running with the land An executory promise made between a grantor and a grantee to which they and subsequent owners of the land are bound.

Cover Under the Uniform Commercial Code, a remedy of the buyer or lessee that allows the buyer or lessee, on the seller's or lessor's breach, to purchase the goods from another seller or lessor and substitute them for the goods due under the contract. If the cost of cover exceeds the cost of the contract goods, the breaching seller or lessor will be liable to the buyer or lessee for the difference. In obtaining cover, the buyer or lessee must act in good faith and without unreasonable delay.

Cram-down provision A provision of the Bankruptcy Code that allows a court to confirm a debtor's Chapter 11 reorganization plan even though only one class of creditors has accepted it. To exercise the court's right under this provision, the court must demonstrate that the plan does not discriminate unfairly against any creditors and is fair and equitable.

Crashworthiness doctrine A doctrine that imposes liability for defects in the design or construction of motor vehicles that increase the extent of injuries to passengers if an accident occurs. The doctrine holds even when the defects do not actually cause the accident.

Creditor A person to whom a debt is owed by another person (the debtor).

Creditor beneficiary A third party beneficiary who has rights in a contract made by the debtor and a third person. The terms of the contract obligate the third person to pay the debt owed to the creditor. The creditor beneficiary can enforce the debt against either party.

Creditors' composition agreement An agreement formed between a debtor and his or her creditors in which the creditors agree to accept a lesser sum than that owed by the debtor in full satisfaction of the debt.

Crime A wrong against society proclaimed in a statute and, if committed, punishable by society through fines and/or imprisonment—and, in some cases, death.

Criminal act *See Actus reus*

Criminal intent *See Mens rea*

Criminal law Law that defines and governs actions that constitute crimes. Generally, criminal law has to do with wrongful actions committed against society for which society demands redress.

Cross-examination The questioning of an opposing witness during the trial.

Cumulative voting A method of shareholder voting designed to allow minority shareholders to be represented on the board of directors. With cumulative voting, the number of members of the board to be elected is multiplied by the total number of voting shares held. The result equals the number of votes a shareholder has, and this total can be cast for one or more nominees for director.

Cure Under the Uniform Commercial Code, the right of a party who tenders nonconforming performance to correct his or her performance within the contract period.

Cyber crime A crime that occurs online, in the virtual community of the Internet, as opposed to the physical world.

Cyber hate speech Extreme hate speech on the Internet. Racist materials and Holocaust denials disseminated on the Web are examples.

Cyber mark A trademark in cyberspace.

Cyber stalker A person who commits the crime of stalking in cyberspace. Generally, stalking consists of harassing a person and putting that person in reasonable fear for his or her safety or the safety of the person's immediate family.

Cyber terrorist A hacker whose purpose is to exploit a target computer for a serious impact, such as the corruption of a program to sabotage a business.

Cyber tort A tort committed in cyberspace.

D

Damages Money sought as a remedy for a breach of contract or for a tortious act.

Debenture bond A bond for which no specific assets of the corporation are pledged as backing; rather, the bond is backed by the general credit rating of the corporation, plus any assets that can be seized if the corporation allows the debentures to go into default.

Debtor in possession (DIP) In Chapter 11 bankruptcy proceedings, a debtor who is allowed to continue in possession of the estate in property (the business) and to continue business operations.

Declaratory judgment A court's judgment on a justiciable controversy when the plaintiff is in doubt as to his or her legal rights; a binding adjudication of the rights and status of litigants even though no consequential relief is awarded.

Decree The judgment of a court of equity.

Deed A document by which title to property (usually real property) is passed.

Defalcation The misuse of funds.

Defamation Any published or publicly spoken false statement that causes injury to another's good name, reputation, or character.

Default The failure to observe a promise or discharge an obligation. The term is commonly used to mean the failure to pay a debt when it is due.

Default judgment A judgment entered by a court against a defendant who has failed to appear in court to answer or defend against the plaintiff's claim.

Defendant One against whom a lawsuit is brought; the accused person in a criminal proceeding.

Defense That which a defendant offers and alleges in an action or suit as a reason why the plaintiff should not recover or establish what he or she seeks.

Deficiency judgment A judgment against a debtor for the amount of a debt remaining unpaid after collateral has been repossessed and sold.

Delegatee One to whom contract duties are delegated by another, called the delegator.

Delegation The transfer of a contractual duty to a third party. The party delegating the duty (the delegator) to the third party (the delegatee) is still obliged to perform on the contract should the delegatee fail to perform.

Delegation doctrine A doctrine based on Article I, Section 8, of the U.S. Constitution, which has been construed to allow Congress to delegate some of its power to make and implement laws to administrative agencies. The delegation is considered to be proper as long as Congress sets standards outlining the scope of the agency's authority.

Delegator One who delegates his or her duties under a contract to another, called the delegatee.

Delivery In contract law, the one party's act of placing the subject matter of the contract within the other party's possession or control.

Delivery ex ship Delivery from the carrying ship. A contract term indicating that risk of loss will not pass to the buyer until the goods leave the ship or are otherwise properly unloaded.

Delivery order A written order to deliver goods directed to a warehouser, carrier, or other person who, in the ordinary course of business, issues warehouse receipts or bills of lading [UCC 7–102(1)(d)].

Demurrer *See* Motion to dismiss

De novo Anew; afresh; a second time. In a hearing *de novo*, an appellate court hears the case as a court of original jurisidction—that is, as if the case had not previously been tried and a decision rendered.

Deposition The testimony of a party to a lawsuit or a witness taken under oath before a trial.

Destination contract A contract for the sale of goods in which the seller is required or authorized to ship the goods by carrier and deliver them at a particular destination. The seller assumes liability for any losses or damage to the goods until they are tendered at the destination specified in the contract.

Dilution With respect to trademarks, a doctrine under which distinctive or famous trademarks are protected from certain unauthorized uses of the marks regardless of a showing of competition or a likelihood of confusion. Congress created a federal cause of action for dilution in 1995 with the passage of the Federal Trademark Dilution Act.

Direct examination The examination of a witness by the attorney who calls the witness to the stand to testify on behalf of the attorney's client.

Directed verdict *See* Motion for a directed verdict

Disaffirmance The legal avoidance, or setting aside, of a contractual obligation.

Discharge The termination of an obligation. (1) In contract law, discharge occurs when the parties have fully performed their contractual obligations or when events, conduct of the parties, or operation of the law releases the parties from performance. (2) In bankruptcy proceedings, the extinction of the debtor's dischargeable debts.

Discharge in bankruptcy The release of a debtor from all debts that are provable, except those specifically excepted from discharge by statute.

Disclosed principal A principal whose identity is known to a third party at the time the agent makes a contract with the third party.

Discovery A phase in the litigation process during which the opposing parties may obtain information from each other and from third parties prior to trial.

Disparagement of property An economically injurious falsehood made about another's product or property. A general term for torts that are more specifically referred to as slander of quality or slander of title.

Disparate-impact discrimination A form of employment discrimination that results from certain employer practices or procedures that, although not discriminatory on their face, have a discriminatory effect.

Disparate-treatment discrimination A form of employment discrimination that results when an employer intentionally discriminates against employees who are members of protected classes.

Dissenting opinion A written opinion by a judge or justice who disagrees with the majority opinion.

Dissolution The formal disbanding of a partnership or a corporation. It can take place by (1) acts of the partners or, in a corporation, of the shareholders and board of directors; (2) the death of a partner; (3) the expiration of a time period stated in a partnership agreement or a certificate of incorporation; or (4) judicial decree.

Distribution agreement A contract between a seller and a distributor of the seller's products setting out the terms and conditions of the distributorship.

Distributorship A business arrangement that is established when a manufacturer licenses a dealer to sell its product. An example of a distributorship is an automobile dealership.

Diversity of citizenship Under Article III, Section 2, of the Constitution, a basis for federal court jurisdiction over a lawsuit between (1) citizens of different states, (2) a foreign country and citizens of a state or of different states, or (3) citizens of a state and citizens or subjects of a foreign country. The amount in controversy must be more than $75,000 before a federal court can take jurisdiction in such cases.

Divestiture The act of selling one or more of a company's parts, such as a subsidiary or plant; often mandated by the courts in merger or monopolization cases.

Dividend A distribution to corporate shareholders of corporate profits or income, disbursed in proportion to the number of shares held.

Docket The list of cases entered on a court's calendar and thus scheduled to be heard by the court.

Document of title Paper exchanged in the regular course of business that evidences the right to possession of goods (for example, a bill of lading or a warehouse receipt).

Domain name The series of letters and symbols used to identify site operators on the Internet; Internet "addresses."

Domestic corporation In a given state, a corporation that does business in, and is organized under the law of, that state.

Domestic relations court A court that deals with domestic (household) relationships, such as adoption, divorce, support payments, child custody, and the like.

Donee beneficiary A third party beneficiary who has rights under a contract as a direct result of the intention of the contract parties to make a gift to the third party.

Double jeopardy A situation occurring when a person is tried twice for the same criminal offense; prohibited by the Fifth Amendment to the Constitution.

Double taxation A feature (and disadvantage) of the corporate form of business. Because a corporation is a separate legal entity, corporate profits are taxed by state and federal governments. Dividends are again taxable as ordinary income to the shareholders receiving them.

Dram shop act A state statute that imposes liability on the owners of bars and taverns, as well as those who serve alcoholic drinks to the public, for injuries resulting from accidents caused by intoxicated persons when the sellers or servers of alcoholic drinks contributed to the intoxication.

Due process clause The provisions of the Fifth and Fourteenth Amendments to the Constitution that guarantee that no person shall be deprived of life, liberty, or property without due process of law. Similar clauses are found in most state constitutions.

Dumping The selling of goods in a foreign country at a price below the price charged for the same goods in the domestic market.

Durable power of attorney A document that authorizes a person to act on behalf of an incompetent person—write checks, collect insurance proceeds, and otherwise manage the disabled person's affairs, including health care—when he or she becomes incapacitated. Spouses often give each other durable power of attorney and, if they are advanced in age, may give a second such power of attorney to an older child.

Duress Unlawful pressure brought to bear on a person, causing the person to perform an act that he or she would not otherwise perform.

Duty of care The duty of all persons, as established by tort law, to exercise a reasonable amount of care in their dealings with others. Failure to exercise due care, which is normally determined by the "reasonable person standard," constitutes the tort of negligence.

E

E-commerce Business transacted in cyberspace.

E-contract A contract that is entered into in cyberspace and is evidenced only by electronic impulses (such as those that make up a computer's memory), rather than, for example, a typewritten form.

E-money Prepaid funds recorded on a computer or a card (such as a *smart card*).

Early neutral case evaluation A form of alternative dispute resolution in which a neutral third party evaluates the strengths and weakness of the disputing parties' positions; the evaluator's opinion forms the basis for negotiating a settlement.

Easement A nonpossessory right to use another's property in a manner established by either express or implied agreement.

Emancipation In regard to minors, the act of being freed from parental control; occurs when a child's parent or legal guardian relinquishes the legal right to exercise control over the child. Normally, a minor who leaves home to support himself or herself is considered emancipated.

Embezzlement The fraudulent appropriation of money or other property by a person to whom the money or property has been entrusted.

Eminent domain The power of a government to take land for public use from private citizens for just compensation.

Employee A person who works for an employer for a salary or for wages.

Employer An individual or business entity that hires employees, pays them salaries or wages, and exercises control over their work.

Employment at will A common law doctrine under which either party may terminate an employment relationship at any time for any reason, unless a contract specifies otherwise.

Employment discrimination Treating employees or job applicants unequally on the basis of race, color, national origin, religion, gender, age, or disability; prohibited by federal statutes.

Enabling legislation A statute enacted by Congress that authorizes the creation of an administrative agency and specifies the name, composition, purpose, and powers of the agency being created.

Encryption The process by which a message (plaintext) is transformed into something (ciphertext) that the sender and receiver intend third parties not to understand.

Entrapment In criminal law, a defense in which the defendant claims that he or she was induced by a public official—usually an undercover agent or police officer—to commit a crime that he or she would otherwise not have committed.

Entrustment The transfer of goods to a merchant who deals in goods of that kind and who may transfer those goods and all rights to them to a buyer in the ordinary course of business [UCC 2–403(2)].

Environmental impact statement (EIS) A statement required by the National Environmental Policy Act for any major federal action that will significantly affect the quality of the environment. The statement must analyze the action's impact on the environment and explore alternative actions that might be taken.

Environmental law The body of statutory, regulatory, and common law relating to the protection of the environment.

Equal dignity rule In most states, a rule stating that express authority given to an agent must be in writing if the contract to be made on behalf of the principal is required to be in writing.

Equal protection clause The provision in the Fourteenth Amendment to the Constitution that guarantees that no state will "deny to any person within its jurisdiction the equal protection of the laws." This clause mandates that state governments treat similarly situated individuals in a similar manner.

Equitable maxims General propositions or principles of law that have to do with fairness (equity).

Equity of redemption The right of a mortgagor who has breached the mortgage agreement to redeem or purchase the property prior to foreclosure proceedings.

Establishment clause The provision in the First Amendment to the U.S. Constitution that prohibits Congress from creating any law "respecting an establishment of religion."

Estop To bar, impede, or preclude.

Estoppel The principle that a party's own acts prevent him or her from claiming a right to the detriment of another who was entitled to and did rely on those acts. *See also* Agency by estoppel; Promissory estoppel

Estray statute A statute defining finders' rights in property when the true owners are unknown.

Ethical reasoning A reasoning process in which an individual links his or her moral convictions or ethical standards to the particular situation at hand.

Ethics Moral principles and values applied to social behavior.

Evidence Proof offered at trial—in the form of testimony, documents, records, exhibits, objects, and so on—for the purpose of convincing the court or jury of the truth of a contention.

Ex parte **contact** Communications with an administrative agency that are not placed in the record.

Ex ship *See* Delivery ex ship

Exclusionary rule In criminal procedure, a rule under which any evidence that is obtained in violation of the accused's constitutional rights guaranteed by the Fourth, Fifth, and Sixth Amendments, as well as any evidence derived from illegally obtained evidence, will not be admissible in court.

Exclusive distributorship A distributorship in which the seller and the distributor of the seller's products agree that the distributor has the exclusive right to distribute the seller's products in a certain geographic area.

Exclusive jurisdiction Jurisdiction that exists when a case can be heard only in a particular court or type of court, such as a federal court or a state court.

Exclusive-dealing contract An agreement under which a seller forbids a buyer to purchase products from the seller's competitors.

Exculpatory clause A clause that releases a contractual party from liability in the event of monetary or physical injury, no matter who is at fault.

Executed contract A contract that has been completely performed by both parties.

Execution An action to carry into effect the directions in a court decree or judgment.

Executive agency An administrative agency within the executive branch of government. At the federal level, executive agencies are those within the cabinet departments.

Executor A person appointed by a testator to see that his or her will is administered appropriately.

Executory contract A contract that has not as yet been fully performed.

Export To sell products to buyers located in other countries.

Express authority Authority expressly given by one party to another. In agency law, an agent has express authority to act for a principal if both parties agree, orally or in writing, that an agency relationship exists in which the agent had the power (authority) to act in the place of, and on behalf of, the principal.

Express contract A contract in which the terms of the agreement are fully and explicitly stated in words, oral or written.

Express warranty A seller's or lessor's oral or written promise, ancillary to an underlying sales or lease agreement, as to the quality, description, or performance of the goods being sold or leased.

Expropriation The seizure by a government of privately owned business or personal property for a proper public purpose and with just compensation.

F

F.A.S. Free alongside. A contract term that requires the seller, at his or her own expense and risk, to deliver the goods alongside the ship before risk passes to the buyer.

F.O.B. Free on board. A contract term that indicates that the selling price of the goods includes transportation costs (and that the seller carries the risk of loss) to the specific F.O.B. place named in the contract. The place can be either the place of initial shipment (for example, the seller's city or place of business) or the place of destination (for example, the buyer's city or place of business).

Family limited liability partnership (FLLP) A limited liability partnership (LLP) in which the majority of the partners are persons related to each other, essentially as spouses, parents, grandparents, siblings, cousins, nephews, or nieces. A person acting in a fiduciary capacity for persons so related could also be a partner. All of the partners must be natural persons or persons acting in a fiduciary capacity for the benefit of natural persons.

Federal form of government A system of government in which the states form a union and the sovereign power is divided between a central government and the member states.

Federal question A question that pertains to the U.S. Constitution, acts of Congress, or treaties. A federal question provides a basis for federal jurisdiction.

Federal Rules of Civil Procedure (FRCP) The rules controlling procedural matters in civil trials brought before the federal district courts.

Federal system A system of government in which power is divided by a written constitution between a central government and regional, or subdivisional, governments. Each level must have some domain in which its policies are dominant and some genuine political or constitutional guarantee of its authority.

Fee simple An absolute form of property ownership entitling the property owner to use, possess, or dispose of the property as he or she chooses during his or her lifetime. On death, the interest in the property descends to the owner's heirs; a fee simple absolute.

Fee simple absolute An ownership interest in land in which the owner has the greatest possible aggregation of rights, privileges, and power. Ownership in fee simple absolute is limited absolutely to a person and his or her heirs.

Fellow-servant doctrine A doctrine that bars an employee from suing his or her employer for injuries caused by a fellow employee.

Felony A crime—such as arson, murder, rape, or robbery—that carries the most severe sanctions, usually ranging from one year in a state or federal prison to the forfeiture of one's life.

Fiduciary As a noun, a person having a duty created by his or her undertaking to act primarily for another's benefit in matters connected with the undertaking. As an adjective, a relationship founded on trust and confidence.

Fiduciary duty The duty, imposed on a fiduciary by virtue of his or her position, to act primarily for another's benefit.

Filtering software A computer program that includes a pattern through which data are passed. When designed to block access to certain Web sites, the pattern blocks the retrieval of a site whose URL or key words are on a list within the program.

Final order The final decision of an administrative agency on an issue. If no appeal is taken, or if the case is not reviewed or considered anew by the agency commission, the administrative law judge's initial order becomes the final order of the agency.

Firm offer An offer (by a merchant) that is irrevocable without consideration for a period of time (not longer than three months). A firm offer by a merchant must be in writing and must be signed by the offeror.

Fitness for a particular purpose *See* Implied warranty of fitness for a particular purpose

Fixture A thing that was once personal property but that has become attached to real property in such a way that it takes on the characteristics of real property and becomes part of that real property.

Flame An online message in which one party attacks another in harsh, often personal, terms.

Force majeure (pronounced mah-*zhure*) **clause** A provision in a contract stipulating that certain unforeseen events—such as war, political upheavals, acts of God, or other events—will excuse a party from liability for nonperformance of contractual obligations.

Foreclosure A proceeding in which a mortgagee either takes title to or forces the sale of the mortgagor's property in satisfaction of a debt.

Foreign corporation In a given state, a corporation that does business in the state without being incorporated therein.

Foreseeable risk In negligence law, the risk of harm or injury to another that a person of ordinary intelligence and prudence should have reasonably anticipated or foreseen when undertaking an action or refraining from undertaking an action.

Forgery The fraudulent making or altering of any writing in a way that changes the legal rights and liabilities of another.

Formal contract A contract that by law requires for its validity a specific form, such as executed under seal.

Forum A jurisdiction, court, or place in which disputes are litigated and legal remedies are sought.

Franchise Any arrangement in which the owner of a trademark, trade name, or copyright licenses another to use that trademark, trade name, or copyright, under specified conditions or limitations, in the selling of goods and services.

Franchisee One receiving a license to use another's (the franchisor's) trademark, trade name, or copyright in the sale of goods and services.

Franchisor One licensing another (the franchisee) to use his or her trademark, trade name, or copyright in the sale of goods or services.

Fraud Any misrepresentation, either by misstatement or omission of a material fact, knowingly made with the intention of deceiving another and on which a reasonable person would and does rely to his or her detriment.

Fraud in the execution In the law of negotiable instruments, a type of fraud that occurs when a person is deceived into signing a negotiable instrument, believing that he or she is signing something else (such as a receipt); also called fraud in the inception. Fraud in the execution is a universal defense to payment on a negotiable instrument.

Fraud in the inducement Ordinary fraud. In the law of negotiable instruments, fraud in the inducement occurs when a person issues a negotiable instrument based on false statements by the other party. The issuing party will be able to avoid payment on that instrument unless the holder is a holder in due course; in other words, fraud in the inducement is a personal defense to payment on a negotiable instrument.

Fraudulent misrepresentation (fraud) Any misrepresentation, either by misstatement or omission of a material fact, knowingly made with the intention of deceiving another and on which a reasonable person would and does rely to his or her detriment.

Free exercise clause The provision in the First Amendment to the U.S. Constitution that prohibits Congress from making any law "prohibiting the free exercise" of religion.

Frustration of purpose A court-created doctrine under which a party to a contract will be relieved of his or her duty to perform when the objective purpose for performance no longer exists (due to reasons beyond that party's control).

Full faith and credit clause A clause in Article IV, Section 1, of the Constitution that provides that "Full Faith and Credit shall be given in each State to the public Acts, Records, and Judicial Proceedings of every othere States." The clause ensures that rights established under deeds, wills, contracts, and the like in one state will be honored by the other states and that any judicial decision with respect to such property rights will be honored and enforced in all states.

Full warranty A warranty as to full performance covering generally both labor and materials.

Fungible goods Goods that are alike by physical nature, by agreement, or by trade usage. Examples of fungible goods are wheat, oil, and wine that are identical in type and quality.

G

Garnishment A legal process used by a creditor to collect a debt by seizing property of the debtor (such as wages) that is being held by a third party (such as the debtor's employer).

General jurisdiction Exists when a court's subject-matter jurisdiction is not restricted. A court of general jurisdiction normally can hear any type of case.

General partner In a limited partnership, a partner who assumes responsibility for the management of the partnership and liability for all partnership debts.

General partnership *See* Partnership

Genuineness of assent Knowing and voluntary assent to the terms of a contract. If a contract is formed as a result of a mistake, misrepresentation, undue influence, or duress, genuineness of assent is lacking, and the contract will be voidable.

Good faith Under the Uniform Commercial Code good faith means honesty in fact; with regard to merchants, good faith means honesty in fact *and* the observance of reasonable commercial standards of fair dealing in the trade.

Good faith purchaser A purchaser who buys without notice of any circumstance that would put a person of ordinary prudence on inquiry as to whether the seller has valid title to the goods being sold.

Good Samaritan statute A state statute that provides that persons who rescue or provide emergency services to others in peril—unless they do so recklessly, thus causing further harm—cannot be sued for negligence.

Grand jury A group of citizens called to decide, after hearing the state's evidence, whether a reasonable basis (probable cause) exists for believing that a crime has been committed and whether a trial ought to be held.

Grant deed A deed that simply recites words of consideration and conveyance. Under statute, a grant deed may impliedly warrant that at least the grantor has not conveyed the property's title to someone else.

Grantee One to whom a grant (of land or property, for example) is made.

Grantor A person who makes a grant, such as a transferor of property or the creator of a trust.

Group boycott The refusal to deal with a particular person or firm by a group of competitors; prohibited by the Sherman Act.

Guarantor A person who agrees to satisfy the debt of another (the debtor) only after the principal debtor defaults; a guarantor's liability is thus secondary.

H

Habitability *See* Implied warranty of habitability

Hacker A person who uses one computer to break into another. Professional computer programmers refer to such persons as "crackers."

Hearsay An oral or written statement made out of court that is later offered in court by a witness (not the person who made the statement) to prove the truth of the matter asserted in the statement. Hearsay is generally inadmissible as evidence.

Hirfindahl-Hirschman Index (HHI) An index of market power used to calculate whether a merger of two businesses will result in sufficient monopoly power to violate antitrust laws.

Historical school A school of legal thought that emphasizes the evolutionary process of law and that looks to the past to discover what the principles of contemporary law should be.

Homestead exemption A law permitting a debtor to retain the family home, either in its entirety or up to a specified dollar amount, free from the claims of unsecured creditors or trustees in bankruptcy.

Horizontal merger A merger between two firms that are competing in the same market.

Horizontal restraint Any agreement that in some way restrains competition between rival firms competing in the same market.

Hot-cargo agreement An agreement in which employers voluntarily agree with unions not to handle, use, or deal in nonunion-produced goods of other employers; a type of secondary boycott explicitly prohibited by the Labor-Management Reporting and Disclosure Act of 1959.

Hung jury A jury whose members are so irreconcilably divided in their opinions that they cannot come to a verdict by the requisite number of jurors. The judge in this situation may order a new trial.

I

Identification In a sale of goods, the express designation of the goods provided for in the contract.

Illusory promise A promise made without consideration, which renders the promise unenforceable.

Immunity A status of being exempt, or free, from certain duties or requirements. In criminal law, the state may grant an accused person immunity from prosecution—or agree to prosecute for a lesser offense—if the accused person agrees to give the state information that would assist the state in prosecuting other individuals for crimes. In tort law, freedom from liability for defamatory speech. *See also* Privilege

Implied authority Authority that is created not by an explicit oral or written agreement but by implication. In agency law, implied authority (of the agent) can be conferred by custom, inferred from the position the agent occupies, or implied by virtue of being reasonably necessary to carry out express authority.

Implied warranty A warranty that the law derives by implication or inference from the nature of the transaction or the relative situation or circumstances of the parties.

Implied warranty of fitness for a particular purpose A warranty that goods sold or leased are fit for a particular purpose. The warranty arises when any seller or lessor knows the particular purpose for which a buyer or lessee will use the goods and knows that the buyer or lessee is relying on the skill and judgment of the seller or lessor to select suitable goods.

Implied warranty of habitability An implied promise by a landlord that rented residential premises are fit for human habitation—

that is, in a condition that is safe and suitable for people to live in.

Implied warranty of merchantability A warranty that goods being sold or leased are reasonably fit for the general purpose for which they are sold or leased, are properly packaged and labeled, and are of proper quality. The warranty automatically arises in every sale or lease of goods made by a merchant who deals in goods of the kind sold or leased.

Implied-in-fact contract A contract formed in whole or in part from the conduct of the parties (as opposed to an express contract).

Impossibility of performance A doctrine under which a party to a contract is relieved of his or her duty to perform when performance becomes impossible or totally impracticable (through no fault of either party).

Imposter One who, by use of the mails, telephone, or personal appearance, induces a maker or drawer to issue an instrument in the name of an impersonated payee. Indorsements by imposters are not treated as unauthorized under Article 3 of the Uniform Commercial Code.

In pari delicto At equal fault.

In personam jurisdiction Court jurisdiction over the "person" involved in a legal action; personal jurisdiction.

In rem jurisdiction Court jurisdiction over a defendant's property.

Incidental beneficiary A third party who incidentally benefits from a contract but whose benefit was not the reason the contract was formed; an incidental beneficiary has no rights in a contract and cannot sue to have the contract enforced.

Incidental damages Damages resulting from a breach of contract, including all reasonable expenses incurred because of the breach.

Indemnify To compensate or reimburse another for losses or expenses incurred.

Independent contractor One who works for, and receives payment from, an employer but whose working conditions and methods are not controlled by the employer. An independent contractor is not an employee but may be an agent.

Independent regulatory agency An administrative agency that is not considered part of the government's executive branch and is not subject to the authority of the president. Independent agency officials cannot be removed without cause.

Indictment (pronounced in-*dyte*-ment) A charge by a grand jury that a named person has committed a crime.

Indorsee The person to whom a negotiable instrument is transferred by indorsement.

Indorsement A signature placed on an instrument for the purpose of transferring one's ownership rights in the instrument.

Industry-wide liability Product liability that is imposed on an entire industry when it is unclear which of several sellers within the industry manufactured a particular product. *See also* Market-share liability

Informal contract A contract that does not require a specified form or formality in order to be valid.

Information A formal accusation or complaint (without an indictment) issued in certain types of actions (usually criminal actions involving lesser crimes) by a law officer, such as a magistrate.

Information return A tax return submitted by a partnership that only reports the income earned by the business. The partnership as an entity does not pay taxes on the income received by the partnership. A partner's profit from the partnership (whether distributed or not) is taxed as individual income to the individual partner.

Infringement A violation of another's legally recognized right. The term is commonly used with reference to the invasion by one party of another party's rights in a patent, trademark, or copyright.

Initial order In the context of administrative law, an agency's disposition in a matter other than a rulemaking. An administrative law judge's initial order becomes final unless it is appealed.

Injunction A court decree ordering a person to do or refrain from doing a certain act or activity.

Innkeeper An owner of an inn, hotel, motel, or other lodgings.

Innkeeper's lien A possessory or statutory lien allowing the innkeeper to take the personal property of a guest, brought into the hotel, as security for nonpayment of the guest's bill (debt).

Innocent misrepresentation A false statement of fact or an act made in good faith that deceives and causes harm or injury to another.

Insider A corporate director or officer, or other employee or agent, with access to confidential information and a duty not to disclose that information in violation of insider-trading laws.

Insider trading The purchase or sale of securities on the basis of "inside information" (information that has not been made available to the public) in violation of a duty owed to the company whose stock is being traded.

Insolvent Under the Uniform Commercial Code, a term describing a person who ceases to pay "his debts in the ordinary course of business or cannot pay his debts as they become due or is insolvent within the meaning of federal bankruptcy law" [UCC 1–201(23)].

Installment contract Under the Uniform Commercial Code, a contract that requires or authorizes delivery in two or more separate lots to be accepted and paid for separately.

Insurable interest An interest either in a person's life or well-being or in property that is sufficiently substantial that insuring against injury to (or the death of) the person or against damage to the property does not amount to a mere wagering (betting) contract.

Intangible property Property that is incapable of being apprehended by the senses (such as by sight or touch); intellectual property is an example of intangible property.

Integrated contract A written contract that constitutes the final expression of the parties' agreement. If a contract is integrated, evidence extraneous to the contract that contradicts or alters the meaning of the contract in any way is inadmissible.

Intellectual property Property resulting from intellectual, creative processes. Patents, trademarks, and copyrights are examples of intellectual property.

Intended beneficiary A third party for whose benefit a contract is formed; an intended beneficiary can sue the promisor if such a contract is breached.

Intentional tort A wrongful act knowingly committed.

International law The law that governs relations among nations. International customs and treaties are generally considered to be two of the most important sources of international law.

International organization In international law, a term that generally refers to an organization composed mainly of nations and usually established by treaty. The United States is a member of more than one hundred multilateral and bilateral organizations, including at least twenty through the United Nations.

Interpretive rule An administrative agency rule that is simply a statement or opinion issued by the agency explaining how it interprets and intends to apply the statutes it enforces. Such rules are not automatically binding on private individuals or organizations.

Interrogatories A series of written questions for which written answers are prepared and then signed under oath by a party to a lawsuit, usually with the assistance of the party's attorney.

Investment company A company that acts on behalf of many smaller shareholder-owners by buying a large portfolio of securities and professionally managing that portfolio.

Invitee A person who, either expressly or impliedly, is privileged to enter onto another's land. The inviter owes the invitee (for example, a customer in a store) the duty to exercise reasonable care to protect the invitee from harm.

Irrevocable offer An offer that cannot be revoked or recalled by the offeror without liability. A merchant's firm offer is an example of an irrevocable offer.

Issue The first transfer, or delivery, of an instrument to a holder.

J

Joint and several liability In partnership law, a doctrine under which a plaintiff may sue, and collect a judgment from, one or more of the partners separately (severally, or individually) or all of the partners together (jointly). This is true even if one of the partners sued did not participate in, ratify, or know about whatever it was that gave rise to the cause of action.

Joint liability Shared liability. In partnership law, partners incur joint liability for partnership obligations and debts. For example, if a third party sues a partner on a partnership debt, the partner has the right to insist that the other partners be sued with him or her.

Joint stock company A hybrid form of business organization that combines characteristics of a corporation (shareholder-owners, management by directors and officers of the company, and perpetual existence) and a partnership (it is formed by agreement, not statute; property is usually held in the names of the members; and the shareholders have personal liability for business debts). Usually, the joint stock company is regarded as a partnership for tax and other legally related purposes.

Joint tenancy The joint ownership of property by two or more co-owners in which each co-owner owns an undivided portion of the property. On the death of one of the joint tenants, his or her interest automatically passes to the surviving joint tenants.

Joint venture A joint undertaking of a specific commercial enterprise by an association of persons. A joint venture is normally not a legal entity and is treated like a partnership for federal income tax purposes.

Judgment The final order or decision resulting from a legal action.

Judgment n.o.v. *See* Motion for judgment n.o.v.

Judgment rate of interest A rate of interest fixed by statute that is applied to a monetary judgment from the moment the judgment is awarded by a court until the judgment is paid or terminated.

Judicial lien A lien on property created by a court order.

Judicial process The procedures relating to, or connected with, the administration of justice through the judicial system.

Judicial review The process by which courts decide on the constitutionality of legislative enactments and actions of the executive branch.

Jurisdiction The authority of a court to hear and decide a specific action.

Jurisprudence The science or philosophy of law.

Justiciable (pronounced jus-*tish*-a-bul) **controversy** A controversy that is not hypothetical or academic but real and substantial; a requirement that must be satisfied before a court will hear a case.

K

King's court A medieval English court. The king's courts, or *curiae regis*, were established by the Norman conquerors of England. The body of law that developed in these courts was common to the entire English realm and thus became known as the common law.

L

Laches The equitable doctrine that bars a party's right to legal action if the party has neglected for an unreasonable length of time to act on his or her rights.

Larceny The wrongful taking and carrying away of another person's personal property with the intent to permanently deprive the owner of the property. Some states classify larceny as either grand or petit, depending on the property's value.

Last clear chance A doctrine under which a plaintiff may recover from a defendant for injuries or damages suffered, notwithstanding the plaintiff's own negligence, when the defendant had the opportunity—a last clear chance—to avoid harming the plaintiff through the exercise of reasonable care but failed to do so.

Law A body of enforceable rules governing relationships among individuals and between individuals and their society.

Lawsuit The litigation process. *See* Litigation

Leasehold estate An estate in realty held by a tenant under a lease. In every leasehold estate, the tenant has a qualified right to possess and/or use the land.

Legal positivists Adherents to the positivist school of legal thought. This school holds that there can be no higher law than a nation's positive law—law created by a particular society at a particular point in time. In contrast to the natural law school, the positivist school maintains that there are no "natural" rights; rights come into existence only when there is a sovereign power (government) to confer and enforce those rights.

Legal rate of interest A rate of interest fixed by statute as either the maximum rate of interest allowed by law or a rate of interest applied when the parties to a contract intend, but do not fix, an interest rate in the contract. In the latter case, the rate is frequently the same as the statutory maximum rate permitted.

Legal realism A school of legal thought that was popular in the 1920s and 1930s and that challenged many existing jurisprudential assumptions, particularly the assumption that subjective elements play no part in judicial reasoning. Legal realists generally advocated a less abstract and more realistic approach to the law, an approach that would take into account customary practices and the circumstances in which transactions take place. The school left a lasting imprint on American jurisprudence.

Legal reasoning The process of reasoning by which a judge harmonizes his or her decision with the judicial decisions of previous cases.

Legislative rule An administrative agency rule that carries the same weight as a congressionally enacted statute.

Levy The obtaining of money by legal process through the seizure and sale of property, usually done after a writ of execution has been issued.

Liability Any actual or potential legal obligation, duty, debt, or responsibility.

Libel Defamation in writing or other form (such as in a videotape) having the quality of permanence.

License A revocable right or privilege of a person to come on another person's land.

Licensee One who receives a license to use, or enter onto, another's property.

Lien (pronounced leen) An encumbrance on a property to satisfy a debt or protect a claim for payment of a debt.

Lien creditor One whose claim is secured by a lien on particular property, as distinguished from a general creditor, who has no such security.

Life estate An interest in land that exists only for the duration of the life of some person, usually the holder of the estate.

Limited jurisdiction Exists when a court's subject-matter jurisdiction is limited. Bankruptcy courts and probate courts are examples of courts with limited jurisdiction.

Limited liability Exists when the liability of the owners of a business is limited to the amount of their investments in the firm.

Limited liability company (LLC) A hybrid form of business enterprise that offers the limited liability of the corporation but the tax advantages of a partnership.

Limited liability limited partnership (LLLP) A type of limited partnership. The difference between a limited partnership and an LLLP is that the liability of the general partner in an LLLP is the same as the liability of the limited partner. That is, the liability of all partners is limited to the amount of their investments in the firm.

Limited liability partnership (LLP) A form of partnership that allows professionals to enjoy the tax benefits of a partnership while limiting their personal liability for the malpractice of other partners.

Limited partner In a limited partnership, a partner who contributes capital to the partnership but has no right to participate in the management and operation of the business. The limited partner assumes no liability for partnership debts beyond the capital contributed.

Limited partnership A partnership consisting of one or more general partners (who manage the business and are liable to the full extent of their personal assets for debts of the partnership) and one or more limited partners (who contribute only assets and are liable only to the extent of their contributions).

Limited warranty A written warranty that fails to meet one or more of the minimum standards for a full warranty.

Liquidated damages An amount, stipulated in the contract, that the parties to a contract believe to be a reasonable estimation of the damages that will occur in the event of a breach.

Liquidated debt A debt that is due and certain in amount.

Liquidation (1) In regard to bankruptcy, the sale of all of the nonexempt assets of a debtor and the distribution of the proceeds to the debtor's creditors. Chapter 7 of the Bankruptcy Code provides for liquidation bankruptcy proceedings. (2) In regard to corporations, the process by which corporate assets are converted into cash and distributed among creditors and shareholders according to specific rules of preference.

Litigant A party to a lawsuit.

Litigation The process of resolving a dispute through the court system.

Loan workout *See* Workout

Long arm statute A state statute that permits a state to obtain personal jurisdiction over nonresident defendants. A defendant must have "minimum contacts" with that state for the statute to apply.

M

Magistrate's court A court of limited jurisdiction that is presided over by a public official (magistrate) with certain judicial authority, such as the power to set bail.

Mailbox rule A rule providing that an acceptance of an offer becomes effective on dispatch (on being placed in a mailbox), if mail is, expressly or impliedly, an authorized means of communication of acceptance to the offeror.

Main purpose rule A rule of contract law under which an exception to the Statute of Frauds is made if the main purpose in accepting secondary liability under a contract is to secure a personal benefit. If this situation exists, the contract need not be in writing to be enforceable.

Majority *See* Age of majority

Majority opinion A court's written opinion, outlining the views of the majority of the judges or justices deciding the case.

Maker One who promises to pay a certain sum to the holder of a promissory note or certificate of deposit (CD).

Malpractice Professional misconduct or the failure to exercise the requisite degree of skill as a professional. Negligence—the failure to exercise due care—on the part of a professional, such as a physician or an attorney, is commonly referred to as malpractice.

Manufacturing or processing-plant franchise A franchise that is created when the franchisor transmits to the franchisee the essential ingredients or formula to make a particular product. The franchisee then markets the product either at wholesale or at retail in accordance with the franchisor's standards. Examples of this type of franchise are Coca-Cola and other soft-drink bottling companies.

Mark *See* Trademark

Market concentration A situation that exists when a small number of firms share the market for a particular good or service. For example, if the four largest grocery stores in Chicago accounted for 80 percent of all retail food sales, the market clearly would be concentrated in those four firms.

Market power The power of a firm to control the market price of its product. A monopoly has the greatest degree of market power.

Marketable title Title to real estate that is reasonably free from encumbrances, defects in the chain of title, and other events that affect title, such as adverse possession.

Market-share liability A method of sharing liability among several firms that manufactured or marketed a particular product that may have caused a plaintiff's injury. This form of liability sharing is used when the true source of the product is unidentifiable. Each firm's liability is proportionate to its respective share of the relevant market for the product. Market-share liability applies only if the injuring product is fungible, the true manufacturer is unidentifiable, the unknown character of the manufacturer is not the plaintiff's fault.

Market-share test The primary measure of monopoly power. A firm's market share is the percentage of a market that the firm controls.

Marshalling assets The arrangement or ranking of assets in a certain order toward the payment of debts. In equity, when two creditors have recourse to the same property of the debtor, but one has recourse to other property of the debtor, that creditor must resort first to those assets of the debtor that are not available to the other creditor.

Material alteration *See* Alteration

Material fact A fact to which a reasonable person would attach importance in determining his or her course of action. In regard to tender offers, for example, a fact is material if there is a substantial likelihood that a reasonable shareholder would consider it important in deciding how to vote.

Mechanic's lien A statutory lien on the real property of another, created to ensure payment for work performed and materials furnished in the repair or improvement of real property, such as a building.

Mediation A method of settling disputes outside of court by using the services of a neutral third party, called a mediator. The mediator acts as a communicating agent between the parties and suggests ways in which the parties can resolve their dispute.

Member The term used to designate a person who has an ownership interest in a limited liability company.

Mens rea (pronounced *mehns ray*-uh) Mental state, or intent. A wrongful mental state is as necessary as a wrongful act to establish criminal liability. What constitutes a mental state varies according to the wrongful action. Thus, for murder, the *mens rea* is the intent to take a life; for theft, the *mens rea* must involve both the knowledge that the property belongs to another and the intent to deprive the owner of it.

Merchant A person who is engaged in the purchase and sale of goods. Under the Uniform Commercial Code, a person who deals in goods of the kind involved in the sales contract; for further definitions, see UCC 2–104.

Merger A contractual and statutory process in which one corporation (the surviving corporation) acquires all of the assets and liabilities of another corporation (the merged corporation). The shareholders of the merged corporation receive either payment for their shares or shares in the surviving corporation.

Meta tags Words inserted into a Web site's key words field to increase the site's appearance in search engine results.

Minimum-contacts requirement The requirement that before a state court can exercise jurisdiction over a foreign corporation, the foreign corporation must have sufficient contacts with the state. A foreign corporation that has its home office in the state or that has manufacturing plants in the state meets this requirement.

Minimum wage The lowest wage, either by government regulation or union contract, that an employer may pay an hourly worker.

Mini-trial A private proceeding in which each party to a dispute argues its position before the other side and vice versa. A neutral third party may be present and act as an adviser if the parties fail to reach an agreement.

Mirror image rule A common law rule that requires, for a valid contractual agreement, that the terms of the offeree's acceptance adhere exactly to the terms of the offeror's offer.

Misdemeanor A lesser crime than a felony, punishable by a fine or imprisonment for up to one year in other than a state or federal penitentiary.

Misrepresentation   A false statement of fact or an action that deceives and causes harm or injury to another. *See also* Fraudulent misrepresentation (fraud); Innocent misrepresentation

Mitigation of damages   A rule requiring a plaintiff to have done whatever was reasonable to minimize the damages caused by the defendant.

Money laundering   Falsely reporting income that has been obtained through criminal activity as income obtained through a legitimate business enterprise—in effect, "laundering" the "dirty money."

Monopolization   The possession of monopoly power in the relevant market and the willful acquisition or maintenance of the power, as distinguished from growth or development as a consequence of a superior product, business acumen, or historic accident.

Monopoly   A term generally used to describe a market in which there is a single seller or a limited number of sellers.

Monopoly power   The ability of a monopoly to dictate what takes place in a given market.

Moral minimum   The minimum degree of ethical behavior expected of a business firm, which is usually defined as compliance with the law.

Mortgage   A written instrument giving a creditor (the mortgagee) an interest in (a lien on) the debtor's (mortgagor's) property as security for a debt.

Mortgage bond   A bond that pledges specific property. If the corporation defaults on the bond, the bondholder can take the property.

Mortgagee   Under a mortgage agreement, the creditor who takes a security interest in the debtor's property.

Mortgagor   Under a mortgage agreement, the debtor who gives the creditor a security interest in the debtor's property in return for a mortgage loan.

Most-favored-nation status   A status granted in an international treaty by a provision stating that the citizens of the contracting nations may enjoy the privileges accorded by either party to citizens of the most favored nations. Generally, most-favored-nation clauses are designed to establish equality of international treatment.

Motion   A procedural request or application presented by an attorney to the court on behalf of a client.

Motion for a directed verdict   In a jury trial, a motion for the judge to take the decision out of the hands of the jury and direct a verdict for the moving party on the ground that the other party has not produced sufficient evidence to support his or her claim; referred to as a motion for judgment as a matter of law in the federal courts.

Motion for a new trial   A motion asserting that the trial was so fundamentally flawed (because of error, newly discovered evidence, prejudice, or other reason) that a new trial is necessary to prevent a miscarriage of justice.

Motion for judgment *n.o.v.*   A motion requesting the court to grant judgment in favor of the party making the motion on the ground that the jury verdict against him or her was unreasonable and erroneous.

Motion for judgment on the pleadings   A motion by either party to a lawsuit at the close of the pleadings requesting the court to decide the issue solely on the pleadings without proceeding to trial. The motion will be granted only if no facts are in dispute.

Motion for summary judgment   A motion requesting the court to enter a judgment without proceeding to trial. The motion can be based on evidence outside the pleadings and will be granted only if no facts are in dispute.

Motion to dismiss   A pleading in which a defendant asserts that the plaintiff's claim fails to state a cause of action (that is, has no basis in law) or that there are other grounds on which a suit should be dismissed.

Multiple product order   An order issued by the Federal Trade Commission to a firm that has engaged in deceptive advertising by which the firm is required to cease and desist from false advertising not only in regard to the product that was the subject of the action but also in regard to all the firm's other products.

Municipal court   A city or community court with criminal jurisdiction over traffic violations and, less frequently, with civil jurisdiction over other minor matters.

Mutual assent   The element of agreement in the formation of a contract. The manifestation of contract parties' mutual assent to the same bargain is required to establish a contract.

Mutual fund   A specific type of investment company that continually buys or sells to investors shares of ownership in a portfolio.

Mutual rescission   An agreement between the parties to cancel their contract, releasing the parties from further obligations under the contract. The object of the agreement is to restore the parties to the positions they would have occupied had no contract ever been formed. *See also* Rescission

N

National law   Law that pertains to a particular nation (as opposed to international law).

Natural law   The belief that government and the legal system should reflect universal moral and ethical principles that are inherent in human nature. The natural law school is the oldest and one of the most significant schools of legal thought.

Necessaries   Necessities required for life, such as food, shelter, clothing, and medical attention; may include whatever is believed to be necessary to maintain a person's standard of living or financial and social status.

Necessity   In criminal law, a defense against liability; under Section 3.02 of the Model Penal Code, this defense is justifiable if "the harm or evil sought to be avoided" by a given action "is greater than that sought to be prevented by the law defining the offense charged."

Negligence   The failure to exercise the standard of care that a reasonable person would exercise in similar circumstances.

Negligence *per se*   An act (or failure to act) in violation of a statutory requirement.

Negligent misrepresentation   Any manifestation through words or conduct that amounts to an untrue statement of fact made in circumstances in which a reasonable and prudent person would not have done (or failed to do) that which led to the misrepresentation. A representation made with an honest belief in its truth may still be negligent due to (1) a lack of reasonable care in ascertaining the facts, (2) the manner of expression, or (3) the absence of the skill or competence required by a particular business or profession.

Negotiation   In regard to dispute settlement, a process in which parties attempt to settle their dispute without going to court, with or without attorneys to represent them.

Nominal damages   A small monetary award (often one dollar) granted to a plaintiff when no actual damage was suffered.

Nonconforming goods   Goods that do not conform to contract specifications.

No-par shares   Corporate shares that have no face value—that is, no specific dollar amount is printed on their face.

Notary public   A public official authorized to attest to the authenticity of signatures.

Notice-and-comment rulemaking   An administrative rulemaking procedure that involves the publication of a notice of a proposed rulemaking in the *Federal Register*, a comment period for interested parties to express their views on the proposed rule, and the publication of the agency's final rule in the *Federal Register*.

Notice of Proposed Rulemaking   A notice published (in the *Federal Register*) by an administrative agency describing a proposed rule. The notice must give the time and place for which agency proceedings on the proposed rule will be held, a description of the nature of the proceedings, the legal authority for the proceedings (which is usually the agency's enabling legislation), and the terms of the proposed rule or the subject matter of the proposed rule.

Novation The substitution, by agreement, of a new contract for an old one, with the rights under the old one being terminated. Typically, there is a substitution of a new person who is responsible for the contract and the removal of an original party's rights and duties under the contract.

Nuisance A common law doctrine under which persons may be held liable for using their property in a manner that unreasonably interferes with others' rights to use or enjoy their own property.

O

Objective theory of contracts A theory under which the intent to form a contract will be judged by outward, objective facts (what the party said when entering into the contract, how the party acted or appeared, and the circumstances surrounding the transaction) as interpreted by a reasonable person, rather than by the party's own secret, subjective intentions.

Obligee One to whom an obligation is owed.

Obligor One that owes an obligation to another.

Offer A promise or commitment to perform or refrain from performing some specified act in the future.

Offeree A person to whom an offer is made.

Offeror A person who makes an offer.

Opening statement A statement made to the jury at the beginning of a trial by a party's attorney, prior to the presentation of evidence. The attorney briefly outlines the evidence that will be offered and the legal theory that will be pursued.

Operating agreement In a limited liability company, an agreement in which the members set forth the details of how the business will be managed and operated.

Operation of law A term expressing the manner in which certain rights or liabilities may be imposed on a person by the application of established rules of law to the particular transaction, without regard to the actions or cooperation of the party himself or herself.

Opinion A statement by the court expressing the reasons for its decision in a case.

Optimum profits The amount of profits that a business can make and still act ethically, as opposed to maximum profits, defined as the amount of profits a firm can make if it is willing to disregard ethical concerns.

Option contract A contract under which the offeror cannot revoke his or her offer for a stipulated time period, and the offeree can accept or reject the offer during this period without fear that the offer will be made to another person. The offeree must give consideration for the option (the irrevocable offer) to be enforceable.

Order for relief A court's grant of assistance to a complainant. In bankruptcy proceedings, the order relieves the debtor of the immediate obligation to pay the debts listed in the bankruptcy petition.

Ordinance A law passed by a local governing unit, such as a municipality or a county.

Original jurisdiction Courts having original jurisdiction are courts of the first instance, or trial courts—that is, courts in which lawsuits begin, trials take place, and evidence is presented.

Output contract An agreement in which a seller agrees to sell and a buyer agrees to buy all or up to a stated amount of what the seller produces.

P

Parent-subsidiary merger A merger of companies in which one company (the parent corporation) owns most of the stock of the other (the subsidiary corporation). A parent-subsidiary merger (short-form merger) can use a simplified procedure when the parent corporation owns at least 90 percent of the outstanding shares of each class of stock of the subsidiary corporation.

Parol evidence A term that originally meant "oral evidence," but which has come to refer to any negotiations or agreements made prior to a contract or any contemporaneous oral agreements made by the parties.

Parol evidence rule A substantive rule of contracts under which a court will not receive into evidence the parties' prior negotiations, prior agreements, or contemporaneous oral agreements if that evidence contradicts or varies the terms of the parties' written contract.

Partially disclosed principal A principal whose identity is unknown by a third person, but the third person knows that the agent is or may be acting for a principal at the time the agent and the third person form a contract.

Partner A co-owner of a partnership.

Partnership An agreement by two or more persons to carry on, as co-owners, a business for profit.

Partnership by estoppel A judicially created partnership that may, at the court's discretion, be imposed for purposes of fairness. The court can prevent those who present themselves as partners (but who are not) from escaping liability if a third person relies on an alleged partnership in good faith and is harmed as a result.

Par-value shares Corporate shares that have a specific face value, or formal cash-in value, written on them, such as one dollar.

Past consideration An act done before the contract is made, which ordinarily, by itself, cannot be consideration for a later promise to pay for the act.

Patent A government grant that gives an inventor the exclusive right or privilege to make, use, or sell his or her invention for a limited time period. The word *patent* usually refers to some invention and designates either the instrument by which patent rights are evidenced or the patent itself.

Payee A person to whom an instrument is made payable.

Penalty A sum inserted into a contract, not as a measure of compensation for its breach but rather as punishment for a default. The agreement as to the amount will not be enforced, and recovery will be limited to actual damages.

Per curiam By the whole court; a court opinion written by the court as a whole instead of being authored by a judge or justice.

Per se A Latin term meaning "in itself" or "by itself."

Per se **violation** A type of anticompetitive agreement—such as a horizontal price-fixing agreement—that is considered to be so injurious to the public that there is no need to determine whether it actually injures market competition; rather, it is in itself (*per se*) a violation of the Sherman Act.

Perfect tender rule A common law rule under which a seller was required to deliver to the buyer goods that conformed perfectly to the requirements stipulated in the sales contract. A tender of nonconforming goods would automatically constitute a breach of contract. Under the Uniform Commercial Code, the rule has been greatly modified.

Perfection The legal process by which secured parties protect themselves against the claims of third parties who may wish to have their debts satisfied out of the same collateral; usually accomplished by the filing of a financing statement with the appropriate government official.

Performance In contract law, the fulfillment of one's duties arising under a contract with another; the normal way of discharging one's contractual obligations.

Periodic tenancy A lease interest in land for an indefinite period involving payment of rent at fixed intervals, such as week to week, month to month, or year to year.

Personal jurisdiction *See In personam* jurisdiction

Personal property Property that is movable; any property that is not real property.

Petition in bankruptcy The document that is filed with a bankruptcy court to initiate bankruptcy proceedings. The official forms required for a petition in bankruptcy must be completed accurately, sworn to under oath, and signed by the debtor.

Petitioner In equity practice, a party that initiates a lawsuit.

Petty offense In criminal law, the least serious kind of criminal offense, such as a traffic or building-code violation.

Pierce the corporate veil To disregard the corporate entity, which limits the liability of shareholders, and hold the shareholders personally liable for a corporate obligation.

Plaintiff One who initiates a lawsuit.

Plea In criminal law, a defendant's allegation, in response to the charges brought against him or her, of guilt or innocence.

Plea bargaining The process by which a criminal defendant and the prosecutor in a criminal case work out a mutually satisfactory disposition of the case, subject to court approval; usually involves the defendant's pleading guilty to a lesser offense in return for a lighter sentence.

Pleadings Statements made by the plaintiff and the defendant in a lawsuit that detail the facts, charges, and defenses involved in the litigation; the complaint and answer are part of the pleadings.

Police powers Powers possessed by states as part of their inherent sovereignty. These powers may be exercised to protect or promote the public order, health, safety, morals, and general welfare.

Policy In insurance law, a contract between the insurer and the insured in which, for a stipulated consideration, the insurer agrees to compensate the insured for loss on a specific subject by a specified peril.

Positive law The body of conventional, or written, law of a particular society at a particular point in time.

Positivist school A school of legal thought whose adherents believe that there can be no higher law than a nation's positive law—the body of conventional, or written, law of a particular society at a particular time.

Possessory lien A lien that allows one person to retain possession of another's property as security for a debt or obligation owed by the owner of the property to the lienholder. An example of a possessory lien is an artisan's lien.

Potential competition doctrine A doctrine under which a conglomerate merger may be prohibited by law because it would be injurious to potential competition.

Potentially responsible party (PRP) A potentially liable party under the Comprehensive Environmental Response, Compensation and Liability Act (CERCLA). Any person who generated the hazardous waste, transported the hazardous waste, owned or operated a waste site at the time of disposal, or currently owns or operates a site may be responsible for some or all of the clean-up costs involved in removing the hazardous chemicals.

Power of attorney A written document, which is usually notarized, authorizing another to act as one's agent; can be special (permitting the agent to do specified acts only) or general (permitting the agent to transact all business for the principal).

Precedent A court decision that furnishes an example or authority for deciding subsequent cases involving identical or similar facts.

Predatory pricing The pricing of a product below cost with the intent to drive competitors out of the market.

Preemption A doctrine under which certain federal laws preempt, or take precedence over, conflicting state or local laws.

Preemptive rights Rights held by shareholders that entitle them to purchase newly issued shares of a corporation's stock, equal in percentage to shares presently held, before the stock is offered to any outside buyers. Preemptive rights enable shareholders to maintain their proportionate ownership and voice in the corporation.

Preference In bankruptcy proceedings, property transfers or payments made by the debtor that favor (give preference to) one creditor over others. The bankruptcy trustee is allowed to recover payments made both voluntarily and involuntarily to one creditor in preference over another.

Preferred stock Classes of stock that have priority over common stock both as to payment of dividends and distribution of assets on the corporation's dissolution.

Prejudgment interest Interest that accrues on the amount of a court judgment from the time of the filing of a lawsuit to the court's issuance of a judgment.

Preliminary hearing An initial hearing used in many felony cases to establish whether or not it is proper to detain the defendant. A magistrate reviews the evidence and decides if there is probable cause to believe that the defendant committed the crime with which he or she has been charged.

Prenuptial agreement An agreement made before marriage that defines each partner's ownership rights in the other partner's property. Prenuptial agreements must be in writing to be enforceable.

Preponderance of the evidence A standard in civil law cases under which the plaintiff must convince the court that, based on the evidence presented by both parties, it is more likely than not that the plaintiff's allegation is true.

Pretrial conference A conference, scheduled before the trial begins, between the judge and the attorneys litigating the suit. The parties may settle the dispute, clarify the issues, schedule discovery, and so on during the conference.

Pretrial motion A written or oral application to a court for a ruling or order, made before trial.

Price discrimination Setting prices in such a way that two competing buyers pay two different prices for an identical product or service.

Price-fixing agreement An agreement between competitors in which the competitors agree to fix the prices of products or services at a certain level; prohibited by the Sherman Act.

Prima facie case A case in which the plaintiff has produced sufficient evidence of his or her conclusion that the case can go to to a jury; a case in which the evidence compels the plaintiff's conclusion if the defendant produces no evidence to disprove it.

Primary liability In negotiable instruments law, absolute responsibility for paying a negotiable instrument. Makers and acceptors are primarily liable.

Principal In agency law, a person who agrees to have another, called the agent, act on his or her behalf.

Principle of rights The principle that human beings have certain fundamental rights (to life, freedom, and the pursuit of happiness, for example). Those who adhere to this "rights theory" believe that a key factor in determining whether a business decision is ethical is how that decision affects the rights of others. These others include the firm's owners, its employees, the consumers of its products or services, its suppliers, the community in which it does business, and society as a whole.

Privatization The replacement of government-provided products and services by private firms.

Privilege In tort law, the ability to act contrary to another person's right without that person's having legal redress for such acts. Privilege may be raised as a defense to defamation.

Privileges and immunities clause Special rights and exceptions provided by law. Article IV, Section 2, of the Constitution requires states not to discriminate against one another's citizens. A resident of one state cannot be treated as an alien when in another state; he or she may not be denied such privileges and immunities as legal protection, access to courts, travel rights, or property rights.

Privity of contract The relationship that exists between the promisor and the promisee of a contract.

Pro rata Proportionately; in proportion.

Probable cause Reasonable grounds to believe the existence of facts warranting certain actions, such as the search or arrest of a person.

Procedural due process The requirement that any government decision to take life, liberty, or property must be made fairly. For example, fair procedures must be used in determining whether a person will be subjected to punishment or have some burden imposed on him or her.

Procedural law Rules that define the manner in which the rights and duties of individuals may be enforced.

Procedural unconscionability Occurs when, due to one contractual party's vastly superior bargaining power, the other party lacks a knowledge or understanding of the contract terms due to inconspicuous print or the lack of an opportunity to read the contract or to ask questions about its meaning. Procedural unconscionability often involves an *adhesion contract*, which is a contract drafted by the dominant party and then presented to the other—the adhering party—on a take-it-or-leave-it basis.

Product liability The legal liability of manufacturers, sellers, and lessors of goods to consumers, users, and bystanders for injuries or damages that are caused by the goods.

Product misuse A defense against product liability that may be raised when the plaintiff used a product in a manner not intended by the manufacturer. If the misuse is reasonably foreseeable, the seller will not escape liability unless measures were taken to guard against the harm that could result from the misuse.

Profit In real property law, the right to enter onto and remove things from the property of another (for example, the right to enter onto a person's land and remove sand and gravel therefrom).

Promise A declaration that something either will or will not happen in the future.

Promisee A person to whom a promise is made.

Promisor A person who makes a promise.

Promissory estoppel A doctrine that applies when a promisor makes a clear and definite promise on which the promisee justifiably relies; such a promise is binding if justice will be better served by the enforcement of the promise. *See also* Estoppel

Promoter A person who takes the preliminary steps in organizing a corporation, including (usually) issuing a prospectus, procuring stock subscriptions, making contract purchases, securing a corporate charter, and the like.

Property Legally protected rights and interests in anything with an ascertainable value that is subject to ownership.

Prospectus A document required by federal or state securities laws that describes the financial operations of the corporation, thus allowing investors to make informed decisions.

Protected class A class of persons with identifiable characteristics who historically have been victimized by discriminatory treatment for certain purposes. Depending on the context, these characteristics include age, color, gender, national origin, race, and religion.

Proximate cause Legal cause; exists when the connection between an act and an injury is strong enough to justify imposing liability.

Proxy In corporation law, a written agreement between a stockholder and another under which the stockholder authorizes the other to vote the stockholder's shares in a certain manner.

Proxy fight A conflict between an individual, group, or firm attempting to take control of a corporation and the corporation's management for the votes of the shareholders.

Public figures Individuals who are thrust into the public limelight. Public figures include government officials and politicians, movie stars, well-known businesspersons, and generally anybody who becomes known to the public because of his or her position or activities.

Public policy A government policy based on widely held societal values and (usually) expressed or implied in laws or regulations.

Public prosecutor An individual, acting as a trial lawyer, who initiates and conducts criminal cases in the government's name and on behalf of the people.

Puffery A salesperson's often exaggerated claims concerning the quality of property offered for sale. Such claims involve opinions rather than facts and are not considered to be legally binding promises or warranties.

Punitive damages Money damages that may be awarded to a plaintiff to punish the defendant and deter future similar conduct.

Q

Quantum meruit (pronounced *kwahn*-tuhm *mehr*-oo-wuht) Literally, "as much as he deserves"—an expression describing the extent of liability on a contract implied in law (quasi contract). An equitable doctrine based on the concept that one who benefits from another's labor and materials should not be unjustly enriched thereby but should be required to pay a reasonable amount for the benefits received, even absent a contract.

Quasi contract A fictional contract imposed on parties by a court in the interests of fairness and justice; usually, quasi contracts are imposed to avoid the unjust enrichment of one party at the expense of another.

Question of fact In a lawsuit, an issue involving a factual dispute that can only be decided by a judge (or, in a jury trial, a jury).

Question of law In a lawsuit, an issue involving the application or interpretation of a law; therefore, the judge, and not the jury, decides the issue.

Quiet enjoyment. *See* Covenant of quiet enjoyment

Quitclaim deed A deed intended to pass any title, interest, or claim that the grantor may have in the property but not warranting that such title is valid. A quitclaim deed offers the least amount of protection against defects in the title.

Quorum The number of members of a decision-making body that must be present before business may be transacted.

Quota An assigned import limit on goods.

R

Ratification The act of accepting and giving legal force to an obligation that previously was not enforceable.

Reaffirmation agreement An agreement between a debtor and a creditor in which the debtor reaffirms, or promises to pay, a debt dischargeable in bankruptcy. To be enforceable, the agreement must be made prior to the discharge of the debt by the bankruptcy court.

Real property Land and everything attached to it, such as foliage and buildings.

Reasonable care The degree of care that a person of ordinary prudence would exercise in the same or similar circumstances.

Reasonable doubt *See* Beyond a reasonable doubt

Reasonable person standard The standard of behavior expected of a hypothetical "reasonable person." The standard against which negligence is measured and that must be observed to avoid liability for negligence.

Rebuttal The refutation of evidence introduced by an adverse party's attorney.

Receiver In a corporate dissolution, a court-appointed person who winds up corporate affairs and liquidates corporate assets.

Recording statutes Statutes that allow deeds, mortgages, and other real property transactions to be recorded so as to provide notice to future purchasers or creditors of an existing claim on the property.

Red herring A preliminary prospectus that can be distributed to potential investors after the registration statement (for a securities offering) has been filed with the Securities and Exchange Commission. The name derives from the red legend printed across the prospectus stating that the registration has been filed but has not become effective.

Redemption A repurchase, or buying back. In secured transactions law, a debtor's repurchase of collateral securing a debt after a creditor has taken title to the collateral due to the debtor's default but before the secured party disposes of the collateral.

Reformation A court-ordered correction of a written contract so that it reflects the true intentions of the parties.

Regulation Z A set of rules promulgated by the Federal Reserve Board to implement the provisions of the Truth-in-Lending Act.

Rejection In contract law, an offeree's express or implied manifestation not to accept an offer. In the law governing contracts for the sale of goods, a buyer's manifest refusal to accept goods on the ground that they do not conform to contract specifications.

Rejoinder The defendant's answer to the plaintiff's rebuttal.

Release A contract in which one party forfeits the right to pursue a legal claim against the other party.

Relevant evidence Evidence tending to make a fact at issue in the case more or less probable than it would be without the evidence. Only relevant evidence is admissible in court.

Remainder A future interest in property held by a person other than the original owner.

Remanded Sent back. If an appellate court disagrees with a lower court's judgment, the case may be remanded to the lower court for further proceedings in which the lower court's decision should be consistent with the appellate court's opinion on the matter.

Remedy The relief given to an innocent party to enforce a right or compensate for the violation of a right.

Remedy at law A remedy available in a court of law. Money damages are awarded as a remedy at law.

Remedy in equity A remedy allowed by courts in situations where remedies at law are not appropriate. Remedies in equity are based on settled rules of fairness, justice, and honesty, and include injunction, specific performance, rescission and restitution, and reformation.

Remitter A person who sends money, or remits payment.

Replevin (pronounced ruh-*pleh*-vin) An action to recover specific goods in the hands of a party who is wrongfully withholding them from the other party.

Reply Procedurally, a plaintiff's response to a defendant's answer.

Reporter A publication in which court cases are published, or reported.

Repudiation The renunciation of a right or duty; the act of a buyer or seller in rejecting a contract either partially or totally. *See also* Anticipatory repudiation

Requirements contract An agreement in which a buyer agrees to purchase and the seller agrees to sell all or up to a stated amount of what the buyer needs or requires.

Res ipsa loquitur (pronounced *rehs ehp*-suh *low*-quuh-duhr) A doctrine under which negligence may be inferred simply because an event occurred, if it is the type of event that would not occur in the absence of negligence. Literally, the term means "the facts speak for themselves."

Resale price maintenance agreement An agreement between a manufacturer and a retailer in which the manufacturer specifies the minimum retail price of its products.

Rescind (pronounced reh-*sihnd*) To cancel. *See also* Rescission

Rescission (pronounced reh-*sih*-zhen) A remedy whereby a contract is canceled and the parties are returned to the positions they occupied before the contract was made; may be effected through the mutual consent of the parties, by their conduct, or by court decree.

Residuary The surplus of a testator's estate remaining after all of the debts and particular legacies have been discharged.

Respondeat superior (pronounced ree-*spahn*-dee-uht soo-*peer*-ee-your) In Latin, "Let the master respond." A doctrine under which a principal or an employer is held liable for the wrongful acts committed by agents or employees while acting within the course and scope of their agency or employment.

Respondent In equity practice, the party who answers a bill or other proceeding.

Restitution An equitable remedy under which a person is restored to his or her original position prior to loss or injury, or placed in the position he or she would have been in had the breach not occurred.

Restraint on trade Any contract or combination that tends to eliminate or reduce competition, effect a monopoly, artificially maintain prices, or otherwise hamper the course of trade and commerce as it would be carried on if left to the control of natural economic forces.

Restrictive covenant A private restriction on the use of land that is binding on the party that purchases the property originally as well as on subsequent purchasers. If its benefit or obligation passes with the land's ownership, it is said to "run with the land."

Retained earnings The portion of a corporation's profits that has not been paid out as dividends to shareholders.

Retaliatory eviction The eviction of a tenant because of the tenant's complaints, participation in a tenant's union, or similar activity with which the landlord does not agree.

Reverse To reject or overrule a court's judgment. An appellate court, for example, might reverse a lower court's judgment on an issue if it feels that the lower court committed an error during the trial or that the jury was improperly instructed.

Reverse discrimination Discrimination against majority groups, such as white males, that results from affirmative action programs, in which preferences are given to minority members and women.

Reversible error An error by a lower court that is sufficiently substantial to justify an appellate court's reversal of the lower court's decision.

Reversionary interest A future interest in property retained by the original owner.

Revocation In contract law, the withdrawal of an offer by an offeror. Unless an offer is irrevocable, it can be revoked at any time prior to acceptance without liability.

Right of contribution The right of a co-surety who pays more than his or her proportionate share on a debtor's default to recover the excess paid from other co-sureties.

Right of first refusal The right to purchase personal or real property—such as corporate shares or real estate—before the property is offered for sale to others.

Right of redemption *See* Equity of redemption; Redemption

Right of reimbursement The legal right of a person to be restored, repaid, or indemnified for costs, expenses, or losses incurred or expended on behalf of another.

Right of subrogation The right of a person to stand in the place of (be substituted for) another, giving the substituted party the same legal rights that the original party had.

Right-to-work law A state law providing that employees are not to be required to join a union as a condition of obtaining or retaining employment.

Robbery The act of forcefully and unlawfully taking personal property of any value from another; force or intimidation is usually necessary for an act of theft to be considered a robbery.

Rule of four A rule of the United States Supreme Court under which the Court will not issue a writ of *certiorari* unless at least four justices approve of the decision to issue the writ.

Rule of reason A test by which a court balances the positive effects (such as economic efficiency) of an agreement against its potentially anticompetitive effects. In antitrust litigation, many practices are analyzed under the rule of reason.

Rule 10b-5 *See* SEC Rule 10b-5

Rulemaking The process undertaken by an administrative agency when formally adopting a new regulation or amending an old one. Rulemaking involves notifying the public of a proposed rule or change and receiving and considering the public's comments.

Rules of evidence Rules governing the admissibility of evidence in trial courts.

S

S corporation A close business corporation that has met certain requirements as set out by the Internal Revenue Code and thus qualifies for special income tax treatment. Essentially, an S corporation is taxed the same as a partnership, but its owners enjoy the privilege of limited liability.

Sale The passing of title from the seller to the buyer for a price.

Sale on approval A type of conditional sale in which the buyer may take the goods on a trial basis. The sale becomes absolute only when the buyer approves of (or is satisfied with) the goods being sold.

Sale or return A type of conditional sale in which title and possession pass from the seller to the buyer; however, the buyer retains the option to return the goods during a specified period even though the goods conform to the contract.

Sales contract A contract for the sale of goods under which the ownership of goods is transferred from a seller to a buyer for a price.

Scienter (pronounced *sy-en-*ter) Knowledge by the misrepresenting party that material facts have been falsely represented or omitted with an intent to deceive.

Search warrant An order granted by a public authority, such as a judge, that authorizes law enforcement personnel to search particular premises or property.

Seasonably Within a specified time period, or, if no period is specified, within a reasonable time.

SEC Rule 10b-5 A rule of the Securities and Exchange Commission that makes it unlawful, in connection with the purchase or sale of any security, to make any untrue statement of a material fact or to omit a material fact if such omission causes the statement to be misleading.

Secondary boycott A union's refusal to work for, purchase from, or handle the products of a secondary employer, with whom the union has no dispute, for the purpose of forcing that employer to stop doing business with the primary employer, with whom the union has a labor dispute.

Securities Generally, corporate stocks and bonds. A security may also be a note, debenture, stock warrant, or any document given as evidence of an ownership interest in a corporation or as a promise of repayment by a corporation.

Self-defense The legally recognized privilege to protect one's self or property against injury by another. The privilege of self-defense protects only acts that are reasonably necessary to protect one's self or property.

Seniority system In regard to employment relationships, a system in which those who have worked longest for the company are first in line for promotions, salary increases, and other benefits; they are also the last to be laid off if the work force must be reduced.

Service mark A mark used in the sale or the advertising of services, such as to distinguish the services of one person from the services of others. Titles, character names, and other distinctive features of radio and television programs may be registered as service marks.

Service of process The delivery of the complaint and summons to a defendant.

Settlor One creating a trust.

Sexual harassment In the employment context, the granting of job promotions or other benefits in return for sexual favors or language or conduct that is so sexually offensive that it creates a hostile working environment.

Sham transaction A false transaction without substance that is undertaken with the intent to defraud a creditor or the government. An example of a sham transaction is the sale of assets to a friend or relative for the purpose of concealing assets from creditors or a bankruptcy court.

Share A unit of stock. *See also* Stock

Shareholder One who purchases shares of a corporation's stock, thus acquiring an equity interest in the corporation.

Shareholder's derivative suit A suit brought by a shareholder to enforce a corporate cause of action against a third person.

Sharia Civil law principles of some Middle Eastern countries that are based on the Islamic directives that follow the teachings of the prophet Mohammed.

Sheriff's deed The deed given to the purchaser of property at a sheriff's sale as part of the foreclosure process against the owner of the property.

Shipment contract A contract for the sale of goods in which the seller is required or authorized to ship the goods by carrier. The buyer assumes liability for any losses or damage to the goods after they are delivered to the carrier.

Short-form merger A merger between a subsidiary corporation and a parent corporation that owns at least 90 percent of the outstanding shares of each class of stock issued by the subsidiary corporation. Short-form mergers can be accomplished without the approval of the shareholders of either corporation.

Short-swing profits Profits made by officers, directors, and certain large stockholders resulting from the use of nonpublic (inside) information about their companies; prohibited by Section 12 of the 1934 Securities Exchange Act.

Signature Under the Uniform Commercial Code, "any symbol executed or adopted by a party with a present intention to authenticate a writing."

Slander Defamation in oral form.

Slander of quality (trade libel) The publication of false information about another's product, alleging that it is not what its seller claims.

Slander of title The publication of a statement that denies or casts doubt on another's legal ownership of any property, causing financial loss to that property's owner.

Small claims courts Special courts in which parties may litigate small claims (usually, claims involving $2,500 or less). Attorneys are not required in small claims courts, and in many states attorneys are not allowed to represent the parties.

Smart card Prepaid funds recorded on a microprocessor chip embedded on a card. One type of *e-money*.

Sociological school A school of legal thought that views the law as a tool for promoting justice in society.

Sole proprietorship The simplest form of business, in which the owner is the business; the owner reports business income on his or her personal income tax return and is legally responsible for all debts and obligations incurred by the business.

Sovereign immunity A doctrine that immunizes foreign nations from the jurisdiction of U.S. courts when certain conditions are satisfied.

Spam Bulk, unsolicited ("junk") e-mail.

Special warranty deed A deed in which the grantor only covenants to warrant and defend the title against claims and demands of the grantor and all persons claiming by, through, and under the grantor.

Specific performance An equitable remedy requiring exactly the performance that was specified in a contract; usually granted only when money damages would be an inadequate remedy and the subject matter of the contract is unique (for example, real property).

Spot zoning Granting a zoning classification to a parcel of land that is different from the classification given to other land in the immediate area.

Standing to sue The requirement that an individual must have a sufficient stake in a controversy before he or she can bring a lawsuit. The plaintiff must demonstrate that he or she either has been injured or threatened with injury.

Stare decisis (pronounced *ster-*ay dih-*si-*ses) A common law doctrine under which judges are obligated to follow the precedents established in prior decisions.

Statute of Frauds A state statute under which certain types of contracts must be in writing to be enforceable.

Statute of limitations A federal or state statute setting the maximum time period during which a certain action can be brought or certain rights enforced.

Statute of repose Basically, a statute of limitations that is not dependent on the happening of a cause of action. Statutes of repose generally begin to run at an earlier date and run for a longer period of time than statutes of limitations.

Statutory law The body of law enacted by legislative bodies (as opposed to constitutional law, administrative law, or case law).

Statutory lien A lien created by statute.

Statutory period of redemption A time period (usually set by state statute) during which the property subject to a defaulted mortgage, land contract, or other contract can be redeemed by the debtor after foreclosure or judicial sale.

Stock An equity (ownership) interest in a corporation, measured in units of shares.

Stock certificate A certificate issued by a corporation evidencing the ownership of a specified number of shares in the corporation.

Stock option *See* Stock warrant

Stock warrant A certificate that grants the owner the option to buy a given number of shares of stock, usually within a set time period.

Stockholder *See* Shareholder

Strict liability Liability regardless of fault. In tort law, strict liability may be imposed on defendants in cases involving abnormally dangerous activities, dangerous animals, or defective products.

Strike An extreme action undertaken by unionized workers when collective bargaining fails; the workers leave their jobs, refuse to work, and (typically) picket the employer's workplace.

Subject-matter jurisdiction Jurisdiction over the subject matter of a lawsuit.

Subpoena A document commanding a person to appear at a certain time and place or give testimony concerning a certain matter.

Subrogation *See* Right of subrogation

Subscriber An investor who agrees, in a subscription agreement, to purchase capital stock in a corporation.

Substantial evidence test The test applied by a court reviewing an administrative agency's informal action. The court determines whether the agency acted unreasonably and overturns the agency's findings only if unsupported by a substantial body of evidence.

Substantial performance Performance that does not vary greatly from the performance promised in a contract; the performance must create substantially the same benefits as those promised in the contract.

Substantive due process A requirement that focuses on the content, or substance, of legislation. If a law or other governmental action limits a fundamental right, such as the right to travel or to vote, it will be held to violate substantive due process unless it promotes a compelling or overriding state interest.

Substantive law Law that defines the rights and duties of individuals with respect to each other, as opposed to procedural law, which defines the manner in which these rights and duties may be enforced.

Substantive unconscionability Results from contracts, or portions of contracts, that are oppressive or overly harsh. Courts generally focus on provisions that deprive one party of the benefits of the agreement or leave that party without remedy for nonperformance by the other. An example of substantive unconscionability is the agreement by a welfare recipient with a fourth-grade education to purchase a refrigerator for $2,000 under an installment contract.

Suit *See* Lawsuit; Litigation

Summary judgment *See* Motion for summary judgment

Summary jury trial (SJT) A method of settling disputes in which a trial is held, but the jury's verdict is not binding. The verdict acts only as a guide to both sides in reaching an agreement during the mandatory negotiations that immediately follow the summary jury trial.

Summons A document informing a defendant that a legal action has been commenced against him or her and that the defendant must appear in court on a certain date to answer the plaintiff's complaint. The document is delivered by a sheriff or any other person so authorized.

Superseding cause An intervening force or event that breaks the connection between a wrongful act and an injury to another; in negligence law, a defense to liability.

Supremacy clause The provision in Article VI of the Constitution that provides that the Constitution, laws, and treaties of the United States are "the supreme Law of the Land." Under this clause, state and local laws that directly conflict with federal law will be rendered invalid.

Surety A person, such as a cosigner on a note, who agrees to be primarily responsible for the debt of another.

Suretyship An express contract in which a third party to a debtor-creditor relationship (the surety) promises to be primarily responsible for the debtor's obligation.

Syllogism A form of deductive reasoning consisting of a major premise, a minor premise, and a conclusion.

Symbolic speech Nonverbal conduct that expresses opinions or thoughts about a subject. Symbolic speech is protected under the First Amendment's guarantee of freedom of speech.

Syndicate An investment group of persons or firms brought together for the purpose of financing a project that they would not or could not undertake independently.

T

Tag A key word in a document that can serve as an index reference to the document. On the Web, search engines return results based, in part, on the tags in Web documents.

Taking The taking of private property by the government for public use. Under the Fifth Amendment to the Constitution, the government may not take private property for public use without "just compensation."

Tangible property Property that has physical existence and can be distinguished by the senses of touch, sight, and so on. A car is tangible property; a patent right is intangible property.

Tariff A tax on imported goods.

Technology licensing Allowing another to use and profit from intellectual property (patents, copyrights, trademarks, innovative products or processes, and so on) for consideration. In the context of international business transactions, technology licensing is sometimes an attractive alternative to the establishment of foreign production facilities.

Tenancy at sufferance A type of tenancy under which one who, after rightfully being in possession of leased premises, continues (wrongfully) to occupy the property after the lease has been terminated. The tenant has no rights to possess the property and occupies it only because the person entitled to evict the tenant has not done so.

Tenancy at will A type of tenancy under which either party can terminate the tenancy without notice; usually arises when a tenant who has been under a tenancy for years retains possession, with the landlord's consent, after the tenancy for years has terminated.

Tenancy by the entirety The joint ownership of property by a husband and wife. Neither party can transfer his or her interest in the property without the consent of the other.

Tenancy for years A type of tenancy under which property is leased for a specified period of time, such as a month, a year, or a period of years.

Tenancy in common Co-ownership of property in which each party owns an undivided interest that passes to his or her heirs at death.

Tenancy in partnership Co-ownership of partnership property.

Tender An unconditional offer to perform an obligation by a person who is ready, willing, and able to do so.

Tender of delivery Under the Uniform Commercial Code, a seller's or lessor's act of placing conforming goods at the disposal of the buyer or lessee and giving the buyer or lessee whatever notification is reasonably necessary to enable the buyer or lessee to take delivery.

Tender offer An offer to purchase made by one company directly to the shareholders of another (target) company; often referred to as a "takeover bid."

Third party beneficiary One for whose benefit a promise is made in a contract but who is not a party to the contract.

Tippee A person who receives inside information.

Tombstone ad An advertisement, historically in a format resembling a tombstone, of a securities offering. The ad informs potential investors of where and how they may obtain a prospectus.

Tort A civil wrong not arising from a breach of contract. A breach of a legal duty that proximately causes harm or injury to another.

Tortfeasor One who commits a tort.

Toxic tort Failure to use or to clean up properly toxic chemicals that cause harm to a person or society.

Trade dress The image and overall appearance of a product—for example, the distinctive decor, menu, layout, and style of service of a particular restaurant. Basically, trade dress is subject to the same protection as trademarks.

Trade fixture The personal property of a commercial tenant that has been installed or affixed to real property for a business purpose. When the lease ends, the tenant can remove the fixture but must repair any damage to the real property caused by the fixture's removal.

Trade libel The publication of false information about another's product, alleging it is not what its seller claims; also referred to as slander of quality.

Trade name A term that is used to indicate part or all of a business's name and that is directly related to the business's reputation and goodwill. Trade names are protected under the common law (and under trademark law, if the name is the same as the firm's trademarked property).

Trade secret Information or a process that gives a business an advantage over competitors who do not know the information or process.

Trademark A distinctive mark, motto, device, or implement that a manufacturer stamps, prints, or otherwise affixes to the goods it produces so that they may be identified on the market and their origins made known. Once a trademark is established (under the common law or through registration), the owner is entitled to its exclusive use.

Treasury shares Corporate shares that are authorized by the corporation but that have not been issued.

Treaty An agreement formed between two or more independent nations.

Treble damages Damages consisting of single damages determined by a jury and tripled in amount in certain cases as required by statute.

Trespass to land The entry onto, above, or below the surface of land owned by another without the owner's permission or legal authorization.

Trespass to personal property The unlawful taking or harming of another's personal property; interference with another's right to the exclusive possession of his or her personal property.

Trespasser One who commits the tort of trespass in one of its forms.

Trial court A court in which trials are held and testimony taken.

Trustee One who holds title to property for the use or benefit of another (the beneficiary).

Tying arrangement An agreement between a buyer and a seller in which the buyer of a specific product or service becomes obligated to purchase additional products or services from the seller.

U

U.S. trustee A government official who performs certain administrative tasks that a bankruptcy judge would otherwise have to perform.

Ultra vires (pronounced *uhl*-trah *vye*-reez) A Latin term meaning "beyond the powers"; in corporate law, acts of a corporation that are beyond its express and implied powers to undertake.

Unanimous opinion A court opinion in which all of the judges or justices of the court agree to the court's decision.

Unconscionable (pronounced un-*kon*-shun-uh-bul) **contract or clause** A contract or clause that is void on the basis of public policy because one party, as a result of his or her disproportionate bargaining power, is forced to accept terms that are unfairly burdensome and that unfairly benefit the dominating party. *See also* Procedural unconscionability; Substantive unconscionability

Undisclosed principal A principal whose identity is unknown by a third person, and the third person has no knowledge that the agent is acting for a principal at the time the agent and the third person form a contract.

Unenforceable contract A valid contract rendered unenforceable by some statute or law.

Uniform law A model law created by the National Conference of Commissioners (NCC) on Uniform State Laws and/or the American Law Institute for the states to consider adopting. If the state adopts the law, it becomes statutory law in that state. Each state has the option of adopting or rejecting all or part of a uniform law.

Unilateral contract A contract that results when an offer can only be accepted by the offeree's performance.

Union shop A place of employment in which all workers, once employed, must become union members within a specified period of time as a condition of their continued employment.

Unitary system A centralized governmental system in which local or subdivisional governments exercise only those powers given to them by the central government.

Unliquidated debt A debt that is uncertain in amount.

Unreasonably dangerous product In product liability, a product that is defective to the point of threatening a consumer's health and safety. A product will be considered unreasonably dangerous if it is dangerous beyond the expectation of the ordinary consumer or if a less dangerous alternative was economically feasible for the manufacturer, but the manufacturer failed to produce it.

Usage of trade Any practice or method of dealing having such regularity of observance in a place, vocation, or trade as to justify an expectation that it will be observed with respect to the transaction in question.

Usurpation In corporation law, the taking advantage of a corporate opportunity by a corporate officer or director for his or her personal gain and in violation of his or her fiduciary duties.

Usury Charging an illegal rate of interest.

Utilitarianism An approach to ethical reasoning in which ethically correct behavior is not related to any absolute ethical or moral values but to an evaluation of the consequences of a given action on those who will be affected by it. In utilitarian reasoning, a "good" decision is one that results in the greatest good for the greatest number of people affected by the decision.

V

Valid contract A contract that results when elements necessary for contract formation (agreement, consideration, legal purpose, and contractual capacity) are present.

Validation notice An initial notice to a debtor from a collection agency informing the debtor that he or she has thirty days to challenge the debt and request verification.

Vendee One who purchases property from another, called the vendor.

Vendor One who sells property to another, called the vendee.

Venue (pronounced *ven*-yoo) The geographical district in which an action is tried and from which the jury is selected.

Verdict A formal decision made by a jury.

Vertical merger The acquisition by a company at one stage of production of a company at a higher or lower stage of production (such as a company merging with one of its suppliers or retailers).

Vertical restraint Any restraint on trade created by agreements between firms at different levels in the manufacturing and distribution process.

Vertically integrated firm A firm that carries out two or more functional phases (manufacture, distribution, retailing, and so on) of a product.

Vesting The creation of an absolute or unconditional right or power.

Vicarious liability Legal responsibility placed on one person for the acts of another.

Virtual courtroom   A courtroom that is conceptual and not physical. In the context of cyberspace, a virtual courtroom could be a location on the Internet at which judicial proceedings take place.

Virtual property   Property that, in the context of cyberspace, is conceptual, as opposed to physical. Intellectual property that exists on the Internet is virtual property.

Void contract   A contract having no legal force or binding effect.

Voidable contract   A contract that may be legally avoided (canceled, or annulled) at the option of one of the parties.

Voidable preference   In bankruptcy law, a preference that may be avoided, or set aside, by the trustee.

Voir dire (pronounced *vwahr deehr*)   A French phrase meaning, literally, "to see, to speak." In jury trials, the phrase refers to the process in which the attorneys question prospective jurors to determine whether they are biased or have any connection with a party to the action or with a prospective witness.

Voting trust   An agreement (trust contract) under which legal title to shares of corporate stock is transferred to a trustee who is authorized by the shareholders to vote the shares on their behalf.

W

Waiver   An intentional, knowing relinquishment of a legal right.

Warehouse receipt   A document of title issued by a bailee-warehouser to cover the goods stored in the warehouse.

Warehouser   One in the business of operating a warehouse.

Warranty   A promise that certain facts are truly as they are represented to be.

Warranty deed   A deed in which the grantor guarantees to the grantee that the grantor has title to the property conveyed in the deed, that there are no encumbrances on the property other than what the grantor has represented, and that the grantee will enjoy quiet possession of the property; a deed that provides the greatest amount of protection for the grantee.

Warranty disclaimer   A seller's or lessor's negation or qualification of a warranty.

Warranty of fitness   *See* Implied warranty of fitness for a particular purpose

Warranty of merchantability   *See* Implied warranty of merchantability

Warranty of title   An implied warranty made by a seller that the seller has good and valid title to the goods sold and that the transfer of the title is rightful.

Waste   The abuse or destructive use of real property by one who is in rightful possession of the property but who does not have title to it. Waste does not include ordinary depreciation due to age and normal use.

Watered stock   Shares of stock issued by a corporation for which the corporation receives, as payment, less than the stated value of the shares.

Wetlands   Areas of land designated by government agencies (such as the Army Corps of Engineers or the Environmental Protection Agency) as protected areas that support wildlife and that therefore cannot be filled in or dredged by private contractors or parties.

Whistleblowing   An employee's disclosure to government, the press, or upper-management authorities that the employer is engaged in unsafe or illegal activities.

White-collar crime   Nonviolent crime committed by individuals or corporations to obtain a personal or business advantage.

Will   An instrument directing what is to be done with the testator's property on his or her death, made by the testator and revocable during his or her lifetime. No interests in the testator's property pass until the testator dies.

Willful   Intentional.

Winding up   The second of two stages involved in the termination of a partnership or corporation. Once the firm is dissolved, it continues to exist legally until the process of winding up all business affairs (collecting and distributing the firm's assets) is complete.

Workers' compensation laws   State statutes establishing an administrative procedure for compensating workers' injuries that arise out of—or in the course of—their employment, regardless of fault.

Workout   An out-of-court agreement between a debtor and his or her creditors in which the parties work out a payment plan or schedule under which the debtor's debts can be discharged.

Writ of attachment   A court's order, prior to a trial to collect a debt, directing the sheriff or other officer to seize nonexempt property of the debtor; if the creditor prevails at trial, the seized property can be sold to satisfy the judgment.

Writ of *certiorari* (pronounced sur-shee-uh-*rah*-ree)   A writ from a higher court asking the lower court for the record of a case.

Writ of execution   A court's order, after a judgment has been entered against the debtor, directing the sheriff to seize (levy) and sell any of the debtor's nonexempt real or personal property. The proceeds of the sale are used to pay off the judgment, accrued interest, and costs of the sale; any surplus is paid to the debtor.

Wrongful discharge   An employer's termination of an employee's employment in violation of an employment contract or laws that protect employees.

Z

Zoning   The division of a city by legislative regulation into districts and the application in each district of regulations having to do with structural and architectural designs of buildings and prescribing the use to which buildings within designated districts may be put.

Table of Cases

Index

West's Online Research Guide—LAW and ETHICS
Updates and Additions at http://www.westbuslaw.com

General Legal Resources

ABA Section on Business Law	http://www.abanet.org/buslaw/home.html
Academy of Legal Studies in Business	http://www.alsb.org/
Counsel Quest	http://www.CounselQuest.com/
Court TV Online	http://www.courttv.com/
FindLaw	http://www.findlaw.com/
Hieros Gamos	http://www.hg.org/
Law News Network	http://www.lawnewsnetwork.com/
Legal Information Institute (LII)	http://www.law.cornell.edu/

Legal Terms

Everybody's Law Dictionary (Nolo Press)	http://www.nolo.com/dictionary/wordindex.cfm

Court Cases

Bankruptcy Court Opinions (FindLaw)	http://www.findlaw.com/casecode/bankruptcy.html
Federal Circuit Court Opinions (FindLaw)	http://www.findlaw.com/casecode/courts/index.html
Federal District Court Opinions (FindLaw)	http://www.findlaw.com/casecode/district.html
State Court Opinions (FindLaw)	http://www.findlaw.com/casecode/state.html
Supreme Court Cases (1893-Present) (FindLaw)	http://www.findlaw.com/casecode/supreme.html
Supreme Court Cases (1937-1975) (Fedworld)	http://www.fedworld.gov/supcourt/index.htm
Supreme Court Cases (1990-Present) (LII)	http://supct.law.cornell.edu/supct/
The Oyez Project Audio recordings of key Supreme Court cases (Northwestern University)	http://oyez.nwu.edu/
West's Case Updates	http://www.westbuslaw.com/topic_index.html

Acts, Codes, Treaties, and the Constitution

Code of Federal Regulations (LII)	http://www4.law.cornell.edu/cfr/
GATT (The Trading Floor)	http://trading.wmw.com/gatt/
NAFTA (Wiretap)	gopher://wiretap.spies.com/11/Gov/NAFTA
Securities Acts (University of Cincinnati)	http://www.law.uc.edu/CCL/sldtoc.html
State Codes (FindLaw)	http://www.findlaw.com/casecode/state.html
U.S. Code (LII)	http://www4.law.cornell.edu/uscode/
U.S. Constitution (USConstitution.net)	http://www.usconstitution.net/
Uniform Commercial Code (LII)	http://www.law.cornell.edu/ucc/ucc.table.html

Alternate Dispute Resolution

ABA Section on Dispute Resolution	http://www.abanet.org/dispute/home.html
American Arbitration Association	http://www.adr.org/
Guide to ADR (Hieros Gamos)	http://hg.org/adr.html

Ethics

Institute for Global Ethics	http://www.globalethics.org/
Institute for Business and Professional Ethics (DePaul University)	http://condor.depaul.edu/ethics/
Legalethics.com	http://www.legalethics.com/